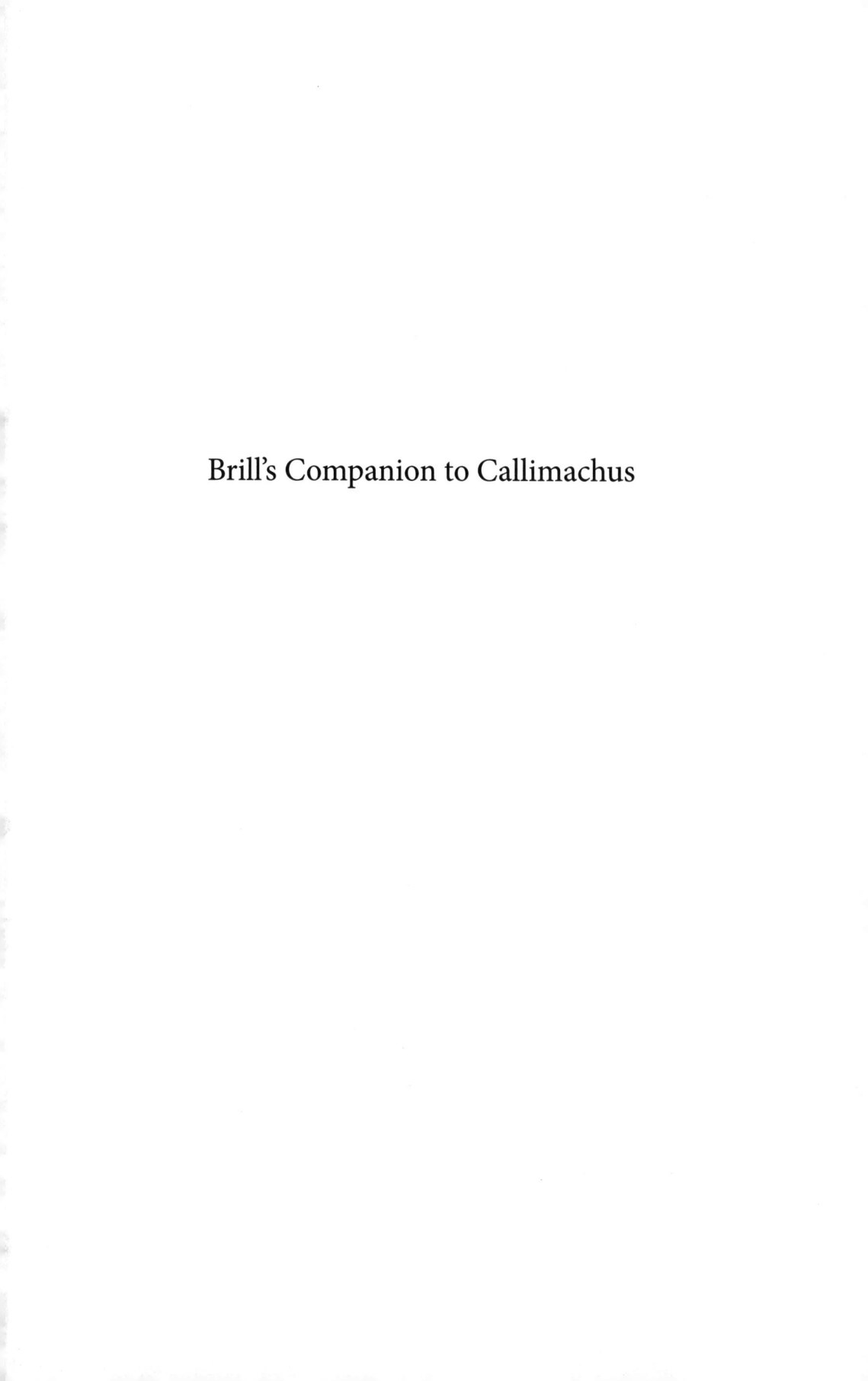

Brill's Companion to Callimachus

Brill's Companion to Callimachus

Edited by

Benjamin Acosta-Hughes
Luigi Lehnus
Susan Stephens

BRILL

LEIDEN • BOSTON
2011

Cover illustration: Black granite statue of a Ptolemaic queen (59.1 inches high). 3rd century BC. Discovered at Canopus. Image reproduced courtesy of the HILTI Foundation. Photograph by Christoph Gerigk.

This book is printed on acid-free paper.

Library of Congress Cataloging-in-Publication Data

Brill's companion to Callimachus / edited by Benjamin Acosta-Hughes, Luigi Lehnus, Susan Stephens.
   p. cm.
   Includes bibliographical references and index.
   ISBN 978-90-04-15673-9 (hardback : alk. paper) 1. Callimachus—Criticism and interpretation. 2. Greek poetry, Hellenistic—Egypt—Alexandria—History and criticism. I. Acosta-Hughes, Benjamin, 1960– II. Lehnus, Luigi. III. Stephens, Susan A. IV. Title: Companion to Callimachus.

PA3945.Z5B75 2011
881'.01—dc22

2011011254

The titles published in this series are listed at brill.nl/bccs.

ISSN 1872-3357
ISBN 9789004156739

Copyright 2011 by Koninklijke Brill NV, Leiden, The Netherlands.
Koninklijke Brill NV incorporates the imprints Brill, Global Oriental, Hotei Publishing, IDC Publishers, Martinus Nijhoff Publishers and VSP.

All rights reserved. No part of this publication may be reproduced, translated, stored in a retrieval system, or transmitted in any form or by any means, electronic, mechanical, photocopying, recording or otherwise, without prior written permission from the publisher.

Authorization to photocopy items for internal or personal use is granted by Koninklijke Brill NV provided that the appropriate fees are paid directly to The Copyright Clearance Center, 222 Rosewood Drive, Suite 910, Danvers, MA 01923, USA.
Fees are subject to change.

MIX
Paper from responsible sources
FSC
www.fsc.org FSC® C008919

PRINTED BY A-D DRUK BV - ZEIST, THE NETHERLANDS

CONTENTS

Contributors ix
Abbreviations xvii

Introduction 1
   Susan Stephens

PART ONE

THE MATERIAL AUTHOR

1. Callimachus Rediscovered in Papyri 23
   Luigi Lehnus

2. The *Aetia* through Papyri 39
   Giulio Massimilla

3. Callimachus as Fragment 63
   Annette Harder

4. The *Diegeseis* Papyrus: Archaeological Context, Format, and
   Contents 81
   Maria Rosaria Falivene

5. Callimachus Cited 93
   Filippomaria Pontani

6. Callimachus' Philology 118
   Nita Krevans

7. Callimachus and His *Koinai* 134
   Peter Parsons

PART TWO
SOCIAL CONTEXTS

8. Dimensions of Power: Callimachean Geopoetics and the Ptolemaic Empire 155
Markus Asper

9. Callimachus on Kings and Kingship 178
Silvia Barbantani

10. Callimachus' Queens 201
Évelyne Prioux

11. Poet and Court 225
Gregor Weber

12. The Gods of Callimachus 245
Richard Hunter

13. Callimachus and Contemporary Religion: The *Hymn to Apollo* 264
Ivana Petrovic

PART THREE
SOURCES AND MODELS

14. Digging Up the Musical Past: Callimachus and the New Music 289
Lucia Prauscello

15. Callimachus and Contemporary Criticism 309
Allen J. Romano

16. Callimachus' Muses 329
Andrew Morrison

17. Callimachus and the Atthidographers 349
Giovanni Benedetto

18. Callimachus and Fable 368
    Ruth Scodel

19. Proverbs and Popular Sayings in Callimachus 384
    Emanuele Lelli

PART FOUR
PERSONAE

20. The Poet as a Child 407
    Adele-Teresa Cozzoli

21. Speaking with Authority: Polyphony in Callimachus'
    Hymns 429
    Marco Fantuzzi

22. Other Poetic Voices in Callimachus 454
    Christophe Cusset

23. Individual Figures in Callimachus 474
    Yannick Durbec

24. Iambic Theatre: The Childhood of Callimachus Revisited .. 493
    Mark Payne

PART FIVE
CALLIMACHUS' AFTERLIFE

25. Roman Callimachus 511
    Alessandro Barchiesi

26. Callimachus and Later Greek Poetry 534
    Claudio De Stefani and Enrico Magnelli

27. *Arte Allusiva*: Pasquali and Onward 566
    Mario Citroni

Epilogue 587
  Benjamin Acosta-Hughes

Bibliography 603
Index Locorum 659
Index Rerum 684

CONTRIBUTORS

BENJAMIN ACOSTA-HUGHES is Professor of Greek and Latin at the Ohio State University. He is the author of *Polyeideia: The Iambi of Callimachus and the Archaic Iambic Tradition* (2002) and of *Arion's Lyre: Archaic Lyric into Hellenistic Poetry* (2010). With Susan Stephens he is the coauthor of *Callimachus in Context: From Plato to Ovid* (Cambridge, forthcoming).

MARKUS ASPER is Professor of Classics at the Humboldt University of Berlin. He has authored monographs on Callimachus' poetic metaphors and the genres of Greek science writing, and has published an edition of Callimachus with German translation. He has published papers on Callimachus, Apollonius of Rhodes, Greek mathematics, archaic law and the emergence of standardized forms of argument, the earliest forms of Greek prose, Galen and his readers, and narratives in science.

SILVIA BARBANTANI is currently a Researcher teaching Greek Language and Classical Philology at the Università Cattolica del Sacro Cuore (Milan and Brescia). Her publications include *ΦΑΤΙΣ ΝΙΚΗΦΟΡΟΣ: Frammenti di elegia encomiastica nell'età delle guerre galatiche* (2001), *The Glory of the Spear* (2007), and "Idéologie royale et littérature de cour dans l'Égypte lagide" in *Des rois au Prince* (2010).

ALESSANDRO BARCHIESI is Professor of Latin Literature at the University of Siena at Arezzo and at Stanford. His recent research includes editing the *Oxford Handbook of Roman Studies* (with W. Scheidel) and work in progress for his Sather Lectures (2011) on Italy in Virgil's *Aeneid*. Most of his previous publications deal with the major Augustan poets and their poetics, with frequent reference to Callimachus and his influence.

GIOVANNI BENEDETTO is Associate Professor of Classics at the University of Milan. His research interests concern Hellenistic poetry and the history of its interpretation in classical scholarship of the eighteenth and nineteenth centuries (*Il sogno e l'invettiva: Momenti di storia dell'esegesi callimachea*, 1993) and the history of classical studies. He has written the commentary to most *epitymbia* in the editio princeps of the epigrams of Posidippus (PMilVogl 8.309).

MARIO CITRONI is Professor of Latin Literature at the Istituto Italiano di Scienze Umane, Florence. His publications include *Poesia e lettori in Roma antica* (1995) and studies of literature and society and literature and contemporary *mentalité* in the Roman world, as well as on ancient literary epigram. He is editor of *Memoria e identità: La cultura romana costruisce la sua imagine* (2003). He is currently working on literary canons in ancient literature and on the origin of the concept of the classic.

ADELE-TERESA COZZOLI is Associate Professor of Greek Literature at the University of Rome III. Her interests include fifth-century theater, in particular Euripides' fragmentary plays; she has edited Euripides' *Cretans* with translation and commentary (2001). She has also authored numerous articles on Hellenistic poetry and is editor of two conference volumes on Callimachus and one on the Argonautic tradition. Recently she has turned her attention to the distinctive features of the Hellenistic intellectual, erudition, and literary polemic.

CHRISTOPHE CUSSET is Professor of Greek at the École Normale Supérieure, Lyon; his principal interests are Hellenistic poetry, didactic poetry, New Comedy, and the Greek novel, with particular focus on intertextuality and poetics. He is the author of *La Muse dans la bibliothèque* (1999) and *Ménandre; ou, La comédie tragique* (2003), has published several conferences on Hellenistic poetry and has created an online journal for Hellenistic studies at www.aitia.revues.org. He is currently preparing an edition of Euphorion and a commentary on Theocritus *Idyll* 6.

CLAUDIO DE STEFANI teaches Greek Literature at the Università degli Studi II, Naples. He has published widely on Hellenistic and late Greek poetry, Greek and Arabic medicine, and Byzantine poetry. His works include an edition and commentary of the first book of Nonnus' *Paraphrase of St. John's Gospel* (2002) and a critical edition of Paul the Silentiary's ecphrastic poems (2011). He is currently preparing critical editions of Galen's *De differentiis febrium* and Aelius Aristides' *Orations 17–25*.

YANNICK DURBEC teaches at the Thiers Lycée in Marseilles and is a Research Scholar associated with the CNRS (UMR 6125) at the Maison Méditerranéenne des Sciences de l'Homme, Aix-en-Provence. He is the editor of *Callimaque: Fragments poétiques* (2006) and is currently co-editing a collection of fragmentary poets of the third century BC. He is the author of numerous articles on Hellenistic poetry.

MARIA ROSARIA FALIVENE is Associate Professor of Papyrology at the University of Rome II Tor Vergata. Her principal fields of study include both literary and documentary papyrology, Alexandrian poetry, and the history of the administration of Greco-Roman Egypt. She takes a special interest in the Greek-speaking intelligentsia of Egypt in the Hellenistic period and in the reconstruction of Greek libraries and archives on the basis of their surviving papyrus fragments.

MARCO FANTUZZI is Visiting Professor of Greek Literature at Columbia University and Professor of Greek Literature at the University of Macerata and at the Graduate School of Greek and Latin Philology of the University of Florence. He is the author of *Bionis Smyrnaei Adonidis epitaphium* (1985), *Ricerche su Apollonio Rodio* (1988), *Tradition and Innovation in Hellenistic Poetry* (with R. Hunter, 2004), articles on Greek and Latin metrics and literary criticism, Hellenistic poetry, and Greek drama. He has also edited (with T. Papanghelis) *Brill's Companion to Greek and Latin Pastoral* (2006).

ANNETTE HARDER is Professor of Ancient Greek Language and Literature at the University of Groningen. She has written on Greek tragedy and published a number of mythographic papyri and various articles on Hellenistic poetry. She organizes the biennial Groningen Workshops on Hellenistic Poetry and has edited several volumes of the series Hellenistica Groningana. She has also published a Dutch translation of a selection of Callimachus' poetry, and her edition with introduction and commentary of Callimachus' *Aetia* will appear in 2011.

RICHARD HUNTER is Regius Professor of Greek at the University of Cambridge and a Fellow of Trinity College. His research interests include Hellenistic poetry and its reception in Rome, ancient literary criticism, and the ancient novel. His most recent books are *The Hesiodic Catalogue of Women: Constructions and Reconstructions* (2005), *The Shadow of Callimachus* (2006), *Wandering Poets in Ancient Greek*

Culture (with Ian Rutherford, 2009), and *Critical Moments in Classical Literature* (2009). Many of his essays have been collected in *On Coming After: Studies in Post-Classical Greek Literature and Its Reception* (2008).

NITA KREVANS is Associate Professor in the Department of Classical and Near Eastern Studies at the University of Minnesota. Her research interests include the history of the book in antiquity, Hellenistic poetry, and the reception of Hellenistic models in Latin literature. Her most recent publications are a study of epigram arrangement in papyrus collections and an essay on book burning and poetic deathbeds.

LUIGI LEHNUS is Professor of Classics at the University of Milan. His research interests extend from late-archaic Greek literature to Hellenistic and Roman poetry, and to the modern history of classical scholarship. He is currently preparing a new edition of the fragments of Callimachus.

EMANUELE LELLI collaborates with the University of Rome I "La Sapienza." He is the author of *Critica e polemiche letterarie nei Giambi di Callimaco* (2004) and *Callimachi Iambi XIV–XVII* (2005), *Volpe e leone: Il proverbio nella poesia greca* (2006), *I proverbi greci: Le raccolte di Zenobio e Diogeniano* (2006), and of *L'agricoltura antica*: Geoponica di Cassiano Basso (2009).

ENRICO MAGNELLI is Assistant Professor at the University of Florence. He has published widely on Greek poetry from the Hellenistic to the Byzantine period, on Attic comedy, and on Greek meter, including *Alexandri Aetoli testimonia et fragmenta* (1999) and *Studi su Euforione* (2002). He is currently preparing a monograph on the use of Homer in Greek comedy and satyr plays, a critical edition of Greek epigrams by poets of the imperial period and late antiquity (with Gianfranco Agosti), and an edition with commentary of the fragments of Euphorion.

GIULIO MASSIMILLA is Associate Professor of Greek Literature at the University Federico II in Naples. He is the author of a two-volume critical edition, with commentary, of Callimachus' *Aetia* (1996, 2010). He has written on archaic Greek lyric, Hellenistic poetry, imperial Greek epic, and Greek literary papyri.

ANDREW MORRISON is Senior Lecturer in Classics at the University of Manchester. He is the author of *The Narrator in Archaic Greek and Hellenistic Poetry* (2007) and *Performances and Audiences in Pindar's Sicilian Victory Odes* (2007), and coeditor of *Ancient Letters* (2007). He is currently working on Apollonius' use of historiography (especially Herodotus) and a commentary on selected poems of Callimachus.

PETER PARSONS, Regius Professor of Greek Emeritus at Oxford University, has worked extensively in literary papyrology. He is the author, with Hugh Lloyd-Jones, of the *Supplementum Hellenisticum* (1983) and an editor of *The Oxyrhynchus Papyri*.

MARK PAYNE is Associate Professor in the Department of Classics, the John U. Nef Committee on Social Thought, and the College at the University of Chicago. He is the author of *Theocritus and the Invention of Fiction* (2007), *The Animal Part: Human and Other Animals in the Poetic Imagination* (2010), and articles on ancient and modern poetry and poetics.

IVANA PETROVIC is Senior Lecturer at the Department of Classics and Ancient History at the University of Durham. Her *Von den Toren des Hades zu den Hallen des Olymp: Artemiskult bei Theokrit und Kallimachos* (2007) studies contemporary religion in Hellenistic poetry. She has co-edited volumes on the Roman triumph (2008) and on Greek archaic epigram (2010), and published papers on Greek (especially Hellenistic) poetry, Greek religion, and magic. She is currently working on a commentary on Callimachus' *Hymn to Artemis*.

FILIPPOMARIA PONTANI is Associate Professor of Classical Philology at the University of Venice "Ca' Foscari." His publications include works on a wide range of Greek and Latin authors, as well as on humanistic Greek (Greek epigrams of Angelo Poliziano, 2002; Marcus Musurus, 2003; Budé's *Homeric Studies*, 2007) and the history of Homeric exegesis and reception (Heraclitus' *Quaestiones Homericae*, 2005; the manuscript tradition of Greek exegesis to Homer's *Odyssey*, 2005; unknown introductions to Homer, 2005 and 2009; a Byzantine portrait of Homer, 2005). He is currently working on an edition of ancient and Byzantine *Odyssey* scholia (vols. 1 and 2 [covering Books 1–4], 2007–10).

LUCIA PRAUSCELLO is Lecturer in Classics at the University of Cambridge and Fellow of Trinity Hall. She is the author of *Singing Alexandria: Music between Practice and Textual Transmission* (2006) and has published various works on archaic and Hellenistic poetry, drama, and the sociology of Greek music.

ÉVELYNE PRIOUX is a Research Professor at the Centre National de la Recherche Scientifique and teaches ancient art history in the Department of Art History at the University of Paris Ouest–Nanterre–La Défense. She is the author of *Regards alexandrins: Histoire et théorie des arts dans l'épigramme hellénistique* (2007) and of *Petits musées en vers: Épigramme et discours sur les collections antiques* (2008).

ALLEN J. ROMANO is Assistant Professor of Classics at the Florida State University. His major research interests and recent publications include work on tragedy, Greek epigram, and Hellenistic elegy. He is currently engaged in a book-length study of aetiological myth in Greek poetry and drama.

RUTH SCODEL is D.R. Shackleton Bailey Collegiate Professor of Greek and Latin at the University of Michigan. She has published widely in Greek literature, particularly on Homer and tragedy. Her books include *Credible Impossibilities: Conventions and Strategies of Verisimilitude in Homer and Greek Tragedy* (1999), *Listening to Homer* (2002), *Epic Facework: Self-Presentation and Social Interaction in Homer* (2008), and an *Introduction to Greek Tragedy* (2010).

SUSAN STEPHENS is Sara Hart Kimball Professor in the Humanities and Professor in the Department of Classics at Stanford University. She is the author of *Seeing Double: Intercultural Poetics in Ptolemaic Alexandria* (2003), and with Benjamin Acosta-Hughes of *Callimachus in Context: From Plato to Ovid*.

GREGOR WEBER is Professor of Ancient History and Direktor des Instituts für Europäische Kulturgeschichte at the University of Augsburg. His publications include *Dichtung und höfische Gesellschaft* (1993), *Kaiser, Träume und Visionen in Prinzipat und Spätantike* (2000), and *Pseudo-Xenophon: Der Staat der Athener* (2010). He is editor of *Kulturgeschichte des Hellenismus* (2007) and *Kulturbegegnungen im ptolemäischen Alexandreia* (2010), and is coeditor of *Propagand—Selbstdarstellung—Repräsentation im römischen Kaiserreich des 1. Jahrhunderts n.Chr.* (2003), *Antike und moderne Demokratie* (2004), *Traum und res publica* (2008), and the *Gnomon* Bibliographische Datenbank.

ABBREVIATIONS

The texts of Callimachus are from Pfeiffer (Pf.) or Massimilla (M.). In the non-technical papers some papyrological sigla (e.g., half brackets) have been omitted from Greek texts. Papyrological abbreviations follow Checklist of Greek, Latin, and Coptic Papyri, http://scriptorium.lib.duke.edu/papyrus/texts/clist.html. Brief citations are ordinarily placed within text; longer comments expressed as footnotes.

AP	*Anthologia Palatina*
APl	*Anthologia Planudea*
CA	J.U. Powell, *Collectanea Alexandrina* (Oxford, 1925)
DK	H. Diels and W. Kranz, *Die Fragmente der Vorsokratiker* (6th ed. Berlin, 1951–1952)
FGE	D.L. Page, *Further Greek Epigrams* (Cambridge, 1981)
FGrHist	F. Jacoby, *Die Fragmente der griechischen Historiker* (Berlin and Leiden, 1923–1958)
GDRK	E. Heitsch, *Die griechischen Dichterfragmente der römischen Kaiserzeit* (Göttingen, 1963–1964)
GLP	D.L. Page, *Greek Literary Papyri I.* (Cambridge, MA 1942)
GP	A.S.F. Gow and D.L. Page, *The Greek Anthology. Hellenistic Epigrams* (Cambridge, 1965)
GVI	W. Peek, *Griechische Vers-Inschriften* (Berlin, 1955)
H.	A. Hollis, *Callimachus: Hecale. Introduction, Text, Translation, and Enlarged Commentary* (2nd ed. Oxford, 2009)
ICret	M. Guarducci, *Inscriptiones Creticae* (Rome, 1935–1950)
IEG	M.L. West, *Iambi et Elegi Graeci* (2nd ed. Oxford, 1989–1992)
IG	*Inscriptiones Graecae* (Berlin, 1873–)
IGUR	L. Moretti, *Inscriptiones Graecae Urbis Romae* (Rome, 1968–1990)
IME	E. Bernand, *Inscriptions métriques de l'Égypte gréco-romaine* (Paris, 1949)
KA	R. Kassel and C. Austin, *Poetae Comici Graeci*. 8 vols. (Berlin, 1983–).
LDAB	*Leuven Database of Ancient Books* http://www.trismegistos.org/ldab/

LSJ	H.G. Liddell et al. *A Greek-English Lexicon* (9th ed. Oxford, 1940)
M.	G. Massimilla, AITIA. *Libri primo e secondo.* (Pisa and Rome, 1996). *Libro terzo e quarto.* (Pisa and Rome, 2010).
M.-W.	R. Merkelbach and M.L. West, *Hesiodi Fragmenta* (3rd ed. Oxford, 1990)
MP[3]	*Catalogue des papyrus littéraires grecs et latines* http://promethee.philo.ulg.ac.be/cedopal/indexanglais.htm
OGIS	W. Dittenberger, *Orientis Graeci Inscriptiones Selectae* (Leipzig, 1903–5)
PEG	A. Bernabé, *Poetarum Epicorum Graecorum.* (Leipzig, 1987–2007)
Pf.	R. Pfeiffer, *Callimachus*, 2 vols. (Oxford, 1949–1953)
PCG	See KA
PMG	D.L. Page, *Poetae Melici Graeci* (Oxford, 1962)
PMGF	M. Davies, *Poetarum Melicorum Graecorum Fragmenta* (Oxford, 1991–)
Powell	See *CA*
RE	A. Pauly, G. Wissowa, and W. Kroll et al., eds. *Real-Encyclopädie der classischen Altertumswissenschaft.* (Stuttgart-Munich, 1894–1980)
SEG	*Supplementum Epigraphicum Graecum* (Leiden, 1923–)
SGO	R. Merkelbach and J. Stauber, *Steinepigramme aus dem griechischen Osten.* 5 vols. (Munich, Leipzig, 1998–2004)
SH	H. Lloyd-Jones and P.J. Parsons, *Supplementum Hellenisticum* (Berlin and New York, 1983)
SSH	H. Lloyd-Jones, *Supplementum Supplementi Hellenistici* (Berlin, 2005)
SLG	D.L. Page, *Supplementum Lyricis Graecis* (Oxford, 1974)
Sk.	O. Skutsch, *The* Annals *of Q. Ennius* (Oxford, 1985)
SVF	H. von Arnim, *Stoicorum Veterum Fragmenta.* (Leipzig, 1903–1924)
Syll	W. Dittenberger, *Sylloge Inscriptionum Graecarum* (3rd ed. Leipzig, 1915–1924)
TGF	A. Nauck, *Tragicorum Graecorum Fragmenta* (2nd ed. Leipzig, 1889)
TrGF	B. Snell, R. Kannicht, and S. Radt, *Tragicorum Graecorum Fragmenta* (Göttingen, 1971–2004)
West	See *IEG*
Σ	Scholion

INTRODUCTION

Susan Stephens

Abstract

The introduction provides a survey of Callimachus' extant poetry; an assessment of the evidence for his life; discussion of the differences between Cyrene, the oldest Greek city in North Africa, and Alexandria, the foundation of which occurred only fifty years before Callimachus began writing, and how these places are represented in his poems. It concludes with a brief discussion of the current directions of scholarship on Callimachus and the rationale for the topics discussed in this volume.

Callimachus was the most important poet of the Hellenistic age, because of his engagement with ideas about poetry, his wide-ranging generic experimentation, and his self-conscious stance as a poet between a performed art and the emerging possibilities of the text.[1] His was a singular moment in the transition from the classical world of old Greek cities to the new foundation of Ptolemaic Alexandria—a megacity that attracted people of diverse ethnicities from many locations around the Mediterranean (Scheidel 2004). Callimachus took advantage of the freedoms and challenges that this new environment provided to experiment at the boundaries of the inherited literary past. Whether we regard his various statements on poetry as serious and systematic, as playful, or as *captatio benevolentiae*, he was unique in his expression of interest in what constituted poetic excellence, and these statements in combination with his compositions in multiple genres provoked frequent and continuous imitation. Yet of his poetic oeuvre, which would have exceeded what we now have of Theocritus, Aratus, Posidippus, and Apollonius combined, only his six hymns and around sixty of his epigrams have survived intact. The rest has been reduced to numerous citations in later Greek lexicons and handbooks or, beginning in the late nineteenth century, has been discovered on papyrus fragments.

---

[1] For example, his *Aetia* opens with Apollo addressing him as singer—ἀοιδός—at the very moment when first he placed his writing tablet on his knees (fr. 1.21–24 Pf.)

The Poetry

Celebrated for his elegance, learning, and generic experiment, Callimachus is noted also for the remarkable scope of his poetic output both in its size and in the range. What follows is an outline of his poetic oeuvre.

The Hymns

Callimachus' six *Hymns* have survived intact because they were collected and transmitted along with the *Homeric Hymns*, the Orphic hymns, and those of Proclus. The manuscript containing them was brought to Italy from Constantinople between the fourteenth and the early fifteenth century (Bulloch 1985: 71 n. 1); it is no longer extant, but all known manuscripts of these hymns descend from that single archetype. Papyrus finds of Callimachus' *Hymns* confirm the order in which they appear in the manuscript tradition. That confirmation, although by no means conclusive, lends credence to scholarly assertions that this was the arrangement of the poet himself. Internal references militate against their having been composed at the same time. These hymns are usually categorized as literary, meaning that they were never intended for performance,[2] though there are dissenters from this judgment.[3] Each hymn features a single Olympian divinity—Zeus, Apollo, Artemis, Delos (Apollo), Athena, Demeter. The first four have a strong focus on childhood. All address the deity in the second person singular (usually referred to as *Du-Stil*) and include traditional features: the narrative of birth and divine accomplishments. Three hymns are mimetic, as if the speaker and audience were attending a ritual event. The poems have very strong intertextual links with the *Homeric Hymns* (particularly the *Homeric Hymns to Dionysus, to Demeter*, and *to Apollo*), and with Hesiod and Pindar. *Hymns* 1–4 and 6 are written in hexameters; *Hymn* 5 in elegiacs. The dialect of the first four is epic-Ionic; the last two are in Doric. (On the *Hymns*, see the chapters by R. Hunter, M. Fantuzzi, and C. Cusset.)

---

[2] See Furley and Bremmer 2001: 1.45–47; Fraser 1972: 1.652–53. Bing (1988b and 2009: 106–115) and Depew (1989, 1993, and 1998) state what is still the majority position.

[3] See, e.g., Alan Cameron 1995: 24–70.

Hymn 1, "To Zeus" (96 lines), begins with Callimachus expressing his doubt about how to hymn Zeus: Was he born in Arcadia, or in Crete? The poet opts for an Arcadian birth, after which the infant is immediately transferred to Crete, where his growth is prodigious. Zeus then assumes the prerogatives of the king of the gods, taking Olympus for his portion by virtue of his superior might. He has charge of kings, the most important of whom is Ptolemy. This hymn is generally taken as the earliest, the king of line 86 being identified with either Ptolemy I (who died in 282) or, more likely, Ptolemy II at the beginning of his reign. (See S. Barbantani.) The poem has close textual affinities with contemporary philosophical views about Zeus as expressed in Aratus' opening of the *Phaenomena*, in Euhemerus,[4] and in Antagoras of Rhodes (Cuypers 2004).

Hymn 2, "To Apollo" (113 lines), begins with a hushed anticipation of the epiphany of the god and an exhortation to a chorus of young men to hymn him. The poem includes events from the childhood, youth, and finally marriage of the god to the nymph Cyrene. The central section describes the origins of the Carneia, a festival of Apollo brought to Cyrene from Sparta by the first immigrants, and this section encourages belief that the hymn was written for Cyrene. This hymn is most famous for its sphragis (105–113), in which Apollo, in support of the poet, spurns Envy with his foot and announces his preference for pure drops of water carried from a spring, not the Assyrian river that carries garbage in its great stream. (See I. Petrovic and M. Fantuzzi.)

Hymn 3, "To Artemis" (268 lines), is a diffuse and complicated narrative that begins with the child Artemis asking her father, Zeus, for a number of gifts, including eternal virginity, her weapons of the hunt, the care of women in childbirth, and choruses of mountain nymphs. Zeus's amused response includes even more gifts, including cities under her protection and cult titles. The bulk of the poem is taken up with a catalogue of her many cult sites and titles.[5]

Hymn 4, "To Delos" (326 lines), recounts Leto's flight through the eastern Mediterranean as she searches for a place to give birth. The hostility of Hera prevents other islands from providing her shelter, but Delos, a wandering island, agrees. In the course of Leto's wandering, the unborn Apollo prophesies from his mother's womb that the

---

[4] He is also alluded to polemically in *Iambus* 1.
[5] See Bing and Uhrmeister 1994 and I. Petrovic 2007.

Macedonian Ptolemy (II) will be born on Cos, come to rule Egypt, and will defeat the Gauls (lines 162–95); the event referred to took place in 275 BC. After Apollo's birth Delos is fixed in the sea; song bursts forth, and the poem ends with a description of the mythological origins of the festival of the Delia.[6] The hymn has close affinities with Pindar's *Hymn* 1 and *Paean* 7b and Bacchylides 17.

Hymn 5, "To Athena" (142 lines), is also called *the Bath of Pallas* (*Loutra Pallados*) from its subject matter. The poem opens with the invisible narrator summoning the Argive women to an annual rite in which they process the Palladium to the sea in order to wash it. (The Palladium was the statue of Athena that Ajax took from its sanctuary when Troy was sacked; he brought it to Argos.) The central section of the poem contains a cautionary tale directed at Argive men, who are urged to avert their eyes from the sacred event. Callimachus tells of the blinding of Tiresias, who accidentally caught sight of Athena bathing in the woods (lines 55–130). This poem is the only one of the group in elegiacs; as in the next hymn, the dialect is Doric. (See P. Parsons.)

Hymn 6, "To Demeter" (138 lines), has notable affinities with the previous hymn (Hopkinson 1984a: 13–17). The poem also opens with an unseen narrator summoning the women for a rite, in this case for Demeter, which has elements of the Thesmophoria and the Mysteries. The participants' fasting is juxtaposed with the enclosed tale of Erysichthon, whose sacrilege in attempting to cut down a sacred grove of Demeter is punished with an all-consuming hunger (lines 25–115).

The Epigrams

Callimachus' epigrams were quite admired in antiquity, and according to Athenaeus (15.669c) they formed part of the school curriculum. They include erotic, sympotic, dedicatory, and funerary types, and a few express literary opinions. To judge from the practice of other epigrammatists, Callimachus probably organized his own epigrams into at least one poetry book; but if he did, it has not survived (Gutzwiller 1998: 183–190). The epigrams we have today were included in later Hellenistic and Byzantine collections and were subsequently reassembled from sources like the *Palatine Anthology* and the *Planudean Anthology*, or occasionally from ancient sources like Athenaeus.

---

[6] The poem has often been read metapoetically: see especially Bing 1988b.

A.S.F. Gow and D.L. Page's edition of 1965, *The Greek Anthology: Hellenistic Epigrams*, contains sixty-three epigrams and seven fragments attributed to Callimachus, with extensive commentary. (Their numbering of these epigrams is designated "GP.") Rudolf Pfeiffer (1949–53) also prints sixty-three, though not in the same order.

The Aetia

Callimachus' most influential work was the *Aetia* (*Origins* or *Causes*), an elegiac poem arranged in four books of approximately a thousand to fifteen hundred lines each, with both a prologue and an epilogue. It consisted of a series of interlocked accounts (*aitia*) that explained certain features of cult. Now only about a thousand lines survive, in more than two hundred separate papyrus fragments. (For the geographic range of the *Aetia*, see M. Asper; for its organization, constituent *aitia*, and themes, see G. Massimilla; for editorial reconstruction, see M.A. Harder.)

There are two recent editions of the *Aetia*:

Callimaco: Aitia, libri primo e secondo (Pisa, 1996) and *Aitia, libro terzo e quarto* (Pisa, 2010), Giulio Massimilla's Italian edition, with text, extensive commentary, and translation of the *Aetia*, is now complete in two volumes. Massimilla has renumbered the fragments, which are cited with the designation "M." or "Mass." (See his discussion in this volume.)

Callimachus, Aetia: Introduction, Text, Translation and Commentary (Oxford, forthcoming). Annette Harder's English edition of the *Aetia* has extensive introductory material, text, very detailed commentary, and translation. As much as possible, Harder has retained the earlier numeration of the *Aetia* fragments according to Pfeiffer (1949), adding a, b, or c where necessary, and the *Supplementum Hellenisticum* (Lloyd-Jones and Parsons 1983).

The Iambi

The *Iambi* was a metrically heterogeneous collection of short poems that insert themselves into the iambic tradition by, in the opening poem, bringing back the archaic iambicist Hipponax from Hades to attack the poet's critics, but with a milder style of invective. (Hipponax was known for the extreme vitriol of his personal attacks; Callimachus adopts a much softer, moralizing tone.) There were at least thirteen *Iambi*: the first and thirteenth form a clear ring composition—the first by introducing Hipponax chastising the critics as its frame, and the thirteenth by introducing critics who chastise Callimachus' imitation of Hipponax. Callimachus' targets range from literary critics (*Iambi* 1 and 13) to sexually irresponsible behaviors (3, 5, 9, 11); we find animal fables (2, 4), descriptions of statuary (6, 7, 9), a birthday poem (12), and an epinician (8). The meters include traditional choliambic (1–4, 13), epodic (5, choliambic and iambic dimeter; 6 and 7, iambic trimeter with ithyphallics), brachycatalectic iambic trimeter (11), and catalectic trochaic trimeter (12).

The poems have been reconstructed from papyrus fragments and from a later prose summary (the Milan *Diegeseis*) of Callimachus' poetry that gives the order of the individual stories within the *Aetia*, the *Iambi*, and other now fragmentary poems. (See M.R. Falivene.) The most extensive papyrus of the *Iambi*, POxy 7.1011, also contained parts of *Aetia* 3 and 4, followed by an epilogue. These precede *Iambi* 1–4, 12, and 13, though with many lacunae. The *Epilogue* to the *Aetia* states in its final line αὐτὰρ ἐγὼ Μουσέων πεζὸν [ἔ]πειμι νομόν (fr. 112.9 Pf.), "but now I am proceeding to the pedestrian pasture of the Muses"; this has been taken to mean that Callimachus, having completed the *Aetia*, now turned to writing the *Iambi*.[7] The fact that the title Ἴαμβοι heads this group of poems in the papyrus indicates that it was conceived as a unit, most likely arranged by the author himself.

For recent editions of the thirteen *Iambi* see:

Callimachus' Book of Iambi (Oxford, 1999). Arnd Kerkhecker's English edition of the *Iambi* follows Pfeiffer's numbering. It provides some new readings and extensive notes. All thirteen *Iambi* are treated, though the poems are not presented as continuous texts.

Polyeideia: The Iambi *of Callimachus and the Archaic Iambic Tradition* (Berkeley and Los Angeles, 2002). Benjamin Acosta-Hughes' English treatment of the *Iambi* presents the texts with facing translations and some textual notes, accompanied by interpretive essays. He discusses *Iambi* 1–7, 9, 12, and 13.

---

[7] A less likely alternative (once proposed by Wilamowitz) is that Callimachus is now turning from poetry to prose. P. Knox (1985a and 1993) suggested that fr. 112 was the epilogue to an original edition of *Aetia* 1 and 2, and that the last line of the fragment was one of literary intent, not a reference to an already accomplished work. For summaries of the scholarship on these positions, see Massimilla 2010: 519–520 and M.A. Harder, forthcoming *ad* fr. 112.9.

The Μέλη

Four poems immediately follow the *Iambi* in the *Diegeseis*, without an additional title. Therefore, some scholars consider that these poems also belong to the iambic collection. (The fact that these four were also occasional poems is not an impediment, since apparently *Iambi* 8 and 12 were as well.) Also part of the debate is whether Horace's collection of seventeen epodes resulted from his knowing a book of seventeen *Iambi*. Rudolf Pfeiffer treated these four poems separately in his great edition of Callimachus (1949–53), identifying them with the Μέλη ("Lyrics") that the *Suda* attributed to Callimachus (T 1 Pf.).[8]

Fragment 225 Pf. Ἡ Λῆμνος τὸ παλαιόν, εἴ τις ἄλλη was, according to the Milan *diegesis*, the first line of this poem, which "he speaks to beautiful boys." It was written in the phalaecian meter; its length is not known. The subject matter was the legend of the Lemnian women who had murdered their menfolk. No other lines survive, and the relationship of the boys to the Lemnian women is opaque, though in view of *Hymns* 5 and 6, the story may have been apotropaic.

Fragment 226 Pf. The *Pannychis* or "Night Revel" was, according to the ancient metrician Hephaestion, written in the fourteen-syllable "Euripidean" meter. It was a drinking song for the Dioscuri. Fragments of nine lines survive.[9]

Fragment 228 Pf. The *Apotheosis of Arsinoe* was written in archebouleans. Parts of seventy-five lines from this poem survive. Its subject matter was the death of Arsinoe II and her subsequent transport into the heavens by the Dioscuri. The poem opens with the poet asking Apollo to lead the singers; and the whole of Egypt is portrayed as mourning the dead queen. It was in part modeled on Andromache's lamentation for Hector.[10] (See É. Prioux.)

Fragment 229 Pf. The *Branchus* was written in catalectic choriambic pentameters. Only thirteen lines survive. Branchus was a young shepherd whom Apollo loved, and on whom he bestowed the gift of prophecy. Branchus is credited with founding the cult of Apollo at Didyma, near Miletus. In the fragment that we have he is described

---

[8] The proponents of a collection of thirteen *Iambi* include Acosta-Hughes 2002: 4–9 and 2003, and Kerkhecker 1999: 271–282; those who argue for seventeen include Alan Cameron 1995: 163–172 and Lelli 2005a. D'Alessio 2007 leaves the question open.

[9] The poem and its subject matter are treated extensively by Bravo 1997: 103–117.

[10] D'Alessio 2007: 665–666 and nn. 26, 29.

as transplanting a shoot from Apollo's laurel at Delphi in the new precinct at Didyma.

For these four poems, see Emanuele Lelli's recent reedition with translation and extensive commentary (in Italian), *Callimaco: Giambi XIV–XVII* (Rome, 2005).

The Hecale

The *Hecale* was a hexameter poem of around a thousand to twelve hundred lines, of which less than a third survives, in well over a hundred fragments. For this reason, to reconstruct it has proved even more challenging than Callimachus' other major poems. The *Hecale* relates the story of Theseus' defeat of the Marathonian bull. On his way to accomplish that task, Theseus takes shelter from the elements in the hut of an old woman named Hecale, who shares her meager provisions with the hero and relates her life story. The next day, when he returns with the bull in tow, he finds that she has died; as a result he establishes a shrine to Zeus Hecalius, an annual feast in her honor, and names the local deme after her. The poem exhibits very strong Homeric elements: its central theme of hospitality has numerous echoes of Odysseus and Eumaeus from the *Odyssey*, at the same time owing much to Attic tragedy (Ambühl 2004). There is also a long exchange between two birds who narrate the early history of Attica. Callimachus made extensive use of the Atthidographers for his local history of Attica in this poem. (See G. Benedetto.) The *Hecale* has long been claimed as an example of an epyllion or miniature epic, supposedly popularized in the Hellenistic period.[11]

Adrian Hollis' *Callimachus: Hecale* (2nd ed.: Oxford, 2009), with extensive introduction, text, and detailed commentary, is now the standard for this poem. Hollis' reordered and renumbered fragments of the *Hecale* are now cited with the designation "H."

Other Fragments

Other fragmentary poems that contribute to our understanding of Callimachus' poetic interests include:

Fragments 378 and 379 Pf. In what was apparently a hexameter treatment of the invasion of the Gauls the poet mentions Galatea, the

---

[11] The category has occasioned considerable controversy. For various views, see Ziegler 1966; Alan Cameron 1995: 437–453; Fantuzzi and Hunter 2004: 191–199; Hollis 2006.

Nereid whose coupling with the Cyclops Polyphemus produced their eponymous ancestor, Galates. Another fragment mentions Brennus, who led the Gauls' attack against Delphi in 279/8 BC. For the importance of the Gauls in Hellenistic poetry, see S. Barbantani (this volume and 2001).

Fragments 381 and 382 Pf. The *Ibis* was, according to the *Suda* (T 1 Pf.), a scurrilous attack (in either elegiacs or hexameters) on Apollonius of Rhodes, though few scholars accept that verdict today. It was imitated in elegiacs by Ovid, but nothing of the Greek original remains (Alan Cameron 1995: 225–228).

Fragment 384 Pf. Fragments from sixty lines survive of what was an elegiac epinician written for Sosibius (Fuhrer 1992: 139–204).

Fragment 388 Pf. This is the remnant of an elegiac poem that mentions Magas, king of Cyrene, and his daughter Berenice II. She later married Ptolemy III (Chiesa 2009).

Fragment 392 Pf. All that remains is the opening line from what appears to be a poem on the marriage of Arsinoe II.

Titles of Other Poems

The *Suda* (T 1 Pf.) attributes a number of other poems to Callimachus about which we have no further information: "The Arrival of Io," "Semele," "The Foundation of Argos," "Arcadia," "Glaucus," "Hopes," satyr plays, tragedies, comedies.

Callimachus in Alexandria

Callimachus was from the old Greek city of Cyrene, about 535 miles to the west of Alexandria. In these lines from a funerary epigram, ostensibly for his father, he claims to be related to the distinguished general of the same name, who is attested in other sources (Laronde 1987: 118, 129):

> Ὅστις ἐμὸν παρὰ σῆμα φέρεις πόδα, Καλλιμάχου με
> ἴσθι Κυρηναίου παῖδά τε καὶ γενέτην.
> εἰδείης δ' ἄμφω κεν· ὁ μέν κοτε πατρίδος ὅπλων
> ἦρξεν, ὁ δ' ἤεισεν κρέσσονα βασκανίης.

> Whoever walks by my tomb, know that I am the child and father of Callimachus the Cyrenean. You would know both. One once led the armies of his homeland; the other sang beyond the reach of envy.
>
> *Ep.* 21 Pf. = *APl.* 7.525

In the Cyrenean section of his *Hymn to Apollo* Callimachus refers to Cyrene as "my city" and to "our kings" (lines 65 and 68). Nonetheless, the bulk of his poetry seems to have been produced in Alexandria, or at least to have had a very strong Alexandrian focus. Those texts for which we have secure external support for a date belong in the reign of the second Ptolemy (Philadelphus, 283–246 BC) or early in the reign of the third (Euergetes, 246–221). These include the *Hymn to Delos* (lines 171–87), which alludes to the defeat of Gaulish mercenaries in 275 BC (see S. Barbantani); and the first line from a poem that seems to have been written for the marriage of Arsinoe II to her full brother, Ptolemy II (fr. 392 Pf.)—hence their title Sibling Gods (Θεοὶ Ἀδελφοί)—a marriage that occurred between 278 and 274 BC. Callimachus also wrote on Arsinoe II's death (fr. 228 Pf.), which occurred in 270 BC. Two other fragmentary poems that have been incorporated into the *Aetia* feature Berenice II, the daughter of Magas the king of Cyrene. (Magas was dead by 246 BC.) The *Victory of Berenice,* at the opening of *Aetia* Book 3, commemorates the queen's chariot victory at the Nemean Games in either 245 or 241 BC; the *Lock of Berenice,* at the end of *Aetia* Book 4, commemorates her marriage to Ptolemy III Euergetes in 246. (See É. Prioux.) Further information comes from Athenaeus (6.252c): namely that Callimachus recorded in his *Pinakes* that one Lysimachus wrote on the education of Attalus. However, the first Pergamene king so named took the throne only in 241; if Athenaeus' statement is accurate, then Callimachus must still have been writing in 240, and possibly even later.[12] He also wrote an elegiac epinician for Sosibius (frr. 384 and 384a Pf.). Consensus now identifies this Sosibius with the notorious advisor of Ptolemy IV, which if correct must mean that the poem could not have been written much before 240 and was possibly written as late as 230.[13] In light of these data, Callimachus' birth probably fell around 305, and his death sometime after 240.

One of the most distinctive features of the new city was its Library. Probably established under Ptolemy I with the assistance of Demetrius of Phalerum (Erskine 1995 and Bagnall 2002), it had an ambitious

---

[12] For a thorough canvass of the chronological possibilities, see Lehnus 1995.

[13] Another option is recorded by Athenaeus (4.144c), who claims that this elegy was for a Sosibius who wrote a tract on kingship for Cassander. Since Cassander died in 297 BC, a poem for this man would require a much earlier compositional date. But the number of athletic victories with which Callimachus credits Sosibius suggests a political rather more than a literary figure. See Asper 1997: 5; D'Alessio 2007: 680–681; Lehnus 1995: 12.

program of collecting books from throughout the Greek-speaking world. Although he was never its librarian,[14] Callimachus must have produced his taxonomic masterpiece, the *Pinakes*, by taking advantage of the wide range of Greek literature flowing into Alexandria. The *Pinakes* was a list of previous writers organized by genre; it included biographies and listed their works with incipits. (See N. Krevans.) Callimachus' extensive prose output (frr. 403–66 Pfeiffer) included tracts on the winds, barbarian customs, birds, nymphs, islands, and rivers, and at least one (Πρὸς Πραξιφάνην, fr. 460 Pf.) that seems to have been about the critique of poetry. (See A. Romano.)

Further details of Callimachus' life are uncertain. The *Suda* claims that he was a schoolmaster (γραμματικός) in the Alexandrian suburb of Eleusis (T 1 Pf.), but a Byzantine source (Tzetzes: T 4c Pf.) asserts that he was a νεανίσκος τῆς αὐλῆς ("a youth of the court"), a rank of sufficiently high status to seem unsuited to the position of a schoolmaster.[15] Alan Cameron argues persuasively that other members of his family were highly placed, including a number who were known to be Cyrenaic philosophers.[16] Another ancestor, Anniceris, according to Diogenes Laertius (3.20), ransomed Plato from the Syracusan tyrant Dionysius, a story that, however apocryphal, again suggests a Cyrenean family of some wealth and connections.

Why or when Callimachus moved from Cyrene to Alexandria is not known, and whether he lived primarily in one or the other city is equally unclear. Between 275 and 246 the two cities were technically at war. Probably this did not require all traffic between the two cities to cease entirely; more likely some exchange was allowed to continue at least sporadically, especially in the long period of the betrothal of Magas' daughter Berenice to Ptolemy II's son. But where Callimachus spent these years is not known, though his poem on the death of Arsinoe probably means that he was in Alexandria at least in 270. Very few data survive from Alexandria itself, but good documentary evidence from elsewhere in Egypt indicates that individuals from Cyrene and Cyrenaica formed a very large immigrant group in the early Ptolemaic

---

[14] POxy 10.1241, which provides a list of early heads of the Library, does not include Callimachus.
[15] Alan Cameron 1995: 3–5. He makes the point that there would have been no Greek schools in Egypt before Ptolemy I arrived, and therefore the term γραμματικός in the third century probably meant "scholar" (n. 16).
[16] 1995: 7–12, following A. Laronde and C. Meillier. See especially Alan Cameron's nn. 26 and 29 (pp. 7–8).

period, and there is no reason to assume a different pattern for Alexandria. Thus Callimachus' frequent references to Cyrene and Libya in his poetry are not necessarily indicative of his location: he may have been writing in and for Cyrene, or his references may have been intended to recall the homeland for the Cyrenaean community in Alexandria.

Callimachus' connection with Cyrene and Alexandria is not in doubt, but assertions that he traveled elsewhere are more problematic. However, an Athenian inscription listing contributors to a special levy to aid the state includes the name Callimachus, without further qualification. It has recently been redated to a period well within our poet's lifetime (around 247 BC), and therefore it may indicate both his presence in Athens, and, as the editor of the text argues, his distinction, since he is identified without any ethnic and is followed by "Lycon philoso[pher]" (Oliver 2002: 6). Whether or not we choose to believe that the Callimachus of the Athenian inscription is the poet, the find does illustrate the fluid state of Callimachus' biography as well as his poetry; every new discovery on papyrus or stone, of a new intertext,[17] or of a scholium in a medieval manuscript,[18] may require us to reassess our previously held ideas.

One of the most distinctive features of Callimachus' poetry is his interest in cult, which regularly manifests itself in descriptions of statues, rites, and temples. Alexandria is no exception, as he clearly took an interest in some of the earliest of the city's monuments. In the first *Iambus* he conjures up the long-dead Hipponax, who returns from the underworld to chastise quarrelsome critics in Alexandria, summoning them to a temple "outside the walls." (This is the earliest reference that we have to Alexandria's walls.)[19] According to the Milan *diegesis*, this temple was Parmenio's Serapeum. This was not the Great Temple of Serapis built under Ptolemy III, but an earlier shrine, the existence of which is independently attested by a papyrus letter of 253.[20] The Cape Zephyrium temple dedicated by Callicrates of Samos to Arsinoe-Aphrodite appears in the Nautilus Epigram (*Ep.* 5 Pf. = 14 GP) as well as in the elegiac *Lock of Berenice*. It was in that temple that the lock

---

[17] See B. Acosta-Hughes, in this volume, on the reading μαῖα δ' ἀνάσσης in the *Epilogue* to the *Aetia*.
[18] See Pontani 1999 on πολλάκ]ι in fr. 1 Pf.
[19] McKenzie 2007: 41 n. 38.
[20] *Dieg.* VI 3-4 (Pfeiffer 1949-53: 1.163) and PCairZen 59355. See Fraser 1972: 1.270-71.

was dedicated, thence to be translated into the heavens (fr. 110.56–57 Pf.). Callimachus related another catasterism, this time from the precinct of Arsinoe's mortuary temple. Again, from the Milan *diegesis* of the now fragmentary *Apotheosis of Arsinoe* we learn that Callimachus mentioned the altar and precinct of Arsinoe near the Emporium, from which the Dioscuri carried her up after her death.[21] This mortuary temple, later described by Pliny (*NH* 34.148), seems to have had a vaulted ceiling, somehow magnetized so that a statue of the dead queen could be seen to levitate (apparently attracted by the iron in her hair). A dedication "to the Canopic god" in *Epigram* 55 Pf. (= 16 GP) must refer to the temple that Ptolemy III and Berenice II dedicated to Serapis at Canopus.[22] Another epigram (*Ep.* 37 Pf. = 17 GP), describing a dedication to Serapis by a Cretan from Lyctus, most likely refers to the same Canopic shrine of Serapis, or perhaps to the Serapeum in Alexandria.

Callimachus did not write in a vacuum: Ptolemaic Alexandria was a fertile, thriving poetic environment, in part because imperial patronage strove to make it so; in part because the new city provided opportunities in so many different venues, not the least of which was the newly established Library. Callimachus' poetry reflects various elements of this new space. Demetrius of Phalerum, for example, apparently collected the fables of Aesop. It is unlikely to be coincidence that Callimachus uses Aesop in his own poetry. (See R. Scodel.) Callimachus locates Euhemerus in Alexandria in his first *Iambus* (fr. 191.10–11 Pf.: the old man scribbling his unrighteous books). Author of the *Sacred Register*, Euhemerus was famous (or notorious) for his claims that Zeus and other gods had first been mortals and subsequently came to be worshipped for their benefits to mankind.

Callimachus' most important poetic contemporaries included Theocritus of Syracuse, the inventor of the bucolic genre. Associated with Sicily and Cos, he was among the earliest Hellenistic poets, and his residence in Alexandria belongs, probably, between the 280s and the 270s. His *Encomium of Ptolemy II* (*Idyll* 17) and *Heracliscus* (*Idyll* 24) share numerous verbal and thematic parallels with Callimachus' *Hymn to Zeus* and *Hymn to Delos*.

---

[21] *Dieg.* X 11–13 (Pfeiffer 1949–53: 1.218).
[22] The temple was famous, and a fragment attributed to Apollonius' poem on Canopus (fr. 1 Powell) is thought to describe its columns.

Apollonius of Rhodes, whose surviving poem is the epic *Argonautica*, is also credited with foundation poetry. Thought to have been a native Alexandrian and a slightly younger contemporary of Callimachus, he followed Zenodotus as head of the Alexandrian Library. There are numerous intersections between the *Argonautica* and Callimachus' *Aetia*, not the least of which is the fact that the *aitia* of Callimachus' poem apparently begin with the Argonauts on Anaphe, the location of a long episode at the end of the *Argonautica*.[23]

Aratus of Soli (ca. 315–240 BC) wrote the *Phaenomena*, a didactic treatment of Eudoxus' astronomy that was subsequently of great influence in Latin poetry. He probably wrote in the court of Antigonus Gonatas of Macedon; whether he was ever in Alexandria is moot. Nonetheless, the proem to Zeus in the *Phaenomena* and Callimachus' *Hymn to Zeus* are interconnected, even if priority cannot be established (Cuypers 2004: 100).

Epigrammatists from a variety of locations also achieved prominence during this period. Their epigrams, often imitating earlier stone inscriptions, were beginning to be collected into books of verse.[24] The most important of these writers were Asclepiades of Samos and Posidippus of Pella. A roll of more than a hundred epigrams of Posidippus, datable to the late third century BC, was published as recently as 2001.[25] A surprising feature of this new collection was its emphasis on the Ptolemies, especially their queens. The epigrams of Posidippus too share many features in common with Callimachus' *Aetia*.[26]

The exact chronology of all of these poets will continue to be disputed, not least because they clearly wrote in response to each other's texts; and even when allusive priority may seem clear, we know so little about strategies of informal poetic exchange or what may have constituted formal publication that any assertions need to be made with extreme caution. Their obviously shared subjects testify to a rich and very interactive poetic environment and the growing importance of the text as a viable poetic and ideological medium.

---

[23] See M.A. Harder in this volume and 2002a: 217–223.
[24] For Hellenistic epigram, see Gutzwiller 1998 and Bing and Bruss 2007.
[25] For essays on the epigram collection, see Gutzwiller 2005.
[26] See Fantuzzi 2005. Posidippus was identified as one of the Telchines in the Scholia Florentina on the *Prologue* to the *Aetia*. See Alan Cameron 1995: 185–232, and Stephens 2005.

The Organization of This Companion

The lacunose and evolving status of many of Callimachus' poems presented an unusual challenge to us as editors of this *Companion* and accounts in part for why a handbook on this author, despite his importance, makes an appearance so much later than those devoted to his contemporaries. The circumstances of his survival have dictated many of the individual solicitations for this volume. Approximately a third of the chapters are devoted to explaining how our present corpus of Callimachus has come about and what the guiding assumptions have been in collecting book fragments or editing papyrus fragments. The contributors provide information on Callimachus' linguistic experiments, his use of nonpoetic sources, and the relationship of his prose writings to his poetic corpus. We have also emphasized the importance of his contemporary social context. Since so much of his surviving poetry is about and for the Ptolemies, we have included contributions that focus on these kings and queens; but equally important are his divinities, his interest in cult, and contemporary literary-critical and musical trends. The contributors also discuss a number of the characteristic features of his poetics. Among ancient poets Callimachus probably uses the widest range of sources, borrowing from traditions of archaic and classical poetry, as well as from prose; he experiments with a large number of voices, from the narrating ego to speaking poets of the past, to mythological subjects, divinities, historical figures, trees, birds, and even objects like Berenice's lock of hair, which is the main character in the final elegy of the *Aetia*.

In the selection of topics, we have made a conscious effort to avoid, insofar as is feasible, merely repeating or summarizing material that is easily accessible in recent scholarship, where it has necessarily been set out with deeper and more nuanced arguments. For this reason we do not include chapters on Callimachus' relationship to individual Greek precursors like Homer or Hesiod or Pindar; we do not have chapters devoted to particular genres like hymns or *iambi*, though discussions of individual poems and the generic assumptions that inform them may be found throughout as appropriate for specific topics.[27] We have

---

[27] For the *Hymns*, see especially the contributions of M. Fantuzzi, R. Hunter, and C. Cusset; for the *Iambi*, see especially those of L. Lelli, M. Payne, and R. Scodel.

avoided repeating the work of recent scholars on Callimachus and his poetic contemporaries, and we have no chapters devoted to such questions as performance versus text, intertextuality, or audience,[28] or the poet's relationship to non-Greek Egypt[29]—though, again, discussion of such topics is interwoven into many of the chapters. We have given considerable thought to shaping this *Companion* to capture recent developments in Callimachean scholarship, especially the growing trend toward reading his poetry within its political, social, and art-historical contexts, and to take account of recent publications of new commentaries on the *Aetia,* the *Hecale,* and the *Iambi.* We have included conflicting interpretive positions, since there can be no one, canonical approach to this most Protean of authors.

The chapters have been grouped into sections of the book as follows. "The Material Author" begins with a history of papyrological discovery (L. Lehnus); this section continues with a summary of the papyri that represent Callimachus' most extensive work, the *Aetia,* and a reconstruction of its narrative (G. Massimilla). Thereafter A. Harder discusses the editorial processes (and possible pitfalls) of working with Callimachus' papyrus fragments, and M.R. Falivene narrates the discovery and the nature of the Milan *Diegeseis,* a prose summary of Callimachus' poems that has considerably clarified our understanding of the order and content of the individual tales within the *Aetia* as well as other fragmentary poems. Prior to the recovery of so many of Callimachus' texts on papyri in the nineteenth and twentieth centuries, much of his poetic work, and all his prose, was known primarily through citation: F. Pontani focuses on the process and habits of mind that result in citation and how it contributes to our modern text; N. Krevans discusses Callimachus' rich and varied prose oeuvre, which is now almost entirely lost. In a period that distinguished elevated and spoken language, P. Parsons' chapter centers on the poet's engagement with the evolving *koine,* or popular Greek, the dialect now most widely associated with the Hellenistic period.

The next section, "Social Context," surveys selected aspects of Callimachus' work in terms of Ptolemaic geopoetics, the Alexandrian court, and religious cult. Beginning from M. Asper's consideration of the

---

[28] See, e.g., Alan Cameron 1995; Bing 1988b and 2009; Asper 1997; Fantuzzi and Hunter 2004; and the chapters in M.A. Harder, Regtuit, and Wakker 1993 and 2004.

[29] See most recently Selden 1998 and Stephens 2002b and 2003.

Ptolemaic empire as it is reflected in Callimachus' poetry, the discussion turns to figures of power in Callimachus: kings (S. Barbantani), queens (É. Prioux), and courtiers and court society (G. Weber). R. Hunter looks at the gods that we find in Callimachus, and I. Petrovic considers inscriptional evidence to assess the cult practices described in the *Hymn to Apollo*.

The contributions in the following section, "Sources and Models," turn to Callimachus' intellectual environment. L. Prauscello considers Callimachus from the perspective of the hugely popular New Music of the later fifth and early fourth centuries; A. Romano, in light of the development of contemporary literary criticism. A. Morrison looks at Callimachus' debt to earlier epic and lyric poets through the lens of the Muses, contrasting previous claims for poetic authority with Callimachus' reappropriation of these traditional figures. G. Benedetto analyzes Callimachus' use of the Athenian prose chroniclers (known as Atthidographers), particularly in the *Hecale*. R. Scodel (on fable) and E. Lelli (on popular sayings) examine Callimachus' deployment of folkloric and vulgate features of language and culture within more elevated poetic settings.

Callimachus is a master at speaking in a variety of poetic voices, as the chapters in our next section illustrate, "Personae". In her analysis of Callimachus and the Italian poet Giovanni Pascoli, A.T. Cozzoli foregrounds Callimachus' manipulation of the imagery and imagination of childhood. M. Fantuzzi illustrates how Callimachus constructs his self-consciously authoritative persona, particularly in the hymns; C. Cusset elucidates how Callimachus makes the voices of earlier poets audible through his own. Y. Durbec turns his attention to the astonishing variety of characters—mythological, historical, and contemporary—who inhabit these poems. In his turn, M. Payne also considers Callimachus' poetics of childhood, with particular emphasis on the *Iambi* and the influence of tragedy and tragic models.

The chapters comprised in "Afterlife," the volume's final section, engage with Roman, Greek, and modern aspects of Callimachean reception. A. Barchiesi discusses the presence of Callimachus as a distinct feature of Roman poetry. C. de Stefani and E. Magnelli present a detailed and compelling case for the extensive influence of Callimachus in later Greek poetry. In his study of G. Pasquali's often cited (if not read) *Arte allusiva*, M. Citroni follows the development of the term and the concept of allusion that lies behind it, ideas that still underpin scholarly views of Callimacheanism.

Finally, in his "Epilogue," B. Acosta-Hughes sketches out a number of features of Callimachus' style that dovetail with modern poetic sensibilities, particularly in comparison with a much later Alexandrian poet, C.P. Cavafy.

Collected Editions of Callimachus

Because the assembly of Callimachus' fragmentary texts is a continuing process, and therefore the numerical designations for the fragments are increasingly complex, we have appended a brief list of the most recent modern sources and editions, with an explanation of their contents where necessary.

Callimachus (Oxford, 1949–53). This two-volume edition (in Latin) by Rudolf Pfeiffer remains the standard. It contains testimonia, all the fragments (of both prose and poetry), the hymns, and the epigrams. It is conventional to cite Callimachus' fragments by Pfeiffer's numbering (designated "Pf.").

Supplementum Hellenisticum (Berlin, 1983). Edited by H. Lloyd-Jones and P.J. Parsons (in Latin), this volume contains fragments of Callimachus that were discovered after Pfeiffer's edition was published, including the papyrus text of the *Victory of Berenice*; it also includes a revised text of fragment 260 Pf. Fragments from this collection are regularly identified with the designation *SH*.

Supplementum Supplementi Hellenistici (Berlin, 2005). Edited by H. Lloyd-Jones (in Latin), as the title states, this publication supplements the previous collection of fragments of Hellenistic poets. It contains a few new fragments of Callimachus that came to light after the *Supplementum Hellenisticum* was published; it is regularly identified with the designation *SSH*.

Callimaco (4th ed.: Milan, 2007). Giovan Battista D'Alessio's two-volume Italian edition of Callimachus contains an extensive introduction, brief but very helpful notes, and translation. It is currently the most up-to-date collection of Callimachus' complete works. D'Alessio follows the numbering in Pfeiffer and *Supplementum Hellenisticum* where possible.

Kallimachos, Werke: Griechisch und Deutsch (Darmstadt, 2004). Markus Asper's German edition has an extensive introduction to and text of the complete works, including prose fragments, with facing translation and brief notes. He renumbers the fragments (though he also attaches Pf. and *SH* numbers).

Callimaque: Fragments poétiques (Paris, 2006). Yannick Durbec's French edition, with a brief introduction, text, facing translation, and brief notes, contains the *Aetia, Iambi, Hecale,* and the larger hexameter and elegiac fragments, as well as the unplaced poetic fragments. He renumbers the fragments (though he also attaches Pf. and *SH* numbers).

Editors' Note

Benjamin Acosta-Hughes is responsible for translating Cusset, Durbec, and Prioux from the original French; James Kierstead (Stanford University) is responsible for translating Weber from German and Cozzoli from Italian; and Susan Stephens, for translating Lelli from Italian. We would like to acknowledge the work of Paul Psoinos in preparing the bibliography and copy-editing, and Mark Wright (Ohio State University) for checking of references. Donald Mastronarde came to our aid at a crucial moment in the final stages of editing, and we would like to acknowledge, as always, his kind generosity. Finally, we are most grateful to our editors at Brill Press for their help and support.

PART ONE

THE MATERIAL AUTHOR

CHAPTER ONE

CALLIMACHUS REDISCOVERED IN PAPYRI

Luigi Lehnus

ABSTRACT

This chapter discusses the reemergence of Callimachus' remains from the time of Henri Estienne (Stephanus) to the end of twentieth century. From Stephanus to Thomas Stanley to Vulcanius and Anna Fabri fragments were gathered very slowly. However, Bentley's Utrecht edition of 1697 provided a dramatic increment both in quality and in quantity. After that, the scholar who most contributed to the assemblage of Callimachus fragments was L.C. Valckenaer, whose *Callimachi elegiarum fragmenta* were published in 1799. Otto Schneider's edition of 1873 was only partially successful, but by that date Alphons Hecker at Groningen had made substantial advances by discovering a number of new fragments from the *Hecale*, formulating the law that still carries his name, and by suggesting that a polemic prologue should open the *Aetia*. Papyri have allowed twentieth century scholars from Wilamowitz to Pfeiffer and beyond to reconstruct full sections of *Aetia*, *Iambi*, and the *Hecale*. The chapter ends with an up-to-date list of papyri containing fragments of Callimachus' lost works.

Henricus Stephanus was the first to attempt a collection of Callimachus' fragments. His 1577 edition of Callimachus, ostensibly complete for its time, contained no more than a dozen scattered pieces, but this was soon increased to eighty-four by Bonaventura Vulcanius (Antwerp and Leiden, 1584), thanks chiefly to the admission of entries (fifty-seven of them) from the *Etymologicum magnum*. This number was considerably augmented by the end of the seventeenth century by Anna Fabri (Mme. Dacier, 1675) and by Sir Thomas Stanley (Stanleius).[1] Single-handedly, Richard Bentley nearly finished the work by bringing the total up to 417 fragments (1697),[2] which he had gathered from the widest range of sources—mostly grammarians, lexicographers, and

---

[1] Stanley's collection survives in several manuscripts.
[2] Note that Dirk Canter had already collected 837 fragments of Euripides by 1571; cf. Collard and Cropp 2008: xxiii–xxiv.

scholia.³ Bentley's collection was further supplemented by J.A. Ernesti's Καλλίμαχος ὅλος (1761: frr. 418 to 463),⁴ while further new fragments were added by both C.J. Blomfield (1815) and Otto Schneider (1873). The latter rejected Blomfield's *Spicilegium fragmentorum*,⁵ and started a new series from fragment 464 to fragment 573, to which he added 393 "fragmenta anonyma," only 266 of which were to be subsequently accepted by Rudolf Pfeiffer.⁶

The numbering and disposition of the fragments proceeded rather randomly after Bentley. Schneider—whose edition Wilamowitz styled a μέγα κακόν⁷—tried to introduce order while retaining Bentley's numeration, but to do so he resorted to a score of transpositions, suppressions, additions, and cross-references, which resulted in a rather artificial layout and produced a book that was unwieldy. Schneider's own theory concerning the structure of the *Aetia*—namely that according to an alleged testimony of Hyginus the contents were grouped as "agones" (Book 1), "urbium conditores" (Book 2), "inventores" (Book 3) and "sacrorum publicorum causae" (Book 4)⁸—has long been disproved; to say the least, it heavily underestimated Callimachus' striving for variety. Bentley's contention, accepted by Valckenaer (1799: 1–32), that Callimachus' *Elegies* and his work entitled *Aetia* were two separate entities had already been disproved. But the eighteenth century was also the age when, in the wake of Bentley and thanks to the doctrine

---

[3] He was falsely accused of having pillaged Stanley's unpublished work in a scurrilous pamphlet called *A Short Account of Dr. Bentley's Humanity and Justice to Those Authors Who Have Written before Him: With an Honest Vindication of Tho. Stanley, Esquire, and His Notes on Callimachus* (London, 1699). The anonymous accuser has now been identified as Abednego Seller (1646?–1705), a nonjuror (i.e., Jacobite) divine of the Church of England, embittered against bishop E. Stillingfleet and his protégé Bentley in the aftermath of the Glorious Revolution; cf. Lehnus 1991b.

[4] Ernesti, himself not a first-rate scholar, owed much, as he allowed, to the Dutch (of German origin) David Ruhnkenius, who had checked manuscripts of the Greek *Etymologicum* in Paris. Things proved more difficult with the less easily appeased L.C. Valckenaer—otherwise the only contemporary who, if properly asked, would have been able to contribute a flood of new material from lexicographers and grammarians.

[5] Fragments 464 to 507: "pauca tantum nominavit certa incertis miscens Blomfieldus" (Schneider 1870–73: 626).

[6] A few of those remaining have ended up among the *Frustula adespota ex auctoribus* in Lloyd-Jones and Parsons 1983.

[7] Manuscript jotting by Wilamowitz on the frontispiece of his *Handexemplar* of O. Schneider 1873 (now in the Institut für Klassische Philologie, Humboldt University Library, Berlin). "Illius editionis vitia manifestiora sunt virtutibus" (Pfeiffer 1949–53: 2.xlvii). I was able to inspect the Berlin Wilamowitz-Handbibliothek in spring 2000 thanks to the kindness of Prof. Wolfgang Rösler and Prof. Thomas Poiss.

[8] Cf. Hyg. *Fab.* 273–277, and see already Rauch 1860.

of the great *Batavi* (Tib. Hemsterhuis, Ruhnkenius, Valckenaer), fragmentology established itself as a scientific discipline (suffice it to evoke L.C. Valckenaer's masterpiece, the *Diatribe in Euripidis perditorum dramatum reliquias* of 1767), and people at last began to make extensive use of the wealth of information streaming out of the late-antique and Byzantine grammarians. (Valckenaer again deserves mention for his epoch-making 1739 editon of the synonymic lexicon of Pseudo-Ammonius.)

Considerable progress with single sections of the lost Callimachus (*Hecale*, the *Prologue* to the *Aetia*, and the *Dream, Linus and Coroebus,* and *Acontius and Cydippe*) resulted from the activity of scholars like A. Hecker, A.F. Naeke, and Karl Dilthey during the mid-nineteenth century. A.F. Naeke, a pupil of Gottfried Hermann and a professor in Bonn, worked chiefly on the *Hecale* (Naeke 1842–45), and we owe to him some felicitious joinings of fragments and many sensible observations on style and meter.[9] Karl Dilthey in his turn (also coming from the Bonn school) was the first to attempt to reconstruct a single complete elegy[10]—his acclaimed commentary on *Acontius and Cydippe* gave what was to become the canonical definition of Alexandrian poetry but failed to notice that the foundation on which to build was not the Roman Alexandrian Ovid, with his *Heroidum epistulae* 20 and 21, but the late Greek rhetorician Aristaenetus (Dilthey 1863).

A true genius, the ill-fated Alphons Hecker, from Groningen, was the man who did the most for Callimachus' fragments in the period between Bentley and the age of papyri. (Incidentally, both Hecker and Dilthey arrived at the idea of producing a new collection.) Hecker not only saw that what he described as a "prologus galeatus" ("polemical prologue") should definitely feature in Callimachus' poems; he realized that such a prologue opened not the *Hecale*, as had been previously surmised by Naeke, but the *Aetia*, as we now know from POxy 17.2079. Indeed, in his doctoral dissertation, Hecker also formulated the law that now bears his name, "regula Heckeriana" (Hecker 1842: 133):

> Nam illud urgemus nullum in Suidae lexico legi versum heroicum alibi non inventum, qui non in Hecale olim affuerit, adeo ut non nisi gravissimis argumentis aliis poëtis aliisve carminibus vindicari possint, i.e. si de iis certiores nos fecerit disertum veteris scriptoris testimonium. Talibus

---

[9] Otherwise he erred in following Plutarch's *Life of Theseus* as a frame for reconstructing the whole poem.
[10] After Philipp Buttmann, in fact.

autem indiciis, si adhuc inedita in lucem proferantur, vel jam e tenebris eruta nos latuerint, vix dubitamus nostras conjecturas firmatum iri.

I insist on affirming that in the *Suda* lexicon no hexameter, found only there and not elsewhere, occurs that cannot be derived from the *Hecale*. It follows that these hexameters can be attributed to other authors or works only on the basis of substantial proof: that is, only if a different attribution is explicity provided to us in the testimony of an ancient author. I am certain that my conjectures will be confirmed by this rule if passages as yet unedited come to light in the future, or any that escaped my notice although already uncovered from obscurity.

Alphons Hecker believed that the *Suda* was drawing directly from a surviving exemplar of Callimachus' *Hecale*; it was R. Reitzenstein who subsequently pointed out that the Byzantine lexicon derived its wealth of information not from the poem but from a commentary on the *Hecale* written (probably in the fourth century AD) by the grammarian Salustios, very possibly the same man who was responsible for the commentary on Sophocles (cf. Reitzenstein 1890–91: 13–17.) In fact, Hecker's *trouvaille* has yielded up to two hundred quotations coming with varying degrees of certainty from the epic poem of Callimachus; and—as an impressive countercheck—no passages attributed to the *Hecale* under Hecker's rule have so far needed to be reassigned to the *Aetia*.

By the end of the nineteenth century Reitzenstein's discovery of the *Etymologicum genuinum* A (cod. Vatic. gr. 1818) presented us with the last large source of Callimachean fragments from indirect tradition (even if no complete critical editon of the *Etymologicum* is yet available).[11] World War I had just broken out when Ida Kapp, a pupil of Wilamowitz, in her Berlin dissertation "Callimachi *Hecalae* fragmenta" performed the last service of the pre-Pfeiffer era in the rescue of lost Callimachus (Kapp 1915).

Papyri

Since the end of the nineteenth century our knowledge of Callimachus has been radically changed by the discovery of papyri.[12] (The first

---

[11] Cf. Reitzenstein 1897.
[12] On the finds of Callimachus papyri, see Casanova 2006. I am much obliged to Dr. Valentina Millozzi for showing me her unpublished dissertation, Urbino, 2000/2001; thanks are also due to Prof. M. Rosaria Falivene, who fostered that invaluable piece of work.

ancient witness to the text of Callimachus to be discovered, however, was not a papyrus at all but a wooden tablet, the so-called Tabula Vindobonensis, published by Theodor Gomperz in Vienna in 1893.)[13] As of June 2008, I counted sixty to sixty-three papyri,[14] preserving parts of the *Aetia*, *Iambi* (+ '*Lyrics*'), *Hecale*, and other poems of Callimachus as yet unidentified. A first group appeared on the eve of the Great War (the most important of which was POxy 7.1011, published in 1910 by A.S. Hunt) and had as an immediate consequence the definitive rejection of the already mistrusted Schneider. A new edition was badly needed, and that was happily entrusted to Rudolf Pfeiffer, an adoptive pupil of Diels and Wilamowitz and a student of Otto Crusius in Munich; it was an epochal choice. Pfeiffer wrote (1921: praefatio):

> Ottone Crusio praeceptore, quem morte repentina et praematura nobis ereptum esse cum multis maxime maereo, assentiente et cohortante hanc editionem parare coepi, cum gravi vulnere affectus e bello infelicissimo redieram: quantum illius viri humanissimi disciplinae et benevolentiae debeam, hoc loco dicere non possum. Grato animo nominandus est in primis Hermannus Diels, qui schedas suas, quibus iamborum multa supplementa commendaverat, liberalissime mihi per litteras transmisit, deinde gratias ago quam maximas Eduardo Schwartz, Udalrico de Wilamowitz, Paulo Maas, qui operam meam multis adiuverunt consiliis.

> I began to prepare this edition with the consent and at the urging of my teacher Otto Crusius (whom I among many others lament as having been taken from us by an unforseen and premature death) when, upon suffering a grave wound, I returned a veteran of that most unfortunate war. I cannot explain how great is my debt to the teaching and kindness of that most humanistic gentleman. Among the first to whom I owe a debt of gratitude is Hermann Diels, who with great generosity transmitted to me by letter the files to which he had entrusted many conjectures in the *Iambi*. And I here render my greatest thanks to Eduard Schwartz, to Ulrich von Wilamowitz, and to Paul Maas, who aided my work with much advice.

---

[13] PRain VI; cf. Gomperz 1893: 3–12. The Tabula was found near Arsinoe in the winter of 1877–78.

[14] Variables include POxy 37.2823, which possibly comes from the *Hecale*; PBerol. inv. 13417, which may belong with POxy 18.2168 (together with PBerol inv. 11629 and PSI 133); and POxy 18. 2171, which may belong with 18.2172. Three more papyri may be related to the lost Callimachus: for POxy 27.2463 (anonymous commentary [on *The Victory of Berenice?*]), see Livrea 1989b and *SSH* 257–258; for POxy 39.2886 (anonymous commentary [on the *Hecale?*]), see *SSH* 948–949 (but cf. also Meliadò 2004); for PMich inv. 3499 (Doric archebuleans on Heracles and Laomedon?), Lloyd-Jones 1974 and *SH* 992.

Pfeiffer's first collection of post-Schneider material appeared in Bonn as an issue of the Kleine Texte series. Besides a few *fragmenta nova minora* chiefly from the *Etymologicum* and from the scholia to Lycophron, the book's most important items were the Tabula Vindobonensis, the great Oxyrhynchus codex 7.1011 containing *Acontius and Cydippe* (fr. 75 Pf.), the *Epilogue* to the *Aetia* (fr. 112), and *Iambi* 1–4, 12, and 13, then POxy 9.1362 (*Icos*, frr. 178–83, possibly from the beginning of *Aetia* 2) and the Berlin and Florence codices,[15] with *Aetia* I and III, 'Lyrics', and the *Hecale*.[16] A reprint including POxy 15.1793 (containing what possibly is *The Wedding of Berenice* and *The Victory of Sosibius*) soon followed (in 1923), under the somewhat misleading subtitle *Editio maior*.[17]

Rudolf Pfeiffer was to work on the fragments of Callimachus for the next three decades, through vicissitudes both general and personal—he was forced to leave Hitler's Germany because his wife was Jewish, and found a refuge in Oxford—achieving with his two-volume epoch-making edition (1949–53) an extremely reliable text of the fragments, the *Hymns*, and the *Epigrams*, and what immediately proved to be and definitely will remain a major milestone in the history of the rediscovery of Callimachus.

Meanwhile volumes 17–20 of the collected Oxyrhynchus Papyri had appeared, full of substantial new texts. Suffice it to mention POxy 17.2079, named *Aetia Prologue* by Hunt (1927; it was in fact Naeke's and Hecker's long-awaited "prologus galeatus"),[18] and the late-antique codex POxy 20.2258, published by Lobel and containing *The Lock of Berenice* and *The Victory of Sosibius* with related scholia,[19] along with important accessions from the Società Italiana in Florence, thanks to the joint efforts of Girolamo Vitelli and Medea Norsa (*Aetia* with *The Lock of Berenice*, *Iambi*, and *Diegeseis*). In Oxford Pfeiffer enjoyed the full cooperation of Edgar Lobel and his own fellow refugee Paul Maas, also a pupil of Wilamowitz (Pfeiffer 1949–53: 1.ix):

> [P]apyrorum Oxyrhynchiarum...apographa sua benignissime transmiserat Edgarus Lobel et ad papyros examinandas me semper admitte-

---

[15] Florence codex now also at Oxford; see no. 9 in the list below.
[16] One cannot exclude the possibility that the order was *Hecale, Aetia, 'Lyrics'*; see "Outlook," below.
[17] Apparently Pfeiffer had no intimation that he was to prepare an *editio maxima*.
[18] Hunt 1927: 45–57; cf. Benedetto 1993: 27–91.
[19] Cf. Lobel, Wegener, and Roberts 1952: 69–107.

bat; quaerenti mihi quamvis molesto nunquam deerat per multos annos vir oculatus, vigilans, integer, sermonis poetarum Graecorum unice peritus, quem ne plagulas quidem perlegere piguit. Ex eorum numero qui me abhinc plus viginti quinque annos in editione parva priore consiliis adiuverant, unus superstes est Paulus Maas—unus instar milium. Officii enim duxit curare, ut carmina elegantiarum plena quantum fieri posset perpolita ederentur; in quo labore vir, artem criticam pulchre callens, non minus ferventi ingenio quam sano iudicio ab operis initio usque ad ultimas schedas corrigendas perseveravit.

Edgar Lobel most generously provided me with his transcriptions...of Oxyrhynchus papyri and always allowed me to inspect them directly; a man of unfailing eye, vigilant, honest, with a unique knowledge of Greek poetic lanaguage, who was even willing to read my proofs to the end, he never shrank from my demands, however annoying these may have been. Among those who more than a quarter-century ago helped me in the preparation of the editio minor with their advice, Paul Maas alone remains—one equal to a thousand. He considered it in fact his duty to bring it about that poetry full of elegance be published in the most perfect way possible, and in this undertaking that great expert of textual criticism persevered from the beginning to the corrections of the final proofs with avid expertise no less than sound judgment.

A constant though slowly decreasing influx of papyri has characterized the time that has passed since 1949, with substantial contributions to the *Hecale* (cf. POxy 23.2376 and 2377), and with a single discovery of great weight that allowed Peter Parsons to reconstruct the epinician overture of *Aetia* 3, named by him *The Victory of Berenice*. (Cf. Parsons 1977.) All the Callimachus papyri not containing any of the *Hymns* come from the triad *Aetia, Iambi* (including the so-called Μέλη, frr. 226–29),[20] and *Hecale*, with the exception of a few courtly pieces like the elegy *The Victory of Sosibius* (frr. 384 and 384a) and the (possible) epithalamium of Berenice II (cf. Hollis 1992b), whereas none of the ghost titles given to Callimachus in the *Suda* is represented. (Nor, for that matter, have any papyri been found of the grammatical works, like the Μουσεῖον and the 120–book Πίνακες.)[21]

If that is roughly the external history of the papyrological recovery of Callimachus, the following synopsis of all the papyri containing remains from the poet's lost works may be of use. The items listed below include essential data and are listed according to their first

---

[20] On the issue of the pertinence of the Μέλη to the *Iambi*, see Alan Cameron 1995: 163–173.

[21] *Suda* κ 227 Adler.

occurrence within the general frame of Pfeiffer's (1949–53) volume 1 and Lloyd-Jones and Parsons 1983.[22]

1. 15 Pf., 195<.1> MP³, I.11 M., 496<.1> LDAB (first half of II)
   POxy 17.2079 [Hunt] and 2167 [Lobel] + PSI 11.1217A [Norsa & Vitelli *bis*]: *Aetia* 1 and (?) 3
2. 24 Pf., 196 MP³, I.18 M., 498 LDAB [Norsa & Vitelli *bis*; Bastianini][23] (II or beginning of III)
   PSI 11.1219: *Diegeseis* of *Aetia* 1
3. 5 Pf., 197 MP³, I.2 M., 462 LDAB [(Milne, in fact) Bell][24] (I)
   PLitLond 181: scholia on *Prologue* and *Dream* (*Aetia* 1)
4. 20 Pf., 197.1 MP³, I.17 M., 486 LDAB [Lobel] (second half of II)
   POxy 20.2262: commentary on *Aetia* 1
5. 29 Pf., 198 MP³, I.21 M., 505 LDAB [Lobel] (III)
   POxy 19.2208: *Aetia* 1 and (?) 3
6. 198.1 MP³, I.26 M., 521 LDAB [Müller; Gronewald] (cod. V/VI)
   PBerol inv. 17057: *Aetia* 1
7. 16 Pf., 195<.2> MP³, I.12 M., 496<.2> LDAB [Norsa & Vitelli *bis*] (II)
   PSI 11.1217B: *Aetia* 1
8. 17 Pf., 200 MP³, I.13 M., 473 LDAB [Wilamowitz] (II)
   PBerol inv. 11521: commentary on *Aetia* 1
9. 32 Pf., 5 Hollis, 201 MP³, I.22 M., 518 LDAB, II.12 M. (cod. second half of IV)
   POxy 18.2168 [Lobel] + PBerol inv. 11629 [Wilamowitz] (?)+ PBerol inv. 13417 [Wilamowitz] + PSI 2.133 [Vitelli]: *Aetia* 1 and 3, Μέλη,[25] *Hecale*
10. 201.1 MP³, I.14 M., 4763 LDAB [Henrichs] (II)
    PMich inv. 3688r: commentary on *Aetia* 1

---

[22] Entries are organized in two sections: first, numberings of papyri from Pfeiffer 1949–53 (Pf.) to Hollis 1990 (2nd edition, 2009) and Massimilla (M.) volume I (1996) or II (2010), and in Mertens and Pack, third edition (MP³), and Leuven Database of Ancient Books (LDAB), followed by chronology (in parentheses), where Roman numerals indicate century (all dates are centuries AD unless otherwise indicated); second, name of collection, item number, and first editor or editors (in square brackets); summary indication of content.

[23] Papyrus revised and reedited by Bastianini 2006.

[24] Cf. Lehnus 2006b.

[25] That PBerol inv. 13417 belongs here is not assured; cf. Pfeiffer 1949–53: 2.xxi.

11. 9 Pf., 202 MP³, I.5 M., 485 LDAB [Lobel] (beginning of II)
    POxy 19.2209: *Aetia* 1+[26]
12. [to be published by Schwendner][27] (II)
    PMich (Cairo) inv. 5475: *Aetia* 1
13. 26 Pf., 205 MP³, I.19 M., 501 LDAB [Lobel] (II/III)
    POxy 20.2263: *Diegeseis* of *Aetia* 1
14. 13 Pf., 203 MP³, I.6 M., 476 LDAB [Hunt] (beginning of II)
    PRyl 13: *Aetia* 1
15. 14 Pf., 205.1 MP³, I.7 M., 484 LDAB [Lobel] (beginning of II)
    POxy 20.2261: *Aetia* 1
16. 18 Pf., 206 MP³, I.15 M., 487 LDAB [Hunt] (II)
    POxy 17.2080: *Aetia* 2
17. 10 Pf., 207 MP³, I.8 M., 488 LDAB [Lobel] (beginning of II)
    POxy 19.2210: *Aetia* 2+
18. 207.1 MP³, I.3 M., 472 LDAB [Meillier] (I)
    PSorb inv. 2248: *Aetia* 2
19. 205.2 MP³, I.24 M., 508 LDAB [Barns] (cod. III/IV)
    PAnt 113: *Aetia* 1 or 2
20. 23 Pf., 207.2 + 207.21 MP³, 495 LDAB, II.9 M. (end of II or beginning of III)
    POxy 18.2173 [Lobel] + PSI 15.1500 (= inv. 1923 [Ozbek] + inv. 2002) [Bastianini]: *Aetia* 3
21. 207.3 MP³, 527 LDAB, II.1 M. [Meillier; Parsons] (end of III BC [after 221] or II BC)
    PLille inv. 76d, 78a–c, 79, 82, 84: *Aetia* 3
22. 6 Pf., 207.4 MP³, 469 LDAB, II.3 M. (I/II)
    PSI 11.1218 [Vitelli *bis*] + POxy 18.2170 [Lobel]: *Aetia* 3 and 4
23. 11 Pf., 208 MP³, I.9 M., 489 LDAB, II.6 M. [Lobel] (beginning of II)
    POxy 19.2212: *Aetia* 3+
24. 22 Pf., 209 MP³, 490 LDAB, II.8 M. [Lobel] (end of II or beginning of III)
    POxy 18.2169: *Aetia* 3

---

[26] Fragment A belongs to the *Rite of Anaphe*; for ascription of fragment B (fr. 118 Pf., 68 Massimilla) to the same *aition*, cf. Livrea 2006b.

[27] I am obliged to Dr. Gregg Schwendner for sending me a copy of the handout that accompanied his paper "Callimachus in a House of Psalms at Karanis," presented at the 29 December 1995 meeting of the American Philological Association. See now Schwendner 2007.

25. 8 Pf., 1 Hollis, 211 MP³, 470 LDAB, II.5 M. (I/II)
PMilVogl inv. 1006 [Gallazzi & Lehnus] + PMilVogl (I, *olim* PRIMI) 18 [Norsa & Vitelli; Vogliano] + PMilVogl inv. 28b [Gallazzi & Lehnus]: *Diegeseis* of *Aetia* 3 and 4, *Iambi* + Μέλη, *Hecale* (to col. XI 7)

26. 31 Pf., 210 MP³, I.23 M., 506 LDAB, II.10 M. [Lobel] (cod. III)
POxy 19.2211: *Aetia* 3

27. 37 Pf., 2 Hollis, 186 MP³, 523 LDAB, II.13 M. [Pfeiffer; Lobel] (cod. beginning of VI)[28]
POxy 20.2258: *Hecale* (from A fr. 9v, fr. 11), *Aetia* 3, *Aetia* 4 (*Lock of Berenice*) + *Victory of Sosibius*

28. 35 Pf., 211.1 MP³, 514 LDAB, II.11 M. [Hunt] (cod. end of IV)
POxy 7.1011 = Bodl. inv. MS. Gr. class. c. 72 (*olim* d. 114) (P)/1–7: *Aetia* 3 and 4, *Iambi*

29. 211.11 MP³, 471 LDAB, II.4 M. [Richter & Parsons] (I/II)
POxy 64.4427: *Aetia* 3

30. 12 Pf., 212 MP³, 491 LDAB, II.7 M. [Lobel] (first half of II)
POxy 19.2213: *Aetia* 3+

31. 1 Pf., 214 MP³, 524 LDAB, II.2 M. [Vitelli *bis*] (I BC)
PSI 9.1092: *Aetia* 4 (*Lock of Berenice*)

32. 217.01 MP³, I.20 M., 499 LDAB [Koenen, Luppe & Pagán] (II/III)
PMich inv. 6235 (1+2): *Diegeseis* of *Aetia* (Book 1?)

33. 217.3 MP³, I.16 M., 461 LDAB [Grenfell & Hunt; Gronewald] (I/II)
POxy 1.14: *Aetia* (1?)

34. 217.2 MP³, I.10 M., 477 LDAB [Gronewald] (beginning of II)
PMich inv. 4761C: *Aetia* (1?)

35. 3 Pf., 216 MP³, I.4 M., 466 LDAB [Grenfell & Hunt] (I)
POxy 11.1362 = Bodl. inv. MS. Gr. class. c. 77 (P): *Aetia* (beginning of Book 2?)

36. 217.1 MP³, I.25 M., 517 LDAB [Barns] (cod. IV/V)
PAnt 3.114: (?) *Aetia* (book uncertain)

37. 2 Pf., 217 MP³, I.1 M., 526 LDAB [Lobel] (I BC / I AD)
POxy 19.2214: *Aetia* (book uncertain)

38. 234.01 MP³, 9945 LDAB [Menci] (I/II)
PHorak 4 = PSI inv. 3191 (*olim* CNR 80) v: glossary to elegiacs[29]

---

[28] Dated ca. 500 AD by Irigoin 1994: 78.
[29] Conveniently included with Italian translation and commentary by D'Alessio 2007: 2.793–801.

39. 4 Pf., 234 MP³, 464 LDAB [Hunt] (end of I)
    POxy 15.1793: elegiacs on Berenice + *Victory of Sosibius*
40. 235 MP³, 465 LDAB [Lobel] (I)
    POxy 23.2375: elegiacs
41. 25 Pf., 218 MP³, 504 LDAB [Grenfell & Hunt] (II/III)
    POxy 11.1363 = Bodl. inv. MS. Gr. class. g. 60 (P): *Iambus* 1
42. 19 Pf., 219 MP³, 475 LDAB [Norsa & Vitelli (fr. b *bis*)] (II)
    PSI 9.1094: scholia on *Iambus* 1
43. 27 Pf., 220 MP³, 502 LDAB [Lobel] (II/III)
    POxy 19.2215: *Iambi* 3 and 4
44. 7 Pf., 222 MP³, 468 LDAB (I/II)
    PSI 11.1216 [Norsa & Vitelli (partially *bis*)] + POxy 18.2171 (?) and 2172 [Lobel]: *Iambi* 4–7 (?)+ *Branchus*[30]
45. 34 Pf., 221 MP³, 511 LDAB [Roberts] (IV)
    PRyl 485: *Iambi* 4 and 5
46. 21 Pf., 223 MP³, 474 LDAB [Grenfell & Hunt] (end of II)
    POxy 4.661: *Iambus* 7
47. [Colomo fr. b][31] (II)
    PLips inv. 290v: scholia on *Iambi* 11 and 12
48. 28 Pf., 224 MP³, 503 LDAB [Lobel] (II/III)
    POxy 19.2218: *Iambus* 12
49. 225 MP³, 478 LDAB [Bonner] (beginning of II)
    PMich inv. 4967: *Iambus* 12
50. (*dub.*) 230.2 MP³, 481 LDAB [Lobel] (II)
    POxy 37.2823: *Hecale*[32]
51. 30 Pf., 3 Hollis, 226 MP³, 507 LDAB [Lobel] (cod. III)
    POxy 19.2216: *Hecale*
52. 4 Hollis, 230.1 MP³, 509 LDAB [Lobel] (cod. III/IV)
    POxy 30.2529: *Hecale*
53. 6 Hollis, 230 MP³, 510 LDAB [Lobel] (cod. III/IV)
    POxy 23.2377: *Hecale*
54. 7 Hollis, 229 MP³, 492 LDAB [Lobel] (II)
    POxy 23.2376: *Hecale*

---

[30] "*PSI* 11.1216 and *POxy.* 18.2171 are pieces of the same roll: the fragments are contiguous. The fragment of the *Branchus* in *POxy.* 18.2172 is in the same hand, and may come from the same 'set' of Callimachus, but need not belong to the same roll" (Kerkhecker 1999: 274; cf. 116 n. 1.).
[31] I am obliged to Dr. Daniela Colomo for showing me this papyrus in advance. See now Colomo 2009.
[32] Cf. Hollis 2009: 141–142.

55. [to be published by N. Gonis; cf. Gonis 2006] (I or beginning of II)
POxy inv. 112/87(b): *Hecale*
56. 36 Pf., 8 Hollis, 227 MP³, 529 LDAB [Gomperz *bis*; Lloyd-Jones & Rea] (IV–V)
TVindob. inv. G HT 6 = PRain VI: *Hecale*
57. 9 Hollis, 227.1 MP³, 463 LDAB [Lobel] (first half of II)
POxy 24.2398: *Hecale*
58. 10 Hollis, 227.2 MP³, 493 LDAB [Lobel] (II)
POxy 25.2437: *Hecale*
59. 33 Pf., 11 Hollis, 228 MP³, 513 LDAB [Lobel] (IV)
POxy 19.2217: *Hecale*
60. 234.1 MP³, 497 LDAB [Montanari *bis*] (II)
PPisaLit 21 = PLettCarlini 21 (formerly PTicinensis 1): commentary on unidentified poem.

As is apparent, different literary types occur here: texts only, texts with scholia, various kinds and levels of commentary, *diegeseis*, a glossary. Texts are either (more commonly) confined to single works or books, or extended to full collections. Of these last—all coming from the late antiquity—something more will be said in the closing section below ("Outlook").

Callimachus' papyri range from the late third or early second century BC (no. 21 above, already containing an interlinear commentary)[33] to the early sixth century (Oxyrhynchus codex, no. 27 above);[34] second to early third century AD is by far the age most represented. Nine of the sixty papyri are in codex form (third to early sixth centuries); most were found in Oxyrhynchus, though the one physically largest, the so-called Milan *Diegeseis* roll, was excavated by Vogliano in the Cantina dei Papiri at Tebtynis.[35] Of the Oxyrhynchus papyri, a few are now co-located between Oxford (Grenfell and Hunt) and Florence (Breccia),[36] coming from the library or libraries of well-educated persons of this period in Greco-Roman Egypt, if not of professional scholars; while one (codex no. 9) is shared by Oxford (Grenfell and Hunt), Florence

---

[33] Similar to the Derveni Papyrus; cf. Messeri-Savorelli and Pintaudi 2002: 47–48.
[34] A fully annotated manuscript, with pages measuring 37 × 28 cm.
[35] On the event, see Gallazzi 2003: 166.
[36] Kôm Ali el-Gâmman: cf. Houston 2007: 337–342.

(Pistelli), and Berlin, as some pages of it were actually bought by German emissaries from a local dealer in Gizeh.[37]

A skillful combination of papyri (texts and *diegeseis*) with testimonia from the indirect tradition allowed Pfeiffer and his successors to restore in a more or less readable form full sequences of elegies from *Aetia* Books 1, 3, and 4. The whole work in its final form opened with an impressive twofold elegy, *Against the Telchines* and *The Dream*, after which Clio informed the poet of how and why the rites of the Graces on Paros happened to be performed without crown or the song of flutes; Calliope followed narrating a threefold elegy describing how the Argonauts had begun in Anaphe a scurrilous rite similar to that of Heracles Buthoenas at Lindus, itself easy to parallel with the episode of the clash between the hero and the Dryopian king Thiodamas (*The Return of the Argonauts and the Rite of Anaphe*, plus *The Sacrifice at Lindus*, plus *Thiodamas the Dryopian*). This first group of elegies was perhaps immediately followed by the tangled *aition* of *Linus and Coroebus*,[38] ending with the foundation of Tripodiscus in the Megarid—to which a further elegy was attached recounting the story of the mortar crown of *Artemis of Leucas*. Then the statue of Athena at Teuthis in Arcadia, with a bandage on its thigh, was introduced (cf. Lehnus 1992 and Hollis 1992c); and that was in turn possibly followed by the tragic story of Artemis Ἀπαγχομένη in the Arcadian town of Caphyae (fr. 187 Pf., 111 M.; cf. Cappelletto 1995).

While content and structure of *Aetia* 2 yet remain to a great extent a mystery,[39] multiple papyrus discoveries have made *Aetia* 3 a fairly coherent read. A new scrap from the Milan *Diegeseis* has now restored either immediately or very soon after the end of *The Victory of Berenice* (frr. 254–68C SH) the *aition* of *Diana Ductrix*.[40] Accordingly, Book 3 now looks as follows: *The Victory of Berenice*, [?...] *Diana Ductrix*, *The Attic Thesmophoria* (fr. 63 Pf.), *The Tomb of Simonides* (fr. 64 Pf.),

---

[37] Manuscript note by A. Vogliano on the title page of his *Handexemplar* of Wilamowitz 1912: 524, now in the library of the Dipartimento di Scienze dell'Antichità, Sezione di Papirologia, Università degli Studi di Milano (pressmark Vgl. III G 49/10.1; information possibly coming from W. Schubart).

[38] Immediate proximity depends on whether Λινδίας can be read in fragments 26–31a *Dieg.* 5 Pf.

[39] That Book 2 opened with papyrus no. 35 in the list above (fr. 178 Pf., 89 M.) has been convincingly argued by Zetzel 1981.

[40] Previously fragment 665 Pf., 159 M. Gallazzi and Lehnus 2001: 11 had designated this *Phalaecus of Ambracia*; now, partially following Bulloch 2006: 500 (*Artemis Hegemone*), I propose to call it *Diana Ductrix*, according to Pfeiffer's Latin usage.

The Fountains of Argos (frr. 65 and 66 Pf.), *Acontius and Cydippe* (frr. 67–75 Pf.), two or three uncertain elegies, *The Nuptial Rite of the Eleans* (fr. 77 Pf.), *The Isindian Guest* (fr. 78 Pf.), *Diana Lucina* (along with *Phrygius and Pieria*, frr. 79–83 Pf.),[41] and *Euthycles the Locrian* (frr. 84 and 85 Pf.).

Eighteen or nineteen elegies appear to have composed Book 4; these are mainly known to us through the *Diegeseis*: (?) *An Uncertain Story* (fr. 86 Pf.), *The Delphic Daphnephoria* (frr. 87–89 Pf.), *Abdera* (fr. 90 Pf.), *Melicertes* (frr. 91 and 92 Pf.), *Theudotus of Lipara* (fr. 93 Pf.), *Limone* (frr. 94 and 95 Pf.), *The Boastful Hunter* (fr. 96 Pf.), *The Pelasgian Walls* (fr. 97 Pf.), *Euthymus* (frr. 98 and 99 Pf.), *The Primordial Statue of Hera on Samos* (fr. 100 Pf.), *A Second Statue of Hera on Samos* (fr. 101 Pf.), *Pasicles the Ephesian* (fr. 102 Pf.), *Androgeos* (fr. 103 Pf.), *Oesydres* (fr. 104 Pf.), *The Dragging of Antigone* (fr. 105 Pf.), *The Roman Gaius* (frr. 106 and 107 Pf.), *The Anchor of the "Argo" Left at Cyzicus* (frr. 108 and 109 Pf.), *The Lock of Berenice* (fr. 110 Pf.), and the *Epilogue* (fr. 112 Pf.). Two remarkable papyri (nos. 31 and 27) preserve large parts of the *The Lock of Berenice* and occasionally allow us to check the existing (Scaliger 1562, Salvini 1749 but before 1729, Barber 1936)[42] retranslations of the Catullan version into Greek (Bing 1997). The transition from the *Epilogue* to the *Iambi*, thanks to the codex POxy 7.1011 (no. 28), had already been known since 1910.

Almost none of this was to be found in Schneider's edition of 1873, produced on the eve of the era of papyri—so that a final remark by M.L. West on the Hesiodic *Catalogue of Women* is relevant here: "There is no other work of ancient literature, *with the possible exception of Callimachus' Aitia*, for which papyri have made such a contribution to the resurrection in outline of a lost composition in several books."[43]

Outlook

Future editors of the complete Callimachus will have to decide in arranging the poems whether they will follow the order of the *Diege-*

---

[41] There is no room here to discuss the relative positions of *Artemis the Goddess of Childbirth* and *Phrygius and Pieria*. With Paul Maas (cf. Lehnus 2009) I am inclined to think that *Phrygius* was a digression from *Artemis* and ignored as such by the *diegetes*. See now Cecchi 2010: 191–193.

[42] Scaliger 1562: critical edition by Tissoni 1993–94.

[43] M.L. West 2008: 29 (emphasis mine). One might add that Kannicht lists seventy-five papyri of Euripides. Homer is obviously out of scale.

seis (with Pfeiffer) or the sequence of the anonymous epigram printed as Pfeiffer's testimonium 23:[44]

Ὑμνῶ τὸν ὑψίζυγον ἐν πρώτοις Δία,
Φοῖβον δ' ἔπειτα, καὶ τρίτην τὴν Ἄρτεμιν,
Δῆλον τετάρτην, εἶτα Λουτρὰ Παλλάδος,
ἕκτην δὲ τὴν Δήμητρα τὴν παλαιτέραν.
μέλπω δὲ γραὸς τῆς φιλοξένου τρόπους
καὶ τὴν τελευτήν, Θησέως τε τὴν ἄγραν
καὶ τῶν μεγίστων Αἰτίων τὴν τετράδα.

I sing first high-throned Zeus, then Phoebus, and Artemis third, Delos fourth, then the Bath of Pallas, and sixth the venerable Demeter. I celebrate with song the character and death of the hospitable old woman, and Theseus' hunt, and the tetrad of the greatest *Aetia*.

If they follow the *Diegeseis*, in which the diptych *Aetia-Iambi* is followed by *Hecale* and by the *Incertae sedis fragmenta*,[45] retaining Pfeiffer's numbers might not in principle be impossible (a parallel may be found in the way Schneider adapted Bentley), despite the increase in number of the fragments, and would entail clear advantages. A beginning with the flamboyant manifesto against the Telchines might come closer to an authentic intention of the poet—quite apart from the fact that Callimachus' books of elegies had been in fact, and were soon considered ("elegia... cuius princeps habetur Callimachus," Quint. 10.1.58), his most ambitious work.

Otherwise, we do not have any evidence of an original arrangement of Callimachus' poetic oeuvre, apart from the poet's own statement that he will pass on directly from the last verse of the *Aetia* to a Μουσέων πεζὸς νομός: that is, to the *Iambi*—which he actually does do from fragment 112.9 (αὐτὰρ ἐγὼ Μουσέων πεζὸν ἔπειμι νομόν) to fragment 191.1 Pf. However, as against the order *Aetia-Iambi-Hecale-Hymns* attested by the *Diegeseis*, there exist three or four converging clues that the customary ordering of Callimachus' poems in late antiquity was epics, elegiacs, and iambics, according to a consolidated scale of poetic values. (Cf. Alan Cameron 1995: 113.) Our first clue arises in the fact that the codex POxy 7.1011 (no. 28), from the end of the fourth century, actually begins with the last seventy-seven verses of what was at least the sixth elegy of Book 3 (*Acontius and Cydippe*). Given that fragment 75 Pf. coincides with pages 151 and 152 of the

---

[44] "Epigr. adesp. saec. VI p. C. vel potius posterioris aetatis" (vv. 1–7), test. 23 Pf.
[45] On the *Aetia* and *Iambi* as a superstructure, see Clayman 1988.

papyrus, and that its pages contain between thirty-seven and forty-two lines each, the missing initial part of the codex must have amounted to some 5,900 verses, far too many for only two and a half books of the *Aetia*; therefore one can reasonably conclude that the *Hymns* and the *Hecale*, or the *Hecale* and the *Hymns*, did precede. Second, the situation is the same with Marianus of Eleutheropolis' (early sixth-century) iambic metaphrasis of the complete works of Callimachus (*Iambi* excepted, of course), in which the sequence *Hecale-Hymns* opened the collection (*Suda* μ 194 Adler = test. 24 Pf.); and third, the iambic epigram printed as Pfeiffer's testimonium 23 (quoted above: sixth-century at the earliest) lists as the first three titles of a collected edition of Callimachus the *Hymns*, the *Hecale*, and the *Aetia*. Additional, though more uncertain, support for the same pattern comes from the papyrus numbered 27 in the list above (also a codex). It preserves pieces of the *Hymns, Hecale,* and *Aetia* (in addition to the elegiac *Victory of Sosibius*); unfortunately, we are ignorant of the position of the *Aetia*, but since the *Hecale* immediately followed *Hymn* 6, as is confirmed by A fr. 9, it seems odd that the *Hymns* should be placed between the elegies and the *Hecale* instead of preceding the paired *Hecale* and *Aetia*, as in the iambic epigram. "Videmus igitur inde a quarto fere saeculo epica primum locum occupavisse neque veri dissimile est codicem no. 37 [no. 27 above] eundem ordinem servavisse," concluded Pfeiffer (1949–53: 2.xxxviii).

The Leipzig Scholia, a part of which has been recently published by Daniela Colomo (2009), will increase to a degree our knowledge of the mysterious *Iambus* 11 (no. 47 above), while further details will be added by the papyri numbered 12 and 55 in the list above. More promising results might be obtained by a dedicated study of the Florentine glossary PHorak 4 (no. 38 above);[46] though in general it does not seem that new papyri capable of altering our present picture of the lost Callimachus are on the horizon. (Of course, one never knows.) However, if a further full edition of the fragments is contemplated, disposition according to the late-antique pattern would have to be weighed anew, though at the risk of introducing a fourth, completely new numeration, after Bentley, Pfeiffer, and Asper.[47]

---

[46] A paper on this was announced by R. Luiselli for *Eikasmos*.
[47] Cf. Asper 2004. A fifth, if we consider Hollis for the *Hecale* and Massimilla for the *Aetia*.

CHAPTER TWO

THE *AETIA* THROUGH PAPYRI

Giulio Massimilla

ABSTRACT

Papyri have shown that Callimachus adopted two different techniques of composition in the first and second halves of the *Aetia*. Accordingly, I have first outlined the contents of Books 1 and 2, and highlighted some of their most important features, i.e. the subjects, the arrangements, and the respective lengths of the single elegies, as well as the tone and the structure of the conversation between "Callimachus" and the Muses, and its treatment as a narrative framework. Then I have outlined the contents of Books 3 and 4, and called attention to some of their most significant aspects, i.e. the relative lengths, the aetiological relevance, and the mutual connections of the single elegies, as well as the various narrative voices selected by Callimachus and his inclination to set his many-sided poetic persona in the foreground.

Papyri have decisively increased our knowledge of the *Aetia*. They have shed new light not only on the texts of many passages already known through the medieval indirect tradition (Massimilla 2006a), but also on the structures of the single books. Among other things, they have shown that Callimachus adopted two different techniques of composition in the first and second halves of the *Aetia*. Accordingly, I will treat Books 1 and 2 together under one heading and Books 3 and 4 together under another.[1]

Books 1 and 2

The first two books of the *Aetia* share a narrative framework. Callimachus relates that, during a dream he had as an adolescent, he found

---

[1] I quote the fragments of the *Aetia* in accordance with the numbering I have used in my editions of Books 1 and 2 (Massimilla 1996) and of Books 3 and 4 (Massimilla 2010). The translations into English of most of the Greek passages are those of Trypanis 1978 (often adapted). The translations of the passages that have come to light more recently and of the less complete ones are my own. I refer to the internal sections of the *Aetia* by the conventional titles given to them by modern editors.

himself on Mount Helicon in Boeotia (frr. 3-4). He says that, having met the Muses there, he asked them questions on the origins of customs and rites, and in turn received the goddesses' answers. It is difficult to follow the unfolding of the plot within this framework, for two reasons. First, the texts have come down to us in a fragmentary state. Second, it is very often impossible to reconstruct the contents of the missing parts, as the topics of the conversation between the Muses and the secondary narrator-narratee Callimachus (this sense being hereafter signaled with the name in quotation marks, "Callimachus") are forever changing.[2] Yet we can point out the most extensive and interesting passages.

Book 1

The most noteworthy passages are as follows.

1.1. Fragment 1 (= fr. 1.1-40 Pf.): *Against the Telchines* (or: *Prologue*). Callimachus defends his poetry against malicious criticism and states his artistic views.

1.2. Fragment 2 (= fr. 1a.12-30 Pf. [lemmata]): *Invocation to the Muses*. Perhaps this short section was a part of the *Prologue* (Massimilla 1996: 231-33).

1.3. Fragments 3 and 4 (= frr. 1.41-45 Pf. + 2a Pf. [lemmata] + 696 Pf. + 2 Pf.): *The Dream*. Callimachus relates that, when he was an adolescent, he was raised onto Mount Helicon during a dream, and began a conversation with the Muses there. The talk between the Muses and "Callimachus" forms the *aitia* of the first two books.

1.4. Fragments 5 through 9.18 (= frr. 3-7.18 Pf. + SH 249A verso): *The Graces* (first *aition*). This section explains why at Paros the Graces are worshipped without flutes and garlands. We begin with "Callimachus'" question to the Muses.[3] Clio replies that Minos, while performing a sacrifice to the Graces at Paros, learned that his son, Androgeos, had died (cf. *Schol. Flor.* 30). Without interrupting the ceremony, Minos put a stop to its flute and took off his garland as signs of his mourning, thereby giving rise to the Parian custom. Taking her cue from this story, Clio next recounts the genealogy of the Graces: "Cal-

---

[2] Cf. fr. 1.3, οὐχ ἓν ἄεισμα διηνεκές ("not a uniform and continuous poem").
[3] Fr. 5, κῶς ἄν[ις αὐλῶν] | ῥέζειν καὶ στεφέων εὔαδε τῷ Παρίῳ ("Why did it please the Parians to sacrifice [to the Graces] without flutes and garlands?").

limachus" mentions three different traditions of their birth, but Clio corrects him, stating that the Graces are daughters of Dionysus and Coronis, a Naxian Nymph (cf. *Schol. Flor.* 30-35). An invocation to the Graces that we read near the end of the *aition* (fr. 9.9-14) is apparently uttered by Callimachus himself, who temporarily interrupts the narrative framework in this passage. Here he begs the Graces to give long-lasting fame to his elegies.

1.5. Fragment 9.19 through fragment 23 (= fr. 7.19-34 Pf. + *SH* 249A recto + frr. 8-21 Pf. + fr. 352 Pf. + *SH* 250): *The Return of the Argonauts and the Rite of Anaphe* (second *aition*). This section explains why the cult of Apollo on Anaphe, an island of the Sporades, is characterized by abuse and insults. We have the question of "Callimachus" to the Muses (fr. 9.19-21), regarding the cults both of Apollo at Anaphe and of Heracles at Lindus (treated in the following *aition*), which resembles Lindian Apollo's in its abusive character. Calliope replies (fr. 9.22): the Argonauts, being overtaken by a very dark night during their return from Colchis, disembarked at Anaphe thanks to Apollo, who caused a prodigious light to shine for their safety;[4] the following morning, the Argonauts performed a makeshift sacrifice to Apollo and were teased for it by Medea's Phaeacian maidservants. A playful exchange of insults and abuse ensued, which has remained in this rite.

1.6. Fragments 24 and 25 (= frr. 22 and 23 Pf.): *The Sacrifice at Lindus* (third *aition*). This section explains why at Lindus, on Rhodes, curses against Heracles are uttered during the ceremonies in his honor. "Callimachus" has already asked his introductory question at the beginning of 1.5. The answering Muse remains Calliope: at Lindus Heracles met a farmer, seized one of his oxen, and devoured it; unable to defend himself, the farmer cursed him. Ever since, the Lindians have sacrificed to Heracles while cursing him, immolating a bull in his honor without cutting it up. This elegy contains a prayer to Heracles (fr. 25.21-22) that may be spoken by Callimachus outside the narrative framework of the exchange with the Muses.

1.7. Fragments 26 and 27 (= frr. 24 and 25 Pf.): *Thiodamas the Dryopian* (fourth *aition*). While passing through the Aetolian land of the Dryopes with his small son, Hyllus, Heracles met King Thiodamas and asked him for something that the child might eat. When Thiodamas

---

[4] The very name of the island is related to the verb ἀναφαίνειν ("to reveal").

refused and insulted him, Heracles killed one of his oxen and ate it with Hyllus. War ensued, and the Dryopes were defeated. Heracles compelled them to establish themselves in the Peloponnese, where they took the name *Asineis* ("Not Harmful").

1.8. Fragments 28 through 34 (= frr. 27, 28, 26, 29, 30, 31, 31a Pf.): *Linus and Coroebus*. (We do not know how far this *aition* was from 1.7.) This section explains why the Argives name one of their months "Lamb Month"—during which they kill dogs—and recalls the origin of Tripodiscus, a city in the Megarid. Psamathe, daughter of the Argive king Crotopus, being seduced by Apollo, gave birth to Linus. Entrusted to a shepherd, the child grew up among the lambs but was torn to pieces by the king's dogs. (This explains the Argives' custom during Lamb Month.) When Crotopus learned of this clandestine birth, he put Psamathe to death, and Apollo avenged her by sending a baby-snatching monster to Argos. The hero Coroebus killed this monster, but Apollo then sent plague upon Argos. Coroebus traveled to Delphi in order to purify himself and was given a tripod there, being directed to build a temple to Apollo and to found a new city where the tripod slipped from his hands. Accordingly he founded Tripodiscus, in the Megarid. At some point in this elegy (fr. 30.5–8) Callimachus seems to be speaking outside the narrative framework.

1.9. Fragments 35 through 38 (= frr. 31b–e Pf.): *Artemis of Leucas* (*aition* placed immediately after 1.8). This section explains why the statue of Artemis in Leucas has a mortar on its head. We have the transition from the previous *aition* and the question of "Callimachus" to the Muses. While sacking the sanctuary of Artemis on Leucas, some Epirotes found a statue of the goddess wearing a golden crown. In mockery they removed it, replacing it with a mortar. The next day the Leucadians put a new crown on the statue instead of the mortar, but the following morning they found that it had fallen off. It proved useless to nail the crown in place, as they found it on the ground again the next two days also. Consulting the Delphic Oracle, they were told that Artemis wanted the mortar back on her statue's head.

Book 2

The order of the fragments in this book is unknown. The most noteworthy passages are as follows.

2.1. Fragment 50.1–83 (= fr. 43.1–83 Pf.): *The Sicilian Cities*. This section explains why the founder of the Sicilian city Zancle is worshipped without being named. "Callimachus" asks his question (vv. 18?-27) and adds a long digression about the other Sicilian cities he knows of, which by contrast honor their founders by name (vv. 28-55). Again the Muse Clio answers him (we have her entire speech, vv. 56-83): the two founders of Zancle, Perieres of Cyme and Crataemenes of Chalcis, argued because they both wished to be the city's patron. When they consulted the Delphic Oracle, they were told that neither of them should be considered the founder. Therefore, since that time, the magistrates at Zancle invite the patron to the ritual feast without naming him, and they tell him that he may be accompanied by other heroes also.

2.2. Fragment 50.84-133 (= fr. 43.84-133 Pf.): *Haliartus and Crete* (*aition* placed immediately after 2.1). This section explains why the Boeotian city Haliartus celebrates the Cretan festival of the Theodaisia and why incense (στυρόν) grows only round about Haliartus and in Crete. We have the transition from the previous *aition* with another question from "Callimachus" (beginning at line 84; the text is very broken after line 92, it is not clear where this question ends). As it seems, a Muse said that Haliartus and Crete are so connected because Rhadamanthys moved from Crete to the district of Haliartus, where he resided and was buried.

2.3. Fragments 51 through 55 (= frr. 44-47 Pf. + *SH* 252 +fr. 475 Pf. + *SH* 253): *Busiris and Phalaris.* Busiris, a king of Egypt, and Phalaris, a tyrant of Acragas, visited their cruelties upon their very advisers. In the case of Busiris, the king's first victim was the Cypriote seer who in a period of drought advised the king to sacrifice any foreigners coming to Egypt on the altar of Zeus. In the other case, the first man to be roasted alive in the bronze Bull of Phalaris, as it was called, was the inventor of this instrument of torture. Within this elegy we perhaps have the end of a Muse's speech. (Fr. 55.14. But it is not certain that fr. 55 belongs to 2.3.)

2.4. Fragment 60 (= fr. 51 Pf.; probably the last line of the book). Athens is praised for its unique mercy.[5]

---

[5] Οὕνεκεν οἰκτείρειν οἶδε μόνη πολίων ("since it is the only town that knows how to pity").

Book 1 or Book 2

Here the inclusion in Book 1 or Book 2 is certain only for fragments 98 and 99. However, since the contents of most elegies of Book 3 and of nearly all the elegies of Book 4 are known to us, it is likely that many fragments from the *Aetia* that cannot be attributed with certainty to any particular book belong in fact to Book 1 or Book 2. Obviously we do not know their respective placements. The most noteworthy passages are as follows.

1/2.1. Fragments 89 through 96 (= frr. 178–85 Pf.): *Icos*. During a banquet in Alexandria, Callimachus asks the merchant Theugenes, a native of the island Icos, in the Sporades, why Peleus is worshipped there. Theugenes tells him that this is so because Peleus died on Icos. There are good reasons for supposing that this elegy belongs to Book 2 and immediately precedes 2.1. As it seems, "Callimachus" tells the Muses of his conversation with Theugenes.[6]

1/2.2. Fragment 97 (= fr. 186 Pf.): *The Hyperboreans*. Here Callimachus describes the journey of the offerings that the Hyperboreans send to the Delian shrine of Apollo, and he perhaps says that Orion tried unsuccessfully to rape a Hyperborean girl. The end of a Muse's speech may be recognized in verse 30. In verse 31 a prayer to Artemis begins, possibly spoken by Callimachus outside the narrative framework of the conversation with the Muses.

1/2.3. Fragment 98 (= fr. 625 Pf. + *SH* 238). The content of this fragment is uncertain. We may have the end of a Muse's speech in verse 4 and a new question of "Callimachus" in verses 5–7. The Muse Erato begins to speak in verse 8. The aetiological myth somehow regards Sicyon and its mythical king Epopeus.[7]

1/2.4. Fragment 99 (= *SH* 239). The content of this fragment is also uncertain. All that is apparent is that verses 6–10 deal with poverty (Massimilla 1996: 436).

1/2.5. Fragment 110 (= fr. 667 Pf. + *SH* 276): *The Bandaged Statue of Athena at Teuthis*. This section explains why in the Arcadian town Teuthis the statue of Athena formerly had a bandage on her thigh. At the time of the Trojan War a general from Teuthis, who had come to

---

[6] See Świderek 1951: 234 n. 18; Massimilla 1996: 400; Fantuzzi and Hunter 2004: 80–81; Morrison 2007: 183–184.

[7] See Hollis 1990b and 1992a: 13; Borgonovo 1996; Robertson 1999.

join the Greek forces gathered in Aulis, argued with Agamemnon and decided to go back to Arcadia with his men. When Athena, assuming a human appearance, tried to dissuade him, he became furious and wounded her on the thigh. On returning to his fatherland, he had a vision of the wounded Athena. His town was then struck by famine. The inhabitants of Teuthis consulted the oracle of Dodona and were ordered to appease Athena by raising a statue to the goddess with a bandage on her thigh.

A Conversation between Peers

In the conversation between the Muses and "Callimachus" it does not always happen that they teach and he learns. Sometimes "Callimachus," reversing the topos of inspiration, takes pride in being a *poeta doctus* and shows off his culture to the Muses.[8] In the passage that I have designated 1.4 above (*The Graces*) he acquaints them with three different traditions of the Graces' parentage, which prove to be erroneous. In 2.1 (*The Sicilian Cities*), on asking the Muses to tell him why the founder of Zancle is worshipped without being named, he launches into a digression and lists—amid a great store of geographical, historical, and mythological learning—the other Sicilian cities that he knows of where instead the founders are honored by name. The digression is longer than Clio's answer, which follows it.

Moreover, if (as is highly likely) the banquet described in 1/2.1 (*Icos*) comes immediately before the talk between "Callimachus" and the Muses in 2.1, "Callimachus" proves to be even more self-sufficient. In a leisurely manner he tells the Muses that he had a place at the banquet and informs them of what he learned there.

Thus, the conversation between the Muses and "Callimachus" takes place in an atmosphere of equality and intimacy. Before beginning to speak, Clio makes herself comfortable, resting her hand on the shoulder of one of her sisters.[9] The talk between the nine goddesses and the learned adolescent may perhaps have been described as a λέσχη, a "chat" (fr. 3.10).

---

[8] See Hutchinson 1988: 44–45; M.A. Harder 2004: 68.
[9] Fr. 50.56–57, ὡς ἐφάμην· Κλειὼ δὲ τὸ [δ]εύτερον ἤρχ[ετο μ]ύθ[ου] | χεῖρ' ἐπ' ἀδελφειῆς ὤμον ἐρεισαμένη ("So I said. And Clio went on to speak a second time, resting her hand upon her sister's shoulder").

Subjects and Arrangement of the Elegies

The *aitia* are markedly different from one another, with regard to both their geographical settings and their mythical events. In addition to the contents of the most important and extensive passages collected in the outlines above, many other subjects emerge from the great number of minor fragments.

The arrangement of the *aitia* does not conform to any particular plan either, as one may see in three series of *aitia* that papyri have brought to light (1.4 to 1.7 [*The Graces* through *Thiodamas the Dryopian*], 1.8 and 1.9 [*Linus and Coroebus* and *Artemis of Leucas*], 2.1 and 2.2 [*The Sicilian Cities* and *Haliartus and Crete*]) and in the section on Busiris and Phalaris (2.3). In some of these fragments we find *aitia* with similar contents next to each other. The cults of Apollo at Anaphe and of Heracles at Lindus, for example, both abuse their objects of worship (1.5 and 1.6), and Heracles' encounter with the Lindian farmer is very like the one with Thiodamas (1.6 and 1.7).[10] The stories of Busiris and Phalaris both portray cruel rulers and their deservedly punished advisers (2.3).

Yet elsewhere consecutive *aitia* show no thematic link. From the cult of the Graces at Paros, established by Minos, we pass to the cult of Apollo at Anaphe, set up by the Argonauts (1.4 and 1.5). From the Argive story of Linus and Coroebus we pass to the statue of Leucadian Artemis (1.8 and 1.9). From the anonymous worship of the founder at Zancle we pass to connections between Crete and the Boeotian city of Haliartus (2.1 and 2.2).

Relative Lengths of the Elegies

The lengths of the single *aitia* vary. We learn this by comparing 1.5 (*The Return of the Argonauts*) and 2.1 (*The Sicilian Cities*), the only two elegies whose lengths, thanks to papyri, can be determined with any confidence. The first of these occupied more than 120 lines, whereas the second merely twenty-six (if Clio's answer alone is taken into account, fr. 50.58–83) or perhaps about sixty-six (if the question of "Callimachus" and his digression are also counted, fr. 50.18?–83).

---

[10] Cf. *Schol. Flor.* 51–52.

Structure of the Talk between "Callimachus" and the Muses

Although we cannot always ascertain how long the questions of "Callimachus" may have been, a number of passages allow us to see his variety. Whereas 1/2.3 (?Sicyon and Epopeus) probably contains a question of only three lines (fr. 98.5–7), in 2.1 (*The Sicilian Cities*) the real question of about ten lines (fr. 50.18?–27) is followed by a long digression (fr. 50.28–55) and thus reaches a total length of (probably) thirty-eight lines. The next question (in 2.2, *Haliartus and Crete*) must have been quite long also, as it covered at least nine lines (fr. 50.84–92). Questions vary not only in their length, but also in their form. The usual pattern is for a question to be set in direct speech and to introduce the *aition* that immediately follows. But this convention is twice varied: in fragment 9.19–21 "Callimachus" asks the Muses two questions at the same time, thus introducing the two following *aitia* (1.5 and 1.6, *The Return of the Argonauts* and *The Sacrifice at Lindus*),[11] and in fragment 50.84–92 (2.2, *Haliartus and Crete*) the question is set in indirect speech.

The Muses alternate in answering "Callimachus." Clio recounts the *aitia* regarding the Graces (1.4) and Zancle (2.1). Calliope relates the pair of *aitia* about the cults of Apollo at Anaphe and of Heracles at Lindus (1.5 and 1.6).[12] Erato retails an *aition* about Sicyon and Epopeus (1/2.3). In a tiny fragment, which may belong to Book 2 (fr. 76.3), perhaps the name of Polymnia can be read.[13] So far as we know, the Muses neither spoke in a fixed order nor related *aitia* somehow consistently with their domains. In this connection we may note solely that the account of the foundation of Zancle (2.1) is entrusted to Clio, the Muse of history.

Twice we see that the Muses' speeches are introduced briefly, by a single pentameter (frr. 9.22 and 98.8, 1.5 [*The Return of the Argonauts*] and 1/2.3 [?Sicyon and Epopeus]). But in fragment 50.56–57 (2.1, *The Sicilian Cities*) the introduction takes up a distich, as it is adorned with a picturesque detail: while beginning to talk, Clio rests her hand on the shoulder of one of her sisters (Ehlers 1933: 32 n. 78).

---

[11] See Fantuzzi and Hunter 2004: 45; Hutchinson 2003: 50 = 2008: 47.

[12] If fr. 141 is Callimachean, we have there the beginning of another speech by Calliope.

[13] Fr. 140 (possibly Callimachean) contains the beginning of the speech of a particular Muse, but we do not know which one.

Moreover, the only two passages where we can be sure that Callimachus is marking the end of a Muse's speech are very concise: "Thus she spoke" (1.9 [*Artemis of Leucas*], fr. 35) and "So she ceased to speak" (2.2 [*Haliartus and Crete*], fr. 50.84). Fragment 98.4 (1/2.3 [?*Sicyon and Epopeus*]) may contain a charming variant of this pattern: there Callimachus perhaps says that the Muse "withdrew her hand from the golden lyre."[14]

There are only two cases extant of transition from one *aition* to another. The first (1.8 [*Linus and Coroebus*] to 1.9 [*Artemis of Leucas*], fr. 35) is very simple: "Thus she spoke, and straightaway my spirit asked them again."[15] The second (2.1 [*The Sicilian Cities*] to 2.2 [*Haliartus and Crete*], fr. 50.84) has a more complex form, because a parenthetical clause expands upon it: "So she ceased to speak, but I wanted to know this too—for indeed my secret wonder grew—why…"[16]

A Flexible Framework

The first *aition* (1.4, *The Graces*) invokes the Graces at its end (fr. 9.9–14). Since the goddesses are invited here to "wipe their hands upon the elegies" and to make them famous (Bing 1988b: 18), it is likely that Callimachus speaks the prayer in his poetic persona, temporarily interrupting the narrative framework of a conversation between the Muses and "Callimachus."[17] But we must bear in mind that 1.4 is closely linked, in both its position and its content, with the *Prologue*, the *Invocation to the Muses*, and *The Dream* (1.1 to 1.3). Therefore Callimachus' invocation of the Graces here is most appropriate to the context.

Then there are two fragmentary passages where we cannot exclude the possibility that Callimachus similarly steps outside the narrative framework: the prayer to Heracles in the *aition* about Lindus (1.6, fr. 25.21–22)[18] and the invocation of Artemis in the elegy concerning the Hyperboreans (1/2.2, fr. 96.31). Another uncertain instance of the

---

[14] Χρυσ]είης χεῖρ᾽ ἀ[ν]έπαυσε λύρη[ς (uncertain text). See Lloyd-Jones and Parsons 1983: 91.

[15] Fr. 35, τὼ]ς μὲν ἔφη· τὰς δ᾽ εἶθαρ ἐμὸς πάλιν εἴρετο θυμός. Here ἐμὸς…θυμός ("my spirit") is equivalent to "Callimachus."

[16] Fr. 50.84–87, ὣ]ς ἡ μὲν λίπε μῦ[θ]ον, ἐγὼ δ᾽ ἐπὶ καὶ [τὸ πυ]θέσθαι | ἤ]θελον—ἦ γάρ μοι θάμβος ὑπετρέφ[ετ]ο—…κῶς κτλ. See Fantuzzi and Hunter 2004: 59–60.

[17] See D'Alessio 1996: 385; Fantuzzi and Hunter 2004: 52–53.

[18] See Hutchinson 1988: 43 n. 35.

framework's possible interruption occurs in a fragment of the Linus and Coroebus *aition* (1.8, fr. 30.5–8), where a male subject (probably Callimachus) says, "I sing continuously." Some readers have thought that here the poet is making a programmatic statement outside the narrative framework, but it is also possible to see these scant remains as part of the conversation between the Muses and "Callimachus" (Massimilla 1996: 303–4).

Therefore the only certain interruption of the narrative framework appears in the quasi-proemial invocation to the Graces. But the framework is nevertheless flexible, and it can accommodate contents of various descriptions. A brilliant proof of this flexibility is seen in the group consisting of 1/2.1 (*Icos*) and 2.1 (*The Sicilian Cities*). There, as it seems, "Callimachus" tells the Muses what he learned when he attended a banquet in Alexandria. If this reconstruction is correct, the stratification of narrative levels becomes considerably deeper, transitioning from the oneiric Heliconian scenery to the vivid setting of a lively banquet.

Books 3 and 4

In the last two books of the *Aetia* the narrative framework of a conversation with the Muses disappears. The elegies are now separate from one another, without explicit connections. Proof of this is seen in the fact that, when papyri contain the end of one *aition* and the beginning of the next, we find no narrative transitions.[19] This differing narrative strategy in the last two books distinguishes them markedly from the first two and greatly influences the planning and development of the single elegies.

The overall structure of Books 3 and 4 can be more easily reconstructed than can that of Books 1 and 2. As a matter of fact, the summaries of the *aitia* provided by the Milan *Diegeseis* for a large part of Book 3, right up to its conclusion (that is, at least two-thirds of the poems that made it up), and for the whole of Book 4 allow us almost always to know the order of the elegies, often to outline their contents, and frequently to read their incipits, with a degree of completeness

---

[19] Cf. the transitions from fr. 162 to fr. 163, from fr. 165 to fr. 166; and (in more precarious textual conditions) from fr. 174 to fr. 175, from fr. 180 to fr. 181, from fr. 185 to fr. 186, from fr. 195 to fr. 196, from fr. 198 to fr. 199. See Pfeiffer 1949–53: 2.xxxv.

that becomes progressively greater as we approach the end of the *Aetia* (see PMilVogl 1.18). Moreover, right up to the present papyri pertaining to Book 3 continue to be discovered, bringing to light conspicuous sections of it. The second half of the *Aetia*, therefore, offers a more complete picture than does the first. Let us look at it.

Book 3

Fragments 143 through 156, representing the first elegy of the book, follow one upon another and belong to its first *aition*. For the series of *aitia* that began with the second elegy, however, and closed before the next series for which we have evidence, we have no information. The fragments from number 159 to the end of the book form a continuous sequence of poems. I have arranged them in an order that reflects the *Diegeseis*, diverging only in the arrangement of fragments 182 + 183–85 + 186–87. The outline of the book is as follows.

3.1. Fragments 143 through 156:[20] The *Victory of Berenice* (proem and first *aition* of the book). Callimachus praises Queen Berenice II, whose horses have won the chariot race at the Nemean Games. An aetiological myth regards the foundation of these games by Heracles, slayer of the Nemean Lion. Callimachus describes the hero's stay at the house of the old farmer Molorchus before and after fighting the lion.[21]

Fragments 157 and 158 (= frr. 61 and 62 Pf.). It is uncertain whether either of these fragments (one concerning Pythagoras; the other, a Delphian village) belongs here within the section of text set between 3.1 (*The Victory of Berenice*) and 3.2 (*Phalaecus of Ambracia*). In fact these fragments could also belong somewhere amid the three unknown *aitia* intervening between 3.6 (*Acontius and Cydippe*) and 3.10 (*The Nuptial Rite of the Eleans*).

---

[20] The constituent fragments of this *aition* are assembled from many sources: fr. 143 (= fr. 383 Pf. + *SH* 254); fr. 144 (= fr. 674 Pf. + PSI 15.1500); fr. 145 (= fr. 54 Pf. = *SH* 266); fr. 146 (= fr. 55 Pf. = *SH* 267); fr. 147 (= fr. 56 Pf. = *SH* 267A); fr. 148 (= frr. 176 Pf. + 372 Pf. + 590 Pf. + 711 Pf. + 722 Pf. + *SH* 257); fr. 149 (= fr. 177 Pf. = *SH* 259); fr. 150 (= *SH* 260); fr. 151 (= frr. 333 Pf. + 557 Pf. + *SH* 260A); fr. 152 (= *SH* 262); fr. 153 (= *SH* 263); fr. 154 (= fr. 57 Pf. = *SH* 264); fr. 155 (= fr. 58 Pf. = *SH* 268); fr. 156 (= fr. 59 Pf. = *SH* 265).

[21] Fr. 144 (corresponding to PSI 15.1500) has only recently come out: see Ozbek et al. 2005; Bastianini 2008.

In all likelihood we must place here fragments 64 and 65, whose position within the *Aetia* is uncertain. In these fragments we find remnants of three consecutive elegies, as described immediately below.

Onnes and Tottes (frr. 65 + 64.1–3 = frr. 115 Pf. + 114.1–3 Pf.). This section tells the story of the brothers Onnes and Tottes, Cabiri who freed Miletus of the tyrant Amphitres. The poem ends with a reference to the aniconic statue of Apollo in Miletus.

The Statue of Apollo at Delos (fr. 64.4–17 = fr. 114.4–17 Pf.). This short elegy contains a dialogue between the statue of Delian Apollo and an anonymous interlocutor who questions it about its distinctive features.

An Uncertain Thracian Story (fr. 64.18–25 = fr. 114.18–25 Pf.). This section perhaps explains the mythical origin of a breed of Argive horses (Massimilla 1996: 383–84).

3.2. *Fragments 159 and 160* (= frr. 665 Pf. + 60 Pf. = SH 268A): *Phalaecus of Ambracia*. While besieging Ambracia, the tyrant Phalaecus was killed by a lioness because he picked up her cub. Callimachus probably wrote that Artemis caused Phalaecus to lift up the cub and that therefore the grateful Ambraciotes erected a statue of the goddess beside a lioness.[22]

3.3. *Fragments 161 and 162* (= PMilVogl 1.18, col. Y, 8 [lemma] + fr. 63 Pf.): *The Attic Thesmophoria*. An aetiological myth, apparently regarding Demeter's anger toward a girl, has a ritual outcome that is explicit at the end of the elegy: from then on, virgins may not be present at the Mysteries of Demeter during the Attic Thesmophoria.

3.4. *Fragment 163* (= fr. 64 Pf.): *The Tomb of Simonides*. The poet Simonides, now dead, relates how a general impiously demolished his tomb at Acragas and paid the penalty for his sacrilege.

3.5. *Fragments 164 and 165* (= frr. 65 and 66 Pf.): *The Fountains of Argos*. This elegy regards the four fountains of Argos, named for four daughters of Danaus, and the different ritual uses of their waters.

3.6. *Fragments 166 through 174* (= frr. 67–75 Pf.): *Acontius and Cydippe*. The clan of the Acontiadae in the Cean city Iulis owes its origin to a mythical occurrence that Callimachus relates at length. Acontius, a young man of Ceos, fell in love with a Naxian girl named

---

[22] The inclusion of *Phalaecus of Ambracia* in the *Aetia* and its assignment to this point in the third book are recent developments, ensuing from the publication of a new fragment of the *Diegeseis*. See Gallazzi and Lehnus 2001: 7–13, 17–18.

Cydippe. Resorting to an unusual trick, he made her swear an oath by Artemis that led her to marry him.

3.7. Fragment 175 (= POxy 7.1011, fol. 1 [recto], 78 + fr. 76.2–3 Pf.): first unknown *aition*. The subject cannot be determined.

3.8. Fragment 176 (= PMilVogl 1.18, col. Z, 30 [lemma]): second unknown *aition*. Again, the subject cannot be determined.

3.9. Fragment 177 (= PMilVogl 1.18, col. Z, 39 [lemma]): third unknown *aition*. Once again, the subject cannot be determined.[23]

3.10. Fragments 178 through 180 (= frr. 76.1, 77, 77a + 158.1 Pf.): *The Nuptial Rite of the Eleans*. An Elean nuptial rite in which an armed man is present is apparently the outcome of the aetiological myth related in this elegy. Needing men because so many Eleans had died during his war against Augeas the king of Elis, Heracles made the wives of the fallen Eleans lie with his soldiers and thus become pregnant. The story of the war against Augeas was also linked to Heracles' founding the Olympic Games.

3.11. Fragment 181 (= frr. 78 Pf. + 158.2–3 Pf.): *The Isindian Guest*. The people of the Ionian city of Isindus are excluded from the Ionian festivals because once upon a time an Isindian guest killed his host, a certain Aethalon.

3.12. Fragment 182 (= fr. 79 Pf.): *Artemis the Goddess of Childbirth*. Three different reasons are given to explain why women in labor pains call on the virgin goddess Artemis.

3.13. Fragments 183 through 185 (= frr. 81, 80 + 82, 83 Pf.): *Phrygius and Pieria*. Phrygius, a young king of Miletus, upon seeing the girl Pieria of Myus during a festival in honor of Artemis, fell in love with her and promised to grant her all she desired. Pieria took the opportunity to ask him whether the long hostility between Miletus and Myus might end, and she achieved her aim. The elegy probably ends with the aetiological outcome of the myth: from then on, Ionian women traditionally express the wish that their husbands may respect them as Phrygius respected Pieria.

3.14. Fragments 186 and 187 (= frr. 84 and 85 Pf.): *Euthycles the Locrian* (last *aition* of the book). Euthycles, an Olympic victor of

---

[23] The discovery of 3.7, 3.8, and 3.9 between 3.6 and 3.10 also results from a new fragment of the *Diegeseis*; see Gallazzi and Lehnus 2001: 13–18. We cannot rule out the possibility that between *Acontius and Cydippe* (3.6) and *The Nuptial Rite of the Eleans* (3.10) there were two—not three—unknown *aitia*.

Epizephyrian Locri, was unjustly accused of treason by his fellow citizens, who defiled his statue. When Locri was beset by famine, the Delphic Oracle said that this misfortune befell the Locrians because they dishonored Euthycles. Therefore the Locrians revered the statue of Euthycles, dedicated an altar to him, and established a cult in his honor at the beginning of the month.[24]

Book 4

The *Diegeseis* guarantee the sequence of the *aitia* throughout the entire book. Fragment 215, the *Epilogue* of the *Aetia*, is not attested in the *Diegeseis* Papyrus, but its final position is guaranteed by POxy 7.1011. For many elegies we only have the incipits, as recorded in the *Diegeseis*. The outline of the book is as follows.

4.1. Fragment 188 (= fr. 86 Pf.): fourth unknown *aition* (first *aition* of the book). The subject cannot be determined. We know, however, that this poem began with an invocation to the Muses.[25]

4.2. Fragments 189 through 191 (= frr. 87–89 Pf.): *The Delphic Daphnephoria*. The rite known as the Delphic Daphnephoria, when a boy travels from Delphi to the Thessalian Valley of Tempe and returns to Delphi crowned with leaves of the laurel (*daphne*) tree, commemorates the acts of purification performed by the young Apollo immediately after killing the *Python* at Delphi.

4.3. Fragment 192 (= fr. 90 Pf.): *Abdera*. This elegy regards a purification rite performed at Abdera in which a slave is abused as a scapegoat (φαρμακός), being stoned and banished beyond the boundaries.

4.4. Fragments 193 through 195 (= fr. 91 Pf. + SH 275 + fr. 92 Pf.): *Melicertes*. A ritual killing of babies and blinding of mothers in honor of Melicertes, performed in times past by the Leleges on the island of Tenedos and later suppressed, originated after the corpse of Melicertes was washed up on the island.

---

[24] The sequence 3.13–3.14 (*Phrygius and Pieria* to *Euthycles the Locrian*) is attested in POxy 19.2212, whereas the *Diegeseis* Papyrus has the sequence 3.12 followed by 3.14 (*Artemis the Goddess of Childbirth* followed by *Euthycles the Locrian*), probably preceded by 3.13 (*Phrygius and Pieria*). See Massimilla 2010: 397.

[25] We cannot exclude the possibility that fr. 188 belongs to *The Delphic Daphnephoria* (4.2), which in that case would be the first elegy of the book. See Pfeiffer 1949-53: 1.95.

4.5. Fragment 196 (= fr. 93 Pf.): *Theudotus of Lipara*. While besieging the island of Lipara, the Tyrrhenians (i.e., the Etruscans) promised to sacrifice to Apollo the strongest of the Liparenses if the god would make them victorious. After winning a victory, they sacrificed a warrior named Theudotus.[26]

4.6. Fragments 197 and 198 (= frr. 94 and 95 Pf.): *Limone*. On discovering that his daughter, Limone, had a secret lover, an Athenian man locked her up in her room with a horse, which killed her. He also speared her seducer and tied his corpse to a horse, which dragged it throughout the city. The elegy ends with the aetiological outcome of the story: since then a certain Athenian place has been called "of the Horse and of the Girl."

4.7. Fragment 199 (= fr. 96 Pf.): *The Boastful Hunter*. On killing a boar, a hunter said that those who surpass Artemis in hunting are not bound to dedicate their prey to her. Therefore he dedicated the head of the boar to himself, hanging it in a poplar tree. He went to sleep under the tree, and the boar's head fell and killed him. This story was probably set in Italy.

4.8. Fragment 200 (= fr. 97 Pf.): *The Pelasgian Walls*. The ancient Pelasgian Walls of Athens relate that they were built by the Tyrrhenians.

4.9. Fragments 201 and 202 (= frr. 98 and 99 Pf.): *Euthymus*. Euthymus of Epizephyrian Locri, an Olympic victor in boxing, freed the Bruttian city Temesa from a tribute—the ritual rape of young maidens—that had been enjoined upon it by "the Hero," the ghost of a shipmate of Odysseus. Euthymus got heroic honors. Two statues representing him were struck by lightning at Locri and at Olympia on the same day as proof of his sacredness. This story was possibly the *aition* from which the proverb "The Hero of Temesa" is derived.

4.10. Fragment 203 (= fr. 100 Pf.): *The Primordial Statue of Hera at Samos*. At first the statue of Hera on Samos was only a rough plank, credited with an Argive origin. Only later did it become anthropomorphic.

4.11. Fragment 204 (= fr. 101 Pf.): *The Other Statue of Hera at Samos*. A more recent statue of Hera on Samos has a vine winding round her hair and a lion skin at her feet. These symbols indicate the goddess' triumphs over Dionysus and Heracles, illegitimate sons of Zeus.

---

[26] It is extremely unlikely that one more elegy separated *Theudotus of Lipara* (4.5) from *Limone* (4.6). See Massimilla 2010: 429–430.

4.12. Fragment 205 (= fr. 102 Pf.): *Pasicles of Ephesus*. Pasicles, the governor of Ephesus, was pursued at night by some men, who were having difficulty with the pursuit in the dark. When they arrived at the Temple of Hera, Pasicles' mother, who was a priestess there, heard the uproar and ordered a lamp to be brought out. Thanks to its light the attackers succeeded in killing Pasicles.

4.13. Fragment 206 (= fr. 103 Pf.): *Androgeos*. Here we learn that Minos' son Androgeos is the so-called Hero of the Stern. The name is somehow related to the ancient Athenian port of Phalerum.

4.14. Fragment 207 (= fr. 104 Pf.): *The Thracian Oesydres*. The Parians, after killing a Thracian named Oesydres, underwent a long siege, probably laid to their colony Thasos. They consulted the Delphic Oracle and were ordered to pay as a fine whatever pleased the Bisalti (a Thracian people, to whom Oesydres presumably belonged).

4.15. Fragment 208 (= fr. 105 Pf.): *The Dragging of Antigone*. After her brothers had killed each other, Antigone dragged the body of Polynices to the funeral pyre of Eteocles. But the flames split into two, thereby confirming the eternal enmity between the brothers. This myth has two aetiological outcomes. In one Callimachus probably said that a certain place in Thebes has since then been called "The Dragging of Antigone." In the other he related that the prodigious splitting of the flames still takes place whenever sacrifices are made to Eteocles and Polynices together.

4.16. Fragments 209 and 210 (= frr. 106 and 107 Pf.): *The Roman Caius*. While the Peucetii (by which name the Etruscans are possibly meant here) were laying siege to Rome, a Roman soldier named Caius attacked and killed their leader, himself sustaining a wound in the thigh. When later he complained about his limp, his mother's scolding induced him to take courage again.

4.17. Fragments 211 and 212 (= frr. 108 and 109 Pf.): *The Anchor of the "Argo" Left at Cyzicus*. While sailing to Colchis, the Argonauts disembarked at Cyzicus to take on fresh water. At the foot of the fountain Artacia they left the stone that they had been using as an anchor, since it was too light, and took a heavier one aboard. The first stone was later dedicated to Athena.

4.18. Fragment 213 (= fr. 110 Pf.): *The Lock of Berenice*. In this elegy the constellation known as the Lock of Berenice provides the *aition* of its name. When Berenice II's husband, Ptolemy III, had left Alexandria to wage war against Syria, the queen vowed to dedicate a lock of her hair to the gods upon his safe return. When Ptolemy returned,

Berenice kept her promise. But as soon as the lock had been cut and offered, Aphrodite sent Zephyrus to fetch it and transformed it into a new constellation. Despite the magnificence of its present condition, the Lock would prefer to be back on Berenice's head.[27]

4.19. Fragment 215 (= fr. 112 Pf.): *Epilogue* (end of the *Aetia*). Callimachus quotes a passage from the beginning of the *Aetia* that describes the meeting between Hesiod and the Muses on Mount Helicon beside the spring Hippocrene (1.3, *The Dream*: fr. 4.1–2). Then he takes leave of a goddess (perhaps Cyrene, the eponymous heroine of his native land) and of Zeus. Finally he marks the transition from the *Aetia* to the book of the *Iambi*, which followed in his collected works.[28]

Book 3 or Book 4

Fragments 216 through 250 (= frr. 138–74 Pf.) are papyrus scraps, probably belonging to Book 3. Fragment 251 (= fr. 175 Pf.) is a somewhat larger papyrus scrap that may belong to Book 3 or to Book 4. The little we can read of it is perhaps compatible with 4.15 (*The Dragging of Antigone*).

Respective Lengths of the Elegies

The last eight elegies of Book 3 together with the whole of Book 4 totaled some 1,300 lines, as we infer from POxy 7.1011.[29] A stichometric sign in POxy 19.2213 shows that in all likelihood the thousandth line of Book 3 was to be found within its final *aition* (3.14, *Euthycles the Locrian*). These two facts in combination indicate that Books 3 and 4 consisted of approximately a thousand lines each and that the last eight elegies of Book 3 occupied some three hundred lines.

As the outline proposed above shows, seventeen elegies can be located in Book 3 (3.1, *Onnes and Tottes, The Statue of Apollo at Delos, An Uncertain Thracian Story*, and the poems 3.2 through 3.14). Since

---

[27] Fr. 214, which deals with Lesbos and certainly belongs to Book 4, cannot be confidently assigned to any of the elegies mentioned above. Yet it might belong to *Melicertes* (4.4). See Massimilla 2010: 509–510.

[28] Fr. 215.9, αὐτὰρ ἐγὼ Μουσέων πεζὸν [ἔ]πειμι νομόν ("but I will pass on to the pedestrian pasture of the Muses").

[29] See Pfeiffer 1949–53: 2.xxii–xxiii; but note that 32 pages of POxy 7.1011—not 34 pages, as Pfeiffer writes—are missing between fr. 175.3 (3.7) and fr. 215.1 (4.19).

we know that Book 4 probably contained eighteen *aitia* before the *Epilogue* (see the outline above), it is plausible that the seventeen recognizable elegies of Book 3 accounted for all or most of its contents. This means that the approximately three hundred lines of the last eight poems of Book 3 had to suffice for the second half of that book, or slightly less. Thus it seems that some poems included in the first half were quite long. This is in fact confirmed by 3.1 (*The Victory of Berenice*) and 3.6 (*Acontius and Cydippe*). Especially 3.1, the great elegy that opens Book 3, is of a most unusual length: in all probability it ran to about 240 lines, filling almost a quarter of the whole book. The elegy 3.6 was very long also, at least 150 lines. Within Book 4, we see that the last *aition* (4.18, *The Lock of Berenice*) reaches considerable length, ninety-four lines, in keeping with its prominent position at the end of the entire *Aetia*, where it is also meant to be a companion piece to 3.1 (*The Victory of Berenice*). Some elegies are instead very short. *The Statue of Apollo at Delos* (fr. 64.4–17) amounts to fourteen lines; 3.4 (*The Tomb of Simonides*) covers eighteen lines or slightly more, and 3.5 (*The Fountains of Argos*) is of roughly the same length. Those two short poems, 3.4 and 3.5, precede the long 3.6 (*Acontius and Cydippe*). Callimachus probably arranged the *aitia* similarly elsewhere also, alternating long and short ones.

Aetiological Aspects

As I have tried to highlight in the outlines proposed above, almost all the elegies of Books 3 and 4 may be referred back to a basic *aition*. We see that sometimes the aetiological outcome is expressly mentioned at the end of a poem: this is the case with 3.3 (*The Attic Thesmophoria*: cf. fr. 162.9–12), 3.13 (*Phrygius and Pieria*: cf. fr. 185), and 4.6 (*Limone*: cf. fr. 198.4–5). We see also that some elegies begin by mentioning what will be explained in the following lines (3.12 [*Artemis the Goddess of Childbirth*], 4.11 [*The Other Statue of Hera at Samos*], 4.13 [*Androgeos*]). A peculiar development is found in 3.12, where we would expect to learn why women in labor call on the virgin goddess Artemis: in fact, to judge by the *diegesis*, three different explanations of this custom were proposed, without any of them being given priority.

Some poems apparently lack an aetiological core, especially in Book 4 (3.4 [*The Tomb of Simonides*], 4.5 [*Theudotus of Lipara*], 4.7 [*The Boastful Hunter*], 4.12 [*Pasicles of Ephesus*], 4.14 [*The Thracian Oesydres.*], 4.16 [*The Roman Caius*]). But we must bear in mind that when our information about an elegy depends solely or mainly on its *diegesis*, we cannot be certain about the absence of this element, since the *Diegeseis* are at times textually damaged; and even when well preserved, they often provide superficial or incomplete information.[30] Yet the fact that a poem such as *The Tomb of Simonides* (3.4) offers no *aition*, even though it is well preserved and almost complete, leads us to suppose that here and there some elegies did not hinge on aetiology (Körte 1935: 236).

Connections among Elegies

Callimachus chose to frame the second half of the *Aetia* within two elegies recently written in honor of Berenice II (3.1 [*The Victory of Berenice*] and 4.18 [*The Lock of Berenice*], see Parsons 1977: 50). Moreover, in the *Epilogue* (4.19) he refers explicitly to *The Dream* at the beginning of the *Aetia* (1.3), quoting almost verbatim a passage about Hesiod's meeting the Muses on Mount Helicon.[31]

It is possible to spot other connections between the beginnings and the ends of Books 3 and 4. The two elegies that open and close Book 3 (3.1 [*The Victory of Berenice*] and 3.14 [*Euthycles the Locrian*]) refer to Panhellenic games, the Nemean and the Olympic, respectively (Fantuzzi and Hunter 2004: 46–47). The first line of Book 4 (4.1) apparently refers simultaneously to the *Epilogue* (4.19), to the beginning of Book 3 (3.1, *The Victory of Berenice*), and to the *Prologue* of the *Aetia* (1.1).[32]

Furthermore, in the *Epilogue* (4.19) Callimachus mentions first the Graces and then the Heliconian Muses, deliberately reversing the order chosen at the beginning of the *Aetia*, where he speaks first about the

---

[30] For an attempt to identify the aetiology of 4.12 (*Pasicles of Ephesus*), see Stroux 1934: 313 n. 21.

[31] Cf. fr. 4.1–2, ποιμ₁ένι μῆλα νέμ₁οντι παρ' ἴχνιον ὀξέος ἵππου | Ἡσιόδ₁ῳ Μουσέων ἑσμὸ₁ς ὅτ' ἠντίασεν ("when the swarm of the Muses met the shepherd Hesiod tending sheep by the footprint of the fiery horse"), and fr. 215.5–6, τῷ Μοῦσαι πολλὰ νέμοντι βοτά | σὺν μύθους ἐβάλοντο παρ' ἴχν[ι]ον ὀξέος ἵππου ("[Hesiod] with whom the Muses spoke, as he tended his many sheep by the footprint of the fiery horse"). See Massimilla 2010: 516.

[32] At the beginning of Book 3 (fr. 143.1–2) Callimachus names Zeus and addresses Berenice. At the end of Book 4 (fr. 215.8) he greets Zeus and begs him to safeguard Ptolemy and Berenice. The beginning of Book 4 (fr. 188, incomplete text) contains an invocation to the Muses and a mention of sovereignty and of song: in this, it is formally similar to the beginning of Book 1 (fr. 1.1–3). For this last point, see D'Alessio 1996: 500.

Muses in his invocation of them (1.2) and in *The Dream* (1.3) and then about the Graces in the first *aition* (1.4). In a similar chiastic arrangement, a story about the *Argo*'s outbound voyage to Colchis (4.17, *The Anchor of the "Argo"*) precedes the last *aition* (4.18, *The Lock of Berenice*), mirroring how *The Return of the Argonauts* (1.5) follows the first *aition* (1.4, *The Graces*).

It is clear that in order to endow his extremely heterogeneous collection with a certain unity, Callimachus has created a network of cross-references between the beginnings and the ends not only of the whole *Aetia* but also of its second half and of its third and fourth books singly. Similar links sometimes apply also to elegies within Books 3 and 4. Resemblances in subject matter allow us to recognize connections between *aitia* in immediate sequence as well as among others more widely separated. It is important, however, to use caution in this regard. As for sequences of poems, when our information about the order of the elegies depends upon the *Diegeseis* alone, we must not have too much faith in the reliability of that source. We know that in at least one case a sequence of poems attested by the *Diegeseis* (3.12–14, probably preceded by 3.13) differs from what we find in another papyrus (POxy 19.2212, with the sequence 3.13–14). The same papyrus (POxy 19.2212) seems to preserve, after *The Statue of Apollo at Delos* (fr. 64.4–17), not *An Uncertain Thracian Story* (fr. 64.18–25), as in POxy 19.2211, but some different elegy (Massimilla 1996: 131). We get the impression that the very nature of the *aitia* of Books 3 and 4, disconnected as they are each from the next and lacking any narrative links, has exposed them to instability in the order of their transmission. Therefore we cannot be sure that the order of the elegies, as witness the *Diegeseis* (or other papyri also), always reflects Callimachus' intention.

Besides that, when seeking to perceive connections among widely separated poems, we should avoid being too subtle. We must bear in mind that, in all likelihood, Books 3 and 4 of the *Aetia* include several poems that Callimachus had previously composed (Parsons 1977: 50). So it seems implausible that, by including (partly, at least) preexistent pieces, he could or would wish to create too many very complicated internal connections.

Let us now consider sequences of elegies with similar subject matter. In Book 3 two consecutive poems concern statues of Apollo (the second one conspicuously so): *Onnes and Tottes* (fr. 65 + fr. 64.1–3) and *The Statue of Apollo at Delos* (fr. 64.4–17). Artemis is the protagonist of 3.12 (*Artemis the Goddess of Childbirth*) and plays a prominent role in 3.13 (*Phrygius and Pieria*).[33] In Book 4 both 4.2 (*The Delphic Daphnephoria*) and 4.3 (*Abdera*) deal with purification rites. At the same time 4.3, because of its macabre subject, is similar to 4.4 (*Melicertes*), 4.5 (*Theudotus of Lipara*), and 4.6 (*Limone*).[34] More specifically, both 4.4 and 4.5 are concerned with human sacrifices carried out by non-Greek peoples. The elegies 4.10 and 4.11, describing two statues of Hera on Samos, clearly form a pair. To them we may join 4.12 (*Pasicles of Ephesus*), which also has to do with Hera.[35]

Let us also take into account here connections among elegies that do not fall in immediate sequence. In Book 3, both 3.1 (*The Victory of Berenice*) and 3.10 (*The Nuptial Rite of the Eleans*) portray Heracles as the founder of Panhellenic games, the Nemean and the Olympic, respectively. Book 3 also gives unusual prominence to *eros* in two poems (3.6 [*Acontius and Cydippe*] and 3.13 [*Phrygius and Pieria*]) that look very like each other for their happy endings and for the important role that Artemis plays in them (Fantuzzi and Hunter 2004: 47). But we note that in order to create a significant element of *variatio*, Callimachus chooses contrasting points of view in these two elegies, giving a central and active role to the male character in 3.6 and to the female in 3.13.

In Book 4 both 4.5 (*Theudotus of Lipara*) and 4.8 (*The Pelasgian Walls*) tell stories referring to the "Tyrrhenians," by which name the Etruscans are meant in 4.5 and the Pelasgians in 4.8. Etruscans may possibly be meant in 4.16 also (*The Roman Caius*).

Other connections may be recognized between Books 3 and 4. *Onnes and Tottes* (fr. 65 + fr. 64.1–3), 4.5 (*Theudotus of Lipara*), and 4.14 (*The Thracian Oesydres*) share warfare as their subject and show Apollo in a significant role. Both 3.14 (*Euthycles the Locrian*) and 4.9 (*Euthymus*) center on Olympic victors of Epizephyrian Locri and relate that their statues became objects of worship.[36]

---

[33] See Fantuzzi and Hunter 2004: 47; Massimilla 2010: 399.
[34] See Herter 1937: 139; Świderek 1951: 232.
[35] See Norsa and Vitelli 1934: 14 n. 1; Herter 1937: 139; Mras 1938b: 54; Świderek 1951: 232.
[36] Olympic victors—especially if from Magna Graecia—and their statues seem to have been a recurrent topic within the second half of the *Aetia*. See Lehnus 1990b: 286–291; Massimilla 2010: 411, 414.

Narrative Voices

In the second half of the *Aetia*, with the oneiric conversation with the Muses no longer in play, Callimachus can freely select and manage the narrative voices of the single elegies. Thus, although (as it seems) most of the poems have a primary external narrator, some are entirely set in the mouths of internal narrators, in accordance with a format deriving from epigrammatic poetry. So speak the dead poet Simonides (3.4), the Lock of Berenice (4.18), probably the Pelasgian walls of Athens (4.8), and perhaps the scapegoat of Abdera (4.3). Internal narration is also to be found, but in dialogue form, in *The Statue of Apollo at Delos* (fr. 64.4–17), which consists entirely of a conversation between the statue and an anonymous interlocutor, without any narrative links.[37]

Callimachus in the Foreground

Callimachus often sets his own persona in the foreground. In the two poems that open and close the second half of the *Aetia* (3.1 [*The Victory of Berenice*] and 4.19 [the *Epilogue*]) his status as court poet comes prominently to light. Here Callimachus depicts himself as an enthusiastic praiser of Berenice's Nemean victory (3.1, frr. 143 and 144) and as a suppliant who prays to Zeus for the monarchs' prosperity (4.19, fr. 215.8). But in the *Epilogue* Callimachus gives prominence to other aspects of his persona also: perhaps his attachment to his native land, Cyrene (fr. 215.2–4 and 7), and certainly his status as *poeta philologus*, who marks the transition from the *Aetia* to the book of *Iambi* (fr. 215.9).

In a passage of *The Victory of Berenice* (3.1, fr. 154) Callimachus explicitly draws our attention to his narrative strategies. Here, taking his inspiration from Pindar, he invites the reader to bridge a conspicuous narrative gap and thereby reduce the length of the poem. The device is the more remarkable for also emphasizing Callimachus' unwillingness to dwell on well-known myths and for shaping a double aposiopesis, first of Callimachus in his own poetic persona and then of a character in the story he is telling (Heracles in conversation with Molorchus).[38]

---

[37] See M.A. Harder 2004: 68–69; Morrison 2007: 197–199.
[38] Αὐτὸς ἐπιφράσσαιτο, τάμοι δ' ἄπο μῆκος ἀοιδῇ· | ὅσσα δ' ἀνειρομένῳ φῇ[σ]ε, τάδ' ἐξερέω· | "ἄττα γέρον, τὰ μὲν ἄλλα πα[ρὼν ἐν δ]αιτὶ μαθήσει, | νῦν δὲ ... πεύσῃ..."

Callimachus' many-sided persona comes prominently to light in the long fragment 174, which preserves the last seventy-seven lines of *Acontius and Cydippe* (3.6) in very good textual condition. In verses 4–9, where Callimachus is on the point of recalling the secret marriage of Zeus and Hera, he stops short (again in the style of Pindar) and, interrupting the main narrative, explains and comments on his self-censorship: he heatedly reminds his own soul that the gods' secrets must not be revealed, blames it for its imprudent loquacity, and ironically remarks that learning is a serious evil if one fails to curb his tongue. Further on, in verses 44–49, Callimachus puts forward his opinion (δοκέω) that Acontius, after finally managing to marry Cydippe, would not have given up his first night with her for anything in the world, adding that all who know how difficult love can be would support this judgment. At last, in the long final part of the poem (vv. 50–77), Callimachus sets his scholarly research in the foreground: he names the historian Xenomedes of Ceos as his source in *Acontius and Cydippe* (3.6) and gives an account of the information that Xenomedes provided about the most important myths of Ceos. At the end of *Melicertes* (4.4) also Callimachus mentions his source—here probably the historian Leander of Miletus. (Cf. fr. 195.2–3.)

In *Acontius and Cydippe* (3.6) and *Melicertes* (4.4) Callimachus insists, not without reason, that his sources are ancient and truthful.[39] His Muses are the volumes of the Alexandrian Library.

("[The reader] may suggest to himself, and cut short the song's length. But I will relate all [that Heracles] answered to the questions [of Molorchus]: 'Father, old man, the rest you will learn while present at the feast, but now you will hear...'"). See Massimilla 2010: 289–291.

[39] Cf. fr. 174.54 (ἀρχαίου Ξενομήδεος, "of old Xenomedes"), fr. 174.66 (γέρων, "old man"), fr. 174.76 (πρέσβυς ἐτητυμίῃ μεμελημένος, "old man, lover of truth"); and fr. 195.2–3, Λε]ανδρίδες εἴ τι παλαιαί | φθ[έγγ]ονται...ἱστορίαι ("if Leander's old *Histories* speak truth").

CHAPTER THREE

CALLIMACHUS AS FRAGMENT

Annette Harder

Abstract

To a large extent Callimachus' works have survived only in fragments and, due to the whims of the transmission, our knowledge of these works is far from complete and rather uneven. This chapter investigates the implications of the fact that a poem survives only in fragments, with a focus on Callimachus' *Aetia* as a case study. Distinguishing between various categories of evidence (testimonia, book-fragments and papyrus-fragments) it offers examples of the dangers and pitfalls of this kind of transmission and discusses the ways in which one can deal with a fragmentary poem in a responsible and profitable manner. It also shows that the rather diverse material offers much more than just "text" of the *Aetia* and helps to provide a basis for further interpretation and informs us about the work's reception and readership.

To a large extent Callimachus' works have survived only in fragments. Thus we have fragments of the *Aetia*, the *Hecale*, the *Iambi*, and some lyrical fragments such as *The Apotheosis of Arsinoe* or *The Victory of Sosibius*.[1] This means that of these poems we possess knowledge of a special kind—not only less complete but also distributed rather unevenly, because of the whims of their transmission—and therefore fundamentally different from our knowledge of complete poems such as the *Hymns* and the *Epigrams*.

For example, in the case of the *Aetia*, on the one hand we have some large chunks of text, as in the long fragment of the love story *Acontius and Cydippe* in *Aetia* 3 (fr. 75). From this fragment we can get a good idea about Callimachus' meter, language, style, and narrative technique, and generally about the experimental character of his work. We are also thus able to form an opinion about his attitude as

[1] The standard edition is still that of Rudolf Pfeiffer 1949–53, with additions in the *Supplementum Hellenisticum* (Lloyd-Jones and Parsons 1983). For editions with translations and some notes, see D'Alessio 2007 (in Italian) or Asper 2004 (in German). My own edition with commentary will appear in 2011.

an Alexandrian scholar-poet, about his playfulness and sophistication, and about the more serious concerns lurking behind all this. Also, thanks to a century of papyrus finds, we have now enough material to create a picture of the *Aetia* as a whole and to form some idea about its structure and concerns. On the other hand, many questions remain, even about better-preserved parts of the *Aetia* such as the story of Acontius and Cydippe, and there are numerous small scraps among the *Fragmenta incerta* that defy interpretation. We even have a number of not-so-small scraps that are almost as hard to understand as the small ones, such as the tantalizing fragment 93 about a human sacrifice to Apollo following the siege of the small island Lipara in *Aetia* 4,[2] the beginning of which is still unclear and a matter of debate, or the vexed lines about long and short poems in the *Prologue* of the *Aetia* (fr. 1.9–12).[3]

All this material adds up to more or less complete lines of roughly one-tenth of the *Aetia* (i.e., ca. 600 lines out of ca. 6,000) and many parts of lines, often not much more than a few letters or single words. Apart from these fragments of the actual text there are also a certain number of testimonia, including scholarly material on the *Aetia* of a subliterary nature, such as commentaries and summaries. Rather paradoxically, the *Aetia* has been studied so much by several generations of scholars, particularly since the first papyrus fragments turned up, that in spite of all the limitations one gets the impression that somehow we still know the *Aetia* quite well. In a way we do, too, because thorough investigation of all the fragments has taught us a great deal. Even so, there is also a danger of assuming that we know more than we actually do and filling in gaps without any solid basis.

In this chapter I will investigate the implications of the fact that a poem survives only in fragments and focus on Callimachus' *Aetia* as a case study. I will give some examples of the dangers and pitfalls of this kind of transmission, discuss the ways in which one can deal with a fragmentary poem in a responsible and profitable manner, and show how much the fragments actually have to offer. I will draw attention to the various categories of evidence—testimonia, book fragments, and papyrus fragments—and by way of illustration I will also adduce some

---

[2] See, e.g., Massimilla, forthcoming.
[3] See recently, e.g., Bastianini 1996; Luppe 1997; Spanoudakis 1998; C.W. Müller 1998: 36–40 and 2002: 237; Hunter 2006b; Tsantsanoglou 2007.

examples of the treatment of fragments from the recent as well as the more distant past.[4]

Testimonia

If we take a look at the testimonia to the *Aetia* in the second volume of Rudolf Pfeiffer's edition (1949-53), we find a small group of texts that have in common the fact that they tell us something about the *Aetia* or its reception. Such testimonia are of considerable importance and nowadays usually form an integral part of editions of fragmentary texts.[5]

In the case of Callimachus we find testimonia that tell us facts about his works, such as an epigram that offers a list of Callimachus' works, including in line 7 τῶν μεγίστων Αἰτίων τὴν τετράδα ("the four books of the very substantial *Aetia*": *test.* 23).[6] Another anonymous epigram is an important testimonium for the structure of the *Aetia*. It tells us that the *Aetia* was presented as a dream about gods and heroes and that this dream brought Callimachus from Libya to Mount Helicon, where the Muses answered his questions and told him aetiological stories (*test.* 27). More recent evidence, however, also shows that one should be careful in taking everything in the testimonia at face value, as thanks to papyrus finds we now know that the dialogue with the Muses was the narrative framework only of *Aetia* 1 and 2, and not of Books 3 and 4.

Other testimonia give some indication of the work's reception, positive as well as negative. A passage about an iambic paraphrase of Callimachus' works by the Roman Marianus in the late fifth or early sixth century AD suggests that the poet was still considered important at that time and that it seemed worthwhile to make the contents of his work more widely accessible (*test.* 24). On the other hand, other testimonia indicate that at some stage the *Aetia* was also considered antiquarian, difficult, and devoid of human interest: a poem of Martial's tells

---

[4] For other publications on the way one can approach fragments of Greek literature, see Radt 2002b; Parsons 1982; Prins 1999: 23-73. On the specific demands on scholars who edit and collect fragments and write commentaries on them, see Most 1997 and Stephens 2002a.

[5] As in, e.g., the editions of the fragments of Aeschylus, Sophocles, and Euripides: see the volumes of *TrGF*.

[6] Except when specified otherwise, testimonia and fragments are cited according to their numbers in Pfeiffer 1949-53.

Mamurra that if he is not interested in getting to know himself he should read the *Aetia*, where he will find the monsters of mythological stories but nothing about human nature (*test.* 25a), and Clement of Alexandria in the late second or early third century AD considers the *Aetia* an obscure poem suitable for exercising the interpretive skills of grammarians (*test.* 26). Martial and Clement of Alexandria create the impression of a rather dry and unattractive work, but they probably had reasons of their own for judging rather one-sidedly, and one should therefore treat such evidence as theirs with some caution.

Apart from these testimonia referring to the *Aetia* as a whole we also have a number of passages that somewhat misleadingly appear as supposed fragments in modern editions. Strictly speaking these passages are not fragments but testimonia, because they do not contain any actual text of Callimachus' works but rather tell us something about certain parts of those works. Fragment 8, placed in the story of the Argonauts at Anaphe, where the Argonauts landed after a frightening darkness on their homeward journey and founded a ritual for Apollo Aegletes, is an example of such a testimonium. In this testimonium the scholia to Euripides *Medea* 1334 discuss the location of the death of Apsyrtus at Medea's hands. They tell us that in Euripides Medea killed her brother at the hearth at home, that in *Argonautica* 4.452–81 she killed him at the altar of Artemis (i.e., on a small island on the Argonauts' homeward journey), and that in Callimachus she did so at home in her native country. The precise reference of this testimonium is not entirely certain, because the scholia mention only Callimachus and not the work, but the story of the Argonauts in *Aetia* 1 (frr. 7–21) seems a very likely location. In this story we read that Aeetes began an angry speech in which he seems to have accused and threatened the Argonauts at their departure ὡς ἴδεν ἔργα θυγατρ[ός ("when he saw the deeds done by his daughter": fr. 7.27), and ancient scholia on this passage show that some kind of killing was mentioned in this passage of the *Aetia* (Pfeiffer 1949–53: 1.19 line 24 ἔκτανον). Thus a small piece of evidence leads to the interesting conclusion that in his story of the Argonauts Callimachus took a position on a mythographical issue dealt with by several poets, namely the location of the killing of Apsyrtus, and that he followed the tradition of the tragedian and differed from the version of Apollonius Rhodius. As the interaction between Callimachus and Apollonius—who may have written before or after Callimachus or even at the same time in continuous interaction—

in general and in the story of the Argonauts at Anaphe in particular is the object of much scholarly interest, this is valuable information (M.A. Harder 2002a: 217-23).

Under the heading of testimonia one should also consider the scholia and summaries found on papyrus, which have been printed but not systematically numbered in Pfeiffer's edition. These too can be of great importance and make valuable contributions to our knowledge of the *Aetia*.

Thus, for example, the *Scholia Florentina* (Pfeiffer 1949-53: 1.3ff.) help us to reconstruct the beginning of *Aetia* 1 and to locate a number of fragments in this part of the work. These scholia contain the first line of the *Prologue*, followed by comments and summaries of part of its contents and a description of the beginning of the story of Callimachus' dream about his dialogue with the Muses on Mount Helicon. Then they quote the first line of the first aetiological story of the *Aetia*, the story of the Graces on Paros (frr. 3-7), followed by a summary and some comments, and after that the first line and a summary of the next group of stories, those about Apollo and the Argonauts at Anaphe, Heracles and the Lindian farmer, and Heracles and Thiodamas, also with various comments. These comments offer intriguing additional information, such as a list of people who may be lurking behind the Telchines of fragment 1.1 (Pfeiffer 1949-53: 1.3) or information about the sources Callimachus used for his story of the Graces, the Argive historians Agias and Dercylus (Pfeiffer 1949-53: 1.13).

These scholia also tell us something about the structure and organization of the stories. We read that in the story of the Graces on Paros Callimachus also asked the Muses about the Graces' parentage and, before hearing their answer to his question about the cult on Paros, told them what he himself knew about the different traditions on this point (Pfeiffer 1949-53: 1.13). The scholia also tell us that Callimachus combined two scurrilous rituals, for Apollo on Anaphe and for Heracles at Lindus, in one question to the Muses (Pfeiffer 1949-53: 1.17; cf. also fr. 7.19-21). They also seem to say that after the Muses told the story of the Lindian farmer whose ox Heracles slaughtered and ate, Callimachus himself added another, somewhat similar but more flattering story, about Heracles and Thiodamas, whose ox Heracles killed in order to feed his starving son, Hyllus. Besides, Heracles subsequently punished Thiodamas, together with his people, for his inhospitable and rude behavior (Pfeiffer 1949-53: 1.31).

All this information from the scholia is precious evidence, as we learn much about the first part of the *Aetia*. We observe the prominence of programmatically important divinities such as the Muses, the Graces, and Apollo. We become aware of a great deal of attention for the Ptolemies' ancestor Heracles, who appears first as a rather boorish glutton and is then, as it were, rehabilitated by appearing as a solicitous father looking after his son and as a civilizer of mankind transporting Thiodamas' Dryopians to the Peloponnese, where they mingle with other people and lose their villainous character. We may also notice that immediately at the beginning of the *Aetia* Callimachus' treatment of the Ptolemies is by no means slavishly flattering and that his attitude toward the Muses is not that of a dependent mouthpiece either, as he is telling them things also (as can be seen in the story of the Graces, discussed above).

Another important source of information is the *Diegeseis* papyrus (Pfeiffer 1949-53: 1.71-123, where its *diegesis* is quoted with each aetiological story), which offers summaries of most of the stories in *Aetia* 3 and 4 and helps us to form a picture of the outlines, composition, and content of these two books. This papyrus has enabled us to locate many fragments within these two books. Thus we know, for example, that the love story *Acontius and Cydippe* (frr. 67-75) was part of *Aetia* 3, that *The Lock of Berenice* (fr. 110) stood at the end of *Aetia* 4, and that there was very little room for *The Victory of Berenice* except at the beginning of *Aetia* 3. As to the overall composition of these two books we can also see that Callimachus did not use the format of the dialogue with the Muses here but placed the stories next to each other without any such framework. Even so, however, he reminded his readers of the lively interaction of direct discourse by letting many of the stories begin with a question (e.g., fr. 79 with a question to Artemis as a goddess of childbirth) or a second-person address (e.g., fr. 84 addressed to the story's main character, Euthycles of Locri) or by letting unusual characters speak about themselves in an epigrammatic fashion, such as the dead poet Simonides (fr. 64), the lost Pelasgian Walls of Athens (fr. 97), or the Lock of Berenice, transformed into a constellation (fr. 110).[7] As to the books' content it also becomes clear that there were certain groups of related stories. Thus there is a focus on statues of Hera in fragments 100 and 101 and on human sacrifice and capital punishment in some rather grim stories

---

[7] See Krevans 1984.

in fragments 90–95, where we find descriptions and explanations of a scapegoat ritual in Abdera, a sacrifice of babies whenever there was an emergency on Tenedos, a human sacrifice after the siege of Lipara, and the killing of a girl and her adulterous lover in Athens.

On a smaller scale also this kind of subliterary material can offer valuable information, as for example in the *London Scholia* 45 (Pfeiffer 1949–53: 1.7) and the scholia to fragment 2a.5–15 (Pfeiffer 1949–53: 2.102), where we learn that at the beginning of the *Aetia* Callimachus used the noun δεκάς rather obscurely to indicate that someone was added to the nine Muses. The *London Scholia* seem to mention only Arsinoe as a candidate, but the other scholia discuss three possibilities: the first of them still obscure, the second Apollo Musagetes, and the third Arsinoe.

There are also texts that are relevant for the *Aetia* but not identified as testimonia or fragments in Pfeiffer's edition. Such texts include, for example, the letters of Aristaenetus, an epistolographer dated to the late fifth and the early sixth century AD who in his letters 1.10 and 1.15 offers summaries of two love stories in *Aetia* 3, *Acontius and Cydippe* (frr. 67–75) and *Phrygius and Pieria* (frr. 80–83). These letters have long been used as a source for Callimachus' stories, but only in the course of the last century could one use papyrus fragments of both stories to verify earlier conclusions (M.A. Harder 1993c). Careful comparison of the material has shown that although on the whole Aristaenetus is following Callimachus rather closely, there are also important differences, and that one should be cautious when using Aristaenetus for reconstructing Callimachus' work in detail. When, for instance, we compare Aristaenetus 1.10.81–88 with fragment 75.12–19, about the illnesses that affect Cydippe when her father is trying to marry her off to another man instead of Acontius, there are close similarities between the two texts overall, but we also find considerable differences in, for example, the description of Cydippe's three illnesses. In fragment 75.12–19 this description is fairly explicit (epilepsy, quartan fever, a debilitating cold), whereas Aristaenetus 1.10.84–88 leaves out the details, merely speaking in general terms three times about Cydippe's falling ill. Similarly, Aristaenetus leaves out the learned digression on epilepsy's being wrongly regarded as a sacred disease in fragment 75.12–14 as well as Callimachus' summary of his source, the Cean history of Xenomedes, at the end of the story in fragment 75.53–77. It is precisely some of the elements that we now regard as typical of Callimachus (interposing in his own poems and drawing attention to his status as an Alexandrian scholar), and as therefore of particular interest, that Aristaenetus leaves out. Thus some caution is needed in using this kind of testimonium.

Even more caution is necessary when one tries to draw inferences about Callimachus' verse from the work of Latin poets. Even in an obvious case such as Catullus 66, which was intended as a translation of Callimachus' *Lock of Berenice* (fr. 110), there are several small differences, as in for instance Catullus 66.45–46, "cum Medi peperere nouom mare, cumque iuuentus | per medium classi barbara nauit Athon" ("when the Medes made a new sea, and when their young men sailed straight through Mount Athos with their barbarian fleet"), where Catullus leaves out the reference to the rather obscure "ox piercer of your mother, Arsinoe," in fragment 110.45–46, βουπόρος "Ἀρσινόη͜ις μ͜ητρὸς σέο, καὶ διὰ μέ[σσου | Μηδείων ὀλοαὶ νῆες ἔβησαν Ἄθω ("the ox piercer of your mother, Arsinoe, and the destructive ships of the Medes went straight through Mount Athos"), as papyrus finds have now revealed. So long as we had only the text of Catullus, no one would have guessed what Callimachus actually wrote.

Summarizing, one may say that the testimonia are varied and of great importance for our knowledge of the *Aetia*, both regarding its overall structure and reception and concerning all kinds of details of its contents. They must, however, be treated with caution, as we cannot always know whether the testimonia are really based on accurate firsthand knowledge of a passage or work that we think they may refer to, whether the author of the testimonium really understood the text he was referring to, or whether he had considerations of his own that made him create a picture that was not quite accurate.

Book Fragments

The so-called book fragments of ancient authors are other authors' literal quotations of bits of text—sometimes only a single word—from antiquity until well into the Byzantine period. Until about a century ago the book fragments were our main source for the text of Callimachus. After a number of scholars had collected them, Otto Schneider published the fragments available in 1873 in the sturdy second volume of his text of Callimachus, which became the standard edition of its time (O. Schneider 1870–73).

It is in the nature of the book fragments that whoever may quote them always does so for a particular purpose. The fact that his interests are not necessarily the same as ours can at times be frustrating—for instance, because we would want to locate and interpret a given fragment in its context, but the author tells us nothing about it because he is interested in only an unusual word or metrical feature. On the other hand, when we survey the various fragments of a given work as a group, we may get a picture of certain features of the work, as well as of the elements in it that interested ancient authors or of their views of the work's literary or other aspects.

A closer scrutiny of the book fragments in *Aetia* 1 may illustrate this point (and fragments of the other books also fit with this picture):

1. One of the reasons for quoting from the *Aetia* was to illustrate aspects of the elegiac meter. Thus, for instance, we owe a large part of fragment 3 to Hephaestion, who wants to give an example of a pentameter of thirteen syllables.
2. Callimachus' vocabulary was generally considered difficult and unusual. Accordingly, many of his usages are adduced in scholia on various authors as illustrations for some unusual or typically poetic phrasing (e.g., fr. 24.7, quoted in the scholia on Apollonius Rhodius) or are explained in ancient lexicons, such as the lexicon of Hesychius or the *Etymologicum genuinum* (e.g., fr. 22); or grammarians may comment on their spellings, as for example in fragment 19, where Choeroboscus comments on the form Μελαντείους. We find comments on Callimachus' use of words also, as in fragment 5, where the scholia on the *Iliad* maintain that he confuses θύος ("sacrifice") with θύον ("incense"), or in fragment 10, where the scholia on Apollonius Rhodius refer to Callimachus' use of μαστύς as an unusual word for "search."
3. Other quotations are due to remarks on syntax, grammar, or style. Thus the grammarian Apollonius Dyscolus quotes fragment 6, οἱ δ' ἕνεκ' Εὐρυνόμη Τιτηνιὰς εἶπαν ἔτικτεν ("and others said that Titanian Eurynome was their mother"), as an example of Callimachus' "annoying" habit of confusing the word order; and fragment 28, τόν σε Κροτωπιάδην ("you, the grandson of Crotopus"), as an example of Callimachus' adopting the Attic usage of placing an article before a personal pronoun.
4. Often, too, we have quotations thanks to the fact that a fragment may help to illustrate some point of history or geography. Thus fragment 4, about Minos' expansion over the Cyclades, is due to Cyril of Alexandria's illustrating the notion that Minos was not

content to rule over Crete alone, and two of the sources of fragment 15 quote it to adduce evidence for the two harbors of Corcyra. Less often we find fragments such as 27 and 41 in the *Florilegium* of Johannes Stobaeus, where they are quoted for their moral content.

Thus we see that the *Aetia* became an object of study for a great variety of scholars who were interested in metrical, linguistic, or literary aspects of the poem but also regarded it as serious evidence for various kinds of antiquarian or moral knowledge. It is also interesting, particularly because of the epigram of Martial's discussed above (test. 25a), that Stobaeus quotes only a few fragments of the *Aetia*, whereas his *Florilegium* is full of moralizing fragments from Greek tragedy, especially the plays of Euripides. This suggests that although one should probably not consider the *Aetia* devoid of human interest, it usually did not adopt a moralizing tone with easily quotable statements or advice in the field of human nature—a notion that is confirmed by the papyrus fragments.

On the whole, then, working with book fragments is not always easy and requires a good deal of caution. Moreover, their locations may very often be uncertain. Ideally an author's quotation would include the poet's name and the title of his work, possibly identifying besides what part of the work is being quoted, as in fragments 32 and 33, Καλλίμαχος ἐν πρώτῳ Αἰτίων ("Callimachus in the first book of the *Aetia*"); but more often we find only the name of the poet, as in fragments 4 and 5. This means that one must find other methods for locating a fragment and has to be very cautious when doing so. Preferably there is external evidence to support a location. Thus many book fragments have found a home because they happen to overlap with later papyrus finds: we see, for example, that many quotations from the *Aetia* have now been placed in the *Prologue* (fr. 1) because they overlap with it.

Another good example of the use of external evidence for the location of a fragment thanks to later papyrus finds is fragment 4, καὶ νήσων ἐπέτεινε βαρὺν ζυγὸν αὐχένι Μίνως ("and Minos extended his heavy yoke over the islands' neck"), about Minos extending his rule over the Cyclades. In Schneider's edition this fragment appeared as number 467, and Schneider considered that it belonged to the story of Androgeos in *Aetia* 4. (Cf. now fr. 103, about Androgeos as Hero of the Stern in Phalerum.) Thanks to the *Scholia Florentina* (Pfeiffer 1949–53: 1.13), however, we now know that *Aetia* 1 contained a story about Minos sacrificing to the Graces on Paros. In the summary of this story it is stated explicitly that Minos sacrificed on Paros θαλασσοκρατο(ῦν)τι ("ruling the seas"). Therefore the location of fragment 4 in the story of the Graces on Paros is very likely to be right. In a similar way Lobel could locate fragment 22, τέμνοντα σπορίμην αὔλακα γειομόρον ("a farmer cutting a furrow fit for sowing") about a farmer plowing his land, in the story of Heracles and the Lindian farmer, whereas Schneider regarding fragment 491b thought about the somewhat similar story of Heracles and the uncivilized farmer Thiodamas. It is now clear from a papyrus (fr. 24) that the story of Thiodamas contained a different description of a plowing farmer, so that there would be no room in it for fragment 22. Even so, though both examples are quite convincing, they are not as certain as the cases where there is a real overlap. One should always bear in mind the possibility that Callimachus mentioned Minos' expansion or a plowing farmer also in a part of the *Aetia* that we know nothing about.

The interpretation and location of the fragments can also present problems because of a lack of context. It often takes careful arguing and great knowledge of Hellenistic and later Greek poetry to reach a convincing conclusion. A good example of successful interpretation and location is fragment 10, μαστύος ἀλλ' ὅτ' ἔκαμνον ἀλητύι ("but when they grew tired by the wandering of their search"). The first to see that these words must refer to the Colchians pursuing the Argonauts on their homeward journey was the Dutch scholar Alphons Hecker (1842: 44–46), who saw that the fragment must refer to the Colchians because of an allusion to it in Dionysius the Periegete 489-90, Κόλχων υἷες... ἔστ' ἐμόγησαν | ἴχνια μαστεύοντες ἀλήμονος Αἰητίνης ("when the sons of the Colchians grew tired, searching the traces of the wandering daughter of Aeetes"); Hecker connected this allusion with the Colchians who founded Polae on the Adriatic coast (fr. 11). This idea derives further support from Lycophron, *Alexandra* 1021-26, Κρᾶθις δὲ γείτων ἠδὲ Μυλάκων ὅροις | χῶρος συνοίκους δέξεται Κόλχων Πόλαις, | μαστῆρας οὓς θυγατρὸς ἔστειλεν βαρὺς | Αἴας Κορίνθου τ' ἀρχός, Εἰδυίας πόσις, | τὴν νυμφαγωγὸν ἐκκυνηγετῶν τρόπιν, | οἳ πρὸς βαθεῖ νάσσαντο Διζηροῦ πόρῳ ("but neighboring Crathis and the land of the Mulaces will receive within their boundaries, as inhabitants of Polae, those of the Colchians whom the hard leader of Aea and Corinth, the husband of Eiduia, sent to search for his daughter, hunting for the ship that carried the girl on it, who settled near the deep stream of Dizerus"—also about the Colchians who founded Polae), and Apollonius, *Argonautica* 4.303-4, Κόλχοι δ' αὖτ' ἄλλοι μὲν ἐτώσια μαστεύοντες | Κυανέας Πόντοιο διὲκ πέτρας ἐπέρησαν ("some of the

Colchians, searching in vain, sailed out of Pontus through the Cyanean Rocks"), and 1001–3, στρατὸς… | Κόλχων, οἳ Πόντοιο κατὰ στόμα καὶ διὰ πέτρας | Κυανέας μαστῆρες ἀριστήων ἐπέρησαν ("an army of Colchians, who sailed through the mouth of Pontus and through the Cyanean Rocks, searching for the heroes"). These passages, from similar contexts, all recall Callimachus' phrasing.

An example of a fragment that is hard to interpret and locate is fragment 603, σκέρβολα μυθήσαντο ("they spoke abusive words"). Following a suggestion of Pfeiffer's on fragment 603, Enrico Livrea on *Argonautica* 4.1726–27 argued that, as both *Argonautica* 4.1727, κερτομίῃ καὶ νεῖκος ἐπεσβόλον ("mockery and scurrilous quarrel," from the story of the Argonauts at Anaphe), and Callimachus fragment 603 are reminiscent of *Iliad* 20.202, κερτομίας ἠδ' αἴσυλα μυθήσασθαι ("to speak mocking and unseemly words"), fragment 603 too must refer to the scolding at the end of the story of the Argonauts at Anaphe. The idea is attractive but not so cogent as Hecker's, and in fact Pfeiffer himself also remarked *ad loc.* that this reference to abusive language would also be conceivable elsewhere.

Papyrus Fragments

The papyrus fragments have changed our view of the *Aetia* drastically. Compared with book fragments they offer a very different kind of text, because there has been no previous selection of the fragments by a specific author. What the papyri offer us is simply what survived in the sands of Egypt or what was cut up for mummy cartonnage in antiquity and rescued in modern times. This means that we get an arbitrary collection of bits of texts from all over the *Aetia*.

In the course of the twentieth century, research on the papyri and with it the reception of the Callimachean fragments has gradually changed its character. The first scholars working on the papyri were busy with the basics of publishing the fragments, which were often damaged and hard to read. The task to establish what Callimachus wrote was the first job that had to be dealt with, and we see how the first editions of the papyri are, as it were, surrounded by numerous small articles in periodicals in which scholars added their suggestions for reading or supplementing the text.[8] There are also the remains of

---

[8] See, e.g., Housman 1910; Hunt 1910b; A. Platt 1910.

a lively correspondence between scholars who sent each other cards and letters with suggestions.[9] In this way the texts gradually improved and eventually found their way into Pfeiffer's edition of 1949–53. In this edition the papyrus fragments and all the subliterary material were collected from all the different volumes and periodicals in which the texts had been first published, and the papyrus fragments were combined with the book fragments, for which at that time Otto Schneider's edition of 1870–73 was still the main source. Besides, thanks to the subliterary material in particular, Pfeiffer had been able to organize most of the material into the four books of the *Aetia*, preceded by the *Prologue* and followed by an *Epilogue*. With Pfeiffer's text one could for the first time survey the *Aetia* as a whole and be certain that the picture presented in his edition was based on solid evidence and could be a trustworthy basis for further research. Since then a number of other papyri have been published, such as the impressive fragments of *The Victory of Berenice* in 1976 (*SH* 254–68C), and these could be located in the *Aetia* as it appeared in Pfeiffer's edition or could at least be related to it in a meaningful manner.

After Pfeiffer the *Aetia* kept presenting problems on a basic level, because consisting of fragments it still contained many lacunae or loose ends and gaps, where the text was hotly disputed for a long time and still is not established or explained with certainty—such as fragment 1.9–12, a passage to which scholars keep returning, often with some profit but never yet with a convincing solution. (See above, n. 3.) Even so, there was also room now for further investigation of issues such as the literary technique, content, or function of the *Aetia*.

In this respect the first reactions to some of the larger fragments have been somewhat disappointed. In the early twentieth century scholars judged rather severely about the large fragment of the love story of Acontius and Cydippe (fr. 75): they thought that it did not show much art and was rather second-rate,[10] learned but without much emotion.[11] Somewhat later also *The Lock of Berenice* (fr. 110) at first was faced with the judgment "steifer, gekünstelter und lebloser…als alles, was wir sonst von Kallimachos haben" (Ziegler 1937: 37).

---

[9] On this kind of material, many traces of which we see also in Pfeiffer's notes and apparatus, see, e.g., Lehnus, 2006a and 2006b.
[10] See, e.g., Puech 1910, especially 259 and 274.
[11] See, e.g., Graindor 1911: 63–64.

In the course of the second half of the twentieth century, however, and particularly its last decades, opinions of the *Aetia* and of Hellenistic poetry in general gradually changed. Now the fragments of the *Aetia* have been much studied, and it has become clear that they can teach us a great deal, not only about Callimachus' language and style but also about his views on poetry, his interaction with other poets, and the position he assumes in the literary tradition and in the cultural and political environment of Alexandria.[12] Also, now that we have more of the *Aetia* and understand it better, it has become more evident how large the debt of Roman poets is to the *Aetia* and how they have been inspired by it in various ways, both in small details and in the overall structure of works.[13] Altogether, one could say that the *Aetia*, though preserved only in fragments, has become more than mere fragments because of its impact on Callimachean and Latin scholarship.

Apart from the actual text, the papyri as a group also have a story to tell about the *Aetia*. It is quite striking that we have so many papyri from this work, and in fact Callimachus belongs among the top ten authors represented by papyrus finds in Oxyrhynchus.[14] A survey of the papyrus finds, moreover, shows that Callimachus was read not only in Oxyrhynchus but also in other provincial towns such as Antinoopolis and Hermopolis, as well as in villages in the Fayum such as Karanis and Tebtynis. Furthermore, we have remains of annotated editions with basic comments between the lines (the Lille Papyrus of *The Victory of Berenice*) or extensive comments in the margins (POxy 20. 2258, containing *The Lock of Berenice*) as well as a number of so-called subliterary papyri related to the *Aetia* that contain scholia, varying from a fairly basic level in the London Scholia to a more advanced level in the *Scholia Florentina*, and summaries of most of the last two books of the *Aetia* in the *Diegeseis*. All this material helps to show that all through antiquity attempts were made to make the *Aetia* accessible at various levels. When we survey the papyrological evidence, it becomes clear that the *Aetia* was well read and considered important.

Working with papyrus fragments also has its difficulties and pitfalls. The establishment of the actual text is often far from easy if a papyrus is damaged and lacunose, as is often the case. On the whole the frag-

---

[12] See, e.g., M.A. Harder 1990, 2002a, 2003, and 2007.
[13] Out of the many publications on this topic, see, e.g., Wimmel 1960; George 1974; Puelma 1982: 221–46 and 285–304; R.F. Thomas 1983; and Hunter 2006a: 5–8, 88–90.
[14] See Krüger 1990: 214–15; M.A. Harder 2002b: 77.

ments of Callimachus have been edited with great care, and in Pfeiffer's edition and the *Supplementum Hellenisticum* we have a sound basis for the text. Even so scholars have sometimes been tempted to supplement the text and to extend it in ways that are not really justified by the evidence. Although they sometimes add the warning "e.g." to their supplements, this is still to be regretted, because it makes it difficult for the reader to disassociate himself from the text as presented and to have an unbiased view of the fragment. Sometimes the supplements suggested are rather fanciful and unlikely for various reasons, so that it is easy to reject and forget them. In fact the more attractive supplements are the most dangerous.

Thus, for example, in fragment 186.13–15 we find the text supplemented as ἔνθεν] ἐπὶ πτολιάς τε καὶ οὔ[ρεα Μηλίδος αἴης | στέλλο]υσιν Νάου Θῆτες ἀ[νιπτόποδες | Ζηνός,] ὅτις φηγοῦ [("whence the servants with unwashed feet of Zeus Naios, who…oak, bring [*sc.* the sacrifices of the Hyperboreans for Apollo] to the towns and mountains of the Malian land").[15] This is an attractive supplement, as it gives the kind of sense that one would expect in this passage, which describes how the sacrifices of the Hyperboreans were handed over from one people to the next until they reached the sanctuary of Apollo at Delos. There is also ample support for it in *Iliad* 16.234–35, for example, where the Selloi, the priests of Zeus at Dodona, are also called ἀνιπτόποδες, and in Callimachus' *Hymn to Delos* 287–88, δεύτερον Ἴριον ἄστυ καὶ οὔρεα Μηλίδος αἴης | ἔρχονται ("second, they go to the town of Irium and the mountains of the Malian land"), which refers to the same stage in the transport of the Hyperborean sacrifices. Still Pfeiffer seems right not to print the supplement in his text, because its very attractiveness and plausibility can be misleading and prevent us from considering other possibilities and from remembering that a poet such as Callimachus may have been more creative and original in his phrasing than we, as non-native speakers of a later age, can imagine.

Another apparently plausible supplement in a passage about the catasterism of the Lock of Berenice in fragment 110.63–64 was printed in Pfeiffer's text and from there made it into the later editions of Marinone (2nd ed., 1997), Asper (2004), and D'Alessio (4th ed., 2007). This supplement should, however, be considered critically. In Pfeiffer's edition the passage is as follows: ὕδασι] λουόμενόν με παρ' ἀθα[νάτους ἀνιόντα | Κύπρι]ς ἐν ἀρχαίοις ἄστρον [ἔθηκε νέον ("Cypris placed

---

[15] See Barber and Maas 1950: 96.

me, washed in the water, going up to the immortals, as a new star among the old"). In this line it is hard to see how the two participles λουόμενον and ἀνιόντα should be connected, as there is no connective particle and no way for one of them to be subordinate to the other. As long as one keeps the supplement ἀνιόντα, the present tense λουόμενον is also hard to explain, because the bathing is not simultaneous with ἀνιόντα or with the catasterism. In favor of ἀνιόντα one may point to passages like Theocritus 22.9–10, οὐρανὸν εἰσανιόντα | ἄστρα ("stars going up into heaven"), and to the translation in Catullus 66.63–64, "uuidulam a fluctu cedentem ad templa deum me | sidus in antiquis diua nouom posuit" ("the goddess placed me, going wet from the floods to the temples of the gods, as a new star among the old ones"). In the latter passage, however, *cedentem* is unproblematic, because we do not have the difficulty of two participles. Thus ἀνιόντα should be seriously questioned, and one may consider solving the difficulties by assuming that Catullus did not translate quite literally and supplementing ἀνάγουσα, for example (suggested to me by R.R. Nauta), at the end of the line. This could be translated as: "[By lifting me up] to the immortals while I was being washed in the sea, Cypris made me into a new constellation among the old ones," a pattern that recalls fragment 632, for instance, Ζεὺς δὲ εἰς οὐρανὸν αὐτὴν [*sc.* Callisto] ἀναγαγὼν πρώτην κατηστέρισεν ("Zeus lifted her up into heaven and made first her into a star").

Location of papyrus fragments can be difficult too, as with the book fragments. In some cases the papyri are big enough to justify conclusions, as in the case of the long fragment from the love story of Acontius and Cydippe, which, as we know from the *Diegeseis*, belonged in *Aetia* 3 (fr. 75). In other instances there is an overlap with a fragment attributed to a certain book of the *Aetia*, as in *Supplementum Hellenisticum* 252. This is a small strip of papyrus, which overlaps with fragment 46 about Perillus first using the murderous bronze bull he invented for Phalaris for roasting strangers. From the context of fragment 45 (which tells us that Phalaris imitated the inhospitable behavior of Busiris) in the scholia on *Alexandra* 717 we know that Callimachus told this story in *Aetia* 2. Alternatively, we may have a testimonium referring to a passage in a papyrus, as in fragment 43.70–71, about the ζάγκλον with which Cronus castrated his father. The scholia on *Alexandra* 869, ζάγκλον δὲ παρὰ τοῖς Σικελοῖς τὸ δρέπανον. μέμνηται δὲ καὶ Καλλίμαχος ἐν β' Αἰτίων ("the Sicilians call the sickle ζάγκλον. Callimachus speaks about this in Book 2 of the *Aetia*"), very probably refer to this passage and thus help to locate the papyrus containing fragment 43 about the anonymous ritual for the founders of Zancle in *Aetia* 2.

With other fragments, particularly but not exclusively the smaller ones, location is often impossible if there is no overlap with a quotation or help from testimonia, and accordingly Pfeiffer's edition has a fairly large section of *Fragmenta incerta*. Quite often these fragments have inspired attempts at location, which are sometimes quite plausible, as in, for example, the case of fragment 178, which has been attributed to the beginning of *Aetia* 2 because it contains a symposiastic setting that recalls fragment 43.12–17 from that book. In other cases the attempts are far more speculative and should be regarded skeptically, as in, for example, the case of fragment 118. Pfeiffer tentatively considered this fragment—which seems to contain some references to building, a temple, Apollo, and amphictyons—a description of a series of temples of Apollo in Delphi in chronological order. Recently Livrea (2006b) argued that the fragment was about the temple built by the Argonauts on the small island of Anaphe after they had been rescued by Apollo. The most important of his arguments was that POxy 19.2209B 1–11, containing fragment 118, is written in the same hand as 19.2209A, which contains fragment 21 from the story of the Argonauts in *Aetia* 1. However, according to Lobel (see POxy 19.2209), who published this papyrus, these fragments were probably not written at the same time, as the hand in 2209B is "neither so heavy nor quite so large" as 2209A, and they were not found in the same place. Therefore we have no means of knowing which book of the *Aetia* this fragment comes from. Livrea's arguments concerning the contents are inconclusive, because the contents are scanty: one cannot really exclude Livrea's interpretation, and it is certainly justified to question Pfeiffer's attempt at explanation; but as the remains of at least the first five lines suggest a rather technical description of building, the traditional explanation still seems to account somewhat better for the fragment's contents, and one should draw no hasty conclusions.

At the end of this section it may be good to draw attention to a very well-argued and successful treatment of new papyrus material, the location of the fragments of *The Victory of Berenice* at the beginning of *Aetia* 3 by Parsons (1977) and the addition of fragment 177, about Molorchus and his mousetraps, to this part of the *Aetia* by Livrea (1979). Their results, now generally accepted, led within three years after the publication of the fragments of *The Victory of Berenice* to interesting new views on the structure of the *Aetia*, where the last two books now turn out to be framed by two poems for Berenice II, with *The Victory of Berenice* at the beginning of Book 3 and *The Lock of Berenice* at the end of Book 4. They also brought new insights into Callimachus' way of writing court poetry, as it turns out that in the epinician poem for Berenice the emphasis probably was not so much on her famous ancestor Heracles' killing of the Nemean Lion but rather on the poor, obscure farmer Molorchus' fighting the mice who invade his home and destroy his meager possessions.

Conclusion

In this chapter the implications of the fragmentary state of the *Aetia* have been explored from various angles in order to give a picture of Callimachus as fragment. We have seen that the rather diverse material has a great deal to contribute to the overall picture and that in fact it offers much more than just text of the *Aetia*. It also forms the basis for further interpretation and informs us about the work's reception and readership, and it helps us besides to form an impression of the fate of the *Aetia* in the course of several centuries.

We have also seen that there are a number of problems and pitfalls when one is working with fragmentary texts and that this affects an unpredictable poet such as Callimachus in particular. In order to reach solid results we must either have indisputable evidence (as in many cases we fortunately do) or rely on careful and unbiased thinking, always bearing in mind the possibility that we have got hold of the wrong end of the stick.

Although we would gladly possess much more or in fact all of the *Aetia*, this demanding character of a fragmentary work also has its advantages. It means that almost every scrap of text has been studied at length and that by means of much close scrutiny scholars have been able to acquire a great deal of knowledge about the *Aetia* in spite of—or perhaps thanks to—its fragmentary character. Thanks to all the efforts of many generations of scholars it may be precisely as a fragment that the *Aetia* has become a well-known and much-appreciated work of poetry from which we can get a very good impression of Callimachus' sophisticated genius, in which playful distance and serious involvement went hand in hand, and which inspired many poets of later generations.

CHAPTER FOUR

THE *DIEGESEIS* PAPYRUS: ARCHAEOLOGICAL CONTEXT, FORMAT, AND CONTENTS

Maria Rosaria Falivene

ABSTRACT

The *Diegeseis* papyrus preserves what is left of fourteen columns (Y, Z, I–XII) of the original roll of *diegeseis* ('summaries') of Callimachus' oeuvre. It was unfinished in antiquity: its writer failed to go beyond *Hymn* 2. Although it is now missing the first half of what must have contained summaries to the first three books of the *Aetia*, it is essential in retrieving the framework within which Callimachus' fragments can once more find their proper place. This paper retraces the possible archaeological links connecting the *Diegeseis* papyrus to the other literary papyri found by Achille Vogliano and Gilbert Bagnani in or near the *cantina dei papiri* at Tebtynis in 1934. Considerations about provenance, format and contents lead to suggestions about the origin and purpose of the *Diegeseis* papyrus, and of the text it preserves.

> *By about half past ten on March 14—we had been working from six o'clock—my foreman brought me some baskets and ropes that were being found in the cellar. We both went down into it and worked alongside the two men who were digging, while at the same time I sent to the camp for boxes. In another quarter of an hour we realized what we had found. A layer a couple of feet deep right over the cellar floor was one solid mass of papyri, old baskets, ropes, palm fibre, and old mats, an ideal medium for the preservation of papyri.*

Archaeological Context

The epigraph to this chapter is from Gilbert Bagnani's 1934 report about the find (in Begg 1998: 206),[1] of about a thousand papyri in

---

[1] Vogliano indicated different dates: 21 and 22 March, then 27 March, finally 23 March. See discussion in Gallazzi 2003: 167 n. 101. Gallazzi himself favors 21 March as the actual date of the find.

the so-called Insula of the Papyri, at the site of ancient Tebtynis (near modern Umm-el-Breigât, in the Fayum). A more recent assessment reckons the number of papyri that have been found at about 750, including anything from mere fragments to entire rolls (Gallazzi 1990 and 2003: 166).

The other main actor on the Tebtynis scene in 1934 was Achille Vogliano. On his very first trip to Egypt, he had arrived in Cairo on 24 January, reaching the Fayum no sooner than 28 February: he was the head and sole member of the newly established (in December 1933) archaeological mission of the University of Milan.[2] Pursuant to his apparently unwritten agreement with Carlo Anti,[3] Vogliano engaged Bagnani, whom he described as "reluctant" (1937: XIV n. 1), in some very determined, if methodologically unsound,[4] papyrus hunting,which in a couple of weeks led to the extraordinary discovery of what has since been known as the Cantina dei Papiri.[5] According to Vogliano (1937: 66), the future PMilVogl 1.18 "almost surfaced" amid the thirty-centimeter stratum of papyri covering the cellar floor. Within a few days of its being found, it was placed in a metal box (provided by David L. Askren)[6] and transferred to Cairo, there to be photographed "on a Sunday afternoon" by an Italian phographer (Vogliano 1937: XII). Before pictures could be taken, the papyrus must obviously have been unrolled and restored: some information on the procedure adopted at the time can be gleaned from Stewart Bagnani's letters to his mother (who was herself wintering in Cairo), including one of 26 March:

> I am sleepy and rather gaga on account, as it seems to me, of having done nothing but clean, stick together, and frame paps for years!

---

[2] Gallazzi 2003: 139 and 154, respectively.

[3] In his capacity as head of the Italian Archaeological Mission to Egypt, Anti had been in charge of the Tebtynis excavations since 1928 (Gallazzi 2003: 136–139).

[4] Vogliano himself was aware of this, or later became so (Vogliano 1937: XV n. 2, quoted by Gallazzi 2003: 171).

[5] After Anti's return to Italy upon his appointment as dean of the University of Padua in October 1932, Bagnani had been acting as the field director on the Tebtynis site (Begg 1998: 195; Gallazzi 2003: 137).

[6] David L. Askren: "La prima sera attorno al nostro tavolo di lavoro, compresi del nostro stesso entusiasmo, stavano due ospiti non inoperosi: il dottor Askren, un medico missionario degli Stati Uniti, da trent'anni stabilito nel Faiyûm...ed il rappresentante inglese della Barclay's Bank a Medinet el Faiyûm. Tutti aiutarono la causa nostra" (Vogliano 1937: XII). See also Gallazzi 2003: 145 n. 43.

and another of 29 March:[7]

> We have decided to stop the digging when this group of houses is finished which will be in about five days' time. I am profoundly thankful as then Gil can get his photos and cataloguing done peacefully to say nothing of the packing of all those foul little things. Could you get me boxes of Meta[ldehyde]. Four of 5'0. I want them for ironing paps. Just post them to the bank.

The photos were presently sent by air mail to Girolamo Vitelli, in Florence, who was to prepare the editio princeps. On 12 May 1934, permission was obtained for the papyrus itself to be sent to Italy. (Rudolf Pfeiffer [1949–53: 2.xii] would be able to inspect it in Florence in October 1935.) About half the papyri from the same find followed a couple of months later, reaching the Civici Musei del Castello Sforzesco on 26 October. The remaining ones would be sent no sooner than 1938 (Gallazzi 2003: 173–174); a few were returned to Cairo after publication, including PMilVogl 1.18, which is presently exhibited in the Egyptian Museum (Room 29). Excellent reproductions are also available on line:[8] it may be useful to inspect them alongside the very accurate plates provided in the edition of Vogliano (1937), which obviously represent an earlier stage in the preservation of the papyrus.

The vast majority of the papyri from the 1934 Tebtynis excavations—many of them still unpublished—are documents belonging to several archives or dossiers whose dates range between the second half of the first and the late second century AD,[9] and whose connection, if any, with the literary papyri found at the same site remains to be determined.[10] For the time being, it seems worthwhile to try retracing the possible archaeological links connecting the literary papyri found on that occasion, as the former seem to be consistent with a philological

---

[7] Quoted in Begg 1998: 201 (and n. 31 on the uses of metaldehyde); see also Gilbert Bagnani's report in Begg 1998: 206.

[8] http://ipap.csad.ox.ac.uk (Centre for the Study of Ancient Documents/Photographic Archive of Papyri in the Cairo Museum).

[9] These include the archives of the descendants of Patron (see Clarysse and Gallazzi 1993), the descendants of Pakebkis, Kronion, the family of Harmiusis, Diogenis, and Turbo. See Gallazzi 2003: 166. For more information on each archive, see: www.trismegistos.org/Archives s.vv.

[10] Van Minnen 1998 (an important contribution to the study of literary texts, both Egyptian and Greek, from Tebtynis), p. 166: "Whether the literary texts belonged to one of these archives or ended up in the 'cantina' independently of them is unclear."

connection, in that some, at least, of these papyri share a scholarly attitude toward texts.

Among the published literary papyri from the 1934 Tebtynis excavation, PMilVogl 6.262, part of a commentary on Nicander's *Theriaca*, deserves first consideration here. It is recorded as found in the Insula of the Papyri (Insula 1 in the aerial view from 1935; reproduced in Gallazzi 2003: 190 fig. 4)[11] at the end of March—that is, after the discovery of the Cantina dei Papiri—and provides a link to other literary papyri that were found, along with documentary texts, in the so-called Street of the Papyri (numbered 4 in the 1935 aerial view) before the Cantina was discovered. These literary papyri include another fragment (PMilVogl 2.45 + 6.262 = *SH* and *SSH* 563A) of the same commentary on Nicander's *Theriaca*, and some scholia minora on the *Iliad* (PMilVogl 3.120). A mythological compendium listing Zeus's mistresses (PMilVogl 3.126, reedited by Salvadori 1985) was most probably also found in the Street of the Papyri—unless it was retrieved from the Cantina along with the Callimachean *Diegeseis*,[12] in which case the association of these two papyri would be especially close, and consistent with their contents: both are included among the "ancient readers' digests" that Monique van Rossum-Steenbeek (1998) studied a few years ago. Literary texts found in the Street of the Papyri were probably blown there by the wind from one or another of the four rooms in Insula 2 (immediately north of the Insula of the Papyri, alias Insula 1; see the 1935 aerial view). According to Bagnani's excavation daybook, this is where work started on 4 March 1934, and where on the following day papyri were retrieved from a thick layer of ash in the southernmost room at the southeastern corner of Insula 1 (Bagnani in Begg 1998: 198), among them a prose anthology compiled during the reign of Hadrian (PMilVogl 1.20),[13] a Euripides papyrus,[14] and Apollodorus of

---

[11] Plan of the site: Gallazzi and Hadji-Minoglou 2000: 39; Bagnall and Rathbone 2004: 148.

[12] PMilVogl 2.47 (*Acta Alexandrinorum*) was certainly found in the Cantina. All these data are elicited from Gallazzi 1990 (note especially p. 286, on PMilVogl 3.126) and Gallazzi 2003: 156–69.

[13] It comprises a section on the so-called Flower of Antinous (Vogliano 1937: 176).

[14] According to Gallazzi 2003: 157 n. 71, "versi euripidei non si trovano fra il materiale recuperato in quell'ambiente," but the future PMilVogl 2.44 (a hypothesis to Euripides' *Hippolytus*) would fit very well into the picture: note that it, too, is reckoned among Van Rossum Steenbeek's (1998) "readers' digests." See also Barrett 1964: 95–96 and 431–32; Luppe 1983.

Athens' *Grammatical Inquiries into Book XIV of the "Iliad"* (PMilVogl 1.19), of which only the title at the end is preserved, followed by the note ΣΩΣΥΟΥ. This last has been plausibly interpreted as referring to the Sosii, famous booksellers in Rome (Turner 1968: 51). The fact that this book or its exemplar may have been produced in Rome also reflects on other books found in its company: Are we dealing with volumes reaching the Fayum via Rome, whether because they themselves or their exemplars were produced there, or because their readers had connections to the capital? This question also applies to PMilVogl 1.18, since Roman literati of the first and second centuries AD showed considerable interest in Callimachus.

Medea Norsa and Girolamo Vitelli's (1934) editio princeps of the newly unearthed Callimachean *Diegeseis* Papyrus appeared within a few months of its being found. There followed a host of reviews and other contributions,[15] which soon necessitated a revised edition. When Vitelli died, in 1935, Vogliano took it upon himself to produce one. The papyrus thus became number 18 in *Papiri della Reale Università di Milano*, volume 1 (1937),[16] which included two additional fragments, both pertaining to the beginning of the preserved portion of the original roll (Vogliano 1937: 114).

As it presently stands in Cairo, the roll measures 139 centimeters in length by 30 centimeters in height, consisting of the twelve columns numbered I to XII by Norsa and Vitelli in their editio princeps, plus what was left of a preceding column (designated Z in Vogliano's second edition); a central gap, caused by worms eating the roll from

---

[15] Vogliano (1937: 67–68 n. 2) lists eighteen of them, besides referring in the *Addenda* (p. 274) to Herter 1937. A more comprehensive list is found in Lehnus 2000b: 78–79.

[16] Hence the acronym P. PRIMI, later superseded by *P. Milano Vogliano*, which is now the title in general use for the whole series. For reviews of Vogliano's edition and further discussion, see Pfeiffer 1949–53: 2.xii–xiii; Lehnus 2000b: 79. An anticipation of Vogliano's edition (*Dal I° volume dei papiri della R. Università di Milano*) was presented at the Fourth International Congress of Papyrology, held in Florence in April 1934. Vogliano himself was not present, having gone back to Egypt, where he spent little more than a week at the Tebtynis site before moving on to Medînet Mâdi (Gallazzi 2003: 174–175). Anti, on the other hand, read his paper "Scavi di Tebtynis (1930–1935)," which was later published in *Atti del IV Congresso Internazionale di Papirologia* (Florence, 1935), 473–78 (Begg 1998: 208–209).

the outside, narrows down toward its inner, best-preserved portion,[17] which coincides with the end of the text.[18]

In 2001 two more fragments from the same roll were identified in Milan "tra il materiale della Collezione Milano Vogliano" (Gallazzi and Lehnus 2001: 7): they are inventoried as PMilVogl inv. 28b and 1006, measuring 1.7 centimeters by 8.6 centimeters and 4.0 centimeters by 6.2 centimeters, respectively. As the editors saw,[19] PMilVogl 28b connects precisely to the bottom left of column Z in the main part of the roll. The other fragment, PMilVogl inv. 1006, completely detached and preserving part of a column's upper margin, has been convincingly placed to the left of column Z, being assigned to the top of the preceding column (Y). To sum up: we now have what remains of fourteen columns (Y, Z, I–XII) of the original roll of the *Diegeseis* to Callimachus oeuvre.

PMilVogl 1.18, written in a basically bilinear, expert, but informal hand with cursive tendencies, occasionally betrays chancery training.[20] Because of its archaeological context—namely the dated documents with which it was found—it can be safely dated between the second half of the first and the first half of the second century AD (Pfeiffer 1949–53: 2.xxviii); palaeography supports this dating. The back is blank.

Format

The layout of the *Diegeseis* roll is quite carefully planned, though the plan is executed with an increasing approximation as the work approaches the end (which in fact it fails to reach). Column width varies around an average of 9 centimeters. Column height is on average

---

[17] By taking the dimensions and shape of this gap into account, one can assess the number and cross-section of the successive volutes, or coils, of the roll: D'Alessio 2001.

[18] After last being opened in antiquity, the book had been rerolled properly, from right to left, so that it would open again from the beginning.

[19] Gallazzi and Lehnus 2001, reproductions on Tafel 1.

[20] Cursive tendencies: note ligatured diphthongs AI, EI; often rounded Π; Y often in one movement, though in two possible shapes; short second vertical stroke of H, this letter being often drawn in a single movement. Chancery training: note elongated C especially, but not exclusively at end of line (cols. III.5, 39, 40; IV.4, 8, 13; VIII.4; IX.5, 15; X.18 in title and below passim; XII.7, 13); emphatic A (IV.30; VI.3; VII.25, 31; X.22); enlarged K (III.12, VII.22); very rapid Ξ (IV.38); elongated Y at end of line (IX.26, 27).

21 centimeters. Upper and lower margins are approximately 4 centimeters and 5 centimeters, respectively. The columns show a downward slant to the left (Maas's law) that is quite regular and consistent from one column to the next, creating the impression that the slant was intentional.[21] In the ideal format, or template, of this book roll each *diegesis* dealing with one of Callimachus' poems begins with a quotation of the first line (incipit), written in *ekthesis* with enlarged initial letter or letters underlined by a *paragraphos* and followed by an empty space to distinguish it from what follows; the end of each *diegesis* is then marked by a very long *paragraphos*, decorated with a hook on its left end, and by a blank space clearly separating it from the next *diegesis*. This format is applied somewhat inconsistently— perhaps most noticeably, the *ekthesis* device is abandoned from column VII.25—and variably: for instance, the enlarged initial in column VIII.1 occurs amid a *diegesis* and a decidedly unimportant word.

There are initial titles (in midline and midcolumn): in col. II.9, a Δ surmounted by a horizontal stroke (i.e., the Greek numeral 4) refers to the beginning of the section devoted to *Aetia* Book 4; in col. X.18 the title "[sc. *diegesis*] of the *Hecale*" is marked out by horizontal lines above and below it, and two strokes on the sides.[22] Something resembling a main title is found above column VI: unlike the two just mentioned, it refers to what precedes it. (It is here that the term *diegesis* appears [*The Diegeseis of the Four (Books) of Callimachus' "Aetia"*: col. VIa–b], which Norsa and Vitelli reasonably extended to the whole work.) This title does not fit the layout of the text as presented in PMilVogl 1.18: it is, strictly speaking, a *subscriptio* and should be found at the right end of a roll. A possible explanation could be that it did in fact originally belong with a separate roll of the *Diegeseis* to Callimachus' *Aetia*, part of the complete edition, in more than one volume, of the *Diegeseis* to Callimachus' poems. If so, it would have no place in the layout initially envisaged by a compiler reducing two volumes into one, but it might have been inserted by him, on second thought and in the upper margin, as it turned out to be useful in order to mark the transition from the *Aetia* to the *Iambi* (beginning, with no title of its own, at col. VI.1). No title signals any distinction between col. IX.38

---

[21] A very accurate description of the layout of PMilVogl 1.18 can be found in Van Rossum-Steenbeek 1998: 75–76. On Maas's law, see Johnson 2004: 91–99.

[22] A short diagonal to the left; on the right a different sign, cut short but otherwise similar to the long *paragraphos* marking the end of each *diegesis*. See below.

(end the *diegesis* to *Iambus* 13) and col. X.1, the incipit of the first of four 'lyric' poems, which may therefore be seen as belonging with the *Iambi* (Lelli 2005a). Finally, no distinction is made between the end of the *Hecale* section (col. XI.7) and the *diegesis* to the *Hymn to Zeus* (col. XI.8): any attempt at explanation would be entirely speculative here, but it seems appropriate to remark that the compiler may have interrupted his work, left it unfinished, and had no time or wish to deal with this last layout problem (Bastianini 2000).

Contents

As it presently stands, PMilVogl 1.18 preserves a dozen or so *diegeseis* for *Aetia* Book 3 (cols. Y-II.8; Gallazzi and Lehnus 2001: 18) and all those to Book 4 (cols. II.9-V), followed by the *diegeseis* to the *Iambi* (cols. VI.1-IX), the four ensuing 'lyric' poems (col. X.1-17), the *Hecale* (cols. X.18-XI.7), the *Hymn to Zeus* (col. XI.8-19), and the *Hymn to Apollo* (cols. XI.20-XII.3). There is considerable variation in the length of the different *diegeseis*, possibly because some poems are more straightforward, easier to summarize, than others.

According to a famous distinction of Plato's (*Rep.* 392d-394d), taken up by Aristotle (*Poet.* 1448a20-24), *diegesis* means "narration without mimesis": that is, told from the point of view of the author rather than of the characters. This is exactly what each *diegesis* in PMilVogl 1.18 does, narrating what a poem is about while reducing it to the third person of its author and to sheer facts. By the same token, in the *diegesis* to *Iambus* 6 (col. VIII.25-31) the verb *diegeomai* is used of the poet who "reports" the dimensions and costs of Phidias' Zeus of Olympia, thereby reducing a celebrated work of art to, as it were, its basic ingredients.

The *Diegeseis* Papyrus was not meant to be an ambitious scholarly work; rather, it is a user-friendly text, meant for studying, understanding, and possibly teaching the poetry of Callimachus.[23] But its lack of distinction in handwriting and format, mirrored by its characteristic clumsiness in both spelling and syntax as regards contents, should not disguise the fact that these *diegeseis* are firmly rooted in the tradition of Callimachean exegesis. As Paul Maas first observed, Rudolf Pfeiffer

---

[23] "A careful summary of a long and complex work with a few scholarly references may be of service even to serious readers" (Alan Cameron 1995: 123 n. 96, adducing Vladimir Nabokov's *Lectures on "Don Quixote"* in support of his argument).

eventually agreed, and Alan Cameron more recently restated,[24] the same template used in PMilVogl 1.18 can be detected in PSI 11.1219, POxy 20.2263, and PMich inv. 6235. The first two of these papyri certainly concern *Aetia* Book 1, as the third may possibly also.[25] This makes a strong a priori argument in favor of their descending from one original, variously transmuted in later versions to suit the needs, uses, and related tastes of particular readers, or groups of readers, of Callimachus' poetry. In other words, these four papyri, taken together, provide the material for a case study in the basics of *Parallelüberlieferung*.

The beginnings of Callimachean exegesis may well go back to Callimachus' school—if not to Callimachus himself, who was certainly very good at self-promotion. A very well-known Lille papyrus (PLille inv. 76d, 79, etc., preserving fragments of a line-by-line commentary to *The Victory of Berenice*) provides evidence of very early, detailed, ambitious exegetical work on Callimachus' poetry. Dated on palaeographical grounds to the second half of the third (Turner: 250–210 BC) or early second century BC (Cavallo), it is, in Eric Turner's authoritative judgment (1987: 126), "the most beautiful example of a Ptolemaic book-hand that I know." That is, it cannot have had an origin distant in time, or possibly in space,[26] from such first-generation Callimacheans as Hermippus, Istrus, Stephanus, and Callimachus' nephew and namesake. The commentary, however, appears to be "of the most jejune kind and rarely goes beyond paraphrase" (Turner 1987: 126). The Lille Papyrus may be a case of *Parallelüberlieferung* at a very early stage, or else its apparent naïveté may be misleading: Hellenistic scholarly prose can admittedly be disappointing, the usual explanation for this being that earlier Hellenistic treatises have come down to us through less worthy epigones;[27] alternatively, scholarship in the third century BC may have accorded with methods of composition, patterns of circulation, techniques of explanation, and other scholarly habits altogether different from what modern readers tend to prefer.

---

[24] Maas 1934: 437 and 1937: 159 (with reference to PSI 11.1219 and the *Diegeseis* roll, the only two papyri in this group to have been published at the time); Pfeiffer 1949–53: 2.xxviii and n. 2 (*contra* himself, Pfeiffer 1934: 5); Alan Cameron 1995: 120–126 (widening the scope of Maas's observation to include PMich inv. 6235).

[25] Editio princeps of the Michigan papyrus (about the *aition* on King Teuthis and Athena "of the Bandaged Thigh"): Koenen, Luppe, and Pagán 1991. For possible attribution to *Aetia* Book 1: Lehnus 1992; Hollis 1992c. For summaries, see Massimilla 1996: 439–441; D'Alessio 2007: 570 n. 41.

[26] Its high "bookish" quality may even suggest an origin in Alexandria itself.

[27] Alan Cameron 1995: 192, with reference to Stephanie West's work on Didymus.

There may also exist internal or external evidence in favor of the inbred origin, as it were, of Callimachean exegesis. As regards internal evidence, it has long since been observed that the device of introducing each *diegesis* by quoting the first line of the relevant poem ultimately derives from the catalogue (*Pinakes*) of the Library of Alexandria, and this latter enterprise was of course Callimachus' lifework, and most certainly his school's also (Maas 1937: 156). On the other hand, at least one attestation of Callimachus' commenting on himself may provide a piece of external evidence: a fragment from his *Hypomnemata* (fr. 464 Pf.) deals with Adrastea (Nemesis), a deity also appearing in his poetry (*Hecale* fr. 116 H. = 299 Pf., and possibly fr. 176 H. = 687 Pf.). Perhaps Callimachus' *Hypomnemata* was a commentary to the poet's own oeuvre and, if so, the foundation for all or most of the later critical work on it, including commentaries and a collection of prose abstracts for each of his poems—of which, apparently, "Duae...'redactiones,' ut ita dicam, extant: altera uberior et paulo doctior...altera brevior et simplicior in P.Med."[28] In my opinion, this could explain the presence, even in the "brevior et simplicior" version of the *Diegeseis*, of a few circumstantial pieces of information that, one assumes, would not have been readily available to a critic writing the first work on particular poems long after the date of their composition. The most easily detected instances are column VI.3–4 (in *Iambus* 1, a reference to the "so-called Sarapideum of Parmenio" as the meeting place for the *philosophoi* or *philologoi* in Alexandria); column VII.20–21 (in *Iambus* 5, on the schoolteacher Apollonius or, "according to others," Theon); and column X.10–13 (in fr. 228 Pf., a dedication to the deified Arsinoe of an altar within a sacred precinct "near the Emporium" in Alexandria). As for the "uberior et paulo doctior" version (represented in this case by PSI 11.1219), there is of course the all-too-famous instance of the identity of the Telchines in the *Prologue* to the *Aetia*.

There are further tokens of inherited scholarly accuracy. We may consider the quite specific expressions employed in the *Diegeseis* Papyrus with reference to genre and occasion: ἐπίνικος (col. VIII.21–22, with reference to *Iambus* 8); τοῦτο γέγραπται εἰς ἕβδομα θυγατρίου (col. IX.25, with reference to *Iambus* 12); παροίνιον (col. X.6, denoting the second lyric poem); ἐκθέωσις Ἀρσινόης (col. X.10, presumably referring to the occasion of the third lyric poem, the dedication

---

[28] Pfeiffer 1949–53: 2.xxviii. "P.Med." is Pfeiffer's siglum for PMilVogl 1.18.

of an altar and sacred precinct to the deified Arsinoe). Several terms for the poet's activity are also precisely appropriate: Callimachus "tells the story of" the Pelasgian Walls in Athenian territory (ἱστορεῖ, col. IV.2);[29] in *Iambus* 1 he "puts up the fiction" of Hipponax coming back from Hades (ὑποτίθεται, col. VI.2); he "blames" the values of his time in *Iambus* 3 (καταμέμφεται, col. VI.34); he "assails [a schoolteacher, whether Apollonius or Theon] in iambics" in *Iambus* 5 (ἰαμβίζει, col. VII.21); he "reports the exact dimensions and costs" of the Phidian Zeus in *Iambus* 6 (διηγεῖται, col. VII.27); in *Iambus* 13 he "counters those who blame him for experimenting with too many genres" (πρὸς τοὺς καταμεμφομένους αὐτὸν ἐπὶ τῆι πολυειδείαι ἁπάντων φησὶν ὅτι κτλ., col. IX.33); he "talks to the *jeunes garçons en fleur*" (πρὸς τοὺς ὡραίους φησίν) and "sings a hymn and prays," respectively, in the first and second of the four lyric poems (ὑμνεῖ καὶ παρακαλεῖ, col. X.1–2 and 7–8); and he "leads a choral dance" to celebrate the epiphany of the god in the *Hymn to Apollo* (προτερατευσάμενος...ἐπιλέγει, col. XI.21–25).

At the opposite chronological end, the latest avatars of Callimachean exegesis have reached us through codices F and At (both dating from the early fifteenth century; Pfeiffer 1949–53: 2.125 [*Addenda*]), and through Ianos Lascaris (Pfeiffer 1949–53: 2.lxxvi–lxxix). For *Hymns* 5 and 6, the scholia are preceded by abstracts that, however short,[30] clearly belong to the same tradition as the *Diegeseis* of PMilVogl 1.18. The abstract to *Hymn* 5 shares with the *Diegeseis* Papyrus (col. XI.18–19) an apparently improper use of the adverb ἐκεῖσε in lieu of ἐκεῖ. The same adverb is also found in a scholion to *Hymn* 4.165, the historical character of which connects it with the abstract to *Hymn* 6. Ptolemy II Philadelphus is the subject of both the scholion and the abstract: from the scholion to *Hymn* 4.165 we learn that he grew up in Cos, whereas the abstract to *Hymn* 6 informs us that Ptolemy imported the ritual described therein from Athens.[31] Once more, this is circumstantial evidence, ultimately deriving from a source very near in time to Ptolemy II

---

[29] Cf. col. II.12 (ἱστορία, with reference to "the first elegy" in *Aetia* Book 4) and PSI 11.1219 fr. 1.35.

[30] This brevity is seen especially in the *diegeseis* to *Hymns* 1 and 2, apparently lost in the medieval tradition but preserved in PMilVogl 1.18; they were nevertheless deemed incomplete by Pfeiffer 1949–53: 2.41 (here following Vogliano 1937: 144).

[31] Despite Hopkinson's skepticism (1984a: 32–33), this may well coincide with the πανηγυρίς at Alexandrian Eleusis mentioned by Satyrus in his *Demes of Alexandria* (POxy 27.2465 fr. 3 col. II.4–11).

and Callimachus, and to Theocritus as well: in fact, a similar piece of information concerning Ptolemy's birth in Cos (enriched by a reference to his mother, Berenice I) also appears in a scholion to *Idyll* 17.58. Such matter-of-fact historical information on Ptolemy II and the Ptolemaic royal family is found already in the line-by-line commentary of the Lille Papyrus (PLille inv. 82.1.2–6), pointing to one authoritative source dating from the third century BC. As suggested above, this may have been the Callimachean *Hypomnemata*.

Midway, as it were, between the *Diegeseis* Papyrus and the early fifteenth-century manuscripts F and At, continuity in the tradition of the *diegeseis* during late antiquity may be confirmed by certain verbal parallels between the *diegesis* of the *Hecale* in PMilVogl 1.18 and what little survives of a summary of the same poem in POxy 20. 2258.[32] At this stage of its transmission, continuity of the exegetical lore could be insured, if at all, only by its migration into the margins of books in the new format, the codex. This meant assembling into the margins material that used to be available in separate book rolls containing commentaries to and abstracts from an author's main text. Theocritus' medieval manuscript tradition may be adduced to illustrate this point: each *Idyll* is in fact provided with an abstract that is remarkably similar to a *diegesis* in PMilVogl 1.18; the scholia then follow, just as with Callimachus *Hymns* 5 and 6. As set forth by Pfeiffer (1949–53: 2.lxxviii), the scholia to Callimachus cannot have differed much from those to Theocritus.

To this date, the *Diegeseis* Papyrus is the best-preserved testimony for ancient criticism on the whole of Callimachus' poetry. It also provides the main framework within which a large number of Callimachus' fragments can be assigned their place, notwithstanding the puzzle, still unsolved, of the order in which several parts of Callimachus' oeuvre succeeded one another according to the author's intention, and according to editors in later antiquity.

---

[32] Alan Cameron 1995: 125, with reference to Hollis 1990a: 65–66.

CHAPTER FIVE

CALLIMACHUS CITED

Filippomaria Pontani

Abstract

Most of Callimachus' fragments have come down to us as brief quotations by other literary authors or in grammatical works and lexica: this paper attempts a brief survey of the ways and forms of Callimachus' indirect tradition, a vital topic for scholars and editors from Angelo Poliziano to Rudolf Pfeiffer, and one that has dramatically affected (all the more so before the papyri came to light) their ability to construct an adequate image of the poet. It demonstrates how Callimachus' poetry inspired less enthusiasm among Greek prose writers (with the possible exception of Plutarch) than among erudite commentators of other Hellenistic poets, of Pindar and Homer (among them Theon and Didymus); and how in Byzantium Callimachus lived on in lexica, but also in the works of the archbishop Michael Choniates, possibly the last reader of his *Aetia*.

> *Help me find her; she*
> *Is out there somewhere*
> *Now, one of those flakes*
> *Of white on the waves*
> *Which play with her as*
> *With my straining eyes.*
> —J. Hollander, *After Callimachus*

Callimachus' Traces: The First Modern Collectors

Ὡς αἰεὶ τὸν ὁμοῖον ἄγει θεὸς εἰς τὸν ὁμοῖον.[1] The first modern scholar to scan ancient authors looking for quotations from or information on Callimachus' lost poems was the "father of philology" Angelo Poliziano (1454–1494), himself a ποιητὴς ἅμα καὶ κριτικός,[2] a great admirer of

---

[1] *Od.* 17.217, "so does God ever draw like to like." This αἶνος Ὁμηρικός is quoted by Callimachus in fr. 178.9–10 Pf.

[2] Pfeiffer 1949–1953: 2.xliii. The Greek definition actually applies to Philetas (Strabo 14.2.19 = *test.* 11 Spanoudakis), but Strabo 17.3.22 (*test.* 16 Pf.) calls Callimachus

the Cyrenean,[3] and the *editor princeps et translator* of *Hymn* 5 in the first *Centuria* of his path-breaking philological work *Miscellanea* (published in 1489).[4]

This encounter between two *spiritus magni* was neither fortuitous nor occasional: after brilliantly detecting and patiently picking out—from epigrams, ancient scholia (to Apollonius Rhodius, to Aratus, and to Callimachus' own *Hymns*), Latin authors (Catullus, Pliny the Elder, Statius, Hyginus, Apuleius, and especially Ovid), and Byzantine lexica (e.g. the *Suda*)—various items of information concerning the *Hecale* and *The Lock of Berenice* (see *Miscellanea* 1.24 and 1.68), Poliziano devoted to the *Aetia* an entire chapter (no. 10) of the unfinished second *Centuria* of the *Miscellanea*, a work that remained unknown until its rediscovery in 1962.[5]

In order to defend the unanimously transmitted reading "Aetia" in Martial 10.4.12 ("legas Aetia Callimachi") against the silly emendation "Ethea" proposed by Domizio Calderini (a man who also deserved blame for placing Latin love elegy "in the shadow of Callimachus"),[6] Poliziano appealed not only to the unanimous authority of the manuscripts that he had examined (unmasking Calderini's unreliability in this respect) but also to various clues to the existence and nature of a poem with that title: first and foremost the epigrams now collected as *Anthologia Palatina* 11.275.2 (= test. 25 Pf.) and 7.42.7–8, and the literary criticism contained in Clement of Alexandria's *Stromateis*

ποιητὴς ἅμα καὶ περὶ γραμματικὴν ἐσπουδακώς, "poet and also concerned with language."

[3] Lines 426–433 of the *Silva Nutricia* (Bausi 1996: 207–208) are devoted to Callimachus, but see also the Callimachean imitation in Poliziano's Greek epigram 23 (F. Pontani 2002: 106–107).

[4] *Miscellanea* 1.80 (Politianus 1553: 288–295). See, e.g., Bulloch 1985: 58–59 and Pette 1981. Another reference to Callimachus' *Hymn* 1.8 is to be found in *Miscellanea* 1.35 (Politianus 1553: 256).

[5] Branca and Pastore Stocchi 1978: 213. See Harder 1989, with full examination of Poliziano's sources and *modus operandi*; Bing 1997: 78–79.

[6] *Miscellanea* 1.80 (Politianus 1553: 289): "Iam illud quoque miror, cur et Domitius et alii quidam post illum, quocumque momento, quacumque occasione scribere audeant, hoc aut illud imitatione Callimachi dictum fuisse a Propertio, cum praeter hymnos pauculos nihil prorsus extet ad nos poetae istius, nec autem plane quicquam quod amoris argumenta contineat." ("I also wonder on which grounds Domizio, and others after him, dare affirm in any occasion and circumstance that Propertius had written this or that in imitation of Callimachus, while in reality nothing at all of this poet has come down to us beyond a couple of hymns, at any rate nothing that pertains to the subject of love.") For a modern evaluation of Calderini and of the Roman school of philology, see Campanelli 2001: 49–72.

(5.8.50, = *test.* 26 Pf.; see below), but also quotations of Callimachean material in more remote technical sources such as Priscian's *Grammar* (1.11 and 30; 2.12 = fr. 61 Pf.), Stephanus of Byzantium's *Ethnika* (α 470 Bill. = fr. 37.1 Pf.), John Lydus' *De mensibus* (4.1 = fr. 33 Pf.), and the *Suda* (μ 194 = test. 24 Pf.).[7] He also believed that this poem owed its title to the fact that "causas rerum multarum plerunque fabulosas afferat, sicuti solet Ovidius," probably an implicit reference to Ovid *Fasti* 1.1-2.[8]

The achievement of bringing to light the title and some elements of what we now judge Callimachus' most important poem was to remain buried in a couple of sentences written by Poliziano's pupil Pietro Crinito, who in 1498 published an incomplete and often unreliable summary of the second *Centuria*.[9] Yet that achievement—taken together with the similar but less impressive studies devoted to Eupolis in *Miscellanea* 1.91, to Euripides' *Cresphontes* in *Miscellanea* 2.47, and to Sappho in the unpublished *Praelectio* on Ovid *Heroides* 15—certainly amounts to one of Poliziano's most significant contributions in regard to ancient literature, inaugurating sound methodological and epistemological foundations for the practice of fragment collection down to the present day.[10]

In particular, Poliziano anticipated a preliminary answer to the *desiderium* of many European philologists who could not content themselves with the *Hymns* alone.[11] And as a matter of fact, the correct

---

[7] In the autograph manuscript edited by Branca and Pastore Stocchi 1978, Poliziano's marginal note to the end of this paragraph reads: "Vide Ammonium grammaticum," which implies that the Italian humanist had eventually become aware of the six quotations from Callimachus in Ammonius' *De adfinium vocabulorum differentia*.

[8] "It provides the causes of many things, most frequently fabulous ones, as is common in Ovid." On the parallel established by Poliziano between Callimachus and Ovid, see Bausi 1996: xxiv–xxv.

[9] Crinito's letter to Alessandro Sarti, indexing some of the topics of the second *Centuria*, was published as no. 22 in Book 12 of Poliziano's *Epistulae* in his Aldine *Opera* of 1498 (the direct antecedent of Politianus 1553, where the letter appears on pp. 180-182): see Branca and Pastore Stocchi 1978: 59-65. Crinito adds *suo Marte* a reference to "Valerius Probus," namely to Ps.-Prob. *in Verg. Georg.* 3.19 = fr. 54 Pf.

[10] See Dionisotti 1997: 22 and 26-27: "The range of his [*sc.* Poliziano's] reading, in all manner of rare and unpublished Greek and Latin texts, enabled him to pronounce with unique authority on what was or was not preserved, and made his essays in fragment-collection impressively exotic.... The suggestion is that classical scholarship as a whole is like a collecting of fragments, a piecemeal reconstruction of the ancient world."

[11] I.B. Pius, preface to Crucius 1509 (*corrige* Pfeiffer 1949-1953: 2.lxxvi), c. A VIr: "Ex hoc tam infelici naufragio quota hymnorum Callimachi pars superfuit? unde

understanding and *Erläuterung* of Martial's allusion to the "Aetia Callimachi" was immediately regarded as such an important feat of philology that no later than 1501 another Italian humanist, the Calabrian Aulo Giano Parrasio, devoted a whole page of his commentary on Claudian's *De raptu Proserpinae* to a vehement polemic on his own priority over anyone else (clearly Poliziano, or rather Crinito's summary, is meant) in this discovery.[12]

Parrasio substantiated his claim by invoking the testimony of his old students Mario Equicola and Tideo Acciarini, and by listing a couple of references to the *Aetia* in Servius (*in Aen.* 1.408 = fr. 189 Pf., and *in Aen.* 7.778 = fr. 190 Pf.) and Priscian (2.12 = fr. 61 Pf., the same passage quoted by Poliziano), as well as Ovid's allusion in *Fasti* 1.1 (probably already implied, though not quoted, by Poliziano, as we have just seen). Parrasio's entire note (on the adjective "Trinacria" in *De raptu Proserpinae* 1.141) takes its cue from the mention of the *Aetia* in Stephanus of Byzantium 635.11 M. (fr. 40 Pf.), but by far the most interesting evidence that Parrasio mentioned—certainly his own *trouvaille*, and one that was not to be exploited for a long time to come—are the numerous quotations of the *Aetia* in the Homeric scholia.[13]

---

ut ab Achillis hasta manus eius, ab Herculis vestigio corporatura, perinde et ab hoc hymnorum libello Battiadae ratiocinamur ingenium felicissimamque foecunditatem." ("How much of Callimachus' hymns has survived this unfortunate catastrophe? From this small book of hymns we can figure out the Battiad's intelligence and felicitious skill just as (we can reconstruct) the strength of Achilles' arm from his spear, and the size of Heracles' body from his footprint.") Pius is here paraphrasing lines 1–8 of Ianos Lascaris' very sophisticated Greek epigram Εἰς τοὺς Καλλιμάχου ὕμνους, which framed the 1494 editio princeps of the *Hymns* (*Ep.* 21 in Meschini 1976). See also the preface to Gelenius 1532 (linking Callimachus' fate with Menander's): "Quid vetat minutissimas quoque tantorum ingeniorum reliquias toto complecti pectore? maxime si tales sint, ut ob sui precium non una cum caeteris perisse videantur, perinde ac si ex incendio quopiam horribili gemmae dumtaxat unionesve incolumes eripiantur." ("What prevents us from embracing wholeheartedly even the smallest relics of such conspicuous geniuses? All the more so if it is clear that they did not perish with the rest on account of their extraordinary value, much in the same way as gems or big pearls recovered intact from a terrible fire.")

[12] Some selected philological notes from the Claudian commentary (first published in Milan in 1501) were later reprinted at the end of the Paris edition Parrhasius 1567, from which I quote: I refer to pp. 217–218. But other quotations from Callimachus appear on pp. 44 (fr. 178.11–12 Pf., from Macrobius), 183 (*Hymn* 1.6–7), and 189 (fr. 411 Pf., from Pliny).

[13] Parrhasius 1567: 218: "Ex Ætiis praeterea Callimachi vetustus et innominatus interpres Homeri, qui in publica Vaticana bibliotheca Romae legitur, saepissime testimonium petit" ("Furthermore, an old and anonymous exegete of Homer, who can be

Thus, from the very beginning of classical philology (and until just before the papyri came to light)[14] the pastime of collecting Callimachus' fragments as quoted by ancient authors attracted the most brilliant philological *ingenia*, eager to *parturire vultum* of an author whose renown—especially thanks to the vital and often controversial mediation of Latin sources[15]—was by no means matched by the size and weight of his direct manuscript tradition. One reason for this interest lay obviously in a growing awareness of Callimachus' massive presence in Latin poetry and culture. But another reason may have lain in the surprising fact that—leaving aside his metrical, linguistic, and thematic influence in later Greek poetry[16]—Callimachus was not often quoted in antiquity by erudite and literary authors, whereas he was definitely one of the favorite poets (if not the favorite, after Homer) of lexicographers, grammarians, and philologists.[17]

In other words, collecting the fragments of Callimachus is a remarkably difficult task, one that still even today requires familiarity with a large number of obscure treatises, unpublished lexica, and scarcely legible marginalia. The charm of this editorial task clearly has appealed to scholars from Angelo Poliziano to Luigi Lehnus, and in what follows we shall try to outline what underlay it, namely the forms and purposes of citations from Callimachus, from the second century BC down to the early thirteenth century AD.[18]

---

read in the public Vatican library at Rome, offers many quotations from Callimachus' *Aetia*"). This must be a reference to the D scholia to the *Iliad* (Σ D A 609, B 145 and N 66 carry open references to the *Aetia*), and a good candidate might be Vat. gr. 33, one of the four independent manuscripts of that scholiastic corpus, certainly kept in the Vatican Library at least since 1475. See Devreesse 1965: 47, Van Thiel 2001.

[14] I simply mention the names Henri Estienne, Richard Bentley, Anne Dacier (the notes of these scholars were collected in the splendid variorum edition of Graevius 1697), Ludwig Valckenaer, Adolf Hecker: see Lehnus 2002: 1-5 and 28-29, Benedetto 1993 and 1997.

[15] "Callimachus' name has always been made to stand, almost by metonymy, for things beyond his own poetry" (Hunter 2006a: 146). On Callimachus' fortunes in Roman poetry, see Barchiesi in this volume. Here it may be noted that two humanists active in Rome in the second half of the fifteenth century chose the name Callimachus because they considered him (on the basis of his Roman imitators) as the antonomastic champion of elegy and epigram: I refer to Filippo Buonaccorsi, alias Callimachus Experiens (see Kumaniecki 1958: 69) and to the Sicilian Angelo Callimaco (see Schizzerotto 1973).

[16] On this subject, see De Stefani and Magnelli in this volume.

[17] Pfeiffer 1949-1953: 2.xxvi: "A grammaticis certe nullus alius poeta praeter Homerum tam saepe laudatur."

[18] Readers looking for an exact, systematic overview of the sources of Callimachean indirect tradition, with special attention to grammarians and lexica, and with clear

Callimachus' Scholarly Works

Most of the eight hundred books ascribed to Callimachus by the *Suda* (κ 227 = test. 1 Pf.) appear to have been scholarly works: none of them (with the possible exception of the Θαυμάτων συναγωγή transmitted by the paradoxographer Antigonus: fr. 407 Pf.) survives in any direct tradition ancient or medieval. (See frr. 403–466 Pf.) Yet the importance of these works in different fields can hardly be overrated: one thinks of his foundation and systematization of Greek literary history (Callimachus' *Lebenswerk* was the Πίνακες, in 120 books, frr. 429–453 Pf., a mine of information on literary genres and individual authors for Dionysius of Halicarnassus, Athenaeus, Diogenes Laertius, and no doubt many others; see Blum 1977) and of his substantial progress in various other disciplines, such as ethnography (Βαρβαρικὰ νόμιμα, surfacing in Photius' lexicon; Ἐθνικαὶ ὀνομασίαι, known to Athenaeus) and natural history. (Περὶ ὀρνέων was very often used by Athenaeus, but also by scholiasts on Aristophanes, Apollonius Rhodius, and Lycophron; Περὶ ποταμῶν, by Strabo; Περὶ ἀνέμων, by Aratus' commentator Achilles Tatius.)

There is no evidence that any of Callimachus' scholarly works was still extant beyond the third century of our era, and we can rule out any having survived the Middle Ages. Like most reference works, even these writings—for all the reverence and authority that they enjoyed[19]—were doomed to be replaced by other manuals and then to be excerpted or forgotten in the *Verfall* of classical culture and instruction. The extant author who manifestly appears to have profited most from them—but who was, on the other hand, not very sensitive to Callimachus' poetry—is Athenaeus, to whom we also owe the quotation of what has since become a motto of Alexandrian poetics: μέγα βιβλίον μέγα κακόν (Athen. *Epit.* p. 72a = fr. 465 Pf.).

Callimachus' philological activity was devoted primarily to Homer, and although that did not lead to an edition or commentary, it was part and parcel of his poetry, as recent studies have clearly pointed out (see Rengakos 1992 and 1993; Tosi 1997). But this link was already clear

---

indication of the editions available and the degree of their reliability, are referred to Lehnus 2000b.

[19] There were exceptions: Dionysius of Halicarnassus opened his treatise *On Dinarchus* (1) by stating that neither Callimachus nor the Pergamene grammarians had written anything ἀκριβές on this orator (fr. 447 Pf.; see also Phot. *Bibl.* 265, 491b31 = fr. 446 Pf.).

in antiquity: a passage of Porphyry of Tyre's *Homeric Questions* (1.4, p. 15.11 Sod.) blames τὸν δοκοῦντα ἀκριβέστατον καὶ πολυγράμματον Καλλίμαχον for confusing in his poetry (fr. 383.10 Pf.) the two Homeric words ἁματροχιά and ἁρματροχία (*Il.* 23.422, 505).

Callimachus' Poetry: Citations in Literary Works

Papyrological evidence attests that Callimachus' poems were exceptionally widespread in Egypt in all eras and that they circulated in comprehensive books at least until the sixth century AD. Callimachus' success in terms of papyrological finds outdoes even beloved authors like Menander and Euripides, and certainly surpasses by far other poets such as Apollonius Rhodius and Theocritus;[20] indeed, POxy 20. 2258 shows that in the mid-sixth century beautiful copies of his *opera omnia* were produced, enriched with learned marginal scholia.[21]

Unlike less popular Hellenistic poets (see Magnelli 1999a: 44–45), Callimachus was read in schools: this is attested during the first century AD by Statius' father (*Silvae* 5.3.156-60, where Callimachus appears along with other purportedly obscure authors such as Lycophron, Sophron, and Corinna) and by Quintilian's canon of readings for the orator (*Inst. orat.* 10.1.58), and then later by Marcus Aurelius, who in 143 "meminit se legere apud magistrum" *Aet.* fr. 2.1-2 Pf.,[22] and by Athenaeus, who recalls in *Deipnosophistae* 15.669c–d his perusal of *Epigram* 43 Pf. (= 13 GP). Indeed, according to Clement of Alexandria, Callimachus (together with Euphorion and Lycophron) had written works that served merely as γυμνάσιον εἰς ἐξήγησιν γραμματικῶν παισίν,[23] or school exercises, and the truth of this statement will be

---

[20] See, e.g., Lehnus 2000c: 36; Montevecchi 1973: 359–394, esp. 383–384, where the author remarks that we have no papyri of Callimachus' *Epigrams* despite their evident popularity. On Apollonius' success among school readers and commentators, see Bowie 2000: 8–9. However, the quantitative aspect of papyrological finds and publications should be handled with great caution: see Harder 2002b: 77–78.

[21] See Porro 1985 (esp. 178–183) and the essays by Lehnus and Massimilla in this volume. I am more confident than Porro about the plausibility of identifying in POxy 20.2258 a good late-antique antecedent to what will become medieval scholiastic corpora: see F. Pontani 2005: 96–100, with further bibliography.

[22] On Statius, see Hollis 2009: 34. Marcus Aurelius' letter is now 1.4.7 among Fronto's epistles; for Synesius' reference to the same passage, see also below, n. 39.

[23] Clem. Alex. *Strom.* 5.8.50 = test. 26 Pf., already mentioned as a pivotal passage by Poliziano in *Miscellanea* 2.10 and again at 2.57. See above, "Callimachus' Traces: The First Modern Collectors."

seen below.[24] Yet it is self-evident that Callimachus' place in school syllabi, however secure down to the sixth century,[25] is conceivable only at an advanced level,[26] a position that exposed him to the threats of waning literacy, especially since, so far as we know, he did not enter any of the canons of lyric or elegiac poets from the Antonine era down to Themistius and the early Byzantine age, when Lycophron was chosen as the champion of difficult poetry.[27]

The number of significant Callimachean quotations in prose authors, by comparison, is not so great as one might expect. Two admirers of our poet are Strabo and Plutarch, both variously indebted to previous *Mittelmenschen* (for the former, chiefly Apollodorus). Strabo (9.438 = fr. 200a Pf.) praises Callimachus—using the poet's own words—as πολυίστωρ, εἴ τις ἄλλος, καὶ πάντα τὸν βίον, ὡς αὐτὸς εἴρηκεν, οὔατα μυθεῖσθαι βουλόμενος ("a very learned man—if any other man was—who throughout his life, as he himself wrote, wanted the ears to speak", fr. 178.30 Pf.; but both Pfeiffer and Radt emend to βουλομένοις ἀνέχων and construe as "who lent his ears to those who wanted to speak").[28] Strabo knows myths from the *Hymns*,[29] words from the *Epigrams*,[30] and details from *Iambi* 6 and 10,[31] but—in the wake of Apollodorus, who is certainly his source here—he also makes the most of the *Aetia* concerning the travels of Odysseus and of the Argonauts.[32]

---

[24] The very idea of paraphrasing in 6,810 iambic lines Callimachus' major works, apparently accomplished by Marianus of Eleutheropolis at the turn of the sixth century (*Suda* μ 194 = test. 24 Pf.: the works involved are of course the *Aetia*, *Hymns*, *Hecale*, and *Epigrams*), is a remarkable witness to the poet's nature as γυμνάσιον, or suitable school material!

[25] Lightfoot 1999: 94–96. But was it so firm outside Egypt? See N.G. Wilson 1983: 20.

[26] See Cribiore 2001: 201–202 (with an interesting reference to the coupling of two difficult poets, Pindar and Callimachus, in Palladas *AP* 9.175 = test. 82 Pf.). I am thus less confident than Hollis (2009: 35) that "knowledge of his work was common to pagans and Christians of any education."

[27] See Irigoin 1952: 94–100; Canfora 1995. On Lycophron, see Magnelli 2003; A. Pontani 2000.

[28] This judgment may go back to Asclepiades of Myrlea, who spoke of Callimachus as πολυίστορος ἀνδρὸς καὶ ἀξιοπίστου, "a learned and trustworthy man" (Ach. Tat. *In Arat. isag.* p. 59.5 de Maria).

[29] Strabo 8.3.19 on Thera's foundation, 10.4.12 on Britomartis.

[30] Strabo 14.638 = *Ep.* 6 Pf. = 55 GP on Creophilus of Samos, 17.805 = fr. 715 Pf. on δρόμοι in Egyptian temples.

[31] See, respectively, Strabo 8.353–54 on Phidias' Olympian Zeus and 9.438 on Artemis Kastnietis.

[32] See, respectively, Strabo 1.44 and 7.299 (frr. 13 and 470 Pf.) and Strabo 1.46, 5.216, 10.484 (frr. 7.23–26 and 11 Pf.); see Benedetto 1993: 179 n. 18.

Plutarch is perhaps the only ancient Greek writer who not only betrays direct familiarity with Callimachus but also refers to his poetry not merely in order to display his erudition. Certainly, there are references to mythographical or historical motifs,[33] but at times Plutarch's rumination of Callimachus' verse seems to grant the Cyrenean poet the status of a real mine of expressive and semantic cores: in *de exilio* 602f the line *Aetia* fragment 1.10 Pf. is quoted in a recommendation not to measure with gross units such as the *schoinos*;[34] the quasi-proverbial βροντᾶν οὐκ ἐμὸν ἀλλὰ Διός (*Aet.* fr. 1.20 Pf.), "to thunder is not my task, but Zeus'" appears as the adulator's typical insincere dictum in *de adulatione et amico* 54d; the lover's kiss on his beloved's threshold (*Ep.* 42.5-6 Pf. = 8.5-6 GP) is a paradigm of passion in *De cohibenda ira* 455b-c; and finally, turning to the spurious *Consolatio ad Apollonium*, the line pondering the length of human life is a perfect argument for a consolation (see *Cons. ad Apoll.* 113e = fr. 491 Pf., also quoted by Cic. *Tusc.* 1.93, and probably parodied by Emperor Tiberius: see below, "Callimachus' Poetry: Commentators and Grammarians"), and the sad distich on worldly evils (*SH* 253.1a-1, cf. *Cons. ad Apoll.* 115a) a paradigm of our daily toils.

Yet the Cyrenean is altogether absent from the authors of the Second Sophistic, from the rhetors, from the novelists,[35] and—quite surprisingly, given his interest for ethnography and geography (he appears dozens of times in Stephanus of Byzantium)—from Pausanias (who may allude to *SH* 276 in 8.28.4-6). Nor does he occur in the most important extant treatise of literary criticism, *On the Sublime*.[36]

---

[33] Most remarkably Plut. *Mul. virt.* 253f on Phrygius and Pieria (frr. 80-83 Pf.); *Parall. min.* 315c = fr. 45 Pf. on Phalaris; *Quaest. conv.* 677a-b = fr. 59 Pf. on Nemea's celery crown (crowns were a popular motif to be looked for in Callimachus: see the passages of Tertullian's *De corona*—probably depending on Varro—quoting frr. 59.2, 89, 101; *inc. auct.* 804 Pf.); fr. 158 Sandb. = fr. 100 Pf. on Hera's statue on Samos (quoted by Eusebius *Praep. ev.* 3.8.1).

[34] It is no coincidence that this was one of the few cases in which the context of the quotation demonstrably helped modern editors (namely Hecker, before the discovery of POxy 17. 2079) reconstruct the sense of Callimachus' text: see Benedetto 1993: 179 n. 16.

[35] With the possible exception of Hld. *Aeth.* 4.19.3, behind which Bulloch 1985: 80, detected a reference to *Hymn* 5.78. But simple allusions are often hard to prove: another interesting instance is Philo Judaeus *Leg. ad Gaium* 95: see Pfeiffer 1949-1953 on fr. 114.8. On the comparatively low relevance of Apollonius Rhodius in sophistic prose, philosophers, and novelists, see Bowie 2000: 1-7.

[36] See esp. *Subl.* 33, with references to Apollonius, Eratosthenes, and Theocritus; on this, Hunter 2006a: 3 n. 7. Callimachus is also rarely quoted in rhetorical handbooks:

Athenaeus is more interested in his erudite works, quoting poetry only from indirect sources: he is typically keen on curious information—mostly derived from Pamphilus' *Onomasticon*—concerning olives (2.56c), kinds of fish (7.284c, 318b, 327a), drinking and sympotic habits (10.442f, 11.477c, 15.668c).[37] Diogenes Laertius quotes Callimachus' epigrams on philosophers (1.80, 2.111, 9.17; the only exception is 1.23–28, with information on Thales drawn from Callimachus' first *Iambus*, see also Diodorus Siculus 10, fr. 11 C.-S. on Pythagoras), as does Sextus Empiricus (*Math.* 1.309 = fr. 393.3–4 Pf.). Even Gellius quotes only one passage, and probably at second hand (4.11.2 = fr. 553 Pf.; see Lightfoot 1999: 85). Unlike Euripides and Menander, Callimachus—by far less gnomic and moralizing a poet—remains virtually unknown to paroemiographers and florilegia,[38] and yet the occasional occurrences of his verse are of gnomic character in Aelian (*VH* 8.9; cf. *NA* 7.11: fr. 2.5 Pf., but see also fr. 64.7–14 and fr. 302.1 Pf. = 103.1 H.), Artemidorus (4.84, p. 300.16–17 Pack: fr. 475 Pf. = *SH* 253.11), and (?Pseudo-)Lucian (*Amores* 48 = fr. 571 Pf.), whereas they affect only tangentially lexical matters in Galen. (See frr. 43.41 and 550–552 Pf.)

Turning from polymaths to Christian authors: Cyril of Alexandria quotes Callimachus on Minos' cruelty (*In Iul.* 6, *PG* 76.792B = *Aet.* fr. 4 Pf.); Callimachus' fellow citizen Synesius probably refers to *The Dream* in the *Aetia*;[39] but again Clement of Alexandria is the key figure: he briefly refers to *Iambus* 4,[40] quotes polemically in his *Protrepticus* two pagan rites known from the *Aetia* (2.29.4, 38.3), and—following some lost intermediate source—introduces the Callimachean lines on man made of earth (frr. 192.1–3 and 493) as the first poetic quotation of *Stromateis* 5.4, a section devoted to showing how Greek wisdom actually depends on Judaeo-Christian doctrines (in this case particularly *Genesis* 2.7; see also Euseb. *Praep. ev.* 13.13.23).

---

for example, Demetrius' *On Poems* probably quoted *Ep.* 7.3–4 Pf. = 57.3–4 GP, and Ps.-Trypho quoted fr. 194.13 Pf.

[37] Diehl 1937: 339–344. Lehnus 2000c: 27: "Ateneo è raramente implicato nella trasmissione di Callimaco." Erudite details from Callimachus appear often in Pliny (frr. 14, 99, 107, 249–250, and 579–585 Pf.), and Seneca probably quoted him for information on Egypt: see Pfeiffer 1949–1953 on fr. *inc. auct.* 811.

[38] The paroemiographers also have some spurious material, and Stobaeus very few items, especially concerning the ages of man (remarkably frr. 27, 41, 43.12–17 Pf.).

[39] See Hollis 2002: 37–43; Alan Cameron 1995: 369–370. On Callimachus and Synesius, see also *SSH* 308B; and Pfeiffer 1949–1953 on fr. 602.3 for Cyrene as μήτηρ.

[40] Or 'Iambus' 17? See Clem. Alex. *Strom.* 5.8.48 (fr. 194.28–31 Pf.), with Alan Cameron 1995: 170 and Lelli 2005a: 7 n. 16.

In the sixth century, Procopius of Gaza may or may not allude to Callimachus' narration of the story of Demophoon and Phyllis (*Epist.* 47 G.-L. = fr. 556 Pf.; the quotation might as well derive from Herodian *Mov. λέξ.* 915.17 Lentz), but two epistles by Aristaenetus (1.10, 1.15) derive definitely from episodes of *Aetia* Book 3 and show the author's deep enthusiasm for and study of Callimachus' poetical work. (Remarkably enough, these are the only instances of nonadulterine love affairs in Aristaenetus' entire collection.) Finally, the only Greek historian to quote Callimachus is Theophylact Simocatta (early seventh century), whose work opens with a dialogue between Philosophy and History, the latter proclaiming she will reveal to her friend any good she might inquire about, as the Cyrenean prescribes (*Hist.* pp. 20.9–20.11 de Boor = fr. 620 Pf.).[41]

It looks as if attention to Callimachus was mostly occasional and rarely affected the core of his poetry. (What a difference, indeed, from the poets who took him as a model of style and subject!) Only two texts enjoyed a wide and ongoing popularity among writers and philosophers: I am referring to the passage of *Hymn* 1 on Zeus's alleged death on Crete (1.6–10), lines that were variously praised, parodied, or alluded to by many Christian authors,[42] and to the famous epigram on Cleombrotus, quoted (for example) by Cicero, Sextus Empiricus, and many Neoplatonic philosophers.[43] It should come as no major surprise that precisely the epigrams—because of their size, immediacy, and chiefly their better state of preservation—have been the works most representative of Callimachus in his *Nachleben* down to the present day.[44]

---

[41] See N.G. Wilson 1983: 59. Theoph. Simoc. *Epist.* 65.4 Zanetto, as the editor suggests, may contain a subtle allusion to the opening of Call. *Ep.* 31 Pf. = 1 GP.

[42] The proverbial beginning of *Hymn* 1.8, Κρῆτες ἀεὶ ψεῦσται, "Cretans always lie" (on which see Cuypers 2004), actually a quotation from Epimenides fr. 1 DK, prompted some exegetes (but not, e.g., John Chrysostom [*PG* 62.676D] or Epiphan. *Panar.* 2.169.13 Holl [= *PG* 41.793B–C], who states that Callimachus is quoting Epimenides, and may be the source of Phot. *Amphil.* 151.27–30 Westerink) to believe that the line quoted by Paul in *Titus* 1.12, Κρῆτες ἀεὶ ψεῦσται, κακὰ θηρία, γαστέρες ἀργαί, "Cretans always lie, nasty beasts, savage stomachs" belonged in fact to Callimachus, not to Epimenides: this misunderstanding earned our poet the title of προφήτης! See Jo. Dam. *PG* 95.1028B, and already Theodoret *PG* 82.861.17.

[43] See Spina 1989, G.D. Williams 1995. The sixth-century Aristotelian commentator David *In Ar. Categ.* p. 125.7 Busse also quotes *Hymn* 6.3–4. On the fortune of Callimachus' *Epigrams* in antiquity, see, e.g., Parsons 2002: 102–3.

[44] I refer to Y. Bonnefoy's *L'apport d'un poème à Callimaque* (on *Ep.* 13 Pf. = 31 GP), to J. Hollander's poem quoted as the epigraph to this chapter (in *Poetry*

But what do authors think of Callimachus? The literary evidence points to a decreasing popularity of our poet (and of the more conspicuous aspects of his poetics) throughout the imperial age and late antiquity. Whereas Menander is described as the "divine poet" rivaling Homer,[45] Callimachus' pedigree appears less exciting: even leaving aside the criticism on theological matters that ended up in Aëtius' doxography,[46] and the playful mockery by epigrammatists such as Martial, Philip of Thessalonica, Antiphanes, and Apollonius,[47] Callimachus becomes a symbol of prolixity in Lucian (*De conscr. hist.* 57.9-10 = test. 78 Pf.), a symbol of insignificance against Homer's greatness in Eunapius,[48] a symbol of poor critical skill in Longinus and Proclus,[49] a symbol of poetry's ambiguity and deceitfulness in Choricius,[50] a symbol of elliptical style in Photius and the unnamed κριτικοί he mentions as his source.[51]

The most remarkable example of an anti-Callimachean stance is provided by the bishop Severianus of Gabala, who in early fifth-century Alexandria could tolerate (ἀπεδέχετο μετρίως) other poets but was fond of ridiculing Callimachus, to the point of spitting repeatedly on his books (οὐκ ἔστιν ὅτε οὐ κατέσκωπτε τὸν Λίβυν ποιητήν· ἀνιώμενος δὲ ἐπὶ μᾶλλον, ἤδη πολλαχοῦ καὶ τῷ βιβλίῳ προσέπτυε).[52] Whether

---

123.2 [1973]: 64; on *Ep.* 41 Pf. = 4 GP), to Hadrian's erotic imagery as outlined by M. Yourcenar (*Tellus stabilita*, in *Mémoires d'Hadrien*).

[45] See Aristophanes of Byzantium *apud IG* 14.1183c, but later also Sen. *Brev. vitae* 2.2, "maximus poetarum"; Hier. *Epist.* 58.5; Auson. *Protr. ad nep.* 45-47; Canfora 1995: 156-158.

[46] Ps.-Plut. *Plac. philos.* 880d-f = Aët. 1.7.1-3 Diels = frr. 586 and 191.9-11 Pf.

[47] Mart. 10.4.9-12 = test. 25a Pf.; *AP* 11.321, 322, 275 = test. 69, 71, 25 Pf. For the imperial age, see Lightfoot 1999: 88-91 and Alan Cameron 1995: 475.

[48] Eunap. *Vit. soph.* p. 494 Boiss. = test. 84 Pf. But already Pollianus' mocking epigram (*AP* 11.130.5-6) implies that Callimachus and Parthenius were not highly regarded poets, as opposed to the cyclic ones: see Alan Cameron 1995: 396-99, Lightfoot 1999: 84.

[49] Procl. *In Plat. Tim.* 1.90.25 Diehl = test. 86 Pf., probably derived from Cassius Longinus fr. 34 Patillon and Brisson. But it should not be forgotten that Proclus himself (*In Plat. Remp.* 125.29) resorted to *Hymn* 4.84-85 (on the Nymphs' weeping over dying oaks) in order to exemplify—and defend—the gods' empathy with their προνοούμενοι, something Plato had vehemently criticized in Homeric poetry.

[50] Chor. *Or.* 32.24, dating from before 526 AD: Call. *Ep.* 26.3-4 Pf. = 47.3-4 GP.

[51] Phot. *Epist.* 166.181-85 LW = test. 90 Pf.: Photius is here discussing the style of Paul's epistles.

[52] Damasc. *Vita Isid.* fr. 282, pp. 227.10-227.12 Zintzen = *Suda* σ 180 = test. 85 Pf. (That fr. 283 Zintzen = *Suda* κ 705 should also refer to Severianus' criticism of Callimachus is to my mind very doubtful.) The passage is mentioned by Lehnus 2002: 27 n. 119. (See also ibid. 56.) Λίβυς ποιητής occurs only here, in Phot. *Epist.* 166 (see

this idiosyncratic hatred derived from Platonic sympathies,[53] or from obscure doctrinal stances,[54] or from other reasons we do not know; it might be suggested, however, that Severianus' unconventional gesture distorted, in a ludicrous way, Callimachus' own verse, if we believe that fragment 779 Pf., πάντων δ' ἔπτυσε πουλὺ κάτα, "he spat much upon all", belongs to the Cyrenean.[55]

Not too frequently—and sometimes not too favorably—quoted by Greek prose authors, Callimachus seems to have rarely entered the aesthetic world of literati as an artist, a creator of metaphors, stories, or images: he was seldom used to back an assumption, to adorn a phrasing, to lend authority or charm to a special passage. Even if poets such as Gregory of Nazianzus and Nonnus certainly read and imitated him,[56] and his influence on the development of poetry in Greece and Rome is undeniable, it is not always obvious that the rationale of his *Nachleben* in prose authors was remarkably different from that of his rival Antimachus, who—despite Hadrian's fondness for him (Cass. Dio 69.4.6 = *Suda* α 527 = Antim. test. 31 Matthews)—decayed "into a mere quarry for lexicographers and grammarians in search of linguistic rarities."[57]

This state of affairs has interesting epistemological consequences, in that the context of Callimachean quotations hardly ever helps modern philologists reconstruct the spirit, the meaning, and the context of

---

above, n. 51), but also in Epiphan. *Panar.* 2.169.13 Holl (= *PG* 41.793B-C). Yet some link between Damascius and Photius might be argued from the occurrence in *Vita Isid.* fr. 276 Zintzen (= *Suda* υ 166, on Hypatia) of the same etymology of κριτικός from κρίνειν as in Phot. *Epist.* 166.184-85.

[53] As surmised by Bandini 1763: 20, who joins this passage with Proclus' criticism mentioned above.

[54] It should be remarked that, however keen on classical literature (especially Isocrates: see Damasc. *Vit. Isid.* fr. 282, p. 227.3-9 Zintzen), Severianus was by no means gentle with the poet of Κρῆτες ἀεὶ ψεῦσται (see above, n. 42), though he probably took him to be Epimenides rather than Callimachus (*Fragm. in epist. ad Tit.* 344.15 Staab).

[55] I shall not indulge in further speculation on either wording or context: ἐπὶ μᾶλλον (or ἔτι μᾶλλον) could be the end of a hexameter, but it is well attested in Damascius' own *usus scribendi* as well; the pentameter might read ἤδη καὶ πάντων ἔπτυσε πουλὺ κάτα, although πάντων is not secured by the sources of fr. 779 Pf.

[56] On this topic, see Alan Cameron 1995: 334-336 (especially for the relationship with Antimachus); Hollis 2002; and again De Stefani and Magnelli in this volume.

[57] Matthews 1996: 75, and 72-74 for the harsh judgments of various authors on Antimachus' style. See also Magnelli 2002: 125: "Il nostro autore [*sc.* Euphorion] non sembra aver mai suscitato interesse se non come fonte di parole rare o irregolari e di notizie peregrine."

Callimachean words or lines;[58] indeed it might even prove misleading or inexact.[59]

Callimachus' Poetry: Commentators and Grammarians

I shall not take up here the much-debated issue of when Hellenistic poets became the objects of exegetical and philological activity in their own right.[60] It can be assumed that Hellenistic poets—and above all Callimachus—were actually known and studied by Alexandrian critics, and above all students of Homer, partly for help in the constitution of the Homeric text, partly in order to highlight polemically their differences from epic diction.[61] There is as yet little evidence that a running commentary or *hypomnēma* on their poetical works was produced before the Augustan age.[62]

---

[58] This has been brilliantly stated for the proem by Benedetto 1993: 179–180, who rather insists on the importance of indirect references (in Latin poetry, epigrams, etc.) for the construction of Callimachus' image.

[59] For the general problem of indirect tradition, and for a wise and careful reevaluation of its importance in reconstructing and ordering the fragments of ancient poets, I refer the reader to Nicosia 1976: 23–26 and 254–270, Tosi 1988 (on p. 84 the representative case of Call. fr. 631 Pf.; see also the review by Kleinlogel 1991), and Radt 2002a. Massimilla 2006a has an overall assessment of the importance of papyri in the constitution of Callimachus' text. In some cases, however, single details may prove very useful: thus, Emanuele Lelli has recently argued for the (otherwise debated) existence of *Iambi* 14–17 on the basis of a reference to fr. 217 Pf. in the *Etymologicum genuinum* (AB s.v. Κεραιίτης, from Orus' Περὶ ἐθνικῶν) and to fr. 555 in *EGud* 239.18 Stef.: see Lelli 2005a: 7–10.

[60] The best systematic introductions to the topic of commentators and grammarians in regard to the poetry of Callimachus remain Pfeiffer's *Prolegomena* (Pfeiffer 1949–1953: 2.xxvi–xxxiii) and Diehl 1937. Here I shall follow a less comprehensive approach, focusing on some key moments. The debate regarding when Hellenistic poets became objects of exegetical and philological study was opened by Montanari 1995, whose optimistic views have been partly refuted by Rengakos 2000. More recently, see Montanari 2002.

[61] See Rengakos 2000 for a detailed examination of references in Homeric scholia of Alexandrian origin.

[62] Significant clues are listed by Montanari 1995: 47–49 and partly again in Montanari 2002: 74–77: the scholia to the Oyster Riddle (*SH* 983–984) and to Callimachus' *Victory of Berenice* (*SH* 254–261), both in Ptolemaic papyri (PLouvre inv. 7733v and PLille 76, 78a–c, 82, 84, 111c); Demetrius Chlorus writing on Nicander, perhaps in the first century BC (Steph. Byz. 375.10 M. = Plut. fr. 115 S. = Theon fr. 46 Guhl). Two other interesting items may rather belong to the Περί literature: Timarchus' work on Eratosthenes' *Hermes* (Athen. 11.501e; on Timarchus' date, see *Suda* α 3419; Alan Cameron 1995: 188 and 244–245; but Susemihl read Τιμαχίδας instead) and the treatise of Dionysius of Phaselis (a follower of Aristarchus) Περὶ τῆς Ἀντιμάχου ποιήσεως (*Vita Nicandri* 1; Matthews 1996: 67–68).

As far as Callimachus is concerned, I shall refrain from tackling the complicated issues of chronology and genre posed by exegeses on papyri, chiefly the *Diegeseis* and the Lille Papyrus of *The Victory of Berenice*. Limiting the inquiry to indirect sources, we do not know if the Hedylus mentioned by the *Etymologicum genuinum* (α 551 L.-L. = Call. test. 45 Pf.) as the author of a work Εἰς τὰ ἐπιγράμματα Καλλιμάχου (see *SH* 458) should be identified with the poet Hedylus of Samos, perhaps belonging to the first half of the third century BC.[63] Also very uncertain is the existence of a commentary (on the *Hecale*?) by one Nicias, or by the well-known Augustan grammarian Aristonicus.[64]

Work on Callimachus was carried out well before the Augustan age, as the wealth of references in (for example) Aristophanes of Byzantium, Apollodorus of Athens, and Philoxenus shows.[65] But there is no proof that this work was systematic. The man generally credited with the merit of inaugurating a line-by-line exegesis to Hellenistic poets is the grammarian Theon of Alexandria, who worked in Rome probably between 50 BC and 20 AD.[66] From information scattered in the Byzantine etymologica we learn that Theon wrote commentaries to the *Aetia* (*EGen* β 207 and α 1316 L.-L. = frr. 42 and 261 Pf.) and possibly to the *Hecale* (see *EGen* α 1198 = fr. 274 Pf. = 45 H.) and to the *Iambi* (*EGud* 239.18 Stef. = fr. 555 Pf.): it is widely assumed that he produced a *kommentierte Gesamtausgabe* of Callimachus' poetry. (See Wendel

---

[63] Alan Cameron 1995: 224–225 and Parsons 2002: 102 identify the two Hedyli (already von Radinger, *RE* 7.2 [1912]: 2592–2593), whereas Gow and Page 1965: 2.153 do not and in 2.289 judge the hypothetical existence of this commentary "surprising."

[64] The textual problem (Ἀριστόνικος [or οὕτω Νικίας Her.] ἐν ὑπομνήματι †ἐκάλεσ᾽ ἐπὶ στοιχείου† [ἐκάλεσεν ἐπὶ στίου Her.]) lies in the text shared by Ammon. *adf. voc. diff.* 352 and Her. Phil. o 132 Palm. = fr. 470b Pf.: discussion in Montanari 2002: 68–70.

[65] See Pfeiffer 1949–1953: 2.xxxi and frr. 224 and 543 Pf. (= Ar. Byz. frr. 25A and 48E Slater, known from Eustathius; Aristophanes had also written a book on Callimachus' Πίνακες: see fr. 453 Pf.); frr. 13, 114.8, 238.11, 305, 466, 702 Pf. (Apollodorus, especially his very influential Περὶ θεῶν; see Rengakos 2000: 333–334). Callimachus occurred quite often in Philoxenus' Περὶ μονοσυλλάβων ῥημάτων but also in other minor works of the same grammarian: all references occur in the Byzantine etymologica. See Theodoridis' edition *ad indicem* and Pfeiffer 1949–1953 on fr. 23.15. See also Varro's quotations, frr. 722 and 723 Pf.

[66] Date tentatively reconstructed by Alan Cameron 1995: 191–92 (who dates Didymus 81–80 BC). *Suda* α 3215 gives the grammarian Apion as Theon's διάδοχος and Dionysius of Halicarnassus' contemporary, but Guhl 1969 on the contrary believes Theon to be Didymus' senior, and at least two generations older than Apion.

1934: 2055.) Through other sources, we know that Theon produced commentaries on archaic poets (Pindar, Alcman, Stesichorus, etc.) but also on Theocritus, Apollonius Rhodius, Nicander: it is likely that the bulk of our scholia to these Hellenistic poets rests precisely on Theonian material, even if the present state of the scholiastic corpora reflects later developments.[67]

This state of affairs explains extraordinarily well the large number of references to Callimachean words and phrases in the scholiastic corpora to the other Hellenistic poets, especially to Apollonius Rhodius (a number more significant, e.g., than in the scholia to the dramatic poets).[68] Even if it is not always right to reconstruct bits of Callimachean exegesis from those scholia, and even if Callimachus was certainly quoted independently by many ancient scholiasts,[69] in many cases the relationship is obvious, and similar explanations will definitely go back to one and the same source, namely Theon.[70]

Theon's commentary was an important witness to earlier scholarship and was in its turn the basis for later exegesis (see the cases of Epaphroditus and Sallustius below) and lexicography: it certainly increased the amount of Hellenistic material in the lexica of Seleucus (an important source for the Byzantine etymologica: see frr. 231.2,

---

[67] For similar situations, I note the names Theaetetus and Amarantus for Theocritus, Diphilus of Laodicea and Plutarchus for Nicander, Lucillius of Tarrha and Sophocleius for Apollonius, Sextion and Philogenes for Lycophron. See Wendel 1920 and 1932, Leone 2002: xvii–xx.

[68] The scholia to Aristophanes and Euripides offer quite a few references to Callimachus, mostly concerned with the description of mythical or divine figures, or with geographical matters, odd *Realien*, or rare words. (But see, e.g., fr. 73 Pf. on lovers carving their names on trees, or fr. 604 Pf. with Callimachus' polemic against dithyrambs and New Music.) On Sophocles, see below, n. 88.

[69] The most direct witnesses are the quotations in commentaries to other authors on papyrus, listed by Pfeiffer 1949–1953: 2.xxvi (Antimachus, Euphorion, Thucydides). Commentaries on Hellenistic poets were known to Virgilian exegetes (see, e.g., frr. 54 and 696–99 Pf.), and Callimachean material obviously surfaces in the farrago of the scholia on Ovid's *Ibis*. See frr. 381–382 and 661–665 Pf.

[70] See already Pfeiffer 1949–1953: 2.xxvii n. 4 and 2.xxx. On the wealth of Callimachean references in the scholia to Apollonius Rhodius (especially for mythographical and lexical issues), Lycophron, and Theocritus, see Diehl 1937: 367–373, 377–381, 388–392. A reconstruction of Theon's commentary, sometimes bold but more often sound, has been attempted by Bongelli 2000. It is interesting to note that already Poliziano had detected Theon as a major source for the fragments of *The Lock of Berenice*: see *Miscellanea* 1.68 (Politianus 1553: 282), with quotations from Theon "Arati eiusdem interpres" (but the commentator on Aratus might in fact be the astronomer Theon: see Schiano 2002) and from the scholia to Apollonius Rhodius "ex Lucilio Tarrheo, Sophocleo ac Theone collectis."

275, 359, 527a Pf.), Pamphilus (a source for Athenaeus, and probably for Hesychius too: see Pfeiffer on fr. 423), Erotian, and Epaphroditus, all writing in the first century AD. The synonymic lexicon of Philo of Byblus (now known chiefly through the versions of Herennius Philo and Ammonius) contained a number of—very often polemic— quotations of Callimachean linguistic peculiarities.[71] In the early second century, the lexicographers most keen on Callimachus were Pollux and Diogenianus, the latter himself a primary source of Hesychius (ca. 500 AD).

Theon's commentary, with its later accretions and abridgments, was excerpted in the fifth century in Orus' Περὶ ἐθνικῶν (a source for the *Etymologicum genuinum* but also for Stephanus of Byzantium; see, e.g., fr. 42 Pf.), in Methodius' lexicon (an important source for letter α of the *Etymologicum genuinum*: see Pf. 1949–1953 on fr. 274), and through the mediation of other grammarians (such as Soranus *On the Parts of Human Body* and Helladius: see frr. 263 Pf. = 80 H., 383.16 Pf., 500 Pf.) in Orion's *Etymologicum* (also a source for the *Etymologicum genuinum*). Thus, the large number of Callimachean quotations in Byzantine etymologica—perhaps the most important source for us today—is rooted in a continuous lexicographical and exegetical tradition that had Theon as its starting point but was by no means confined to him.[72]

Theon owes his success in lexica to the fact that he was primarily concerned with the etymology,[73] accentuation, and meaning of difficult words, as well as with some geographical and mythographical issues. There is no evidence that Theon ever addressed broader literary or historical issues, or that he understood Callimachus' verse against the background of Hellenistic or earlier poetry, with respect either to its subject matter or to matters of genre. This limit Theon shares with many others ancient exegetes of Greek poetry, which is why most references to Callimachus concern the meaning and etymology of the

---

[71] For all this, see again Pfeiffer 1949–1953: 2.xxx–xxxi. On the historical development of Greek lexicography, see the overviews by Alpers 1990 and 2001.

[72] On the sources of the *Etymologicum genuinum*, see specifically Pfeiffer 1949–1953: 2.xxix–xxx and Diehl 1937: 408–412, Bongelli 2000: 287–288; more generally Reitzenstein 1897 (esp. pp. 25 and 326 on the presence of Callimachean material in Methodius and Orus). Further information and bibliography on Byzantine lexica in F. Pontani 2005: 152–156 and 179–181.

[73] See Diehl 1937: 320–326, Wendel 1934: 2057–2058. Bongelli 2000: 288–289 seeks to define a typology of Theonian etymology, but her attempt seems far-fetched.

countless lexical gems that embellished his verse.[74] This limitation also explains why the typology of Callimachean quotations in ancient scholia is so often disappointing for anyone wishing to reconstruct the context of Callimachean poetry. (See above, "Callimachus' Poetry: Citations in Literary Works.")

But not all scholiastic corpora are equally disappointing. Whether slightly older or slightly younger than Theon (see above, note 66), Didymus Chalcenterus, the most prolific grammarian of antiquity, never dealt *in extenso* with Hellenistic poetry but could boast an intimate knowledge of Callimachus' oeuvre. This appears not only from a couple of quotations in fragmentarily known commentaries to Demosthenes and Homer,[75] but also in what is commonly regarded as one of his most important exegetical achievements, namely the commentary to Pindar (see Irigoin 1952: 67–75 and 102–105): as Diehl (1937: 381–86) remarked long ago, Pindaric scholia—demonstrably built upon Didymus' *hypomnemata*—display a peculiar approach to Callimachean material, in that they often quote longer passages (sometimes two or three lines, not just one word) with remarkable correctness, they show virtually no interest in etymology or lexical matters, they turn to *res et nomina*, and they proceed from nonmechanical associations (in terms of imagery and aesthetic and literary values) from the Pindaric to the Callimachean context.

Some examples. The inextricable link between ἀρετή and ὄλβος, a characteristic ideal of Pindar's world, is also found in *Hymn* 1.95–96 (Σ *Ol.* 2.96f, *Pyth.* 5.1a). Poetry must not be composed for money (no ἐργάτις Μοῦσα, as in fr. 222 Pf.: see Σ *Isthm.* 2.9b) and becomes immortal only if assisted by the Χάριτες (fr. 7.13–14 Pf.: Σ *Nem.* 4.10a). Callimachus is an authority on Italian music (fr. 669 Pf. = Σ *Ol.* 10.18b). There are of course in these scholia a series of learned quotations concerning toponyms and myths (Gela, Thera, Cyrene, Phocis, Perilaus, etc.), but many references are not obvious: see, for example,

---

[74] Other topics include the identification of toponyms and local cults—esp. in the scholia to Dionysius Periegetes and Lycophron (Diehl 1937: 377–381)—and astronomical matters in the scholia to Aratus (Diehl 1937: 373–375). Achilles Tatius' Εἰσαγωγή obviously quotes *Iambus* 1 on Thales and the epigram on Aratus himself (27 Pf. = 56 GP; see pp. 7.19–22 and 59.5–9, 61.22–25 de Maria). See also fr. 387 (on Berenice), p. 21.23 de Maria.

[75] See Harding 2006, col. XIV, 33–35, with quotation of fr. 495 Pf. on the toponym Ὀργάς. Didymus' commentary on *Od.* 14.6 quoted the occurrence of περίσκεπτος in *Ep.* 5.8 Pf. = 14.8 GP: see *EGen* AB s.v. περισκέπτω = *EM* 664.49.

fragment 23.19-20 Pf. on Heracles' self-chosen toils (Σ *Nem.* 3.42c); fragment 1.36 Pf. shows Enceladus, not Typhon, beneath Etna (Σ *Ol.* 4.11c); fragment 673 Pf. is quoted as a parallel for Cyrene's much-debated κᾶπος Ἀφροδίτας, "garden of Aphrodite" (Σ *Pyth.* 5.31). Even the reference to the etymology of ῥαψῳδός from ῥάβδος is elegantly motivated with Callimachus fragment 26.5 Pf. (Σ *Nem.* 2.1d). See also fragments 384.35-36 and 672 Pf.

According to Jane Lightfoot, it is "just possible that Theon took part in the Tiberian craze."[76] For all the chronological doubts surrounding Theon and Didymus, it seems unlikely that they should be linked with the reign of Tiberius, the emperor credited by our sources with a special fancy for difficult and if possible obscure Hellenistic poets—he even urged grammarians to write books on them, and on Augustus' death he performed rare funerary rituals following a passage of the *Aetia*.[77]

Be that as it may, between the early empire and the revival of Hellenism under Hadrian we know of some exegetical activity: sometime in the mid-first century AD Archibius, the father of the Homeric lexicographer Apollonius Sophista,[78] wrote a commentary on Callimachus' *Epigrams* (*Suda* α 4105 = test. 44 Pf.; no fragment extant); more important, Epaphroditus of Chaeronea (22-97 AD), besides listing Callimachean words in his Λέξεις, wrote a commentary on the *Aetia* (we know only about *Aetia* Book 2: see frr. 52 and 53 Pf.), probably largely relying on Theon's work and not unlike it in approach;[79] Nicanor of Alexandria wrote a treatise on the interpunction of Callimachus (*Suda* ν 375 = test. 43 Pf.).

The golden age of Greek grammar in the Antonine period entailed a series of references to Callimachus in the most successful manuals of the time: Apollonius Dyscolus continuously refers to Callimachean examples—often juxtaposing them to Homeric lines—for

---

[76] Lightfoot 1999: 81. On Theon's linking role between Alexandrian and Roman philology, see Wilamowitz 1921: 162-163.

[77] The key passage here is Suet. *Tib.* 70: "fecit et Graeca poëmata imitatus Euphorionem et Rhianum et Parthenium, quibus poëtis admodum delectatus scripta omnium et imagines publicis bibliothecis inter veteres et praecipuos auctores dedicavit, et ob hoc plerique eruditorum certatim ad eum multa de his ediderunt." See Magnelli 2002: 109-12. On Tiberius and Callimachus (with a very acute remark on Suet. *Tib.* 62.6 as a "rovesciamento" of fr. 491 Pf.), see La Penna 1987.

[78] Himself a source for Callimachean fragments: see most conspicuously Ap. Soph. 10.13 Bekk. = fr. 192.15-17 Pf., 125.34 = fr. 24.17 Pf.

[79] See Wilamowitz 1921: 187-90; Diehl 1937: 326-330.

syntactical constructs and for the morphology of adverbs and conjunctions.[80] (See, e.g., fr. 474 Pf., against Trypho.) Herodian's Καθολικὴ προσῳδία—to judge from its only extant fragment—was full of Callimachean vocabulary,[81] and to be sure many Callimachean quotations in later grammarians such as Georgius Choeroboscus (early ninth century, one of our most important sources *überhaupt*), concerning aberrant declensions or rare orthographies, go back precisely to Herodian's works.[82] Hephaestion's handbook of Greek meter contains a large number of Callimachean examples (alas, focused exclusively on prosody, not on semantic units), both in regard to special forms of hexameters or elegiacs and in regard to more unusual meters.[83]

Like Didymus' Pindaric scholia, the exegetical scholia to Homer, mainly compiled from commentaries of the early imperial age, sometimes provide interesting contexts for Callimachean quotations. Whereas the so-called VMK scholia (chiefly Didymus, Herodian, and Aristonicus) focus on textual problems, on the use of prepositions and conjunctions, on etymology, or on single linguistic items, the bT scholia to the *Iliad* display a deeper interest for Callimachus' poetry: for example, fragment 6 Pf. is quoted by Apollonius Dyscolus (Herodian's father) for the preposition οὕνεκα but by the T scholia on *Iliad* 18.398–99b for the presence of Eurynome; the T scholion on *Iliad* 14.172b quotes fragment 196.45 Pf. as an instance of synaesthesia; Callimachus' use of the optative formula ὤφελε (fr. 696 and *Ep.* 17.1 Pf. = 45.1 GP) is underlined twice (Σ AT on *Il.* 1.415b and Σ T on *Il.* 24.254); peculiar usages of common words like τεῖχος or κόλπος recall Callimachus (frr. 635 and 7.9–10 Pf.: see Σ bT on *Il.* 22.56a and 22.80c); the bT scholia on *Iliad* 22.452–53 find the same image of knees suddenly blocked by fear or emotion in Callimachus' *Hymn* 5.83–84, and the T scholion on *Iliad* 16.235 quotes fragment 631 Pf. as a comparable example of religious seclusion. In the scholia to the *Odyssey* it is more difficult to draw typological distinctions, and some of the most valu-

---

[80] See Pfeiffer 1949–1953: 2.xxxi; Diehl 1937: 346–355.
[81] Hunger 1967 has four likely fragments of Callimachus (frr. 44–47 Hunger, on the accent of words with particular endings; the first, which makes an entire line, is now *SH* 275), but the lemma Καλλίμαχος often appears in the margins where the text of the palimpsest cannot be properly read.
[82] This holds true even if Lentz' reconstruction of Herodian's work is methodologically flawed and unreliable: see Dyck 1993: 772–794.
[83] Hephaestion drew directly on Callimachus: Diehl 1937: 330–338.

able Callimachean quotations seem to proceed from morphological (Σ *Od.* 3.380, 14.199) or syntactical (Σ *Od.* 2.50, 136) interests.[84]

Two other commentators of Callimachus are obscure grammarians of unknown date: Astyages, who lived possibly in the fifth century AD, wrote a *hypomnema* on the Cyrenean.[85] Sallustius, who played a decisive role in the transmission of Sophoclean scholia,[86] also wrote a commentary on the *Hecale* (*EGen* α 1279 = fr. 240 Pf. = 29 H., but see also frr. 235 and 741 Pf. = 9 and 179 H.) and possibly on the *Hymns*. (Comparison of Σ *Hymn* 2.89 with Steph. Byz. α 75 Bill. suggests that Sallustius may indeed be the direct source of the scholia to the *Hymns* preserved in our manuscripts.) All this does not help us date him, although he must probably be distinguished from the identically named author of Περὶ θεῶν, and the second century or the early third is a more likely date than the fourth.[87] Be that as it may, Sallustius' commentary on the *Hecale* not only was known to the *Etymologicum genuinum* (where Theonian material ended up, though indirectly; see above) but also was a major source for the compiler (or compilers) of the *Suda* in the tenth century, which beautifully explains the rationale behind the so-called Hecker's law ("all hexameters quoted only by the *Suda* belong to Callimachus' *Hecale*"), the only mechanical system yet discovered for identifying and classifying Callimachean quotations in grammatical authors.[88]

---

[84] See Montanari 1979; F. Pontani 1999.

[85] *Suda* α 4259 = test. 42 Pf. This Astyages might be the same as the Astyagius quoted as an authority on the pronoun by Pomp. *In Donat.* 5, pp. 209 and 211 Keil, and by Σ Lond. Dion. Thr. pp. 546–547 Hilg.: see Kaster 1988: 149 and 385–386. Another terminus ante quem is Orion, who quotes him for the etymology of Ἡρακλῆς (Heracles) in p. 164.5 Sturz (whence *EGud* 248.1 Sturz).

[86] De Marco 1952: xx–xxvii; Diehl 1937: 386–388. His hypothesis to *Oed. Col.* circulated in papyri of the late fourth century AD: see Luppe 1985: 94–96 and 103.

[87] See Wilamowitz 1921: 198–200, Diehl 1937: 445–446; an updated overview of the problem in G. Ucciardello's article in the *Lessico dei grammatici greci antichi*. Sallustius may be the same grammarian who also wrote *hypomnemata* to Herodotus and Demosthenes. (See *Suda* σ 60.) On him, see also Pfeiffer 1949–53: 2.xxviii–ix.

[88] Hecker's law has been confirmed by the papyrological finds, except for a few cases that can mostly be easily explained: see Hollis 2009: 41–44. On the sources of the *Suda*, and on the formal typology of its quotations, see the detailed (and often optimistic) analysis by Diehl 1937: 392–407. On the vain quest for a mechanical method, see Diehl 1937: 305–306; Pfeiffer 1949–1953: 2.xxxiii–xxxiv; Benedetto 1993: 89–90.

Callimachus in Byzantium

Like Sappho and Menander, Callimachus is one of those authors whose books still circulated in the sixth or even the seventh century AD but then apparently—and quite surprisingly—disappeared (except for the *Hymns*, which were joined together with those of other authors in the successful collection of this genre).[89] Callimachus lived in Byzantium mostly as a fragmentary author, and most quotations from him—with a couple of very dubious exceptions[90]—do not proceed from reading him independently.[91]

But unlike Sappho, whose survival down to the Fourth Crusade has been often assumed on no firm ground (see F. Pontani 2001 and Reinsch 2006), and like Hipponax, whose *Iambi* were still read by John Tzetzes in the mid-twelfth century (and by him alone, and by no one after him),[92] a copy of Callimachus' poetical works (besides the *Hymns*)[93] was certainly extant in the high Byzantine era. If the chances that Eustathius of Thessalonica ever had access to such a book are not very great (we know that the archbishop used to draw on remote and often no longer extant grammatical sources),[94] and the same holds true

---

[89] Quite puzzling is what we know about the Armenian translation of "Callimachus and Andronicus" mentioned (together with translations of Plato and Olympiodorus) by the learned nobleman and poet Gregorius Magister in a letter written from Constantinople to his friend Sargis of Ani (mid-eleventh century): see Leroy 1935: 280 and 289–291 (who believes that Callimachus' *Pinakes* is meant here); N.G. Wilson 1983: 164; Canfora 1995: 163–64.

[90] The title of *AP* 7.154, referring to the story of Coroebus in *Aetia* 1 (fr. 29 Pf.) was probably added by Constantine Cephalas but may well rely on a preexisting tradition. Some scholia to Eusebius, Lucian, and (chiefly) Pausanias containing references to lost Callimachean lines have been thought to go back to the man who copied them, namely the learned archbishop Arethas of Caesarea (early tenth century), but "scepticism is in order: there is nothing to prove that these references are due to Arethas himself" (N.G. Wilson 1983: 131 [see also pp. 122 and 125]). See also Diller 1983: 152; Hollis 2009: 38; no help comes from the obscure and corrupt passage listed as Call. *Hec.* test. 19 H.

[91] No proof of direct knowledge is given either by Cazzaniga 1968 (see Hollis 2009: 353–54) or by Gentile Messina 2000 (who does not even problematize the alleged echo of *Acontius and Cydippe* in the twelfth-century historian John Cinnamus, and who does not mention the real possibility that the latter was rather drawing on Aristaenetus' *Epist.* 1.10).

[92] Masson 1962: 42–52; Degani 1984: 80–81 and 70–82 on Hipponax' *Nachleben*, in some aspects comparable to Callimachus'.

[93] On *Hymn* 6.50–52 clearly paraphrased in Mich. Chon. 1.349.22 Lambros, see Hollis 2002: 49.

[94] See Van der Valk 1971: xci: "Callimachi quoque Hymni Eustathio sunt noti, cum cetera opera poëtae, quae hic illic ab eo afferuntur, e fontibus tantum cognoverit."

for John Tzetzes (see Irigoin 1960: 444), on the other hand the archbishop of Athens Michael Choniates (†1222) repeatedly quoted (or alluded to) passages from the *Aetia* and the *Hecale*, which he could hardly have found anywhere else but in a complete copy.[95]

Like Tzetzes with Hipponax, Choniates never openly named Callimachus (he once spoke of παλαιός τις: *Epist.* 174.37), nor did he refer to the manuscript where he had found so rare an author: the latter fact is quite surprising for a man so keen on his library, and so sad at its loss the day after the Latin Conquest of Athens in 1205.[96] But it should be borne in mind that the former archbishop still quoted Callimachean lines in the exile of his later years,[97] which makes it at least possible that he never parted with his precious Callimachus, perhaps one of the very few transliterated copies of this author that ever existed, and perhaps the last copy of our author to be preserved in history.[98]

Even in places where Van der Valk is in doubt about Eustathius' source, one will have to infer secondhand citation from some grammatical text: see, e.g., *In Iliadem* 522.15 (fr. 2.5 Pf.; from the *Suda*?), 629.55 (fr. 544 Pf.), 870.6 (fr. 1.31 Pf.; from Pollianus' parody in *AP* 11.130?), 781.52 (and 985.56, and 1372.2, and *In Od.* 1778.27: fr. 203.1 Pf.; from *scholia pleniora* to Soph. *Oed. Col.* 1621?); 1271.34 is interesting because it quotes fr. 291.3 Pf. (= 113.3 H.), also occurring in Tzetzes *Hist.* 8.834 and *Epist.* 34 Leone, and already in Olympiodorus' commentary to Aristotle's *Metaphysics*. Secondhand derivation becomes even more likely when a single word is involved, as in frr. 542, 549, and 545 Pf. (*in Il.* 630.19, ἐλαχός; 380.14, ἐφολκός; 437.21, Ὑδατοσύδνη derives from Apollodorus' Περὶ θεῶν). The one intriguing passage is *In Il.* 1317.19, where Call. fr. 1.26 Pf. (also in Olympiod. *In Plat. Phaed.* p. 31.3 Norvin; picked up by Eustathius also in *Prooem. in comm. Pind.* 23.1 and in *Op. min.* p. 268.42 Wirth) and fr. 1.28 Pf. (nowhere else in extant sources) are quoted together, as if the author had found them in a continuous context: but this association might as well go back to a lost anthology or gnomological source. On Eustathius' *Zitierweise*, see also Pfeiffer on frr. 547 and 620.

[95] The doubts expressed by Bulloch 1985: 81–82 must be dismissed: no lexicographical source could possibly account for the quality of the *Aetia* quotations, and one wonders what parallels can be adduced for the alleged "Byzantine digest [*sc.* of the *Hecale*] which preserved some of the Callimachean vocabulary." See also Pfeiffer 1922: 113–20; Hollis 2002: 49–51 and 2009: 39.

[96] See Mich. Chon. *Epist.* 146; N.G. Wilson 1983: 205.

[97] Choniates lived on the island of Ceos from 1205 until 1216, then from 1217 until 1222 he retired to the monastery of St. John Prodromus at Mendenitsa, near Thermopylae: see Kolovou 1999: 7–23.

[98] One cannot help noting that all the texts exhibiting references to Callimachus (save the προσφώνημα to Demetrius Drimys) belong to the period after 1204. It is thus quite doubtful that—as critics have hitherto assumed—Michael's manuscript of Callimachus perished in the sack of Athens during the Fourth Crusade (an otherwise traumatic event for the preservation of Greek culture: see, e.g., N.G. Wilson 1983: 218).

Apart from the echoes in Choniates' own hexameter poetry (the *Theano*)[99] and the solemn appeal to Hecale's hospitality in his public oration for the arrival in Athens of the imperial praetor Demetrius Drimys (1183-1184),[100] the epistles are the typical venue where the Byzantine *Gelehrte* displays all his stock of quotations (often taken "nicht aus unterhaltsamer Bettlektüre, sondern aus der Disziplin des Schulalltags") and amuses himself by deliberately altering their wording. (See Pfeiffer 1922: 119; Kolovou 1998: 130-131 and 2001.) As a matter of fact, Callimachus represents the exception among the pagan authors whom Choniates prefers, who all belong to the routine of the Byzantine curriculum (Homer, Hesiod, Aeschylus, Sophocles, Euripides, Pindar, Theocritus, Lycophron, perhaps Aratus), so that Adrian Hollis' doubt whether Choniates "expected his addressees to recognize his allusions or was playing a solipsistic game" is more than justified.[101]

Some examples. I shall leave aside the generic allusions to the Telchines (*Epist.* 128.4) and to peculiar myths (*Epist.* 111.65-66 and 80) and concentrate on four irrefutable instances of poetic memory. When mourning in a letter to Georgius Bardanes (ca. 1206-1208) the decay of Greece after Latin Conquest, Choniates sadly compares the rough and incomprehensible utterances of the ignorant Latins with the braying of nine-year-old donkeys (*Epist.* 110.54-55: οἷα κανθήλιοι ἐννεάμυκλοι; see fr. 650 Pf.). When complaining in a letter to Euthymius Tornices (ca. 1208) about the terrible food he is eating in Ceos, he alludes with specific adjectives (ἄνοψος, αὐχμηρά) to Hecale's poor dining table (*Epist.* 103.64-65: fr. 252 Pf. = 82 H.). In a very learned epistle of thanks to John Apocaucus, written from Mendenitsa (ca. 1217), Choniates refers to the Minotaur and to his death by the hand of Theseus, who κορύνῃ θάτερον τῶν κεράτων ἠλόησεν (*Epist.* 173.159-60; see *SH* 288.1 = fr. 69.1 H.), "with his club crushed one of

---

[99] See *Theano* 337-342 (test. 35 Pf. = 14 H.); Bornmann 1973; Nikolaou 1985; Magnelli 1999b: 230 (who detects some echoes from the *Hymns*). Further possible echoes of the *Hecale* are detected by Hollis 1997c and 2002: 49-51; less convincingly again Hollis 2000.

[100] See the very opening of Choniates' learned προσφώνημα, 1.157.5 and 159.8 Lambros = test. 36 Pf. = test. 15 Hollis; and the ingenious speculation of Hollis 1997a.

[101] Hollis 2002: 50. But for the same reason Hollis' comparison in n. 64 with the case of Lycophron—on whom see above, n. 27—is misleading.

the two horns".¹⁰² A couple of years later, in one of his latest letters, Choniates complains about the drawbacks of old age, whose weight he compares, in the wake of "an ancient author" (παλαιός τις), to that of Sicily heaped by Zeus on the Giant Enceladus (*Epist.* 174.36–40: *Aet.* fr. 1.33–36 Pf.).

Keen on single words as well as on images, on myth as well as on style, Michael Choniates emerges from these few instances as one of the few Greek prose authors of all times to have read Callimachus so deeply as to be able to quote his verse subtly as a stylistic device and as a rhetorical ornament to his own prose, applying a typical Byzantine approach to an author who must have been a rarity in his time. (He was unknown even to Michael's brother, the exceptionally learned historian Nicetas Choniates). It belongs to the irony of history that one of the most reactive readers of Callimachus' oeuvre was also the last.

---

¹⁰² See Lloyd-Jones and Rea 1967: 134. Hollis 2009: 39–40 aptly points to Michael's use in his own verse (*Εἰς τὸν μονόκερων* 6: 2.393 Lambros) of the rare adjective οἰόκερως occurring in the same Callimachean line.

CHAPTER SIX

CALLIMACHUS' PHILOLOGY

Nita Krevans

Abstract

This essay surveys Callimachus' scholarly writings. Although the exact titles and contents of Callimachus' prose treatises are still disputed, his scholarship can be divided into four main categories: bibliography, paradoxography, aetiology, and onomastics. These categories frequently overlap, however, and scholarly comments, notes, and theories may be found everywhere in Callimachus' poetry as well as in the (largely lost) prose works. The survey concludes by considering Callimachean scholarship as part of a larger Alexandrian intellectual project and offers several models for understanding the Hellenistic impulse to collect, label, and annotate the collective past of Greek-speaking peoples.

> *Philologer. One whose chief study is language;*
> *a grammarian; a critick.*
> *Philology. Criticism; grammatical learning.*
>
> —Samuel Johnson, *A Dictionary of the English Language.*

The traditional range of activities described by the word "philology" has not changed much since Samuel Johnson's day, and, in modern usage, is often narrowed even further to refer specifically to classical scholarship. Grammar, syntax, textual criticism, allusion hunting, commentaries: these are the central tasks of the philologist. The earliest generation of Alexandrian scholars (many, like Callimachus, also poets in their own right) fits this narrower definition well: Zenodotus and Aratus edit Homer; Alexander Aetolus and Lycophron work on dramatic texts; Philetas and Simias compile glosses.[1]

---

[1] Pfeiffer 1968: 89–92, 105–122; Lycophron and Alexander Aetolus are said to have "edited" (διώρθωσαν) comedy and tragedy, respectively, but the evidence for these editions is problematic; in the case of Lycophron, the scholiastic tradition suggests glosses on comedy rather than a full edition.

In the case of Callimachus, philology has a broader mandate. In fact, were this chapter to confine itself to Callimachus' views on Homeric readings or to his critical evaluations of other poets, most of it would be concerned with his poetry. Unlike his predecessors, Callimachus did not produce editions of Homer or tragedy. He certainly read and responded to those editions, but his responses are encoded in cleverly framed citations of rare or disputed words within his own poems. A typical example: Callimachus creates a superlative from a rare variant of a Homeric epithet and uses it to modify a new word that clarifies his view of its meaning.[2] Similarly, most of his positions on the literary controversies of his day are found in famous programmatic passages in his poems: the *Prologue* to the *Aetia; Iambus* 13; the envoi to the *Hymn to Apollo*. We even see him, like a commentator, offering up a typical scholiast's series of alternative explanations as part of the first episode in the *Aetia*: "but some say that the Titaness Eurynome bore [the Graces]" (fr. 6 Pf.); the *Scholia Florentina* (*ad* frr. 5–7 Pf.) tell us that the poet offers three possible genealogies, all eventually rejected by his divine informant Clio in favor of a fourth explanation.

Of Callimachus' prose scholarly works now known to us (including those known only by title), only a few seem to fit the classic picture of Johnson's philologer. The list of his works in the *Suda* includes the title *Pinax of the Glosses and Writings of Democritus*. Nothing survives beyond this title, and although it does specify glosses, they are part of a larger project, which scholars like Rudolf Blum (1991: 143–150) envision as a precursor to the more famous *Pinakes*: a combined bibliography and technical lexicon of the philosopher's work. A second work, *Against Praxiphanes*, may have indicted the Peripatetic writer Praxiphanes for his views of the poet Aratus. To supplement the meager information provided by this title and the one brief reference to its content (fr. 460 Pf., attesting that Callimachus praised Aratus in this work), Praxiphanes obligingly appears in the *Scholia Florentina's* list of Telchines as an opponent of Callimachus' poetry. Modern scholars continue to argue about the exact nature of Callimachus' criticism of

---

[2] Fr. 548 Pf., θηλύτατον πεδίον ("fertile plain"); Callimachus takes a variant adjective (θηλυτεράων at *Il.* 21.454, 22.45; the vulgate has τηλεδαπάων, "far-off") modifying the word "islands" and transfers it to modify the word "plain" to make clear his view of its meaning ("fertile" as opposed to "women-ruled"). See Rengakos 1993: 142–143, with further references; Pfeiffer 1949–1953 *ad loc.* and 1968: 139.

Praxiphanes in this treatise; it is clearly a literary dispute, but the evidence is so thin that attempts to be more specific are difficult.[3]

Three further titles may also belong in the philologer group. *Hypomnemata*, used three times in citations of Callimachean scholarship, is a general word for a commentary. The content of these citations, however, overlaps so markedly with the designated topics of other titles (*On Nymphs, Barbarian Customs, On the Rivers of the Inhabited World*) that it is possible that that the term *hypomnemata* is a generic designation rather than a title. (See Blum 1991: 136; Krevans 2004: 182.) The meaning of the title Περὶ λογάδων (fr. 412 Pf.) is uncertain; *On the Selections* has been suggested (Pfeiffer 1949-1953 *ad loc*). The citation, from a scholion to Theocritus *Idyll* 2, describes a garland of apples worn by Dionysus. Finally, the *Suda* lists the title *Mouseion*. Rudolf Pfeiffer (1949: 339) includes this title in what he calls the *Fragmenta grammatica*, on the analogy of the rhetorical anthology of the same name by Alcidamas, but Blum (1991: 161 n. 5) points out that all the other known prose treatises of Callimachus have specific, concrete titles.

The remainder of Callimachus' prose scholarship can be divided into four main categories: bibliography, paradoxography, aetiology, and onomastics. Bibliography is represented by three *pinax* ("list," "table," "tablet") titles: *Pinax of the Glosses and Writings of Democritus, Pinax and Register of the Dramatic Poets in Order from the Beginning*, and the monumental *Pinakes of All Those Preeminent in Literature and of Their Writings, in 120 Books*. Paradoxography is the best-preserved item; Antigonus of Carystus includes in his own book of wonders a lengthy excerpt from Callimachus' *Collection of Marvels throughout the World by Location* (Antig. Hist. mirab. 129-173; text in Musso 1985: 59-71.). The aetiological books treat cities' foundations (*Foundations of Islands and Cities and Their Name Changes*), sacred games (*On Contests*), and non-Greek rituals (*Barbarian Customs*). Treatises on nomenclature range from natural phenomena (*On Winds, On Birds*) to geography (*On the Rivers of the Inhabited World*), myth (*On Nymphs*), and local terminology (*Local Month Names*, likely a subsection of *Local Nomenclature*).

---

[3] Brink 1946; Pfeiffer 1968: 95; Alan Cameron 1995: 376. Lefkowitz 1981: 125 argues that the title of the treatise could well have generated the name Praxiphanes in the scholiast's list of enemies For further discussion, see Romano in this volume.

It is not easy to reconstruct the content and shape of these treatises. Many works survive only as titles, and even these titles (as in the case of *Local Month Names*) may be subsets of other, larger works or alternative names for something else we already know. There is also a certain amount of overlap between the different subjects specified by the titles. For example, the paradoxographical work (*Collection of Marvels throughout the World by Location*) includes anecdotes of strange behavior by birds, but there is also a separate treatise on birds and their names; meanwhile, the only surviving fragment of *On Nymphs* (fr. 413 Pf.) concerns a spring that shatters pottery vessels dipped into it—in other words, a water marvel like those in the *Collection of Marvels*. The treatises on nomenclature sometimes include aetiological material (cult practices, omens), whereas the study of cities' foundations also discusses cities' names. Finally, it is clear even from the meager testimonia that the scope of many of these treatises is broader than their titles may suggest. The *Pinakes* includes not only conventional bibliographic data for authors, such as lists of titles, *Echtheitskritik*, and stichometric totals, but also biographical information; some of the onomastic works contain, in addition to the aetiological digressions already noted, descriptions of topography and natural phenomena.[4]

Bibliographic Works

Blum, in his study of the three *pinax* titles and their influence, sees Callimachus as the inventor of bibliography.[5] It is true that the two smaller works have clear precedents in the earlier scholarly tradition. The *Pinax and Register of the Dramatic Poets in Order from the Beginning* is obviously based on Aristotle's *Didascaliae*, a record of the dramatic competitions in Athens (whose chronology Callimachus attacks in fr. 454 Pf.).[6] The title and the emphasis on chronology in the few citations that we have show that this work, unlike the later *Pinakes*,

---

[4] Krevans 2004: 181–182 provides a list of all the titles of the prose works, with a summary of the content of the relevant fragments and the possible instances where cited titles may in fact be subsections of other known works.

[5] Blum 1991: 244; see also Lehnus 1995 on the combination of biography and criticism. Alan Cameron 2004: 26–27 states that Callimachus' treatises inaugurate the practice of systematic citation of sources, this being one of many *prōtos heuretēs* claims for Callimachus the scholar that will be noted in this chapter.

[6] Pfeiffer 1968: 81, 132.

is primarily a record of the competition rather than a bibliography of dramatic texts.[7] The table of Democritean glosses and writings also has precedents in the glosses of the scholar-poets Philetas and Simias.[8]

The 120-volume *Pinakes*, however, is unprecedented in size, scope, and organization. The title emphasizes the encyclopedic, universal nature of these *Lists*: "of All Those Preeminent in Literature." The list is author-centered—contrast the transmitted title of the Democritus *pinax*—and the fragments and testimonia (frr. 429–453 Pf.) allow us to envision something of the range of material covered, as well as the different types of information supplied for each entry.[9] The *Pinakes* was subdivided by genre: there are specific references to sections on law, oratory, and "miscellaneous" (frr. 430–435 Pf.), and other citations prove that the work included all types of poetry, philosophy, medicine, and even cookbooks.[10] Within each section, authors were listed alphabetically (fr. 435 Pf.).[11] Entries were not merely lists of titles but provided detailed bibliographic information. For many titles Callimachus also provided an incipit (frr. 433, 434, 436, 443 Pf.); the instability of titles in antiquity meant that the opening words were often used instead or in addition, and it seems that Callimachus himself assigned titles to certain works that had no well-accepted label at the time (frr. 432, 443, 448 Pf.).[12] Stichometric totals (frr. 433, 434 Pf.) give the exact size of the work listed; this tally may be a check against poor copies or forgeries. A concern with the latter can be seen in Callimachus' frequent engagement with problems of attribution (frr. 437, 442, 444–447, 449 Pf.), a serious issue in an era when royal patronage of an enormous library offered incentives to forgers.[13]

---

[7] On the distinction between this table and the larger *Pinakes*, see further F. Schmidt 1922: 49; Regenbogen 1950: 1423; Blum 1991: 137–142.

[8] This work, attested only by title, has been variously interpreted. Some believe it was a subsection of the *Pinakes* proper; others believe that it was a collection not of glosses but of maxims (which would add paroemiography to Callimachus' scholarly *polyeideia*). See the careful discussion of Blum 1991: 143–150, with further references.

[9] On the *Pinakes*, see further F. Schmidt 1922; Regenbogen 1950; Pfeiffer 1968: 127–134; Blum 1991.

[10] E.g., lyric poets, *SH* 293; drama, fr. 451 Pf.; philosophy, fr. 442 Pf.; medicine, fr. 429 Pf.; cookbooks (in the "miscellaneous" section), fr. 435 Pf.

[11] Although one fragment does not a system make, later lists and catalogues invariably follow this same organizational method; see Blum 1991: 155 and Pfeiffer 1968: 129.

[12] On ancient titles, see Nachmanson 1941; Gardthausen 1922: 78–82 points out that alphabetical ordering would require that works with no titles be assigned one.

[13] Forgeries: Fraser 1972: 1.325, 2.481 n. 151. A detailed examination of Callimachean *Echtheitskritik* can be found in Slater 1976.

Athenaeus (who supplies more than a third of the *Pinakes* fragments) gives us this citation, which, although from an exotic source, shows the typical format of Callimachus' entries (Athen. 13.585b = fr. 433 Pf.):

Γνάθαινα...καὶ νόμον συσσιτικὸν συνέγραψεν, καθ' ὃν δεῖ τοὺς ἐραστὰς ὡς αὐτὴν καὶ τὴν θυγατέρα εἰσιέναι, κατὰ ζῆλον τῶν τὰ τοιαῦτα συνταξαμένων φιλοσόφων. ἀνέγραψε δ' αὐτὸν Καλλίμαχος ἐν τῷ τρίτῳ πίνακι τῶν Νόμων καὶ ἀρχὴν αὐτοῦ τήνδε παρέθετο· 'ὅδε ὁ νόμος ἴσος ἐγράφη καὶ ὅμοιος,' στίχων τριακοσίων εἴκοσι τριῶν.

Gnathaena...wrote a *Rulebook for Dining*, which her lovers and her daughter's lovers had to follow when visiting, in imitation of the philosophers who have put together similar [rules]. Callimachus recorded it in the third *pinax*, "Of Laws," and quoted its incipit: "This rule has been written as equal and fair." Lines: three hundred twenty-three.

Thus far the *Pinakes* look like an extraordinarily large and careful library catalogue, and some scholars indeed have identified the work as an exact index of the holdings of the Library at Alexandria.[14] But Callimachus also included biographical information about the authors (frr. 429, 430, 438, 453 Pf.); this, in combination with the full title's emphasis on authorial achievement, signals that the *Pinakes* was not simply a library catalogue. Rather, the work appears to have been designed as what Blum (1991: 239) calls "a national biobibliography"—an encyclopedia of Greek literature. Later imitators, beginning with Callimachus' own pupil Hermippus and continuing with the *Suda* (the main source for our knowledge of Callimachus' prose work), maintain this same combination of title list and *vita*, still found today in standard reference works such as the *Oxford Classical Dictionary*. The aggressive separation of authorial biography from poetic text that the New Critics propounded in the middle of the last century was battling a two-thousand-year-old tradition of transmitting literary history.

The *Pinakes*, then, enshrines Callimachus as a *protos heuretes*, or "inventor", of bibliography. Its massive scale and the wide variety of authors included are balanced by a concern with exact attributions, precise quotations, and accurate line counts. This combination of vast size and careful detail in turn requires an elaborate and consistent

---

[14] E.g., Gardthausen 1922: 76–77; recent discussions agree with Pfeiffer 1968: 128 in distinguishing the *Pinakes* from the specific holdings of the Alexandrian Library. The confusion may stem in part from the earlier belief that Callimachus served as the head of the Library, corrected by the publication of POxy 10.1241; see Fraser 1972: 1.333.

set of organizational principles governing everything from generic labels (oratory? philosophy?) to the exact spelling of an author's name or book's title as part of an alphabetical list. An impulse to collect a complete set of something (which will be seen again in Callimachus' other prose works) is inseparably bound to an impulse to arrange that collection.

Paradoxography

Callimachus' *Collection of Marvels throughout the World by Location* (frr. 407–411 Pf.) is the only one of his prose treatises preserved in anything like its original form. Antigonus of Carystus, a near contemporary of Callimachus, inserts a large excerpt paraphrased from the *Collection of Marvels* into his own wonder book (fr. 407 Pf.).[15] Although Antigonus rearranges the order of the items (Callimachus grouped them by location; Antigonus, by type of marvel),[16] the forty-four examples give a good overview of Callimachus' material. Most are water marvels: springs that cure disease, springs that kill the drinker, rivers that burst into flame, salt water that tastes sweet.[17] Each entry cites a source—well-known fourth-century writers such as Theophrastus, Theopompus, Eudoxus, and so on—and gives a brief description of the marvel.[18] At the end of the water marvels Antigonus includes some miscellaneous entries in other categories (plants, birds, minerals). The remaining fragments from Callimachus' work cited in other sources (frr. 408–411 Pf.) are entirely consistent with Antigonus' material: two further water marvels, a cave that fills with wind, and some odd crows.

One of the more sophisticated entries is a description of an Ethiopian spring (fr. 407. XVII): "Ctesias says there is one in Ethiopia

---

[15] *Hist. mirab.* 129–173; some believe Antigonus used an epitome of Callimachus, but see Pfeiffer 1949–1953 *ad loc.*; on the identification of Antigonus as Antigonus of Carystus, Fraser 1972: 2.657–2.658 n. 62.

[16] That Callimachus arranged his *Collection of Marvels* by location is clear not only from the transmitted title but also from an additional title, *On the Marvels and Wonders of the Peloponnese and Italy*, listed under Callimachus' name in the *Suda*; this must be a section of the larger work.

[17] A series of these water marvels appears in Ovid *Met.* 15.308–36.

[18] As Fraser 1972: 1.454–55 points out, the list of sources for the marvels in wonder books remains constant during the long lifetime of this genre.

that has water that is red like cinnabar, and those who drink from it become madmen." This is a double marvel: the water has two unusual properties, its color and its effect on the drinker. The comparison of the color to cinnabar is significant: the name can refer either to the poisonous mineral extract red mercury or to the plant sap known as Dragon's Blood (*LSJ* s.v. κιννάβαρι); both substances are psychotropic, although the latter's effect is mild. This specificity as to the water's deep red hue ("like cinnabar") leads subtly to the second marvel: not only is it the wrong color; it has an effect like poison (the mineral) or a drug (the plant sap). Thus the comparison also governs the water's second, more malevolent feature. It is tempting to see the double-edged simile as Callimachean. And yet Antigonus does not hesitate to expand the entry with an additional source of his own: "Philo, author of the *Ethiopica*, also describes this."

Antigonus' willingness to rearrange Callimachus' material and add further references of his own is very different from the care with which Callimachus himself treated the books and authors listed in the *Pinakes* but is in keeping with the basic principles of paradoxography in the surviving collections:

1. The marvels are attested not from personal observation but by reference to an earlier, written scholarly source.
2. The marvels are natural, not man-made.
3. The marvels are of interest as a group, organized in sets. The method of arranging the marvels changes from compiler to compiler: as we saw, Callimachus grouped by location, whereas Antigonus uses the type of marvel (water, stone, etc.).
4. No rational explanation of the supposedly unnatural phenomenon is provided, even though many of the sources are well-known Peripatetic naturalists such as Theophrastus.
5. The presentation of the marvel is brief and unadorned.[19]
6. Later collections incorporate earlier ones wholesale, often verbatim.

---

[19] Although there are later verse paradoxographers such as Archelaus and Callimachus' own nephew, also named Callimachus. On the development of paradoxography, see Fraser 1972: 1.770–74; Ziegler 1949. More recently, Gabriella Vanotti (2007, *non vidi*) provides a discussion of the genre and its origins in the introduction to her edition of the pseudo-Aristotelian *De mirabilibus auscultationibus*.

As he did with the *Pinakes*, Callimachus built on an earlier Peripatetic tradition but went far beyond it. And just as Blum argues that Callimachus invented bibliography, Pfeiffer argues that Callimachus invented paradoxography. Although earlier discussions of natural phenomena existed, Callimachus was the first to select and organize them in this fashion, and all later examples of the genre follow his model.[20]

Paradoxography is one of the more obscure genres of Hellenistic scholarship, but its importance for the Alexandrian poets should not be underestimated. We find an interest in natural marvels in Callimachus' Nautilus Epigram (*Ep.* 5 Pf. = 14 GP), in parts of Apollonius' *Argonautica* (e.g., the Clashing Rocks, 2.317–23), and in works like Nicander's *Theriaca*. The recently published epigrams of Posidippus are exceptionally rich in wonder formulas (using words like θαῦμα, θαυμάσιον, τειρατοεργόν, etc.).[21] In paradoxography, science is converted into ecphrasis: stop, look, and wonder.[22]

Aetiology

Only a few small citations survive from the prose aetiological treatises. The lone citation from *On Contests* (fr. 403 Pf.) deals with the Actian Games. *Barbarian Customs* is also represented by only one item (fr. 405 Pf.), noting that the inhabitants of Phaselis sacrificed pickled meat to a local hero. *Foundations of Islands and Cities and Their Name Changes* is known by title only.

We may be able to expand these scanty remains slightly: there is a reference to calculating time by Olympiads (fr. 541 Pf.) that may belong to *On Contests*, and a notice in Pliny (*NH* 4.65) citing Cal-

---

[20] Pfeiffer 1968: 134–35. Fraser, who dates the pseudo-Aristotelian *De mirabilibus* (see above, n. 19) very early in the Hellenistic period, argues that Callimachus' work is a revision of this Peripatetic predecessor, but even he concedes that Callimachus gave the genre its definitive form (Fraser 1972: 1.454, 771; see also Richardson 1994: 15–16; Asper 1997: 211–212).

[21] Nos. 13.2, 15.7, 17.2, 19.10 AB. A more detailed comparison of the bird and stone epigrams in the Milan papyrus to the Hellenistic wonder books may be found in Krevans 2005: 88–92.

[22] Alan Cameron 1995: 353 points out that the famous Callimachean quote ἀμάρτυρον οὐδὲν ἀείδω (fr. 612 Pf.: "I sing nothing unattested"), usually read as the pledge of a writer who composes poetry with footnotes, is more likely a challenge issued in conjunction with the presentation of something that is difficult to believe. Perhaps one of the wonders? Also, Bulloch 1985: 161–162 compares fr. 612 Pf. with the disclaimer in the *Hymn to Athena*, l. 56: μῦθος δ' οὐκ ἐμός, ἀλλ' ἑτέρων.

limachus on the original name of the island of Andros (fr. 580 Pf.) could derive from the treatise on names of islands and cities. In both cases, however, it is equally tempting to assign the fragments to Callimachus' poetic corpus. The *Aetia* includes several episodes featuring sacred games: *The Victory of Berenice*, the stories of the Olympic victor Euthycles (frr. 84, 85 Pf.) and the boxing champion Euthymus (frr. 98, 99 Pf.); perhaps also the episode about Elean marriage rites, which opens with a reference to Zeus of Pisa and includes a Heracles myth related to the founding of the Olympic Games (frr. 76, 77 Pf.). By the same token, Book 2 of the *Aetia* contained a long episode on Sicilian cities (fr. 43 Pf.), and Book 1 a description of the wanderings of the Argonauts (fr. 7.19-fr. 21 Pf.); both could easily have contained information about island names. Thus Pfeiffer, in his commentary on the references preserved in Pliny, wonders why some Callimachean island names preserved in Pliny are assigned to Callimachus the poet whereas others are assigned to Callimachus the scholar.[23]

There are earlier precedents for all three treatises. Duris of Samos also wrote a work called *On Contests*; Hellanicus (among others) wrote a *Barbarian Customs*, and many authors—possibly including the polyeidetic Ion of Chios—wrote prose *ktiseis*, or foundation narratives.[24] More generally, the interest in local history and ethnography during this period can be seen everywhere in Callimachus' poetry, which makes frequent use of sources like Timaeus (on Sicily), Agias and Dercylus (writers of an *Argolica*), and the Atthidographers.[25] In a startling departure from earlier poetic practice, Callimachus even cites prose historians by name in his verse. The most famous example is his praise of the historian Xenomedes of Ceos in the *Acontius and Cydippe* episode of *Aetia* Book 3. After naming the historian as his source (fr. 75.54-55 Pf.), Callimachus then concludes the episode by tracing a line of poetic inspiration from Xenomedes, whom he calls πρέσβυς ἐτητυμίῃ μεμελημένος ("an old man careful of the truth"), to his own Muse, Calliope (fr. 75.76-77 Pf.). A second example is more tentative: a figure named either Leandrius or Maeandrius is named

---

[23] "Haec distinctio fundamento caret": Pfeiffer 1949-1953 *ad* fr. 580.

[24] Duris and Hellanicus: Pfeiffer 1949-1953 *ad* frr. 403, 405. On Ion of Chios and Callimachus, see Acosta-Hughes 2002: 88-89; on his foundation narrative and its genre, see Bowie 1986: 32-33; on foundation narratives more generally, Schmid 1947.

[25] On Timaeus, see Fraser 1972: 1.763-67; Agias and Dercylus are cited by the *Scholia Florentina ad* fr. 7 Pf. and by the *diegesis* to fr. 26 Pf.; on Callimachus' use of the Atthidographers, see Benedetto in this volume.

in a poorly preserved piece (fr. 92.2 Pf.) of the *Melicertes* episode of *Aetia* Book 4.[26]

Nomenclature

The five treatises that I have grouped under this heading may not all belong here.[27] Even though the surviving fragments of the works on winds, birds, rivers, and nymphs sometimes focus closely on rare terms and names, this focus could be a distortion imposed by our informants, who are often lexicographers like Hesychius (fr. 419 Pf., *On Birds*) or scholiasts trying to gloss a specific name or word in their text. The scholia to Aristophanes' *Birds*, for example, furnish six of the citations from the treatise *On Birds*, and three more are from scholia on Homer, Lycophron, and Apollonius. Scholia also supply two of the three citations from *On the Rivers of the Inhabited World*. Thus although many of the bird entries deal with rare bird names or variants, one fragment (fr. 428 Pf.) discusses the *krex* (corn crake) as an ill-omened bird for newlyweds to see, and another (fr. 418 Pf.) includes an explanation of the origin of the name of the owl.

In two cases we have only one firmly attested fragment, a paucity of evidence that makes the reconstruction of a work's content nearly impossible. In the first case we can at least say that the fragment certainly does not concern nomenclature: the lone citation from *On Nymphs* (fr. 413 Pf.) is, as noted earlier, about a spring with miraculous properties and could easily fit into the *Collection of Marvels throughout the World by Location*. In the other case, however, the only surviving piece of *On Winds*, Callimachus is quoted in the midst of a detailed discussion about the formation of various epithets for winds (fr. 404 Pf.). Pfeiffer himself (1968: 135) suggests that *On Winds* and *On Birds* may have been subsections of *Local Nomenclature* but is conspicuously silent about the books on nymphs and rivers.

The treatise *On the Rivers of the Inhabited World* is perhaps the most problematic; Pfeiffer assigns a Callimachean mention of the

---

[26] Pfeiffer 1949–53 reads Leandr- and connects this reference to fr. 88, a scholion to Apollonius' *Argonautica* (*ad* 2.705–11) that mentions a scholar whose name is either Leandrius or Maeandrius. More recently Polito 2006 argues for this latter figure, Maeandrius of Miletus, as the authority mentioned here.

[27] On Hellenistic lexicography more generally, see Tosi 1994; and on Callimachus' scholarly practice, pp. 149–150.

intoxicating properties of the Phrygian river Gallus (fr. 411 Pf.) to the *Collection of Marvels*, but notes that others place it in the rivers book; another fragment (fr. 458 Pf.) is a scathing critique of the water quality in the Eridanus; a citation claiming to be from Callimachus' *Rivers of Asia*, clearly a section of the work on rivers, says merely that Callimachus discusses the river (fr. 459 Pf.). Only one fragment (fr. 457 Pf.) seems to center on the name of a river.[28]

The two titles that clearly do indicate a focus on nomenclature are probably one work: *Local Month Names* (the literal translation of the title is *Appellations of the Months according to Peoples and Cities*) looks like part of *Local Nomenclature*, just as *Names of Fishes*, listed in the *Suda* as a work of Callimachus, is shown to belong within this treatise by Athenaeus' specific description of it as a "part" of the larger work (fr. 406 Pf.). For these books, whether they are two or one, we have only one surviving citation (Athenaeus' discussion of fish names, Athen. 7.329a = fr. 406 Pf.). Luckily it is a long and detailed citation, showing clearly that this work was concerned not merely with rare fish but specifically with different local terms for the same one, as for example "the *ozaina* [a "fetid polypus" according to *LSJ*] is the *osmylion* in Thurii."

The topic of local nomenclature is again one treated in Callimachus' verse. An episode in the *Aetia*, for example, explains why the Argives named a month "Lamb Month" (frr. 26–31 Pf.; *Dieg.* Pf. 1949–1953: 2.107–8). Pfeiffer therefore believes that an unassigned fragment (fr. 521 Pf., a reference in the *Etymologicum genuinum* to Callimachus' discussion of the name of a Rhodian month) may come from Callimachus' verse, even though its subject perfectly matches the title of the prose treatise.[29] But it also seems plausible that a scholar from Cyrene living in an Egyptian city whose official documents used Macedonian month names would have a keen interest in the various calendars used around the Greek world.

---

[28] Weber 1993: 316 links the fondness of Hellenistic poets for "catalogue-sequences" with scholarly compendia such as these and, in particular, points to Callimachus' treatise *On the Rivers of the Inhabited World* in conjunction with the list of rivers in his *Hymn to Zeus* 18–27; Romano (in this volume) speculates that the treatise *On the Rivers of the Inhabited World* or the group of water marvels may have included discussions of water sounds, a common metaphor for poetry in Callimachus and others.

[29] Pfeiffer 1949–1953 *ad* fr. 521 Pf.; he points out that Rhodes appears in several places in the *Aetia*, for example, and that the etymologist prefers poetic sources.

More generally, the interest in collecting local names and terms can be seen as an inversion of the project of the *Pinakes*. The latter attempts to define a national literature; these treatises aggressively insist on the varieties of Greekness and their indissoluble ties to specific places. As the Koine emerged and local alphabets disappeared, these linguistic idiosyncrasies became valuable antiques, as worthy of preservation as the texts of poets, orators, and historians gathered in the Library.[30] Daniel Selden points out that Greeks in Alexandria during Callimachus' lifetime retained their original citizenship in their home city; legal identification still used the ethnic (e.g., "Callimachus of Cyrene") as well as the patronymic. "In effect," Selden observes, "every time a person signed his name, he re-acknowledged that he was an alien."[31] He thus sees the preoccupation with origins (aetiology) in Callimachus' prose texts as fundamentally linked to place ("locative") as well as to an earlier time (Selden 1998: 319–323).

Callimachean Scholarship and the Alexandrian Pathology

Can we, in fact, make sense of Callimachus' prose works as the coherent expression of a particular intellectual moment?[32] Two influential paradigms have been invoked to explain the self-conscious pedantry of Hellenistic literature; although they primarily address Callimachus' poetry, it is certainly reasonable to attempt to apply them to his prose, especially given the close connections, noted throughout this chapter, between the themes of his poetry and the subjects of his prose works.

The first paradigm, found in the work of Peter Bing, imagines a sense of "rupture," a chasm between a majestic literary past and the "discontinuity and isolation" of the modern poet living in Alexandria (Bing 1988b: 56–75). From this point of view, Callimachus' scholarly works could be seen as attempting to seize and preserve a vanishing world, a linguistic and textual archive of carefully embalmed artifacts

---

[30] On the mixture of dialects in Callimachus' poetry and their relationship to spoken Greek in Alexandria, see Parsons in this volume.

[31] Selden 1998: 294, 298; his point is developed further by Stephens 2003: 241–250, a discussion of the place of Egyptians within Greek ethnicity.

[32] Parsons (in this volume) offers a unique view of Callimachus' scholarly oeuvre when he points out the numerous parallels between the poet's treatises and a late third-century-BC teacher's notebook.

from a dead culture. Aetiology is central to this model, because it reveals both "an awareness of the enormous gulf separating past and present, and the desire to bridge it" (Bing 1988b: 71). Equally important is the *Pinakes*, which, in Bing's view (1988b: 37), represents the world of books, the new "real world" that has for the Alexandrian scholars replaced the outside world, with its limitations of geography and ethnicity. The attempt to capture and freeze the achievements of the past, then, responds to anxiety about chronological discontinuity.

Selden takes a different view. As noted above, Selden focuses not on temporal isolation but on physical dislocation. He replaces "rupture" with "alienation"—in the legal as well as the psychological sense—and reads Callimachus' poetry as a textual version of the polyglot population of Alexandria. For example, he sees the *Aetia* as "a vast compendium of different, independent local traditions"; "the poem refuses to homogenize," preferring "a heteronomy of individual cults, beliefs and rites" (Selden 1998: 358). Callimachus' decision to use location as an organizing principle for several treatises (*On the Rivers of the Inhabited World, Collection of Marvels throughout the World by Location, Local Nomenclature*) would, for Selden, reflect the Hellenistic awareness of spatial discontinuity. In his model, then, Callimachus' regional lexica and themed collections from local histories would come to the fore; the *Pinakes*, with its idealized Panhellenism, would recede into the background.[33]

Both models thus frame Hellenistic literature as in essence a neurotic reflex, and Callimachus' scholarship can be understood as part of this reflex. The impulse to collect and organize books, birds, rivers, marvels, nymphs, winds, place names, and local dialects is an impulse born of loss. Whether Callimachus the scholar aims to create a virtual world of books (Bing) or to maintain the Polyhellenism of the Greek world before Alexander (Selden), his research is a form of intellectual self-medication. There is a certain truth to this picture that any modern student of the ancient world can recognize.

---

[33] The notion of Greekness, for Selden, is further complicated by Alexandria's double identity as both an Egyptian and a Greek city; this dichotomy is explored in detail by Stephens 2003, and her reminder (pp. 249–250) that the Ptolemies collected Egyptian, Jewish, and Persian texts for the Library in addition to Greek books offers a useful foil to the determined Hellenocentrism of the *Pinakes*.

In addition to—not instead of—these models, I would like to propose a third paradigm for Callimachean philology: the parade. Callimachus and his fellow scholars, were, after all, not the only Hellenistic collectors. The Ptolemies bought (or confiscated) books for their Library.[34] They recruited scholars for the Museum. They collected art.[35] There was even a zoological garden in the palace precinct full of rare birds and animals (Fraser 1972: 1.515).

Royal collecting goes hand in hand with display, and we have detailed information about at least one: the so-called Grand Procession of Ptolemy Philadelphus. This event probably took place in 275/4 BC in association with the Ptolemaea, a quadrennial festival in honor of Ptolemy Soter.[36] Callixenus of Rhodes wrote an account of the celebration, and a portion of it is preserved in Athenaeus.[37] Although the surviving text describes only a few sections of the parade (notably the procession of Dionysus), certain of its general features are clear. First, many objects were not only exceptionally rich (e.g., gold, purple) but were also oversized: Callixenus mentions a tripod forty-five feet tall (Athen. 5.202c) and a gold horn of the same length (5.202e); these are dwarfed by a 135-foot-long thyrsus and 180-foot-long phallus (5.201e). Objects of normal size are "magnified" by appearing in enormous quantities (3,200 gold crowns: 5.202d). A second feature of the parade is the uniqueness or rarity of its animals or objects. Chariots drawn by pairs of ostriches, antelopes, and hartebeests appear (5.200f); there is a mechanical statue of Nysa that stands up, pours a libation, and sits back down, carried on a cart drawn by sixty men (5.198f); camels bear loads of rare spices (5.201a). The most interesting item in the parade, for our purposes, is the procession of Ionian cities, "which, situated in Asia and the islands, had been subdued by the Persians" (Rice 1983: 21). These cities follow a cart containing statues of Ptolemy and Alexander and a figure representing Corinth (5.201d–e). The cities

---

[34] Their acquisitive zeal became legendary; see Galen's story that books were confiscated from all ships docking in Alexandria and copied; the Library kept the originals and returned the copies to the visitors (*Comm. 2 in Hippocr. libr. 3 epidem.* 239 = F. Schmidt 1922: test. 28).

[35] Ptolemaic art collections: Plut. *Arat.* 12–13 on gifts of art to Ptolemy Philadelphus. Callixenus of Rhodes (*apud* Athen. 5.196e) describes a pavilion set up by Philadelphus with hundreds of statues and paintings inside; more on Callixenus below.

[36] I follow the dating of Foertmeyer 1988.

[37] Athen. 5.197c–203b; see the edition of Rice 1983, with introduction and commentary.

are represented by women, crowned with gold and wearing costly gowns and jewels.[38] Ellen Rice (1983: 109) believes that these personified cities must have been individually identified by placards.

The parade, as a statement about royal power, makes several obvious claims. The use of gold, silver, and purple asserts wealth; the oversized cult objects simultaneously project devotion to Dionysus and the unlimited nature of divine (and royal) strength. The rare objects and animals suggest royal control over distant and exotic lands. (Rice [1983: 93] emphasizes the allusion to Alexander's conquest of India in the spice-laden camels.) Finally, the personified Ionian cities are both a historical reminder of Alexander's victory over the Persians, which restored the cities to their former rights, and an assertion of the legitimacy of Greek states in the eastern Mediterranean.

If we see the royal act of collection and display as an assertion of authority, then it is not unreasonable to see scholarly collection and display as a similar project. Some Callimachean treatises display rare or exotic objects (*Collection of Marvels, Local Nomenclature, Barbarian Customs*). Some emphasize encyclopedic completeness or enormous size (*Pinakes, On the Rivers of the Inhabited World*). Some offer sets of images from the Greek past (*On Contests, Foundations of Islands and Cities and Their Name Changes*). Perhaps those images do serve, in part, to express nostalgic longing. But like the procession of Ionian cities in Philadelphus' parade, they also serve to remind us that what is lost may be regained.

---

[38] Rice 1983: 105–109 discusses the particular significance of the wording of this passage, which seems to refer to the League of Corinth and its role in Alexander's conquest of Persia.

CHAPTER SEVEN

CALLIMACHUS AND HIS *KOINAI*

Peter Parsons

ABSTRACT

This chapter sets out to survey the various linguistic registers that might be expected in the poet's mind and in the minds of his original readers, between the actual *koine* Greek that they spoke, as exemplified in the documentary papyri, and the 'poetic *koine*' that they inherited, as illustrated by contemporary glossaries and scholia and similar educational materials. Their Hellenic education offered Egyptian Greeks lists of literary words, which did not respect generic boundaries; their study of Homer will have taught them that *glottai* and a mixing of dialects are proper to epic. In this climate, Callimachus may have seemed less wayward than he does to us.

Callimachus' poetry speaks with an individual voice; and from a formalist standpoint one might represent that voice as an idiolect formed by taste and ambition from two main strands, the diachronic (and mainly written) tradition of Hellenic poetic diction and the synchronic (and partly spoken) conventions of Hellenistic day-to-day communication. Both strands are complex, one complexity being dialect—historically, the original Greek dialects and their relation to genre; among the poet's contemporaries, the survival of inherited dialects and the birth of regional *koinai*.

Roman Jakobson, in a famous phrase, defined poetic language as "an act of systematic violence upon ordinary language." This simple polarity does not do justice to the nuances. Callimachus' readers will recognize more random perversion than systematic violence; and "ordinary language" needs to cover a whole spectrum of ordinariness, from high literary to low colloquial. This chapter sets out to survey the various registers that might be expected in the poet's mind and in the minds of his original readers: their potential understanding of his language, and his of theirs.

Callimachus' literary inheritance has received much scholarly attention on the basis of other surviving texts. We need of course to recognize that we possess at most 5 percent of the literature that he read, so that the hunt for intertextualities should not press too hard on the few foxes that remain in the covert; further papyri of (say) Simonides or Pindar, favorite poets and prestigious exemplars of the paid Muse in the service of despots, will certainly reveal more, as has already happened for Theocritus. But Callimachus' linguistic ambience has enjoyed less interest, even though Egypt provides a unique resource in the pile of documentary texts surviving from the third century BC.[1] Above all we have the nearly two thousand items of the Zeno Archive, dating from circa 260–240 BC.[2] These are the accumulated papers of Zeno of Caunus, a Greek immigrant who worked for Apollonius the chief minister of Ptolemy II Philadelphus; they were discovered on the site of Philadelphia in the Fayum, where Zeno served as manager (256–248) of the great estate that Apollonius had received from the king. These and the smaller finds exemplify *koine* at more than one level—the sometimes nearly illiterate language of private letters, the formalized Greek of business and administration. At the same time we find, mingled with the documents, remains of literary and subliterary texts that illustrate the taste and resources of Egyptian Greek readers, and remnants of educational materials (textbooks and exercises) that give a view of the formative structures and expectations of the Hellenic diaspora. No doubt Callimachus' own schooling had followed similar lines, which he himself will have maintained in his early career as γραμματοδιδάσκαλος in Alexandrian Eleusis.

This documentation has its limits. Alexandria, later to be called Ἀλεξάνδρεια ἡ πρὸς Αἰγύπτῳ, "Alexandria next to Egypt," can be seen as a world on its own; certainly scholars later attributed to the so-called Alexandrian dialect features that were in fact common to the *koine*, or at least the Egyptian *koine*, as a whole. (See Fraser 1972: 1.107–108; Fournet 2009.) The site preserves no papyri; those few that we have survive only because they were taken and left elsewhere. Beyond Alexandria comes ἡ χώρα, "the country," all the rest of Egypt: the northern part, the Nile Delta, which takes in two-thirds of the cultivatable land, preserves papyri only in rare circumstances (the groundwater is too high); but from Memphis southwards for eight hundred miles the dry climate does make survival possible, either in direct finds like the Zeno Archive or indirectly in mummy casings made of cartonnage (a flexible cardboard composed of recycled papyri torn up and glued

---

[1] The pioneering paper of Dr. Schwendner ("Standard and Poetic in Callimachus: Archaeology of Lexical Style") remains unpublished. I am most grateful to him for allowing me to refer to it.
[2] Complete lists and word index in Pestman 1981.

one on top of another). Cartonnage has a special importance for this early phase of Greek Egypt. In many places papyri collected in rubbish dumps layer upon layer; the lowest layers, containing the earliest papyri, were most exposed to rising water. For this reason, and others, papyri of the third and second centuries BC are relatively rare. In this same period, however, the Egyptian Greeks adopted the practice of mummification, with cartonnage mummy cases, and a whole number of interesting literary texts have been recovered by resolving such cases, which survived in drier conditions. Any one case can yield both literary and documentary texts, and the (often dated) documents provide a kind of context for the literary pieces, but not a strong enough context to prove that all the pieces came from the same archive or even the same village. The provenance of the case may or may not be related to the provenance of the papyri it contains; thus the famous cartonnage of Abusir el-Melek contained documents from Alexandria, 150 miles away, though again we cannot know whether they were specially transported there for recycling or simply kept there by some Alexandrian resident.

Almost all our material, then, comes from the backwoods; and there has been some tendency for historians of Hellenistic literature to ignore it, as a pallid footnote to the glories of Alexandria and its poets, whose gaze is directed always to the north. This snobbery is misplaced. Greek settlers on the fringe naturally missed Greek education and Greek lifestyle. In an early case reported by Diodorus (18.7.1), they gratified their nostalgia by trying to return home. However, there is evidence enough (for example, at Ai Khanoum) that most set about rebuilding Hellas *in partibus*. It could be argued that the Hellenic institutions well attested in Roman Egypt took time to construct and do not in themselves prove that the Egyptian Greeks of the early Ptolemaic period maintained any level of Greek culture. But in fact there is anecdotal evidence to suggest that the *chora* was in no sense a desert of the beaux arts.

Thus the Zeno Archive includes twin epitaphs (one in elegiacs, one in iambics) on a hunting dog, received in Philadelphia but composed elsewhere and sent to Zeno in the form of a letter (*SH* 977). Texts of Archilochus and Euripides probably derive from the same find of documents.[3] Zeno's brother Epharmostus takes delivery of books by Callisthenes (PColZen 2.60). Zeno is asked to send Demeas, the local

---

[3] PZenPestm 14–15; Pestman 1981: 189.

gymnasiarch, the texts "if you have already had them transcribed, so that we may have something to occupy us, since we don't even have any one to talk to" (PCairZen 4.59588—if τὰ βυβλία are books, not documents), and to bring together as many people as possible for the benefit of the visiting Mnesitheus (PCairZen 4.59603), an expert, it seems, on "the poet": that is, Homer. One correspondent quotes Aeschylus (PCairZen 4.59651); a schoolboy writes out ὦ ἄνδρες δικασταί, and before it a mock hexameter, "As many as the ships Achilles had, so many drops you owe" (PCairZen 4.59535; MP³ 1794)—no doubt the tears, or the blood, that he owes to the schoolmaster's cane. From the same new town, Philadelphia, and the same period, we have also four ostraca written by one and the same hand (Cribiore 1996: nos. 232–235), which together contain short extracts from Homer, Theognis, Euripides, Pseudo-Epicharmus, and New Comedy: the medium and the sententiousness of the texts suggest a school.

At the same time, the *chora* had an appetite for contemporary literature. The *Riddle of the Oyster* (*SH* 983), with its learned and elaborate commentary, is said to have been found at Memphis. Four notable collections of epigrams come to us from cartonnage found in or near the Fayum: the Vienna *Pinakes* kept company with documents from the Arsinoite nome (Parsons 2002: 118–120); the Posidippus Papyrus (PMilVogl 8.309) was accompanied by documents from that same nome and the Heracleopolite; *Supplementum Hellenisticum* 961 and 985 derive from cartonnage excavated in the same area (Gurob). The earliest papyrus of Callimachus, PLille 76 (*SH* 254–269), also comes from cartonnage recovered near the ancient Magdola in the Fayum. It is true that the provenance of the cartonnage (demonstrated by its findspot or its documentary content) does not prove the provenance of its literary content; and some editors continue to insist that bibliographically elaborate literary texts must come from Alexandria. Even if that were certainly true, it would not follow that these texts reached the *chora* only as scrap. But the fact that there are five instances undermines skepticism: Why should these books not have been imported, or indeed manufactured, for the enjoyment of local readers? Indeed, the government may well have encouraged Greek culture, as a way of encouraging Hellenic solidarity. Ptolemy II, around 256 BC, granted exemption from the salt tax to the standard functionaries of *paideia*, teachers of letters, athletic trainers, artists of Dionysus, victors in certain games (PHal 1.260–65; see D.J. Thompson 2007.) Ptolemy IV built his temple to Homer, celebrated in an epigram that soon after was being read and copied in Memphis (*SH* 979). At some stage (though the dates assigned vary from Ptolemy I to Ptolemy VI) the processional avenue of the Memphite Serapeum took on a hemicycle of Greek culture heroes, including (though not all the identifications are certain) Pindar, Hesiod, Homer, Protagoras, Thales, Heraclitus, and Plato (Hölbl 2001: 281–283; McKenzie 2007: 119–120).

In short, when we find Callimachus copied and glossed in the Lille Papyrus, we can reasonably take this as an encounter with a reader two hundred miles from the salons of the capital, reading Callimachus within a generation of his death.

As a first stage, we need to clarify the different varieties of Greek that may have furnished Callimachus' mind. I exclude here the native Egyptian language: even if we believe that Callimachus shows knowledge of pharaonic texts, we should assume that he relied on (oral or written) translations (Stephens 2003: 45–49). With his readers, things may have been different (see below.)

Koine

In the background is the lingua franca, ἡ κοινὴ διάλεκτος. Its spoken form is by nature not recoverable, but in Egypt at least the documents do allow a worm's-eye view of local language behavior. The Greek immigrants to Egypt brought their dialects with them: the Elephantine marriage contract of 311 BC (PEleph 1), in which the parties come from Cos, still shows some Doric features. But on the whole the old dialects disappear quite rapidly—disappear, that is, from written communication, though of course we can easily visualize a society in which (as in Germany or Italy now) even educated people spoke dialect at home and wrote standard Greek for business; it remains a question whether, when they spoke standard Greek, they spoke it with a dialect accent. To judge from the more formal documents, the standard is a basic Attic-Ionic, with a tendency (already apparent in Thucydides) to eliminate features peculiar to Attic. In the third century, at least, there is some flexibility: thus τέσσαρες is common, but τέτταρες also occurs. Doric vocalization survives, fossilized, in certain proper names and military terms. One must reckon with individual choices: thus isolated Doric σᾶτες "this year" in otherwise normal contexts.[4] Of course

---

[4] PCairZen 3.59346, 59406. On dialectal variations in *koine*: Bubeník 1989.

there will have been many gradations of accent and correctness in the space between Low *koine* (as a native Egyptian might speak it for basic communication) and High *koine* (as an author might write it for the Panhellenic community), and within the literary uses of High *koine*.[5] Despite the schoolmasters, analogical innovations in accidence like ἐσχάζοσαν and πέφρικαν take root soon enough to emerge in Lycophron (*Alex*. 21, 252).

Koine is inherited from the more limited world of the fourth century. In Egypt it faces the hazards of a minority language. Vocabulary is easiest to judge, and no doubt easiest to acquire at local level, for convenience or as an exoticism or simply to designate something newly encountered: months, measures, plants, artifacts. The Egyptians who learned Greek may have adapted its phonemes and even its syntax to their own first language, and some of these adaptations may have spread back to those whose first language was Greek. Certainly as time goes by (and some of Callimachus' first readers will have been born in Egypt) we have to reckon with a new kind of dialect, the regional *koine*. Low-grade writing, above all in private letters, shows an Egyptianizing phonemic confusion between δ and τ, and ρ and λ, alongside the internal confusions caused by phonetic assimilation (as of ει to ι, etc.) and the gradual replacement of the pitch accent. Since our only evidence is written, we cannot tell whether this affected only the uneducated: it is entirely possible that the educated spoke Greek with a distinctive Egyptian accent but wrote it according to the artificial norms of orthography beaten into them at school.

School played a central role. However much importance the Egyptian Greeks attached to their Hellenic origins, there was always the danger of going native, as typological anecdotes show. The Eretrians deported to Babylonia by Darius spoke Greek until Herodotus' time (Hdt. 6.119) but gave up Greek script within a century of their deportation (Philostr. *VA* 1.24); the Greeks of Tomi on the Black Sea spoke, to Ovid's ear, with a Scythian accent (*Trist*. 5.2.67–68, 5.7.51); later, Dio of Prusa would find the people of Olbia speaking a barbarous Greek, yet knowing Homer by heart (*Or*. 36.9). The schoolmasters of the *chora* had to provide for those whose first language was Greek, as

---

[5] Rydbeck 1967. These uses include professional literature—for example, medical texts—with whose technicalities Callimachus will have been acquainted (Zinato 1975).

well as for Egyptians learning the language of the new masters (Clarysse 1998; D.J. Thompson 2007). The two poles appear neatly in a fragment of a grammar dealing with prepositions and with cases: the back was reused by one or more very poorly literate hands to write a Greek-Egyptian glossary (with both languages in Greek letters: PHeid inv. 414, published by Quecke 1997). Their efforts say much about the intellectual preoccupations of the age and its educators, of whom Callimachus was one.

We can get a feel for all this by looking back from the Guéraud-Jouguet Schoolbook (Guéraud and Jouguet 1938; MP³ 2642), a substantial fragment of a textbook or a teacher's notes datable in or not long after the reign of Ptolemy IV (221–205 BC). It contains (1) a syllabary, first two letters, then three; (2) within this, apparently a list of Macedonian months; (3) a list of rare monosyllables; (4) a list of Greek gods; (5) a list of rivers, Greek but also barbarian; (6) a list of personal names, in two, three, four, and five syllables, mostly epic and mythological, the syllabification marked by double points; (7) two short passages of Euripides, also syllabified; (8) with the heading ἔπη, a short passage of the *Odyssey*; (9) epigrams on a fountain celebrating (probably) Ptolemy III and Berenice II, and a temple of Homer built by Ptolemy IV; (10) three passages of New Comedy about cooks; (11) a table of squares and a table of subdivisions of the drachma.

Of these elements, the syllabary (1) carries over from the fourth century: reading lessons traditionally began with the class reciting βα, βε, βη, βι, βο, βυ, βω, and so on through the alphabet.[6] The list of months (2) maintains the Macedonian calendar, which had to fight a losing battle with the Egyptian; at a higher level Callimachus collected Μηνῶν προσηγορίαι κατὰ ἔθνος καὶ πόλεις (Pfeiffer 1949–53: 1.339). The list of rivers (5) represents general knowledge, perhaps also the wider horizons of the Greek world after Alexander; at a higher level Callimachus had written περὶ τῶν ἐν τῇ οἰκουμένῃ ποταμῶν (frr. 457–59 Pf.).[7] The list of rare monosyllables (3) belongs in the systematic progression from short to long words; at the same time it contains some epic items, and some like στράγξ that suggest the later

---

[6] So Aratus *AP* 11.437 (2 GP) makes the unfortunate Diotimus teach his pupils beta-alpha, not alpha-beta.

[7] So PBerol inv. 13044 (= MP³ 2068), a chrestomathy of the second or first century BC published in Diels 1904, includes lists of the largest islands, mountains, and rivers.

tongue twisters. (See below.) The list of personal names (6) and the passages from Euripides (7) teach the rules of syllabification, which are so firmly rooted that they govern the copying of literary texts for the next millennium. It may be also that these exercises, and indeed the tongue twisters, aim to enforce correct enunciation.

The *Odyssey* passage (8), the epigrams (9), and the passages from New Comedy (10) represent an anthology that progresses from epic to elegiac to iambic. The choice is not random. First, Homer and the *Odyssey*: it may be worth noting, with due allowance for accidents of preservation and doubtful datings, that in this period papyri of the *Odyssey* are nearly as common as papyri of the *Iliad*, a marked contrast with the Roman period, when the *Iliad* is much more popular. Some scholars argue that Callimachus chooses Odyssean themes by way of refusing Iliadic heroics; but if so, his preference may simply chime with the public's. After Homer we have an epigram on the divinity of Homer (*SH* 979) and a speech from Strato (fr. 1 KA) in which the comic cook uses Homeric diction, such that his master needs to look the words up in the dictionary of Philetas. At the same time the two epigrams celebrate monuments erected by the Ptolemaic dynasty. That is striking. Fifty years on, the papers of Ptolemy son of Glaucias and his schoolboy brother will include epigrams by Posidippus on the Pharos and the nearby Temple of Arsinoe II (115, 116 AB); and of the three papyri of Callimachus surviving from the Ptolemaic period, two contain dynastic material (*The Victory of Berenice* and *The Lock of Berenice*). Homer represents the inherited culture; the Ptolemies, the new. When the Greeks of the *chora* chose to read recent or contemporary literature alongside the established classics, they may have been showing their patriotism.[8]

Dialects

The ancient reader of Homer recognized in his text a διάλεκτος that he contrasted with his own language, ἡ κοινὴ or ἡ ἡμετέρα διάλεκτος. We need to remember that Greek *dialektos* does not coincide exactly with our "dialect" (Morpurgo Davies 1987), a term that has hierarchical implications; nor is it clear how far Greeks distinguished dialect

---

[8] For other dynastic and patriotic verse circulating in the third century: *SH* 961 (marriage of Arsinoe II?); 958 and 969 (Galatian War; see Barbantani 2001).

(which may extend to accidence and vocabulary) from accent (largely a matter of phonetics and intonation). More generally, the study of Greek dialects, real and literary, and the relationship between them, suffers from well-known difficulties. For spoken language we rely on contemporary inscriptions. For literary language we rely on the text as transmitted in papyri (relatively few before the Roman period) and medieval manuscripts. Unfortunately, the inscriptions mostly contain formal matter, and their language may be correspondingly formal—that is, archaic—and the manuscript transmission shows itself divided and inconsistent, especially in phonetic and morphological details where the meter cannot decide the original reading. Later lexicographers too comment on dialect usages, especially in vocabulary, and this tradition no doubt goes back at least to the fourth century BC. In most cases, however, we have no way to check what they say about real dialects, and some reason, besides, to think that what they say about literary dialects may rest on theory rather than information, so that, for example, a Doric text may have been edited to make it look more Doric (Cassio 2007).

More difficult still is the question of how dialects functioned in daily life. Athens, perhaps, had been linguistically more uniform; the philosopher Theophrastus, who came originally from Lesbos, took great pains to master Attic, but he betrayed his foreignness by being too perfect (Theophr. 7A–B F.). Dialect was for outsiders, or for professionals (the doctor in Menander's *Aspis* 433–464 speaks Doric, or perhaps mock Doric with lapses, since proper doctors come from Cos or Sicily). Even in the melting pot of Alexandria some dialects stood out. The Syracusan ladies in Theocritus' *Idyll* 15 speak Doric, perhaps Syracusan Doric, which may be more or less broad according to their mood; the passerby who tells them off for "broadening everything" himself utters in Doric (*Id.* 15.87–88), perhaps because he finds their accent more annoyingly broad than his own; or more likely, I think, because he parodies their accent as a way of reinforcing his insult.[9] Callimachus too will have brought with him Cyrenean dialect, which scholars have traditionally classified in the Strong Doric group:[10] How and when did he use it? Did he speak dialect in émigré circles but

---

[9] On possible variations within the ladies' own dialect: Stanford 1968; Ruijgh 1984. In general: Hinge 2009.

[10] It proves very tenacious: at Cyrene dialect inscriptions outnumber those in *koine* as late as the first century BC; see Dobias-Lalou 1987. As usual, we have no means of

koine at court, where the sovereign may have been at home in Macedonian? Did he, in a familiar way, unite with *koine* some phonemes and words and intonations recalling his homeland? In a performance of *Hamlet*, we can tell by ear whether the hero is American or English, though the words are the same. Imagine a recital at which Apollonius Rhodius, Callimachus, and Theocritus took turns reading from Homer: Would the listener have been able to identify their geographical origins? When someone in Epicharmus' *Pyrrha* quotes Homer, the verse comes (as transmitted) with Doric vocalization.[11]

Things look different if we accept C.J. Ruijgh's theory that the literary Doric of Theocritus and of Callimachus' *Hymns* 5 and 6 represents the spoken language of Cyrenean émigrés like Callimachus in Alexandria, a form of Cyrenean Doric with some adaptation to local conditions. Since this supposed subdialect represents a local social construct, we cannot object that it differs in some respects from the language of Cyrene itself.[12] If the theory were true, we should see Callimachus springing a double surprise in these hymns: archaic form realized in contemporary speech. However, the visible unreliability of the manuscripts undermines the whole structure, and there are philological objections as well, so that Ruijgh's view has not found general acceptance (Molinos Tejada 1990; Abbenes 1995). Nonetheless, the dialect of these poems must have struck the Cyrenean ear as oddly familiar, perhaps even as a counter to the Ionic-Attic tradition—Homer as transmitted through Athens—that now, as *koine*, provided the basic standard of discourse.

At the same time, we should not overstress dialectal differences. In speech, it may be that different dialects were mutually incomprehensible; in writing the conspicuous difference might lie in vocabulary, with a standard set of phonetic and morphological markers providing the surface cover. It has been said of *Hymns* 5 and 6 that "every line in these poems could be 'translated' into epic dialect without damage to the metre (and almost every line into Attic κοινή...)" (Hopkinson 1984a: 44). At the same time, Greek categories may be more complex than ours. Thus, when we talk of Callimachus' mixing dialects, we need to remember that the Alexandrian interpreters recognized

---

telling how archaic was the language of inscriptions in relation to that normally spoken, or indeed how far the formal language was rearchaized later.

[11] Epich. fr. 113.415 KA, noted and discussed by Cassio 2002: 72.
[12] The theory: Ruijgh 1984. The reality: Dobias-Lalou 2000.

Homer's dialect as mixed: the Homeric scholia refer to more than thirty local subdialects as well as to our broad traditional classification. Eventually his biographers will believe that Homer traveled the whole of the Greek world and mixed together elements from every one of its dialects ([Plut.] *De Hom.* 2.8 Kindstrand).

For a given poem, the poet might choose his dialect to suit the genre, or the subject, or his personal voice (Kerkhecker 1991: 27–34):

1. *Genre*. Callimachus inherited a literary tradition that exhibited identifiable dialects partly corresponding to different genres, or particular authors, which in turn corresponded to some extent with different traditions of performance. Code switching between meters, forms, and dialects is part of his technique. So it is that those who objected to his πολυείδεια objected to the variety of his dialects, Ἰαστὶ καὶ Δωριστὶ καὶ τὸ σύμμεικ[τον (*Iamb.* 13: fr. 203.18 Pf.). But of course he may make his effect by disappointing generic expectation rather than satisfying it. *Hecale* shows the proper dialect for hexameter narrative and for its Athenian setting. But the *Iambi*, which begin in the meter and Ionic dialect of Hipponax, later move over to dialects dictated by subject matter.

2. *Subject*. The geography of a narrative, the source of a myth, the character of an internal speaker (ethopoeia), the background of an audience (imagined or actual) may attract a particular dialect. In the *Aetia*, the basic Ionic makes no concessions to the Sicilian tomb of Simonides or the famous springs of Argos (frr. 64–66 Pf.). Among the *Hymns*, which revive an Ionic genre, the second sticks to the epic language, though many scholars have connected it with a Cyrenean Carneia, whereas the fifth chooses Doric in tribute to its Argive setting, and elegiacs out of sheer perversity. In the *Iambi*, the generic voice of Hipponax gives way to Doric for an Elean guide (*Iamb.* 6), for an epinician and an Aeginetan (*Iamb.* 8), and for Connidas of Selinus in his tomb (*Iamb.* 11); Aeolic Aenus draws in Aeolic elements (*Iamb.* 7). Alexandrian intellectuals gathered at the "shrine outside the wall" (fr. 191.9 Pf.) might find the mix of accents familiar from day-to-day life. Then, within the general dialect, there may be elements especially suitable to the particular environment. Thus *Hymn* 5 has features that may be specifically Argive (Bulloch 1985: 26). Thus in *Hecale* the poet adds some specifically Attic words to the Ionic mix, underlining his command of Athenian geography and institutions: in Hecale's cottage Theseus sits on a stool, ἀσκάντης; the wine is mixed

with warm water, μετάκερας; the bread is taken from the breadbin, ἐκ...σιπύηθεν (frr. 29, 34, 35 H.). All three words occur commonly in Attic Comedy, and Callimachus borrows them for this scene, with added sophistication: μετάκερας appears in tmesis; σιπύη takes the fossilized suffix -θεν, very familiar with Attic deme names.

3. *Personality.* There is also the possibility of a personal voice: Callimachus sometimes uses Doric in poems of friendship (Kerkhecker 1999: 169–70). The use of Doric in itself may have gradations. Indeed, if we think a Cyrenean reading Homer aloud might pronounce him with a Cyrenean accent, we could also regard translatable poems like *Hymns* 5 and 6 as written versions of the poet's personal utterance—a record of accent rather than of dialect in the wider sense.

Poetic Koine?

In our experience of our own language as standard usage, we can recognize a parallel language distinguished by poeticisms—exotic vocabulary, archaic accidence—which together might be said to form a poetic *koine*, exemplified once upon a time by amateur sonneteers and still current in the versifying of Valentine cards. For the age of Callimachus, we can turn to two sources of information: occasional poetry and educational texts.

Occasional poetry shows mostly in inscriptions on stone that answer recurrent social needs (epitaphs, honorifics, religious dedications). Most of those from Egypt can be found in the edition of Étienne Bernand, *Inscriptions métriques de l'Égypte gréco-romaine* (Paris, 1969). (A general collection of the Greek verse inscriptions of the third century BC remains a desideratum.) Taken together they illustrate the linguistic norms (heavily Homeric) favored by the epigrammatists, the standard clichés of the formal genres to which most of them belong, and the limitations on the metrical form of such performances. This material has special relevance for the appreciation of Callimachus' epigrams, for it shows not only the conventions among which the poet moved but also his ways of handling, transcending, and disappointing them (Parsons 2002: 114–115).

The education of poets and of their readers centers on the study of literary texts, and part of this study relates to the meaning of difficult words. That of course goes back at least to the fifth century. In the background will be the Ἄτακτοι γλῶσσαι of Philetas (frr. 29–59 K.), circulating from about 300 BC, famous enough to make a joke in Strato (fr. 1.43 KA): the few surviving fragments suggest that it explained Homeric glosses, technical terms, and dialect expressions. Descendants included Zenodotus' Γλῶσσαι (Homer only? alphabetical order) and Aristophanes of Byzantium's Λέξεις (alphabetic? classical prose and poetry; Alexandrian dialect also?). (See Pfeiffer 1968: 115, 198.) Most of the evidence relates to the language of the Homeric poems, which had already a long tradition with schoolteachers. So in Aristophanes' *Banqueters* the father questions the reprobate son about the meaning of κόρυμβα and ἀμενηνὰ κάρηνα, described as Ὁμήρου γλῶτται (fr. 233 KA). The fruit of such discussions finds a place both in scholarly commentaries and in the more basic Homeric dictionaries and Homeric vocabularies that papyri commonly attest for the Roman period. It multiplies also into the work of Hellenistic poets, who sometimes use Homeric *glossai* in contexts that make clear which disputed reading or meaning they endorse (Rengakos 1992, 1993); in this, Antimachus may have set a precedent (Wyss 1936: 67–68, 101). In this context, a poet may create *glossai* as well as borrow them. So Callimachus took the archaic oddity πλαγκτοσύνη (only *Od.* 15.343) and combined it with the archaic suffix –τύς already revived by Antimachus (*Aet.* fr. 26.7 Pf., 30 M.). (See R. Schmitt 1970: 72–73.)

However, difficult words were not treated simply as hazards: they could be considered an essential characteristic of certain kinds of poetry. Γλῶτται play a central part in Homeric linguistics at least from the time of Democritus' περὶ Ὁμήρου ἢ ὀρθοεπείης καὶ γλωσσέων (68 B 20a DK): in that title the contrasted items seem to correspond to Aristotle's distinction, λέγω δὲ κύριον μὲν ᾧ χρῶνται ἕκαστοι, γλῶτταν δὲ ᾧ ἕτεροι.... τὸ γὰρ σίγυνον Κυπρίοις μὲν κύριον, ἡμῖν δὲ γλῶττα, "I mean by 'standard word' one that every group uses, and by *glotta* one that others use.... So *sigunon* ['spear'] is standard for Cypriotes, but a *glotta* for us" (*Poet.* 1457b3). Aristotle later in the same work identifies *glottai* as specially suited to "heroic" verse: τῶν δ' ὀνομάτων τὰ μὲν διπλᾶ μάλιστα ἁρμόττει τοῖς διθυράμβοις, αἱ δὲ γλῶτται τοῖς ἡρωικοῖς, αἱ δὲ μεταφοραὶ τοῖς ἰαμβείοις, "Of words, compounds most suit dithyrambs; *glōttai*, heroic verses; and metaphors, iambic verse" (*Poet.* 1459a8–10). Too many of them may produce a frigid effect (*Rhet.* 1406a7); but τὰ διπλᾶ καὶ [τὰ] ἐπίθετα πλείω καὶ τὰ ξένα μάλιστα ἁρμόττει λέγοντι παθητικῶς, "compound words and numerous epithets and strange words most suit someone speaking emotionally" (1408b11). At this stage *glossai* need not be Homeric:

they may be, like Aristotle's σίγυνον, current but regional. Such, presumably, were Callimachus' Ἐθνικαὶ ὀνομάσιαι (fr. 406 Pf.), which included local (Chalcedonian and Athenian) names of fish; his works about winds, months, and birds (fr. 404 Pf., p. 339; frr. 414–428 Pf.) may have had similar scope. Discussion of *glossai* as a category continued in an anonymous *Poetics* that circulated in Egypt in the late third century.[13]

This sort of enterprise, lists of words with or without explanations, appears in several papyri from the *chora* that provide more evidence for the poetic *koine*. There are simple lists of words, general lexica, and glossing scholia to particular authors. So, in the cartonnage recovered at El Hibeh, the same mummy yielded an alphabetical lexicon (PHib 2.175 = MP³ 2122) that glosses many Homeric words but also δέπαστρον (known to us only from Antimachus); a list of lines from Homer, each followed by a comparable line of Archilochus, a systematic juxtaposition of two generic archetypes;[14] and a treatise on poetic diction (poetry admits εὐχή but not προσευχή).[15]

First, the explanation of a single author: the Lille mummy contains, as well as the Callimachus, fragments of a commentary on *Odyssey* 16 and 17, datable perhaps to the later third century BC. In this the lemmata most often introduce single glosses; here and there, longer paraphrases.[16] Glossing is the primary function, and no doubt these early papyri contain remnants of pre-Alexandrian interpretation of Homer. There had also been interpretation in a wider sense: such is a dialogue that discusses the dramatic logic of minor characters in the *Odyssey* (Circe and Irus)—another topic that may be relevant to Callimachus' handling of his Odyssean material.[17]

Second, lists of words with explanations: several papyri datable to the middle or late third century BC contain alphabetical glossaries of poetic words, often from Homer but with a clear admixture from

---

[13] PHamb 128 (= MP³ 2289.1), sometimes assigned to Theophrastus. But see Schenkeveld 1993.

[14] PHib 2.173 (= MP³ 136). Slings 1989 relates this text to later works on plagiarism (κλοπή).

[15] PHib 2.183 (= MP³ 2296).

[16] PLille inv. 83, etc., published in Meillier 1985 (= MP³ 1211.01). Cf. PStrasb inv. G 2374 (= MP³ 1185), with Van Rossum–Steenbeek 1997.

[17] PGiessenKuhlmann 2.9 (= MP³ 1215); another piece of the same work in a later papyrus, PLondLit 160 (= MP³ 1214).

other sources.[18] One of these glossaries includes rarities known to us only from Hesychius and two words that it distinguishes as Athenian.[19] An ostracon (but written in a literate hand) explains a scatter of rare words, with examples: σοῦσα "ropes" from Homer and Antimachus; ὧρος, "year", from Homer and Hipponax.[20]

Third, simple lists: a private paper from the Zeno Archive tabulates rare, poetic, and literary words and phrases, perhaps notes from private reading (PCairZen 4.59534 = MP³ 2137). The Guéraud-Jouguet Schoolbook lists monosyllables for the beginning reader, but those include the epic κῆρ and λάξ, the hardly attested κλάγξ, and the mysterious κνάξ, which in the formula κναξζβιχθυπτησφλεγμοδρωψ will be familiar to later schools as tongue twister and writing exercise (every letter of the alphabet once), attributed to Thespis and enshrined in the legend of Branchus, as Callimachus knows (fr. 194.30 Pf.).[21] Most striking is a list of 120 compound adjectives, not alphabetical but roughly grouped by common elements or semantic similarity. These are not γλῶτται but διπλᾶ in Aristotle's sense, and indeed some of the adjectives have a known ancestry in lyric poetry. Perhaps the work served as a Roget of inherited riches. As it happens, at least one epithet, ἁλίζωνος, first turns up in Callimachus (fr. 384.9 Pf.).[22]

Taken together, these oddments throw considerable light on the verbal environment of educated men during and after their education. The *glossai* chosen for explanation do not derive exclusively from the *Iliad* and *Odyssey*. Antimachus plays a part, and beyond epic we find words from iambus, lyric, and tragedy listed or adduced. This suggests that the pattern we find in Hesychius, of collecting and explaining unusual words without distinction of genre, goes back to the generation of Callimachus, and probably indeed to the generation of Philetas.

---

[18] In addition to PHib 2.175, note PHib 1.5 + PRyl 1.16 + PHeidSieg 180 + PLondLit 90 (= MP³ 2124.1; for an overview of the remains, see PHeidSieg pp. 60–62), a large-scale glossary of words in omicron copied on the back of a New Comedy: non-Homeric ὄθροον (next in Hesychius), ὀθνιότυμ[βος (next in Manetho Astrol.), various forms of ὀθνεῖος (tragedy, commonly in hexameter poetry from Callimachus, Apollonius, and Theocritus on; discussed by Aristophanes of Byzantium fr. 274 Slater).

[19] PBerol inv. 9965, published in Poethke 1993 (= MP³ 2121.01): βλάξ μῶρος Ἀθηναῖοι, βλε[ι]μ[ά]ζει βαστάζει Ἀθηναῖοι (both items, in reverse order, in Hesychius).

[20] OBerol inv. 12605, published in Wilamowitz-Moellendorff 1918 (= MP³ 2131); see S. West 1967: 260–263.

[21] Cribiore 1996: 39–40; Thespis *TrGF* 1.1 F 4.

[22] PHib 2.172 (= *SH* 991; = MP³ 2129). See Pfeiffer 1968: 78–79.

Of course we can guess that new factors encouraged this systematic interest in the byways of language: a synchronic appreciation of the wide range of dialects and foreign languages more easily encountered in the new Hellenistic world, and a diachronic accumulation of literature more or less archaic now being sorted and interpreted as a common inheritance of Hellenism. But we may also guess that such improving vocabularies, general thesauri of poetic diction, were available already in Callimachus' formative years.

The techniques of Homeric commentary could be applied also to contemporary poets. The Lille Papyrus of *The Victory of Berenice* (*SH* 254; see above), which takes us to Middle Egypt hardly more than a generation after the poet's death, represents an early example. The small, neat, serifed script looks quite professional; but the copy is remarkable for its notes of explanation, written at the same size as the text and by the same hand at irregular intervals within the poem, set off only by indentation. The author solves briefly cryptic references to Proteus and Archemorus (*SH* 254.5, 7), and explains at length the genealogy of Berenice (1–2), and the complex expression "front runners" (9–10), combining Homer and Bacchylides; he does not think it necessary to explain "Helen's island" (254.5) or "Danaus' well" (260A.4). He glosses a whole series of rare words but also αἰνολέων, whose αἰνο- should be familiar from Homer; on the other hand, he neglects to gloss the dialect ἀέκων or the rare λητιαί or the unusual sense of ἑρμαίου (257.4, 5, 16). This seems eclectic enough to be personal: Does it represent the private preparation of a Fayum schoolteacher?

Koine *and Poetry*

But the *koine* may have a closer connection with Callimachus' poetry than simply translating his *glossai*. His original reader may have noticed that in some places Callimachus was avoiding the everyday, or adopting it with a context to show it off, or most interestingly employing it in an older or more literary sense than its normal usage. I give some examples rather at random.

Aetia fragment 24.6–7 Pf. (26 M.): δεκάπ[ο]υν δ' εἶχεν ἄκαιναν ὅγε, | ἀμφότερον κέντρον τε βοῶν καὶ μέτρον ἀρούρης, "and he [Thiodamas] held a ten-foot pole, both a goad for his oxen and a measure of his field." Ἄκαινα begins as something pointed (root ἀκ-), such as the Pelasgian lance at *Argonautica* 3.1323, where scholia deduce that the word is Thessalian; it comes to indicate a measure of length and of area, attested for Asia Minor, said by metrologists to be Egyptian but never found in Egyptian documents. Callimachus thought the Thessalian word suitable for his Dryopian story, constructing a metrical scholion on its meanings. The second explanation, μέτρον ἀρούρης, plays with a specifically Egyptian usage: traditionally ἄρουρα means "field," but in Egypt it is a technical term of every land survey, an area one hundred cubits square. By adding μέτρον Callimachus gently underlines his archaism.

SH 254.1: νύμφα, κασιγνήτων ἱερὸν αἷμα θεῶν, "bride, sacred blood of the Sibling Gods." Berenice II, here addressed, figured for dynastic purposes as the child of Ptolemy II and his sister Arsinoe II. Their formal titulature had appeared, in the form Θεῶν Ἀδελφῶν, in the date clause of every document of the last twenty-five years. The poet reverses the elements and replaces the commonplace ἀδελφῶν by a word known not from documents but from Homer and tragedy, glossed in our Homeric scholia.

SH 259.33: ἱπόν τ' ἀνδίκτην τε μάλ' εἰδότα μακρὸν ἀλέσθαι, "the press and the jumper that knew well how to make a long leap"—these are parts of Molorchus' mousetrap. The second word looks like a *nomen agentis* from the archaic verb ἀν(α)δικεῖν, and archaic perhaps it was, since Callimachus proceeds to gloss it. So, when the very similar [α]νδικτο( ) turns up four centuries later in the tax rolls of Karanis (PMich 4.223.2665), apparently as a rendering of the Egyptian proper name Πανπῖν, "Man of the Mouse," Herbert Youtie (1970) concluded that the tax clerk was an *érudit manqué* who relieved his boredom by adding a Callimachean reference to his register. Perhaps. Or was it that the word continued current in some form, a technical term, not a poetic oddity? We know that archaic, colloquial, and poetic may coincide.

Iambi fragment 203.54–55 Pf.: τὴν γενὴν ἀνακρίνει | καὶ δοῦλον εἶναί φησι καὶ παλίμπρητον, "he questions my birth and says I am a slave and sold on." The poet's enemy tries to prove him a slave. Meter and Ionic diction (including the form γενή) belong to Hipponax. But there is a deliberate contrast with two current technicalities. Παλίμπρατος, "resold," does not occur in the documents, and it has a wider future as an insult, "sold over and over," "shop-soiled"; but the verb παλιμπρατεῖν does, in the tax code issued under the name of Ptolemy Philadelphus in 259 BC and the clause relating to Alexandrian retailers under the state oil monopoly (PRev 47.16). Ἀνακρίνειν is the documentary term used of official inquiries and interrogations: in the Roman period, indeed, the technical term for the examination of slaves to determine their status (Bieżuńska-Małowist 1977: 54-63).

Apotheosis of Arsinoe fragment 228.9 Pf.: ἀμετέρα] βασίλεια φρούδα, "our queen is gone." Ptolemaic queens in documents have the title βασίλισσα, and no doubt that was common usage (Theoc. *Id*. 15.24); but Callimachus (and poetry in general) avoided it. At the same time, Dr. Schwendner observes, βασίλεια was applied to the deified Arsinoe II, as a cult title borrowed from Hera. Here, therefore, the older word also chimes with current usage.

Hecale fragment 251 Pf. (35 H.): ἐκ δ' ἄρτος σιπύηθεν ἅλις κατέθηκεν ἑλοῦσα, "from the breadbin she took enough loaves and put them down." Σιπύη has a life in Attic Old Comedy, but it appears also (in the spelling συπύας) in a contemporary list of household goods and provisions, between jars of pickle and water pots (PCairZen 1.59014 fr. B 14). That gives an extra piquancy to the epic phrasing and the mythic rusticity.

Hecale fragment 248 Pf. (36 H.): γεργέριμον πίτυρίν τε καὶ ἣν ἀπεθήκατο λευκὴν | εἰν ἁλὶ νήχεσθαι φθινοπωρίδα, "the ripened olive and the bran olive and the pale autumn olive that she stored away to swim in brine." Of these varieties, the first remains an object of scholarly curiosity to Didymus and beyond. But the last makes a double gesture. Φθινοπωρίς trumps the more homely φθινοπωρινός, which in Zeno's accounts distinguishes autumn sesame from summer sesame. Εἰν ἁλὶ νήχεσθαι paraphrases the everyday term κολυμβάς (PCairZen 3.59501 R9), as Callimachus himself points out at *Iambi* fragment 194.77 Pf.

Hecale fragment 261.3 Pf. (71 H.): κατὰ δρόμον Ἀπόλλωνος, "at the running track of Apollo," the crow meets Athena by the Lyceum. This use of δρόμος is said in the *Suda* to be Cretan. But Callimachus knows another specialized usage, for the processional avenue of an Egyptian temple; in fragment 715 Pf., ὁ δρόμος ἱερὸς οὗτος Ἀνούβιδος, the Egyptian deity makes it plain.

Hymn to Zeus lines 19-20: ἔτι δ' ἄβροχος ἦεν ἅπασα | Ἀζηνίς, "and all Azenis was without water." The adjective looks rare (attested for us only once, in Euripides), but, it is familiar in the documentary papyri, for it describes land that has not been watered by the flooding Nile: Callimachus' verse brings primeval Arcadia together with Egyptian bureaucracy.

Hymn to Artemis line 50: ἱππείην τετύκοντο Ποσειδάωνι ποτίστρην, "they [the Cyclopes] wrought for Poseidon an equine trough." Ποτίστρα occurs first here; later we find it only in prose, and commonly in the documentary papyri to mean "pond" or the like (-τρίς already at PCairZen 5.59825.19). As Fritz Bornmann observes (1968: xliii and 29) the prosaic word, qualified by the poetic adjective, gives an earthy twist to the heroic labors of the Cyclopes.

Hymn to Demeter line 1: τῶ καλάθω κατιόντος ἐπιφθέγξασθε, γυναῖκες, "as the basket goes home, women, add your cry!" Neil Hopkinson notes (1984a: 77) that κάλαθος is attested chiefly in prose literature, and indeed the word occurs in a private letter to Zeno (PRyl 4.556.10, "14 baskets for the wool") and in later documents. Callimachus could have used κάνεον (Attic κανοῦν), a Homeric word but still current and familiar from the dynastic cult, in which the κανηφόρος of Arsinoe II played a leading role. Perhaps the more homely word was more Argive—or more alienating.

Callimachus' language, that is, has its references in life and in literature and in scholarship. It is a unique synthesis, and there is some temptation to see it as a revolutionary synthesis, because it follows so soon upon the geopolitical transformation of the Hellenic world. However, much of the new is not new as such. Antimachus and Philetas had already blazed a trail in poetry and lexicography. The Derveni Papyrus has shown that verbal scholarship goes back well into the fourth century; the *Meropis* (*PEG* 1.131–35) hints at a wider tradition of local myths and mutant Homerisms. This chapter has tried to illustrate, above all from papyri, how Callimachus' contemporaries in Ptolemaic Egypt may have reacted to his work, to the use that he made of the poetic *koine* that they inherited and the actual *koine* that they spoke. Their education offered them lists of literary words, which did not respect generic boundaries. Their study of Homer will have taught them that *glottai* and a mixing of dialects are proper to epic, so that Callimachus may have seemed more Homeric to them than he does to us. They took pride in their new kingdom, which Callimachus celebrated in his court poetry. They flourished in a melting pot of new perspectives and cultural surprises, where a poetics of πολυείδεια may have seemed all the more at home.

PART TWO

SOCIAL CONTEXTS

CHAPTER EIGHT

DIMENSIONS OF POWER: CALLIMACHEAN GEOPOETICS
AND THE PTOLEMAIC EMPIRE

Markus Asper

ABSTRACT

The paper offers a political reading of, mainly, the *Aetia* and *Iambi*, arguing that Callimachus creates Ptolemaic dimensions of space and time in these poems. First, many of the places prominently mentioned or described extensively by Callimachus may have had special political relevance for Ptolemaic politics. This seems to be the case with, e.g., Miletus, Athens and Attica, Ceos, Cos, and Rome. Further the Callimachean practice of juxtaposing episodes that are set at different places, propels a reader, in his imagination, through the Hellenistic world as if travelling by rocket. These mind-travels in *Aetia* I, *Aetia* III–IV and *Iambi* (plus *Mele*) map a Callimachean 'geopoetics'. From such a perspective, the *Aetia* and *Iambi* assume features of a 'Panhellenic reader', that is a corpus of texts that presents the world from a Ptolemaic perspective. The chapter also explores an equivalent approach to the presentation of time in Callimachus (his 'chronopoetics').

Recent years have seen new approaches to the performance and circulation of Alexandrian poetry. One could almost say that since the mid-1990s Callimachus and his fellow court poets have left the ivory tower that modern scholarship had erected for them.[1] Although the notion of an elitist readership is still dear to many, at least some scholars no longer assume that Alexandrian poets wrote exclusively for a tiny, bookish, and infinitely erudite audience. Such an assumption would require that these poets were writing only for themselves. Wider audiences must have found something attractive in these poems that cannot have consisted wholly of subtle intertextual references that only a tiny minority of actual readers could have completely appreciated. What was it in these poems, then, that attracted larger audiences? This chapter suggests that part of the attraction may have been the close

---

[1] E.g., Hunter 1993: 4–5; Alan Cameron 1995: 3–70; Selden 1998; Asper 2001: 94–108; Stephens 2003: 238–257; Hunter 2006a: 4.

connection of aesthetics and politics. What follows explores such a combination, namely a certain way of talking about places in poetry, for which I will use the term "geopoetics" here.[2] In brief, I shall argue that Callimachus created Ptolemaic dimensions of space and time in his poems.[3]

Geopoetics and Politics: Knowing Places

First, the creation of Ptolemaic space: Callimachus mentions hundreds of place names in his narratives. As such, these places are usually part of the commonly accepted plots of these narratives. Only the selection of the stories, their arrangement, and, perhaps, minor alterations or decisions between several versions are Callimachus'. Most of the places in question, however, still existed in the time of the poet and his contemporary readers. It seems natural to assume that the place names mentioned must have elicited some response on the audience's part and that this response would have been affected by the politics of the day. I do not suggest that this was the case with every single place mentioned. Five examples will show, however, that behind the mythological narrative a political present often looms.

1. Miletus, in Ionia, since it was founded quite late in comparison with the major centers of the Mycenaean world, is not a prominent city in the major cycles of Greek myth. Thus, in poems for which the topics are mostly taken from such cycles, the prominence of Miletus in Callimachus' *Aetia* and *Iambi* is quite remarkable.[4] The city provides the setting for the (almost entirely lost) love story *Phrygius and Pieria* in *Aetia* 3 (frr. 80–83 Pf.; see Ehrhardt 2003: 282), for the scenes concerned with Thales in *Iambus* 1 (fr. 191.52–77 Pf.), and for the story known as *Branchus* (fr. 229 Pf.) that explains the aetiology of Apollo's oracle at the temple of Didyma, near Miletus. Besides the immediate appeal of these stories, did the place resonate with Ptolemaic audiences? It probably did. During the third

---

[2] K. White defines it loosely as "a higher unity" of poetry and geography (1992: 174). A. Barchiesi has, in his Gray Lectures on "Virgilian Geopoetics" (Cambridge 2001), introduced the term into classical studies.

[3] For similar approaches, compare Bing 2005: 121–127, who speaks of "politics and poetics of geography" (on time, see p. 135). See also Stephens 2005: 231.

[4] As Wilamowitz had already observed; see Ehrhardt 2003: 283.

century, the Ptolemies tried to gain influence in Miletus in order to use it as a power base for their aspirations in the Aegean and western Asia Minor, efforts that were mainly directed against the Seleucids. Already in 294 BC, Ptolemy I had signed a treaty with the Milesians to the effect of mutual friendship (Huss 2001: 205). In 279/8 Ptolemy II donated land to the *demos* of Miletus.[5] Despite these signs of favor, in 260 the Milesians defected to the Seleucids. This was certainly a failure of Ptolemaic foreign policy and certainly also a topic of general concern in Alexandria, precisely at the time when Callimachus composed these poems and precisely among his readership.

2. Athens and Attica provide the setting of the *Hecale*, a poem that makes use of local Athenian writings in order to convey a realistic flair to a readership less familiar with the area. Eratosthenes turned in his *Erigone* an Athenian local legend into an aetiological epyllion. With their double wanderings, both Icarius and Erigone give their author presumably ample opportunity to call to mind, and his audiences to remember, Attic topography. The parallels with the *Hecale* are quite obvious (see Rosokoki 1995: 17–20). Except for Athenian immigrants, was anybody in Alexandria interested in reading about Athens? Many people were, I assume. Throughout the greater part of the third century, Athens was at the center of the Ptolemies' intentions to tackle the Antigonids' power in central Greece. Ptolemy II signed a truce with the Athenians in 268 to this effect (Huss 2001: 271–281). At this time, the Macedonians controlled Piraeus and various parts of Attica while the Ptolemies backed Athens against their archenemies under the slogan "Liberty for All Greece." To liberate Athens from Antigonid siege was one of the most important Ptolemaic goals of these years, eventually achieved forty years later by Ptolemy III in 229 (Huss 2001: 357). During these years, Athenian lore must have struck a chord with Alexandrian audiences. Those who read about Hecale and Theseus must have readily recognized the place names of current campaigns. As we know now, Callimachus himself was at Athens in 248/7 donating a huge sum of money toward an Athenian defense project. In turn, the Athenians honored him as their

---

[5] For Miletus and the Ptolemies, see Huss 2001: 262; Ehrhardt 2003: 286–289.

benefactor (Oliver 2002: 6–8). Doubtless he acted on behalf of his royal sponsors.

3. The little island of Ceos, some forty miles southeast of Athens, provides the setting for the novelesque story *Acontius and Cydippe* (*Aetia* 3, fr. 65–72 Pf.). The story ends, somewhat surprisingly, as an aetiology of contemporary Ceos.[6] The end of the little narrative mentions the four towns of Ceos and, along with them, the ruling families, whose founding ancestor turns out to be Acontius. Modern readers have always been struck by the bold, self-referential way in which Callimachus lets his narrative end in footnotelike fashion. Nonetheless, perhaps the average reader was less interested in the somewhat obscure Xenomedes and the highbrow games that Callimachus plays on him than in Ceos itself: for the island probably played a crucial role in the struggle against Antigonus in 267–265. Its main harbor, Coresia (fr. 75.74 Pf.), had (just?) been renamed Arsinoe.[7] Although this must remain speculative, members of the families of Ceos mentioned in Callimachus may have been well known in Alexandria. Certainly later, in 227, a citizen of Ceos, Hegesias, served as an ambassador at Alexandria (Huss 2001: 435). As in the case of Miletus, for Ptolemaic audiences of the 260 and 250s Ceos certainly held a significance besides its role in the love story *Acontius and Cydippe*—it probably reminded them of the Ptolemies' imperial intentions in Greece.

4. In at least one case, Callimachus explicitly plays upon the relation of myth and geographical present assumed here: in a famous scene from *Hymn* 4, the unborn Apollo tells his mother, who is desperately looking for a place to give birth, and the reader that the island Cos is inappropriate, because the birth of another god, namely Ptolemy II, is due to happen there in the future (*Hymn* 4.162–204) and in the reader's past (308 BC). The unborn Apollo launches into a vivid description of Ptolemy's future glory that is, in fact, present time for audience and poet. Throughout much of the third century, the island of Cos is one of the places outside Egypt most closely associated with the Ptolemies: it had been their major naval base in the Aegean since at least 313 (Huss 2001: 173–174). After the sea battle of Leucolla (an unknown place on Cos, in 255), Antigonus

---

[6] Ceos is also the setting of *Ep.* 5 Pf. = 14 GP. See Weber 1993: 257.
[7] On Coresia-Arsinoe and the campaign against Antigonus, see Walbank in Hammond and Walbank 1988: 284; Huss 2001: 275.

Gonatas threatened Ptolemy's power in the Aegean for some years. The Ptolemies may have even withdrawn from the island. After the late 250s, however, Ptolemy seems to have regained power over what he considered his island.[8] Thus, the praise of Apollo not only is a casual reference to Ptolemy's place of birth but touches upon one of the key places of Ptolemaic power, written in the very years when the island's strategic position was key to the struggles against the Antigonids. The triumphal spirit of the passage might well celebrate the state of affairs after 250. For the audience, the glorious present became suddenly visible in the midst of the ancient myth of Apollo's birth.

5. When we move our attention from the East to the West, two passages in the *Aetia* come to mind that relate aetiological stories about places far removed from Ptolemaic power: famously, Callimachus mentions Rome (*Aetia* 4, frr. 106–107 Pf., discussed below). In addition, *Aetia* 2 opens with a long catalogue of Sicilian cities and their founding sagas (fr. 43 Pf. = 50.1–83 M.). Simply to assume that a general antiquarian interest was responsible for these passages would leave open the question of how any broader audience could have appreciated these topics. The perspective changes radically when one realizes that the Ptolemies had sent an embassy to Rome already in the 270s and were monitoring the First Punic War closely.[9] Probably any narrative treatment of Rome or Italian cities that were involved in what became the Punic War would have elicited a response that showed the same characteristics as the examples adduced so far: for Ptolemaic audiences, contemporary politics provides a background to the narrative treatment of places in aetiological myth.

One could think along the same lines concerning places and names from the Peloponnese and, naturally, Cyrene.[10] Whenever Callimachus

---

[8] On Ptolemaic Cos, see further Theocritus 17.64–72; Sherwin-White 1978: 90–112; Buraselis 1982: 147–151, 170–172; Walbank in Hammond and Walbank 1988: 291–293, 595–599; Huss 2001: 285, 302–303.

[9] On Rome and the Ptolemies, see, e.g., Lampela 1998: 56–58; Huss 2001: 294–295 n. 332.

[10] Ptolemy II tried to gain influence in the northern and eastern Peloponnese in the late 250s: for example, he had contacts with Argos, favored the Sicyonians' revolt against Macedonian rule, and sought influence in the Achaean League. See Urban 1979: 12, 33–38; Huss 2001: 302.

On Cyrene, Apollonius, and Ptolemaic rule, see the remarks of Hunter 1993: 152–153.

or Apollonius singles out a place for detailed geographical description or mentions it prominently, one should ask what the role of this particular place would have been in the actual politics of the time. The time of Callimachus and his peers was a period of Ptolemaic engagement over almost all Greece. Viewed from this perspective, the many place names in his works might sum up to a geography of Ptolemaic power or, at least, of the Ptolemies' aspirations to power. Certainly these place names provide a way of reconstructing spontaneous responses from any audience, especially any larger audience, of that time. An interest in geography was shared not only by ruler and poet but, obviously, by contemporary audiences and readers alike.[11] One might go even further and maintain that the poets' interest in geography is merely a reflection of the audience's. From this point of view, the elaborated aetiologies of Callimachus told, in a way, the poetically distorted prehistory of current politics.[12] Again, I am not saying that each and every single place mentioned must have elicited such a response. Nonetheless, below the superficial impression of antiquarianism and seemingly disinterested fascination with geographical information, there is a background of contemporary geopolitics—transformed into geopoetics.

Geopoetics and Space: Going Places

The political aspect of geopoetics relies on the fact that a place mentioned in the context of a mythological narrative may have been of political importance in the audience's world. There is a second aspect of geopoetics, however, that for lack of a better term I will call "spatial" here: a reader of fiction is usually absent from the place or the time where the fictionalized event takes place. In order to become absorbed in the act of reading one must, to a certain extent, bridge this gap. Reading Callimachus is no exception. Anyone who reads the works of Callimachus travels through an imaginary Greece—not, however, in a well-organized, predictable way but on a zigzagging route that

---

[11] See Meyer 2001: 234; compare Weber 1993: 316–319.
[12] A splendid example (*Hymn* 3.197–240) had already caught Wilamowitz's eye (1924: 2.58–59): there, most of the cult places of Artemis mentioned are located in areas recently occupied by the Ptolemies. See also Weber 1993: 316–317.

includes constant surprise takeoffs and sudden landings.[13] In the following discussion, I will try to map some of these routes.

As far as we can still tell, the episodes of *Aetia*, for example, are set in the following places in this order: after *Prologue* and invocation, readers find themselves on Mount Helicon, in Boeotia (frr. 1.41–2 Pf. = frr. 3, 4 M.); the islands of Paros (frr. 3–7.18 Pf. = 5–9.18 M.), Corcyra (frr. 7.19–16 = 9.19–18 M.), Anaphe (frr. 17–21 Pf. = 19–23 M.), and Rhodes (Lindus, frr. 22, 23 Pf. = 24, 25 M.); then Aetolia (frr. 24, 25 Pf. = 26, 27 M.), Argos (frr. 27–31 Pf. = 28–34 M.), and the island of Leucas (frr. 31a–e Pf. = 35–38 M.). It is not certain but probable that Argos and Leucas followed immediately after Aetolia. In further fragments from Book 1 that are not part of the episodes known so far, the reader comes across Cilicia, Lesbos, and Sicily, among other locales. Of course, these are only the places where the main part of the narrative is set. Many more place names show up, with no less irregularity: for example, in the fragments preceding the story associated with Corcyra, Colchis and the modern-day Croatian coast are prominent. There is no discernible geographical pattern that would make the series of places predictable or that would at least prepare the reader for what might come next. Such a pattern famously structures the Homeric Catalogue of Ships; and, still in Hellenistic poetry, generally the genre of the *periplus* recommended itself for structuring geographical diversities.[14] In the *Aetia*, however, readers are forced to jump at the end of one story and are deliberately kept unaware of where they will land next. While reading through the poem, the reader's mind, hopping from place to place, travels through mainland Greece. Readers who are perhaps less familiar with Greek geography may want to visualize these imaginary travels. They would end up with roughly the schema of Figure 8.1.

Of course, this is not to suggest that Callimachus used a map. (If he had done so, his map would have looked quite different.)[15] What Figure 8.1 shows, however, is his apparent desire to arrange the order of his stories aiming at a maximum of geographical discontinuity, albeit within the old Greek world. Readers would have experienced a

---

[13] See the survey in Harder 2003: 294–296.
[14] On Apollonius' use of *periplus*, see Meyer 2001: 219–220.
[15] The symmetrical clarity of the diagram is based on exact maps that did not exist in Callimachus' time.

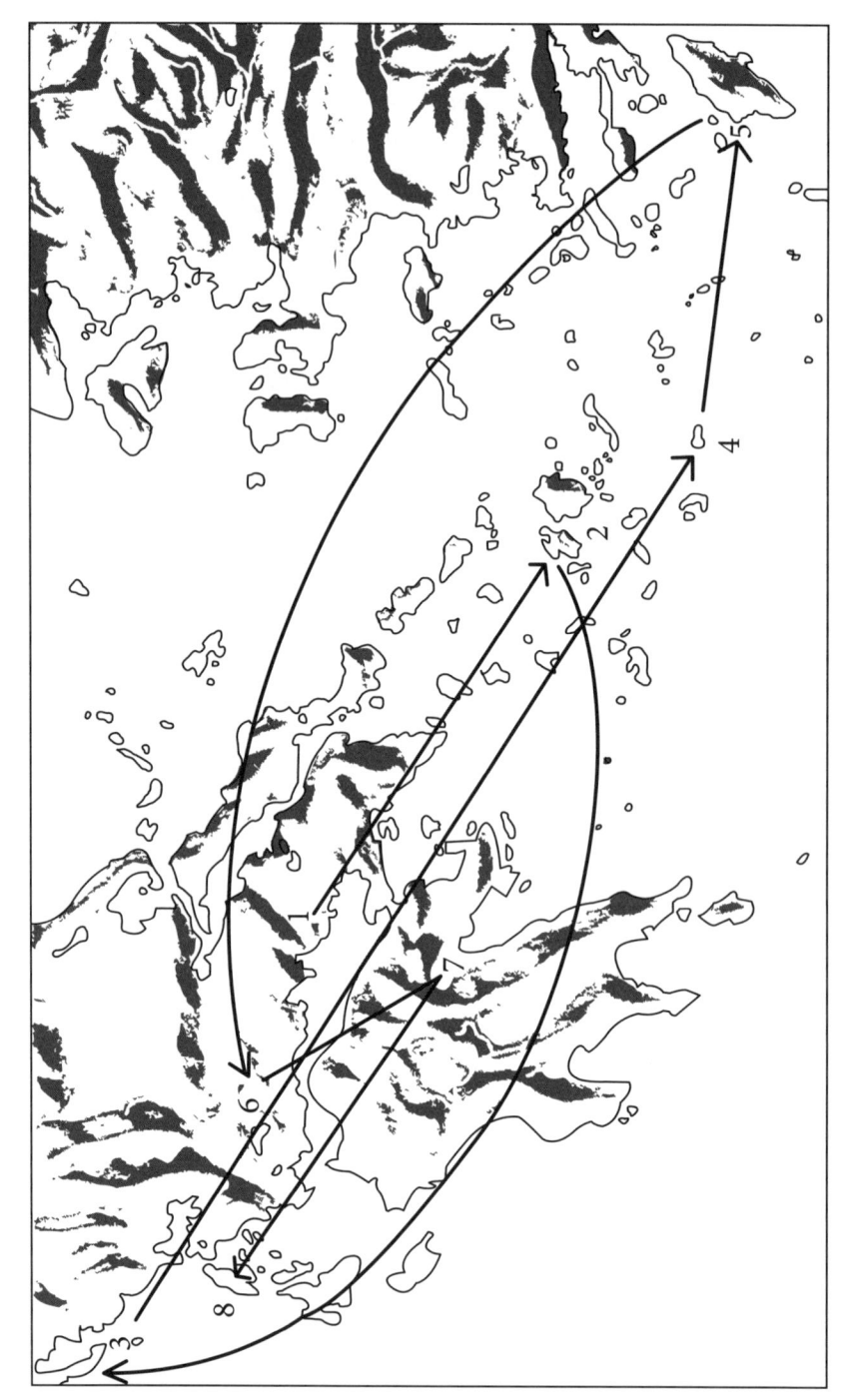

Fig. 8.1. Mind-traveling in *Aetia* I: *1*, Mt. Helicon (Boeotia); *2*, Paros; *3*, Corcyra; *4*, Anaphe; *5*, Rhodes; *6*, Aetolia; *7*, Argos; *8*, Leucas.

notion of traveling through geographically discontinuous spaces, especially if their mental maps would have contained merely hodological concepts (Meyer 2001: 229–230). Obviously, I take it for granted that Callimachus wrote mainly for a reading public,[16] which does not preclude the performance of single episodes of the *Aetia* or shorter poems, like single *iambi* or hymns, in an oral setting.[17] Nonetheless, it would destroy the impression of geographical discontinuity to assume the performance of single episodes as a regular mode of perception.

In *Aetia* 1, there are only eight episodes of which the geographical setting and the relative position are still clear from the fragments. Is the impression of geographical discontinuity merely a product of chance? How do these travels look when we have a chance to survey a longer stretch of Callimachean poetry? *Aetia* 3 and 4 provide splendid material for such an approach: first, these paired books were apparently designed as a single complex for readers, which seems to be the message of their framing narratives concerning Berenice II. Second, thanks to the Milan *Diegeseis*, sufficient knowledge is available about the plots of twenty-seven stories (ten in *Aetia* 3, seventeen in *Aetia* 4) that follow one after another without even the connecting device of the Muses' dialogue. Here the sense of unexpected transportation must have struck the reader even more strongly. *Aetia* 3 begins with the two-layered celebration of Berenice's victory at Nemea that is at the same time an *aition* of the Nemean Games, focusing on Heracles (*SH* 254–272). Then follow, united by a large papyrus, three short aetiological narratives set in Attica (fr. 63 Pf.), Agrigentum (fr. 64 Pf.), and Argos (frr. 65, 66 Pf.) before the *diegetes* takes over, summing up the story *Acontius and Cydippe*—which is, although partly set in Naxos, mostly about Ceos (frr. 67–75 Pf.). After a comparatively minor gap of perhaps three narratives (see Gallazzi and Lehnus 2001), we find ourselves in Elis (frr. 76, 77a Pf.: Olympia), then in Ionian Isindus (fr. 78 Pf.). An *aition* about Artemis of uncertain local affiliation follows (fr. 79 Pf.: perhaps Ephesus?), then the love story *Phrygius and Pieria*, set in Miletus (frr. 80–83 Pf.), and a narrative located in Calabrian (Epizephyrian) Locri (fr. 84–85Pf.), which ends *Aetia* 3. Book 4 begins with the explanation of the *Daphnephoria* (frr. 86–89),

---

[16] See Asper 2001: 94–95.
[17] Both forms of publication seem plausible, at least, for the *Hymns*, *The Lock of Berenice*, and Pfeiffer's Μέλη (frr. 179–82, now sometimes regarded as *Iambi* 14–17; see Acosta-Hughes 2003).

a procession from Delphi to Thessalian Tempe and back. (To judge from the fragments, most of the story was set in Delphi.) Then we find ourselves in Thracian Abdera (fr. 90 Pf.), on the island Tenedos and, perhaps, on Lesbos (frr. 91, 92 Pf.), on Lipara (fr. 93 Pf.), and after that in Athens (Limone, frr. 94–95 Pf.). There follows a story about the death of a bragging hunter: its geographical setting is not important, and since the *diegesis* does not give a local affiliation, Callimachus may not even have mentioned it. (However, scholars have sometimes assumed a setting somewhere in Italy: fr. 96 Pf.) Definite places are again part of the ensuing narratives: the Athenian acropolis (fr. 97 Pf.), Calabrian Temesa (frr. 98, 99 Pf.), and Hera's famous sanctuary on Samos—twice (frr. 100, 101 Pf.)! After that, the reader is transported to Ephesus (fr. 102 Pf.), to Piraeus (fr. 103 Pf.), to the island Thasos (fr. 104 Pf.), probably to Thebes (*The Dragging of Antigone*: fr. 105 Pf.) before suddenly arriving at Rome (frr. 106, 107 Pf.). Toward the end of the book a story from the Argonautic traditions leads us to Cyzicus (frr. 108, 109 Pf.) before the book ends with the famous *Lock of Berenice* (fr. 110 Pf.), beginning in Alexandria and mentioning Canopus.[18] The reader's mind, quite well adjusted to long-distance travel by now, would have to perform, more or less, the translocations sketched in Figure 8.2. (Now we need a map covering almost the whole Mediterranean.)

Not surprisingly, the three main areas of Greek settlement and, therefore, of Greek collective memory present the three geographical foci in this map. It becomes very clear, however, that Callimachus is not interested in a geographical pattern—the three Ionian narratives set in Isindus, Ephesus, and Miletus (Fig. 8.2, nos. 7–9) that are grouped together are the only exception. Instead, he makes his reader constantly change between West and East. Furthermore, the last place visited is Alexandria, where a greater part of the implied readership was actually reading these poems. If it is acceptable that the first *aition*, which combines praise for Berenice with an aetiological story centered on Nemea, also possesses some Alexandrian background, then by the end of *Aetia* 4 the reader will have come full circle, after having followed the poet on a wild tour through Greece.

---

[18] Although the *Epilogue* mentions the Hippocrene and refers back to the Helicon scene at the beginning of *Aetia* 1, it does not seem to have any real geographic significance.

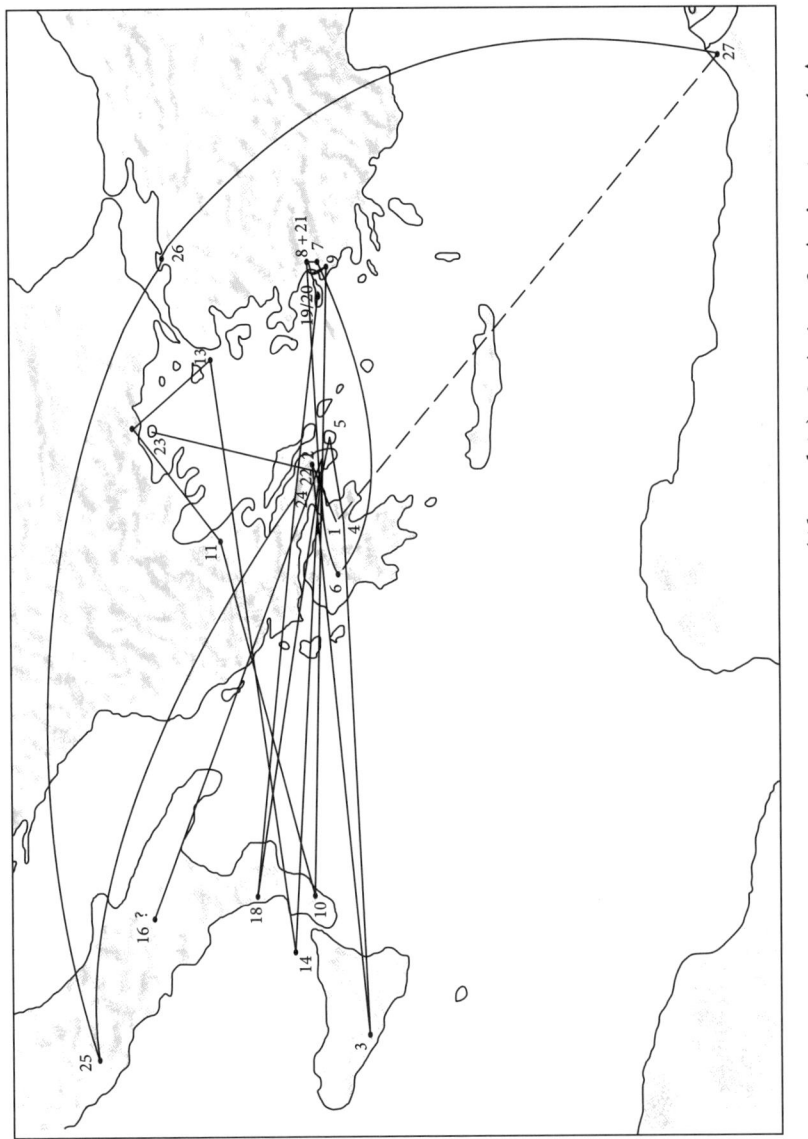

Fig. 8.2. Mind-traveling in Aetia III-IV: *1*, Nemea (Alexandria); *2*, Attica; *3*, Agrigentum; *4*, Argos; *5*, Ceos,...; *6*, Elis; *7*, Isindus; *8*, Ephesus(?); *9*, Miletus; *10*, Locri in Calabria; *11*, Tempe (Thessaly); *12*, Abdera; *13*, Tenedos; *14*, Lipara; *15*, Athens; *16*, somewhere in Italy; *17*, Athens; *18*, Temesa in Calabria; *19*, *20*, Samos; *21*, Ephesus; *22*, Piraeus; *23*, Thasos; *24*, Thebes; *25*, Rome; *26*, Cyzicus; *27*, Alexandria and Canopus.

Is there a poetic design in this arrangement, which seems to aim, again, at a maximum of geographic discontinuity? There is only one more text that we could look at in order to frame the impressions derived from the *Aetia*: the *Iambi*.[19] The *Iambi* contained at least thirteen poems that, almost certainly, the poet himself arranged. Readers would have thus perceived them as a poetic complex. For the sake of my argument, I include the four Μέλη here, because they would at least have been read after the *Iambi* in the collected works that the *diegetes* follows, whether or not Callimachus saw them as part of the actual poetry book of *Iambi*. Of its seventeen stories, one (fr. 192 Pf.) does not have any setting, so far as we can know. Seven and a half have settings dispersed all over the Greek world: the setting of *Iambus* 6 (fr. 196 Pf.) is Olympia; *Iambus* 7 (fr. 197 Pf.) takes place in Aenus, in Thrace; *Iambus* 8 (fr. 198 Pf.), on Aegina; *Iambus* 10 (fr. 200 Pf.), in Aspendus, in Pamphylia; *Iambus* 11, in Selinus, in Sicily; fragment 226 Pf. on Lemnos; and fragment 229 Pf. in Miletus.[20] I count as half a setting the story of *Iambus* 1 (fr. 191 Pf.), which unfolds a story centered on Miletus within an Alexandrian frame. The surprise, however, comes with the remainder of the settings: the remaining eight and a half plots are set in Alexandria (frr. 193–95, 199, 202–3, 227–28 Pf.; obviously the half is *Iambus* 1, fr. 191 Pf.).[21] This result is immediately clear from the mixed character of the *Iambi*: fables and parables that convey moral or mock-moral points aimed at Alexandrian audiences interchange with aetiological stories. These stories continue either in the spirit of the *Aetia* (fr. 228 Pf.) or perhaps even assume the character of a parodic countergenre (fr. 196 Pf.) that refers the reader back to the preceding books.[22] Naturally, the latter are set somewhere in the Greek world, whereas the former are firmly rooted in Alexandria. An

---

[19] I find it hard to believe that the *Hymns* were arranged as a poetry book by the poet himself. Compare, however, Hunter and Fuhrer 2002: 176–179; Depew 2004: 117, 134–135.

[20] It is an argument not made, so far, in favor of including the so-called Μέλη into the *Iambi* that Miletus-centered poems at the beginning and the end would provide a frame for this poetry book.

[21] Those poems that have no specific setting but target apparently real persons whom the reader could identify I take to be set in Alexandria. Admittedly, the plot of the fable in *Iambus* 4 is set on Lydian Mt.Tmolus, but the frame is Alexandrian. Since the fable in no way depends on local elements (unlike *Iambus* 1), I count it as Alexandrian.

[22] The concept of the *Iambi* as a countergenre of the *Aetia* was first explored by Clayman 1988.

attempt at visualization must result, accordingly, in a different picture, as seen in Figure 8.3.

The *Iambi*, then, show a different geopoetical structure than the *Aetia*: the reader's mind does not travel freely and chaotically through a half-fictitious and half-utopian space that one might call Panhellenia but returns again and again to contemporary Alexandria. The *Iambi* are overtly Alexandrian, much more so than the *Aetia*. They focus on aetiologies only secondarily and therefore are mostly free to address directly the reader's present.

In all these texts, most episodes in the narrative take place somewhere other than where the neighboring episodes are situated. Transitions are generally harsh. The intended harshness of these sudden changes from episode to episode doubles the effect: we find eastern islands next to western cities, rivers in the north next to Peloponnesian mountains, references to Athens next to local lore of Cyrene, all mixed and arranged in a completely unpredictable order. Some of the longer hymns are similar in effect, especially *Hymns* 3 and 4. Now and then in this Panhellenic kaleidoscope, usually at important points in the overall composition, Ptolemaic Alexandria comes into focus as well: most remarkably at the beginning of *Aetia* 3 and at the end of Book 4 with the two episodes concerning Berenice. Thus, the entire compound presents a multifaceted macrocosm that is united in only one respect: it is Greek, viewed from an Alexandrian perspective.

The works of Callimachus, especially the *Aetia*, the *Iambi*, and also the longer hymns certainly have a Panhellenic impact: the reader rediscovers all the different parts of Greece, their myths and history, their place names, their local heroes, cults, and festivals, and sometimes even local words—for example, the names of the months in Argos (fr. 26 Pf. = 30 M.). It is not difficult to imagine the impact on an Alexandrian reader: every Greek in Egypt could probably find some story here relating to that part of the old world where his family came from. Moreover, he would have experienced his family's origins as being juxtaposed and connected to other parts of old-time Greece in ways he had never thought of. For such readers, the thrill of reading Callimachus might have in a sense consisted of transportation to places that were part of Greek cultural memory. In this context, the so-called mimetic hymns of Callimachus come to mind: besides the strong integration of the reader into the worshipping group, these texts also transport their audiences to a place far beyond the confines of Alexandria: to Argos in the case of *Hymn* 5, perhaps to Cyrene in

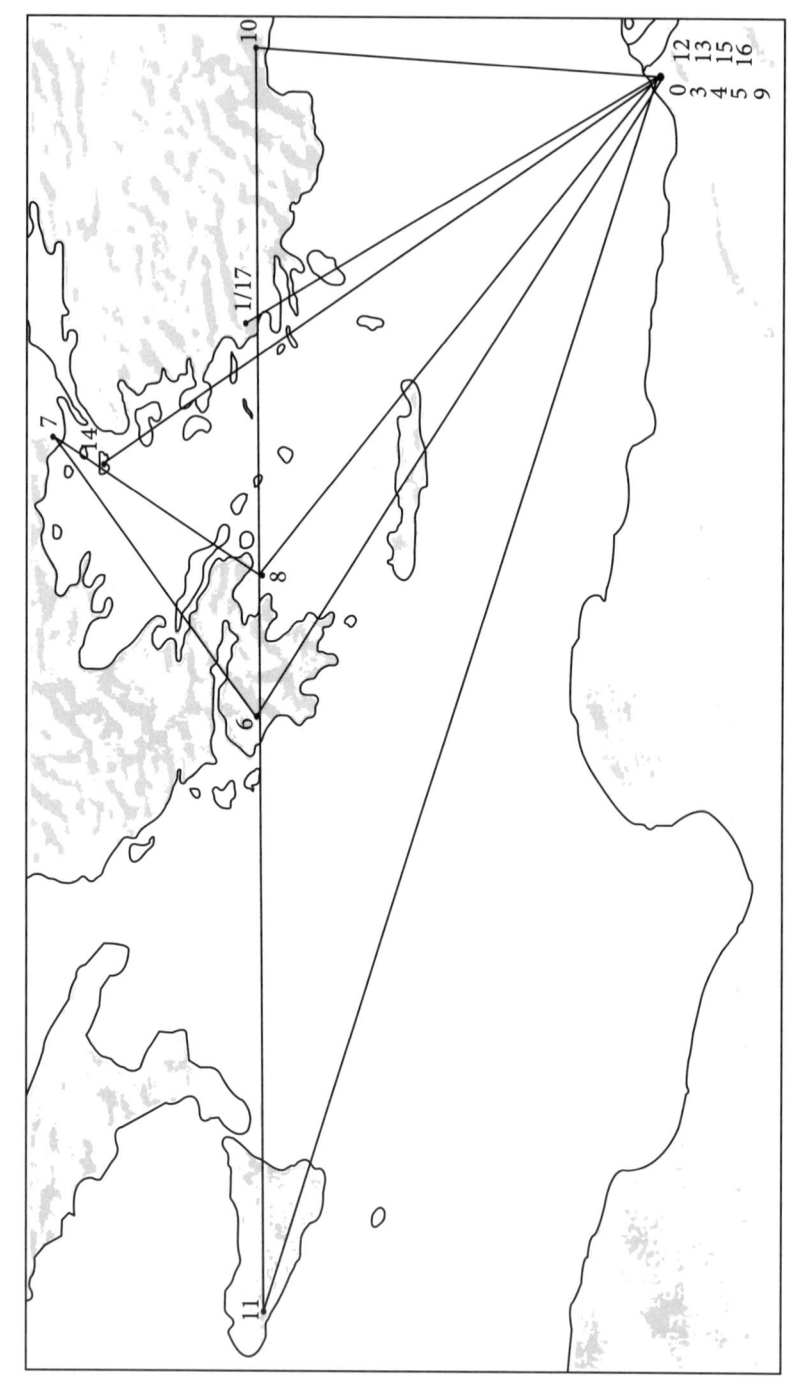

Fig. 8.3. Mind-traveling in *Iambi*: *0, 1*, Alexandria/Miletus; *2*, —; *3–5*, Alexandria; *6*, Olympia; *7*, Aenus (Thrace); *8*, Aegina; *9*, Alexandria; *10*, Aspendus (Pamphylia); *11*, Selinus; *12, 13*, Alexandria; *14*, Lemnos; *15, 16*, Alexandria; *17*, Miletus.

Hymn 2. In the *Hymn* (6) *to Demeter* and the *Hymn* (2) *to Apollo*, one could make the case even for generic settings, meaning that the rituals described have international and universal qualities that enable worshippers from different places to imagine the local rituals of the places where they or their parents used to worship. All this, however, by means of aetiology and the Ptolemaic voice present in many of these poems, would have directed the reader straight to the present and to the new regime with its Panhellenic aspirations.

As from so many other perspectives, the *Aetia* and the *Iambi* (and perhaps the *Hymns*) are also admirable compositions if we try to see them as a Panhellenic reader with the subtitle *What Does It Mean to Be Greek in Ptolemaic Alexandria?* Reading these texts must have triggered a powerful feeling of inclusion, entirely in line with the Ptolemies' attempts to create a new Greek ethnic identity. (See below.) From this perspective, poems such as the *Aetia*, the *Iambi*, and the *Hecale*, as far as Panhellenism is concerned, appear to mirror the aspirations of the royal dynasty that sponsored Callimachus and his poetic contemporaries.[23]

Occasionally, Panhellenism even shows up in the texts: near the end of *Aetia* 3, Callimachus tells a story that has surprised many readers because it involves Rome. The aetiological gist of the narrative that tells of the heroic bravery of the Roman Caius in battles against the barbarian Peucetii is not clear. The first verse of the episode, which is also the only (partly) surviving verse, turns the story into a model of bravery for "all Hellas": Ὧδε[....]γείνεσθε Πανελλάδος, ὧδε τελέ[σ]σαι. Although the antecedent of the genitive Πανελλάδος is lost,[24] the force of the appeal is rather obvious: it aims at inclusion. This is one of the very few stories in the *Aetia* about barbarians,[25] directed as an example toward a Panhellenic audience.[26] A notion of the unity of all Greeks is created, not least by the exclusive strategy of comparing them with two kinds of barbarians: the paradigmatic Caius and his Peucetian enemy.

---

[23] For the Panhellenism of the Successor kings, see Bosworth 2002: 246.
[24] Barber and Maas 1950 suggested Ὧδ' ἐ[σθλοί]; D'Alessio 2007:521 n. 29, Ὧδ' ἔ[ρκος].
[25] Perhaps similarly fr. 11.5–6 Pf. (the language of the Colchians contrasted with Greek).
[26] Compare Posidippus 116.8 AB: appeal to Ἑλλήνων θυγατέρες.

The famous Banquet of Pollis (frr. 178–85 Pf.) inscribes reading-acts of spatial geopoetics into the geopoetic text of the *Aetia* itself, thereby indicating at least one way in which Callimachus anticipated his readership. Here, the scene that Callimachus sketches out in order to introduce his lost aetiological narrative tells about the Panhellenic aspects of geopoetics: in Alexandria an immigrant from Athens, Pollis, celebrates Athenian holidays with all their religious connotations (fr. 178.1–4 Pf.), as many expatriate Athenians would have done. This man, however, also uses the holidays for a Panhellenic purpose, if one may exaggerate just slightly: he invites immigrants from other parts of Greece (fr. 178.5–7 Pf.).[27] Here they sit and drink, newly immigrated Alexandrians: the host, the Callimachean narrator Theugenes from Icos, and their peers. What are they talking about? Aetiological lore from the parts of Greece from which they come. The banqueters entertain one another with these stories, and this occasion provides the hook for Callimachus to hang his aetiological story on. Geographic diversity provides the background against which ethnic unity is celebrated. I take the entire scene to be a mirror for Callimachus' intended readers. Here, spatial geopoetics is shown, as it were, in action, humorously exaggerated, with its identity-enhancing implications.

The impact of spatial geopoetics is slightly different from that of political geopoetics: in the latter, behind the aetiological myth, a present becomes visible that is more Ptolemaic than it seems at first glance. In addition to aetiology in itself, this political present draws the audience into the story and, at the same time, makes the story relevant for Ptolemaic audiences. In order to experience the Ptolemaic present, all one needs to know is the name of the place and its strategic or political importance. Spatial geopoetics, on the other hand, creates a notion of the world in the reader's mind:[28] while following the text and trying to imagine where the narrative takes place in relation to the narratives preceding and following, the reader experiences a geopoetic version of a Ptolemaic world. This world is all-inclusive as far as Greek readers are concerned.[29]

---

[27] One wonders whether the hospitality theme present here and in other episodes of the *Aetia* (see Harder 2003: 298) also has some affinity with Ptolemaic self-presentation. See Herodas 1.26–32; Theocritus 14.58–68.

[28] This response presupposes readers, because the whole of the *Aetia* or *Iambi* has to be appreciated. Recitations of single episodes will not produce the same effect.

[29] See Hunter 1993: 152–169—e.g., p. 159 on the *Argonautica*: "the ultimate triumph of a Panhellenic crusade."

Chronopoetics: Creating Ptolemaic Time

Callimachus not only created (or made his readers imagine) a two-dimensional geopoetic version of the Ptolemaic empire. He also provided his readers, by similar poetic means, with a dimension in time. For the sake of terminological consistency, one might use the term "chronopoetics." Obviously, the constant aetiological references in all these poems are a common denominator not only of the *Aetia* but also of Callimachus' *Iambi* and *Hymns*. Even in his shorter, autonomous works—for example, the *Hecale* and the *Branchus*—aetiology is the background against which the stories unfold. The same is true for Apollonius' *Argonautica*, which, in part, reads like a string of aetiological stories explaining place names and cults along the shores of the Mediterranean. Both poets also authored full-blown κτίσεις, (aetiological) legends about the foundations of poleis and sanctuaries.[30] Nor was this interest in continuities a purely poetic phenomenon: in Hellenistic times, one finds a revival of interest in local history, often in the guise of restoring heroic cults, in many places.[31] As in the case of places and place names, it is preferable to explain aetiological lore on such a scale by something more specific than merely the term "antiquarianism."[32] Rather, it is the construction of continuities that aetiology aims at, of the feeling that the present is firmly rooted in the past. The sheer mass, the juxtaposition, and the chaotic arrangement of all the aetiological stories create a Panhellenic dimension of time that emerges from a common past and is both ethnically and politically inclusive.[33] This dimension is further enhanced by the many links between these stories, most of which have to do either with the Argonauts or with the Trojan War and its many aftermaths. The time structure of the *Aetia* would probably warrant a closer look.[34] Here, let it suffice to

---

[30] For Callimachus, among the lost prose works a collection of Κτίσεις νήσων καὶ πόλεων καὶ μετονομασίαι is attested (Pfeiffer 1949–1953: 1.339); for Apollonius we have scarce fragments of the κτίσεις of Alexandria, Caunus, Cnidos, Naucratis, Rhodes, and Lesbos (*Collectanea Alexandrina* ed. Powell, pp. 5–8; see, however, Krevans 2000: 83). Photius' summary of Conon (*Bibl.* cod. 186) may give an impression of this aetiological subgenre.

[31] See Alan Cameron 1995: 49, with material.

[32] See Harder 2003: 290–291 with nn. 1 and 5; Hunter and Fantuzzi 2004: 49–50. On the role of aetiology in general, see the excellent remarks of Stephens 2000: 208–209.

[33] One aspect of shared time is, of course, identity: compare Veyne 1983: 87, who understands aetiology as creating political identities.

[34] See the groundbreaking survey in Harder 2003: 296–299.

point out that, exactly as we have seen in the poem's geographical aspects, the juxtaposition of various eras creates a totality of time. In the *Aetia* there are episodes from all the major time layers of heroic myth (Heracles, Theseus, the Argonauts, the Trojan War, the *Odyssey*), interspersed with episodes from later times (e.g., the foundation myths of Sicilian cities in *Aetia* 2; Pasicles at Ephesus, who is datable to the mid-sixth century BC; and Simonides' tomb in *Aetia* 3), and, of course, the Ptolemaic layer of the events that frame the last two books.[35] Not by chance, the last episode of Book 4, *The Lock of Berenice* (fr. 110 Pf.) reaches into the reader's present. Therefore, besides the notion of continuous time that is typical for aetiological constructs,[36] readers experience an impression of a continuous stretch of interlocking time spans that reach from heroic times into their own present.[37] For them, the construct of a collective, Panhellenic memory of events and shared narratives emerges.

It is quite interesting to compare the time structure of the *Argonautica* with that of the *Aetia*: in the former, the notion of an evolving past, albeit narrated discontinuously, provides the temporal background to the geographic aspects of the story.[38] Apollonius, however, does not provide a focus for this evolution in the time of the reader. Except for the present implied by aetiologies (εἰσέτι καὶ νῦν...), no Ptolemaic perspective emerges directly from the story.[39] In Callimachus' *Aetia*, on the other hand, although there is no notion of an evolution or of a transformation of mythological time, all the discontinuous stories, taken together, add up to cover more or less the entire history of Greece, ending in and culminating at Ptolemaic Alexandria. (Fifth-century Athens is marked by silence.) Thus, in an unexpected way,

---

[35] As far as I can see, only the fifth and fourth centuries are not covered. It would be rewarding to investigate the time structure of the *Aetia* in light of what we know about Hellenistic chronography. Damastus of Sigeum (5 *FGrHist*) comes to mind.

[36] Compare Stephens 2000: 208, who links the prominence of aetiology in Alexandrian poetry to "the colonizing dimension of the Ptolemaic rule."

[37] Hunter 1993: 162–169 has made a similar point for the less obvious time structure of the *Argonautica*.

[38] See Clauss 2000: 20 and passim, who describes the "evolutionary" concept of time in Apollonius.

[39] Compare Hunter 1993: 105; and Stephens 2000: 203–204, who considers the *Argonautica* to provide a Ptolemaic past. Even in her view, however, Apollonius would be working with analogues rather than with an explicit Ptolemaic focus. See also Stephens 2003: 171–237.

the *Aetia* does create history.[40] In this sense, Ovid's *Metamorphoses* is even closer to the *Aetia* than one would expect at first glance. (One wonders about the time structure of Nicander's *Heteroeumena*, too.)[41] As was the case with the dimension of space, the *Iambi* allows for an even stronger sense of an Alexandrian present than does the *Aetia*. On the other hand this present is less closely tied to the Ptolemies. In the *Hymns*, most clearly in the mimetic ones, the continuity of myth and present is obvious, because they are essentially prayers.

Through the dimensions of both time and space, Callimachus' works delivered to the Greek reader of his day a certain notion of being included. Geopoetics and chronopoetics combined not only refer to the Ptolemaic empire in an affirmative way. They also create a literary analogue of the ideological pretensions of this empire: namely to be the only legitimate present that emerges from the string of stories and, thus, to aspire to Panhellenic power in the created geographical space.

Two visual testimonies illustrate how well this fits in with an imperial notion of space and time on behalf of the Ptolemies: first, the famous procession of Ptolemy II paraded personifications of Panhellenic space (see below, n. 58) and time. (Mentioned are the Morning Star, the Evening Star, the Year, the Penteris.)[42] Second, the so-called Archelaus Relief features two persons as allegories of inhabited space (*oikoumene*) and of time—and these seem to be cryptoportraits of Arsinoe III and Ptolemy IV.[43]

Ptolemaic Exclusions: Writing Out Egypt

I hope that it has become evident how one may read some of Callimachus' works as an attempt to create a Greek cosmos for Greek readers. The geopoetic practice is, without a doubt, targeted at creating a Panhellenic experience through the act of reading. From this perspective,

---

[40] Compare, again, Hunter 1993: 166–168: "The 'creation of history' is indeed a prime concern of Ptolemaic poetry, as it must have been of the Ptolemies themselves."

[41] Frr. 38–67 Gow and Scholfield: at least, fr. 40 mentions Battus; all others are about purely mythological characters. Nonetheless, chronological order is quite an obvious way to arrange such material. Of Parthenius' *Metamorphoses* too little is left (fr. 24 Lightfoot) to infer anything about an underlying structure.

[42] See D.J. Thompson 2000: 375–376, who reads the symbolism rather as referring to "festival time." See p. 376 for an Antiochian parallel.

[43] See I. Petrovic 2006: 19, 20 n. 28.

this kind of poetry is Ptolemaic to a degree that transcends the level of conventional court poetry: here, continuity in time and geographical comprehensiveness combine to create an inclusive universe of Ptolemaic space and time.[44]

Nonetheless, as the Peucetii fragment noted above demonstrates, there are also exclusive strategies at work here. This is made clear by the almost complete absence of contemporary Egypt or Egyptians in Alexandrian poetry. In all of what is left of Callimachus, there is only one aetiological story that deals with the legendary Egyptian king Busiris (fr. 44 Pf.). This story began with the word *Aiguptos*. Nonetheless, since the story is about Heracles killing Busiris, it must remain uncertain whether there was much of contemporary Egypt in it. I suspect that the story goes back to Herodotus (2.45) rather than to Egyptian lore. A parallel case is the mention of Egypt as the direction of the cranes' flight (in the crane metaphor in the *Prologue*: fr. 1.13 Pf.), which adapts a Homeric simile (*Iliad* 3.3–6—where Egypt is not explicitly mentioned, however). This was part of the traditional Greek image of Egypt. Aside from these, we come across only three minor mentions of Egypt and Egyptians.[45] When Callimachus mentions Egyptian gods in his dedicatory epigrams, these are of course Hellenized: Isis is the daughter of Inachus—that is, identified with Io.[46] The Ptolemies at Alexandria are never mentioned within any explicit Egyptian framework.

Apart from those mentioned, there are no unambiguous references to Egypt or Egyptians in Callimachus: no Egyptian names of persons or places, no descriptions or explanations of Egyptian rituals, and, most remarkably, no mention of Egyptian myths. Although some of this lore would have been accessible in Greek (e.g., through Manetho's work on Egyptian festivals, or even Herodotus' Egyptian *logos*),[47] Callimachus leaves all this untouched in his poems, especially in the *Aetia* and *Iambi*. The same is true for the so-called grammatical writings, many of which assemble long lists of oddities concerning place names

---

[44] For a general description of such constructive practices among the Successor kings, see Bosworth 2002: 4.

[45] The only real one is the δρόμος ἱερὸς Ἀνούβιδος (fr. 715 Pf.). An allusion to the Apis bull (fr. 154.16 *SH*; compare fr. 655 Pf.) and the Nile in fr. 384 Pf. are part of "intertextual Egypt"; see Stephens 2003: 10. A fourth instance would be the probably spurious fr. 811 Pf.

[46] Sarapis in *Ep.* 37 Pf. = 56 GP; Isis-Io in *Ep.* 57 Pf. = 18 GP.

[47] Manetho: *FGrHist* 609 F 14, 15 (Περὶ ἑορτῶν).

or remarkable phenomena (*paradoxa*) concerning some river or place. The place names are collected from all over Greece, but unless I am mistaken, not a single one among them is Egyptian.

What about his fellow court poets, then? Apollonius' heroes leave relics and foundations wherever they travel, from the Black Sea coast to modern Serbia and Libya, but they never touch Egyptian soil.[48] Once, Apollonius refers to Egyptian priests, but his remark reads more like a reference to Herodotus than to the real-life possibility of consulting with actual Egyptian priests;[49] in fact, this probably is a reference to Herodotus.[50] Theocritus mentions Egyptians, once, as criminals who used to rob and murder Greek travelers at night until Ptolemy II put an end to this (*Idyll* 15.46–50). Otherwise, as a Theocritean scholar once remarked: "Theocritus seems to participate...with Callimachus in a conspiracy never to reveal that Egypt is not a Greek land" (Griffiths 1979: 85). Today, we would make an exception for poems that touch upon kingship ideology.[51] The new Posidippus does not change the picture, either: in this collection, one finds a number of fairly adulatory epigrams, mostly referring to Berenice's victories and Arsinoe's sanctuary. However, this is all arranged into a strictly Greek, even Pindaric, framework.[52] Egypt is mentioned only once (*Ep.* 115.3 AB), without reference to cultural elements at all. In Alexandria itself, however, let alone farther south, contemporary Egypt was by no means invisible (Scheidel 2004: 25). In other words, the court poets seem to exclude non-Greek traditions and surroundings in their poems. The poetic practice of exclusion is intended to create a fictitious contemporary world that is exclusively Greek. To this poetic world, then, are added aspects of space and time by the geopoetic strategies that I have described above.

---

[48] Compare, however, Stephens 2000: 198–203, who explores Egyptian connotations of both Colchis and Libya in Apollonius.

[49] *Argon.* 4.259–60. See Stephens 2000: 210; Scherer 2006: 26; compare Hunter 1993: 164. Behind the remark about Sesostris (*Argon.* 4.272–79) there may stand Herodotus, too (2.103.2–104.1; see Stephens 2000: 199).

[50] See Clauss 2000: 27. What we are facing here is "intertextual Egypt" (Stephens' concept; see, e.g., 2002b: 245): that is, knowledge on Egypt taken from the Greek tradition; and for Herodotus, Pelling 1990: 50.

[51] Especially *Idyll* 17; see Stephens 2003: 122–170.

[52] Compare *Epigrams* (Austin and Bastianini) 74 (Callicrates and the Theoi Adelphoi), 78 (Olympic victories of Ptolemies), 79 (of Berenice, parallel to *Aetia* 3 *init.*); perhaps 80–82, 87, 88. *Epigrams* *113 and *114 are dedicatory, written for the dynasty. *Epigram* 119 is about Arsinoe Zephyritis; *141, about Berenice I. See also Stephens 2004a: 81–85 and 2005: 234.

This is not to deny that Ptolemaic kingship ideology has, partly, a pharaonic background, as, among others, Ludwig Koenen, Daniel Selden, and, most recently, Susan Stephens have convincingly shown.[53] Doubtless, Hellenistic court poets integrated Egyptian elements of pharaonic ideology into their praise of contemporary kings.[54] The practice, however, seems to have been on the one hand quite restricted; on the other hand we sense a desire on the part of the poets to keep these passages understandable in purely Greek terms.[55] To adopt Stephens' metaphor, it may be possible to see double sometimes, but it is hardly ever necessary.

Conclusion: Panhellenic Poetry for Ptolemaic Readers

Geopoetic and chronopoetic practices appeal to (or sometimes even create) Panhellenic identities.[56] As such, one can understand these poetic practices as conceptually framed by the dynasty's ideological Panhellenism[57] (as demonstrated by, e.g., the Museum, and performed, e.g., in the famous procession of Ptolemy II).[58] In addition, the creation and use of Panhellenic concepts tallies well with Ptolemaic measures to unify the heterogeneous Greek population in Egypt, while

---

[53] See, e.g., Koenen 1993: 81–113; Selden 1998: 331–354, 401–402; Stephens 2003: 74–121 (on Callimachus).

[54] In Callimachus, the pertinent texts are mainly passages in the *Hymns* to Zeus, Apollo, and Delos, and *The Lock of Berenice*. The texts have been most recently discussed in Stephens 2003: 74–121.

[55] A typical case: *Hymn* 1.87–88 has parallels in Egyptian hymnic language (Stephens 2003: 112 n. 114) but also in Greek: compare *Homeric Hymn to Hermes* 17–19, 43–46. Thus, Egyptian hymnic language influenced Greek probably already earlier.

[56] Therefore, archaic Panhellenism (see, e.g., Nagy 1990: 37) may have suggested itself for references.

[57] See the brief and excellent remarks in Hunter 2006a: 5–6.

[58] The Museum: e.g., Cambiano 1988: 82; Erskine 1995: 42–43; Too 1998: 122–123; Shipley 2000: 242–243; Asper 2001: 101.

The Grand Procession: according to Callixenus (*FGrHist* 627 F 2, quoted by Athenaeus) the symbolism of the procession was definitely Greek and decidedly Panhellenic. Compare, e.g., 201e: προσηγορεύοντο δὲ πόλεις αἵ τε ἀπ' Ἰωνίας καὶ ⟨αἱ⟩ λοιπαὶ Ἑλληνίδες ὅσαι τὴν Ἀσίαν καὶ τὰς νήσους κατοικοῦσαι ὑπὸ τοὺς Πέρσας ἐτάχθησαν ("They were called by the names of cities, some from Ionia, and the rest Greek, as many as were established in Asia and on the islands and were ruled by the Persians"). Here, we get a glimpse of the combination of Panhellenism and liberation ideology. On the Greeks as target audience, see Rice 1983: 106–107; D.J. Thompson 2000: 368; implicitly Hazzard 2000: 66–75.

at the same time maintaining to a large extent the separation of Greeks and Egyptians in social and institutional terms.[59]

To return to the beginning: besides the poetic qualities of these poems, their Panhellenic appeal to an all-Greek readership may well have been the reason that made them interesting to so many readers. They conjured up and transported a certain identity. Geopoetic design and chronopoetic perspective made them carriers of Panhellenic concepts that were by no means restricted to Ptolemaic readers.[60] Romans and cultural Greeks of imperial times may have reacted to these inclusive features in an even stronger way. Paradoxically, it was perhaps precisely those elements in Alexandrian poetry that reacted to the specific historical context of their primary audiences that made them become classics.

---

[59] This separation marked a change from the interior politics of Ptolemy I and probably reached its peak during the reign of Ptolemy II. (Compare Hazzard 2000: 108-9.) See Shipley 2000: 219-223; on separation and Greek ethnic heterogeneity, see Asper 2001: 97-101 and 2004: 14-20; Scheidel 2004: 25. The matter is, however, controversial: compare, e.g., Gruen 2006: 308-312.

[60] One could perhaps even understand the intertextual richness of the texts in question, often seen as their distinctive feature, as being a part of chronopoetics.

CHAPTER NINE

CALLIMACHUS ON KINGS AND KINGSHIP

Silvia Barbantani

Abstract

In *Aetia* fr. 1.3–5 Pfeiffer Callimachus complains that his adversaries, the Telchines, accuse him of not writing "one continuous poem in many thousands of verses," celebrating "kings and heroes." Callimachus did choose to celebrate kings and heroes, but in poetry that is subtle, brief, allusive, learned, and ironic. Contemporary kings occur particularly in the hymns to Zeus, Apollo, and Delos, while queens are more prominent in the *Aetia*. Hesiod is Callimachus' most important Greek model in constructing an image of the just king from whom wealth, prosperity and peace flow. A number of scholars have also argued that Egyptian models of kingship may be in play as well, though filtered through Greek texts.

In one of the most controversial passages in the *Prologue* to his *Aetia* (fr. 1.3–5 Pf. = 1 M.), Callimachus complains that his adversaries, the Telchines, accuse him of not writing "one continuous poem in many thousands of verses" celebrating "kings and heroes." This is generally understood to mean contemporary kings and heroes of old. The Telchines, then, identify two main strategies of a narrative poem: the mythical (chosen by Apollonius in his *Argonautica*) and the historical,[1] in praise of living kings. What Callimachus rejects is not the content proposed by the Telchines but the modality of treatment of this material: a single lengthy poem, describing in detail, and possibly in chronological order, deeds of the protagonist. Callimachus did choose to celebrate kings and heroes, but in poetry that is subtle, short, allusive, learned, and ironic, without the overt adulation of encomia or the grand style of epic. Contemporary kings occur, particularly in the hymns to Zeus, Apollo, and Delos, but only rarely in the *Aetia*, where queens are more prominent, if we are to judge from the extant fragments. Hesiod is Callimachus' most important Greek model in constructing an image of the just king from whom wealth, prosperity,

[1] See, for example, POxy 30.2520, an epic poem on Philip II.

and peace flow. A number of scholars have also argued that Egyptian models of kingship may be in play as well, though filtered through Greek texts.

The Aetia

Poems for Berenice II, the daughter of Magas, king of Cyrene, who married Ptolemy III Euergetes, open Book 3 and close Book 4 of the *Aetia*. In *The Victory of Berenice*, which opens *Aetia* 3 (fr. 383 Pf. + SH 268C), Ptolemy II Philadelphus occurs only tangentially, joined with his sister-wife, Arsinoe II, as the dynastic parents of Berenice II with the title "Sibling Gods."[2] After the marriage with his sister, but probably only after her death in 270 or 268 BC, Ptolemy II assumed the title of Philadelphus and was worshipped together with his spouse.[3] It has been argued that Ptolemaic endogamy should be seen only as an Egyptian phenomenon, though the poets look to Zeus and Hera for a model of the sibling marriage.[4] Probably Egyptian royal ideals resonate with Ptolemaic politics. Certainly conjugal love is exploited as a royal virtue, as it guarantees the birth of a legitimate successor.

Ptolemy III appears in *The Lock of Berenice* (fr. 110 Pf.), the elegy that closes the *Aetia*, not so much as a victorious warrior (as he is portrayed in the Adulis and Canopus decrees, *OGIS* 54 and 56) but as the beloved spouse of Berenice II, who with the sacrifice of her lock and her ardent prayers obtains his safe homecoming after his victory in the Third Syrian War. Conjugal love between the rulers, the true subject of the poem, is stressed as a guarantee of dynastic stability. In Catullus' version of *The Lock of Berenice* Ptolemy appears as a successful warrior as well as the object of his wife's affection, and his enterprises are presented mainly from the woman's point of view (*Carmen* 66.11-12, 20, 35-36). The same royal couple may have been mentioned in the first

---

[2] Line 3: κασιγνήτων...θεῶν. The only other place where a similar epithet appears, Philadelphoi, is the ambiguous fr. 507 Pf.: φιλαδελφίων† ἄτμενος †ᾗ ἀδείμων. See Lehnus 1996b: 146-147; D'Alessio 2007: 710-711; Pfeiffer (comm. ad loc.) considers it part of an elegy for a courtier.

[3] Also in plastic arts: see the monument dedicated to the Siblings by Callicrates at Olympia *OGIS* 26 and 27; Hintzen-Bohlen 1992: 77-81).

[4] Koenen 1993: 161-164; Carney 1987; Criscuolo 1990; Ager 2005; Rolandi 2006; however, according to Hazzard 2000, the main concern of Philadelphus in marrying his sister was not to conform to pharaonic habits but to gather around himself the dispersed family descended from the "Savior Gods", *Theoi Soteres*, Ptolemy I Soter and his wife Berenice I.

line of *Aetia* 4 (fr. 86.1 Pf.), Μοῦ]σαί μοι βασιλη[ἀεί]δειν, and they certainly occur in the *Epilogue* of the *Aetia* (fr. 112.8 Pf.), where the poet asks Zeus to protect the house of his lords (presumably Ptolemy III and Berenice II), whom he designates by the lofty Homeric term ἀνάκτων ("lords"). But nowhere in what we have of the *Aetia* does the king seem to be singled out as an individual; rather he is present only as part of the royal couple.

Fragmentary Poems

Although we know from Posidippus' *Hippica* that Ptolemaic kings were passionate competitors in the equestrian games (PMilVogl 8.309), we have no epinician elegy by Callimachus for a king. In the elegiac epinician for the powerful courtier Sosibius (fr. 384 Pf.), the monarch remains in the background as a recipient of the glory earned by his loyal and beneficent subject (ll. 53–58).[5] Sosibius won in the double run (*diaulos*: fr 384.39–41 Pf.), probably at the Ptolemaia, the festival instituted in honor of Ptolemy I.[6] In the poem Callimachus pays homage to the deceased and deified Soter, father of the reigning king, addressing him directly at lines 40–41: Λαγείδη, παρὰ σοὶ πρῶτον ἀεθλοφορεῖν | εἱλάμεθα, Πτολεμαῖε, τεῇ π[...]ρ ἡνίκ᾽ ἐλεγχ[("We chose to compete for the first time [in the *diaulos*] by you, O Lagid Ptolemy, when to you...O F[athe]r ?..."). In another fragment (fr. 388 Pf.), which may have been a epinician for Berenice II, there is mention of her wedding and her heroic deeds. In *The Victory of Berenice* the married queen had already been adopted by the Sibling Gods, but in this poem she is still unmarried, and her natural father, Magas, the king of Cyrene and Ptolemy II's half brother, is named (l. 8). The *basileus* appearing at lines 3–4, however,]. νη βασιλῆα σὲ...πρ.[.]. δ᾽ ἀκρω[|]...πάντων πά[ν]τα τελειότατε ("king...most wholly accomplished of all"), might as easily refer to Zeus, the king of the gods (Call. *Hymn* 1.57), as to the Cyrenaean sovereign.

The name of Ptolemy II, who was responsible for the suppression of a Celtic mercenaries' revolt in Egypt, does not appear in the extant frag-

---

[5] Cf. the praise of an officer in SP 3.111 (third century BC; see Parsons 1996; C. Austin and Stigka 2007): among other virtues, he is φιλοβασιλεὺς...ἐν πίστει μέγας...φιλέλλην ("king's friend...great in trust...philhellene").

[6] The festival is not named, but the most likely hypothesis is that Callimachus refers to the Ptolemaia; see D'Alessio 2007: 687 n. 23.

ments of the *Galatea*, but the Celtic king Brennus, leader of the hordes attacking Delphi in 279 BC, is prominently named in a fragment attributed to the same poem (fr. 379 Pf.): "[the warriors] whom Brennus guided from the western sea to overthrow the Greeks." Although there are only a few lines surviving, the mythological context seems clear: Galatea was the Nereid mother of Galatas, the eponymous ancestor of the Galatians (also called Gauls, or Celts); therefore it is reasonable to imagine that hiding under a mythological veil were the recent events of the Galatic Wars (280–278 BC).[7] The Galatians are featured again in the *Hymn to Delos*, where their defeat in Greece and in Egypt is seen as righting the cosmic order. In that hymn Callimachus adopts a majestic, celebratory tone suitable to the genre; in the *Galatea* he may have chosen an aetiological approach to the contemporary event.

The Hymns

Callimachus' most explicit praise of kings is to be found in the first (*To Zeus*), second (*To Apollo*), and fourth (*To Delos*) of the six hymns of his collection. These are balanced by three others devoted to female deities, possibly representing aspects of the royal women (see Depew 2004.) Like encomia, the hymns included a narrative section, the aretalogy of the god, or a specific episode of his or her life.[8] The development of a royal dynastic theology and the proliferation of civic cults in honor of the Benefactor and Savior Gods contributed to blurring the boundary between the two genres.[9] Hymns refer clearly to the Ptolemaic court pantheon, with any shift between analogy and identification of gods and rulers often being imperceptible.[10]

---

[7] So Pfeiffer 1949–1953: 1.xxxix, followed by Fraser 1972: 1.659; Meillier 1979: 55; Nachtergael 1977: 184–185; Petzl 1984; Bing 1998b; and D'Alessio 2007: 675 n. 1. Alan Cameron 1995: 66, 281–282, suggested that the poem was performed in the competition of the Soteria in Delphi. Frr. 378 and 379 Pf. also belong to the poem; Livrea 1998: 31–33 has found a possible echo of the *Galatea* in late-antique poetry. On the sources of the Galatea myth, see Pfeiffer 1949–1953: 1.304–5; Lightfoot 1999: 531–535.

[8] Pavese 1991: 169–173; on the relationship between *Idyll* 17 and the *Homeric Hymns*, see Gow 1950: 2.325; Cairns 1972: 106.

[9] On the royal cult organized by the poleis, see Habicht 1970; Gauthier 1985: 39–53; Bringmann 1993: 7–24 and 1995.

[10] Hunter and Fuhrer 2002: 164–175. Bing 1988b: 126 was the first to argue that *Hymns* 2 and 3 are companion pieces; cf. Erler 1987. *Hymn* 3.121–37, modeled on Hes. *Op*. 225–247, offers again a model for the good king.

Only in the *Hymn to Delos* is the identification of the monarch certain. Ptolemy II Philadelphus is easily recognizable by virtue of his birth on Cos. For the *Hymn to Zeus* and the *Hymn to Apollo* the identity of the monarch is uncertain. However, in each of these three hymns the poet articulates a facet of his own poetics: "praise poetry involves a negotiation of identity and authority; on the part of the poet, it involves the ability to recognize, represent and embellish the god's status and prior relationship to the poet and the group for whom s/he speaks. On the part of the god, hymns set out to construct a divine complicity in the performance of praise itself" (Depew 2004: 118). The court poet could not choose a better occasion to advertise his own authority and value as a servant of the Muses than with a hymn or encomium to the king and to the gods who grant the ruler power, riches, and prosperity, therefore obliging him to extend generosity toward his loyal ministers and subjects, including poets. (On the virtues praised in hymns, see Weber 1993: 204–243.)

The Hymn to Zeus

Hymn 1, the shortest, typifies Callimachus' rejection of long works in honor of kings and heroes.[11] When it comes to praise of the greatest deity, Zeus, the poet bids an abrupt farewell (*Hymn* 1.91, 94),[12] refusing to deal with the god's innumerable *erga*—after all, who could (l. 92)? There has been considerable debate on the date of the poem, on the identification of the king hidden under the character of the titular god, and on the role of the poet as speaker of truth, as presented in lines 1–9 and 55–69.

The hymn is generally interpreted as a celebration of Philadelphus' accession to coregency with his father, Ptolemy Soter,[13] on 12 Dystrus

---

[11] For general comments: McLennan 1977; Hopkinson 1984b; Clauss 1986; Haslam 1993; Stephens 2003: 77–114. On the hymn's sources, see Cozzoli 2006. On the many voices of the poet in this hymn, see Lüddecke 1998. On Zeus's birth, see Ambühl 2005: 235–245.

[12] This happens also in the *Hymn to Apollo*, where the god himself cuts the poem short by kicking away Phthonos; see Haslam 1993: 115–116.

[13] Iust. 16.2.7. See Clauss 1986: 155–170; Stephens 2003 and 1998: 171–183; *contra*, Meillier 1979: 61–78; Laronde 1987: 366; Carrière 1969. According to Lehnus 1993: 76, Callimachus was probably born in 303 BC; therefore he was a younger contemporary of his patron, Ptolemy II.

285 BC (= 15/16 December).¹⁴ These events coincided with the Basileia, an Alexandrian festival in honor of Zeus Basileus.¹⁵ The incipit of the hymn, inviting libation (ll. 1-2), suggests the context of a symposium (whether fictional or a formal court gathering), which traditionally opened with three libations: one to Olympian Zeus, one to the Heroes, and one to Zeus Soter.¹⁶ Zeus appears immediately as a great and eternal ἄναξ whose earthly hypostasis is the ruler. If the hymn was created for and performed at the ceremony of accession, the king was likely to be present.

Ptolemy Philadelphus was elevated to coregent despite being the youngest of several brothers: Magas and Ptolemy Ceraunus were sons of Ptolemy Soter and Eurydice, whereas Ptolemy II was the issue of Soter and his second wife, Berenice I. Inserting the myth of Zeus's accession to the throne (ll. 55-62), Callimachus rejects the Homeric tradition of the division of cosmic power through drawing lots (*Il.* 15.186-93; cf. Pind. *Ol.* 7.54), following instead the Hesiodic tradition (*Theog.* 881-885) whereby Zeus's brothers, Hades and Poseidon, spontaneously offer him supreme power.¹⁷ Callimachus, like Hesiod (*Theog.* 453-457, 478) makes Zeus younger than Poseidon and Hades, whereas according to Homer Zeus is older than Poseidon (*Il.* 13.355, 15.166).¹⁸ If this really is a reference to Philadelphus' rule, the poem

---

[14] So Koenen 1977; Clauss 1986. Alexander may have been crowned at the Basileia in Memphis in 331 BC. According to Weber 1993: 172, the Basileia as royal festival was founded as a commemoration of the death of Ptolemy I (dead in 283/2).

[15] Ptolemy II's accession as sole ruler was celebrated in 282 BC, some weeks later than the Basileia: that is, on 25 Dystrus 282 BC (6/7 January), the same coronation day as his father. (See Koenen 1977: 58-62 and 1993: 73 n. 114.) He reigned alone from 282 to 246 BC.

[16] Cf. Athen. 15.692f-693c; *Paean Erythraeus in Seleucum* Powell, *CA* 140.1: opening libations to Apollo; Pindar *Isthm.* 6.8-9 and *Prosodion* fr. 89a SM.

[17] In the Augustan age, the tradition reemerges in Egypt in one of the four epigrams on the Pillar of Ptolemagrius from Panopolis (Bernand 1969: no. 114): the poems are a Hellenistic *summa* of royal theology, presenting the Roman emperor as Zeus King of the World: of these four epigrams, the first is dedicated to Poseidon and recalls the division of the world among the three divine brothers; the second, to Zeus "Caesar" αὐτοκράτωρ, βασιλεύς, king of the universe; the third, to Ares (the poet presents himself as a servant, or θεράπων, of Caesar and Ares); and the fourth, to Pan and Apollo. See Criscuolo 2000, www.telemaco.unibo.it/epigr/agrios.htm.

[18] McLennan 1977: 95-99. The discrepancy may be due to the fact that Poseidon and Hades, though older than Zeus, were vomited up (reborn) later by Cronus thanks to Zeus's intervention. As Clauss 1986 noticed, Callimachus' poem is also heavily indebted to the *Homeric Hymn to Hermes*: the reconciliation between Apollo and Hermes in *HH Hermes* 423b-35 is due to Hermes' singing a theogony.

must date from very soon after his accession to the throne. Ptolemy II's older half brothers resented their father's choice and contested Philadelphus' position after Soter's death. The hymn treats subjects suitable to an early date—the birth and the accession of Zeus to power—and his just rule can be understood as both an *aition* and a wish for the young king. Zeus is given royal prerogatives in spite of the fact that he is presented as a newborn child in the first half of the hymn: he is addressed as "Father Zeus"(*Hymn* 1.7, 43) at the very moment when the beginning of his life is narrated. However, there are only faint allusions to his deeds (ll. 3, 57, 66–67). Wilamowitz (1924: 2.11), followed by many other scholars, read in Callimachus' refusal to sing of Zeus's *erga* a hint of the very young age of the actual dedicatee of the poem, Ptolemy II, who at the time of the hymn had no exploits yet.

Apollonius also treats the birth of Zeus and the establishment of his power in the *Argonautica* (1.507–11, 730–34; 2.1233–34). The collection of *Homeric Hymns* does not include a major hymn to Zeus although Pindar composed one (fr. 29 SM). It is possible that Pindar's hymn was placed first in the Hellenistic edition of his poems,[19] and its aporetic incipit may well have inspired Callimachus. The topos of doubt is similarly part of the fragmentary *Homeric Hymn to Dionysus*, which likewise stands first in the collection of the *Homeric Hymns*.[20] Other allusions to previous and contemporary literature are detectable in the opening lines of the poem: line 5, ἐν δοιῆι μάλα θυμός ("my heart is in doubt"), coincides with line 1 of the *Hymn to Eros* by Antagoras of Rhodes, a contemporary poet active at the court of Antigonus Gonatas.[21] At line 8, Κρῆτες ἀεὶ ψεῦσται was attributed in antiquity to Epimenides of Crete,[22] but this proverb also echoes the contemporary views of Euhemerus, who also appears in Callimachus' *Iambus* 1 (Spyridakis 1968).

---

[19] Fantuzzi and Hunter 2004: 371. D'Alessio 2005 and 2009 thinks that Pindar's *Hymn* 1 was dedicated to Apollo. Cf. also Pind. *Pyth.* 1, where the cosmic order created by Zeus is kept by the tyrant Hieron, victor over the barbarians; cf. Hunter and Fuhrer 2002: 168–172.

[20] The *Hymn to Dionysus* opens with various false traditions of the god's birth to which the poet contrasts his own true one, rejecting the ψευδόμενοι (l. 6). This hymn stands first in the Homeric collection in the best codex, the Mosquensis (West 2001).

[21] McLennan 1977: 31–32. Cuypers 2004: 96–101 reads this hymn as an Academic antagonist to the Stoic celebration of Zeus by Aratus and Cleanthes.

[22] Cuypers 2004: 102–105. Epimenides probably is also alluded to in *Iambus* 12. On the weight of the Epimenidean tradition in Callimachus, see Cozzoli 2006: 124–128.

The main model for Callimachus is Hesiod, who describes the birth of Zeus in *Theogony* 467–506 and treats justice and kingship both human and divine in his *Works and Days*. That Hesiod had always been a central model for Callimachus is evident from the dream sequence that follows the *Prologue* of the *Aetia*, where Callimachus recalls the Boeotian poet at the moment of his poetic investiture.[23] Hesiod, the ancient "servant of the Muses" consecrated on Mount Helicon, became a point of reference for all the Alexandrian poets. Hesiod was the first to sanction with his poetic *auctoritas* the interdependent relationships among kings, Muses, and poets,[24] and to have provided the image of the city governed justly.[25]

The heavily Hesiodic elements in Callimachus' *Hymn to Zeus* (esp. ll. 79–90) find a resonance in a later *Hymn to Isis* of Isidorus found in Egypt.[26] In Isidorus the kings who abide with Isis are rich, powerful, victorious, and bringers of domestic peace. Similar Hesiodic echoes occur in Theocritus *Idyll* 17.77–120. "Both poems [Isidorus' and Theocritus'] clearly reflect both traditional Greek ideas and aspects of Egyptian royal ideology, and they shed light upon a kind of lingua franca of praise which turns up in many different guises all over the Hellenistic world."[27] In Apollonius' *Argonautica* (4.110, 1177–79, 1201–2), Alcinous is an earthly manifestation of Zeus's pure justice, as his wise sister-wife Arete is an avatar of Hera.

Truth and lies.

Ancient poets were true in no respect. They said that the son of Cronus divided the residences in three, drawing lots. But who would leave to chance the possession of Olympus or Hades, except an utter fool? In fact it is reasonable to chance for equal portions, but those are worlds apart. May my fictions persuade the listener's ear! Not chance was it that made you lord of the gods, but the deeds of your hands, your might, and the power that you placed next your throne.

Callimachus *Hymn* 1.60–67

---

[23] Fr. 2 Pf. = 4 M.; *Scholia Florentina* 16–19; *AP* 7.42. See Wilamowitz 1924: 2.92–96; Bing 1998b: 70–71; Alan Cameron 1995: 362–371; Pretagostini 1995b: 168–171. Dependence on Hesiod: Reinsch-Werner 1976: 24–73.

[24] *Theog.* 80–103. See Brillante 1994: 14–26; Hunter 1996: 81.

[25] *Op.* 213–247. A testimony to Hesiod's significance as a master of wisdom in linking civil harmony and the fertility of the land comes from a stele on Mt. Helicon dated to the third century BC: see Hurst 1996: 57–71; Veneri 1996: 73–86.

[26] See especially Isid. *Hy.* 3.1–18; Vanderlip 1972: 49–50.

[27] Fantuzzi and Hunter 2004: 352–354. Callimachus reuses the same Hesiodic passage in *Hymn* 3.121–35.

Callimachus here adapts the proem of the *Theogony* to create his own conception of truth poetry.[28] The power of poetry to convey truth, but also lies that can disguise some elements of truth, is a particularly important issue for a court poet, because it bears on the veracity and value of his statements about the nature of monarchy. The hymn is structured around two lies: in the first section of the hymn Callimachus exposes the lie of the Cretans on the birth of Zeus (*Hymn* 1.4–14); in the second, the lie of the acquisition of power by Zeus (ll. 55–65). The first claim, against a Euhemerist interpretation of the gods, comes early in the poem and lays the foundations for the poem's second part, where the poet articulates the kingly attributes of Zeus and the divine attributes of the human king. Moreover, the statements about poetic doubt, truth telling, and lies (ll. 7–8, 65–66) acquire a new light if considered from the perspective of the Egyptian world that Ptolemy now ruled as pharaoh at the same time as he ruled the Greeks as *basileus*: "He [Callimachus] presents himself as devising fictions, as experimenting with a variety of inherited traditions in order to construct a lineation for the king of the Nile, who is neither Greek nor Egyptian, but both."[29]

A bicultural monarchy. So far I have concentrated on Ptolemy as a Greek king, but he ruled over Egypt and Egyptians as well as Greeks. A number of scholars (most recently Susan Stephens, in the greatest detail) have argued that Callimachus deliberately fashioned his *Hymn to Zeus* in conformity with features of Egyptian cosmology salient for kingship:

> Arcadia provides a primordial Greek landscape for Zeus' birth, the contours of which are made to resemble Egypt, in that the arid land comes to be watered at the time of the birth of the divine child. The Cretan landscape has associations with Near Eastern dying gods on the one hand, but also the Euhemerist tradition that demotes the Olympic pantheon to culture heroes.

In Callimachus' first hymn (line 66), the naming of Zeus as "king of bees" (ἐσσῆνα) employs a very rare Greek word that may be intended

---

[28] See Serrao 1977: 228–229; Clauss 1986; Alan Cameron 1995: 371; Pretagostini 1995b: 163–165.
[29] Stephens 2003: 113. Truth and lies differ in accordance with cultural perspective: a Greek lie may contain an Egyptian truth and vice versa. (E.g., Osiris is a dying god.) There are competing truths: Ptolemy is both a mortal and a god; the kingship is both Greek and Egyptian. And for the citations that follow, pp. 107–109.

to translate an Egyptian term, the hieroglyphic symbol of the bee that designates the king of Lower Egypt; but it is mainly via Hesiod that:

> [Callimachus] adumbrates the ideological essentials of Egyptian kingship: the link between the king and the god, the victory over chaos personified as a cosmic enemy, and the maintenance of cosmic harmony or justice. Not surprisingly, Hesiod's texts exhibit demonstrable links with the ancient Near East, and particular patterns of kingship.

The phrase Πηλαγόνων ἐλατῆρα used of Zeus in *Hymn* 1.3, has also been linked with the implicit addressee of the poem, the king, though its meaning remains a subject of debate: ἐλατῆρα means "driver of chariots," "charioteer," in Homer and Pindar (*Ol.* 4.1, of Zeus as charioteer) but also "driver away"; "Pelagonians" may be either the Earth-born Titans (γηγενείς) or human beings (if we accept the reading of the manuscripts, Πηλογόνων, "Mud-born"). The most economical suggestion, if not entirely convincing, is Adolf Köhnken's, reading the expression simply as "shepherd of human beings," a variation of the Homeric formula for hero kings, ποιμένα λαῶν ("shepherd of the people").[30] According to James Clauss, the epithet refers to Ptolemy Philadelphus' being able to "drive away" those who contest his claim to the throne, whereas G.R. McLennan proposes a very unusual meaning, "router of the Pelagonians [Macedonians],"[31] reading the line as praise of Ptolemy Soter as victor over Demetrius Poliorcetes. If an allusion to the Titans should be read here (cf. Hes. *Theog.* 820: Zeus drives away Titans from Olympus), in line with the Hesiodic *fil-rouge* running through the hymn, the verse may anticipate Callimachus *Hymn* 4.174, where Ptolemy II conquers the "late-born Titans": that is, the Celts or Galatians. (Cf. also the Hellenistic hymn on PChic col. VI, 13, where the god's victory over the Giants is recalled in line 14.)[32] In Hesiod, Zeus's defeat of Typhoeus (the Egyptian Seth, Horus' adversary) and the Titans demonstrated his capacity for maintaining rule and order: Ptolemy's Galatian enterprise was yet to come (275/4?), though his

---

[30] See Köhnken 1984, with a possible allusion also to Hermes, who "drives away" the cows, ἐλατῆρα βοῶν, in the *Homeric Hymn to Hermes* 3, 14, 265, 377.

[31] Clauss 1986: 162–163; McLennan 1977: 27–28. For "Pelagonians" meaning Macedonians, see Strabo 7.39f.; Steph. Byz. s.v. Πηλαγονία; Philod. *De piet.* 248v Schober.

[32] Powell 1925: 84 considers this a hymn to Zeus or to Apollo. See Meliadò 2008; Barbantani 2008. Cf. *GDRK* I² 22 (*GLP* fr. 135, pp. 542–544) on the victory of Diocletian and Galerius over the Persians, where the two emperors are assimilated to Zeus and Apollo in the act of crushing the Giants (fr. 1 verso).

father and brothers, like Zeus's older brothers, spontaneously accepted his rule before he had actually performed any deeds.

The description of Zeus, who while still a child devises everything to perfection (*Hymn* 1.57), is echoed by a description of Ptolemy as a king well able to accomplish whatever he devises immediately or, at most, by the end of the day.[33] If the monarch here paralleled with Zeus is young Ptolemy II, Callimachus may have had in mind also the *Homeric Hymn to Hermes* 17–19, where Hermes, born in the morning, steals the cattle of his half brother Apollo on the same day, then is reconciled with him (Clauss 1986: 160–167). Again, a concept found in traditional Greek poetry has parallels within Egyptian culture: the idea that a deed is accomplished as soon as the king thinks it was a feature of Egyptian hymns and royal inscriptions, where it described the power of the god and, by extension, of the pharaoh (Stephens 1998: 171–83 and 2003: 112). Theocritus, praising Ptolemy Soter in the encomium addressed to his son, expresses a similar concept (*Idyll* 17.13–15):

> From his ancestors what a man for accomplishing a great deed was Ptolemy son of Lagus, when in his mind he had conceived a decision that no other man would be able to think.

This also reprises the Hesiodic topos of the protection granted by Zeus to the kings. (Compare *Idyll* 17.74–75 with *Hymn* 1.69–86.)[34] Nothing is closer to Zeus than rulers (*Hymn* 1.80). The power of the kings is absolute and, like that of Zeus, is based on *bia* and *kratos*, Force and Power (l. 67). Then the Homeric explicit at lines 95–96 ("Without virtue, wealth cannot enhance men, | nor virtue without prosperity. Give us virtue and wealth.") reprises line 84 ("you have bestowed abundant wealth on them") and expresses a Hesiodic (*Theog.* 96; cf. *Hymn* 1.84) as well as a Pindaric concept,[35] familiar also in Egyptian culture: the coincidence between the prosperity of the land and the personal virtue of all its inhabitants, but especially of the king.

---

[33] Cf. also *Hymn* 4.162–70, widening the horizon over which Ptolemy extends his rule.

[34] For relationships between encomiastic poems by Callimachus and Theocritus, see Pretagostini 2000b: 157–159.

[35] See scholia to Pind. *Ol.* 2.96f and *Pyth.* 5, 1a.172 Drachmann, in which these final lines of Callimachus' hymn are quoted.

Zeus is also a giver of wealth:[36] in the Hellenistic monarchies, riches were used to manifest the king's munificence, or *euergesia*, toward his subjects and, of course, to his Friends; therefore the poet twice asks the god (*Hymn* 1.94, 96)—in the person of the king—for virtue and prosperity (ἀρετή, ἄφενος, cf. Theognis 30, 129-130 West). There is an echo here of Theocritus *Idyll* 17.95, but Theocritus at line 135 instructs Ptolemy to ask the god directly for these gifts, without the poet as intermediary.[37] Like the king, *Philoi*—that is, his courtiers of highest rank in every field (administration, army, culture; cf. *Hymn* 1.69)[38]—were expected to exercise benevolence and generosity. Callimachus states the same idea firmly in the epinician elegy for the influential minister Sosibius (fr. 384.57-58 Pf.). The subtext of the last section of the hymn is clear: Zeus endows kings with gifts and prerogatives, and protects them (*Hymn* 1.81-84); Ptolemy excels among kings (ll. 85-90); the poet ranks next to the king (cf. Hes. *Theog.* 94-96); and so Callimachus, the only poet capable of properly lauding the king of the gods—and his own master—doubtless excels among poets.

The Hymn to Apollo

The god celebrated in *Hymn* 2 is explicitly presented as patron of Callimachus' home town, Cyrene, where a majestic temple to Apollo had been dedicated and the festival of the Carnea had a long tradition, going back to the Spartan ancestors (*Hymn* 2.71).[39] Since Cyrene is honored and beloved by the god of poetry more than other cities (ll. 95-96), the Cyrenaean Callimachus wishes to be honored above any other poet (ll. 28-29). Alan Cameron (1995: 64) suggested that Callimachus' *Hymns* could be performed in festivals and public ceremonial occasions—in this case, a setting in Cyrene would be appropriate. Most scholars, however, prefer to think that in this poem, as

---

[36] Δῶτορ ἑάων ("granter of wealth", *Hymn* 1.91) occurs only with reference to Hermes in *Odyssey* 8.335 and *Homeric Hymns* 18.2 and 29.8: another reference to the *Homeric Hymn to Hermes* and its story.

[37] On beneficence as the capital element of the monarchic ideology, see Erler 1987 and Bringmann 1993; on the same theme in Theocr. *Id.* 17, see Hunter 1996: 86-89.

[38] McLennan 1977: 107 suggests that here the *philoi* are the literary associates of Callimachus.

[39] For the relationship between Call. *Hymn* 2 and Pindar *Pyth.* 4 and 5, see Calame 1993 and Ambühl 2005: 337-348. See Lehnus 1994a: 197-201 for Apollo's exceptional role as founder—*archegetes* and *ktistes* (man and god are *sunoikisteres*) of Cyrene.

well as in the other mimetic hymns, the poet is creating the fiction of ritual performance.[40]

Hymn 2 contains only two short but quite overt references to the nature of monarchy and to rulers—who, however, remain unnamed. The identification of these characters has a decisive relevance for the dating of the poem. The king is presented as an avatar of Apollo in lines 25–27 (cf. Theocr. *Id.* 22.212):

> ἰὴ ἰὴ φθέγγεσθε· κακὸν μακάρεσσιν ἐρίζειν.
> ὃς μάχεται μακάρεσσιν, ἐμῷ βασιλῆι μάχοιτο·
> ὅστις ἐμῷ βασιλῆι, καὶ Ἀπόλλωνι μάχοιτο.
>
> Cry *Hie! Hie!* It is bad to strive with the Blessed.
> He who fights with the Blessed Ones would fight with my king;
> and whoever fights with my king would fight also with Apollo.

An explicit reference to the kings of Cyrene, in the person of the founder, Battus, occurs in lines 65–68:

> Φοῖβος καὶ βαθύγειον ἐμὴν πόλιν ἔφρασε Βάττῳ
> καὶ Λιβύην ἐσιόντι κόραξ ἡγήσατο λαῷ,
> δεξιὸς οἰκιστῆρι, καὶ ὤμοσε τείχεα δώσειν
> ἡμετέροις βασιλεῦσιν· ἀεὶ δ' εὔορκος Ἀπόλλων.
>
> Phoebus, too, revealed to Battus my city of fertile soil, and as a raven guided the people entering Libya, auspicious to the founder, and swore that he would give walls to our kings. Always Apollo keeps his promises.

A scholion to line 26 reads (scholia to *Hymn* 2.25–26; Pfeiffer 1949–1953: 2.50): "The reference is to Ptolemy Euergetes. It is because he is *philologos* that the poet honors him like a god." Many scholars have taken this to mean that the Ptolemy in question is actually Philadelphus,[41] because *philologos* is more characteristic of him: he was primarily responsible for the development of the Library and the Museum. But others prefer to give credit to the scholiast and see Euergetes in the reference to "my king,"[42] possibly because Callimachus had an affectionate reverence for his wife, Queen Berenice II. The portrayal of the nymph Cyrene in the *Hymn to Apollo* 91–92 may allude to the manly deeds of Berenice, both on the athletic field and in the

---

[40] E.g., F. Williams 1978: 2–3; Depew 1993.
[41] E.g., Wilamowitz 1924: 2.80, 87; Lehnus 1993: 100; Depew 2004: 125.
[42] E.g., Pfeiffer 1949–1953: 1.xxxviii–xxxix; Weber 1993: 221.

political arena.[43] The passionate love that moves Apollo toward Cyrene is also paralleled by the strong conjugal bond between the king and his loyal consort, which is the subject of *The Lock of Berenice:* in addition to praying for her husband's safe return from the battlefield, Berenice brought him as dowry the riches of her city and her fleet, enabling him to launch the Third Syrian War.

If this reconstruction is correct, the *Hymn to Apollo* should be dated after the wedding of the Euergetae in 246 BC. P. Smotrytsch (1961: 662), however, would date the poem to the 260s, when Berenice was still engaged to Ptolemy III and fighting against her mother, Apama: in lines 25–27 Callimachus would then be addressing the two factions tearing apart Cyrene after the death of Magas, endorsing Ptolemaic control over the city. The future tense in line 28 would imply that the poet is seeking the protection of the young Euergetes in the future; and Euergetes, who was coregent with his father, Ptolemy II, would be the equivalent of Apollo, "sitting to the right of Zeus" (*Hymn* 2.29). Cameron alone would date the hymn to the 270s, identifying "my king" as the last independent Cyrenaean king, Magas, father of Berenice II (Alan Cameron 1995: 408–409). Consensus has it that the king in lines 26–27 is a contemporary of Callimachus, and not the original Battus, the founder of the city, also named in line 65.[44] "Battus" was used generically for any Cyrenaean ruler and never became a proper name:[45] the dynasty of the first Battus died out in the fifth century BC with Arcesilas IV, a patron of Pindar. Callimachus proudly styled

---

[43] Smotrytsch 1961: 664–665; F. Williams 1978: 79. Young Berenice, engaged to Ptolemy III, rebelled against her mother, Apama, a partisan of the Seleucid faction, who wanted her to marry instead Demetrius the Fair. Apparently Berenice II had Demetrius killed and married Euergetes in 246 BC. Equestrian victories of Berenice II are celebrated by Callimachus in *Aetia* 3 (*The Victory of Berenice*) and by Posidippus 78, 79, 82 AB.

[44] *Contra* S. White 1999: 177. As Apollo's designated ἀρχηγέτης, the founding hero was an earthly representative of the god. In this case there is no correspondence between divine attributes and prerogatives of the Ptolemaic king: whereas Apollo liked to found new cities (*Hymn* 2.56–57), the Ptolemies would found only one new polis in Egypt, Ptolemais. On Ptolemaic settlements outside of Egypt, see Mueller 2006.

[45] See the scholia to Pind. *Pyth.* 4.60–65, 105–106 Drachmann; cf. Hdt. 4.155. Pindar *Pyth.* 5, where the line between Apollo in Sparta and in Cyrene is traced, gives the etymology of Battus, whose dynasty is prophesied in Pind. *Pyth.* 4.9. "Revival of either royal name could then suggest royalist pretensions, whether during the period of independence or under the subsequent reign of Magas and the Ptolemies"—a sort of patriotic claim for Greeks of Dorian ancestry surrounded by natives (S. White 1999: 173–175).

himself "Cyrenaean" (*Ep.* 21.2 Pf. = 29 GP) and "Battiades" (*Ep.* 35.1 Pf. = 30 GP), not necessarily boasting a royal lineage but as a sign of loyalty and affection toward his homeland: "Battiadae" at *Hymn to Apollo* 96 may well refer to all Cyrene's citizens or simply to its ancient monarchs. In conclusion, "our kings" in line 68 does not necessarily refer to the same ruler as in line 26: the possessive suggests that the former named may be the long-extinct dynasty of the Battiads, or the mythical founders of Cyrene;[46] the latter, the actual patron of the poet in Alexandria, Ptolemy II or III. Apparently Callimachus did not see any break in continuity in the traditions of his homeland, considering the successors of Lagus (whether Magas or Euergetes) no less worthy than the descendants of Battus (in the past) as Cyrenaean rulers, and their legitimate successors. It must be noted, in any case, that references to "Battiadae" (l. 96), "my city" (l. 65), or "my king" and "our kings" (ll. 26, 68) are spoken not necessarily by the poet *in propria persona* but by a chorus, ideally present at the cultic ceremony, or by the poet as representative of the community, a generic feature in archaic choral lyric performance:[47] the central section of the poem (especially ll. 71–72) is heavily indebted to Pindar's *Pythian* 5, which celebrates Arcesilas and traces a continuity in the worship of Apollo from Sparta to Libya.

"Callimachus' Apollo is indeed the divine model for the poet, just as Zeus of the *First Hymn* is the divine model for the king.... The *Hymn to Apollo* thus forms a close counterpoint to the *Hymn to Zeus* in its debt to Hesiod's *Theogony* (94–103)" (Hunter and Fuhrer 2002: 153; cf. Depew 2004: 121). As a patron of poets, Apollo serves as a correlative for the poetic patronage of rulers. *Hymn* 2, like *Hymn* 1, explicitly considers the nature of poetry and the role of Callimachus himself as a court poet, whether at Alexandria or Cyrene. In line 31 the king should be "an easy subject of songs" like Apollo, and like the Cyclades in *Hymn* 4.4.

---

[46] Cf. Cahen 1930: 46–47, 69–70; Laronde 1987: 362–364; Hunter and Fuhrer 2002: 156–157; Morrison 2007: 108–109.

[47] On the poetic persona in the mimetic hymns, see Gelzer 1982; Bulloch 1984 (esp. 215–220); Falivene 1990; Pretagostini 1991b; M.A. Harder 1992; Depew 1993. Here Morrison 2007: 132–133 suggests a strict parallel with the narrator's claim about his own ancestry in Pind. *Pyth.* 5. Calame 1993: 50: "in imitation of the intimate relation that is established between Phoebus and the young chorus who celebrates him, an affinity is suggested between 'my king,' the narrator/speaker's sovereign, and the divinity protecting him."

The poem ends abruptly with an *Abbruchsformel* in which Apollo takes the part of the speaker (Callimachus) and rejects Phthonos. This is not the place to explore the meaning of these famous lines.[48] Let us say only that the two moments converge, the political and the poetic: "The final link in his chain of enmities and favor given and received identifies both Ptolemy and Apollo as joint sponsors of choral performance, and of the poet" (Henrichs 1993: 146). Zeus in *Hymn* 1 and Apollo in *Hymn* 2 are presented as divine role models for the king and the poet, respectively, even though Apollo himself, as in the *Hymn to Delos*, can also be seen as a divine figure for the king.

The Hymn to Delos

Hymn 4, the *Hymn to Delos*,[49] is modeled on the *Homeric Hymn to Apollo* (recalling the defeat of Pytho in the Delphic section)[50] and Pindar's *Paeans* 5 and 7. The longest and most complex of Callimachus' *Hymns*, this is the only one in which reference to the king is unambiguous for modern reception; in this section praise of Philadelphus is uttered by Apollo, the god of poetry (*Hymn* 4.165–90):

> But another god is due her [Cos] by the Moirai, from highest lineage of the Saviors; beneath his diadem shall come—not displeased to be ruled by a Macedonian—both the internal lands and those that are set in the sea, as far off as the sunset and whence the swift horses carry the sun. And he shall have the characteristics of his father (170). And one day he will face an enterprise in common with us, in the future, when against the Hellenes rising the barbarian sword and Celtic war, the late-born Titans from the farthest West, will rush like snowflakes, and numerous (175) as the stars when they flock most thickly in the sky; [...] and Crisaean Plains and the valleys of Hephaestus will be under siege, and shall behold thick smoke of their burning neighbor, and no longer by hearsay only; (180) but already beside the temple they will see the ranks of the enemy, and already beside my tripods the sword and impious belts and hostile shields, which shall cause an evil journey for the foolish tribe of the Galatians. Some of them will be an offering to me; others, (185) after seeing their wearers perish amid fire, will be set beside the Nile as a prize for the king who toiled so much. O Ptolemy who will be, these are the

---

[48] For the concluding lines of this hymn the bibliography is immense: see at least Bundy 1972; F. Williams 1978: 85–99; Bing 1986; Alan Cameron 1995; Kofler 1996.

[49] General comments: Fleming 1981; Hopkinson 1985; Mineur 1984 (esp. 180–194); Schmiel 1987; Bing 1988b: 91–146; Gigante Lanzara 1990 (esp. 124–133); Meillier 1996; Barbantani 2001: 188–195; Vamvouri Ruffy 2005: 245–283; Ukleja 2005.

[50] Fantuzzi and Hunter 2004: 355–356.

prophecies of Phoebus for you. You will greatly praise him who still in his mother's womb was prophet every day in the future (190).

Apollo foresees the birth of "another god" and refuses to be born in Cos in order to leave the little island the honor of being the exclusive homeland of the future king. Cos also had a key role in the propagandistic exploitation of the Galatian Wars, which offered Philadelphus an opportunity to boast a majestic enterprise as a guarantee of his kingship, as the slaying of Python had been for Apollo.

The Galatian revolt in Egypt. The passage above alludes to Philadelphus' suppression of a mutiny of Celtic mercenaries, the only other evidence for which are a scholion to the *Hymn to Delos* and a passage in Pausanias (1.7.2). The taming of rebellious barbarians gains significance in connection with the much more dangerous invasion of mainland Greece by Galatian hordes in 279/8 BC, followed by a sequence of attacks and battles in Thrace and Asia Minor that continued until the first half of the second century BC. Military enterprises undertaken during the Galatian Wars achieved the status of legend even among contemporaries, and their fame spread to the farthest reaches of Alexander's former empire.[51] These victories offered aspiring *basileis* like Antigonus Gonatas in Macedonia and Attalus I in Pergamum a means of justifying their accession to the throne and provided monarchs who were already established in power, like Antiochus I in Asia Minor, a way of solidifying the position that they had inherited from their predecessors.[52] Ptolemy II did not have the chance to take part in any of these glorious battles, but he could not miss so splendid a propagandistic opportunity.

In *Hymn* 4, the attack on Delphi is presented as an event contemporary with the local Delphic commemoration of Apollo's victory over Python in order to underline the parallel between the chthonic powers once defeated by the god and the "New Titans" assaulting the

---

[51] On the Galatian Wars: Nachtergael 1977; Strobel 1991 and 1994; Barbantani 2001.

[52] The Hellenistic king must reign over a "spear-won land", χώρα δορίκτητος (cf. *SH* 922.9, Ptolemy I, son of "Lagus, renowned for his spear", δ[ο]ρικλειτοῖο Λαάγου; *SH* 979.6–7, Ptolemy IV king worthy "in spear and Muses", ἐν δορὶ καὶ Μούσαις). See also Call. *Hymn* 1.74, ἴδρις αἰχμῆς ("skilled with the spear"); Theocr. *Id.* 17.56 and 103, αἰχμητὰ Πτολεμαῖε ("spearman Ptolemy") and ἐπισταμένος δόρυ πάλλειν ("knowing how to brandish the spear").

sanctuary,[53] and (potentially) the territories controlled by Ptolemy II. Apollo, in his prophecy, defines the fight against the Galatians as a "common cause" (l. 171) with Ptolemy Philadelphus, the "other god" mentioned in line 165. (Cf. *Hymn* 2.27.) Following the apotheosis of his parents (the "Saviors": i.e., the divinized Ptolemy I and Berenice I), Ptolemy was moving from the rank of ἡμίθεος to a divine status,[54] which would have been completed after the death of his wife (270: divinization of the couple of the *Philadelphoi*). The prophecy of the god while still in the womb concludes with a vision of Ptolemy's enterprise in such ambiguous and oracular terms as to suggest an episode of epic proportions. The syntactical continuity between Brennus' descent into Greece and the extermination of the rebellious mercenaries inserts a marginal event (three lines are devoted to it, ll. 185–187) into the broad context of cosmic history, where victory over the forces of chaos was assured by the help of the Olympian gods.

The news of the victory at Delphi arrived in Egypt via the island of Cos, birthplace of Ptolemy Philadelphus: Cos was the first Greek community to commemorate it with a decree celebrating the Delphic and Aetolian success over the invaders.[55] The prominence of Cos in *Hymn* 4 may reflect this event and probably indicates that the poem was written before the defeat of the Ptolemaic fleet around this island (ca. 262/1) and the end of the Chremonidean War, when Ptolemy lost control over it (lower terminus ca. 253 BC).[56] In any case, the poem, with its celebration of the Cyclades, belongs to a period when Ptolemaic influence in this archipelago was at its height, as stated also by Theocritus *Idyll* 17.90. But the exact date of the hymn is by no means certain.[57] The terminus post quem is obviously the revolt of the Galatian mercenaries whom Ptolemy II enrolled through a *Philos* named

---

[53] For the chronology of the procession in the Valley of Tempe and the lacunose ll. 177a–b, 178: Mineur 1979; Bing 1986 and 1988b: 129–130; Gigante Lanzara 1990: 128.

[54] Also promoted by Theocr. *Id.* 17, a true hymn to the king. Cf. l. 7, ὑμνήσαιμι.

[55] *Syll.*³ 398. See Nachtergael 1977: 401–403. Representatives of Ptolemaic Egypt were invited to the Delphic Soteria.

[56] Weber 1993: 303. Bing (1988: 93) proposes 259 as terminus ante quem of this hymn, since at l. 19 Corsica is still said to be Carthaginian, as it was no longer after being conquered by Cn. Cornelius Scipio in that year.

[57] Griffiths 1977–1978 places it before the death of Arsinoe and Theocr. *Id.* 17, *ante* 271.

Antigonus.[58] The occasion for the enrollment was, according to Pausanias, the revolt of Ptolemy's half brother Magas (Chamoux 1956: 20–21, 29), which cannot be dated precisely but probably fell between 277 and 274. Magas' attack against Alexandria was soon stopped by a raid of the nomads against Cyrene; apparently only after Magas' withdrawal did the Galatian mercenaries revolt, and they were defeated before the First Syrian War broke out between Ptolemy and Antiochus I. We can therefore hazard for *Hymn* 4 a date around 276/5 BC, on the grounds that in order to be effective as an encomium the hymn was likely to have been composed and performed not much later than the event described.

No other Ptolemaic poetic work survives celebrating this event, with the possible exceptions of *SH* 958 and Callimachus' *Galatea*. (For *SH* 958, see Barbantani 2001.) The theme of barbarian invasion of Greek sacred spaces appears also in Callimachus' *Hymn* 3.251–58, an allusion to the Cimmerian attack on the rich sanctuary of Ephesus. *Hymns* 3 and 4 may have been composed in the same period: both contain a Herodotean topos, the divine retribution that follows upon the hubris of the invaders (*Hymn* 3.252) and prevents their safe return home (cf. *Hymn* 4.184.) *Hymns* 3 and 4 both rhetorically exaggerate the numbers of the enemy: the Galatians are like snowflakes (*Hymn* 4.175–76);[59] the Cimmerians, like grains of sand (*Hymn* 3.253). It is, however, difficult to establish a relative chronology between *Hymn* 4 and Theocritus' *Idyll* 17.[60] Although the latter seems to be later than the First Syrian War, it lacks any allusion to the Galatian revolt, which, if it had already happened, very likely would have been pressed into service for this encomium. The celebration of the suppression of the Galatian revolt in Egypt and its link with the Delphic victory in 279, achieved with the decisive role of the Aetolians, is significant also for the maintenance of good relations between Philadelphus and the powerful sanctuary of Apollo. Immediately before the descent of the Galatians into mainland

---

[58] On the episode, see bibliography and discussion in Barbantani 2001: 188–203.

[59] Cf. *Il.* 3.222, 19.357. Geffcken 1902: 28 thinks that *Or. Sib.* 5.464–67 refers to the same episode.

[60] According to Griffiths 1977–1978 and Hunter 1996: 82 n. 21, *Hymn* 4 precedes *Id.* 17 (271), whereas Mineur 1984 believes that *Hymn* 4 is later. Ambühl 2005: 348 remarks upon the complementarity of *Hymn* 4 and *Id.* 17: in Callimachus the praise is a future prospect, whereas Theocritus sings the prophecy fulfilled in the present; in *Hymn* 4, Cos waits for the god reserved to her (ll. 165–166), whereas in Theocr. *Id.* 17.66–67 Cos wishes to be venerated as is Delos, the island of Apollo.

Greece and after the death of Ptolemy I Soter (283), Ptolemy II asked the Delphic Amphictiony to accept the new festival that he had founded in honor of his father, the Ptolemaia (cf. Hazzard 2000: 28–32, 66); however, so far as we know Philadelphus did not send troops to Greece to fight Brennus, although his rivals Antiochus I and Antigonus did (Paus. 10.20.5). In spite of his failure to do so, Delphi granted Alexandria the right of *promanteia* (*Syll.*³ 404) and accepted as *proxenos* an Alexandrian courtier, Sostratus. About 247/6, when the Aetolians reorganized the Soteria created thirty years before, the Ptolemies were invited to participate (Nachtergael 1977: 228–229).

The Galatians as new Titans. The attacks of the Celts functioned for contemporary dynasts as a reenactment of the Persian Wars, in which the whole social order was threatened. The exploitation of anti-Persian feelings, still vivid in Egypt, was useful to Philadelphus in the legitimation of his power, both with his Greek and with his Egyptian subjects. The memory of the deeds of Alexander, the conqueror of Persia, was very much present in the court poetry of the age of Philadelphus and was exploited in public pageants like the Grand Procession (Callix. *apud* Ath. 5.201d; Rice 1983: 102–111, 191). Ptolemy II was presenting himself as heir to the Philhellenic and anti-Persian politics of Alexander, the man who in Theocritus *Idyll* 17.19 is represented as punishing the Persians and standing next to Ptolemy I, the founder of the dynasty.

According to Greek sources, the Galatians had in common with the Persians the sacrilegious attitude that would, following the Hesiodic and Herodotean principle of retribution, lead to the fate already experienced by the Medes. In the *Hymn to Delos* the Galatians are not named explicitly, but they have become "late-born Titans."[61] The ethnic Γαλάται appears only in line 184. Their designation as Titans is motivated by their physical appearance (Paus. 10.20.7; Liv. 7.10.9; Gell. 9.11), but also by their similarities to the mythical opponents of the gods, the Titans and the Giants, in their impiety and lack of restraint. The Galatians' arrival from the far West, a place of access to the chthonic world and inhabited by monstrous creatures, is underlined in Callimachus fragment 379 Pf., from the *Galatea*. The direct

---

[61] *Hymn* 4.174. Ὀψίγονοι, "Late-born" (cf. *Il.* 3.353, 7.87) is opposed to προτερηγενέας Τιτῆνας "earlier-born Titans" in Antim. 41a7 Matthews and to Τιτῆσι μέτα προτέροισι θεοῖσιν in Hes. *Theog.* 424.

collision between βαρβαρικὴν μάχαιραν and Ἑλλήνεσσι in *Hymn* 4.172–73 is expressive, and its meaning politically noteworthy: whereas Delphic propaganda later tried to convince the Greeks that the attack was mainly directed at the sanctuary, Callimachus, although concentrating on the Apollo episode, constructs the threat as hovering over all the Greeks, therefore making Ptolemy's deed a common cause with the reaction of the entire Greek world against the invaders.

The Galatians are seen by Callimachus as a moving forest of weapons (*Hymn* 4.183–84), to which is attributed the character of the warriors carrying them: the μάχαιρα, the φάσγανον, the military belts, and especially the shields are here personified (as often in an *ex-voto*) in the lines relating the extermination of the mercenaries.[62] The shields are an element of continuity between the Delphic enterprise and that near Alexandria. In both cases they were exhibited as a trophy: consecrated by the Aetolians in Delphi to the savior god Apollo, they were exhibited as a victory prize by Ptolemy.[63] Judging from the use that Greek citizens and other Hellenistic monarchs made of enemy shields,[64] those of the defeated mercenaries were probably exhibited as a trophy also in Egypt, where they were represented under the feet of the Egyptian god Bes (Perdrizet and Picard 1927; Nachtergael 1977: 190–191). In Egypt the attention to the Galatian shields could also have been motivated by the dynastic legend according to which the infant Ptolemy I was exposed in a shield and saved by a divine eagle (*Suda* λ 25 Adler; Nachtergael 1977: 189). Ptolemaic coins show the image of the shield from the first year of Philadelphus' reign, and these clearly cannot be associated with the suppression of the revolt (though they might reflect the dynastic legend). The golden and silver shields adorning the royal tent during the Grand Procession of the Ptolemaia,[65] however, probably do evoke the Celtic shields.

---

[62] For weapons used to represent feelings to their owners, cf. *AP* 6.131.3, *ICret.* 4.243.

[63] Paus. 10.19.4. On the use of the Galatic shield, see bibliography in Barbantani 2001: 194–196. See Meillier 1996: 141–144 for the affinity between *Hymn* 4 and the epinician.

[64] Paus. 1.4.6; 10.18.7, 10.21.5; *AP* 6.130; Nachtergael 1977: 196–197.

[65] Athen. 5.196f; Studniczka 1914: 89–91. Hazzard 2000 sets the procession in 262 BC; Förtmeyer 1988, between December 275 and February 274, just before the First Syrian War. Some date it to 270 (e.g., Rice 1983), just after this conflict.

Greek-Egyptian elements. Just as in the *Hymn to Zeus*, elements of the narrative are constructed to appeal to both the Greek and the Egyptian audience. In the *Hymn to Delos* the syncretistic elements are more obvious than in other poems, even though "the poem attempts to interpret in Greek terms and for a Greek audience a conception of monarchy which, in some of its most conspicuous features, was shaped by Egyptian customs" (Bing 1998b: 132).

Ptolemy appears wearing the characteristic *diadema* of Hellenistic monarchs (*Hymn* 4.166–68: μίτρη), sported also by the divinized Alexander in Theocritus *Idyll* 17.18–19 (Hunter 2003c: 115). The king reigns over ἀμφοτέρη μεσόγεια (l. 168), "both continents," Asia and Europe (a stock *iunctura* in praise poetry: cf. Isid. *Hy*. 3.13 Vanderlip) but this phrase can also hint at another, common to Egyptian royal titulature, "Upper and Lower Egypt." Cos, where Ptolemy was born, is defined in *Hymn* 4.160 as a "primeval island," like the birthplace of Horus (the floating island Chemmis: Hdt. 2.156) and Zeus.[66] In the *Hymn to Delos* the child Apollo is born when the river Inopus is swollen by a subterranean flow from the Nile (ll. 206–8).

The contests between Apollo and the Python and between Zeus and the Titans have analogues in Egyptian mythology with the struggle between Horus, the divine child with whom the pharaoh is identified, and Seth, god of the desert and of death.[67] Even the use of fire in destroying the Galatian prisoners has parallels in pharaonic tradition.[68] (It is, though, most likely that the Galatians threw themselves into the flames, in a ritual mass suicide, just as the Galatians defeated in Delphi did.)[69] According to Peter Bing (1998b: 131–132; cf. also Weber 1993: 217, 306–307, 376–388), the superimposition of the king's image on

---

[66] Stephens 2003: 114–121, 180–181: the birth of Horus, like that of Apollo, was preceded by the wanderings of his mother, Isis.

[67] The Egyptian serpent Apophis is also defeated by Horus. Ptolemy V is assimilated to Horus, slayer of the ἀσεβεῖς, in *OGIS* 90.11, 27 (the Rosetta Stone); the identification with Hermes, also proposed in the stele, in Egyptian terms is an equivalence with Thoth, another benefactor god.

[68] Koenen 1983: 174–175 and 1993: 81–84. Plut. *Is*. 73.380d relates that in Egypt human beings are burned alive as a sacrifice to Typhon. In the Egyptian tradition, rebels against the pharaoh are ἀσεβεῖς, working for Typhon-Seth: the second-century BC version of the *Oracle of the Potter* (cf. POxy 22.2332.9, third cent. AD) imagines that the "Typhonians" are set on fire by the reigning king; at the time of Philadelphus, a version of this oracle calls the impious *zonophoroi*. Cf. the Galatians in Call. *Hymn* 4.183: ζωστῆρας ἀναιδέας.

[69] Launey 1949–1950: 498; Weber 1993: 307 n. 1 is skeptical.

that of Apollo engaged in the fight with underworld forces should be considered as part of a cultural project promoted by the Ptolemaic court: that is, the translation, in terms acceptable for the Graeco-Macedonian population, of some Egyptianizing aspects of the ideology and practice of the Ptolemaic government (e.g., as the foundation of order, or *maat*).[70]

There is also a striking note on the ethnic provenance of the king, which occurs only here in Callimachus but is more common in Posidippus:[71] in *Hymn* 4.167 the poet asserts that all the lands "do not refuse to have a Macedonian king." The king is styled as (almost) a Greek sovereign, in order to present him properly as a savior of the Ἕλληνες in line 171. In Hellenistic poetry, "Hellene" is used only as opposed to non-Greeks, and in his surviving works Callimachus uses the terms "Hellene" (fr. 379 Pf.; *Hymn* 4.172) and "barbarian" (in the adjectival form βαρβαρικός) only in the context of the Galatian invasion.[72]

Stripped of its contingent elements in *Hymn* 4, the suppression of the Galatian mercenaries' revolt assumes a universal significance in a pharaonic interpretation of the world not very different from the Hellenistic or Augustan interpretation: the divine and the royal victory over destructive forces are part of the same equilibrium, which also allows the court poets to create and experiment in peace—and possibly to pay appropriate tribute, in the form of encomia, to the monarch responsible for this peaceful condition. If Delos first salutes Apollo as a god (*Hymn* 4.6), and Apollo—who in turn recognizes Ptolemy as a god—would praise Callimachus or the chorus for celebrating Delos (ll. 9–10), the hope is that the king also would commend his loyal poet (Bing 1988b: 119).

---

[70] See Faraone and Teeter 2004.
[71] D.J. Thompson 2005; Stephens 2004a and 2005. Van Bremen 2007: 173 rightly argues that the primary reason for the ethnic claim was the rule of the epinician genre, which included the statement of the winner's homeland.
[72] Hunter 1991: 85, 87 n. 19. Cf. *SH* 969.7: φῦλα μὲν Ἑλλήνων (Barbantani 2001: 111–114).

CHAPTER TEN

CALLIMACHUS' QUEENS

Évelyne Prioux

Abstract

The *Victoria Berenices*, the *Coma Berenices* and the *Ektheosis Arsinoes* probably contributed, as did a series of texts and allusions scattered throughout Callimachus' work (mostly in the *Aetia*, the *Epigrams* and in occasional poems), to the formation of a court ideology in which the queens, Arsinoe II and Berenice II, were quite prominent: such pieces were probably intended to reinforce a coherent contemporary ideology in the circle immediately surrounding the royal couple. Around poems that one might define as dynastic and allusions that, brief or cryptic though they may be, are nonetheless clearly also dynastic, one may also note, in Callimachus' œuvre, a nebula of texts that concern mythological figures, divinities, and places that were of interest to the queens. Callimachus promotes, whether in textual detail or in overall architecture of his work, representations of the royal family that affirm dynastic continuity among the first three Ptolemaic generations. He also plays on the integration of Egyptian elements, but takes care to present these in a 'Hellenized' form in seeking out, through Archaic or mythological precedents, events similar to those established in the contemporary setting of the Alexandrian court.

The *Epilogue* of the *Aetia* is addressed to the figure of a female sovereign (fr. 112.2 Pf.: ἀνάσσης, "queen"), bearing witness to the importance of the queen in the work that the poet has just finished; and thus one of Callimachus' earliest pieces gives pride of place to Arsinoe II as the new queen of Egypt. To the extent that we can judge from its first and only surviving line (fr. 392 Pf.: Ἀρσινόης, ὦ ξεῖνε γάμον καταβάλλομ' ἀείδειν, "stranger, I strike up Arsinoe's wedding-song"), it was an epithalamium for the marriage of Ptolemy II and Arsinoe, which surely dates to 277/6 BC. Thirty years later, an important turn in the poet's career came in 246 with the marriage of Ptolemy III to

I wish to thank B. Acosta-Hughes for translating this chapter into English; he and Susan Stephens provided generous help and stimulating comments while I was writing this essay. The research for this paper is part of the ANR CAIM project.

Berenice daughter of Magas, a princess who had grown up in Cyrene, Callimachus' own city of origin. (Lelli 2005b.) Shortly after this wedding, Callimachus composed the two poems that subsequently were to frame Books 3 and 4 of the *Aetia*, thus reinforcing the ties between this work and praise of the Lagid queens: *The Victory of Berenice* and *The Lock of Berenice*. These two poems probably contributed, as did a series of texts and allusions scattered throughout the poet's work, to the formation of a court ideology in which the queens were quite prominent. The importance of their political and religious role was surely inspired in part by that exercised by the Egyptian queens, but the incestuous marriage of Arsinoe II and her brother Philadelphus, if inspired by Egyptian models, was a serious breach of Greek and Macedonian cultural conventions. In this context Callimachus turned to Greek myth and, by the ingenious use of archaic examples, provided Greek precedents for events that the contemporary audience may have thought unheard of.

Poems on Queens

Of the poetry that is now extant,[1] we have two poems that explicitly celebrate queens: *Epigram* 5 Pf. concerns the dedication of a nautilus in the Temple of Aphrodite-Arsinoe, erected at Cape Zephyrium, near the Canopic mouth of the Nile; and *Epigram* 51 Pf. celebrates a Berenice as a fourth Grace among Graces. Aside from these, we have important fragments of three other poems in which Callimachus celebrates queens: *The Victory of Berenice*, *The Lock of Berenice*, and *The Apotheosis of Arsinoe*.

The Victory of Berenice is the title that modern scholars have given to the poem that opens Book 3 of the *Aetia*. The poet begins by proclaiming that he will offer a song to Zeus and to Nemea in thanks for the victory that Berenice II has won in chariot racing at the Nemean Games. He then describes the arrival of the news of this victory in Egypt and introduces the image of the Egyptian women occupied in weaving and possibly offering their work to celebrate the queen's victory. The elegy continues with the narrative of Heracles' adventures

---

[1] For a list of the fragments relating to Arsinoe II composed by Callimachus and his contemporaries, see Lelli 2002: 10.

immediately before and immediately after his fight with the Nemean Lion. Callimachus' main interest was the meeting between Heracles and Molorchus, the humble host who gives him shelter before his battle with the lion. In keeping with Molorchus' status, Callimachus narrates an unexpected *aition:* Molorchus' invention of the mousetrap, for use against the rodents that have invaded his hut.[2] The poem plays on the protocols of Pindaric epinician while constantly frustrating readers' expectations: Berenice's victory is implicitly compared with Heracles' combat with the Nemean Lion—a combat that is not quite narrated but is mischievously replaced with that of Molorchus against the mice.[3]

The Lock of Berenice, which is the last poem of *Aetia* 4 (D'Alessio 2007: 522 n. 32), is known to us from a fragment that has been reconstructed from *PSI* 1092 and POxy 20. 2258C (fr. 110 Pf.), the summary of the *diegesis*, and Catullus' translation into Latin (*Carmen* 66). In POxy 20.2258, *The Lock of Berenice* seems to be a separate elegy immediately preceding *The Victory of Sosibius* in the layout of the codex. This fact, in addition to the differences between fragment 110 Pf. and Catullus' translation, has led some commentators to posit that *The Lock of Berenice* circulated as an occasional poem before being reworked by Callimachus with a view to including it within Book 4 of the *Aetia*. The poem is an elegy spoken by the lock of hair that Berenice II dedicated for her husband's safe return from the Third Syrian War: after it was cut to become a dedicatory offering, the lock became a constellation. The elegy opens with the narrative of the astronomer Conon's discovery of the lock now placed in the night sky. The lock then narrates the departure of the king for war and the queen's sorrow, her vow, and the king's victorious return. The lock says that it left the queen's head unwillingly, comparing itself to the peninsula of Acte, separated from Athos by the canal dug on Xerxes' orders for the passage of his fleet. There follows a recounting of the lock's ascent into the sky thanks to Aphrodite and its position among the other constellations. Still regretting that it could not remain on the queen's head, the lock asks that Berenice offer the lock of perfumes.

---

[2] The order of the fragments is uncertain; see especially Hollis 1986, who suggests that *SH* 259 (= fr. 177 Pf.) originally stood at the opening of an *aition* and that the epinician frame was added later. Contra, see Livrea 1989b: 146–47.
[3] For these interlocked stories, see Gutzwiller 2007: 66.

The Apotheosis of Arsinoe (fr. 228 Pf.) is one of four songs (frr. 226–29 Pf.) that were apparently added at the end of Callimachus' collection of thirteen *Iambi*, though they do not seem in any way to belong to that poetic genre.[4] The title and the subject are provided by the *diegesis:* the dead queen was borne to heaven by the Dioscuri, and her mortuary temple, the *Arsinoeum*, was constructed near the Emporium of Alexandria. After voicing a wish to be guided in his song by Apollo and the Muses (fr. 228.1–4 Pf.), the poet evokes the heavenly course of the deified Arsinoe (ll. 5–6) and her funeral rites in Alexandria (ll. 7–39), and then shifts perspective to Philotera, the deified sister of Ptolemy II and Arsinoe. Philotera sees a column of smoke rising from Alexandria. In her anxiety she sends Charis to Mt. Athos, from there Charis reports that Philotera's sister has died (lines 40–75).

Besides these pieces that allow us to analyze how Callimachus elaborated the queens' images and the ideology of the court, there are scraps of other poems. Fragment 392 Pf., mentioned above, is the opening of a poem composed for the marriage of Arsinoe II and Ptolemy II Philadelphus. Fragments 387 and 388 Pf., with which it may be possible to join fragments 385 and 386 Pf., attest the existence of other elegies on Berenice II now lost. Fragment 388 names Berenice and Magas and mentions a wedding;[5] fragment 387, which may be from the same elegy, speaks of (line 2) "Berenice's star," thus linking with *The Lock of Berenice*.[6]

If the elegies and epigrams that we have mentioned constitute the cardinal elements of Callimachus' discourse on the queens, there are also fleeting allusions found throughout Callimachus' work in which one may detect a close correspondence with Lagid ideology. The royal presence may be suggested in an isolated word from a very fragmentary passage of *The Dream* at the opening of the *Aetia* (fr. 3 M. δεκ]άς, with scholia, PLitLond 181.45, and POxy 20. 2262: fr. 2a.10–15) and, more explicitly, in the *Epilogue* of the same work (fr. 112 Pf.). Two other Callimachean passages may allude to Sotades' obscene verses on

---

[4] On these four poems, see Acosta-Hughes 2003. For the stylistic and generic characteristics of fr. 228 Pf., see Lelli 2002: 25–27.

[5] On this fragment, see Gelzer 1982: 19.

[6] Hollis 1992c proposes an ingenious reconstruction for frr. 387 and 388. See also Jackson 2001, who has provided overwhelming evidence for these fragments' Callimachean origin. For the relevance to Berenice's biography, see, e.g., Gelzer 1982: 17–18.

the incestuous pairing of Ptolemy II and his sister: *Aetia* 3 fragment 75.4–9 Pf. and *Hymn to Demeter* 63.[7] A justification of the union of brothers and sisters may also be found in *Epigram* 1 Pf. Fragment 101 Pf., whose subject is one of the cult statues of Hera on Samos, can be viewed in the context of the iconography of the double horn of plenty, a symbol that Ptolemy II chose for his sister-wife. Another example is fragment 227 Pf., a song in honor of the Dioscuri that seems to form a diptych with fragment 228 Pf., *The Apotheosis of Arsinoe*. Finally, *Epigram* 47 Pf., which concerns the dedication of a saltcellar to the Cabiri, can be related in interesting ways to Arsinoe II as founder of temples and as herself a new divinity honored in cult. Other passages of interest specifically concern Berenice II. One especially significant example comes from Callimachus' *Hymn to Apollo*, evoking the love of Apollo and Cyrene—which, scholars have argued, presented through the myth a way to celebrate Berenice's courage.

In addition to pieces that we may identify as dynastic and allusions that, however brief or cryptic, are nonetheless clearly also dynastic, there exists in Callimachus' oeuvre a nebula of texts that concern mythological figures, divinities, and places that were of interest to the queens. From the start we must emphasize that of the divinities whom Callimachus mentions and celebrates none is identified completely with the queens. It is tempting to see points of contact that link his *Hymn to Artemis, Bath of Pallas*, and *Hymn to Demeter* to Lagid queens:[8] it is also true that the figures of Artemis and Athena are well represented in the *Aetia* in the evocation of their cults. The manner in which these goddesses are presented, as well as their experiences and their powers, are always ambiguous, leaving a large margin of uncertainty and a need for caution in establishing links to specific royal figures; it would be illusory, for example, to interpret every allusion to Hera or Athena as directly corresponding to a particular queen.

---

[7] See Pretagostini 1984, 1991a; Fuhrer 1988: 64–66; Weber 1998–99: 171–172; H. White 2000: 187–188; Giangrande 2004; Durbec 2005a; Prioux 2009b.

[8] See the suggestive work of Depew 2004; Gutzwiller 2007: 70–71. For identifications of Callimachus' *Hymns* 1–4 with the Ptolemaic royal family, see Fantuzzi in this volume. See also S. Müller 2009: 243–244 on a possible comparison of Berenice and Leto in Posidippus *Ep.* 40 AB.

Working Out a Dynastic Discourse

In a thorough study, S. Müller (2009) has recently observed the various carefully orchestrated processes and political acuity with which Ptolemy II guaranteed the succession to the throne of his son Ptolemy III. He repudiated his first wife, Arsinoe I (daughter of Lysimachus of Macedon), who was thought to have conspired against him (schol. Theocr. *Id.* 17.128; S. Müller 2009: 91). He chose to avoid multiple wives, which could have created problems of legitimacy at the moment of succession. He entered into a marriage with his full sister Arsinoe II, who was no longer of an age to bear children, and so avoided having issue who could have contested the inheritance of Ptolemy Euergetes, his son by Arsinoe I. There is, too, the notable absence of a wedding for Philotera, the sister whom Ptolemy II apparently preferred to leave without a husband, perhaps to avoid the risk of creating another branch of an already contentious family. It may also be added that the king did not take another wife after the death of Arsinoe II.

Whether or not one agrees with the details of this strategy, or on the degree of political acumen that Müller suggests, it is clear that in his dynastic poems Callimachus, by his choice of images and words, elaborates a continuity that linked the second (Philadelphus and Arsinoe) and third (Berenice II and Euergetes) generations of the Ptolemies as parents and children.[9] *The Victory of Berenice* thus speaks of Berenice as the "blood" (αἷμα) of the Theoi Adelphoi (*SH* 254 + fr. 383.2 Pf.; S. Müller 2009: 101), and *The Lock of Berenice* calls Arsinoe the "mother" (μητρός) of Berenice (fr. 110.45 Pf.; Koenen 1993: 98), presenting Ptolemy III and Berenice II as brother and sister although they were in fact cousins.[10] A double imaginary filiation occurs in the final distich of *The Lock of Berenice* as we know it from POxy 20. 2258 (= fr. 110.94a–b Pf.), the form of the elegy that probably circulated independently of the *Aetia*. Here Arsinoe is described as φίλη τεκέεσσι ("dear to her children"). *The Lock of Berenice* equally reinforces the dynastic discourse in that it sets a high value on the resemblance between Berenice II and Arsinoe II and the similarity of their destinies. The lock, which enjoys catasterism thanks to Aphrodite-Arsinoe, evidently

---

[9] See Gelzer 1982: 18, who elaborates the fine distinctions between the strategies employed in *The Lock of Berenice* and in *The Victory of Berenice*.

[10] Cf. Catull. 66.22; Koenen 1993: 97, remarking on Callimachus' humor in this passage.

follows the path of Arsinoe, whose own deification was related in *The Apotheosis of Arsinoe*, and by synecdoche prefigures the deification of Berenice II, worthy heir of her "mother" Arsinoe.

Filial love and the connections and resemblances between successive generations come to occupy a central place in the ideological apparatus of the Ptolemies and in the presentation that Callimachus gives of the royal family (Koenen 1993: 112). He does the like with the fraternal and conjugal love that unites the royal couple, which becomes the subject of several images and scenes in Alexandrian court poetry (Gutzwiller 1992a: esp. 368). Theocritus and Callimachus evoke the bridal chambers of royal couples and pretend to share with the reader, in a studied intrusion, the supposed intimacy of their princes.[11] A passage of Theocritus *Id.* 17 suggests that the thematization of the royal couple's love served to guarantee that their children "resembled" their father, and were therefore true heirs,[12] thereby inscribing by the same strategy the fiction that made Ptolemy III and Berenice II the children of Arsinoe II. To suggest the royal couple's love, *The Lock of Berenice* unveils a desirable spouse and evokes the sensuality of her perfume. Parallel scenes are probably reflected in the *Lithica* of Posidippus, who describes, at the heart of his imaginary jewelry cabinet, containers for cosmetics in all likelihood intended for use by the queen.[13] As B. Acosta-Hughes has shown (2010: 63–75), Callimachus' allusions to the queen's cosmetics are on a par with a set of intertextual references to poems of Sappho, in particular to fragment 94 V., where we find, with erotic connotations, images of violets, perfume, and the theme of separation from a loved one that are taken up in *The Lock of Berenice*. The double motif of conjugal and fraternal love is further highlighted by a play on the lock's origin and, in Callimachus' poem, a masculine speaker (βόστρυχον: fr. 110.8 Pf.): the lock, which can play a double role as the absent royal husband lamenting his separation from his queen, significantly evokes the lament of his "sisters," the other royal

---

[11] Theocr. *Id.* 17–39–42, 128–130; and Catull. 66.11–14. See S. Müller 2009: 137; Gutzwiller 2007: 70–71.

[12] See Gutzwiller 1992a: 365; also Koenen 1993: 62 and Stephens 2003: 155–156, who link this to Egyptian tradition.

[13] Posidippus 11 and 12 AB. See Kuttner 2005: 149–151. For the perfumes in *The Lock of Berenice*, see Holmes 1992 and especially Jackson 2001, who links perfume with the first Ptolemies' interest in the natural resources of the Red Sea and the Trogodytic coastline. For Arsinoe II's and Berenice II's interest in perfumes, see Apollonius Mys apud Athenaeus 16.688f–689a. For perfume in Theocr. *Id.* 15, see Foster 2006. For the connections between cosmetics and the milieu of the court, see Prioux 2009a.

locks (κόμαι...ἀδε[λφεαί, fr. 110.51 Pf.), thus doubling the motif of the love that Berenice II and Ptolemy III have for each other, the supposed brother and sister separated by the Third Syrian War (Acosta-Hughes 2010: 65–69).

If the poems in their details present Berenice II as the daughter of Arsinoe II, the structure itself of the *Aetia* and the arrangement of individual poems throughout the work appear to converge in emphasizing dynastic continuity between the second and third generations of the Ptolemies. It can be effectively argued that the ring composition and carefully placed echoes encourage the reader to juxtapose and compare the different poems of particular relevance to the queens. Although the extent of the chronological arc corresponding to the composition and edition of the four books of the *Aetia* is the subject of much debate, we should nonetheless emphasize that the final edition of this work, the ensemble made up of Books 3 and 4, opened with *The Victory of Berenice* and closed with *The Lock of Berenice*. Another frame is formed by the evocation of a tenth Muse at the opening of the *Aetia*, in *The Dream* (fr. 3 M.), and by the reference to a female "sovereign" (ἀνάσσης: fr. 112.2 Pf.) and the "house of the sovereigns" (οἶκον ἀνάκτων: fr. 112.8 Pf.) in the *Epilogue*. The ancient commentaries (PLitLond 181.45, POxy 20. 2262, fr. 2a.10–15 Pf.) suggest seeing Arsinoe II as the tenth Muse.[14] If we suppose that the *Epilogue* (fr. 112 Pf.) also dates to an early period of the *Aetia*, then the same queen would recur in the work's final lines. The fact that the tenth Muse and the sovereign were not further defined allows an eventual slippage in sense with Berenice II's arrival on the scene (Gelzer 1982: 23–24; D'Alessio 2007: 541 n. 67).

Another effect of this echo, and a quite remarkable one, has to do with the links between the four so-called *Μέλη* (frr. 226–29 Pf.) and the four books of the *Aetia*, particularly their opening poems. Acosta-Hughes (2003) has called attention to the interplay of correspondences between the two series. If his argument is correct, the reader would thus be invited to find resemblances between *The Apotheosis of Arsinoe*, the third of the four *Μέλη*, and *The Victory of Berenice*, which begins *Aetia* 3.

As we have seen, Callimachus, whether in textual details or in the overall architecture of his work, promotes representations of the royal

---

[14] Koenen 1993: 93–94; Lelli 2002: 15–16; S. Müller 2009: 197; Acosta-Hughes 2010: 75, 80.

family that affirm dynastic continuity among the first three Ptolemaic generations. These representations of the royal family are also occasions to celebrate the various roles assigned to the queens within the empire of the Ptolemies. Callimachus adumbrates at least four: their patronage of the arts, their χάρις ("thanks," "grace," "beauty"), their military and diplomatic skills, and certain symbolic functions within the bilingual culture of Ptolemaic Egypt.

The role of the queen as patron of the arts may be introduced by the motif of the tenth Muse in *The Dream*. Equally, *The Victory of Berenice* suggests that Berenice II shared Callimachus' taste for an aesthetic centered on λεπτότης, "finesse." This elegy's opening juxtaposes Callimachus offering his song to Nemea and to Zeus in thanks for Berenice's victory with Egyptian women who are weaving material, probably with the intention of offering it to Berenice. The women's weaving may be understood as a double sign of finesse and polish (λεπταλέους ἔξυσαν: fr. 383 Pf. + SH 254.15), images that, if they convey the character of a real offering, will also have a metapoetic dimension (e.g., Prioux 2007: 51–56 and n. 97). This supposition is confirmed later in the poem, where the heroic narrative of Heracles' battle with the Nemean Lion seems to have been ignored in favor of a description of the battle joined between the humble Molorchus and the mice that infest his house. No doubt the queen appreciated the charm of this unexpected substitution (Gutzwiller 2007: 66), and one is tempted to see here, with A. Ambühl (2005: 97), Callimachus placing a programmatic poem under the protection of Berenice.

As patrons of the arts, the queens are also associated with the notion of χάρις and the image of the three Graces. Further, the symbolic value of χάρις probably facilitated an aesthetic discourse that had ramifications for the ethical and political order. It certainly would have included the recognition of sensual beauty and the queens' power of seduction, features that occupied a central place in the ideological apparatus of the first Ptolemies. (For the ethical, political, and aesthetic dimensions of the three Graces in Callimachus, see Prioux 2007: 190–214, 224–228, 234–237). The importance that Callimachus accords the image of the Graces as a political and aesthetic emblem appears notably in a compliment addressed to one of the Berenices (*Ep.* 51 Pf.):[15]

---

[15] Theocritus employs the expression ἀρίζηλος Βερενίκη in *Id.* 17.57 to evoke Berenice I. Callimachus' epigram is addressed to a different Berenice, either Berenice

Τέσσαρες αἱ Χάριτες· ποτὶ γὰρ μία ταῖς τρισὶ τήναις
ἄρτι ποτεπλάσθη κῆτι μύροισι νοτεῖ.
εὐαίων ἐν πᾶσιν ἀρίζηλος Βερενίκα,
ἃς ἄτερ οὐδ' αὐταὶ ταὶ Χάριτες Χάριτες.

Four are the Graces. For amid the other three just now a new one has been fashioned, still moist with perfume, Berenice, splendid, blessed among all, without whom the very Graces would not be Graces.

The characterization of Berenice as a fourth Grace parallels that of Arsinoe as the tenth Muse (Bertazzoli 2002). Again we find the motif of seduction associated with the perfume that Berenice used after her marriage. The last verse may have political overtones if one considers that the dance of the three Graces could be interpreted as a representation of the three gestures of exchange (giving, receiving, returning) and that it soon became an image, in philosophical circles, of relations between one who benefits and one who is benefited (Azoulay 2004). In *De beneficiis* Seneca criticizes Chrysippus' explanation of the symbolism of the three Graces in his *Περὶ Χαρίτων*, "On the Graces." We learn there that Chrysippus had exploited the figures of the three Graces to didactic purpose, based on a systematic equivalence between Χάρις and χάρις, Grace and grace or favor. SVF 2.1082 = Sen. *De beneficiis* 1.3.3–4.5). If third-century ideas of χάρις as emblematic of a prince's generosity are largely unknown to us, Seneca's *De beneficiis*, which responds to treatments from the Hellenistic period, bears witness to a tight articulation between generosity and the idea of power: the danger of encountering human ingratitude should never discourage a prince from great generosity (Inwood 1995). Without wishing to attribute to Callimachus a theory that is largely from a later era, we can assume that certain features of these political reflections on the notion of χάρις were already circulating within courts at the beginning of the Hellenistic period and that they would have been especially welcome in the context of royal euergetism. If this hypothesis is justified, the last line of *Epigram* 51 Pf. could signify that the queen, a figure full of grace and aesthetic sensibility, also dispenses benefits, thus fulfilling in an essential way a role given to the king—who should, as does Delian Apollo, dispense benefits and favors (fr. 114b Pf.). This play on the association between Grace and power may have been taken

---

Syra or, more probably, Berenice II. His use of the adjective ἀρίζηλος in *Ep.* 51.3 Pf. was perhaps intended to reinforce the resemblance of the queens across generations.

up also in *The Apotheosis of Arsinoe*, where Philotera, deified sister of Ptolemy Philadelphus and Arsinoe seeks aid from Charis, the wife of Hephaestus (fr. 228.47, 66 Pf.).

In other passages of his oeuvre, Callimachus hints at the role of the Ptolemaic queens in war and diplomacy.[16] Berenice's character, strength of spirit, and courage are underscored in Catullus' version of *The Lock of Berenice* with the adjective *magnanimam* (*Carm.* 66.26), which is generally thought to allude to her role, before her marriage, in thwarting her mother's conspiracy to prevent her marriage with Ptolemy III (and the reunification of Cyrene and Egypt). In *The Victory of Berenice* the implicit comparison between Heracles as victor over the Nemean Lion and Berenice as victor at the Nemean Games may symbolize the role of the queen with the prophetic name "Victory-Bringing" in the defense of Egypt's interests. The implicit comparison of Berenice with Heracles also resonates with a passage of Callimachus' *Hymn to Apollo* in which the nymph Cyrene, Apollo's bride, kills the monstrous lion ravaging Eurypulus' flocks (*Hymn* 2.90–96). The resulting reciprocal χάρις joined Apollo to Cyrene's inhabitants (Barbantani in this volume), and the couple Cyrene and Apollo may be an avatar of Berenice II and Ptolemy III (Merkelbach 1981: 34). The name Eurypylus, moreover, bears potential connections to the royal house: Triton introduces himself to the Argonauts by this name when he helps them cross the Syrtes (Pind. *Pyth.* 4.32; A.R. 4.1561), and this is also the name of a mythical king of Cos, which may in turn permit an allusion to the father of Ptolemy III, Ptolemy II, who was born on that island. The image of the lion serves to indicate the queen's martial valor directly in *The Victory of Berenice*, and it may serve a like function indirectly in the *Hymn to Apollo*.

Some fragments are probably indicative of Arsinoe's diplomatic role regarding the West, especially Rome and Magna Graecia.[17] In other passages Callimachus looks eastward, taking up imagery inherited from the age-old conflict between Europe and Asia and applying it, apparently, to recent conflicts between the Ptolemies and the Seleucids.

---

[16] For visual and literary representations alluding to the symbolic roles exercised by Arsinoe II and Berenice II in the military domain, see S. Müller 2009: 216–229, especially on Posidippus, Ep. 36 AB, and the Thmuis mosiacs; Merriam 1993 on Aphrodite Areia in A.R. 1.730–68.

[17] See Mattingly 1950; Gigante 1997; L.-E. Rossi 1997; Prioux 2009c; and S. Müller 2009: 278–280.

The image of this conflict between Europe and Asia developed in Greek literature and art after the Persian Wars,[18] and its transposition into an Egyptian context was certainly encouraged by the history of conflicts that saw pharaonic Egypt opposed to Persia: the Ptolemies were effectively able to present themselves as restoring the grandeur of Egypt after several centuries of Persian domination. Several texts, among them Callimachus' *Lock of Berenice* and the *Lithica* of Posidippus, appear to use this theme in veiled form (Selden 1998: 326–354; Prioux 2008: 180–182).

I would like to return here to a particularly enigmatic passage of *The Lock of Berenice* that compares the lock, severed from the queen's head, to the peninsula of Acte, severed from Athos by the canal cut by Xerxes to allow the passage of his fleet. This comparison provides the occasion for a brief geographic enigma (fr. 110.44–46 Pf.):[19]

ἀμνά]μω[ν Θείης ἀργὸς ὑ]περφέ[ρ]ετ[αι,
βουπόρος Ἀρσινόης μητρὸς σέο, καὶ διὰ μέ[σσου
Μηδείων ὀλοαὶ νῆες ἔβησαν Ἄθω.

The brilliant descendant of Thia has risen up, the ox-piercer of Arsinoe, your mother, and through the middle of Athos pass the dire ships of the Persians.

Thia's descendant is probably Helius, who rises here over Athos. Catullus' rendition indicates that at this point Callimachus compared the lock, severed by iron, with Athos, pierced by the canal that Xerxes constructed at the Isthmus of Acte to allow a passage for his fleet. As to the problematic "ox-piercer of Arsinoe," G.L. Huxley (1980) ingeniously proposed seeing here an allusion to how the shadow of Athos arose like the needle in a sundial, going on to touch several different points of the Aegean. A fragment of Sophocles (fr. 776 Radt) actually shows that the shadow of Athos was known to touch the back of the statue of a cow on Lemnos at a certain time of year. The reference to the

---

[18] See, e.g., the opening of Herodotus Book 1, or consider the paintings of the Stoa Poecile in Athens (Paus. 1.15–16). Cf. Prioux 2008: 274.

[19] Cf. Catull. *Carm.* 66.43–46: *ille quoque euersus mons est quem maximum in oris | progenies Thiae clara superuehitur, | cum Medi peperere nouum mare cumque iuuentus | per medium classi barbara nauit Athon*, "even that mountain was overthrown, greatest in the region, which Thia's bright offspring crosses, when the Medes brought forth a new sea and barbarian youth sailed though the middle of Athos." On the passage, see G.L. Huxley 1980; and Koenen 1993: 98–99, who points out that βουπόρος may also mean "obelisk." For the analysis proposed here, see Prioux 2010: 158–160.

Persian Wars and the shadow cast by the monument has always been a source of contention among commentators: at first blush it is not obvious what may link Berenice's lock with Athos and the Persian Wars. But I think this comparison should be understood within the frame of a more general discourse that recalls the conflict between Europe and Asia to herald its (supposed) conclusion with the Third Syrian War and the dedication of the lock. That this war brought about the annexation of Asia to Egypt was surely the explicit content of the lost verses immediately preceding our passage. At least Catullus' rendition suggests this: *captam Asiam Aegypti finibus addiderat*, (*Carm.* 66.36). The reference to Chalcidice, an area that plays, it seems, a central role in defining relations of Europe and Asia (Braccesi 2001a: 115), probably results from the desire to inscribe the Third Syrian War into the frame of an abridged universal history that would allow Ptolemy III to appear as the author of an ultimate resolution to an age-old conflict.

Indeed the reference to Athos implicates a famous episode of the Persian Wars, and the term βουπόρος may evoke the Bosporus. This "Cow's Passage" was the waterway between Europe and Asia named for Io, who traversed the limits of both continents in her wanderings after being turned into a heifer. The term βουπόρος allows Callimachus to allude to the adventure of Io, the ancestor of Danaus, an Argive princess whose kidnapping by Phoenician pirates was narrated in Herodotus 1.1–2 and in Lycophron's *Alexandra* 1291–1301 as the first manifestation of an ages-long hostility between Europe and Asia. Io in Egypt was equated with Isis. In creating the βουπόρος Ἀρσινόης, Callimachus allows himself at the same time a learned allusion to a statue on Lemnos mentioned by Sophocles, a discreet nod to the assimilation of Isis and Arsinoe, and a comparsion that allows him to inscribe the Third Syrian War in the frame of universal history marked by age-old conflicts between Europe and Asia.

As D. Selden has shown, *The Lock of Berenice* probably sought to represent the queen as the guarantor of world order. To do so, Callimachus would have played on the underlying presence of a series of allusions to Egyptian religion and the traditional roles played by pharaonic couples in the struggle against the forces of chaos (with which all enemies were equated, but particularly Asia). In Selden's reading, Callimachus' elegy takes into account knowledge of the Egyptian *sphaira* "vault of heaven." The placement of *The Lock of Berenice* is anything but fortuitous, as the position that the lock assumes thanks to Aphrodite puts her near Ursa Major, the part of the sky where, in Egyptian religion, the nightly battle between order and chaos was played out (Selden 1998: 343–344). Ursa Major in fact corresponds to the constellation that the Egyptians called the Bull's Thigh, or Seth's Thigh, the constellation that strives to bring about chaos in the world. The sky maps that we have from Egyptian sanctuaries show this same constellation surrounded by a series of entities endeavoring to limit or control Seth's movements: a falcon-headed god that immediately recalls Horus and a female hippopotamus that, on some sky maps, bears the name Isis (Neugebauer and Parker 1969: 183–191, 190–191). The falcon-headed god menaces Seth's Thigh with a spear; the female hippopotamus holds it with a rope, thus stabilizing world order by assuring that the Bull's Thigh remains enchained. By introducing Berenice's lock among these stars, Conon, the discoverer of this new constellation, took care to make Berenice symbolically the new guarantor of harmony in the world. Once placed by Ursa Major, Berenice's lock could also take part in the fight against the forces of chaos and help to contain Seth's destructive movements. As Selden points out, in Egyptian documents, this struggle against the forces of chaos is directly linked to the function of the pharaoh, whose duty it was to restrain the menace represented by the lands situated to the east of Egypt. Berenice's lock would thus be considered an entity that contributes to guaranteeing world order and establishing the power of Egypt in the face of enemy forces. Callimachus' presentation of the queens thus rests on underlying Egyptian elements that a court audience would certainly have understood.[20]

Callimachus and Royal Incest

If it is possible to find Egyptian elements underlying a certain number of Hellenistic poems designed to express Lagid court ideology, the poets found themselves equally confronted with the necessity of justifying the incestuous marriage of Ptolemy II and Arsinoe II to a Greek and Macedonian audience. For poets under the protection of

---

[20] For other examples, see Stephens 1998 and 2003; whereas Selden's reading of *The Lock of Berenice* focuses on the Isiac model for Ptolemaic queens, Llewellyn-Jones and Winder 2010 study the Hathoric model, which apparently was specifically promoted by Berenice II. For comparable strategies in Theocritus, see Reed 2000. See Prioux 2008: 177–198 for discussion of certain allusive elements of *The Lock of Berenice* found in Posidippus' *Lithica*.

the Ptolemies, it was a matter of Hellenizing this royal incest, particularly through highlighting mythic precedents: an incest that the king had manifestly borrowed from Egyptian tradition, and one that included the wish of guaranteeing, through endogamy, dynastic perpetuity (S. Müller 2009). The model to which the poets turned was of course the couple Zeus and Hera,[21] but the use of comparisons between the incestuous marriage of the new kings and the *hieros gamos*, "holy marriage," varies considerably from one poet to another; an obvious contrast is the tone and directness at the end of *Idyll* 17 (*Encomium of Ptolemy*), where Theocritus presents Iris preparing the bed of Zeus and Hera (ll. 133–134), whereas Callimachus' treatment is much more allusive and humorous (Koenen 1993: 97).

Callimachus took care to introduce references to the *hieros gamos* of Zeus and Hera (*Iliad* 14.292–351) or implicit comparisons between Arsinoe and Zeus' sister-wife into his *Aetia* through small touches and fleeting allusions (Prioux 2009b). For instance, when Berenice's lock relates how it was borne by Arsinoe's winged horse Zephyrus, it specifies that the deified queen is ἰοζώνου ("with violet sash"). As Acosta-Hughes (2010: 64–65) has observed, this adjective is formed on two models: ἰόκολπος ("with lap of violet"), attested exclusively in Sappho, where the adjective appears most frequently as an attribute of Aphrodite (e.g., fr. 103.3–4 V.), and πορφυρόζωνος ("with purple sash"), attested exclusively in Bacchylides (11.48–49), where it refers to Hera. The intertextual construction of this adjective suggests a double comparison between Arsinoe on the one hand and Aphrodite and Hera on the other; we might add that Arsinoe was also associated with the violet and with Hera in an epigram attributed to Lycophron, where the letters of Arsinoe's name are rearranged to yield "Hera's violet" (Ἀρσινόη becoming Ἥρας ἴον; cf. Eust. 46.3–5). The motif of Hera's ζώνη, or girdle, may further evoke the enchanted gift that Aphrodite gives Hera in *Iliad* 14.181.[22] In truth, the image that we find in this passage of *The Lock of Berenice* may recall an allegorical interpretation of Zeus' and Hera's love as representing the arrival of spring:[23]

---

[21] This model is equally found in monuments: at Olympia, Ptolemy II's admiral Callicrates of Samos had had a monument erected with columns and statues that required a direct comparison between the couple Hera-Zeus and Arsinoe II–Ptolemy II. See Hintzen-Bohlen 1992.

[22] See Pfeiffer fr. 110.54 *ad loc.*; Acosta-Hughes 2010: 65.

[23] *Heracl. Alleg. Hom.* 39. See also Russell and Konstan 2005: xii; Plut. *Quom. adul. poet. aud. deb.* 19e–20b.

Arsinoe is in effect served by Zephyrus, the θῆλυς or "fertile" wind (fr. 101.53 Pf.; Acosta-Hughes 2010: 68). In this passage there is a coherent nexus of allusions that makes Arsinoe a figure identifiable as Aphrodite and Hera and that highlights images of fertility, perhaps inspired by allegorical readings of *Iliad* 14. The ideological range of these images is probably motivated by the wish to present the queen as guarantor of the fertility of the kingdom,[24] a discourse that surely complements Ptolemy II's choice of the horn of plenty as image for his royal spouse.

For Callimachus' court audience the motif of the *hieros gamos* might be relevant in fragments 100 and 101 Pf., which are two *aitia* of the cult statues of Hera on Samos.[25] This pair of fragments may be a diptych for the queen in the same way that the pair formed by fragments 114a and 114b Pf. (descriptions of cult statues of Apollo) may be for the king. In each case the evocation of an aniconic image is followed by an allegorical interpretation of an archaic statue and at least for the second fragment a political reading seems possible. The image of Delian Apollo was probably meant to describe the mercy and justice of Ptolemy II compared with Horus-Apollo. The choice of Samian Hera seems to me dictated by the intention of furnishing a match for fragment 114b Pf.: Samos is associated with the birth of Hera as Delos is with the birth of Apollo, and the poet proposes an allegorical interpretation that allows a review of the divine figure. In the case of Hera, there is an explanation why a vine snakes through the goddess' hair and why a lionskin lies stretched out at her feet (fr. 101 Pf.). The similarity with the context and subject matter of fragment 114b Pf. suggests the possibility of a political reading for fragment 101 Pf. as well.

There are indeed other points of contact between this image and other representations that Callimachus and his contemporaries have left of Arsinoe II. The theme of the *hieros gamos* is very likely present, as Samos was sometimes represented as being the place where the first union of Zeus and Hera occurred (Hollis 1976: 145): the statue of Hera at Samos was elsewhere involved in rites commemorating the *hieros*

---

[24] The fact that Arsinoe was past childbearing age when she married her brother suggests that this fecundity is symbolic and connected to the fertility of the Egyptian land guaranteed by the annual Nile flood. This motif could be connected to the theme of fertility in the *Lithica* of Posidippus. See Casamassa 2004: 243–244.

[25] For a comparison with the archaeological sources and with the iconographic material, see Prioux (forthcoming).

gamos of the divine couple (Elderkin 1937: 424). Callimachus further indicates that the Hera of fragment 101 Pf. bears vine and *lionskin* because she received homage from Dionysus and Heracles, illegitimate sons of Zeus; this situation may recall for us the honors that Ptolemy III Euergetes—a king who would be happily compared to Dionysus and to Heracles and who was the son not of Arsinoe II but of Arsinoe I—had given to his father's new wife. And further, the fruits associated with Dionysus and Hera, the grape and the pomegranate, were brought together in the representations that coins have given us of Arsinoe's double horn of plenty.[26]

Allusions to the *hieros gamos* of Zeus and Hera allow justification of royal incest, but they also allow the suggestion that the royal couple rises above humanity precisely because of behavior ordinarily prohibited that nonetheless imitates divinity. This idea occurs notably in the opening of *The Victory of Berenice*, where Berenice II, imagined as the offspring of hierogamy, is presented (line 2) as κα[σιγνή]των ἱερὸν αἷμα θεῶν, "the holy blood of the sibling gods" (S. Müller 2009: 129). Allusions to the hierogamy of Zeus and Hera in *Iliad* 14 also allow the possibility of representing in Greek terms an Egyptian practice that the Ptolemies borrowed from pharaonic tradition in supporting the identification of the royal couple with the divine Egyptian couple Isis and Osiris.

In addition to these allusions to hierogamy, *Epigram* 1 Pf. may bear witness to a different attempt to represent this incestuous union, here as a choice taken from wisdom literature that echoes precepts formulated in a Greek milieu. At least this is the suggestion of P. Bleisch (1996) in an elegant analysis of this text that reproduces an exchange between Pittacus and an Atarnean stranger who has come to ask for his advice. To the stranger, who hesitates between a marriage that would unite him with a wife of higher station and one that would unite him with an equal, Pittacus suggests marriage with "her who corresponds with him by birth." Bleisch argues that οὕτω καὶ σύ, Δίων, "so you too, Dion," in the final line of the epigram is an anagram for the dual Δι(ο)νυσιακῶ and would predispose his audience to apply this formulation to the royal couple, who as "descendants of Dionysus" had carried out marriage between equals to an extreme degree. The reader would thus understand Callimachus' text as insinuating that the royal pair

---

[26] See S. Müller 2009: 375, who notes the parallel with fr. 101 Pf.

merely followed the counsel of one of the Seven Sages. The exaggeration of this idea, which depends for its effect on humor and absurdity, probably constituted the means by which Callimachus' compliment could be received and shared with good humor by the Alexandrian elite (Bleisch 1996: 462, 468).

From Queen to Goddess

The implicit comparisons between the queen and Hera, which allow reformulating royal incest with images borrowed from Greek culture, demonstrate how Callimachus' oeuvre contributes to an image of a divinized Arsinoe. To complete the picture sketched out with Hera, we turn now to the representations of Arsinoe II as Aphrodite or Helen, with the addition of a few remarks, if only fleeting, on the assimilation of the queen with Isis-Io.

If in Callimachus the kings seem especially to accede to divine status through references (sometimes ambiguous) in the *Hymns*, the queens are openly represented as the recipients of offerings mentioned in *Epigram* 5 Pf. (Selenaea's offering of a nautilus) or in *The Lock of Berenice* (the lock, "taken up" (line 55) by Arsinoe-Aphrodite and offered (line 8) to "all the gods"). Selenaea's nautilus and Berenice's lock form a sort of pair, as both these offerings were probably made at the Temple of Arsinoe situated on Cape Zephyrium. They belong with a series of epigrams attributed to Posidippus of Pella and Hedylus of Samos that also describe offerings made in the same temple.[27]

Selenaea's epigram on the nautilus suggests the powers of Arsinoe-Aphrodite Zephyritis: not only the protection that she accords to navigation, for which the nautilus—compared through its anatomy with a miniature sailing vessel—is in one sense a symbol, but also the role that she plays for young women on the eve of marriage.[28] This same epigram also inserts allusions to the personal history of Arsinoe and celebrates the maritime power of the Lagids and the extent of their empire. Selenaea comes from Smyrna (*Ep.* 5.12 Pf.)—which under the name Eurydicea was one of the foundations of Lysimachus of Macedon, Arsinoe's first husband (Strabo 14.1.37; S. Müller 2009: 269)—and

---

[27] See most recently S. Müller 2009: 206–249, with the previous literature. See also Hedylus *Ep.* 4 GP = Athenaeus 11.497d; and for the cult at Cape Zephyrium, see Posidippus *Ep.* 12 and 13 GP respectively, PFirminDidot and and Athenaeus 7.318d.

[28] See especially Gutzwiller 1992b; Selden 1998: 309–313; S. Müller 2009: 268–269.

the nautilus was gathered up through her care on "the shores of Iulis" (*Ep.* 5.7 Pf.). Since Iulis, a city on the island of Ceos, is not situated on the shore, it is likely that Selenaea had put into port at Coresia, a Lagid naval base that had taken the name Arsinoe during the reign of Ptolemy II.[29]

So *Epigram* 5 Pf. combines allusions to the divine status of Arsinoe-Aphrodite, protectress of sailors and of future brides, with geographical references to the Lagid empire. This is a game comparable to that at the center of *The Lock of Berenice*, in the passage that evokes the help brought by Arsinoe-Aphrodite and her servant Zephyrus to the future constellation (fr. 110.51–58 Pf.). The motifs of favorable wind and of the lock "bathed" by Arsinoe-Aphrodite (λουόμενον: fr. 110.63) recall the goddess' role as protectress of navigation, while the allusion to Epizephyrian Locri surely celebrates the role of Arsinoe in state diplomacy. Two further observations permit the reader to see the easy parallelism between *Epigram* 5 Pf. and *The Lock of Berenice*. On the one hand, the last two verses of *The Lock of Berenice* (fr. 110.94a–b), which are no doubt from the initial version of the poem and were probably removed prior to its insertion into the *Aetia*, suggest reading the whole poem as a hymn to Arsinoe-Aphrodite. These two verses highlight the importance of the image of the queen as a goddess accepting the offering of a song associated with a dedication that had taken place in her sanctuary (Koenen 1993: 113). On the other hand, if one accepts the reading proposed by S.B. Jackson (2001), the lock could evoke, through its association with expensive cosmetics and its passage through the waters in which it is "bathed" (λουόμενον), a new wonder arisen from the sea that would serve as a pair with the nautilus, namely a coral known under the name of Ἴσιδος πλόκαμος, "lock of Isis," which came from the Red Sea and was used as an erotic talisman. If indeed a recollection of this coral is present in the text, it would add to the instances identifying the deified queen with Isis.

I believe that other identifications of Arsinoe with divine figures arise in lines 4–6 of *The Victory of Berenice*. In this passage Proteus, who was honored in a temple on Pharos, gladly receives the news of Berenice's victory. This news comes directly from Argos, the land of Danaus the descendant of Io, who was metamorphosed into a cow:

---

[29] See D'Alessio 2007: 221 n. 13. For Arsinoe as the name of Coresia under Ptolemy II, see L. Robert 1960: 146–147 on *IG* 12.5.1061.

ἁρμοῖ γὰρ Δαναοῦ γῆς ἀπὸ βουγενέος
εἰς Ἑλένη[ς νησῖδ]α καὶ εἰς Παλληνέα μά[ντιν,
ποιμένα [φωκάων], χρύσεον ἦλθεν ἔπος.

Just now from the land of cow-born Danaus
to the island of Helen and the Pallenean prophet,
shepherd of seals, a golden word has come.

Proteus, who intervenes to prevent the abduction of Helen to Troy, is as a result tied to Helen's fortunes and to those of Menelaus in Egypt. Here through the reference to the island of Pharos he is associated as much with the land of Egypt as he is with Chalcidice through evocation of the peninsula of Pallene. One might suggest that Proteus' double geographic connection with Pallene and with the island of Pharos recalls, at the heart of the praise of Berenice, the destiny of her mother-in-law, Arsinoe II, a queen who completed a journey of distance much like that of Proteus: daughter of Ptolemy I, Arsinoe left Alexandria to marry the Thracian king Lysimachus, then returned to Egypt to marry Ptolemy II, just as Proteus left Egypt to dwell in Pallene and then returned to Egypt.[30]

Indeed the three verses quoted just above appear coded in their rapport with the divine status of Arsinoe II. There is clearly much more behind the reference to Danaus, Io, and Helen than simple mythological allusion. Danaus, king of Egypt and descendant of the Argive princess Io, recalls direct links that exist between Io and Egypt. As a princess, Io arrives in Egypt after her wandering in bovine form and there becomes assimilated to Isis, as Arsinoe II will also be.[31] And as we will see at the conclusion of this chapter, Arsinoe was in all likelihood assimilated to Helen—which means that the two queens mentioned in this passage are mythological precedents indirectly evoking the divinity of Arsinoe II.

This reading may find confirmation in the second passage where Callimachus evokes the figure of Proteus, *The Apotheosis of Arsinoe* (fr. 228 Pf.). Here the reference to the god of Pharos occurs in a geographic dream space that unites Thrace and Athos to Alexandria in the

---

[30] Proteus may have constituted a parallel for the Ptolemies in that he was both a king and a god, well established on the site of the future Alexandria; see Prioux 2010.

[31] An allusion to the identification of Io with Isis may be strengthened by the inclusion a little later in this passage of a reference to the Apis bull, whom the Greeks identified with Epaphus the son of Io; see Stephens 2003: 8–9.

course of the same vision.³² The *diegesis* to fragment 228 Pf. indicates that the dead Queen Arsinoe was borne heavenward by the Dioscuri and that a sanctuary and altar were founded near the Emporium. The shore, the sea, and the area of Pharos occur in a lamentation in honor of the dead queen pronounced at Alexandria itself, as the first part of the poem suggests: line 15 mentions a ceremony held around the altars of Thetis on an island (Pharos), and line 39 introduces Proteus as a silent auditor of lamentation. As in the elegy on Berenice's victory, he hears words as true as will be his own predictions: Πρωτῆϊ μὲν ὧδ᾽ ἐτύμοι κατάγο[ντο φᾶμαι (fr. 228.39 Pf.: "thus true words were carried to Proteus").

The appearance of Proteus marks a point of transition in the poem, which up to this point has been in direct discourse. The transition is marked by the particles μέν...δέ (lines 39–40) and by the brusque focalization at line 40, from the point of view of a spectator far removed from the scene: the dead and deified Philotera,³³ who has come from visiting Demeter in Sicily, and who, as she crosses over the waters (near Lemnos?), from a distance perceives the smoke of the funeral pyre. She asks Charis to go the summit of Mount Athos to look out and discover the source of the smoke (lines 47–51). As Charis turns her eyes toward Pharos, she replies that the smoke is coming from Alexandria.

The figure of Proteus, like that of the Dioscuri, brings the image of Helen to mind, as evoked at the opening of *The Victory of Berenice*. Helen takes us back to Egypt at the time of the Trojan War, but also to Lagid propaganda that probably assimilated Arsinoe II to a new Helen.³⁴ We should remember that Helen had been assimilated, since at least the time of Herodotus, to Aphrodite Xene (probably a version of Astarte venerated as protectress of the seas. This Aphrodite was precisely the one venerated in the *temenos* of Proteus at Memphis (Hdt 2.112; G. Castagna 1981). In *The Apotheosis of Arsinoe*, the double reference to Proteus and Helen could thus recall on the one hand the divine status of Helen and her assimilation to Aphrodite and on the

---

³² For the geographical allusions that connect the two to Arsinoe, see Lelli 2002: 9.

³³ For the cult of Philotera, which is associated with Demeter, see Fraser 1972: 1.229.

³⁴ See, e.g., Basta Donzelli 1984; Foster 2006; and Prioux 2010. On the correspondences between Helen and Arsinoe II in Callimachus, see D'Alessio 2007: 694–695 n. 36.

other hand the triangulation between Arsinoe, Aphrodite, and Helen. With the Dioscuri we encounter the famous Savior Gods—protectors of seafaring to whom the Pharos at Alexandria may have been dedicated[35]—but also the personal history of Arsinoe, who as the wife of Lysimachus and queen of Thrace had dedicated a round temple to the Great Gods of Samothrace, the Cabiri, who were divine forces assimilated to the Dioscuri (McCredie, Roux, and Shaw 1992). The Cabiri are, like Helen, indirectly lined to the figure of Proteus, since they were thought to be the children of Hephaestus and Cabiro, daughter of Proteus (Strabo 10.3.21 = *FGrHist* Pherecydes 3 F 48).

Several passages in Callimachus' oeuvre suggest that the poet was very well informed about the traditions concerning the Cabiri: one elegy of the *Aetia* is dedicated to Onnes and Tottes, their Milesian equivalent (fr. 115 Pf.); *Iambus* 9 deals humorously with the Cabiri of Samothrace; and *Epigram* 47 Pf. takes an interest in the Cabiri of Samothrace as protectors of seafaring. The epigram expands on the metaphor of a storm of debts and evokes the dedication of a saltcellar to these deities. Arsinoe's role is implicit, as founder of the temple and in her association with the Cabiri/Dioscuri as protectors of sailors.

In *The Apotheosis of Arsinoe*, just as in *The Lock of Berenice*, reference to Athos and to Chalcidice is associated, directly or otherwise, with Lemnos, an island close to Samothrace known to have hosted a cult of the Cabiri (frr. 110.45 and 228.44 Pf.). In *The Apotheosis of Arsinoe*, a text that tells how the Dioscuri raised the dead queen to heaven, Philotera asks the aid of Charis, the wife of Hephaestus, who was the father of the Cabiri. It is surely significant that Arsinoe is invoked with the formula ὦ δαίμοσιν ἁρπαγίμα ("you who were taken up by the daimons": fr. 228.46 Pf.): the substantive δαίμοσιν can evidently designate the Cabiri, gods of Samothrace, while the term ἁρπαγίμα, "object of seizure" may recall the substantive ὑφαρπάγιμον, which Stesichorus appears to use for Helen.[36]

The poem that precedes *The Apotheosis of Arsinoe* is a sympotic song in honor of the Dioscuri (fr. 227 Pf.) sung on the occasion of a nocturnal festival (Acosta-Hughes 2003). According to the *diegesis*,

---

[35] For the debates over the identification of the Savior Gods, to whom the Pharos was dedicated—Is "Savior Gods" a designation of the Dioscuri or of the royal couple Ptolemy I and Berenice I, or is this an ambiguous reference to both pairs?—see Guimier-Sorbets 2007.

[36] Cf. *PMGF* S104.13. For the parallels, see D'Alessio 2007: 665 n. 26.

this song celebrated the Dioscuri and their sister Helen in bidding them accept a sacrifice. These two poems, fragments 227 and 228, probably played on the assimilation of Helen and Arsinoe, and on the allusions to the religious iconography of the Dioscuri and the Cabiri (Basta Donzelli 1984: 306).

A series of images studied by F. Chapouthier (1935), the earliest of which can be dated to the third century BC, shows the Dioscuri or the Cabiri flanking a goddess whom they serve. The original of this series is an image of the Dioscuri flanking Helen, but numerous variations soon occur: Cabiri or Dioscuri flank Cybele, Demeter, or Hecate; the Dioscuri flank Isis;[37] the Dioscuri flank Tyche. Interestingly, the image of the goddess is occasionally replaced by one of the new goddesses created by the Lagid regime. Callimachus' text may be illustrated by a coin preserved in a private collection that clearly fits this series: a golden double octodrachma showing on the obverse a portrait of Arsinoe wearing a veil and crown and on the reverse the double horn of plenty—an emblem of Arsinoe II—between two *piloi* raised above stars representing the Dioscuri, with the legend ΑΡΣΙΝΟΗΣ ΦΙΛΑΔΕΛΦΟΥ.[38] The same iconography is used on a monetary issue of Ptolemy III in memory of his sister Berenice Syra, wife of Antiochus II of Syria, assassinated in 246: a golden decadrachma bearing on the obverse the queen's portrait and on the reverse a horn of plenty between two stars with the inscription ΒΕΡΕΝΙΚΗΣ ΒΑΣΙΛΙΣΣΗΣ (Chapouthier 1935: 265–266). Again we find the symbol of the queen flanked by the Dioscuri. Even if the date of this monetary issue is uncertain (between 246 and 222 BC), the link with the Third Syrian War and with the ideology that guided the composition of *The Lock of Berenice* is clear, as the Third Syrian War was meant precisely to avenge the assassination of Berenice Syra.

In conclusion, the compliments addressed to the queens occur principally in the *Aetia*, in the *Epigrams*, and in occasional poems that are often very badly preserved, in contrast to the praise of the kings that appears especially in the *Hymns*. The strategies by which Callimachus celebrates the kings and the queens are thus differentiated first by their placement in the poet's oeuvre. They are also thematically distinct,

---

[37] This iconography should be compared with the text of POxy 9.1380, which identifies Isis with the Great Goddess of the Mysteries of Samothrace.
[38] For this issue and its rapport with the text of Callimachus, cf. Hazzard 1995: 423–424 and pl. II, 10.

with, notably, the recurrence of celestial journeys in the poems on the queens, or with the repeated setting of an offering made to the queens raised to divine status. In the passages relating to the queens, Callimachus makes use of different techniques probably intended to assure a coherent contemporary ideology in the circle immediately surrounding the royal couple. Thus he plays on the integration of Egyptian elements, but he takes care to present these in a Hellenized form in seeking out, through archaic or mythological precedents, events similar to those established in the contemporary setting of the Alexandrian court. Intertextuality is thus often a tool that strengthens the discourse at hand. Moreover, Callimachus' humor imbues his verse, a humor that itself reinforces his ideological perspective, both engaging the reader and illustrating the generosity of princes tolerant of certain forms of free speech (see Prioux 2009b).

Two important questions remain for further inquiry. First, there are the differences distinguishing the poems that focus on Arsinoe II from those focused on Berenice II. As far as our evidence allows us to surmise, praise of Berenice occurs primarily in poems dedicated to Berenice herself, whereas praise of Arsinoe occurs primarily in diffuse allusions that suggest political allegory. There are counterexamples in both cases: the episode of the nymph Cyrene in the *Hymn to Apollo* for Berenice; for Arsinoe *The Apotheosis of Arsinoe* (fr. 228 Pf.) and the epithalamium for her marriage to Ptolemy II (fr. 392 Pf.). Does the impression of the whole that we take from the preserved corpus, a small part of a once vast oeuvre, correspond to a real tendency in the poet's treatment of the queens, or is it simply a chance result of papyrological discovery? Second, one would like to know whether the thematic coherence that exists at certain points in the work of Posidippus and Callimachus (epithalamia for Arsinoe, offerings at the Temple of Arsinoe–Aphrodite Zephyritis, Panhellenic victories of Berenice) bears witness simply to the two court poets' emulation of each other or is in response to commands addressed at the same time to different poets, perhaps by such figures as Callicrates of Samos.

CHAPTER ELEVEN

POET AND COURT

Gregor Weber

ABSTRACT

Beginning from an overview of Hellenistic monarchy this conribution turns first to Ptolemy I and his need for a royal court to establish himself in Egypt. Intellectuals in a variety of areas at the Ptolemaic court contributed in a major way to this development, intellectuals who were also in large part also friends of the King. We should understand Callimachus and his work in this context: the court with its personalities and events gave him material for poetic creation, and ensured its reception. The variety of his work can be understood as a reflection of the character of the court as political, administrative, intellectual, and social center—for Callimachus and his fellow poets were informed by the court's structures of communication and interaction. These structures also make it possible for us to consider the contexts of publication and performance, as well as audience.

When Alexander the Great died in July 323 BC, not only had he failed to settle his succession, but it was also an open question how the Greek world would develop in the newly conquered regions of his vast empire.[1] At first Alexander's closest confidants split the satrapies up among themselves and governed them on behalf of Alexander's son (also named Alexander) and feeble-minded half brother, Philip III Arrhidaeus, but soon enough there was a state of constant warfare among the Successors. In this series of conflicts, all the other combatants would invariably combine against the one who appeared to be the strongest at the time, resulting in a constant reduction in the number

---

Throughout this chapter, volume 6 of W. Peremans, *Prosopographia Ptolemaica* (Louvain, 1968), will be abbreviated as *PP* VI. I thank Benjamin Acosta-Hughes for the invitation to contribute to this volume, which I gladly undertook, especially because of the memory of our time studying together in Freiburg. I thank also Jürgen Malitz and Susan Stephens for several important suggestions. Christopher Schliephake helped with bibliography and proofreading.
[1] Possible options: Weber 2007a: 256–258.

of contestants.[2] After Alexander's son and sister died, a new state of affairs emerged, in that each of the main players one after another proclaimed himself king, or rather was so acclaimed by his troops.[3] This step was to prove rich in consequences, since kings like Lysimachus, Seleucus, Antigonus, and Ptolemy were now faced with a difficult task: they had to present themselves in the lands they occupied as legitimate rulers and win acceptance among the various peoples, or else establish robust structures for their rule, since they were each still exposed to the attacks of their competitors. As different as their relationships with their kingdoms appeared in detail, all the new Hellenistic monarchs were faced with a similar situation. What was crucial in the establishment of Hellenistic monarchies is encapsulated in the entry Βασιλεία in the *Suda*, a Byzantine lexicon of the tenth century AD: οὔτε φύσις οὔτε τὸ δίκαιον ἀποδιδοῦσι τοῖς ἀνθρώποις τὰς βασιλείας, ἀλλὰ τοῖς δυναμένοις ἡγεῖσθαι στρατοπέδου καὶ χειρίζειν πράγματα νουνεχῶς.[4] The Hellenistic king had first of all to be a successful military general;[5] a king could manage his so-called πράγματα only if he had reliable helpers beneath him, had set up an administrative and political center, and could deploy adequate financial resources, which he had to draw from his own territory. These were essential to pay for troops, mostly mercenaries, as well as for a residence that could be the foundation for satisfactory royal self-fashioning—for a king required a whole infrastructure compartmentalized in accordance with his needs, with rooms for audiences, feasts, and symposia, as well as storerooms and living quarters.[6] Besides all this, he had to keep an eye on his acceptance as a Graeco-Macedonian king (βασιλεύς) and deport himself, whether through military aid, foundations, financial expenditure, or other acts of generosity, as Savior (Σωτήρ) and Benefactor (Εὐεργέτης) before the Greek public. Hellenistic monarchy, therefore, entailed personal rule and centered on the king's affairs (τὰ πράγματα) and on his household (οἶκος; Virgilio 1994: 163–164).

---

[2] This phase lasted, with shifting coalitions, for a good fifty years, till 272 BC; see further Braund 2003; Bosworth 2006; Malitz 2007: 23–36.

[3] On the Year of the Kings ((306/5 BC), see Plut. *Demetr.* 18 and P. Köln 6.247 with O. Müller 1973; Gehrke 2003: 39 and 167–168; M.M. Austin 2006: no. 44.

[4] Translation in M.M. Austin 2006: no. 45: "Monarchy. It is neither descent nor legitimacy which gives monarchies to men, but the ability to command an army and to handle affairs competently." See further on this Gehrke 2003: 46–49.

[5] Hence the title of Gehrke 1982.

[6] The evidence is reviewed by Nielsen 1999, though often with excessively confident identifications; see Vössing 2004: 100–106.

The development of a court soon came to be seen as an indispensable ingredient in the organization of a kingdom; moreover, as an expanded version of the royal household it represented the spatial center that the king inhabited.[7] From here he administered the fate of his sovereign territory, and here, in festivals and other performances, he put his kingdom on show.[8] Above all, though, the king surrounded himself with people who helped him cope with his various duties, on whom he could rely, and in whose company he appeared on many different occasions: these were the king's Companions (φίλοι), who, along with the royal family, the royal servants, and individuals residing on a temporary basis at the court (ambassadors, for instance), made up court society. Among these Companions the king also convened the royal council (συνέδριον), and made public displays of communality at feasts (συνουσίαι) and drinking parties (συμπόσια).[9] It goes almost without saying that such gatherings were a locus of conflicts, since within the court circle (which was in no sense hermetically sealed to outsiders) there was fierce competition for royal favor.[10] The king in his turn had to fulfill expectations, and thus minimize potential threats, through donations of land and money, the distribution of prestigious priesthoods, or the dedication of statues (Habicht 1958: 4, 10–12; Seibert 1991). Even members of the royal family could represent a source of anxiety, since the existence of pretenders to the throne born from different marriages could lead to friction in the absence of clear rules of succession. (Ogden 1999 is fundamental here.) How the new elite

---

[7] On what follows: Weber 1993: 20–32; Herman 1997; Weber 1997; Winterling 1998: 661–662. It is illuminating that the phrases τὸ βασίλειον or τὰ βασίλεια, which at first meant only "the royal" and required an explanatory noun, came to limit a specific space belonging to the king. At the same time the word αὐλή ("court"), which seems to have emerged first in the context of Hellenistic courts, had similar spatial connotations while also containing within its field of meaning the idea of court society (Funck 1996: 52). The royal court in Pella had already been specially constructed, even though the norm under Alexander, if we disregard the final stage of his expedition in Babylon, was really a traveling court. The nature of the court as a military camp, imposed by the necessities of war, meant that the royal tent (σκηνή)—equipped with everything that was required for organization and representation—became a visual and symbolic center.

[8] See on this Weber 2007c: 102–111. Luxury (τρυφή) would become one of the characteristic features of the Hellenistic monarchs in comparison with the Roman *nobiles*; see on this Heinen 1983.

[9] On the forms of court life, see Weber 1997: 43–46; Asper 2004: 7–9; Strootman 2005b: 191–92. On the symposium and the rich tradition of anecdotes associated with it, see Vössing 2004: 86–92.

[10] On the competition, see Polybius 4.874–85 with Herman 1997: 210–211; Meissner 2000: 9–10 nn. 27, 28.

was made up—what regions and social classes the king's Companions came from, what functions they had been installed to fulfill, and whether members of the former native upper class were represented— was consequently of great concern to every royal court.[11]

If we look more closely at the actions of Ptolemy I in the light of these considerations, peculiarities emerge. Ptolemy was the son of a Macedonian named Lagus, and as a member of Alexander's bodyguard was a member of his closest circle of friends (σωματοφύλακες). In the apportioning of the satrapies in the wake of Alexander's death, he secured Egypt and not only defended his sovereign territory but was also able to extend it to include Cyrene, part of Asia Minor, and a number of the Aegean islands.[12] Problems within the family, which resulted from passing over the older Ptolemy Ceraunus (Lightning Bolt), the king's son by Eurydice, in favor of a younger Ptolemy who was the result of the king's marriage to Berenice, were not replicated in subsequent dynastic history (Malitz 2007: 34–37). Ptolemy I had come upon considerable financial resources in Egypt, which he invested shrewdly in various projects.[13] One initiative concentrated on recruiting mercenaries and putting the defense of Egypt on an effective footing. He also endeavored to win the good will of the Egyptian priestly elite from the beginning through donations and funds for repair work to sanctuaries.[14] Connected to this courting of the priestly class is another peculiarity of the Ptolemaic regime in Egypt, the "dual-faced" nature of the monarchy, in which Ptolemy was both *basileus* and pharaoh.[15] Ptolemy had next to strive to get as many Greeks and Macedonians as possible as settlers, traders, and so forth, and as many experts in a

---

[11] The pattern of interaction between the king and these various circles of acquaintances did not remain constant throughout the Hellenistic period but went through several different phases, on which see Weber 2007c: 114–116. On the equality of relations between βασιλεύς and φίλοι, at least at the beginning of the period, see Weber 1997: 42–43; *contra*, Meissner 2000. On the type of the flatterer (κόλαξ), who is often mentioned in accounts of the court as viewed from outside, see Kerkhecker 1997: 130–132; Vössing 2004: 93–100.

[12] Hölbl 1994: 14–31; Huss 2001: 97–212. In comparison with the other Successors, Ptolemy confined himself from the beginning to Egypt and made no claims on Alexander's empire as a whole.

[13] According to Diod. 18.14.1 these consisted of 8,000 talents, which Cleomenes of Naucratis had accumulated there as his predecessor (Legras 2006). Similar sums were available to the founders of the Attalid dynasty.

[14] Cooperation seemed a good idea to both sides; for the range of measures, see Huss 1994.

[15] For this the term *monarchie bicéphale* has been introduced; see Peremans 1987.

variety of areas: for example, agricultural science, finance, and so on. To them, he was their βασιλεύς and had to fulfill their expectations. At the same time he fulfilled the role of pharaoh for the indigenous Egyptians, since in Egyptian theology such a figure was indispensable for the preservation of the natural order.[16] Subsequent Ptolemaic rulers also submitted themselves to this requirement, though their behavior vis-à-vis Egyptian culture and the Egyptian elite changed somewhat over time. Finally, Ptolemy must have hurried along the construction of Alexandria as his capital and royal city (while residing until 311 at the latest in Memphis), although separate phases of construction can hardly be discerned there any longer. Because of this, Strabo's detailed description of Alexandria is of some importance:[17]

ἔχει δ' ἡ πόλις τεμένη τε κοινὰ κάλλιστα καὶ τὰ βασίλεια, τέταρτον ἢ καὶ τρίτον τοῦ παντὸς περιβόλου μέρος· τῶν γὰρ βασιλέων ἕκαστος ὥσπερ τοῖς κοινοῖς ἀναθήμασι προσεφιλοκάλει τινὰ κόσμον, οὕτω καὶ οἴκησιν ἰδίᾳ περιεβάλλετο πρὸς ταῖς ὑπαρχούσαις.... τῶν δὲ βασιλείων μέρος ἐστὶ καὶ τὸ Μουσεῖον, ἔχον περίπατον καὶ ἐξέδραν καὶ οἶκον μέγαν ἐν ᾧ τὸ συσσίτιον τῶν μετεχόντων τοῦ Μουσείου φιλολόγων ἀνδρῶν. ἔστι δὲ τῇ συνόδῳ ταύτῃ καὶ χρήματα κοινὰ καὶ ἱερεὺς ὁ ἐπὶ τῷ Μουσείῳ τεταγμένος τότε μὲν ὑπὸ τῶν βασιλέων νῦν δ' ὑπὸ Καίσαρος. μέρος δὲ τῶν βασιλείων ἐστὶ καὶ τὸ καλούμενον Σῆμα, ὃ περίβολος ἦν ἐν ᾧ αἱ τῶν βασιλέων ταφαὶ καὶ ἡ Ἀλεξάνδρου· ἔφθη γὰρ τὸ σῶμα ἀφελόμενος Περδίκκαν ὁ τοῦ Λάγου Πτολεμαῖος κατακομίζοντα ἐκ τῆς Βαβυλῶνος.

The city has magnificent public precincts and the royal palaces, which cover a fourth or even a third of the entire city area. For just as each of the kings would from a love of splendor add some ornament to the public monuments, so he would provide himself at his own expense with a residence in addition to those already standing.... The Museum also forms part of the royal palaces; it has a covered walk, an arcade with recesses and seats, and a large house, in which is the dining hall of the learned members of the Museum. This association of men shares common property and has a priest of the Muses, who used to be appointed by the kings but is now appointed by Caesar. The so-called Tomb is also part of the royal palaces; this was an enclosure in which were the tombs of the kings and of Alexander. For Ptolemy son of Lagus got in ahead of Perdiccas and took the body from him when he was bringing it down from Babylon.

---

[16] On the ideology of the Graeco-Macedonian monarchy: Gehrke 1982; M.M. Austin 1986; Virgilio 2003; Ma 2003. On Egyptian ideas: Koenen 1993; Schloz 1994; Stephens 2003: 20–73; Blöbaum 2006: 277–280; Edelmann 2007: 22–26.

[17] Strabo 17.1.8 with M.M. Austin 2006: no. 292; Weber 2007c: 99–103. On the palace: Nielsen 1999: 131–138 with no. 20.

The geographer's final remark refers to a remarkable coup on the part of Ptolemy: by taking Alexander's corpse into his possession and keeping it close to him, so to speak, by burying it at first at Memphis and then later in Alexandria, he proved himself a legitimate Successor.[18] Of lasting importance is the erection of the Museum, which also included a library. Demetrius of Phalerum, who had come from Athens to Alexandria in exile, may have had a part in the initiative for the founding of this institution.[19] Ptolemy, who had himself written about Alexander's campaigns,[20] doubtless reinforced a previous tendency toward Aristotelian scientific learning, while now under royal patronage a real research institute was established, the like of which was not to be found anywhere else in the Greek world.[21] Ptolemy II continued his father's initiatives, so that it is sometimes unclear which measures go back to which Ptolemy. The kings spared no expense and tried to bring the best scholars in all fields of knowledge to Alexandria; these scholars could pursue research in their areas of inquiry undisturbed, in the best working conditions. The consequences were threefold. First, new foundations were laid in many intellectual disciplines. Second, the most prominent scholars served as guardians of Greek culture and powerfully reiterated its significance. Third, and most important, they increased by their activities the prestige and reputation (κλέος) of the Ptolemaic kings in the Greek world.[22] Lasting advances were made under the Ptolemies, for example in medicine and anatomy (with human vivisection), astronomy (with an observatory), engineering (with innovative equipment), and biology (with a zoological garden).[23] Above all, every book that could possibly be possessed was bought—or

---

[18] Besides Diod. 18.28.2, Curt. 10.10.20 with Schlange-Schöningen 1996. The cult of the deified Ptolemies followed almost immediately after the cult of the dead Alexander, starting with Ptolemy II Philadelphus and his biological sister, Arsinoe II, as Θεοὶ Ἀδελφοί (Huss 2001: 325–327).

[19] *PP* VI 16104 with Weber 1993: 77–78; Erskine 1995: 40. In the opinion of Bagnall 2002: 349–351, the relationship between the Museum and the Library is far from clear. There are discussions of the topography in Rodziewicz 1995 and McKenzie 2007.

[20] *PP* VI 16942: *FGrHist* 138 with Ellis 1994: 17–22; Ameling 2001: 533.

[21] Fraser 1972: 1.305–35; Weber 1993: 82–86; Asper 2004: 12. On the patronage of intellectuals by monarchs, which was already not unusual in archaic and classical times, see Weber 1992. On Alexander's example, see Weber 2007a: 240–241, 252–253.

[22] On the competitive aspect: Weber 1995 and 1997: 27–29, 45–46.

[23] For a comprehensive treatment, see Weber 1993: 84–85; Huss 2001: 317–319; Scholz 2007: 162–167.

stolen—for the Library.[24] In order to receive proper treatment by philologists, its contents, which under Ptolemy II must have encompassed a good two hundred thousand papyrus rolls, had first to be catalogued (Ps.-Aristeas 10; Vössing 1997: 641). This achievement is inseparably connected with the name of Callimachus, who produced a comprehensive catalogue of authors (with biographies) and works in 120 books.[25] Callimachus was never chief librarian but between the 280s and the 240s BC he was among the most influential intellectuals of the Ptolemaic royal court.[26] This status brings us back to the question of the composition of court society: that is, of the actual surroundings in which Callimachus found himself and produced both his multifaceted scholarly work and also his poetry.

In the context of continuing military challenges, especially in periods of intensive conflict with the Seleucids and Antigonids,[27] Ptolemy reached out in the first instance (and in accordance with his personal judgment and current requirements) to people who were part of his own entourage at the time, who came from Macedonia but also from the Greek city-states (πόλεις) and tribes (ἔθνη). (For an overview, see Strootman 2005b: 187–188.) Selection mechanisms presumably included personal acquaintance through previous work on the general staff and references from other people; also conceivable are self-introductions by adventurers and individuals who had been exiled from their πόλεις.[28] Military, administrative, and diplomatic capabilities seem to have been among the prerequisites necessary for

---

[24] Erskine 1995: 39–40. The goal was to collect Greek texts and also the most important books in foreign languages (Ps.-Aristeas 9–10; Athen. 1.3a; Plin. NH 30.4; with Vössing 1997: 641–642); on Egyptian books, see Legras 2002: 987–988; on the significance of Houses of Life for Egyptian literature, see Legras 2001: 130–140.

[25] The full title runs: Πίνακες τῶν ἐν πάσῃ παιδείᾳ διαλαμψάντων καὶ ὧν συνέγραψαν. The attestations: frr. 429–453 Pf. and SH 292–293 with Erskine 1995: 45; Asper 2004: 12–13, 49–50. Admittedly, whether or not the Πίνακες were identical with the Library catalogue is still a controversial question. See Bagnall 2002 and Krevans, this volume.

[26] On the construction of the chronological framework, see Asper 2004: 3–5. On the list of chief librarians (POxy 10.1241): Weber 1993: 83; Vössing 1997: 641. I leave to one side the question of whether Callimachus actually came to court as a royal page, as the νεανίσκος τῆς αὐλῆς in Tzetzes (CGF p. 31 Kaibel) suggests (Alan Cameron 1995: 3–5; Asper 2004: 5).

[27] On the period of the first three Ptolemies, see Hölbl 1994: 36–42, 46–53.

[28] At times we are confronted by considerable methodological problems, since—especially at the beginning of the Hellenistic period—the status of a φίλος is often not explicitly remarked upon (Weber 1993: 133 n. 5).

qualification for the core group of intimates.²⁹ Remarkably, prestige in literature, science, and art also played an important role, as references to the most prominent scholars in individual disciplines make clear. We know of several mathematicians, astronomers, philosophers, historians, and geographers from this period.³⁰ Along with other intellectuals, the chief librarian often performed the duties of tutor to the king's children, and well-known examples of royal tutors are Philetas of Cos, Strato of Lampsacus, and Zenodotus of Ephesus.³¹ Such men had a special relationship of trust with the king. Their appointment also demonstrated the significance of the Greek education (παιδεία) they transmitted. A few scholars were multitalented and active in several branches of learning at the same time; above all, though, they dedicated themselves to poetry.

A developed aristocracy—that is to say, a nobility of birth who owned a part of the land and also lived there—was not a feature of the beginning of the Ptolemaic era in Egypt. Instead we have a new, artificially created elite, which like the king was a foreign imposition on a conquered land, and which was based mostly at court—that is to say, in the capital city.³² And this would essentially remain the case under later Ptolemaic rulers. We know the names of several people with broad official remits from the over thirty-year reign of Ptolemy II, although the mass of individual attestations does not permit us to put together concrete groups that would have attended court at particular times.³³ The royal family itself is well documented, and apart from that we know the names of a few royal mistresses (ἐρώμεναι), such as Bilistiche.³⁴ Among those explicitly called φίλοι are Dionysius of Lampsacus and his son Apollodorus, the Athenian politician Glaucon,

---

²⁹ On the especially important military, in which there were a few Macedonians, see Weber 1993: 133–135.

³⁰ See Weber 1993: 136–137 with the documents and numbers from PP VI.

³¹ Philetas: PP VI 16724; Strato: PP VI 14656; Zenodotus: PP VI 14648; others: Meissner 1992: 493–497; Weber 1993: 74–75 with nn. 3 and 4, as well as 134, 418; Hose 1997: 51–52. On Philip and Alexander as exempla, see Weber 2007a: 240 n. 57.

³² It is not possible to describe living arrangements at court any more precisely, but in view of the levels of competition already mentioned, continual efforts at greater proximity to the king among the φίλοι can safely be assumed.

³³ Many of the people with military experience were not permanently at court but were brought in according to need: Weber 1993: 138–148.

³⁴ On her and other women, see Weber 1993: 138–139 with n. 3. Chronological certainty is difficult, although it seems reasonably certain that Ptolemy II did not marry again after the death of his sister-wife, Arsinoe II, on 9 July 270 BC: see Weber 1993: 138–148.

the nauarch Callicrates of Samos, Pelops of Macedonia, and Sostratus of Cnidus. (For all these people, see Weber 1993: 138–148.) The finance minister (διοικητής) Apollonius is not explicitly referred to as a φίλος, although his closeness to the king is not in doubt.[35] The number of intellectuals with verifiable links to the court shows a remarkable increase under Ptolemy, including the medicals Erasistratus of Ceos and Herophilus of Chalcedon, the mathematicians Archimedes of Syracuse and Conon of Samos, a few philosophers, grammarians, and geographers, but above all the poetic colleagues of Callimachus: Alexander Aetolus, Apollonius Rhodius, Asclepiades of Samos, Lycophron of Chalcis, Philicus of Corcyra, and Posidippus of Pella.[36] While for some of these figures a definite position in the Library is attested, for others all we have to go on are fragments of their works. It is, moreover, unclear whether Herodas of Cos, Theocritus of Syracuse, or even Sotades of Maronea really belonged to the inner court circle (Weber 1998–1999: 162–165). The well-known remark from the *Silloi* of Timon of Phlius about bookworms quarreling in the birdcages of the Muses in any case makes clear that arguments and competition— and surely not just over literature—were the order of the day.[37]

A comparable list could be compiled for the court under Ptolemy III (Weber 1993: 149–154). Besides family members it was especially Sosibius of Alexandria, Hippomedon of Sparta, Dositheus, and Antiochus who were trusted by the king with important tasks. In the circle of intellectuals the figure of Eratosthenes was outstanding, who had not only the titles of chief librarian and royal tutor to his name but also some impressive achievements in geography.[38] Also involved were numerous other doctors such as Philip and Xenophantus, historians such as Demetrius of Byzantium or Satyrus of Callatis, astronomers like Dositheus of Pelusium, and the epigrammatist Dioscorides. In

---

[35] His activity is well known through the archive of his steward Zeno. (Apollonius owned an enormous δωρεά in the Fayum: Weber 1993: 143–144 with n. 3.) In his case we can even make out a smaller, personal court (Swiderek 1959–1960); also of interest in this connection is the fact that Zeno ordered two funerary epigrams for his deceased hunting dog Tauron, presumably in Alexandria (*SH* 977; Weber 1993: 153–154, 294–295; Parsons 2002: 103–104).

[36] For a summarized biography, see Weber 1993: 420–426, where a stay at the court in Alexandria is inferred for several poets from their work.

[37] *SH* 786 with Weber 1993: 87–95; Alan Cameron 1995: 31–33; Di Marco 2002: 592–593; Asper 2004: 11; see Stephens 2005 for references to the other side of the debate.

[38] *PP* VI 14645 = 16515, besides Weber 1993: 427; see also Geus 2002: 26–30, according to whom Eratosthenes did not belong to the φίλοι.

addition, we often have to take the presence of artists and architects of various types in court society into account (Weber 1993: 137–138 n. 5, 148 n. 1, 152 n. 1; von Hesberg 1981: 112; S. Schmidt 2004), although here explicit named attestations (as in the case of Ctesibius) seldom crop up.[39]

Now, there are a few people who for several reasons stand out in court society. First of all, there are those whose especially close ties to the king are immediately plain: Callicrates, Glaucon,[40] Medeius, Pelops, and his brother Taurinus, as well as Sosibius and Dositheus, all fulfilled the functions of the eponymous priests of Alexander and of the Θεοὶ Ἀδελφοί, while Bilistiche was known to have held the office of the κανηφόρος (processional bearer of the sacred basket) of Arsinoe.[41] These offices brought with them an extraordinary level of prestige; bestowing recognition and honor on the individual selected, they simultaneously demonstrated his loyalty to the state (Hauben 1989; Weber 1993: 140–143). Further, a few individuals from this circle were remarkable for their dedication of enormous monuments: this is true of Sostratus, who built the hundred-meter-high Lighthouse (Φάρος) of Alexandria,[42] as well as of Callicrates, who founded for the royal couple a temple complex of Isis and Anubis (as well as a separate temple in honor of Arsinoe in the aspect of Aphrodite Euploea) in Canopus, near Alexandria.[43] For another thing, not a few members of Ptolemaic courtly society received mentions in the poetry produced by figures linked to the court. But we know as a rule very little else about the circumstances of the time, so that it is impossible to say whether we are dealing with poetry written to order or whether it was a custom of the court to celebrate certain people beyond the king and his family in

---

[39] *PP* VI 16546 with von Hesberg 1987; Weber 1993: 144 n. 6.

[40] *PP* VI 14596 with Weber 1993: 139 n. 7. Glaucon was honored by Ptolemy III with a statue in Olympia (*Syll.*³ I 462; *SEG* 32.415, 33.406; with Criscuolo 2003: 320–322).

[41] PCairZen 2.59289, so Clarysse and van der Veken 1983: no. 40 = *PP* VI 14717 and IX 5066.

[42] *PP* VI 14632 with Weber 1993: 140 n. 3. Pliny *NH* 36.18 seems certain that Sostratus was the architect, whereas the Ptolemaic rulers supplied the funds for the monument and dedicated it; but the whole issue is still mired in controversy; see Weber 2007c: 115. According to Bing 1998 only the statue of Zeus that crowns the Lighthouse is by Sostratus. Sostratus did dedicate a statue of Ptolemy II in Delphi: see Kotsidu 2000: 146.

[43] *PP* VI 14607 with Weber 1993: 139 n. 8; Kerkhecker 1997: 134. Besides this, Callicrates dedicated statues of Ptolemy II and Arsinoe II in Olympia (Bing 2002–2003: 252–253).

poetry. In any case, the court with its goings-on and its cast of people represented a veritable reservoir of material for poets.[44] Because of the system of patronage, it is not surprising that the reigning king, his wife, and other members of his family were featured in poems of the most diverse genres. Sometimes praise occurred in a perfectly direct way, though often discretion was preferred, especially in Callimachus and in contrast to Theocritus, for example.[45] This also applies to the aforementioned Bilistiche, to whose Olympic victory there may be a cryptic allusion in an epigram attributed to Asclepiades (35 GP).[46] That the poets mention each other (directly or indirectly) is understandable, although we cannot always with any certainty link to the court the persons named.[47] As for other people, we can begin with Callimachus, who concludes the fourth and final book of his *Aetia* with *The Lock of Berenice* (fr. 110 Pf.). In 245 BC, Berenice II dedicated a lock of hair in the Temple of Arsinoe Zephyritis after Ptolemy III, whom she had recently married, returned home safely from the Third Syrian War against Seleucus II.[48] When the astronomer Conon came across an unfamiliar constellation in the night sky and was unable to find it on his charts, it occurred to him that it might be the lock of Berenice transformed into stars. Callimachus, who has the lock itself speak, gives to Conon—and of course to the queen as well, who like the poet himself came from Cyrene—a prominent place in the *aition* of this catasterism, thereby underlining his importance, although declining to give us any further biographical details about the astronomer. (On the poem's structure, see Weber 1993: 266–267; Marinone 1997.) In an epinician ode (frr. 384 and 384a Pf.), Callimachus celebrates the

---

[44] The place in which court society, with all its cultural trappings, was located—that is, the court as a physical structure within the βασίλεια—is no more specific a representation, not even through the work of Callimachus; in this connection, only two passages deserve citation: the description of the inside of the palace in Theocritus *Id.* 15 and the naming of the Μουσῆιον in Herodas 1.31 (Weber 1993: 199–201, 284, 320–321).

[45] Weber 1993: 199–335; on Arsinoe II, see the summary by Lelli 2002: 10. See also the contributions of Barbantani and Prioux in this volume.

[46] *PP* VI 14717 with Weber 1993: 269–270; Alan Cameron 1995: 244–246; Criscuolo 2003: 319–320; Stephens 2005: 247–248.

[47] See the material in Weber 1993: 285–293, esp. Call. *Ep.* 33 GP = 10 Pf. (Timarchus, *PP* VI 16792), *Ep.* 34 GP = 2 Pf. (Heraclitus, *PP* VI 16689), *Ep.* 57 GP = 7 Pf. (Theaetetus, *PP* VI 16692), with the epigrams of Hedylus and Dioscorides; there are also several passages in Callimachus' *Iambi* that refer to colleagues.

[48] On the historical context, Huss 2001: 341–354; on reactions in visual culture, Kuttner 1999: 112–113.

victory of Sosibius at the Isthmian and Nemean Games as well as in Athens and Alexandria. This Sosibius is identical to the man mentioned in the sources as a φίλος of Ptolemy III, so that the work is to be dated later than *The Lock of Berenice*.[49] The most interesting lines are those containing a direct characterization of the honorand (fr. 384.53-56):

> καὶ τὸν ἐφ' οὗ νίκαισιν ἀείδομεν, ἄρθμια δήμῳ
> εἰδότα καὶ μικρῶν οὐκ ἐπιληθόμενον,
> παύριστον τό κεν ἀνδρὶ παρ' ἀφνειῷ τις ἴδοιτο
> ᾧτινι μὴ κρε[ί]σσων ᾖ νόος εὐτυχίης.

> And him (sc. Sosibius) we celebrate for his victories, knowing friendly to the people and forgetting not the poor, a thing so rarely seen in a rich man, whose mind is not superior to his good fortune (Trypanis).

Sosibius is represented here as a man of the people, who fulfills perfectly the ideal of the *euergetes*. We do not know what relation this representation has to the historical Sosibius, and a description of this sort is hardly a first in literary history, but it may allow us a wished-for glimpse of court life from the outside. Finally, the Philip mentioned in *Epigram* 3 GP (= 3 Pf.) could be identical to the doctor named as a member of the royal court.[50]

People from the world of the court are also mentioned in the epigrams of Posidippus. This is the case for Sostratus of Cnidus, who is mentioned in relation to the construction of the Φάρος in *Epigram* 11 GP (= 115 AB). Although nothing is said about his patronymic or his coming from Cnidus, the epigram is clearly tailored to the uses of the new construction and the glory of the king (Weber 1993: 332-334). Above all, the nauarch Callicrates of Samos is thought worthy of being honored in several ways: his dedication of the Temple of Arsinoe Zephyritis is poeticized in *Epigrams* 12 and 13 GP (= 116 and 119 AB); he is named in his function as royal nauarch; but most important is the description of his dedication as "a shrine that is a safe harbor from all the waves" (116.8 AB, ἱερὸν παντὸς κύματος εὐλίμενον), which highlights the use of the temple (administered by its priestesses) by those traveling to or from Egypt.[51] Additional relevant material is

---

[49] Fuhrer 1992: 139-204; Weber 1993: 209-212 on the identification of the man; Kerkhecker 1997: 14-15. On the intention: Fantuzzi 2005: 265-266.
[50] *PP* VI 16640 with Weber 1993: 295.
[51] Weber 1993: 258-259; Barbantani 2001: 44-47; Bing 2002-2003. The dedication of a seashell in this temple, which Call. *Ep.* 14 = 5 Pf. alludes to (Stephens 2005:

to be found among the new epigrams attributed to Posidippus: *Epigram* 39 AB, which also mentions the nauarch in connection with the temple of Arsinoe Zephyritis. This accumulation of evidence is more than fortuitous and it allows us to conclude that Callicrates was clearly eager to promote the new cult that he had established.[52] Finally, *Epigram* 74 AB makes reference to a Delphic oracular response to Callicrates, in gratitude for which he dedicated a bronze chariot to the Θεοὶ Ἀδελφοί; the connection with the royal couple, doubtless his patrons, becomes the more obvious when we learn that Callicrates was the first eponymous priest of this cult in 272/1. (On the dating, see Bing 2002-2003: 250-251; D.J. Thompson 2005: 279.) *Epigram* 95 AB refers to the dedication of a bronze statue for Apollo by one Medeius son of Lampon from Olynthus. This must have to do with the doctor and priest named above, who also undoubtedly belonged to the inner circles of the court,[53] though admittedly we have no further details about this person and his actual activities at court. Another epigram attributed to Posidippus is *SH* 978, preserved only in fragments, which talks about a watered enclosure with a statue of Arsinoe in the middle.[54]

Hedylus alludes to a golden rhyton in the form of the Egyptian god Bes that was placed as a dedication in the Temple of Arsinoe Zephyritis (*Ep.* 4 GP). Ctesibius had equipped it with a device that played music as it poured out wine (Weber 1993: 259; Lelli 2002: 18; Ambühl 2007: 284). Ctesibius is important for the Ptolemaic court because a

---

245-246), is also relevant here, although Callicrates is not mentioned; this goes for Dioscorides too: *Ep.* 14 GP.

[52] For a detailed treatment, see Ambühl 2007: 278-285. We leave to one side here the question of whether Callicrates was aiming "to mediate between the new world and the old" (Bing 2002-2003: 254)—that is, between the Egyptian and the Greek world—and whether there was a well-defined intellectual program behind his actions, or whether he simply combined individual ideas according to his personal preferences.

[53] This identification is considered secure on the basis of the combination of documents set out by Bing 2002. On the identification of the nomarch Etearchus with the victor in the chariot races mentioned in *Ep.* 76 AB, see D.J. Thompson 2005: 279-280.

[54] *FGE* anon. 151a = *113 AB, with Weber 1993: 295, 332; Barbantani 2001: 51-52; D.J. Thompson 2005: 271. But this text is relevant in this connection only if one reads Βα[λάκρου or Βά[κχωνος instead of βα[σιλεῖς in line 3, thus linking the monument to a high-ranking individual in the Ptolemaic court. The like also applies to *SH* 969, a fragmentary elegy whose connection with Egypt (other than simply mentioning the country by name) is not secure (Weber 1993: 310 n. 3, 315). Barbantani (2001 passim and 2007: 20 with n. 6) argues for an allusion to a Ptolemaic general, possibly the Lycian Neoptolemus (*PP* VI 15224).

few of his innovative mechanical inventions were set up to help draw crowds during the Grand Procession (πομπή) of Ptolemy Philadelphus at the Ptolemaia described by Callixenus (probably to be dated to 279/8 or 275/4).

These poems, particularly the epinicians and epigrams, have a common feature in the clear association of named figures with the king and royal family; in his own poetry, particularly of these two genres, Callimachus aligns himself with this program. These poems are part of a larger system, one that at least in one aspect—namely the connection with the court—is self-referential but at the same time through the larger worldwide community of poets could develop a considerable impact abroad. The focus is of course hardly surprising, as the βασιλεύς represented the center of attention for all members of the court. Poetic representation of the generosity of the φίλοι or praise of the talent (τέχνη) of intellectuals in a certain area in turn increased the king's prestige.

My description of the courtly society up to this point may have given the impression that it was a purely Greek community in all its parts. And yet if we bear in mind the concept of a *monarchie bicéphale*, the question of the relationship between the Ptolemies on the one hand and their court on the other is revealed as nothing less than central.[55] First of all, it was necessary for Ptolemy I on pragmatic grounds to be able to fall back on experts who were either themselves Egyptian or were extremely well informed about Egypt in order to have any understanding of the temple organizations, the Egyptian pantheon, the theology, and the practical execution of the cult in a way that was in any case already seen as normal under the Achaemenids and Alexander.[56] That there were Egyptians in Alexandria is not disputed;[57] nor is the fact that intensive contact with the priestly elite was the norm in the context of the celebration of Egyptian rites in the temples (Clarysse

---

[55] Weber 1993: 23–24 with nn. 2 and 3. The relationship between king and indigenous subjects seems to have been different in the case of the Seleucids and even the Antigonids (Weber 1997: 40–42); on the situation at the time of Alexander's death, Weber 2007a: 242–256, making the point that what Alexander would have wanted had he lived longer is virtually impossible to ascertain.

[56] Huss 2001: 213–218; Legras 2002: 966–967, 989–990; Verhoeven 2005: 279–280. On the degree of understanding that was actually achieved, and on interpreters or translators, see Weber 1993: 143 n. 2; Thissen 1993: 241; Wiotte-Franz 2001: 63–71.

[57] Stephens 1998: 168, 179; Hunter 2003c: 46–47 on the material finds from the city harbor.

2000). If we follow the literary tradition, it would appear that an Egyptian priest named Manetho, who came from Sebennytus in the Nile Delta, and was even referred to as a φίλος, composed an *Egyptian History* in Greek (Αἰγυπτιακά).[58] It is probably safe to assume that this work was supposed to make Egyptian culture, religion, and history more accessible to the Greeks, though the exact role of its author and his precise intentions are as fiercely contested as its date.[59] The careful analysis of a number of monuments in hieroglyphics has brought to light additional material, which admittedly brings with it a number of interpretive problems: for instance, with regard to the literary genre of autobiography.[60] People tend to claim in writing about themselves that they had a close relationship with the king—that is to say, a position at court. Petosiris, the high priest of Thoth from Hermopolis, boasted of the king's favor and his exceptional popularity among the ladies-in-waiting at court; at the same time he made reference to his outstanding capacities in the fields of architecture and jurisprudence, and moreover evinced an interest in the Greek language and the Greek literature of his day.[61] The governor of the city of Memphis, whose name is not known but who was simultaneously a priest of Ammon, also served Ptolemy as an advisor (Derchain 2000: 18-19; Verhoeven 2005: 280-281), as did the priest and general Djed-Hor; one Nectanebus served as a general, as did Wennofer, who remarks that the king took his advice.[62] From the time of Ptolemy II we have the priest Senoucheri, son of a Greek named Jason, who claims to have been a member of the "secret chamber" in Alexandria and to have been esteemed by the king on account of his wisdom, eloquence, loyalty, and trustworthiness.[63] Also worth noting are Smendes the son

---

[58] *FGrHist* 609 with *PP* VI 14614; Weber 1993: 134 with n. 4; Legras 2002: 974-977; H.H. Schmitt 2005: 670.

[59] He is usually dated to the reign of Ptolemy II: Verhoeven 2005: 281. It is possible that he corrected the account of Hecataeus of Abdera (Legras 2001: 136).

[60] Legras 2002: 969-970 has identified fifteen individuals, of whom four belong to the reign of Ptolemy I, three to the reign of Ptolemy II, and one other to the reign of Ptolemy III; see further Verhoeven 2005. On Egyptian autobiography, see Derchain 2000: 14-15.

[61] *PP* III 5406 with Legras 2002: 979-983; Baines 2004: 45-48; Verhoeven 2005: 280.

[62] On Djed-Hor, see Derchain 2000: 23; Legras 2002: 969 n. 31. On the others, see D.J. Thompson 1992: 324 with n. 2; Hölbl 1994: 29; Stephens 1998: 168.

[63] Derchain 2000: 23-29 with an analysis of all his responsibilities; Legras 2002: 983-985; Verhoeven 2005: 281. We also know that he distinguished himself in the foundation of the cult of the Θεοὶ Ἀδελφοί in Upper Egypt. Whether the name of

of Pchorchonsis, priest in Thebes and royal advisor with the title "First after the King," and, also under Ptolemy III, Amasis the son of Smendes, also a priest in Thebes as well as a functionary in Memphis and Hermopolis (Legras 2002: 972).

It must be confessed that the relationships that these various individuals had with the king can hardly be precisely defined, and that the question of whether they really belonged to upper-class society cannot now be decisively settled. The fundamental problem is that for some of these functions we have no Greek descriptions, and so with regard to titles such as "The King's Brother" or "The King's Relative," for example, it is not clear to what extent we are dealing with personal closeness as is implied in the word φίλος (Huss 1994: 92; Hölbl 1994: 29; Collombert 2000: 48). But even though we are not talking about a very large group in terms of numbers, there is nonetheless one significant enough finding: the Greek sources transmit to us a picture of upper-class society that consists predominantly of Greeks and Macedonians. That nevertheless members of the Egyptian elite brought with them wide-ranging intellectual capabilities should remain beyond question.[64] However, the question arises whether from this finding we can draw any conclusions that can contextualize the poetry of the period. This is especially relevant for the issue of what impact elements of Egyptian culture had on the work of Callimachus and his contemporaries, and what sorts of intentions were bound up with this process, has been the subject of some debate in the scholarly literature.[65] In any event, precisely because several of the Egyptians known to us by name in the king's circle are also known to have been influenced by Greek culture and were thus clearly oriented toward the culture that was dominant politically, it becomes difficult to attest whether they contributed any fundamentally different perspectives to the poets who may have absorbed their influence.[66] Nonetheless one must allow that there is a

---

his father can be brought together with the *Argonautica* of Apollonius of Rhodes is doubtful (Legras 2002: 984 with n. 117).

[64] Whether we should go so far as Legras 2002: 991 and consider that membership of the Museum was open to Egyptians seems questionable. What is certain is that several of the individuals attested by name have taken up various elements of Greek culture—for example, in their tombs (Baines 2004: 46–47).

[65] For the proactive and conceptually wide-ranging employment of Egyptian material, see Koenen 1993; Selden 1998; Stephens 2002b and 2003. *Contra*, Weber 1993: 371–388; Hose 1997: 47 n. 3; Asper 2004: 16–20; Goldhill 2005; Effe 2007: 263. For a different take, see Hunter 2003c: 46–53.

[66] The Greeks saw "no necessity to take these representations of their sovereign for the sake of his Egyptian subjects as an integral part of their own understanding of

difference between Egyptian members of the administrative elite and figures like Manetho, who could contribute at a literary level.

This brings us at last to the question what place Hellenistic poetry had in life at court during the time of Callimachus, bearing in mind first of all the apparent fact that in some (though by no means all) of the texts people are mentioned who we can assume were actually present at court. If we look at the poetry of the period in this way, we come up against a sobering discovery: in the extant work of Callimachus we have no concrete indication how the poems were supposed to be performed or appreciated. The poems of his contemporaries are no more helpful in this regard. The scene described in Theocritus *Idyll* 15.22–24, 60, 65–86, in which a section of the royal palace is opened to the public for the festival of Adonis, and Arsinoe II hires a female singer for a hymn, is clearly exceptional. For this reason, most scholars have ruled out a concrete performance context within the framework of an appropriate festival for Callimachus' hymns or his epigrams. It has been argued that since the poetry of Callimachus and his contemporaries is distinguished by such a high level of complexity and by such an abundance of allusions, only a purely literary audience would have been in a position to appreciate the literature of the *poetae docti* at all (Hunter and Fuhrer 2002; Ukleja 2005: 17–19, 278; Effe 2007: 263–264). On the other hand when the hymns are considered in the context of divine epiphanies, which were one of the definitive elements in Hellenistic religion, it becomes impossible to rule out public performance. For the hymns come stylistically, in the Hellenistic period, to focus even more on gods, as part of cultic honors for kings and in aretalogies, in the interest expressed in old cults, and in the scenic presentation of cult images.[67] Therefore, it would seem to make sense to posit several different dimensions of performance or appreciation of poetry in this period, as well as several different levels in its understanding or interpretation (Weber 1993: 101–130; Asper 2004: 14–15; Effe 2007: 278). This means that despite the difficulty and verbal complexity of the poetry, which have often been remarked upon, there are also certain elements (names, key ideas, descriptions) that could

---

themselves as Greeks;" those who felt moved to integrate must therefore have been an "Egyptian elite with Hellenizing tendencies:" so Asper 2001: 103 with n. 140. On Petosiris, see Hölbl 1994: 29.

[67] I. Petrovic 2007: 138–139, 270–271, and *passim*. On the dating and on possible occasions for performance: Vestrheim 2005.

probably be grasped among a wider readership.[68] And this is all the more so in view of the fact that the different literary genres serving a diverse audience must be strictly distinguished from one another. Hellenistic literature certainly did not consist entirely of exclusivist, highbrow literature. Even within individual genres—for example, the epigram—various purposes and goals seem to have been envisaged for different works.[69] That individual works were later brought together and through being read in conjunction could produce reciprocal allusions is no more an obstacle to this way of thinking than the idea that texts produced by poets at court in Alexandria were read by colleagues abroad.[70] The hypothesis that solely through reading did the epigrams and epinicia of Callimachus and other poets reach the members of courtly society mentioned in such works may be right in certain cases but should by no means be generalized.

If we think on the one hand of the symposia that the βασιλεύς held with his closest circle, at which a profoundly competitive, not to say agonistic environment existed,[71] and on the other hand of the many elements of Ptolemaic self-fashioning and self-representation operative in Alexandria, then it becomes clear that we are dealing with a rich and varied culture of festivals. Such a culture had various different addressees in mind, being capable of restricting itself exclusively to an elite circle or of orienting itself toward the masses, so that it often becomes very difficult to identify a definite target audience. The occasions for festivals of the close inner circle (which also could aim to have a corresponding effect outside that sphere) were most often found on dates that had something to do with the king and his dynasty: festivals in the king's honor (above all his birthday), festivals for the queen, for members of the dynasty both living and dead, for its patron deities, and finally in celebration of military victories.[72] Besides the like of these, we can take for granted that the festivals associated with the

---

[68] Asper 2001: 95–96 sees aetiologies (for a broad readership) and intertextualities (for a small one) as the main distinguishing features of Hellenistic poetry.

[69] See Parsons 2002: 103–104; Meyer 2005: 130–143 on epigrams for readers and listeners.

[70] On Aratus: Weber 1995: 309–310. Besides this, there are various ways of determining how the literature of the time was received in the χώρα (Parsons 2002: 109–110).

[71] Völcker-Janssen 1993: 78–81; Alan Cameron 1995: 71–103; Bing 2000: 144–147; Hose 1997: 54–55; Barbantani 2001: 16–17, 41–43; Vössing 2004: 154–158.

[72] On all types of festivals, see Weber 1993: 170–182; Perpillou-Thomas 1993: 151–163. On victories of the royal family: D.J. Thompson 2005: 273.

traditional Greek gods, whose cults were imported into Alexandria, were also celebrated. That the known Greek festivals were linked to processions, sacrifices, hymns, and competitions should also be taken into account when appropriate.

A glance at the diplomats and special envoys who came from all parts of the Greek world, and whose names are often recorded after visits to the royal court, makes clear that we should envision a literary audience that possessed a very high level of education.[73] The scene portrayed in Theocritus *Idyll* 15 alludes in the first instance to the fact that the Ptolemies possessed an exorbitantly large royal palace (as we know from other sources), which encompassed not only the Museum, the Library, and the royal residence itself, but also extensive parkland (Sonne 1996; Nielsen 2001). Temporary, movable structures could be put up inside for festivals: one famous instance included Ptolemy II's cavernous festival marquee, which according to Callixenus contained 130 couches (κλῖναι) and was decorated with huge sculptures of eagles (a symbol of Ptolemaic rule) as well as other figures and friezes. "This was probably the customary context in which the king displayed to foreign delegates at the festival his wealth and divine ancestry, and the secure state of his rule, before crowds of cheering Alexandrians."[74] What was extraordinary about these arrangements was that these structures were to be used on only one occasion, or perhaps a few, but were in any case not designed for permanent installation. On such occasions we should probably imagine various performances of light entertainment (Vössing 2004: 158–165), but also (bearing in mind the kind of competition described above) poetic recitation of parlor pieces. It was in precisely in environments like this that the king could be especially approachable (Hose 1997: 54).

The πομπή described by Callixenus did admittedly have different dimensions to it and a different target group.[75] It served to draw people toward a constructed image of the monarch and at the same time projected outwards the ideology of his rule in a spectacular way. At this festive event, among all the other things happening, the mechanical

---

[73] Weber 1993: 135–136 with n. 1; 145–146 with nn. 4–6; 150–151 with nn. 6 and 7; 154–164; 166–167.

[74] Vössing 2004: 107–110, 115–116 (for the quotation, see p. 110); Athen. 5.196a–97b with von Hesberg 1989, 1996; Pfrommer 1999: 69–75.

[75] Athen. 5.197c–203b with Rice 1983; Köhler 1996: 35–45; Pfrommer 1999: 62–68; D.J. Thompson 2000.

inventions of Ptolemaic scholars were exhibited at the same time that the Ptolemaic conception of monarchy was being communicated impressively through the statues of Alexander and Ptolemy I, and the personifications of Corinth and of other city-states. Above all, though, there was the separate guild or company of Dionysiac ritual experts, who played an essential role in organizing and running the festivals associated with the cults of the ruler and the dynasty—and who counted poets among their number (Le Guen 2001: 2.34–36, 89; Aneziri 2003: 115–118, 240–242). Their priest, Philicus of Corcyra, belonged to a group of tragic poets at court, although it seems safe to assume that their dithyrambic performances were directed at a rather broader audience.[76]

In the Ptolemaic court, Callimachus found himself in an environment that offered him and his fellow poets an inexhaustible abundance of material and inspiration for poetry, but also—so we can assume—an atmosphere with a permanent resonance. An engagement with the literary heritage of the past and at the same time an incorporation of debates about contemporary trends in literature and about tradition and innovation in the various literary genres can easily be identified in his work (Fantuzzi and Hunter 2004); this engagement furthered the attempt to make his own cultural identity more secure. But material and inspiration for poetry were also found in the people of the place and the events that they were involved in, as well as from the research that was carried on in the Museum. The multifaceted nature of the content is fundamentally related to the character of the court as a political and administrative center, and also one closely implicated in the public representation of the monarch.[77] Poets, too, were influenced by the structures of communication and interaction that were part of the workings of the court (Hunter and Fuhrer 2002: 165). That the head of the οἶκος who happened to be in power at the time, his family, and his close associates had a central position there is hardly surprising in view of the structure of Hellenistic monarchies in general and of the unique power relations in Egypt in particular. It is all the more remarkable, in contrast, how subtly and sensitively Callimachus deals with this context in his poetry (Hose 1997: 63–64).

---

[76] On their priest Philicus of Corcyra (*PP* VI 16725): Weber 1993: 424; Bing 2000: 142. After looking at his elaborate hymn (*SH* 677), we may well speculate that Philicus felt at home in both poetic worlds.

[77] Weber 2007c: 110–11. This observation in no way compels us to see the poet as part of a well-oiled propaganda machine, as Dunand 1981 seems to imply.

CHAPTER TWELVE

THE GODS OF CALLIMACHUS

Richard Hunter

ABSTRACT

This paper explores the presentation of the divine in Callimachus, and the differences and similarities in this matter from earlier poetry, through three case studies. First, how poets, both archaic and Hellenistic themselves fashion the divine and cultic world represented in their poetry, and how cult is used to link the present with the mythical past; secondly, the paper sets forth a reading of Callimachus' *Sixth Iambus* to explore the importance of statues in Hellenistic poetry, an importance without real parallel in archaic poetry; finally, the paper considers the representation of experience of the divine and of epiphany through a comparison between the *Homeric Hymn to Dionysus* and Callimachus' so-called mimetic hymns.

The theology of Hellenistic poetry remains an area of uncertainty and promise: What kind of language are we to use to describe the poets' encounter with, and representation of, the divine? Does one size fit all? Are we to expect consistency from the poets or from any one poet? How does the Hellenistic representation differ from—if it does—and exploit the archaic and the classical? This chapter addresses these and other questions through three brief soundings in the poetry of Callimachus. If only the tip of the iceberg is visible here, I hope, however, that some sense of the mass that lies suppressed will also emerge.

Creating Gods

In a famous passage of his second book Herodotus describes the development of the Greek conception of the gods and its debt to Egypt.[1] The Greeks inherited the names of most of their gods from the ancient Pelasgians, who had by their own account taken them from the barbarians (i.e., according to Herodotus, from the Egyptians); but the

[1] For helpful introductions to the passage and its links to contemporary speculation, cf. Burkert 1985b; Rosalind Thomas 2000: 274–282; Graziosi 2002: 180–184.

elaborations beyond the names were largely the work of Hesiod and Homer:

> From where each of the gods came into being [ἐγένοντο], whether they had all existed for all time [αἰεί], and what they looked like in appearance, the Greeks were unaware until, so to speak, the day before yesterday; for I think that Hesiod and Homer lived four hundred years and not more before me. It is they who created divine genealogies [ποιήσαντες θεογονίην] for the Greeks, gave the gods their special names [ἐπωνυμίας],[2] distributed honors and crafts among them, and told us of their appearance.[3] The poets who are said to have preceded these men in fact came after them, in my opinion. The source for the first part of this account [i.e., the taking over of foreign names] is the priestesses at Dodona, but I myself am responsible for the part about Hesiod and Homer.
>
> Herodotus 2.53

The influence of early hexameter poetry on Greek thinking about the gods and on actual religious practice can indeed hardly be exaggerated,[4] but it is the terms in which Herodotus expresses himself that are first of interest. It was, says Herodotus, the two great poets who taught the Greeks where the gods came from; the verb ἐγένοντο is studiedly ambiguous, but with θεογονίη immediately following—and Herodotus can hardly not be thinking of Hesiod's *Theogony* (cf. vv. 46, 108, εἴπατε δ' ὡς τὰ πρῶτα θεοὶ καὶ γαῖα γένοντο. "tell how first the gods and earth were born")—we most naturally think of parentage and birth. The disjunctive question that the poets solved for the Greeks is in fact the same quasi-paradox that Callimachus places at the head of the *Hymn to Zeus*:

> πῶς καί νιν, Δικταῖον ἀείσομεν ἠὲ Λυκαῖον;
> ἐν δοιῇ μάλα θυμός, ἐπεὶ γένος ἀμφήριστον.
> Ζεῦ, σὲ μὲν Ἰδαίοισιν ἐν οὔρεσί φασι γενέσθαι,
> Ζεῦ, σὲ δ' ἐν Ἀρκαδίῃ· πότεροι, πάτερ, ἐψεύσαντο;
> "Κρῆτες ἀεὶ ψεῦσται"· καὶ γὰρ τάφον, ὦ ἄνα, σεῖο
> Κρῆτες ἐτεκτήναντο· σὺ δ' οὐ θάνες, ἐσσὶ γὰρ αἰεί.

---

[2] This is usually understood either of cult names, such as Σμινθεύς for Apollo in the opening scene of the *Iliad* (cf. further below), or of formulaic epithets, such as "far-shooting" of Apollo in the same scene.

[3] Here Herodotus is probably thinking of epic anthropomorphism in general, as well as the special physical features of each god (Zeus's dark locks, Hera βοῶπις, etc.).

[4] Burkert 1985a: 119–125 are familiar and influential pages.

How shall we hymn him, as Dictaean or Lycaean? My heart is very much in doubt, as his origin [*genos*] is disputed. Zeus, some say that you came into existence on the Idaean mountains; some, Zeus, say in Arcadia: Which group, father, are lying? "Cretans are always liars"; for the Cretans even devised a tomb for you, Lord, but you did not die, for you are for all time.

Callimachus *Hymn to Zeus* 4–9

Zeus was indeed born but is (also) forever.[5] Callimachus is thus taking upon himself the role that Herodotus ascribed to his great predecessors; the *Hymn to Zeus* is in fact Callimachus' *Theogony* (as the *Theogony* is also Hesiod's *Hymn to Zeus*),[6] and Callimachus, like Hesiod and Homer before him, is fashioning the gods before our eyes.

In the *Theogony* it is Zeus who distributes honors and functions to the Olympians (vv. 73–74, 111–112, 885, etc.), though there is in fact no consistent program of distribution carried out through the poem;[7] in the *Iliad*, by contrast, Poseidon famously reports how Zeus, Hades, and he himself divided the cosmos among themselves by lot (15.187–193). The distribution that established the current order may in fact be seen as the central subject of all cosmogonic and theogonic poetry: Hermes' first song for Apollo tells of "the immortal gods and the dark earth, how they first came into being [γένοντο] and how each received his share [λάχε μοῖραν]" (*Homeric Hymn to Hermes* 427–428). Herodotus' description of how Hesiod and Homer "distributed honors and crafts [among the gods]" thus ascribes a Zeus-like function to the poets; this is not merely an example of the trope, particularly familiar from later poetry, whereby poets are said to have done what their characters in fact did, but it is rather a powerful dramatization of the central role that Herodotus ascribes to the poets. Whether or not Herodotus also had what we call the *Homeric Hymns* in mind cannot be known, but it is certainly the case that the major hymns are centrally concerned with the birth, honors, and spheres of activity of the deities. In the *Hymns* of Callimachus, and particularly in those to Zeus, Apollo, and Artemis, the division of honors and spheres of activity is also a persistent and explicit theme. In the *Hymn to Zeus*, after having rejected the Iliadic

---

[5] On the significance of γένος in v. 5, cf. Cuypers 2004: 97. Cuypers also discusses (pp. 104–105) the relationship of this paradox to contemporary views (e.g., those of Euhemerus) in which Zeus really did die; cf. also Stephens 2003: 90–91.

[6] Cf. Hunter and Fuhrer 2002: 167–168.

[7] Cf. M.L. West 1966 on lines 112–113.

story of the division of the cosmos (vv. 60–67), the poet recounts how Zeus "chose" the particular group of mortals (city-governing kings) under his special control, leaving other groups to "lesser gods," and how the actions of those kings mirror the actions of Zeus himself (as, of course, the actions of mortal poets mirror those of Apollo); in the *Hymn to Apollo* a central section is devoted to the manifold τέχναι that the god has as his portion (ἔλαχε), and Artemis' initial encounter with Zeus in the hymn in her honor is precisely to do with her τιμαί and τέχναι. The explicitness of these hymns on this subject and the repeated concern with how myriad individual parts form a single Olympian whole presumably reflects not merely the systematization of the archaic system, but also reflection upon that systematization.

Homer and Hesiod did not just create the genealogies of the gods; they also created ways of talking about divine action and about the interactions between men and gods. For later Greeks it will hardly have been an accident that the very first such interaction in the *Iliad* is Chryses' prayer to Apollo (whose genealogy is also repeatedly stressed: *Il.* 1.9, 36); G.S. Kirk (in his commentary *ad loc* 1.37–42) notes that this is a prayer that "follows the regular religious pattern," but what is actually interesting is that we here see that "regular" pattern being created before our eyes. The fact that Chryses' *da quia dedi* prayer sounds familiar becomes part of the passage's didactic force,[8] just as it also teaches us who Apollo's parents were. The poets literally taught later Greeks how to worship the gods by such paradigmatic scenes of prayer, sacrifice (e.g., *Od.* 3.1–66), and cultic song, no less than they gave to (educated) Greeks a way of thinking about divine action. In the first divine intervention in the human action, Apollo comes down "like night," the arrows clanking in the quiver on his back (vv. 46–47); it is not merely ancient scholars who have wondered how literally all this is to be taken: the verses, like the account of Apollo's shooting the mules and dogs that immediately follows, precisely problematize the ways of speaking about divine action. Are these verses metaphorical, or does divine action always lend itself to more than one mode of description (which is also, of course, interpretation)? Is such ambiguity of characterization fundamental to the very conception of super-

---

[8] Pulleyn 1997: 16–38 considers whether prayers of this form were indeed a Homeric construct or had purchase in real life. For very many Greeks, however, these verses may well have been the first introduction to how to pray.

natural action? So much later Homeric criticism, like so much later religious history, takes its cue from interpretive directions to which Homer himself gave the impetus.

In the *Homeric Hymns* the links between paradigmatic scenes of a divine past and the human present are often visible. It is, for example, clear that the scene of Olympian festivity in the *Homeric Hymn to Apollo* (vv. 187–206) provides a pattern for human celebration of the god, just as the pattern of the original Delphic paean and procession of which the hymnist tells was repeated every year. (Cf., e.g., Furley and Bremer 2001: 1.14–15; Fantuzzi and Hunter 2004: 365–366.) So too in Callimachus' *Hymns*, which are rooted both in the poetry of the past and also in contemporary cultic practice, the past breaks through and embraces us at every point. The Cyrenean rites for Apollo that "we" are now performing, for example, were witnessed immemorially long ago by Apollo himself (*Hymn to Apollo* 90–95). At the end of the *Hymn to Delos* the poet tells of a tree-biting rite in the god's honor:

> Ἀστερίη πολύβωμε πολύλλιτε, τίς δέ σε ναύτης
> ἔμπορος Αἰγαίοιο παρήλυθε νηὶ θεούσῃ;
> οὐχ οὕτω μεγάλοι μιν ἐπιπνείουσιν ἄῆται,
> χρειὼ δ' ὅττι τάχιστον ἄγει πλόον, ἀλλὰ τὰ λαίφη
> ὠκέες ἐστείλαντο καὶ οὐ πάλιν αὖτις ἔβησαν,
> πρὶν μέγαν ἢ σέο βωμὸν ὑπὸ πληγῇσιν ἑλίξαι
> ῥησσόμενον καὶ πρέμνον ὀδακτάσαι ἁγνὸν ἐλαίης
> χεῖρας ἀποστρέψαντας· ἃ Δηλιὰς εὕρετο νύμφη
> παίγνια κουρίζοντι καὶ Ἀπόλλωνι γελαστύν.

> Asterie of many altars and many prayers, what merchant sailor on the Aegean passes you by in his speeding ship? Such strong winds never urge him on; never must he make so swift a voyage! Quickly they furl the sails and do not go on board again before they have gone around your great altar while being beaten with blows and have bitten the sacred trunk of the olive, their hands held behind their backs. The nymph of Delos devised this as a game and source of laughter for the young Apollo.
> Callimachus *Hymn to Delos* 316–324

The rite has been practiced since the god was a baby, and it is something that every passing sailor does, however urgent his business. Moreover, there are here two presents, that of cultic practice and that of the hymn we are hearing or reading. As the poet is about to take his leave of the island, a parallelism is suggested between the passing sailors and the poet on his own journey: as the sailors never pass by without paying their respects, so the poet has not forgotten Delos. (Cf. v. 8.) The sailors will then continue on, but will do so having pleased the god; so too will the poet, who thus solves in yet another new way (cf. the end of the *Hymn to Apollo*) the eternal problem of when to stop hymning the god.

The relationship of past and present is again central to, but configured differently in, the reverent silence with which songs in praise of Apollo must be heard, a silence authorized by figures from the distant past, Thetis and Niobe, who nevertheless bring their potentially disruptive mourning into the present (*Hymn to Apollo* 20–24). Behind this latter passage may lie the famous opening of Pindar's *Pythian* 1, in which both Zeus's eagle and "violent Ares," two creatures unlikely to lower their guard, respond with quiet calm to the music of the Apolline lyre, whereas "those whom Zeus does not love," including the Giant beneath Etna, are panicked by the sound; when Callimachus draws the moral from the case of Niobe that "it is a bad thing to compete with the blessed ones" and establishes a clear parallelism between such opposition to Apollo and opposition to "my king" (vv. 25–27), he may be contracting and sharpening the clear parallelism that *Pythian* 1 draws between Zeus and Apollo and Hieron of Syracuse. (For another Callimachean use of this passage of Pindar, cf. Hunter 2006a: 95.)

The interaction between past and present is in fact probably nowhere as dynamic as in poems in honor of the gods; epic poetry tells of heroes whose deeds still have a powerful meaning for their cities as well as a general didactic force, but it is gods whose favor and attention are always urgently sought in the present. Stories about the past are therefore told because of their relation to, and power to work in, the present. Callimachus' revelation of what poetic myths are for is particularly on show in celebrating the new gods of the Ptolemaic house. Philadelphus' newly deceased sister-wife, Arsinoe, and her sister Philotera play the roles of Persephone and Demeter in *The Apotheosis of Arsinoe* (fr. 228 Pf.; cf. Hunter 2003c: 50–53), and the running together of Apollo and Ptolemy and the mingling of the past history of Delos with the contemporary history of the Delian and Cycladic league in the *Hymn to Delos* are a sharply explicit use of this traditional power of song. Somewhat similar is the association between Zeus and "our ruler" (v. 86) in the *Hymn to Zeus*. Whether or not Callimachus understood the βασιλῆες, who are praised in Hesiod's *Theogony* (vv. 80–103) and who have a special relationship with the Muses and with poets, to have been Hesiod's patrons (cf. M.L. West 1966: 44–45), it is not a very big step from there to the encomium of the poet's king in the *Hymn to Zeus*. Hellenistic ruler cult has an obvious importance also for the related subjects of the two remaining sections of this chapter, the centrality of statues and of ideas of epiphany to Callimachean poetry and Hellenistic religious life.

Seeing Gods

Some five hundred years after Herodotus, Dio Chrysostom expanded on Herodotus' insight in his *Olympic Oration* (*Or.* 12), in which he discourses upon the sources of human conceptions of the divine. These are said to be, first, an innate sense of divinity that is common to all human, rational beings and without which all other sources have no validity and, second, the ideas we acquire from the poets, lawgivers, artists, and philosophers. In the second part of the speech Dio puts into the mouth of Phidias, the sculptor of the colossal image of Zeus at Olympia, a defense of his representation of the god and a contrast between the resources and limitations of the plastic arts and the freedom enjoyed by poets, a contrast taking its start not just from the familiarity, by Dio's time, of the analogy between the verbal and plastic arts but also (chapters 25–26) from the commonly cited anecdote in which Phidias admitted that the inspiration for his Zeus had come from Homer's description of Zeus nodding assent to Thetis' request at *Iliad* 1.528–30.[9] Both the setting and the role of Phidias are entirely appropriate to the subject of the discourse, as the Zeus at Olympia was by common consent, with the only possible rival being Phidias' own Athena Parthenos on the Athenian Acropolis, the closest man had come to the representation of divinity, and it was a statue that itself, just like the poetry of Homer from which it was derived, was argued to have influenced human notions of the divine; as Quintilian (12.10.9) puts it, "the beauty of the statue seems to have added something more to the inherited sense of the divine [*recepta religio*], so exactly did the majesty of the work equal the god." So too, Cicero traces the pattern for Phidias' two great masterpieces not to any human likeness, but rather to a mental image of perfect beauty that he compares to Platonic Forms (*Orator* 2.8–10). The sight of Phidias' Zeus produces a religious awe even in dumb animals (Dio 12.51); it can provoke us to

---

[9] Cf. Strabo 8.3.30 (on which see further below). Most of the ancient sources on Phidias' Zeus are collected in Overbeck 1868: 125–136; and cf. Lapatin 2001: 79–86.

contemplation of the divine, just as do the Homeric verses on which it is based (Strabo 8.3.30).

Phidias' Zeus is therefore a very special case of the complex and ambiguous relationship throughout Greek antiquity between, on the one hand, gods and our conceptions of them and, on the other, the images and representations of them that men create.[10] Callimachus' best-known exploration of this productive tension is the *Hymn to Athena* (cf. Hunter 1992b), but this is also the background against which we must view the poem devoted precisely to Phidias' Zeus, namely *Iambus* 6.[11] According to the *diegesis*, the poem, addressed to an acquaintance who was sailing off to see the statue,[12] consisted of a detailed description of it, an account of how much it cost, and the fact that the artist was Phidias the Athenian, son of Charmides. The only verse that remains from the first part of the poem is in fact the opening verse, but it has much to tell us:

Ἀλεῖος ὁ Ζεύς, ἁ τέχνα δὲ Φειδία.

The Zeus is Elean; the artwork Phidias.

Callimachus fr. 196.1 Pf.

In our sources the people of Elis are always very closely associated with the building and protection of the statue—after all, they commissioned it—but "Elean" is nowhere else used of Zeus.[13] The form suggests a cult title, and it obviously evokes the very cult title of the statue itself, Ὀλύμπιος, meaning both "Olympian" (i.e., dwelling on Mt. Olympus) and (unusually) "of Olympia"; the local epithet both prefigures the pedantic *akribeia* that is to be a hallmark of the poem and humorously downgrades the majesty of the Panhellenic Olympian god to that of a local divinity.

The chiastic arrangement of the opening verse opposes Zeus to "the artwork": that is, principally, the statue (cf. Kerkhecker 1999: 150),

---

[10] There is a large bibliography: guidance can be found throughout Tanner 2006; and with particular regard to poetic exploitations of the relationship, cf. also Kassel 1983.

[11] Recent discussion in Manakidou 1993: 238–242; Acosta-Hughes 2002: 288–294; Kerkhecker 1999: 147–181; Prioux 2007: 114–121.

[12] This fact cannot be confirmed from the remains of the poem itself (cf. Kerkhecker 1999: 174), though the existence of an addressee is confirmed by vv. 45–46 and 62.

[13] At fr. 76.2 Pf. (= 175.2 M.) Zeus is apparently given the epithet Πισαῖος, "of Pisa" (cf. Pfeiffer 1949–1953 *ad loc.*); for Zeus and Elis, cf. fr. 77 Pf. (= 179 M.).

though the word choice also suggests the skill of the craftsman. That opposition, however, evokes a central element in the Greek sense of the divine, and Callimachus will have expected his readers to wonder what such an opposition might actually mean: In what sense can "the Zeus" be "Elean" but the statue be "Phidias'"? If we obviously have "the playful identification of god and statue,"[14] issues of divine identity are also in play. Diogenes Laertius reports a story concerning Stilpo of Megara (late fourth and early third century BC):

> They say that he argued concerning the Athena of Phidias in the following way: "Is Athena [daughter] of Zeus a god?"; when the interlocutor agreed, he said, "This one at any rate is not of Zeus but of Phidias," and when this too was agreed, he said, "Then she is not a god." When he was summoned before the Areopagus, he did not deny that he had said this, but claimed that he had argued correctly, for she was not a god, but a goddess, and it was the males who were gods. Nevertheless, the Areopagites ordered him to leave the city immediately.
> Diogenes Laertius 2.116 (= Stilpo fr. 12 Giannantoni)

Stilpo is playing here with a number of linguistic issues, but one of them is the force of a genitive when it is attached to the name of a god; this is not just a play with the apparent polyvalency of the genitive case, but it also draws attention to the problematic relationship of god and statue. So does the opening verse of *Iambus* 6 by evoking the possibility of, while avoiding, saying "Zeus of Phidias," with all the theological complications that that would bring. There is perhaps some further indication that these implications of Callimachus' verse were appreciated in antiquity.

The earliest account of, though not reference to, the Seven Wonders of the World that survives from antiquity is an essay ascribed in the principal manuscript to Philo of Byzantium, though there is general consent that this cannot be the writer on mechanical subjects of the late third-early second century BC; the essay on the Seven Wonders is now generally dated to late antiquity.[15] In the account of Phidias' Zeus, Philo too plays with both questions of paternity and the relation between god and statue:

---

[14] Kerkhecker 1999: 150. For the Stilpo anecdote that follows, cf. Stewart 1998: 271–273; Lapatin 2010: 126–127.

[15] The most recent edition is Brodersen 1992; cf. also Hercher 1858. Kroll's short notice in *RE* 20.54–55 remains the most helpful account.

In heaven Cronus is Zeus's father; in Elis it is Phidias: the one was engendered by immortal nature; the other by the hands of Phidias, which alone are able to give birth to gods. Blessed is he who alone beheld the ruler of the cosmos and was able to show the Wielder of the Thunder to others. If Zeus is ashamed to be called [the son] of Phidias,[16] art [τέχνη] was the mother of the image of him.... Therefore we only wonder at the other of the Seven Wonders, but this one we also worship: as a work of art it is remarkable [παράδοξον]; as a representation [μίμημα] of Zeus it is holy.[17] The labor that went into it wins praise, but its immortality wins our honor.

Philo of Byzantium, *Seven Wonders* 3.1.3

Callimachus' poem seems to have been well known in antiquity,[18] and we should not rule out faint echoes of it here. Philo will, of course, have had access to other sources as well. His praise of Phidias ("Blessed is he...") is picked up at the end of the section on the Zeus of Olympia, as he apostrophizes the lucky period to which Phidias belonged:

You could show to men visions [ὄψεις] of the gods; a man who had seen them would not be able to look at images from other times (3.4).[19]

Both observations seem very close to a bon mot about Homer that Strabo (8.3.30) quotes in the same connection, "the only man to see or to show the images [εἰκόνες] of the gods," a bon mot that could easily within Strabo's text be understood to refer to Phidias rather than Homer and has indeed been so understood in modern times.[20]

If a direct debt to Callimachus cannot be established with certainty, Philo's essay does have one very striking link to *Iambus* 6. The wit of Philo's description of the Zeus at Olympia is that it tells us absolutely nothing about what the statue looked like; Philo's sketches of the other Wonders may be vague and given to cliché, "nicht...eine Beschreibung, sondern...eine rhetorische Plauderei" as Kroll (*RE* 20. 54) puts it, but there is in each of them some attempt at detailed description, usually

---

[16] Brodersen softens the force of this ("Man mag sich scheuen, von Zeus als Sohn des Pheidias zu sprechen"), but I do not see any grammatical or thematic justification for that.

[17] Accepting the conjecture ὅσιον for the transmitted ὅμοιον.

[18] It is cited at Strabo 8.3.30: "Certain writers have given an account of the measurements of the statue, and Callimachus recorded them in an iambic poem." Cf. Pausanias 5.11.9; Kerkhecker 1999: 166–167.

[19] The sense and the text are not absolutely clear.

[20] Radt's assertion *ad loc.*, "εἰκόνας δείξας könnte nicht von einem bildenden Künstler gesagt sein," seems improbable at best, and is almost disproved by Philo.

involving quantitative numerical description. Philo, however, offers no help whatsoever with the Zeus, and as such this case might seem the furthest removed from the stated purpose of his essay. He begins by observing the extraordinary labor involved in actually visiting the Seven Wonders, a task that would take a whole lifetime, whereas:

> Education [παιδεία] is an amazing possession and wonderful gift, because it releases a man from traveling and shows him beautiful things in his own home, by giving eyes to the soul. What is most amazing is that the man who has gone to the places and seen things once goes away and forgets, for he does not take in the details [τὸ ἀκριβές] of the works, and his memory of each part fades; whereas the man who has studied the marvel and the craftsmanship of its construction through writing [ὁ δὲ λόγῳ τὸ θαυμαζόμενον ἱστορήσας καὶ τὰς ἐξεργασίας τῆς ἐνεργείας] has observed the whole of art's creation as in a mirror and preserves impressions of each image that cannot be wiped out, for he has seen amazing things with his soul. My account will be convincing if my speech vividly [ἐναργῶς] explores each of the Seven Wonders and persuades the hearer to assent to the fact that it has brought him the impression of personal observation [θεωρία].
>
> Philo of Byzantium, *Proem* 2–3

There is much here that could be said about the philosophical and rhetorical background of Philo's observations, but two points will suffice in the current context. The stated purpose of Philo's essay is to remove the necessity of seeing the Wonders in person; some have argued that the wit of *Iambus* 6 too lies precisely in the fact that it offers an alternative to autopsy, one ironically addressed to someone just setting off to see the statue. Philo does not explicitly say that he has not seen the Wonders, but that would seem to be the natural inference to draw from the prologue: he too is a beneficiary of the same παιδεία that he offers his readers. As for Callimachus, it may well be that we are to understand that the speaking voice in *Iambus* 6 belongs to someone who himself has never been to Olympia; this would fit not merely with the stay-at-home persona familiar from elsewhere in Callimachus' works but, more important, with the whole conception of the poem. The statue is reduced to a series of measurements, and those measurements could be acquired from a book more easily than by autopsy or by reliance on local guides; the apparently dismissive ἀπέρχευ, "go forth", with which the poem ends suggests that the proposed trip will be a waste of time, because the addressee now knows all that there is to be known about the statue. Callimachus is here Herodotean in his concern with exactness of description, down to the cost of the statue,[21] but anti-Herodotean in his rejection of autopsy.

If Callimachus and Philo both offer an alternative to autopsy, their strategies for so doing seem utterly different. Philo ends his essay with what might seem a paradoxical appeal to the significance of vision:

> And Phidias has so far surpassed Olympus as vividness [ἐνάργεια] is better than guesswork [ὑπόνοια], knowledge [γνῶσις] than investigation [ἱστορία][22] and autopsy [ὄψις] than report [ἀκοή].

Philo's appeal to autopsy may seem to undermine his own project of making a visit to the Wonder unnecessary, but there may be more at stake here than just rhetorical incompetence. It was a familiar observation that no description of the statue could do it justice; it was a work that called forth thoughts of the divine, and it is to this metaphysical level that Philo's rhetorical sleight of hand appeals. This is a work that can be "seen with the soul" only, through a particularly potent form of *phantasia*: in refusing to describe it in any banal, physical way, Philo is in fact making clear the most important fact about Phidias' Zeus.[23] Just as Cicero's Phidias took his pattern for the statue from a mental image (*Orator* 2.8–10), so the statue itself can be grasped only as a mental image; we still need autopsy, but it is not autopsy as normally understood.[24] Callimachus' strategy in this regard is utterly different. If Philo is right that the onetime visitor to one of the Wonders will be unable to grasp τὸ ἀκριβές, "the details," then Callimachus has averted this danger by an excess of accurate detail; whereas, however, Philo's silence seems to point to the overwhelming impact of the statue, Callimachus' detail shuts the metaphysical out: "The statue's visual impact is ignored. The standard elements of ἔκφρασις are avoided. The measurements do not convey the viewer's experience. The poem frustrates all such expectations."[25]

---

[21] Cf. Holford-Strevens *apud* Kerkhecker 1999: 161 n. 78. The broken v. 47 with its οὐ λογιστὸν οὐδ'... may have contained a Herodotean expression of doubt.

[22] I am unsure of the exact meaning here, and this may be thought to sit oddly with τὸ θαυμαζόμενον ἱστορήσας in the poem.

[23] Whether or not Philo did in fact know anything serious about the statue (cf., e.g., Brodersen 1996: 69) is therefore a secondary question.

[24] The discussion of *phantasia* at Philostratus VA 6.19.2 is particularly relevant here.

[25] Kerkhecker 1999: 168. It is worth noting that, in his discussion of the sophist Acacius, Eunapius (497 = XVII Giangrande) draws a contrast, apparently descending from Libanius himself, between, on the one side, the sublimely inspired (and hard

Nothing in what survives of *Iambus* 6 appears to evoke the famous verses of *Iliad* 1 that were widely believed to have been Phidias' inspiration. Nevertheless, the familiarity of the anecdote allows the suspicion that Callimachus wants us to recall these verses, and the contrast between the epic and the iambic representation then carries a potent generic charge. The Homeric verses are characterized by a richness of poetic epithets (κυανέῃσιν, ἀμβρόσιαι, ἀθανάτοιο) and vocabulary (ἐπερρώσαντο, ἐλέλιξεν), whereas the *Iambus* offers a prosaic vocabulary in its description of the parts of the statue, homely touches such as the hare and the tortoise (v. 22, whatever the reference might be), and—so far as the remains allow us to see—a very limited descriptive range (χρύσιον, 25; ἅγιον, 29; etc.); in Homer the god acts in a moment of sublime movement; in Callimachus the god remains very unsublimely stationary. Homer's Zeus could not possibly be a statue, whatever inspiration it provided for Phidias, whereas Callimachus challenges us to (be able to) remember that his Zeus really is a δαίμων (v. 37). Homer in fact has very little reference to images of gods, but the most famous such passage is instructive in the present context.

In *Iliad* 6 the Trojan women offer a robe to the image of Athena, together with a prayer that she should save them from the rampaging Diomedes. The god, however, does not grant the prayer: ἀνένευε δὲ Παλλὰς Ἀθήνη (v. 311).[26] This passage may well have been in Callimachus' mind when he reworked Zeus's proud assertion to Thetis, which immediately precedes the nod that inspired Phidias, at the end of the *Hymn to Athena*:

οὐ γὰρ ἐμὸν παλινάγρετον οὐδ' ἀπατηλόν
οὐδ' ἀτελεύτητον, ὅ τι κεν κεφαλῇ κατανεύσω.

Whatever I confirm with a nod of my head cannot be withdrawn and neither deceives nor lacks fulfillment.

Homer *Iliad* 1.526–527

---

to explain) skill of Homer and Phidias and, on the other, the careful learning and *akribeia* of Libanius. Here perhaps is a later echo (or at least analogy) for the humorous contrast that lies at the heart of *Iambus* 6; for the use of Callimachean ideas in such later texts, cf. Hunter 2008b: 536–558).

[26] Aristarchus athetized this verse, and one of the reasons (not necessarily Aristarchan) that the A scholia offer is "the idea of Athena nodding refusal is ridiculous [γελοῖα]." If this refers, as it seems to, to the statue, then the question of the relationship between god and statue was, for later interpreters, directly thematized: Athena herself, like Zeus in *Iliad* 1, certainly could nod, but the idea of the statue doing so is absurd.

ὣς φαμένα κατένευσε· τὸ δ' ἐντελές, ᾧ κ' ἐπινεύσῃ
Παλλάς, ἐπεὶ μώνᾳ Ζεὺς τόγε θυγατέρων
δῶκεν Ἀθαναίᾳ πατρώια πάντα φέρεσθαι,
λωτροχόοι, μάτηρ δ' οὔτις ἔτικτε θεάν,
ἀλλὰ Διὸς κορυφά. κορυφὰ Διὸς οὐκ ἐπινεύει
ψεύδεα   αι θυγάτηρ.
ἔρχετ' Ἀθαναία νῦν ἀτρεκές κτλ.

> So saying she nodded in confirmation. Whatever Pallas confirms with a nod will be fulfilled, since Zeus gave to her alone of his daughters that she should have all her father's privileges, and it was no mother who gave birth to the goddess, but the head of Zeus. Zeus's head does not nod untruths '...' daughter. Athena is really coming out now.
> Callimachus *Hymn to Athena* 131–137

If Homer's Zeus could not be a statue, Callimachus' nodding Athena is both a statue and a goddess who speaks and bathes in mountain streams.

Juxtaposed to *Iambus* 6 is (in the same meter) *Iambus* 7, in which an image of Hermes, a minor work (πάρεργον) of Epeius, the creator of the Trojan Horse, tells of its many vicissitudes before ending up in the Thracian city of Aenus. (See now Petrovic 2010.) The pointed contrast with the Panhellenic grandeur of Phidias' Zeus is obvious, but the pairing, together with *Iambus* 9, which is a conversation with an ithyphallic statue of Hermes, points to the importance of the materiality of Callimachus' gods, and in this Callimachus offers us a glimpse of the Hellenistic religious world, which is far from being simply a poetic fiction. This was indeed a world full of gods, and the most visible sign of those gods was their images and the festivals that celebrated them, both of which take center stage in the poetry of the high Alexandrian period. The Graces whom Callimachus asks to bestow immortality upon his elegies are both gods with birth narratives and stories to tell (Schol. Flor. p. 13 Pf., p. 76 M.) and statues of beautiful women, sometimes nude and sometimes wearing fine, delicate clothes (fr. 7.9–11 Pf. = 9.9–11 M.). Probably in Book 3 of the *Aetia* Callimachus presented a conversation with the cult statue of Apollo on Delos in which the god-statue explained the symbolic significance of why he was represented carrying the Graces in his right hand and his bow in the left (fr. 114 Pf. = 64 M.).[27] The papyrus that preserves the first part of this conversation seems to conclude with the end of the preceding *aition*, in which πολυγώνιε χαῖρε, "Hail, you of many corners" (fr. 114.2 Pf.), suggests

---

[27] In addition to the standard commentaries, cf. Pfeiffer 1952; Manakidou 1993: 225–235; Borgonovo and Cappelletto 1994; D'Alessio 1995a.

that this was a conversation with, or an account of, an aniconic image of a god, and Pfeiffer made the very attractive suggestion that this was in fact one of the blocks of stone that represented Apollo in a Milesian cult of the god; if so, πολυγώνιε presumably plays with the frequent, and Callimachean (cf. *Hymn to Apollo* 68–70), association of the god's name with πολύς.[28] Be that as it may, such a juxtaposition of a rude stone to the elaborate image of the Delian god bearing "the lovely Graces" both recalls the juxtaposition of *Iambi* 6 and 7 and reminds us that Callimachus' gods tend to be local rather than Panhellenic, or rather, as in the *Hymn to Artemis*, to be the sum of myriad local parts (cf. Hunter and Fuhrer 2002: 148); if Callimachus was here influenced by prose handbooks about local cults, he himself may well have influenced subsequent scholarly tradition, as witness, for example, the Ἐπιφάνειαι Ἀπόλλωνος (*Appearances of Apollo*) of his follower Istrus (*FGrHist* 334 F 50–52).[29] Moreover, both the emphasis on materiality and the multiplicity of divine images, both anthropomorphic and aniconic, may from a literary point of view be seen as in part a reaction to Herodotus' stress, from which I began, on the role of Hesiod and Homer in shaping the Greek divinities; those grand epic figures have been replaced by *real* divinities made of tangible substances such as marble and wood.

Examples could be multiplied from across the Callimachean corpus. In Book 4 of the *Aetia* poems devoted to two images of Hera on Samos were juxtaposed (frr. 100, 101 Pf. = 203, 204 M.). The first *aition* involved the oldest aniconic wooden representation of Hera on the island:

οὔπω Σκέλμιον ἔργον εὔξοον, ἀλλ' ἐπὶ τεθμόν
  δηναιὸν γλυφάνων ἄξοος ἦσθα σανίς·
ὧδε γὰρ ἱδρύοντο θεοὺς τότε· καὶ γὰρ Ἀθήνης
  ἐν Λίνδῳ Δαναὸς λιτὸν ἔθηκεν ἕδος.

Not yet was the finely carved work of Scelmis, but in the old manner you were a plank that had not been carved with chisels. This is how they set up gods in those days: at Lindus Danaus had set up a simple image of Athena.

Callimachus fr. 100 Pf.

---

[28] Cf. Hunter and Fuhrer 2002: 163. For πολυγώνιε, cf. also Alan Cameron 1995: 168, with further bibliography.
[29] Cf. Dillery 2005: 511–512. The whole of Dillery's discussion is important for setting Hellenistic poetry against the wider background of the interest in and recording of cultic history.

If the representation of Hera changed over time from an aniconic plank to anthropomorphic form, can she be said to be "forever," αἰεί, like Callimachus' Zeus? The historical interest in change over time ("That's how they represented gods at that time") is, moreover, both typical of Callimachus' age and speaks to the concern with particularity that is everywhere the hallmark of his treatment of the divine. That said, there clearly are differences of nuance between, on the one hand, the divine statues of the *Aetia* and the *Iambi* and, on the other, the gods of the hexameter *Hymns* that may appear as statues but that remain recognizably also the gods of poetic tradition.

Experiencing Gods

Statues are to be seen, though usually in circumstances and times determined by the god and his or her attendants; and central too to the presentation of the divine in the *Hymns* of Callimachus is the concept and imagining of divine epiphany, as indeed we know it to have been to the practice of Hellenistic religion. Albert Henrichs has noted that the sense of anticipation that (in particular) the hymns to Apollo and Athena create represents with some accuracy the experience of cultic participants.[30] Here too Callimachus is building not just upon archaic lyric but also upon the foundation of the *Homeric Hymns*, which narrate and explore epiphany in various ways, not all of which have always been fully appreciated.[31] In this final section, I want to consider some of the archaic roots of a poetic form that has always seemed quintessentially Callimachean.

The *Homeric Hymn to Dionysus* (no. 7) seems to look forward to Callimachus in various ways;[32] the date of this poem is uncertain, however suggestive a link with Exekias' famous depiction of Dionysus and the dolphins (ca. 530 BC) may be, but there is no good reason not to consider it archaic. The poem begins with an epiphany:

---

[30] Henrichs 1993: 142–145; the subject has been much discussed, but cf. also Petrovic 2007: 142–181.

[31] Cf., e.g., Fantuzzi and Hunter 2004: 364–366 on the *Homeric Hymn to Apollo*; the discussion of the hymns of Isidorus there also contains much of relevance to the present chapter.

[32] On the narrative pattern shared between this hymn and Callimachus' tale of Erysichthon, cf. Bulloch 1977: 99–101.

ἀμφὶ Διώνυσον Σεμέλης ἐρικυδέος υἱόν
μνήσομαι, ὡς ἐφάνη παρὰ θῖν' ἁλὸς ἀτρυγέτοιο
ἀκτῇ ἔπι προβλῆτι, νεηνίῃ ἀνδρὶ ἐοικώς
πρωθήβῃ·

I will celebrate Dionysus, the son of glorious Semele, how he appeared by the shore of the unharvested sea, on a steep headland, looking like a young man in the prime of youth.

Homeric Hymn to Dionysus 1–4

Here is a very familiar narrative pattern: Dionysus "appears" to those who do not know or recognize him and demonstrates his divinity; in the *Bacchae* of Euripides his purpose is to become ἐμφανὴς δαίμων to mortals. Both Ovid (*Met.* 3.572–700) and Nonnus (*Dion.* 45.103–69) acknowledged this affinity to later narratives by embedding their versions of the pirate story into the story of the destruction of Pentheus.[33] Games of recognition are here, as they always are with Dionysus, fundamental. We recognize the god both because of what the hymn's singer tells us and because of our familiarity with narrative patterns, but the Tyrrhenian pirates do not. Knowledge of the Lycurgus-Pentheus pattern, together with the unsettling lack of geographical specificity as the narrative of this *Hymn* begins—Where is the "steep headland"?—and the god's announcement of his name, genealogy, and nature (ἐρίβρομος) at the conclusion of the narrative (vv. 55–57) makes us wonder in fact whether we are to understand that this is Dionysus' first appearance or that every appearance of Dionysus is in some senses the first. As in the *Bacchae*, Dionysus is both a new god and immemorially old.[34] (The sea is already οἶνοψ, v. 7.) Do we know the god, or can you only understand this poem if you put yourself in the position of an audience that has never heard the name Dionysus, let alone Semele?

Whereas the terrified sailors (ἐκπληγέντες, v. 50) leap overboard, where they are transformed into dolphins, the god restrained the σαόφρων (v. 49) steersman who realized (νοήσας, v. 15) that they had

---

[33] Ovid introduces the character of Acoetes, who may or may not be the god, so that even we readers, let alone Pentheus, do not recognize the god, or are not sure whether we do; Bömer's rather sad survey of modern discussion of the question reveals nothing so clearly as how successfully Ovid has achieved this effect.

[34] I am in fact tempted to take πρώτιστα in v. 35 as "for the first time," but I doubt that many will follow me.

captured no ordinary young man,[35] made him "all blessed" (πανόλβιος, v. 54), and revealed his identity to him. This pattern, including the urging of the worshipper θαρσεῖν (v. 55), is strikingly reminiscent of what (little) we know of initiation into Mystery cults;[36] the steersman is now in the happy position of the initiate into Demeter's cult at Eleusis:[37]

> ὄλβιος ὃς τάδ' ὄπωπεν ἐπιχθονίων ἀνθρώπων,
> ὃς δ' ἀτελὴς ἱερῶν ὅς τ' ἄμμορος, οὔ ποθ' ὁμοίων
> αἶσαν ἔχει φθίμενός περ ὑπὸ ζόφῳ εὐρώεντι.
>
> Blessed is he of men upon the earth who has witnessed these things; he who is uninitiated or who has no share in the holy things enjoys no similar fate after death in the moldy dark.
> *Homeric Hymn to Demeter* 480-482

The epiphanic revelation toward which the *Homeric Hymn to Dionysus*, like so many hymns (including some of Callimachus'; on this pattern, see esp. García 2002), has been moving represents also the revelatory sight offered to the blessed. The god's θάρσει (v. 55) finds parallels in texts that there are reasonable grounds for thinking reflect encouragement to those undergoing initiation,[38] and the god's revelation of himself in pity (v. 53) for a mortal may make us think of Isis appearing to Lucius: "adsum tuos miserata casus, adsum fauens et propitia" (Apuleius *Met.* 11.5).

This pattern will also make us ask who speaks the closing verses:

> χαῖρε, τέκος Σεμέλης εὐώπιδος· οὐδέ πη ἔστιν
> σεῖό γε ληθόμενον γλυκερὴν κοσμῆσαι ἀοιδήν.
>
> Hail, child of fair Semele! It is not possible for him who forgets you to adorn sweet song.
> *Homeric Hymn to Dionysus* 58-59

At one level, these verses are obviously spoken by the hymn's singer as he greets and bids farewell to the god, but after what has preceded we may also sense the voice of the steersman acknowledging the ἐμφανὴς

---

[35] The participle may of course mean no more than "when he saw this" (M.L. West), but the choice of the verb remains suggestive; García 2002: 17-20 has the steersman having "an insight" and discusses other examples of this verb in the context of hymnic recognition.
[36] Cf., e.g., Lada-Richards 1999: 236-237, 319. I hope it will not need stressing that I am not suggesting that this text is actually a mystical or initiatory one.
[37] Cf. also *Homeric Hymn to Demeter* 486-489.
[38] Cf. Seaford on Eur. *Ba.* 607; Joly 1955; Lada-Richards 1999: 86-87, 93 n. 188.

δαίμων in front of him and the divine favor he has been shown. (Note the ironically laden δαίμων of v. 31.) The steersman and the poet are in fact in the same position in having received the god's χάρις. (Cf. v. 55.) The narrative of an epiphany of the god in the timeless past, the mingling of voice, the interaction between the divinity praised and the hymnist doing the praising, however appropriate to the nature of Dionysus,[39] and the evocation of cultic practices all look forward to the so-called mimetic *Hymns* of Callimachus.

In Callimachus' *Hymn to Apollo* the worshippers are waiting for the god to appear—their situation is thus very different from that of the pirates who capture Dionysus—but here too the epiphanic revelation will be limited to a blessed group:[40]

ὠπόλλων οὐ παντὶ φαείνεται, ἀλλ' ὅτις ἐσθλός·
ὅς μιν ἴδῃ, μέγας οὗτος, ὃς οὐκ ἴδε, λιτὸς ἐκεῖνος.
ὀψόμεθ', ὦ Ἑκάεργε, καὶ ἐσσόμεθ' οὔποτε λιτοί.

Apollo does not appear to everyone, but only to the good. He who sees him, that man is great; he who does not see him, that man is of no account. We shall see, Far-Worker, and we shall never be of no account.
Callimachus *Hymn to Apollo* 9–11

That this is not just a pious hope is made clear by the end of the poem, in which Apollo does actually appear (with startling suddenness) to Callimachus' readers to confirm their poetic principles. The exchange between Phthonos and Apollo took place somewhere in an unspecified past, but just as the final address of the hymnist in the *Homeric Hymn to Dionysus* picks up the immediately preceding words of the god, in part perhaps in a kind of cultic repetition and in part to link the present experience of the hymnist (and his audience) to the story that has just been narrated, so the closing verse of the Callimachean hymn both salutes the appearance of the god (χαῖρε) and (on the most probable interpretation) links the alleged present experience of the poet—μῶμος, "criticism," "blame"—to the past just narrated; if Apollo speaks like Callimachus, then Callimachus' dismissal of Blame is in its turn a very Apolline act.

---

[39] There are analogous phenomena in the *Homeric Hymns* to Apollo and Demeter, but in neither case is the closeness of the hymnic voice to that of the figure in the narrative who has received the god's favor as marked as in the *Hymn to Dionysus*.

[40] On such language in the *Hymn to Apollo*, cf. now Petrovic forthcoming.

CHAPTER THIRTEEN

CALLIMACHUS AND CONTEMPORARY RELIGION: THE *HYMN TO APOLLO*

Ivana Petrovic

ABSTRACT

This paper aims to illustrate the significance of contemporary religious practices for Callimachus' poetry, by focusing on his *Hymn to Apollo* and reading it in the context of metrical and prose sacred regulations such as *programmata*, oracular responses, the Cyrenaean purity regulation, and the inscriptional hymns of Isyllus and Philodamos from Scarpheia. Each of these classes of text resonates in Callimachus' poetry and contributes to its rich tapestry of influences and allusions. Finally, the paper considers the Cyrenaean context of Callimachus' *Hymn to Apollo* as well as the connection of Callimachus' family to the cult of Apollo in Cyrene, arguing that the personal relationship Callimachus forges with Apollo in this hymn resembles the subscriptions accompanying hymns inscribed in sanctuaries. These texts also record divine approbation of the poets and list and various honors the sanctuaries have bestowed on them.

Callimachus' attitude toward religion was extensively discussed in the twentieth century. The question was often posed whether Callimachus believed in the Olympian gods, and the answers varied from abso-

---

The following abbreviations are used throughout this paper:
Edelstein = Edelstein, E.J. and L. Edelstein, eds. 1945. *Asclepius: A Collection and Interpretation of the Testimonies*. Baltimore.
I. Lindos = Blinkenberg, C. 1941. *Lindos. Fouilles et Recherches, II. Fouilles de l'Acropole. Inscriptions*. Berlin.
EGBR = *Epigraphic Bulletin for Greek Religion*.
LSAM = Sokolowski, F. 1955. *Lois Sacrées de l'Asie Mineure*. Paris.
LSCG = id. 1969. *Lois Sacrées des Cités Grecques*. Paris.
LSS = id. 1966. *Lois Sacrées des Cités Grecques. Supplément*. Paris.
NGSL = Lupu, E. 2005. *Greek Sacred Laws. A Collection of New Documents*. Leiden, Boston.
PW = Parke, H.W. and D.E.W. Wormell. 1956. *The Delphic Oracle*. 2 Vols. Oxford.
SGO = Merkelbach, R. and J. Stauber, eds. 1998–2004, *Steinepigramme aus dem Griechischen Osten*. 5 Vols., Munich, Leipzig.

lute denial to emphatic affirmation.[1] More recently, the consensus has been that Callimachus perceived Olympian gods as literary figures,[2] and his hymns were discussed as literary experiments devoid of any *Sitz im Leben*. Excellent studies have been devoted to their narrative strategies and relationship with literary predecessors, but the religious dimension of the *Hymns* has tended to be sidelined. However, current scholarship is paying more attention to the social context of Hellenistic poetry. Callimachus' relationship to contemporary religion has been reassessed,[3] with the conclusion that, like all Hellenistic poets, Callimachus too was deeply interested in and often commented on the politics and religion of his age. In order to illustrate the significance of contemporary religious practices for Callimachus' poetry, this chapter will focus on his *Hymn to Apollo*, reading it in the context of metrical and prose sacred regulations and inscriptional hymns. Each of these classes of text resonates in Callimachus' poetry and contributes to its rich tapestry of influences and allusions.[4]

Greek Sacred Regulations

It is an often-repeated truism that Greek religion had no sacred book. But the lack of one, single Panhellenic scripture does not mean that the Greeks had no sacred texts at all. In fact, they had a plethora of texts that regulated and prescribed the performance of religious rituals. Most of these sacred regulations are epigraphically transmitted.[5] The corpus of Greek sacred regulations is generically extensive, consisting of laws of state, official contracts, calendars, decrees, treaties,

---

[1] Nikitinski 1997: 15–23 provides an overview of scholarship on the personal religiosity of Callimachus. For denial, see Stähelin 1934: 62; affirmation, Meillier 1979: 195, and Fraser 1972: 1.662.
[2] See excellent observations in Hunter 1993: esp. 29, 33–34.
[3] Hunter 1993, and Hunter and Fuhrer 2002, announced a renewed interest in the context of Callimachus' *Hymns*. Henrichs 1993 provides valuable comments on epiphany in the *Hymns*. Stephens 2003: 74–121 discusses how the *Hymns* react to Egyptian cults and mythology. Vamvouri Ruffy 2005 interprets the *Hymns* in the context of inscriptional cult poetry. Petrovic 2007 discusses the reception of contemporary religion in Theocritus and Callimachus.
[4] The following discussion is based on Petrovic forthcoming.
[5] The term *Leges sacrae*, which has been used as a *terminus technicus* for the epigraphically transmitted sacred regulations, has recently been questioned, mainly because of their generic heterogeneity. I shall refer to them as sacred regulations. On sacred regulations in general, see Guarducci 1967–78: 4.3–45; Parker 2004; Lupu 2005: 3–112; On the terminology, I. Petrovic and A. Petrovic 2006: 151–154, with further literature.

public records, building inscriptions, *horoi* ("boundary stones"), sepulchral, and dedicatory inscriptions, oracular responses, terms of tenure for priesthoods to be sold, decisions of private associations, and purity rules. Their thematic heterogeneity is also considerable: some texts regulate the minutiae of a specific component of a ritual, such as the procession or the sacrifice; others devote themselves entirely to specifying the sacrificial animal and the division of its meat or to recording priestly prerogatives. Cult calendars list the festival days throughout the year. Purity rules enumerate the sources of pollution and the methods of achieving ritual purity as a necessary prerequisite for entry into the sacred space. Most sacred regulations are prescriptive in nature, as they provide the participants of rituals with a set of rules regulating conduct in a sacred space.

Together with hymns, sacred regulations provide the script for Greek rituals: sacred regulations are prescriptive; hymns, performative texts. Hymns tend to address aspects like *aitia* of certain rituals or festivals, descriptions of the deity, and specifications of divine powers and areas of influence, which the sacred regulations leave unspecified. Hymns enable the worshippers to create a system of reference where each deity has its own domain and spheres of influence, whereas the sacred regulations enable the worshippers to honor each individual god in an appropriate manner.

Callimachus' mimetic hymns describe the rituals and even provide instructions for the participants, thus crossing the boundary between prescriptive and performative texts.[6] However, there are also sacred regulations that reach into the domain of cult hymns—metrical regulations. These texts are not as numerous as the prose regulations. In the corpora of Greek inscriptions, twenty-nine texts are composed in meter.[7] They range from the fourth century BC to the third century AD. Most are composed in hexameters, but there are also some in elegiacs.[8] The content of these texts seems to determine their form: twenty of twenty-nine texts are oracular responses, all but one (*SGO* 1.04.01.01) in hexameters. Of five texts in elegiac couplets, one is a dedicatory

---

[6] Callimachus quotes sacred regulations most extensively in his mimetic hymns. See Petrovic forthcoming.

[7] See the catalogue and the discussion of the material from the Greek East in I. Petrovic and A. Petrovic 2006.

[8] Hexameters: *SGO* 1.01.09.01, 1.01.19.01–02; 1.01.19.05–08; 1.01.20.03; 1.01.23.02; 1.02.01.02; 1.03.02.01; 1.06.02.01; 2.08.01.01; 2.09.01.01; 3.16.31.01; 4.17.06.01; 4.17.18.01; 4.18.19.01; 11.02.02.01. Elegiacs: *SGO* 1.01.17.01; 2.09.07.01; *LSS* 108; *I.Lindos* 2.484; 487. *SGO* 1.04.01.01 is composed in a mixture of meters.

epigram (*SGO* 2.09.01.01) and the other four are *programmata*—regulations concerning ritual purity.

Sacred regulations in the form of oracular responses were ubiquitous in the Greek world, because oracles were perceived as highest authorities in respect to sacred legislation. Most transmitted oracular responses pertain to religious matters. Apollo was consulted as a mediator between humans and the gods, and his oracles often regulated cult foundations, specified the sacrifices and other offerings, provided ritual ordinances, rights of sanctuary, and immunity, specified the patron deities of cities, ritual customs, and similar matters.[9] Apollo's oracular centers in Delphi and later in Clarus and Didyma were consulted as the chief authorities in order to approve change in existing rituals and introduce new cults.[10] Apollo's instructions regarding the cults were usually inscribed, at first as a prose summary in which the oracular response was embedded in the text of a decree. From the Hellenistic period onwards, there is an increased tendency to inscribe the full oracular response in hexameter verse. By prefacing the inscription with a prose summary of the question that the community posed to the god and then providing a full response in meter, the impact of divine words was increased. Apollo's personal attention to the cult minutiae of a polis must have been perceived as an indicator of the cult's importance. On the other hand, the practice of inscribing the words of the god in full also corresponds to a Hellenistic tendency to record divine words and deeds. It is also in the early Hellenistic period that we witness an increased tendency to collect and inscribe instances of epiphanies of the gods, and to collect and publish divine aretalogies.[11] Finally, this is the period when the first instances of inscribed *programmata* probably appear. *Programmata* are texts providing cathartic regulations and determining the right of entry to a *temenos*. They use the topoi of oracular responses (gnomic statements, demand for ritual purity) and their formal characteristics (metrical form, direct address of the reader, imperatives).[12] However, whereas the inscriptions containing genuine oracular responses are preceded by a summary of the

---

[9] Fontenrose 1978: 11–57. On Apollo as mediator between gods and men in religious matters, see Parke and Wormell 1956: 1.320–27; Parker 2000.

[10] On Apollo's oracles in Clarus and Didyma, see Parke 1985; Fontenrose 1988; Busine 2005.

[11] On recording epiphanies in the Hellenistic period, see I. Petrovic 2007: 152–170; on aretalogies, 162–168, both with further literature.

[12] I. Petrovic and A. Petrovic 2006: 176–177.

question and a title θεὸς ἔχρησεν, which clearly mark them as divine announcements, *programmata* do not provide any information about their origin or the source of their authority.

The earliest known programma was inscribed above the portal of the Temple of Asclepius at Epidaurus, probably in fourth century BC:[13]

ἁγνὸν χρὴ ναοῖο θυώδεος ἐντὸς ἰόντα
ἔμμεναι· ἁγνεία δ' ἐστὶ φρονεῖν ὅσια.

> He who goes inside the sweet-smelling temple must be pure. Purity is to have an honest mind.

Purity regulations were ubiquitous in Greek sanctuaries, addressing very mundane matters. They provide lists of objects that are prohibited in sanctuaries and enumerate different sources of pollution, such as sexual intercourse, menstruation, contact with a corpse, or even certain foods, listing the number of days the polluted should keep away from the sanctuary and the ways they can purify themselves.[14] They are composed in prose and have no literary pretensions. The elegiac couplet from Epidaurus is strikingly different, as it simply states that in order to enter the *temenos* one must be pure, and then goes on to define purity not as lack of physical pollution but as a state of mind.[15] Furthermore, this text poses an important question: Who can identify those who do not φρονεῖν ὅσια? The metrical form of the inscription suggests a divine oracle, and the fact that the speaker is not identified further strengthens the impression that it is the god himself speaking.

The Epidaurus inscription is the earliest recorded of several similar *programmata*. One from Euromus (*SEG* 43. 710 = *SGO* 1.01.17.01) was inscribed on the door pillar of the entrance to the Temple of Zeus Lepsynus:[16]

---

[13] Edelstein T 318. Translation Parker 1983: 322–323. The text is not transmitted epigraphically but is quoted by two late writers (Porphyry *De abstinentia* 2.19 = Clemens Alex. *Strom.* 5.13.3 p. 334.24 St.). On this text, see Parker 1983: 322–325 and Chaniotis 1997. Bremmer 2002 proposed a new, later date for this inscription based on its use of the terms ἁγνός and ὅσιος; but see J. Mylonopoulos' objections in *EGBR* 2002: no. 15.

[14] For a catalogue and discussion of purity regulations as a group, see Parker 1983: 37 with n. 3 and 352–356. See also Parker 2004: 63–64; Lupu 2005: 14–18; 77–79.

[15] Nock 1958: 418 argued that the sanctuary of Asclepius was following the Delphic practice of inscribing moral maxims. On purity of mind in Greek religion, see Chaniotis 1997.

[16] The inscription is dated to the second century BC by Errington 1993: 29–30 and to the second century AD by Voutiras 1998: 148. The text is quoted here after *SGO* 1.01.17.01.

εἰ καθαράν, ὦ ξεῖνε, φέρεις φρένα καὶ τὸ δίκα[ι]ον
ἤσκηκες ψυχῇ, βα[ῖ]νε κατ' εὐίερον·
εἰ δ' ἀδίκων ψαύεις καί σοι νόος οὐ καθαρεύει,
πόρρω ἀπ' ἀθανάτων [ἔ]ργεο καὶ τεμένους·
οὐ στέργει φαύλους [ἱ]ερὸς δόμος, ἀλλὰ κολάζει,
τοῖς δ' ὁσίοις [ὁ]σίους ἀντινέμει [χάριτας].

If you bring a pure mind, Stranger, and if you have practiced justice in your soul, come to this place of sanctity. But if you touch the unjust, and if your mind is not pure, stay far away from gods and their sanctuary. The holy house does not approve of villains; it castigates them and gives pious deserts to the pious in return.

Several *programmata* have been found in Rhodes: *LSS* 108, from Lindus, is dated to the first century AD and quotes the first line of the Epidaurian inscription verbatim; *I.Lindos* 2.484, from the imperial period, is a metrical building inscription with elements of divination that stress the importance of a clear conscience. *I.Lindos* 2.487 = *LSS* 91 is from the third century AD. The text consists of a prose inscription in twenty lines with detailed purity regulations, and the second part is a metrical programma:

Τάν ποτ' Ὀλύμπον ἔβας ἀρετάφορον· εἴσιθι τοιγὰρ
εἰ καθαρὸς βαίν(ε)ις, ὦ ξένε, θαρραλέως·
εἰ δέ τι πᾶμα φέρ(ε)ις, τὸν ἀπάμονα κάλλιπε ναόν,
στεῖχε δ' ὅπᾳ χρήζ(ε)ις Παλλάδος ἐκ τεμένους.

Having trodden the virtuous path toward Olympus, enter—that is to say, if you are coming pure, Stranger, enter without fear. But if you are carrying blame with you, leave the blameless temple and go wherever you want, but stay away from Athena's precinct.

All these texts insist on purity of mind and urge the impure to leave the sacred precinct. Some even threaten the impure of mind with punishment and promise rewards for the just.[17] These inscriptions also bear a close resemblance to priestly proclamations (*prorrheseis*) at the beginning of rituals.[18]

---

[17] Cf. *SGO* 1.01.17.1.5–6; *LSS* 91.3–4.
[18] Dickie 2001 and 2004 discuss literary evidence that testifies that at the beginning of some rituals, most notably the Eleusinian rites, the priests urged the impure to leave the sacred precinct. See also Chaniotis 2006, discussing an inscription from Philadelphia that explicitly states that the presence of an impure person disturbs the performance of rituals (*LSAM* 20.36–41).

Programmata and the Beginning of the Hymn to Apollo

The beginning of Callimachus' *Hymn to Apollo* bears a striking resemblance to *prorrhēseis* and *programmata* both thematically (insistence on purity of mind, threats to the unjust) and formally (direct address, imperatives, and unidentified but possibly divine authority behind the statement). The *Hymn to Apollo* opens with a voice announcing that the laurel sapling is shaking and that the very temple of Apollo trembles. The impure are urged to leave the sacred precinct (2: ἑκὰς ἑκὰς ὅστις ἀλιτρός). The word ἀλιτρός, "sinful" or "wicked," has a strong connotation of hubris. The idea that the impure of mind should stay away from the temple is additionally strengthened in lines 9–11:[19]

> ὡπόλλων οὐ παντὶ φαείνεται, ἀλλ' ὅτις ἐσθλός·
> ὅς μιν ἴδῃ, μέγας οὗτος, ὃς οὐκ ἴδε, λιτὸς ἐκεῖνος.
> ὀψόμεθ', ὦ Ἑκάεργε, καὶ ἐσσόμεθ' οὔποτε λιτοί.
>
> Not on everyone, but only on the noble shines Apollo's light. He who has seen the god is great; he who has not is of no account. We will see you, Lord who shoot from afar, and never be of no account!

The prerequisite for witnessing the epiphany of Apollo is ritual purity.[20] The setting of the poem is a religious festival; the speaker and his audience are located in a sacred space. Callimachus' emphasis on a special type of purity—that of the mind—bears a strong resemblance to the stipulations in *programmata*.

Another characteristic of the opening of this hymn that connects it to *programmata* is the uncertainty regarding the speaker. The excited voice is probably the same as the one commanding the impious to leave the sacred space. "Begone, begone, whoever is impure!" might well be the warning of the speaker, who is perhaps reading the inscription on the temple doors, or indeed impersonating or reproducing the voice of the god himself.[21]

---

[19] Translations of Callimachus are after Nisetich 2001.
[20] Williams 1978: 23–24 *comm. ad vv.* 9–16 argues that epiphanies are often restricted to special recipients and quotes literary parallels for depiction of a sudden arrival of a deity. However, in this hymn, the arrival of the deity is expected, since its setting is a religious festival.
[21] Dickie 2002: 115–116 argues that the beginning of the *Hymn to Apollo* evokes a *prorrhesis*.

The Hymn to Apollo *and the Cyrenean Purity Regulation*

One further inscription that sheds more light on Callimachus' presentation of Apollo is the Cyrenean Purity Regulation.[22] This is a lengthy and detailed document from the late fourth century BC that stipulates how Cyreneans should keep pure in religious rituals. It is the only Greek text of this type claiming divine authority. Perhaps not surprisingly for Cyrene, a city that was from its very foundation exceptionally closely connected to the Delphic Oracle, its set of purity regulations is characterized as an oracle of Apollo. The law opens with the following statement (A 1-3):

> Ἀ]πόλλων ἔχρη[σε·] | [ἐς ἀ]εὶ καθαρμοῖς καὶ ἁγνήιαις κα[ὶ δε|κατ]ήιαις χρειμένος τὰν Λεβύαν οἰκ[έν.]
>
> Apollo issued an oracle: [The Cyreneans] shall inhabit Libya for ever, observing purifications and abstinences and tithes.

It is probably not coincidental that in the final part of Callimachus' *Hymn to Apollo* we also find a divine approbation and utterances concerning purity. It is the very hymn that is approved by Apollo, who uses the criteria of purity in order to pass judgment on various poetic compositions (*Hy.* 2.105-113):

> ὁ Φθόνος Ἀπόλλωνος ἐπ' οὔατα λάθριος εἶπεν·   105
> 'οὐκ ἄγαμαι τὸν ἀοιδὸν ὃς οὐδ' ὅσα πόντος ἀείδει.'
> τὸν Φθόνον ὡπόλλων ποδί τ' ἤλασεν ὧδέ τ' ἔειπεν·
> 'Ἀσσυρίου ποταμοῖο μέγας ῥόος, ἀλλὰ τὰ πολλά
> λύματα γῆς καὶ πολλὸν ἐφ' ὕδατι συρφετὸν ἕλκει.
> Δηοῖ δ' οὐκ ἀπὸ παντὸς ὕδωρ φορέουσι μέλισσαι,   110
> ἀλλ' ἥτις καθαρή τε καὶ ἀχράαντος ἀνέρπει
> πίδακος ἐξ ἱερῆς ὀλίγη λιβὰς ἄκρον ἄωτον.'
> χαῖρε, ἄναξ· ὁ δὲ Μῶμος, ἵν' ὁ Φθόνος, ἔνθα νέοιτο.
>
> Envy whispered into Apollo's ear: "I don't like a poet who doesn't sing like the sea." Apollo kicked Envy aside and said: "The Assyrian river rolls a massive stream, but it's mainly silt and garbage that it sweeps along. The bees bring water to Deo not from every source but where it bubbles up pure and undefiled from a holy spring, its very essence." Farewell, Lord! Let Criticism go where Envy's gone!

---

[22] *SEG* 9.72 = *LSS* 115. See on this regulation Parker 1983: 332-351 and 2004: 63-64; Chaniotis 1997: 145-148; Rhodes and Osborne 2003: 494-505. I quote their text and translation.

The much-discussed final passage of the hymn has often been interpreted as a statement of poetics, and numerous literary texts have been discussed in this context,[23] but thus far it has not been related to the metrical and nonmetrical sacred regulations. If this complex passage deals with Callimachus' poetic preferences and can be viewed as a veiled comment on the various modes of imitation and emulation of previous poets, it also owes much to local Cyrenean inscriptions, oracular sacred regulations, and the *programmata* from the great Panhellenic sanctuaries. A reading that considers these texts as well contributes to our understanding of the closing of this hymn without silencing other voices that resound in it.

At the end of the *Hymn to Apollo*, the god himself proclaims a purity regulation. Not only the divine authority and the topic but also the specifications regarding the gifts to the gods resemble the Cyrenean text, which contains stipulations regarding the pure and impure sacrifice. This notion plays a very important role in the final passage of the *Hymn to Apollo*. The poetic vehicle of a deus ex machina proclaiming his preferences in a statement that juxtaposes several types of water and rates them according to their purity resembles the following specifications of the Cyrenean Purity Regulation (*LSS* 115 A 26–31):

> αἴ κα ἐπὶ βωμῶι θύσηι ἰαρῆιον, ὅ τι μὴ νόμος θύεν, τ[ὸ] | ποτιπίαμμα ἀφελὲν ἀπὸ τῶ βωμῶ καὶ ἀποπλῦναι καὶ τὸ ἄλλο λῦμα ἀνελὲν ἐκ τῶ ἰαρῶ καὶ τὰν ἴκ|νυν ἀπὸ τῶ βωμῶ καὶ τὸ πῦρ ἀφελὲν ἐς καθαρόν· | καὶ τόκα δὴ ἀπονιψάμενος, καθάρας τὸ ἰαρὸν καὶ | ζαμίαν θύσας βοτὸν τέλευν, τόκα δὴ θυέτω ὡς νόμ[ος.]

> If someone sacrifices at an altar a victim that it is not customary to sacrifice, he is to remove from the altar the fat that remains and wash it away, and remove from the sanctuary the rest of the filth, and take away the ash from the altar and the fire to a pure place; and then, when he has washed himself and purified the sanctuary and sacrificed as a penalty a full-grown animal, let him sacrifice according to custom.

This part of the cathartic law of Cyrene basically treats a noncustomary victim as pollution for both the sacrificer and the shrine (Parker 1983: 339). Here, as in the *Hymn to Apollo*, we encounter Apollo rejecting the impure and demanding a pure sacrifice. In the *Hymn*, the purity

---

[23] See Asper 1997: 109–120 for a thorough analysis of the metaphors employed in this passage; Williams 1978: 90–99 and Alan Cameron 1995: 403–407 for two different interpretations. See now also Cheshire 2008.

regulations are applied not to the animal sacrifice but to the hymn itself, which is a gift to the god. Both utterances are oracular—in the cathartic regulation this is stated at the beginning; in the *Hymn to Apollo* it is suggested by the setting and vocabulary.

The vocabulary used in the sacred regulation is also evoked in the hymn—note the usage of the words λῦμα (*LSS* 115.28) and λύματα in *Hymn* 2.109; καθαρή in *Hymn* 2.111 and καθαρὸν (*LSS* 115.29); καθάρας (*LSS* 115.30).

Programmata *in the Final Part of the* Hymn to Apollo

The closing of the hymn evokes the beginning through an elaborate ring composition: Apollo appears—this time as a literary critic—and uses his foot again, not to pound on the temple door (l. 3) but to kick Envy (l. 107). At the beginning, the impure are urged to leave the sacred space (l. 2), but they have obviously not obeyed, since Envy is offering a blatant display of impurity of mind by criticizing the poet and his gift to the god—the hymn (l. 106).

The Delphic motif subtly evoked at the beginning with the mention of the laurel sapling (l. 1) and sustained throughout the hymn by several references to Delphi and its oracles escalates in a powerful crescendo in the final part of the hymn. Apollo is actually speaking now, and he speaks in a mode very similar to Delphic oracles: he does not directly respond to the criticism of Envy but uses elaborate metaphors and opaque speech. He refers to the topic most typical of the Apolline oracular responses—he specifies the types of sacrifice that gods approve of and discusses ritual purity. In doing this, Apollo uses the very metaphors actually employed in two *programmata*. Good parallels are to be found in two epigrams in Book 14 of the *Palatine Anthology* listed under the heading χρησμὸς τῆς Πυθίας, as oracular responses attributed to Delphic Apollo.[24] These texts are in fact *programmata* and have been classified as oracular responses because they, just like all other *programmata*, emulate the style and formal characteristics of oracles.

---

[24] *AP* 14.74 = PW 591; *AP* 14.71 = PW 592. See Parke and Wormell 1956: 2.XVII and I. Petrovic and A. Petrovic 2006: 176–177.

Let us consider first *Palatine Anthology* 14.74:

Ἱρὰ θεῶν ἀγαθοῖς ἀναπέπταται, οὐδὲ καθαρμῶν
χρειώ· τῆς ἀρετῆς ἥψατο οὐδὲν ἄγος.
ὅστις δ' οὐλοὸς ἦτορ, ἀπόστιχε· οὔποτε γὰρ σὴν
ψυχὴν ἐκνίψει σῶμα διαινόμενον.

> The sanctuary of gods is open for the virtuous; I do not even require cleansing—because to virtue clings no pollution. But whoever is wicked in heart—away with you! Because never will bathing your body purge the filth of your soul.

Here the idea that the most important purity is that of the mind is reiterated, as is the implication that the impure will be driven away from the sanctuary. This is exactly what happens to Envy in the *Hymn to Apollo*.

The second *programma* uses the same metaphors as Callimachus (*AP* 14.71):

Ἁγνὴς πρὸς τέμενος καθαρός, ξένε, δαίμονος ἔρχου
ψυχὴν νυμφαίου νάματος ἁψάμενος·
ὡς ἀγαθοῖς ἀρκεῖ βαιὴ λιβάς· ἄνδρα δὲ φαῦλον
οὐδ' ἂν ὁ πᾶς νίψαι νάμασιν Ὠκεανός.

> Stainless in respect of your soul, Stranger, come to the pure precinct of the deity after you have washed yourself with water sacred to Nymphs. For the virtuous just a drop will suffice, but him who is wicked will not wash the streams of the whole Ocean.

In the *Hymn to Apollo*, Φθόνος displays hubris by criticizing the hymn offered to the god. Apollo reacts by defending the hymn and drives him out of the *temenos* because he does not obey the purity regulations and does not display purity of mind. The closing passage of the *Hymn to Apollo* elaborates the general motif of *programmata* (demand for purity of mind, which is first attested in the inscription from Epidaurus) and even employs the same metaphors as *Palatine Anthology* 14.71.3–4, where λιβάς is juxtaposed to ὠκεανός. The motif of *programma* at the beginning of the hymn is thus reiterated at its very end.

It is very difficult to date the *programmata* from the *Anthology*, which raises the question of possible Callimachean influence on these texts. In the case of *Palatine Anthology* 14.74 this scenario is conceivable, but it is very unlikely for 14.71. The latter, in fact, demonstrates the greatest similarity to Callimachus' hymn, but it addresses someone who is about to enter the sacred space and is not already there.

It addresses the worshipper as a stranger (l. 1), which is typical for *programmata* but does not feature in Callimachus' hymn. It mentions water sacred to the Nymphs (l. 2), which does not feature in Callimachus' hymn at all. Rather than seeing Callimachean influences in *Palatine Anthology* 14.71 and 74, I suggest that they and Callimachus' opening and closing passages drew from the common source and are indebted to the traditional topoi of *programmata*.

Gifts to the Gods

In previous scholarly discussions of the ending of *Hymn to Apollo*, much has been made of Callimachus' use of water metaphors and the parallels that this passage displays with the *Reply to the Telchines* (F. Williams 1978: 85–99), but not enough attention has been paid to the fact that in both passages Apollo refers to religious rituals and gifts to the gods. The very metaphors Callimachus employs (ocean and the drop of water) occur in the *programmata* and are related to the purification rituals. Further, the final section of the hymn also mentions the ritual of bearing water for Demeter (*Hy.* 2.110–112):

> Δηοῖ δ' οὐκ ἀπὸ παντὸς ὕδωρ φορέουσι μέλισσαι,
> ἀλλ' ἥτις καθαρή τε καὶ ἀχράαντος ἀνέρπει
> πίδακος ἐξ ἱερῆς ὀλίγη λιβὰς ἄκρον ἄωτον.
>
> The bees bring water to Deo not from every source but where it bubbles up pure and undefiled from a holy spring, its very essence.

Μέλισσαι, apart from simply meaning "bees," was a *terminus technicus* for priestesses of Demeter.[25] This meaning is noted in a Pindar scholion (ed. Drachmann, vol. 2, *ad P.* 106c):

> μελίσσας δὲ τὰς ἱερείας, κυρίως μὲν τὰς τῆς Δήμητρος, καταχρηστικῶς δὲ καὶ τὰς πάσας, διὰ τὸ τοῦ ζῴου καθαρόν.
>
> Bees are priestesses, properly of Demeter; but the term is misapplied to all priestesses because of their pure life.

Frederick Williams represents the general stance of the scholarship regarding this passage (1978: s.v. 110): "We may be pleased to get rid of the priestesses and to restore the poetical simplicity of the passage;

---

[25] On μέλισσαι as priestesses, see Chamoux 1953: 267.

on the other hand, we have to confess that we are not able to see why the bees offer their tiny drops of water to Demeter." I do not see why we should want to get rid of the priestesses,[26] especially considering the fact that this meaning is implied not only by mentioning Demeter but also by mentioning a sacred spring (*Hy.* 2.112). Most important, if we take μέλισσαι to mean "priestesses," the passage makes more sense: the hymns were gifts to the gods, as were sacrifices, statues, and other offerings. The priestesses who bring water to Demeter are thus equivalent to a poet who writes a hymn for Apollo. If we want to understand the closing passage of the hymn as self-reference, then the parallels—priestesses:water:Demeter :: poet:hymn:Apollo—make excellent sense.

Oracular Metrical Sacred Regulations and the Hymn to Apollo

The final part of the *Hymn to Apollo* is composed in the oracular style. Its meter, language, and metaphors correspond to oracular responses. The topic too is perfectly in keeping with the transmitted oracles—it is a ἱερὸς νόμος, a sacred regulation referring to the gifts for the gods. Specifying sacrifices for the gods was one of the main functions of the Delphic Oracle, but it also determined other gifts for the gods, such as temples, statues, clothes—even hymns. Since most oracular responses are transmitted as a paraphrase and not verbatim, we seldom find instances of oracles actually specifying the length and vocabulary of hymns. But those we do find—even though the texts are significantly later than Callimachus' *Hymn to Apollo*—are worth taking into consideration and comparing to Callimachus' text.[27]

One oracular response that does specify the type of hymn Apollo approves of was recorded in Didyma in the second or third century AD (*SGO* 1.01.19.01). Apollo rebukes those who offer hecatombs or statues made out of precious metals and states that hymns are the best possible offering for the gods.[28] Apollo then goes on to specify the type of hymn he likes most:

---

[26] Scholars who discuss the possible religious connotations of the bees in this passage seem to want to put them aside. See Asper 1997: 115 n. 27.

[27] Oracles of Apollo were traditional institutions, and it is highly unlikely that their decisions regarding sacred matters would have changed significantly over the centuries.

[28] This sentiment is very similar to the general idea of Callimachus' *Iambus* 12.

ὦ μέλεοι, τί μοι] εἰλιπόδων ζατρεφεῖς ἑκατόμβαι
[λαμπροί τε χρυ]σοῖο βαθυπλούτοιο κολοσσοὶ
[καὶ χαλκῷ δεί]κηλα καὶ ἀργύρῳ ἀσκηθέντα;
[οὐ μὴν ἀθ]άνατοι κτεάνων ἐπιδευέες εἰσίν,
[ἀλλὰ θεμιστ]είης, ᾗπερ φρένας ἰαίνονται.   5
[αἰὲν δ' εὐσεβ]ὲς ὕμνον ἐμοῖς μέλπειν παρὰ σηκοῖς
[παῖδας ὅπως κ]αὶ πρόσθεν, ὅταν μέλλῃ φάτιν ἄξων
[ἀμφαίνειν ἀδ]ύτων· χαίρω δ' ἐπὶ πάσῃ ἀοιδῇ
[κεῖ τε νέη τ]ελέθῃ· πολλὸν δ' εἴπερ τε παλαιή·
[ἀρχαίη δέ τ]ε μᾶλλον, ἐμοὶ πολὺ φέρτερόν ἐστιν.   10
[τῆς δὲ θεοφ]ροσύνης ἔσται χάρις αἰὲν ἀμεμφής.
[ὕμνοις πρῶτον] ἐγὼ πολυκηδέας ἤλασα νούσους
[οὐλομένων] ἀλεγεινὰ δυσωπήσας λίνα Μοιρῶν.

You miserable people, what use is there for me of your hecatombs of well-fed oxen, shining statues made of precious gold, sculptures made from bronze and silver? Immortals do not require material possessions, but what is ordained b divine law, this cheers their hearts. It is always correct for the youths to sing a hymn in my precinct, just as they did before, whenever the axis is about to send forth an oracle from my innermost sanctuary. I am delighted by every song: even if a new song has been composed, very much by an old one, but even more by the ancient one—I find it so much better. Gratitude for a wisely chosen gift will always be without reproach. Indeed it was with the hymns that I chased away grievous diseases after abashing the troubling threads of the accursed Moerae.

In this oracular response, Apollo instructs the worshippers to perform hymns if they want to cheer his heart. His taste is decidedly un-Callimachean, since the god professes a preference for the old and traditional song, and even employs Homeric language in order to express this idea (ll. 8–10): χαίρω δ' ἐπὶ πάσῃ ἀοιδῇ (...) ἀρχαίη δέ τ]ε μᾶλλον, ἐμοὶ πολὺ φέρτερόν ἐστιν.[29] Nevertheless, both this oracle and Callimachus' hymn feature Apollo as a literary critic who passes judgment on poetry. In these two texts Apollo reviews existing compositions, but there are other oracular responses in which the god also offered helpful hints for the future composers of hymns. In a response of the Delphic Apollo inscribed in the third century AD in Tralleis, in Caria (SGO 1.02.02.01), the god advises the citizens to protect themselves from earthquake by sacrificing to Poseidon. After specifying the type of sacrifice (ll. 7–9), Apollo also determines the epithets that should be used in hymning the god (ll. 9–13):

---

[29] Πολὺ φέρτερόν ἐστιν = Il. 1.169 = Od. 12.109 = Od. 21.154. See R. Harder 1956: 90.

καλείσθω
εἰνάλιος, τεμενοῦχος, ἀπότροπος, ἵππιος, ἀργής·
ὧδε, πόλις, δὲ ὑμνεῖτε δεδραγμένον εἶφι βεβῶτα·
οὗ τε βάθρῳ κύκνειον ὅσοι γέρας ἀμφινέμεσθε,
ἐν χορῷ εὖ αἰνεῖν Σεισίχθονα καὶ Δία μείλαξ.

Let him be invoked as the one of the sea, holder of the *temenos*, averter, the one of the horses, the bright one: in this manner, city, you should hymn him with the swan's gift, him who is moving forcefully, clutching [something/gifts?] in his hands; at his base all you who live around, you young men, should hymn beautifully the Shaker of the Earth and Zeus.

This and similar inscriptions testify that oracles were consulted in order to find out how exactly to hymn the gods. But we have even closer parallels to Callimachus' hymn in the form of inscriptions that record the oracles' enthusiastic approval of hymns submitted for review. Particularly interesting and chronologically close to Callimachus are the epigraphically transmitted paeans that have actually been approved by the Delphic Apollo.[30] We have several early records of the Delphic Oracle signifying approval of existing hymns: in the late fourth century BC, or during the third,[31] Isyllus, son of Socrates, from Epidaurus composed (or hired a poet to compose) a paean to Apollo and Asclepius to be performed at a festival of Apollo Maleatas and Asclepius. Isyllus also composed a sacred regulation in hexameters for the festival. He had a certain Astylaidas consult the Delphic Oracle in order to inquire whether the paean should be inscribed. The Delphic sanctuary approved the inscribing of the hymn and thus also expressed its satisfaction with the poetic compositions:[32]

Ἴσυλλος Ἀστυλαΐδαι ἐπέθηκε μαντεύσασθα[ί] οἱ περὶ
τοῦ παιᾶνος ἐν Δελφοῖς, ὃν ἐπόησε εἰς τὸν Ἀπόλλωνα
καὶ τὸν Ἀσκληπιόν, ἦ λώϊόν οἵ κα εἴη ἀγγράφοντι
τὸν παιᾶνα. Ἐμάντευσε λώϊον οἵ κα εἶμεν ἀγγράφοντι
καὶ αὐτίκα καὶ εἰς τὸν ὕστερον χρόνον.

Isyllus commissioned Astylaidas to consult the oracle in Delphi about the paean that he composed for Apollo and Asclepius, whether it would be beneficial for him to inscribe the paean. The oracle responded that

---

[30] On the epigraphically transmitted paeans, see Käppel 1992, Furley and Bremer 2001, Kolde 2003, Fantuzzi 2010. Vamvouri Ruffy 2005 discusses Callimachus' attitude toward hymnic tradition, including the epigraphic hymns.

[31] Several dates have been proposed for this inscription. See the discussion in Kolde 2003: 257–263, who dates this inscription to the beginning of the third century BC.

[32] Furley and Bremer 2001: 1.227–230 (translation); 2.180–183 (text).

it would be beneficial both immediately and afterwards for him to inscribe [it].

By encouraging Isyllus to inscribe the text so that "it would be beneficial both immediately and afterwards," the oracle acted not only as a religious institution but also as a literary critic.

The best example for a close cooperation of Apollo with a poet, where Apollo acted as a lawgiver of the hymns, is a Delphic inscription of a paean for Dionysus by Philodamos from Scarpheia dated to or shortly after 340/39 BC.[33] The text of the paean is followed by a very interesting subscription:[34]

Θ[ε]ο[ί]· Δελφοὶ ἔδωκαν Φιλοδάμ[ωι Αἰν]ησιδάμου Σκαρφεῖ καὶ τοῖς ἀδελφοῖς Ἐπιγένε[ι] Ι..ντίδαι αὐτοῖς καὶ ἐκ[γόνοις] προξενίαν προμαντείαν προεδρίαν προδικ[ίαν] Ι [ἀτέ]λειαν ἐπι[τιμ]ὰν καθ[άπερ Δε]λφοῖς ἄρχοντος Ἐτυμώνδα βουλευόντων Ι...]ειστωνος Καλλικρα[ατίδου (...) [ἐπεὶ Φιλόδαμος καὶ τοὶ ἀδελφο]ὶ τὸμ παιᾶνα τὸν εἰς τὸν Διόνυσον Ι [ἐποίησαν...12 letters missing....κατὰ τ]ὰν μαντείαν τοῦ Θεοῦ ἐπαγγείλα[ν]τ[ος...35 letters missing....]...αι τυχἀγαθᾶι.

Philodamos and his brothers have composed a paean for Dionysus "according to the oracular instruction of the god," and it has been so pleasing to Delphi that they have received many splendid honors as a reward.[35] Apollo not only approved the hymn; he almost dictated it to the poet—half of Philodamos' composition is relating a Delphic oracle. The oracle is yet another example of a sacred regulation.[36] It commands the Amphictyons to receive the hymn and to make a public sacrifice, to finish Apollo's temple and set up precious statues, to establish a sacrifice and dithyramb competition in honor of Dionysus, and to erect a statue of Dionysus on a chariot (ll. 105-49):[37]

Ἐκτελέσαι δὲ πρᾶξιν Ἀμ-   IX 105
φικτύονας θ[εὸς] κελεύ-
ει τάχος, ὡ[ς Ἑ]καβόλος

---

[33] Käppel 39 = Furley and Bremer 2.5. Käppel 1992 offers a detailed overview of scholarship of this hymn (pp. 211-218) and a literary analysis (pp. 222-284). See also Rutherford 2001: 131-136; Furley and Bremer 2001: 1.121-28 and 2.52-84; Vamvouri Ruffy 2005: 103-106 and 187-206; and Fantuzzi 2010.

[34] Furley and Bremer 2001: 2.57.

[35] Aristonous, who composed a paean to Apollo in the fourth century BC, was also honored in a manner similar to Philodamos (Käppel 42 = Furley and Bremer 2.4).

[36] Only Furley and Bremer 2001: 1.127 and 2.82 briefly note the similarity of the poem to the sacred regulations.

[37] Text and translation follow Furley and Bremer 2001: 1.122-23 and 2.55-56.

μῆνιν ε[. .] κατάσχηι,
—Εὐοῖ ὦ [ἰὸ Β]άκχ', ὦ ἰὲ Παιάν—
δε[ῖξαι] δ' ἐγ ξενίοις ἐτεί-   110
οις θεῶν ἱερῶι γένει συναίμωι
τόνδ' ὕμνον, θυσίαν τε φαί-
νειν σὺν Ἑλλάδος ὀλβίας
πα[νδ]ήμοις ἱκετείαις.
...
Πυθιάσιν δὲ πενθετή-   XI
ροις [π]ροπό[λοις] ἔταξε Βάκ—
χου θυσίαν χορῶν τε πο[λ-
λῶν] κυκλίαν ἄμιλλαν
—Εὐοῖ ὦ ἰὸ Βάκχ', [ὦ ἰὲ] Παιάν—   135
τεύχειν.
...
Ἀλλὰ δέχεσθε Βακχ[ια]σ-   XII
τὰν Διόνυσ[ον, ἐν δ' ἀγυι-]   145
αῖς ἅμα σὺγ [χορ]οῖσι κ[ι—
κλήισκετε] κισσ[οχ]αίταις
—Ε[ὐο]ῖ ὦ ἰὸ Βάκχ', ὦ ἰὲ [Παιάν]—
Πᾶσαν [Ἑλ]λάδ' ἀν' ὀ[λβί]αμ

> The god commands the Amphictyons to execute the action with speed, so that he who shoots from afar may restrain his anger—Euhoi, o, io Bacchus, o ie Paean!—and to present this hymn for his brother to the family of the gods, on the occasion of the annual fest of hospitality, and to make a public sacrifice on the occasion of the Panhellenic supplications of blessed Hellas.—Ie Paean! Come, O Savior, and kindly keep this city in happy prosperity!

[Lines 115–130: Regulations concerning the temple of Apollo and the statues to be set up in it.]

> To the organizers of his quadrennial Pythian festival the god has given the command to establish in honor of Bacchus a sacrifice and a competition of many dithyrambs—Euhoi, o, io Bacchus, o ie Paean!

[Lines 136–43: Regulations concerning the statue of Bacchus and the establishment and furnishing of his sacred grotto.]

> Come on, then, and welcome Dionysus, god of the bacchants, and call upon him in your streets with dances performed by people with ivy in their hair who sing *Euhoi, o, io Bacchus, o ie Paean!* all over blessed Hellas.

Philodamos has incorporated an oracle with specific regulations pertaining to his own hymn into his text and in this respect offers the closest parallel to Callimachus' *Hymn to Apollo*. Philodamos' paean demonstrates remarkable generic self-awareness, since it provides two justifications of its own generic status as a paean as being ordained by Apollo.[38] Dionysus' hymn is not a paean but a dithyramb. By presenting Apollo and the Muses, who hymn Dionysus with a paean on Olympus (ll. 53-63), Philodamos appropriates the genre for Dionysus on a mythical level. On the cultic level, the justification for the genre is Apollo's oracle, which is related in the second half of the poem. According to the oracle, Philodamos' hymn, essentially a paean, must be performed at Theoxenia (ll. 110-12).

Whereas in Philodamos' hymn Apollo approves of the generic experiment and allows a paean to be performed for Dionysus, in Callimachus' hymn Apollo approves of Callimachus' innovative poetics and accepts his hymn as a gift. In both hymns, Apollo appears as a literary critic.[39] In both hymns, Apollo is represented as angry and ready to punish those who disobey his words: In Philodamos' paean, the god is threatening and commands a swift execution of his orders ὡ[ς Ἑ]καβόλος | μῆνιν ε[..] κατάσχηι,[40] "so that the god who shoots from afar may restrain his anger" (ll. 107-08). In Callimachus' hymn, divine anger is represented in action, as Apollo kicks Envy with his foot (l. 107). Finally, the mimetic elements in Philodamos' hymn are also very similar to Callimachus' mimetic hymns, since Philodamos' composition also refers to and addresses its own performers and audience (ll. 146-49): "Call upon him in your streets with dances performed by people with ivy in their hair who sing *Euhoi, o, io Bacchus, o ie Paean!* all over blessed Hellas."[41]

Commentators on Callimachus' *Hymn to Apollo* have often singled out the final part of the hymn as a controversial testimony of narrator's self-confidence, since here Callimachus presents a defense of his

---

[38] Käppel 1992: 277-284; Rutherford 2001: 135. Käppel 1992: 280 compares Philodamos' generic self-awareness with Callimachus' *Iambus* 1 but not with his *Hymn to Apollo*.

[39] In Philodamos' paean, Apollo regulates a religious syncretism as well, since he incorporates the worship of Dionysus into the already-thriving cult of Apollo. Rutherford 2001: 135 notes that in this hymn, religious and generic syncretism go hand in hand.

[40] On the text, see Furley and Bremer 2001: 2.75-76.

[41] On self-reference in Philodamos' paean, see Käppel 1996: 268-270; Vamvouri Ruffy 2005: 190-196. Neither comments on the similarity with reference to festivals in Callimachus' mimetic hymns. Albert 1988: 71 n. 205 and 76 n. 225 dismisses Philodamos' paean as comparandum for Callimachus, since it does not feature comments regarding the change of scenery.

own poetics as divine words (and deed!). The inscriptions discussed above, however, provide an important social context: many Apolline oracles actually take an interest not only in prescriptive ritual texts but also in performative texts—the hymns. Like Philodamos, Callimachus inserts a divine approbation of his poetry in the very text of his hymn.[42] Apollo as a divine lawgiver of the hymn was not his invention. In fact, Philodamos' hymn goes much further than Callimachus in asserting its own significance and divine approval: it even emphasizes its own status as an inscribed text that has to be presented to the family of the gods as a testimony of Dionysus' divine status at Delphi (110–112): δε[ῖξαι] δ' ἐγ ξενίοις ἐτεί | οἷς θεῶν ἱερῶι γένει συναίμωι | τόνδ' ὕμνον, "[Apollo orders] to present this hymn for his brother to the family of the gods on the occasion of the annual fest of hospitality."[43] Not only does Philodamos' hymn have a divine origin in Apollo's prophecy and favorable review; it has divine readers. Is it imagining the gods invited to the Theoxenia festival as gathering around the stone, carefully reading Philodamos' inscriptional hymn in order to find out about the recent mergers and acquisitions at the Delphic sanctuary? When it comes to bold assertion of the powers of poetry, Philodamos has far surpassed Callimachus. The fact that Philodamos' hymn was cult text, performed annually at Delphi,[44] ought to instill more caution with scholars who emphatically deny any such possibility for Callimachus' hymns. Philodamos' hymn is a very important early example of a poem that is comfortable not only with being both a performative and a literary text but also with drawing attention to and creatively exploring its status as an inscription.

The Role of the Speaker

The setting of the *Hymn to Apollo* is the festival of the Carneia at Cyrene. Its narrator comments upon the signs of the epiphany and urges the chorus to sing the hymn. The role of the speaker has been much discussed, thus far without consensus.[45] However, if we follow

---

[42] *Pace* Vamvouri Ruffy 2005: 64–65, who singles out the closing passage of the *Hymn to Apollo* as essentially different from the epigraphic hymns.
[43] See Furley and Bremer 2001: 2.77 comm. *ad loc.*
[44] On the performance context, see Käppel 1992: 208–211.
[45] See I. Petrovic 2007: 134–139 for an overview of scholarship on this matter.

the analogy relating to different gifts to the gods from the final section of the hymn (priestesses bring pure droplets of water to Demeter, poet gives hymn to Apollo), then the narrator does shape his role as very similar to that of a priest of Apollo. Like a priest, he has to sacrifice a pure offering to the god, only in his case the offering is not a pure sacrificial animal but a pure hymn.

There are further hints in this poem and external evidence that testify that Callimachus' family had close ties to the Cyrenean cult of Apollo. In lines 69–71, the narrator refers to several cult titles of Apollo and asserts that he personally calls Apollo "Carneius," explaining that this is his ancestral custom (*Hy.* 2.71): αὐτὰρ ἐγὼ Καρνεῖον· ἐμοὶ πατρώιον οὕτω.

He also stresses the role Apollo played in founding the city and how the god personally led Battus, the founder of the colony (ll. 65–96). Here Callimachus alludes to several legendary Delphic oracles. According to the traditional account, Apollo's role in the foundation of Cyrene was unique: the Pythia addressed Battus, who came to consult her on other matters, and urged him to found a colony in Libya.[46] Callimachus, too, stresses the personal bond his ancestor Battus had with Apollo. Because of the god's benefactions, the Battiads honored Apollo more than any other god (ll. 95–96): Οὐδὲ μὲν αὐτοί | Βαττιάδαι Φοίβοιο πλέον θεὸν ἄλλον ἔτισαν. This verse should be understood quite literally. According to Françoise Chamoux (1953: 217–219), the Battiads, the first kings of Cyrene, were very probably the priests of the city's chief deity, Apollo. After the establishment of a republican government (in 439 BC), this priesthood of Apollo became an eponymous magistracy.[47] The records of the priests, preserved in the accounts of the *demiourgoi* (*SEG* 9.11–44), make it clear that this important position was often monopolized by the leading families in Cyrene (Sherk 1992: 271). This is probably the reason why Ptolemy I Soter limited the position to those men who had not occupied it before and were older than fifty in a *diagramma* containing the new constitution of Cyrene (*SEG* 9.1.23–25). This magistracy was so prestigious, that even the Ptolemaic king Euergetes II held the office of Cyrenean priest of Apollo.[48]

---

[46] PW 39. On the Cyrenean foundation legend, see Calame 1988 and 1993; Nicolai 1992; Vamvouri Ruffy 2005: 117–119.
[47] Cf. *SEG* 9.11–13; Chamoux 1953: 217, 301–302; Sherk 1992: 270–272.
[48] Cf. Athen. 12.549e–f = *FGrHist* 234 F 9. See on this Sherk 1992: 271.

Alan Cameron (1995: 7-8) argues that a certain Androcles, son of the general Callimachus who is mentioned in lines 84 and 87 of Ptolemy I Soter's *diagramma* as an ephor and *nomothetes*, was actually a son of the general Callimachus whose family tree was partly reconstructed by André Laronde (1987: 118, no. 3) and the father or uncle of the poet Callimachus. Both Françoise Chamoux (1960: xxxiii) and Luigi Lehnus (1993: 76) argue for the general Callimachus as grandfather of the poet. If this assumption is correct, then the family tree reconstructed by Laronde (1987: 118, no. 3) is actually the family tree of the poet Callimachus. Anniceris (born no later than 415) had three recorded sons: Philo (born no later than 385), Callimachus (born no later than 380), and Peithagoras (born no later than 372). According to Cameron, Callimachus had two recorded sons, Androcles and Theudorus. Either could have been the father of the poet Callimachus.

The poet's granduncle Peithagoras was an eponymous priest of Apollo in 321 BC. Philo, Callimachus' other paternal granduncle, participated in the renovation of Apollo's sanctuary in Cyrene and rebuilt the great altar of Apollo (Laronde 1987: 110-112).

The connection of Callimachus' family to the cult of Apollo in Cyrene is remarkably strong. Not only does Callimachus underline his personal relationship with Apollo as a poet by depicting the god uttering a prophecy in defense of his hymn; he also stresses the close ties his whole family has with the god—ἐμοὶ πατρώιον οὕτω. Note also how he takes great care to depict the altars of the god with ever-burning offerings in lines 80-84. One of these great altars was erected by his paternal granduncle Philo. The large letters of the dedicatory inscriptions are still visible (Laronde 1987: 111 fig. 34). So, in a way, Callimachus depicts himself almost on a par with Battus—the *oikistes* received oracles from Apollo directly, and so did the poet; Battus was probably a priest of Apollo, erected a beautiful sanctuary to the god, and instituted the Carneia in Cyrene,[49] but Callimachus can make a similar boast: Philo, his paternal granduncle, erected a monumental altar for the god; Peithagoras, his other paternal granduncle, was Apollo's priest. And the poet himself composed a hymn approved directly by the god.

---

[49] *Hymn to Apollo* 77-78: δεῖμε δέ τοι μάλα καλὸν ἀνάκτορον, ἐν δὲ πόλῃ | θῆκε τελεσφορίην ἐπετήσιον.

The personal ties the poet forges with Apollo in this hymn resemble the subscriptions accompanying hymns inscribed in sanctuaries that record divine approbation and various honors the sanctuaries have bestowed on the poets. Comparison of Callimachus' hymn with inscriptional evidence demonstrates that religious discourse deeply resonates in the *Hymn to Apollo*. Callimachus is interested in the way inscriptional hymns shape and negotiate the relationship of the gods with poets and alludes not only to previous hymns within a literary tradition but also to prescriptive and performative inscriptions in sanctuaries.[50] Local Cyrenean cult is very important for understanding the way Callimachus presents Apollo and even for interpreting passages that have previously been discussed as pertaining to poetics only. In this hymn, religion and poetics are inseparable.

---

[50] Callimachus also displays a vivid interest in visual representations of the divine, often mentioning and discussing divine images. See on this I. Petrovic 2010, with further literature.

PART THREE

SOURCES AND MODELS

CHAPTER FOURTEEN

DIGGING UP THE MUSICAL PAST: CALLIMACHUS AND THE NEW MUSIC

Lucia Prauscello

ABSTRACT

'New Musical' gestures were still an active force that contributed to defining poetic (and at times ideological if not overtly political) allegiances in Ptolemaic Alexandria. This paper investigates if and how Callimachus ever engaged with this strand of the poetic legacy. A close reading of some programmatic passages (*Ia.* 13.43–5, *Aetia* fr. 1. 35–8) suggests that approaching Callimachus from the side of a 'Dionysian poetics' may present some surprises. To investigate some of the ways in which Callimachus negotiates his own Apollo by exploiting the musical/literary tradition of rivalry between Apollo and Dionysus may help us to understand better, within a historically oriented perspective, some features of the few surviving occurrences of Dionysus in Callimachus' poetry (especially the Delphic Dionysus). Confrontation with Plato's theorizing on chorality and its cultic affiliations (particularly in the *Laws*) will also prove to be an important critical tool to interpret Callimachus' own choices.

According to Aristotle knowledge of truth may require, from time to time, some embarrassing acknowledgements: even wrong steps may contribute to a broader understanding (*Met.* 993b10–14). As the climax of his argument, Aristotle cites an example from the domain of *mousike*, whose centrality in shaping the Greeks' social and cultural identity makes it perhaps the closest Greek equivalent to our own modern idea of culture. "If there had been no Timotheus," says Aristotle, "we would be without much of our lyric poetry; on the other hand, if there had been no Phrynis, there would have been no Timotheus" (*Met.* 993b15–16).[1] Apologetic as Aristotle's words may sound, they make it clear that Timotheus' wrong step has unavoidably shaped the present

---

My warmest thanks to Giovan Battista D'Alessio, Richard Hunter, Peter Wilson, and Richard Rawles for their invaluable criticism and suggestions.

[1] Εἰ μὲν γὰρ Τιμόθεος μὴ ἐγένετο, πολλὴν ἂν μελοποιίαν οὐκ εἴχομεν· εἰ δὲ μὴ Φρῦνις, Τιμόθεος οὐκ ἂν ἐγένετο.

we are living in. The revolutionary spin brought into fifth-century BC Athenian culture by the so-called New Music (its professionalism, demagogic virtuosity, cross-genre contamination, and unorthodox Dionysiac revival)[2] was then still a controversial heritage to be reckoned with long after its heyday, and this well beyond the limit of dramatic poetry (cf. Aristotle's use of μελοποιία).[3] Unrestrained, intoxicated inspiration, verbal wizardry, and the spread of a Dionysiac mood far beyond traditionally Dionysiac genres are the overarching charges ascribed to the New Music and its epigones from Old Comedy down to Plato and Middle Comedy.[4] In Antiphanes' comedy *Tritagonistes*,[5] the appraisal of the contemporary poetic climate post–New Music is the following (fr. 207.7–9 KA):[6] οἱ νῦν δὲ κισσόπλεκτα καὶ κρηναῖα καὶ | ἀνθεσιπότατα μέλεα μελέοις ὀνόμασιν | ποιοῦσιν ἐμπλέκοντες ἀλλότρια μέλη. "Ivy-twisted" (κισσόπλεκτα), "fountainy" (κρηναῖα), "flower-flitting" (ἀνθεσιπότατα) songs that resort to pitiful vocabulary and weave "ventriloquizing melodies" (ἀλλότρια μέλη)[7] are the present legacy, under the sign of Dionysus, left by the New Music.[8] Wine and its intoxicating power, another central element of New Musical inspiration (and especially its reception), do not feature explicitly in Antiphanes' catalogue of the hallmarks of Dionysiac music. Plato's description of poetic inspiration in *Ion* 534a4–b2 may play some role

---

[2] For the ideological debate triggered by the New Music in the second half of the fifth century, see Csapo 2004 and P. Wilson 2004. On Timotheus, see now Csapo and Wilson 2009. On the archaizing Dionysiac roots of the New Dithyramb, cf. Csapo 2000 and 2003.

[3] Phrynis (ca. 460–400 BC) died two decades before Aristotle's birth; Timotheus' *floruit* must be dated, according to the Parian Marble, to 398 BC. See Hordern 2002: 3.

[4] For a useful survey and discussion of the main passages of Plato and Old Comedy, see now Fearn 2007: 186–199, with previous bibliography. For the sustained engagement of Middle Comedy with New Music, see Nesselrath 1990: 241–266 and Dobrov 2002.

[5] Most likely to be dated not very much after the death of the New Dithyrambist Philoxenus of Cythera (380/79 BC); see Pickard-Cambridge 1968: 134.

[6] Lines 1–6 are a not unambiguous eulogy of Philoxenus' poetry: see Dobrov 2002: 184–185.

[7] The precise meaning of ἀλλότρια is much debated: cf. Fongoni 2005: 96–97, Conti Bizzarro 1993–1994: 156, Barker 1984: 1.95. Programmatic passages (unquoted by previous scholarship) like Pind. *Pae*. C2.12 Rutherford (= *Pae*. VIIb.12 Maehler, ἀλ]λοτρίαις ἀν' ἵπποις) and Ar. *Vesp*. 1022 (οὐκ ἀλλοτρίων ἀλλ' οἰκείων Μουσῶν στόμαθ' ἡνιοχήσας), but also *Lyr. adesp*. 923.4 *PMG* (ἀλλοτρίαις δ' οὐ μίγνυται μοῦσαν ἀρούραις) seem to me to suggest that ἀλλότριος is here the antonym of what we would call original poetic creativity.

[8] For the heavy Dionysiac veneer of these lines, cf. Fongoni 2005.

in this respect,⁹ but κρηναῖα may indirectly subsume it:¹⁰ springs or streams of wine (as well as milk and honey) are traditionally associated with Dionysus' epiphany.¹¹ Closer to Alexandria and down to the third century BC, the picture of Philoxenus' poetry drawn by Machon (fr. 9.14–17 Gow) and Hermesianax (fr. 7.69–74 *CA*) testifies to the lasting strength of this literary and cultic affiliation.¹²

The social conditions for the production and transmission of poetry in third-century BC Alexandria differ greatly from the world of the classical polis: the written word has mostly outdone song, and performance scenarios have been reshaped accordingly.¹³ Nevertheless, choral performances—paeans, dithyrambs, hymns, encomia, even fully fledged drama—never disappeared from public life: as recent important studies have shown, Hellenistic Alexandria, and more generally the whole Greek Hellenistic world, went on being, even if on a more local basis, intensely musical.¹⁴ Callimachus' poetry itself, especially the *Hymns* but also the *Aetia*, actively contributes to construing a readership that is asked to experience in the present or share in the memory the image of an ever-dancing, ever-singing world.¹⁵ The New Musical discourse was absorbed within and adapted to these changed circumstances. The semantic instability inherent in the New Dithyrambic language of inclusive multiplicity (*polychordia, polyphonia, polyeideia*), its crossing and recrossing generic boundaries, together with its pronounced mimetic quality, became part of the new

---

⁹ Murray 1997: 116 notes that "it is striking that P[lato] makes no mention of wine here, despite its special association with Dionysus...and with poetry." As I shall try to show later on, Plato's reluctance to associate Dionysiac inspiration with wine is part of his broader philosophical agenda in defining the role of poetry.

¹⁰ The primary sphere of reference is, of course, that of poetic inspiration: cf., e.g., Pind. fr. 94b.76–78 Maehler, Call. *Ep.* 28.3 Pf. (= 2.3 GP), *Hy* 2.110–12. Cf. Poliakoff 1980: 42–43.

¹¹ Cf., e.g., Eur. *Ba.* 142, ῥεῖ δ' οἴνῳ; 707, καὶ τῇδε κρήνην ἐξανῆκ' οἴνου θεός.

¹² On the relationship between these two passages and its possible import for Callimachus' aesthetic of λεπτότης, see Cairns 2000, with the corrigendum of Hordern 2000.

¹³ Hunter 1996: 3–7 offers an updated, balanced view on the subject; cf. also Fantuzzi and Hunter 2004: 17–26.

¹⁴ See P. Wilson 2003a: 164–167 and D'Alessio forthcoming for the dithyramb. Further, D'Alessio is planning a study of choral performances in general during the Hellenistic and early imperial periods; cf. also Cairns 1992: 14–16. For tragedy, see now Nervegna 2007.

¹⁵ For the cultic imagination and the audience reception construed within the fictionalized world of the *Hymns*, quite apart from their modality of performance, see Hunter and Fuhrer 2002: 147–149.

literary scene. As observed by Marco Fantuzzi and Richard Hunter (2004: 21), "the reconfiguration of the generic system was, therefore, not only a poetic choice for the Alexandrians, but also a historical necessity rooted in the experience of the fifth and fourth centuries."

New Musical gestures were thus still an active force that contributed to defining poetic (and at times ideological if not overtly political) allegiances in Ptolemaic Alexandria. One evident case is Theocritus' portrait of Simonides in *Idyll* 16.44–46. Negotiating between patronage and immortality of the poetic expression *per se*, Theocritus appeals to the "epinician" Simonides who immortalized his Thessalian patrons αἰόλα φωνέων | βάρβιτον ἐς πολύχορδον (*Id.* 16.45–46, "tuning his varied songs to the *barbiton* of the many strings").[16] The antiquarian gesture of epinicians sung to the *barbiton*,[17] the language of ποικιλία and innovation (polychordy), are elements that suggest that Theocritus is here figuring Simonides "as a professional musician and poet of the 'modern' time,'" a New Musical "virtuoso instrumentalist like the famous Timotheus" (Hunter 1996: 101–102). Likewise, Orpheus' musical triumph with his deafening Thracian lyre over the Sirens (and Apollonius' over Homeric epic) in *Argonautica* 4.902–11 is described by Apollonius Rhodius in such a way as to recall, no doubt provokingly, pieces of standard criticism directed against New Music: the overpowering of vocal song by instrumental music, the confusion of voices, "the breaking down of the link between rhythmical and linguistic structures" (Hunter 1996: 146–147).

A shorthand version of New Music reduced to few distinctive features but still identifiable as such in third-century BC Alexandria would most probably list fluid generic boundaries, ecstatic inspiration, and last but not least, Dionysus, the democratic god of theater and wine. Did Callimachus ever engage with this strand of the poetic legacy? If we leave aside, for the time being, Callimachus' generic experimentalism, at first sight the only possible answer may seem to be a straightforward denial. Callimachus, if anything, always sides with Apollo: his whole poetic production is crossed by a network of poetic, religious, and political associations that constantly assimilate his poetry and

---

[16] For a detailed analysis of how in *Id.* 16 different portraits of Simonides (the choral poet and the elegist) are sophisticatedly intertwined by Theocritus in a nexus of overlapping images, see Rawles 2006: chap. 4.

[17] The *barbiton* was a piece of musical archaeology for a third-century-BC reader: cf. Bundrick 2005: 24.

his persona to Apollo.[18] The contention of the present chapter is that approaching Callimachus from the side of Dionysus may present some surprises. To chase up some of the ways in which Callimachus negotiates his own Apollo by exploiting the musical and literary tradition of rivalry between Apollo and Dionysus may help us to understand better, within a historically oriented perspective, some features of the few surviving occurrences of Dionysus in Callimachus' poetry—especially the Delphic Dionysus. Confrontation with Plato's theorizing on chorality and its cultic affiliations, particularly in the *Laws*, will also prove to be an important critical tool to interpret Callimachus' own choices. Comprehensiveness in charting Callimachus' critical response to such traditions will not be attempted here: instead I would like to focus on some passages whose interpretation may suggest future lines of inquiry in approaching an apparently unpromising topic like Callimachus and the New Music.

Iambus 13: How Many Ions?

Before starting to look for Callimachus' Dionysus (or Dionysuses), let us first turn our attention to *Iambus* 13 (fr. 202 Pf.), and in particular to the use and abuse, both ancient and modern, to which Callimachus' mention of Ion of Chios has been exposed.[19] The Milan *diegesis* (IX 32–38) tells us that in *Iambus* 13 Callimachus is replying to those who censured him for his πολυείδεια by "claiming that he is imitating Ion the tragic poet" (35–36: φησιν ὅτι | Ἴωνα μιμεῖται τὸν τραγικόν). The programmatic nature of *Iambus* 13 has attracted huge scholarly interest.[20] The precise nature of the charge (πολυείδεια, writing in multiple genres, or generic contamination, or both), its target (the *Iambi*, or Callimachus' whole poetic output), and the scope of the imitation of Ion have been widely discussed and do not need repeating here. Let us just say that there seems to be a general consensus that Callimachus, by way of adopting and at the same time ironically exposing a Socratic persona, is here constructing his own literary history through

---

[18] See especially Bassi 1989, Calame 1993, and Hunter and Fuhrer 2002: 150–157 on Callimachus' *Hymn to Apollo*, and Slings 2004 on the *Hymn to Delos*.

[19] For a recent critical survey, see Henderson 2007, esp. 39–44.

[20] The fullest account is by Acosta-Hughes 2002: 60–103. See also Hunter and Fantuzzi 2004: 15–17, Hunter 1997, Kerkhecker 1999: 250–270, Depew 1992, and most recently Steiner 2007a.

what has been called "a strategy of obliquity" (Hunter 1997: 44): the evocation of a model (in this case, the threefold Ion: Ion of Chios, Plato's character in the *Ion*, the eponym of the Ionians) is simultaneously also the exposure of its inadequacy.[21]

Why, then, is Ion of Chios invoked in *Iambus* 13? First of all, Callimachus is answering the Platonic criticism "one genre, one poet" aired in lines 31–32: the fifth-century polymath Ion of Chios practiced different genres (dramatic and nondramatic, monodic and choral),[22] and the charge against him is, if you like, serial generic consistency, certainly not generic contamination (*Iamb*. 13.43–45):[23]

]οὐχὶ μοῦνον εξ [
ο]υς τραγῳδοὺς ἀλλὰ κα[......].ν
π]εντάμετρον οὐχ ἅπαξ [. ἐ]κρουσε

] not only he[xameter verses[24]...] the (?) tragedians but [...]...the pentameter he did not strike[25] once

From the scanty remnants of these verses Callimachus must, then, have been referring to at least three spheres of poetic expertise of Ion of Chios: hexametric poetry, whatever this may have been,[26] elegiacs, and tragedy. Why did Callimachus choose Ion of Chios as a model to be adopted and at the same time to be differentiated from? Though confined to the rank of second-best in pseudo-Longinus *On the Sublime* 33.5, Ion (poet, philosopher, prose writer) was far from neglected as a subject of literary and scholarly interest before and after Callimachus' time: Arcesilaus of Pitane, Baton of Sinope, Aristarchus too, to mention just a few, directed their exegetic interest to Ion.[27] Callimachus himself joined in this scholarly interest (cf. his *Pinakes* and fr. 449 Pf.), and traces of a direct engagement with Ion's texts are

---

[21] Cf. Acosta-Hughes 2002: 87–89; for Ion's aliases in *Iamb*. 13, see above all Hunter 1997: 46.

[22] See Leurini 1985: 5–9 on the *Suda* entry: it is most likely that the testimonia on Ion of Chios go back to Callimachus' Πίνακες.

[23] See Fantuzzi and Hunter 2004: 17 with n. 63.

[24] I am reading ἐξά[μετρ(α) with Wilamowitz: for possible alternatives, see Kerkhecker 1999: 265 and Acosta-Hughes 2002: 66 *ad loc.* and 88.

[25] The translation follows Gallavotti's supplement ἀ[νέ]κρουσε: cf. Kerkhecker 1999: 264 n. 82 and now also Asper 2004: 252.

[26] Acosta-Hughes 2002: 88 mentions as possible candidates Ion's hymns or encomia, or the κοσμολογικός mentioned by the scholia to Ar. *Pax* 835–837a Holwerda (= test. 8 Leurini).

[27] For scholarly interest on Ion in Hellenistic times, see Leurini test. 20–33. See also Leurini 1985: 11 n. 11.

clearly discernible in his own poetic works.[28] But what was Ion's poetry about, and how did he position himself in relation to the New Musical trends (Euripides, Timotheus, etc.) of his own age? The evidence here is far from unambiguous, and this instability of Ion's poetic allegiances may well have been what Callimachus was looking for, especially as a reaction to the Platonic mask of his critics (*Iamb.* 13.31–32).

If we turn back to *Iambus* 13, immediately after the reference to Ion in lines 43–45 we find the mention of a "Lydian *aulos*" and of some "strings," obviously referring to a musical instrument (*Iamb.* 13.47, Λυδὸν] πρὸς αὐλὸν λ.......καὶ χορδάς). Scholars have usually interpreted this line as referring to Ion's "poetic performances at the symposium" (Kerkhecker 1999: 264). This may well be the case,[29] but it is worth noticing, with Pfeiffer,[30] that the Lydian mode and its relaxed sympotic world seems to have been one of the privileged themes of Ion's dramatic poetry as well. In his satyr drama *Omphale* we find mentioned Lydian ψάλτριαι (fr. 26a Leurini) and the musical curiosity of the Λυδὸς μάγαδις αὐλός (fr. 26b Leurini),[31] whereas elsewhere (fr. 42 Leurini) we have an *aulos* pouring forth a Λύδιος ὕμνος. On the face of it, one could read these lines simply as common satyric targets, and this is certainly part of what is going on.[32] Lydian hymns, sympotic setting, playing the *magadis* or *pectis* have a well-attested literary pedigree at least since Pindar (fr. 125 M),[33] but what is more interesting is that they are also what Ion's contemporary the New Dithyrambist Telestes ostensibly reinterprets and advertises as hallmarks of the New Musical wave (frr. 808 and 810 *PMG*). In his *Asclepius* (fr. 806 *PMG*: probably a dithyramb), Telestes goes so far as to describe the Lydian "strain" (νόμος) played on the *aulos* as the "antagonist of the Dorian Muse" (Δωρίδος ἀντίπαλον μούσας)—that is, the opponent of the traditional Hellenic music.[34] We know too little about Ion's *Omphale* to

---

[28] Cf. Leurini 1985: 12–13 on Callimachus' reuse in fr. 242 Pf. of the rare παλαίθετος and κᾶλον attested before, respectively, only in Ion frr. 26a and 31 Leurini.

[29] The qualification τραγικός in *Dieg.* IX 35–36 is clearly nothing more than a scholarly label.

[30] Pfeiffer 1949–53: 1.208 *ad* fr. 202.47; cf. also Acosta-Hughes 2002: 66.

[31] On this instrument, see M.L. West 1992b: 73 n. 108.

[32] Cf. Power 2007: 197: "the usual comic themes are here: Lydianizing, luxurious softness, transvestism."

[33] For the possible interchangeability of the terms *magadis* and *pectis*, see Barker 1988.

[34] On the ideological agenda underpinning Telestes' *Asclepius*, see the brilliant analysis by P. Wilson 2003b: 191–192.

be able to interpret Ion's stance there: ironic though he may have been, what is nevertheless clear is that Ion was engaging in and reacting to the contemporary debate on musical discourse (elitist string instruments vs. demotic wind instruments, Greekness vs. otherness).

This is most evident if we turn to his elegies. In fragment 93 Leurini (= fr. 32 West²) the speaking *I* addresses the relatively new eleven-stringed lyre, provided with a "ten-step arrangement" of its strings (δεκαβάμονα τάξιν ἔχουσα) and "concordant crossroads of tuning" (συμφωνούσας ἁρμονίας τριόδους), and praises its increased harmonic and melodic possibilities if compared with the traditional seven-string lyre (ll. 2–3, πρὶν μέν σ᾽ ἑπτάτονον ψάλλον διὰ τεσσάρα πάντες | Ἕλληνες, σπανίαν μοῦσαν ἀειράμενοι, "before all Greeks plucked you, of the seven notes, through the span of the octave, raising a poor music"). The eleven-string lyre was not brought to prominence first by Ion, nor, presumably, by Timotheus.[35] Yet Timotheus' vaunt of having "awakened the *kithara* with eleven-stringed measures and rhythms" (*PMG* 791.229–31, νῦν δὲ Τιμόθεος μέτροις | ῥυθμοῖς τ᾽ ἑνδεκακρουμάτοις | κίθαριν ἐξανατέλλει) contributed to the fact that in fifth-century Athens "the trope of the lyre with too many strings became a potent symbol, an expression of the unnatural development of the instrument's proper range, and, by easy extension, of the breaking of all aesthetic and social boundaries" (P. Wilson 2004: 287). The social and cultural tensions underlying the appropriation of the eleven-string *kithara* can hardly have escaped the philo-Cimonian Ion, who criticized the democratic Themistocles for not having learned to sing or to play the lyre (fr. 106 Leurini = Plut. *Cim.* 9.1).[36] Callimachus' Delian Apollo is the god of the proper seven-stringed lyre. Apollo's birth and the invention of the musical instrument are one and the same event in the cosmic and human history sketched in *Hymn* 4.253–55: the swans leave the Maeonian Pactolus and fly in a circle (ἐκυκλώσαντο) seven times (ἑβδομάκις) around Delos; "hence later the child god strung his lyre with seven strings, that many were the times the swans sang over the birth pangs. But the eighth time they did not sing: Apollo sprang out to life" (ἔνθεν ὁ παῖς τοσσάσδε λύρῃ ἐνεδήσατο χορδάς| ὕστερον, ὁσσάκι κύκνοι ἐπ᾽ ὠδίνεσσιν ἄεισαν·|

---

[35] M.L. West 1992b: 24.
[36] Cf. Ford 2002: 194.

ὄγδοον οὐκέτ' ἄεισαν, ὁ δ' ἔκθορεν). The number seven was, of course, traditionally associated with Apollo,[37] but it is difficult not to see in the redundant, emphatic litotes of line 254 (ὄγδοον οὐκέτ' ἄεισαν) a reference to the improper *polychordia* of the past musical tradition.[38] The invention of the seven-stringed lyre and Apollo's epiphanic birth establish the correct way of singing and playing: "Apollo will honor the chorus who sings according to his liking" (*Hy.* 2.28–29, τὸν χορὸν ὠπόλλων, ὅ τι οἱ κατὰ θυμὸν ἀείσει | τιμήσει). How should we then interpret Ion's take on the ἑνδεκαχόρδος λύρα? Ion, we may remember, was also a composer of dithyrambs, and quite fashionable ones (test. 8–11 and frr. 82–84 Leurini): in Aristophanes' *Peace* 832–837 Ion is clearly associated with the kind of dithyrambic poets ridiculed in *Birds*; he is one of the διθυραμβοδιδάσκαλοι (l. 829) met by Trygaeus in his ascension to Olympus who spend their time flitting about collecting preludes "of the air-haunting-swiftly-soaring kind" (ll. 830–31, ξυνελέγοντ' ἀναβολὰς ποτώμεναι | τὰς ἐνδιαεριαυρινηχέτους τινάς).[39] Within this context, Tim Power has recently advanced an attractive suggestion for Ion's praise of the eleven-string lyre: far from embracing the demotic politics of polychordy, elitist Ion would have provokingly appropriated the New Musical eleven-string *kithara* as a spurning gesture of conservatism, drawn to it because "its very esotericism, its intellectual, anti-popular snob appeal made good sense within the symposium's ideology of exclusivity" (Power 2007: 188). This reading dovetails nicely with a social trend well attested in the fourth century BC (cf., e.g., Amphis' *Dithyrambus* fr. 14 KA) and possibly already operating in fifth-century Athens:[40] in fragment 93 Leurini, just as in Amphis fragment 14 KA, we can detect, in P. Wilson's words (2000: 70), the "clearly elitist attitude which sees dithyrambic poets bringing tit-bits from the cultural riches of the upper-class private world of pleasure into the public world of the mob." Ion's double standards make him an ideal mouthpiece for a do-it-yourself literary history.

---

[37] Mineur 1984: 208–209 and 211.
[38] McKay 1962: 166. Mineur's objection to McKay's argument is abundantly superseded (1984: 211). The Pythian Apollo invoked in the embedded paean of Timotheus' *Persians* (202–205, 236–240) is asked to bestow his protection on Timotheus' eleven-stringed rhythms.
[39] Translation after Sommerstein 1985: 81.
[40] See Prauscello 2006: 62–65.

If we turn to Ion's sympotic elegies (frr. 89–93 Leurini) and lyric poems with sympotic settings (fr. 86 Leurini), we see that they are an uninterrupted Dionysiac revelry staged within the (at times transgressed) boundaries of sympotic propriety:[41] philo-Spartan innuendos, Dionysiac intoxication (fr. 89.2 Leurini, αὕτη γὰρ πρόφασις παντοδαπῶν λογίων, "this [i.e., Dionysus or wine] is the prompting of all kinds of writers"), and apparently mocking gestures at conventions make Ion, once more, a difficult case to pin down. Ion's overt propensity for a wine aesthetic is most probably something from which Callimachus would have distanced himself,[42] but its potential as ironic retort against "those not unlearnedly inspired" (*Iamb.* 13.66, μὴ ἀμαθῶς ἐναύονται) could hardly be left unexploited by Callimachus.[43] Ion's *polyeideia* is, then, only one part of Callimachus' argument: Ion's Dionysiac inspiration, his ambiguous engagement, both in tragedy and in elegies, with contemporary musical discourse, and his presenting himself as a different poet on different occasions (the trendy dithyrambist who appeals to the mob and the elitist symposiast) makes him a good (mis)match for Callimachus' notorious defiance of any easy categorization and his intentional misreading of past literary tradition.

Looking for Dionysus: Delphi in Delos

Siding with Apollo in Ptolemaic Alexandria was not an unavoidable choice, not even for a native of Cyrene.[44] To sing a god in an age when kings are living gods is simultaneously a political and a religious act; in the new order of the world to declare theological allegiances becomes a trope for expressing not only generic and literary affinities but also allegiance to or dissent from the contemporary cultural propaganda.[45] Of course, Apollo and his sacred geography (Delos, Delphi, Cos) may be an attractive way to bridge the gap between mythical past and his-

---

[41] See the recent discussion by Katsaros 2007.

[42] For Callimachus' collaborative construction of himself as water drinker, see now Fantuzzi and Hunter 2004: 448–449, with previous bibliography (n. 15). On Ion's attitude to wine and its cultural and social significance within fifth-century Athenian dramatic festivals, see now Stevens 2007.

[43] For the frequent transference of αὔω and its compounds from the sphere of fire to that of water drawing in poetic contexts, see Borthwick 1969.

[44] For the overwhelming importance of the cult of Apollo at Cyrene, see Nicolai 1992.

[45] See especially Stephens 2003: 127–128.

torical present (the Delian and Cycladic leagues) and to praise the new Apolline god Philadelphus.[46] But it was Dionysus that the Ptolemies claimed as their divine ancestor, and it was Dionysus as god of wine and theater who played a prominent public role thanks to the Artists of Dionysus sponsored by royal patronage: all this at the apparent expense of the chthonic side of Dionysus-Osiris.[47] As such, Dionysus, especially the Indian Dionysus and god of wine, was very much a catalyst of cultural tensions: if Euphorion's *Dionysus* (frr. 13-18 CA) was probably celebratory in content and scope, Eratosthenes, Callimachus' pupil, in his *Erigone* (frr. 22-27 CA) and elsewhere may as well have exhibited a more critical approach toward the use of the myth of Dionysus by the Ptolemies.[48]

Where, then, is Dionysus in Callimachus, and above all, what kind of associations does his Dionysus (or do his Dionysuses) evoke?[49] An inherently multiple god like Dionysus is unlikely to yield to a single point of view, and it is thus not surprising that this is the case also in Callimachus. According to the *Suda* (test. 1. 11 Pf.), Callimachus wrote a *Semele*, and Dionysiac subjects or contexts are not entirely lacking in what is preserved down to us.[50] More specifically, if we look at the preserved occurrences of Dionysus in Callimachus' extant work,[51] two very different Dionysuses seem to emerge from the background. If we leave apart the traditional joint mention of Dionysus (wine) and Demeter (staple) in *Hymn* 6.70-71 and the oath by Dionysus and Pan in the homoerotic *Epigram* 44.2 Pf. (= 9.2 GP),

---

[46] See Fantuzzi and Hunter 2004: 355-359 and Stephens 2003: 114-121, both on *Hymn* 4.

[47] For the cult of Dionysus at Alexandria and its promotion by the Ptolemies, see the classic Fraser 1972: 1.202-8 (esp. 202 and 205 on how the chthonic element under the royal patronage "had largely dropped off"), and now Stephens 2003: 245-246, Hunter 2006a: 43-44.

[48] On Euphorion's *Dionysus*, see Clúa 1991; on Eratosthenes' criticism, see Pàmias 2004, who focuses especially on the *Catasterisms*.

[49] Haslam 1993: 125 n. 33 observes that the absence of a hymn to Dionysus in Callimachus is indeed "notable."

[50] The occasion of fr. 178 Pf. is the celebration, at Alexandria, of the Attic Anthesteria; a Dionysus-Osiris is probably mentioned in fr. 383.16 Pf., εἰ͜δυῖ͜αι φαλιὸν τ͜ι͜α͜ῦ͜ι͜ρον ἰηλεμίσαι. (Cf. Henrichs 1975: 143 n. 18.) Fr. 503 Pf. included the "Macedonian history" of Argaeus and his victory against the Illyrians thanks to the Dionysiac *mimallones*. (Cf. also fr. 743 *inc. auct.* Pf.) Dionysus may have had some role also in the treatment of the *Oinotropoi* maidens in fr. 188 Pf. (see D'Alessio 2007: 2.566-67 n. 37); from *Dieg.* IV 30 Pf. we also know that at the feet of the statue of the Samian Hera there was a lionskin, booty of Heracles and Dionysus, "bastards" of Zeus.

[51] Henrichs' survey (1975: 143) is a useful starting point.

we have a relatively coherent picture: alongside the rival Dionysus, patron of (the mostly contemporary) dramatic poetry (*Ep.* 7.2 Pf. = 57.2 GP; *Ep.* 8.2 Pf. = 58.2 GP; *Ep.* 48.5 Pf. = 26.5 GP;[52] cf. also *Iamb.* 1.6–8;[53] *Hec.* fr. 85 H. = 305 Pf.: Dionysus Limnaeus as the oldest recipient of χ‚οροστάδας... ἑορτάς),[54] we find Dionysus the brother of Apollo buried by his sibling at Delphi (fr. 50.117 M. = 43.117 Pf.; fr. 110.9 M.[55] = 667 Pf. + *SH* 276; fr. *inc. sed.* 643 Pf.; cf. also fr. *inc. sed.* 517 Pf.). Callimachus' gods, as often noted, are Panhellenic divinities rather than local gods, and the Delphic Dionysus fits well into this picture. There are anyway other elements worth considering. First, Delphi is one of the not very many places where the cults of Apollo and Dionysus are seen as not antagonistic but rather productively interacting with each other.[56] The address to Apollo Pythius and the reference to paeans

---

[52] These epigrams have received detailed treatment by Fantuzzi 2006a and 2007. Particularly interesting are especially *Epp.* 7 and 8 Pf.: in *Ep.* 8 Callimachus' poetics of the βραχυσυλλαβίη is represented as the winning option over the bombast of theatrical performances by way of paradoxically appropriating the god (Dionysus) of his rivals. Pasquali 1986: 1.304–05 made the attractive suggestion that the dramatic contests presupposed in *Ep.* 7 Pf. are neither tragic nor comic but dithyrambic, quoting Timoth. fr. 802 *PMG* as possible source of allusion.

[53] The text is highly lacunose: the contemporary (οἳ νῦν) *philologoi* or *philosophoi* are just like foolish seabirds (]κέπφ[), "crazed at the sound of the flute [| of Dio]nysus" (κα]τηύλησθ' οἱ με[| Διω]νύσου: Acosta-Hughes' translation). The syntactical link of Διω]νύσου at l. 7 with the following mention of the Muses and Apollo (equally in the genitive) at l. 8 is unclear. (See Kerkhecker 1999: 20, 22.) The presence of the verb καταυλέομαι in conjunction (?) with Dionysus is, however, suggestive. (Cf. Acosta-Hughes 2002: 42.) In Pl. *Laws* 7.790e1–3 (following the text of England 1921: 2.241 *ad loc.*) the mothers fascinate (καταυλοῦσι) the babies who cannot sleep "like the priestess who casts a spell on the mad frenzies" (with reference to Corybantic rites). In Pl. *Rep.* 8.561c7–d1 the person who is μεθύων καὶ καταυλούμενος is opposed to the ὑδροποτῶν καὶ κατισχναινόμενος (the second one linked to a "philosophic way of life"); for the deceiving power of music expressed by καταυλέω, cf. also Pl. *Rep.* 3.441a5.

[54] For Callimachus' hostility toward contemporary tragedy, cf. also *Ep.* 49 Pf. = 27 GP, *Iamb.* 2.11–12 (= fr. 192 Pf.), οἱ τραγῳδοὶ τῶν θάλασσαν οἰ[κεύντων] | ἔχο[υ]σι φωνήν (on which cf. Acosta-Hughes 2002: 187–188 and D'Alessio 2007: 1.594 n. 46); frr. 215 (τραγῳδὸς μοῦσα ληκυθίζουσα) and 219 Pf. (οὐ πρῷν μὲν ἡμῖν ὁ τραγῳδὸς ἤγειρε), fr. 219 Pf. perhaps belonging to the lost section of *Iamb.* 13. On Callimachus' relationship with tragedy (according to the *Suda* = test. 1.12 Pf. he composed satyr plays, tragedies, and comedies), see Richard Thomas 1979. For Callimachus' censure of dithyramb, see fr. 604 Pf., νόθαι δ' ἤνθησαν ἀοιδαί (referring to New Musical dithyrambs according to Fearn 2007: 212) and fr. 544 Pf. (Archilochus).

[55] For Μεθυμναίο‚υ... κυθηγενέος as a likely reference to Dionysus Zagreus, see Henrichs 1975: 140 n. 3, followed by Massimilla 1996: 445 *ad loc.*

[56] See Burkert 1985a: 224–225, Cavalli 1994, Clay 1996, and most recently Detienne 2001 and Fearn 2007: 170–174.

and Delphic choruses in Bacchylides' second dithyramb (16.8–13)[57] clearly emphasize "the separation but also the complementarity between the cults of Apollo and Dionysus at Delphi" (Fearn 2007: 172). The New Musical construction of an ideological polarity of Dionysus' *aulos* versus Apollo's *kithara* never applied to Delphi: Sacadas of Argos won in the first Pythian Games at Delphi playing Apollo's fight with the Dragon to the *aulos* (Paus. 2.22.8), and Strabo 9.3.10 informs us of an "ancient contest" at Delphi where *kitharodoi* sang paeans to Apollo.[58] Callimachus' description of the Crane Dance at Delos (*Hy.* 4.312–13, σὸν περὶ βωμὸν ἐγειρομένου κιθαρισμοῦ | κύκλιον ὠρχήσαντο) thus does not need to be interpreted as an antiquarian relic of the originally citharodic *Ur*-dithyramb: circular dances to the accompaniment of the *kithara* around Apollo's temple may well be paeans. In fact it is at Delphi that circular choruses for Dionysus (dithyrambs) and Apollo (paeans) come closest to each other in terms of modality of performance.[59] Philodemus' paean to Dionysus (no. 39 Käppel = *CA* pp. 165–171) for the inauguration of the sixth temple at Delphi (340/39 BC) is most interesting in this respect. In lines 59–60 the Muses crown the newly arrived Dionysus with ivy and dance around him (κύκλῳ): the circular dance for Dionysus merges into a paean, and it is Apollo who starts the song (l. 63, [κα]τᾶρξε δ' Ἀπόλλων).[60] The sustained assimilation of Dionysus to Apollo in Philodemus' paean shows how at Delphi "generic syncretism" (a paean for Dionysus) was linked to religious syncretism, and this most probably from quite an early time.[61]

Most important, and closer in space and time to Callimachus' world, two inscriptions from Cyrene dating to about 335 BC and mentioning dithyrambs have been recently linked to a festival in honor of Apollo

---

[57] Bacch. 16. 8–13 Maehler,]δ' ἵκηι παιηόνων | ἄνθεα πεδοιχνεῖν, | Πύθι' Ἄπολλον. | τόσα χοροὶ Δελφῶν | σὸν κελάδησαν παρ' ἀγακλέα ναόν.

[58] On the modality of performance of paeans at Delphi (*aulos* and *kithara*), see Rutherford 2001: 79–80 with n. 41.

[59] For κύκλιος χορός as a general label expressing modes of performances rather than cultic (Dionysiac) affiliations, see P. Wilson 2007b: 167–168 and Fearn 2007: 165–177. For dithyrambs at Delphi, see Kowalzig 2007b: 57 with n. 5.

[60] See Käppel 1992: 246.

[61] Cf. Rutherford 2001: 131–136 (esp. 131 with n. 14), with discussion of previous bibliography on the subject. For a syncretism of Apollo and Dionysus already in classical times, see Eur. fr. 477 K. (*Licymnius*), δέσποτα φιλόδαφνε Βάκχιε, Παιὰν Ἄπολλον εὔλυρε, and Aesch. fr. 341 Radt, ὁ κισσεὺς Ἀπόλλων, ὁ βακχειόμαντις. It may be worth noticing that Callimachus knew Euripides' *Licymnius* well enough to notice Aristophanes' lost opportunity for referring to it: cf. fr. 455 Pf. (= scholia to Aristoph. *Av.* 1242).

(*SEG* 9.13 and 48.2052).[62] The special relationship of Cyrene with Delphi, from its very foundation and throughout the whole Hellenistic period, is well known:[63] what is more relevant is that epigraphic and archaeological evidence from Cyrene testifies also to the privileged relationship that in Cyrenaïca the cult of Dionysus enjoyed with Delphian Apollo at least from the first century BC.[64] Callimachus fragment 517 Pf. (καὶ Δελφὸς ἀνήρ ἐμοὶ ἱεροεργός), perhaps belonging to a lost poem on Cyrene, fits well the bill.[65]

Apollo and Dionysus were not so far apart from each other in classical Athens either: Peter Wilson has shown how at the Thargelia, the most important civic festival in honor of Apollo, Dionysiac and Apolline features intertwined.[66] In the Sanctuary of Apollo Pythius, whose cult Peisistratus greatly promoted as a backup for the poor relationship of Athens with Delphi, a contest of cyclic choruses (κύκλιοι χοροί) was annually held in honor of Apollo. A testimony from Theophrastus' *On Drunkenness* (fr. 576 Fortenbaugh = fr. 119 Wimmer) attests to the fact that in Athens Apollo Delius was identified with the Apollo Pythius of the Thargelia,[67] and this joint worship well reflects the Thargelian influence on the choral contest held at the Delia under Athenian control.[68] Apollo Delius in Athens was, then, strictly linked to the Delphic Apollo, brother of Dionysus.[69]

---

[62] Ceccarelli and Milanezi 2007: 197–199, with reference to the Apollo Carneius of the Taranto krater (Taranto, Nat. Mus. IG 8263); cf. also D'Alessio forthcoming. It is also relevant that "the theatres of Cyrene and Delos were built in the sanctuary of Apollo."

[63] The Pythium at Cyrene dates back at least to the mid-sixth century BC: see Lehnus 1994a: 203 with nn. 92 and 93.

[64] See Ceccarelli and Milanezi 2007: 196 with n. 19.

[65] Cf. Lehnus 1994a: 203–204 and D'Alessio 2007: 2.713 n. 34.

[66] See P. Wilson 2007b. I am heavily indebted to his treatment of the Thargelia.

[67] πυνθάνομαι δ' ἔγωγε καὶ Εὐριπίδην τὸν ποιητὴν οἰνοχοεῖν Ἀθήνησι τοῖς ὀρχησταῖς καλουμένοις. ὠρχοῦντο δὲ οὗτοι περὶ τὸν τοῦ Ἀπόλλωνος νεὼν τοῦ Δηλίου τῶν πρώτων ὄντες Ἀθηναίων καὶ ἐνεδύοντο ἱμάτια τῶν Θηραικῶν. ὁ δὲ Ἀπόλλων οὗτός ἐστιν ᾧ τὰ Θαργήλια ἄγουσι. ("I have information that even Euripides the poet poured wine at Athens for the so-called Dancers. These, who are among the foremost Athenians, used to dance around the Temple of Apollo Delius and wear Theran garments. This Apollo is the god in whose honor they celebrate the Thargelia.") On the connection of the young Euripides and Delian Apollo, see below. Matthaiou has recently made a strong case for identifying the Athenian Pythium with the Temple of Apollo Delius: see Matthaiou 2003; see also P. Wilson 2007b: 176–177.

[68] See P. Wilson 2007b: 175–178.

[69] For the relationship between Delphi and Delos, see Bruneau 1970: 114–139 (esp. on the second-century-BC Athenian promotion of the ancient cult of Apollo Pythius

What has all this to do with Callimachus? In *Aetia* fragment 1.35–38 M. (= fr. 1.35–38 Pf.) Callimachus, according to a well-defined poetic code, wishes a rejuvenating process for himself and his poetry. Old age (γῆρας, l. 33) is a burden (βάρος, l. 35) to him, since it crushes him down just as Sicily crushes upon Enceladus-Typhon (ll. 35–36). But his comfort is that the Muses do not abandon in old age those whom they cherished as children (ll. 37–38, Μοῦσαι γὰρ ὅσους ἴδον ὄθματι παῖδας | λοξῷ, πολιοὺς οὐκ ἀπέθεντο φίλους). The programmatic importance of these lines and their intertextual dialogue with past poetic tradition (Hesiod, Plato, Euripides) have been amply and perceptively discussed.[70] In particular, the relevance of the second stasimon of Euripides' *Madness of Heracles* (ll. 636–700: the wish for rejuvenation of the elder Thebans and their musical old age) was noted already by Pfeiffer, and more recent studies have shown its interpretative payoff not only for lines 36–38 but for the entire *Prologue* to the *Aetia*.[71] Giulio Massimilla and Giovan Battista D'Alessio have convincingly argued that the intertextual dialogue with lines 691–694 of *The Madness of Heracles* (παιᾶνας δ' ἐπὶ σοῖς μελάθροις | κύκνος ὣς γέρων ἀοιδὸς | πολιᾶν ἐκ γενύων | κελαδήσω) strongly suggests that the winged creature (*Aet*. fr. 1.39 M. = Pf., πτερόν) that is most active in song (fr. 1.40, ἐνεργότατος) when death is approaching is not the cicada but the swan.[72] What I would like to draw attention to is the very idiosyncratic nature of the second stasimon of *The Madness of Heracles* not only within the musical microcosm of Euripides' homonymous tragedy but also within the whole fifth-century-BC tragic corpus. Euripides' *Madness of Heracles* is pervaded by images of destructive Dionysian music, a tendency that has been rightly related "to a broader religious anxiety concerning a perceived inefficacy or irrelevance of traditional ritual forms—including most importantly musical forms" (P. Wilson 1999–2000: 439). The domineering music of *The Madness of Heracles* is that of the violent, destroying Dionysiac *aulos*, which accompanies the onset of Heracles' folly (ll. 894–95, δάιον τόδε | δάιον

---

at Delos). The Temple of Apollo Pythius at Delos dates from as early as the 280s BC (Bruneau 1970: 123).

[70] Cf. Scodel 1980a, Alan Cameron 1995: 174–184; Acosta Hughes and Stephens 2002, Fantuzzi and Hunter 2004: 72–76.

[71] See Pfeiffer 1928. Cf. now Basta Donzelli 1991 and Massimilla 1996 *ad* ll. 36 and 39. Massimilla 1996: 248 sees reminiscences of *HF* also in fr. 5 (= 3 Pf.).

[72] Massimilla 1996: 230–231 and D'Alessio 2007: 2.377 n. 25. Cf. also M.A. Harder 2002a: 209 with n. 25.

μέλος ἐπαυλεῖται).[73] Yet the picture offered by the second stasimon is remarkably different. Let us consider lines 673–694:

οὐ παύσομαι τὰς Χάριτας
ταῖς Μούσαισιν συγκαταμει-
    γνύς, ἡδίσταν συζυγίαν.   675
μὴ ζῴην μετ' ἀμουσίας,
αἰεὶ δ' ἐν στεφάνοισιν εἴην·
ἔτι τοι γέρων ἀοιδὸς
κελαδῶ Μναμοσύναν,
ἔτι τὰν Ἡρακλέους   680
καλλίνικον ἀείδω
παρά τε Βρόμιον οἰνοδόταν
παρά τε χέλυος ἑπτατόνου
μολπὰν καὶ Λίβυν αὐλόν.
οὔπω καταπαύσομεν   685
Μούσας αἵ μ' ἐχόρευσαν.

παιᾶνα μὲν Δηλιάδες
⟨ναῶν⟩ ὑμνοῦσ' ἀμφὶ πύλας
  τὸν Λατοῦς εὔπαιδα γόνον,
εἱλίσσουσαι καλλίχοροι·   690
παιᾶνας δ' ἐπὶ σοῖς μελάθροις
κύκνος ὣς γέρων ἀοιδὸς
πολιᾶν ἐκ γενύων
κελαδήσω·

I shall not cease mixing the Graces with the Muses, a most sweet union. May I never live a life without song; may I always be crowned with garlands! Though an older singer, I still sing Mnemosyne; I still sing Heracles' victory song in the presence of Bromius, giver of wine, of the song of seven-stringed lyre, and the Libyan pipe. Never shall I stop the Muses, who set me dancing!
The Maidens of Delos sing a paean around the temple's doors for the fair son of Leto, whirling in circle their foot in their lovely dances. And I, an old singer, like a swan will sing paeans about your house from my hoary throat.

Though a "joy of premature rejoicing," and as such only an illusory moment of peace within the plot of *The Madness of Heracles*, this second half of the stasimon not only reaffirms the regenerative and rejuvenating power of music but also confronts us with one of few passages where the lyre and *aulos* are paired "in a very rare tragic image

---

[73] The perverted Dionysiac music of *HF* and its social import has been discussed in detail by P. Wilson 1999–2000: 432–439.

of harmonious union. They are partners in celebration, not enemies" (P. Wilson 1999-2000: 435).[74] In lines 682-84 the seven-stringed lyre, the Libyan *aulos*, and Dionysus "giver of wine" harmoniously coexist in the extemporized epinician performed by the Theban elders (ll. 680-81, τὰν...καλλίνικον ἀείδω). In the immediately following lines the chorus' self-referentiality takes the form of choral projection (ll. 687-94): the Theban elders explicitly compare their present "epinician" performance to the paean of the Delian Maidens in honor of Apollo.[75] The Dionysiac music of the previous stanza finds its ideal mirror and counterpart in paeans in honor of Apollo at Delos. This projection should certainly have reminded the Athenian audience of the civic *theoria* with a chorus of male dancers that Athens regularly sent to Delos. On the basis of Theophrastus fragment 576 F. (see above) Albert Henrichs has persuasively suggested that the Dancers (ὀρχησταί) mentioned by the philosopher may be identified with these theoric dancers, for whom the young Euripides is said to have poured wine and who we are told danced at Athens around the Temple of Apollo Delius—that is, Apollo Pythius.[76] It is ultimately under the aegis of Delphi and Delos that Dionysian and Apolline music can be reconciled.

Even more interesting, the second stasimon of Euripides' *Madness of Heracles* is repeatedly echoed by Plato in Book 2 of the *Laws* when within a digression on drunkenness the philosopher proposes to discuss the "right music" (ὀρθότης τῆς μουσικῆς: cf. 642a, 655d, 657c) and how a religiously proper χορεία organized on a civic basis is the only way to educate exemplary citizens.[77] Accordingly, feasts (ἑορταί) have been established by the gods out of pity (οἰκτίραντες) for human sufferings: the gods assigned to mankind the Muses, Apollo Musagetes, and Dionysus as συνεορταί, in order that they may set people right by associating with the gods (653d1-5). Gods are συγχορευταί, who lead human choruses linking men with one another by means

---

[74] For the other few passages in tragedy where the distance between Apollo and Dionysus is reduced (esp. Soph. *Tra.* 205-220 and *Aj.* 693-705), cf. Henrichs 1994-1995: 73-85 and Kowalzig 2007a: 232-242. It is worth emphasizing that the Apollo in whom the Cretan Pan and Dionysus merge in the *Ajax* is Apollo Delius (702-703, ἄναξ Ἀπόλλων ὁ Δάλιος εὔγνωστος).

[75] Fundamental on the whole passage is Henrichs 1996.

[76] Henrichs 1996: 59 n. 39.

[77] For the parallelism between the second stasimon of *HF* and *Laws* 665b-667b, with specific reference to the Chorus of Dionysus, see P. Wilson 1999-2000: 435 n. 29.

of song and dance (654a). It is within this conceptual frame that the necessity of song and dance for the whole civic community independently of age, sex, and social status is reasserted,[78] and the whole civic body is exhorted to change constantly their songs and seek variety (ἀεὶ μεταβαλλόμενα καὶ πάντως παρεχόμενα ποικιλίαν) so as to inspire the singers with an insatiable desire for song (665c). The Plato of the *Laws* is a Plato who is desperately trying to reintegrate and to productively absorb music, and especially its Dionysiac component, in his second-best city.[79] And the way he is trying to do it is, in allegiance with a whole poetic tradition,[80] by revaluing the positive effect of wine by making it a φάρμακον bestowed by Dionysus to old age so that the elders may become young again and dance and sing in a kind of renewal of the *paideia* they enjoyed while young (666a–c). Those who have reached the age of forty (and as such belong to the Chorus of Dionysus, according to Plato) and join the *syssitia* (which, within the discursive frame of the *Laws*, are, remarkably, presented as part of a festival in honor of Dionysus)[81] must "invoke the other gods and especially Dionysus to join in the initiation rite and play of the old, the wine, which he bestowed to men as a helper and medicine against the dryness of old age, so that we may become young again" (666b 3-7, καλεῖν τούς τε ἄλλους θεοὺς καὶ δὴ καὶ Διόνυσον παρακαλεῖν εἰς τὴν τῶν πρεσβυτέρων τελετὴν ἅμα καὶ παιδιάν, ἣν τοῖς ἀνθρώποις ἐπίκουρον τῆς τοῦ γήρως αὐστηρότητος ἐδωρήσατο τὸν οἶνον φάρμακον, ὥστε ἀνηβᾶν ἡμᾶς).[82] The thematic and verbal affinities with the second stasimon of *The Madness of Heracles* are startling:[83] in his attempt at integrating Dionysus' songs into Magne-

---

[78] Larivée 2003: 36 n. 26 has emphasized how 665c closely recalls passages from Euripides' *Bacchae*.

[79] Belfiore 1986 and Panno 2007 (esp. chap. 1) are an excellent guide in this respect. On Plato's previous attitude to Dionysiac music (especially the dithyramb), see Fearn 2007: 199 n. 113, 202–212.

[80] It is particularly interesting that in defending the right of the elders to dance and sing, Plato spectacularly redeploys to his own agenda the lyric poets' complaint about his inability to dance because of old age (the "my knees cannot bear me" motif: cf. *Laws* 664d, οὐ γὰρ δυνατοὶ φέρειν ᾠδάς, and cf. Sappho fr. 58.15 V., γόνα δ' [ο]ὐ φέροισι. Giovan Battista D'Alessio brings to my attention also Alcman fr. 26 *PMGF*, οὔ μ' ἔτι...γυῖα φέρην δύναται.

[81] See again Belfiore 1986: 434–436.

[82] Cf. also Panno 2007: 154–159. At 657d1-6 we are told that the musical festivals are established τοῖς δυναμένοις ἡμᾶς ὅτι μάλιστ' εἰς τὴν νεότητα μνήμην ἐπεγείρειν.

[83] Cf. especially *HF* 646, τᾶς ἥβας ἀντιλαβεῖν, and 663, δίδυμον ἂν ἥβαν ἔφερον, cf. *Laws* 666b7, ὥστε ἀνηβᾶν ἡμᾶς; *HF* 682, παρά τε Βρόμιον οἰνοδόταν, cf. *Laws* 666b4-6.

sia's social and religious organization Plato has significantly echoed a passage where Dionysus and Apollo Delius and Pythius are already συγχορευταί. Further on (828a–835a) the Athenian stranger will specify that the Delphic Apollo must be considered the νομοθέτης of every kind of ἑορταί, including athletic and poetic or musical contest.[84] Finally, it is also worth noticing that Plato's obsessive interest in the *Laws* for the ὀρθή μουσική under the patronage of Dionysus represents in itself a significant shift if compared with Pindar's fragment 32 Maehler. (Apollo performs at the wedding of Cadmus and Harmonia "performing correct music", μουσικὰν ὀρθὰν ἐπιδεικνύμενος: as noted by D'Alessio, in an unpublished paper, "Plato has moved the ὀρθὰ μουσικά from the realm of Apollo to that of Dionysus.")

The second stasimon of *The Madness of Heracles* was, then, already a foundational passage for Plato's theorizing on the ideal form of χορεία: it was his final attempt at facing historically and more pragmatically the musical reality left by the New Dithyramb and its descendants. It seems to me highly likely that the role played by the second stasimon of *The Madness of Heracles* in shaping Plato's reformed musical world in the *Laws* must have been present to Callimachus:[85] its resurfacing in the *Prologue* of the *Aetia* is at the same time also a critical response to Plato's own response. And it is a response that, as often in Callimachus, is at the same time a form of critique. Massimilla already suggested the importance of the second stasimon of *The Madness of Heracles* also as a link to the first *aition* (frr. 5–8 M.),[86] where Clio, in reply to Callimachus' question about the "true" genealogy of the Graces, would have mentioned Dionysus and the Naxian nymph Coronides. (Cf. *Schol. Flor.* 29–32 *ad* frr. 5–9 M.) This answer is perhaps just another Hesiodic lie,[87] but what is still more interesting is that the chorus of old men in Euripides' *Madness of Heracles* will celebrate the Graces (and Muses) not only with both lyre and *aulos* (ll. 683–84) but also with crowns (l. 677, αἰεὶ δ' ἐν στεφάνοισιν εἴην), whereas the distinctiveness of the Parian cult of the Graces, Callimachus' first *aition*, is just the fact that their celebration rejects both the *aulos* and the crowns (cf.

---

[84] On Plato and Delphi, see Delcourt 1955: 272–280.
[85] For Callimachus' engagement with Plato's *Laws* in the *Prologue* of the *Aetia* and elsewhere, see already Stephens 2002: 244, and Acosta-Hughes and Stephens forthcoming.
[86] Massimilla 1996: 248.
[87] See Fantuzzi and Hunter 2004: 56–57.

fr. 5 M. = 3 Pf., [...] κῶς ἄγ[ις αὐλῶν] | ˻ῥέζειν καὶ στεφέων εὔαδε τῷ Παρίῳ˼). After having alluded in *Aetia* fr. 1 M. (= fr. 1 Pf.) to one of the very few passages in tragedy where there is an allegiance between Dionysus and Apollo (or *aulos* and *kithara*), Callimachus rectifies it retrospectively (no *aulos* and crowns, after all) by choosing as his first *aition* the *aulos*-free, garland-free cult of the Graces at Paros.[88] As with the case of Ion of Chios, Callimachus' engagement with the heritage left by the previous literary tradition is, once again, typically elusive and multifaceted: Delphi in Delos, Apollo in Dionysus.

---

[88] For the importance of the cult of Apollo Delius at Paros, see Rubensohn 1968, and Kowalzig 2007b: 73–74 for the Delium of Paros and Naxos. On the relationship between Paros and Delos, see now Constantakopoulou 2007: 46–47. On the relevance of the cult of Dionysus at Paros, cf. Zaninovic 1994: 213, with previous bibliography.

CHAPTER FIFTEEN

CALLIMACHUS AND CONTEMPORARY CRITICISM

Allen J. Romano

ABSTRACT

Callimachus imagines his poetry as the target of contemporary critics on more than one occasion: e.g., *Aet.* fr. 1 Pf. (= 1 M), *Iamb.* 13, *Hy. Apollo* 105–13. Though such examples dramatize Callimachus' relationship to contemporary criticism as largely adversarial, his foregrounding of aesthetic conflict conceals considerable overlap and interplay of ideas with contemporary strands of literary criticism. Situating Callimachus against the fragmented (and often post-Callimachean) record of Hellenistic literary criticism surviving in sources such as "Demetrius" *On Style*, euphonist criticism preserved in Philodemus and reflected in Dionysius of Halicarnassus, and theories of poetic composition by the likes of Neoptolemus of Parium reveals in Callimachean poetry a complex interweaving of contemporary debates about the nature of poetry.

It is a peculiar irony of literary history that Callimachus' literary polemics, in retrospect, stand as confident pronouncements on poetic aesthetics when Callimachus went to such great lengths to pretend that he was, among other things, a light, childlike cicada and clearly on the receiving side of literary judgment and instruction. *Aetia* fragment 1 Pf. (= 1 M.), a prominent site for modern reconstruction of Callimachus' views toward his own poetic craft, begins not from a statement of critical principles, but rather from the assumption that poetry elicits a critical response: "Telchines mutter at my song."[1] Similarly, other well-worn passages underlying familiar modern constructions of Callimachus as Alexandrian literary critic *par excellence* depict poet and poetry as critical target (e.g., *Iamb.* 13, *Hy. Apollo* 105–113). These examples dramatize Callimachus' relationship to contemporary criticism as largely adversarial, but the situation is not so easily schematized. Callimachus' foregrounding of aesthetic conflict

---

[1] Cf. Fantuzzi and Hunter 2004: 446–447.

conceals considerable critical overlap and interplay of ideas. In what follows, I examine what we can know about Callimachus' debts and contributions to the literary criticism of his age and, more important, how such interactions shaped his poetry. I draw examples especially but not exclusively from *Aetia* fragment 1, a bellwether for previous views of Callimachean poetics and a passage whose explanation frequently drives interpretation of the Callimachean corpus.[2]

Hellenistic Criticism

Despite Callimachus' apparent explicitness about criticism and his privileged role as model for later poets, the story detailing Callimachus' relationship to the literary criticism of his own age is not easily reconstructed.[3] In an ideal world we might imagine juxtaposing Callimachean poetry, Callimachean prose on literary matters, and then the treatises of literary critics. We would view one set of texts through the lens of the others and vice versa, back and forth between poetic practice and critical principles. Unfortunately, our evidence resists this exercise. Of Hellenistic literary criticism, the most relevant material is lost (e.g., Praxiphanes, Peripatetic treatises, and the prose of Philetas, Eratosthenes, and Callimachus himself). What is fully extant is of problematic date (Pseudo-Demetrius *On Style*). Other texts may preserve key elements of late fourth-century and early third-century critical insights but are post-Callimachean, often significantly so, and it is difficult to separate new principles from inherited ones (Pseudo-Longinus *On the Sublime*, Dionysius of Halicarnassus, probably Pseudo-Demetrius). Finally, crucial material for the present investiga-

---

[2] Good points of entry to the copious bibliography are Acosta-Hughes and Stephens 2002; Asper 1997 (especially 209–246); Alan Cameron 1995; Fantuzzi and Hunter 2004: 66–76; and Massimilla 1996: 199–231. I follow Alan Cameron 1995: 104–132 in considering fragment 1 an integral part of the original publication of *Aetia* 1 and 2.

[3] For Hellenistic literary criticism generally, see Grube 1965: 103–149; Kennedy 1989: 194–219; Russell 1981: 34–51; as it overlaps with philosophy, Asmis 1998; Fraser 1972: 1.480–494; Schenkeveld and Barnes 1999; with scholarship, Fraser 1972: 1.447–479; Pfeiffer 1968: 87–104; Rengakos 1993; and with rhetoric, Classen 1995; Russell 2006. The thumbnail sketch in Porter 2006b: 334–338 captures much in a short space. For comparison of Hellenistic criticism and poetry, see Gutzwiller 2007: 202–213 and Fantuzzi and Hunter 2004: 444–461. Too 1998: 115–150 is derivative of Pfeiffer 1968.

tion, the critics preserved in the charred rolls of Philodemus, present us with texts papyrologically more difficult and conceptually more laborious than Callimachus' own poetry.[4] Callimachean idiosyncrasies further muddy the waters. In contrast to his evocation of previous historians, philosophers, and poets by name in his poems, he does not refer so directly to any specific literary critic. On the other hand, Callimachean poetry collapses some temporal distinctions while exaggerating others. He can become a new Hipponax in *Iambus* 1, but he casts contemporaries as antiquated sorcerers in *Aetia* fragment 1.[5] It is also far from certain, and often quite unlikely, that Callimachus' poetic practice consistently follows his self-presentation.[6] In short, Callimachean habits specifically resist tidy disentanglement of our two categories, criticism and poetry.

Given these necessary cautions, there were ample conduits for both direct and indirect interaction between Callimachus and Hellenistic literary critics working at multiple intellectual centers and royal courts during the third century.[7] Cultivation of literary judgment occupied an important place in Hellenistic παιδεία. As a passage of Dionysius Thrax (ca. 170–ca. 90 BC) makes clear, κρίσις is the highest form of response to literature but may utilize all aspects of γραμματική.[8] Put simply, the function of this κρίσις is to distinguish good poetry and the principles that set good poetry apart from bad, often with the

---

[4] Translations of Philodemus best reflect the underlying choices of reconstruction; since the present essay does not attempt to contribute to discussion of the complexities of Philodemus, all translations are from Janko 2000 except where noted otherwise.

[5] Callimachus frequently praises the new and disparages the old (fr. 75.54 Pf., παρ' ἀρχαίου Ξενομήδεος; fr. 92.2, Λε]ανδρίδες εἴ τι παλαιαί; *Hy. Zeus* 60; cf. Ovid *Fasti* 1.7).

[6] E.g., the Telchines' charge that Callimachus did not compose poems on kings and heroes soon rings false as Jason and Heracles figure in the early episodes of *Aetia* 1 (fr. 7.19–fr. 23 Pf. = fr. 9.19–fr. 25 M.). Cf. Acosta-Hughes and Stephens 2002: 242.

[7] The most important figures for Callimachus may be not his immediate contemporaries but rather his teachers and their contemporaries. Thus Theophrastus' work on poetry may have been known directly or through contemporary reactions. Callimachus' own teacher, Hermocrates of Iasus, wrote a work entitled *On Accents*. The nature of this work is not clear, but accentuation plays an important role in later criticism. Philodemus preserves part of Pausimachus' scheme (Janko 2000: 183 n. 1).

[8] *Ars Gram.* 1: "the assessment of the poems [κρίσις ποιημάτων], which is the finest of all the parts of the craft [ἐν τῇ τέχνῃ]." Cf. *Schol. in Dion. Thrax* 170.5, 303.28, 471.34–35, 568.15 Hilgard; Pseudo-Longinus *Subl.* 6.1. For connections of this late Hellenistic treatise to earlier works, see Pfeiffer 1968: 267–270; for later material, cf. Lallot 1989: 20–26. On κρίσις generally, see Too 1998: 9–12; Ford 2002: 1–22; Laird 2006b: 31–32.

added goal of using this discernment and these principles of discernment to authenticate existing works and to create good poetry oneself.[9] Frequently the practice of literary κρίσις cleaves to larger projects of philosophical ethics, rhetorical persuasion, and grammatical commentary in an intellectual world defined by competition for resources, patronage, and students among individual philosophers, philosophical schools, rhetoricians, and intellectual centers. The exercise of ancient criticism attests to interaction among the various schools and their ideas, and it is likely that Callimachus had some knowledge of the main strands of criticism, even if we cannot determine, in most cases, that he was acquainted with specific treatises or critics.

Peripatetic Criticism and Pseudo-Demetrius On Style

Our ancient sources identify at least one potential connection. We are told that the Peripatetic Praxiphanes (ca. 340–mid-3rd century) was one of the Telchines (*Schol. Flor.* 7) and that Callimachus wrote a prose work entitled *Against Praxiphanes* (fr. 460 Pf.).[10] Praxiphanes himself wrote works entitled *On Poems* and *On Poets*, both no longer extant.[11] Callimachus likely knew other early Peripatetic works on poetry, but these too have not survived.[12] Although Callimachus himself was not a Peripatetic (*contra* Wilamowitz and emphasized by C. O. Brink), Callimachus' prose output has a suspiciously Peripatetic flavor (e.g., *On*

---

[9] Ford 2002: 82; Porter 2006b: 317–318.

[10] Before discovery of the Scholia Florentina, Πρὸς Πραξιφάνην was thought to mean *On Praxiphanes*, and the work was supposed to be a form of homage to a like-minded critic. Cf. Massimilla 1996: 200, Brink 1946: 12–14. The scholiast may have counted Praxiphanes among the Telchines as an inference from Callimachus' work. It is doubtful that the testimony of the Latin translation of the *Life of Aratus* preserves an authentic record of Praxiphanes and Callimachus meeting (*pace* Alan Cameron 1995: 210).

[11] Philodemus *On Poems* 5.21.28 Mangoni: Περὶ Ποιη[μά]των. Diog. Laert. 3.8: Περὶ Ποιητῶν. Cf. Brink 1946: 21; Janko 1991; Mangoni 1993: 47–95.

[12] Heraclides of Pontus (fourth cent. BC, alive in 322): *On Poetry* and *On Poets*. Theophrastus (ca. 370–ca. 284): *On Rhetoric, On Poetry, On Comedy, On Lexis, On Hupokrisis*. Cf. Innes 1985 for connection to later Hellenistic theories of style. Aristoxenus (born ca. 370): numerous works on music likely relevant to euphonic theorizing (Janko 2000: 175–181). Demetrius of Phalerum (born ca. 350): see below. Dicaearchus of Messana (fl. 320–300): works on Homer, *On Musical Contests*. Phanias of Eresus (fl. 320): *On Poets*. Chamaeleon of Heraclea (ca. 350–after 281): *On the Iliad, On Alcman, On Sappho, On Stesichorus, On Simonides, On Lasus, On Anacreon, On Satyrs, On Comedy, On Thespis, On Pleasure*. Hieronymus of Rhodes (third cent. BC): *On Poets, On Citharodes, On the Tragedians*. Cf. Podlecki 1969, Blum 1991: 47–48.

Birds, On Winds), and it seems that a strand of Peripatetic activity had a home in Alexandria.[13] Insofar as the *Pinakes* recorded biographical information and literary history, they would parallel Peripatetic modes of literary criticism.[14] So too, fragments of the *Pinakes* make clear that Callimachus passed judgment on the authenticity of individual works, an activity that would fall under the purview of κρίσις.

Evidence for an important extension of Peripatetic criticism is the fully extant *On Style* attributed to Pseudo-Demetrius, a work that bears witness to the fundamental role of stylistic criticism in the Hellenistic period. Most scholars would date it to the second century BC but are quick to acknowledge that it reproduces older material and is thus a significant witness to post-Aristotelian criticism. The dating of *On Style* to the mid-third century by G.M. Grube and now Richard Janko is attractive but problematic.[15] Unfortunately then, the extant treatise cannot be attributed to Callimachus' contemporary Demetrius of Phalerum, a figure who has numerous points of contact with Callimachus. Not only did he spend the end of his life in Alexandria and thus likely was an old man to Callimachus' relative youth, but many of his authentic works are frustratingly suggestive of similar interests.[16] For example, he is credited with works entitled *On Old Age* and *On Dreams*, two topics that figure prominently in the opening of the *Aetia*.[17] Stobaeus (3.1.172) preserves a selection of the sayings of the Seven Wise Men made by Demetrius, recalling *Iambus* 1. So too Callimachus may have used Demetrius' collection of the fables of Aesop in constructing the *Iambi*.[18] Like many Peripatetics, Demetrius also wrote works on rhetoric (probably containing stylistic comments relevant to literary criticism) and Homer (Montanari 2000: 403). It is not surprising, then, that the extant *On Style*, a work that accords strikingly

---

[13] Brink 1946: 12; Pfeiffer 1968: 67; Janko 1991.

[14] Blum 1991 rightly emphasizes the philological knowledge required to produce the *Pinakes* but overstates the probable similarity of the actual product, whose nature is highly debatable (Pfeiffer 1968: 127–128), to Peripatetic literary treatises. Cf. Krevans 2004: 173–174.

[15] Janko 2000: 176 n. 6; Grube 1961: 39–56, 133–163. Morpurgo-Tagliabue 1980 advocates second century BC; Schenkeveld 1964 a 1st-century-AD reworking of earlier material.

[16] Life in Alexandria: Diog. Laert. 5.78 = Hermippus fr. 58 W.; cf. Sollenberger 2000. For Demetrius' literary output and problems, see especially Montanari 2000.

[17] Diog. Laert. 5.81. Del Corno 1969: 138 questions the authenticity of *On Dreams*.

[18] Acosta-Hughes 2002: 173; Matelli 2000: 433–438.

well with Peripatetic practice and draws on earlier Peripatetic sources, should have been attributed to this famous Demetrius.[19] *On Style* distinguishes four styles (grand, elegant, plain, forceful) and their faulty mirrors (arid, affected, frigid, unpleasant), an idiosyncratic scheme compared with more common distinctions of either two (plain and grand)[20] or three styles (low, middle, high).[21] It is unfortunate that the dating of Pseudo-Demetrius *On Style* is problematic; we cannot know whether points of contact indicate Callimachean borrowing, inspiration, or a shared (Peripatetic) source.

Aetia fragment 1 showcases Callimachus' use of terminology and metaphors drawn from stylistic criticism. Scholars have long noted his appropriations of Aristophanes' stylistic vocabulary.[22] The imagery of the bountiful Demeter, the long lady, slender verses, and large lady (ll. 9–12) and later the fat sacrifice, slender Muse, broad path, narrow route, and weight of old age that burdens the poet like an island (ll. 23–28, 35–36), develop stylistic oppositions of weightiness, grandeur, and magnitude to lightness, thinness, and sparseness. Richard Hunter rightly adduces a passage from Philodemus *On Poems* 5 (7.25–9.28 Mangoni), possibly drawn from Heraclides, that similarly contrasts poetry on the basis of style. He notes that the *Aetia* prologue "plays provocatively with familiar terms of literary discussion, drawn in fact from many areas and 'genres', as part of the production of a paradigmatically 'light' poem" (Fantuzzi and Hunter 2004: 72). Divergences in stylistic schemes as evidenced here and in the extant *On Style* exemplify the debate dividing Callimachus and Praxiphanes. Of Callimachus' *Against Praxiphanes* we hear only that in it he praised Aratus for being a good poet and knowledgeable (fr. 460 Pf.: ὡς πολυμαθῆ καὶ ἄριστον ποιητήν). This may be a later generalizing characterization of specific stylistic praise of Aratus. (Cf. *Ep.* 27 Pf. = 56 GP.)[23] The meager fragments of Praxiphanes suggest that stylistics was

---

[19] As has long been recognized, the distinctive use of the term ψυχρός to describe the "frigid" style (114–127, vs. "swelling") is an Aristotelian inheritance (*Rhet.* 1405b34ff). There is frequent quotation of Aristotle, Praxiphanes (57), Demetrius of Phalerum himself (289).

[20] Aristophanes' *Frogs* and frequently later (e.g., Cic. *Brutus* 201).

[21] *Rhet. ad Her.* 4.8.1 and Cicero *De or.* 3.177, 199, 310–312.

[22] E.g., Wimmel 1960: 115; Pfeiffer 1968: 137–139; O'Sullivan 1992; Acosta-Hughes and Stephens 2002: 246–247.

[23] Cf. Gow and Page 1965: 2.208–209 on τρόπος and λεπταί.

a major concern.[24] We know almost nothing of Praxiphanes' dialogue on poetry except that it depicted a conversation of Isocrates and Plato (Diog. Laert. 3.8). Plato is a touchstone for Callimachean poetry,[25] and Isocrates was later praised for his style in terms that may recall Callimachean aesthetics (cf. Dion. Hal. *Comp.* 23). More specifically, the Florentine scholiast reports that the Telchines (including Praxiphanes) criticized Callimachus for his "thin" (ἰσχνός) style and lack of magnitude (*Schol. Flor.* 8-9). The idea goes back at least to Aristophanes, whose Euripides characterizes his own style in these terms (*Frogs* 939-943), and *On Style* devotes a section to the ἰσχνός style (190-239).[26] The charge of plain style is, however, a misreading of Callimachus' practice, particularly in the *Prologue* to the *Aetia*. That he denies grand style does not imply that he chooses plain style. Even in the *Hecale*, where Callimachus seems to employ a plainer style in keeping with the humble content, he employs novel arrangement and word choice that undercuts a monostylistic label.[27] Indeed, we find elements of *On Style*'s plain, grand, and elegant styles all used for distinct purposes by Callimachus. The *Aetia* too cannot be reduced to a single stylistic category, as Callimachus acknowledges at the end of the poem (fr. 112 Pf.). Without entering the fray of debate about what future publication the πεζὸν νομόν of the Muses anticipates,[28] we can note that in looking back to the Hesiodic shepherding scene (fr. 2) the phrase also continues the stylistic tenor of fragment 1. In claiming to turn to another type of song, Callimachus refashions the traditional hymnic close implying transition to another song, marked frequently by the key phrase αὐτὰρ ἐγώ (e.g. *HH Demeter* 495, *HH Apollo* 546, *HH Hermes* 580; cf. Simonides *fr.* 11.20-21 West²). To such a traditional closing gesture, Callimachus adds a keyword from hymnic priamel. His pun on νομός/νόμος ("pasture"/"tune") itself echoes the play on this word in the opening of the *Homeric Hymn to Apollo* (20: νομοί of song) and thus Callimachus conflates the beginning and end

---

[24] E.g., fr. 13 Wehrli (= Ps.-Dem. *On Style* 55-58). Cf. Brink 1946: 19-25; Podlecki 1969: 124-125.
[25] S. White 1994, Acosta-Hughes 2002: 85-86.
[26] Heracleodorus may refer to this style as well: *On Poems* 1.197.4. Pausimachus maligns ἰσχνοφωνία (*On Poems* 1.96.3-6), "stuttering" according to Janko (2000: 303 n. 8 and 425 n. 3).
[27] For example, *Hec.* fr. 1 H. displays a "programmatically creative tension...between matter and manner" (Fantuzzi and Hunter 2004: 198). Cf. Hollis 2009: 10-15.
[28] Cf. Alan Cameron 1995: 154-156; Knox 1985a and 1993.

of the poetic god's signature hymn. The concluding lines answer the charge of unadorned (πεζός) style with a tongue-in-cheek rebuttal that matches the tone of fragment 1. The reference to a future song that is πεζός makes the point that the preceding poem has been, through to its endpoint, the opposite.

Stoics, Epicureans, and Κριτικοί

In addition to Peripatetic theorizing, Callimachus may have known something of the developing Stoic criticism. Distinctively Stoic is the subordination of literary aesthetics to ethics and the acceptance of poetry as a form of wisdom (σοφία) and of craft (τέχνη), principles embodied in the *Hymn to Zeus* by Callimachus' contemporary Cleanthes (331–232 BC).[29] Aristo of Chios, possibly the Stoic critic whose views are recorded in Philodemus *On Poems* 5, was also active during Callimachus' lifetime (Asmis 1990: 149–151). On the other hand, Epicurus (341–270) famously rejected literary and musical theory, but later Epicureans took up his views on aesthetic pleasure in works related to poetry, most notably Philodemus (ca. 110–ca. 40/35).[30] Among the critics of varying affiliation preserved (and attacked) by Philodemus are a number of Callimachean contemporaries who put special emphasis on the role of sound and euphony in the discernment of good poetry. Andromenides and Neoptolemus of Parium may have been active toward the end of Callimachus' life, and Megaclides of Athens nearer the beginning.[31] Heracleodorus (late third or early second century), Pausimachus of Miletus (ca. 200), and Crates (second century) write after Callimachus' death but confront critical issues that predate their own writings. If we connect this later euphonic theorizing with Peripatetic musical criticism, as Janko argues, then one source for these ideas was likely Heraclides of Pontus, a pupil of both Plato and Aristotle in the late fourth century.[32] The last of these critics, Crates,

---

[29] Cf. Thom 2005; Asmis 2007.

[30] Asmis 1992a and 2006; Sider 1995.

[31] According to Eustathius, Aristophanes of Byzantium (ca. 257–280) referred to Neoptolemus. Tatian (*Or. adv. Gr.* 31.130 = Eusebius *Praep. Ev.* 10.11.3) lists Megaclides after Ephorus and Philochorus (ca. 340–267/61) and with Chamaeleon (ca. 300). Cf. Janko 2000: 140.

[32] Janko 2000: 134–138. There are multiple avenues for Callimachean awareness of the main lines of euphonic criticism. Heraclides remarks upon Lasus of Hermione's famous sigmaless *Hymn to Demeter*, the centerpiece of a poetic contest between Lasus

resided at the Pergamene court and was a contemporary and foil of Aristarchus. The antithesis of Pergamum and Alexandria is familiar, reified in contrasts like analogy/anomaly and κριτικός/γραμματικός.[33] Although these are second-century divisions, and definitively post-Callimachean, they likely had roots in the third century, when the main lines of argument had not been delineated so sharply.

The so-called κριτικοί advocated judgment of poetry based primarily or, in some cases, solely on the quality of poetic sound and its proper arrangement (σύνθεσις). Recovering this strand of Hellenistic criticism is an immense labor that requires reading through layers of heavily damaged and exceptionally fragmentary papyri, through Philodemus' hostile report and biases, around Crates' mischaracterizations of his predecessors, and then using only fragmentary tidbits of text to reconstruct an original that would, even in its unmediated state, have presented considerable interpretive difficulties.[34] To echo Asmis' assessment, any reconstruction is a working hypothesis (Asmis 2002). Despite these difficulties, these fragments attest to one of the most distinctive advances in Hellenistic literary criticism.

A central assertion of euphonist criticism was that judgment (κρίσις) of poetry depends upon hearing. As Crates put it, "the natural difference that exists in poems is discerned by the hearing."[35] It is this emphasis on pleasing sound as a measure of poetic excellence that drew the attack of Philodemus: "It is a sorry proposition to emphasize the euphony that supervenes on the arrangement of words and to attribute the judgment of this [arrangement] to the exercise of hearing" (*On Poems* 5.23.26–33 Mangoni). For Philodemus' targeted κριτικοί, pleasure in hearing a poem comes not immediately from its

---

and Pindar (Porter 2007b). If Callimachus knew something of this specific back-and-forth on poetic sound, then his treatment of sound as criticism may also owe something to a poetic model.

[33] The terminology here masks a complex history. Crates seems to be resuscitating an older label to mark the contrast with grammarians of Alexandria. Callimachus' predecessor Philetas was, according to Strabo 14.2.19, both κριτικός and ποιητής, but the distinction with grammarian is elided in the *Suda*, where he is γραμματικὸς κριτικός. For Philodemus' use of the term, see Schenkeveld 1968, Blank 1994, Porter 1995b, Janko 2000: 125–127.

[34] See especially Porter 2007a and Janko 2000: 11–47.

[35] *On Poems* 5.27.17–21 Mangoni. Cf. 5.24, where Philodemus says that "Crates misunderstands the view of Heracleodorus and those who share them; for they praise not the composition but the sound that supervenes upon it."

thoughts (διάνοια) but only in thoughts as mediated by its sounds.[36] Further, there should be a pleasing and fitting (πρέπον) connection between meaning and form. (For example, Andromenides: "[The poet must] also adopt words suited to the actions" and "every [critic says that] '[words] that imitate[?] badly do not have character.,'" *On Poems* 1.169.16–18 and 15.20–21.) The poet could thus achieve excellence by proper and pleasing arrangement (σύνθεσις) of the smallest units of sound (Janko 2000: 162–164). (For example, Heracleadorus: "One verse is good, the other bad, [although they are] composed from the same words," PHerc 1676 col. II, 12–13, 16–17.) Next, sound is the distinctive province of the poet; where matters of diction are shared (κοινά) by composers of history, rhetoric, and philosophy as well as poetics, sound is distinctive (ἴδιον) for poetry. (For example, in a summary of Andromenides: "It is the function of poets not to say what nobody else has, but to say it in a way in which nobody of those who are not poets would express it," *On Poems* 1.131.8–12 and 167.16–20.)

Manipulation of sound and showcasing of euphony are particularly pointed in the opening of the *Aetia*. Callimachus depicts critics who "grumble at" (ἐπιτρύζουσιν) his song; he, by contrast, advocates a type of poetry that is refined, pure, and clear-sounding. He reinforces this contrast with expert manipulation of sound and sense connections. Callimachus puns on the Telchines' name in the word "to melt" (τήκ[ειν]), which plays the Telchines' occupation (smelters) off of the harsh sounds of tau and kappa (Acosta-Hughes and Stephens 2002). In lines 13–14, he bids the harsh and military sound of the cranes leave Egypt and return to Thrace. As he states by way of contrast later, "the nightingale is sweeter" (l. 16: ἀ[ηδονίδες] δ' ὧδε μελιχρ[ό]τεραι). He says he will not thunder like Zeus (l. 20: βροντᾶν οὐκ ἐμόν, ἀλλὰ Διός). The word βροντᾶν itself resonates and captures the type of sound Callimachus is rejecting.[37] If this image evokes the story of Hesiod frag-

---

[36] Heracleodorus (*On Poems* 1.33.1–5): "Even if what is said is unintelligible, [the sound] is the cause of comprehension and of signification even in the midst of people making a din." Cf. Asmis 1992a: 159; Janko 2000: 121.

[37] Elsewhere Callimachus develops the common criticism of tragic sound as bombastic (e.g., Ar. *Clouds* 1367, Dem. *De cor.* 262; cf. Arist. *Rhet.* 1403b31–35, Diod. Sic. 15.7, Ps.-Plut. *Vit. X orat.* 848b). In *Iambus* 2 Callimachus mocks tragic actors for the booming sound of their voices. In *Iambi* fr. 215 Pf. the term λήκυθος activates a metaphor of aural criticism shared by Aristophanes, Callimachus, and his near contemporary Andromenides (cf. schol. Hephaest. 5 p. 122.21–23 Cornsbruch). Janko 2000: 389 n. 2, recognized previously by Sider 1992.

ment 27 M.-W., then the sound imagery is even more pointed. In the Hesiodic story, Zeus punishes Salmoneus for acting as an impostor and attempting to imitate Zeus's thundering with the sound of chariots. In fragment 1, Callimachus casts himself as a possible Zeus, the legitimate noisemaker whose thundering would mark punishment of other, illegitimate, thunderers. As usual, Callimachus gets to have it both ways. He asserts mastery of thundering while rejecting thundering as a preferred mode of song. Philodemus attributes to Pausimachus a series of observations about syllable and accent arrangement that likely are not original to this late critic.[38] For example, Pausimachus prefers open, light syllables (e.g., κύκλος) to closed, heavy syllables without accent (χαλκὸν) and a hierarchy of euphony from easily pronounceable letters to more difficult ones (*On Poems* 1.88). In the contrast of this thundering line (l. 20) with his expressions about good poetry (ll. 30, 33), Callimachus employs such principles of aural arrangement to create euphonous lines that contrast with the resounding thunder. Similarly, in a key couplet Callimachus claims at lines 30–31 that he will "sing among those who love the shrill sound [λιγὺν ἦχον][39] of the cicada, not the din of asses. Let another bray [ὀγκήσαιτο] like the long-eared beast." These lines, connecting sound and sense, end with the onomatopoeic ὀγκήσαιτο. The word imitates the sound of the ass and produces a relatively rare (and therefore striking) spondaic end to the line (Fantuzzi and Hunter 2004: 71 n. 101). The "long-eared" (οὐλ[α]χύς) donkey amusingly signals the importance of the aural, and the ensuing shift in focus to vision (l. 37: ὄθματι παῖδας | μὴ λοξῷ, "favorable eye") also frames the sound effect. The word ὀγκήσαιτο recalls ὄγκος ("weight"), a contemporary stylistic term. Ὄγκος signals the grand or, less charitably, swollen style, in contrast to the plain and thin.[40] A provocative passage of Andromenides suggests one possible euphonic extension: "A word exhibits beauty when the syllables shine forth densely woven with letters and the mouth grasps and hurls weighty syllables of the most resplendent notes" (*On Poems* 1.21 and 181.8–22). Andromenides seems to find positive value in weightiness, whereas the musical critic Heraclides (Ath. 14.624e)

---

[38] Janko 2000: 175–188. The essentials of this system recur in later sources as well.
[39] For this musical term, cf. Janko 2000: 229 n. 5.
[40] E.g., Ps.-Dem. *On Style* 36, 66, 77, 120. Pseudo-Longinus *Subl.* 3.1 similarly describes tragedy as "naturally grand and permitting bombast [ὄγκος]."

characterized ὄγκος negatively as specific to the Aeolian mode.[41] Callimachus' manipulation of the term refashions this critical debate. He strips ὄγκος of all possible grandeur by packaging it in the harsh sound of the braying ass. The sound effect imitates the idea and thus would seem to follow solid euphonist principles for good poetic sound; however, heard amid Callimachus' larger set of ideas, the clash of weightiness and the ass in depicting Callimachus' rival poets and potential critics casts them not just as purveyors of bad sound but as fools who confuse harsh braying with grandeur.

In all these examples, Callimachus uses sound to play medium off message. Not only does he show himself an expert manipulator of poetic sound, but he also foregrounds sound as the basis of criticism very much like euphonist critics. This is not confined to *Aetia* fragment 1. *Epigram* 8 Pf. (= 58 GP) contrasts the short speech of a winner (l. 2: νικῶ) with the longer speech of the loser (l. 4: σκληρὰ τὰ γιγνόμενα). Σκληρά is a musical term (Aristoxenus fr. 87 Werhli), and Callimachus again makes the medium match the message by having the losing poet use a harsh-sounding word and the winning poet a more euphonic one.[42] Finally, Callimachus pointedly describes poetry with water metaphors (e.g., *Hy. Apollo* 105–113, *Ep.* 28 Pf. = 2 GP). Water sounds are a particular favorite for κριτικοί and later commentators.[43] Callimachus' prose work on rivers (fr. 457–59 Pf.) and on wonders (fr. 407 Pf.), insofar as it drew from poetic sources, may reveal Callimachus himself a commentator on these types of effect. At *Hymn to Apollo* 105–113, Envy tells Apollo, "I don't like a poet who doesn't sing like the sea" (l. 106: οὐκ ἄγαμαι τὸν ἀοιδὸν ὃς οὐδ' ὅσα πόντος ἀείδει). The well-studied image works in multiple spheres at

---

[41] Heraclides goes on to note more subtly that "this does not mean malice but is, rather, lofty and confident." Cf. Ps.-Dem. *On Style* 38.

[42] Cf. Fantuzzi 2007: 486–487. The sound effect in Hesiod *Theogony* 839 (σκληρὸν δ' ἐβρόντησε) anticipates this usage. The echoing of Callimachus *Ep.* 28 Pf. = 2 GP (ἐχθαίρω/χαίρω/σικχαίνω, ὧδε καὶ ὧδε, μισέω/πίνω, ναίχι καλὸς καλός/ἄλλος ἔχει) creates a related effect. In line 1, κυκλικόν may have the sense of "going round" (*AP* 9.559, Dion. Hal., Ps.-Dem. *On Style* 20.1), as attested in descriptions of dithyramb (cf. Fantuzzi and Hunter 2004: 20–21) rather than "cyclic epic" (Alan Cameron 1995: 396). For Callimachus to say that he hates the "cyclic" poem is a pointed joke, as going round is precisely what the epigram itself does.

[43] Pausimachus (Philodemus *On Poems* 1.108 and 93) cites *Il.* 17.265 and 17.122, Heracleodorus (PHerc 1676 col. VII, 8–11) on Euripides (fr. 330b Kannicht), Andromenides (Philodemus *On Poems* 1.18 and 178) on *Il.* 2.209–11 (cf. Dion. Hal. *Comp.* 16.1, schol. *Il.* bT 209–10).

once.⁴⁴ It equates song with the flow of water and the poet as source of song with the source of water (cf. Plato *Laws* 4.719c), and it draws obliquely on the contrast of water and wine salient elsewhere (*Aet.* fr. 178.11-12 Pf. = 89.11-12 M.). The metaphor also extends to sound. The opening of the poem begins, in imitation of the *Homeric Hymn to Apollo*, with loud sounds heralding the god's arrival and the call for silence at lines 17-21 pointing explicitly to the effect. Parallel to the aural emphasis at the opening, the close of the poem contrasts differing water sounds. The antithesis of Callimachean pure water (ll. 111-12: καθαρή τε καὶ ἀχράαντος...ἄκρον ἄωτον) and the muddy torrent of the Assyrian river (l. 109: λύματα γῆς καὶ πολλὸν ἐφ' ὕδατι συρφετὸν ἕλκει) opposes too the sound of these water flows, one loud and rushing like Homeric descriptions of water and the other not. This contrast, moreover, reworks the equation of Homer and Oceanus found elsewhere, typically interpreted as a metaphor that depicts Homer as the font of all poetry and wisdom (F. Williams 1978: 98-99). Homer is the resounding model of poetry, the Ocean that can rush boomingly; by contrast, Callimachus fashions himself a small and therefore quiet trickle. In choosing this metaphor, given the preeminent role of Homeric sound as an object of literary criticism, Callimachus makes his poetry a critical object on par with the special treatment accorded Homer in the very act of defining the newness of his own practice.⁴⁵

Criticism alone did not prompt Callimachus' attention to sound. Antimachus, the metric of Hellenistic aesthetic taste, was criticized in part for the sound of his poetry. As Nita Krevans (1993: 156-159) notes, Aratus' use of παχέα (*Phaen.* 953) for sound accords with the use of the word πάχιστον at *Aetia* fragment 1.23. Aratus, like Callimachus, was also attuned to euphonic effects in Homer. For example, continuing the focus on water, Aratus' passage on seafaring (*Phaen.* 287-299) employs solid euphonic principles and includes an echo (περικλύζοιο θαλάσσης) of one of the most famously aqua-imitative Homeric phrases, πολυφλοίσβοιο θαλάσσης. To reach even further back to another crucial poetic model for Callimachus, Pindar frequently makes striking use of sound, and later commentators pick up

---

⁴⁴ Alan Cameron 1995: 363-366; Crowther 1979; Kahane 1994; Knox 1985b; F. Williams 1978: 86-99.
⁴⁵ It may not be inconsequential that an important model for this passage as well as for *Aet.* fr. 1, Timotheus *Persae* fr. 791.202-40, calls on Apollo to ward off μῶμος (210) and focuses especially on sound and music. Cf. F. Williams 1978: 86.

on it (e.g., *Dith.* 2).⁴⁶ Callimachus' use of sound effects capitalizes on this poetic habit. That careful arrangement of sound offers opportunity for displaying poetic skill is nothing new; however, by Callimachus' time such moments have attracted the attention of commentators, and thus a tour de force passage like *Aetia* fragment 1 or the *Hymn to Apollo* 105–113 uses this habit of critical attention to sound in order to assert itself as a poem that merits selection and inclusion—that is, κρίσις—alongside the works of Homer and others.

Predecessors, Pupils, and Neoptolemus of Parium

The tutors of Ptolemy Philadelphus (Zenodotus of Ephesus, Philetas of Cos, and Strato of Lampsacus) were also points of contact with critical writings and figures such as Duris (ca. 340–ca. 260 BC), his brother Lynceus, Hermippus (third century), and Satyrus (third century) wrote works on literature that may have included some form of literary criticism. The Cyrenaics, philosophers in closest proximity to Callimachus both through his native Cyrene and by their presence in Alexandria, have left nothing that might be considered literary criticism; however, they may have been an important secondhand conduit for ideas, including literary criticism, generated in the other Hellenistic philosophical schools (Fraser 1972: 1.480–82). Still other critics likely drew from Callimachus as much as or more than they contributed to his poetic production; however, in many cases these younger contemporaries may make explicit the terms of Callimachean-era debates. For example, according to the *Suda*, Eratosthenes (ca. 285–194) was a fellow Cyrenean and pupil of Callimachus as well as of the Stoic Aristo (Pfeiffer 1968: 153–154). Although his work on literary criticism does not survive, Eratosthenes claimed that the poet tries to "move the soul, not to teach" (ψυχαγωγίας, οὐ διδασκαλίας: Strabo 1.1.10). He frames succinctly the crucial fault line of Hellenistic debates over poetic usefulness, striking an Aristotelian note in pointed contrast to contemporary Stoics who followed Plato in denying the emotions a favored role in poetry.⁴⁷

---

⁴⁶ Porter 2007b: 6–7 cites a fourth-century Peripatetic treatise, PBerol 9571v.
⁴⁷ Strabo 1.2.3; cf. 1.2.17. Connections of Eratosthenes to philosophers (Solmsen 1942) may also be conduits for literary criticism. For some clues to emotional language in Callimachus, see M.A. Harder 1990: 303–309.

One of the most important developments of Hellenistic literary theory is the division and analysis of poetic art (ποιητική) through its constitutive parts. Like most strands of Hellenistic literary criticism, our post-Callimachean evidence points to Callimachean-era debates. Though the specific schemes of division vary widely, critics separated, roughly speaking, elements of form (poem, ποίημα; diction, λέξις; arrangement, σύνθεσις) from elements of content (poetry, ποήσις; idea, διάνοια; theme, ὑπόθεσις).[48] Contrasts between form and content appear in Plato and Aristotle and recur frequently in Hellenistic criticism.[49] In the later Hellenistic period, Posidonius employs the distinction of poem and poetry (fr. 44 Kidd = Diog. Laert 7.60).[50] By contrast, Neoptolemus of Parium proposed a threefold division of ποίημα ("poem," the medium), ποίησις ("poetry," the message), and ποιητής ("poet," the intent), the "most comprehensive classification of poetry known from antiquity."[51] Neoptolemus insisted upon the independence of these three elements as coequal perspectives on poetic art.[52] Thus one can speak of the σύνθεσις (arrangement) of the whole poem separately from the ὑπόθεσις (plot, meaning) of the same poem. Unlike later critics, he did not subordinate poetic form to content (ποίημα to ποίησις), and he took the counterintuitive step of separating the poet (ποιητής) from other parts of the art. Andromenides likely shared this tripartite scheme, which may derive from Theophrastus.[53]

---

[48] Dion. Hal. *Comp.* 3 sums it up: σύνθεσις is to ἐκλογή as ὀνόματα are to νοήματα.

[49] Praxiphanes contrasts λόγος vs. λέξις (fr. 12 Wehrli). Aristo of Chios at Philodemus *On Poems* 5.14.12; see further Porter 1995a: 98–102. Mangoni speaks of poems with good σύνθεσις and good διάνοια. This distinction can be seen in Plato (e.g., *Ion* 530b10–c4 διάνοια vs. ἔπη, *Rep.* 378d) and Aristotle.

[50] I.G. Kidd 1988: 2.1.198 notes that Posidonius' development of this distinction is idiosyncratic in importing the Stoic logical term σημαντικόν.

[51] Asmis 1998: 391. *On Poems* 5.14.5–11 Mangoni. "He presents the person who possesses the poetic art and its potential as an aspect of the art of poetry, alongside the verse and the composition" (Janko 2000: 152). Neoptolemus was long known as the source for Horace's theory of poetics in the *Ars Poetica* (according to Porphyry). The story is likely more complex. See especially Porter 1995a; Asmis 1992c; and Brink 1963.

[52] It is clear that he expressed some sorts of connections among the various elements, but the interpretation of the relevant passage is highly contested. See Porter 1995a: 104–105.

[53] Janko 2000: 153–154, following Rostagni, suggests that Andromenides is the link confirming a Theophrastean origin for the system. However, the fact there is no evidence in Theophrastus for this view (as Asmis notes) makes this conclusion highly suspect. So too, Asmis 1992c: 227 n. 100, *contra* Janko 2000; Porter 1995a: 146–147 rightly points out that Crates' acceptance of a tripartite scheme is also far from assured.

These classifications underlie the more pressing questions about articulation of the components. For Stoic critics, for example, elements of form should follow from content. A similar principle of appropriate coordination of form and content looms large in Pseudo-Demetrius *On Style*. For Posidonius and Philodemus, form and content cannot be separated, and therefore form reflects the more important element, content. Euphonic critics did not banish content completely but asserted that one could judge content through arrangement alone. This is itself a radical step, but one that accords well with critical debates about these matters. Neoptolemus' system, on the other hand, opens up the possibility of proceeding differently between elements of form, elements of content, and, in the category he adds, the poet. Asmis proposes that ποίημα, ποίησις, and ποιητής map to the educational progression of a poet from training in verbal composition to the ability to fashion plots and characters to a poetic intent to move and benefit listeners.[54] Like Callimachus, Neoptolemus was a poet as well as a critic, though very little of his poetry survives.[55] Neoptolemus' division of poetic art may reflect his own poetic training and in doing so propose a model of poetic production for the practicing poet as much as it does a model of literary κρίσις.

The distinction between ποίημα and ποίησις is not one of size, strictly speaking, but it did frequently map to the antitheses of big versus small and complete versus incomplete. Often under the spell of Aristotelian ideals of unity and completeness, later critics tend to slip into subordination of a notionally smaller unit of analysis, ποίημα, to the larger, complete notion of ποίησις (e.g., Philodemus 11.26–12.13).[56] In *Aetia* fragment 1, Callimachus uses this slippage in reverse. If we imagine the issues that Neoptolemus raises in light of *Aetia* fragment 1, metaphors of size signal in part the sorts of distinctions that Neoptolemus later stresses. The critique of composing poetry "little by little" (l. 5: ἐπὶ τυτθόν) points to ποίημα, form and its arrangement. So too, Callimachus' depiction of himself "like a child" (l. 6: παῖς ἄτε) matches

---

[54] Asmis 1992c: 217–218. Cf. Brink 1963: 73.

[55] He wrote a mythological poem on Dionysus (Athen. 3.82d = FGrH 702 F 3 = fr. 1 Mette) and a poem *On Witticisms* (Stob. 4.52.24 = FGrHist 702 F 5: Περὶ ἀστεισμῶν).

[56] Asmis 1992c: 213–24. Philodemus, reacting against the implication that ποίημα is a small work, must square the circle and argue that short poems such as epigrams, which he himself writes, can in fact be ποίησις (*On Poems* 5.37.2–38.15 Mangoni; cf. Sider 1997: 28–31).

Neoptolemus' placement of ποίημα as the first element of poetic art. Apollo's injunction to keep the Muse slender (ll. 23–24) reflects ποίημα first and is appropriate to Callimachus as child. In light of distinctions between ποίημα and ποίησις, the charge of rejecting heroes and kings (ll. 3–5) evokes not genre but more specifically theme and ποίησις (Rosenmeyer 2006). In short, Callimachus begins his poetics from formal elements, with σύνθεσις and ποίημα, rejecting the charge of not foregrounding content or ποίησις. He proceeds from discussion of poetic form to content and eventually to poet in Apollo's instructions and his own rejuvenation.

Callimachus seems at his most explicitly size-ist when he invites his audience to judge the wisdom of poetry by τέχνη and not by the Persian chain (ll. 17–18: αὖθι δὲ τέχνῃ | κρίνετε,] μὴ σχοίνῳ Περσίδι τὴν σοφίην). The key terms of this passage have a rich poetic heritage in which archaic poets singled out wisdom and craft as criteria for both creating and judging poetry. Pindar, for example, opposes the poet by nature and the poet of craft.[57] A traditional reading of *Aetia* fragment 1.17–18 stresses the Platonic contrast of τέχνη and ἐνθουσιασμός.[58] Callimachus has it both ways. Apollo's teaching of Callimachus casts divine inspiration in terms of craft and answers explicitly the Platonic critique of poetic inspiration. This exposes an important strand of Callimachus' response to previous literary criticism, but the preference for Plato also obscures the relevance of Hellenistic elaborations of τέχνη. Late Hellenistic critics tend to emphasize the important role of experience (ἐμπειρία) and the quality of teachability central to poetic τέχνη. For example, Philodemus glosses τέχνη as "a faculty or disposition arising from observation of certain common and fundamental things that extend through most particular instances, a faculty that grasps and produces an effect such as only a few who have not learned the art can accomplish, and doing this firmly and surely, rather than conjecturally."[59] Elsewhere Philodemus defines τέχνη in terms of what is similar (cols. 16.32–17.23) and, drawing on Zeno (col. 30.25–28), defines τέχνη in terms of imitation: "to imitate well the [poems] of Homer and [others] who have been similarly handed down" (Asmis

---

[57] *Ol.* 2.83–88; cf. *Ol.* 9.100–102 and 3.40–42.

[58] For the contrast, Murray 2006. Cf. Fantuzzi and Hunter 2004: 1–17. Russell 1981: 38 describes Callimachus' approach as "craftsmanlike" and unphilosophical.

[59] *On Rhetoric* 2 = Pherc 1674 col. xxxviii p. 123.5–19 Longo. Blank 1995: 179–180 discusses the flexibility of Philodemus' use of the term τέχνη.

1992b: 409). This sense of τέχνη as recognizing and reproducing what is similar fits well the dual use of the term as both means of evaluating and means of producing poetry. *Aetia* fragment 1.17–18 would imply that one should judge poetry by selection and proper arrangement of ideas. But in the distinction between form and content Callimachus cuts off this straightforward reading. Σχοῖνος is a particularly well-chosen word. First, there is a mismatch between the thought and the word. The term σχοῖνος can refer to an aphrodisiac (schol. Lycophron *Alexandria* 832). The erotically charged encounter with Apollo at the beginning of *Aetia* 1 recalls aspects of the symposium in the way that it makes Callimachus a young boy gazed upon by older, envious men. Cast in the meter of sympotic poetry, this scenario colors the opening, and the term σχοῖνος picks up this resonance. The explicit contrast is also complex. There is a sound resonance in the idea of σχοῖνος, "reed," highlighting the preference for "reedy" sound, typically "shrill" (λιγύς). This terminology corresponds perhaps to Pindar *Dithyramb* 2.2, "stretched out like a rope." But σχοῖνος as "reed" and "rope" also implies being interwoven. Finally, Pseudo-Demetrius *On Style* 54 cites another Schoenus, the place named in *Iliad* 2.497 as part of a "long chain of connectives" that acquire weight (ὄγκος) despite being small. The idea of measuring by τέχνη instead of being drawn out uses both common poetic tropes and conflates them with more specialized discourse. In the contrast of τέχνη and σχοῖνος, Callimachus paradoxically combines two terms that may, in certain contexts, refer to similar processes.[60]

Conclusion

This discussion does not exhaust the resonance of contemporary literary criticism by any stretch. Many issues fall under the heading of philosophy or rhetoric. For example, we can note in passing that ethical concerns underlie Callimachus' *Iambi* and might be adduced for other Callimachean works as well.[61] So too, the biographical method utilized in contemporary philosophical (particularly Peripatetic) writing resonates with Callimachus' practice of poetic autobiography at

---

[60] Hunter 1993 argues for an analogous procedure at work in the collocation of ἕν and διηνεκές, harmonizing two terms antithetical in Aristotelian criticism.
[61] Acosta-Hughes 2002: 205–264; Kerkhecker 1999: 294; Clayman 1980: 70.

the beginning of the *Aetia*.⁶² A number of prominent concepts in Hellenistic criticism, such as ἐνάργεια ("vividness"), φαντασία ("image," "imagination"), and other elaborations of classical μίμησις have been well studied in the context of Hellenistic realism and the connections between poetry and art. "Vividness" may well have significance in *Aetia* fragment 1 (l. 40: ἐνεργότατος), but the context is unclear. Finally, allegory has a prominent place in ancient criticism from the earliest poetry through prose of the sixth and the fifth century (e.g., Theagenes of Rhegium, Metrodorus of Lampsacus) and into the later Hellenistic period. Although Aristotle and the Alexandrians do not exploit allegory as much as Crates and Stoic critics, it still has an important place in Alexandrian poetry.⁶³ These interactions between Callimachus and the contemporary critical scene are not insignificant and, at a minimum, point to the depth of Callimachean engagement with contemporary criticism both in its details and in its outlines.

In the *Politics*, Aristotle mentions Zeus as an ideal critic who judges music but does not perform it himself (1339b6).⁶⁴ Callimachus and his contemporaries often cast their patron and model critic as Zeus (e.g., *Hymn to Zeus*, Theocritus *Idyll* 17), but in *Aetia* fragment 1 he rewrites the paradigm by characterizing the Telchines in marked contrast to Zeus's ideal critic. Though Callimachus has given to subsequent ages a literary "aesthetics," a κρίσις, the more important consequence of his particular engagement with literary criticism, in the context of his own poetry, lies in the transformation of his audience into critics favorably disposed to his poetry. In an important sense, ancient criticism was an inherently hostile practice that had at its root the potential for censorship, banishment, and, in the archaic metaphor, starvation.⁶⁵ Callimachus packages his poetry with its critical reception foregrounded. This is a deeply traditional poetic gesture, familiar in Theognis' praise of both poetic skill and audience discernment (e.g., 681-82 W) and in Hesiod's ventriloquism of the Muses, who "speak false things like true things" (*Theogony* 26-28).⁶⁶ Hesiod, for example, has a special

---

⁶² Momigliano 1971: 65-84; Too 1998: 132-133.
⁶³ *Contra* Kennedy 1989: 86-87 and Pfeiffer 1968: 140, 237-238. Gutzwiller 2007: 209-212 provides a more sober assessment, emphasizing the importance of allegory for understanding the construction of ecphrases in particular. See also Slings 2004.
⁶⁴ Ford 2002: 290-291. Cf. *Pol.* 1340b23-25.
⁶⁵ Cf. Asmis 1995; Too 1998: 169-173.
⁶⁶ Cf. Theognis 19, 769-772, 789-794; Pindar *Ol.* 2.84; Bacchylides *Odes* 3.85; *Il.* 2.484-87; *Od.* 8.487-91; *WD* 202.

relationship with the Muses, but like the audience he is at their mercy and thus, in some way, on the same side as the audience. Callimachus weaves into his poetry the terms of contemporary literary debate for a similar purpose, to situate his critics with him ("among the cicadas") as ideal listeners for his particular style of poetry. Contemporary criticism furnishes fresh material, but these are old tricks.

CHAPTER SIXTEEN

CALLIMACHUS' MUSES

Andrew Morrison

Abstract

This paper examines the relationship Callimachus has with the Muses by investigating their role and function in a number of different texts, especially the *Aetia*. The Muses are an important way for poets to talk about the qualities of their own poetry and in *Aetia* 1–2 Callimachus builds on the depiction of the Muses in earlier poets and their capacity to provide inspiration or information to portray himself as participating in an active and engaged conversation with the individual Muses in turn. The individualized Muses in *Aetia* 1–2 reflect the ongoing process of specialization as to the province of each Muse which led to the traditional division into the 'Muse of History', etc. Callimachus did not persist with the framework of the Muse-dialogue in *Aetia* 3–4, but we should not think of Callimachus as therefore rejecting the Muses in *Aetia* 3–4, but as showing the relationship of poet to Muse from a different perspective from that in *Aetia* 1–2.

Callimachus is famous as a poet who portrayed himself as having a particularly close relationship with the Muses (though, as we shall see, he is not the first or only poet to do so). This special relationship Callimachus depicts as having begun early and lasted long, as the aged Callimachus, the narrator in the *Prologue* to the *Aetia* puts it:

.......Μοῦσαι γὰρ ὅσους ἴδον ὄθματι παῖδας
μὴ λοξῷ, πολιοὺς οὐκ ἀπέθεντο φίλους.

...because the Muses do not send away their friends when they're old, if they looked on them favorably as children.
                                                            Aetia fragment 1.37–38 Pf.=M.

But despite this close association there are considerable problems in getting a clear sense of the character of Callimachus' Muses: accidents of preservation have left us without complete texts of those poems in which the Muses featured most heavily, the *Aetia* and (to a lesser extent) the *Iambi*;[1] while the Muses in Greek literature more generally

---
[1] Those texts that survive complete (the *Hymns* and the *Epigrams*) are much lighter on Muses.

are themselves hard to pin down, their character and function varying a great deal from poet to poet (cf. Murray 2005: 147), as we might expect from goddesses who in part allow poets to talk about the peculiar character of their own poetry and its composition. (Cf. de Jong 1987: 46 on Homer.) Nevertheless, it is still possible to see the different roles Callimachus can make his Muses play, and it is also important to take into account those places where other poets (or genres) may have turned to the Muses but Callimachus does not.

At the start of the *Iambi* the first voice we hear is not that of a narrator invoking a Muse to begin a narrative,[2] but that of an archaic poet returned from the dead demanding to be listened to himself: Ἀκούσαθ' Ἱππώνακτος ("Listen to Hipponax!" *Iambus* 1.1). Accordingly Hipponax functions in the *Iambi* as a good example of what Marco Fantuzzi and Richard Hunter (2004: 3) have called a "poet-guarantor": an illustrious predecessor used to authorize a particular poetic tradition and the legitimacy of the new Hellenistic addition to it. Hipponax himself marks out what is to be different about this new iambic poetry—it does not "sing of the battle with Bupalus" (*Iambus* 1.3-4). This use of an earlier poet to represent a type of poetry and articulate one's relationship with it is part of a wider Hellenistic pattern,[3] one advertising the fact that the Muses are not the only source of poetic authority available to Callimachus. Hellenistic poets were able, as genre and situation required, to emphasize either that their poetry was a *techne* or "craft" (which one might learn from an expert predecessor) or that it was inspired by or derived from the Muses (or similar artistic deities such as Apollo).[4] *Iambus* 13, which may be the final poem of the *Iambi* (and in any case looks back to *Iambus* 1),[5] also concerns the nature of inspiration and dependence on one's poetic forerunners. Here Callimachus portrays himself as responding to criticism of his poetry, which mixes dialects (*Iambus* 13.17-18) and which has not begun from traveling for

---

[2] This might from one point of view reflect archaic *iambus* itself, in which we find poems (e.g., Archil. frr. 168, 185 W.) that begin not with Muse invocations but first-person statements by the primary narrator about his intention to tell particular narratives. Cf. Morrison 2007: 78.

[3] Cf., e.g., Lycidas in Theocritus *Idyll* 7 or Hipponax in Herodas' *Mimiambus* 8, with Fantuzzi and Hunter 2004: 4-5.

[4] On the background to these different conceptions of the nature of poetry (which could, if necessary, be combined), see Fantuzzi and Hunter 2004: 1-4.

[5] Cf., e.g., Acosta-Hughes 2002: 89-91 on the connections between *Iambi* 1 and 13. On the question of the number of *Iambi* (13 or 17), see Kerkhecker 1999: 271-282; Acosta-Hughes 2002: 9-13; Morrison 2007: 200.

inspiration to the home of Hipponactean choliambic poetry, Ephesus (*Iambus* 13.12–14). At the very end of the poem (and hence perhaps the very end of the book of *Iambi*) Callimachus echoes the very words his critic used against him in lines 12–14:

ἀείδω
οὔτ' Ἔφεσον ἐλθὼν οὔτ' Ἴωσι συμμείξας,
Ἔφεσον, ὅθεν περ οἱ τὰ μέτρα μέλλοντες
τὰ χωλὰ τίκτειν μὴ ἀμαθῶς ἐναύονται.

...I sing, neither going to Ephesus nor mixing with the Ionians: Ephesus, whence those who want to give birth to limping lines are not unskillfully inspired.

Iambus 13.64–66

Despite the fragmentary state of the poem it seems clear that Callimachus does not need to travel to Ephesus because Hipponax has himself come to Alexandria in the very first poem (cf. Fantuzzi and Hunter 2004: 16), in which Hipponax recommends (and authorizes) an iambic poetry very different from what he himself produced.[6] The repeated words of the critic in *Iambus* 13 (τὰ χωλὰ τίκτειν, "to give birth to limping [things/lines]") sound as if they are recommending something highly undesirable, the birth of deformed creatures, and it may be that Callimachus repeats them precisely to highlight the problematic terms in which his critics conceive of the production of poetry (see Acosta-Hughes 2002: 77–78). Callimachus is not limiting himself to "limping lines," or choliambs (as the metrical variety of the *Iambi* has shown by the time we've reached *Iambus* 13), nor to iambic poetry. He portrays poetry as a *techne*, which means he is not restricted to one genre:

τίς εἶπεν αὐτ[....]λε..ρ.[....].   30
σὺ πεντάμετρα συντίθει, σὺ δ' ἡ[ρῷο]ν,
σὺ δὲ τραγῳδε[ῖν] ἐκ θεῶν ἐκληρώσω;
δοκέω μὲν οὐδείς, ἀλλὰ καὶ το.δ..κεψαι...

Who said...you compose pentameters, you hexameters, you have been allotted tragedy by the gods? No one, I think, but...

Iambus 13.30–33

These lines seem both to allude to the poet Ion of Chios, famous for having worked in a wide variety of genres (cf. *Dieg.* IX.35–36), and also to reject how Socrates in Plato's *Ion* characterizes poetic ability

---

[6] Prominent in the fragments of Hipponax are sexual and scatological material, as well as invective and abuse. Cf., e.g., frr. 78, 84 W.

as tied to the particular type of poetry ἐφ' ὃ ἡ Μοῦσα αὐτὸν ὥρμησεν ("to which the Muse drives him [*sc.* a poet]," 534c2–3) and no other, because (as Socrates sees it) a poet composes when he is ἔνθεος and ἔκφρων ("inspired" and "out of his mind," 534b5) rather than through *techne* (534b7–8).[7]

One might expect, then, that the *Iambi* would have little room for the goddesses of inspiration themselves. But *Iambus* 13 itself begins with an invocation to the Muses along with Apollo, which was probably placed in the mouth of Callimachus rather than his critic (cf. Kerkhecker 1999: 252–253; Acosta-Hughes 2002: 70):

Μοῦσαι καλαὶ κἄπολλον, οἷς ἐγὼ σπένδω...

Beautiful Muses and Apollo, to whom I pour libations...

Iambus 13.1

Furthermore both the critic (Μοῦσαι, *Iambus* 13.22) and Callimachus himself (Μούσας, *Iambus* 13.26) mention the Muses, and Callimachus probably makes a further reference to them toward the end of the poem, when he characterizes the critic's behavior as leading to the departure of females whom in all likelihood we should identify with the Muses (cf. Kerkhecker 1999: 266; Acosta-Hughes 2002: 97):

φαύλοις ὁμι[λ]εῖ[ν....].ν παρέπτησαν
καὐταὶ τρομεῦσαι μὴ κακῶς ἀκούσωσι.

...to have anything to do with bad people...they flew past, afraid they too would be criticized.

Iambus 13.58–59

Even in the *Iambi* the allegiance of the Muses is important, and it is clear that the prominence of Hipponax at the beginning of the collection does not mean that the Muses are rejected. The presence or absence of the Muses remains a way of talking about the quality of one's poetry (cf. Callimachus' critics at the beginning of the *Aetia*, the Telchines who are "no friends of the Muse," *Aetia* fr. 1.2 Pf. = 1.2 M.), and it also suggests that the Muses, while not the only way for Callimachus to provide authority for the content, manner, or genre of a poem, can also represent more than simply the divine possession of an

---

[7] Cf. Depew 1992: 327 and 1993: 64; Acosta-Hughes 2002: 82–89.

inspired poet. To obtain a clearer picture of Callimachus' Muses and their varying roles we must turn back to the *Aetia*.

Here too we find a poetic predecessor whose example Callimachus engages with, but one who himself played a crucial role in shaping later poets' view of the Muses. Book 1 of the *Aetia* moves from the *Prologue* to a scene strongly recalling Hesiod's meeting with the Muses in the *Theogony*. The situation in Callimachus appears to be that the primary narrator, an older Callimachus, gives an account of a dream he had about meeting with and talking to the Muses on Mount Helicon as a boy,[8] with an explicit reference to Hesiod's own meeting (cf. Hesiod's description of himself ἄρνας ποιμαίνονθ' Ἑλικῶνος ὑπὸ ζαθέοιο, "shepherding lambs under sacred Helicon," *Theog.* 23):[9]

ποιμένι μῆλα νέμοντι παρ' ἴχνιον ὀξέος ἵππου
Ἡσιόδῳ Μουσέων ἑσμὸς ὅτ' ἠντίασεν.

when, as he tended his sheep by the quick horse's foot mark, the swarm of Muses met Hesiod the shepherd.
                              Callimachus fragment 2.1–2 Pf. (= 4.1–2 M.)

Hesiod's meeting with the Muses forms part of the opening Hymn to the Muses at the start of the *Theogony*, which portrays the Muses as dancing goddesses (cf. *Theog.* 3–4, 7–8) who use their beautiful, untiring, immortal voices (cf. *Theog.* 39–40, 43) to sing a song that reflects the theogonic focus of the wider poem:

θεῶν γένος αἰδοῖον πρῶτον κλείουσιν ἀοιδῇ
ἐξ ἀρχῆς, οὓς Γαῖα καὶ Οὐρανὸς εὐρὺς ἔτικτεν,
οἵ τ' ἐκ τῶν ἐγένοντο, θεοὶ δωτῆρες ἐάων·

First in the song they sing of the august race of gods from the beginning, those whom Earth and wide Heaven engendered, and those who were born from them, gods, givers of blessings.
                                              Theogony 44–46

These goddesses have taught Hesiod καλὴν... ἀοιδήν ("beautiful song," *Theog.* 22), given him a staff of laurel, and breathed into him αὐδὴν | θέσπιν ("divine voice," *Theog.* 31–32):

---

[8] Cf. κ]ατ' ὄναρ σ(υμ)μείξας ταῖς Μούσ[αις, "talking with the Muses in a dream," Schol. Flor. 16; ἀ]ρτιγένειος ὤν, "with my first beard," Schol. Flor. 18.
[9] Cf. Parsons 1977: 49; M.A. Harder 1988: 2.

ἵνα κλείοιμι τά τ' ἐσσόμενα πρό τ' ἐόντα,
καί με κέλονθ' ὑμνεῖν μακάρων γένος αἰὲν ἐόντων,
σφᾶς δ' αὐτὰς πρῶτόν τε καὶ ὕστατον αἰὲν ἀείδειν.

...in order that I might celebrate future things and things past, and they ordered me to sing of the race of the blessed who are forever, and of themselves first and last always to sing.

Theogony 32–34

Accordingly, Hesiod tells of their own birth from Mnemosyne (Memory) and Zeus, nine like-minded (ὁμόφρονας, *Theog.* 60) maidens, whom he names as Clio, Euterpe, Thalia, Melpomene, Terpsichore, Erato, Polymnia, Urania, and Calliope (*Theog.* 77–79). It is these Muses with whom Callimachus portrays himself as having his dream conversation in *Aetia* book 1. The first to speak is Clio (Schol. Flor. 30), who tells him about the worship of the Graces on Paros as well as their genealogy (Schol. Flor. 30–32), a Hesiodic topic with which to begin, and one that also points the audience to the Graces of the *Theogony*, placed close to the Muses on Olympus by Hesiod (*Theog.* 64–65).

Clio gives her account in the first place in response to a question put by Callimachus about Parian ritual, κῶς ἄγ[ις αὐλῶν | ῥέζειν καὶ στεφέων εὔαδε τῷ Παρίῳ ("how is it that it pleases the Parian to sacrifice without garlands or [pipes]?" fr. 3 Pf. = 5 M.), which provides us with a good example of the kind of topic in which the Callimachus of *Aetia* books 1 and 2 is interested: the origins of Greek rituals and customs (particularly strange or anomalous ones). It is also clear that Callimachus himself made a further contribution to this opening exchange with Clio by listing suggested genealogies for the Graces (Schol. Flor. 32–35) before their birth from Dionysus and the nymph Coronis was confirmed by Clio. Hence we can see that the situation portrayed in *Aetia* books books 1 and 2 was one of genuine dialogue between Callimachus and the Muses—Callimachus does not simply ask a straightforward question and passively receive an answer. Nevertheless, Annette Harder (1988: 3–5) has suggested (persuasively) that we should see the invocations of the Muse in Homeric epic as well as the requests at the end of the Hesiodic Hymn to the Muses as antecedents for the dialogue in *Aetia* book 1.

At *Iliad* 14.508–510, for example, we have an address to the Muses (Μοῦσαι Ὀλύμπια δώματ' ἔχουσαι, "Muses who dwell on Olympus," 508) with an imperative "tell to me now" (ἔσπετε νῦν μοι, 508) followed by what is effectively the content of a question (ὅς τις δὴ πρῶτος βροτόεντ' ἀνδράγρι' Ἀχαιῶν | ἤρατ', "who was first of the Achaeans to carry off gory spoils," 509–510) and then the implied answer: Αἴας ῥα πρῶτος Τελαμώνιος ("Telamonian Ajax was the first," 511).[10] Hesiod's Hymn to the Muses exhibits a similar pattern, although on a much larger scale, where his invocation, praise, and genealogy of the Muses lead to the imperatives to the Muses as to the subject matter of his song at the close of the hymn:

κλείετε δ' ἀθανάτων ἱερὸν γένος αἰὲν ἐόντων,
οἳ Γῆς ἐξεγένοντο καὶ Οὐρανοῦ ἀστερόεντος,
Νυκτός τε δνοφερῆς, οὕς θ' ἁλμυρὸς ἔτρεφε Πόντος.

Tell of the holy race of the immortals who are forever, those born of Earth and starry Heaven, and of murky Night, and those whom briny Pontus reared.

Theogony 105–107

ταῦτά μοι ἔσπετε Μοῦσαι Ὀλύμπια δώματ' ἔχουσαι
ἐξ ἀρχῆς, καὶ εἴπαθ' ὅτι πρῶτον γένετ' αὐτῶν.

Tell these things to me, Muses who dwell on Olympus, from the beginning, and say which of them first came into being.

Theogony 114–115

We then hear (the beginning of) the answer: ἤτοι μὲν πρώτιστα Χάος γένετ'· ("first of all was the Chasm," *Theog.* 116). Here the responding utterance is not explicitly that of the Muses, who are invoked as a group, in marked contrast to the situation in *Aetia* book 1, where each of the Muses appears to have spoken in turn. This latter pattern is strongly suggested by fragment 43.56 Pf. (50.56 M.), where Clio speaks for the second time (Κλειὼ δὲ τὸ [δ]εύτερον ἤρχ[ετο μ]ύθ[ου]), in an *aition* that we can place in Book 2. We can also observe Calliope speaking in fragment 7.22 Pf. (9.22 M.), Erato in *SH* 238.8 (fr. 98.8 M.: Ἐρατὼ δ' ἀνταπάμειπτο τά[δε, "Erato answered in turn as follows"), and perhaps Polymnia in fragment 126.3 Pf. (76.3 M.):].πολυμ[.

These individualized Muses in *Aetia* books 1 and 2 reflect an ongoing process of specialization as to the province of each Muse that begins with Hesiod's naming of the nine in the *Theogony* and develops further through the picture that the Platonic Socrates presents in the *Phaedrus*,[11] where the dead cicadas who were once men report to the Muses on how mortals honor them with activities appropriate to

---

[10] Cf. also for explicit Homeric questions to the Muses *Il.* 2.761–62, 11.218–20, 16.112–13.

[11] On which see in general Murray 2002.

each: Terpsichore through choral dancing, Erato through erotic matters, and so forth (259c5–d7).[12] By the imperial period we can see that the traditional division of the Muses into the Muse of Epic, Muse of History, and so on has become established, but this clearly derives from a process well under way in the Hellenistic period, as suggested by the iconography of the Muses visible in *The Apotheosis of Homer* by the sculptor Archelaus of Priene.[13] However, we cannot say very much with certainty about the different narrative styles or subject matter of the individual Muses in *Aetia* books 1 and 2, because we do not have enough of each Muse's answers (cf. Massimilla 1996: 33). It is also almost impossible to tell to what extent the order in which Hesiod names the Muses, Plato's account in the *Phaedrus*, or the individual portrayals of other poets have shaped the organization of *Aetia* books books 1 and 2. It is suggestive (but no more) that the first two Muses to speak are Clio (named first in Hesiod's list at *Theog.* 77–79) and Calliope, whom Hesiod names last and calls προφερεστάτη ... ἁπασέων ("greatest of all," *Theog.* 79). Calliope is also the senior Muse in Plato's *Phaedrus* (259d3) and cited more frequently than the other Muses in early poetry (e.g., Alcman *PMG* 27, Sappho fr. 124 V., Bacch. 5.176–178).[14] Clio too is more prominent in earlier poetry than most of her sisters (e.g., at Bacch. 3.3; 12.1–3; 13.9, 228–231; Pind. *Nem.* 3.83). To judge by the frequency with which Bacchylides describes himself in relation to Urania (cf. χρυσάμπυκος Οὐρανίας | κλεινὸς θεράπων, "golden-headbanded Urania's glorious servant," Bacch. 5.13–14; also Bacch. 4.8, 6.11, 16.3) and the fact that she is the next oldest after Calliope in the *Phaedrus* (259d3–4), we might expect her to have spoken early in the order in the *Aetia*, but there is no evidence in the fragments to support this possibility.

The picture Callimachus presents of his interaction with the Muses is a very different one from that in the *Iliad* or the *Theogony*, in part because he does not present the Muses as his sole source of information or as the originators of the whole of the content of his song: contrast the dependence of Hesiod on the theogonic knowledge of the Muses, who have initiated him in this type of poetry (*Theog.* 32–34), or the explicit association of the Muses with knowledge and the narrator with ignorance at *Iliad* 2.485–486. At various points Callima-

---

[12] See Murray 2004: 374–375.
[13] See Murray 2004: 383 and 2005: 153, on the basis of Cohon 1991–92.
[14] Cf. Murray 2002: 42–43.

chus himself professes knowledge about customs and practices from around the Greek Mediterranean, such as the various Sicilian cities (including Gela, Minoa, Leontini, and Eryx) in which the founder is commemorated by name in the corresponding festival (fr. 43.46-55 Pf. = 50.46-55 M.). Here he marks his knowledge with the repeated οἶδα ("I know," ll. 46, 50), but this is information he appears to have derived from sources other than the Muses. What he seeks from Clio is explanation for the anomaly of the anonymous reference to the founder at Zancle and Messene rather than the entire account of the relevant Sicilian customs.

We can perhaps see one of the alternative sources for Callimachus' knowledge of the origins of Greek rituals in the symposium he depicts in fragment 178 Pf. (89 M.), if the suggestion is correct that this should be placed within the *Aetia* at the beginning of Book 2.[15] If this fragment formed part of the dream conversation with the Muses, it appears that Callimachus narrated his own earlier conversation with one Theugenes at a sympotic imitation in Alexandria of the Athenian festival of the Aiora, in memory of Erigone daughter of Icarius (fr. 178.3-6 Pf. = 89.3-6 M.). This earlier Callimachus was as interested in the origins of Greek customs and rituals as the Callimachus who is in conversation with the Muses. His question to Theugenes about the Ician worship of Peleus resembles the questions of Callimachus to the Muses, such as that concerning the celebration of the Cretan Theodaisia in Boeotia:

Μυρμιδόνων ἐσσῆνα τ[ί πάτριον ὔ]μμι σέβεσθαι
Πηλέα, κῶς Ἴκῳ ξυν[ὰ τὰ Θεσσαλι]κά

The Myrmidons' prince, Peleus: Why is it your ancestral custom to worship him? How are Thessalian things related to Icos?
      Callimachus fragment 178.23-24 Pf. (= 89.23-24 M.)

Κ]ισσούς‹σ›ης παρ' ὕδωρ Θεοδαίσια Κρῆ[σσαν ἑ]ορτὴν
ἡ] πόλις ἡ Κάδμου κῶς Ἁλίαρτος ἄγ[ει;

How is it that by the waters of Cissousa the Cretan festival of Theodaisia is celebrated by Haliartus, the city of Cadmus?
      Callimachus fragment 43.86-87 Pf. (= 50.86-87 M.)

---

[15] Cf. Zetzel 1981: 31-33; Alan Cameron 1995: 133-137; and now Fantuzzi and Hunter 2004: 80-81 for the history of the suggestion. Alan Cameron 1995: 134-135 suggests that the symposium in fr. 178 Pf. ends with the comments in fr. 43.12-17 Pf. = 50.12-17 M. about Callimachus recollecting only what he had heard at a symposium.

Callimachus, however, is not the first poet to reveal that there are other ways of coming to know of facts or narratives (cf. in general Morrison 2007: 73–90). In Solon, for example, the Muses are present not as the source for the narrator's knowledge of the condition of the polis but as deities to whom he prays for success and good reputation (much as one might do to Zeus or Athena).[16] Anacreon does not need to invoke the Muses for the sympotic subject matter of his poetry, nor does Theognis require them in his dealings with Cyrnus. (When they appear, it is in a mythological context, in lines 15–18.) This is part of a wider pattern in archaic and early classical poetry in which the Muses are the sources of mythological narratives,[17] but are not required when poets are telling of contemporary people or events.[18] Hence Simonides in his Plataea Elegy characterizes Homer as dependent on the Muses for his account of the Trojan War but invokes the Muse as his own ἐπίκουρος or "auxiliary," which portrays his own contribution as at least equal to that of the Muses (cf. Aloni 2001: 95):

οἷσιν ἐπ' ἀθά]νατον κέχυται κλέος ἀν[δρὸς] ἕκητι
  ὃς παρ' ἰοπ]λοκάμων δέξατο Πιερίδ[ων
πᾶσαν ἀλη]θείην

on whom [sc. the Greeks who conquered Troy] undying glory was poured by the grace of the man who received [the whole truth] from the [violet]-haired Pierides

Elegies fragment 11.15–17 W.

ἀλλὰ σὺ μὲ]ν νῦν χαῖρε, θεᾶς ἐρικυ[δέος υἱέ,
  κούρης εἰν]αλίου Νηρέος· αὐτὰρ ἐγώ[
κικλήισκω] σ' ἐπίκουρον ἐμοί, π[ολυώνυμ]ε Μοῦσα,
  εἴ πέρ γ' ἀν]θρώπων εὐχομένω[ν μέλεαι·

[But you] now farewell, famed goddess' [son], she who is marine Nereus' [girl], but I [call on] you as my auxiliary, Muse [of great name], [if] men's prayers [concern you at all].

Elegies fragment 11.19–22 W.

---

[16] On the stress in Solon on poetry as the creation of the poet rather than divine inspiration, see Noussia 2001: 49–50.

[17] For the Muses as inspiring such mythological narratives, see Stesichorus *PMG* 210.1 and in general Morrison 2007: 79–81.

[18] Cf. Ibycus *PMG* S151.23–48, in which he contrasts the Trojan War (on which the Muses can easily sing but mortals cannot) with his own contemporary subject, Polycrates.

The latter passage recalls (and internalizes) the ends of *Homeric Hymns* and their function as proems for epic song,[19] but it also marks the move from a mythological subject to one from the recent past (the battles against the Persians) and hence to a different relationship with the Muses. But some poets go further still. Pindar, for example, who can similarly portray the Muses as working alongside the poet to produce the song (e.g., *Ol.* 3.4–5),[20] regularly also cites as the source of his narrative "what men say" with no reference to the Muses, as in the following examples:[21]

> ἅ τοι Ποσειδάωνι μι-
> χθεῖσα Κρονίῳ λέγεται
> παῖδα ἰόπλοκον Εὐάδναν τεκέμεν.

She [*sc.* Pitana] is said to have coupled with Poseidon son of Cronus and given birth to violet-haired Evadna.
Olympian 6.28–30

> φαντὶ δ' ἀνθρώπων παλαιαί
> ῥήσιες, οὔπω, ὅτε χθό-
> να δατέοντο Ζεύς τε καὶ ἀθάνατοι…

The ancient sayings of men tell that when Zeus and the deathless ones were dividing up the earth, not yet…
Olympian 7.54–56

> φαντὶ γὰρ ξύν' ἀλέγειν
> καὶ γάμον Θέτιος ἄ-
> νακτα, καὶ νεαρὰν ἔδειξαν σοφῶν
> στόματ' ἀπείροισιν ἀρετὰν Ἀχιλέος·

…because they say that the king [*sc.* Zeus] with others honored the marriage of Thetis, and wise men's mouths have displayed to those unknowing of it the young excellence of Achilles.
Isthmian 8.46a–48

In part such statements about what "they say" are a way of talking about existing narrative traditions, particularly earlier poetic versions, which is explicit in the use of "they say" in *Isthmian* 8, in the last of the passages quoted above (the σοφοί or "wise men" are clearly poets).

---

[19] See further Parsons 1992: 32.
[20] See further on Pindar and the Muses Morrison 2007: 84–89.
[21] Cf. Scodel 2001: 124. This use of a "they say" statement or the like to attribute a narrative to tradition is not exclusive to Pindar (cf. Sappho fr. 166 V.; Alcaeus frr. 42.1, 343 V.; Bacch. 5.57, 5.155, fr. 20A.14), but he does seem particularly fond of it: cf. also *Ol.* 2.28, 9.49; *Pyth.* 1.52, 2.22, 6.21; *Nem.* 7.84, 9.39; *Pae.* 12.9; *Dith.* 1.15.

But they also remind us that in Greek poetry before the Hellenistic period the picture of the relationship between Muses and poets is not uniformly one of dependence of poet on Muse, and that the Muses are not universally presented as the only medium for poets to gain access to the events of the distant mythological past. The references to tradition and to the narratives of earlier poets form an antecedent to the use of "poet-guarantors" such as Hipponax in the *Iambi*, which we examined above.

When we consider the alternative sayings that can provide narrative material for earlier poets, it is also striking that the alternative to the Muses that Callimachus presents in fragment 178 Pf. (89 M.) should be another conversation. In gathering the knowledge on display in *Aetia* books 1 and 2 both the exchange with Theugenes and the conversation with the Muses replace the Library and its texts with a setting that privileges an oral mode of communication over the more bookish research that very probably stands behind the erudition of the poem,[22] and that may itself reflect the language of orality and speech in Callimachus' poetic predecessors. Nevertheless, the impression created of Callimachus and the Muses is very much one of a learned scholar in discussion with even more erudite Muses, one who seeks (as Gregory Hutchinson 1988: 44 has put it) "from superior authority the solution of some recondite problems about anomalies and curiosities." Their similarity, and the pronounced shift in the relationship between poet and Muse as compared with Homer or Hesiod, is apparent from the beginning of Calliope's reply in fragment 7 Pf. (9 M.):

Αἰγλήτην Ἀνάφην τε, Λακωνίδι γείτονα Θήρῃ,
 π]ρῶτ[ον ἐνὶ μ]νήμῃ κάτθεο καὶ Μινύας,
ἄρχμενος ὡς ἥρωες ἀπ' Αἰήταο Κυταίου
 αὖτις ἐς ἀρχαίην ἔπλεον Αἱμονίην

The Shining One and Anaphe, neighbor of Laconian Thera, first set down in your memory, and the Minyans, beginning with how the heroes sailed back from Cytaean Aeetes to ancient Haemonia.
  Callimachus fragment 7.23–26 Pf. (= 9.23–26 M.)

Here we can observe that Calliope uses language that recalls the typical language of narrators at the beginning of songs (e.g., μνήσομαι,

---

[22] Cf. Morrison 2007: 187; and for the interaction of oralist and literary elements in the *Aetia*, see Bruss 2004.

"I shall recall," at the beginning of several *Homeric Hymns*)[23] but also reverses the normal request of poet to Muse to sing of a particular topic, and in a sense reveals and domesticates the process of inspiration of the poet by the Muse: almost *Don't forget what I'm going to tell you* (cf. D'Alessio 1996: 2.386 n. 49). Further differences in the situation in *Aetia* books 1 and 2 follow from the fact that the Muses themselves take over as narrators of particular *aitia* rather than providing the inspiration for the primary narrator's own narrative. Because of the uncertainty over the attribution of several fragments to particular speakers in *Aetia* books 1 and 2, it is difficult to talk with certainty about the precise character of the Muses' narratives; but it seems likely that in some ways the Muses' way of telling stories recalls that of Callimachus himself. There are, for example, possible addresses by the Muses to characters in a narrative at fragments 23.2–7 Pf. (25.2–7 M.: to Heracles),[24] 24.2–6 Pf. (26.2–6 M.: also to Heracles),[25] 27 Pf. (28 M.: to Linus),[26] 28 Pf. (29 M.: again to Linus), and 37 Pf. (44 M.: to Athena). Such apostrophes, and the explicit expression of narratorial judgment passed on Heracles at fragment 23.6 Pf. (25.6 M.: to Heracles), ἐσσὶ] γὰρ οὐ μάλ' ἐλαφρός ("because you are not very clever"), would make the Muses' own narratives resemble the emotionally engaged manner that we see Callimachus himself employ (cf., e.g., fr. 43.84–85 Pf. = 50.84–85 M., on his reaction to Clio's speech).[27]

The most extensive surviving Muse's speech from books 1 and 2 of the *Aetia* is that of Clio about Zancle in fragment 43 Pf. (50 M.). Here we can see something of the relaxed and familiar nature of the Muses' conversation with Callimachus in the detail that Clio is resting her

---

[23] Cf., e.g., *HHAp.* 1, *HHom.* 7.2. At the beginning of the Iliadic Catalogue of Ships the narrator states that he would not be able to tell of the mass of men who came to Troy εἰ μὴ...Μοῦσαι | μνησαίαθ' ("unless...the Muses were to recall," *Il.* 2.492) their names.

[24] This fragment concerns the reasons why at Lindus they accompany their sacrifices to Heracles with abuse, one of Callimachus' questions at fr. 7.20–21 Pf. = 9.20–21 M., which suggests that the speaker is a Muse (probably Calliope) responding to Callimachus. See Massimilla 1996: 285, although Hutchinson 1988: 45 and 47 thinks Callimachus is speaking.

[25] For a Muse as the speaker here, see Massimilla 1996: 294. Hollis 1982: 118 suggests that the emotional language in this fragment is more appropriate in the mouth of Callimachus.

[26] Cf. Massimilla 1996: 299, 302.

[27] On the use of emotional and evaluative language in the *Aetia*, see further Morrison 2007: 185–186, 192–197.

hand on her sister's shoulder (fr. 43.57 Pf. = 50.57 M.) as she begins her response, but we see also the extent of the Muses' knowledge:

ἀλλήλοις δ' ἐλύησαν· ἐς Ἀπόλ[λωνα δ' ἰόν]τες
εἴρονθ' ὁπποτέρου κτίσμα λέγοιτ[ο νέον.
αὐτὰρ ὁ φῆ, μήτ' οὖν Περιήρεος ἄ[στυ]ρ[ον εἶ]ναι
κεῖνο πολισσούχου μήτε Κραταιμέ[νεος.
φῆ θεός· οἱ δ' ἀΐοντες ἀπέδραμον, ἐ[κ δ' ἔτι κεί]νου
γαῖα τὸν οἰκιστὴν οὐκ ὀνομαστὶ κ[αλε]ῖ,
ὧδε δέ μιν καλέουσιν ἐπ' ἔντομα δημ[ι]οεργοί·
"ἵ]λαος ἡμετέρην ὅστις ἔδειμε [πόλ]ιν
ἐρ]χέσθω μετὰ δαῖτα, πάρεστι δὲ καὶ δύ' ἄγεσθαι
κ]αὶ πλέας· οὐκ ὀλ[ί]γως α[ἷ]μα βοὸς κέχυ[τ]αι."

There was discord between them. Going to Apollo they asked to which of them the new colony should belong. But he declared that the townlet should have as its city guardian neither Perieres nor Crataemenes. The god spoke, and having heard him they went off. From that day still the land does not summon its founder by name; rather, the magistrates summon him to the sacrifice as follows: "Whoever built our city, may he be favorable; let him come to the banquet, and it is permitted to bring two or more guests. Not meanly has the blood of an ox been poured out."
Callimachus fragment 43.74–83 Pf. (= 50.74–83 M.)

Here Clio knows not only the details of the quarrel between the founders of Zancle and how this has led to their not being named in the sacrifice, but even the precise form of words employed at the ritual because of their peculiar anonymity. Before the passage quoted above she also includes a scholarly parenthesis about the sickle that Cronus used to castrate his father (κεῖθι γὰρ ᾧ τὰ γονῆος ἀπέθρισε μήδε' ἐκεῖνος | κέκρυπται γύπῃ ζάγκλον ὑπὸ χθονίῃ, "there, you see, is hidden in a cave in the ground the sickle that that one used to prune the genitals of his father," fr. 43.70–71 Pf. = 50.70–71 M.), which also functions as an allusion to the etymology of Zancle ("Sickle").[28]

The picture Callimachus presents of learned Muses in conversation with an erudite Alexandrian interlocutor on a range of obscure and peculiar Greek rituals and customs fits in well with Penny Murray's suggestion that in the Hellenistic period the Muses develop into goddesses who preside not simply over song and dance but over the whole of scholarship, learning, and education (see Murray 2004: 385–86). It is also worth remembering when considering the role of the Muses in *Aetia* books 1 and 2 that Callimachus was working in an institution,

---

[28] Cf. Morrison 2007: 195.

the Alexandrian Museum ("Shrine of the Muses") and its associated Library, which was formally at least directed at the worship of the Muses and under the direction of a priest (cf. Fraser 1972: 1.315-16; Erskine 1995: 38-40). This in itself is part of the development of the Muses into goddesses of learning, which may in turn have been influenced by the Musea ("Muse sanctuaries") of the Athenian Academy and Lyceum (cf. Erskine 1995: 39-40; Murray 2004: 378), but it serves to reinforce the very different relationship between poet and Muses with which Callimachus plays in *Aetia* books 1 and 2 (especially the investigative quality of their enterprise and their shared interests and erudition), particularly if the first audience of the poem was itself made up of members of the Museum and received it within the Museum itself.

Before turning to the second two books of the *Aetia* it is useful to compare two passages from Callimachus' *Hymns* that resemble the treatment of the Muses in *Aetia* books 1 and 2. In contrast with their invocation at the beginnings of several *Homeric Hymns*,[29] which form one of Callimachus' chief models,[30] the Muses in fact hardly feature at all in the *Hymns* of Callimachus. The Muses are named as such only in the *Hymn to Delos* (ll. 5, 7, 82, 252), the most important passage being that in which the narrator asks the Muses a question:

ἐμαὶ θεαὶ εἴπατε Μοῦσαι,
ἦ ῥ' ἐτεὸν ἐγένοντο τότε δρύες ἡνίκα Νύμφαι;
"Νύμφαι μὲν χαίρουσιν, ὅτε δρύας ὄμβρος ἀέξει,
Νύμφαι δ' αὖ κλαίουσιν, ὅτε δρυσὶ μηκέτι φύλλα."

---

[29] Cf. *HHMerc.* 1, *HHVen.* 1, *HHom.* 9.1, 14.2, 17.1, 19.1, 20.1, 31.1-2 (Calliope named), 32.1, 33.1 (the last two examples are to plural Muses; the rest, to a single Muse).

[30] As far as we can tell the Muses were also not prominent in the *Hecale*, which begins Ἀκταίη τις ἔναιεν Ἐρεχθέος ἔν ποτε γουνῶι ("An Actaean woman lived once on a hill of Erechtheus," fr. 1 H.), a striking divergence from Homer, and Greek epic in general, where it is normal to invoke a Muse. It may be that the Muse received a mention in the following lines: "tell her story, Muse," or "tell how she and Theseus met"; but in any case her removal from the first line is significant. It may be, however, that the absence of a Muse invocation is part of a strategy of narratorial unobtrusiveness in the *Hecale* (on which see Morrison 2007: 191 n. 471), in marked contrast to the other Hellenistic epic that marginalizes the Muses, the *Argonautica*, which begins with a bold first-person statement—μνήσομαι ("I shall recall," A.R. 1.2). The absence of Muses may also be meant to advertise the difference between the *Hecale* and archaic epic, which is also clear from the first word of the first line—"an Actaean woman" (cf. Lynn 1995: 7-8 and Fantuzzi and Hunter 2004: 198-199), inverting the "man" (ἄνδρα, *Od.* 1.1) of the *Odyssey*—and from the "once upon a time" opening that gives the *Hecale* the feel of a folktale, very different from epics beginning with the Muses.

> My goddesses, tell me, Muses, is it true that oaks are born at the same time as their Nymphs? "The Nymphs are glad when the rain makes the oaks grow, and the Nymphs lament when the oaks no longer have leaves."
>
> *Hymn* 4.82–85

It appears that the Muses themselves reply in lines 84 and 85 (cf. Mineur 1984: 117), and in one sense this question-and-answer pattern reminds us of the *Aetia*, but it is also important to note that here the question is asked of and answered by the Muses as a whole, a rather different arrangement from the speeches of the individualized Muses in *Aetia* books 1 and 2. Nevertheless it may be that we are meant here to recall the situation of the *Aetia*, and the close relationship of Callimachus and the Muses there depicted: it is certainly striking that the narrator here should refer to the Muses as "my goddesses," as this use of a possessive pronoun with Muses being invoked has no precedent (cf. Mineur 1984: 118). The closest parallel is the description of a single Muse by Pindar as μᾶτερ ἀμετέρα ("my mother") at the beginning of *Nemean* 3, where he is invoking her as ὦ πότνια Μοῦσα ("O Queen Muse").[31] But we cannot be sure of the relative chronology of *Aetia* books 1 and 2 and the *Hymn to Delos*.

It may be that we should read the question to the Muses in the *Hymn to Delos* against the background of a similar question in the preceding *Hymn to Artemis*:

> τίς δέ νύ τοι νήσων, ποῖον δ' ὄρος εὔαδε πλεῖστον,
> τίς δὲ λιμήν, ποίη δὲ πόλις; τίνα δ' ἔξοχα νυμφέων
> φίλαο καὶ ποίας ἡρωΐδας ἔσχες ἑταίρας;
> εἰπέ, θεή, σὺ μὲν ἄμμιν, ἐγὼ δ' ἑτέροισιν ἀείσω.
>
> Which now of the islands, which hill pleases you most? Which harbor, which city? Which nymph do you love most, and which heroines do you have as companions? You tell me, Goddess, and I will sing it to others.
>
> *Hymn* 3.183–86

These questions are to Artemis herself but treat her very much like a Muse: formally the questions resemble some of those implicitly put to the Muses in Homer (e.g., Ἔνθα τίνα πρῶτον τίνα δ' ὕστατον ἐξενάριξαν | Ἕκτωρ τε Πριάμοιο πάϊς καὶ χάλκεος Ἄρης; "Then whom first and whom last did Hector son of Priam and bronze Ares slay?" *Il.* 5.703–704), and line 186 figures Artemis as the source of knowledge

---

[31] Cf. Morrison 2007: 151–152.

for which the poet will act as a conduit to the audience through his song, which is the traditional relationship of poet to Muse, as at Pindar, fragment 150 S.-M., μαντεύεο, Μοῖσα, προφατεύσω δ' ἐγώ ("Muse, you prophesy, and I shall interpret"), and Theocritus *Idyll* 22.116–17, εἰπέ, θεά, σὺ γὰρ οἶσθα, ἐγὼ δ' ἑτέρων ὑποφήτης | φθέγξομαι ("Tell, goddess, because you know, and I shall speak as the interpreter for others"). Why should Callimachus depict Artemis as a Muse?

The narrator of the *Hymn to Artemis* is unusually garrulous for a Callimachean narrator, and this may be a response to the fact that he declares at the beginning of the hymn that it is "no small thing for those singing to forget her" (*Hymn* 3.1) and closes with the need to avoid her anger and a catalogue of those unfortunates who have provoked it (*Hymn* 3.260–67): he thus tries to crowbar as much praise as possible into the hymn.[32] Perhaps the Muselike invocation is another strategy to avoid giving Artemis offense and reinforces the final request to her to receive the narrator's song graciously (*Hymn* 3.268). But the joke may be on Artemis, who is not normally closely associated with music or song—her hymn is sandwiched between two for her twin brother (and rival),[33] Apollo (the *Hymn to Apollo* and the *Hymn to Delos*), who is a musical god and often closely associated with the Muses. Both the *Hymn to Apollo* and the *Hymn to Delos* seem systematically to marginalize Artemis, and it may be that the invocation to the Muses themselves at *Hymn* 4.82–85 should prompt us to recall the Muselike (but inappropriate?) invocation of Artemis in the preceding hymn.[34]

Let us return to the *Aetia:* Callimachus did not persist with the framework of the Muse dialogue of *Aetia* books 1 and 2 in the second two books of the poem.[35] In *Aetia* 3 and 4 we find instead discrete sections (such as *The Victory of Berenice, SH* 254–268, or the narrative of *Acontius and Cydippe*, frr. 67–75 Pf.), which were probably without an outer connecting frame.[36] Book 3 begins not with the Muses but with Berenice (i.e., Berenice II, the Cyrenaean wife of Ptolemy III

---

[32] On the verbosity of the narrator of *Hymn* 3, see Morrison 2007: 138–147.

[33] For their rivalry, see *Hymn* 3.83, 250; and Haslam 1993: 115.

[34] For a more positive view of the role of Artemis as a patroness of song in *Hymn* 3 (with reference to 3.136–37), see Bing and Uhrmeister 1994: 26–28. On the marginalization of Artemis in *Hymn* 4, see Morrison 2007: 147–149.

[35] Alan Cameron 1995: 138 suggests this is because Callimachus may have awakened from his dream at the end of *Aetia* book 2: cf. *SH* 253.7, 14.

[36] For useful comments on the structure of the *Aetia* as a whole and in particular *Aetia* 3 and 4, cf. Fantuzzi and Hunter 2004: 44–49.

Euergetes), in a section celebrating her victory in the chariot race at Nemea:

Ζηνί τε καὶ Νεμέῃ τι χαρίσιον ἕδνον ὀφείλω,
 νύμφα κα[σιγνή]των ἱερὸν αἷμα θεῶν,
ἡμ[ε]τερο [......] εων ἐπινίκιον ἵππω[ν.
 ἁρμοῖ γὰρ Δαναοῦ γῆς ἀπὸ βουγενέος
εἰς Ἑλένη[ς νησῖδ]α καὶ εἰς Παλληνέα μά[ντιν,
 ποιμένα [φωκάων], χρύσεον ἦλθεν ἔπος.

To Zeus and to Nemea I owe a wedding gift of thanks, O Bride, Holy Blood of the Sibling Gods, our...victory song of horses. Because just now from the ox-born land of Danaus to the [isle] of Helen and the Pallenian seer, shepherd of [seals], came a golden word.
Fragment 383 Pf. + SH 254. 1–6 (= 143. 1–6 M.)

Berenice operates here as a surrogate Muse: she is addressed in a quasi-divine capacity as "Holy Blood of the...Gods" (SH 254.2) and stands in the place normally occupied in poetry celebrating athletic or equestrian success by various gods, including the eponymous nymphs of various cities and the Muses.[37] Berenice in fact frames the second half of the *Aetia*: the final *aition* is *The Lock of Berenice* (fr. 110 Pf.), in which Callimachus tells of the astronomer Conon's discovery among the stars of a lock of Berenice's hair, which she dedicated in fulfillment of a vow to do so should Ptolemy III return victorious from war. Should we read Berenice's prominence in *Aetia* 3 and 4 as usurping the role of the Muses in the earlier part of the poem? It may be rather that we are simply to see Berenice as another Muse, but one who provides the content for Callimachus' poem in a different manner (through her own achievements). It is relevant in this connection that Callimachus adds her to the Graces:

Τέσσαρες αἱ Χάριτες· ποτὶ γὰρ μία ταῖς τρισὶ τήναις
 ἄρτι ποτεπλάσθη κἤτι μύροισι νοτεῖ.
εὐαίων ἐν πᾶσιν ἀρίζηλος Βερενίκα,
 ἇς ἄτερ οὐδ' αὐταὶ ταὶ Χάριτες Χάριτες.

The Graces are four: because in addition to those three, one
 has just been shaped and is still wet with unguents.
Happy and conspicuous among all Berenice,
 without whom not even the Graces themselves are Graces.
Epigram 51 Pf. (=15 GP)

---

[37] Cf. Morrison 2007: 196. For the Muses at the beginning of epinician odes, see Pind. *Ol.* 10; *Pyth.* 4; *Nem.* 3 and 9. Victors are rarely addressed at the start of such poems: cf. *Isthm.* 4 *init.*; Bacch. 5 *init.*

The Graces, of course, are closely associated with the Muses in Greek poetry (e.g., Hes. *Theog.* 64–65), and in particular in *Aetia* books 1 and 2, where the first *aition* told by a Muse concerns the Graces (frr. 3–7.18 Pf. = 5–9.18 M.) and is followed by a request from Callimachus to guarantee his poem's long-lasting success:

ἔλλατε νῦν, ἐλέγοισι δ' ἐνιψήσασθε λιπώσας
χεῖρας ἐμοῖς, ἵνα μοι πουλὺ μένωσιν ἔτος.

Now be favorable, and upon my elegies wipe your glistening
hands, so that they may endure for me for many years.
Callimachus fragment 7.13–14 (= 9.13–14 M.)

We should then think of Callimachus not as rejecting the Muses in *Aetia* 3 and 4, nor even perhaps of him asserting greater independence, but as showing the relationship of poet to Muse in a different perspective from that in *Aetia* books 1 and 2. (Cf. in general Morrison 2007: 196–197.) In the tale *Acontius and Cydippe* from *Aetia* 3, for example, Callimachus points us back to how Calliope began her *aition* in *Aetia* book 1 at fragment 7 Pf. (= 9 M.):

Κεῖε, τεὸν δ' ἡμεῖς ἵμερον ἐκλύομεν
τόνδε παρ' ἀρχαίου Ξενομήδεος, ὅς ποτε πᾶσαν
νῆσον ἐνὶ μνήμῃ κάτθετο μυθολόγῳ,
ἄρχμενος ὡς...

Cean, we heard of this love of yours
from ancient Xenomedes, who once the whole
island set down in a memoir about its mythology,
beginning with how...
Callimachus fragment 75.53–56 Pf.

Here the description of Xenomedes' history is strongly reminiscent of Calliope's injunction to Callimachus, ἐνὶ μ]νήμῃ κάτθεο...| ἄρχμενος ὡς ("set down in your memory...beginning with how," fr. 7.24–25 Pf. = 9.24–25 M.). Now, however, Callimachus presents himself as having direct access to a work of scholarship (Xenomedes' history of Ceos), which is again later explicitly the source for his narrative: it is thence that the story comes ἐς ἡμετέρην...Καλλιόπην ("to our Calliope," fr. 75.76–77 Pf.). In one sense to discover that (after all) Calliope was reading comically exposes what Jon Bruss calls the "oralist fiction" of the conversation with the Muses in books 1 and 2 of the *Aetia*, a conversation that itself (of course) Callimachus writes down. (Cf. Morrison 2007: 197 n. 493.) It also suggests that we need to reinterpret the relationship of poet and Muses that we saw in *Aetia* books 1 and 2—we are being allowed to see here what appears to be a more realistic picture of the processes of research and composition that stand behind the *Aetia* as compared with the dream conversation of *Aetia* books 1 and 2. The different ways Callimachus uses the Muses to articulate his relationship with earlier poetry and scholarship perhaps came together at the very end of *Aetia* 4 in the so-called *Epilogue* (fr. 112 Pf.),[38] where the image of Hesiod tending his sheep on Helicon is repeated from the beginning of *Aetia* book 1, and where Callimachus announces his intention to pass on to the Μουσέων πεζὸν…νομόν ("Muses' prose pasture," fr. 112.9 Pf.),[39] which may be a reference to the kind of scholarship on which he and his Muses have drawn deeply throughout the four books of the *Aetia*.[40]

---

[38] Knox has suggested that this originally stood at the end of *Aetia* book 2. On this model it was transferred to the end of *Aetia* 4 by Callimachus (Knox 1985a: 64–65) or an editor (Knox 1993; Alan Cameron 1995: 154–160).

[39] There may also have been an address to a Muse in the closing section of the *Aetia* at fr. 112, beginning in line 3, which may have ended with the imperative "Farewell" in line 7, though this is controversial—cf. Pfeiffer 1949–53: 1.124.

[40] Cf. Hutchinson 2003: 58 n. 31 on the possibility that the reference here is not to the *Iambi* but to prose works of scholarship.

CHAPTER SEVENTEEN

CALLIMACHUS AND THE ATTHIDOGRAPHERS

Giovanni Benedetto

ABSTRACT

This chapter illustrates the role played by the local chronicles of Athens and Attica within Callimachus' oeuvre. In recent years research on Callimachus has increasingly stressed the importance of local antiquities as an essential part of the connective tissue of Callimachean poetry. Among local chronicles of the Greek world used as sources by Callimachus particularly relevant were the Atthidographers, the authors of a series of histories (*Atthides*) composed between the end of the fifth century and the middle of the third century BC that chronicled the Athenian and Attic past. After tracing a history of the modern studies about Atthidography from Wilamowitz to Jacoby, the paper examines the role of some Atthidographers in Callimachus' poetry, especially in the *Aetia* and *Hecale*. It also considers the decisive contribution of Callimachus and his school (in particular Istrus) to the definition and preservation of the Atthidographic tradition until Philochorus.

Hecale and Her Attic Roots

Research on Callimachus has stressed more and more the importance of local antiquities as an essential part of the "connective tissue" of Callimachean poetry (cf. Lehnus 1999: 205; Ragone 2006: 74). Among Callimachus' sources the local historians played an important role in the *Aetia*: "the very subject-matter of the *aitia* comes largely from prose, from local historians," and their use in a dialogue with the Muses "increases the complexity of the relationship in the work between prose and poetry" (Hutchinson 2003: 48). Thus Callimachus' interest in antiquities is interwoven into the whole of his activity as scholar and poet.[1]

---

[1] For the fundamental and lifelong link of Callimachus with history and myths of Cyrene, see Lehnus 1994a.

The clearest evidence we have about the authors of local histories used by Callimachus attests Xenomedes of Ceos (explicitly mentioned in fr. 75.54–55 Pf.), the Argives Agias and Dercylus (Lehnus 2004a), and Meandrius of Miletus.[2] Among local chronicles of the Greek world a prominent part was certainly reserved for Attica, and within Callimachus' oeuvre Attica is primarily relevant for the *Hecale*, but also in the *Aetia* every book contained something about the region (Hollis 1992a: 6). The *Hecale* itself was likely to have been an *aition* of the local cult of Zeus Hecaleius;[3] Callimachus' attention was probably drawn to it by a work of the last and most important of the Atthidographers, Philochorus, quoted by Plutarch in his *Life of Theseus* (*FGrHist* 328 F 109), at the end of the chapter where we find the story of both the encounter between Theseus and Hecale and the institution of a cult of Zeus Hecaleius.

According to the definition that opens Felix Jacoby's *Atthis* (1949), Atthidographers were "the group of writers who from the closing years of the fifth century BC down to the end of the Chremonidean War in 263/2 BC narrated the history of Athens and of Athens alone"—a series from Hellanicus of Lesbos to Philochorus, who died in the aftermath of the Chremonidean War.[4] *Atthis* is the title commonly used for the chronicles of the Atthidographers. Modern work on them starts from the chapter "Die Atthis" in the first volume of Wilamowitz's *Aristoteles und Athen* (1893). "With incomparable courage and quickness of mind"[5] Ulrich von Wilamowitz-Moellendorff (1848–1931) wrote his book after F.G. Kenyon's publication of the papyrus of Aristotle's *Athenaion politeia* (January 1891). The pages of "Die Atthis" in *Aristoteles und Athen* concern the sources of the first section of the newly discovered Aristotelian treatise, namely the part dealing with the most ancient Athenian history and the various phases of the *politeia* up to the restoration of democracy in 403 BC. In Wilamowitz's view the account of Aristotle is based, especially but not exclusively in the chronological

---

[2] See Polito 2006. For the chronicle of Athanadas of Ambracia as source in *Aetia* 3, see Lehnus 2004b: 29; about Sicyon, see Puricelli 2004; survey of prose sources in the poetry of Callimachus in Krevans 2004: 178–181.

[3] Hollis 1992a: 4, who notes that this is a cult "for which we do not at present have any evidence unconnected with Philochorus and Callimachus."

[4] Jacoby 1949: 1. See also the definitions given by Harding 1994: 1 and 2008: 1.

[5] Pfeiffer 1968: 82. Among older works, still worth mentioning is Boeckh's essay "Über den Plan der Atthis des Philochoros" (1832) = Boeckh 1871: 397–429.

parts, on an *attische Chronik* developed by a group of interpreters of sacred law, the ἐξηγηταί. From the chronicle of the *exegetai*, according to Wilamowitz published around the year 380 by an anonymous editor ("den herausgeber der exegetenchronik"),[6] arose the first *Atthis*, of Hellanicus, and from him all subsequent Atthidographers.

To the features of the original *Atthis*, the primeval chronicle source of the Atthidographic tradition, Wilamowitz attributed a particular disposition "to fix the antiquities of the city cult, and to interpret them, mostly through aetiological sagas."[7] Two years after the publication of the *Athenaion politeia* and in the same year as *Aristoteles und Athen*, another papyrus find gave Wilamowitz the opportunity to perceive traces of the activity of the Atthidographers in the very poetry, set in an Attic milieu, of the greatest among Alexandrian poets, Callimachus. In 1893 Theodor Gomperz published the edition of the Tabula Vindobonensis, a wooden tablet containing about sixty verses in four columns from Callimachus' *Hecale* (now frr. 69, 70, 73, 74 H.). *Über die Hekale des Kallimachos*, the study written by Wilamowitz in that same year, focuses on columns II–IV. They contain a fascinating dialogue between two birds, one of them a crow and the other probably a younger crow.[8] Gomperz had already recognized as the subject of the birds' conversation the story of the banishment of the crows from the Acropolis by order of Athena. According to Antigonus of Carystus, the story was mentioned by the Atthidographer Amelesagoras (now *FGrHist* 330 F 1). Callimachus tells here an αἴτιον, strictly connected to Attic primordial history and presented through the dialogue of the birds.

The source of the episode is commonly considered to have been Amelesagoras (Hollis 2009: 7, 227, 229). A rich and lively discussion involving several generations of scholars has led currently to a largely shared vision of the *Vogelszene*. The episode needs to be read with reference to the myth of Erichthonius and the daughters of Cecrops, and is at the same time probably to be connected with the news of

---

[6] About Wilamowitz's book and his theory of the chronicle kept by the *exegetai*, see Chambers 1985: 226–229.

[7] Wilamowitz 1893b: 1.279, noting that the chronicle was especially attentive to "die altertümer der städtischen cultes im weitesten sinne zu fixiren und, meist durch aetiologische sagen, zu erläutern."

[8] About the identity of the second bird, the listener, see most recently Moscadi 2003.

Hecale's death, which is still unknown to Theseus.[9] Among contributions to the interpretation of the newly published Tabula Vindobonensis, Wilamowitz's article stands out for its clarity and breadth of view, particularly in the pages devoted to the astonishing verses set *im Vogelreiche*. Through their elucidation Callimachus' sensibility for Attic stories is made clear. Commenting on verses 13–14 from the third column, Wilamowitz notes that Gomperz's brilliant reconstruction of the verses αὐτὰρ ἐγὼ τυτθὸς παρέην γόνος, ὀγδοάτη γάρ | ἤδη μοι γενεὴ πέλεται (cf. fr. 73.13–14 H.)[10] finds support in the Athenian *Königsliste* given by Philochorus: Aegeus, "under whom the crow tells her story," is named as eighth king after Cecrops (Wilamowitz 1893b: 734). Consequently, as Adrian Hollis puts it, "it would be appropriate enough for the crow born in the reign of Cecrops to be in her eighth generation under Aegeus" (Hollis 2009: 242).

Almost nothing survives from the Atthidographers about Aegeus, the father of Theseus. They both appear at the very beginning of the *diegesis* preserving the argumentum of the *Hecale*: "having escaped the attempt on his life by Medea, Theseus was being carefully guarded by his father, Aegeus, who had not expected the youth's sudden arrival from Troezen" (translation Nisetich 2001: 3). In the absence of any fragment of the Atthidographers about Theseus' birth, his childhood, and his deeds on the way from Troezen to Athens (Harding 2008: 54), Plutarch's *Life*, much more than the version in Apollodorus, offers a coherent thread for reconstructing the entire story of Theseus.[11] The value of this work is unique, since "no extant author of antiquity ever attempted to make a reasonable and sensible history out of the corpus of fables surrounding a legendary figure" (Frost 2005: 81–82).

The *Life of Theseus* displays a large number of quotations from Plutarch's sources, a good third of which come from the Atthidographers, especially the first (Hellanicus) and the last (Philochorus).[12] A question much discussed since the nineteenth century is how much

---

[9] See Hollis 2009: 225; D'Alessio 2007: 1.316–21; Fantuzzi and Hunter 2002: 273; Asper 2004: 301, 303. Kerkhecker 1993 dwells on obscurities and doubts arising from the entire *Vogelszene*; about the absence of Erichthonius' name, see now Skempis 2008.

[10] "But I was a tiny chick then, [eight] generations ago," transl. Nisetich 2001: 17.

[11] Ward 1970: 7–24, with iconographic material. For the copious modern bibliography about Theseus, see the discussion of Walker 1995.

[12] Six from Philochorus and five from Hellanicus: list of passages in Frost 2005: 83–84.

direct knowledge Plutarch had of the Atthidographers. It is commonly thought that Philochorus was the only Atthidographer whose work was still available in Plutarch's time: open to question is whether Plutarch read Philochorus' *Atthis*,[13] finding there the opinions of other Atthidographers as well, or made use only of the Συναγωγὴ τῶν Ἀτθίδων written by Istrus in the second half of the third century as "something of an anthology of the Atthidographers."[14] What matters for the *Hecale* is the significance of Plutarch's *Life* as storehouse of the Atthidographic tradition about Aegeus and Theseus, revised by Philochorus and Istrus. Istrus is quoted in the *Life of Theseus* only once, in chapter 34, though that entire chapter perhaps should be regarded as an excerpt from his work (cf. Jacoby 1954: 1.633). Plutarch mentions "Istrus in Book 13 of his *Attica*" for his "original and entirely extraordinary story" about the abduction by Hector of Aethra, the mother of Theseus (*FGrHist* 334 F 7).[15] Moreover, Plutarch's catalogue περὶ γάμων Θησέως in chapter 29 of the *Life* is generally acknowledged as deriving from Istrus, who according to Athenaeus "in Book 14 of the *Attica* gave a list of Theseus' women" (*FGrHist* 334 F 10).[16] From Istrus again probably comes what in the same context is said about Theseus' father, Aegeus,[17] who likewise "had many wives... and associated with a great number of women outside of wedlock" until "he took Aethra, the daughter of Pittheus, and after her Medea" (trans. Harding 2008: 69).

The *diegesis* reveals that *Hecale*'s first verse was Ἀκταίη τις ἔναιεν Ἐρεχθέος ἔν ποτε γουνῷ ("once there lived an Attic woman in the hill country of Erechtheus"). Hollis has connected to it fragment 231 Pf., thus masterfully restoring the beginning of Callimachus' *Hecale*, with the aid of a passage from Michael Choniates (Hollis 1997a and 2009: 425). The poem opened in the name of Hecale,[18] along with Erechtheus, a "founding father" of Athens (Harding 2008: 47). On the

---

[13] See Ampolo 1988: XLVI–XLVII, and now Costa 2007: 175–176.
[14] Dillery 2005: 509, with the convenient addition that "preciously little is known" about Istrus and his works. See now Berti 2009.
[15] Translated in Harding 2008: 68–69.
[16] Ἴστρος γοῦν ἐν τῇ τεσσαρεσκαιδεκάτῃ τῶν Ἀττικῶν καταλέγων τὰς τοῦ Θησέως γενομένας γυναῖκάς φησιν...: transl. Harding 2008: 69.
[17] Cf. Berti 2009: 88. "Primi viderunt Wilamowitz et Wellmann" in the eighties of the nineteenth century: see Schwartz 1917: 95.
[18] See McNelis 2003: 156: "Theseus' labors are not the focus of the poem. In fact, as the first verse of the poem indicates, Hecale is Callimachus' interest." For the possibility that the *Diegeseis*' system of quoting the first line of the text may go back to Callimachus' *Pinakes*, see Alan Cameron 2004: 58.

basis of the witness of the *diegetes*, who starts his summary with Theseus escaping Medea's plot (φυγὼν τὴν ἐκ Μηδείης ἐπιβουλήν), it is possible to infer that after the mention of Hecale and her hospitality (frr. 1 and 2 H.) the story continued to present the arrival of Theseus in Athens. Traces useful to shed light on "the most obscure part of the poem" (Hollis 2009: 427), Theseus' Troezenian years, can probably be discerned by means of the Atthidographic material rearranged in the first part of Plutarch's *Life*. With fragment 132 H., ἐπήλυσιν ὄφρ' ἀλέοιτο φώριον ("in order to avoid the onslaught of thieves") it is interesting to compare Plutarch's description of Theseus' grandfather and mother, Pittheus and Aethra,[19] unsuccessfully trying to convince Theseus not to reach Athens along the usual road from Troezen, "for it was difficult to make the journey to Athens by land, since no part of it was clear *nor yet without peril from robbers and malefactors*."[20] To the same context it is reasonable to attribute fragment 17 H., where we find, exactly as in Plutarch's *Theseus*, a strict connection between the paradigmatic value of Heracles' Labors for the young hero (cf. fr. 17.3 H.) and his willingness to face the struggles awaiting him on the way to Athens (cf. Plut. *Thes*. 7.2: τοὺς ἐμποδὼν ἄθλους): hence Theseus' prayer to Aegeus in *Hecale* fragment 17.4 H. ("Father, let me go, and you would later receive me back safe").

Several lexicographical sources have preserved the end of a verse, in enjambement with the following hemistich, where Medea, πολύθρονος ("of many poisons", fr. 3 H.), is caught in the very moment when "she realized that he [*sc*. Theseus] was Aegeus' son": ἡ δ' ἐκόησεν τοὔνεκεν Αἰγέος ἔσκεν (fr. 4 H.). That the unspecified subject is Medea can be argued from comparison with Plutarch's *Life of Theseus* 12.2. Medea is there introduced as living in Athens with Aegeus, whom she has promised by her sorcery to relieve of his childlessness. She immediately perceives the true identity of the young stranger, whom Aegeus fails to recognize. Old and fearful of sedition, the king is easily induced by Medea to poison the foreigner during a banquet.[21] As part of the

---

[19] Cf. D'Alessio 2007: 1.347 n. 141; Asper 2004: 325.
[20] Transl. Perrin 1914, with a change; see also *Thes*. 6.7. All subsequent translations from the *Life of Theseus* are Perrin's.
[21] Cf. Plut. *Thes*. 12.3: προαισθομένη δὲ περὶ τοῦ Θησέως αὕτη, τοῦ δ' Αἰγέως ἀγνοοῦντος, ὄντος δὲ πρεσβυτέρου καὶ φοβουμένου πάντα διὰ στάσιν, ἔπεισεν αὐτὸν ὡς ξένον ἑστιῶντα φαρμάκοις ἀνελεῖν.

Atthidographic tradition the story was doubtless in Philochorus (cf. Ampolo 1988: 213); Plutarch found it either there or through Istrus.[22]

In consideration of the role of Atthidography as a major source in the *Life of Theseus*, "we may fairly assume that most of what Plutarch says about Aegeus would have been found in the *Atthis*" (Harding 2008: 50–51). Examination of Plutarch's *Life* seems in particular to suggest that in Philochorus' *Atthis* "the latter part of Aegeus' reign mainly consisted of exploits of Theseus."[23] In the *Hecale* a "crisis characteristic of tragedy" (Hutchinson 1988: 61), joining father and son, must have been the recognition of Theseus on the point of drinking the deathly potion prepared for him by Medea. Suddenly Aegeus sees the sword he had left many years earlier in Troezen among the γνωρίσματα intended for Aethra's child. We can follow the scene in Plutarch's words (*Thes.* 12.4–5):

> Theseus, on coming to the banquet, thought best not to tell in advance who he was, but wishing to give his father a clue to the discovery, when the meats were served, he drew his sword, as if minded to carve with this, and brought it to the notice of his father. Aegeus quickly perceived it, dashed down the proffered cup of poison, and after questioning his son, embraced him, and formally recognized him before an assembly of the citizens.

Plutarch's lively account is the best framework for connecting the few scattered remains presumably coming from this part of the Callimachean poem (frr. 7–15 H.): from Aegeus' scream (fr. 7 H.: "Stop, Child: do not drink!") to the ἀναγνώρισις of Theseus, in a series of episodes supposedly found by Plutarch (and Callimachus?) in Philochorus (Ampolo 1988: 213). The Philochorean origin of this section in the *Life of Theseus* seems at least partly assured by the chapters immediately following. Chapter 13 is devoted to the war against Theseus, newly declared Aegeus' heir, waged by the sons of Pallas, brother of Aegeus, "exasperated...that Theseus should be prospective king

---

[22] That the fundamental source of Plutarch's biography of Theseus is not Philochorus but a later general tradition, with variants and learned quotations, perhaps Istrus' Συναγωγὴ τῶν Ἀτθίδων, was held by Jacoby 1954: 1.305; but see now Berti 2009: 24–25. Elsewhere, however, Jacoby 1954: 2.339 maintains that source of the story of the Marathonian Bull in Plut. *Thes.* 14 is "a kind of general tradition about Theseus, and we do not gain anything by calling it Istrus."

[23] Jacoby 1954: 1.432. The events pertaining to Aegeus' reign were probably treated in the second book of Philochorus' *Atthis*: see Costa 2007: 24–25.

although he was an immigrant and a stranger." A scholion to Euripides' *Hippolytus* affirms that Philochorus treated the theme in similar terms (*FGrHist* 328 F 108). Uncertain as Plutarch's precise source may be,[24] what especially interests us is the possibility that Callimachus may have alluded in the *Hecale* (fr. 5 H.) to the version asserting that Aegeus' true father was not King Pandion but Scirus (Hollis 2009: 426). The Atthidographic information conveyed in *Life of Theseus* 13.1 indeed bears witness to the claim of the sons of Pallas, the Pallantidae, that Aegeus "was only an adopted son of Pandion and in no way related to the family of Erechtheus," and thus a usurper. *Life of Theseus* 17.6 explicitly quotes Philochorus about a Scirus of Salamis in connection with the institution of the Kybernesia (*FGrHist* 328 F 111), "an obscure festival for helmsmen that...shows Philochorus' interest and knowledge of little-known cults" (Harding 2008: 60). It is therefore worthwhile to note that Σαλαμῖνος κτίσις was the title of one of the many works of Philochorus, and that Callimachus in the *Hecale* mentioned Salamis with its primeval name, Kolouris (or Koulouris; cf. fr. 91 H.), "presumably found in one of the Atthidographers."[25]

At the end of chapter 14 for the first time in his *Life of Theseus* Plutarch cites Philochorus, with regard not simply to Theseus and the Marathonian Bull but more specifically to the honors granted by Theseus to Hecale "as a return for her hospitality" (τὰς εἰρεμένας ἀμοιβὰς τῆς φιλοξενίας).[26] In this case too, as with the Kybernesia in chapter 17, the mention of Philochorus is connected to the reminiscence of a minor Attic cult,[27] probably to be considered "the starting point and the center of the narrative," as Jacoby observed.[28] The fragments that can plausibly be assigned to the conclusion of the poem seem to concern funeral and posthumous honors for Hecale (frr. 79–83 H.),

---

[24] About the likely provenance from Philochorus, see Jacoby 1954: 1.432–34; Ampolo 1988: 214; Harding 2008: 54.

[25] Alan Cameron 1995: 443. Hollis 1992a: 4 thinks that Callimachus' source about Scirus and Kolouris in the *Hecale* may well have been the Σαλαμῖνος κτίσις of Philochorus.

[26] For the suggestion that Callimachus could actually have used the noun ἀμοιβαί for the "recompense" that Hecale received in return for her hospitality, see Hollis 2002: 50.

[27] And of the pertinent festival Hecalesia?

[28] Jacoby 1954: 1.436; see now Harding 2008: 56. Jacoby stresses that Plutarch evokes the authority of Philochorus not for the adventure against the Marathonian Bull "but *only* for the honor conferred on Hecale by Theseus in the cult of Zeus Hecaleius" (italics mine).

again not without intriguing affinities with particular elements in Plutarch's *Theseus*—including the possibility, noticed by Hollis, of detecting Hecale's new demesmen, "under the lead of Theseus" (cf. Plut. *Thes.* 14.3: τοῦ Θησέως κελεύσαντος), as subject of fragment 169 H., Βριλησσοῦ λαγόνεσσιν ὁμούριον ἐκτίσσαντο ("they founded...bordering on the flanks of Mount Brilessus"), in one of the last lines of the poem.[29] No less interesting is the fact that part of Philochorus' *Atthis* was devoted to the local history of the Attic demes (Hollis 1992a: 4).

Hollis gives up any attempt to place the fragments according to a narrative order after fragment 83; the following fragments 84–92 are gathered around their connection to *res Atticae*. A systematic survey, still lacking, of all the discernible links between fragments of the *Hecale* and fragments (or echoes) of the Atthidographers would take great advantage of a full use of the commentaries of Pfeiffer, Jacoby, and Hollis. Fragment 179 (*inc. auct.*), the last in Hollis' edition, leads us back to Attic cults, and to Istrus ὁ Καλλιμάχειος, the last upholder (or the anthologist) of the Atthidographic tradition. A scholion to Aristophanes' *Lysistrata* says that Istrus (*FGrHist* 334 F 27) referred to the ἐρσεφορία as a "procession for Herse [or Erse],"[30] one of Cecrops' three daughters: if, as fragment 179 seems to show, Callimachus did indeed mention the Attic festival Hersephoria and connected it with Herse daughter of Cecrops,[31] it would be another clue about the relevance in the *Hecale* of the story of Erichthonius' birth, one of the most important of the Athenian myths, at the core of the *Vogelszene* in fragments 73 and 74 H.[32]

Atthidographers and the Aetia

In 1949, in the same year as volume 1 of Pfeiffer's edition of Callimachus, Felix Jacoby published *Atthis*, the book about the Atthidographers on which he worked at Oxford during World War II as an exile from Nazi Germany. What would become *Atthis* was originally just the introduction to a complete treatment of the Atthidographers, with

---

[29] Hollis 2009: 326: see also Hollis 1997b: 112 and, about fr. 83, 2009: 433.
[30] Transl. Harding 2008: 28; see also Berti 2009: 167–173.
[31] After Hollis 1990: 229 and 332, see now Hollis 2009: 435.
[32] For other connections of the episode with the Atthidographic tradition, see, e.g., Θριαί in fr. 74.9 H. and Philoch. *FGrHist* 328 F 195.

a collection of the fragments and a commentary.[33] At instance of the publisher the greater part of that material had to be cut out, finally finding its place some years later within *Die Fragmente der griechischen Historiker* (Jacoby 1954). What makes Jacoby's *Atthis* particularly relevant in connection with our subject is the suggestion therein present, and still generally accepted,[34] that it was Callimachus, while working at the *Pinakes*, who first catalogued under the title Ἀτθίς "those books that gave the local chronicle of Athens." Of these works we do not know the original titles assigned by their authors, from Hellanicus to Philostratus. Why would Callimachus have chosen to enter in his catalogue the Attic local chronicles as Ἀτθίδες? According to Jacoby this was the title of Amelesagoras' work (quoted by Antigonus of Carystus precisely as Ἀμελησαγόρας ὁ Ἀθηναῖος ὁ τὴν Ἀτθίδα συγγεγραφώς, *FGrHist* 330 F 1). Amelesagoras' *Atthis*, likely used by the Cyrenean poet as source for the episode of the crow in the *Hecale*,[35] would have induced Callimachus to extend the same title to the other, similar Attic local chronicles (Jacoby 1949: 85).

With his tale about the banishment of the crows from the Acropolis because of Athena's wrath, the *Atthidenschreiber* Amelesagoras permitted Gomperz (1893: 11) to infer that columns III and IV of the Tabula Vindobonensis referred to "die Verbannung der Krähe von der Akropolis als Strafe für ihre unwillkommene Meldung." Amelesagoras' fate has been an odd one. He was the first of the Atthidographers to be connected with a Callimachean passage in the attempt to interpret difficult verses of the *Hecale* from the newly published Tabula Vindobonensis. Although he had been relegated to the "Pseudepigrapha" in *Die Fragmente der griechischen Historiker*, Amelesagoras has nevertheless regained a central position in Jacoby's reconstruction of the Atthidographic tradition thanks to Callimachus[36]—namely because of the use that the Cyrenean scholar-poet could have made of the *Atthis* of that "mysterious" author (Hollis 2009: 7).

---

[33] Reconstruction of the genesis of Jacoby's *Atthis* in Chambers 1990. As Clarke 2008: 177 emphasizes, "almost sixty years after its publication, Jacoby's *Atthis* remains the one serious, systematic, and substantial attempt to approach even a fraction of the material which makes up the fragments of local Greek historiography."

[34] See, e.g., Schepens 2001: 22; Harding 2008: 1.

[35] That Callimachus used Amelesagoras' book in the *Hecale* is considered "a fact hardly to be doubted" by Jacoby 1949: 85.

[36] For the status of Amelesagoras as a source for Callimachus, see now Berti 2009: 17–18.

Amelesagoras' fragment narrates the myth of the birth of Erichthonius, with his custody entrusted to the daughters of Cecrops and the succeeding punishment of the Cecropides by Athena. It is interesting to encounter Ion, a figure mythologically connected to Erechtheus—in origin presumably the same as Erichthonius[37]—in another of the papyrological discoveries of the beginning of the twentieth century, concerning in this case Callimachus' *Aetia*. Ion is mentioned as ancestor of the Ionians ('Ἰάονες) in the last lines of a commentary to what is now Callimachus fr. 7.23-29 Pf. (part of the *Return of the Argonauts and the Rite of Anaphe*). Preserved by a Berlin papyrus, and therefore known as the Commentarius Berolinensis, it was published in 1912 by Wilamowitz with the help of W. Schubart. We owe to Wilamowitz the restorations in the left margin of the papyrus, accepted in Pfeiffer's *Callimachus* (1949-53: 1.19):

> Now he has named all the Hellenes *in common* Ia[ones], after the Athenians. For these (i.e. the Athenians) were formerly called Iaones. [And] Homer, whenever he mentions 'Ionians with trailing tunics' (*Iliad*: 13.685), means the Athenians. For originally they used to wear [tunics] that reached to their feet after the fashion of the Persians, [S]yr[ians, and Kar]khe[d]onians. Kleidemos reports this in the *Atthis*. He has called the Hel[lenes Athenians], (naming the whole) from the part, as Pindar (says) 'Athens pillar of H[ellas]'. And the Iaones got their name [from Ion], son of Xouthos, son of Aiolos, son of He[llen].
> (Translation, Harding 2008: 43)

The erudition of the scholiast is prompted by the need to explain Ἰήονες in the Callimachean text (= fr. 7.29 Pf.). The reference to Cleidemus is most probably a product of the scholiast himself, not supported by the Callimachean text. Almost a century after its publication, the Commentarius Berolinensis remains the only papyrus preserving parts of Callimachus' works, and of any of his ancient commentators, where we find explicit reference to an *Atthis* in some connection (although probably indirect or inaccurate) with a Callimachean passage. So far as we can infer from the papyrus fragment, it seems inappropriate to consider Cleidemus a source of Callimachus like Xenomedes of Ceos (evoked by Callimachus himself in *Aetia* fr. 75.54-55 Pf.) or Agias and

---

[37] Cf. Hollis 2009: 226 and Harding 2008: 47. The relation between the two was discussed also in antiquity: see Carlier 2005: 127-128.

Dercylus (cited three times by ancient interpreters of the *Aetia*).[38] It is nonetheless curious to see the Commentarius Berolinensis, transmitted by a papyrus of the second century AD, still quoting the work of a minor local historian active six centuries earlier, one called by Pausanias, a contemporary of the Berlin papyrus, "the earliest among those who wrote about the customs of the Athenians" (*FGrHist* 323 T 1: ὁπόσοι τὰ Ἀθηναίων ἐπιχώρια ἔγραψαν ὁ ἀρχαιότατος).[39]

It is possible in fact to detect between Callimachus and Cleidemus a link stronger and more relevant than the mention of the latter in the Commentarius Berolinensis devoted to the *Aetia*. The survival for several centuries of at least part of the work of Cleidemus and other earlier Atthidographers is very likely the result of the vast literary activity of Istrus, who received the epithet ὁ Καλλιμάχειος in antiquity (*FGrHist* 334).[40] "Neither Plutarch nor Pausanias can be supposed to have consulted [Cleidemus'] original" (Jacoby 1954: 1.60): access for them and their contemporaries to the oldest *Atthides* was achievable mostly (or only) through the Συναγωγὴ τῶν Ἀτθίδων of Istrus, already mentioned. Speculations about Istrus and his work, in particular as an Atthidographer, have not been lacking among scholars of the nineteenth and the twentieth century: from the suggestion that Istrus was *Hauptquelle* for the use of the Atthidographers in Plutarch's *Life of Theseus*,[41] to the idea that "the keen interest of Callimachus in Attic myths, and indeed in aetiological legends generally, renders it probable that he employed Istrus in collecting the material which he incorporated in his *Aetia* and his *Hecale*" (cf. Pearson 1942: 139), to the recent "guess" by Alan Cameron that Istrus or Philostephanus may be the author of the *Diegeseis*.[42]

Beyond Istrus' influence, important as it seems to have been, it is possible to catch sight of a deeper relation between the Callimachean

---

[38] Lehnus 2004a: 204–208; see Ambühl 2005: 63 n. 124 for the possible derivation from the same source of the character of Molorchus in the *Victory of Berenice*.

[39] For the dating of Cleidemus, see Jacoby 1954: 1.58; Harding 1994: 10–13. Most recently Harding 2008: 7: "Precisely when he wrote is not certain, but it was before the middle of the fourth century."

[40] The epithet is common to Hermippus and Philostephanus too, and may be considered proof of immediate relationship with Callimachus and his work: Bollansée 1999: 97–98.

[41] Hypothesis of G. Gilbert 1874, seen with favor by the most recent editor of Philochorus, Costa 2007: 176.

[42] Cf. Alan Cameron 2004: 65–66. About several aspects of Istrus' industrious work, see Jackson 2000.

tradition of learning and the historiographic commitment of the Atthidographers. "The enduring interest of the Atthidographers in etymologies and *aetia*" was stressed long ago as one of their main features.[43] Jacoby (1949: 128-148) devoted pages to aetiology as a fundamentally important method of inquiry and explanation for the Atthidographers' "treatment of the subject-matter." As Jacoby remarked, "the uncommonly great number" of *aitia* in the fragments of the Atthidographers not only makes them "the main substance of the tradition for the time of the kings and for the archaic period" but reveals also a broader "historical function of the aitia," even a political one.[44] In this respect it may be interesting to compare recent attempts to explain Callimachus' aetiological attitude as something more, and more political, than the expression of mere antiquarian interests (see Harder 2003).

Among the fragments *incerti libri* from the *Aetia* in Pfeiffer's great edition of 1949-53 there is fragment 178, about thirty verses transmitted by POxy 11.1362, for which (*dubitanter*) Pfeiffer suggests a location in the initial part of *Aetia* Book 3. In "one of the better preserved individual episodes in the *Aetia*,"[45] the reader is transported to a symposium, part of the Athenian feast of the Antestheria celebrated at the home of an Athenian, Pollis, but probably in Alexandria.[46] At the party Callimachus "shared a couch"[47] with Theugenes, a native of the island of Icos. After a preamble exalting "the dignity of conversation above the triviality of drinking" (Hutchinson 1988: 27), Callimachus finally asks this Ician guest, as if he were one of the Muses, about a particular point (an αἴτιον) referring to the religious traditions of the tiny island of Icos (fr. 178.21-24 Pf.).[48] Questions of this sort are of course inherent to the very concept of the *Aetia*, "a poem dealing principally

---

[43] Pearson 1942: 156, who further specifies: "a legacy inherited from the old Ionian historians."
[44] Jacoby 1949: 143-145. Well known, and today usually considered with skepticism, is Jacoby's view of the *Atthides* as strongly conditioned by the political and ideological views peculiar to each Atthidographer. See in general Orsi 1995.
[45] Alan Cameron 1995: 133, at the beginning of an important discussion of fr. 178.
[46] For a reconstruction and analysis of the whole scene, see Fantuzzi and Hunter 2002: 97-104.
[47] Transl. Nisetich 2001: 86: "I shared a couch with him, purely | by chance" (= fr. 178.8-9 Pf.: ᾧ ξυνὴν εἶχον ἐγὼ κλισίην οὐκ ἐπιτάξ).
[48] "[Theugenes,] do tell me in answer to my question what my heart yearns to hear from you: Why is it the tradition of your country to worship Peleus, king of the Myrmidons? What has Thessaly to do with Icos?" (transl. Trypanis 1978).

with the events which explain particular religious customs."[49] Originally put forward about sixty years ago, the suggestion that fragment 178 Pf. (and the following frr. 179–85) may belong to *Aetia* Book 2 has in recent years gained consensus.[50] The banquet at Pollis' should be put immediately before fragment 43 Pf.[51] More firmly identified is Callimachus' source about the antiquities of Icos, the book of Ἰκιακά attributed by Stephanus of Byzantium to the Attidographer Phanodemus (*FGrHist* 325 T 7), who lived in fourth-century Athens, receiving unusual marks of honor for his political or diplomatic activity,[52] and writing an *Atthis* of at least nine books. That the source used by Callimachus could be only Phanodemus, "for it seems improbable that there should have existed another book about this insignificant island," was affirmed by Jacoby (1954: 1.175): a view that has strongly influenced Callimachean scholarship.[53] The fragments of Phanodemus' *Atthis* (called Ἀττικὴν ἀρχαιολογίαν by Dionysius of Halicarnassus, *FGrHist* 325 F 13) are overwhelmingly on antiquarian and religious matters,[54] and therefore particularly in accordance with the themes treated by Callimachus during the conversation with Theugenes at Pollis' party, and indeed in the whole poem.

The mention of Icos in POxy 11.1362 was for the first time connected with Phanodemus' *Iciaca* by L. Malten in an important article published in 1918, dealing with the interpretation of the new Callimachean papyrus and the *convivium apud Pollida* there preserved. In fragment 178.27 Pf., εἰδότες ὡς ἐνέπου[σιν ("as those who know inform me"), Malten saw "a kind of veiled citation of the source,"[55] namely

---

[49] Hutchinson 1988: 28. The attribution of POxy 11.1362 to the *Aetia* does not depend on any ancient quotation but rests exclusively on "the obvious aetiological drift" of the scene, remarked already in the editio princeps: cf. Dettori 2004: 35.

[50] For a review of the interpretations of the fragment, see most recently Dettori 2004: 36–37.

[51] Cf. Fabian 1992: 315, with some hesitation; Alan Cameron 1995: 133–135; Massimilla 1996: 400; D'Alessio 2007: 1.316–21; Fantuzzi and Hunter 2002: 101; Hutchinson 2003: 50.

[52] Cf. Jacoby 1954: 1.172; the inscriptions attesting the honors accorded to Phanodemus are recorded by Chaniotis 1988: 329–330.

[53] Jacoby's position is embraced especially by Fabian 1992: 322–323; in the same direction but more cautiously, D'Alessio 2007: 560 n. 23; Fantuzzi and Hunter 2002: 103.

[54] Cf. Rhodes 1990: 78; Dillery 2005: 509; and more generally Jacoby 1949: 55. A sketch of what we know about Phanodemus in Harding 1994: 28–30.

[55] Transl. Jacoby 1954: 1.175 of Malten's (1918: 171) "eine Art verschleierten Quellencitats."

Phanodemus: an allusion not different in its purpose from the explicit mention of Xenomedes as *auctoritas* for the story of Acontius and Cydippe. Some years after Malten's article, a rich and detailed chapter in Rudolf Pfeiffer's *Kallimachosstudien* (1922) would be devoted to the myth of Erigone in the context of the Athenian Anthesteria. Pfeiffer traced the Atthidographic tradition, especially from lexicographical sources, and Phanodemus is not absent in his survey. Worth noting is his caution in treating Phanodemus as *the* source of Callimachus[56]—a caution clearly perceivable also in the edition of 1949–53: in fragment 178.27, εἰδότες ὡς ἐνέπου[σιν, interpreted by Malten as alluding to Phanodemus' *Iciaca*, Pfeiffer prefers to discern a reference to "seamen" (ἁλίπλοοι), as the origin of the accounts heard by Callimachus about the little island of Icos.[57] Still more cautious the recent edition of M. Asper, who sees line 27, εἰδότες ὡς ἐνέπου[σιν, simply as an indication that "the narrator refers to (unknown to us and probably) unmentioned authorities" (Asper 2004: 191).

If Phanodemus is usually connected with the symposium at Pollis' because of the *Iciaca* quoted by Stephanus of Byzantium, according to Athenaeus he was interested also in the Anthesteria (cf. *FGrHist* 325 F 11), and in particular in the ritual of the second day of the festival (the *Choes*), whose origin Phanodemus ascribes to Demophon son of Theseus.[58] Not surprisingly, Callimachus too was interested in Demophon, as we know from fragment 556 Pf., νυμφίε Δημοφόων, ἄδικε ξένε ("bridegroom Demophon, unjust guest"), *incertae sedis*, but "e fonte Attico (fort. Atthide aliqua)."[59]

Between Polis and Kingdom

Amelesagoras, Cleidemus, Phanodemus: the three Atthidographers were associated with Callimachean passages by reason of texts published between 1893 (Tabula Vindobonensis) and 1915 (POxy 11.1362), in the first wave of papyrological discoveries that would during the twentieth century change the knowledge and appraisal of the works

---

[56] Pfeiffer 1922: 106–107; and see Jacoby 1954: 1.185.
[57] Cf. Massimilla 1996: 415; Fantuzzi and Hunter 2002: 119 n. 147.
[58] Translation of the fragment, and commentary, in Harding 2008: 75–76. A brief reference to Phanodemus' fragment in Pfeiffer 1922: 105 and Pfeiffer *ad* Call. fr. 178.2.
[59] Pfeiffer 1949–53 *ad loc.*; cf. D'Alessio 2007: 2.725 n. 63.

of Callimachus. Among the three, only Cleidemus is de facto present in a Callimachean papyrus, the Commentarius Berolinensis published in 1912. The mention of Cleidemus probably originates not from Callimachus' text but from the erudition of the scholiast. Generally recognized as sources of Callimachus in two salient points of the *Hecale* (the *Vogelszene*) and of the *Aetia* (Pollis' banquet) respectively, the Atthidographers Amelesagoras and Phanodemus actually do not figure at all in papyri or fragments from Callimachean works. They have been invoked by modern scholars for good and convincing reasons but are still largely the fruit of conjecture and philological skills. Plutarch's chapter from the *Life of Theseus* quoting Philochorus has been of fundamental importance in the history of the recovery of the *Hecale* from Politian onwards.[60] Chapter 14 of Plutarch's *Theseus* remains our most important witness for a direct link between a work of Callimachus and an Attidographer, but its evaluation is not immune from uncertainty.[61] If it seems "beyond doubt" that Philochorus was Callimachus' inspiration for the story of Hecale,[62] less clear is how long before Philochorus that story was part of the tale of Theseus and the Marathonian Bull. We do not know in which work Philochorus dealt with Theseus and Hecale. Since Philochorus wrote a special book about Marathon and the Tetrapolis, Jacoby suggested that he related the story of Hecale "in detail in the book about the Tetrapolis, more succinctly in the *Atthis*."[63]

Recent years have seen attempts made to detect traces of Attic color derived from comedy, used by Callimachus to strenghten the local dimension proper to the *Hecale*.[64] Frequent attention has been

---

[60] About Politian and fragments of Callimachus, see Harder 1989; N.G. Wilson 1992: 107–108; Bing 1997: 78–79. For a view of the history of scholarship on Callimachean fragments from the Italian humanists to the nineteenth century, see Benedetto 1993.

[61] As Hutchinson 1988: 56 n. 64 notes, "it is not clear exactly what Plutarch ascribes to Philochorus in *Thes.* 14."

[62] See most recently Harding 2008: 56. Cf. especially Jacoby 1954: 1.435 ("fairly certain") and Hollis 1992a: 3–4.

[63] Jacoby 1949: 128: cf. moreover Jacoby 1954: 1.435; Hollis 1990a: 6 n. 8; Lehnus 1993: 92. Remnants of Philochorus' Περὶ τῆς Τετραπόλεως in FGrHist 328 F 73–75; about Philochorus as author of a work in two books that was probably the first Olympiad chronicle ever written, see Christesen 2007: 304–307.

[64] Alan Cameron 1995: 443–444, referring also to Hollis' studies. For the "pickled olive which Theseus drank, too" in *Iambus* 4 (fr. 194.77 Pf.) as allusion to the hospitality scene of *Hec.* fr. 36.4 H., see Kerkhecker 1999: 105–106; Acosta-Hughes 2002: 191–192.

directed toward the *Aetia* in order to collect new evidence about Attic presences in the poem, such as *aitia* built up around problems of early Attic mythology,[65] or passages like fragment 63 Pf. (*The Attic Thesmophoria*).[66] Without here reviewing the suggestions found in Pfeiffer's edition about possible connections between Callimachean fragments (chiefly *incertae sedis*) and Atthidographic erudition or Athenian subjects, it may suffice to recall fragment 51 Pf., οὕνεκεν οἰκτείρειν οἶδε μόνη πολίων.[67] According to its source (a scholion to Sophocles' *Oedipus at Colonus*), the fragment is to be connected with the traditional praise of Athens as φιλοικτίρμων and ἱκεταδόκος, "compassionate to suppliants." Fragment 51 Pf. is usually considered to be the last verse of *Aetia* 2.[68] Such an outstanding mention of Athens at the very end of the second book of the *Aetia*, and the role in the architecture of the book presumably reserved to Pollis, Callimachus' Athenian friend, may even induce us to consider *Aetia* 2 "un libro segnatamente ateniese o attico"[69]—a particularly intriguing remark if combined with two observations that Hollis made some years ago. Finding a tribute to Athens like fragment 51 Pf. at the end of *Aetia* Book 2 appears particularly significant if put in association with the hypothesis that the original version of the poem (ca. 270 BC?) contained only two books. At the same time it could be seen in the context of the "official interest which the Ptolemies took in Athens throughout the third century BC," with their involvement on the side of Athens in the Chremonidean War.[70]

The end of the Chremonidean War (ca. 262 BC) simultaneously marked the fall of Athenian independence under Macedonian rule, and the ceasing of Atthidography with the death of Philochorus.[71] The Atthidographer died, according to the *Suda*, "caught in an ambush by Antigonus, since he was accused of having inclined toward Ptolemy's reign" (*FGrHist* 328 T 1: ἐτελεύτησε δὲ ἐνεδρευθεὶς ὑπὸ Ἀντιγόνου,

---

[65] Cf. Hollis 1990b; Borgonovo 1996; D'Alessio 2007: 2.441 n. 49.
[66] Still quite obscure: see Bulloch 2006: 505.
[67] "Since she is the only town which knows how to pity" (transl. Trypanis). For Theseus protector of suppliants in the fragments of the Atthidographers, see Harding 2008: 70–71.
[68] A broader *Epilogue* in Nisetich 2001: 93–95; see also Lehnus 1993: 85. For a list of potential Athenian *aitia*, see D'Alessio 2007: 2.575 n. 49.
[69] Borgonovo 1996: 53 n. 27; and see already Lehnus 1993: 82–83.
[70] Hollis 1992a: 6; and the remarks of Asper 2004: 37–38.
[71] A synchronicity emphasized especially by Jacoby 1949: 107–109.

ὅτι διεβλήθη προσκεκλικέναι τῇ Πτολεμαίου βασιλείᾳ). In all probability the *Suda*'s words must be interpreted as referring to the fact that Philochorus fell victim to Antigonus Gonatas after the conquest of Athens by Macedonian troops, possibly in conjunction with retaliations following the capitulation of the town.[72] As cause for the murder the Byzantine lexicon explicitly states Philochorus' backing of Ptolemy's βασιλεία. The information probably conceals a reference to the involvement of the king in the war (Habicht 1997: 143; Huss 2001: 273), and notably to Ptolemy Philadelphus' generals who helped the Athenians fighting against Antigonus Gonatas. In the famous Athenian decree proposed by Chremonides from which the war received its name, mention is made of a συμμαχία of Athens with Ptolemy. The decree praises with particular emphasis Philadelphus and especially his sister-wife, Arsinoe II, since "King Ptolemy, following the policy of his ancestors and of his sister, conspicuously shows his zeal for the common freedom of the Greeks."[73]

It seems in fact opportune to read the likely decisive role played by the Alexandrian milieu in preserving wholly or in part Philochorus' *Atthis* and the entire Atthidographic tradition in the light of the historical and political circumstances that closely joined Athens and the Ptolemies during the third century BC.[74] Especially through the Συναγωγὴ τῶν Ἀτθίδων of Istrus, "grammarian in the Callimachean sense,"[75] Callimachus' work and influence appear strongly linked to the Atthidographers and their fate. According to Jacoby, as we have seen, the title *Atthis* for the Attic local chronicles goes back to Callimachus, who in his *Pinakes* could have chosen to extend to all of them the heading of Amelesagoras' work. If it was truly Callimachus who imposed and made long-lasting the title Ἀτθίς, he may perhaps

---

[72] Costa 2007: 8; Jacoby 1954: 1.220 discusses the possibility that the death of Philochorus may have occurred "in the critical years before the Chremonidean War" by intervention of the Macedonian party in Athens opposed to the alliance with Ptolemy II; on the contrary, Pearson 1942: 107–108 thought that Philochorus was executed "perhaps not until some years" after Antigonus' victory.

[73] English translation in M.M. Austin 1981: 95. For the problem of the dating of the beginning of the Chremonidean War, see different positions in Shipley 2000: 125 and Huss 2001: 271.

[74] See Costa 2007: 5–6. For an overview of Athens and the Ptolemies, see Habicht 1994: 140–163.

[75] Together with Hermippus and Philostephanus, see Jacoby 1954: 1.619; Pfeiffer 1968: 150–151.

have taken it from Philochorus rather than from the obscure Amelesagoras.[76]

The author of that *Atthis*, "the latest *Atthis* known to us" (Jacoby 1949: 107), was bound to arouse the enduring interest of Callimachus and his school: in a way, Philochorus too lived "between *polis* and kingdom."[77] We do not know whether Philochorus was "connected with the group of intellectuals who planned the Chremonidean War," as one modern scholar supposed.[78] Certainly if he placed his trust in Ptolemy Philadelphus' power (the *Suda*'s Πτολεμαίου βασιλεία), it was for his country's sake: "always full of that noble love for his country, its gods and its liberty, to which he bore witness with his life and by his death," as Wilamowitz saw him.[79]

---

[76] The suggestion of Costa 2007: 13, who thinks also that the *Suda*'s knowledge about Philochorus' life and works may come from the *Pinakes* of Callimachus; see also Harding 1994: 34. For Callimachus' alleged residence in Athens, see Fraser 1972: 2.463–64 and the recent audacious proposal of Oliver 2002.

[77] Like Callimachus: Lehnus 1993. For Philochorus, see Meissner 1992.

[78] Pearson 1942: 107. "If Antigonus had him executed or murdered, he must have been among the leaders of the movement," Jacoby 1954: 1.222 observes.

[79] Wilamowitz 1893a: 1.288 in the English translation of Jacoby 1954: 1.237. See Habicht 2006: 285–288 for epigraphic evidence that has recently turned up demonstrating that Antigonus Gonatas was the recipient of godlike honors bestowed upon him by the Athenians some time after the Chremonidean War, and most recently O'Neil 2008.

CHAPTER EIGHTEEN

CALLIMACHUS AND FABLE

Ruth Scodel

ABSTRACT

Callimachus used fables because they linked archaic iambic poetry and Hellenistic popular philosophy, and Greek with Egyptian and other Near Eastern cultures. They also invited characteristically Callimachean combination of an apparently simple voice with perplexing shifts and turns. All three of Callimachus' surviving fable passages are difficult. *Iambs* II and IV present fables whose context, and thus targets, are obscure; while the olive seems superior to the laurel, it is not certain whether the reader should agree with the laurel's rejection of the bramble's right to comment. The programmatic proem of the *Aetia* alludes to Aesop 184 Perry, but the fable is entangled with many other allusions that complicate any straightforward message. The genre rests on essentialist premises (a donkey cannot be other than a donkey) that in the Callimachean context are always ambiguous.

The fable is a brief narrative that most often describes typical behaviors for a didactic purpose.[1] Its characters, except sometimes gods, are nameless and generic. Typically, these characters include animals or plants, partially anthropomorphized. They speak, reason, and engage in human social behaviors—they make friends, argue, show hospitality, and make war. At the same time, they display those attributes of their species that are most salient from a human perspective. Fabulistic lions are brave and fierce; foxes, cunning; frogs, noisy. Predators are usually predators; and prey, prey. They thereby represent human types. Indeed, the pseudo-Aristotelian treatise *On Physiognomy* criticizes simpleminded uses of animal likenesses to understand human characters: "Those who make physiognomic claims on the basis of animals do not properly select their signs. For one cannot just go through the form of each animal and say that whoever is similar to this animal in body will be similar also in soul" (805b10–14). Nonetheless, the

---

[1] There is a full survey of Greek fable in Van Dijk 1997.

treatise does comment on human somatic features that indicate traits of character by their similarity to specific animals—so, for example, being swollen around the ribs indicates talking too much without point, like frogs and cows (810b15–16). What in fable is metaphorical could be literal in speculative thought.

The fable surely came to Greece from the Near East (M.L. West 1997: 319–320). The form traveled easily, however, and it is firmly established in Greek culture by the time of our earliest literary texts. Although people presumably told fables for education and entertainment, fables were not an independent genre in the literature of archaic and classical Greece. When fables appear, they are embedded in other texts belonging to other genres and take their point from context. Although the moral of most fables in pre-Hellenistic Greek literature is usually obvious, the application is usually off the record, left for the hearer to infer, or spoken by a character within the fable itself.

Although the extant fragments of Hipponax, Callimachus' overt model in his *Iambi*, do not include any fables, Archilochus clearly used fables freely. Demetrius of Phalerum, the Peripatetic and tyrant of Athens, created the first collection of fables late in the fourth century BC or early in the third. It is not at all clear what this collection was intended to be: Demetrius may have intended it as a resource for later orators or authors, or as a work of scholarship, or as a contribution to literature, and its contribution to the later collections of fables is very uncertain— but Callimachus surely had access to it (Adrados 1999: 410–496).

Fables concern human universals. The Homeric epics include no fables, probably because the external narrator rarely comments, while Homeric characters are contained within the heroic world. Homeric characters deploy an alternative kind of story-with-a-point: when they need to move others to a particular course of action, they tell stories about heroes of another generation, or about themselves. They compare a present situation not to a recurrent type in human life but to singular events in the idealized past. The heroes thus remain a little removed from ordinary people. Yet Homer comes close to fable sometimes when he speaks in his own voice, in similes. The simile of the boys who molest a wasps' nest near a road, so that the wasps later attack an innocent passerby, is very like a fable in structure and tone (*Il.* 16.259–65). The first surviving Greek literary text to present itself not as narrative about a remote past but as an intervention in the contemporary world, Hesiod's *Works and Days*, also offers the first fable in Greek literature, the Hawk and the Nightingale (*Op.* 202–212).

Because moderns typically encounter a selection of Aesop's fables as children and see them as moralizing stories, we do not always realize how worldly-wise, even cynical (in the modern sense), Greek fables often are. The characters of fable are consistently greedy, shortsighted, deceitful, and boastful. While there are certainly fables that encourage the keeping of promises or warn of vengeance against injustice, the single most common moral of the Aesopic fable is that you need to be very careful: the fox disguises himself as a doctor when the birds are sick. The fable is a powerful tool of satire, and the moral is often not entirely "moral" but is an insight into the way of the world. Hesiod's fable of the Hawk and Nightingale has perplexed interpreters because its overt moral seems contrary to the poetic argument: a hawk, having seized a nightingale, tells the bird to stop crying, because it is pointless to argue with superior force. The hawk will eat her or not, as he chooses. Yet the fable makes excellent sense if we understand it as telling its addressees, the corrupt kings who are judging the dispute between Hesiod and his brother, not how they should behave but how they typically behave and how they will behave now if Hesiod does not convince them to act otherwise. Judges exist to uphold justice, an alternative to the rule of force; but if they do not follow justice, they are themselves hawks. Recommendations not to oppose superior force are common in Greek literature, but those who make them are unsympathetic oppressors or their subordinates (Aegisthus at Aes. *Ag.* 1624, Talthybius at Eur. *Tro.* 726–739). This fable at least seems to offer the kings a choice whether to resemble the characters or not. Fables often have a bias toward a conservative view of the social order. The hawk is simply being a hawk, and animals in fable that try to disguise themselves as something else always fail.

It is not hard to understand why Callimachus would have been interested in fable. It offers a link between archaic iambic poetry and Hellenistic popular philosophy, which frequently deployed fables for their liveliness and satiric edge. The genre unites Greek with Egyptian and other Near Eastern cultures (M.L. West 1969). And it invites a characteristically Callimachean rhetorical maneuver, the combination of an apparently simple voice with perplexing shifts and turns.

Two of Callimachus' *Iambi* consist mostly of fable narrative. Fable is also a significant subtext in the programmatic proem of the *Aetia*. All three passages are difficult to interpret, though for different reasons. The fable allusion in the *Aetia* proem does not straightforwardly transmit the original fable, and it is entangled in a web of other allusions.

The actual fables in the *Iambi* present pragmatic difficulties; we do not quite understand them, because Callimachus has not provided enough context for them. They are not set off from any particular application, like the fables in a collection; the poems present the fables as communication from one person to another in a specific situation. However, the poems do not explain what that situation is. The reader assumes that the narrator tells them for a reason, but we cannot be entirely sure what that reason is. Fable is always potentially ambiguous, and Callimachus makes this ambiguity salient.

Iambus 2 has a generically characteristic opening:

> Ἦν κεῖνος οὑνιαυτός, ᾧ τό τε πτηνόν
> καὶ τοὐν θαλάσσῃ καὶ τὸ τετράπουν αὔτως
> ἐφθέγγεθ' ὡς ὁ πηλὸς ὁ Προμήθειος.

> It was that time in which the winged being, and the one in the sea, and the four-footed one alike spoke just as the mud shaped by Prometheus [i.e., humanity]

Since there is no dramatic situation, the reader assumes that the speaker is Callimachus. Similarly, it ends by ascribing the story to Aesop:

> ταῦτα δ' Αἴσωπος
> ὁ Σαρδιηνὸς εἶπεν, ὅντιν' οἱ Δελφοί
> ᾄδοντα μῦθον οὐ καλῶς ἐδέξαντο.

> These things Aesop of Sardis said, whom the Delphians, when he sang his tale, did not receive graciously.

The intervening story, reconstructed from the fragments and the *diegesis*, runs as follows: in the time of Cronus and the beginning of Zeus's reign, animals could talk. However, the swan went on an embassy to Zeus to ask to be freed of old age, and the fox (presumably a member of the embassy) complained that Zeus was unjust. Zeus therefore took away the animals' voices and gave them to human beings (who already could talk more than they needed to: Callim. fr. 192.8–9 Pf.). As a result, people are both talkative and storytellers, and some show animal characteristics in speech:

> καὶ κυνὸς [μ]ὲ[ν] Εὔδημος,
> ὄνου δὲ Φίλτων, ψιττακοῦ δε[
> οἱ δὲ τραγῳδοὶ τῶν θάλασσαν οἰ[κεύντων
> ἔχο[υ]σι φωνήν· οἱ δὲ πάντες [ἄνθρωποι
> καὶ πουλύμυθοι καὶ λάλοι πεφ[ύκασιν
> ἐκεῖθεν, ὠνδρόνικε.

And Eudemus has a dog's, Philto a donkey's, and...a parrot's, and the tragedians have the voice of those who live in the sea. And all people are thereby both full of stories and talkative, Andronicus.

The fable is superficially aetiological: it explains why people talk so much. There is an addressee, Andronicus, but we know nothing about him, and the poem tells us nothing. The address implies some context in which Callimachus tells the story, some reason why Andronicus needs to understand why people are so talky, but the poem does not provide it. So the reader's only context for the poem is the poem that has preceded it.

The poem also does not inform us about Eudemus, who has a dog's voice, or Philto, who has a donkey's. These are not the names of famous people, and they are surely pseudonyms. Although Callimachus' first audience may have known to whom these pseudonyms referred, any wider audience could not possibly know, and the poem as it stands in the collection must be intended to be effective without that knowledge. The false names rescue the poem from being abuse of the archaic iambic kind, just as Hipponax in the first poem attacks the scholars without naming names (Kerkhecker 1999: 44).

Callimachus probably found this fable in the collection of Demetrius of Phalerum, but it is not in the extant fable collections. E. Lelli (2004: 39–40) treats it as a direct adaptation of 228 Hausrath (240 Perry), but this is unlikely. In this fable, after Prometheus has created humans and animals, Zeus finds that there are too many animals as compared with people, and so orders Prometheus to reconfigure some animals as human. This story explains why some people, despite their human form, have beastlike souls. Lelli uses the difference between the *iambus* and the fable to argue that the *iambus* is literary polemic, since Callimachus has replaced moral qualities with the voice. Although this fable is unlikely to be the source of Callimachus' poem, to which it has only a very general resemblance, the general similarity indeed points to the importance of the voice in the *iambus*. Callimachus does not imagine a transfer of soul from animal to human, or associate the animal quality in the human with anything visible, as physiognomy does: he locates the animal quality in the voice.

The fable is slightly confusing from the start. The two animals who participate in the embassy are the swan and the fox. Callimachus consistently associates the swan with music and with Apollo (*Iambus* 4.47–48, *Hymn to Apollo* 5, *Hymn to Delos* 249, *Hecale* 56). The fox is, of course, a common character in fable, not only as trickster but also as victim of injustice in the celebrated fable of Archilochus, *The Fox and the Eagle*. The fox's complaint of Zeus's injustice sounds like an expression of his frustration that Zeus is not listening to his petition. Yet Callimachus himself hopes in the *Aetia* that his poetry will win him an escape from the burdens of old age (fr. 1.33-34 Pf.). So if the animals are justly punished, it is not for what they feel and want but for their failure to use speech adroitly enough, to say the right thing at the right time. Yet the poem ends by attributing the story to Aesop, who spectacularly failed at precisely this skill. Aesop's fables to the Delphians did not improve their behavior but only got him killed.

The animals evidently lose not their voices but the capacity for articulate speech, since dogs, donkeys, and parrots are not quiet. What, then, do people acquire: a tendency to say the kinds of things the animals once said, or a sonic resemblance? Callimachus is unlikely to be referring to the literal qualities of the voice—since fish do not make noises, it would be difficult to extract any point of this kind from his comment on the tragedians—but to characteristics that would be perceptible in literary texts. Callimachus calls people *polymythoi*, prone to storytelling, as well as *laloi*, talkative, which surely means that Zeus has transferred content. The parrot-person presumably repeats what others have said. Style seems implicated, too, since animal qualities are easy to see in it. Philto probably does not bray but talks stupidly, or writes poetry that is so pointless and also lacking in euphony that it is reminiscent of braying. Eudemus may be a Cynic, who adopts doggy attitudes to social norms and loudly harangues everybody. So what does it mean that the tragedians have the voice of the inhabitants of the sea, and are the tragedians poets, or (more likely) actors? Callimachus has expressly said that fishes could talk. Since they now make no sound at all, we may assume that for some reason the transfer from animal to human was more complete in their case: the tragedians have not only their ability to use sounds intelligibly but their vocal capacity. As a result, the tragedians would be noisier than anyone else; they talk all the time (Greek acting was very much a vocal art.) And perhaps, since we have no sense of what fish would say if they spoke, tragedians make no sense.

The poem has a variety of complex connections with *Iambus* 1, and these are more significant because the collection of *Iambi* is the only context the fable has. In the story of the cup of Bathycles in that poem,

Thales, given a golden cup left to the wisest among men, sends it to another of the Seven Sages, and it makes the round of all seven before returning to Thales, who dedicates it to Apollo. The Sages, according to Plato, are memorable precisely because they were not talkers:

> οὗτοι πάντες ζηλωταὶ καὶ ἐρασταὶ καὶ μαθηταὶ ἦσαν τῆς
> Λακεδαιμονίων παιδείας, καὶ καταμάθοι ἄν τις αὐτῶν τὴν σοφίαν
> τοιαύτην οὖσαν, ῥήματα βραχέα ἀξιομνημόνευτα ἑκάστῳ εἰρημένα·
> οὗτοι καὶ κοινῇ συνελθόντες ἀπαρχὴν τῆς σοφίας ἀνέθεσαν τῷ
> Ἀπόλλωνι εἰς τὸν νεὼν τὸν ἐν Δελφοῖς, γράψαντες ταῦτα ἃ δὴ
> πάντες ὑμνοῦσιν, Γνῶθι σαυτόν καὶ Μηδὲν ἄγαν.

> These men were all emulous of and lovers and students of Spartan culture, and one could understand their wisdom as of that kind, consisting in memorable brief statements that each one made. They also went together to dedicate a first fruits offering of their wisdom to Apollo at his temple in Delphi, writing the inscriptions everybody celebrates, "Know yourself" and "Nothing in excess."
>
> *Protagoras* 343a–b

Iambus 2 ends with an allusion to Aesop's poor reception at Delphi: traditionally, Aesop told a fable against the Delphians' (proverbial) greed, and they put a golden cup from the sanctuary among his possessions and executed him for temple robbing. Hipponax in *Iambus* 1 has compared the crowd he confronts with the Delphians at a sacrifice (Callim. fr. 191.27 Pf.) as well as with wasps, so the reader is primed to remember the greedy Delphians and perhaps also the golden cup in Aesop's story. Callimachus' lines suggest but do not explicitly state that the story Callimachus has repeated from Aesop is among those that aggravated the Delphians.

But it is not clear why the fable of *Iambus* 2 should be so profoundly offensive, except to the individuals who are selected for particular mockery. And there is a certain ambiguity in the position of Aesop. It is because of the animal additive to their speech that people are "full of *mythoi*." Yet it is a *mythos* that Aesop sings to the unreceptive Delphians. The fabulist thus does not stand outside the point of his fable. He tells a story instead of speaking briefly and directly, and so himself exemplifies the practice he explains.

Iambus 4 presents a similar problem of the speaking situation. Somebody addresses the son of Charitades, who is named Simus, according to the *diegesis*: Εἷς—οὐ γάρ;—ἡμέων, παῖ Χαριτάδεω, καὶ σύ ("You're one of us, son of Charitades—Isn't that what you think?"). After four poorly preserved lines, the speaker invites Simus to hear his fable: ἄκουε δὴ τὸν αἶνον. He then tells a story that he attributes to the ancient Lydians about a quarrel that took place on Mount Tmolus, in Lydia, between a laurel and an olive. Each tree makes a speech in praise of herself. The olive claims to hear the conversation of two birds (at least one is a crow) sitting in her branches. These, in direct speech, praise the olive over the laurel, because she was directly created by Athena, while the laurel has grown like all other trees; because she is so useful, producing food, drink, and ointment; and because suppliants carry her branches. Although this last is the third fall for the laurel, which would make the olive the winner in a wrestling match, the crow, even though someone (presumably the olive, unless we are to imagine that the laurel or the speaker of the poem interrupts the olive's speech) scolds it for talking inappropriately, adds that the olive that sheltered Leto when she gave birth to Apollo is honored by the Delians.

As the laurel prepares to respond angrily, a nearby bramble intervenes to suggest that they should not quarrel, lest they give joy to their enemies. The laurel then turns angrily to the bramble, echoing the opening lines of the poem:

ὦ κακὴ λώβη,
ὡς δὴ μί᾽ ἡμέων καὶ σύ; μή με ποιήσαι
Ζεὺς τοῦτο.

You lousy disgrace, so you are one of us? May Zeus not bring that about!

The final lines, which may have clarified the social setting of the fable, are too mutilated to explain much. They do make clear, however, that the final section was short compared to the fable. There is a disjuncture between the frame and the fable, since the frame is occupied exclusively, as far as we can tell, with the rebuke of Simus and offers very little information about the quarrel that has prompted Simus' intervention, whereas the fable is mostly concerned with the quarrel itself and ends with a few lines abusing the bramble. The fable in *Iambus* 4 is very long; the trees' speeches are extensive self-eulogies, and the emphasis seems to be as much on the rhetoric of the argument as on its outcome. We cannot, therefore, interpret the poem simply in accordance with the moral of the fable, that the quarrels of the nobles invite the base to pretend to be better than they are, for that moral does not require any amplification of the quarrel. As a speech, it is indeed odd, for the speaker seems to be carried away in repeating the arguments of the laurel and olive. Although the overt point is that Simus does not belong in this discussion at all, the speaker talks to him at great length, and in detailing the quarrel within the fable he effectively includes him even in rejecting him. Insofar as the poem is directed at Simus, the point must be not just that he lacks standing to intervene but that the quarrel is genuinely meaningful and is not to be settled simply by declaring it ended. If we imagine the speaker's original opponent as another addressee of the fable (for he has surely not disappeared during this long speech to Simus), we may wonder if the speaker extends the arguments of laurel and olive at such length as a way of continuing the original argument (Kerkhecker 1999: 112–114). If that is so, the social interaction has gone from one extended argument, between people who are represented by olive and laurel, to another, between the speaker and Simus. The external audience may read the whole poem as a miniature social comedy. It both demonstrates and deconstructs the moral of the second *Iambus*. The speaker is a typical talkative human. He cannot stop talking even to tell an intruder that he does not want him in the conversation. On the other hand, within the world of fable, even trees turn out to be garrulous.

The fable of *Iambus* 4 has a close parallel in the fable tradition (233 Hausrath, 213 Perry). Here a pomegranate and an apple argue, in some manuscripts over their fruit, in others about their beauty. A bramble intervenes and says, "Friends, let us finally stop fighting." Although it has been argued that Callimachus is the source of the fable, that seems unlikely (Edmunds 2001a: 94–95). However, we cannot assume, either, that Callimachus found this exact fable in Demetrius or elsewhere and himself decided to use laurel and olive instead of apple and pomegranate. The fable is likely to have had many variants.

The competition between nonhuman contenders is a typical Greek and Near Eastern form of folk narrative. Corinna offers a contest between Cithaeron and Helicon; Himerius 20 (Perry 432) has Helicon compare herself to Cithaeron in order to persuade the Nymphs to leave Apollo alone and come home. Thus, the competition can either be the sole point of the narrative, or it can be incorporated into a larger story. It appears in both Greek fables and in those of other ancient cultures. Perry 14 concerns a dispute between a fox and monkey about nobility of birth; 20 Perry is a similar dispute between a fox and a crocodile. A lion and a boar fight over who should first drink from a spring—until they notice the vultures waiting.

The narrative move from elegant or useful plants to the bramble is also likely to be traditional. In Judges 9:8–15, Jotham, the only survivor of Abimelech's massacre of the sons of Jerobaal, tells a fable to the men of Shechem about how the trees decided to select a king. They offered kingship to the olive, the fig, and vine in succession, but none of these wanted to leave its present honorable and useful function, so they went to the bramble. The bramble said, "If you are acting honorably in anointing me king over you, come and take shelter in my shade; but if not, may fire issue from the thorn bush and consume the cedars of Lebanon!" Here it is the olive, fig, and vine that are satisfied with their condition and have no desire to compete with one another, whereas the thorn, representing Abimelech, shows its aggressiveness.

Callimachus does not define any single basis for his trees' rivalry. They are not arguing about which is more beautiful or more useful, but about which is in some absolute sense best. As a result, within the poem the standards of evaluation are themselves potentially in contention. The birds explicitly decline to evaluate the trees on the basis of the gods by whom they are especially loved. Apollo favors the laurel; Athena, the olive; both are great gods. The laurel denigrates the olive for its use in funerals, whereas the olive claims to be happy and proud in this role. For the reader, there is no obvious basis from which to allegorize the fable. We cannot easily say what the debate is actually about. The *diegesis* says that the poet was in an argument with a rival when Simus happened by and tried to intervene. A rival would most obviously be a poetic rival, and this interpretation invites attempts to distinguish the laurel, olive, and perhaps bramble as different poets, poetic schools, or poetic genres; but nothing in the *diegesis* gives us reason to think that its author knew more about the poem's occasion than the poem itself implies.

Most recent scholars think that the olive is the clear winner (e.g., Fantuzzi and Hunter 2004: 13). Still, this is not quite certain. There is no real external judge, since the poem is ambiguous about the status of the direct speech of the crow: the olive claims to hear the birds, and the direct speech simply follows. The reader will probably assume that that the speech of the bird (or birds: there is no way to know whether there are changes of speaker within this section) is embedded in the olive's speech, but it is possible that the frame narrator is himself providing the reader's access. The laurel's aggressive tone and overt disparagement of the olive stand in contrast with the olive's ironic and detached style, and the olive's speech is more tightly organized than the laurel's, which seems to move randomly from one point to the next. The laurel attacks the olive as slavish in appearance, and in general the laurel presents itself as consistently elevated, whereas the olive celebrates her more modest and useful qualities along with her own links with divinity and the Olympic Games.

The birds who appear in the speech of the olive seem to have flown into this poem from the *Hecale*, where a crow, apparently warning another bird against the dangers of reporting bad news, delivers an extended digression on the story of the daughters of Cecrops (frr. 70–74 H., at least 82 lines). Not only do the talking birds evoke the *Hecale* by their presence; they use Athena's creation of the olive, mentioned in the *Hecale* (70.9–11), as an argument, and their praise of the olive's usefulness specifies the same humble food Hecale serves Theseus in that poem and explicitly mentions Theseus (*Iamb.* 4.76–77).[2] The crow is remarkably well informed about Attic material, although this fable takes place in Lydia. In contrast, the laurel's final outburst strikes a distinctly Lydian note:

].ς οὐ μὰ Φοῖβον, οὐ μὰ δέσποιναν,
τῇ κ]ύμβαλοι ψοθεῦσιν, οὐ μὰ Πακτ[ωλόν....

Not by Phoebus, not by the Mistress for whom cymbals resound, not by the Pactolus....

Since the olive hears voices that come directly from Callimachus' poetry, it is easy to guess that the olive is Callimachus and that the birds, who are Callimachean characters, judge rightly. And the olive in her own voice points out that laurel forms the crown for winners at the Pythian Games, whereas the olive crowns victors at Olympia, games greater than the Pythian.

Still, we should be a little careful. The birds, after all, may exist only in the olive's speech and are not trustworthy external witnesses. Although some readers take the olive's rebuke of the crow as a demonstration of the birds' independence of the olive, one could as easily see it as cunning artifice, as the olive pretends to be offended by speech she herself invents. Throughout, the olive's modesty is feigned. Her arguments are not all beyond dispute. For example, the crow speaks of the olive that gave rest to Leto (*Iambus* 13.62 repeats this); yet Callimachus' *Hymn to Delos*, though it twice mentions the holy olive (262, 322), has Leto give birth leaning against the palm (210). The chorus of Euripides' *Iphigenia in Tauris* (1099–1102) lists laurel, palm, and olive

---

[2] Hollis 2009: 174, *ad* fr. 36.4–5 Pf.

as the trees of Delos, though it is the last that is "dear to the birth pain of Leto." The function of different sacred trees on Delos was open to varying traditions; an argument based on such a potentially disputed point is not strong. Again, the crow claims that Athena made the olive grow, whereas the laurel just grows like other trees; but the story of Daphne, which makes the laurel also a miraculous growth, was probably known to Callimachus (Phylarchus had a version: 81 F 32 *FGrH*). The very dependence of the birds' speech on the *Hecale* complicates the force of their verdict: if the olive is Callimachus, he wins by making his own poem the basis for judgment. The contest clearly proves that the olive is a better rhetorician than the laurel, but not perhaps more than that.

Also, the laurel within the fable, in rebuking the bramble, assumes the role of the speaker in the frame, which might prompt a reader to guess that the laurel represents Callimachus, since nothing in the extant fragment marks the speaker of the poem as anyone else. Then there is the position of the bramble. Her call for peace is reminiscent of the Hipponax of the first *Iambus*, and the bramble is a plausible symbol for iambic poetry. Simus means "snub-nosed" (in Greek terms, ugly), whereas Charitades is possibly a significant name for a poet, a "son of delight." If the bramble is intruding in a quarrel where she does not belong, so did the birds; yet the olive has invited the birds' participation as enthusiastically as the laurel rejects the bramble's. Still, the bramble's call for restraint, lest the trees become "sources of joy for our enemies" (Callim. fr. 194.98–99 Pf.—a reason the bramble does not provide in the original fable) is slightly absurd: Who are the enemies of the trees who would be happy to hear that they are quarreling? Although the people they represent may have enemies who would be pleased to hear that they are quarreling, the warning simply makes no sense in the world of trees, and the advice ludicrously evokes Nestor's speech to Achilles and Agamemnon at *Iliad* 1.255–58.

The reader may well decide, after hearing the fable, that the speaker of the poem is not its implied author. In that case, the joke is on the speaker and the laurel. Both, by reacting so furiously to the unworthy outsider, show how pointless the quarrel really is: whether or not the olive is actually superior to the laurel, the laurel itself recognizes that she and the olive are actually members of the same group. Oddly enough, the bramble's intervention accomplishes exactly what it seems to intend—ending the argument—but by deflecting the laurel's resentment onto itself.

It is very probably the laurel that at the beginning of the fable's narrative (lines 9-10) is shaking with anger:

καλόν τε δένδρε[ον
σείσασ[α] τοὺς ὄρπηκ[ας...

The beautiful tree...shaking its branches...

This is reminiscent of the first line of Callimachus' *Hymn to Apollo*, where the laurel branch shakes at the imminent arrival of the god (ἐσείσατο δάφνινος ὄρπηξ). The laurel also refers to Branchus' healing of the Ionians (lines 28-32); the poem sometimes considered *Iambus* 17, a hymn to Apollo and Zeus, is called *Branchus* and includes in its surviving lines the foundation of the altar to Apollo at Didyma "near the branches of the laurel" (11). The speech of the olive has strong affiliations with the *Hecale*, and there are traces of the laurel's in other poems of Callimachus (cf. Acosta-Hughes 2002: 199-203).

It may be that all three figures of the fable are aspects of Callimachus' own poetry: the fable presents a debate of *Hymn* and *Elegy* that *Iambus* interrupts. That would at least give some point to the Attic connections of the olive and the laurel's awareness that it is in Lydia, since in *Iambus* 13 the poet defends himself for writing choliambics when he has not gone to Ephesus. *Iambus* 4 stresses his mastery of stories from different locations.

In the *Aetia*, Callimachus claims that he has followed the advice Apollo gave him when he was a boy, to take a narrower but less well-trodden poetic path (lines 26-28):

ἑτέρων ἴχνια μὴ καθ' ὁμά
δίφρον ἐλ]ᾶν μηδ' οἶμον ἀνὰ πλατύν, ἀλλὰ κελεύθους
ἀτρίπτο]υς, εἰ καὶ στεινοτέρην ἐλάσεις.

Drive your chariot not along the common tracks or the broad trail, but on untrodden ways, even if you have to drive a narrower road.

He then defines himself through the contrast between two animals, the cicada and the donkey:

τῷ πιθόμη]ν· ἐνὶ τοῖς γὰρ ἀείδομεν οἳ λιγὺν ἦχον
  τέττιγος, θ]όρυβον δ' οὐκ ἐφίλησαν ὄνων.
θηρὶ μὲν οὐατόεντι πανείκελον ὀγκήσαιτο
  ἄλλος, ἐγ]ὼ δ' εἴην οὐλ[α]χύς, ὁ πτερόεις,
ἆ πάντως, ἵνα γῆρας ἵνα δρόσον ἣν μὲν ἀείδω
  πρώκιον ἐκ δίης ἠέρος εἶδαρ ἔδων,
αὖθι τὸ δ' ἐκ]δύοιμι, τό μοι βάρος ὅσσον ἔπεστι
  τριγλώχιν ὀλοῷ νῆσος ἐπ' Ἐγκελάδῳ.

I obeyed him. For we sing among those who love the piercing sound of the cicada, not the clamor of asses. Let someone else bray just like the animal with the ears, but may I be the light one, the winged one—oh, absolutely, so that old age and dew—so that I can sing with morning dew from the bright air as my diet, and I can shed age, which lies on me as a weight as great as the three-cornered island lies on wicked Enceladus.
(*Aet.* fr. 1.29–36 Pf.)

The juxtaposition between donkey and cicada evokes Aesop 184 Perry. A donkey, enchanted by the song of cicadas, asked what they ate that enabled them to sing so beautifully. They answered dew—that cicadas eat only dew is frequently attested in Greek—whereupon the donkey tried to do the same, and starved to death. The fable is about keeping to one's proper nature and not attempting what is impossible. Yet in Callimachus, the donkey is not trying to be a cicada, but is a rival—some people actually like the donkey's noise more than the cicada's song. The word Callimachus uses for "bray," ὀγκήσαιτο, probably puns on the stem ὄγκος, literary "weight," another term for the size and pretension Callimachus avoids.

When the poet says that he sings "among those" who have loved the cicada's song, does he mean that he is among a group of poets who have sought to be cicadas, or is he complimenting his audience, particularly his patrons, for their good taste in preferring him? Again, where the context concerns the appreciation of poetry, when Callimachus goes on to refer to the donkey as the "beast with ears," the original readers would probably have the recalled the proverb "a donkey heard the lyre, and wiggled its ears" (of those who have no real appreciation)—so familiar a saying that it could be abbreviated to "donkey/lyre."[3] Yet the line in which the donkey's ears are mentioned is not about the reception of poetry, but about its production. Both fable and proverb are handled so that poet and critic are not distinguished. The fable and proverb are important to the understanding of the passage, but not in a straightforward way.

The allusions in these lines pull in different directions. Tithonus, who became a cicada because he had immortality without eternal youth, haunts the passage. Callimachus further alludes to Plato's myth of the cicadas in the *Phaedrus*, where the cicadas are men who starved to death because they were so lost in music and poetry, and became

---

[3] Lelli 2006a: 184 notes the proverb here but says nothing about its force. Callimachus alludes to it also at fr. 32.5–7 Pf.

the eternal spies of the Muses on Earth. Old age is in turn conceived as a weight, which further bends the image of the donkey, the beast of burden. At the same time the weight is that of Sicily on Enceladus. Sicily is the home of Theocritean pastoral, where the cicada is at home, but Enceladus is a Giant who fought the gods, and a subject of the kind of poetry Callimachus does not compose.[4]

Callimachus has not escaped old age yet; he longs to be the cicada, but this is an aspiration, not a certain reality. Indeed, it is a wish that hovers at the edge of impiety; it was precisely such a request that made Zeus angry at the swan in *Iambus* 2. He has evoked the fable in which the donkey dies by seeking the impossible. So in the next couplet he tries to justify his hope, or redefines it so that it is possible:

........Μοῦσαι γ[ὰρ ὅσους ἴδον ὄθμα[τ]ι παῖδας
μὴ λοξῷ, πολιοὺς] οὐκ ἀπέθεντο φίλους.

For the Muses, whomever they look at not askance as children they do not cast them aside when grey.

Aetia fr. 1.37–38

Scholars have guessed that the missing beginning of line 37 is οὐ νέμεσις, the text of the parallel lines in *Epigram* 21—meaning either than one cannot treat Callimachus' hope of escape as wrong, because it is based on the relationship he has had with the Muses since he was a child, or that he recognizes that he should not be angry that he has become old, since the Muses provide him with consolation (see M.A. Harder forthcoming).

Even though the fable belongs in an imaginary world of talking animals and trees, the genre aggressively polices the boundary between reality and unhealthy fantasy. Fables are about facing the way the world is, and they are often essentialist: if you are a donkey, you cannot pretend to be anything else; if you are a bramble, a quarrel between noble trees does not allow you to escape your status; if you have the voice of a dog, Zeus gave you that voice. Yet in the *Aetia*, this is a boundary the poet wants to mark in order to cross it. In the real world, people are usually more like donkeys than like cicadas, but they can avoid the donkey's folly by accepting their limits. Callimachus points to those limits and then hopes to ignore them—in part. Accepting that he cannot actually turn into a cicada and shed his skin, he still expects

---

[4] On the complex web of allusion, see Acosta-Hughes and Stephens 2002: 251–253.

that the Muses' love will lighten his burden. That is typical of his use of fable. By evoking the genre, he claims a grounding in a real social world, a practical knowledge of life. His opponents would do well to listen to the everyday wisdom of fables and stop arguing about poetry, which they do not understand. Yet the fable is never the last word. Being always embedded, given to a secondary speaker or linked with allusions to canonical literary texts, it lacks any final authority.

CHAPTER NINETEEN

PROVERBS AND POPULAR SAYINGS IN CALLIMACHUS

Emanuele Lelli

Abstract

Callimachus employs numerous proverbs and popular expressions suitably adapted to the diversity of his literary genres. In his *Hymns* we find especially Homeric and Hesiodic *sententiae*, which are elevated in tone. In his *Aetia* there are proverbs that serve as the basis for an *aition*, as well as numerous proverbs of less formal tone. In the *Epigrams* often the proverb provides the poet with an effective cap and closure. In the *Iambi* there are many colloquial expressions and popular proverbs connected with *realia* and animals. Finally, the proverb is employed by Callimachus (probably as *senex*) in autobiographical (fr. 178; 193 Pf.) or poetological (fr. 1 Pf.) contexts, to emphasize moments of reflection.

The proverb is a concise and concrete expression of popular folk wisdom that is very often transcultural. Though inherently prosaic, elevated forms of the proverb, occurring as sententiae or maxims, can be found in almost all Greek poetry. The formal collecting of proverbs in antiquity began with Aristotle and his school (Theophrastus, Clearchus, and Dicearchus), included the Stoic Chrysippus, and extended to Alexandria (for example, Aristophanes of Byzantium).[1] Although it is not clear whether Callimachus, in his prose writing, participated in this formal study of proverbs, he did in fact profit from the rich and fascinating proverbial imaginary in his own poetic production. His use of the material of proverbs offers us an excellent insight into how he incorporates philology into his poetry and, as we might expect, the aetiological dimension of the proverb often surfaces in his verses.

Numerical references to Tosi's 1991 collection of proverb types are usually given in text. *DPI* = C. Lapucci, *Dizionario dei Proverbi Italiani* (Florence, 2006).

[1] For recent treatments, see Tosi 1994; Mariño-Sánchez-Elvira and García Romero 1999: 11–26; Lelli 2006b: 16–26 and Lelli 2006a: 135–185.

In his choice and deployment of proverbial material, Callimachus seems to observe the hierarchy of ancient literary genres, the norms of which were by the Alexandrian age now fixed. It was a question of the *prepon*, then, that induced Callimachus to assign sententiae and *mots* from a Homeric and Hesiodic matrix to the high genres of his production (as the *Hymns*) while assigning more explicitly popular proverbs to less distinguished genres such as epigrams and *iambi*. Not surprisingly, there were occasional deviations from this practice that accord with the general Alexandrian tendency to contravene the 'rules' of genre.

The Hymns and the Hecale

The hexametric *Hymns* and *Hecale* remained even for the revolutionary Callimachus the highest of the formal poetic genres. The proverbs of a popular cut (with animal protagonists or natural elements) are only rarely incorporated herein, and for specific functions. Expressions that are more formally gnomic occur somewhat more frequently, and these are sententiae of Homeric and Hesiodic influence. For example, the *Hymn to Zeus* opens the collection of the *Hymns* with the name of the heavenly sovereign (Ζηνός). Callimachus' motif of beginning with Zeus (*Hymn* 1.1), previously attested in Pindar (*Nem.* 2.1–3), is present in all of classical culture, and reveals its sententious nature finally in the modern: one thinks, for example, of Italian: "non si comincia ben se non dal cielo" ("One does not begin well unless from heaven", Tosi 805).

Another example, which is already in Homer (*Il.* 17.98–99), is the clearly proverbial motif that there is no way to fight against the gods. Variants of the sentiment are attested from Theognis to Menander,[2] and in all Latin and Christian cultures (Tosi 1496), not to mention the similar but more generalizing sentiment of Hesiod (*Op.* 210). The Callimachean formulation (*Hymn to Apollo* 25)—

ἰὴ ἰὴ φθέγγεσθε· κακὸν μακάρεσσιν ἐρίζειν.
ὃς μάχεται μακάρεσσιν, ἐμῷ βασιλῆι μάχοιτο·

Say *Hie! Hie!* It is a bad thing to quarrel with the Blessed Ones. He who quarrels with the Blessed Ones would quarrel with my king.

---

[2] Theogn. 687, *Monost.* 341; and cf. Apost. 8.89c.

—elegantly superimposes the divine plan on the royal. This sententious motif, *ubi maior, minor cessat*,[3] serves as a functional justification of Hellenistic royalty, for the wishes of rulers are juxtaposed to the wishes of the gods. In this way sententiae that shared the Homeric and Hesiodic tradition, and were known to all, serve to strengthen the poetic message.

Even if Callimachus was clearly aware that expressions that are too popular are inconsistent with the hymnic-epic style, however skillfully redeployed, nevertheless he did introduce dissonant and humorous moments into the six *Hymns*. And it is appropriate, and characteristic of these moments, that the poet inserts proverbial expressions with a more obviously popular coloring. This is the case, in the *Hymn to Demeter*, in the section that highlights the grotesque elements of Erysichthon's character (McKay 1962, Bulloch 1977). The insatiable hunger that struck Erysichthon compelled him to eat everything in sight, but without taking any nourishment, so that he was reduced to "skin and bones" (*Hymn* 6.93). "Skin and bones" is an idiomatic expression well known from diverse sources and continuing into modern culture. An even more proverbial tone concludes the section (*Hymn* 6.116–17): Callimachus uses the famous ἐμοὶ κακογείτονες ἐχθροί. A maxim previously in Hesiod (*Op.* 348), and diffused through ancient and modern culture (Tosi no. 1374),[4] it underlines the turn to the more common tone of the passage on Erysichthon.

Thus the treatment that Callimachus reserves for the proverbial and sententious elements of his hexametric work seems clear. A few proverbs, but none with an extremely popular flavor, function in the *Hymns* to reinforce elements of the characters who are given humorous treatment; maxims from the Homeric and Hesiodic matrix impart a slightly more elevated tone. However, true and proper proverbs are entirely lacking in the *Hecale*.

Aetiological Paroemiography and the Aetia

Proverbs and proverbial expressions are well represented in the *Aetia* and employed in quite precise functions. Our philologist, first of all,

---

[3] Frequently attested in Tosi nos. 1264–65. See also M.L. West 1978: 209.
[4] For additional ancient attestations, see M.L. West 1978: 244. In modern times, compare, for example, Italian "chi ha mal vicino, ha mal mattino" (Pitré 1870: 153).

is enamored of the origin of a proverb, often wrapped in the mystery or the legacy linked to a particular anecdote, as for example scarcely known rites and individuals, minor legends recovered by the learned in the search for truth.

Among the first questions that the poet poses to Calliope are those on the origins of two curious rites that demanded insults from the celebrants (fr. 7.19–20 Pf.):

κῶς δέ, θεαί .[...] μὲν ἀνὴρ Ἀναφαῖος ἐπ' αἰσ[χροῖς
ἡ δ' ἐπὶ δυ[σφήμοις] Λίνδος ἄγει θυσίην;

Why, Goddesses, does on the one hand a man from Anaphe make sacrifice with obscenities, and on the other a man from Lindus with insults?

The second of these rites, from the Rhodian city of Lindus, had become proverbial; in the paroemiographers,[5] it is recorded in a form very similar to Callimachus' phrase: Λίνδοι τὴν θυσίαν; παροιμία ἐπὶ τῶν δυσφήμως ἱερογούντων, "Lindians at the sacrifice; proverb about those sacrificing with blasphemy."

In contrast, it is difficult to say precisely which *aition* Callimachus focuses on in one of the last elegies of Book 4 (frr. 98–99 Pf.). The event concerns Euthymus of Locri, a boxer who put to an end the custom of sacrificing a virgin to the legendary Hero of Temesa, a companion of Odysseus. (His name, according to some sources, was Polites.) This companion was abandoned at Greek Bruttium, where he was stoned to death, and afterwards became a demon who had to be appeased with this tribute. The story seems clearly to be connected with a female rite of passage, but the connection with third-century reality remains obscure, as does the motive for Callimachus' interest in the legend (see Visintin 1992). Certainly, by Callimachus' era a proverb must have been in circulation that traced its origin from this material; "the hero of Temesa" occurs in Strabo (6.1.5) and Pausanias (6.6), and subsequently is recorded in the paroemiographers,[6] with an obscure explanation, ὅτ' ἀπαιτῶν τις αὐτὸς ὕστερον προσοφείλων εὑρέθη, ὁ ἐν Τεμέσῃ γέγονεν ἥρως ("When someone demanding a payment is later himself found owing a debt, he was the 'hero in Temesa' ").

A significant digression that displays a connection between proverb and *aition* occurs in the elegy *Acontius and Cydippe* when the girl

---

[5] Zenob. 4.95; Diogenian. 6.15, and cf. 7.96.
[6] Plut. *Prov.* 2.31; Zenob. Ath. 3.175; *Suda* o 64.

falls ill for the first time (fr. 75.13–15 Pf.): "The sickness came that we banish onto wild goats, and we falsely say it is sacred." In the brief compass of the distich, the poet has here devised a way to insert a variant of the proverbial expression κατ' αἶγας ἀγρίας, well attested in the paroemiographers and lexicographers,[7] both to display the expression's origin and to underline, with a rationalizing erudition, its folkloric and popular aspect—ψευδόμενοι δ' ἱερὴν φημίζομεν ("we falsely say it is sacred")—following the trail of Hippocratic scientific doctrine.

As already noted, aetiology occurs throughout Callimachus' work, and is not limited to the *Aetia*; rather, it is a frequent feature of his poetry, an ingrained concession to an art that is erudite and self-conscious of its erudition. The proverb, rare, strange, for us often obscure because of its popular rather than textual origins, offers the opportunity for the poet to show his learning and at the same time to create the effect of making poetry from even a proverbial observation, sometimes a true and proper lesson. One example would be *Iambus* 11. Callimachus introduces the protagonist of the proverb ἁρπαγὰ τὰ Κοννίδα to speak directly—or, better, his voice, which through the medium of his own epitaph corrects the form of his name. This is one of the most colorful anecdotes in the corpus of the paroemiographers (Zenob. 1.11; and see Bühler 1999: 373–380). The pungent matter of the story, a pimp who leaves his inheritance for plunder, guaranteed a long fascination with the anecdote from the province of Magna Graecia;[8] and further, the onomastic question, which probably concerned the correct spelling of an indigenous name,[9] contributes to sustain the poet's interest in this proverb, enough to dedicate the entire poem to it. An *aition*, then, iambic and proverbial at the same time.

In fragment 229 Pf. (*Iambus* 17) we have the scene of Apollo attracted to the shepherd Branchus and trying to steal a kiss from him. Pretending that he is a goatherd, he ends up milking a billy goat, thus revealing his own inexperience and, at the same time, his divine nature (fr. 217 Pf.).[10] This constitutes the origin of a proverb: "to milk a billy

---

[7] Diogenian. 5.49; Hesych. κ 1123, παροιμία λεγομένη εἰς ἀγρίας αἶγας τρέφειν. Cf. Philod. *Ad contubern.* 1.3 (= *PHerc* 1005, col. VII 8–10); Philostr. *Heroic.* 2, p. 179 K.

[8] So Timaeus *FGrHist* 566 F 148, probably Callimachus' source.

[9] Another interest well attested in Callimachus: Lelli 2007.

[10] Pfeiffer hesitantly assigns fragment 217 to *Iambus* 1; see Lelli 2005a: 6–10 for reasons to locate it in the *Branchus*.

goat" (τράγον ἀμέλγειν), well noted in a series of *adynata*, proverbially useless actions (Diogenian. 7.95; Apost. 17.32a), which has found here, now ironically, its own later mythological exegesis.

One of Callimachus' *Epigrams*, transmitted by Diogenes Laertius (1.79), a true and proper epigrammatic *aition*, is based on one of the *sententiae* attributed to Pittacus and was subsequently included in the paroemiographers and lexicographers.[11] The expression τὴν κατὰ σαυτὸν ἔλα, "drive along your own track" offers, as a rule for marriage, interesting comparisons with proverbs both ancient and modern, from the Sardinian "cojaudi cum pares tuos" ("Marry with your equals," which is glossed "that is, of age and situation")[12] to the Tuscan "il parentado dev'essere pari" ("The marriage ought to be equal").

A final instance of Callimachus' interest in the aetiology of proverbs is worth mentioning. Φασηλιτῶν θῦμα is a geographical proverb for a cheap and bloodless sacrifice; according to Photius, Callimachus discussed this saying in his *Customs of the Barbarians*, claiming that the proverb originated because "the Phaselitans sacrificed salted fish to Cylabra" (fr. 405 Pf.).

In addition to including proverbs for their aetiological value, Callimachus was quite conscious also of the expressive and stylistic potential of proverbs and *sententiae*, and he exploited them in a broad range of functions. To understand this better, let us return to the *Aetia*. The artistic function detectable in Callimachus' use of proverbs is the connotative, aiming to characterize a person or a context. In the *Dream* (fr. 2.5 Pf.) the reader encounters a well-known motif clearly intended to recall the wise figure of Hesiod, whose analogous sententious verse Callimachus has intentionally redeployed. Hesiod warned corrupt kings: οἷ τ' αὐτῷ κακὰ τεύχει ἀνὴρ ἄλλῳ κακὰ τεύχων ("a man devising evil for another devises evil for himself," Hes. *Op.* 265).[13] Callimachus, in his construction of the persona of Hesiod, chooses to characterize him in an appropriately gnomic way—Eustathius comments (*ad Od.* 21.64): Τὸ δὲ "οἷ τ' αὐτῷ" ἀρχὴ γέγονε γνωμικοῦ, πρῶτα μὲν Ἡσιόδῳ, εἶτα καὶ Καλλιμάχῳ, τοῦ εἰπόντος, ὡς ὁ τεύχων ἑτέρῳ κακὸν ἑῷ ἥπατι τεύχει ("οἷ τ' αὐτῷ was the beginning of a gno-

---

[11] *Suda* τ 522 (attributed also to Chilon); Diogenian. 8.46; Apost. 9.89; cf. Plut. *Lib educ.* 19.
[12] Spano 2004: 203.
[13] The motif is probably of Near Eastern origin (M.L. West 1978: 222 and Alster 2005: no. 50). Tosi nos. 266, 268.

mic verse, first in Hesiod, then in Callimachus, saying..."). Thus Callimachus reinforces the image of Hesiod as a wise man and preceptor that continues throughout the Hellenistic period.

If a motif with a prestigious tradition is appropriate to connote Hesiod, to construct the image of a less legendary—and more acquisitive (cf. fr. 222 Pf.)—figure, Simonides (who in one of the initial elegies of *Aetia* 3 laments the profanation of his tomb in Agrigentum during the work of fortifying the city wall), the poet uses, in a significant opening *sedes*, a well-known and popular proverb, also in the ambit of Magna Graecia (fr. 64.1-2 Pf.):

> Οὐδ᾽ ἄ]ν τοι Καμάρινα τόσον κακὸν ὀκκόσον ἀ[ν]δρός
> κινη]θεὶς ὁσίου τύμβος ἐπικρεμάσαι·
>
> Not even Camarina would threaten such a great evil as tearing down a pious man's tomb.

The proverb, which has an oracular origin,[14] falls into a well-attested series of prohibitions against moving an object, which, if violated, could provoke harm or sudden alteration in situation.[15] The proverb's descendant, in this case, connotes perfectly the persona of Simonides. It retains elements of the wise man from the biographical tradition, but at the same time the characteristics that we also read in his own fragments, popular and proverbial expressions that allow the modern critic to catch a glimpse of the author's proximity to the origins of literary epinician, characterized also by elements pertaining to the more spontaneous forms of improvised victory songs[16]—and that ought to have reminded Callimachus, if only by contrast, of Pindar above all, whose preference for gnomic expression is well known.

Other personae in the *Aetia* take on a distinctive character through the use of familiar popular proverbs. This is the case of the celebrated lock of Berenice, which, when it has ascended into the heaven among the stars, grieves to be far from the queen, and declares without fear of impiety one of the most famous Greek proverbs: Παρθένε, μὴ] κοτέσῃ[ς, Ῥαμνουσιάς· οὔτ]ις ἐρύξει | βοῦς ἔπος (fr. 110.71-72 Pf. and Addendum). From the end of the archaic period and in subse-

---

[14] Zenob. 5.18; and compare *AP* 9.685; Luc. *Pseud.* 32. The proverb occurs also in *Sibylline Oracle* 3.737.
[15] One thinks of Ἀνάγυρον κινεῖν (Zenob. 2.55).
[16] Cf. frr. 507, 509, and 512 *PMG*.

quent Greek literature,[17] there is a long discussion of the saying "an ox upon my tongue," with various ideas of its origin. The one that is most plausible seems to lie in popular folklore: comparison with the Calabrian proverb: il bue ha la lingua grossa, e non può parlare, "The ox has a large tongue and cannot speak" (Mosino 1996-7) provides an obvious parallel (well contextualized in the conservative society of southern Italy) and clarifies the genesis of the expression, for which the hypothetical archetype ought to be: "I have become like an ox, who cannot speak." Callimachus for his part alludes to the proverb in a more subtle way that nonetheless characterizes the lock by its speech as obviously not aristocratic, even though belonging to a royal head.

Besides the two functions already discussed—characterizing a persona or a context, and the *aition* explaining a proverb—the proverb in the *Aetia* has a further use. It may lighten the tone in a context that is too solemn. A clear example occurs at the end of the first *aition* of Book 1, where Callimachus takes leave of the Graces by addressing them thus (fr. 7.9-14 Pf.):

]ες ἀνείμον[ες] ὡς ἀπὸ κόλπου
μητρὸς Ἐλειθυίης ἤλθετε βουλομένης·
ἐν δὲ Πάρῳ κάλλη τε καὶ αἰόλα βεύδε᾽ ἔχουσαι
.....ἀπ᾽ ὀστλίγγων δ᾽ αἰὲν ἄλειφα ῥέει.
ἔλλατε νῦν, ἐλέγοισι δ᾽ ἐνιψήσασθε λιπώσας
χεῖρας ἐμοῖς, ἵνα μοι πουλὺ μένωσιν ἔτος.

Naked with Eleithuia's favor you emerged from your mother's womb, but in Paros you stand wearing finery and shimmering tunics, and ointment always flows from your locks. Come now and wipe your anointed hands on my elegies that they may live for many a year.

The reference here seems unquestionably to be to the proverb "naked as the day you were born," recorded in the paroemiographers, in the biblical tradition, and well attested in Latin literature.[18] Here the descendant of the proverbial allusion comes to assume a more disengaged tone, at the poet's final leave-taking: a tone, moreover, already announced by the quite humble reference to the glue (κόλλῃ) in the preceding verses, and reaffirming the pragmatic image of the Muses, who "wipe their hands anointed with oil" on the poet's elegies. As on other

---

[17] Theogn. 815; Aesch. *Ag.* 36; Strattis fr. 72 KA.
[18] Diogenian. 4.2; Greg. Cypr. 1.82; Apost. 5.72. For the biblical tradition, see Ecclesiastes 5.14, Job 1.21; for the Latin tradition, see Lucil. 623 Marx; Apul. *Met.* 1.14.

occasions, the image that the poet wishes to give of his own work is inclined to a dismissive and disingenuous tone, one that is self-ironizing, a position that is sometimes facilitated by the use of a proverb.

The Epigrams

His ample recourse to proverbs and idiomatic expressions seems to confirm that the epigrammatic genre constitutes, for Callimachus, the terrain of refined literary exercise, not elevated in the hierarchy of ancient literary genres. Indeed, the significant presence of proverbial elements distinguishes the *Epigrams* of Callimachus from those of his contemporary Alexandrians. This may well be because Callimachus was neither an *epigrammatopoios* by profession, as was Posidippus,[19] nor an author exclusively devoted to epigrams, as was Asclepiades. For the Cyrenean, the epigram could not have constituted anything more than a refined *parergon*, in contrast to works of greater literary and scientific engagement like the *Aetia* and the *Hymns*. But Callimachus was the first to perceive and to bring to fruition the proverb's enormous potential to bring the brief epigrammatic text to its conclusion in a concise and witty manner.

And this is much more relevant—contrary to what we might expect—if we consider that the use of proverbs and sententiae in inscribed epigrams is scarcely of consequence.[20] It seems to me that this disparity confirms the intentionality of Callimachus' abundant recourse to the proverb in another of his *Epigrams*, a literary experiment that reveals the poet's desire to characterize his place within a very popular genre, distanced from his more refined Alexandrian contemporaries (preoccupied, perhaps, with raising the epigram to a more prestigious stylistic level) and also distanced from the great many (for us anonymous) local epigrammists who insert Homeric turns of phrase to ennoble their commissioned verses.

---

[19] I have attempted to delineate the pragmatic distance between the two authors in Lelli 2005b.

[20] The funerary epigram is limited to a few themes: "It is a good thing to die for one's country"; "Whom the gods love die young". As Bruno Gentili stressed in the "Discussion" in Labarbe 1967: 384, "The development of gnomic themes parallels the more literary direction of the epigram, one more ready to accept themes and motifs from tragedy, rhetoric, and philosophy."

If Callimachus is above all an erotic epigrammatist, it is easy to see that for his erotic production (as is appropriate) he has reserved an abundant use of proverbs. Among the love oaths most famous in Greek literature is without doubt that of Callimachean Callignotus for Ionis (*Ep.* 25 Pf.):

> Ὤμοσε Καλλίγνωτος Ἰωνίδι μήποτ' ἐκείνης
> ἕξειν μήτε φίλον κρέσσονα μήτε φίλην.
> ὤμοσεν· ἀλλὰ λέγουσιν ἀληθέα τοὺς ἐν ἔρωτι
> ὅρκους μὴ δύνειν οὔατ' ἐς ἀθανάτων.
> νῦν δ' ὁ μὲν ἀρσενικῷ θέρεται πυρί, τῆς δὲ ταλαίνης
> νύμφης ὡς Μεγαρέων οὐ λόγος οὐδ' ἀριθμός.

> Callignotus swore to Ionis that he would never hold any man or woman more dear than her. He swore. But they speak truly that the oaths of those in love cannot reach the ears of the immortals. Now he burns with passion for a man, and of the wretched bride there is, "as of the Megarians, neither account nor number."

The motif of the lover's oath disregarded by the gods seems directly modeled on a mode of proverbial speech recorded in the paroemiographers and lexicographers: εἰς θεῶν ὦτα ἦλθεν· ἐπὶ τῶν οὐ λανθανόντων ἐφ' οἷς ἔπραξαν.[21] Callimachus' interjection "they speak truly" (λέγουσιν ἀληθέα) provides a clue of how the author understands the motif. (See also fragment 178.15 Pf., discussed below.) The oath of Callignotus, moreover, is as false as it is cruel to the poor girl, who now is "of neither account nor number," like the Megarians (*Ep.* 25.6 Pf.: ὡς Μεγαρέων, οὐ λόγος, οὐδ' ἀριθμός). This last expression is one of the numerous proverbs derived from oracles now found in the paroemiographers,[22] and variously employed. One finds this famous Delphic response (1Parke-Wormell) given to the inhabitants of more than one Greek city for their vainglory after a victory of little importance. According to the version attributed to Mnaseas, a writer of the Hellenistic period credited with a tract *On Oracles* (fr. 58 Cappelletto), it was given to the Achaean city of Egia; according to another source,[23] Megara. Thus the proverb offered the poet the possibility of employing a jocular tone in his text, relieving the erotic tension of the situation,

---

[21] Zenob. 3.49; Diogenian. 3.37; cf. *DPI* 2856: "Oaths of lovers count little and are worth less."

[22] Zenob. 1.48; Diogenian. Vind. 1.21; *Suda* υ 108; Tzetz. *Chil.* 9.864–87 L.; and see Bühler 1987: 270–276.

[23] Dinias *FGrH* 306 F6. The same expression occurs in Theocr. *Id.* 14.48–49.

and, for the philologist, of taking a position on the paroemiographic variants, confirming one or another exegetic tradition.

In *Epigram* 43 Pf., for example:

> Ἕλκος ἔχων ὁ ξεῖνος ἐλάνθανεν· ὡς ἀνιηρόν
> πνεῦμα διὰ στηθέων—εἶδες;—ἀνηγάγετο,
> τὸ τρίτον ἡνίκ' ἔπινε, τὰ δὲ ῥόδα φυλλοβολεῦντα
> τὠνδρὸς ἀπὸ στεφάνων πάντ' ἐγένοντο χαμαί·
> ὤπτηται μέγα δή τι· μὰ δαίμονας· οὐκ ἀπὸ ῥυσμοῦ
> εἰκάζω, φωρὸς δ' ἴχνια φὼρ ἔμαθον.

> The stranger had a wound that went unnoticed. How he expelled a painful sigh from his chest! Did you notice? When he had his third drink, the roses, dropping their petals from the man's garland, all fell on the ground. He is well done, by the gods! Not without reason do I infer: as a thief, I know a thief's tracks.

The speaker declares that he is well aware that he has been a victim of the "wound that went unnoticed," which afflicted his visiting guest. Ὤπτηται μέγα δή τι is clearly an idiomatic and colloquial expression; μὰ δαίμονας, one would not guess at random; φωρὸς δ' ἴχνια φὼρ ἔμαθον is a very old and popular variant of the proverb "Like recognizes like" attested from Aristotle and continuously into modern culture, where one might say: "to understand like thieves at the marketplace," (Quartu 1993: 252) or even "One devil knows another" (Tosi nos. 243, 273).

Menexenus in *Epigram* 44 Pf., who is initially—and proverbially—presented as "a fire under the ashes," reveals all the potential destructiveness of his capacity to insinuate himself slowly into the heart of the *persona loquens*.

> Ἔστι τι ναὶ τὸν Πᾶνα κεκρυμμένον, ἔστι τι ταύτῃ
> ναὶ μὰ Διώνυσον πῦρ ὑπὸ τῇ σποδιῇ.
> οὐ θαρσέω· μὴ δή με περίπλεκε· πολλάκι λήθει
> τοῖχον ὑποτρώγων ἡσύχιος ποταμός.
> τῷ καὶ νῦν δείδοικα, Μενέξενε, μή με παρεισδὺς
> †οὗτος οσειγαρνης† εἰς τὸν ἔρωτα βάλῃ.

> There is something hidden, by Pan; there is some fire there, by Dionysus, under the ashes. I am not brave. Do not embrace me. Often unnoticed the quiet river undermines the wall. I am afraid now, Menexenus, that...slip in and cast me down in love.

This is yet another proverb functioning in an erotic key, in a formulation that—if in antiquity is less well attested, though corresponding to "gutta cavat lapidem" ("A drop of water hollows a stone", Tosi nos. 214, 898)—finds an apt comparison in the modern "l'acqua cheta rovina i ponti" ("Silent water ruins bridges") (Kaczynska 2001).

In Callimachus' repertory of proverbs that have an erotic function, the most famous is τὸν φιλέοντα φιλεῖν. It is found earlier in Hesiod (Hes. *Op.* 353) and is the archetype for numerous erotic examples of a *lex talionis*—when the punishment fits the crime (Tosi no. 1303): Callimachus employs it as the preamble to *Epigram* 52 Pf., addressed to Theocritus:

Τὸν τὸ καλὸν μελανεῦντα Θεόκριτον, εἰ μὲν ἔμ' ἔχθει,
τετράκι μισοίης, εἰ δὲ φιλεῖ, φιλέοις.

If Theocritus, whose cheeks are fairly growing dark, hates me, may you hate him four times as much; if he loves me, may you love him as much.

The Iambi: A Festival of Proverbs

Iambus is the literary genre in which more than any other the protagonist is the *I* of the poet: in Callimachus' book of *Iambi* there is a greater externalization of his literary convictions and his artistic ideas. By means of invective, allegorical fables, metaphors, disguises, and cryptic jesting—the traditional characteristics of the genre—the poet stages the literary polemics of the Museum in such a way that one may easily glimpse the biased position of the author, a polemic neither generic nor typecast but almost always timely and personal; diverse poems of the first thirteen *Iambi* take up questions of literary criticism.[24]

But traditional *iambus*, besides being the genre of personality, was also the genre of the popular, and of the lowborn, of the fable, and of the quotidian—in a word, of folklore. Callimachus realized the best of these aspects and, as an Alexandrian poet, scholar, and anthropologist *ante litteram*, went in search of what could color the texts of his *Iambi* in a popular mode, combining together elements in themselves heterogeneous, but also artistically (and anthropologically) consonant on a connotative level, including antiquarian elements, of gastronomy and costume, of magic and superstition. He uses proverbs and colloquial expressions, accurately selected from the very low and unsententious, with animal protagonists, *Realien*, persons from anecdotes, and

---

[24] I believe at least six (1–5 and 13); see Lelli 2004.

geographical peculiarities, often not without satisfaction for their scholarly rarity. Callimachus uses them to confer on the *sermo* of his *Iambi* a folkloric cast that serves to recall the popular coloration of archaic *iambus* while adding savor for the audience of philological poets of the Museum. The poet found in the use of the proverb a formidable instrument, one very congenial to his own polemic, to lambaste this or that adversary, to ridicule malevolent critics or opposing schools.

If *Iambus* 1 is the manifestation of the collection's metaliterary point of view, it also manifests the point of view that Callimachus assigns to proverbs and proverbial expressions in the production of his *Iambi*. A proverbial image, in fact, opens *Iambus* 1 (and the whole collection): the philologists who gather before the Serapeum, summoned by Hipponax *redivivus*, are apostrophized as κέπφοι (fr. 191.6 Pf.), birds not very well identified, though the ancient evidence does indicate that the κέπφος is a proverbial symbol for coarseness and stupidity. According to the scholion on Aristophanes' *Peace* 1067, the κέπφος is a "guileless creature" (εὐῆθες ζῷον), said of men who were irrational or senseless (ἀλογίστων).

Also in *Iambus* 1, a proverbial expression returns in line 27 to delineate the image of philological folly (fr. 191.27 Pf.):

ὤπολλον, ὦνδρες, ὡς παρ' αἰπόλῳ μυῖαι
ἢ σφῆκες ἐκ γῆς ἢ ἀπὸ θύματος Δελφ[οί,

O Apollo, men, like flies around a goatherd, or wasps from the earth, or Delphians at the altar,…

A "Delphic sacrifice," as is clear from the interpretation of *Appendix Proverbiorum* 1.95, was an image drawn from the world of the sacred. The paroemiographer offers as a lemma a probable comic trimeter (Δελφοῖσι θύσας αὐτὸς οὐ φαγῇ κρέας, "At Delphi the sacrificer himself does not eat the meat") with the comment παρόσον τοὺς ἐν Δελφοῖς θύοντας συνέβαινε διὰ τὸ πλῆθος τῶν ἑστιωμένων αὐτοὺς μηδένος γεύεσθαι ("In respect to those sacrificing at Delphi, it happens that because of the plethora of feasters they themselves taste nothing"). Callimachus introduces Hipponax in the first verses of *Iambus* 1 with another expression centered on a religious taboo (fr. 191.2 Pf.):

Ἀκούσαθ' Ἱππώνακτος· οὐ γὰρ ἀλλ' ἥκω
ἐκ τῶν ὅκου βοῦν κολλύβου πιπρήσκουσιν.

Listen to Hipponax. For I have come from where they sell an ox for a penny.

Cited by Pollux 9.72 as Callimachean (the poet alludes to the same idea in *Epigram* 13.6 Pf., Πελλαίου βοῦς μέγας εἰν Ἀίδῃ), the image has an idiomatic and colloquial nature, as seems reinforced by comic and lexicographic citations (Ar. *Peace* 1200; Pherecrates fr. 86 KA; Phot. 314.17). The popular motif of the inconsequential value of things in the afterlife is related,[25] also, to a form of taboo that prohibits openly naming Hades.

Callimachus' Hipponax employs another idiomatic expression, λευκὴ ἡμέρα, to indicate metaphorically old Bathycles' dying day (fr. 191. 32, 35–37 Pf.):

ἀνὴρ Βαθυκλῆς Ἀρκάς...τῶν πάλαι τις εὐδαίμων
ἐγένετο, πά[ν]τα δ' εἶχεν οἷσιν ἄνθρωποι
θεοί τε λευκὰς ἡμέρας ἐπίστανται.

> Bathycles, a man of Arcadia,...was one of the blessed of old, and he had everything that men and gods know as happy days.

This manner of speaking has its origin in popular usage:[26] to mark each day as happy or unhappy with, respectively, a white or a black pebble, which only at the end of life would be compared in order to weigh the balance of one's existence. The anecdote soon took on a proverbial valence, as numerous attestations make clear, as well as its presence in the paroemiographers (*App. Prov.* 3.60; and cf. Mac. 5.57).

The final section of *Iambus* 1 is where the Hipponactean paroemiographic libido most rages. (It is also quite lacunose.) Here Hipponax, presented at first as one who would "not sing any longer of the Bupalian battle," suggesting an *iambus* without personal attacks, reveals himself at the end as the Hipponax of old, who takes aim—perhaps directly, perhaps allusively—not at Bupalus but at the poet-philologists of the Museum, and who vents his spleen polemically and aggressively, in the manner of Hipponax, before having to return to Hades (*Iambus* 1.98; cf. 34–35). He does this by unleashing a proverbial repertory without precedent—and not particularly faithful to the historical Hipponax.

Alcmeon is first evoked in *Iambus* 1.78–79: to be "mad as Alcmeon" is well attested in the comedians,[27] although it is not recorded in the paroemiographers. Then alluding to a new adversary, Callimachus' Hipponax exclaims: "Pay attention! The Corycian hears you!" The

---

[25] Rehrenboeck 1987: 55–57; Caccamo Caltabiano and Radici Colace 1987.
[26] For the significance and origin of the expression, see Di Marco forthcoming.
[27] Antiphanes fr. 189. 9 KA; Timocl. fr. 6.12 KA.

inhabitants of Corycus in Asia Minor had a notorious habit of eavesdropping on the conversations of sailors and telling pirates what they learned. Finally, their trick was discovered, and ἐκράτησεν ἡ παροιμία ἐπὶ τῶν δοκούντων μὲν λάθρα πράττεσθαι, εἰς γνῶσιν δὲ ἐρχομένων ("The proverb refers to those seeming to do something secretly but being detected").[28] Here, perhaps, is artistic espionage?

There is no shortage of proverbial inserts in *Iambus* 4, which stages the fable of a contest between a laurel, an olive, and a bramble, botanical metaphors for a dispute between the poet (the olive) and his rivals. The manner in which the olive cuts short the debate with the laurel employs one of the most famous proverbs of antiquity, as well as of modern times, "Silence is golden" (ἀλλ' ἄριστον ἡ σιωπή, fr. 194.59 Pf.), in origin already in the Bible and attested in diverse variants (Tosi nos. 16–19).

The next example, in *Iambus* 13, is addressed to a broad array of detractors who complain that the poet cultivates too many literary genres and mixes amid them an inconvenient variety of styles. Callimachus here employs a proverbial expression that aids in the exegesis of the complex piece (fr. 203.61–62 Pf.):

τοῦδ' οὕνεκ' οὐδὲν πῖον, ἀ[λλὰ] λιμηρά
ἕκαστος ἄκροις δακτύλοις ἀποκνίζει,
ὡς τῆς ἐλαίης, ἣ ἀνέπαυσε τὴν Λητώ.

For this reason each one scratches off nothing rich but famine-causing bits with his fingertips, like those from the olive that gave rest to Leto.

The expression "touch with fingertips" was widely used to indicate a surface approach.[29] Here Callimachus, the father of the poetry of *labor limae* and of metaphors of professional dedication,[30] addressed it to those who sarcastically criticized him. For their part, the malevolent portrayed the iambic poet as a dangerous figure (similar, perhaps, to the image in *Iambus* 1.83–86), one whom you should fear, and they did it by using a proverbial expression, ἐς κέρας τεθύμωται (fr. 203.52 Pf.). "He has inflated his horns" indicates the attitude of someone proud and angry, drawing from the image of an angered bull.[31] Horace bor-

---

[28] Zenob. 4.75; Phot. 171.17 P.; *Suda* τ 813, Menander fr. 137 KT; Dioxippus fr. 2.1 KA.
[29] Cf. Ar. *Lys.* 435–444; Eur. *IA* 950–951; and for the Latin *primoribus digitis*, see Plaut. *Bacch.* 675, *Poen.* 566. See Tosi no. 156.
[30] This is delineated in Lelli 2001.
[31] See Otto 1890 s.v. *cornu*. Cf. Plato *Resp.* 586b; Plut. *Quaest. Rom.* 71; Diogenian. 7.89.

rows not only the popular expression but also Callimachus' literary-critical context (*Sat.* 1.4.34, "faenum habet in cornu, longe fuge").[32]

In the *Iambi*, however, the proverb is not univocal in function or used solely in metaliterary contexts. The folkloric cast of Callimachus' language, in fact, is often achieved through the grafting of expressions drawn especially from the more popular types of proverbs. This is the case with the passage, unfortunately incomplete, in *Iambus* 6, a *propemptikon* for a friend wanting to visit Olympia, in which λαγὸς χελύναν (fr. 196.22 Pf.) more than likely recalls the proverb "before the turtle beats the hare," among the most famous of paroemiographic *adynata*.[33] Similarly, we find the expression τὸν πυραμοῦντα λήψεται ("He will take the cake," fr. 227.6 Pf.) with which *Iambus* 15 designates the rewards for those who manage to stay awake the entire night of the festival honoring the Dioscuri and Helen.[34]

Proverbs between Poetry and Life

Callimachus is among the authors of Greek literature who talk to us about themselves, their poetic world, and their relationships with others. These personal revelations are almost inevitably filtered by metaphor, the facade of the *persona loquens*, through allusion or literary play. Occasionally, however, the poet surprises us with his personality, seemingly without disguise and without masks: these are moments when the narrator reveals himself to his audience, openly and (apparently) with irony, moments in which he seems to recall lived experiences. In these passages, a Callimachus emerges, who opens himself to the reader, who seems to reveal his deep convictions, his own strengths and weaknesses: the passion and pride, self-irony and stubbornness. In these passages—and here is the surprise—the poet who speaks of himself does not go in search of daring metaphors or unusual images. Rather, one finds the most natural form of conversation, a plainer style and a more popular mode of communication: in a word, the proverbs. The proverbial Callimachus opens a window on himself that at first glance differs from the revolutionary (and aristocratic) experimenter

---

[32] Cf. Cozzoli 1996b: 142–144; Kerkhecker 1999: 265–266.
[33] Diogenian. 7.57; Apost. 16.76; cf. Lib. *Epist.* 72.
[34] The proverbial milieu is guaranteed by Ar. *Knights* 277 and *Thesm.* 94, and the scholion on the latter passage; see also Artemidorus 1.72.

to whom we are accustomed: this is a Callimachus (*senex?*) who speaks through proverbs, perhaps mildly, but not without effectiveness. Callimachus, once again, knew how to reach his readers, offering an image of disenchanted but reassuring wisdom.

The *aition* on the cults of Icos, inserted into the frame of the so-called Banquet of Pollis (fr. 178 Pf.), is one of the passages in which Callimachus shows himself in a most spontaneous and ordinary manner. The poet, speaking in the first person, reminisces about a symposium, held probably in Alexandria, at the house of an Athenian named Pollis, who was celebrating his native festival of the Anthesteria abroad.

The symposium, a setting of intimate sociability, induces confidentiality, especially upon encountering a person with whom one feels an immediate accord (fr. 178.9–10 Pf.):

ἀλλ' αἶνος Ὁμηρικός, αἰὲν ὁμοῖον
ὡς θεός, οὐ ψευδής, ἐς τὸν ὁμοῖον ἄγει.

But Homer's saying is not false: god always brings like to like.

The wording echoes *Odyssey* 17.218; this expression is among the most famous in the ancient proverb repertory,[35] and it serves as a meaningful introduction to the dialogue between the two men.

An atmosphere of intimacy is established immediately. After the introductions and a few glasses of wine, Callimachus enters into a conversation, asking his new acquaintance for information about distant lands that he himself has never visited.[36] He does this with a phrase that is most likely proverbial, as is suggested by the formula that it introduces (fr. 178.15–16 Pf.):[37]

ἦ μάλ' ἔπος τόδ' ἀληθές, ὅ τ' οὐ μόνον ὕδατος αἶσαν,
ἀλλ' ἔτι καὶ λέσχης οἶνος ἔχειν ἐθέλει.

Indeed this is a true mot, that wine needs its portion not only of water but even of conversation.

Callimachus characterizes himself by a similar trait in his short but incisive self-epitaph: "one who knows when to mix laughter with

---

[35] Callimachus has employed the motif seen in *Epigram* 43.6 Pf. in a witty variant.
[36] See Massimilla 1996: 399–400. A list of benefactors to the city of Athens, registered under the archonship of Diomedon (248/7 BC), lists one Callimachus, tentatively identified by Oliver 2002 as our poet.
[37] See the remarks of Massimilla 1996: 410.

wine" (*Ep.* 35.2 Pf.). Here, in the opening lines, the motif reveals its colloquial idiom, which is reinforced by comparison with the many sayings on wine that induce mirth and song known from modern cultures (Tosi no. 735).

If Callimachus begins by expressing himself in proverbs, the Ician guest maintains the register (fr. 178.32–34 Pf.):

τρισμάκαρ, ἦ παύρων ὄλβιός ἐσσι μέτα,
ναυτιλίης εἰ νῆιν ἔχεις βίον· ἀλλ' ἐμὸς αἰών
κύμασιν αἰθυίης μᾶλλον ἐσῳκίσατο.

> Thrice blessed, truly you are happier than few are if you have a life ignorant of seafaring. But my life is spent more at home on the waves than the seabird.

The sea, danger par excellence in the ancient (and also modern) imagination, offers plenty of material for the paroemiographic repertoire. But here, the evident proverbial coloring adds a noticeable tinge of colloquialism. And this applies to the whole scene. The two guests meet at the symposium; almost by chance, they begin to talk in clichés of their personal affairs between one glass of wine and another. Callimachus here has touched the pinnacle of Alexandrian realism, sketching—thanks to the use of the proverb—a slice of life lived and fondly remembered.

The poet reveals himself, and consequently his poetry, even in sections where he interrupts a fictional narrative and turns to a persona, or the reader, or himself. This is the case in an extradiegetic speech from *Acontius and Cydippe* (fr. 75.4–9 Pf.):

Ἥρην γάρ κοτέ φασι—κύον, κύον, ἴσχεο, λαιδρέ
θυμέ, σύ γ' ἀείσῃ καὶ τά περ οὐχ ὁσίη·
ὤναο κάρτ' ἕνεκ' οὔ τι θεῆς ἴδες ἱερὰ φρικτῆς,
ἐξ ἂν ἐπεὶ καὶ τῶν ἤρυγες ἱστορίην.
ἦ πολυιδρείη χαλεπὸν κακόν, ὅστις ἀκαρτεῖ
γλώσσης· ὡς ἐτεὸν παῖς ὅδε μαῦλιν ἔχει.

> For they say that once upon a time Hera—dog, dog, stop, shameless heart: you would sing even of what is not holy. You are lucky that you have not seen the rites of the dire goddess, since you would have disgorged the story of them as well. Surely, knowing a lot is a bad thing for someone who does not guard his tongue. Really, he is like a child with a knife.

Although much has been written on this piece, it has not been sufficiently stressed, I think, that Callimachus once again has dipped into the proverbial repertory, as always at a moment of emphasis, to express traits by which he characterizes his personality and his poetry. "Much learning, much disgrace," first of all, is a sententious formulation that shares common ground with the proverbial "Who adds knowledge, adds troubles."[38] Indirectly and humorously, one sees the personality of a poet conscious of his learning and taking pleasure in good-natured fun. But Callimachus goes even further. "Like a child carrying a knife" clearly closes the proverbial apostrophe to himself: a self-directed irony in which once again the proverbial imaginary functions in the poet's self-presentation. Like the child holding the knife, Callimachus too is aware of but fascinated by the danger of the powerful weapon of language. And the efficacy of the image is increased because it is proverbial.

Within the metaliterary, Callimachus also seems to have favored the figure of the child:[39] this is not only a step in the direction of the proverbial; it also makes a significant bridge with *Epigram* 1 Pf. (mentioned above), where the refrain in the game that Mytilenean children play with the top functions as a paradigm for the human, and artistic, journey; it also connects with the best-known, most studied, discussed, and imitated passage of Callimachus: the *Prologue* of the *Aetia*. In his *Reply to the Telchines*, Callimachus claims to "write poetry like a child, despite the decades of [his] years" (fr. 1.6–7 Pf.). This is, perhaps, an allusive reminder of the poetological account in fragment 75 Pf., and one that can open the interesting, if hypothetical, prospect of reading the most famous page in Callimachus' extant oeuvre as a distillation of proverbial wisdom.

There is no escape, then, from the attentive eye of the paroemiologist. If Pfeiffer's conjecture of φῦλον ἀ[κανθές (fr. 1.7 Pf.)—which is supported by intertextual references to Antiphanes and Philip (*AP* 11.322 and 11.321, respectively)—is right, then could Callimachus be alluding to the famous proverb ἀκάνθιος τέττιξ ("spiny cicada")?[40] This is certainly a very suitable image for the insensitive and Museless Telchines. This line of argument becomes even more congenial if we consider that Callimachus only a few verses later wishes to become a "cicada [τέττιξ] of the Muses." Nor should it escape notice that, despite the

---

[38] For the Near Eastern and biblical origins, see Tosi no. 340; *DPI* 865.
[39] See Cozzoli in this volume.
[40] Zenob. 1.51, Diogenian. 1.49. The Greek ἀκάνθιος could refer to a type of cicada (Ael. *NA* 10.44). For a discussion, see Spyridonidou-Skarsouli 1995: 311–313.

very personal nature of the metaphor evoked in the contrast of fragment 1.10 Pf. (δρῦν?] πολὺ τὴν μακρὴν ὄμπνια Θεσμοφόρο[ς), its proverbial background could have been partially familiar to most people: one would remember βύβλου...καρπὸς οὐ κρατεῖ, "The fruit of the papyrus is inferior [to the corn]" (originally Aeschylean, and then in the paroemiographers).[41] Also, behind βροντᾶν οὐκ ἐμόν, ἀλλὰ Διός (fr. 1.20 Pf.) could well lurk the proverbial ἀπήντησε κεραυνοῦ βολὴ πρὸς ὑπέρτατον ἄτης, "The thunderbolt strikes a haughty man," which could support the author's *recusatio*; whereas on the other hand the Apollonian dictate to "follow not the broad path taken by all, but paths that are narrow and untrodden" (fr. 1.25-28 Pf.), could encompass more than its undeniably familiar literary tradition. Does this phrase programmatically distort the proverbial "who leaves the old road for the new," well attested in several ancient versions? (Tosi nos. 61, 464). The ass invoked as a symbol of artistic incompetence (fr. 1.30-31 Pf.) certainly brings to mind the famous ὄνος λύρας, and perhaps—if the motif is already old—the equally relevant "A braying ass never arrived in heaven";[42] and, finally, the desire to divest himself of old age and become the cicada (fr. 1.32-36 Pf.) has significant points of contact with the proverbial imagery related to γυμνότερος ληβηρίδος, "more naked than a membrane"—precisely explained by reference to the cicada stripped of its membrane—and is used συνόλως ἐπὶ τῶν ἀποδυομένων τὸ γῆρας ("in general for the shedding of old age"),[43] both with respect to the proverbial Τιθώνου γῆρας (Zenob. 6.18).

It is fascinating to consider that for Callimachus—a Callimachus here certainly *senex*—these allusions were present and in essence part of his culture. One of the most famous passages not only of this poet, but of all Greek literature, takes on a different flavor: colorful, new, and perhaps unexpected; here are the proverbs, with the power arising from tradition, that substantiate the argumentation of the Alexandrian revolution.

---

[41] Zenob. 2.73; Aesch. *Suppl.* 761; Lelli 2004: 27-28.
[42] *DPI* 4862, attested in diverse regional variants.
[43] Zenob. 2.95; cf. Diogenian. 3.73; Apost. 6.55.

PART FOUR

PERSONAE

CHAPTER TWENTY

THE POET AS A CHILD

Adele-Teresa Cozzoli

ABSTRACT

This chapter examine the poetics of childhood in Callimachus, which is complicated in its operations, and profound in its ideological import, but receives scant attention, particularly from the ancient critics, who fail to recognize its innovative nature or its status as the conscious end point of a long and varied career of poetic experimentation. The central concepts defining this literary tendency have been set out mainly by Bruno Snell (1963: 376–86), such ideas as the childlike, play, seriousness, ingenuousness, amazement, erudition, irony, and humor. Even if many of Snell's ideas on Callimachus now seem outmoded (as for example his claim that there is a total absence of didactic aims), he nonetheless saw very clearly that the poet constructed a certain image of himself as *auctor in fabula*—a self-fashioning, however, that should have been noticeable to any attentive critic, ancient or modern.

> *LUSUS, sapiens ait ille, MAGISTER OPTIMUS*
> —Giovanni Pascoli, *Poemata Christiana, Paedagogium*
>
> *Vecchio è l'aedo, e giovane la sua ode*
> —Giovanni Pascoli, *Il fanciullino. Miei pensieri di varia umanità*. 1903

Homeric epic does not usually represent childhood as a period that might contribute anything to the high seriousness of the heroic ideal. The only descriptions of childhood occur in *Iliad* 6.464–84 and 9.486–91, but in neither of these scenes is there any intention of accurately portraying actual episodes from the lives of children. Homer does also allude to the games of children, normally in similes (e.g., *Il.* 15.360–64, 16.259–65). But whereas modern researchers—as well as Plato and Aristotle[1]—have emphasized the educational function of games in which children's imitation of adult behavior through play constitutes a form of cultural habituation, Homer instead views games as senseless contests lacking any real seriousness. Indeed, even in the more peaceful world of the *Odyssey*, where we might expect more references to

---

[1] E.g., *Rep.* 2.377a–378 and Cerri 1991: 19–37, 58–74; *Poet.* 1448b4–19.

children, there is little trace of them or their play, even though we do meet the verb παίζω, "play," in reference to dancing (*Od.* 23.147), and even though we encounter a description of Nausicaa and her companions playing with a ball (6.100–101).

It is in fact only in the tradition of the *Homeric Hymns* that we have a true picture of a child's impetuous playfulness, linked to music and poetry, in the description of the divine child Hermes, archetype of the subsequent representations of divine children in the Callimachean *Hymns* (Ziegler 1966: 42–52). There is however a relevant passage in the *Iliad*, in the episode of the Shield of Achilles (18.568–72). Homer describes a grape harvest alleviated by a traditional work song. A child plays the *kithara* and sings the song of Linus in a soft voice (λεπταλέηι φωνῆι), and the workers beat their feet in time to his singing. This scene lies behind the final image of another ecphrasis, that in Theocritus' *Idyll* 1, which contains clear parallels with the programmatic *Idyll* 7 (Cairns 1984: 103–105). The unnamed αἰπόλος, urging Thyrsis to sing for him, promises him a κισσύβιον on which one of the three scenes depicted is that of a little boy in a vineyard. The boy should be keeping watch over the vines, but while foxes are snatching the grapes and the boy's lunch, he remains absorbed in the work of making a wicker cage for crickets. He thus symbolizes what seems to have been the highest value of Theocritus' pastoral art, namely ἀσυχία (Serrao 1977: 220; Cozzoli 1994: 95–110). Here the motive of the boy dedicating himself with some seriousness to his pastoral play resonates with the Homeric scene of the boy playing the *kithara* and is nevertheless indicative of a special kind of poetry, pastoral song. Making a wicker cage is undoubtedly a delicate operation; weaving the various strands of asphodel into a whole, however, for the boy is never more than delightful child's play. And in the Hellenistic era, even in the more traditional genres such as epic, children's games gain for the first time a certain representative autonomy. For all its references to Anacreon, Eros' game of dice and the description of the golden ball that Adrasteia gave to the child Zeus in Apollonius (3.114–44), while perhaps symbolic of the universal power of Eros,[2] are not purely allegorical, as they might have been in the archaic period.[3] Apollonius draws our attention first to the everyday nature of the game of dice between two children

---

[2] Cf. Livrea 1982: 39; Hunter 1989a: 113. See also Campbell 1994: 123–126.

[3] Cf. Pretagostini 2007: 169–179. With the image of the ball in fr. 13 Gent. (= 358 *PMG*), Anacreon has already alluded to *Odyssey* 6.100–101. Cf. Pace 1996: 81–86.

and second to the precise description of the marvelous toy, περικαλλὲς ἄθυρμα, created by Hephaestus. The ball is made of golden bands with hoops around each of them, but the connections between the parts are hidden, and blue spirals run over them. The description of the wonderful toy calls to mind the poet's own artistic achievement: the ball, like the poem, has a perfection and grace that depend on connections that tie together its various parts, linkages that though invisible to the untutored eye can be appreciated by the learned observer (κρυπταὶ δὲ ῥαφαί εἰσιν).

The poetics of childhood in Callimachus is even more complicated in its operations, and profound in its ideological import,[4] but receives scant attention, particularly from the ancient critics, who fail to recognize its innovative nature or its status as the conscious end point of a long and varied career of poetic experimentation. The central concepts defining this literary tendency have been set out mainly by Bruno Snell (1963: 376–386), such ideas as the childlike, play, seriousness, ingenuousness, amazement, erudition, irony, and humor. Even if many of Snell's ideas on Callimachus now seem outmoded (as for example his claim that there is a total absence of didactic aims), he nonetheless saw very clearly that the poet constructed a certain image of himself as *auctor in fabula*—a self-fashioning, however, that should have been noticeable to any attentive critic, ancient or modern.

In Callimachus' *Epigram* 1 a stranger from Atarneus asks Pittacus for advice about whether or not he should marry a woman of higher social status than himself. The sage of Mytilene, raising his stick, tells him to listen to the cries that a few children close by are raising while spinning a top and recommends that he "follow in their tracks." The stranger, hearing them exclaim τὴν [sc. βέμβικα] κατὰ σαυτὸν ἔλα, takes their words as an omen and gives up trying to marry into a wealthy household. And so, he concludes, just as he brought home τὴν δ' ὀλίγην...νύμφην, you too should κατὰ σαυτὸν ἔλα. This tale, with its allusive ambiguity between νύμφην and βέμβικα, appears in several sources (Serrao 1977: 225–226), but Callimachus adds to it an additional, literary level of signification. In accordance with the warnings of Apollo in the *Prologue*,[5] and

---

[4] Livrea 1997 refers to a "poetics of the child," which Ambühl 2005 wants to restrict to stories with children as the main characters.

[5] *Aet.* fr. 1.20: βροντᾶν οὐκ ἐμόν, ἀλλὰ Διός, "it is not for me to thunder, but for Zeus"; fr. 1.23-4...ἀοιδέ, τὸ μὲν θύος ὅττι πάχιστον | θρέψαι, τὴν Μοῦσαν δ' ὠγαθὲ λεπταλέην, "singer, raise your sacrificial victim as fat as possible, but your Muse, good man, to be thin."

with the ancient precept of Pittacus, the direct addressee, the stranger from Atarneus is exhorted to take a wife suited to his own status; at the same time, the poet himself shows that he is willing to choose τὴν [sc. ποίησιν] κατὰ σαυτόν, which is appropriate, considering his own nature and inclinations. Old man—child, play—seriousness, and ingenuousness—wisdom represent semantic axes that open to us a further perspective in the reading of the point of the epigram. The old sage does not himself give clear advice but directs his questioner to listen to the exclamations of the children, whose activity, far from empty child's play, is revealed as a source of age-old wisdom.

Giovanni Pascoli's poem *La civetta*, "The Owl" (in the collection *Convivial Poems*) contains a striking number of Callimachean reminiscences, which, although entirely unconscious, are profoundly integrated into the structure of a work based "mimetically on the thematic and linguistic model" of the classical sources:[6]

> O tristi capi! O solo voci! O schiene vaie
> così come la biscia d'acqua!
> Via di costì!" gridava agro il custode
> della prigione. Era selvaggio il luogo,
>   deserto, in mezzo della sacra Atene....
> *Ed anche in terra un gruppo*
> *di su di giù correva, di fanciulli;*
> *strillando anch'essi.* Ed ecco s'aprì l'uscio
> della casa degli Undici, e il custode
> alzò dal tetro limitar la voce.
> Egli diceva: "È per voi scianto ancora?
> Ieri da Delo ritornò la nave
> sacra, e le feste sono ormai finite.
> Non è più tempo di legar col refe
> gli scarabei! Non più, di fare a mosca
> di bronzo!" Un poco più lontano il branco
> trasse, in silenzio. Poi gridarono: "Ohe!
> che parli tu di scarabei, di mosche?
> *È una civetta*."...
>
> Ma Gryllo avvinse con un laccio un piede
> della civetta, e la facea sbalzare
> e svolazzare al caldo sole estivo.

---

[6] It was Pascoli's practice, particularly in the *Convivial Poems* (cf. Leonelli 1989: 42–45 and 2004: 329–333) to transform original texts into a new creation approximating the ancient to the modern, so to speak, in an entirely mimetic way and not eruditely passing off a modern poem for an ancient one.

E dai tuguri altri fanciulli,
figli d'arcieri sciti, figli di metèci,
trassero. *E in mezzo a tutti la civetta
chiudeva apriva trasognata gli occhi rotondi,
fatti per la sacra notte.*

E il coro "Balla" cantò forte "o muori!"
E nel carcere in tanto era un camuso
Pan boschereccio, un placido Sileno
col viso arguto e *grossi occhi di toro.*
Dolce parlava. E gli sedeva ai piedi
un giovanetto dalla lunga chioma,
bellissimo. E molti altri erano intorno,
uomini, muti. Ed a ciascuno in cuore
era un fanciullo che temeva il buio;
e il buon Sileno gli facea l'incanto.
"Voi non vedete ciò ch'io sono. Io sono"
egli diceva *"ciò che di me sfugge
agli occhi umani: l'invisibile. Ora
s'ei guarda, come fosse ebbro, vacilla;
ma non è lui, non è quest'io, che trema:
trema ciò ch'egli guarda, che si vede,
che mai non dura uguale a sé, che muore.
Io, di me, sono l'anima, che vive
più, quanto più vive con sé, lontana
dal mondo, nella sacra ombra dei sensi.
E s'ella parta libera per sempre,
nella notte immortale, ove si trovi
ella con tutto che non mai vacilla,
ella morrà? non vedrà più?"* Qualcuno
"Vedrà" rispose; "Non morrà" rispose.

Poi fu silenzio....
*Ed ecco entrò dall'abbaino un canto
d'acute voci: "Balla, dunque, o muori!"*

For all the variety of sources drawn on in this poem—from the painting by Dufresnoy that served as its initial inspiration (Garboli 2002: 1061), through Aristophanes' *Birds*, to the Platonic dialogues—the dominant influence is exercised by Hellenistic poets as diverse as Herodas and Theocritus.[7] In particular, *La civetta* seems to be reutilizing the oppositions between age and youth, play and seriousness, that were a

---

[7] Cf. the commentary and introduction by Leonelli 2002: 1174–78. For the reuse of the classical past in the *Convivial Poems*, see now Citti 1996: 53–80 and 1997: 99–131; Cerri 2007: 16–31.

hallmark of the Callimachean epigram discussed above, even though Pascoli's poem is formally much more complex. Just as the judgment of the old sage Pittacus is articulated through the voices of the children in Callimachus' poem, so in its Italian reincarnation the voices of children are woven into a conversation between Socrates and his disciples in a parallel construction that is sustained until the final, ominous cry of the bird. The traditional saying underlying Pascoli's poem is found in a fragment of the *Hecale* (fr. 77 H.): "If only you were dead or had danced for the last time!" (αἴθ' ὄφελες θανέειν ἢ πανύστατον ὀρχήσεσθαι),[8] where the imprecation against the owl, in the form of a wish, was probably pronounced by the owl's enemy the crow. As the *Suda* explains (where the fragment was found, α 166, 8 Adler), nocturnal birds could sometimes become the victims of cruel children's games in which the creatures would be exposed to the sun after capture and, removed from their natural nocturnal environment, would move around blindly in an uncertain way as if they were dancing. That Pascoli drew inspiration from this fragment, perhaps together with another (fr. 168 H.), is beyond doubt. But the particular volume that Pascoli had in hand was probably not Otto Schneider's edition of Callimachus (1870–1873) but rather the third part of Bergk's *Poetae Lyrici Graeci* (p. 681, cf. Leonelli 2002: 1175), in which the editor, though he cites the fragment, notes that he failed to include in his *Carmina Popularia* the "puerorum cantilena" about the owl.[9] In both poems, then, the voices of children are the medium for a message of profound philosophical import and of no less than sacred significance.

The manner in which Pascoli reelaborated distant and faded snatches of the Hellenistic poets can be even better understood through his use of the image of the child. Certain fragments seem to have been particularly inspiring for him. When *Reflections on the Art of Poetry* appeared in 1897, soon followed by the second, extended edition of *The Child* in 1903, the *Prologue* to Callimachus' *Aetia* had not yet been discovered in papyrus form (POxy 17.2079); and it would not be published until 1927. Before that, only a few snatches, torn from their context, were known, all quoted by Hephaestion, including the programmatic line

---

[8] The line is not metrical, but it is difficult to see exactly where the textual corruption lies. Pascoli must have read ἢ ὕστατον, Bentley's conjecture, which was accepted by Bergk.

[9] Another popular song, "Εἰρεσιώνη," reworked in the poems *Solon* and *The Final Voyage*, appears on the same page of Bergk and clinches the issue.

παῖς ἄτε, τῶν δ' ἐτέων ἡ δεκὰς οὐκ ὀλίγη (fr. 1.6 Pf.). Gaisford's 1885 edition, the one probably used by Pascoli, printed Porson's conjecture παῖς ἄτε (later confirmed by the papyrus and then adopted by Bergk in his *Adespota Lyrica* [*PLG* 1882, 1355]) for the reading παίσατε found in Hephaestion's manuscripts. The conjecture παῖς ἄτε, however, had already fallen out of fashion by the turn of the twentieth century (it is absent, for example, from the 1906 edition of Cornsbruch), partly because of the judgment of Schneider, who accepted παίσατε, mistakenly attributing an erotic sense to the verb παίζειν and translating "ludite, dum aetas patitur, nam annorum decas non tenuis est," on the basis of a faulty parallel with the *Agatia* (*AP* 5.281.4), in which the middle and final parts of the line (though not the beginning) are reemployed. Though hard proof is lacking, it seems highly probable that Pascoli came across this line of Callimachus printed in Bergk's edition as meaning "like a child, though the decades of my life are not few." Or he could also have come across it in Hephaestion's *Enchiridion*, which Pascoli drew on extensively in his *Rules of Classical Metre* and in which he makes another Callimachean allusion, referring to his own *Letter to Chiarini* as a μέγα βιβλίον and μέγα κακόν (fr. 465 Pf.). Besides fragment 1.6 Pfeiffer, Pascoli seems to have come across another important passage from Book 1 of the *Aetia*, fragment 41 Pf., transmitted by Stobaeus in his discussion of old age: "and old age is gentler to the man | that children love, and accompany like their father [οἷα γονῆα] | hand in hand up to the door of his house." The expression "like their father" makes it clear that—in contrast to the way the verse is reused by Tibullus (1.4.79–80)—the relationship between the old man and the children is not erotic, against the unanimous opinion of ancient and modern commentators. The image of fragment 41 will reappear in *The Child*, reflected in the image of the old man holding hands with a child (italics mine):

> The poet is old, but his poetry young.... And if the eyes with which we look outside of ourselves can see no more, nevertheless the old man sees now only with those wide eyes that are inside him, and he has nothing before him except for the vision that he had as a child and that children tend to have. *And if one had to depict Homer, one should present him as old and blind, guided by the hand by a child, looking round and round as he talks....* You, child, who know not how to reason except in your own way, a childish way that we call profound because suddenly, without having us descend one by one the steps of thought, you transport us into the abyss of truth.... You are the eternal child who sees everything with wonder, everything as if seeing it for the first time.

In the work of this cultivated reader and translator of the most obscure Callimachean fragments,[10] we can make out "flashes of Hellenistic subtlety, realistic details, gentle irony, word games, and slices of childhood," not only in *The Child* but also in *Convivial Poems*. And these may well be "the playthings and jests of a rejuvenated Callimachus," even if "in retraversing the landscapes of myth, nothing remains but a fragile device, last distillation of a reality by now consigned to books and in our age only to be cited, not experienced" (Leonelli 1989: 46). Of course, for technical literary reasons as well as sociohistorical ones,[11] there are significant differences in the poetics of Callimachus and Pascoli. All the same, the similarities are striking. Both pay particular attention to the world of childhood and in particular to child psychology. Both attempt to create a new style and language with which to describe this world. And both try to find material for poetry in the realities of everyday life, just as a child would do, looking at the world with fresh eyes.

A similar aesthetic occurs in another member of Philetas' circle: Theocritus. In *Idyll* 2, an adapted version of Sappho's symptomatology of love is connected to the linguistic limitations of children (Bonanno 1993: 61–67; 1996: 173–175). Simaetha confesses to the moon the effects of the arrival of Delphis at her home: "Then I went colder than ice, and from my brow | sweat dripped like dewdrops, and I could say nothing, not even as much as children | mutter [κνυζεῦνται] in their sleep, turning themselves toward their mothers; | but I became stiff all over my beautiful body, like a wax doll" (*Id*. 2.106–10). Attacks of aphasia, in a sense, reverse the process of language acquisition observed in children, so that Theocritus' use of a verb (κνυζέω) most commonly employed with reference to children is expressive of the sudden infantilization of the lover when confronted with her beloved (Bonanno 1993: 67; 1996: 174). And in *Idyll* 14, the poet compares the behavior of the girl Cynisca to a child's, saying that "she suddenly burst into tears like those | of a little girl, only six years old, who wants to be put in her mother's lap" (*Id*. 14.31–32). But perhaps most significant of all is the reaction of Gorgo in *Idyll* 15. Although hardly imaginable

---

[10] Pascoli kept up to date with new editions of Callimachus as they appeared: he translated, for example, a difficult passage from the *Hecale* contained in the Vienna wooden tablets published by Gomperz only in 1893.

[11] Pascoli was of course also influenced strongly by developments in the Italian and European literature of his day: see Leonelli 1989: 75–87 and 2002: 926–927.

as a child, in quieting the capricious desire of her son to follow her and Praxinoa with the exclamation Μορμώ, δάκνει ἵππος, she projects onto little Zopyrion her own fears as a child (ἐκ παιδός), fears that reemerge during the journey to Ptolemy's palace, when the two friends are confronted with some of the king's horses (*Id.* 15.52–59).[12] Though the use of the image of the scared child being comforted is as old as Plato (who puts it into Socrates' mouth in the *Phaedo*), it is in the Alexandrians that the child first becomes an opportunity for literary exploration, providing the platform for a certain type of introspective analysis and enabling the poet to address even the most hackneyed themes in a rejuvenated spirit.

> The artist is like a child in whom everything produces a sense of wonder. His soul renews itself every day; his joy at the perpetual youth of things has no boundaries. The clouds drifting through the sky, the distant undulation of the mountains, the fire blazing in the fireplace, the trees and flowers that he sees every day all speak new words to him constantly, and constantly reveal to him some new aspect of life. Inspiration is the state that precedes the instant at which his wonder will be granted expression through literary style. If we want to understand artists, we have to think about children.

These remarks, by the art critic and theorist Angelo Conti (*The Blessed Shore* [Milan, 1900], 26), D'Annunzio's "gentle philosopher,"[13] would not have been foreign to the old Callimachus of the *Aetia Prologue*, where the poetics of childhood finally achieves artistic self-consciousness. The *Prologue* was the culmination of the poet's entire personal and poetic life, begun many years previously with the *Dream*, and may even represent a literary last testament.[14] The juxtaposition of the two pieces reveals a sophisticated and studied coherence: though the proem with its Hesiodic coloring does not presuppose the *Prologue*, the *Prologue* was certainly composed to be united with it.[15]

---

[12] Here I use the readings of Latte and Gow, defended by Pasquali (1951: 379) and confirmed by what Gorgo says about her irrational fear of horses as a child. See *contra* Gallavotti 1952: 140.

[13] On the relation between his work and Pascoli's, see Leonelli 1989: 33.

[14] For a reconstruction of Callimachus' literary career, see Lehnus 2000c: 21–44.

[15] Interesting remarks on the links between the *Prologue* and the *Dream* can be found in Alan Cameron 1995, although it should be borne in mind that these do not establish that both were written at the same time. Instead, they suggest that the *Prologue* was composed to be seamlessly attached to the *Dream* (cf. Pretagostini 2007: 13–14; Cozzoli 1998: 135–154; Serrao 1998: 299–300), even though the transition between the two is not direct but mediated through fr. 2, the *Invocation to the Muses*.

In his reply to the Telchines, Callimachus responds to those who have accused him of ending his poems too quickly, like a child (6),[16] and of failing to write a long work glorifying the king and the heroes of old. Instead of replying directly, however, he introduces Apollo, the god of poetry himself, to expound a few key axioms of the art. Right from the beginning of Book 1, in the *Dream*, Callimachus refers to himself as a παῖς ἀρτιγένειος and so returns to being a child again, but now only in a metaliterary fashion, writing poems like a child: that is, exactly in the way that his adversaries had accused him of doing, but also exactly in the way that he himself intended according to his own literary principles. Though the Telchines deprecate his works as immature, the expression παῖς ἄτε is for the poet more compliment than insult. Indeed, this two-word phrase, sharpened by the poet's admission of advanced age in the very same line, has something of the quality of a motto applicable to Callimachus' whole artistic approach. Being childlike, precisely what his enemies find most blameworthy in poetry, is for the poet-philologist a positive prerogative that cannot be renounced (cf. also Acosta-Hughes and Stephens 2002: 240).

For Callimachus, this stance was the end result of a process of literary experimentation that involved all poetic genres and affected all the various levels of a poem, from the structure of an entire work down to the choice of individual words. The elegiac story of the *Aetia* breaks with the cyclical narratives often associated with archaic epic. What we have instead is a radial structure, noticeably different from the forms of the Homeric poems considered archetypal by the Peripatetic school (cf. Serrao 1977: 236–246). The most important example of the new style is the part of *Aetia* Book 1 dedicated to the saga of the Argonauts, which incorporates mythical elements belonging to a strand of the epic tradition stretching back much farther than the Homeric and again in fashion in the third century BC. In this section, the narrative radiates from a central node (Anaphe) in lines of unequal length (Colchian foundations in the Adriatic, Calypso, Circe, Corcyra) that also involve some backward progression in the form of flashbacks to initial events, e.g. embarking, the drawing of lots, the construction of an altar to Apollo at Pagasae (Cozzoli 2007: 143–163). This kind of narrative structure, in its essentials already present in the *Odyssey*, finds

---

[16] Or even of telling his stories like a child, if one accepts the reading ἔ[λεξα suggested by Acosta-Hughes and Stephens 2001: 214–216.

more exact precedents in late archaic lyric, and particularly in a few of the Pindaric odes. If Stesichorus had borne the "weight of heavy epic song" on his lyre in the seventh century (Quint. 10.62), and Antimachus had resuscitated the elegy by making it epic in the fourth (cf. Del Corno 1962: 57-95; Serrao 1979b: 91-98), so Callimachus in the *Aetia* carried out the final subversion of the epic-elegiac mode by a Pindaric fragmentation of narrative structure. The project is signaled by such techniques as the elimination of any distance between the myth of the past and the rite of the present,[17] and the dramatization of the creative act by the frequent intrusion of the narrative voice.[18] Both are part of a profound engagement with lyric poetry, above all with Pindar, in an effort to integrate certain forms and expressions from their original context in lyric into the formerly objective manner of the epic-elegiac genre, which had previously been impervious to their influence. In this way, Callimachus' work foreshadowed many of the characteristics of modern literatures, a foreshadowing that to the traditionalist Telchines must have seemed nothing more than reproachable child's play.

An important stage in Callimachus' struggle to innovate—which reaches its climax in Books 3 and 4 of the *Aetia*—is marked by the *Hecale*. According to a scholiast's comment on the *Hymn to Apollo*, Callimachus wrote the *Hecale* to prove that he could write exactly the kind of epic poem that his detractors accused him of not being up to. But most likely this remark is an example of the common scholiastic habit of turning *post hoc* into *propter hoc*. So the *Hecale* may well be a product of the poet's maturity, when the polemic with the Telchines had been running for quite some time, and after the more radical experiments in epic-elegiac narrative in the *Aetia* had already been published. The innovative aspects are found in the first instance in the form and structure of the work and its language, and then also in its aetiological and epichoric content, which is in some ways decisive in terms of the final aesthetic product, since the poem finishes by assuming the character of local epic. Above all, the narrative structure of the *Hecale* does not conform to Aristotelian precepts. Callimachus has chosen an episode from the saga of Theseus, his reception at the house of the old woman Hecale, that has no effect on the unity of the

---

[17] Cf. Serrao 1979a: 309-10; Fuhrer 1992; Cozzoli 2003: 67-73.
[18] For the technique of introducing dialogue with the Muses, see M.A. Harder 1988 and 1993a.

Theseus legend as a whole, and that could therefore be removed from it without any problems (cf. Aristotle *Poet.* 1451a16–35). The novelty is in the way the story is narrated. Although in view of the fragmentary nature of the work it is difficult to reconstruct the narrative in its particulars, nonetheless in the *diegesis* there is a striking recurrence of the adjective αἰφνίδιον, "suddenly," used to move from one section of the narrative to another. The predilection for this word might be imputed to a stylistic idiosyncrasy on the part of the *diegetes*, but the presence of expressions with a similar meaning in his summary of the *Hecale* (such as "without the father expecting it") makes it appear that the adverb has a distinctive role in the presentation of the narrative; it marks, in fact, the succession of scenes, which are often presented suddenly and without logical links—for example, the sudden return of Theseus, the sudden outbreak of a storm, the unexpected death of the old woman. Such accidental events, which elude any attempts at prediction, are for Aristotle typical of reality or of historiography, which narrates what has happened, and which is to be distinguished from poetry, in which only what should happen is narrated, arranged in a rational way by the intelligence of the ποιητής. Moreover, if fragment 80 H. precedes fragment 69 H. and so probably the entire episode with the crows,[19] then the speaker who addresses Hecale as dead in fragment 80 and celebrates her generous hospitality to all wayfarers cannot but be the poet himself. The narrator himself must therefore have indicated the victorious return of Theseus at some earlier point, in order then to transport the reader again to Mount Brilessus, leaving the final eulogy of the heroine to animals "actant", as in a fairy tale. To the ancient reader accustomed to cyclic epic, such a transition must have seemed nothing less than acrobatic. And since such transitions could not easily be condensed into an epitome, the *diegetes* eliminates any mention of the very un-epic episode involving the talking birds, and at that impasse notes only in a very impressionistic manner "but suddenly [Theseus], having found her dead and groaning because he had been disappointed in his expectation...."[20]

---

[19] As Gonis suggests in his new reconstruction of POxy inv. 112/87bII presented at the conference "Callimachus: One Hundred Years of Papyri" on 9 and 10 June 2005. Cf. Gonis 2006: 29–30.

[20] Rapid changes in narrative direction are rare in Callimachus: cf. the episode involving Heracles and Molorchus in Book 3 of the *Aetia*.

But it is above all the dialogue between the two birds—that is, in the insertion into the narrative context of a fairy-tale, surreal element— that revolutionized the epic generic code. With this innovation the poet achieved a double goal. First, in the speech of the old crow, an eyewitness of the mythical Attic past, he is able to leap over the many generations separating him from that period. And second, he is able to endow the crow, guardian (like all birds for Aristophanes: *Av.* 687–89) of the most ancient secrets about the universe and the natural world, with a competence more typically associated with the Homeric bard: that is, with the ability to sing about great events as if he had actually been present (*Od.* 8.487–91), or about great events at which he has actually been present (*Od.* 11.365–68). In transforming epic, then—in accordance with a schema already utilized in the *Hymns*[21]— Callimachus also transforms the profile of the narrator, who appears here in an entirely antitraditional, folktale, popularizing guise.[22] One aspect of the crow's mythical background is that it was a symbol of bad luck because of the famous κακαγγελία delivered to Athena; another is the tradition that the crow had to beg for food after being punished by Athena, as a result of which a common term for a beggar was κορωνιστής. Indeed, beggars even used to carry crows around with them, as is documented by popular songs that have passed into the literary record, such as fragment 2 Powell, by Phoenix of Colophon. If it is true that for every animal or bird there existed in the ancient world a symbolic interpretation based on the sound of the creature's name or its call (Bettini 2008: 143–159), it may not be too far-fetched to hear in the crow's incessant *craw-craw* an echo of the Greek verb forms χράω, χρή, and χρῄζω, and so to interpret the bird's cry as a desperate plea for help, and by extension as an expression of indigence or poverty. The link is already suggested in Phoenix's poem, in which κορώνη appears in the first line and χρῄζει in the third.[23] The crow, then, may be part of that group of birds that retells its own myth of origin every time it opens its mouth, like the nightingale.

---

[21] On the narrative "I" in the *Hymn to Delos*, see M. Giuseppetti's unpublished dissertation.

[22] We cannot fail to note how near the two poet-philologists, Callimachus and Pascoli, are to each other once again: whereas the former creates a popular bard, the latter integrates the popular element in ancient poetry into his own work as a manifestation of the child.

[23] On the text of this fragment, see now De Stefani 2000.

In Plato's *Phaedo* (60d–61d), Socrates, urged on by orders he hears in dreams, dedicates the last moments of his life to composing μουσική and versifying Aesop's fables: turning, that is, no longer toward the philosophical λόγος but to the more popular μῦθος. What Plato seems to be presenting to us here is a philosopher on the verge of the beyond who has decided to try to "persuade by narrating" myths (Cerri 1991: 53–74), which alone have the power to convince in areas where rational philosophizing has little effect. But this strange little palinode did not go unnoticed by the later tradition. Pascoli, in *The Child*, agrees that poets should construct *mythoi* and not *logoi*, stories rather than arguments, but does not fail to remind us how "difficult it is to content oneself with doing only what one should" and implies that Plato himself may not have resisted temptation altogether successfully in this regard. In a completely different cultural context, Callimachus uncovers capacities and potentialities sufficient for analytic history also in fabulistic and popular stories, transforming *mythos* into *logos* and trespassing on the territories of philosophy and science, fields previously forbidden to poets.[24]

The sense of wonder shared by the child and the poet, though, finds its artistic expression in the fashioning of a new style. Pascoli, following the recommendations of Angelo Conti, employs in the *Convivial Poems* a "heterogeneous linguistic collage";[25] so does Callimachus too, for he includes technical jargon, dialectal forms, and words from the iambic tradition in order to modernize and reawaken the expressive capacities of a language that had been rendered hackneyed by the epic tradition, which had grown stale.[26] His style is thus characterized by the frequent reemployment of forms from both the literary past and the current language (or languages), for us documented now by epigraphical and papyrological sources (Parsons 1993b and this volume).

---

[24] On the science of Hellenistic poetry, see Bonanno 2000: 210–212, 2002: 13–27 and 2004: 451–475, in which she argues that the observation of reality from a scientific point of view is a way of discovering fresh material for poetry from everyday reality.

[25] In Pascoli, one can identify "Hesiodic forms, forms from Greek and Latin lyric, borrowings form Plato and Bacchylides, expressions from the *Greek Anthology* and various Hellenistic authors, and even personal inventions created on the model of classical precedents, the little tricks of the trade of a prodigious forger" (Leonelli 1989: 49); at the same time, Pascoli enjoys inserting naïve dialectal forms that seem to come from the childhood of his people and that reassert his work's fundamental playfulness.

[26] See Bornmann's (1968: xxxv–liv) introduction to the *Hymn to Artemis*, a pioneering analysis of the style of Callimachus.

A good example of Callimachean style can be found in the *Hecale*, in the section in which Hecale offers food to Theseus (fr. 35 H.):

ἐκ δ' ἄρτους σιπύηθεν ἅλις κατέθηκεν ἑλοῦσα
οἵους βουνίτηισιν ἐνικρύπτουσι γυναῖκες.

And taking them from the basket, she placed on the table plenty of loaves
Such as women hide under cinders for cowherds.

As Pfeiffer first noticed, these verses recall a pair of lines in the *Odyssey* (3.479–80):

ἐν δὲ γυνὴ ταμίη σῖτον καὶ οἶνον ἔθηκεν
ὄψα τε, οἷα ἔδουσιν διοτρεφέες βασιλῆες.

Inside, the housekeeper served bread and wine
And the foods that the god-born kings consume.

The modification of the epic model here proceeds on two levels, language and subject matter. On the linguistic level, Callimachus chooses to employ lexical forms attested in other genres like comedy, often dressed up as Homerisms. So ἄρτους, the bread consumed by people of low social status (as opposed to σῖτον) and κατέθηκεν, which replaces the Homeric ἐν...ἔθηκεν, are both words drawn from the iambic and comic traditions (cf. Hipp. fr. Deg. 115.8 and Epich. 71.3 Kaibel.) Similarly σιπύη, a term drawn from Attic comedy, is epicized into the pleonastic Homeric form ἐκ...σιπύηθεν. The dissolution of any barriers between high and low subject matter,[27] epic and comic style, is completed by the final line. The loaves laid out for Theseus are, with olives and legumes, part of the traditional rustic diet and are food more for shepherds than for kings, but Callimachus specifies that they are prepared in a typically Attic way, by being cooked under cinders. Pascoli's child, his fanciullino, constructs a similarly heterogeneous mixture of technical jargon, idioms, Graecisms and Latinisms; indeed, his vitality is partly constituted by this linguistic *polyeideia*, which makes him sound old as well as young, but which also sets the stage for reversals of generic and stylistic expectation, as Pascoli says:

---

[27] Making the great small and the small great are characteristic techniques of all categories of literary irony. On irony in Hellenistic poetry, see Horstmann 1976 and Fantuzzi 1996: 16–35. It is above all the generic conventions of heroic poetry that are subverted (Bonanno 1986: 29–38; Serrao 2000: 55–61).

He discovers the most ingenious similarities and relations between things. He applies the word for the biggest things to the smallest, and vice versa.... He makes things smaller so that he can examine them, bigger so that he can marvel at them.... Nor is his language faulty.... And to every manner he gives a sign, a sound, a color by which he can always recognize what he sees for the first time.

The similarities between Callimachus and Pascoli cannot always be explained in terms of the latter's conscious use of the former, but often derive from a model that both drew upon, at times as an inspirational paradigm, at others as an antitype to be subverted: Plato. Only recently have scholars done justice to Plato's position within the allusive world of Callimachus.[28] Working backward in time, Callimachus progressed from Aristotle to Plato. Aristotle rescued poetry from its condemnation by Plato, restoring it to a position within the highest category of knowledge, but for this purpose he was compelled to furnish it with fixed rules and regulations, rationalizing it, and at the same to limit its field of operation to that of verisimilitude. For this reason, Aristotle was also forced to strip poetry of the inspired, robbing it of the religious qualities that are basic to every genre of ancient literature and reducing the poet from an inspired worshipper to an everyman happening to have the right natural bent.[29] But in the Hellenistic cultural environment there was little room for either the model of poetry condemned by Plato or the one rescued by Aristotle's extensive surgery. The new style of poetry practiced by the poet-philologists of the third century did not correspond in either its form or its content to the poetry produced by the oral culture of the fifth century. (Nor was it intended to.) The ποιητὴς καὶ ἅμα κριτικός was now in a position to move into fields of inquiry that had previously been reserved by the Platonists for philosophy alone. The task that Callimachus gave himself was, in effect, to save poetry without giving up its uniqueness as a form of expression. His task was to raise poetry to the rank of ἐπιστήμη by demonstrating that it could admit of as much accuracy and precision as science when moved out of the realm of opinion and

---

[28] See G.D. Williams 1995: 154–169; Andrews 1998: 1–17; and especially the chapters by Acosta-Hughes and Stephens in Martina and Cozzoli forthcoming.
[29] *Poet.* 1455a30-b and *Rhet.* 1390 b27–31; see Lanza's introduction to his translation of the *Poetics* (1992).

into that of truth.[30] The new style of poetry tended to characterize itself as in essence a τέχνη—one that could, however, apply the instruments of scientific analysis to its own style and subject matter, even if it also wanted to continue to value inspiration and originality almost above all else. In the *Prologue* to the *Aetia*, this value manifested itself in Apollo's order to get out onto untraveled ways, paths that are pure precisely because no one else has passed along them. Unfortunately, the poetry ran up against measurability, one of the key criteria of science and one with which Aristotle had attempted to infuse it. So at the end the high poetry's value, bred by the actual practice of literature as well as by philological study, was fostered by two poets who had a profound influence on Callimachus, both poets' poets and anything but rationalists: Pindar and Aristophanes.

The poetics of childhood, then, involves a recalibration of the persona of the poet in its entirety, redefining him as philologist and scientist as well as bard. Curiosity, stupefaction, wonder, and imagination are shared by both the child and the scientist, because they constitute the conditions of any desire to learn or discover. Albert Einstein, in his autobiography, stressed that every learning experience is born from a sensation of wonder, which we feel when we come up against phenomena that do not agree with our previously untroubled vision of the world. Every time we experience such a sensation, according to Einstein, we are driven to react by searching for explanations, initiating a "continual flight from wonder" (Schilpp 1949: 12–13). But whereas Plato and Aristotle had both considered wonder as a starting point only for those inclined toward philosophy,[31] for Callimachus thirst for knowledge and scholarly zeal are implicit also in poetry. There is a strikingly didactic tone to much of his work, starting with the description of the Muses as those who "see all and know everything" in the *Aetia*, and continuing with the depiction of the Banquet of Pollis, during which the young Callimachus, unfamiliar with travel, entrusts himself to the foreigner Theugenes and to the wisdom "of those who know" (fr. 178.27–30 Pf.). This same relationship between teacher and student is featured in the *Hecale* in the proverbial phrase "as much as the eyes are weak, so much are the ears wise" (fr. 292 Pf.) with which

---

[30] On the poetics of truth, see Serrao 1977 and Bonanno 2004.
[31] *Theaet.* 155d; *Met.* 1.982b12–21; "All philosophy begins with wonder" is quoted by Pohlenz (2005), who considers θαυμάζειν the characteristic activity not only of the philosopher but of the Greeks in general.

the narrator describes the eagerness of a young character to learn and in which he invites him to listen to the advice and stories of others (Cozzoli 2000: 225–32). It is featured again in the same poem when the old, wise crow warns his inexperienced friend about the unpleasant consequences of κακαγγελία by telling the myth of Cecrops and the daughters of Erichthonius (frr. 70–76 H.). In the first few verses of fragment 43 Pf., belonging to Book 2 of the *Aetia*, a banquet is mentioned (perhaps again that of Pollis), but it is made clear that (in contrast to the famous epitaph of Sardanapalus) nothing remains of the crowns, oils, and food, but only what the ears have taken in: in other words, only what Callimachus has learned from the experience. Later in the same fragment, the poet once again shows a desire to learn after the long story of one of the Muses, because "the more he learned, the greater his wonder grew."[32] But ultimately, scientific imagination has to be constrained in principle, just as poetic creativity has to be normalized in style; and Callimachus knows the difference between the naïve curiosity of the child and the scientific wonder of the scholar-poet. He knows, in other words, that the search for truth must be, in the end, a flight from wonder and must involve criteria that can at least evaluate the plausibility of a mythical tale. He is well aware that in the wrong hands "a lot of learning is a dangerous thing for those who cannot hold their tongue," a situation comparable to "a child who has a knife in his hands" (fr. 75.8–9 Pf.). Precisely for this reason, the poet adopts in the judgment of myths the methodology characteristic of Hellenistic science, in which hypotheses were evaluated according to their ability to explain empirical phenomena, which represented the direct consequences of the hypothesized laws as they manifested themselves in the real world (L. Russo 2001: 190–198). Similarly, μῦθοι in Callimachus are evaluated as true αἴτια according to their ability to explain τεκμήρια,[33] real facts or events such as toponyms, festivals, cults, foundations, and monuments that are the direct consequences of the actions commemorated in the mythical tradition (Serrao 1979a: 299; Cozzoli 2006: 119–136).

Callimachus' rethinking of previous ideas about poetry never attained the status of a coherent body of theory but is instead scat-

---

[32] Imagination and intuition are preeminently tools of the scientific philologist; see Pasquali 1964a: 50; Gentili 1992: 1–20.

[33] A concept already present in Thucydides (2.41.4) and later formally defined by Aristotle (*Rhet.* 1357b) as something assumed to be already known.

tered throughout various passages in his works, passages in which different tendencies seem to be in the ascendant at different times. A recourse to images of water, for example, is a constant feature of Callimachus' poetry, one that appears to be overturned by the derisive label ὑδροπόται, which was applied to the poet by his critics (Degani 1995: 106–36). Water is a leitmotif running through all the various phases of Callimachus' poetic career, starting with the first edition of the *Aetia*, in which he seems to be describing the mystical invasion of his soul by the Muses (fr. 1a.20 Pf., the *Invocation to the Muses*), probably provoked by the waters of Aganippe offered to him at one point by the gods when he was a child in an initiation ritual (referred to immediately afterward at fr. 2a.16 Pf.).[34] It would seem, then, that in the first part of his career, Callimachus wanted to revindicate the traditional role of the poet as seer, defending the centrality of creative inspiration within the art of poetry. He wanted, that is, to proclaim himself a poet through and through, or in Theocritus' phrase, "an offspring of Zeus molded on truth," seeking to avoid conforming to imitative models and instead to create in his own right.

But in the *Prologue* to the *Aetia*, there is a change of perspective toward a more nuanced style of writing (and reading), a rejuvenation announced and then immediately realized in metaliterary fashion in the comparison of the poet to a child. Here Callimachus defends the importance and power of the dangerous passion that Plato dismissed as child's play and against which Socrates warned in the *Republic* (607b5–6). Further, he challenges the view of poetry presented by Plato even in the *Phaedrus* and *Ion*, in which the philosopher concedes that the poet is "delicate, winged, and sacred" like the divinely inspired bee but denies him any access to true knowledge. But Callimachus also challenges the Aristotelian tradition and finds a critical model for the definition of his style in the comic categories employed by Aristophanes. Already in the *Frogs*, in fact, the poet's art was "weighed like cheese" (1365–68), applying a quantifiable, therefore scientific, criterion to an aesthetic judgment; in Plato's *Philebus* (55b–56) it is precisely the mathematical criterion of quantity that marks true knowledge, *episteme*, as opposed to mere opinion (Pohlenz 1962: 323). In the *Prologue* to the *Aetia*, Callimachus borrows words, images, and

---

[34] Cf. M.A. Harder 1993b: 11–13. On images of water in Callimachus, see Cozzoli forthcoming.

even scenes from the *Frogs* (cf. Snell 1963: 166; Alan Cameron 1995: 328–331), using them to restore to poetry its dignity as a τέχνη, but one in which the units of scientific measurement are completely overturned from their original and objective values. So in the end, it follows that poetic σοφία, which Aristotle said distinguished those who were ἀκριβέστατοι in their τέχναι, can in fact be measured not in terms of Persian units of length or by specific weight, but only in terms of notions of technical competence proper to the art itself and drawn up by the god Apollo himself.

Two different groups of words turn up again and again in the *Prologue* to the *Aetia* as part of a contrast that Callimachus draws between two kinds of poetry: the outmoded, bombastic poetry appreciated by his detractors, the Telchines, and the harmonious, subtle verse of the poet who, like the cicada, can slough off old age and become a child again. For the former he uses words expressing heaviness and noise like μακρήν, μεγάλη, πάχιστον, πλατύν, and θόρυβον; for the latter, he privileges opposite images, as in ὀλιγόστιχος, ὄμπνια, λεπτόν, λιγύν, and ἐλαχύς. Yet for the latter he also suggests aesthetic superiority despite their implicit inferiority in terms of scale and weight, as clearly shown by evaluative terms such as ὄμπνια, μελιχρότεραι, and λιγύν.[35]

Callimachus, feeling himself in his old age to have become the sonorous little-winged cicada beloved of the Muses, aspires to a second youth, because his attainment of poetic σοφία at some point is foreordained. From the first manifestations of his inclinations toward poetry, Callimachus has kept himself ὅσιος, avoiding both the indelible stain of artistic hybris and "the broad highway," "walking instead on untrodden paths" (D'Alessio 1995b: 143–181). The recovery of youth is thus a reward for someone who, since his actual childhood, worked to obtain the favor of the Muses and of Apollo and to remain artistically childlike, avoiding the hybris of the donkey who competed with the cicada in song (Aesop 184 Perry, cf. Cozzoli 1996a). By contrast, the Telchines are old and will stay that way, since even though they tried to obtain the good will of the Muses, they failed to do so; without the Muses' φιλία, they have no hope of rejuvenation.[36] Above all else, the mythological tradition proves that the Telchines are impi-

---

[35] On the contrast of styles, see Alan Cameron 1995: 328–331; Ziegler 1966: 42–52; Cozzoli 1998: 143–145.

[36] See Acosta-Hughes and Stephens 2002: 238–55; Di Benedetto 2003: 97–119.

ous: originally from Ceos, the story goes, they were led by their practice of magic and mutual emulousness to desire powers greater than those of the gods. As a result, the gods destroyed them. Whereas their mythological predecessors were unworthy of the gods' favor because of their magical hybris, the Telchines who criticized Callimachus at Ptolemy's court are unworthy of the Muses because of a different sort of hybris, a literary kind.[37] They arrogantly seek to imitate the inimitable Homer, and they enviously oppose anyone who, like Callimachus, has dedicated himself to a kind of poetry that contravenes their ideal parameters.

Callimachus, then, spurred by the sharpest of his detractors' accusations, that he is childlike, appropriates and takes ownership of this very childishness; he develops a style in which he evaluates all childhood's positive characteristics linked to philologist, scientist, and poet, and at the end, in the *Prologue* to the *Aetia*, formulates new aesthetic criteria, borrowing his terms from Aristophanes' *Frogs*. Thus the discovery of the mind that Snell almost intuited in Callimachus must be replaced by the poet's appreciation of the perennial ability to marvel that is characteristic of the child, the poet, and the scientist, and by his reconfiguration of poetry in the aspect of a child in order to incorporate within it both poetry and philology, literature and science. However, the only danger in the new style of poetry practiced in Alexandria was that, weighted down with literary erudition, it would come to be just as heavy. But it is precisely in παίζειν, "playing," that the poet's learning can be lightened. In the *Hymn to Delos*, for example, Callimachus, after a long description of the rites and traditions of Delos, remarks that these are all simply παίγνια invented by the nymph of Delos as playthings (γελαστύν) for the child Apollo (κουρίζοντι, 323). In so doing he turns an ironic gaze on his own knowledge and passes swiftly from the role of scientific philologist to one of poet-trickster (Cozzoli 2006: 131–132). In Callimachus' work, then, a playful style of narration, with its sudden shifts from realism to surrealism,[38] its multiplication of perspectives and of compositional centers of gravity, and its linguistic *polyeideia*, dissolves any heaviness and produces instead an effect of alienation and an impression of aerial lightness.

---

[37] On the mythological tradition of the Telchines, see Musti 1999.
[38] On Callimachus' surrealism, see D'Alessio 2007: 10–23; F. Williams 1993: 217–225.

Rapidity, exactness, and lightness of tone were, then, the hallmarks of the new style of poetry developed in the post-oral, bookish environment of Hellenistic Alexandria. These same qualities, however, are equally characteristic of the literature of the postindustrial age and are, according to Italo Calvino, aesthetic values that we should cherish as we move into the third millennium. In the first of his 1988 *American Lectures*, Calvino defends the lightness to which he dedicates himself in his works, taking "weight from the structure of the short story and from its language." He contrasts two different traditions of style in European literature, the weighty style associated with Dante and the light alternative represented by Cavalcanti. Cavalcanti's "agile sudden leap" described in the *Decameron* is then used by Calvino as a way of visualizing his lightness of style. Aristophanes long since compared the contrasting styles of two practitioners of the tragic genre, Aeschylus and Euripides, in the *Frogs*. There, Euripides accuses Aeschylus of using big words and of departing from ordinary language; Aeschylus replies that one must try to find words appropriate to great thoughts. Earlier, Euripides described his innovations in tragedy through the metaphor of weight loss, saying that Aeschylus left the art form bloated with bombastic speeches and swollen diction, and that he himself has slimmed it down with a diet of white beets and verslets (ἐπυλλίοις). In distinguishing two opposed styles of tragedy, the "high-thundering" style of Aeschylus and the "slender" alternative offered by Euripides,[39] Aristophanes sets up the terms of a debate that will be carried on and revolutionized in the Hellenistic period, in which slender poetry develops in antithesis to the severe Homeric tradition. And perhaps in the Hellenistic age other images, just like Cavalcanti's leap, effectively visualize the hallmarks of a new poetry: in the *Prologue* to Callimachus' *Aetia*, the scale rising up and the cicada taking off old age; Philetas himself, worn out by the study of glosses, puts weights on his feet so as not to be picked up by the next gust of wind (cf. Alan Cameron 1995: 488–93). Such images, which depend on the archetypal model of Euripides composing while suspended in the air in Aristophanes' *Acharnians* (398–99), illuminate the light style, making it visible to readers in all eras, just as that aerial writer of our own day, Calvino, has pointed out.

---

[39] Snell 1963: 166–189. On Aristophanes' literary-critical schema in the context of the play, see Bonanno 1998: 79–87.

CHAPTER TWENTY-ONE

SPEAKING WITH AUTHORITY:
POLYPHONY IN CALLIMACHUS' *HYMNS*

Marco Fantuzzi

ABSTRACT

Polyphony in Callimachus is often a strategy of persuasion: adopting a plurality of points of view in the presentation of an argument makes that argument more authoritative—especially when the authority of at least some of these points of view can be taken for granted. This paper investigates a few examples of the frequent overlapping of the authorial voice of Callimachus with different Callimachean voices impersonating or allusively evoking a series of more or less peremptory figures—a literary critic in defense of his poetics, the *vox populi*, the director of a ritual for a god, the god himself, or a series of saviors of the past. The paper concludes with an argument that the editor of Callimachus' *Hymns* (Callimachus himself?) may have hidden behind the authority of Callimachus the "theologian".

Multifaceted Solid Truths

A polyphony operates throughout Callimachus' *Hymns* that makes the persona of the narrator seem insubstantial, thus leading readers often to question the identity and the authority of some of his voices, or even the authority of any narrator at all. In fact these different voices seem, on occasion, to be digressions that fragment the unity of the author and increase authorial irony about the roles he plays. However, they simultaneously validate the multilayered authority of the author as especially reliable. As Aristotle comments about the rhetorical figure of division, to fragment a whole into its constituent parts makes that whole seem greater (*Rhet.* 1.1365a10–15).

Callimachus' metaliterary statements sometimes appear in straightforward and autonomous form, as in the *Prologue* of the *Aetia* or in

This chapter has profited from the advice of M. Asper, R. Hunter, T. Papanghelis, and I. Petrovic, whom I thank. It was mainly written in the earthly paradise of the library of the Center for Hellenic Studies, in Washington, D.C.

Iambus 13. But the *Prologue* and the last poem of the book of *Iambi* (or the last poem in the iambic section if the book included *Iambi* and Μέλη) were, respectively, prefatory and closural spaces of metaliterary validation by the author himself or by a superior authority (e.g., Apollo's voice in the *Prologue* to the *Aetia* or, at a less exalted level, the model of Ion of Chios in *Iambus* 13). They were thus placed at the margins of poetic books that, within the self-contained framework, had their own undisturbed autonomy. In their marginal isolation, they usually presented the poet's *I* in a solipsistic defense against enemy attacks, stressing his isolation from the stupidity of others. The *Prologue* of the *Aetia* also gives voice to a supportive Apollo, which is similar to what we find at the end of the *Hymn to Apollo*. But whereas that entire hymn can be understood as preparation for the concluding moment of consensus between Callimachus and Apollo, in the *Prologue* of the *Aetia* Apollo's appearance comes as a late intervention ex machina, and the god appears at a stage in the text after the poet has been holding the field alone.

Apart from the *Hymn to Apollo*, there are many cases in Callimachus where the characters' action or the action of the authorial *I* coalesces with metaliterary speech, so that they become similitudes or metaphors of each other, and the views of the poet receive an indirect approval by quasi-choral agreement of multiple voices. The example most often quoted of this complex interaction is Callimachus' *Epigram* 28 Pf. (*AP* 12.43 = 2 GP):[1]

> Ἐχθαίρω τὸ ποίημα τὸ κυκλικὸν οὐδὲ κελεύθωι
> χαίρω, τίς πολλοὺς ὧδε καὶ ὧδε φέρει·
> μισέω καὶ περίφοιτον ἐρώμενον οὐδ' ἀπὸ κρήνης
> πίνω· σικχαίνω πάντα τὰ δημόσια.
> Λυσανίη, σὺ δὲ ναίχι καλὸς καλός· ἀλλὰ πρὶν εἰπεῖν
> τοῦτο σαφῶς, ἠχώ φησί τις· "ἄλλος ἔχει."

> I hate cyclic poetry, and get no pleasure from a road crowded with travelers in every direction. I cannot stand a boy who sleeps around, do not drink at public fountains, and loathe everything vulgar. Now you, Lysanies, surely are handsome. But before I have repeated "handsome," Echo's "and some...one else's" cuts me off.

Common erotic preferences drive most people not to prefer promiscuous lovers but to opt for a beloved who is loyal and monogamous; and

---

[1] All the translations of Callimachus' texts are from Nisetich 2001, with occasional modifications.

hygiene leads one to drink from springs of the purest water, though finding fountains or lovers of this sort is much harder and less common than approaching available boys or public wells. The reality of the wide diffusion of the vulgar and a taste for numerous easy lovers nicely converge in the last distich. Many of Callimachus' readers will have remembered that this negative priamel was reminiscent of two quite similar statements in the *Corpus Theognideum*: 579–582,[2]

> I hate a scoundrel [ἐχθαίρω κακὸν ἄνδρα], and I veil myself as I pass by, with as little thought for him as a small bird would have. And I hate a woman who runs around, and a lecher [ἐχθαίρω δὲ γυναῖκα περίδρομον ἄνδρά τε μάργον] who wants to plow a field belonging to another. (Translation from Gerber 1999.)

and 959–962,[3]

> As long as I was drinking myself from the spring's dark water ["Εστε μὲν αὐτὸς ἔπινον ἀπὸ κρήνης μελανύδρου], it seemed sweet and good to me [ἡδύ τί μοι ἐδόκει καὶ καλὸν ἦμεν ὕδωρ]. But now it has become dirty, and water is mixed with earth. I will drink from another spring rather than a river [ἄλλης δὴ κρήνης πίομαι ἢ ποταμοῦ].

Callimachus' epigram seems to propose itself as a new piece of archaic elegy. In this genre the practice of sympotic performance customarily updated previous elegiac material. (At the very least, Theognis updated pieces of Solon, Mimnermus, and Tyrtaeus, and his text was updated after him with the inclusion of many pseudo-Theognidean poems.) Our pseudo-Theognidean Callimachus expresses a new metaliterary voice, which raises the ethical-erotic priamel of Theognis to the intellectual level of poetics. By paralleling promiscuous lovers with traditional Cyclic poetry under the sign of excessive easiness,[4] and uncommon paths with uncommon sources of inspiration as satisfactory difficulty, Callimachus illustrates the desirability of his poetics through the desirability of some widely shared feelings in human life that had already found poetic validation in Theognis. The message of Callimachus the moralist/sympotic epigrammist therefore melds into the message in which Callimachus the poet formulates his poetic

---

[2] With regard to the priamel, cf. Henrichs 1979: 208–211.
[3] This passage has often been interpreted in an erotic sense, with the muddying of the water signifying infidelity, the spring a faithful lover, and the river a promiscuous one. Callimachus seems to have relied on aspects of this allegorical reading: cf. Gomme 1925: 101; van Groningen 1966: 363–364; Alan Cameron 1995: 390.
[4] For the sense of κυκλικός in this epigram, cf. Alan Cameron 1995: 393–399.

credo. This credo thus takes on the obviousness of traditional and self-evident ethical behaviors—which had been also sanctioned by the most famous archaic gnomic poet. Yet Callimachus' epigram allows us to see, in addition to an elitist view of the world, aspects of the nonelitist reality. Apart from the overt statement about Lysanies, the final wordplay covertly replicates nonelitist speech habits like itacistic pronunciation,[5] thus demonstrating that it is all too easy to indulge in vulgar customs—even for Callimachus, who cannot refrain from making popular mistakes or from loving the promiscuous Lysanies. It is left to the reader to conjecture whether Callimachus the poet has been able to maintain his elitism.

In parallel with the erotic (universal) and poetical (particularized) options for exclusivity and elitism suggested in this epigram, another by Callimachus advertises the same existential choices and is based on a similar analogical argument (*Ep.* 31 Pf. = *AP* 12.102 = 1 GP):

> Ὠγρευτής, Ἐπίκυδες, ἐν οὔρεσι πάντα λαγωὸν
> διφᾶι καὶ πάσης ἴχνια δορκαλίδος,
> στίβηι καὶ νιφετῶι κεχρημένος· ἢν δέ τις εἴπηι·
> "Τῆ, τόδε βέβληται θηρίον," οὐκ ἔλαβεν.
> χοὐμὸς ἔρως τοιόσδε· τὰ μὲν φεύγοντα διώκειν
> οἶδε, τὰ δ' ἐν μέσσωι κείμενα παρπέταται.
>
> Up and down the hillsides, on the track of every rabbit, every deer—that is your hunter, Epicydes, braving frost and snow. But if someone says, "There it is, wounded!" he leaves it alone. My passion is like this: expert at chasing what runs away, it passes by what does not.

Here again the exclusive feelings of the hunter who likes to pursue difficult prey validates Callimachus' erotic preference for elusive objects of desire. Though it is essentially a development of the same ideas expressed in *Epigram* 28 Pf., *Epigram* 31 Pf. adds a significant qualification. If, as is probable, the name of the addressee, Ἐπικύδης, is a speaking name ("Illustrious"), it will have reminded the audience that Callimachus' statement is not addressed to everyone and that arduous conquest appeals to those who instinctively pursue glory and distinction; likewise, the negative reference to δημόσια in *Epigram* 28.4 Pf. implies that Callimachus is at variance with the tastes of the mob. Read together, *Epigrams* 28 and 31 Pf. thus construct a traditional ethical or

---

[5] Cf. Hunter 2003b: 480: "The poet's brave words turn out to be a protective barrier which conceal as much as they reveal, and only the operation of echo, which is beyond human control, can unmask the truth. The 'vulgar', embodied in a popular, 'non-elitist' pronunciation which makes the echo possible, triumphs."

behavioral model to frame and justify Callimachus' poetical choices as part of an elitist view of life: he is one who makes the correct choices as a poet, because, broadly speaking, he knows how to choose well, both in love and in life.

Elsewhere in his choice of the untrodden and thus difficult path, Callimachus manages to show that he is in very good company. In the *Hymn to Apollo*, the narrating *I* seems to prepare his audience for Apollo's divine epiphany. But the details upon which he chooses to dwell as a director of the welcoming song for Apollo—the prescription about purity of mind (ll. 2, 9–11) and the features of the song suitable for or preferred by Apollo (ll. 8, 12–23)—are details with which he has also been concerned as a poet in other genres.

The prescription of line 2 (ἑκὰς ἑκὰς ὅστις ἀλιτρός, "begone, begone, whoever is not without sin") restricts participants to those who are not ἀλιτροί. This term has a religious technical sense, "sinful" (dating from *Il.* 23.595), or less probably, a broader sense, "villain," depending on whether misconduct involved the gods or other mortals. In any case, in its ritual context in the hymn, line 2 certainly points to the regulations about purity of mind as a prerequisite for entering temples or participating in rituals for gods; formulated in many inscriptions in both prose and verse, they are called by modern scholars, technically, "programmata," and are found in several temples from the fourth century onwards. (See Petrovic in this volume.) Apart from selecting the audience, this well-paralleled phrase demonstrates Callimachus' competence and authority in allowing only the non-ἀλιτροί access to the sacred space of the temple, and to the presence of Apollo; indirectly, this limitation validates the official role of the speaking voice in the rest of the hymn as directing the rite for Apollo. (The only other substantial voice heard in the hymn, apart from the single line by Momos, will be the reply to Momos by Apollo at the end of the hymn, which silences Momos once for all.) This is especially fitting because Apollo is the god of prophecy, and the majority of the inscriptional programmata in verse had an oracular character, as they purposefully tended to reproduce the authoritative voice of the god, represented in the act of defending his temple or his ritual for the future. At the beginning of the hymn, when the identity of the speaking voice is not yet clear, the audience (or the readers) may not have immediately understood that they observe a narrator-performer directing the ritual. They can only hear of the epiphany of Apollo, demonstrated by the quivering of Apollo's laurel, and of the supposed noise from Apollo's foot, via a third person. Whose voice could utter the second hemistich of line 2?

Is it Apollo himself, paving the way to his epiphany? Already at the end of the *Homeric Hymn to Apollo*, the god left the Cretan founders of his Parnassian temple, after instructing them where and how to proceed with this foundation, with the warning (ll. 538–544):

> Watch over my temple, and welcome the people as they gather here, and <regard> my will above all <...But if on your part> anything wanton is said or done, any insolence [ἠέ τι τηύσιον ἔπος ἔσσεται ἠέ τι ἔργον, | ὕβρις θ'], as is the manner of mortal folk, then you shall have other men as your masters, under whose compulsion you will be subjugated forever. You have your instructions; it is for you to remember them. (Translation from M. West 2003.)

The most intertextually alert readers may have suspected that the speaker of the second hemistich of line 2 in the Callimachean hymn was Apollo, reprising here for his worshippers in the temple of Cyrene the very instructions that he gave in his *Homeric Hymn* to the founders of his temple at Delphi. This identification is facilitated by the end of the Callimachean hymn, where Apollo urges Blame and Envy to leave the scene, following a similar practice of ritual exclusion. (See Bassi 1989.) Of course, readers will by this point have recognized the real identity of the speaker but at the same time acknowledged that there is a perfect accord between the narrator-director of the Apolline Carnea in Callimachus' hymn and the Apollo of the *Homeric Hymn*. This accord, as well as the resulting moral integrity of the author, is restated, again at the level of ritual, in lines 8–11, where Callimachus explicitly lists himself and the chorus of young men whom he directs as among the ἐσθλοί (i.e., non-ἀλιτροί) who are entitled to welcome the epiphany of the god—in other words, the prescription that the ἀλιτροί cannot be present is rephrased in a positive and eulogistic way, thus confirming the poet as master of the song and of his pupil-singers, who merge into a single *we*:[6]

οἱ δὲ νέοι μολπήν τε καὶ ἐς χορὸν ἐντύνασθε.
ὡπόλλων οὐ παντὶ φαείνεται, ἀλλ' ὅτις ἐσθλός·
ὅς μιν ἴδηι, μέγας οὗτος, ὃς οὐκ ἴδε, λιτὸς ἐκεῖνος.
ὀψόμεθ', ὦ Ἑκάεργε, καὶ ἐσσόμεθ' οὔποτε λιτοί.

---

[6] Cf. Calame 1993: 48. Again at l. 97 the *we* listening to the ritual ἰὴ ἰὴ παιῆον may be both the narrator-director of the song and the chorus of young men. According to M.A. Harder 2004: 66–67, "the effect of this merging of voices may be to suggest an enthusiastic crowd taking part in the celebration of Apollo, and it recalls the indeterminacy of the encomiastic voice in Pindar and Bacchylides." See also Morrison 2007: 125–130.

And you, young men, begin the singing and dancing. Not on everyone, but only on the noble shines Apollo's light. He who has seen the god is great; he who has not is of no account. We will see you, Lord who shoot from afar, and never be of no account!

This shift from ritual prescription to prescriptions about the quality of the song for Apollo increases the attention paid to Apollo's musical tastes, paving the way to the central narrative of Apollo's help in the foundation of Cyrene (the city of Callimachus and the singers of his chorus) and to the final opinion expressed by Apollo on poetry. Both narratives reinforce Apollo's favor and protection of Callimachus as director of the song for Apollo and of his poetics in general. In a parallel but opposite direction, a few lines after stating the opportunity of singing for Apollo, Callimachus highlights the superior authority of the poetry that Apollo honors, especially over dirge poetry (ll. 18–24), and in mentioning Thetis' and Niobe's dirges as yielding to Apolline song he reminds us how dangerous it can be not to sing of Apollo,[7] thus opposing him (ll. 25–27):

ἰὴ ἰὴ φθέγγεσθε· κακὸν μακάρεσσιν ἐρίζειν.
ὃς μάχεται μακάρεσσιν, ἐμῶι βασιλῆι μάχοιτο·
ὅστις ἐμῶι βασιλῆι, καὶ Ἀπόλλωνι μάχοιτο.

Sing *Hiē! Hiē!* It is bad to contend with gods. The man who contends with gods would contend with my king. The man who contends with my king would contend with Apollo.

Another generalizing shift, from the authority of Apollo's song to the power of Apollo *tout court*, leads Callimachus at a later stage to exceed the contextual frame of the ritual and song, allowing him in lines 26–27 to suggest the further parallelism between the danger of opposing Apollo or the other gods and the danger of opposing Callimachus' king—an issue that, like the final definition of the best kind of poetry, interests the author Callimachus in general but is not strictly relevant to the ritual, or the song, or the authority of Apollo. We will return to this shift from the authority of Apollo in particular (relevant for the song/ritual being described) to the authority of the god or gods in

---

[7] Niobe is an anti-Apolline character for Callimachus, especially in the *Hymn to Delos* 86–98. There Apollo prophesies the sad destiny of Thebes as a result of its being the birthplace of the Niobids, Niobe's many children, who may exemplify quantity in opposition to the quality of the two children of Leto (Bing 1988b: 117).

general and to the authority of Callimachus' divine king in particular (irrelevant for the song or ritual).

Within this web of authorial voices, which seem to fragment the author but in reality subtly and progressively direct our attention more to the author and his poetic agendas than to the concrete ritual or Apollo himself, Callimachus establishes another implicit point of contact with Apollo: a preference for nonpromiscuous lovers, most clearly expressed in the two epigrams with which we began.

Illustration and motivation of divine epithets are a common motif in the hymns, both Homeric and cultic; and not surprisingly in lines 47–54 Callimachus interprets Apollo's epithet νόμιος in connection with a period of serfdom as a shepherd during the god's youth. (Cf. the parallel of Paris.) More surprising, but in keeping with the Hellenistic delight in discovering erotic overtones in traditional myths, Callimachus identifies this bucolic phase of Apollo's life as a consequence of his love for the young Admetus (l. 49, ἠιθέου ὑπ' ἔρωτι κεκαυμένος Ἀδμήτοιο, "burning with love for the youthful Admetus")—though Callimachus has prepared us with an eroticized description of the god's beauty and his elegant adornment in lines 32–38.[8] We have no reason to believe that Callimachus meant ἀδμήτοιο not as a personal name but as an epithet to be taken with ἠιθέου. (As an epithet, ἀδμήτοιο would serve to specify "marriageable youth," pointing to the fact that he had not yet had sex and thus demonstrating Apollo's accordance with Callimachus' tastes, as expressed in Epigram 28 Pf., discussed above.)[9] It is, however, difficult to escape the temptation to suppose that Callimachus may have hinted at the ambiguity of ἀδμήτοιο, in principle interpretable as an epithet, or at least may have exploited the sense of Ἀδμήτοιο as a speaking name. This eroticized version will also have been a surprise, because it was rare before our hymn; in the version of the myth that is attested from Hesiod onward, and remains the most common after Callimachus, Apollo's serfdom under Admetus is a punishment for killing the Cyclopes.[10]

---

[8] Mention of his "feminine cheeks darkened with down" (l. 37) is particularly homoerotic; see Noussia-Fantuzzi 2010: 381–82.

[9] For the epithet, cf. *LfgrE* s.v. ἄδμητος. See also Depew 2004: 122.

[10] Rhianus (fr. 10 Powell) possibly preceded Callimachus in featuring Admetus in this role, as stated in the scholion on Euripides *Alcestis* 1 (a discussion in Solimano 1970: 260–63), but this cannot be determined with any certainty.

Therefore Callimachus the director of the ritual, Callimachus the hymnodic eulogist of Apollo, and Callimachus the metaliterary defender of his poetics through the voice of Apollo all turn out to be the fruit of a strategic fragmentation of the authorial voice. His *Hymn to Apollo* starts with a phrase concerning ritual purity that could have been—and in fact could seem in the text to be—spoken by Apollo about the requisites of his own cult but was in reality conceived and spoken by the narrator. It includes a hint of Apollo's love for a beloved whose name quintessentially reflects his purity. It finally concludes with a speech by Apollo, who defends the ideal of pure and small-dimensional poetry for the sake of the poet who has directed his ritual and planned the song for him.[11] In fact the poet progressively paves the way in our hymn for the final and only direct appearance of the god in the last lines of the poem (ll. 105-112), which replaces the ritual epiphany suggested at the beginning with a very specific intervention of the god either in defense of the brevity of our hymn—in comparison, for example, with the *Homeric Hymn to Apollo*[12]—or against a criticism of poetry similar to that formulated against Callimachus' poetry in the *Prologue* to the *Aetia*, or more likely both.[13]

The reader is left with an impression that the final validation from Apollo comes to Callimachus' poetry as a consequence of the accord that joins Callimachus and Apollo in diverse aspects of life, from the features of the ritual and of the ritual song to their sexual tastes. Nor should we forget that this final approval by Apollo also strongly corroborates, retroactively, the role of Callimachus as the director of the song, as the parallel example of Isyllus' inscription at Epidaurus clearly shows.

The Epidaurian Isyllus dedicated an inscription of eighty-four lines to Apollo Maleatas and Asclepius in the sanctuary of Asclepius at

---

[11] Callimachus' *Hymn to Apollo* is in a way a prelude to other songs, like the *Homeric Hymns*, both at a narrative and at a metaliterary level: transformed into an applied poetic program, it becomes the source of Callimachus' other songs (Calame 1993: 54).

[12] Alan Cameron 1995: 406.

[13] I am not interested here and now in determining the precise sense of the comparison between the images of the sea, river, and spring, and their symbolic connection with Homer or epic poetry, which are still hotly debated: see Bundy 1972; Asper 1997: 120-125; Morrison 2007: 134-135. What is relevant for me is that, beyond any doubt, "the break-off at the end of the hymn apologises for the brevity of the song, using *phthonos* ('envy') to restate the poem's worth at its end, while portraying the poet under attack from critics" (Morrison 2007: 135-136).

Epidaurus (40 Käppel; *CA* pp. 132–136) not long after the attack of the Macedonian king Philip against Sparta (perhaps Philip II, 338 BC, but more probably Philip III, 317/6 BC, or Philip V, 218 BC).[14] This inscription, constructed around a short paean to both gods (with special emphasis on Asclepius), constitutes an important parallel for the polyphony of authorial voices in Callimachus' poetry. The inscription's final section, in dactylic hexameters (lines 62–84), celebrates Asclepius' power by describing one of his achievements. These lines form an aretalogy, reminiscent of the *Homeric Hymns* in style and form, but the greatness of the god that they recount is presented via personal testimony, shown through an event in Isyllus' own experience, not unlike Callimachus' reporting, as if a witness, Apollo's quarrel with Phthonos about ideal poetry (and Callimachus' poetry). When the Macedonian king marched against Sparta, Asclepius came to the Spartans' aid from Epidaurus. At that moment Isyllus, still a boy, was praying Asclepius to rescue him from his sickness. Asclepius then appeared to him in golden armor and asked the boy to wait until he saved the Spartans from destruction, for their "loyalty to the decrees of Phoebus that Lycurgus imposed upon the city after consulting the oracle" (lines 75–76: Isyllus is a supporter of Sparta's ancestral constitution, and he favors and proposes to the Epidaurians a conservative ideology characterized by the superior authority of the aristocracy). At that point, Isyllus hastened to announce the epiphany to the Spartans, and Sparta was safe. Every section of the inscription—Isyllus' political advice, his ritual prescriptions, the text of the paean, the account of his encounter with Asclepius, and his report to the Spartans—forms part of a strategy of persuasion that builds up Isyllus' political authority through divine validation. His rhetorical strategy strongly resembles that of archaic politicians like Lycurgus—not by accident mentioned by the same Isyllus as protected by Apollo, the other god to whom the inscription is dedicated—or Zaleucus of Locri, whose code of laws, according to ancient doxography, would have found favor at Locri because he asserted that Athena constantly appeared to him and instructed him in his legislation.

Eulogy of the god and encomiastic propaganda in favor of "my king" are thus strongly interlaced in Callimachus' idea of religious discourse, as they were also in Isyllus' inscription. The hymnic genre, in fact, splendidly enhances eulogistic intentions on the author's behalf.

---

[14] On Isyllus' inscription, see Kölde 2003; Fantuzzi 2010.

By adopting the authoritative position granted to him in the *Hymns* by virtue of his role as religious poet, Callimachus could easily deal with his kings qua gods. At the same time, Callimachus could have no better strategy to enhance his own role as a poet, and his prospects of gratitude from the king, than with a hymn to the gods—one of whom, Zeus, was in Hesiodic terms responsible for granting the ruler power. Analogical comparisons between the leadership of kings in the human world and the supreme leadership of Zeus among the gods had not been rare in classical Greece. (Pindar's *Pythian* 1, for example, established an especially close analogy between Zeus's and Hieron's kingly power and peaceful effectiveness.)[15] But thanks to the frame of the hymnodic genre Callimachus can afford to take a step forward in the direction of a more radical equalization—after all, the organization of the cult of divine kings was from its very beginning modeled on the worship of the Olympian gods. (See Chaniotis 2003: 488–489.) The way Callimachus constructs his eulogy presupposes the traditional though unstable distinction between hymns for gods and encomia for mortals as the two possible forms of eulogy (most clearly formulated, e.g., by Plato *Resp.* 10.607a or *Leg.* 801e) and at the same time blurs the borders between these two subgenres, with the result that the poet becomes automatically able to emphasize the divine nature of his seemingly human laudandi.

Apart from equating the power of his king with Apollo's power in the *Hymn to Apollo*, but leaving unspecified the reason for this equation, he also introduces Apollo himself in the *Hymn to Delos* to announce his special connection with Ptolemy II, and to proclaim the divinity of the latter. While still in Leto's womb, Apollo bars his mother from giving birth to him on Cos, because another god is destined to be born on that island, and after legitimizing the divinity of Ptolemy's parents he outlines, thanks to his prophetic powers, Ptolemy's future sphere of influence (ll. 162–8):

> No, Mother, do not bear me there. There is nothing, to be sure, wrong with the island, nor do I have anything against it, shining and rich in flocks if any island is. It is only that some other god is meant by the Fates to belong to it, sprung of the high race of Savior Gods [ἀλλά οἱ ἐκ Μοιρέων τις ὀφειλόμενος θεὸς ἄλλος | ἐστί, Σαωτήρων ὕπατον γένος]: beneath his diadem will come—not unwilling to be governed by a Macedonian—both the two lands deep in earth's interior...

---

[15] So Bing 1988b: 139–141; Hunter and Fuhrer 2002: 168.

One of the most peculiar features of the *Homeric Hymns*' narrative strategies was to systematize the role of the individual gods in terms of acquisition and redistribution of their well-structured *timai*, so that the actions and events that occurred among the gods and that are celebrated by the poet can be shown to have permanent consequences in the present and can explain why the world is the way it is (the "politics of Olympus": Clay 2006: 11). We can therefore easily understand how authoritative Apollo's words are in Callimachus' *Hymn to Delos*. Within a speech that is a prophecy—and Apollo's prophecies are, of course, infallible (see Vamvouri Ruffy 2005: 254–255)—the god first of all ratifies Ptolemy's divinity (via the divinity of his parents, as Theocritus also does in *Idyll* 17). After this elevation of Ptolemy's status, Callimachus' Apollo describes Ptolemy's sphere of influence (ll. 166–170). He also implicitly links Ptolemy's power to his and Apollo's ξυνὸς ἄεθλος, "common war", against the Galatae, who marched against Delphi in the winter of 279/8.[16] In fact, the Galatae are called ὀψίγονοι Τιτῆνες ἀφ' ἑσπέρου ἐσχατόωντος, "late-born Titans of the far West" (l. 174). The Titans belonged to the last generation of pre-Olympian gods, whose enmity to Zeus and the other Olympians is most often evoked in other theological poetry, as their defeat, together with the defeat of the Giants, was considered the final achievement through which Zeus, Apollo, and the Olympian gods established their everlasting power (e.g., *HHApoll*. 334–339 and Hesiod *Theog*. 390–394, 617–719; they are also probably hinted at in l. 3 of Callimachus' *Hymn to Zeus*: see Sistakou 2009: 237–238). The Galatae are defined as ὀψίγονοι Titans in opposition to the previous Titans, as if they were members of the same species but needed to be distinguished from each other. The opposition is made even stronger and more evident, as the older Titans were usually labeled πρότεροι, προτερηγεῖς, or παλαίτεροι (or παλαιότεροι) in comparison with the Olympian gods.[17]

In Callimachus' *Hymn to Zeus* the encomiastic discourse also surfaces as a continuation or update of a religious-theological discourse that does not belong to the hymnodic tradition—there was no major *Homeric Hymn to Zeus*; the only one in the collection, the twenty-third, is four lines long—but refashions, in a temporal regression, the

---

[16] On the chronology of the hymn and the Galatian War, see Barbantani in this volume.
[17] Cf., respectively, Hes. *Theog*. 424, 486; Pherenicus, *SH* 671.3-4; and Antim. fr. 41a.7 Matthews; Aesch. *Eum*. 721; Callim. fr. 177.8 Pf.

authoritative voices of the Hellenistic Antagoras, the fifth-century Epimenides, and the archaic Hesiod. All of them, once they are made relevant for the "Zeusological" issues discussed by Callimachus, establish him as an authority in the field and also become supporters of his eulogistic discourse on Ptolemy, which relies on and expands his discourse about Zeus. The debated issue of the birthplace of Zeus, subject of the hymn's first half, introduced in line 4 (πῶς καί νιν, Δικταῖον ἀείσομεν ἠὲ Λυκαῖον; "How are we to sing of him, as Dictaean, or Lycaean?"), is promptly glossed with the statement ἐν δοιῆι μάλα θυμός, ἐπεὶ γένος ἀμφήριστον (l. 5: "My soul is divided in two, because his birth is an object of disagreement"). This endows the problem with a philosophical dimension, as line 5 probably includes an almost exact quotation of the question with which the contemporary philosopher Antagoras of Rhodes began his *Hymn to Eros* (fr. 1 Powell):[18]

> ἐν δοιῆι μοι θυμός, ὅ τοι γένος ἀμφιβόητον,
> ἤ σε θεῶν τὸν πρῶτον ἀειγενέων, Ἔρος, εἴπω,
> τῶν ὅσσους Ἔρεβός τε πάλαι βασίλειά τε παῖδας
> γείνατο Νὺξ πελάγεσσιν ὑπ' εὐρέος Ὠκεανοῖο·
> ἤ σέ γε Κύπριδος υἷα περίφρονος, ἠέ σε Γαίης,
> ἤ Ἀνέμων, κτλ.

> My mind is in doubt, since your birth is disputed, whether I am to call you, Love, the first of the immortal gods, the eldest of all the children whom Erebus and queenly Night brought to birth in the depths beneath wide Ocean; or are you the child of wise Cypris, or of Earth, or of the Winds?

Antagoras discussed the parentage, and thus the essential nature of Eros, and used for this theme the noun γένος. By reverting to an alternative meaning (taken in the sense "birthplace," not in the more usual sense "birth"), Callimachus situates his discussion about Zeus's birthplace, which in reality has a rather narrow mythological concern, within the frame of the cosmological and ontological questions that were being explored by his contemporaries—the Academic philosopher-poet Antagoras (about Eros), the Stoic philosopher-poet Aratus (about Zeus himself, in the proem and elsewhere in the *Phaenomena*),

---

[18] The relative chronology of Antagoras and Callimachus is not clear, though most modern scholars opt for the former's anteriority. Cuypers 2004: 96–97 provides especially strong arguments in favor of Antagoras' priority. The poem was also attributed to Crantor. (See Cuypers 2004: 99–101.) My argument depends not upon the author but upon the text.

and the philosopher-poet Cleanthes of Assus (author of a hymn to Zeus developing an allegorical interpretation of this god). Finally, by replacing the epithet used by Antagoras, ἀμφιβόητον,[19] with ἀμφήριστον, "object of discord or disagreement," Callimachus may employ a window allusion that evokes, behind Antagoras, Hesiod *Works and Days* 11–13:[20]

> οὐκ ἄρα μοῦνον ἔην Ἐρίδων γένος, ἀλλ᾽ ἐπὶ γαῖαν
> εἰσὶ δύω· τὴν μέν κεν ἐπαινήσειε νοήσας,
> ἣ δ᾽ ἐπιμωμητή· διὰ δ᾽ ἄνδιχα θυμὸν ἔχουσιν.
>
> There was not just one birth of the Strifes after all, but upon Earth there were two Strifes. One of these a man would praise once he got to know it, but the other is blameworthy; and they have thoroughly opposed spirits.

This text, which introduces the two different Erises, one good and one bad, who are sisters generated by Night,[21] may have been perceived by Callimachus as the model for Antagoras' two Eroses, one of whom was generated by Night. (See Antag. fr. 1.4 Powell.) Certainly the two primeval forces of love and strife are similar, not only in their dual nature, as we see in the *Works and Days* and in Antagoras, but in that their names differ from each other by only one letter. In this way, Callimachus would have imposed his own literary and philosophical interpretation on his model Antagoras, highlighting the dependence of Antagoras' philosophical or cosmological interests on the protocosmological author Hesiod, whose relevance is absolutely crucial in the second part of the Callimachean *Hymn to Zeus*.

Once Callimachus elevates his quandary by imbuing it with a philosophical aura, he proceeds to express his own choice among the versions of Zeus's birthplace, for which he relies on the authority of the late-archaic sage Epimenides, evoked once again through a quotation. Callimachus' argument behaves like a reductio ad absurdum. Between the two possible birthplaces that Callimachus decides to consider, Arcadia and Crete, the first cannot be true, because since the Cretans show the tomb of Zeus on their island, they must deny that Zeus is immortal; therefore they must also lie when they say that Zeus was born in Crete. Apart from other fallacies (see Cuypers 2004: 104–105), Callimachus'

---

[19] Or ἀμφίσβητον, if we accept the widespread conjecture suggested originally by Meineke; but see, most recently, Stephens 2003: 80.

[20] With line 13, cf. Antag. fr. 1.1 Powell: ἐν δοιῆι μοι θυμός. The category of "window allusion" was first theorized by R.F. Thomas 1986b: 188–189.

[21] *Op.* 17, and see also the discussion by Blümer 2001: 235–239. Translations of Hesiod are from Most 2006.

syllogism is open to the main objection that the Cretans may well be wrong about the death of Zeus but correct about the birthplace. But he seems to preclude this objection in line 8, quoting the first three words—Κρῆτες ἀεὶ ψεῦσται—of a hexameter by another poet-philosopher who sang in poetry of the birth of Zeus, Epimenides (DK B1):

> Κρῆτες ἀεὶ ψεῦσται, κακὰ θηρία, γαστέρες ἀργαί.
> The Cretans, always liars, evil beasts, idle bellies!

The probative effect of the quotation is enhanced by the fact that Callimachus does not introduce these three words as Epimenidean but inserts them into the text immediately after asking (ll. 6-7): "Zeus, they say you were born on the heights of Ida, and then again, Zeus, in Arcadia: Which ones, Father, are lying?" In this way the reader is compelled to ponder a bit, to remember Epimenides, and eventually to recall the unsignaled quotation from him in order to avoid the impression that the phrase was an authoritative answer from Zeus, and that Zeus (not Callimachus) used Epimenides as an informant about himself.[22] Yet when readers remember that the maxim was Epimenides', they will also remember that Epimenides is Cretan and thus a liar: Is Epimenides, therefore, really capable of uttering a truthful sentence? The irony of this argumentation comes as no surprise:[23] Callimachus is aware that choosing among versions of a myth means adopting a ψεῦδος ("fiction", l. 65), though tentatively the one that most resembles the truth.

Callimachus limits his quotation to the first hemistich of line 8, where the generalizing ἀεί is relevant to support his argument as it excludes the possibility that the Cretans can sometimes be truthful; but of course every ancient reader will have been encouraged to remember the rest of Epimenides' line, where the inclination to ψεύδεα is connected to a fondness for the "stomach", γαστήρ, a motif found already in the *Odyssey* but made most famous in Hesiod *Theogony* 26-27[24]—a passage that is remodeled by Callimachus in line 50, and to which we will return. Does Callimachus, through this possible window reference, implicitly affirm the primacy of Hesiod over the authority of Epimenides, as he had perhaps done with Antagoras and himself?

---

[22] See Hopkinson 1984b: 140; Bing 1988b: 76-77; Goldhill 1986: 27; Lüddecke 1998: 16-17; Barchiesi 2001: 118.
[23] An irony well-highlighted by Goldhill 1986: 27.
[24] The motif of Cretan mendacity had its literary birth, of course, in *Odyssey* 13-19.

Once the issue of Zeus's birthplace is settled, Callimachus observes of the baby Zeus that ἔτι παιδνὸς ἐὼν ἐφράσσαο πάντα τέλεια (l. 57: "though you were young, your thoughts were mature")—a remark reprised in ring composition for Callimachus' king at line 86, which highlights the generosity of Zeus's gifts to the kings, and this specification is justified in particular through the ability of "our rulers", ἡμέτερος μεδέων (cf. ἐμὸς βασιλεύς of the *Hymn to Apollo* l. 26), to accomplish everything in the fastest and most effective way (ll. 85–90):

πᾶσι μέν, οὐ μάλα δ᾽ ἶσον. ἔοικε δὲ τεκμήρασθαι
ἡμετέρωι μεδέοντι· περιπρὸ γὰρ εὐρὺ βέβηκεν.
ἑσπέριος κεῖνός γε τελεῖ τά κεν ἦρι νοήσηι·
ἑσπέριος τὰ μέγιστα, τὰ μείονα δ᾽, εὖτε νοήσηι.
οἱ δὲ τὰ μὲν πλειῶνι, τὰ δ᾽ οὐχ ἑνί, τῶν δ᾽ ἀπὸ πάμπαν
αὐτὸς ἄνην ἐκόλουσας, ἐνέκλασσας δὲ μενοινήν.

On all, but not the same amounts. We can infer as much from our lord's case, for he outstrips them all by far. By evening he completes what he conceived at dawn—his greatest plans, by evening; his smaller ones, at once. Others take a year for this, several years for that; while for others you yourself utterly deny accomplishment and crush desire.

Although for the contemporary reception "my king" would necessarily have been understood as whoever was on the throne when the poem circulated, leaving the king anonymous coincides with a broad advertisement of the new ideology of divinized monarchy.[25] The passage has as its aim a general justification of the king's power, but also a more specific consideration about Zeus's power is constructed at the end in such a way that it could fit both Ptolemy I and Ptolemy II. Zeus having rapidly attained maturity, the poet presents his control of heaven as the result of an agreement between his brothers about assigning him the most desirable share in consideration of his surprising precocity, despite the fact that he was younger than his brothers and sisters (ll. 58–59):

τῶι τοι καὶ γνωτοὶ προτερηγενέες περ ἐόντες
οὐρανὸν οὐκ ἐμέγηραν ἔχειν ἐπιδαίσιον οἶκον.

That is why your brothers, older than you, did not grumble when you took heaven for your special home.

---

[25] The generality of the celebration of Ptolemy's broad and wealthy empire gives the impression that Callimachus transcends the horizon of his *laudandus*, and his eulogy acquires a universal breadth: see Barchiesi 1994: 441; see also Depew 2004: 120 n. 19.

Callimachus is careful in stating the idea that Zeus's supreme power was the fruit not of chance but of merit. Though the parallelism remains implicit, whoever "my king" was, he was greatly favored in the allotment of his kingdom, just like Zeus—and this could be either Ptolemy I or Ptolemy II. If the king alluded to was Ptolemy Soter, Callimachus referred to the division of Alexander's empire among his Diadochi; if this king was Ptolemy Philadelphus, the comparison with Zeus and his older brothers was even more to the point, since Philadelphus became the successor to the throne despite the fact that he was the youngest of Soter's sons.[26]

But different opinions existed: some poets claimed that these divine spheres of influence were determined by lot. Callimachus' lines 60–67 most emphatically strike a blow against the authors who favored this idea:

> δηναιοὶ δ' οὐ πάμπαν ἀληθέες ἦσαν ἀοιδοί·
> φάντο πάλον Κρονίδηισι διάτριχα δώματα νεῖμαι·
> τίς δέ κ' ἐπ' Οὐλύμπωι τε καὶ Ἄϊδι κλῆρον ἐρύσσαι,
> ὃς μάλα μὴ νενίηλος; ἐπ' ἰσαίῃ γὰρ ἔοικε
> πήλασθαι· τὰ δὲ τόσσον ὅσον διὰ πλεῖστον ἔχουσι.
> ψευδοίμην, ἀίοντος ἅ κεν πεπίθοιεν ἀκουήν.
> οὔ σε θεῶν ἐσσῆνα πάλοι θέσαν, ἔργα δὲ χειρῶν,
> σή τε βίη τό τε κάρτος, ὃ καὶ πέλας εἷσαο δίφρου.

> The ancient poets, however, had no regard for truth at all: they said that lots decided homes for the gods three ways: but who would draw lots over Olympus and Hades—who but someone completely naïve? It makes sense to draw for equal shares: here they are as far apart as they could be. May I tell lies that persuade the ear of the listener! It was not chance that made you king of gods, but the deeds of your hands, the might, the power you stationed by your throne.

With this polemical statement, Callimachus aligns himself with some archaic poets—first of all Hesiod[27]—against other *aoidoi* of the past, supposedly not always truthful, among whom was Homer. Hesiod stressed that Zeus's supreme power was a privilege conceded to him by all the gods (*Theog.* 881–885). In contrast, in the *Iliad*, where Zeus

---

[26] For Ptolemy I, see Carriere 1969. For Ptolemy II, see Clauss 1986; Alan Cameron 1995: 10; Stephens 2003: 77–79; Barbantani in this volume.

[27] The idea occurs also in Solon fr. 25 GP, πολλὰ ψεύδουσιν ἀοιδοί ("singers lie about many things," quoted as an "old proverb" by Ps.-Plato *Just.* 374a and ascribed to Solon only by the scholiast), Xenophanes DK 21 B 1.22, and Pindar *Ol.* 1.28–29, *Nem.* 7.20–23.

was the elder son of Cronus, he obtained control of the sky by lot (15.187–193; esp. 15.192). Callimachus' agreement with the Hesiodic version on the origins of Zeus's supreme power is crucial for the whole poetics of this hymn as a text that at the same time celebrates the birth and enthronement of this god and the divine nature of another supreme power, Ptolemy. This emphasis may depend on a quasi-historical evaluation of Hesiod's own poetic project: "the emergence of the 'just' Zeus in the *Theogony* provides the necessary or logical divine counterpart to the 'just' king who rules over the human condition in the *Works and Days*. The one guarantees the other."[28]

Though the source on the origin of Zeus's sphere of influence for which lines 58–59 opt is certifiably Hesiodic in constrast to Homeric, Callimachus has not yet explicitly spoken in a Hesiodic voice. However, line 65, where Callimachus generalizes the reason for his option, alludes openly to the most famous passage at the beginning of Hesiod's *Theogony* (ll. 26–28), where the Muses admit that apart from truthful narratives they can also author narratives defined as ψεύδεα ἐτύμοισιν ὁμοῖα:

> ποιμένες ἄγραυλοι, κάκ' ἐλέγχεα, γαστέρες οἶον,
> ἴδμεν ψεύδεα πολλὰ λέγειν ἐτύμοισιν ὁμοῖα,
> ἴδμεν δ' εὖτ' ἐθέλωμεν ἀληθέα γηρύσασθαι.
>
> Field-dwelling shepherds, ignoble disgraces, mere bellies: we know to tell many lies similar to truth, but we know to sing reality, when we will.

Another example of the overlapping of different voices that characterizes Callimachus' *Hymns*, line 65 is more than a simple justification by Callimachus the mythographer of the version he adopts about the origin of Zeus's power: it constitutes a real manifesto of the poetics of verisimilitude of Callimachus the defender of his poetics, and it updates in a rationalist direction the polarity of truth or fiction (or deception) presented by Hesiod's Muses. The precise meaning of Hesiodic ὁμοῖα is the subject of debate.[29] But in Homer and Hesiod it seems always to point to the perceptual, not the ontological, dimension of the equivalence (see Nagy 2010); and therefore it is not far from the sense "resembling" and imparts to ψεύδεα a negative connotation—the fic-

---

[28] Stephens 2003: 86, developing Detienne 1996: 44–45.
[29] The term can imply some kind of "equivalence", and thus a positive significance for ψεύδεα as "fictions equivalent to reality." See Heiden 2007; previously the most complete discussion was P. Pucci 1977: 8–27.

tions of the Muses may seem equivalent to truth in the eyes of the still uninitiated Hesiod, but they are not necessarily equivalent in ontological terms. In any case Hesiod's ἐτύμοισιν ὁμοῖα specified an audience-oriented sense for the Muses' ψεύδεα (or could be understood to do so by a Hellenistic reader), focused on what would seem to be the effect or the impression of verisimilitude that these ψεύδεα provoke in an audience. On the one hand, Callimachus resumes this Hesiodic orientation for the audience: line 65 strengthens the idea that what matters for Callimachus is the logical effect of persuasion on those who listen to his poetry. Yet he divides the two options that the Hesiodic Muses ascribe to themselves between two different agents—other epic poets and himself—and does not directly include ἀληθέα among his own tasks, though he accuses the δηναιοὶ ἀοιδοί (l. 60) of lacking truth (οὐ πάμπαν ἀληθέες)[30] and shows himself up-to-date in the debate about telling suitable lies that exercised Plato and Aristotle (see, e.g., *Resp.* 377e, *Poetics* 1460a18–26).

The allusive background of the Hesiodic voice is consistent, and it remains undisturbed by the overlapping echo of other voices in the next passage (ll. 70–80):

εἵλεο δ' αἰζηῶν ὅ τι φέρτατον· οὐ σύ γε νηῶν
ἐμπεράμους, οὐκ ἄνδρα σακέσπαλον, οὐ μὲν ἀοιδόν·
ἀλλὰ τὰ μὲν μακάρεσσιν ὀλίζοσιν αὖθι παρῆκας
ἄλλα μέλειν ἑτέροισι, σὺ δ' ἐξέλεο πτολιάρχους
αὐτούς, ὧν ὑπὸ χεῖρα γεωμόρος, ὧν ἴδρις αἰχμῆς
ὧν ἐρέτης, ὧν πάντα· τί δ' οὐ κρατέοντος ὑπ' ἰσχύν;
αὐτίκα χαλκῆας μὲν ὑδείομεν Ἡφαίστοιο
...Φοίβου δὲ λύρης εὖ εἰδότας οἴμους·
"ἐκ δὲ Διὸς βασιλῆες," ἐπεὶ Διὸς οὐδὲν ἀνάκτων
θειότερον, κτλ.

You chose the greatest of men to favor: not for you the master mariner, the wielder of arms, or even the poet; you simply left other matters for other, smaller gods to attend to and took into your care the rulers of cities, under whose hand are the farmer, the spearman, and everything. What does not fall under the ruler's might? Smiths, for example, belong,

---

[30] Nagy 1990: 44–45 argues that Callimachus evokes the Homeric intertext to demonstrate that the profession of Hesiod's Muses may have been intended to oppose the lack of concern for truth on the part of venal itinerant poets dealing with local traditions versus Hesiod's pursuit of an overarching Panhellenic tradition. (See also Nagy 2009: 276–277.) Possibly Callimachus' opting for the poetics of *pseudea* at least in part depends on his awareness that he was mainly dealing with local myths that were not included in a "Hesiodic" *koine*.

in our songs, to Hephaestus...and those skilled in the lyre's moods to Phoebus. But "kings are from Zeus," and there is nothing godlier than Zeus's lords, etc.

These lines update—not without perfecting it with an argumentative explanation in the second hemistich of line 79 and in line 80—the famous statement of the Hesiodic Muses in *Theogony* 94–96:

ἐκ γάρ τοι Μουσέων καὶ ἑκηβόλου Ἀπόλλωνος
ἄνδρες ἀοιδοὶ ἔασιν ἐπὶ χθόνα καὶ κιθαρισταί,
ἐκ δὲ Διὸς βασιλῆες.

It is from the Muses and far-shooting Apollo that men are singers and citharists on Earth, but from Zeus that they are kings.

The explicit quotation of Hesiod is thus the *sphragis* of Callimachus' ontological definition and eulogy of monarchy, ratifying that the essence of his ideal monarchy quite closely parallels, and is sanctioned by, Hesiod's idea of monarchy.

Mythical Details and Editorial Choices

Finally, I would like to consider what may be a set of intertextual markers that belong first of all to the voice of Callimachus the theologian but have the potential to suggest the theological legitimacy of the specific ordering of the first four poems in what becomes the collection of the *Hymns*. These may have been adopted by the editor of the *Hymns* (whether Callimachus or a later scholar) to construct the first four poems as enacting the first family of Olympus.

The incipit of the *Hymn to Zeus* consists of a rhetorical question (ll. 1–3):[31]

Ζηνὸς ἔοι τί κεν ἄλλο παρὰ σπονδῇσιν ἀείδειν
λώϊον ἢ θεὸν αὐτόν, ἀεὶ μέγαν, αἰὲν ἄνακτα,
Πηλαγόνων ἐλατῆρα, δικασπόλον Οὐρανίδῃσι;

Zeus—What better theme when toasting him than the god himself, ever great, ever lord, who put the Pelagonians to flight and gave justice to the sons of Uranus?

Scholars have often debated whether this hymn was performed (at least initially) at a real symposium, or a ritual libation within a solemn festi-

---

[31] The syntax of Ζηνός is ambiguous: I prefer to take it with λώϊον, but cf. Lüddecke 1998: 12–13.

val for Zeus[32]—though certainly the absence of a definite article before σπονδῆισιν does not instill confidence that the performance was tied to a specific time or space. (See M.A. Harder 1992: 390.) More salient than conjecture about the concrete correspondence between reference to the symposium and the context of performance seems the fact that this opening may have been or have been adopted as a prompt or motivation for the first position of the *Hymn to Zeus* in the series of the *Hymns*, as it unavoidably evokes the traditional custom of pouring the first sympotic libations to Zeus. This custom is first explicitly presented in Ion (*IEG* 27.5–7):[33]

> σπένδοντες δ' ἀγνῶς Ἡρακλεῖ τ' Ἀλκμήνηι τε
> Προκλέι Περσείδαις τ' ἐκ Διὸς ἀρχόμενοι,
> πίνωμεν, παίζωμεν, κτλ.

> And so making pure libation first to Zeus and then to Heracles and Alcmena, to Procles and the children of Perseus, let us drink, let us play, etc.

This sympotic enforcement of Zeus's primacy may simply specify the tradition, probably autonomous, that Zeus was the most suitable first theme of song within a song or a series of songs. This nonsympotic tradition dates back at least to Terpander, Alcman, and Pindar (respectively, *PMG* 698 and 29; *Nem.* 2.1–5 and 5.25) and is reflected in the incipits of Theocritus *Idyll* 17 and of Aratus' *Phaenomena*.[34] It is not clear whether these archaic poets presupposed a connection between the motif of the primacy of Zeus as theme of song and the sympotic practice of pouring libations first of all to Zeus, or were unaware of this custom: the two traditions may have had parallel existences and geneses. But that at least some of the ancients connected the two practices is proved by a note to the first line of the *Phaenomena* from the Περὶ ἐξηγήσεως (p. 34.15–18 Martin), a fragment of the commentary of Achilles (third century AD) that has reached us together with the scholia to Aratus:

---

[32] The fact that Callimachus' lines seem to allude to the *prosodion* of Pindar fr. 89a, τί κάλλιον ἀρχομένοισ(ιν) ἢ καταπαυομένοισιν ἢ βαθύζωνόν τε Λατώ | καὶ θοᾶν ἵππων ἐλάτειραν ἀεῖσαι; "What is more noble when beginning or ending than to sing of deep-bosomed Leto and the driver of swift horses?"—compare Callimachus' Πηλαγόνων ἐλάτειρα in l. 3—has led some scholars to suppose that Callimachus is here trying to recreate the context of a processional song; but the absence of any subsequent mention of a suitable festival context works against such a suggestion: cf. Tandy 1979: 13.

[33] See also at least Poll. *Onom.* 6.15; Σ Pind. *Isthm.* 6.8; Σ Pl. *Phileb.* 66d.

[34] On these two texts' relative chronology, see Fantuzzi 1981; Kidd 1997: 162–163.

This incipit is also most convenient for the poets, because also in the symposia people used to mix three bowls, and the first was for Olympian Zeus [ἐπεὶ καὶ ἐν τοῖς συμποσίοις τρεῖς κρατῆρας ἐκίρνων, καὶ τὸν μὲν πρῶτον Διὸς Ὀλυμπίου], the second for the Dioscuri and the Heroes, and the third for Zeus Soter.

Although the exact relationship of Aratus' poem to sympotic speech is moot,[35] the case of Callimachus' *Hymn to Zeus* is quite different, as the symposium is explicitly mentioned, and in the absence of any relevance to the theme or of any continuation in the poem, the Callimachean σπονδαί of line 1 were exposed to the destiny of being interpreted in connection with the first position assigned to the *Hymn to Zeus* in Callimachus' book of *Hymns*.

The primacy of Zeus was of course beyond discussion and hardly needed remotivation on the occasion of this poem, as he was supreme ruler of the Greek pantheon and the god for the Macedonian kings.[36] However, whether the symposium was the actual place of performance or only evoked fictionally, it does provide a context that Callimachus as editor (or a later editor of Callimachus) could easily have redeployed as a potential validating device for placing the *Hymn to Zeus* first. In fact, this placement would have been felt as also belonging to the long religious and literary tradition that accorded the first sympotic libation to Olympian Zeus. If we doubt that Callimachus himself arranged his book of *Hymns*, we may suppose that his intelligent editor correctly understood Callimachus' fondness for interweaving self-validating voices in his *Hymns* and set the poem to Zeus first in the collection because the mention of the symposium seemed to him a ready-made prompt for this choice.[37]

A similar argument can be made in the case of the *Hymn to Apollo* 29: δύναται γάρ, ἐπεὶ Διὶ δεξιὸς ἧσται, "his is the power, who sits at the right hand of Zeus". The phrase accounts for the power of Apollo—a power that in turn usefully explains why Apollo can greatly reward his singers—because sitting near someone in power means some assimilation of that power. (See, for example, Theocr. *Idyll* 17.18–19.) But at the same time the text of the *Hymn to Apollo* sits next to the *Hymn*

---

[35] See Maass 1892: 317–320; Erren 1967: 14–15; Kidd 1997: 163.

[36] The first poem in the edition of Pindar's *Hymns* by Aristophanes of Byzantium has often been supposed to be a hymn to Zeus. But it could also have been for Apollo: so D'Alessio 2009.

[37] On the question whether Callimachus edited his *Hymns*, cf. Hopkinson 1984b: 147–148; Hunter and Fuhrer 2002: 176–181.

to Zeus in the collection transmitted to us—in a papyrus roll, more graphically than in a modern book or late-antique codex, the *Hymn to Apollo* would begin in the column on the immediate right of the end of the *Hymn to Zeus*, and line 29 of the *Hymn to Apollo* could easily have fallen somewhere toward the end of the first column of this poem.

Furthermore, in *Hymn* 3, the *Hymn to Artemis*, which follows the *Hymn to Apollo* in our collection, Callimachus (or an editor) may also have taken his direction from the passage where the text observes about the goddess οἱ δέ σ' ἐφ' ἕδρην Ι πάντες ὁμῶς καλέουσι· σὺ δ' Ἀπόλλωνι παρίζεις (ll. 169–170: "all the gods clamor for you to sit beside them, but it is by Apollo that you take your place"). In fact, this passage too could easily point to the physical location of this hymn in the collection.

Finally the *Hymn to Delos*, which as a poem on the birth of Apollo concerns Leto no less than Apollo, concludes with a final combined mention of Apollo and Leto that, at least in the form transmitted by the manuscripts and accepted by all modern editors,[38] also includes an address to Artemis: ἱστίη ὦ νήσων εὐέστιε, χαῖρε μὲν αὐτή, Ι χαίροι δ' Ἀπόλλων τε καὶ ἣν ἐλοχεύσαο Λητώ (ll. 325–326: "Fare well, flourishing hearth of islands, farewell to you and to Apollo and she whom you, Leto, bore!"). This reference is unexpected, as the goddess is passed over in silence for most of the poem, apart from lines 229 and 292. It is also cryptic, because in line 326 Artemis is not even called by name. Therefore there have been several attempts to remove the phrase. (See Ukleja 2005: 285–290.) But mentioning Artemis unexpectedly may have been intended as a final surprise. (See D'Alessio 2007: 1.172.) Alternatively, by mentioning her at least once together with Apollo, Callimachus may have intended to link the *Hymn to Artemis* and the *Hymn to Delos* as a pair of texts for the brother and sister gods by a strategy parallel to the frequent mentions of Apollo in the *Hymn to Artemis*. (See Ukleja 2005: 300–301.) Besides, the combined mention of Apollo, Leto, and Artemis has a precedent in the *Homeric Hymn to Apollo* 14–15 and 158–159, for example. Finally, the absence of the goddess' name in line 326 may reflect her polyonymy, for she is called by different names in the other two passages of the hymn that mention her (*Artemis*, 229; *Oupis*, 292). In any case, line 326, though not necessarily written with this sense, could also be easily understood as a sort of *sphragis* to the

---

[38] For a discussion of the line and of the various unnecessary attempts at emending it, see Gigante Lanzara 1990: 178.

sequence of *Hymns* 2–4 or more generally to the small portrait gallery of the family of Zeus and Leto depicted in the first four hymns.

It is not clear if Callimachus read the *Homeric Hymns* in a collection whose structure resembled the sequence now found in the manuscript tradition. Certainly the present order of the *Homeric Hymns* does not reflect a purposeful succession of the poems, neither in literary nor in theological terms. Our collection begins with the short *Homeric Hymn to Dionysus*, the literary ambitions of which are modest, and Callimachus may have read this as the first of the *Homeric Hymns*, as he seems to reflect its opening in the interrogative form of his own,[39] and in lines 5–8 on the variant versions of Zeus's birth and the danger of lies.[40] I suggest that Callimachus the hymnic poet, whom we have seen so carefully handling the "politics of Olympus" in the wake of the *Homeric Hymns* and exploiting such a politics for his own encomiastic or poetological purposes, could also be validating at least a part of the organization of his own collection of *Hymns* in terms of this politics—thus outdoing his model in this respect. My interpretation does not require all the poems' being composed at the same time or belonging to any overarching project involving a motivation for the order of all the *Hymns* in the final book—nor does it presuppose that the four phrases considered above from the first four hymns were conceived for the purpose of ordering the book.

Callimachus may well have written simply to acknowledge the politics of Olympus and its attendant power structure, establishing the primacy of Zeus, or the seat of Apollo at the side of Zeus and of Artemis at the side of Apollo, or the role of Leto as the mother of Apollo and Artemis in the *Hymn to Delos* 326. But he may also have reused this theological discourse to support the order of the first four poems in

---

[39] No other *Homeric Hymn* includes authorial questions, apart from the beginning of the *Homeric Hymn to Dionysus* and the end of the Delian part of the *Homeric Hymn to Apollo*: see Morrison 2007: 116.

[40] *Homeric Hymn to Dionysus* 1–6, "For some it was at Dracanus, some on windy Icarus, some on Naxos, O scion of Zeus, Bull god, and some at Alpheus the deep-swirling river that Semele conceived and bore you to Zeus, whose sport is the thunderbolt; but others, Lord, say that it was at Thebes you were born. All false! The father of gods and men gave you birth [ἄλλοι δ' ἐν Θήβῃσιν ἄναξ σε λέγουσι γενέσθαι | ψευδόμενοι· σὲ δ' ἔτικτε πατὴρ ἀνδρῶν τε θεῶν τε]"; Callim. *Hymn to Zeus* 4–10, "How are we to sing of him? As Dictaean, or Lycaean? I hesitate between the two: each has its champions. Zeus, they say you were born on the heights of Ida, and then again, Zeus, in Arcadia: Which ones, Father, are lying? [πότεροι, πάτερ, ἐψεύσαντο;]... In Parrhasia, then, Rhea bore you." See Hunter and Fuhrer 2002: 172–173.

his book, when and if at a later stage he edited his book of *Hymns*. The autonomous, noneditorial, nonsystematic origin of these four remarks on the hierarchical location of first four gods (Zeus, Apollo, Artemis, and Leto), which were reinterpretable as editorial prompts, would also explain why we do not find comparable remarks in *Hymns* 5 and 6. Simply put, where there were such remarks already existing in his texts, Callimachus the editor (or Callimachus' editor) would have followed their lead in arranging the succession of the poems.

My interpretation does not require that Callimachus himself made such editorial reuse of these phrases. But it seems to me that if the structure of the book was the initiative of a later editor, and not of the author, then such an editor understood and reproduced very well the dynamics of self-validation in Callimachus' polyphony. He would have found in Callimachus' religious discourse—about the primacy of Zeus, or the reciprocal location of Apollo side by side with Zeus and of Artemis side by side with Apollo, or the reference to Leto as the mother of Apollo and Artemis—an excellent authorial prelude to his own editorial work; therefore he would have set Zeus first, and close to him his two children by Leto, followed by the *Hymn to Delos*, where Leto is featured together with Apollo, and her being the mother of Artemis is also at least briefly remembered at the end.

Either Callimachus simply operated in a Callimachean way when editing his own work, relying on his previous religious (*cum* metapoetic) discourse as the guide in validating the arrangement of his first four hymns; or some later editor intervened with a post-Callimachean, hyper-Callimachean application of Callimachus' usual strategy. In either case the coincidence between the hierarchical correctness of the placement of the first four gods on one hand, and on the other the sequence of the first four hymns, will have had an added value for the most erudite readers, as they will have found in the voice of the editor of Callimachus' *Hymns* another small fragment of the self-validating polyphony that the text of Callimachus' *Hymns* educated them to detect and appreciate.

CHAPTER TWENTY-TWO

OTHER POETIC VOICES IN CALLIMACHUS

Christophe Cusset

Abstract

This chapter discusses Callimachus' strategy of employing the voices of earlier poets to augment his own poetic discourse. The Alexandrian poet invokes his illustrious models either by building a complex path of intertextual allusions or by actually staging the figure of these earlier poets, some of whom can even take the place of Callimachus himself. By juxtaposing the examples of Hesiod, the tragedians, and Hipponax, this chapter illustrates the different ways in which Callimachus co-opts independent poetic voices for his text.

Callimachus, who goes to great lengths to sing nothing unattested (fr. 612 Pf.), is a virtuoso at multiplying poetic voices in his own discourse and at recalling earlier poets in a variety of ways, whether by constructing sometimes complex strands of allusion that are gradually woven into an intertextual web or by actually evoking those poets, whose words then compete with Callimachus' own. In what follows, I consider the variety of ways that Callimachus inserts poetic voices, taking as examples Hesiod, tragic poets, and Hipponax.

In Competition with Hesiod?

For an erudite poet like Callimachus who inscribes himself into Homer's poetic tradition, Hesiod's voice at once comes forth clearly as a first model for the renewal of Homeric poetry and as a poetic resource that competes with the Homeric model. Hesiod actually demonstrates how to renew poetry without distancing himself from the poetic tradition. Thus when Callimachus characterizes Aratus as the new Hesiod (*Ep.* 27.1 Pf. = 56.1 GP), this is no superficial compliment that he offers to the poet of the *Phaenomena*. For Callimachus this standard is the best one for the new poetic he promotes, and he knows exactly what he's doing here, as he himself takes the position of a new Hesiod at the opening of the *Aetia*. Here Callimachus recounts that he was borne in a dream from his native Libya as far as Helicon, where the

Muses came to visit him. This encounter replays, with necessary variation, that of Hesiod himself with the Muses (now ten, perhaps with the addition of Arsinoe to their troupe) on the same Mount Helicon, thus giving Callimachus' aetiological poem the look of a *Theogony* for modern times (fr. 2 Pf. = 4 M.):

ποιμ₁ένι μῆλα νέμ₁οντι παρ' ἴχνιον ὀξέος ἵππου
Ἡσιόδ₁ῳ Μουσέων ἑσμὸ₁ς ὅτ' ἠντίασεν
μ]έν οἱ Χάεος γενεσ[
]ἐπὶ πτέρνης ὑδα[
τεύχω₁ν ὡς ἑτέρῳ τις ἑῷ ₁κακὸν ἥπατι τεύχει
]ῷ ζώειν ἄξιον α[
].εν πάντες σε· τὸ γα[
].δε πρήσσειν εὐμα[
]. . ιπὰ .'[..].[

When the swarm of Muses encountered the shepherd Hesiod pasturing his flocks by the trace of the Swift horse, to him the coming of Chaos (...) by the water of the hoof (...) as doing ill to another does ill to one's own heart (...) to live worthily (...) all you (...) to do easily (?)

In this fragment, Callimachus places the figure of Hesiod shepherding his flocks near the river Hippocrene to some advantage at the opening of lines 1 and 2; he shows him in close company with the Muses, who make him a new sort of hero.[1] The portrayal takes up in new terms what Hesiod said of himself (*Theog.* 22-23: αἵ νύ ποθ' Ἡσίοδον καλὴν ἐδίδαξαν ἀοιδήν, ἄρνας ποιμαίνονθ' Ἑλικῶνος ὕπο ζαθέοιο). But it is less the figure of the poet Hesiod, as he appears in his own poetry, than the poetry itself that appeals to Callimachus;[2] for example, the evocation of Chaos (l. 3) looks back to the Chaos of Hesiod's *Theogony*, whereas verse 5 alludes to that poet's *Works and Days*. Hesiod the poet is now Hesiod the poetry.

The dialogue that Callimachus engages in with the Muses serves as the narrative frame of the first two books of the *Aetia*, a poem that comes in a sense to take off from the *Theogony*, which has nothing to say of cults rendered to gods. After the Hesiodic song on the birth of the gods, Callimachus proceeds to a more human sphere in speaking of the birth of cults that humans render to the same gods—genealogical discourse naturally gives way to the aetiological. In answer to the poet, who wants to know why some people sacrifice to the Graces without

---

[1] Fantuzzi and Hunter 2004: 51.
[2] Alan Cameron 1995: 129-130; Barchiesi 1997b: 232-233; Fantuzzi and Hunter 2004: 53-54.

flute or garlands (fr. 3 Pf. = 5 M.), Clio explains that this practice is tied to Minos' mourning upon learning of his son's death (fr. 4–5 Pf. = 6–7 M.). The Muse then turns to a genealogical discourse (as though to take up the Hesiodic manner) to tell the origin of the Graces: but rather than choose the Hesiodic tradition, which makes the Graces the daughters of Zeus,[3] Callimachus prefers a new version that gives them Dionysus and the nymph Coronis as parents.

This is a good example of the ambiguous rapport between Callimachus and Hesiod: the Alexandrian poet presents himself as a new Hesiod, who like him converses with the Muses, having the Muses in their own voices recount what they know; yet what results does not agree with the Hesiodic discourse, which claimed through its divine inspiration to be the truth (*Theog.* 26–28). How are we to believe the Muses here if they contradict themselves as they wander from one poet to the other? Further, Callimachus ends by addressing not the Muses but the Graces in the hope that his elegies may be successful (fr. 7 Pf. = 9.1–18 M.): the Alexandrian poet is less concerned with knowledge than with the beauty, the elegance, of the verses. Callimachus can thus, without fear of contradiction or incoherence, invoke Hesiod's voice to make that same voice say what it in fact did not, since for him the value of poetry does not abide in its content only, as it did for his predecessor.

We find the same ambiguity in Callimachus' *Hymn to Zeus*, which opens his collection of hymns in the manner of Aratus' *Phaenomena*, whose Hesiodic character Callimachus extols. Though the two celebrations of Zeus take quite different forms, they resemble each other in their relationship to Hesiod. For composing a hymn to Zeus is very much a sign of allegiance to the Hesiodic tradition. The principal focus of the *Theogony*, inspired by the Muses, is effectively to tell of Zeus's power. In its general theme, the *Hymn to Zeus* is thus clearly Hesiodic—as it is characterized also by the specific choice of Zeus's birth, for which Hesiod (*Theog.* 453–506) is the first complete extant version.

The incipit of Callimachus' poem immediately leads the audience back to Hesiod: the term Οὐρανίδῃσι (l. 3) for the gods occurs for the first time at *Theogony* 486, precisely in the context of the narrative of

---

[3] It is certainly Hesiod (*Theog.* 907–11) whom we should recognize behind the anonymous designation of fr. 6 Pf. = 7 M.: οἱ δ' ἕνεκ' Εὐρυνόμη Τιτηνιὰς εἶπαν ἔτικτεν.

Zeus's birth, which Callimachus retains as the principal theme of his poem (Tandy 1979: 56; McLennan 1977: 28–29). At his birth Zeus is replaced with a stone offered to his father, Cronus, to satisfy his appetite; and Cronus is designated by this double apposition (*Theog.* 486):

Οὐρανίδῃ μέγ' ἄνακτι, θεῶν προτέρῳ βασιλῆι.
The powerful lord, son of Uranus, first king of the gods.

Taking up the Hesiodic term Οὐρανίδῃ, a clear intertextual marker though in a new metrical sedes, Callimachus elaborates Hesiod's μέγ' ἄνακτι in the preceding verse (Reinsch-Werner 1976: 51), which now qualifies not Cronus but his son, as though the poet sought to establish Cronus' absence from the beginning. The name Cronus appears only elsewhere, late in this hymn, at line 53—and even there only to mark his exclusion as the Curetes' noise makes him oblivious to the infant Zeus's crying.

After posing his initial rhetorical question, what better to celebrate than Zeus at the god's rites, Callimachus asks under what name he should sing of Zeus. In search of the true version of the god's birth, he feigns forgetfulness at having just alluded to Hesiod and preference for the Arcadian over the Cretan version of Zeus's birth that Hesiod chooses (*Theog.* 477). However, the current Cretan version is discredited by the Cretans' reputation for lying,[4] equally as Hesiod's discredited version rests on peculiar reasoning that allows Callimachus to use Hesiod's text legitimately while at the same time not following the archaic poet's version of the story. And this is what the new geographic frame of Arcadia for Zeus's birth shows: if the beginning of the narrative does not take place in Crete as it does in Hesiod, it happens nonetheless in a setting both mountainous (ὄρος) and wooded.[5] Callimachus' text from the beginning invites a close comparison of the poet's free use of his Hesiodic model. The following period, which evokes the site where Rhea gives birth to Zeus, presents two good examples (ll. 11–14):

ἔνθεν ὁ χῶρος
ἱερός, οὐδέ τί μιν κεχρημένον Εἰλειθυίης
ἑρπετὸν οὐδὲ γυνὴ ἐπιμίσγεται, ἀλλά ἑ Ῥείης
ὠγύγιον καλέουσι λεχώϊον Ἀπιδανῆες.

---

[4] Cf. the citation of Epimenides (fr. 5 Kinkel) that Callimachus makes at line 8: but his line is a variation on *Theog.* 26–28, where the Muses thrash out lies!
[5] Cf. *Hy.* 1.10–11 and *Theog.* 484; Reinsch-Werner 1976: 31.

This is why this sacred place neither animal nor woman in need of Eileithyia frequents, but the Apidaneans call it Rhea's ancient childbed.

We should compare these verses to lines 801–6 of the *Theogony*, which articulate the trials reserved for any immortal who perjures himself swearing upon the river Styx:[6]

> εἰνάετες δὲ θεῶν ἀπαμείρεται αἰὲν ἐόντων,
> οὐδέ ποτ' ἐς βουλὴν ἐπιμίσγεται οὐδ' ἐπὶ δαῖτας
> ἐννέα πάντα ἔτεα· δεκάτῳ δ' ἐπιμίσγεται αὖτις
> εἰρέας ἀθανάτων οἳ Ὀλύμπια δώματ' ἔχουσιν.
> Τοῖον ἄρ' ὅρκον ἔθεντο θεοὶ Στυγὸς ἄφθιτον ὕδωρ
> ὠγύγιον, τὸ δ' ἵησι καταστυφέλου διὰ χώρου.

> For nine years he is kept far from the immortal gods; he mingles neither in their councils nor in their banquests for nine full years. Only in the tenth may he come to take part in the interactions of the immortals, masters of the Olympian palaces. So earnest is the oath the gods swear by the the eternal and ancient water of Styx, which flows through rocky country.

The stylistic frame of the anaphora οὐδέ... οὐδέ, displaced from objects to subjects of action, allows the Alexandrian poet to construct his rewriting of the original: he uses the verb ἐπιμίσγεται (l. 13), which does not occur in the Homeric corpus but appears twice here in Hesiod (ll. 802, 803); this marked repetition awakens the reader's attention to Hesiodic innovation, and Callimachus clearly has this innovation in mind in choosing the same metrical position as in *Theogony* 802. Nonetheless a change of construction preserves the intertextual variation: Callimachus employs ἐπιμίσγεται with the accusative, μιν, at line 12,[7] unlike Hesiod, who turns to a prepositional phrase with ἐς or ἐπί.

Ὠγύγιον constitutes a second intertextual curiosity.[8] Callimachus is clearly recalling Hesiod in using the term as an adjective, in the neuter accusative and at the beginning of the verse. The poet is engaging in a philological dispute about this word (Tandy 1979: 30–33, 71–72). For, as when he uses the adjective παλαιότατον (l. 40) of the ὕδωρ of the river Neda, who turns out to be a child of Styx (ll. 35–36), Cal-

---

[6] I leave out of consideration here the other concurrent hypotext: *Od.* 7.244–47.
[7] Elsewhere we find the dative: *Hy.* 4.39; Apollonius of Rhodes *Arg.* 3.658. See *Od.* 7.246–7 (αὐτῇ | μίσγεται).
[8] The use of χῶρος in enjambment at line 11, which in itself is not unusual, here reinforces the association with Hesiod, who has one of the five occurrences of this word at verse end (*Theog.* 806).

limachus is surely suggesting an interpretation of Hesiod's expression ὕδωρ | ὠγύγιον applied to the waters of Styx: ὠγύγιος would have to be taken in the sense "ancient." The comparison of these two lines of Callimachus with the Hesiodic hypotext shows on the one hand how the Alexandrian poet uses his own text as a hermeneutic labyrinth for his reader to traverse, on the other hand the extent to which Callimachus brings several authorial voices into play in a poetic discourse that is truly polyphonic. Whereas Hesiod's voice evolves with certain syntactic and lexical modalities, Callimachus—who at the same time recalls such other poetic voices as Homer or Pindar[9]—arranges the whole by letting one principal, dominant voice stand out, that of his new poetic diction.

This same Arcadia, mythically not Hesiodic, but very much Hesiodic textually, is the object of another geographic excursus at lines 19–21:

> ἔτι δ' ἄβροχος ἦεν ἅπασα
> Ἀρκαδίη· μέλλεν δὲ μάλ' εὔυδρος καλέεσθαὶ
> αὖτις·

It was still dry, Arcadia, but later it was to be called very well watered.

Even if here Callimachus uses the lyric adjective εὔυδρος, opposed to ἄβροχος, which comes rather from tragedy (Eur. Hel. 1485), this opposition seems to correspond to a Hesiodic fragment that is based on the same evolution from aridity to abundance of water in relation to Argos (fr. 128 M.-W.):

> Ἄργος ἄνυδρον ἐὸν Δανααὶ θέσαν Ἄργος ἔνυδρον.

The Danaids, from a waterless Argos, have made Argos well watered.

The rewriting appears summary and distant. Callimachus seems to be content with an outline of an idea and vague Hesiodic memories in his text, without ever being slave to a hypotext, but without ever hiding that hypotext either. For even if Arcadia is not the birthplace of Zeus according to Hesiod, Callimachus strives to give a Hesiodic patina to this land. The geographic displacement assures the originality of his poetic creation and authorizes the recourse to a diffused rewriting. All the variations and distortions in relation to a hypotext, either given or presumed, mark the work of an erudite poet, but even more the

---

[9] For the relationship between Callimachus and Pindar, see especially Smiley 1914; Newman 1985; Fuhrer 1988 and 1992; Lord 1990; Depew 1998, especially 160–178.

pleasure he takes in it. This opposition of dryness versus wetness that Callimachus develops here seems to have as its goal the clarification of a wordplay on the description of the Peloponnesians, and in particular the Arcadians, as Ἀπιδανῆες in the earlier passage that evokes the god's place of birth. This name, Ἀπιδανῆες, by false etymology, designated the Arcadians as the men "without springs" (ἀ-πῖδαξ) or "without drink" (ἀ-πίνειν).[10] Taken up by a chain of names, Callimachus clarifies here the name that the Arcadians themselves give to the place, Arcadia; yet at the same time there occurs a Hesiodic substrate transfer from one text to another, as the name Arcadians is retrospectively elucidated by lines 19–20, which go back to a Hesiodic schema (ἄνυδρον… ἔνυδρον is equivalent to ἄβροχος… εὔυδρος). The discrete presence of Hesiod is elsewhere straightaway confirmed by the variation on the name Rhea: the nominative Ῥέη (l. 21), which is morphologically opposed to the genitive Ῥείης (l. 13) but seems closer to an imaginary etymology from ῥεῖν (Hopkinson 1984c), is a rare form for which we find only two occurrences before Callimachus, namely in the *Homeric Hymn to Demeter* (459) and the *Theogony* (467: παῖδας ἑοὺς κατέπινε Ῥέην δ' ἔχε πένθος ἄλαστον). This last instance occurs in the narrative of Zeus's birth, in a context close to the Callimachean one: Rhea, who suffers because Cronus devours her children, turns in her distress to her mother, Gaia (469–471). In a similar manner in Callimachus' poem, Rhea, upon giving birth, addresses her mother, Gaia, to be able to bathe her newborn child. This trivial request allows the Alexandrian poet to set himself at some distance from his model.

The bathing, at first impossible (l. 16), then occurs several lines later (ll. 32–33):

ἐκ δ' ἔχεεν μέγα χεῦμα· τόθι χρόα φαιδρύνασα,
ὦνα, τεὸν σπείρωσε.

There poured forth an abundant stream; so she washed your body, Lord, and swaddled you.

The clausula χρόα φαιδρύνασα (l. 32) is Hesiodic, borrowed with morphological variation from the *Works and Days* (753–754):

Μηδὲ γυναικείῳ λουτρῷ χρόα φαιδρύνεσθαι
ἀνέρα·

A man should not bathe his body in the bathwater of a woman.

---

[10] Von Jan 1893: 80; D'Alessio 1996: 66.

The verb φαιδρύνεσθαι occurs only once in Hesiod, and only once in Callimachus. In spite of the morphological variation, the homotaxis of the expression confirms the rewriting.[11] Callimachus plays with Hesiod's voice to give it, in spite of itself, contradictory utterances. The passage from the *Works and Days* occurs in a list of varied advice relating to prohibitions or ritual observances. Now, Callimachus has first proclaimed (ll. 15–17) that Rhea, upon giving birth, looks for water to wash off the afterbirth and to bathe the body of her newborn (τεὸν δ' ἐνὶ χρῶτα λοέσσαι, l. 17). But when the water is found (l. 32), the mother's bath is passed over in silence. The reader must mentally supply Rhea's bathing in order to understand Callimachus' game. If we respect the order of events in lines 15–17, Zeus's bath (l. 32), implicitly occurring after his mother's, comes into contradiction with the very Hesiodic formulation that it indicates, namely, that a man not bathe in the water used by a woman after childbirth (see Reinsch-Werner 1976: 38–39). What are we to make in this situation of Hesiod's moral proscriptions, if Zeus himself transgresses their commandments?

After the bath, Zeus is entrusted to the tender care of the nymph Neda. The nymph gives Callimachus an opportunity to renew his complex games of allusion with the archaic poet. Neda is the link between Callimachus' Arcadia and Hesiod's Crete: it is to Crete that she takes the new god, but even though this narrative seems to come from Hesiod's version, the semantics at first suggest a rejection of Hesiod. Line 34 accumulates forms foreign to Hesiod,[12] in an alliterative chain heavy with kappas that associates Crete with secrecy and the hidden, and Callimachus plays on this secrecy in constructing his own version of Zeus's birth. He then brings Hesiod back in an unexpected way: though unknown in Hesiod's world, the nymph Neda is qualified to be a member of Callimachus' through the apposition πρωτίστῃ γενεῇ (l. 36), which clearly reformulates the Hesiodic expression προτέρη γενεή (*Op.* 160).[13] And as we saw earlier, it is this very Neda, whose name is given to nascent flowing water, who confirms the semantic links between ὠγύγιον (l. 14) and παλαιότατον (l. 40): she is decidedly the most Hesiodic of nymphs!

---

[11] Tandy 1979: 103. Hesiod's expression is taken up again by Apollonius of Rhodes (3.832), Moschus (2.31), and Oppian (*Cyneg.* 2.355).
[12] Κευθμός is Homeric (*Il.* 13.28), whereas κευθμών is Hesiodic (*Theog.* 158); κρύφα is Pindaric (*N.* 9.33); παιδεύω is not epic.
[13] The expression is notably present as a Hesiodic signal in Aratus, whom Callimachus terms a new Hesiod: Effe 1970; Fakas 2001: 56–57.

The last episode of the narrative of Zeus's birth, the sojourn on Mount Dicte, is structured by a play on Κυρβάντων (l. 46) and Κούρητες (l. 52):[14] it is here that the alliterative chain in kappa observed above finds its full realization. For Crete, the place where Zeus lies hidden away (κρύφα), is peopled by the Meliae and their companions (named first at l. 46) the Κύρβαντες,[15] who are, through an etymological wordplay, partly implicit in κρύπτω, "those who hide" Zeus from his father after his birth, while under the name Κούρητες they are occupied with the *kouros* that Zeus represents (κουρίζοντος, l. 54). The Meliae serve above all to introduce, by a new wordplay with μέλι, the evocation of the sweet honey (γλύκυ κηρίον, l. 49) that the bee Panacris produces. To tell of this liquid's appearance Callimachus again takes up Hesiod's voice in a manner both slightly trivial and humorous (l. 50):

γέντο γὰρ ἐξαπιναῖα Πανακρίδος ἔργα μελίσσης.

For in a moment the work of the bee Panacris was accomplished.

The use of γέντο recalls Hesiod's use of this form in the sense of ἐγένετο in the narrative of Aphrodite's birth (*Theog.* 199):

Κυπρογενέα δ', ὅτι γέντο πολυκλύστῳ ἐνὶ Κύπρῳ·

Cyprogenea, because she was born on wave-bathed Cyprus.

This passage tells of the spectacular birth of an immortal being.[16] A bee's production of honey in Callimachus' text seems a posteriori much more trivial and banal. The ironic displacement from divine order to the simple dawn of nature's benefits produces a distancing effect vis-à-vis the archaic hypotext.

In the course of the hymn, Callimachus evokes the god's youth as well as his attributes in continually resorting to Hesiodic allusions (Cusset 1999: 316–318). At the end of this sequence, with the granting of kingship to Zeus, there occurs a new use of reference to Hesiod (ll. 66–67):

---

[14] Κούρητες (l. 52) maintains an etymological association with κουρίζοντος (l. 54). According to Reinsch-Werner 1976: 44–46, the onomastic game that structures verses 46–54 rests on Hesiodic reminiscences, notably on fr. 123 M.-W., which evokes the Curetes as sprightly dancers (φιλοπαίγμονες ὀρχηστῆρες).

[15] The Meliae according to Hesiod are nymphs born as a result of the castration of Uranus (*Theog.* 187); but Callimachus elsewhere (fr. 598 Pf.) assigns them another origin, making them the descendants of Melia, the daughter of Ocean.

[16] We find the same usage in the context of Pegasus' birth at *Theog.* 282–283.

Οὔ σε θεῶν ἐσσῆνα πάλοι θέσαν, ἔργα δὲ χειρῶν,
σή τε βίη τό τε κάρτος, ὃ καὶ πέλας εἴσαο δίφρου.

No, it was not choice of lots that made you king of the gods, but the works of your arms, your energy and your strength; this is why you set them at the side of your throne.

The final expression of line 66, ἔργα δὲ χειρῶν, set off by the bucolic diaeresis, doubly recalls the text of the *Theogony*. For one thing, the fact that his kingship is due to the strength of his arms recalls Hesiod's proclamation in the narrative of Zeus's birth that the son of Cronus drove his father from his throne (βίῃ καὶ χερσὶ δαμάσσας | τιμῆς ἐξελάειν, *Theog.* 490–491). What Hesiod proclaims is an event already accomplished in Callimachus. The Alexandrian poet does not totally reconcile his expression with Hesiod's, however, but deliberately seeks out the provocation of rare usage with the word ἐσσῆνα, explained as "king of the bees" (*EM* 383.30). Now, the similarity of this clausula with that in line 50 (ἔργα μελίσσης) is a revealing sign of the lexical game Callimachus puts into play here (McLennan 1977: 103). This sign is again one of ironic rewriting: Zeus is made king (of the bees) by the work of his hands since honey is associated in his childhood with the nursing of Amalthea (l. 49). Further, if for the idea Callimachus refers to the Hesiodic narrative of Zeus's birth, he is also working with line 677 of the *Theogony*, which occurs in the narrative of the battle of the Titans and the Hundred-Handed Ones. Each camp competes in force and shows "the work of its hands and of its force" (χειρῶν τε βίης θ' ἅμα ἔργον). So the Hesiodic voice mingles with itself and becomes diffused (apparently) freely at the will of verbal associations. But beyond wordplay there are in question more serious matters of the reading of literary tradition. Moreover, we can judge this in line 67 of Callimachus' *Hymn to Zeus* by the effects produced through variations and condensation of the Hesiodic reference to lines 385–88 of the *Theogony*:[17]

καὶ Κράτος ἠδὲ Βίην ἀριδείκετα γείνατο τέκνα,
τῶν οὐκ ἔστ' ἀπάνευθε Διὸς δόμος οὐδέ τις ἕδρη,
οὐδ' ὁδὸς ὅππη μὴ κείνοις θεὸς ἡγεμονεύῃ,
ἀλλ' αἰεὶ πὰρ Ζηνὶ βαρυκτύπῳ ἑδριόωνται.

---

[17] McLennan 1977: 105; Reinsch-Werner 1976: 58–59; Tandy 1979: 151–152.

She gave birth also to Power and Force, remarkable children. Zeus has neither home nor seat without them, nor is there route where the god is not their guide, but ever have they their place by heavy-sounding Zeus.

Callimachus condenses these four lines into one by suppressing the central verses that offer for his purpose only unnecessary detail. For Callimachus, κράτος and βίη are not divine powers that accompany Zeus but only divine qualities of Zeus himself, as the determinant before each of their names indicates. Further, Callimachus transposes the order of the two names, so that βίη more distinctly marks the juncture between the two hypotexts. The final image (εἴσαο), unexpected, reintroduces the Hesiodic perspective in the personification of κράτος and βίη. The two qualities are presented in a concrete context (l. 67, πέλας...δίφρου) that accentuates the material aspect of Zeus's divinity. Thus the two hemistichs produce a striking contrast between the abstract qualities of Zeus on the one hand and their concrete representation in the Hesiodic tradition on the other.

The end of the hymn progressively evolves from a celebration of Zeus to a praise of Ptolemy, associating celestial Zeus and terrestrial Zeus (Hunter and Fuhrer 2002: 169). The Alexandrian poet again makes use of the authority of Hesiod's voice to assure the link between the two forms of kingship (Fantuzzi and Hunter 2004: 353). We should note first (l. 79) a practice actually quite rare in Callimachus[18]—exact citation. He reproduces the first hemistich of *Theogony* 96:

> Ἐκ γάρ τοι Μουσάων καὶ ἑκηβόλου Ἀπόλλωνος
> ἄνδρες ἀοιδοὶ ἔασιν ἐπὶ χθόνα καὶ κιθαρισταί,   95
> ἐκ δὲ Διὸς βασιλῆες·

> For it is from the Muses, you know, and far-shooting Apollo that there are singers and *kitharistai* upon the earth; and from Zeus, kings.

The citation is remarkable not only for Callimachus' fidelity to the Hesiodic text but even more with respect to the original context. For lines 76–79 of the *Hymn to Zeus* concern the allocation of various human activities in terms of the gods who preside over them—artisans belong to Hephaestus, soldiers to Ares, hunters to Artemis, poets to Apollo, kings to Zeus—and Hesiod also mentions the poets as a category (*Theog.* 95). The distortion of the citation is thus limited in

---

[18] It is actually rather well represented in the *Hymn to Zeus*, since Callimachus cites Antagoras with a few variations (l. 5), Epimenides (l. 8), and the end of a *Homeric Hymn* (l. 96).

opposition to Callimachus' habitual practice, and, doubtless, the range of Hesiod's voice is stronger, as if Callimachus had suddenly become more serious than usual.

Lines 82–83 take up again this capricious intertextual style more typical of Callimachus:

> ...ἐπόψιος οἵ τε δίκῃσι
> λαὸν ὑπὸ σκολιῇσ' οἵ τ' ἔμπαλιν ἰθύνουσιν·
>
> ... watching over those who lead the people with crooked decrees or, contrarily, those who lead them with upright ones.

These lines are effectively a mosaic of expressions that we find here and there in Hesiod but whose fracture does not permit establishing an exact hypotext: we can invoke line 250 of the *Works and Days* (σκολιῇσι δίκῃσιν) or line 7 of that same poem (ἰθύνει σκολιὸν). Here Hesiodic color prevails his values. Callimachus' writing here suggests a secret diffusion and a dissemination deaf to Hesiod's voice; in the Alexandrian text, Hesiod's voice is also sometimes muted.

Tragic Voices in Callimachus

The *Suda* attributes tragedies and comedies to Callimachus, but their existence remains hypothetical. Callimachus certainly kept close to such tragic authors as his friend Theaetetus (*Ep.* 7 Pf. = 57 GP),[19] who seems to have followed the "pure path" (καθαρὴν ὁδόν, l. 1)[20] of Callimachus' aesthetic without being recognized publicly for his qualities as a poet. If Callimachus sings his praises, the stance from which he does so is completely opposed to the judgment of dramatic competitions. But this "pure path" of Theaetetus, which brings him close to the poetry of Callimachus and Pindar, could certainly by its very purity be contrasted with the essence of tragedy. It is not certain whether a poetry written with an eye to scenic performance is compatible with Alexandrian preciousness. Callimachus brings elsewhere a severe censure to bear upon tragedy that perhaps confirms this notion (*Iambus* inc. sed. fr. 215 Pf.):

> ἥτις τραγῳδὸς μοῦσα ληκυθίζουσα...
>
> The tragic Muse, who in her inflated declamation...

---

[19] Wilamowitz 1924: 123–125; A. Giannini 1962: 60–63; Meillier 1979: 123–124.
[20] On this image, see Asper 1997: 29.

Pfeiffer suggests attaching this choliambic line to *Iambus* 13, which is essentially polemic: Callimachus defends himself here against his detractors.[21] From this perspective, Callimachus would set his poetry (or the true poetry) in opposition to the turgid character of tragic style, or the style of a certain type of tragedy. Are we to understand this as a wholesale rejection of tragedy on Callimachus' part? Even though classical tragedy has only a faint intertextual resonance in his work, Callimachus does not shut the tragic voice out of his poetic space completely.

The richness of Aeschylus' language and his great capacity for linguistic invention had to interest our poet, as his frequent lexical borrowings from Aeschylus show. But it appears that this lexical interest does not evolve into a larger interest on the level of the text (A. Giannini 1962: 51–53). The resultant intertextual effects bear only on particular words from the diction of this tragic poet and agree with the erudition of the Alexandrian poet ever careful to elucidate rare or difficult words from classical texts. Let us consider a few examples.[22]

In the opening of the *Hymn to Zeus*, the term ἐλατῆρα (l. 3) serves to qualify the god as "he who has driven out" the Giants, sons of Earth, confused with the Titans. (Cf. Hes. *Theog.* 820.) The noun ἐλατήρ, which occurs already in Pindar (*Ol.* 4.1–3) and Homer (*Il.* 4.145, 11.702, 23.369), no longer has the sense here of "he who drives" a chariot or horses, corresponding to the simple verb ἐλαύνω, but has the sense "he who drives out," "he who expels," corresponding to the composite verb ἐξελαύνω. Here Callimachus imitates Aeschylus' verbal invention, for the latter had already created the adjective ἐλατήριος (*Cho.* 968), with the same meaning. In the *Hymn to Delos*, the noun ἰχθυβολεὺς (l. 15) is equally a Hellenistic recreation,[23] taken from the composite ἰχθυβόλος, no doubt first formed by Aeschylus (*Sept.* 131).

When he borrows more directly from Aeschylus, Callimachus nonetheless preserves his own inventiveness. At line 77 of the *Hymn to Zeus*, the rare term τευχηστής seems to come directly from the description in the *Seven against Thebes* of Polynices' shield, which bears the figure of a warrior engraved in gold (χρυσήλατην... ἄνδρα τευχηστὴν, l. 644). If τευχηστής for Aeschylus is an adjective, Callimachus turns it into a noun, in contrast to other Hellenistic repetitions that follow

---

[21] On *Iambus* 13, see Dawson 1950: 130–149; Kerkhecker 1999: 250–270; Acosta-Hughes 2002: 60–103.
[22] See the list—not exhaustive—in A. Giannini 1962: 52 n. 18.
[23] Leonidas of Tarentum (*AP* 7.504.2) and Nicander (*Ther.* 793). See Gigante Lanzara 1990: 74.

the tragic poet's usage (A.R. *Arg.* 3.415; Tryphiodor. 534). Thus Callimachus' rapport with Aeschylus is ambiguous: without doubt the first to use this Aeschylean term again, he renders a sort of homage to his predecessor while at the same time challenging him through a use of the word different from the original.

At line 112 of the *Hymn to Apollo* the term λιβάς, which belongs to the stock vocabulary of tragedy,[24] is not a priori specifically from Aeschylus. However, the term λιβάς is certainly associated from the time of Aeschylus on with the image of a spring that Callimachus, in turn, takes up at the conclusion of the hymn, a conclusion whose metaliterary value has often been noted:[25] in that passage Callimachus is making a judgment on good and bad poetry. It is further worth noting that Callimachus uses this tragic diction in a manner first found in Aeschylus and that this λιβάς derives from a "sacred spring," πίδακος ἐκ ἱερῆς, a variation in turn of the Homeric expression πίδακος ἀμφ' ὀλίγης (*Il.* 16.825), where πίδαξ is a *hapax*. Thus it is tragic language, notably Aeschylus', that serves here to designate good poetry, something that should cause us to question Callimachus' alleged disparagement of tragedy.

The use of the adverb πρυμνόθεν at line 35 of the *Hymn to Delos* is more complex. Unknown in Homer, this adverb occurs for the fist time in the *Seven against Thebes* (ll. 71, 1056), where it has the metaphorical sense "completely," "from top to bottom." The sense Callimachus gives it here corresponds closely but not exactly: the adverb here means "fundamentally," "profoundly." The other Alexandrian poets, however, eschew this use of the word, giving it rather the sense of the Homeric adverbial πρύμνηθεν, "from the stern."[26]

The sole instance in the hymn *On the Bath of Pallas* is the composite χρυσεοπήληξ in the invocation to the goddess at line 43. This descriptive epithet is to all appearances suggested by the adjective χρυσοπήληξ applied to Ares in apostrophe (*Sept.* 106).[27] Callimachus doubly sets himself apart from Aeschylus with the morphological variation χρυσεο-/χρυσο- and by the divinity described by the adjective. Ares is replaced by Athena, though also as viewed as a warrior: she

---

[24] Aesch. fr. 72 Radt (κρήνης ἀφθονεστέρα λιβάς) and *Pers.* 613 (λιβάσιν ὑδρηλαῖς παρθένου πηγῆς μέτα); Soph. *Phil.* 1216; Eur. *Andr.* 116.
[25] See especially Köhnken 1981; Lord 1990: 74–117; Asper 1997: 109–125.
[26] Aratus 343; A.R. *Arg.* 4.911. See Cusset 1999: 46.
[27] The form χρυσοπήληξ occurs in Euripides apropos of the Spartans (*Phoen.* 939). See R. Schmitt 1970: 80 n. 5.

destroys cities (l. 43, περσέπτολι) and takes pleasure in the noise of shields (l. 44).

There are, however, exceptional cases where Callimachus very explicity solicits Aeschylus' tragic voice. Fragment 301 Pf. (= 117 H.) of the *Hecale* provides a rare example:

> βουσόον ὅν τε μύωπα βοῶν καλέουσιν ἀμορβοί.
>
> The ox goad that their drivers usually call *myops*.

Callimachus relies here on lines 307–8 of the *Suppliants:*[28]

> ΒΑ. Βοηλάτην μύωπα κινητήριον.
> ΧΟ. Οἶστρον καλοῦσιν αὐτὸν οἱ Νείλου πέλας.
>
> *The King.* A maddening *myops* that pursues the oxen.
> *Coryphaeus.* Near the Nile people call it "gadfly"!

Both passages offer a lexical equivalence between μύωψ and another noun: οἶστρος in Aeschylus, βουσόος in Callimachus. Yet in the two passages, the problematic μύωψ is not introduced in the same way: in Aeschylus, the king, Pelasgus, rather naturally uses the term, and the chorus then gives a translation; whereas Callimachus uses the explanatory adjective βουσόος first, a variation inspired by the metaphorical use of βοηλάτης in Aeschylus.

In this case, where the intertextual rapport appears more developed, it is significant that the recurrence bears on a lexical question: it is precisely from words, from verbal invention, that Callimachus' poetic discourse works out renewal. Even if the poetic universes of Aeschylus and Callimachus remain largely foreign to each other, even if their thematic fields only rarely cross and their literary agendas do not agree, even if their poetic objectives diverge and their receptions have nothing in common, we find in both a common love of words and of the propagation of literary material. There is no reason for Aeschylus' voice not to echo in Callimachus, for in its own way it offers an alternative to Homeric discourse, to the epic tradition that it transposes into a tragic framework, much as Callimachus does in turn in his hymns and his elegies. Nevertheless, the distance that Callimachus maintains from Aeschylus may result from a divergence in their poetic theories, resting on the profound opposition between φύσις et τέχνη (A. Gian-

---

[28] In turn, it seems to be imitated by Apollonius at *Arg.* 3.276–77 (Hollis 1990a: 303; Cusset 1999: 155–156).

nini 1962: 53). For we know the critique that Ovid already maintains on this subject regarding Callimachus (*Amores* 1.15.11–15):

> *Viuet et Ascraeus, dum mustis uua tumebit,*
> *Dum cadet incurua falce resecta Cesces.*
> *Battiades semper toto cantabitur orbe,*
> *quamuis ingenio non ualet, arte ualet;*
> *Nulla Sophocleo ueniet iactura cothurno.*

> The poet of Ascra will live, so long as the grape swells for the vintage, so long as Ceres falls at the stroke of the curved sickle. The son of Battus will ever be sung throughout the earth, though his strength be not native talent, but art. No harm will come to the Sophoclean buskin.

In this passage Ovid praises a certain number of poets whose fame is nowhere near fading. The succession in this poetic ensemble is Hesiod, Callimachus, Sophocles: if the tragic poet garners fame without blemish, Callimachus, here evoked out of chronological order between Hesiod and Sophocles, will surely know fame without end, but there is a restriction on the praise. For Ovid, Callimachus cultivated art at the cost of talent, of natural genius. The sequence and the formulation of these lines allow the reader to understand that Sophocles, by contrast, has a true genius, a true poetic *physis*. Ovid is not speaking of Aeschylus here, but one is inclined, in light of the critique that Aristophanes makes of Euripides' art to Aeschylus' benefit in the *Frogs*, to set up the same opposition between the arts of Callimachus and of Aeschylus, an opposition that rests in part on that of λεπτότης (Callimachean) and σεμνότης (Aeschylean).[29]

Euripides' influence is no doubt more important in the Hellenistic period than the other tragedians', as the number of pieces transmitted and the close rapport of Euripides and New Comedy prove.[30] However, Euripides does not appear to have a privileged intertextual presence in Callimachus: Euripides' tragic voice in general appears only in the very scattered rare lexical borrowings, more often composite forms.[31] There

---

[29] On this last opposition, see Prioux 2007: 108–113.
[30] Katsouris 1975; Hurst 1990; Cusset 2003.
[31] See ἐνδυτός (*Hy.* 2.32 and *Ba.* 111, etc.), κακόγλωσσος (*Hy.* 4.96 and *Hec.* 661), βαρύθυμος (*Hy.* 4.215 and *Med.* 176), δυστοκέες (*Hy.* 4.242 and Eur. fr. 863 N²), μεταστείχω (*Hy.* 6.9 and *Hec.* 509, *Suppl.* 90), φιλότεκνος (*Hy.* 6.83 and *HF* 636, *Phoen.* 356, 965). In addition to characteristic repetitions of composite terms, one could call attention to certain specific usages that perhaps go back to the tragic language of Euripides: the imperative ἄνωγε used for ἄνωχθι (fr. 628 Pf.) could refer back to *Or.* 119 (cf. Pfeiffer 1949–53: 1.425; A. Giannini 1962: 56); ἄργος (fr. 299.2 Pf.) is used in

is, however, a major exception to this (Meyer 2005: 193-195) the direct citation of a line from the *Bacchae* in *Epigram* 48 Pf. (= 26 GP):

Εὐμαθίην ᾔτεῖτο διδοὺς ἐμὲ Σῖμος ὁ Μίκκου
ταῖς Μούσαις· αἱ δὲ Γλαῦκος ὅκως ἔδοσαν
ἀντ' ὀλίγου μέγα δῶρον. ἐγὼ δ' ἀνὰ τῇδε κεχηνώς
κεῖμαι τοῦ Σαμίου διπλόον ὁ τραγικός
παιδαρίων Διόνυσος ἐπήκοος· οἱ δὲ λέγουσιν
'ἱερὸς ὁ πλόκαμος', τοὐμὸν ὄνειαρ ἐμοί.

> Simus son of Miccus, in dedicating me to the Muses, asked that I be gifted at study; they, like Glaucus, gave him great benefit for his little offering. And I, the Dionysus of tragedy, remain there gaping twice as much as the Samian as I hear litanies of schoolboys reciting, "Sacred is the lock"—much good this does me!

This poem was meant to mark the occasion of the dedication of a theater mask on the part of a certain Simus. Callimachus takes pleasure here in playing on the effects of the uttered and the unuttered word. The fictitious speaker is the mask itself, which, rather than as usual bearing the word of another, becomes the subject of its own discourse. But this discourse is not pronounced by a living voice. It highlights the written: the mask cannot speak, as its mouth is forever gaping (l. 3, κεχηνώς); the poet rather speaks in its place. The tenor lent to the mask continues the play with the spoken word: the mask, whose mouth is henceforth useless, is entirely dedicated to listening (l. 5, ἐπήκοος). What he hears is exactly what he himself was wont to utter, namely the tragic verses that the pupils recite in class. It is here that Callimachus (l. 6) cites *Bacchae* 494: ἱερὸς ὁ πλόκαμος. The origin of the citation agrees with the mask that presents itself as a representation of Dionysus (ll. 4-5). But the status of this citation is a very particular one: the expression remains detached from the rest of the sentence and has only value in itself as representing tragedy in general. In the end any tragic phrase could take the place of the mask's voice now definitively absent, the mask for the future dedicated for exposi-

---

the sense of πεδίον as at *Elec.* 1; γοερός (*Hy.* 5.94) should be compared with *Hec.* 84 and *Phoen.* 1567, where it has the sense "groaning," in contrast to Aesch. *Ag.* 1176, where it means "which causes groaning" (Bulloch 1985: 206); σιωπηλός (*Hy.* 2.12 and *Hy.* 4.302) is attested in poetry before Callimachus only at *Med.* 320; ὑδέοιμι (fr. 371 Pf.) could find a precedent in the sense "sing" in *Hypsipyle* (POxy 852 fr. 1, col. III, 15), but see Bond 1963: 72-73.

tion. There is thus in Callimachus' citation from Euripides something other than the citation itself—whether from the absence of the actual hypotext, or on the contrary the presence of the entire tragic corpus.

The New Voice of Hipponax

Lyric poetry was at Alexandria object of the same attention and same interest as the rest of earlier poetic production. In the cases of Pindar, Archilochus, and Sappho, interest grows from the third century on (Masson 1962: 35–36). In the case of Hipponax in particular, we can cite the treatise, composed in several books, of Lysanias of Cyrene, Callimachus' contemporary and compatriot, *On the Iambic Poets*, from which Athenaeus culled several fragments that cite Hipponax a number of times (7.304b, 9.388b). Another student of Callimachus a little later wrote a *Life of Hipponax*. In this context, it is not surprising to find that Callimachus shows a deep knowledge of the Ephesian poet. This familiarity is especially evident in the first *Iambus*, where Callimachus causes his worthy predecessor to come back directly from Hades to address his invective against an assembly of *philologoi* doubtless gathered (*Dieg.* VI 1.3–4) at the Serapeum of Alexandria:

Ἀκούσαθ' Ἱππώνακτος· ͺοὐ γὰρ ἀλλ' ἥκω
ἐκ τῶν ὅκου βοῦν κολλύͺβου πͺιπρήσκουσιν,
φέρων ἴαμβον οὐ μάχην ͺἀείδͺοντα
τὴν Βοͺυπͺιάλͺειοͺν [.].νἀ.[…ἄ]νθρωπος

Listen to Hipponax; for truly I come from down there, where they buy an ox for a penny, and I bring an *iambus* that does not sing of the war against Bupalus…man…

The discursive positioning is not far from that of certain epigrams written for poets where the deceased frequently address future readers of the epitaphs. Yet the declamatory context is quite different, and nothing allows us a priori to expect Hipponax's abrupt opening remark. In this surprising opening (Kerkhecker 1999: 15–18), which, taking up the *Reply to the Telchines* in another form, might well be an ironic counterpoint to the very Hesiodic apparition of the Muses to the poet on Mount Helicon in the *Aetia*, to the extent that one finds in the two episodes the same dream function (Lelli 2004: 7), Callimachus recalls in his fashion the topos of the *katabasis*, which he transforms into an *anabasis*. In the manner of a famous hero's descent into Hades to meet there with celebrated and important figures of the past, in the same way Hipponax comes to find a circle of philologues. And to the inversion of idea of communication between the worlds of the living and of the dead corresponds no doubt a reversal of values of the figures implied in the episode.

But whatever judgment one brings to bear on Hipponax, two aspects of the aggressive opening address of the poet *redivivus* should be underlined. He uses the Ionic dialect (cf. l. 2, ὅκου, πιπρήσκουσιν), and at the same time the typical Hipponactean meter of the iambic trimeter scazon, the last foot "limping", each line concluding with three long syllables. There is every ground to assume that these two formal characteristics that Callimachus retains are not purely gratuitous but are true intertextual indications, especially as they are combined with a poetic technique that perfectly echoes the style of Hipponax, as the designation of the poet himself in the first person shows.[32] But just how far are we to push the issue of the authenticity of Hipponax's voice? In thus having a vanished poet speak, is Callimachus making a pastiche of a master's style, or is he going as far as making an exact citation?[33] In general one is inclined to agree with Pfeiffer in considering that what we have here is a very Alexandrian imitation of Hipponax, for the following reasons: the opening verse is never attributed to Hipponax in ancient citations; Callimachus never cites an author textually to this extent; the expression οὐ γὰρ ἀλλά did not occur in Ionic. Kerkhecker, in reviewing these criteria, already showed that the third could be questioned, as we find οὐ γὰρ ἀλλά not only also in Herodas (6.101) but already in the Hippocratic Corpus (*Art.* 69). Kerkhecker, however, remains convinced by the first two arguments. We think it possible to revisit these arguments again here.

First of all the argument *ex silentio* has only a very limited demonstrative force. It frequently happens that the citation of a hypotext in a secondary author is attributed in the end to the latter either because it passed unnoticed in the original hypotext or because the hypertextual setting is closer in time and so remembered for that reason. Further, the use of the third person to designate Hipponax, in spite of its being a mannerism, though indeed found in Hipponactean self-reference,

---

[32] Cf. Hippon. frr 32.4, 37, 117.4 W.; Acosta-Hughes 2002: 37–38.
[33] Ardizzoni 1960: 6–10; D'Alessio 1996: 579 n. 6; Kerkhecker 1999: 28–31.

may have militated against attributing the citation to its true author: the citation appears thus objectified.

As to the second argument, namely that Callimachus never cites a hypotext without modifying it in some way, we have just seen in the case of *Epigram* 48 Pf. (= 26 GP) at least one counterexample with the citation of a hemistich from the *Bacchae*. Nothing, then, prevents us from considering that Callimachus is here citing Hipponax.[34] The comparison of the two Callimachean passages is of interest in another regard. For the mask, inasmuch as it is the speaker of the epigram, makes itself the bearer of a tragic expression of Euripides that the mask itself would once have served to transmit but of which it is now only the passive auditor. Hipponax, in turn, in that he is the speaker of the *iambus*, while at the same time making himself the "bearer of an *iambus*" (φέρων ἴαμβον, l. 3) of a new kind, could also be the bearer of an expression that the poet Hipponax himself uttered at one time. Inasmuch as he is a literary figure fictively returned from Hades, Hipponax could very well cite the text that the real poet wrote some centuries earlier. The distance between the past age of the true Hipponax and the present of his literary double introduced into a foreign, Alexandrian setting is of the same order as that separating the mask hung in a schoolroom from its earlier theatrical career. In the same way that the mask, a tragic theatrical object, can cite from a tragedy that it can no longer voice itself, so the character of Callimachus (*Hipponax*) can cite from the verses of Hipponax, which Hipponax himself can no longer utter.[35]

For Callimachus, the multiplicity of poetic voices in the heart of his work is not only a way of inscribing himself into the literary tradition but also a way of thinking about what his own writing represents as the reflection of what poetry gives from itself to itself.

---

[34] Uncertainty about the status of the citation results in uncertainty about whether this opening line should be attributed to Hipponax or not: Masson 1962 attributes it without hesitation to the Ephesian poet, but other editors of Hipponax do not follow him in this.

[35] On the discursive strategies of Callimachus in this verse, see Acosta-Hughes 2002: 36–41.

CHAPTER TWENTY-THREE

INDIVIDUAL FIGURES IN CALLIMACHUS

Yannick Durbec

Abstract

This chapter analyzes the various types of characters that occur in Callimachus' oeuvre. Unlike a more traditional mythography or cosmogony, the Callimachean poetic landscape is home to a surprising variety of figures. Among them are characters drawn from mythological and heroic realms, like Theseus and Heracles; kings, and queens, but equally commoners, like Molorchus and Hecale; the Olympic victors Euthymus of Locri and Euthycles; philosophers and charlatans; and love-struck couples like Acontius and Cydippe. As his poetry is geographically diffuse, it is equally so in terms of its individuals and their stories, a mirror of the tremendous variety of tones in the early culture of a new city in Egypt ruled by Macedonian warlords and home to a heterogeneous populace.

Numerous individual actors populate Callimachus' poetry. Some may belong to mythical times, with the Trojan War as the divide, and others are anchored in the classical and archaic periods: we find couples in love, authors, athletes, even rulers. We have even at least one figure of generic type, the Roman Gaius, and possibly a second in Phoenix. For this reason the present chapter makes no claim to be exhaustive. It is my purpose rather to analyze the various types of characters that occur in Callimachus' oeuvre, especially if they play a metapoetic role. Divinities, mythical protagonists involved with divinities, and contemporaries of Callimachus do not figure in this study, since other chapters of this *Companion* are devoted to them.

Several chronological strata emerge when one undertakes a catalogue of these figures, the result of Callimachus' taste for aetiology, which is a constant of his work, extending well beyond the *Aetia*. I have, therefore, organized my discussion along temporal lines—whether they have a biographical reference such as the Olympic victor Euthycles or are purely mythological like Heracles—and along two interdependent axes. How the individual figure is imagined and the complexity of his representation are subjects of my analysis, along with the role given him by Callimachus in the poet's own discourse on literature.

Heracles and Theseus

The period prior to the Trojan War is marked in the extant work of Callimachus by the preeminence of three great mythological cycles, explorations of the borders of civilized and savage worlds that belong to mythic prehistory: those of Heracles, Theseus, and the Argonauts. How Callimachus structured his "Argonautica" segment of the *Aetia* will not occupy us here, as the fragments offer too little for certainty.[1] Nor will other mythological figures like Tydeus (fr. 523 Pf.), Danaus and his daughters (frr. 65–66 Pf.), or even Perseus (fr. 655 Pf.), if the fragments are too small for useful observations. However, an analysis of Callimachus' writing on the figures of mythological epic, perceived through the prism of choral lyric, tragedy, and comedy, as well as the analysis of the intertextual relations the poet establishes with his contemporaries, allow us to highlight certain aspects of Callimachus' poetic.[2]

We find, for example, that Heracles is an important figure in Callimachus' poetry, usually treated humorously. He appears especially in the *Aetia*, in Book 1 (frr. 22–23 and 24–25 Pf.) and in Book 4 (*SH* 254–268c and frr. 76–77 Pf.). Alcmene's son is mentioned for the first time in the collection in the course of the narrative of the *aition* of the sacrifice made in his honor at Lindus, a sacrifice that was traditionally accompanied by curses. The poet questions the origin of this rite (fr. 7.19–20 Pf.), and Calliope responds to him (frr. 22–23 Pf.).

---

[1] *Iambus* 8, which gives the *aition* of the Hydrophoria, and one of the last poems (frr. 108–109 Pf.) of *Aetia* 4, on the anchor left by the Argonauts at Cyzicus, are both summarized in their essentials by the Milan *Diegeseis* (VIII 21–32 and V 33–39, respectively). The summaries name no one individual but evoke the Argonauts collectively, just as in the opening of the *Argonautica* of Apollonius of Rhodes 1.1–2. (Cf. Fantuzzi and Hunter 2002: 123–125.) Fr. 7.6-7 Pf. also mentions "the Minyans" and the "heroes." Callimachus presents Aeetes in a speech full of rage following the departure of the Argonauts from Colchis. His words recall, as Harder (2002a: 218–219) observes, Apollonius of Rhodes 1.212–236, but with an important difference: in Callimachus the sovereign speaks in direct discourse; in Apollonius his speech is related by an external narrator. Jason is likewise presented through his words in the prayer he addresses to Apollo. (Cf. Albis 1995.) A fragment of uncertain context, fr. 668 Pf., names one of the Argonauts, Erigonus son of Clymenes. (Cf. Pind. *Ol.* 4.19–22.) Harder 2002a: 217–223 has observed that in the case of *Aetia* 1 the ritual at Anaphe is the second *aition* of the collection, whereas in *Arg.* 4 the anchor's abandonment is the next-to-last *aition*—a placement that cannot be accidental, since it is an inverted realization of what we find in Apollonius. My observations on the individual figures, slender though they are, reflect the same structural analysis.

[2] On the specific traits of humor of Hellenistic poets, cf. Giangrande 1975.

From other sources we know that the cult at Lindos was of Heracles Bouthoinas,[3] an epithet that alludes to the hero's voracity, an aspect that found much favor in comedy and that may be recalled in the representation of the animal as not yet cut up into serving pieces in line 23.15: θέντες ἀμίστυλλον ταῦρον ἐπισχα⁸[(Barigazzi 1976: 235). The comic traits of Heracles are developed in a quadruple comparison,[4] which extends over six lines (fr. 23.2–7 Pf.):[5]

ὡ]ς ὁ μὲν ἔνθ' ἤρᾶτο, σὺ δ' ὡς ἁλὸς ἦχον ἀκούει
Σ]ελλὸς ἐνὶ Τμαρίοις οὔρεσιν Ἰκαρίης,
ἠι]θέων ὡς μάχλα φιλήτορος ὦτα πενιχροῦ,
ὡς ἄδικοι πατέρων υἱέες, ὡς σὺ λύρης   5
—ἐσσὶ] γὰρ οὐ μάλ' ἐλαφρός, ἃ καὶ λίνος ουσεχελέξ..—,
λυ]γρῶν ὡς ἐπέων οὐδὲν [ὀπι]ζόμ[εν]ος,

One the one hand he cursed, but you—just as the Selloi in the Tmarian mountains listen to the sound of the sea, as the wanton ears of youths hear impecunious lovers, as irresponsible sons hear their fathers, as you hear the lyre (for you were not easy, and what Linus could not...)—thus heeding nothing of the baneful words.

Through a series of negative examples, of those who cannot hear, these three distichs elaborate Heracles' lack of concern for the curses of the animal's owner. The fourth introduces Heracles himself into the comparison: "as you the lyre." Heracles' inability to learn music was proverbial, and the introduction of his ill-fated music teacher,[6] Linus, in the parenthesis,[7] slyly emphasizes the point.[8] We should compare this passage with Theocritus *Idyll* 24.105–134, where while ostensibly the education of the youthful Heracles is under discussion, the true subject is the *paideia* of Ptolemy II. Linus here is no longer a music teacher but rather an instructor of *grammata* (*Id.* 24.105, γράμματα μὲν τὸν παῖδα γέρων Λίνος ἐξεδίδαξεν), and his death is given minimal attention. Pretagostini (2003: 68) has suggested that Theocritus perhaps wished to "return to Heracles the honor that Callimachus' humor in the *Aetia* had to a certain extent compromised."

---

[3] On this cult, cf. Burkert 2001: 90 and n. 31; Massimilla 1996: 285.
[4] Cf. Hunter 2006a: 88–102, especially 91.
[5] Accepting Wilamowitz's conjecture of λίνος in line 6. See Massimilla 1996: 289 n. 6.
[6] On the different versions of Linus' death, cf. Massimilla 1996: 289.
[7] As Pretagostini 2006a: 67 has shown, the "sleight of hand of interpolation" allows ὡς σὺ λύρης to retain its extreme concision as well as its precise meaning.
[8] "The last conveys a decidedly comical impression" (Massimilla 1996: 287).

The following *aition* offers thematic connections with the cult's origin. Fragments 24 and 25 Pf. tell of Heracles' meeting with the unpleasant figure Thiodamas. When the latter refuses the food that Heracles requests for his son, Heracles kills one of his oxen. Subsequent events are known from a scholion to Apollonius of Rhodes: helped by Deianeira, Heracles defeats the Dryopes who have come to the aid of their compatriot Thiodamas. At the end of the fight, defeated, the Dryopians were displaced to the Peloponnese, where they became more civilized. The relationship of these fragments to Apollonius' *Argonautica* 1.1213–1220, long recognized by scholars of both authors, has been interpreted in a number of ways.[9] Callimachus places the episode after the marriage of Heracles and Deianeira;[10] Apollonius, before the Argonauts' expedition. Further, the two poets give quite different pictures of Thiodamas. According to Massimilla (1996: 293), "the imposition of the comic in this episode in the *Aetia* would have led Apollonius to treat the same event seriously and with respect." The comic version in Callimachus' *Hymn to Artemis* (*Hy.* 3.160–161, ἔτι οἱ πάρα νηδὺς ἐκείνη, | τῇ ποτ' ἀροτριόωντι συνήντετο Θειοδάμαντι, "he still had the belly that accompanied him when he encountered Thiodamas at the plow") could thus be read as an analogue of the humorous aspect of this myth in the *Aetia* (*contra* Barigazzi 1976). Callimachus, in the course of his treatment of these two episodes in the mythical biography of Heracles, seems to have taken a certain liberty vis-à-vis a hero that the Ptolemies placed at the beginning of their lineage, whereas Theocritus and Apollonius seem to have suppressed these comic aspects in their own treatments of Heracles.

The type of hymnic greeting that concluded the Rhodian rite evokes the traditional figure of Heracles (fr. 23.19–20 Pf., χαῖρε βαρυσκίπων, ἐπίτακτα μὲν ἑξάκι δοιά, | ἐκ δ' αὐταγρεσίης πολλάκι πολλὰ καμών): "Hail [man] of the heavy staff, you who in suffering accomplished twelve labors imposed upon you and of your own volition often many others." But Heracles of the Twelve Labors is not the one Callimachus privileges, although one of these settings occurs in the *Victory of Berenice* (*SH* 254–268c).[11]

---

[9] Besides Barigazzi 1976, see especially Ardizzoni 1935.
[10] Scholia to Apollonius of Rhodes *Arg.* 1.1212–1219.
[11] The cleansing of the Augean Stables appears in the background of the poem on the seizure of Elis, as the A scholia to *Iliad* 9.700 indicate. However, the fragmentary state of the poem does not let us know whether the labor imposed on the hero

The Heracles who is the protagonist of the myth in the epinician in honor of Berenice's Nemean victory has several affinities with Theseus as Callimachus depicts him in the *Hecale* (Ambühl 2004 and 2005). Both have a foil, Molorchus for Heracles, Hecale for Theseus. Hecale, whose importance is underlined by the economy of a poem that opens with her (fr. 1 H.), and closes with the funeral rites that Theseus accords her (*Dieg.* XI 4-7 and frr. 79-83 H.), appears for the first time in the Atthidographer Philochorus.[12] Callimachus gives her tragic depth. She informs Theseus, in an analepsis, that she was once wealthy (fr. 41 H.), but that a series of catastrophes reduced her to a solitary life in a desolate place (frr. 47-49 and 40.5 H. and note *ad loc.*). This *metabole* conforms to Aristotelian principles.[13] Molorchus, who was to enjoy a great posterity, particularly at Rome, is, it seems, a figure Callimachus created (Parsons 1977). Hecale and Molorchus have similar functions vis-à-vis the two heroes: they are their hosts. The scene at the heart of both poems is a rewriting of the reception of Odysseus by Eumaeus in *Odyssey* 14;[14] by doing so the poet is able to bring a mythological hero into confrontation with daily life in a manner typical of Hellenistic taste (Zanker 1987). Callimachus has substituted the fight against rodents that Molorchus undertakes in his home for the confrontation of Heracles and the Nemean Lion. The passage borders on parody, with a web of epic allusions underpinning the scene. A temporal indication, typical of epic,[15] opens the verses dedicated to the Molorchus' battle (*SH* 259.5-8):

ἀστὴρ δ' εὖτ'] ἄρ' ἔμελλε βοῶν ἄπο μέσσαβα [λύσειν   5
αὔλιος], ὃς δυθμὴν εἶσιν ὑπ' ἠελίου
]ὡς κεῖνος Ὀφιονίδηισι φαείν[ει
]θεῶν τοῖσι παλαιοτέροις.

---

occupied an important place, or rather if it constituted only the point of departure for the narration of earlier episodes: the seizure of Elis, Phyleus' resumption of power, the union of the women of Elis with the soldiers of Heracles. Cerberus' capture was certainly mentioned in the poem, as fr. 515 Pf. attests, presenting the beast in the tortured phrase "Echidna's biting child."

[12] Philochorus *FGrHist* 328 F 109 = Plut. *Theseus* 4.

[13] Aristot. *Poet.* 1451a13-14, 1452a31-32. Ambühl 2004: 26-28 suggests seeing in the *Hecale*'s plot "a genuinely tragic structure" resting on the deception of Theseus, who on his return finds the old woman dead. However, it is rather Hecale herself who represents a tragic character.

[14] On the hospitality theme, see Hollis 2009: 341-354. See also, Ambühl 2004: 32-40.

[15] Fantuzzi 1988: 121-163; Hunter 2006a: 90.

When the star that indicated it was time for the folds was about to release the leather straps from the oxen, who goes at the setting of the sun... when he shines upon the sons of Ophion [the Titans]... the elders of the gods.

A Homeric simile follows. The householder's ear is attuned to hearing the mice just as a stag is on the lookout when he hears a lion (*SH* 259.9-11):

]τηρι θύρην· ὁ δ' ὅτ' ἔκλυεν ἠχ[ήν,
ὡς ὁπότ' ὀκν]ηρῆς ἴαχ' ἐπ' οὖς ἐλάφου
σκ]ύμνος, [μέ]λλ[ε] μὲν ὅσσον ἀκουέμεν, ἦκα δ' ἔλ[εξεν·

...the door; but when he heard the sound, as when near the ears of the timid deer the lion cub roars, he hesitates a bit to listen, then speaks softly.

The comparison is illuminated by the context. The comparisons of Molorchus to a stag and of a mouse to a lion create a comic effect, reinforced by the designation of the mouse's tail as ἀλκαίαις (*SH* 259.23), a rare term used for a lion's tail.[16] In line 29 the mice are described as σίνται, a word that in the *Iliad* is used of a lion (*Il.* 11.481, 20.165) or a wolf (*Il.* 16.353). The inversion of characteristics of heroic combat continues with Molorchus, a man of humble circumstances who in his diction takes on the affect of an epic hero. When he discovers the crime that the undesirable animals have committed, he is seized with a furious passion (*SH* 259.30): μήνατο κεῖνος ἔπι (cf. *Il.* 6.160). The parodic dimension of Molorchus' battle against the mice is a doublet of the comic presentation of Heracles, perpetually hungry and asleep after his victory over the lion, who then in his haste crowns himself not with a more noble wreath like the laurel but with a makeshift local plant, the celery (Ambühl 2004: 29-31).

The displacement of the center of gravity that we observe in the *Victory of Berenice* occurs again in the *Hecale*, where the poet has chosen not the motif of the confrontation with the Bull of Marathon as the poem's center but rather the scene of hospitality (Montes Cala 1989: 245-246). This shift affects the way in which the hero, Theseus, is treated. Theseus is delayed in undertaking his heroic enterprise by a storm that compels him to seek refuge with Hecale.[17] The conquest of

---

[16] Cf. Livrea 2006a for an echo of this passage in Juvenal 8.32-38.
[17] The double temporal indication that opens this passage evokes *SH* 259; cf. Livrea 1992.

the Bull of Marathon, which is an essential to confirm Theseus' status as a hero (Calame 1996: 76–78), is thus deferred and overwhelmed by a "trivialization of the fictional universe" at the heart of a poem with strong epic resonances.[18]

Another mythological episode tied to the Theseus cycle occupies an important place in the *Aetia*, namely the murder of Androgeos and its consequences (frr. 3–7 and 113 Pf.). The murder is not recounted in the surviving verses; therefore we cannot know which version Callimachus followed. Only the reactions of Minos himself survive, who was making a sacrifice to the Graces on Paros when the ghastly news was told to him (frr. 3–7 Pf.). Of the aetiological narrative itself all that remains is the outline of the myth-historical frame remains (fr. 4 Pf., "Minos pressed a heavy yoke upon the neck of the islands") and the gesture of the figure sacrificing at the moment when he is interrupted by the news of his son's death (fr. 5 Pf., "he began to cast the first offering"). The *Scholia Florentina* (*PSI* 11.1219) provide more detail:

Μίνῳ [τ]ῷ Δ[ιὸς κ(αὶ) Εὐρώ-]
πης θαλασσοκρατο(ῦν)τι κ(αὶ) ταῖς Χάρ[ι]σιν ἐν Π[άρῳ θύ-]
οντι Ἀ[ν]δρόγεω τοῦ παιδὸς θάνατος ἀπηγγ[έλλε-]   25
το. ὁ δ(ὲ) οὔτε τ(ῶν) Χαρίτ(ων) τ(ῆς) θυσίας ἠμέλησεν, ἀλ[λ᾽ ἔ-]
θυσεν, οὔτε τοῦ παιδὸς τὸν θάνατον παρενό[μη-]
σεν, τὸν δ᾽ αὐλητ(ὴν) ἐπέσχε κ(αὶ) τὸν στέφανον ἀ[πέ-]
θετο· κ(αὶ) οὕτως π(αρὰ) τοῖς Παρ[ίο]ις τὸ ἔθος ἔμεινε·

Minos, the son of Zeus and Europa, the overlord of the sea, was sacrificing to the Graces on Paros, when news of the death of his son, Androgeos, was brought to him. He did not neglect the sacrifice of the Graces but continued it, and did not lament the death of his son but had the flute player cease and removed his crown. And this continues to be the custom for the Parians.

Fragment 103 Pf. shows the heroization of Androgeos (*Dieg.* V 3–8):

Φησὶν ὅτι ὁ καλούμενος "κατὰ πρύμναν ἥρως" Ἀνδρόγεώς ἐστιν·…πάλαι γὰρ ἐνταῦθα τὸν Φαληρικὸν ὅρμον εἶναι, οὗ τὰς ναῦς ὁρμίζεσθαι πρὶν γενέσθαι τὸν Πειραιᾶ.

[The tablet (*kyrbis*)] says that Androgeos is the "hero of the stern," because in the past the anchorage of Phalerum was where the ships used to anchor before Piraeus was built.

---

[18] For the quote, see Cusset 2001: 237. "Strong epic resonances": see Fantuzzi and Hunter 2002: 270–271.

The *aition* opens with an address to a hero.[19] Callimachus, as at fragment 75 Pf., cites his source, a wooden tablet of the kind that is thought to have preserved the laws attributed to Solon.[20] Androgeos is a figure who draws together several mythic schemes. According to Photius 279.534a, he is the archetype of the *pharmakos* in Athenian rituals:

> The Athenians, afflicted with famine, plague, and other disasters, consulted the oracle, which told them to pay a compensatory tribute to Minos. The death of Androgeos is an *aition* for the instantiation of the famous human tribute that the Athenians sent to the Cretan king until Theseus intervened.

The theme of the *pharmakos* recurs throughout the *Aetia* (Compton 2006: 7–10, 83–86), and we will return to it in the section on athletes, to which category Androgeos belongs. Androgeos also returns us to the Minos episode that began at the opening of *Aetia* Book 1.

The Trojan War

Callimachus does not exploit the Trojan War—at least not as the Homeric poems relate it—but conforms to Hellenistic poetic practice by decentering it.[21] His choice thus often falls upon minor, even unknown figures in the Homeric tradition. A typical such character is Teuthis. Here the war serves as background for an aetiology (cf. Fantuzzi and Hunter 2002: 68–70): a particular feature of Athena's statue set up in the Arcadian city of Teuthis gives the poet the opportunity to develop the history of a little-known king from Homeric tradition and the epic Cycle, in the context of a rewriting of the quarrel of Achilles and Agamemnon. Fragment 110.1–11 M. (= *SH* 276 + fr. 667 Pf.) includes a *parainesis*: a woodsman's career is preferable to a farmer's. The narrative proper begins at line 12 with a myth that lays out how a king of this country once opposed the Atreidae at Aulis. A scholion to Pausanias 8.28.6 allows us to reconstruct the plot: at the time of

---

[19] Androgeos received heroic cult worship at Ceramicus and at Phalerum; cf. Amelesagoras of Athens *FGrHist* 330 F 2; Clem. Alex. *Protr.* 2.40.2; Pausanias 1.2.4.

[20] Cf. Plut. *Solon* 25.2. Hollis 1992a: 8 thinks that the cult of the hero may have been mentioned in "Solon's tablets."

[21] Cf. Sistakou 2004. Harder 2003: 297–298, apropos of the *Aetia*: "The period of the Trojan War is represented by two stories, which are not focusing on the events at Troy, which were familiar from the *Iliad*, but deal with the war from an eccentric point of view."

the Trojan War, Teuthis, or Ornithus, the chief of a Greek contingent coming from Arcadia, came to join the Achaean army at Aulis. As the windless calm continued, Teuthis took Agamemnon to task. Athena, disguised as a Greek warrior, sought in vain to dissuade Teuthis from abandoning the army. Enraged, he struck her with his spear. On his return to Arcadia, the goddess appeared to him in a dream, and the land became barren. The inhabitants consulted the oracle at Dodona, which bade them erect a statue of the goddess with a wound in her side.[22] This quarrel evoked another, which became the subject of the *Iliad*. But for the most famous of the Greeks Callimachus has substituted an unknown who did not participate in the Achaean expedition (Sistakou 2004: 115–117), and thus did not obtain the *kleos* that Callimachus has conferred upon him on the basis of an aetiology that takes the place of recounting a warrior's exploits.

The Archaic and Classical Periods

A number of figures belong to the archaic and classical periods. Some of these appear only in Callimachus' fragments, such as Acontius and Cydippe. The historical accuracy of the poet's treatment of such figures is very difficult to determine, if not impossible.[23] Most characters of this type occur in Books 3 and 4 of the *Aetia*, if one excepts the category of *kritikoi*, who occur especially in the *Iambi*. The catalogue structure of these two books of the *Aetia* and the tendency for poems with strong thematic affinities to occur in pairs is a possible explanation for this apparent temporal dynamic.[24]

With Molorchus or Hecale we have new types of characters entering into the Greek literary patrimony, figures associated with well-known heroes and destined to persist into late works of Greek or Latin. Other figures who appear for the first time in Callimachus have less of an antique setting and greater autonomy. Two poems belonging to *Aetia* 3 reflect Hellenistic poetry's interest in erotic elegy (frr. 67–75 and 80–83 Pf.). They present two erotic couples: Acontius and Cydippe,

---

[22] Hollis 1992c; Massimilla 1996: 439–441; D'Alessio 2007: 570–571 n. 41.
[23] Cf. Harder 2003: 298 n. 28; Lefkowitz 1981; Parsons 1977; Durbec 2005b.
[24] Cf. Krevans 1984: 239–241; Montes Cala 1989: 268–274; Parsons 1977; Durbec 2005b.

and Phrygius and Pieria.²⁵ These poems highlight a number of topoi of erotic elegy. The future lovers meet at the time of a religious festival:²⁶ Apollo's Bouphonia at Delos is the setting for the meeting of Acontius and Cydippe, whereas Phrygius and Pieria see each other for the first time at ceremonies in honor of Nelean Artemis at Miletus. The poet explicitly highlights the beauty of the two young people (cf. Calderón Dorda 1997: 3-4): Cydippe is called *kale* (frr. 67.1-2 and 73.2 Pf.), and the superiority of her beauty over that of her comrades becomes the subject of everyone's praise (fr. 67.11-14 Pf.). Acontius, too, is beautiful, as readers learn indirectly through the homoerotic reactions he arouses (frr. 68, 69 Pf.).

Callimachus indulges in another topos, that of having the lover employ clever rhetoric to persuade his beloved.²⁷ He playfully presents Pieria as superior to Nestor,²⁸ that Homeric paragon of oratory (fr. 184 M. = frr. 80 + 82.20-21 Pf.):

ἔνδει]ξας καὶ Κύπ[ρι]ν ὅτι ῥη[τ]ῆρ[ας ἐκείνου
τ]εύχει τοῦ Πυλί[ου κρ]έσσονας οὐ[κ ὀλίγως.

Having demonstrated that Cypris makes much better orators than the well-known man of Pylos.

In contrast, Acontius is not *polukrotos*, (fr. 67.3 Pf., οὐ γὰρ ὅγ' ἔσκε πολύκροτος). This adjective, a *varia lectio* of *polutropos* (cf. *schol. vet.* A Aristophanes' *Clouds* 260-261), would according to Pardini (1991: 57-70) contrast Acontius with Odysseus, another great Homeric orator: the timid Acontius is "not clever with words"; he has not Odysseus' skillful fluency of speech. This explains the appearance of Eros in his role of *erotodidaskalos* (fr. 67.1 Pf.)—of *praeceptor amoris*, to use Ovid's term (*AA* 2.497).²⁹

One of the consequences of unrequited love is lovesickness, which manifests itself in Acontius' case with a typical desire for solitude

---

²⁵ Phrygius is a Nelead (Plut. *Mor.* 254A, Polyaen. 8.35) who comes to power following the murder of Antheus; cf. Lightfoot 1999: 457. On the erotic theme in Hellenistic elegy, cf. Calderón Dorda 1997; Giangrande 1981b.

²⁶ This theme recurs in the Greek novel (e.g., the *Ephesiaca* of Xenophon of Ephesus). Sánchez Ortiz de Landaluce 1994 has studied the similarities between *Acontius and Cydippe* and the Greek novels.

²⁷ Giangrande 1971: 67-68; Calderón Dorda 1997: 6.

²⁸ A similar role inversion occurs already at Alex. Aetol. fr. 3 Magnelli.

²⁹ Cf. Calderón Dorda 1997: 10-11.

(fr. 72 Pf.).[30] For Cydippe, as the result of her unwitting erotic oath, she experiences four occurrences of increasingly severe illness (fr. 75.16 Pf., δεύτερον; 75.18, τὸ τρίτον; 75.20, τέτρατον), building a dramatic tension that peaks in a polemical definition of the name of the illness (fr. 75.14 Pf., ψευδόμενοι δ' ἱερὴν φημίζομεν, "we falsely call it the sacred disease"). This interruption of the narrative creates a distancing effect that diminishes the pathos of the young girl's misadventures.

Through the prism of erotic narrative, these two *aitia* reflect the historical circumstances of their composition. The synoecism that took place in the third century BC between Miletus and Myontus could have occasioned the legend of Phrygius and Pieria (see Pausanias 7.2.11), which Callimachus would have encountered shortly thereafter (Ragone 2006: 84–86). On the other hand, Callimachus bears witness to the development on Naxos of stories related to the *genos* of the Prometheii after the exile that followed upon the murder of Damasichton (Ragone 2006: 93–94).

Ancient Authors

It is hardly surprising that numerous authors appear by name in a work with a markedly metapoetic character.[31] Callimachus mentions several poets by name or by periphrasis:[32] Homer, Hesiod, Archilochus, Hipponax, Simonides, to name just a few. The *Aetia* and the *Iambi* are constructed around two of these, Hesiod and Hipponax, who are discussed in greater detail by C. Cusset in this volume. Here I want only to elaborate on the role of Hipponax as a figure that Callimachus uses to signal the principal style of the *Iambi*, namely literary criticism accompanied by violent personal polemic (so Lelli 2004). This novel, paradoxical approach underlines the seriocomic character of the *Iambi*, which redefines his relationship to the iambic tradition. He has changed addressee and object of attention but he has preserved their *vis polemica*. In *Iambus* 1 Hipponax brings together the Alexandrian scholars and addresses them directly. He recounts to them a story

---

[30] As is the case of Orpheus enamored of Calaïs in Phanocles fr. 1 Powell.

[31] Lelli 2006a: 178, "Callimachus is certainly among those authors of Greek literature who speak the most about themselves, their poetic world, and their relationships with other poets."

[32] I am not concerned here with the presence of other authors in Callimachus evoked by allusion or rewriting. I am concerned with writers only as individualized figures.

whose implicit moral is an invitation to cease the quarreling that pervades literary communities (Kerkhecker 1999: 39). Three similes and a metaphor characterize the scholars, whether we take them to be philologists or philosophers (fr. 191.26–28 Pf.):[33]

ὤπολλον, ὦνδρες, ὡς | παρ' αἰπόλῳ μυῖαι
ἢ σφῆκες | ἐκ γῆς ἢ ἀπὸ θύματος Δελφ[οί,
εἰληδὸν [ἐσ]|μεύουσιν |· ὤ Ἑκάτη πλήθευς.

O Apollo, the men like flies on a goatherd or wasps from the ground or Delphians from a sacrifice swarm in droves. O Hecate, what a throng!

The *Scholia Florentina* note the Homeric character of two of these comparisons, citing *Iliad* 2.469 and 16.259. These comparisons, which in Homeric epic describe warriors ready for combat, apply here to querulous dependents of the Museum. The story of Bathycles, for which several versions are attested (cf. Diog. Laert. 1.28–33), offers as an ethical model that modest attitude of the Seven Sages,[34] who when offered the leading prize for wisdom refuse it each in turn, each naming one wiser than himself until finally Thales, who comes both first and last, dedicates the prize to Apollo.[35]

Two poets figured in Callimachus not only convey a poetic program: they reflect a major aspect of the Cyrenaean's poetic, his *polyeideia* (cf. Lelli 2004: 126), for which the *Iambi* themselves principally,[36] though not uniquely, are offered as a "defense and illustration." The polymath Ion of Chios, the key figure in *Iambus* 13, is the paradigm for this.[37] In the third book of the *Aetia* the historian Xenomedes, a prose author and thus constitutive of the *polyeideia* that the Cyrenaean poet defends, plays an important role in poetic reflection on elegiac catalogues. Callimachus cites the source of the Cean legends that he evokes in the poem (fr. 75.54–55 Pf.):[38]

---

[33] The original reading of the papyrus that contains *Dieg.* VI 3 is "philosophers", which was then corrected to "philologists". On the respective uses of these terms, cf. D'Alessio 2007: 577 n. 1; Lelli 2004: 7 n. 3.

[34] The lesson proposed for the Greek scholars in Egypt is equally one of unity: cf. Acosta-Hughes 2002: 49. *Dieg.* VI 10–17 preserves the list of Seven Sages given by Callimachus. These are Thales, Bias, Periander, Solon, Chilon, Cleobulus, and Pittacus. This last is the subject of *Ep.* 1 Pf., on the metapoetic character of which see Livrea 1995.

[35] Designating Apollo as the ultimate recipient is perhaps not entirely neutral, as he is the titulary god of Callimachean poetics.

[36] On this point, see most recently Lelli 2005a.

[37] On *polyeideia* and Ion, cf. Leurini 1985 and Acosta-Hughes 2002: 84.

[38] On the meaning of the term *mythologos*, see Bruss 2004: 54–55.

τόνδε παρ' ἀρχαίου Χενομήδεος, ὅς ποτε πᾶσαν
νῆσον ἐνὶ μνήμῃ κάτθετο μυθολόγῳ.

This from old Xenomedes, who once set out the whole island in a myth-historical recollection.

There is a metapoetic point here,[39] as there is in the famous fragment 612 Pf. (cf. Meyer 1993), ἀμάρτυρον οὐδὲν ἀείδω ("I sing nothing unattested"), which supports the declaration at *Hymn* 5.56, μῦθος δ' οὐκ ἐμός, ἀλλ' ἑτέρων ("The story is not mine but another's"). Xenomedes, whose floruit is the second half of the fifth century,[40] is known from other sources.[41] Callimachus fragment 75.50–77 Pf. offers a partial summary of his work, showing what he might have treated but did not.[42] Callimachus is the first poet to cite a prose source by name—one to whom he gives a programmatic status comparable to that of his Hipponax or Hesiod (Krevans 2004: 179–181).

Athletes

Callimachus' interest in athletic competition is not limited to epinician.[43] Other than the poems mentioned here, the Alexandrian poet composed a treatise *On Competitions* (fr. 403 Pf.), for which one of the sources may have been a work of the same name by Duris of Samos (*FGrHist* F 6.33–34).[44] Two episodes of the *Aetia* present Olympic victors with contrasting fates: one, Euthycles (frr. 84–85 Pf.), was the victim of public jealousy, whereas the other, Euthymus (fr. 98 Pf.), received public honors, memorialized by their inscription in a mythological narrative that came to have a certain popularity. These two poems, forming a pair, testify to the particular importance of athletic victors in Greek societies, but also to the narrative treatment for which their lives were the subject.

Aetia 3 opens with the evocation of the Nemean victory of Berenice II and closes with the account of the misadventures of the Olym-

---

[39] On the explicit recall of his source as a component of Callimachean poetics, cf. Magnelli 2006b: 206.

[40] Alan Cameron 1995: 258 n. 103 has contested the traditional dating and proposed rather the beginning of the fourth century.

[41] Cf. *FGrHist* 442: Huxley 1965: 235–245.

[42] On this double movement of demonstration and selection, cf. Fantuzzi and Hunter 2002: 85–86; Magnelli 2006b: 207.

[43] On Callimachus' epinician poetry, cf. among an abundant bibliography Fuhrer 1992.

[44] Cf. Pfeiffer 1949–1953: 1.328.

pic victor Euthycles son of Astycles, of Epizephyrian Locri, in a ring composition of opposites.[45] The diegete's account and POxy 19.2213 fragment 8 (a + b + c + d) lines 1–17, completed by a text of Eusebius (*Praep. Ev.* 5.34.15–16), which gives a very close parallel version, allow us to see the thread of the poem: Euthycles, returning from an embassy with a gift of mules from his host, arouses feelings of jealousy in the hearts of his fellow citizens that lead to their denying him the honors that are his due. But the gods do not let this slight go unpunished, and a famine (or a plague) comes upon the city. This scourge does not cease until the inhabitants, after consulting Apollo's oracle, have reestablished the cult due to the victor. Euthycles' experience comes under the mythic schema of the athletic hero who, because he has become an exceptional individual, suffers the ire of his community.[46]

All that remains of the *aition* dedicated to Euthymus is known from the diegete (*Dieg.* IV 6–17). After a quotation of the first line, Εὐθύμου τὰ μὲν ὅσσα παραὶ Διὶ Πίσαν ἔχοντι ("the great accomplishments of Euthymus at Zeus's Pisa") the tale is summarized as follows:

> In Temesa a hero who was left behind from the ship of Odysseus exacted a tribute from the locals and their neighbors: that they should bring him a couch and a marriageable girl and go away without looking back. In the morning her parents receive a woman, no longer a virgin. The boxer Euthymus put an end to this tribute...

The structure of line 1, with τὰ μέν, indicates that a second development must have been offered at line 2, and the diegete's summary allows us to reconstruct the theme that was introduced: the exploits of Euthymus at Temesa. Pausanias 6.6.4 has an identical anecdote.[47] Euthymus was famous. He was first known as an Olympic victor in boxing, in which he was successful three times, in Olympiads 74, 76, and 77, in the years 484, 476, and 472 BC, respectively.[48] Subsequently, a statue,[49] the work

---

[45] Bulloch's (2006: 503–504) attempt to see symmetry at the heart of *Aetia* 3 is, however, too forced.

[46] Compton 2006: 18, 133, 187 n. 122; Fontenrose 1968: 74, 76–77.

[47] On Pausanias as a reader of Hellenistic poetry, cf. Castelli 1995: 714–715 and n. 12.

[48] POxy 2.222 and Pausanias 6.6.5–6.

[49] The base of this statue (*IvO* 56) has been found near the Eretrians' bull. Pliny *NH* 7.152 reports that Callimachus indicated that another statue had been consecrated to Euthymus by the Locrians. Both statues were struck by lightning on the same day. This event was considered a sign of divine favor, and following a response from the Delphic Oracle, which was consulted about the event, Euthymus received a cult while still alive. This motif, tied to heroic cult, occurs again in the *Life of Euripides* 36–45, which reports that the tragedian's cenotaph in Athens and his tomb in Macedonia

of Pythagoras of Rhegium (cf. Rollet 1994: 338), was set up at Olympia to commemorate his exploits. But it was not so much for his athletic exploits as for having saved Temesa from the 'hero' that Euthymus found lasting fame.[50] The most complete narrative we have is that of Pausanias 6.6.6–10, a text rich in narrative detail (see Visintin 1992). The myth occurs amid numerous accounts of western *nostoi* of Trojan heroes (cf. Braccesi 1994). One of Odysseus' companions was stoned to death for raping a young girl. Left without burial, he came back to terrorize the living until he was finally appeased by an annual offering of a young girl. Euthymus overcame this demonic hero in wrestling and married the young girl who was to be offered to him. Euthymus, who according to Aelian (*VH* 8.18) vanished on the bank of the river Caecinus, was probably honored as a river god in his country (Arias 1987: 1–8).

Contemporary Figures

Other than members of the ruling house, especially Ptolemy II and III, Arsinoe, and Berenice (see Prioux, this volume), several contemporary figures who occupied important positions in their respective communities are mentioned in Callimachus' work. With the exception of Darius II,[51] or the Scopadae (fr. 64 Pf.), who are named only in passing, the remaining powerful figures play central roles in the narratives in which they appear. Several are sovereigns of very negative character, such as Phalaecus, Phalaris, and Amphitres. The punishment that strikes two of them, Phalaecus and Amphitres, and in the case of Phalaris the fate of him who helped the tyrant indulge his cruelty, can have paradigmatic value, but it may also signal a positive development in the relationship of governments and their subjects that belongs to the social and moral progress within the *Aetia* noted by Harder (2003).

The Milan *Diegeseis* recounts the story of the murder of the Ephesian Pasicles (IV 36–V 2; fr. 102 Pf.): Pasicles, the archon of Ephesus,

---

were struck by lightning on the same day (Compton 2006: 141 and n. 32). See also Aelian *VH* 8.8.

[50] In addition to Callimachus and Pausanias, cf. Strabo 6.1.5 (255C); Aelian *VH* 8.18; Eustathius *ad Od.* 1.185, ps.-Plutarch *Proverbs* 2.31, *Suda* 3 p. 509 Adler.

[51] Fr. 381 Pf. = scholion B to Ovid *Ibis* 315. This fragment of the *Ibis* highlights the cruelty and perfidy of the king, who in order to gain the throne swore not to kill his subjects by poison, as his predecessor had done, Darius I; but after gaining power he killed them by shutting them up in a box full of ashes.

was attacked after a banquet. The attackers, having trouble because of the darkness, approached a temple of Hera; Pasicles' mother, a priestess there, ordered a lamp brought out because of the noise of the pursuit. And attackers, happening on the light, killed her son. Ovid *Ibis* 623–624 indicates that Pasicles tried in vain to evade his assassin, a certain Melas or Melanthus. The principal figure of this episode is not presented as a bloody tyrant, but on the contrary as the victim of a pathetic circumstance, as his mother unwittingly delivers him to his assassins by bringing a light that reveals his hiding place. Aelian (*VH* 3.26) gives us some information that suggests a probable identification of the protagonists of this drama: Pasicles was said to have been assassinated by the son of the tyrant Pindar, whose tutor he was (Ragone 2006: 14).

This political murder (the pupil kills his tutor to take power), which is doubled by impiety, as Pasicles is killed in the immediate proximity of a temple of Hera, finds an echo in fragment 115 Pf., mentioning Onnes and Tottes. A passage of Nicolaus of Damascus provides the following story (*FGrHist* 90 F 52 = *Excerpta de insidiis* p. 18.19 de Boor): Amphitres killed his brother Leodamas while the latter was sacrificing in honor of Apollo, and then besieged Assessus, where his victim's children fled for refuge. An oracle told the inhabitants that their salvation would come from Phrygia. One night two brothers, Onnes and Tottes, arrived carrying sacred objects. They demanded that the besieged make and establish sacrifices; then they led out the procession. The army of Amphitres was put to flight, and Amphitres himself was killed. The historical context of this story remains obscure. The reign of Leodamas cannot be dated with accuracy, though the monarchy seems to have lasted in Miletus at least until the eighth century, a date that provides a *terminus ante quem* (Parke 1985: 7). The two stories of Pasicles and of Leodamas have two affinities: a magistrate in one case, and a sovereign in the other, is killed by someone close to him who hopes to seize power, and the murder is a pollution. However, the attempt is successful in the case of Pasicles but fails for Amphitres, who is killed with the help of the Cabeiri Onnes and Tottes.

A very fragmentary scrap from the *Diegeseis* (fr. 160 M.) preserves the account of a lost *aition* that also concerns the theme of despots who were punished (PMilVogl inv. 1006).[52] The diegete tells the story

---

[52] This poem belonged to *Aetia* 3 and was preceded by an *aition* on the Attic Thesmophoria (fr. 63 Pf.); cf. Gallazzi and Lehnus 2001.

of Phalaecus, tyrant of the city of Ambracia, in Epirus. Despised by his subjects, he was killed in the course of hunting by a lioness whose cub he had in his arms. The Ambraciots consecrated a statue to Artemis in gratitude. The most complete account is that of Antoninus Liberalis (*Met.* 4.5). When Apollo, Artemis, and Heracles ask Cragaleus to decide their quarrel over the city of Ambracia, Artemis stakes her claim to sovereignty over the city on the basis of her intervention against the tyrant Phalaecus. Antoninus' source was Athanadas of Ambracia, whom Felix Jacoby dated to the third century BC (*FGrHist* 303 F1), and whose work would have been available to Callimachus. The *aition* of this poem could, according to Gallazzi and Lehnus (2001: 11), recall a specific characteristic of the statue of Artemis of Ambracia. Particular characteristics of certain cult statues are in fact the subject of other poems in the *Aetia* (frr. 35–38 M. = 100 and 101 Pf.).

The cruelty of the tyrant is punished, but one who serves such a sovereign also takes great risks. Phalaris, tyrant of Agrigentum, is the archetype of the bloody autocrat. The bronze maker Perillus, who devised a bronze bull as an instrument of torture for him, was one of its first victims, as several lines of *Aetia* 2 recall (fr. 53 M.), completed by a note from Plutarch (*Par. min.*, *Moralia* 315C). Callimachus may be making the point that in contrast to these figures, life seems to have been benign at Alexandria in the third century BC under the authority of the Ptolemies, at least through the prism of Callimachus' poetry.

Powerful Figures

Two figures merit a special status in studies dedicated to Callimachus' poetic oeuvre, for they both pose a problem of identification that numerous scholars have been unable to resolve. However, it seems that one, Gaius, is generic, and we should not try to identify him with a specific historical individual; whereas the other, Phoenix, is a philological phantom.

In all of Callimachus' extant work a single fragment (fr. 106 Pf.) has a Roman protagonist. *Diegeseis* V.25–32, which preserves the first line of this poem, gives the name of a Roman, Gaius: the diegete says that when the Peucetii were besieging the walls of Rome, Gaius leapt from the walls and killed their leader while being himself wounded in the thigh. Afterwards when he complained to his mother about his limp, she rebuked him, admonishing him for his lack of heart. The issue of identifying this figure is tied to the problem that the dating of this episode in Roman history poses and the identification of the Romans' opponents.[53] The diegete calls this Roman by his praenomen, conforming to Greek convention.[54] Several precise identifications have been suggested: J. Stroux (1934) compares the narrative of the *Diegeseis* with a passage of Cicero that mentions the admonition of a mother to her son,[55] a certain Spurius Carvilius who complains of being afflicted with an infirmity not brought about in glorious combat against an enemy. M. Lechantin (1935) identifies this Spurius Carvilius with the consul of 293 and of 272, who according to the *Fasti triumphales* achieved a victory over the Tarentines. G. De Sanctis (1935: 289–301) rejects this identification, correctly.[56] He in turn offers a hypothesis that is equally unconvincing, because he proposes seeing in Gaius the Roman hero Horatius Cocles. However, as De Sanctis admits, there are numerous differences between the two stories. The aporia to which we are led by an absence of any detail allowing identification suggests, as does S. Mazzarino (1966: 257–271), that we should see in Gaius not a specific individual but a Roman type of exalted martial prowess. This fragment would then be an example of parainetic elegy (D'Alessio 1996: 521 n. 29).

Fragment 64 Pf., also much discussed, evokes the destruction of Simonides' tomb by a certain Phoenix, an "evil warlord of the city." The poem opens with an imprecation (fr. 64.1–2 Pf.) referring to the proverbial misfortune that afflicted the Sicilian city of Camarina.[57] The imprecation applies a posteriori to the impious general who destroyed the poet's tomb to construct fortifications. The general's sacrilegious nature, qualifying him as an ἀνὴρ κακός and σχέτλιον ἡγεμόνα,[58] contrasts markedly with the tradition of respect for strangers for which

---

[53] Cf. most recently Urso 1998; Colonna 2000; and Braccesi 2001.

[54] Aristotle fr. 610 R. (= Plut. *Cam.* 22.4) reports that Rome was saved from the Celts by one Lucius. As Braccesi (2001: 109) remarks, in both cases a very common praenomen serves to designate one who saves his fatherland from attack.

[55] *De or.* 2.249. Stob. 3.7.28 also reports this anecdote of a certain Spartan; Plut. *Mor.* 241 and 331B, of the young Alexander admonishing his wounded father and exhorting him to have courage.

[56] De Sanctis 1935 advances a number of arguments against this identification of the figure Gaius. First of all, Callimachus could not have known a variant of a story concerning an event dated to 272 BC. Further, the *Fasti* do not mention the Peucetii, and Gaius is not the praenomen of the relevant consul.

[57] Cf. Durbec 2006a: 71 n. 208; Lelli 2006b: 152–153; Massimilla 2006b: 37–39.

[58] The expression ἀνὴρ κακός contrasts explicitly with the "holy man" of lines 1–2.

the Agrigentines are famous.[59] The general's name does not survive in Callimachus' text but has been restored based on a passage in the *Suda* (s.v. Σιμωνίδης), which cites Περὶ προνοίας (fr. 63 Hercher):

> The general of the Agrigentines was named Phoenix. They were at war with the Syracusans. Therefore this Phoenix destroyed the tomb of Simonides without care or pity. And he took up these very stones for a wall, and the polis destroyed him. It seems that Callimachus agreed with them [sc. the citizens of the polis].

But this Phoenix, unattested in any other source, could well be but a phantom, and a generic character rather like Gaius. The interpretation attempts to place the episode at the time of the wars against the Syracusan tyrant Agathocles,[60] but Agrigentum was not destroyed during this war. The most satisfactory hypothesis is that of J.A. de Waele (1971: 47–49): what Aelian, or his source, read as a proper name was simply an ethnic marker. The tomb's destruction would have taken place during the course of the capture of the town by the Carthaginians—that is, Phoenicians—under Hannibal in 206 BC.[61]

---

[59] Cf. Diod. Sic. 13.83, who cites Empedocles.
[60] Cf. Pfeiffer 1949–1953 *ad loc.*; Bicknell 1986: 54–60.
[61] Cf. Diod. Sic. 13.86.1. For this hypothesis, cf. also Durbec 2006a: 72–73 n. 211; Livrea 2006c: 53–55; *contra* Massimilla 2006b: 40–43.

CHAPTER TWENTY-FOUR

IAMBIC THEATRE:
THE CHILDHOOD OF CALLIMACHUS REVISITED

Mark Payne

ABSTRACT

Nietzsche calls the child "a holy assent." Callimachus' child poet, on the other hand, has often been read as a figure of dissent, a traumatized refusal of tradition for the sake of a critical ("self-conscious") aesthetic modernity. In this paper I look at who is refusing what from whom in the *Iambi*: who are the parents, who are the children, and what does their childishness have to do with tragedy, performance, and acting out? This analysis of the collection's family dynamics reveals that the paternal anxiety Callimachus' critics have seen in the *Aetia* prologue should be revisited in light of the powerful maternal figures who loom over the child poet in the *Iambi*.

> *Unschuld ist das Kind und Vergessen, ein Neubeginnen, ein Spiel, ein aus sich rollendes Rad, eine erste Bewegung, ein heiliges Ja-sagen.*
> —Friedrich Nietzsche, *Also sprach Zarathustra*

Charles Baudelaire, in his essay "A Philosophy of Toys," makes a strong connection between children's love of mannequins and other such toys, and adults' love of the theater. Something of the child's enjoyment of characters who exist by his own will and for his own pleasure persists, he thinks, in the adult's love of theatrical illusion. There are, however, questions about how the child positions himself with respect to these illusory presences that remain unanswered: Does the child dominate the marionettes that populate his toy theater, or does his play world dominate him? The latter is a danger to which children "of literary or artistic predestination" are particularly liable, so that we are led to ask: Are the adult writer's creations an index of his mastery of the world, or are they a sign of infantile confusion, a willed regression to a time when the boundaries of selfhood could be imagined as rather more fluid than they have become? (Baudelaire 1964: 202).

Callimachus, notoriously, refers to himself as a child in the prologue to the *Aetia* (fr. 1.5-6 Pf.). The first poem of the *Iambi* brings Hipponax back from the dead to speak in the poet's place. How, then, does the use of the dramatic mode relate to the thematics of childhood? Before turning to Callimachus, I want to consider first how Aristotle frames the question. In Book 6 of the *Nicomachean Ethics*, Aristotle defines the arts as a human activity that concerns itself with the coming into being (γένεσις) of things that are capable "either of being or of not being." Things that come into being out of necessity, or according to nature, have their origins in themselves, whereas the origin of an art object is not in the object itself but in its maker (*NE* 6.4.4, 1140a). In Book 9 he considers this fact with respect to the affects involved in benefaction. While we might expect the feelings of the benefited to be stronger than those of their benefactors, the opposite is in fact the case, and, Aristotle claims, this surprising truth can best be understood by looking at artists, and especially poets. The artist conveys the greatest benefit possible—existence—upon his creations, and yet it is nonetheless true that "every artist loves his own work more than that work would love him if it were to come to life." What is true of all artists is especially true of poets, for they dote upon their poems and love them as if they were children, ὥσπερ τέκνα. The apparent paradox is explained by the fact that, although all things love existence, the pleasure of existence is most truly apprehended in action (ἐνέργεια), and creators are the active party in creation, just as benefactors are in benefaction (*NE* 9.7.3-4, 1167b-1168a).

The biological model of poetic invention seems natural enough, and has its parallels in the *Poetics*, where Aristotle speaks of the first poets' "siring" new genres upon whatever raw materials were to hand, ἐγέννησαν τὴν ποίησιν ἐκ τῶν αὐτοσχεδιασμάτων (*Poet.* 1448b). Here poets are fathers, giving form to matter, and initiating the teleological development that will in due course give birth to tragedy and comedy. Yet the two accounts are not exactly symmetrical. The discussion of the affects of benefaction in the *Ethics*, and their origins in the experience of action or passivity, leads Aristotle to a secondary reflection on the relationship between labor and benefaction. Because children involve more effort for the mother than the father, ἐπιπονωτέρα γὰρ ἡ γέννησις, mothers, he claims, love their children more than fathers do—and also because they can be more certain than fathers can that their children are their own (*NE* 9.7.7, 1168a).

Following hard upon the comparison between poets and parents, one wants to feed this piece of information back into the metaphorical matrix. If poets are to their poems as parents are to their children, should we conceive of them as mothers, or fathers? The laboriousness of the creative process Aristotle recommends to the young tragedian in the *Poetics*—plot to be sketched in outline, then expanded with episodes, gestures, and other requisite features (*Poet.* 1455a–b)—suggests the mother's part; anxiety about paternity brings us close to familiar Bloomian and Freudian themes: anxiety of influence and the poet's fear that his poem is not really his own. And if the poet thinks of himself as a child, can he at the same time be a parent of his work, like Nietzsche's child, who is a wheel self-propelled? Finally, if for Aristotle the dramatic mode was how Homer distinguished himself from his rivals, absenting himself from his poems in order to bring forth one character after another (*Poet.* 1460a), should we understand the well-known preference of the Hellenistic poets for literary drama as paternal (Freudian) or maternal (Lacanian) rivalry?[1] Before we consider these questions in the *Iambi*, let us look first at how they have been theorized in scholarship on the *Prologue* to the *Aetia*.

On the Prologue

In the opening lines of the *Aetia*, Callimachus imagines the field of poetic action as a battleground: arrayed against the poet are his enemies, whom he imagines as spiteful and uncomprehending wizards, Telchines. What they accuse him of is poetic immaturity, claiming that he has produced his work in little pieces, like a child (fr. 1.5–6 Pf.): ἔπος δ' ἐπὶ τυτθὸν ελ[| παῖς ἅτε.[2] Child's play is unsustainable

---

[1] On literary drama, see Bulloch 1985: 6 and the discussion in Payne 2007: 10–15. On Plato's Homer as father of all the poets, see Lelli 2004: 133. What is at stake in the Freudian and Lacanian versions of parental rivalry will become clear in the course of my discussion.

[2] I have no new conjecture for the missing word at the end of verse 5 that would make the accusation more precise. The two most popular conjectures, ἑλίσσω, "I roll," and ἐλαύνω, "I drive," are rejected by Acosta-Hughes and Stephens 2001, because of the awkwardness involved in taking ἔπος as the object of either. They propose ἔλεξα instead, where ἔπος would have the sense of "story" or "narrative," rather than "word" or "statement," and the phrase as a whole would mean to narrate discontinuously, as children are nonlinear when telling a story. The general sense of fragmentariness, or piecemeal production, is, however, clear, from ἐπὶ τυτθόν.

production; unlike the poets the Telchines admire, who produce adult-size poems for adult readers, the brevity of Callimachus' productions reveals the imagination of a child,[3] who animates his creations for a little while before dropping them for something else.

Callimachus responds to the accusation of childishness childishly; he defends his poems not by offering a poetics but by claiming that when he was a boy Apollo told him to write the way he writes, and he has continued to do so ever since (21–38); he is just obeying his teacher. If the claim that one's enemies are wizards already sounds childish, this response makes it clear that the entire battle will be conducted on Callimachus' terms. The scene of the child poet with writing tablet on his knee is just the kind of composition by vignette the adult poet has been accused of, and he answers his critics not by reasoning with them, but by out-imagining them. Poetic achievement is enabled by access to childhood powers, whose survival into adulthood is itself enabled by the rejection of adult modes of argument, and obedience instead to the powerful divinities of youth. Those whom the Muses have favored as children, Callimachus claims, will not be abandoned by them as adults, and so *The Dream* follows the *Prologue*, as the adult poet escapes from the old age that oppresses him—as Sicily weighs upon the Titan Enceladus (36)—by staging another little scene in which he once fell asleep and dreamed of meeting the Muses on Mount Helicon, as Hesiod did: his own youth and the youth of poetry come back to life together.[4]

At *Poetics* 1450a Aristotle makes the argument that in the tragedians ontogeny recapitulates phylogeny: as plot was the hard-won achievement of generations of early poets, so the young writer will master diction and character before he learns how to put together a successful story. For Callimachus, access to the early phases of phylogenetic development is a value, but it is a value that can be pursued only by preserving the early phases of ontogenetic development. The way forward is the way back. This, I suggest, is quite unlike the Bloomian-Freudian model of oppression by the past that some schol-

---

[3] On childhood as the characterological expression of the antithesis between large and small that structures Callimachus' poetic thought, see Asper 1997: 148–152.

[4] Alan Cameron 1995: 181–183; Fantuzzi and Hunter 2004: 73–74. As Scodel 1980a has shown, Callimachus stages as poetic fiction the second childhood that was literally granted to Hesiod in some versions of his life.

ars have seen in the *Prologue*'s narrative of poetic childhood.[5] The latter is a familiar, Oedipal, account of the belated poet's relationship to the tradition, a story of adulthood achieved through self-sacrifice and renunciation.[6] Its familiarity is comforting, but it has little to do with the *Prologue*, which, as we have seen, does not contain a sacrificial narrative but instead celebrates the energies of regression. Callimachus does not wait for Zeus to free him from the prison of old age; he gets out of jail free.

If we reject the Bloomian-Freudian story, we must reject along with it the idea of a heroic struggle with scary poetic fathers. This idea is so fundamental to our notions of belatedness that it is hard to imagine how we might do without it. Could it really be that Callimachus is completely unintimidated by his predecessors and finds it all too easy to outdo them? Might he really have the Titanic sense of his own powers that leads him to say of himself later in the *Aetia*: "This guy really is like a child with a knife," ὡς ἐτεὸν παῖς ὅδε μαῦλιν ἔχει (fr. 75.9 Pf.)? According to Baudelaire (cited in Mavor 2007: 233), "the child sees everything in a state of newness; he is always drunk." Is this what Callimachus means by child's play? These are the questions that I want to address in the *Iambi*.

The Articulations of His Book

The *Iambi* begins with a talking ghost, the spirit of the archaic iambic poet Hipponax, who is brought back from the dead by Callimachus

---

[5] "The sequence of thought suggests that the old age which crushes the poet is at one level what *we* have learned to call 'the burden of the past', that consciousness of tradition, of Hesiod, Pindar, Euripides, Aristophanes and the other great figures of the past whose voices well up through Callimachus' verses, a consciousness which hems our every move with qualification, deferral and doubt, and which, like old age, restricts the freedom of action we associate with 'the light one, the winged one'" (Fantuzzi and Hunter 2004: 75, emphasis original). Cf. Acosta-Hughes and Stephens 2002: 246, who cite Bloom's *Anxiety of Influence* and *Map of Misreading* to give a heroic cast to the child poet's self-fashioning as the birth into (Olympian) individuation through strong misreading of the "parent-poems" of his fearsome precursors.

[6] It also underlies the reading of Callimachus' religious poetry in Bulloch 1984, who (p. 229) cites Freud's *The Future of an Illusion*: "Man cannot remain a child forever; he must venture at last into the hostile world." For Bulloch, Callimachus sacrifices classical religious poetry's comforting illusion of gods that care for human beings for a conception of divinity as unconcerned with human beings that, while more frightening, is for that very reason more adult.

to reason with the contentious intellectuals of Alexandria: instead of bickering among themselves, they should learn the lesson of the Seven Sages, each of whom strove to pass on the prize for wisdom to someone other than himself. This is a Hipponax who, as commentators have noticed, has nothing in common with the archaic personage who bore his name. He is public-spirited and lacks aggression; he brings "an iambus that does not sing the Bupalean strife" (1.1–4), having forsworn the hostility to rivals that, in the stories of his life, led him to hound to death with his poems the sculptors who made unauthorized images of him.[7] This Hipponax no longer skewers his adversaries. Deprived of his weapon, he bears the same relation to the iambic tradition as the Polyphemus of Theocritus' *Idyll* 11 bears to Homeric epic; harmless and helpless, both signal a boy poet's mastery of a poetic father. If the Cyclops' impossible anxiety about an Odysseus who is to come—an Odysseus who will blind him and mock him (*Id.* 11.53–79)—points back to Homer as father of the tale, this poetic rivalry is nonetheless all but absent from the poem. It is Sappho's voice that is heard in the Cyclops' song; it is a poet mother whose voice is desired as the child poet's poetic child sings of his desire.[8]

Homer makes a remarkable nonappearance in *Iambus* 6. This strange poem on Phidias' famous statue of Zeus reduces one of the wonders of the Graeco-Roman world to a set of measurements. Figures of size and cost take the place of appreciation, and the poem seems even to misunderstand its rhetorical purpose; what is formally a *propemptikon* ends not with a fulsome *Bon voyage!* but with the briefest of farewells, ἀπέρχευ, whose curtness makes it all too obvious that the poet is happy not to be sharing the journey (6.62).[9] Readers have struggled to find something to admire in the poem, and have sought it in such unlikely places as its "truly impressive variety of measuring techniques," and its humorous staging of "the perversity of the scholar" who imagines size matters.[10] Another popular approach has been to see the Zeus as a

---

[7] See West 1971: 1.109–110 for the ancient testimony. For discussion of its possible significance in an ancient history of medium rivalry, see Miralles 2004: 208–209. On its importance for Callimachus' refocusing of iambic poetry on artistic concerns, see Acosta-Hughes 1996: 210–213, and 2002: 32–35, 281–282.

[8] On the echoes of Sappho, see Hunter 1999: 231–232; Payne 2007: 73–74.

[9] Dawson 1950: 72; Clayman 1980: 34; Kerkhecker 1999: 173–179; Acosta-Hughes 2002: 289.

[10] Clayman 1980: 34; Hutchinson 1988: 27.

setup man for the Hermes of *Iambus* 7, insofar as his bulk represents the kind of supersized literary work the aesthetics of Callimachean slimming has come to do battle with.[11]

Yet why does effacement proceed by disavowal rather than simple replacement? Why is the old god exposed before the new god is set up in his place? Phidias' Zeus was notoriously made out of Homer. Strabo (8.3.30) gives us the lines (*Il.* 1.528–530), and tells us why the sculptor made a hash of them: Homer offers us outlines that enable us to guess at the cloudy majesty of the gods, but Phidias gives us a literal image that blocks our apprehension of their dynamic potentiality. We might connect this discussion of the secondary nature of visual representations with the tales about Hipponax' anger at Bupalus and Athenis for making him look ridiculous in their rendition of scenes from his work. (If we ask how they could have made him look more ridiculous than he made himself look, the answer must be that in their fabrication of discrete scenes from a continuous poetic narrative, the existential meaning of such actions as defecating upon oneself while being beaten by barbarian prostitutes somehow got lost in translation.) But this is not the story I want to take up here. I want to look at a different critical narrative, one that sees poets as opening their minds to anyone who wants to enter them.

Strabo (8.3.30) says there is a witty saying about Homer that "he alone has seen or he alone has shown the likenesses of the gods," κομψῶς δ' εἴρηται καὶ τὸ ὁ τὰς τῶν θεῶν εἰκόνας ἢ μόνος ἰδὼν ἢ μόνος δείξας. Unlike Socrates, Homer does not keep his divine images locked away inside him and show them only to a chosen few (*Symp.* 215a–c, 221d–222a); Homer is an open book. This is what Pseudo-Longinus loves about the archaic poets, and Homer in particular; unlike the Hellenistic writers whose unrelenting precision directs our attention to what they have made, poets of genius show us themselves. To be a great poet is to exist in a condition of constant self-exposure, for "what is out of the ordinary is always closely regarded," θαυμαστὸν δ' ὅμως ἀεὶ τὸ παράδοξον (*Subl.* 35.3–5). The Zeus-Homer equation looks very different from this perspective, for, as Lacan (1992: 60) reminds us, a condition of total contact between the self and the world could be only a state of pain:

---
[11] Lelli 2004: 22 n. 36; Petrovic 2006: 31 and 2010.

Isn't something of this suggested to us by the insight of the poets in the myth of Daphne transformed into a tree under the pressure of a pain from which she cannot flee? Isn't it true that the living being who has no possibility of escape suggests in its very form the presence of what one might call petrified pain? Doesn't what we do in the realm of stone suggest this? To the extent that we don't let it roll, but erect it, and make of it something fixed, isn't there in architecture itself a kind of actualization of pain?

The Hermes of *Iambus* 7 is a god who avoids erection. We learn from the *diegesis* that a wooden statue was fashioned by Epeius, the builder of the Trojan Horse. It was swept into the sea by the swollen flood of the Scamander and carried from the Troad to Aenus in Thrace, where fishermen caught it in their nets. They tried to use it for firewood, but when they could not chop it up with their axes or burn it in one piece, they threw it back into the sea. It was only when they caught it again that they realized there was something fishy about it and set up a cult. How is it that these simple fisher folk were unable to recognize the god when they saw him? It can only be because he was traveling without his phallus. In the similar story about Dionysus Phallen told by Pausanias (10.19.3), the god has features, and a "touch of divinity" about him, with the result that the people of Methymna ask the Pythia of what unfamiliar god he is a likeness rather than discard or attack him. Likewise, the Hermes of *Iambus* 9 is decidedly ithyphallic. If Hermes Perpheraeus can travel the world unnoticed, it must be because he lacks the very thing that normally makes him the center of attention.

This herm is a tease. Not only does he have a missing phallus, not only is he a base without a superstructure,[12] he also sucks the reader into a game of hide-and-seek that ancient readers appear not to have relished. According to Aristotle, the pursuit of Hector in the *Iliad* is a success only because we don't actually see it; if we did, it would be ridiculous (*Poet.* 1460a–b). Likewise, Hera's seduction of Zeus, according to the (bT) scholion on *Iliad* 14.342–351, is poetry that is not meant to be looked at too closely; if you get caught up in trying to picture it to yourself, you'll end up worrying about things like whether talking ghosts have tongues (Meijering 1987: 68–69). This, as Pseudo-Longinus never tires of reminding us, is where the Hellenistic poets went wrong: forcing us to concentrate on what's in the poem gets in the way of imagining the poet (*Subl.* 33). Unlike modern theo-

---

[12] Cf. Dawson 1950: 82 and Clayman 1980: 38 on the swollen form of the epigrammatic convention by which a dedicated cult object narrates its own history.

rists, who relish the prospect of co-creation, helping the poet finish his handiwork seems not to have appealed to ancient ones. Perhaps it was too banausic for them; in any case, they recommend moving swiftly on and not lingering over the details.[13]

There seems to be no end to the teasing of the reader in *Iambus* 7. For Hermes' incompleteness is not just the schematization unavoidable when rendering in words an object that we could encounter in all its missing plenitude if we were somehow able to enter the fictional world to which it belongs. The incompletion of the Hermes may be strictly mimetic, and its aniconicity accidental. Perhaps Epeius ("Wordy"? "Mr. Epic"?) wasn't done with him when he got away.[14] Perhaps in this story it was the crafty father, and not the cunning child, who lost control of the knife in his hand. Perhaps the little fellow was angry with his Dad for spending all his time on the Horse; this, as Virgil reminds us, was a more manly project: as big as a mountain, and with a womb that groaned with real men (*Aen.* 2.15, 52–53, 258). It would be a small wonder, then, if Epeius hadn't spent as much time as he should have on his first child and left him half-finished. Borne off by the swollen Scamander, at any rate, he washes up on the rocks of Aenus, a particularly painful form of exposure, one would think, where he finds his finders are not keepers, and so has to reenact the history of neglect he has suffered at the hands of his father. Such is the story he tells, not entirely cheerfully: "coward," or "spear-fleer," is the tragic epithet he applies to his dad—gone but not entirely forgotten, it would seem.

Bramble between Two Trees

"Spear-fleer," φυγαίχμας, is an Aeschylean *hapax*. The timid elder statesmen of the Persian chorus use it to imagine their helplessness in the face of the unstoppable Greek sailors who are about to ravish their kingdom: "The men of Ionia are no spear-fleers," they worry. "They are manly, all right," Xerxes agrees (*Pers.* 1025–1026). It is one

---

[13] Bing 1995 couldn't be more pleased that Callimachus has invited his readers to participate in an *Ergänzungsspiel*. The joke may be on them, however.

[14] As V. Platt (forthcoming) "Epiphanic Alternatives, 1: The *Xoanon*," observes, it is exceptional for an aniconic statue to have a maker at all, since the unexpected arrival of such objects typically entails ignorance of their parentage. Like exposed infants, they just show up on the doorstep.

of the greatest scenes of misery that tragedy has to offer, as Xerxes and his retainers bewail their fate through almost two hundred lines of antiphonal lament. If this is where Callimachus found the word, he has all but blotted out its affective context.

Tragedy is also concealed in the *agon* of *Iambus* 4. It is a strange kind of contest: two trees, both female, are fighting over which of them human beings love better. Laurel is proud of her associations with priests and seers; she does not know pain and is pleased to have been adopted as a sign of athletic victory, for she herself is pure and holy (25–40). Laurel flaunts her connections with the better class of persons, and we recognize her as the type of hypercompetitive mother whom defeated athletes are ashamed to face (Pindar *Pyth.* 8.86)[15] and who instills feelings of embarrassment in her son towards a father whose social aspirations fall short of her own (Plato *Rep.* 549d–550b). Olive, by contrast, is Good Mommy: she helps out wherever she is needed; she does not shrink from scenes of lamentation, and she is willing to be eaten, even in pickled form, by poor people. As a token of her good nature, she eschews self-praise. She knows that when a person has something nice to say about herself, or something not so nice to say about others, she should pretend someone else is saying it. "So-and-so says" is more polite than "I say," and she therefore has two birds sing her praises. This, for Aristotle, is a lesson we can learn from Archilochus (*Rhet.* 3.17.16, 1418b), and while in his case we might think it is a lesson more honored in the breach than the observance, putting your own words in someone else's mouth is, Aristotle thinks, no more than a ruse, and employed as such by Isocrates, and Sophocles' Haemon, "when he defends Antigone against his father as if someone else were talking."

According to the *diegesis*, this is just what is going on in *Iambus* 4: someone is hiding in the trees, refusing to show himself. For the poem, it claims, began with an explanatory mise-en-scène: the poet was arguing with some unnamed person he thought of as an equal, when Snub-Nose, Σῖμος, the Son of Delight, or of Gratitude, Χαριτάδης, happened along and wanted to join the fray, on the assumption that he belonged

---

[15] It is in an alleyway, λαύρα, like the ones through which they slink, that the old bawd Gyllis of Herodas' *Mimiambus* 1 lives (1.13); here, she claims, Gryllus, a famous athletic victor, is crying and talking baby talk to her, ταταλίζει, in the hope that she will bring him the girl his heart is set on (1.60). On the alleyway as the locus of iambic activities, see Miralles and Pòrtulas 1988: 137.

to the discussion. In response to his intervention, the poet called him a Thracian, because he was a stealer of boys, and went on to tell the "riddle," αἶνος, of the trees, in which Snub-Nose appeared as the Bramble Bush who interrupts Laurel and Olive as they are about to begin round 2 of their dispute, only to be told by Laurel that she is "not one of them" (103). Son of Snub-Nose, Σιμιχίδας, is understood by the scholiasts to Theocritus' *Idyll* 7 to be the bucolic poet's semi-transparent self-naming, since the unnamed goatherd of *Idyll* 3 refers to himself as snub-nosed, and he too is the poet, not too well disguised.[16] Simichidas is a persona "fabricated for the sake of the truth" (*Id.* 7.44), and as Aristotle suggests, such fabrications are sometimes necessary if people are to see through envy to the truth.

It is delightful to imagine Theocritus as "I'm just happy to be here" Bramble, the low character who is barred from the rustic *agon* of *Iambus* 4 and put in his place by Laurel with all the acerbity of Hipponax.[17] Did Callimachus see through the heteronym of *Idyll* 7 and recognize the false modesty of the poet in his youthful protagonist's claim that his poems have reached "the throne of Zeus" (*Id.* 7.93)? Sadly, this is a trail too narrow to follow with confidence, and the road I will take is broader and more obvious, though not so well traveled for all that: Why have the poets the *diegesis* claims the trees represent become old women? What is the connection between contestation and a maternal imaginary? The scene recurs in *Iambus* 12, a poem written for a little girl's birthday. Apollo, the youthful god who is like a father to the boy poet of the *Aetia*, trounces all comers in a competition among the Olympians over who can give Hebe the nicest birthday present at the party that has been arranged for her by her mother, Hera. Athena and Poseidon do their best, but Apollo, whose "chin is still innocent of hair," γένειον ἀγνεύῃ τριχός (12.69), puts on such a good show for the Mother of the Gods that he walks away with first prize.

Callimachus the Boy Poet is to his birthday poem as Apollo the Boy Singer is to his birthday song (Kerkhecker 1999: 247). The unabashed thematizing of precocity is a shift in transparency compared to *Iambus* 4, where the obscurity of persons still just cloaks the naked display of self-praise. We can imagine the tears of Hebe, and the little

---

[16] Payne 2007: 144; cf. Lelli 2004: 77.
[17] On the Hipponactean register, see Edmunds 2001a: 84; Acosta-Hughes 2002: 204.

girl for whom *Iambus* 12 is intended: "It's my party; why is he being such a show-off?" So who does the Boy Poet think is watching him? Who is he trying to impress? And how are we to relate this representation of precocity to the assertion in *Iambus* 13, following hard upon it, that no one can tell Callimachus what kind of poems he ought to write, because he can write them all?

In *Iambus* 13, Callimachus answers a critic whom he has conjured up to accuse him of fathering illegitimate verses. This critic conceives of poetic creation as wedlock to a single Muse, the intended goal of which is the procreation of offspring of a single kind. The terms in which the argument is framed, and the answer Callimachus gives— he has no need to be wedded to a single Muse, nor to go to Ephesus, where Hipponax met his, but can instead work from his knowledge of the tradition—invoke both Ion of Chios, the tragedian who was capable of other kinds of poems too, and (Plato's) Ion of Ephesus, who is silenced by Socrates' demands for a show of poetic *techne*. On this account, the introduction of Ion 1 by a subtle, allusive sleight of hand would be an instantiation of a poetics of learned sophistication that can put to flight the specter of Ion 2 and the poetics of inspiration associated with him.[18]

Callimachus surely does not bring in either Ion in the same way as Homer, according to Aristotle, brings dramatic characters onto the stage of his imaginary theater (*Poet.* 1460a), which is also the way Callimachus brings in Hipponax and Aesop, or Laurel and Olive. The dueling Ions remain offstage, waiting in the wings. So too the *diegesis* asserts that in this poem Callimachus answered his critics in his own voice, defending himself with the claim that he was imitating Ion the tragic poet (Acosta-Hughes 2002: 81–82). Why has Callimachus dropped the ball here? Why does he have recourse to argument instead of the childlike demonstrations of imaginative power with which he answers objections in the *Aetia*? Argument is hardly in keeping with *Iambus* 1's assertion that this is an iambic poetry that will proceed otherwise than by aggression.

I note that the *diegesis* says "Ion the tragedian," not "Ion of Chios": φησιν ὅτι Ἴωνα μιμεῖται τὸν τραγικόν. For although Ion of Chios was a poet successful in a number of genres, he was celebrated for his

---

[18] Kerkhecker 1999: 262; Acosta-Hughes 2002: 85–89; Lelli 2004: 125–127.

achievement in one: tragedy. If we bear this in mind, we will likely recall that, although Callimachus was a poet successful in a number of genres, he is conspicuous for his lack of achievement in one: tragedy. Even if we believe that he composed them, we know he never attained to the order of the Alexandrian Pleiad (Fantuzzi and Hunter 2004: 434). Ion of Chios thus summons the very specter of inspirational poetics he is intended to exorcise. Not being dramatic in *Iambus* 13 represents the failure to be dramatic outside it, in the sense that tragedy is really dramatic, and not just literary drama, imaginative play, or Symbolist theater of the self, "le seul théâtre de notre esprit," as Mallarmé called it.[19] What tragedy represents from this perspective is constraint, everything that stands in opposition to a child poet's sense that he can do as he likes, that his imagination is free to express itself without regard for the opinions of others, and that the regressive energies figured in images of precocity are the best index of what it is to be a poet. For all the invocation of learning, Callimachus remains a poet of childhood, of inspiration, of all that resists reconciliation with reality.

We can now pick up other little hints of a barely concealed resentment of tragedy scattered throughout the *Iambi*. Tragedians have the (silent) voice of fish in *Iambus* 2; Simus, the object of Laurel's aggression in *Iambus* 4, is also the name of the person who erects a monument to tragedy in *Epigram* 48 (48 Pf., *AP* 6.310)—a mask of the tragic Dionysus who, unbeknownst to its dedicator, is just as bored listening to its representative masterpieces as the schoolchildren who spend their days reciting them. The glare that Laurel turns on Simus the Bramble is ludicrous when it is imagined to proceed from an angry tree: "Laurel looked at her from beneath her brows like a bull," τὴν δ' ἄρ' ὑποδρὰξ οἷα ταῦρος ἡ δάφνη | ἔβλεψε (4.101–102). But the taurine stare has a distinguished ancestry, for it is used of Aeschylus in Aristophanes' *Frogs* (804), of Medea in Euripides' *Medea* (92, 187–188), and of Socrates in Plato's *Phaedo* (117b5).[20] Its instances are a brief history of everything a poetics of childhood must turn away from, for no boy poet, no matter how precocious, can join in a discourse about values.

---

[19] Cited in Howe 1990: 100; cf. the discussion in relation to the history of pastoral in Payne 2009.
[20] Edmunds 2001a: 86; Acosta-Hughes 2002: 204. On Callimachus' interest in the *Phaedo*, as witnessed by his epigram on Cleombrotus (*Ep.* 23 Pf., *AP* 7.471), see G.D. Williams 1995.

Supplementary Note

For Lacan, the boy child's fear of a castrating father is an old wives' tale from the Dark Ages of psychoanalysis. If only, Lacan exclaims, "the drama took place at the bloody level of castration," as it does with Cronus and Uranus. Instead, not only does castration not happen; the child figures out at about the age of five that it never will. Instead of a Titanic struggle with a life-threatening ogre, the child must wrestle instead with his knowledge that his father is really quite harmless and ordinary. (If we look for him in literature, we will more likely find him in Menander than in Hesiod.) As the real father fades in importance, mourning for the imaginary father begins. It is the child's yearning for this "someone who would really be someone" that prepares him to be the carrier of maternal ambition and so enables the forms of precociousness that seek approval and satisfaction from her (Lacan 1992: 307–309).

It seems to me that every stage of this process is more useful for thinking about the relationship of Callimachus and other Hellenistic poets to earlier Greek poetry than the Freudian-Bloomian model of paternal authority and paternal menace. The father who can be voiced and staged is no threat at all, and insofar as Callimachus brings in Hipponax and Aesop as fathers of his collection,[21] he makes short work of both, as he does of Homer in *Iambus* 6. One may find the absence of Archilochus more troubling, but I have argued here that it is in places where contestation and precociousness are associated with a female imaginary that we can see the clearest signs of yearning for what the poetics of childhood must ignore. These signs point back to tragedy, and tragedy's paradigmatic place in philosophical discourse about literature and value. Behind the harmless chumps who are given the names Hipponax and Aesop stand Aeschylus, Medea, and Socrates, glaring like bulls. It is in the voice of the mother—the disappointed and ambitious mother who interrupts her child's fun to insist that he outperform his rivals—that they demand an adult-size poem, with an adult-size meaning. The imaginary father—"the father who has fucked the kid up"—speaks only through the mother, and what he says is you

---

[21] On Hipponax and Aesop as co-sponsors of the *Iambi*, introduced as such by its first two poems, see Acosta-Hughes and Scodel 2004.

can't have it both ways (Lacan 1992: 308): there is no poetics of regression that is at the same time a discourse of adulthood.[22]

Let's let Callimachus have the last word. The epitaph he wrote for his father (*Ep.* 21 Pf., *AP* 7.525) has long been a source of scholarly controversy. It starts out like a riddle (1–2): "Be advised: I am the child and the father of Callimachus of Cyrene." But it is a riddle with a simple solution: the poem is spoken by Callimachus' father, and it commemorates the poet's warlike grandfather and the boy poet, his grandson, both of whom have the same name. The name of the father is omitted, but it has been supplied from the funerary epigram for a poet with the patronym Battiades (*Ep.* 35 Pf., *AP* 7.415).[23] This gives us Battus, "Stammerer," Βάττος, as the name of this poet's father, which puts him in same company as "Bramble," βάτος, who also has difficulty getting her words out and is silenced by Laurel the moment she gets up the courage to speak. Bramble, we realize, must have been there all along, tiny in comparison with the trees that tower over her.[24] From a Lacanian perspective, as much as from an Aristotelian one, Callimachus has mothered his own father.

---

[22] As F.B. Farrell 2004: 213–214 would have it. At the end of an outstanding account of what the poetics of regression can accomplish, he insists that we must nevertheless consider its accomplishments in the light of adult tasks: "The point is not to return to an earlier stage, as if that were possible, but to acknowledge loss and to retain what has been lost in attenuated but still satisfying ways."

[23] See Alan Cameron 1995: 78–79; and S. White 1999: 169, who claims the omission "redounds to the honor of the unnamed father," citing Cameron p. 7 at p. 186 n. 2, to dismiss the suggestion of Gow and Page 1965: 2.186 that "there was not very much to say" about him.

[24] F.B. Farrell 2004: 181 discusses imagery of hugeness in literature of maternal regression. Cf. Bulloch 1984: 218 on the first 182 lines of Callimachus' *Hymn* 3, which "play constantly on the incongruous contrast between Artemis' tiny size and the huge, brutish company which she keeps."

PART FIVE

CALLIMACHUS' AFTERLIFE

CHAPTER TWENTY-FIVE

ROMAN CALLIMACHUS

Alessandro Barchiesi

ABSTRACT

This is a rehearsal of the influence and appropriation of Callimachus in Roman letters, intended as introductory reading for students and non-specialists. It includes short case-studies and exemplification, with an emphasis on the agendas, poetics, and rhetoric of Roman poets. The authors discussed are Catullus, Horace, Vergil, Propertius and Ovid. The final section offers some further remarks on two methodological issues that have been highlighted in recent research by Alan Cameron and Richard Hunter. (i) The influence of Callimachean criticism of 'thick' poetry on Roman poets is pervasive: do we have to assume that their reading of Callimachean poetics was identical to ours? (ii) When we employ the labels 'Alexandrian' and 'Hellenistic', are we taking for granted that does categories would make some sort of sense to the Roman reception of Callimachus, and what sort of sense?

Callimachus was read in Italy through the entire late republican and the imperial period, and his poems were influential,[1] but in the context of our *Companion* it is more important to mention that his work is relevant to scholars of Roman poetry in a way that goes beyond measurable borrowings and allusions.[2] This is because the appropriation of Callimachean models is constantly enmeshed with the problems and

---

I am grateful to the editors and to Marco Fantuzzi and Filippomaria Pontani for their comments.

[1] The best guides to the influence of Callimachus on Latin texts are the different approaches of Wimmel 1960; Clausen 1964; Newman 1967; Zetzel 1983; Hopkinson 1988: 98–101; Alan Cameron 1995: 454–483 and *passim*; R.F. Thomas 1993 and 1999 *passim*; Hunter 2006a; Acosta-Hughes and Stephens forthcoming, chapter 4 (made available to me by the authors). Heyworth 1994 is shorter and selective but also very stimulating. On the imperial age, see McNelis 2007, with the bibliography there, and also below on Persius and Martial.

[2] As the temporal distance from the great papyrus discoveries of the early 1900s increases, it is important to remember that the programmatic approach would not have been possible before the discovery of the *Prologue* to the *Aetia*; it is interesting to compare the image of Callimachus in Latin studies before and after the discovery, and Benedetto 1993 is useful for Latinists as well as for Hellenists.

dilemmas of Roman poetics: how to define, express, and control Hellenization; the relationship between poetry and politics or power; poetic careers, patronage, and public; the harmony and tension between programmatic statements and the poems themselves, as they are dynamically experienced and then remembered by readers. In the Augustan age, the effect of those allusions is enhanced by the fact that those Latin poets form a literary society and are likely to allude to their colleagues' recent manipulations and revisions of Callimachus as well as to the Greek texts as we have them. Indeed, one of the main reasons (besides the obvious ones) why we talk about an Augustan age in literature is this mix of cross-reference and reciprocal canonization. The use of Callimachean poetics typically raises questions about patronage, political agendas, and relationship to power that cannot really be addressed in the context of a short chapter and, in any case, are best discussed in a social and cultural framework,[3] not through close readings of individual passages. In this chapter, we will try to address some formal and poetic aspects, apart from consideration of the wider social setting of Roman poetry.

What we discover, on a formal level, is not so much reproduction as creative reuse. As a model to imitate, Callimachus is more difficult (note the implications of Statius *Silvae* 5.3.156–158; note also, from a Greek point of view, Pollianus *AP* 9.130)[4] than any other major Greek author, except for choral lyric, where the fading away of original musical scores and performance conventions increased the sense of a rift. This difficulty in a way intensified an aura of prestige: Catullus and Propertius are particularly proud of being able to handle him as a model. More important, Callimachus was a mentor about creative appropriation through his own operations on Greek models such as Homer, the theater, philosophy, and early lyricists:[5] those were canonical texts for the Romans, and they were able to recognize his art of variation and surprise. This way Callimachus became a poet's poet for the Roman community of literati.

---

[3] For recent discussions of the big picture, see, e.g., Conte 1986; P. White 1993 (with Feeney 1994); Lyne 1995; Citroni 1995.

[4] See Fantuzzi and Hunter 2004: 248.

[5] On those intertexts, see, e.g., Acosta-Hughes 2010; Fuhrer 1992; Acosta-Hughes and Stephens forthcoming.

Propertius as the New Callimachus

Therefore some of the best Callimachean poetry in Latin is unruly, close to our notion of avant-garde, and even dares to test on him intertextual techniques that he himself practiced on earlier Greek models. A short example from Propertius will illustrate this mode of imitation (Prop. 4.8.3–16):[6]

> Lanuvium annosi vetus est tutela draconis:
>   hic ubi tam rarae non perit hora morae.
> qua sacer abripitur caeco descensus hiatu,   5
>   hac penetrat virgo (tale iter omen habet!)
> ieiuni serpentis honos, cum pabula poscit
>   annua et ex ima sibila torquet humo.
> talia demissae pallent ad sacra puellae,
>   cum tenera anguino raditur ore manus.   10
> ille sibi admotas a virgine corripit escas:
>   virginis in palmis ipsa canistra tremunt.
> si fuerunt castae, redeunt in colla parentum,
>   clamantque agricolae "fertilis annus erit."
> huc mea detonsis avecta est Cynthia mannis: 15
>   causa fuit Iuno, sed mage causa Venus.

> Lanuvium is the ancient protectorate of a snake of many years, there where an hour spent on such uncommon tourism is not wasted. For the sacred descent is broken by a blind chasm, where penetrates a maiden (such a journey bears an omen), the honor paid to the hungry serpent, when he demands his annual feed, and twists hisses from the depths of the earth. The girls lowered for these rites turn pale when their youthful hand is grazed by the mouth of the snake. The serpent snatches the food brought for him by the virgin: the very basket trembles in a virgin's grasp. If they have been chaste, they return to the embrace of their parents, and the farmers cry out, "It will be a fruitful year." It was to this place that Cynthia drove off with her clipped ponies: Iuno was the cause, but Venus more so.

The poem is unpredictable, the narrator is quirky, the details of local daily life are vivid, all in the best Callimachean tradition—yet when Callimachus is being visibly used he is also being subverted. The context of Book 4 of Propertius (see below) represents in general a departure from subjective love poetry toward a growing engagement with the tradition of the *Aetia*: thus when the new poem starts with a rare

---

[6] For text, translation, and interpretation, see Heyworth 2007a: 475–477 and 600.

item of Italian antique lore, the snake ritual at Lanuvium, the readers easily accept the idea that Propertius is making good on his promise in the prologue to Book 4: a new Callimachus in the (Propertian more than authentically Callimachean) sense not of amatory elegy but of a poetic aetiology of Rome and Italy based on a close encounter with the *Aetia*. The effect is reinforced by the poet's love for strange details—the sense of age-old memories, the dark snake pit, the horrified girls feeding the snake, their shaking baskets, and the test of virginity destined to the omen of a good year in the countryside (not without a Tibullan touch).[7] Even the considerable amount of sexual innuendo in the ritual description ("penetrat virgo"; the repetition "virgo...virgine...virginis" in lines 6, 11, and 12, completed by "si fuerint castae" in line 13) is potentially a homage to the *Aetia*. The strange nuptial ritual evoked in *Acontius and Cydippe* (fr. 75.1–3 Pf.) is not without its surprises, especially when the sentence "and now the boy had slept with the virgin" turns out to be a reference to a chaste prenuptial rite.

Yet exactly when we think we get the point that this is the long-awaited adaptation of Alexandrian poetry to the world of Italian antiquities, the poem turns on itself and loses contact with Callimachus. While Cynthia is in the Latin neighboring community of Lanuvium, Propertius parties in Rome, in her house on the Esquiline. The details are more lowbrow than in the rather ascetic and selective tradition of Roman elegy: two strippers, a dwarf providing entertainment, wine, and a slave in a supporting role. Comedy—or mime—erupts as Cynthia enters the house and catches the narrator red-handed. In sum, Propertius 4.8 promises Callimachean elegy in the *Aetia* tradition, but only as a feint, then returns to a particularly humble variant of the love poetry that Propertius labeled (in a rather tendentious and different sense) a Callimachean opus back in Book 3. Propertius presumably learned from Callimachus how to ambush models and readers, and here he used Callimachus as his target. In his earlier books, he was practicing already: he was using Callimachus to justify something that Callimachus never contemplated—elegiac poetry about the author's love affair with a woman.

---

[7] My mention of Acontius and Cydippe is purely illustrative: one could also think of rituals involving snakes, virgins, and baskets in the *Hecale*, and more generally of the trend toward strange and shocking rituals suggested by the fragments of Books 3 and 4 of the *Aetia*.

Ennius as a Post-Callimachean?

Familiarity with Callimachus—who never became a curricular author in Roman schools—presumably started, even before the Romans had regular schools, with the poetry of the *Epigrams*, since this was an influential genre in republican Italy and has links with the culture of symposia.[8] The first demonstrable influence of Callimachus is measured in the so-called pre-Neoteric poets (a dangerous label); in the previous generation, Lucilius, a poet of great versatility, must have known and imitated the *Iambi*. In general, even before Lucilius, Roman literature began, unlike Greek archaic poetry, with a boom in multigeneric authors (Mariotti 1965), whereas in Greek poetry before Callimachus multigeneric composition was never mainstream:[9] therefore, Callimachus was a congenial author and potentially a role model because of his *polyeideia*, in spite of the many differences. (For example, the centrality of the theater in republican Rome has no equivalent in the Callimachean outlook.)

Even before, Ennius offers a split picture. In the tendentious perspective of the Augustan poets (Hinds 1998: 52–98), Ennius is an inverted Callimachus, and a complementary defective example: strong on *ingenium*, short on *ars* (Ovid *Trist.* 2.424), whereas Callimachus has universal fame through *ars* but lacks *ingenium* (Ovid *Am.* 1.15.14). In his own time, though, Ennius had been an experimental poet and a leader in the bicultural game of Hellenization and Romanization. It may well be that his polyphonic style and mixing of languages and glosses was in itself indebted to the innovative *koine* of Callimachus.[10] His great epic, the *Annales*, suggests an even greater relevance of Callimachus, this time the *Prologue* to the *Aetia*. If true, this would be a crucial (and very early) episode in the *Fortleben* of Callimachus, but the textual evidence is fragmentary and controversial. Current reconstructions of the *Annales* offer this sequence in the first prooemium (Skutsch 1986): an invocation to the Muses; a dream; an encounter with the Muses; a revelation about Homer in the underworld, with his

---

[8] From a later age, it is suggestive that Call. *Ep.* 42 Pf. (8 GP) is epigraphically attested inside the so-called Auditorium of Maecenas, a place where a culture of wine and poetic performance must have been important.

[9] On Callimachus' interest in maverick poets such as Ion of Chios, note Hunter 1997.

[10] Cf. Parsons in this volume; on the tantalizing *Satires*, cf. A. Russo 2007.

wraith speaking to Ennius and proclaiming him *Homerus redivivus*; the mountain of the Muses and its sources (although there are controversies about Helicon, Parnassus, or both).

Later on, in the procemium to Book 7, there was emphasis on modernity: Ennius contrasted himself with older authors and issued the proud statement "we dared to open up..." (Fr. 210 Sk.: the object is, deplorably, missing; it may have been "gates" or "sources," but the journey and the freshwater imagery would both be compatible with Callimachean programmatics.) Even better, it is possible that Book 15, the last one in a first edition of the *Annales*, closed with the foundation of a Roman temple for the Muses, the first cultic residence for the Greek goddesses ever in Rome—so it ended with the aetiology for the cult of the Muses in Rome (and *Musae* had been the first word of the *Annales*).[11]

Now, it would be dangerous to single out Callimachus as his main model. Admittedly, there are many different cultural strands in the *Annales*—Empedocles, Pythagoreanism, Platonism, Orphism, and a specific south Italian blending of those influences. The Greek models preferentially used by Ennius are various and disparate, but there seems to be a recurring feature: the idea of the Greek abroad and of diasporic identity, an idea crucial to the Hellenism of Callimachus (writing only a couple of generations before Ennius). The model of the *Aetia* may have been crucial, especially for the combination of geopoetics, poetic program, authorial career, dream, speaking Muses, philology and scholarship, and the negotiation of an antique model (Hesiod): even interest in philosophical traditions, a key factor in Ennius, should not be underrated in Callimachus.[12] The fact that Ennius is contrasted with Callimachus in a later age does not terribly matter here. It is usu-

---

[11] Critics usually, and rightly, point to Hesiodic influence, and this would be of course consistent with the tradition of the Callimachean *Dream*; Barchiesi 2001a: 90 adds the observation that Ennius may be thinking, inter alia, of a tradition of Pythagorean readings of Homer (cf. Aristoxenus fr. 91a Wehrli), a tradition at home in a place like Tarentum, the city where Ennius, we usually assume, will have studied Greek (and Oscan) letters.

The end of Ovid's *Fasti* (in the six-book edition published by the poet) suggests a closural reference to the foundation of the Temple of Hercules Musarum at the end of Book 15 of Ennius: the final line, with Hercules harping on the lyre, may be read as a humorous correction of Callimachus *Aetia* fr. 23.5–6 Pf., on Heracles being incompatible with the lyre and even the cause of death for his musical teacher, Linus.

[12] Acosta-Hughes and Stephens forthcoming.

ally objected that the *Annales* was a continuous epic, characterized by inflated style, massive Homerism, inordinate length, and repetition. But this objection is not definitive. The idea of inserting metapoetry and programmatic (even apologetic?) discussions into a national epic is post-Callimachean, although of course not a faithful imitation of Callimachus. Note especially that we don't know how discontinuous Ennian epic may have been. Not a single moment of narrative transition is preserved. Even if we assume the work to have been uniquely large (and there is no confirmation even of that), it cannot have contained all the material that we could extrapolate on the basis of Livy (the almost normative text used by us to reconstruct the historical layout—when it is available: the history covered by Ennius corresponds, at least in theory, and with the addition of a substantial prooemial section, to thirty-seven books of Livy!). The existence of fragments with long direct speeches and descriptions of minute details suggests by contrast the possibility of gaps, or swift bridge passages, or both.[13] In this perspective, the overall effect may have been not so different from that of Ovid's *Metamorphoses*, a text that we usually consider aesthetically antithetic to Ennius and a triumph of asymmetry and of hybridization between Callimachus and the traditions of heroic epic.

But conceivably the use of Callimachean resources for *The Dream* of Ennius indicates a compromise. The *Aetia* had Hesiod, not Homer, in the hard-hat area of programmatic statements; there we know that Hesiod was mentioned as having had a revelation from the Muses, and we gather that Callimachus was identified as a modern Hesiod. The new Homer of Ennius is a Hesiodic, Callimachean, modern Homer—hence the scientific didacticism of the speech of Homer in the Ennian prooemium?[14] This would give edge to the striking invention of the two Homers in Book 1, the ghost and the revenant: the doubling of the archaic model would not be unlike the double take on Hipponax in *Iambus* 1, the aggressive voice from the Ionic past and the revised, modernized Hipponax in Alexandria.

---

[13] Cf. Cicero *Brutus* 76 on the absence of the First Punic War, the longest continuous war in human memory in Graeco-Roman antiquity, and the one already represented in Latin epic by the predecessor and competitor Naevius.

[14] On this and other aspects of Hesiod's Roman reception, see Rosati 2009: 344–346.

Moderns versus Ancients?

For the Romans, one of the main contributions of Callimachus was the development of a critical polarization between ancient and modern. (Other relevant Greek experiments included Ion, Theocritus, the Hellenistic elegists, and post-Theocritean bucolics.)

The prooemium to Ovid's *Metamorphoses* is a famous example of how the opposition can be deconstructed. The gods are being invited to "accompany" or "lead down" (*deducere*) the poem and its story line from the very beginnings of the world to modern times, and it will be a continuous poem (*perpetuum*). *Perpetuum* matches *dienekes*, the ideal of the Telchines in the *Prologue* to the *Aetia*, but if the gods take Ovid's request seriously, the result of the operation of *deducere carmen* will be a *deductum carmen*—the buzzword of neoteric, elegiac, and Callimachean poetry. (Cf. *leptos* and *leptaleos*; Virgil *Ecl.* 6.5, "deductum dicere carmen"; Propertius 3.1.5, in an apostrophe to Callimachus and Philetas, "carmen tenuastis"; Horace *Epist.* 2.1.225, "tenui deducta poemata filo.") If the reader misses the contradiction,[15] a continuous reading of the poem will demonstrate that this is not the epic continuity and fullness envisaged by the Telchines. Ovid will dedicate two half-lines to the foundation of Rome, presumably in order to save space for a list of thirty-seven dogs' names in the Actaeon story.

The new wave of realistic poetry in the Imperial age (Persius, Martial) still treated Callimachean poetry as recent and neoteric, but in a polemical way: Callimachus was now the straw man needed in order to enact a satirical poetics, and Catullus was invoked as a model but dissociated from his Callimachean poetics and mythological imagination.[16] The new twist was that for the 'angry' poets of satire and sarcastic epigram the new-wave poetry of the Callimacheans was in itself out of touch with the reality of Roman life, and therefore outdated.

The opposition between modern and ancient poetics in fact goes back to Catullus, who inaugurated the Roman tendency to identify the passé element with traditional epic about military success. Since Rome was a perpetually belligerent community, this negative pole can

---

[15] The pun was spotted simultaneously by C.D. Gilbert 1976 and by Kenney 1976; it is supported by the important reference to transformation of elegy into epic indicated by Tarrant 1982: 351 and n. 35, in a vindication of *ista* not *istas* in the text of *Met.* 1.2.

[16] See, e.g., Bramble 1974; Mattiacci and Perruccio 2007.

be identified as old-style republican poetry but also as contemporary panegyric (traditional in style but adapted to contemporary circumstances). Thus the Augustan poets were imparting a new significance (whatever the original said or implied about kings and heroes) to the initial opposition of the *Prologue* to the *Aetia*.

Programmatic Writing

In the generation of the Augustan poets, the single most consistent pattern of Callimachean ideas was the opposition of light and heavy, refined and grand. Every single image from the *Prologue* to the *Aetia*, the coda of the *Hymn to Apollo*, and the programmatic epigrams was refracted in many programmatic contexts in Horace, Virgil, Propertius, and Ovid. The idea of Apollo warning Callimachus about the norms of style had been readapted a number of times, and of course every new Latin author was known to engage with the shared Greek model but also with his Latin predecessors. What strikes us the most is the plasticity of the imitations. Not only can Apollo be transformed into a number of alternative mentors; more important, the poets vary the position of the encounter in time and context. In Callimachus, Apollo issues a warning before the poet embarks on his career (*Aetia* prologue) or offers a *viva voce* comment at the end of a text (*Hymn to Apollo*). In Rome, Apollo changes the choice of a genre during its performance (Virgil *Ecl.* 6.3–8), confirms the choice during attempted composition of an epic (Propertius 3.3.13–26), issues a warning about the new direction in a poetic project (Propertius 4.1.3–4, 133–136), criticizes a false start in a poetic career (Horace *Sat.* 1.10. 31–39), discourages the poet from abandoning his chosen genre (Horace *Carm.* 4.15), sabotages a work close to publication (Ovid *Am.* 1.1—although there the function of Apollo is taken over by Cupid). The only frequently shared concept is that Apollo always militates against a higher genre than the one the poet practices, but this sense of a preordained hierarchy is not Callimachean. When those poets are love poets, they combine the Callimachean message with a different strand, itself indebted to recent Greek poetry (Bion and the *Anacreontea*):[17] for a

---

[17] Cf. Fantuzzi 1994; Fantuzzi and Hunter 2004: 181–190.

lover and a poet of love, writing in a higher mode is a physiological impossibility.

The poets compete in adapting the Apolline scenario to their own agenda: a witty example is a passage in Virgil that may have been the first (or second, after Cornelius Gallus?) direct rewriting of the *Aetia* prologue in Latin. The poet (*Ecl.* 6.1–8) sings of *reges* and *proelia*, Phoebus "plucks his ear" (*aurem vellit*) and warns him that a shepherd ought to raise fat sheep but produce a slender song (*deductum dicere carmen*). Apollo calls the singer "Tityrus," and this way we are not allowed to forget that *Eclogue* 6, although anomalous, is still part of the generic frame of *bucolica*. In the *Aetia*, Callimachus was contrasting a "fat victim," always a good idea for a banquet, with a slender Muse: but the singer of the *Eclogues* is a shepherd; hence the conversion from "victim" to "sheep."[18]

The other recurrent factor is related to one particular genre: elegy. While a number of poets participate in the programmatic game through allusions, explicit references to Callimachus are limited to that one genre; either they are in elegiac texts or, in the rare instances of another host genre, they are contextually related to the genre of elegy.[19] This stabilization is not without a certain straining of the Greek model and its originary values. The starting point for Roman elegiac poets seems to be the routinization of Callimachus as a *princeps elegiae* in the formal sense of the word; he can be singled out as the only luminar of elegy, or he can be paired with Mimnermus (cf. Horace, *Epist.* 2.2. 99–101), or Euphorion (cf. discussions of the problem of Virgil *Ecl.* 10.50) or, in Propertius, Philetas of Cos. Since elegy in Augustan Rome is not simply a formal category but the association of form (the distich) and content (love) and form of content (subjective), the Roman authors have a vested interest in extending the umbrella of Callimachus to cover their entire concept of the genre and its values and life choices. Now they seem to be happy with programmatic language indebted

---

[18] Cf., e.g., Hopkinson 1988: 99, and note Horace *Sat.* 2.6.14–15.

[19] Hutchinson 2006b: 9 n. 15. For my present purpose, we can neglect the distinction between elegy and erotic epigram. For explicit quotation of Callimachus and the persistent connection with elegy (or love epigram), or the location of the name in elegiac texts, cf., e.g., Catullus 65.16, 116.2; Horace *Sat.* 1.2.105–108, *Epist.* 2.2.99–101; Propertius 2.34.29–32, 3.1–3, 3.9.43–44, 4.1.64, 4.6.4; Ovid *Am.* 1.15.13–14, 2.4.19–20; *AA* 3.329; *Rem.* 381–382 (cf. 759–760); *Trist.* 2.367–368, 5.4.38; *Ib.* 53; *Pont.* 4.16.32; Statius *Silv.* 5.3.157 (for reference to elegy there, cf. Martial 10.4.11–12).

to the *Aetia* prologue,[20] but very few allusions point to specific texts (let alone programmatic statements) about love in Callimachus. The fact that his only famous subjective love poetry consists of pederastic epigrams is not a good match for the intentions of Propertius and Ovid (although Tibullus in this aspect fits the Callimachean model better);[21] nor is the twinning of Callimachus and Philetas, at least with our modest information on the latter, a very clear indication of how those Hellenistic poets are the legitimate leaders in elegiac poetry— if "elegiac" means "about a centrally positioned *domina*." Ovid, who has a talent for insinuating his voice into his very models and turning them pre-Nasonian, or proto-elegiac, once singles out Cydippe as the representative of "soft, erotic" Callimachean elegy (*Rem.* 381–382: Cydippe is to Callimachus what Achilles is to Homer), and it may well be that his double letters dealing with that unusual story (a pair of elegies representing an exchange between Acontius and Cydippe, of uncertain date and somewhat disputed authorship: printed in our texts as *Heroides* 20 and 21) are a programmatic experiment (Barchiesi 2001c: 219–227), and an attempt to redress the balance—here is finally a Roman elegiac poet who manages to offer an extended reworking of a Callimachean elegy, and one more compatible with the ideology of Roman elegy than previous adaptations or translations such as Catullus' *Lock of Berenice* (*Carm.* 66).[22]

The Dramatization of Poetic Choices

This emphasis on metapoetics has led to a notable evolution in the criticism of Latin poetry (with potential consequences for evaluation of Callimachus in a Ptolemaic context): the idea that programmatics is not limited to prologues and purple passages but infiltrates representations and narratives. Rivers, sources, thin and fat people have been scrutinized as metaliterary symbols. The results are frequently mechanical and sometimes far-fetched, but there is no way of screening out the possibility of such a reading once it is raised. The probability of this incorporation of metapoetry into the narrative is higher when we can demonstrate a contextual function of the ambiguity between

---

[20] For an attempt at fine-tuning the debate, see Hunter 2008b: 534.
[21] Dawson 1950; Bulloch 1973; Cairns 1979.
[22] See Höschele 2009, with bibliography.

referential language and programmatic doublespeak. Here are a few examples from a variety of generic contexts:

1. The hero Aeneas is invested with his mission in the *Aeneid* (3.94–98) by the direct voice of Apollo: the context is reminiscent of the epiphany in the Callimachean *Hymn to Apollo*,[23] so it may be relevant that the divine voice that refused a vast and impure river of songs, and praised pure and selective poetry (Call. *Hymn* 2.105–113), is now authorizing a new kind of epic, vast and sublime but also accountable for Callimachean standards of quality and learning. The echo of Callimachus casts interesting light on the mid-prooemium of the *Aeneid* (7.41–45),[24] where the formal announcement of a higher epic ("maius opus moveo") is cast as a song about "kings and battles", exactly the topic that Virgil had declined by alluding to the *Aetia* prologue back in *Eclogue* 6. Given the suggestive conventions of Roman intertextuality, the use of a formula originating with Callimachean polemics can be either a self-conscious measure of the distance between the various stages of Virgil's career or an invitation to the reader to experience many subtle ways in which this new epic has incorporated not only Homer but Callimachus (through its artistry, the inclusion of nonmartial and erotic themes, the learned exploration of origins, the hints of bucolic aesthetics, the recuperation of the antiquarian past, the avoidance of formulaic style, and more)[25]—more likely, the allusion seeks to have it both ways.

2. The poem by Propertius about a celebration of the battle of Actium has multiple links with Apollo and starts with the invocation of Callimachean water for the poetic ritual (4.6.1–7). Scholars who are aware of this link are usually unresponsive when the victory poem unexpectedly ends with a reference to an old Roman defeat: now, after Actium, it is possible, O Crassus, to walk safely on the dark sands of the Euphrates (Prop. 4.6.83–84):

> gaude, Crasse, nigras, si quid sapis, inter harenas:
>   ire per Euphraten ad tua busta licet.
> Rejoice, O Crassus, if you are sentient, in your heap of black sands:
>   now it is possible to cross the Euphrates and reach your grave.

---

[23] For other Callimachean intertexts, see Barchiesi 1994.
[24] Conte 1986; R.F. Thomas 1986a.
[25] On the exploration of origins, see, e.g., Tueller 2000.

Ovid picks up this detail in his mischievous dry run for a future panegyric on Caesarian victories over Parthian Euphrates (*AA* 1.179):

> Parthe, dabis poenas: Crassi gaudete sepulti.
> Parthian, you will atone: rejoice, you buried Crassi!

For a Callimachean poet, this opportunity, made possible by the settlement of a Roman frontier fort at Zeugma, a crossing point on the Euphrates, in 25 BC (Millar 1993), looks like a mixed blessing,[26] and Crassus—particularly in the plural, "Crassi," encompassing the general and his son, who both fell at Carrhae—is a strangely appropriate name for someone (note the malicious "si quid sapis") who should rejoice in this situation: *crassus*, "thick," "dimwit," had been used by the republican poet Lucilius to express a contrast with *doctus*, "learned," "sophisticated" (Pennacini 1968). By the end of the poem, the celebration of victory is reduced to patriotic one-liners, more reminiscent of military slogans on dice boards than of serious panegyric research, and the celebratory poets—a new kind of company for Propertius as we know him from Books 1–3—are soaked in wine, a hangover not fortified by Callimachean water, at dawn. Their specialization in conquered enemies (e.g., 4.6.77, "paludosos... Sygambros," "the Sygambri with their bogs") again does not sound promising by Callimachean standards.

3. It has not escaped attention that the Ovidian version of the story of Erysichthon, the impious tyrant who is punished by Demeter with insatiable hunger, is based primarily on Callimachus' *Hymn to Demeter* but is an overblown, emphatic version of the Callimachean narrative (*Met.* 8.728–778) (Van Tress 2004). One way to account for this difference is to look at the narrative context with an eye to Callimachean metapoetics (Hinds 2006: 36): it is a common device in Ovid's epic to have inset narrative and internal narrators, but the narrator of the Erysichthon story, Achelous, had been described by Ovid, in a first-person speech loaded with slightly bombastic sublimity (8.530–539), as a river in flood, dragging all sorts of wrecked objects, driftwood, mud, and carcasses in its spate. How likely is this choice to be devoid of malice? The insatiable appetite of Hunger is an anti-Callimachean symbol, just as the operations of Envy (a famous enemy of Callimachus) are a shocking innovation for the plot of Callimachus' *Hecale* in *Metamorphoses* 2.760–835.

---

[26] So Heyworth 1994: cf. Call. *Hymn* 2.108–109, and contrast Cairns 2006.

The *Hecale*, Callimachus' own version of epic, is for Ovid another source of generic impurity: it licenses, through the imitation of a digression in Book 2 of the *Metamorphoses*, the only known episode in a major Roman epic poem with speaking animals—in this case, even as narrators, and loquacious ones; this theme is normally excluded from epic (*Met.* 2.540–632)[27] and reserved in ancient culture to a lowbrow, even servile genre such as the fable, with its various adaptations in prose, *iambus* or diatribe, and satire. In Book 8, when he readapts another unheroic section of the *Hecale*, the rustic dinner, to his own episode of Philemon and Baucis, Ovid pointedly notes that, of all the people present at the tale, Theseus was especially pleased (8.725–726): this must be because he is the guest of another poor and elderly woman farmer in the Callimachean model of this story of hospitality (Kenney 1986: xxviii).

The long tale of Medea in Book 7 features many snapshots of epic and tragedy, including of course a witty abbreviated rewriting of the *Argonautica*, and the entire sequence ends when Medea literally lands into the opening episode of the *Hecale* (the recognition of Theseus: *Met.* 7.401–424): a few lines before, Ovid shows her flying over the island of the envious Telchines (7.365–367: Rhodes, in fact), perhaps hinting that this is not going to be that kind of bad and slow epic.

As we saw above, the procemium to *Metamorphoses* 1 was already creating contrasting expectations about the adaptation of elegy to epic, and the reading of the poem is a dynamic exploration of the possibilities of this new kind of epic. Not all the metapoetical readings that have followed in this wake are equally convincing; yet it is not worth throwing out the baby with the dirty water.

Conversely, the *Fasti* is marked from the beginning as a work in the tradition of the *Aetia*: the topic will be "tempora cum causis Latium digesta per annum" ("times, with their causes, distributed through the Latin year," 1.1). Callimachean reference is present not only in *causis* (i.e., *aitia*) but in the interest in festivals and rituals (cf. the programmatic use of *dies, aras*, 1.8 and 1.13–14), and even in *digesta*, because the fragmentation of the year (contrast "perpetuum...carmen" in *Met.* 1.3–4) dictates the fragmented format of the *Fasti*—and this is of course a poetic legacy of Callimachus. In this work Ovid will exploit

---

[27] Contrast *Iliad* 19.418, and see Hollis 2009: 132 on how later epic examples are influenced by the *Hecale*.

a Callimachean poetics of surface fragmentation and deeper, implicit links and continuities. In this light, the first prooemium links the rejection of martial epic, identified by the *Aeneid*'s titular incipit, *arma* (cf. Hinds 1992 *passim*), and the choice of rituals and holidays as a topic, successfully negotiating the alternative between unwarlike elegy and Caesarian celebration that had been cultivated by the poets of love elegy (young Ovid included): *Caesaris arma canant alii; nos Caesaris aras* (1.13).

The moment when the reader begins to suspect an increasing rapprochement with heroic epic comes when Ovid decides to incorporate in his elegiac poem a sequel to Virgil's story of Dido and Aeneas. The episode (3.543-566) thus carries a considerable burden in the programmatic texture of the *Fasti*. Expectations about Callimachean influence are not disappointed: we follow the exile of Anna, Dido's sister, and she becomes a guest of a king of a small Mediterranean island, a peaceful leader who is an enemy to war: *rex arma perosus | 'nos sumus imbelles'... ait* ("the king, an enemy of arms, said, 'We are unwarlike...'" 3.577-578).

The name of the king is Battus, the royal ancestor who gives to Callimachus his alternative name, *Battiades* (regularly used by Roman poets, especially Catullus and Ovid; Propertius, in his five explicit mentions, always has *Callimachus*). This way the character anticipates in heroic times, but with an Augustan Roman accent, Callimachus' own avoidance of war and of military epic (and in a specifically Callimachean diction: with *arma perosus* compare *Ep.* 28.1, "I hate the cyclic poem").

An invocation of Callimachus within an epic plot is a plug for the poetics of Ovid's *Fasti*, the Augustan text with the strongest claim to be a full-scale imitation of the *Aetia*. Ovid had been taking a cue from the program announced but not systematically performed by Propertius at the start of Book 4 of his elegies: "sacra diesque canam et cognomina prisca locorum" ("I shall sing of rituals, days, and old names of places," 4.1.69).[28] In his edition, Pfeiffer (1949-1953: 1.xxxv) explains that Propertius' Book 4 reproduces the narrative model of *Aetia* 3 and 4, whereas the *Fasti* is based on *Aetia* 1 and 2. This is a

---

[28] Heyworth's OCT (2007b) accepts the conjecture *deos* for *dies*, but the sentence is in any case almost a *suggestio falsi* as far as the Propertian book is concerned; and in favor of *dies*, see the arguments of Hutchinson 2006b *ad loc.*

fundamental insight, but it can be slightly redefined. Propertius and Ovid are both taking into account, in their own ways, the double organization of the *Aetia*. Propertius looks at the separation of elegies in *Aetia* 3 and 4, but his choice of topics is actually closer to the material of *Aetia* 1 and 2. Ovid experiments with the difficult continuous structure of *Aetia* 1 and 2, but there are also effects of separation. If the reader of the *Fasti* is not able to sever some of the sequential episodes one from another, embarrassing effects will arise at the level of Augustan politics and ideology:[29] the choice between the two modes of reading offered by the *Aetia* template turns out to be not a purely formal one.

Poetic Careers: Different Approaches

The other main aspect of Callimachean influence is the use of Callimachus as, so to speak, a first-person voice. Almost all the main triumviral and Augustan poets recur to Callimachus in order to create a sense of a poetic career, and they are very keen to adopt different strategies. Here follow some examples, all extending beyond the limits of a single work or occasional allusion.

Propertius uses Callimachus in a way that suggests a dynamics, not a fixed state. First of all he does not offer much airtime to Callimachus in his Book 1; only in hindsight, after reading the following books, will the reader recuperate some first hints. They seem to connect the poet's voice with the Callimachean character of Acontius from *Aetia* 3: note especially the motif of the solitary lover in 1.18 (Cairns 1969), and the brief but suggestive evocation of the idea of Love the Teacher from the same narrative in the programmatic procemial elegy 1.1 (Acosta-Hughes and Stephens forthcoming). Then at the beginning of Book 2 (1.39–40) he adopts Callimachus as a predecessor, and later on *Callimachi* is the first word of Book 3 (the name of a Greek predecessor being a very unusual and marked choice for the incipit of a Roman text:[30] Gallus and Propertius had been named in the two final distichs of the previous book, 2.34.91–94, in a sequence of elegiac authors);

---

[29] See in general Barchiesi 1997b.
[30] And a very misleading one: Germanicus and Phaedrus begin by quoting Aratus and Aesop, respectively; but they need to activate (at least initially) the idea of a systematic Romanization of their authors.

and *Callimachus Romanus* is the heart of the metapoetic debate in 4.1 (at line 64). In sum, the idea of the Callimachean poet is a dynamic process and a problematic issue. There is in fact a distance from Callimachus, in the first books because the status of Callimachus as an erotic poet is not such an obvious one (and has found too ready an acceptance among Latinists); an elegiac poet who is in many ways more germane to Callimachean influence, Tibullus, finds an easier approach through the imitation of pederastic poetry (cf. Dawson 1950; Bulloch 1973), and there is often a glide from "the Greek poet of love not war" to *princeps elegiae* (itself not an uncontested tradition); in Book 4, because aetiology is supposed to work as an upgrade from and an antidote to love poetry, but the project is sapped by the ambivalent voice of Horus, who is both an Apollo (the two names being interchangeable in Alexandria) and a charlatan, a Callimachean advisor and a butt of Callimachean *iambus*-style irony.

The important point for our discussion is that Callimachus is incorporated into an authorial narrative of metapoetics and career choices. No such neat evolutionary picture can be recuperated from Catullus, but this could be because of the state of our tradition. There is no way of knowing whether the order of poems in our exiguous manuscript tradition is authorial.[31] However, two points seem worthy of attention even if one assumes the ordering to be the result of editorial decisions: the sequence of elegiac poems begins with a poem (*Carm.* 65) which is both a cover letter for the next one and a programmatic text for the choice of writing elegy; now, the next one is the first extant example of an artistic translation of Callimachus in Latin (*Carm.* 66, *The Lock of Berenice*) and *Carmen* 65 itself is marked by an allusion to the Acontius and Cydippe myth as told in the *Aetia*. Then *Carmen* 116, to the best of our knowledge the final poem in the elegiac sequence, and likely to be pointing forward to the composition of iambs (Macleod 1973), mentions explicitly the offering of an adaptation from Callimachus in a more aggressive key. Taken together, those allusions could point to the choice of Callimachus as a programmatic model, a choice consonant with the adoption of Sappho as a model in *Carmen* 51,[32]

---

[31] As, e.g., in Skinner 2003, with special attention to Callimachus as a model in 65–116; for a very skeptical approach to the *Catulli liber*, see Bellandi 2007; for a more nuanced approach, Barchiesi 2005.

[32] On the poetic genealogy Sappho-Callimachus, see Acosta-Hughes 2010. The appropriations of Sappho and of Callimachus as an epigrammatic love poet surface

and with the appropriation of the *Aetia* prologue in the poem contrasting Cinna with the muddy epicist Volusius (*Carm.* 95). Needless to say, Catullus is also using Callimachus in his own short epic, *Carmen* 64. Yet Catullus is different from the later elegiac authors, because he does not need a unified generic matrix. His main contribution to the history of Roman Callimacheanism is his choice of Callimachus as a model good to think with in programmatic contexts; this choice does not imply that other Greek poets, especially the more recent ones (Meleager, Parthenius, various epigrammatists) but also older ones on whom we are less well informed (e.g., Euphorion), are less important to him. Meleager, for example, is imitated in *Carmen* 1 of the *libellus*, just as he will contribute the initial motto to the Propertian collection and to Virgil's *Eclogues* (Gutzwiller 1998: 320–321).

Virgil's approach is subtle and deeply integrated to the choice of an exemplary career: Callimachus is evoked in the programmatic mid-prooemia of the three works (*Ecl.* 6, *Geor.* 3, *Aen.* 7),[33] and the river Euphrates is regularly quoted six lines from the end of a book, as it is in the *Hymn to Apollo* (R.F. Thomas 1999: 320–321). The general impression is that the entire generic evolution from bucolics to didactic to heroic epic is self-conciously punctuated by Callimachean allusions, but there is also a careful attention to poetic autonomy. Virgil never claims Callimachus as a direct, overt model—the way he evokes Theocritus, Hesiod, and Homer, respectively—and apparently stays away from extended imitations. (See on Ovid below.) His use of Callimachus is ambiguous because it has to do with *recusatio* as well as with celebratory poetry, and Virgil wants his poetic triumph both ways. He constructs his very influential model of the Augustan *recusatio* on the basis of the *Aetia* prologue, but he is also able to use Callimachus in order to justify a new and improved approach to grand epic and to praise poetry.

Ovid is the poet who, in addition to the usual buzzwords of Wimmelian poetics (the "dirty river, pure fountain" tradition of Catullus, Virgil, and Propertius), does the most to integrate Callimachus in a clearly articulated literary system. He contrasts Callimachus with Homer and with Ennius. He is also the Roman poet who uses Calli-

---

together in the generation between Lucilius and Catullus; cf. Valerius Aedituus fr. 1 Courtney and Lutatius Catulus fr. 1 Courtney.

[33] R.F. Thomas 1999: 102–111; Conte 1992.

machus the most in actual practice, not just in metapoetic discussions. In the *Metamorphoses* there are sizable continuous narrative sections taken up from the works of Callimachus—and it is hard to prove something like that for Catullus, Virgil, Propertius, or Horace. In the *Fasti*, even the basic idea of the poem is indebted to the *Aetia*—a credential that no other Roman poet flaunts, although of course the poem has a strong autonomy and remains ideologically a very Roman artifact. When all this is said and done, Ovid never claims to be a Roman Callimachus—he seems to be, with Tibullus, the first Roman author of poetry who does not single out any one Greek author as a role model while he engages so many of them. In this sense he deserves to be considered as the first truly imperial poet.

Horace's approach is very different from all the others'. In the *Epodes*, one has the impression that Callimachus is being constructed as a dove in the iambic tradition (Barchiesi 2001b), and thus marginalized, whereas Archilochus is front and center as a classical model: the rare echoes of the Alexandrian *Iambi* are in a mellow mode, very different from the animal spirits of the Archilochean tradition. On the other hand, the entire negotiation with Archilochus (a model larger than life, dangerous, impossible to impersonate) shows that the work done by Callimachus on Hipponax has been deeply absorbed and exploited by Horace; and the *Iambi* are a recurring presence in the Roman tradition of satire, and in Horace's version of it (Freudenburg 1993).

In his lyric poetry, Horace develops a parallel strategy: Alcaeus and Sappho are recentered as classical authors, Callimachean contributions to lyric are not showcased (although they are real),[34] the work done by Callimachus on the lyric canon is appropriated, but the poet's voice pointedly avoids repeating the Callimachean slogans of the *neoteroi* and the elegists, who are the real adversaries or competitors of Horace's lyric project.

It would be easy to compile anthologies of pro-Callimachean and anti-Callimachean statements or sentiments;[35] more important, the references are often dialectically combined in the same passage.[36] For

---

[34] Pasquali 1964b.
[35] The most relevant passages are in Bornmann 1996; cf. also Cody 1976 and Coffta 2002.
[36] For examples of this dialectical reading, see Freudenburg 2001: 37–41; D'Alessio 2006.

example, Horace contrasts Callimachus and Philodemus in *Satire* 1.2.101–110 in ways that suggest that Callimachus is a classic of love poetry (Hunter 2006a: 143); yet he also comments that those "little verses" and their elitist poetics of desire do not have the healing power that a philosophy of life could claim. In *Ep.* 2.2.99–101 it is an upgrade (*plus*) to be a new Mimnermus instead of a new Callimachus, although both models are to be contrasted with Horace's standard as a new Alcaeus. The poet is *inuidia maior* (*Carm.* 2.20.4; cf. Call. *Epigr.* 21.4), yet in other contexts he has a positive approach to *pondus*, "heaviness," "serious" or "weighty" poetry (*Epist.* 1.19.42; 2.2.112; *Ars* 310) and a negative one to lightness; he seems to be pointed when he praises a writer who is like a river, *uemens et liquidus puroque simillimus amni* (*Epist.* 2.2.120)—that is, a big, sweeping, pure river, a paradox in terms of the Callimachean opposition between the Euphrates and the pure drops from the spring. (Cf. the famous "distancing praise" of Pindar in *Carm.* 4.2.5–8.) This model of a poet who is helpful to the community (the crucial new idea in the literary *Epistles*) follows after a critical distancing from the new Callimachuses of elegy. (See above on *Epist.* 2.2.99–101.) Although we should take into account the various strategic situations of each and every context and genre, there is at least one shared aspect: Horace foists on his competitors the mantle of a Callimachean orthodoxy, often to be interpreted as neoteric, elegiac programme, and reserves for himself the freedom to adapt Callimachus to his own agenda, while learning from his approach to the poetic tradition.

Final Questions

Two general questions should be kept in mind. The first is about the difference between interpreting Callimachus in a third-century context and viewing Callimachean poetics through its Roman imitators. The second is the question of periodization in those two different frameworks. If we are still willing to use categories such as Alexandrian and Hellenistic (with all their political baggage and interpretive potential), does it follow that those categories are valid in a Roman emic perspective and can be confidently applied to Roman appropriations of Callimachus? The two key discussions for my final questions are Alan Cameron 1995 and Richard Hunter 2006a.

1. Alan Cameron has brilliantly succeeded in showing that the polemical reference in the *Aetia* prologue is not as straightforward as one would surmise from the Roman imitations: it is not necessarily epic that Callimachus is worried about. This success, however, is my own interpretation of Cameron's results: his own interpretation seems to be that the Romans did not care about epic either (Alan Cameron 1995: 454–483), and that once we manage to fix the meaning of the *Prologue* in its original setting, ancient responses will follow suit. As far as Callimachus' own horizon is concerned, I hasten to add that new papyrological discoveries can always tilt the balance: we still have very little of Hellenistic epic in the papyri; but what if we decide that the lengthy, long-winded *Argonautica* by Cleon of Curium is representative of a wider trend?[37] Still, one aspect of Cameron's position remains convincing (cf. Fantuzzi and Hunter 2004: 69): the enthusiasm of the discovery of the *Aetia* prologue, followed by rediscoveries of the Callimacheanism of Virgil, Propertius, Horace, and Ovid, has generated a Romanized reading of the poetic agenda of Callimachus. This is a valuable critique of previous approaches. Yet Cameron's *pars construens* also shows that the confusion between a historicized reading and a reception-oriented reading is a tenacious one. He has important things to say on Callimachus and elegy (even if I think that the issue of Hellenistic epic has been dismissed too quickly), but at times he seems to claim that the Roman poets must have had the intellectual honesty to read Callimachus the way that he, Alan Cameron, does, and that their *recusationes* do not need the epic tradition, not even as a straw genre. This argument does not provide any extra mileage for the interpretation of Callimachus in a Ptolemaic context, and it severely distorts the agenda of the Roman poets.
2. At the end of a nuanced study of Roman appropriations, a study that answers my first question without collapsing the difference between historicized and Romanized Callimachus, Richard Hunter (2006a: 141–146) raises another important point. How far did the Romans observe the distinction that we make and construct between classical and Hellenistic? And how far did it matter to the

---

[37] On the testimonia, see D'Alessio 2000; F. Pontani 2007.

Augustans that their own age was separated from the great poets of the Hellenistic kingdoms by more than two centuries? It is not just a matter of perception of time, because this leads to the crucial question on whether Callimachus, Theocritus, and the epigrammatists would be perceived as classical models or as latecomers and moderns. Hunter suggests that there was a Roman approach that would respect Ptolemaic Alexandria while promoting aggression against Cleopatra's Alexandria. What is really helpful in his approach is (just as in Cameron's case) his critique of underhistoricized interpretation: it is true that Latinists and even Hellenists have often allowed the categories of Alexandrianism and Hellenistic a power that they cannot claim, as if Propertius and Virgil were responding through the same filter as *fin-de-siècle* Europeans (through ideas of Orientalism, decadence, or avant-garde, languid sensibility). The idea of a positive recuperation of Ptolemaic Alexandria certainly tallies with appropriations where Callimachus is being invoked as a praise poet (cf. Heyworth 1994).

Yet it may be that we are not yet ready to answer this second question, although it remains an important one.[38] We must distance ourselves from the modern category of Alexandrian latecomers when reading Roman imitators of Callimachus, but there are many indications that identifying Callimachus as just another Greek classic simply will not do. We need to take on board Hunter's point about admiration of Alexandria, not just aggression and hatred; but there is still the question of how far appropriations of Callimachus are examples of a more generalized Roman Hellenism or something more special and, so to speak, local. In the light of recent interest in the plurality of Greek cultures within Hellenism, this could be an interesting discussion: How far are the Romans interested in a specific, differentiated approach to, let us say, Athenian, Graeco-Asian, Alexandrian idioms within their own idea of Hellenization?

A thick description of this phenomenon will require careful investigation not only of poetic texts but of many aspects of architecture, material culture, visual experience, and daily life in late republican and Augustan Rome; we will also need to take into account the ideas of moral exemplarity and educational value, and of differ-

---

[38] On ancient classicisms and their construction of the past, see the essays in Porter 2006a.

ent appraisals and evaluations of the Greek past and contemporary achievement. It is also important to bear in mind, because this aspect has been neglected in the enthusiasm of intertextual agnition and recovery of fragments, that a number of Roman poets who are echoing Callimachus (but also Theocritus, Herodas, Posidippus, and others) are doing that in a potentially loaded context: a context in which a model from or about Alexandria is invoked in close proximity with a reference to the Roman conquest of the Ptolemaic kingdom. It is up to us—and it was up to Roman readers back then—to decide whether we want to insulate the poetic references as manifestations of aesthetic preferences or to integrate them into the aesthetics of Roman politics.[39]

The discovery that the prooemial section of *Georgics* 3 is substantially based on the prooemial elegy of *Aetia* 3, *The Victory of Berenice* (R.F. Thomas 1983 = 1999: 68–100), has been a major step in the reappraisal of Callimachean reception at Rome; but not once in his important paper does Richard Thomas mention that the historical context for the Virgilian poem is victory over Alexandria. Yet in Roman culture the idea of appropriating enemy culture and turning it into an instrument of domination has a long history, and Virgilian allusions to Ennius in the same context point toward such triumphal poetics. We should criticize, following Hunter's approach, unreflected and untheorized use of "Alexandrian" as a timeless category of literature; but we also need to take into account contexts where poetry from Alexandria is being appropriated with reference to the conquest of Ptolemaic Egypt.[40]

---

[39] Cf., e.g., Fowler 2009 for the general idea.
[40] For recent examples of this approach, note especially Stephens 2004b; Acosta-Hughes and Stephens forthcoming; Hutchinson 2002, discussing the allusion to Posidippus at the end of Propertius 3.11. I have a paper in progress, "Alexandria in Rome, Rome as Alexandria," where I develop this line of argument more systematically; and see especially the splendid discussion of the *laudes Italiae* of the *Georgics* as an extended, implied syncrisis with Ptolemaic Egypt in Hunter 2008b: 380–382.

CHAPTER TWENTY-SIX

CALLIMACHUS AND LATER GREEK POETRY

Claudio De Stefani and Enrico Magnelli*

ABSTRACT

The paper discusses the various ways in which Greek poets, from the mid-third century BC down to the Byzantine age, exploited Callimachus' language, style, and poetics and how the reception of Callimachus changed over time. Refined Hellenistic authors such as Euphorion and Nicander imitated the Cyrenaean poet in both diction and meter: their Imperial successors proved more selective, integrating a Callimachean heritage into their own (sometimes very different) literary agendas—such is the case of Nonnus, pairing countless borrowings from Callimachus with a markedly un-Callimachean style. Epic parody, inscriptional poems, Christian reworking of Callimachus, and his reception in Byzantine highbrow poetry are also subjects for analysis.

Toward a History of Callimacheanism

"Per totam antiquitatem, immo per medium aevum, ab Apollonio Rhodio usque ad Michaelem Choniaten...poetae Graeci Callimachum imitabantur."[1] The reasons for such great popularity are far from inscrutable. Callimachus was the most influential author of his age: no other contemporary poet appears to have been so deeply concerned with literary debates—or, at least, so inclined to mention them in his verses—so rich in programmatic and metapoetical passages,[2] so strict

---

* We are grateful to Gianfranco Agosti and Valentina Garulli, who read parts of this paper in advance of publication and saved us from several mistakes and omissions; and to the editors, Ben Acosta-Hughes (who greatly improved our English), Luigi Lehnus, and Susan Stephens, for their continuous support and patience.

[1] "Throughout antiquity, indeed throughout the Middle Ages, from Apollonius Rhodius to Michael Choniates...Greek poets were imitating Callimachus." Pfeiffer 1949–1953: 2.xxxiii.

[2] These two features account for Callimachus' influence on Latin poetry as well: Richard Thomas, in his perceptive survey, rightly stated that "the clearest, most obvious, and most publicized, presence of Callimachus at Rome is in his capacity as a pro-

in his metrical technique. In language, style, and compositional strategy, Apollonius and Theocritus were sophisticated as well (the latter possibly even more sophisticated than Callimachus), but the Cyrenaean poet managed to mix the well-known Alexandrian ingredients—erudition, refinement, lightness—into a blend of unrivaled appeal. For any author who wanted to declare his allegiance to third-century Alexandrian aesthetics, or just to count among the elegant, engaging with the poetry of Callimachus was an obvious choice. The real issues are: What exactly did later poets borrow from him, and what exactly were their intentions over time? It is worth investigating how the appropriation of Callimachus' poetry evolved according to the new literary and cultural standards of the following ages. A history of Callimacheanism has not yet been written—though the earnest work of many classical scholars in the last two centuries (above all Otto Schneider and Rudolf Pfeiffer) has made the evidence largely available.

Needless to say, we offer just a small selection. This is not the place for a comprehensive, detailed analysis of Callimachus' reception in Greek poetry of the Hellenistic and imperial ages: that such a task would require a (very un-Callimachean) big book is, we think, self-evident. We have contented ourselves with highlighting a number of relevant instances, representative of the manifold ways in which Callimachus' text was exploited through some fifteen centuries of Greek poetry. Most Callimachean allusions and imitations we deal with in the following pages have been duly recorded in modern editions and commentaries: some of them are new. We have tried to acknowledge our debt to the scholars who preceded us; but when a parallel turns out to be already known, we usually choose to quote standard reference works, without systematically checking the older scholarship simply to ascertain who was the first to point it out in the history of classical philology.[3] Our aim is rather to shed some new light on the evolution of Callimacheanism, illustrating how different authors have looked to the great Alexandrian and integrated his influence into their own poetics.

---

grammatic model" (R.F. Thomas 1993: 199). Hunter 2006a is now the most important study on this topic: see also Barchiesi in this volume.

[3] Notwithstanding, Lehnus 2000b—an invaluable tool in pursuing such research—has been extremely useful to us.

The Hellenistic Age: Allegiance and Extremism

Callimachus' fame spread very rapidly. The keen interest that his contemporaries had in his writings continued to increase in the subsequent generations: from his first pupils and followers down to the end of the Hellenistic age, he enjoyed unrivaled popularity among learned poets. On many of these we will not dwell here, though Eratosthenes, Rhianus, Dioscorides, Moschus, Bion, and Meleager would surely deserve a closer look.[4] Our focus will rather be on four outstanding 'Callimachean' poets—Euphorion, Nicander, Antipater of Sidon, Parthenius—and a quite atypical one, the anonymous author of the *Batrachomyomachia*. All five are of special interest from this point of view. A sixth would be Lycophron, whose links with Callimachus are well known;[5] but we prefer not to treat him, since his chronology is still much disputed and we cannot decide with absolute certainty whether the Lycophron who wrote the *Alexandra* was Callimachus' contemporary, working side by side with Alexander of Aetolia at the Library of Alexandria under the auspices of Ptolemy Philadelphus, or rather a younger poet, well aware of increasing Roman power.[6] Reluctantly, we leave aside Leonidas of Tarentum also, whose chronology is disputed as well.[7]

---

[4] The evidence on Rhianus' relationship with Callimachus is well assessed by Alan Cameron 1995: 297–300 (quoting previous literature); see also Castelli 1998: 22, 27, 30–31, 35–36 (as for *SH* 927b.7, whose ascription to Rhianus is doubtful, note that Bremer 2006 now defends Δηϊώνη in Call. *Hec.* fr. 103 H.). On Dioscorides and Callimachus, see Moll 1920: 5–7; Gow and Page 1965: 2.240; Di Castri 1996: 49–50 and 1997: 61–63, 67; Lelli 2000: 74; Galán Vioque 2001: 184, 355–356. Moschus imitates Callimachus in the *Europa* (Bühler 1960: 74–77, 123, 133; Bornmann 1968: 20, 31; F. Williams 1978: 22–23); in *APl.* 200.2 = 1.2 GP, πήρην δ' εἶχε κατωμαδίην, he appears to have in mind both Call. *Hy.* 6.44 and *Aet.* fr. 24.10 Pf. = 26.10 M. The influence of Callimachus' mimetic hymns on Bion's *Epitaph on Adonis* is discussed by Fantuzzi 1985: 155–156 and by Reed 1997: 15–17 and 24; Bion fr. 9.1 Reed programmatically alludes to Call. *Ep.* 46.3 Pf. = 3.3 GP (Fantuzzi and Hunter 2004: 180–182). On Eratosthenes and Meleager, see below. Add *Epic. adesp.* 4 Powell, a fragment on an impoverished elderly woman, clearly drawing on Callimachus' *Hecale*. Hollis 2009: 29–30 cautiously wonders about Rhianus as its possible author.

[5] Pfeiffer 1949–1953: 2.134 lists some relevant instances; many others can be added. See more recently Gigante Lanzara 1998: 412–414; Schade 1999 *passim*; Durbec 2006b; Hollis 2007: 283–288; Looijenga 2009: 71–78.

[6] For recent surveys on the endless question of Lycophron's date, see Schade 1999: 215–228 and Hurst and Kolde 2008: vii–xxv. Add Fantuzzi and Hunter 2004: 437–439 and Negri 2009, inclined to assign him to Callimachus' age; Musti 2001 and Stirpe 2002, both championing a lower chronology.

[7] Some scholars, among them Gigante 1971: 37–42 and Gutzwiller 1998: 88–89, date Leonidas to the very beginning of the Hellenistic age; Gow 1958: 113–117 and

Too little survives of the *Erigone* of Callimachus' pupil and fellow countryman Eratosthenes to let us ascertain how deeply the *Hecale* may have influenced it.[8] The much more copious remains of Euphorion's poetry allow us to see Callimachus' first true devotee at work. Euphorion, roughly a generation younger than the great third-century Alexandrian poets, was incredibly fond of the Battiad: he draws on him for a large number of rare words, unusual forms, phrases, and themes, often combining allusions to two or more passages in an intertextual play that involves the Callimachean context and requires the reader to know it.[9] Let us quote just one among many illuminating instances, Euphorion fragment 51.8–10 Powell (= fr. 57.8–10 van Groningen):

ἤ που θερμάστραις ἤ που Μελιγουνίδι τοῖαι
μαρμαρυγαί, αἴρησιν ὅτε ῥήσσοιτο σίδηρος,
ἠέρ' ἀναθρῴσκουσι, βοᾷ δ' εὐήλατος ἄκμων.

Such sparklings spring up in the air, either in the furnaces or at Meligounis, when iron is beaten by the hammers and the staunch anvil resounds.

Euphorion has compressed in just three lines no fewer than four Callimachean borrowings from three different works, all related to Hephaestus' forge: first, *Hymn* 4.144, θερμάστραι τε βρέμουσιν ὑφ' Ἡφαίστοιο πυράγρης—note that θερμάστρα, albeit existing before Callimachus, appears nowhere else in surviving Greek literature; second, *Hymn* 3.48, Μελιγουνίς, ἐπ' ἄκμοσιν Ἡφαίστοιο; third, *Hymn* 3.55, ἄκμονος ἠχήσαντος; and fourth, *Aetia* fr. 115.12 Pf. (= 65.12 M.), παρ' Ἡφα⸤ί⸥σ⸤τ⸥οιο καμίνοις | ἔτραφεν αἰράων ⸤ἔργ⸥α διδα⸤ισ⸥κόμε⸤ν⸥οι, the only other extant occurrence of αἶρα (unless one accepts Wilamowitz's αἰρῶν at *Hymn* 3.56).[10] Such a tour de force—possibly enriched with a hint at an antiquarian question, as Euphorion sides with Callimachus (against Philetas?) in assigning Lipara (Meligounis) to Hephaestus rather than to Aeolus[11]—was the best way to show his

---

Gow and Page 1965: 2.308 and 311–312 rather think of the middle of the third century BC. For an updated assessment, see De Stefani 2005: 179–184. On Callimachus and Leonidas, see Pfeiffer 1949–1953: 2.134; Gow and Page 1965: 2.315, 329, 386.

[8] Many scholars assume that Eratosthenes drew on the *Hecale*, and even on the *Aetia* (Pfeiffer 1922: 102–112). Rosokoki 1995: 19–20 and 23–24 is more cautious (too cautious?) on this point. See also Hollis 2009: 345–347. Agosti 1997a points out the Callimachean features of Eratosthenes, fr. 35 Powell.

[9] The evidence is collected and discussed by Magnelli 2002: 22–26, 30.

[10] See Leurini 1992; Magnelli 2002: 24–25, quoting previous literature.

[11] On this point, see Sbardella 2000: 105–106. Callimachus may be involved in a learned dispute with Philetas, but it is unclear whether the mention of Meligounis as

knowledge and command of Callimachean poetry. It is also worth noting that although Euphorion elsewhere plays with Homer's text in various ways already practiced by the Alexandrians and well known to every scholar of Hellenistic poetry—*oppositio in imitando*, subversion, ironical rewriting, and so on—he does nothing of the kind with Callimachus. He may well adapt the Homeric description of Hector's irresistible fury (*Il.* 15.607-608) to a frightened Cerberus subdued by Heracles' power (fr. 51.3-7 Powell = 57.3-7 van Groningen) or turn Agamemnon's abduction of Briseis into the far less serious theft of a silver pot (fr. 8 Powell = 10 van Groningen, alluding to *Il.* 1.324-25 and 356),[12] but his attitude toward Callimachus (and Apollonius) is much more reverential, never inclining toward irony or mockery. He appears to consider the new classics, and especially Callimachus, his true models.[13]

Some decades later, Nicander—at least, the author of the *Theriaca, Alexipharmaca*, and *Georgica*[14]—is as fond of Callimachus as Euphorion was, and his exploitation of Callimachean texts proves as sophisticated as Euphorion's. He may draw on a single passage of his model in different sections of his two extant poems (cf. the lines on the prehistory of Greek rivers in Call. *Hymn* 1.22-27, echoed in *Theriaca* 141-143 and 950), or turn Callimachean *hapax legomena* into *Lieblingswörter* of his own;[15] he even tries to be subtler and more erudite than his great forebear. Consider how Callimachus *Hymn* 2.80-83,

ἰὴ ἰὴ Καρνεῖε πολύλλιτε, σεῖο δὲ βωμοὶ
ἄνθεα μὲν φορέουσιν ἐν εἴαρι τόσσα περ Ὧραι
ποικίλ' ἀγινεῦσι ζεφύρου πνείοντος ἐέρσην,
χείματι δὲ κρόκον ἡδύν,

Aeolus' island in Parth. 2.1 really comes from Parthenius' source, Philetas' *Hermes*, as both Sbardella and Spanoudakis 2002: 105-106 believe; Lightfoot 1999: 383 rather thinks of a mistake by Parthenius himself.

[12] On these and other instances of Euphorion's use of Homer, see Magnelli 2002: 5-21; on the Cerberus fragment see also Dettori 2003: 221-222.

[13] Thus Magnelli 2002: 26, 54-56.

[14] It is unclear whether these poems—and probably all the other fragmentary works ascribed to Nicander, or at least most of them—were written under Attalus III (138-133 BC) or during the last years of the reign of Attalus I (241-197 BC): it is also quite possible that two poets named Nicander existed. For a good assessment of the inconsistent evidence, see Massimilla 2000; on the lower chronology add d'Hautcourt 2001. We do not agree with Alan Cameron 1995: 194-207 in making the author of the *Theriaca* and the *Alexipharmaca* a contemporary of Callimachus and Aratus; see Magnelli 2006d: 187, 201-202.

[15] On both points, see Magnelli 2006d: 187-189, 191 n. 25.

Hie! Hie! Carneius, much-supplicated god. Your altars bear the various flowers gathered by the Seasons in spring, when Zephyrus breathes dew, and in winter sweet saffron,

is reworked in Nicander *Alexipharmaca* 232–234:

...ἢ ἔτι καὶ κλήροισιν ἐπήβολα τοῖά περ Ὧραι
εἰαριναὶ φορέουσιν ἐνεψιήματα κούραις,
ἄλλοτε δὲ στρούθεια.

...or even those belonging to the fields, the kind of girls' playthings the Seasons bear in spring; or again pear quinces.

That Nicander alludes here to the Callimachean *Hymn to Apollo* is evident, but the competent reader could appreciate his choice of a more recherché vocabulary. Not just that Callimachus' bare "flowers" are here turned into "[fruits] belonging to the fields" and "girls' playthings": most remarkable are the occurrences of ἐπήβολος, a Homeric *hapax legomenon* that Hellenistic poets used with various meanings, and ἐνεψίημα, probably coined by Nicander himself with an eye to Callimachus' (and Apollonius') interest in Homeric ἐψιάομαι.[16] It is unnecessary to add other instances among the many already pointed out by scholars.[17] The Colophonian poet competes with his model on the very ground of Alexandrianism: add that he also imitates Euphorion,[18] and here is a nice genealogy of fervent Callimacheans.

Among Hellenistic epigrammatists, Antipater of Sidon (ca. 180–170–ca. 100 BC) appears to be one of those most interested in Callimachus' poetic language. Many an echo of the Battiad can be detected in Antipater's epigrams:[19] the latter's praise of Herinna (*AP* 7.713 = 58 GP) celebrates her "swan's light sound" through a number of Callimachean images and motifs,[20] and his epitaph on Cleinarete is worth quoting in full (*AP* 7.711 = 56 GP):

---

[16] Jacques 1955: 19 pointed out the link between the two passages; for a recent assessment, see Magnelli 2006d: 191. On ἐπήβολος, see Livrea 1973a: 388; on ἐψιάομαι, Rengakos 1994: 92, with further bibliography.

[17] Many are listed by Pfeiffer 1949–1953: 2.136 and recorded by modern editors of both poets (for Nicander, above all Gow and Scholfield 1953 and Jacques 2002 and 2007); see also Magnelli 2006d. On possible Callimachean influence in the final section of the *Alexipharmaca*, see Magnelli 2006c.

[18] Schultze 1888: 46–49; Magnelli 2002: 105–106.

[19] Cf. Pfeiffer 1949–1953: 1.312, 402; Gow and Page 1965: 2.39, 49, 84; Massimilla 1996: 244; Hollis 2009: 325–326.

[20] As Neri 1995 rightly points out. For a detailed commentary on the epigram, see Neri 2003: 198–201.

ἤδη μὲν κροκόεις Πιτανάτιδι πίτνατο νύμφᾳ
  Κλειναρέτᾳ χρυσέων παστὸς ἔσω θαλάμων,
καδεμόνες δ' ἥλποντο διωλένιον φλόγα πεύκης
  ἄψειν ἀμφοτέραις ἀνσχόμενοι παλάμαις
Δημὼ καὶ Νίκιππος· ἀφαρπάξασα δὲ νοῦσος   5
  παρθενικὰν Λάθας ἄγαγεν ἐς πέλαγος,
ἀλγειναὶ δ' ἐκάμοντο συνάλικες οὐχὶ θυρέτρων
  ἀλλὰ τὸν Ἀίδεω στερνοτυπῆ πάταγον.

The saffron-colored nuptial bed was already prepared in the golden chamber for Cleinarete, the bride from Pitana, and Demo and Nicippus, her parents, were eager to grasp the pine torch and lift it up with both hands. But sickness ravished the virgin and took her to the sea of Lethe: and her girlfriends sadly played Hades' din, beating at their bosoms instead of the door of the bridal chamber.

The theme of the girl who dies on the very day of her wedding (or shortly thereafter) was as old as Herinna's *Distaff*, and by Antipater's time had become a commonplace.[21] Yet this epigram, as Pfeiffer noted, is also heavily indebted to Callimachus' *Acontius and Cydippe*: Antipater deliberately reverses the story of the Naxian bride who just before marriage (Call. *Aet.* fr. 75.1 Pf., ἤδη καί ≈ Antip. 1) was struck by a serious disease (Call. fr. 75.11, τὴν δ' εἷλε κακὸς χλόος, ἦλθε δὲ νοῦσος ≈ Antip. 5) and almost died (Call. fr. 75.15, τὴν κούρην Ἀ[ίδ]εω μέχρις ἔτηξε δόμων ≈ Antip. 6) but was finally able to marry Acontius, accompanied by the nuptial song of her friends (Call. fr. 75.42–43, ἥλικες αὐτίχ' ἑταίρης Ι ᾖδον ὑμηναίους ≈ Antip. 7).[22]

Is Antipater to be labeled Callimachean? The answer is complex. That he extols Antimachus (*AP* 7.409 = 66 GP), whose *Lyde* Callimachus once blamed as παχὺ γράμμα καὶ οὐ τορόν (fr. 398 Pf.), and even does this adapting Callimachus' own terminology,[23] need not puzzle us: the praise neither of Herinna nor of Antimachus implies Antipater's militant affiliation to a definite literary trend.[24] What rather distinguishes him from Alexandrian poetry is his 'baroque' style. He fills his verses with unusual words (as Callimachus often does, yet not in his epigrams), redundant epithets, and figures of speech, and some-

---

[21] See Szepessy 1972; Neri 2003: 49–50, 433–434, quoting other literature.
[22] Pfeiffer 1949–1953: 1.77.
[23] Gow and Page 1965: 2.87; Grilli 1979; Knox 1985b: 116; Cucchiarelli 1994: 163–166; Alan Cameron 1995: 332–334. Whether Antipater's epigram in fact refers to either Antimachus' *Lyde* or his *Thebaid*, or even to his whole poetical output, is irrelevant to the present topic.
[24] As Argentieri 2003: 93–94 aptly remarks.

times iterates a conceit just for the sake of expressing it in two different ways—nothing to do with Callimachean concision and lightness.[25] This forms, however, a picture consistent with some features of Euphorion's and Nicander's poetic diction. Euphorion's style and vocabulary perfectly fit a follower of Callimachus; nonetheless he sometimes turns to more peculiar tones (Hermogenes, p. 130 Rabe, charged him with ψυχρότης), erudition ostensibly winning over elegance (Magnelli 2002: 46-53). Nicander's diction is much more idiosyncratic than Callimachus', rich not only in glosses but in metaplasms and morphological peculiarities, and his style often proves quite involved, as if he was taking the practices of Hellenistic learned poetry one step further[26]— note that he even introduces himself as "Homeric" (Ὁμήρειος, *Theriaca* 957), though the epithet is ambiguous and possibly paradoxical.[27] Styles change in time, but this appears not to hinder literary affiliations. Antipater is very different from both Euphorion and Nicander, and presumably does not aim at being altogether 'Alexandrian'; nonetheless his redundant manner is yet another stage in the evolution of Greek Callimacheanism. Euphorion, Nicander, and Antipater all show a keen allegiance to the Cyrenaean poet, though none of them writes like him. And it is remarkable that all three, in spite of some less relevant divergences, write hexameters whose 'inner metric'—that is, the regulation of word ends and sense pauses—is very close to Callimachus' strict standards.[28] It is in the inner metric that Callimachus' metrical technique proved most refined and innovative, and at that time composing verses according to it was an unmistakable sign of adhesion to his reform.

Toward the end of the Hellenistic period, Parthenius of Nicaea plays an important role in our story. Even apart from his (much-disputed)

---

[25] On Antipater's style, see De Stefani 1996: 201-202; Argentieri 2003: 62-67; the old survey by Waltz 1906: 41-60 is still worth reading.

[26] Jacques 2002: xcii-cv and 2007: lxxxix-cx provides the best survey on Nicander's language and style.

[27] According to Jacques 2002: lxxi, Nicander's purpose is to stage Homer as his stylistic model. (But is his poetry Homeric at all?) For other theories, including a new one, see Magnelli 2010: 216-217.

[28] Euphorion's meter: Magnelli 2002: 57-91. Nicander's meter: Brioso Sánchez 1974; Jacques 2002: cxxiii-cxxix; Oikonomakos 2002: 135-152; Magnelli 2006d: 198-201. Antipater's meter: Magnelli 1995: 157-161; Argentieri 2003: 50-59; Magnelli 2007: 179-181. Evidence is available in these studies, and it is unnecessary to present it again here.

influence on Roman poetry,[29] he must have been one of the distinguished Callimacheans of the first century BC: many an echo of the Cyrenaean poet appears in his extant fragments,[30] and it is remarkable that Pollianus, in his well-known epigram against literary plagiarism (*AP* 11.130), chooses Callimachus and Parthenius as representatives of the innovative poetry that he counters to traditional cyclic epic.[31] Yet Parthenius, if we are to trust (to some extent at least) Erycius' bitter words, pushed his militant Callimacheanism beyond the usual horizons of Alexandrian poets and those like them (Erycius, *AP* 7.377.5-6 = 13.5-6 GP):[32]

> ἤλασε καὶ μανίης ἐπὶ δὴ τόσον ὥστ' ἀγορεῦσαι   5
> πηλὸν Ὀδυσσείην καὶ πάτον Ἰλιάδα.
>
> He even went so far in his madness as to call the *Odyssey* mud and the *Iliad* filth.

Erycius' malevolent attack can hardly be taken at face value, and it is most unlikely that Parthenius really dared to slander Homer. Jane Lightfoot (1999: 78) writes that Erycius' remark is "a gross distortion" and that "it would be misguided to take this epigram as evidence that Parthenius expressed, in more forceful terms, 'doctrines' which he derived from the Alexandrians." With the former statement we surely agree, but we remain uncertain about the latter: Erycius'

---

[29] Wendell Clausen, in his important study, pushed his arguments too far in assuming that knowledge of Alexandrian poetry at Rome was mainly due to Parthenius (Clausen 1964; for a more cautious view, see Crowther 1976). Lightfoot 1999: 50-76 provides the best assessment of the topic; see also Fantuzzi and Hunter 2004: 462-467.

[30] Lightfoot 1999: 47 and 559 summarizes the evidence, admirably discussing the relevant passages in her commentary; Cazzaniga 1961: 45-47 can still be read with profit. Callimachean influence may also be detected in anon. *SH* 964, which Spanoudakis 2004 would assign to Parthenius. The elegiac fragments in POxy 69.4711 feature some imitations of Callimachus and interesting structural affinities with Books 3 and 4 of the *Aetia*. Several scholars considered the possibility that these fragments belong to Parthenius' *Metamorphoses* (see Henry 2005: 47; Hutchinson 2006a; Luppe 2006: 55; Magnelli 2006e: 10-11 also found this view appealing, though he has now partly changed his mind), but Reed 2006: 76 deems it unlikely, and Bernsdorff 2007 questions Parthenian authorship with strong arguments.

[31] See Alan Cameron 1995: 396-399; Lightfoot 1999: 84 and 187 (challenging the *communis opinio* that Pollianus in fact likes Callimachus and Parthenius); Nisbet 2003: 188-193.

[32] On this difficult epigram, see Gow and Page 1968: 2.287; Seth-Smith 1981; Bornmann 1993; Lightfoot 1999: 76-80. At line 6 we follow the great majority of editors in printing πάτον, Guyet's emendation for the transmitted βοτόν (P: βάτον J, retained by Lelli 1996: 313-314 as an allusion to Callimachus' *Iambus* 4).

opinion must indeed have originated from something that Parthenius said or wrote (see Bornmann 1993: 88), if not against Homeric poetry, at least against Homer's poor imitators; and it is undeniable that the association of long (epic?) poems with mud and rubbish has obvious Callimachean resonances—Callimachus *Hymn* 2.105-12 immediately comes to mind. Modern scholars have long upheld the view, ill founded though it may be, of a Callimachus fiercely averse to epic poetry as such;[33] it would be unsurprising if late Hellenistic men of letters, albeit knowing Callimachean poetics far better than we do, may occasionally have formed such opinions. Antipater of Thessalonica extols "manly Homer" over the fastidious weakness of learned Alexandrian poets (*AP* 11.20 = 20 GP):[34] Did Parthenius, possibly within some literary quarrel, fall into an opposite kind of extremism, turning his devotion to Callimachus into an unfriendly attitude toward a poetical genre that might be (unduly) regarded as anti-Callimachean?

After Antipater of Sidon's baroque style and Parthenius' strenuous allegiance to Alexandrian poetics, we turn to a literary work of more traditional taste. Jacob Wackernagel's seminal researches have effectively shown that the pseudo-Homeric *Batrachomyomachia* belongs to the late Hellenistic or even early imperial age.[35] This is not a poem that one would expect to draw on Callimachus; yet it displays an evident allusion to the *Prologue* of the *Aetia* (fr. 1.21 Pf. = M., as Apollo instructs the poet ὅτ‚ε πρώτιστον ἐμοῖς ἐπὶ δέλτον ἔθηκα | γούνασι‚ν, "when I first put the tablet on my knees") in lines 1-3:[36]

ἀρχόμενος πρώτης σελίδος χορὸν ἐξ Ἑλικῶνος
ἐλθεῖν εἰς ἐμὸν ἦτορ ἐπεύχομαι, εἵνεκ' ἀοιδῆς
ἣν νέον ἐν δέλτοισιν ἐμοῖς ἐπὶ γούνασι θῆκα.

---

[33] The *communis opinio* about Callimachus' distaste for epic has been deservedly confuted by Alan Cameron 1995, whose arguments are on the whole convincing, and now accepted by most scholars; see also Barbantani 2002-2003.

[34] This may, however, be a harmless joke rather than a venomous attack: see the judicious assessment by Argentieri 2003: 94-98. Antipater of Thessalonica sometimes draws on Callimachus, albeit less frequently than does his Sidonian namesake: see Pfeiffer 1949-1953: 2.128; Gow and Page 1968: 2.39, 51-52, 70-71, 86, 109; Massimilla 1996: 422.

[35] Wackernagel 1916: 188-199. Cf. Glei 1984: 34-36; Fusillo 1988: 41-43; more recently, M.L. West 2003: 229-230. Wölke 1978: 46-70 offers a well-informed story of modern studies on the poem's date.

[36] As already noted in the nineteenth century by commentators on both texts: see Wölke 1978: 59-60. Bliquez 1977: 12 n. 4 still follows Bergk's old theory about *Batr.* 1-3 as "Hellenistic interpolations," apparently unaware of the further Callimachean allusions at lines 116-117 and 180-191—on which, see below.

Beginning from the first column I beg the Heliconian chorus to come into my heart, for the sake of the song that I have just set down in the tablets here on my knees.

It may sound paradoxical that a poem almost entirely made up of Homeric words and phrases should begin under the sign of the *Reply to the Telchines*, Callimachus' renowned claim to originality. In fact, the author of the *Batrachomyomachia* exploits in two different passages another Callimachean text, namely the lines from the *Victory of Berenice* describing Molorchus' mousetraps (one of the most famous occurrences of mice in Greek literature). Callimachus *SH* 259.16–17, with the old farmer preparing "a hidden trap" (κ[ρ]υπτὸν...δόλον) in two snares (π̣αγίδεσσιν), is alluded to at *Batrachomyomachia* 116–117, when an old mouse recounts his son's being killed by men with "a wooden trap that they call a snare" (ξύλινον δόλον...ἣν παγίδα κλείουσι), thus turning Callimachus' light tone into something that, from the mouse's point of view, is quite dreadful. And the Callimachean passage on the wrongdoings of the mice, who drew oil from Molorchus' lamp, kept him awake by night, and chewed up his rags (*SH* 259.22–23, 27–31), is reworked in the *Batrachomyomachia* when an angry Athena expounds first the misdeeds of the mice, who stole her oil and destroyed her robe (ll. 179–182), then those of the frogs, who did not let her sleep (ll. 190–191).[37] It is entertaining to see the Callimachean Molorchus, ἀνὴρ πενιχρός (*SH* 259.25), turned into none other than Athena![38] The *Batrachomyomachia*, for all its archaizing style, proves to be a quite elaborate literary work: "the poem's engagement with the traditions on which it draws is more subtle and sophisticated than has often been assumed."[39] The Molorchus episode in Callimachus had ostensibly ironical nuances, juxtaposing Heracles' fight against the monstrous Nemean Lion and the old farmer's war against the little mice.[40] The author of the *Batrachomyomachia* proba-

---

[37] All these parallels were pointed out by Pfeiffer 1949–1953: 1.148–150 and are recorded in recent editions of the *Batrachomyomachia*.

[38] The humor of this passage is well discussed by Fusillo 1988: 115–117.

[39] Sens 2006: 217, providing an insightful analysis of the poem and its strategies of composition. "The poet is able and inventive" and "does not limit himself to Homeric cliché" (M.L. West 2003: 234).

[40] As Livrea 1979 acutely remarked. His interpretation is now accepted by most scholars: see, e.g., Fuhrer 1992: 69–70; Parsons 1993a: 168; Hunter 2006a: 90; Durbec 2006a: 53 n. 154; D'Alessio 2007: 455 n. 18. Ambühl 2004 effectively illustrates the light, self-ironical tone of the *Victory of Berenice*.

bly realized this and decided to build a parody on a model that is itself quite lighthearted. At that point, his audience would no longer think that the poem's Callimachean opening clashed with its Homeric diction. No fat ladies, no thundering Zeus,[41] no braying donkeys here.

Callimachus on Stone

If refined authors cannot help but take Callimachus into consideration when defining their own poetics, his influence pervades inscriptional poetry as well. No other Greek poet, except Homer and possibly Hesiod, is so often echoed and imitated (even plundered) by the industrious writers of epitaphs, dedicatory epigrams, and the like. From the Hellenistic age down to late antiquity, one finds a fair number of such versifiers either shaping their diction with an eye to Callimachus' text or just picking up one or two phrases from it and adapting them— sometimes quite clumsily—to their own poems.[42] Even in Bactria, at the uttermost end of the Hellenized world, someone was exploiting Callimachean poetry: the acrostic elegy on stone celebrating the deeds of one Sophytus, recently found on the site of ancient Alexandria-in-Arachosia (now Kandahar, Afghanistan), remarkably features two rare Callimachean words in the first three lines, κοκύαι ("ancestors") and τυννός ("little"), both possibly from the *Hecale*.[43]

---

[41] Who in fact proves ineffectual at the end of the poem (ll. 285–91); but we hesitate to see any poetological meaning here.

[42] Kaibel 1878: 692 and Merkelbach and Stauber 1998-2004: 5.332 list a great number of passages. Other instances are recorded by Pfeiffer 1949-53: 1.243, 260; Merkelbach 1969 (on the *Visio Maximi*; see now Brandis 2002, Knuf 2010); Gallavotti 1983: 1-3; D'Alessio 2004b: 43-44; Magnelli 2004a: 53-55; Spanoudakis 2008: 315-322; Agosti 2008b: 197; Massimilla 2010; Garulli (forthcoming). Add *IG* II/III² 3790 = Peek 1980: 21-22 (Athens, first century AD), line 2, Ὠγυγίων υἷες Ἐριχθονιδᾶν, ≈ Call. *Hy.* 5.34; *SGO* 13/11/01.1 (Lycandus, unknown date), κ[αὶ ἐ]μοὶ καταθύμιον ἄνδρ[α], ≈ Call. *Hy.* 5.33; epigram in Clarysse and Huys 1996 (Ain Labakha, second or third century AD), line 4, [ἀ]στέρας ἀμφοτέρους, ≈ Call. *Aet.* fr. 67.8 Pf.; *GVI* 376.2 = Samama 2003: 533 no. 493 (Ostia, second or third century AD), θνή[σ]κιν μὴ [λ]έγε τοὺς ἀγαθούς, ≈ Call. *Ep.* 9.2 Pf. = 41.2 GP; *GVI* 741.4 (Amorgos, third century AD or later), θῆκε δὲ τῷδε τ[ά]φῳ ≈ Call. *Ep.* 58.2 Pf. = 50.2 GP, both on someone drowned at sea.

[43] On this interesting text, first edited by Bernard, Pinault, and Rougemont 2004: 229-332 and dated to either the second or the first century BC, see Merkelbach and Stauber 2005: 17-19; Hollis 2006: 142 n. 8; Garulli 2008: 652-660; Agosti 2008a: 668; Hollis 2009: 434-435; Santin 2009: 276-282.

These anonymous epigraphic poets draw on the *Aetia*, the *Hymns*, the *Hecale*, even the *Iambi*; but genre carries weight, and since the great majority of inscriptional poems are epigrams, those of Callimachus predictably take the lion's share of the imitations. A telling instance is a second-century BC epitaph from Chios describing the tomb of an old country gentleman:[44]

[εἴ σοι] μὴ βαρὺ τοῦτο παραστείχοντι πυθέσθ[αι,]
    [ἴσθι μ]ε Νικίεω παῖδα ἀναπαυόμενον
[.....]να· ζωὴν δὲ ἔλιπον γηραιός, ὁδῖτα,
    [ἕνδε]κα πληρώσας ἑβρομάδας βιότου·
[ἱδρυθεὶ]ς δὲ ἐπ' ἐμῷ τύμβῳ χάλκειος ἀλέκτ[ωρ]   5
    [μάρτυ]ς ἐφέστηκεν σώφρονος ἀγρυπνίης·
[ἦα μὲ]ν ἐκ προγόνων ἀγαθῶν, ἐπὶ πολλὰ γεωργό[ς·]
    [νῦν δ' εἶπ]ας χαίρειν μνῆσαι ὁδοιπορίης.

[If you] do not mind learning this while you walk this way, [know] that I,...son of Nicias, rest here. I parted with life in old age, traveler, after [eleve]n periods of seven years. The bronze cock [fixe]d on my tomb stands here as a [witness] to my wise vigil: [I was] the scion of honest ancestors and spent most of my life as a farmer. [Now bid] me farewell and take care for your journey.

The text runs smooth and (apparently) unpretentious, but a well-read passerby could easily realize that it is a real mosaic of phrases and themes from Callimachus' *Epigrams*. Line 2 (where Merkelbach's supplement is almost certain) blatantly echoes Callimachus' solemn epitaph for his father in his *Epigram* 21.1–2 Pf. (= 29.1–2 GP):

ὅστις ἐμὸν παρὰ σῆμα φέρεις πόδα, Καλλιμάχου με
    ἴσθι Κυρηναίου παῖδά τε καὶ γενέτην.

Whosoever you are who walk near my tomb, know that I am both son and father of a Callimachus from Cyrene.

The real existence of the χάλκειος ἀλέκτ[ωρ] mentioned in the elderly Chian's line 5 we shall not question; yet on a literary level it turns out to be descended from the bronze cock offered to the Dioscuri by one Euainetus in Callimachus *Epigram* 56 Pf. (= 25 GP); and [μάρτυ]ς...ἀγρυπνίης (Robert's supplement is unavoidable) recalls the σύμβολον ἀγρυπνίης of Callimachus' famous epigram in praise

---

[44] First edited by J. Robert 1967; cf. Merkelbach 1970, whose text we print.

of Aratus (27.4 Pf. = 56.4 GP).⁴⁵ These six lines clearly aim at raising the quiet gentleman to the heights of a Battus or an Aratus—though his σώφρων ἀγρυπνία presumably had nothing to do with the latter's literary activity and simply meant, as the first editor noted, that our γεωργός used to wake up at dawn.

In fact, for at least some of these versifiers Callimachus was not just a literary delicacy: by imitating him, they hoped to bestow a most honorific title on their own work—and, in the case of professional poets, on anyone who hired them. A set of three epigrams from Oenoanda, written in AD 238 (*SGO* 17/06/02), celebrates the local γραμματικός Iulius Lucius Pilius Euarestus for having founded and funded quadrennial games in his native town. Euarestus, speaking in the first person, remarks that whereas others posthumously instituted such festivals in Greek cities—he probably had Melicertes and the Isthmian Games in mind—only he achieved this while still living (ll. 19–22):

μοῦνος δ' αὐτὸς ἐγὼν ἔτλην τόδε, καί ῥ' ἐμὸν ἦτο[ρ]
γηθεῖ τερπό‹με›νον χαλκελάτοις ξοάνοις.   20
τοίγαρ μῶμον ἀνέντες ὅσοι φθόνον αἰνὸν ἔχουσ[ιν]
μειμηλοῖς ὄσσοις εἰσίδετ' εἰκόν' ἐμήν.

I alone dared this, and my heart rejoices, pleased by bronze statues.⁴⁶ So lay aside blame, you who feel evil envy, and look at my image with eyes inclined to emulation.

It has been noted that line 21, apart from its awkward syntax, clearly stems from the well-known final line of Callimachus' *Hymn to Apollo* (113, χαῖρε, ἄναξ· ὁ δὲ Μῶμος, ἵν' ὁ Φθόνος, ἔνθα νέοιτο, "Hail, Lord! and let Blame go where Envy has").⁴⁷ The inscription strives to depict Euarestus as not only a wealthy and generous man but above all an

---

⁴⁵ Let us note that μάρτυς in the Chian epigram, just one century later than Callimachus, joins other texts (see Gow and Page 1965: 2.209; Waltz et al. 1974: 226–227) in supporting Ruhnken's σύμβολον in the Callimachean passage—where the indirect tradition reads σύγγονος ἀγρυπνίης and the Palatine manuscript σύντονος ἀγρυπνίη, championed by (among others) Lohse 1967; Alan Cameron 1972; D'Alessio 2007: 1.240 n. 36; Gärtner 2007: 160–162; cf. also Lehnus 1990a: 31.

⁴⁶ Apparently the statues of the winners, ἀρετῆς σύμβολα καὶ σοφίης (l. 16).

⁴⁷ Hall and Milner 1994: 26; Lehnus 2000a: 379–380, rightly noting that Euarestus' epigram supports the reading Φθόνος in Callimachus against the variant Φθόρος (rejected on good grounds by F. Williams 1978: 96–97, Giangrande 1992, and others; we are not persuaded by Blomqvist 1990 and Meillier 1990, who held the opposite view).

innovator (ll. 17-19) and a friend of the Muses (ll. 3-8, 16): nothing better than ending such praise with an allusion to a very famous programmatic closure, written some five centuries earlier by a great poet proud of his originality and ready to dispose of Envy and Blame.

Others were even more concerned with literary affiliation. Of four Greek hymns to Isis composed by an Isidorus in the first century BC and engraved on two pillars of the goddess' sanctuary at Medinet Madi,[48] two are in elegiacs. The author writes in stock epic language and utterly lacks any command of meter;[49] yet his choice of the elegiac couplet probably aims—as scholars have rightly noted—at setting his poems in a tradition of elegiac hymns whose most renowned representative was Callimachus' *On the Bath of Pallas*.[50]

Let us add a few words on Quintus Sulpicius Maximus, a surprisingly young poet who died in AD 94 at the age of eleven. A funeral monument in Rome preserves an ethopoeic poem in forty-three Greek hexameters on Zeus and Phaethon, composed by Maximus himself shortly before his death (*GVI* 1924.1-43 = *IGUR* 1336A), and two Greek epigrams celebrating the talent of this *enfant prodige* (*GVI* 1924.44-63 = *IGUR* 1336C).[51] The first epigram ends with the wish that Maximus may rest in peace in Elysium for the following reason (*GVI* 1924.52-53 = *IGUR* 1336C.9-10):

---

[48] *IME* 175; Vanderlip 1972, with detailed commentary. There is a perceptive analysis of Isidorus' ideology in Fantuzzi and Hunter 2004: 350-363.
[49] "Their metre is execrable" (Lightfoot 1999: 30). Keydell 1953 is still very important on this topic.
[50] That he knew Callimachus is proved by 4.18, γράμμ' ἀναλεξάμενοι, echoing Call. *Ep*. 23.4 Pf. = 53.4 GP. (See Cazzaniga in Merkelbach and Cazzaniga 1965: 300; Vanderlip 1972: 69; Alan Cameron 1995: 151 n. 56.) For a more speculative instance, see Magnelli 2006a: 50. On the other hand, it is hard to find any Callimachean echo in the far better-written anonymous hymn to Isis from Andros (*IG* XII 5, 739 = Peek 1930: 15-22; first century BC?). The only exceptions may be lines 10-11, ἀπόκρυφα σύμβολα δέλτων | εὑρομένα γραφίδεσσι κατέξυσα, ≈ Call. fr. 468 Pf. (though ἀπόκρυφος as "arcane" is not uncommon: see Pfeiffer 1949-53: 2.355), and possibly line 47, λύκος ὠρυκτάς, ≈ Call. *Hec*. fr. inc. 178 H., unless the author rather had in mind Theocr. 1.71, τῆνον μὰν θῶες, τῆνον λύκοι ὠρύσαντο (cf. line 46, ἂν φωλάδες ἔστυγον ἄρκτοι, ≈ Theocr. 1.115, as Gow 1952: 2.25 noted; ὠρύομαι is the *vox propria* for wolves: cf. Arat. 1124; Livrea 1968: 126).
[51] On Maximus' poem, see Diggle 1970: 201-202; Vérilhac 1978-1982: 1.115-121; Fernández Delgado and Ureña Bracero 1991; Döpp 1996; Bernsdorff 1997; Nocita 2000 discusses the monument.

ζωούσας έλιπες γὰρ ἀηδόνας, ἃς Ἀϊδωνεὺς
οὐδέποθ' αἱρήσει τῇ φθονερῇ παλάμῃ.

You left your living nightingales, which Aidoneus will never ravish with his envious hand.

The couplet, as all editors remark, is obviously a variation on Callimachus' lament for his friend Heraclitus of Halicarnassus in *Epigram* 2.5–6 Pf. (= 34.5–6 GP):

αἱ δὲ τεαὶ ζώουσιν ἀηδόνες, ᾗσιν ὁ πάντων
ἁρπακτὴς Ἀΐδης οὐκ ἐπὶ χεῖρα βαλεῖ.

But your nightingales still live, and Hades, snatcher of all, will not lay his hand upon them.

To gain such praise from the fastidious Callimachus was a truly great achievement, and in fact the high quality of the one extant epigram ascribed to Heraclitus (*AP* 7.465 = 1 GP) makes us regret the loss of the rest.[52] Sulpicius Maximus' verses, however good or bad they may seem,[53] are not Callimachean:[54] their tone is quite emphatic (surely because of the influence of rhetoric), and their abundance of epithets has much more to do with the new trends of Imperial poetry than with Alexandrian λεπτότης. But this was not a problem for the epigram's author, who wishes simply to extol Maximus' talent—at the same time choosing for himself the authoritative role of a Callimachus, *arbiter elegantiarum* in decreeing what will survive and what will not—without caring about the fact that he could not be labeled Alexandrian. After all, both the baby poet and his anonymous *laudator* were writing at the end of the first century AD, when imitating Callimachus and using him to lend one's own poetry distinction no longer implied allegiance to true Callimachean poetics, as we will see.

---

[52] As Gow and Page 1965: 2.304 remark, briefly resuming the case for ascribing the epigram to Callimachus' friend rather than to the later Heraclides of *AP* 7.281 and 392. On Heraclitus, see Swinnen 1970 (it is unlikely that *SGO* 01/12/02, the elegy usually called "The Pride of Halicarnassus," was written by him: see Lloyd-Jones 1999: 13 = 230–231 and D'Alessio 2004b: 51); his epigram is well discussed, together with that of Callimachus, by Hunter 1992a. See also Montes Cala 1991: 514–520; Meyer 2005: 119–121.

[53] The judgement of Kaibel 1878: 252 was surely too harsh: "Nos scire iuvat non omnes tunc graecas Musas tam misere balbutiisse. Versus...infimae notae sunt" ("It is good to know that not everyone at that time was so wretchedly babbling in Greek verse. These verses are of the lowest quality").

[54] In spite of one possible, yet not very relevant echo of Call. *Iamb.* fr. 195.26–7 Pf. at *GVI* 1924.33 = *IGUR* 1336A.33, ἴσχε δρόμον (Pfeiffer 1949–53: 1.187).

The Imperial Age: New Trends and Big Books

Callimachus' influence never ceases to flourish throughout the Imperial age. Philip of Thessalonica attacks the grammarians, "soldiers of Callimachus," in an epigram full of Callimachean vocabulary,[55] still declaring his allegiance to ὀλιγοστιχία:[56] Lucillius wittily blends a line from the *Aetia* with its Hesiodic model;[57] Strato of Sardis amuses himself and his audience by subverting Callimachus' programmatic statements in view of his own pederastic perspective.[58] From Babrius to Palladas,[59] from the Orphic *Lithica* to Proclus' *Hymns*,[60] from Naumachius to the anonymous author of an acrostic ethopoeia on Hesiod (POxy 50.3537r),[61] one will scarcely find a competent versifier who is not indebted in some way to Callimachus. It is far from surprising that an elegant poet like Maximus (of Ephesus?), author of Περὶ καταρχῶν, delights in both the *Aetia* and the *Hecale*;[62] yet even the unrefined Orphic *Argonautica*, the clumsy *Manethoniana*, and the highly Homer-

---

[55] Cf. *AP* 11.321 = 60 GP, with Kakridis 1928, Pfeiffer 1949–53: 1.1 and 79, and Gow and Page 1968: 2.362.

[56] The preface to his *Garland* (*AP* 4.2 = 1 GP) has obvious Callimachean overtones: see Lausberg 1982: 41–42; Gutzwiller 1998: 4; Magnelli 2006f.

[57] Lucill. *AP* 11.183.5, being a conflation of Hes. *Op.* 265 and Call. *Aet.* fr. 2.5 Pf. = 4.5 M. (See Massimilla 1996: 245.) The two passages were confused in antiquity (see [Hes.] fr. 373 M.-W.), but it is more likely that the clever Lucillius intentionally mixed them in a window allusion. The same opinion is held independently by Lucia Floridi, whose commentary on Lucillius is forthcoming.

[58] Floridi 2007: 130–132 and 247 provides an excellent discussion of the relevant passages.

[59] On Palladas, see Pfeiffer 1949–53: 1.366. Babrius 47 Luzzatto–La Penna clearly reworks Bathycles' story in Call. *Iamb.* fr. 191 Pf. (Pfeiffer 1949–53: 1.164), and his first proem is inspired by Call. *Iamb.* fr. 192 Pf. (see Kerkhecker 1999: 49 n. 3; Acosta-Hughes 2002: 176 n. 18, 187). Other Callimachean influences are listed by Pfeiffer 1949–53: 2.129; cf. Luzzatto 1975: 42.

[60] [Orph.] *Lith.* 116, αἰνὸν ὄφιν, and 127, πελώριος...θήρ, possibly echo Call. *Hy.* 2.100–101 (both in an Apollinean context); cf. also 197, οἱ δ' ἄρα μιν λήθαιον ἐφήμισαν, ≈ Call. *Aet.* fr. 75.58 Pf., if more speculative. Proclus' *Hymn* 7 (*To Athena*) may be reminiscent of Callimachus here and there: cf. line 7, Παλλάς, Τριτογένεια, δορυσσόε, χρυσεοπήληξ, ≈ Call. *Hy.* 5.43; line 5, πότνια, θυμῷ at line end, ≈ Call. *Hec.* fr. 73.7 H.; line 28, εὖτ' ἐπὶ Κεκροπίδῃσι, ≈ Call. *Hec.* fr. 70.5 H.

[61] Naumachius *GDRK* 29.22 clearly imitates Call. *Aet.* fr. 75.28 Pf. (See Pfeiffer 1949–1953: 1.79; both passages deal with marriage.) Possible Callimachean echoes in the poem of POxy 50.3537r (Hes. test. 95 Most; see Agosti 1997b; Bernsdorff 1999; Miguélez Cavero 2008: 50–52, with full bibliography) are detected by Livrea 1998: 28–31. Dionysius, author of both Βασσαρικά and a Γιγαντιάς, may also owe something to Callimachus: see Livrea 1973b: 58, 63, 114; Hollis 2009: 161 and 303.

[62] Massimilla 1996: 444; Hollis 2009: 295; add Pfeiffer 1949–1953: 1.454, 472 (if fr. inc. auct. 748 is Callimachean indeed: see Massimilla 2004: 23).

izing *Metaphrasis of the Psalms* once wrongly attributed to Apollinarius of Laodicea are not immune to Callimachus' fascination.[63]

Needless to say, literary trends keep changing, and the agenda of Callimachean poets in the Antonine age is not the same as their Hellenistic forebears'. Antipater of Sidon, as we have seen, follows Callimachus in both language and meter. Meleager, a few decades later, is also deeply indebted to Callimachus' poetry,[64] but he has very different metrical standards.[65] The like happens in the Imperial period. The highly refined Dionysius Periegetes, writing under Hadrian, proves very fond of Alexandrian poetry, especially Callimachus and Apollonius.[66] His carefully built hexameters are beyond all charges of incompetence; yet he is so indifferent to Callimachean rules as to violate Naeke's law—avoidance of word break after a spondaic fourth foot, strictly observed by the Cyrenaean[67]—in no fewer than thirty-five lines out of 1,184.[68] Allegiance to Alexandrian models has become more selective, and poets no longer feel obliged, if they imitate them in language, to adopt their meter or, if they imitate their meter, to also employ their language. The Oppians are another telling instance. Oppian of Cilicia, author of the elegant *Halieutica*, in fact contents himself with recalling the Cyrenaean poet here and there, without imbuing his style too

---

[63] Cf. [Orph.] *Arg.* 228, 364, 1251, 1265, 1282, and possibly 1136–1141, with Pfeiffer 1949–53: 1.8, 262; Vian 1987: 100, 166–167; Massimilla 1996: 228; Hollis 2009: 185, 284. [Man.] 6.392, ἄκμοσί τ' ἐξέλκοντες ἔτι ζείοντα σίδηρον, may echo Call. *Hy.* 3.55 and 60; [Man.] 6.690, ἐπιμάρτυροι εἶεν, (≈ 728) may come from either Call. *Aet.* fr. 75.48 Pf. or Homer. (See Rengakos 1994: 87.) On the *Met. Pss.*, see Golega 1960: 52–55, though not all of his parallels are relevant; Hollis 2009: 388; Gonnelli 1988 has a more skeptical view of some allegedly Callimachean borrowings.

[64] See Radinger 1895: 28–33; Wifstrand 1926: 55–57; Pfeiffer 1949–1953: 1.77 and 401; Gow and Page 1965: 2.613–614, 631, 644–645, 652–657, 675–676.

[65] Cf. Magnelli 2007: 180–183. On Meleager's meter, see also Ouvré 1894: 207–233; his prosody is far stricter than his inner metric, as Page 1963 showed.

[66] His several Callimachean imitations are gathered by M. Schneider 1882: 21–24; Pfeiffer 1949–1953: 2.131; Tsavari 1990 *passim*; Hunter 2003a: 344–350 = 2008b: 700–708; Amato 2005: 307–317; Hollis 2009: 388. Counillon 2004 investigates in depth the influence of Callimachus' *Hymn to Delos* on Dionysius; Hunter 2004: 227–228 = 2008b: 729–730 acutely points out the Callimachean origin of Dionysius' statements on literature and knowledge. On Dionysius' pervasive Alexandrianism, see also Bowie 1990: 70–79; Hunter 2003a: 350–356 = 2008b: 708–716; Lightfoot 2008.

[67] On the one possible exception at the much-disputed *Hy.* 4.226, see G. Morelli 1964; Mineur 1984: 195–197; Magnelli 1999b: 232; D'Alessio 2007: 159 n. 79. Two less relevant instances are discussed by Magnelli 2002: 77.

[68] Lines 2, 84, 142, 179, 199, 231, 238, 282, 307, 308, 310 (note the cluster), 332, 333, 423, 464, 471, 487, 564, 571, 603, 662, 725, 730, 754, 822, 865, 871, 876, 894, 911, 912, 970, 1020, 1129, 1161. On Dionysius' meter, see Whitby 1994: 105; M. Schneider 1882: 8–20 is still useful on his prosody.

much with Callimachean imitations. His description of the nautilus (1.338-59) predictably looks back to Callimachus' epigram on the same animal (*Ep.* 5 Pf. = 14 GP);[69] other passages are faint echoes or ornamental borrowings,[70] and even the poetological "untrodden paths" of the *Prologue* to the *Aetia* (fr. 1.27-28 Pf. = M.: κελεύθους | [ἀτρίπτο]υς, with Pfeiffer's unavoidable supplement) are exploited to describe nothing more than wayfarers climbing a rugged hill by night (*Halieutica* 4.68, ἀτρίπτοισι κελεύθοις | πλαζόμενοι).[71] In contrast, pseudo-Oppian, the Apamean poet who wrote the *Cynegetica*, reworks the very same passage from the *Prologue* to the *Aetia* to open his poem in an overtly Callimachean way. Callimachus defends his refusal to sing "the deeds of kings and ancient heroes" (fr. 1.3-5 Pf. = M.) and recounts how Apollo instructed him to follow the above-mentioned "untrodden paths"; the Apamean has Artemis, Apollo's sister, proudly saying (*Cynegetica* 1.20-21),

τρηχεῖαν ἐπιστείβωμεν ἀταρπόν,
τὴν μερόπων οὔπω τις ἑῇς ἐπάτησεν ἀοιδαῖς,

Let us tread a rugged path that no mortal has yet trodden with his songs,

and shortly thereafter bidding him "not to tell of the heroes' race... or of the wars of men" (ll. 28-29, μὴ γένος ἡρώων εἴπῃς...μηδὲ μόθους μερόπων). Calliope also appears as the poet's second instructor (l. 17), thus recalling her role in *Aetia* Books 1 and 2 (cf. fr. 7.22 Pf. = 9.22 M.).[72] Pseudo-Oppian, lacking both lightness in style and refinement in meter, is far inferior to the author of the *Halieutica*; yet "despite his technical deficiencies, the Syrian, paradoxically, owes more to the learned Hellenistic tradition than does the Cilician."[73] And he does not

---

[69] Hopkinson 1994a: 186.
[70] See Pfeiffer 1949-53: 1.270 and 423; Hopkinson 1994a: 196; Massimilla 1996: 213 and 227. Other possible hitherto unnoticed instances include Opp. *H.* 2.367, ἀλλ' αὔτως μογέει κενεὸν πόνον (cf. also 5.169), ≈ Call. *Hec.* fr. 118 H.; Opp. *H.* 1.114, μεταπαύεται ἄλμης, ≈ Call. *Hy.* 4.205.
[71] Pfeiffer 1949-53: 1.5; Massimilla 1996: 221. Rebuffat 2001: 85-86 rightly points out that Oppian's allegiance to Alexandrian poetics is quite mild.
[72] See Hollis 1994b: 157 and the detailed analysis by Costanza 1991. Bartley 2003: 170-178 offers a useful commentary on the whole proem. See also Silva Sánchez 2002: 89-98.
[73] Thus Hollis 1994b: 155, pointing out other Callimachean borrowings in the *Cynegetica*: add C. 4.322-23, πίδακα λεξάμενοι...ἥτ' ὀλίγη, κτλ. ≈ Call. *Hy.* 2.112; here the possible echo conveys no poetological meaning. On the literary ambitions of ps.-

hesitate to display a Callimachean attitude in a poem whose inadequacies Callimachus would surely have scorned.

Quintus of Smyrna, author of a *Posthomerica* in fourteen books, and Triphiodorus with his far shorter *Sack of Troy*, also deserve mention here. Triphiodorus' poem shows that Trojan epic was not itself hostile to Alexandrianism. His 691 hexameters—a kind of 'epyllion'—are full of borrowings from Callimachus, as one could expect from so learned and elegant a poet,[74] and his proem, begging Calliope to expound the sack of Troy "with a speedy song" (line 5, ταχείῃ...ἀοιδῇ), "omitting lengthy speech" (line 3, πολὺν διὰ μῦθον ἀνεῖσα), obviously recalls Callimachean poetics.[75] Quintus, on the contrary, writes a *mega biblion* of quite traditional taste, adopting a smoother version of Homeric language (even deprived of those rare and disputed words that Alexandrian poets were so fond of)[76] and avoiding excessive erudition. He nonetheless knows his Callimachus, occasionally exploiting him. Besides imitating his poems, especially the *Hecale* and the *Hymns*,[77] he ventures to describe his alleged poetical investiture in a very Callimachean way. The passage (12.308–313) is basically modeled on Hesiod's *Theogony*, but when he states that the Muses inspired him

πρίν μοι ⟨ἔτ'⟩ ἀμφὶ παρειὰ κατασκίδνασθαι ἴουλον,
Σμύρνης ἐν δαπέδοισι περικλυτὰ μῆλα νέμοντι,

before down shadowed my cheeks, when I was pasturing my famous flocks in the plains of Smyrna,

he clearly alludes to Book 1 of the *Aetia*, where the Muses met Hesiod μῆλα νέμοντι (fr. 2.1 Pf. = 4.1 M.) and Callimachus himself saw them in a dream when he was ἀρτιγένειος, "just growing his beard" (*Scholia*

Oppian, see also Bartley 2003: 13–14; Hollis 2006: 147–149, 153; Whitby 2007; Lightfoot 2008: 26 ("the heady mix of Callimacheanism and rhetoric in the *Kynegetika*").

[74] Cf. Triph. 78–79, 119, 310, 386, 415, 420, 430, 450–451, 513, 557, 637, 643, 656–659, with Gerlaud 1982 *passim*. Add Triph. 237 ≈ Call. fr. 228.40 Pf. (Pfeiffer 1949–53: 1.220); Triph. 342 ≈ Call. *Hy*. 3.248.

[75] Gerlaud 1982: 103. Note also that Triph. 666–667, ἐγὼ δ' ἅ περ ἵππον ἐλάσσω... ἀοιδήν, may stem from Call. *Aet*. fr. 1.5 Pf. = M., if one reads ἐλ[αύνω rather than ἐλ[ίσσω in the latter passage. See Lehnus 1991a; *contra*, Massimilla 1996: 204, and Pretagostini 2006: 19–20; another supplement is proposed by Acosta-Hughes and Stephens 2001.

[76] García Romero 1989 nonetheless points out a possible instance of Quintus' dissenting from Callimachus on a rare Homeric word.

[77] Imitations of the *Hecale* are listed by Hollis 2009: 390. On two borrowings from the *Hymns*, see Campbell 1981: 135–136 and 173; add Q.S. 1.33–34 ≈ Call. *Hy*. 3.14, in a very similar context: see Bornmann 1968: 12–13 for different parallels.

Florentina p. 11 Pf. = p. 71 M.).[78] In the third century AD even the author of a Homeric poem "in many thousands of lines" (cf. *Aet.* fr. 1.4 Pf. = M.) was unwilling to renounce the distinction that Callimachus' poetry could bestow on him.

It would require a very long chapter to gather and discuss a full dossier about Callimachus' influence on Gregory of Nazianzus. Many instances have been pointed out during the past two centuries,[79] and many others surely remain to be. Let us just note that Gregory's Callimachean ζῆλος operates in many ways. He is quite capable of subtle— and sometimes irreverent—allusive strategies: for example, *Carmina* 1.2.2.302, αἴσχεϊ καγχάζοιεν, ὅσαις τέγος ἀκλήϊστον, where he imitates the beginning of the *Hecale* (fr. 2.2 H.), turning the venerable old woman's "open house" into one of prostitutes;[80] or even, from the same *Carmen* 1.2.2 (a poem containing the most remarkable imitations of the Callimachean epyllion), the lines on Elias and the widow from Sarepta (ll. 172–76):

Ἠλίας δὲ κόραξι τράφη, καὶ γραῖαν ἔθρεψε
Σιδονίην τυτθῇσιν ἐνὶ ψεκάδεσσι βίοιο,
οὔ ποτέ γ' ἐν πενιχρῇ σιπύῃ λήγοντος ἀλεύρου,
καὶ κεράμοιο βρύοντος ἀεὶ τόσον ὑγρὸν ἔλαιον,   175
ὅσσον ἀφύσσετο χερσὶ φιλοξείνοιο γυναικός.

Elias was fed by ravens, and then he in turn fed the old Sidonian woman with modest portions of food: meal was never missing from the poor breadbin, and the jug always provided as much liquid oil as the hospitable woman had drawn with her hands.

Gregory exploits the *Hecale* to rewrite a biblical episode (1 Kings 17.6–16) after the manner of Callimachus, as one may see in *Hecale* fragments 35.1 H., ἐκ δ' ἄρτους σιπύηθεν ἅλις κατέθηκεν ἑλοῦσα, and 80.4 H., φιλοξείνοιο καλιῆς.[81] Some details of the hospitality theme

---

[78] See Vian 1963–69: 3.101 n. 1; Hopkinson 1994a: 106; Massimilla 1996: 243; Bär 2009: 76–78. Quintus echoes the *Prologue* of the *Aetia* elsewhere: see Lehnus 2001: 290.

[79] See Naeke 1842–45: 1.240–249; Cataudella 1928; Wyss 1949: 193 n. 43; Pfeiffer 1949–53: 2.132; Kambylis 1982; Massimilla 1996 *passim*; Tissoni 1997; Hollis 1998 and 2002: 43–49; Simelidis 2009: 30–38, 53–54. Further parallels can be found in recent commentaries on Gregory's poems.

[80] As Zehles and Zamora 1996: 141–142 aptly remark. Cf. Hollis 2009: 138; the parallel was previously pointed out by Ludwich 1887: 238.

[81] See Zehles and Zamora 1996: 107–108; Hollis 2009: 172 and 353. Note the instrumental ἐνί + dative in line 173, a touch of biblical Greek (see Blass, Debrunner, and Rehkopf 1976: §195) in so learned a passage.

are quite similar—the poor widow and her humble meal—but Gregory turns the situation upside down: here we find the extraordinary man feeding the woman who gave him hospitality. Does the allusion convey the message that the deeds of biblical prophets were far greater than those of pagan mythical heroes?

Yet other imitations probably have a true programmatic scope. Gregory opens his (paradoxically huge) collection under the sign of Callimachus: the very beginning of the first poem, ἀλλ' ἀπὸ τῆλε | φεύγετε, ὅστις ἀλιτρός (*Carm.* 1.1.1.8–9), clearly alludes to Callimachus *Hymn* 2.2, and Gregory's καθαροῖσιν | ἠὲ καθαιρομένοισιν (ll. 9–10) matches Callimachus on Apollo's showing himself only to ὅτις ἐσθλός (*Hymn* 2.9).[82] One may even wonder whether Gregory's "small wings" (τυτθαῖς πτερύγεσσι, l. 2) owe something not just to the well-known Platonic motif of the winged soul, or to Anacreon (*PMG* 378),[83] but also to Callimachus' imagery of the poet as cicada—itself of course derived from Plato—in the *Prologue* to the *Aetia*. Be this as it may, the *Reply to the Telchines* appears to be well impressed in Gregory's mind: he often reworks Callimachus' metaphor of the "narrow path,"[84] and at *Carmina* 1.1.11.14–16 he opposes his own ὀλιγόστιχα...γράμματα to the πολλαὶ χιλιάδες ἐπέων of the νήπιοι (ll. 1, 3: cf. νήϊδες at l. 2 of Callimachus' *Prologue*) who do not venerate Christ's incarnation.[85] (Add that in a letter of his he follows Callimachus in blaming Antimachus' alleged prolixity.)[86] It must be said that this is quite at odds with Gregory's literary output: he wrote no long epic poem, but the vastness of his poetical corpus (more than seventeen thousand lines) shows that, despite such commendable aims, he did not really practice ὀλιγοστιχία. Christos Simelidis has acutely pointed out the reasons why Gregory was nonetheless so fond of Callimachean poetics: Callimachus' "reworking of old material with the intention of creating something new certainly appealed to Gregory, who wanted to write a new kind of classicising verse...Like the Hellenistic poets, he was concerned both to indicate his continuity with the literary past and to display his independence from it," striving "to demonstrate his different

---

[82] So Kambylis 1982; see also Sykes in Moreschini and Sykes 1997: 81, and Simelidis 2009: 32–33.
[83] As has been suggested: see Sykes in Moreschini and Sykes 1997: 78.
[84] Massimilla 1996: 222 collects Gregory's passages.
[85] See Wyss 1949: 193 n. 43; Massimilla 1996: 204. Other echoes of the *Reply to the Telchines* in Gregory are listed by Hollis 2002: 43–44.
[86] *Epist.* 54, λέγω...πολὺν τὸν Ἀντίμαχον (test. 27 Matthews).

religious outlook."[87] In Gregory's eyes, the Cyrenaean poet's claim of originality was both a literary and an ethical value—as it was, after all, for Callimachus himself.

It is still possibile to identify further Callimachean influences in Gregory's poems. Some of them may even help to solve textual problems in Callimachus, such as that in a famous passage of *Hymn* 4 (ll. 249-51):

ἡ μὲν ἔφη· κύκνοι δὲ †θεοῦ μέλποντες ἀοιδοί†
Μηόνιον Πακτωλὸν ἐκυκλώσαντο λιπόντες   250
ἑβδομάκις περὶ Δῆλον, ἐπήεισαν δὲ λοχείῃ...

So she spoke; and the swans, †the god's singing minstrels,† leaving Maeonian Pactolus circled seven times around Delos and sang in honor of the childbirth...

There can be little doubt that line 249 is corrupt.[88] Among several emendations hitherto proposed, Meineke's θεοῦ μέλλοντες ἄοζοι ("the god's future servants") stands out for both its cleverness and its elegance.[89] Did Gregory read such a text in his copy of Callimachus? Compare *Carmina* 1.2.1 (ll. 722-23):

...ὥς κεν δὴ μεγάλοιο Θεοῦ τελέθοντες ὀπηδοὶ
γηθόσυνοι μέλπωμεν ἑόρτιον ὕμνον ἄνακτι,

...so that we, having become servants of great God, may gladly sing a festal hymn to the Lord.

Albeit Gregory's primary source is Plato *Phaedrus* 248c, ψυχὴ θεῷ συνοπαδὸς γενομένη, both the song's theme and the shape of line 722 suggest that he was also influenced by this Callimachean passage in some form like the one that Meineke conjectured.[90] Similarly, Adrian Hollis has used Gregory's *Carmen* 1.2.14.101, οὗτος ὁ βρισαύχην,

---

[87] Simelidis 2009: 32–34, the best assessment on tradition and innovation in Gregory's poetry.

[88] See Mineur 1984: 207–208; D'Alessio 2007: 162 n. 82.

[89] Ruhnken already proposed and immediately dismissed ἄοζοι, whereas Reiske tried θεοῦ μέλλοντος ἀΐσσειν. For a detailed survey of all emendations, together with a new one, see De Stefani 1997: 96–98.

[90] So far as we know, this Callimachean echo has hitherto gone unnoticed; Sundermann 1991: 233 simply quotes the Plato passage. We are aware that Gregory's μέλπωμεν may reflect the transmitted μέλποντες in the Callimachean line. One could even revive Ruhnken's θεοῦ μέλποντες ὀπηδοί, closer to Gregory's alleged imitation if less elegant than Meineke's conjecture.

tentatively to solve another notorious crux in Callimachus, *Epigram* 44.6 Pf. (= 9.6 GP).[91] Further discoveries probably await scholars amid Gregory's πολυστιχία.

Nonnus' Jeweled Callimachus

Remarkable as Gregory's ζῆλος Καλλιμάχειος could be, like that of Dionysius Periegetes and Triphiodorus, the greatest champion of Callimacheanism in the imperial age surely was Nonnus of Panopolis. Both his *Dionysiaca* and his *Paraphrase of St John's Gospel* are full of Callimachean echoes and allusions. Much has already been pointed out;[92] much must still lie hidden, especially in the immense poem on the deeds of Dionysus.[93] Callimachus permeates the *Dionysiaca*, providing it with rare myths and elegant phrases, but also inspiring it with humor and, in spite of the poem's size and style, a certain lightness of touch—an 'Alexandrian' refashioning of large-scale epic that is best understood in the light of Nonnus' ambition to surpass Homer rather

---

[91] Hollis 1998.

[92] Keydell 1959, in the *apparatus fontium* of his renowned edition of Nonnus' *Dionysiaca*, quotes Callimachus 147 times. (Montes Cala 1994-95: 64 usefully gathers the evidence.) Other parallels are to be found in O. Schneider 1870-73; in modern Callimachean commentaries (cf., e.g., Pfeiffer 1949-53: 2.136; Massimilla 1996 *passim*; Hollis 2009: 389-390, 426); in both the great Budé edition of the *Dionysiaca* directed by the late Francis Vian and its smaller Italian twin (Gigli Piccardi 2003; Gonnelli 2003; Agosti 2004; Accorinti 2004); in recent commentaries on Nonnus' *Paraphrase* (Livrea 1989a; Accorinti 1996; Livrea 2000; De Stefani 2002; Agosti 2003; C. Greco 2004; Caprara 2005). Further discussions include Lloyd-Jones 1961: 23-24; Cazzaniga 1963: 630-632; Hollis 1976 (142-146), 1992 (13 n. 61), 1994a (43-44, 48-49, 58-59), 1994c, and 2006 (150-151); Tissoni 1994 and 1998: 23-25; Shorrock 2001: 146-152, 165-166; De Stefani 2006: 16-21.

[93] A few examples, not hitherto pointed out: Nonn. *D.* 1.139, ἄστατα νυμφοκόμοιο μετήϊεν ἴχνια ταύρου, ≈ Call. *Hy.* 6.9 (imitated by Nonnus at *D.* 3.324 as well; see Hopkinson 1984a: 88); *D.* 1.231, ἔβρεμε δ' ἠχῇ, ≈ Call. *Hy.* 3.245; *D.* 1.514-15, ἄρμενον...κατέκρυφε κοιλάδι πέτρῃ, ≈ Call. *Hec.* fr. 9 H. (Nonnus rightly interpreting Callimachus' κολουραίη as "hollow"); *D.* 11.54, ἄλλοτε κυκλώσας παλάμας, ≈ Call. *Aet.* fr. 110.53 Pf. (a passage that Nonnus reworks several other times; see Montes Cala 1994-1995: 65-74); *D.* 16.224, παρθενικὴν μέμψασθε, φίλαι δρύες· εἴπατε, πέτραι, ≈ Call. *Hy.* 4.82-85; *D.* 16.399, ἐκ δὲ γάμου Βρομίοιο, ≈ Call. *Aet.* fr. 75.50 Pf.; *D.* 20.320-21, ὅπῃ νόθα τέκνα γυναῖκες | ἀστεροπῇ τίκτουσι, ≈ Call. *Hy.* 4.241-43; *D.* 38.145, τικτομένῳ κελάδησε μέλος πατρώϊος αἰθήρ, ≈ Call. *Hy.* 4.257-58; *D.* 45.306-07, ὀξέϊ θύρσῳ | ἄκρον ὄρος πλήξασα νεοσχιδές, ≈ Call. *Hy.* 1.31.

than just imitate him.[94] Even in one of his most Homeric passages, the catalogue of Dionysus' allies (filling Book 13 entire; the invocation of Homer in lines 49–52 is well known), Nonnus draws on Callimachus for an un-Homeric section on Sicily in lines 309–92, blatantly alluding to the corresponding episode of the *Aetia*,[95] and probably owing much to Callimachean technique.[96] It goes without saying that such an obsession with the Cyrenaean poet operates in many ways and at many levels. Nonnus may use Callimachus to update Homer, for example, at *Dionysiaca* 36.98–100,

> ...μὴ Ἐννοσίγαιος ἀράσσων
> γαῖαν ἱμασσομένην ῥοθίων ἐνοσίχθονι παλμῷ
> ἁρμονίην κόσμοιο μετοχλίσσειε τριαίνῃ,   100
>
> ...fearing lest the Earthshaker, beating the land lashed by the earthquake impact of his waves, might overthrow the order of the universe with his trident,

where he expands *Iliad* 20.62–63, μή οἱ...γαῖαν ἀναρρήξειε Ποσειδάων ἐνοσίχθων,[97] by means of a hitherto unnoticed reworking of Callimachus *Hymn* 4.30–33.[98] And he often blends together echoes from different Callimachean passages, as for example in *Dionysiaca* 2.237–238,

> ὣς φαμένης σκιοειδὲς ἑὸν πτερὸν Ὕπνος ἑλίξας
> εὔνασεν ἀμπνείουσαν ὅλην φύσιν,
>
> So she spoke; and Sleep, moving his shadowy wing, put all breathing nature to rest,

---

[94] On this point, see Vian 1991b; Hopkinson 1994b; Frangoulis 1995; Agosti 2004: 669–675.

[95] D. 13.316–17, from Call. *Aet.* fr. 43.42 Pf. = 50.42 M. (See Vian 1995: 128, 233; Massimilla 1996: 332.) Were Callimachus' text less fragmentary, we could perhaps detect more allusions to it in Nonnus.

[96] "The various sections of Nonnus' catalogue abound with aetiological and anthropological learning" (Hopkinson 1994b: 28). The list of the cities allows him to allude briefly to rare myths without his usual expansion, to contract into some fifteen lines (105–119) the content of Euripides' two plays on Iphigenia, and to etymologize Αὐλίς (111–112); all in all, it is a reworking of the Homeric Κατάλογος in the spirit of Callimachus' list of Sicilian cities.

[97] Gigli Piccardi 1985: 191. On Homer's and Nonnus' theomachies, see Hopkinson 1994b: 24–25; Agosti 2004: 611–614; Frangoulis and Gerlaud 2006: 65–80; Vian 1988 brilliantly illustrates Nonnus' allegorical perspective.

[98] Compare Callimachus' μέγας θεὸς οὔρεα θείνων | ἄορι τριγλώχινι (30–31) and ἐκ νεάτων ὤχλισσε (33). Nonnus apparently identifies the μέγας θεός with Poseidon, and the ἄορ τριγλώχιν with his trident (which is not absolutely secure: see Mineur 1984: 77–78). Note that he imitates this passage at D. 4.455 and 6.290–91 also (O. Schneider 1870–73: 1.261; Keydell 1959: 1.104).

imitating Callimachus *Hymn* 4.234, οὐδ' ὅτε οἱ ληθαῖον ἐπὶ πτερὸν ὕπνος ἐρείσει, but possibly also *Hecale* fragment 74.21 H., τὴν μὲν ἄρ' ὡς φαμένην ὕπνος λάβε, τὴν δ' ἀΐουσαν.[99] Or again, *Dionysiaca* 25.18, Ἀονίης ἀΐω κιθάρης κτύπον· εἴπατε, Μοῦσαι, κτλ. draws on both Callimachus *Hymn* 5.14, συρίγγων ἀΐω φθόγγον ὑπαξόνιον, and *Hymn* 4.82, εἴπατε, Μοῦσαι[100]—a passage that Nonnus appears to have enjoyed very much, if we are to judge from how often he alludes to it in the *Dionysiaca*.[101] Yet Nonnus' most interesting device is his habit of scattering allusions and imitations of his model over a whole episode. He often inserts words or phrases clearly borrowed from Callimachus at the beginning of a narrative section, in order to give the reader a first clue; then, after some lines, he inserts another allusion to either the same passage or another work by the same author, and does it yet again later, so that the whole episode becomes Callimachean. A telling instance is the passage on Cadmus going to Electra's palace (*D.* 3.82–122), sprinkled with three different imitations of the *Hecale*—in the same order that the passages alluded to have in Callimachus' poem.[102]

A Callimachean scene that Nonnus appears to have been very fond of is the beginning of the *Hymn to Artemis*, with the baby goddess asking Zeus to grant her a number of privileges. An obvious imitation is Dionysus' lengthy speech to Nicaea, an Artemis-like hunting girl (Ἄρτεμις ἄλλη, 15.171), in *Dionysiaca* 16.75–143. The first clue comes in line 102, σοὶ κύνας εἰν ἑνὶ πάντας ἐμοῦ τάχα Πανὸς ὀπάσσω, recalling Callimachus *Hymn* 3.90–97, on the dogs that Pan gave to Artemis,[103] and possibly *Hymn* 3.33, τρὶς δέκα τοι πτολίεθρα καὶ οὐχ ἕνα πύργον ὀπάσσω. A few lines later we find a longer Callimachean passage (*Dionysiaca* 16.126–130):

---

[99] On the former passage, see Vian 1976: 176; as for the latter, the Nonnian imitation has not hitherto been pointed out.

[100] Both parallels have apparently gone unnoticed.

[101] Another well-known instance of Nonnus' combinatory technique is the episode of Brongus at *D.* 17.37–86: the poet evokes two Callimachean texts on the hospitality theme, explicitly portraiting Brongus as a new Molorchus (l. 52) and at the same time alluding to the *Hecale* (ll. 54–56 ≈ Call. *Hec.* fr. 36 H.). See Vian 1991a: 592–593 = 2005: 467–468; Hollis 2009: 352.

[102] At the beginning of the episode, l. 89 ≈ Call. *Hec.* fr. 48.5 H., then l. 106 ≈ *Hec.* fr. 68 H., and again l. 119 ≈ *Hec.* fr. 74.9 H.; the detail of the speaking crow evokes both the *Hecale* and A.R. 3.927–39. Pfeiffer 1949–53: 1.241 noticed the cluster of Callimachean echoes; see also Hollis 1976: 145.

[103] Thus Gerlaud 1994: 229, pointing out other Callimachean echoes in the following lines.

δμωίδας ἑξήκοντα χορίτιδας εἰς σὲ κομίσσω,
ὄφρα χορὸν νήριθμον ὀπάονα σεῖο τελέσσω,
ἀμφιπόλοις ἰσόμετρον ὀρειάδος Ἰοχεαίρης,
εἴκελον Ὠκεανοῖο θυγατράσι, μή σοι ἐρίζῃ
Ἄρτεμις ἀγρώσσουσα.   130

> I will bring you sixty dancing maids to complete the innumerable chorus of your servants, as many as those of the Archeress of the mountains, as many as the daughters of Ocean, so that hunting Artemis may not compete with you.

Here lines 126–29 allude to Artemis' request for "sixty dancing Ocean nymphs", ἑξήκοντα χορίτιδας Ὠκεανίνας and ἀμφιπόλους εἴκοσι νύμφας ("twenty nymphs as handmaids") at Callimachus *Hymn* 3.13–15 (the comparison explicitly declares Nonnus' model), and lines 129–30 reverse *Hymn* 3.7, ἵνα μή μοι Φοῖβος ἐρίζῃ, "so that Phoebus may not rival me", adding an echo of *Hymn* 2.60, Ἄρτεμις ἀγρώσσουσα.[104] Another relevant, if less obvious and hitherto unnoticed, instance of Nonnus' exploiting of the same Callimachean episode occurs in *Dionysiaca* 10.292–307, when Dionysus prays Zeus to grant him Ampelus' love:

νεῦσον ἐμοὶ φιλέοντι μίαν χάριν, ὦ Φρύγιε Ζεῦ·
νηπιάχῳ μὲν ἔειπεν ἐμὴ τροφὸς εἰσέτι Ῥείη,
ὡς στεροπὴν Ζαγρῆϊ πόρες, προτέρῳ Διονύσῳ,
εἰσέτι παππάζοντι, τεὴν πυρόεσσαν ἀκωκήν...   295
σεῖο δ' ἐγὼ πρηστῆρος ἀναίνομαι αἰθέριον πῦρ,   298
οὐ νέφος, οὐ βροντῆς ἐθέλω κτύπον...
Ναίω Μαιονίην· τί γὰρ αἰθέρι καὶ Διονύσῳ;   307

> Grant one grace to me in love, O Phrygian Zeus! When I was a child, my nurse, Rhea, told me that you accorded lightning, your spear of fire, to Zagreus, the first Dionysus, while yet a baby... but I refuse your lightning's heavenly fire; I do not want clouds and thunder.... In Maeonia I dwell: What has the sky to do with Dionysus?

Here we find no exact borrowing; yet the theme of the god asking Zeus for his peculiar privileges and refusing more solemn gifts is the same as in the *Hymn to Artemis*, and several phrases in fact rewrite Callimachus' text: line 295 is comparable to Callimachus *Hymn* 3.5 (παῖς ἔτι κουρίζουσα); line 298, to *Hymn* 3.8–9 (οὔ σε φαρέτρην | οὐδ' αἰτέω μέγα τόξον); line 307, to *Hymn* 3.19–20 (σπαρνὸν γὰρ ὅτ' Ἄρτεμις ἄστυ κάτεισιν· | οὔρεσιν οἰκήσω). It is unlikely that Non-

---

[104] Bornmann 1968: 9; Gerlaud 1994: 230.

nus' reworking of the Callimachean episode could escape his most learned readers.[105] Extensive imitations of *Hymn* 3 occur at least twice more in the *Dionysiaca*, one in book 36.48-57, in the first part of Hera's contemptuous exhortation to Artemis to leave the battle of the gods and turn back to her usual hunting;[106] and another in 9.169-83, when both Rhea and Zeus laugh with joy seeing Dionysus' prodigious precocity as a hunter of wild beasts.[107] Nonnus' well-known interest in children and in gods' childhoods may account for his fondness for Callimachus' *Hymn to Artemis*, but we must keep in mind that this very interest, in turn, is a product of Nonnus' literary affiliations. Young heroes and extraordinary children could scarcely fail to evoke Hellenistic poetry, and above all, Callimachus.[108]

These and other instances of large-scale imitation show how Nonnus adapts Callimachus to his own poetics. Rather than just scattering here and there a multitude of intertextual jewels, as Gregory of Nazianzus often does, he tends to rewrite Callimachus into his own baroque, 'jeweled' style.[109] Being an innovator in many elements, including language and meter,[110] he surely felt sympathetic to Callimachean poetry; at the same time, he did not hesitate to update it in his self-confident effort to "compete with both ancient and modern" (*Dionysiaca* 25.27: νέοισι καὶ ἀρχεγόνοισιν ἐρίζων). If Callimachus in his *Iambi* used the poetical mask of a modern, refashioned Hipponax, Nonnus aims at being not just the modern Homer but also the modern Callimachus.

---

[105] Shorrock 2001: 131 offers a very different, poetological reading of this passage.
[106] Cf. l. 48, θηρία βάλλε, ≈ Call. *Hy.* 3.153; l. 49, σκοπέλων ἐπίβηθι, ≈ *Hy.* 3.20; l. 50, ἐνδρομίδας, ≈ *Hy.* 3.16; the mention of hares and deer at lines 54-56 looks back to *Hy.* 3.154-156. (See Bernardini Marzolla 1952: 193; Agosti 2004: 624-625; Frangoulis and Gerlaud 2006: 149.) Frangoulis and Gerlaud 2006: 73 n. 18 rightly add that at the end of the episode, when Apollo rescues his sister, the latter's childish attitude indeed recalls the Callimachean hymn.
[107] D. 9.177, σμερδαλέους δὲ λέοντας ἔτι ζώοντας ἐρύσσας, stems from Call. *Hy.* 3.91-93 (Chrétien 1985: 116). Add that l. 179, on Dionysus' dragging lions "clutching a couple of feet in each hand" (δίζυγας ἀμφοτέρῃσι πόδας παλάμῃσι πιέζων), reworks and even exaggerates the scene of *Hy.* 3.148-51, where the gods laugh at Heracles dragging bulls or wild boars by the hind foot.
[108] Ambühl 2005 is now the standard reference on this topic.
[109] To adopt the definition coined by Roberts 1989 for the Latin poetry of late antiquity.
[110] This obviously does not mean that Nonnian poetry came from nothing, as recent scholarship has deservedly stressed. (See Whitby 1994.) But Nonnus was proud of his achievement: see, inter alia, Agosti 2001: 95-98, who reads—rightly, in our view—*Par. Jo.* 21.142, βίβλους...νεοτευχέας, as a literary seal of the new style.

Nonnus' followers—Pamprepius, Christodorus, Musaeus, Colluthus, John of Gaza, Paul the Silentiary, Julian the Egyptian, Macedonius Consul, Agathias—predictably continue to imitate the Cyrenaean poet.[111] Yet their debt to him is in no way so great as Nonnus': the author on whom they fashion their style and their poetics is none other than Nonnus himself, "the most influential Greek poet since Callimachus."[112] Their exploitation of Hellenistic poetry is due to both their allegiance to Nonnus' literary taste and their command of Greek poetical tradition; none of them appears to be much concerned with giving a true Callimachean flavor to his own verses. The revolution of the new style has now become a trend; and Callimachus, fascinating as he may still be, no longer has a foundational role.

A Glance at Byzantine Poetry

Callimachus survives for centuries after late antiquity, but his influence essentially disappears. Grammarians and lexicographers continue to mention him as a source of rare words, morphological peculiarities, and unknown mythical tales; and prose writers sometimes try to make their orations or their letters more glamorous by inserting into them a brief quotation from his works. (In most cases, direct knowledge of Callimachus' poems is at least very doubtful.)[113] But very few Byzantine poets prove either to be interested in Callimachus or to have read him at all. Leo the Philosopher, one of the outstanding figures in the ninth-century renaissance, may echo the *Aetia* at lines 88–89 of his poem on Job,[114]

---

[111] Pamprepius: Livrea 1992: 149–150; add fr. 4.22 Livrea ≈ Call. *Hy.* 2.19. Christodorus: Tissoni 2000a and 2000b: 67. Musaeus: Kost 1971: 164, 263, 357, 396; Hopkinson 1994a: 138, 153, 163–165; Cucchiarelli 2002 (if καθελκέμεν is to be read at Musae. 288). Colluthus: Livrea 1968: 56, 152, 168–172; Hollis 2006: 154–155; Magnelli 2008: 152, 160. John of Gaza: Pfeiffer 1949–1953: 1.271, 402, adding Io. Gaz. 1.45, γεροντικὸν εἶδος ἀείρων, ≈ Call. *Ep.* 1.7 Pf. = 54.7 GP. Paul the Silentiary: Pfeiffer 1949–53: 2.137; Hopkinson 1994a: 87; De Stefani 2008: 209 and 2010 *passim*. Julian: Pfeiffer 1949–53: 1.306, 359. Macedonius: Madden 1995: 200; Hollis 2009: 180 (less certain). Agathias: Mattsson 1942: 38, 43, 47, 95–96; Viansino 1967: 15–16 (though some of his parallels are not very relevant indeed); Averil Cameron 1970: 22; Marinone 1997: 97; Garulli 2007: 333–334.
[112] Alan Cameron 1982: 227.
[113] See Pontani's excellent assessment in this volume.
[114] *Editio princeps* by Westerink 1986.

ὧδε γὰρ ἐκ μήτρας ὑπὸ ἥλιον ἦλθον ἀνείμων,
χείρεσιν οὔτι φέρων, οὔτ' ἄρ τέκος οὔτε τι ἄλλο,

Thus came I naked from my mother's womb to the light of day, carrying nothing in my hands, neither sons nor anything else,

possibly inspired by the lines on the Graces in Callimachus *Aetia* fragment 7.9–10 Pf. (= 9.9–10 M.):

]ες ἀνείμον[ες] ͵ὡ͵ς ἀπὸ κόλπου
μητρὸς Ἐλειθυίη͵ς ἤλθετ͵ε β͵ο͵υλομένης

...naked, as when you came forth from your mother's womb with the good will of Eileithyia.

Both theme and vocabulary—above all the uncommon ἀνείμων,[115] but also ἀπὸ κόλπου μητρὸς...ἤλθετε ≈ ἐκ μήτρας...ἦλθον—conspire to suggest that Leo may have had Callimachus' verses in mind when rewriting LXX Job 1.21, αὐτὸς γυμνὸς ἐξῆλθον ἐκ κοιλίας μητρός μου, in a more poetic fashion, but obviously this does not mean that he expected his readers to know the *Aetia* as well.[116] And it is hard to say whether the first couplet of a ninth-century epigram in praise of Photius (possibly written by Constantine the Sicilian)[117] was really modeled on Callimachus *Aetia* fragment 112.8–9 Pf. as Paul Maas once assumed.[118] A more intriguing instance comes from the pen of Theodore Prodromus, one of the most learned and competent classicizing poets of the twelfth century. Two lines of his, *Carmina historica* 30.274–75,[119]

---

[115] A Homeric *hapax* (*Od.* 3.348), ἀνείμων after Callimachus appears thrice in Philo (Colson 1941: 544–545), once in Gregory of Nazianzus (*Carm.* 2.2.3.144), four times in Nonnus, and in a handful of passages from Patristic and early Byzantine prose (Eusebius, Cyril of Alexandria, John of Damascus). None of these texts has to do with birth.

[116] For two other passages in Leo's poem a Callimachean model is even more speculative (Magnelli 2004b: 196 n. 75).

[117] Republished by Westerink 1986: 201. The dispute about its author need not detain us here: see Westerink 1986: 197, with previous literature in n. 18; Alan Cameron 1993: 247–248; Lauxtermann 2003: 106–107.

[118] Maas 1921. Mercati 1923–1925: 235 n. 1 = 1970: 1.296 n. 29 was quite skeptical on this point.

[119] Hörandner 1974: 356.

καὶ σμῆνος ἀναρίθμητον ἀθροίσαντες ἐκεῖθεν
κομίζουσι τῷ βασιλεῖ. σῶτερ Χριστέ, τοῦ πλήθους

And gathering from there an immense swarm, they take it to the emperor.
O Savior Christ, what a crowd!

feature striking affinities with Callimachus *Iambi* fragment 191.26–28 Pf.,

ὤπολλον, ὦνδρες, ὡς παρ' αἰπόλῳ μυῖαι
ἢ σφῆκες ἐκ γῆς ἢ ἀπὸ θύματος Δελφ[οί,]
εἰληδὸν [ἐσ]μεύουσιν· ὦ Ἑκάτη πλήθευς

O Apollo, the men swarm round like flies on a goatherd, or wasps springing forth from earth, or the Delphians leaving a sacrifice: O Hecate, what a crowd!

a passage that has not survived in the indirect tradition and is known to us only in POxy 7.1011.[120] Michael Choniates, some fifty years later, was still able to read Callimachus' *Hecale*, *Aetia*, and *Hymns*: Were the neglected *Iambi* also available in twelfth-century Byzantium,[121] at least to so tireless a bookworm as Theodore Prodromus?

Other Callimachean influences on Prodromus' vast poetical corpus are feeble and uncertain:[122] the same applies to the iambic novel *Drosilla and Charicles* by Prodromus' follower Nicetas Eugenianus.[123] The one and only Byzantine poet really fond of Callimachus is Michael

---

[120] This was first noted by Gallavotti 1949: 366; cf. Pfeiffer 1949–53: 1.504.

[121] The epigram written for a late-antique or Byzantine collection of Callimachean texts (test. 23 Pf., once discussed by Reitzenstein 1891) lists the *Hymns*, the *Hecale*, the *Aetia*, the lost *Ibis*, and an obscure riddle-poem concerning Athena but significantly does not mention the *Iambi*.

[122] Theod. Prodr. *Calend. iamb.* 17 March, θεοῦ τὸν ἄνθρωπόν σε τίς μέλψει λόγος; (Acconcia Longo 1983: 117), may or may not be related to Call. *Iamb.* fr. 193.37–38 Pf. Two further doubtful instances are pointed out by Tziatzi-Papagianni 1993–94: 365, 370; add *Tetrast.* VT 32b.2, ἦστο δ' ἐνὶ τριόδῳ (Papagiannis 1997: 2.39), ≈ Call. *Hy.* 6.114 (cf. Thgn. 911, al.); *Tetrast.* VT 218b.3, τό σοι ἐς γάμον ἄρτυνε πατήρ (Papagiannis 1997: 2.228–29; v.l. ἄρτυε), ≈ Call. *Hy.* 6.78 (different syntax; see also *Od.* 4.770–771).

[123] Conca 1990 points out Nic. Eug. 1.243–44, ὀφθαλμὸν λίχνον | ἐπεμβαλεῖ σοι, ≈ Call. fr. 571.1 Pf. (among other parallels) and Nic. Eug. 6.223, βαρύβρομον οἶδμα θαλάσσης, ≈ Call. *Hec.* fr. dub. 370 Pf. (But Nicetas may depend rather on Nonnus and Gregory of Nazianzus, and the fragment's authorship is very doubtful; see Hollis 2009: 321.) We would not rule out the possibilities that Nic. Eug. 3.48–49, ὅμως ἐπειδὴ καρδίαν ἐλαφρύνει | τὸ τοὺς κατ' αὐτὴν ἐξερεύγεσθαι λόγους, echoes Call. fr. 714 Pf. (thus supporting Pfeiffer's brilliant emendation ἐξερύγῃ at l. 4) and that Nic. Eug. 7.199–200, τὰ γοῦν καθ' ἡμᾶς, ὥσπερ ᾔτησας, γύναι, | ἔχεις μαθοῦσα, owes something to Call. *Hec.* fr. 40.3 H.

Choniates (ca. 1138–ca. 1222), the learned archbishop of Athens,[124] who exploits the *Aetia*, the *Hymns*, and above all the *Hecale* very often in both his poetry and his prose, reusing Callimachean words and phrases as well as images and mythical themes. We will not list here the evidence, easily available elsewhere.[125] It has been noted that he never mentions the Cyrenaean poet by name, and some—not to say "most"—of his allusions to Callimachus surely were hard to identify even for the most learned among his (few?) readers.[126] It rather was, we think, a matter of cultural pride no less than of literary taste. Writing such hexameters as ἡσυχίης τόδ' ἄθυρμ' ἐμὸν ἡδέ τε λέσχη μακρά or δουλοσυνάων ἀργαλέα προταμὼν ζυγόδεσμα,[127] Michael could hardly aim at being the Byzantine Callimachus: nonetheless it is reasonable to assume that a man so proud of his education, utterly despising both the ignorant Athenians of his age and, even worse, the Latins, could not but sympathize with the refined poetry and elitist attitude of the great Alexandrian. In the age of the Fourth Crusade, when the very foundations of Greek identity appeared to waver—or better said, the foundations of what educated Byzantine men assumed to be their Greek identity—a nostalgic man of letters found in his Callimachus the symbol of the glorious literary heritage of the past.

---

[124] On him, see Stadtmüller 1934; N.G. Wilson 1983: 204–206; Kolovou 1999; Pontani in this volume.

[125] Michael's borrowings from the *Hecale*, including some not detected before, are carefully recorded by Hollis 2009 (see also Hollis 2002: 49–51); on the *Aetia*, see Pfeiffer 1922: 113–120 and 1949–53: 1.30, 499, 510; Massimilla 1996: 92, 201, 258–259. That he also knew the *Hymns* was suggested by Magnelli 1999b: 230, then demonstrated beyond any doubt by Hollis 2002: 49.

[126] To some extent at least, he was "playing a solipsistic game" (Hollis 2002: 50).

[127] The first and the last line, respectively, of his major poetical output, the *Theano* in 457 hexameters (Lambros 1879–80: 2.375 and 390).

CHAPTER TWENTY-SEVEN

ARTE ALLUSIVA: PASQUALI AND ONWARD

Mario Citroni

ABSTRACT

Pasquali's "Arte allusiva" presupposes the contemporary philological debate, especially in Germany, about the originality of Latin poetry. The theoretical aspect of the question, i.e. that works admittedly modelled on other works may possess their own artistic quality, had been widely discussed by the Italian school of aesthetics. Pasquali's article combines these debates in an original approach. He grants to allusion the full dignity of an artistic process with its own specific prerogatives: allusion evokes a different, more ancient world in a modern text, and thus confronts tradition, recovering and reforming it for a contemporary setting. Allusion appears as peculiar to a production that confronts its own present with a past of artistic traditions possessing a marked significance for authors and public, typically the case for Hellenistic poetry and all Latin literature. Recent theories of intertextuality, and the intertextual analysis conducted today on ancient texts often make reference to Pasquali, reinterpreting the positions that he elaborated in different paths, which are here identified and briefly described.

The concept of allusion, variously recast within the broader frame of intertextuality, is today widely considered an indispensable instrument of literary analysis. Particularly in the study of texts in which the interconnections with a variety of other preexisting texts respond to a clear and determined compositional strategy, the assumption on the critic's part of a method of approach capable of giving an account of the complexity of diverse intertextual dynamics acquires a crucial importance. Such is typically the case with Hellenistic poets, and especially Callimachus, who are emblematic of cultivated poetry in the Western literary tradition, and for whose analysis the intertextual dimension and types of allusion are today, in a sense, the main focus of scholarship.

In classical studies, a pioneering role, or even that of *primus inventor* of an intertextual approach, is usually attributed to Giorgio Pasquali as a result of his article "Arte allusiva" (1942). The image of Pasquali as a pioneer of intertextuality extends even beyond the terrain of classicists. As will become clear in these pages, I too believe that Pasquali's contribution was important and innovative, but it is not easy to determine in what elements its novelty consists and to detect the reasons why his article has come to have such an important position in subsequent scholarly discussion. In the first instance, one must consider that "Arte allusiva" is a short article that appeared in a journal for a nonspecialist readership. *L'Italia Che Scrive* was a monthly journal of book reviews and a few brief articles, designed to give information about contemporary literary production and aspects of intellectual debate. Thus the article appeared in the context of a popular production, a format Pasquali employed sometimes, always in a brief and episodic form. This does not mean that he attributed little importance to the subject; rather he believed in the role of a serious popularization. His student Sebastiano Timpanaro reveals that in the academic year 1940–41, Pasquali held a course on the *Georgics* and a seminar on Ennius in which the central connecting thread was precisely *arte allusiva* (Timpanaro 1973: 190). The article thus mirrored a problem that was at this time very much on Pasquali's mind as a scholar and teacher, but he treated it in a discursive way, without notes or bibliographic references, in a form calculated to arouse the interest of the cultured reader, but not one that allowed systematic depth of treatment: a surprising circumstance for an article destined to become an essential point of reference, if only an initial one, in a refined theoretical debate.

The contents of "Arte allusiva" are often imprecisely cited, overlooking aspects that I find among the most innovative and important; hence it will be useful to summarize the piece briefly. Pasquali begins by sketching in a few lines a typology of the comparisons he usually makes between texts in his philological work. A first category is that of comparisons that involve no relationship of the text under consideration with another text but help the interpreter to understand, in addition to the literal meaning, the multiple connotations of each word or phrase. Among the comparisons that, on the other hand, presuppose a relationship between texts, Pasquali distinguishes three subcategories: reminiscences, which can be conscious or unconscious; imitations, always conscious, that the author may or may not wish to be recognized; allusions (evocations, citations), which the author wishes to be recognized, because only in the recognition itself do these attain the desired effect. The object of Pasquali's discussion is precisely to isolate and describe this final subcategory.

A selection and brief illustration of examples then follows, elucidating Pasquali's idea of this process. This is a feature of all forms of art in all periods. The most important purpose—the only one that Pasquali highlights in the first part of his illustration—is that of evoking, in a new context, a different world: the world connected with the text to which the allusion points. The result is, typically, to bring together in the text the past and the present: "characteristic of allusion...is the presence of the modern in contrast with the ancient or within the ancient, and thus a certain tension that gives movement to the work without breaking up its unity." This happens (in literature, in music, in painting) when a modern text, permeated with the issues and sensibility peculiar to its own period, alludes to a text of an earlier author: the first examples are those of modern Italian poets who introduce quotations or allusions to Greek or Latin texts, or to Dante, and so introduce into their texts the evocation of a different and distant world. But this can also happen through allusions to contemporary texts, and even to those of the same author: in *Die Meistersinger* Wagner introduces a reference to King Mark, a figure in *Tristan*, accompanying it with the return of the musical theme connected with him, and thus "reawakens the world of *Tristan* in a different social and musical setting." This effect of the cohabitation of different worlds can also be obtained through recollection of formal procedures or themes typical of a past period, or of a different artistic school. Pasquali suggests possible combinations of ancient and modern in works of figurative art, and a little earlier he had already found a comparable literary example: the laborious technique of Giosuè Carducci imitated classical meters in the *Odi barbare* (1877): these are thus "allusive already in their meter, which is meant to transport us into another world, that of Horace and Augustus."

Only two pages of the article are taken up with what I have summarized thus far. The remaining six pages are dedicated to allusion in Augustan poetry, in fact almost exclusively in Vergil. Pasquali highlights here too the effect of the coexistence of ancient and modern, but the temporal planes are more complex. In Horace's odes "often the meter is already meant to evoke the world of the Lesbian lyric poets": Pasquali affirms that for him the charm of Horatian lyric lies in precisely this tension or combination between old and new, between the world of ancient Greece and that of contemporary modern Rome. In this regard, he refers to his volume *Orazio lirico*, which, as we shall shortly observe, represents the true moment of the instantiation of Pasquali's idea of *arte allusiva*, and in which he treats in extensive analyses the differing significances that references to Hellenistic poets, or, on the other hand, to poets of archaic and classical Greece, have in Latin poetry. In "Arte allusiva" only in the case of Virgil does Pasquali hint at the different meaning of allusions to Homer, the ancient text that the Latin poet intends to repropose in a new style, in contrast with allusions to Hellenistic poets, which enhance a sense of modernity. Here Pasquali also distinguishes the function of elevation of style through allusions to archaic Latin poets from the function of a personal compliment of allusions to contemporary Latin poets. With this complex interweaving of allusions to various moments and contexts of Greek and Latin literature both past and present, in Augustan poetry the process is "not only widespread, but...fundamental."

A brief reference to Greek poetry confirms the pervasive character of the process in Pasquali's vision. It is earlier than the Hellenistic era (which is thus implicitly identified with the most typical space of allusion in Greek poetry): Euripides, in the *Electra*, alludes to the *Choephoroi*; Aeschylus alludes to precise passages of Homer; Pindar alludes to variants in mythic tradition that had already been expressed in literature; and perhaps one could say something similar even of Homer. And to Homer the whole of Greek poetic language makes conscious reference.

The final section, which occupies more than half of the article, is entirely dedicated to the analysis of Virgilian allusions to passages of two contemporary poets, Varius and Varro Atacinus. Because these are the sole instances where Pasquali has chosen to give a detailed analysis, illustrating and interpreting the variations that Virgil introduces, the attention of those who have discussed this essay has focused specifically on this section. It has been observed that in each case Virgil's reelaboration shows an emulative intent, and on this basis it has often been repeated that Pasquali conceives of allusion as intrinsically connected to a desire to emulate, or even that for Pasquali, allusion is directly the result of emulation. This is not so. The Virgilian examples are important because they provide Pasquali with the opportunity to illustrate concretely how the new text integrates in itself the text to which it alludes, conforming it to new requirements of style and content while preserving its recongnizability. But in these cases it is a question, according to Pasquali himself, of complimentary gestures to a contemporary poet: these are not, therefore, representative of what for Pasquali is the most authentic artistic sense of allusion, namely the evocation of a different, more ancient world, which in the modern context in which it is recalled creates a fascinating sense of tension.

"Allusion is the means, evocation the end," Pasquali declared in the first part of the article. Certainly also when the allusion has this evocative power, the insertion in a new text of features of the text to which it alludes brings with it adjustments of style, sensibility, coloring, that the alluding author, and also the critic, may consider improvements on the original, but which Pasquali, in "Arte allusiva," does not trace back to the concept of emulation.[1]

I underline this point, because in my attempt to identify the elements of novelty in Pasquali's article, and those most likely to stimulate future research, especially in regard to Hellenistic poetry, we will see that these consisted neither in having isolated the concept of allusion, which was already well known, nor in the presumed connection between allusion and an intention to emulate. Rather, Pasquali's contribution lies in surmounting the concept of emulation within the framework of this more ample understanding of the allusive process as a modality peculiar to a production that confronts its own present with a past of artistic traditions possessing a marked significance for authors and public, which is typically the case for Hellenistic poetry and all Latin literature.

The most important forerunner for "Arte allusiva" is Pasquali's own volume *Orazio lirico*. This work, published in 1920 but, as the preface attests, in large part already written before World War I, represents a moment of huge importance in Horatian studies: it is the first, and still not superseded, systematic study of the Hellenistic component in Horace's culture and art. Pasquali put together, through the comparison of an impressive number of texts, a vast reconstruction of the whole of Hellenistic literary culture, in which he placed Horatian lyric. He assumed that Horace's originality derived from the Hellenistic culture that the Roman poet had absorbed and through which he interpreted his archaic lyric models. Richard Reitzenstein had already set forth this concept in 1901, and especially in a 1908 article from which Pasquali drew inspiration.[2] Pasquali emphasizes the idea, which was already cir-

---

[1] The word "emulation" never appears in "Arte allusiva." For the Virgilian passages Pasquali speaks of "variation," of "rendering elocution more refined," of "proceeding further along a path already trodden" by the author to whom allusion is made. In each case, Pasquali attributes this commitment of reelaboration to an act of homage to the poet cited.

[2] Reitzenstein 1901: 69 n. 1 and Reitzenstein 1908, where the similarities between Hellenistic epigrams and Horatian odes are traced back to lost Hellenistic lyric, which

culating in German philology of the period, of the Hellenistic age as the 'modern' age of antiquity, and maintains that Augustan Rome is essentially a Hellenistic city in culture and in custom.

In *Orazio lirico* Pasquali does not use the term "allusione"—he prefers "citazione" ("quotation")—but he constantly affirms that Horace intended his references to Alcaeus, and to other archaic lyric poets, such as Sappho (cf. Pasquali 1920: 504), to be recognizable to the reader, who would appreciate the different artistic result the poet achieved, the autonomous stylistic or thematic route he followed on the basis of his "modern" (that is, "Hellenistic") culture, and thus on the basis of a rapport that entails familiarity and identification with Hellenistic poetry. Toward Hellenistic poets themselves, Horace rarely, according to Pasquali, utilizes the same process: perhaps the sole exception is the reference in *Carmen* 1.3 to the fragment 400 Pf. of Callimachus in lyric meter (Pasquali 1920: 260–278). Normally, he draws from them a stylistic device, or an emotional attitude, that is modern: that is to say, consistent with the Hellenistic culture of Augustan Rome. One of the procedures that Horace derives from Hellenistic poetry is the "quotation" from a text of the past not so much in order to "imitate" it as to "substitute" for it with a corresponding text adapted to the exigencies of a new artistic culture. As examples for Horace, and in general for the Latin poets, of this manner of confronting Greek models, Pasquali points out the opening references to Hipponax in Callimachus' *Iambi* and to Hesiod in the opening of the *Aetia:* these are not poets that Callimachus actually "imitates," but rather he surpasses and substitutes for them with new works different in style and artistic sensibility (Pasquali 1920: 114–115). Pasquali considers the process of the "motto" characteristic of the rapport of Horace with Alcaeus: a "quotation" at the beginning, subsequently developed in an autonomous direction. For this usage also he finds a model in Hellenistic poetry: the "quotation" of Alcaeus in Theocritus 29.[3]

---

could have been Horace's source. We are not able to state anything precisely about the extent or contours of Hellenistic lyric production: to the hypothesis, in itself quite probable, of its influence on Horace, Pasquali gave an excessive elaboration, and he even used the presumed Horatian imitations themselves to try to reconstruct the profile of lost Hellenistic lyrics, exposing himself, entirely in contradiction to his intent, to being suspected of not recognizing Horace's originality. On this question, on the "sources" of *Orazio lirico* and its reception, see in greater detail Citroni 1998. See further La Penna 1964.

[3] Pasquali 1920: 9 (already in Pasquali 1915a: 309).

In *Orazio lirico*, unlike "Arte allusiva," the cases in which the reader is expected to take a reference into account and appreciate its reworking are systematically traced back to the idea of emulation, of surpassing. Pasquali had not yet developed a clear understanding of the fuller idea of allusion as a kind of confluence of ancient and novel that is expressed in "Arte allusiva." In fact the tension between ancient and modern and the coexistence in the same text of the contemporary world and that of the past, achieved through the recognizable recovery of a more ancient text in a new text, is a central theme in *Orazio lirico* too, where as we have seen, it is connected to a vast historical and cultural reconstruction and the interpretation of an artistic era that, conscious of its own modernity, confronts a past in which it recognizes an extraordinary authority and that at the same time it intends to surpass and replace. And in "Arte Allusiva," as we have seen, when he deals with the fascinating effect of the suspension between ancient and modern that he attaches to this procedure, Pasquali makes reference to *Orazio lirico*, where this effect is analyzed in detail in Horace, setting the tone for most of the book.

To go back further, to the sources of the idea of allusion already expressed in *Orazio lirico*, it will be useful to take as our point of reference the motto, a procedure which Pasquali treats at length in the first part of the volume. In several instances, we are able to verify that at the opening of an ode, Horace faithfully translates a verse of Alcaeus, and then proceeds in an autonomous way, or even in contrast to the composition from which the initial reference is taken. Pasquali underlines that every time Horace relies on the fact that the reader will recognize this initial quotation and will appreciate the freedom with which he has transformed the starting point derived from the model. The motto formula happily expresses the idea of an open statement of ideal filiation from an artistic or intellectual point of reference, without any prejudice against the autonomy of the poet's own discourse. The formula has met with success in Horatian studies and is often used with reference to Pasquali, who brilliantly exploited its value.

The process of the motto, in which the fundamental idea of *arte allusiva* is clearly present, was already described in a 1915 article, which Pasquali again takes up at the opening of *Orazio lirico*. Both in this article and later in the volume, Pasquali declares that his own source is Eduard Norden, who in 1909 mentioned this Horatian process, already defining it as a motto, and already indicating that Horace found his model in the Hellenistic poets (with the reference to Theocritus 29 then taken up by Pasquali). But Reitzenstein also, in a

1904 contribution,[4] spoke of a motto from Alcaeus, easily recognizable in Horace, and discussed the process more fully, maintaining that he could see examples in Hellenistic epigram, in a 1908 article that, as we have mentioned, was the starting point for *Orazio lirico*.[5]

Other traces also lead us to Norden. In *Ennius und Vergilius* (1915) he chose as a motto for the last chapter, entitled "De Vergilio Ennii imitatore," the remark of the rhetorician Gallio, recalled by Seneca the Elder (*Suasoriae* 3.7), according to whom Ovid had appropriated many verses of Virgil "non subripiendi causa, sed palam mutuandi, hoc animo, ut vellet agnosci" ("not to steal them, but to take them openly on loan, with the precise intention that they be recognized"). This remark, often cited in recent studies on the theory of allusion as emblematic of the allusive process and of the understanding of it among ancient authors, was thus already highlighted in Norden, who explicitly maintained that this should count as the key to interpreting imitations of Virgil himself by other authors, adding a phrase of Pliny the Elder (*NH praef.* 22), who praises Virgil because he does not hide his models but vies openly with them (Norden 1915: 153–154). Pasquali, reviewing Norden's book in the year of its publication (1915), welcomed the fact that Norden recognized in Virgil this open emulation in relation to his models;[6] and in 1903, when examining one of Virgil's references to Varius, which was to be discussed in "Arte allusiva," Norden himself interpreted it, as Pasquali did subsequently, as a "complimentary quotation," "in accordance with the well-known custom of Hellenistic poets" (Norden 1916 [1st edition 1903]: 292).

In these works of Reitzenstein and of Norden, in which we easily recognize the sphere from which derive the origins of Pasquali's idea of *arte allusiva*, the term "allusion" does not occur (nor does it in *Orazio lirico*): but allusion is clearly not Pasquali's innovation. In a volume by Eduard Stemplinger on imitation and plagiarism in Greek literature, published in 1912, well known at that time and hence probably well known to Pasquali, the author uses *Zitat* ("quotation") and *Anspielung* ("allusion"), and includes *Anspielung* as a term in the subject index. The instances examined, in quick review, are a great many,

---

[4] Reitzenstein 1904: 959. See p. 960 for the association of "modernity" and "Alexandrianism" in Horace that is later developed in Reitzenstein 1908 and especially by Pasquali.

[5] Reitzenstein 1908: 86–87; cf. n. 2 above. On the motto in ancient poetry, see the full treatment of Cavarzere 1996.

[6] Pasquali 1915b: 609 (cf. Pasquali 1994: 1.239).

from archaic lyric (allusions to Homer and Hesiod) to tragedy, Hellenistic poetry, and prose, encompassing very diverse situations of relations between texts, which Stemplinger always, however, traces back to precise and restricted functions: compliment, the reader's pleasure in recognition, exhibition of culture, polemic, parody, emulation.[7] Always at issue are cases in which the reader must recognize the passage to which reference is made in order to gain the desired effect. Nor does Stemplinger claim to introduce a new concept: anyone would know that the ancient principle of imitation or emulation, above all in rhetorical practice, operates openly; the model is exhibited with pride, and with the ambition of being worthy of it or surpassing it (whereas an author is susceptible to being accused of theft if he attempts to hide it).[8]

Both Norden and Pasquali, as we have seen, consider the quotation in terms of homage as a common practice in Hellenistic poetry, referring either to reciprocal reference among contemporary poets, or to reference to poets of the past. And it is certainly in this area that Pasquali first experienced the phenomenon of literary allusion in ancient literature. After very early studies dedicated to later Greek literature, Pasquali soon moved on to devoting himself to Hellenistic poetry. From his student days he had looked to German philology as his point of reference, and had spent periods of study (1908–09) and teaching (1912–15) in Germany. In 1912 he obtained his *Habilitation* in Göttingen with a dissertation on Callimachus (Pasquali 1913), and in these years he published many studies on Callimachus and other Hellenistic poets. *Orazio lirico* is the product of a specialist in Hellenistic culture and takes its place in the dense contemporary panorama of German studies on Hellenistic poetry, in which it was customary to search, especially in the *Hymns* of Callimachus and in Apollonius of Rhodes, for references to rare terms, linguistic peculiarities, textual variants, and problematic places in the text of Homer (and also of Hesiod, the lyric poets, the tragedians), in the belief that the poet

---

[7] Stemplinger 1912. The instances of *Anspielung* are concentrated in the chapters entitled "Komplimentzitate" and "Polemische Zitate" (pp. 196–209) and in a brief paragraph on *aemulatio* (pp. 272–274). Among the instances of quotation as a compliment, we find an example of allusion to Varius in Virgil analyzed by Pasquali in "Arte allusiva." At p. 186, among the issues of self-quotation, is also that of Wagner in *Die Meistersinger*, which we find again in "Arte allusiva."

[8] The many relevant ancient texts are well analyzed by Stemplinger himself. Cf. also Reiff 1959.

on each occasion wanted his reader to understand the preciosity of the reference, and his own interpretive or textual choice.[9] Pasquali's dissertation, which concerns Callimachus' *Hymns*, does not follow this method of working, but he had it here very much in mind. Hans Herter, recapitulating in 1931 this line of Callimachean studies, to which he was giving a new orientation and new perspectives, often uses *Anspielung* and *anspielen*, terms that were in fact already current for these references that invite the reader to engage with the recalled text.[10] "Allusion" is used for this process in Apollonius Rhodius by Gennaro Perrotta, a student of Pasquali, in 1926 (Perrotta 1926: 202).

Yet it remains true that "Arte allusiva" contained important innovations. The formula itself was new, inasmuch as it attributed to allusion the full dignity of an artistic process endowed with its own specific and unique prerogatives. And new too was the importance of the function attributed to the allusive process: the narrow aims of compliment, homage, and an attractive display of learning came to be superseded; and also the aim of emulation, clearly broader, but still inadequate, was superseded, too. Allusion became, as we have seen, a mode of confronting tradition, recovering and reforming it for a contemporary setting. And at the same time it could generate suggestive effects that derived from the suspension between past and present. However, the wider range attributed to the process did not cause it to lose its specificity.

This elevation of perspective in relation to the contemporary context of literary studies was already visible in *Orazio lirico*, where as we have seen the motto was connected with contemporary scholarship's large-scale, thematic claim of Latin poetry's originality, which engaged precisely some of the major figures of classical philology in Germany: Leo, Reitzenstein, Heinze, Norden. A reevaluation of Latin poetry in a reaction against the prejudices of the Romantics, who had much devalued it as an opaque reproduction of the masterpieces of Greek poetry, required the conviction, deeply felt by Pasquali, that also a literature that elaborates given models can be original, and that literary creativity is not necessarily suffocated—indeed, it is normally

---

[9] For Callimachus, see von Jan 1893 and Kuiper 1896. For Apollonius of Rhodes, see already Merkel's edition of 1854.
[10] Herter 1931: 447–448; and cf., e.g., Oppermann 1925: 14 and 32.

enriched—by the experiences that an author has of other intellectual and artistic developments. Hence a positive evaluation of references to Greek authors whom the Roman poets do not "imitate," but renovate in order to substitute for them: through allusion the reader becomes conscious of this artistic and cultural process. Hence Pasquali assimilated the process that occurs among Latin poets in rapport with Greek poets to that which occurs among Hellenistic poets in relation to archaic and classical poets. Hellenistic poetry also was undergoing an analogous process of reevaluation of its supposed marginality in respect to archaic and classical poetry, a reevaluation that could not but consist, also in this case, in a claim of *doctrina* as a component of art.

Italian literary criticism of the first half of the twentieth century was dominated by the prestige of Benedetto Croce, whose idealistic aesthetics attributed value only to the element of intuition, essentially ahistorical, and relegated culture to mere presupposition, to material, in substance irrelevant for judgments about artistic value. Hence derived a diffuse disparaging attitude toward philological work and the search for "sources," even though it boasted, in the study of Italian literature of the medieval period and the Renaissance, results of great value. Pasquali held firmly to his own position, inspired by a rigorous historicism founded on philological data: therefore, his academic prestige notwithstanding, he found himself in a position of relative isolation, and had thorny polemical exchanges with Croce.[11] But the confrontation with idealistic aesthetics, and the debates that circulated on the theme of the relevance of sources from the end of the nineteenth century in Italy, probably contributed to the further widening of the concept of allusion that we find in "Arte allusiva," because these debates must have induced Pasquali to elucidate the difference between his own approach and the concept of a mechanical process of literary derivation of the positivistic kind. In fact the very opening of "Arte allusiva" is a rejection of the term and concept "source" in his answer to an imaginary interlocutor who represents the Crocean conception then dominant and who provokes Pasquali by saying that "the source of poetry is always in the heart of the poet, and never in books that he may have read."

---

[11] On the relationship of Pasquali and Croce, and *il crocianesimo*, also in relation to "Arte allusiva," see Timpanaro 1973; La Penna 1986: xliii–liii.

This Italian debate had already seen the appearance of the idea that on the contrary the source of poetry could very well be in books that the poet had read, and to which he could therefore make explicit reference. Giovanni Pascoli had affirmed this in 1909,[12] but it is not likely that Giorgio Pasquali would have had in mind this isolated assertion by a poet, though a very famous one. It is more important to note that the idea of deriving inspiration from literature itself, and also the idea of the impossibility of an absolute originality in view of the inevitable inheritance of a tradition, was a concept much repeated in European literature, also among the great authors of the Romantic age, which Stemplinger to his credit had underlined. (The theme also recurred in the Italian debate.)[13] In the course of the nineteenth century, the detachment from Romanticism generated poetic programs of cultivated art, in which literary allusion could have great influence (an obvious example is T.S. Eliot), and the learned dimension of the genesis of poetry was often the object of critical attention. In 1933 E.E. Kellett wrote an elegant study on allusion, with examples from English literature and various references to authors from classical antiquity, in which allusion is very clearly identified an artistic process that introduces a diverse atmosphere into a text, and a conditioning of sense, derived from the text to which allusions are made. Kellett affirms at the same time that, in a sense, "all, or practically all, our writing is quotation.... no man can write without employing multitudes of phrases, the associations of which have been fixed long since and cannot be deliberately altered" (1933: 14). Already here the author prefigures the tension between the intentionality of allusion and the governing force of an impersonal tradition that comes to light in the subsequent debate on allusion. In 1944 W.F. Jackson Knight (1944:

---

[12] As noted in Traina 1989: 246–247, where we find further useful references. Cavarzere 1996: 15–16 notes that a similar concept is expressed in a novel of Gabriele D'Annunzio, *Il piacere*, in 1889.

[13] The Italian narrator and critic Vittorio Imbriani in an 1882 text sustained the impossibility of originality, the inevitable dependence of all thought on the thought of others, and formulated a very precise distinction between reminiscence, allusion, citation, imitation, and plagiarism (new attention was focused on Imbriani's text in *Quaderni di Storia* 18 [36] 1992: 141–148). The theme appears occasionally in Croce himself and in Crocean critics (cf. Fubini 1973: 48–49, with a text from 1955 in reference to Pasquali), and even in Croce's attack against "Arte allusiva" (below, n. 15), in which he counters Pasquali, claiming that every product of the human mind emerges necessarily from history dripping with references of all kinds, but what counts is only the original act of artistic creation.

99–105) treated allusion in Virgil with reference to Kellett, to T.S. Eliot and his idea of tradition, and also to the analyses of Livingston Lowes of the process of writing in a "cultured" poet like Coleridge. Allusion became by now an object of considerable interest in European literary criticism, but we cannot follow its subsequent progress here. The English essays that I have mentioned were probably not known to Pasquali (cf. La Penna 1962: 233–234), and neither was the author of *Orazio lirico* known to their authors. Allusion continued occasionally to be the object of scholarly attention, independently of Pasquali, whether in Hellenistic poetry (e.g., Pfeiffer 1955), or in diverse areas of Greek and Latin poetry.[14]

"Arte allusiva" was received with a brief though harsh attack by Croce, who for the reasons mentioned could not appreciate its content.[15] It received little notice, partly because of where it had been published, difficult even for Italian scholars to obtain, unobtainable for non-Italians. Pasquali was accustomed to gathering together some of his not strictly specialized work in volumes of *Pagine Stravaganti*. But *Terze pagine stravaganti* was published in precisely the same year, 1942, when "Arte allusiva" appeared as an article in "L'Italia che scrive," and so "Arte allusiva" had to wait until 1951 to be made accessible to scholars in the volume *Stravaganze quarte e supreme*, as the opening essay. But *Pagine stravaganti* had scarcely any international circulation either. "Arte allusiva" remained known almost exclusively in Italy, where its content came to be diffused largely also through the teaching of Pasquali's many students in university positions. International scholarly interest in "Arte allusiva" came late, through two different venues: first through studies of Hellenistic poetry; then, with much greater resonance, through the study of Latin literature. In both cases the initiative was taken by Italian scholars.

Giuseppe Giangrande, a student of Pasquali's, opened two important articles by referring to "Arte allusiva," one in *Classical Quarterly* of 1967 and one in *L'Antiquité Classique* in 1970, in which, following in the footsteps of Kuiper and Herter, he analyzed a series of passages from Apollonius, and from Callimachus (and from other Hellenistic poets), whose comprehension requires on the part of the reader a

---

[14] E.g., Davison 1955 and Harvey 1957 for archaic Greek poetry, Wigodsky 1972: 3–5 for Virgil. Wigodsky 1972 cites *Orazio lirico* for the motto but ignores "Arte allusiva."

[15] In Croce 1943. See above, n. 13.

comparison with Homeric passages (and in some cases with passages of other authors, even contemporary Hellenistic poets) to whom the author alludes. The first of the two articles (which includes the formula *arte allusiva* in its title) begins with the statement "Alexandrian epic is *arte allusiva par excellence*," which we find again in an even more compelling formulation in the opening of the second article: "Hellenistic poetry is nothing if not *arte allusiva*."[16] From that point the formula *arte allusiva* and the explicit or implicit recall of Pasquali's article become standard usage in the study of Hellenistic poetry. In 1972 also Enrico Livrea began an important article on Apollonius with as strong a statement as Giangrande's: "the allusive technique, as anyone knows, often shows itself to be the raison d'être of Alexandrian poetry" (p. 231). But in Giangrande, in Livrea, and for a long time in subsequent study of Hellenistic literature, the formula is attributed to a very specific type of allusion, one that could not be in itself considered essential to or the raison d'être of that great poetic period. At issue are typically allusions to places in Homer where the text or interpretation was already problematic for ancient exegesis: rare words, textual variants, even morphological or syntactic peculiarities. The reader, to appreciate the desired effect, or even just the sense, had to go back not only to the passage alluded to, but also to the exegetical problem with which the passage was associated. Giangrande defines the allusive processes he studied as "implied grammatical interpretation" and *oppositio in imitando* (or reversal): the latter is a particularly refined device, in which the poet follows a modality opposite to what is present in the text to which he alludes. Giangrande himself claims to derive this formula from the old work of Kuiper. In fact, as we have seen, this very restricted type of allusion was already well known before Pasquali, was not directly studied by Pasquali, and does not correspond to the much broader application that made Pasquali's idea of allusion original and innovative. Much larger perspectives, and new stimuli for the study of Hellenistic poetry itself, were shortly to arise from the relaunching of Pasquali's concept of *arte allusiva* in the study of Latin literature.

An important article by Richard F. Thomas on the *Georgics* in *Harvard Studies* for 1986 opens with a reference to Pasquali and to his "Arte allusiva." Thomas goes back to Pasquali via Giangrande, seeing Hellenistic allusion in the restricted perspective that we have just

---

[16] Giangrande 1967: 85 and 1970: 46, where there is also an opportune reference to *Orazio lirico*.

detailed. Thomas on the one hand claims for the Augustan poets no less an "intellectual and scholarly capacity" than the Hellenistic poets', but then he contrasts the conflation and incorporation of an entire literary tradition, from Homer to Lucretius, that Virgil carries out in his text with the mere exercise in erudition that Thomas attributes to the Hellenistic poets.[17] In fact the instances that Thomas examines do not have a grammatical and philological character but concern associations of sense, atmosphere, and complex connotations derived in the new text from a broad context of passages in Latin and Greek predecessors to which the new text alludes, and these in various ways invest the rapport that Virgil establishes with poetic tradition. On the basis of empirically observing allusion in the *Georgics*, Thomas traces a typology of the process, which he prefers to define as "reference," in that he sees in "allusion" a connotation of playfulness going back to its etymology, a connotation not suited to the phenomenon whose importance he has just underlined. His typology, which encompasses six categories, was to be adopted by Mary Depew in her analysis of Callimachus' *Hymn to Delos* (Depew 1998).

Meanwhile Gian Biagio Conte, in a 1971 article, and then a 1974 book, had begun a new era in the study of allusion, again starting from Pasquali. The impact of these studies in Italy was immediately enormous, and the English edition of 1986 (which also included several subsequent essays) rapidly expanded their international resonance. Conte was among the first to introduce critical attitudes, conceptual categories, and a language more in line with recent developments in literary criticism into the study of ancient texts; he transferred a problem typical of traditional philological work—that of finding a criterion in the utilization of "parallel passages"—to a broad context of reflections from literary theory, always basing his treatment on brilliant analyses of concrete examples. With Conte, and after Conte, discussions about allusion in ancient poets have continually confronted delicate theoretical problems: the relevance of authorial intention, the role of the reader in sense construction, the significance of genre and of literary tradition. The landscape of studies connected with allusion has become vast, now involving and conditioning research on all eras of ancient literature.

---

[17] R.F. Thomas 1986b: 172 and 197–198.

Conte refers to "Arte allusiva" and *Orazio lirico* and to the idea of allusion as evocation of an ancient text within a modern one that, when recognized, brings about a transformation and intensification of sense, and he recognizes in this phenomenon the same efficacy as that of a rhetorical trope. In metaphor, too, the new sense is produced by the presence of a freely evoked image that integrates itself into the discourse and transforms it (Conte 1986: 23-31). Conte defines this type of allusion precisely as "integrative" and in contrast defines as "reflexive" a type of allusion that operates not as a metaphor but as a simile, in that it recalls, in a way quotes, a text while safeguarding its autonomy and its distance from the new text, and while inviting the reader to compare the two different textual situations. This original typology of allusion, based on rhetoric, has shown itself to be a very effective instrument in textual analysis, both in the work of Conte himself and in that of scholars who have subsequently adopted it, among whom recently is H. van Tress in her work on Callimachus' *Hymns* and Ovid's *Metamorphoses*.[18] Other, more specific allusive processes identified and described by Conte have shown themselves very useful for textual analysis, and are now often used by other scholars. Conte's distinction between the exemplary model (the text imitated in a traditional sense) and the code model (or generic model) has also had an important following: the latter is a text whose more general constructive processes are imitated, one that is the generative matrix of a text intended not to imitate but to substitute for the model.

To have traced allusion back to the operative modalities of the rhetorical figure has meant removing the process from the dimension of extemporaneous occasionality, determined by the initiative of particular authors and milieus, and recognizing besides its stable and coherent collocation in the frame of processes characteristic of literary expression. The advantage, immediately testable in Conte's textual analyses, was to be able to compare the effects of allusion with those of other well-known rhetorical processes characteristic of poetic diction. The risk was to lose sight of the specific features of the process of allusion itself.

Conte intended from the beginning to reduce the intentional factor of allusion, interpreting allusion as part of the literary *langue*, founded

---

[18] Van Tress 2004, with on pages 1-21 a useful, concise summary on the state of studies on allusion and intertextuality.

on tradition and thus on memory. The poet could not evade the adoption of expressive modalities, situations, rules already inscribed in tradition—in particular in the tradition of the genre—which he appropriated through the texts present in his memory. From this idea of poetic memory as a system, derived as an original development from critical approaches born in French structuralism, the passage was a short and natural one, in Conte and after, to a reading of allusion within the dimension of intertextuality. Intertextuality was a theoretical frame developed in France toward the end of the 1960s by Julia Kristeva, of the school of Roland Barthes, which rapidly caught on. In this approach the intentional moment is essentially canceled, and each text is inserted into a complex network of recollections, not "intersubjective" between authors but "interobjective" between texts: within such a network each text is generated, and only through it can each text be understood. Literature is a "second-level" production, inevitably constructed from literature itself (an idea that, as we have seen, has quite distant origins). In more recent, poststructuralist versions of intertextuality, in which faith in the existence of a literary system has faded away, the accent is placed rather on the reader, who constructs the sense of the text through renewing the intertextual connections each time through his or her own interpretive strategies.

In this perspective, the risk of loss of identity of the allusive process becomes more concrete. In the traditional vision, the parallel passage is considered relevant to interpretation insofar as it can be considered the result of an intention, and thus can be traced back to a choice of the author, whose personality is expressed in the work. Only this could have been Pasquali's vision: the typology of textual references that he proposes at the beginning of "Arte allusiva," is entirely founded on the existence of intention or lack thereof.[19] Allusion even presupposes a double intention: that of recalling a particular text and that of rendering this reference recognizable. (And it presupposes an evaluation of the capacity of the reader to recognize it.) The difficulty of deciding the intentionality or lack thereof of every textual reference was the common experience of interpreters: the difficulty was so much

---

[19] Cf. above. Yet it is right to remember that in "Arte allusiva" Pasquali shows himself aware of the fact that allusion is contiguous with formal recurrences arising from a generic *langue*: this is suggested by his references to sixteenth-century *Petrarchismo* and to the fact that Homer is the constant source of Greek poetic language, and thus operates as a helping factor in facilitating the allusive process in ancient poetry.

the greater in texts conditioned by a strong formal tradition, which implies that situations and formulas are frequently repeated. The question was already treated by Wilhelm Kroll in his famous *Studien zum Verständnis der römischen Literatur* in 1924 and more recently, and very effectively, by Stephen Hinds.[20] In the context of a growing "crisis of the subject" in the twentieth century, the denunciation of the intentional fallacy had already been energetically advanced long before Barthes proclaimed the "death of the author," finding a delicate point of resistance precisely in allusion (Wimsatt and Beardsley 1946). For allusion, which is identified by a (double) authorial intent, a rigorous anti-intentionality of the type generally assumed in the intertextual approach meant assimilation to any other form of relation between texts, and therefore involved a substantial loss of identity and even of sense. In fact, in studies on ancient authors conditioned by an intertextual perspective, we can find both the use of the term "allusion" for any significant form of relation between texts and the decision to abandon the term completely as inappropriate because of its intentionalistic connotations.[21] This latter tendency has not prevailed: on the contrary, the use of the term "allusion," though affected by the complex tensions arising from this debate, and with the possible different meanings detailed here, is today the most prevalent choice and becoming ever more so.

Through interaction with the intertextual perspective, Conte enhanced his foregoing predisposition to weaken the intentional moment of allusion, which also in some of the more theoretical parts of his writing (not, however, in concrete textual analysis) tends thus to some extent to lose autonomous relevance in respect to the general network of intertextual relations. But he never went so far as to posit the absolute negation of the role of the author, and in his more recent statements on the question, while adopting the formula "intention of the text" (recognizable in the characteristics of a text that orient the reader to an interpretive line between certain determined limits), admits the pragmatic advantages of the critic's adopting at least the conventional presuppositions of intentionality, and recognizes that spaces of authorial intentionality may be usable for the interpretation of poetry written in restricted environments of an audience/authors,

---

[20] Kroll 1924: 150–155; Hinds 1998: 17–51. Cf. also Fowler 1997.
[21] Lyne 1994: 188–189 and 199–200.

those typical of the neoteric and Alexandrian environments, proposing to reserve the term "allusion" for such situations, in which the role of intention can to some extent be recovered.[22]

Within the last thirty years various scholars of ancient literature have rethought these themes on the basis of their work of textual analysis and in interaction with the evolution of general debates on literary theory and critical method. Here I would recall at least the challenging volumes of Stephen Hinds, Joseph Pucci, and Lowell Edmunds, but important theoretical inquiries appear in numerous articles and chapters of edited volumes about ancient literature.[23] It is not possible here to give an account of the various positions expressed, nor either to review the more relevant analyses of situations of intertextuality and allusive processes in the ancient authors that refer, in various ways, to these methodological approaches. The panorama is now simply too vast. But one can observe that for a long time both the theoretical inquiry and the concrete textual analysis based on such inquiry have been practiced almost exclusively by Latinists. This may in part result from the fact that Conte, the promoter and first protagonist of this evolution, is a Latinist; and it may seem natural that reactions to his work, and the motivation to continue it, would be manifested first in his school and then in the same area of study. But a more important motive, and a substantial one, results from the fact that the rapport with models has always been a very significant problem for Latinists. Working on a literature that had long professed itself "derivative"—even in its more elevated achievements—they had systematically to engage with the position that the Roman writers assumed in their relations with their models to understand the very reasons for this artistic production, besides interpreting specific aspects of texts. The nature of Virgil's relationship with Homer, which is emblematic of this large-scale theme, constituted a serious cultural and exegetical problem already for the ancients, and has been a crucial object of reflection in all the subsequent history of the study of Latin literature. It is no accident that Conte himself developed his systematic vision of allusion precisely from the theme of the relationship of Virgil (and Catullus) with Homer (1971 and 1986: 32–39). In the context of this

---

[22] Conte 1994: xix and 135–137; Hinds 1998: 48–51.
[23] Hinds 1998, J. Pucci 1998, Edmunds 2001b. Important theoretical contributions in, among others, Barchiesi 1993 and 1997a; Wills 1996: 15–33; Fowler 1997; Hubbard 1998: 7–18; J. Farrell 2005.

theme, completely traditional in Latin studies, the first, most significant adoptions of this theoretical orientation have been advanced. I refer in the first place to Alessandro Barchiesi's *La traccia del modello* (1984), which makes substantial contributions to the analysis of Virgil's relationship with Homer, making use of the distinction, derived from Conte, between exemplary and generic models, and then to the Virgilian studies of R.O.A.M. Lyne (1987) and of Joe Farrell (1991), in which the concept of allusion is of central importance. We have seen that even in Pasquali the basic significance of "Arte allusiva" has its origins in the same scholar's *Orazio lirico*, and so in the problem of the relationship of the major Roman poets with their Greek models, typical of the study of Latin literature. Another traditional area of Latin studies particularly suitable to the application of an analysis of allusion in systematic terms was that of the Greek and Latin (Catullan and Virgilian) sources of Ovid's mythological poetry. Conte had also worked in this area,[24] and here too Barchiesi has proposed a number of original developments; particularly noteworthy is Barchiesi's analysis of the singular effects created in a particular modality of "reflexive" allusion significant in Ovid and in Hellenistic poetry: reference to a prior text in which is inscribed the future of the event narrated (Barchiesi 1993). The reevaluation of post-Augustan epic is in large part based on a positive understanding of the sense of epigonism as a generator of new poetics, and on the complex allusive and intertextual rapport with the great history of the genre, Greek and Augustan.

Hellenistic poetry has long had ascribed to it a derivative character, this based on its rapport with archaic and classical poetry. The dimension of erudite allusiveness itself has been seen as a sign of narrowness. The new interest in allusions of an erudite character, which we spoke of earlier, was born, in Giangrande and others, from a recognition both of the historical and cultural interest of that erudition, and of the intimate connection between erudition and poetic vocation in the Hellenistic authors. But only in relatively recent years has a real awareness of the complexity of the rapport of Hellenistic literature with earlier tradition developed, in the context of a new understanding of the originality of various poetic trajectories that come into being in a cultural context that is both aware of its own epigonal status and eager for innovation. Herter's well-known study "Kallimachos und Homer"

---

[24] Conte 1974: 35–40 and 1986: 57–63.

(1929) already pointed to this route; but a much more recent acquisition, which we can see well represented in (for example) the general perspective of the research by Marco Fantuzzi and Richard Hunter,[25] is the perception of the multiple scenarios and of the articulated paths of a literature that in the constant confrontation with various periods and genres of the past manages to find profoundly new forms allowing it to represent a spiritually changed world and to operate in new contexts of communication. The understanding of the process through which Hellenistic literature constructs its new identities on the basis of a consciousness of its "coming after"—I allude to the meaningful title given by Hunter to his inaugural lecture at Cambridge in 2001 and to his recent collection of articles on Hellenistic literature (2008b)—very naturally engendered the need to turn to the instruments of analysis and reflection on intertextuality and allusion already developed in the area of Latin literature, where they had served first to search out new responses to the ancient question of its "coming after" in respect to Greek literature. Peter Bing in his *Well-Read Muse*, a book that marks a very important moment in the assertion of this new orientation in the study of Hellenistic poetry, begins his conclusion by referring to Conte; and we have already noted other cases of adoption of the analytic instruments developed by Latinists in recent studies on allusion in Callimachus.[26]

Pasquali and "Arte allusiva" today are often recalled, explicitly or implicitly, in the study of Hellenistic poetry on this path, which, originating from Conte, is very diverse, and certainly more in accord with the substance of Pasquali's thought, than what originated from Giangrande. Because, as we have seen, allusion for Pasquali is not a process of restricted horizon, closed within the confines of an elegantly varied passage, with emulative intent, as some continue to say or to suggest. At times it could be just this, but in its entirety allusion was for Pasquali a phenomenon invested with the essence of the relation of literature with its own past, causing the audience to attend, not only through quotations or echoes of particular passages but also through recalling more general compositive features (e.g., meter), the presence of a meaningful past within a new text—and one conscious of its novelty.

---

[25] Fantuzzi 1993, Fantuzzi and Hunter 2004.
[26] Bing 1988b: 144. I refer to Depew 1998 and Van Tress 2004.

EPILOGUE

Benjamin Acosta-Hughes

ABSTRACT

In responding to the reputation of Callimachus today, and particular in considering the whole of the achievement of the *Brill's Companion to Callimachus*, this epilogue posits that we may best think of Callimachus as the first modern poet, one whose work is consciously, continually aware of another poetry as earlier. He is aware of the poem as text, and of the poem as song; he evokes performative occasion, and at the same time the *labor* of poetic composition, and his own text as object of composition. Callimachus is a poet both of the Archaic past and the post-Alexander present. In this dual character he is comparable to a much later Alexandrian poet, Constantine Cavafy, and it is with a reading of these two figures, so distant in time, if not in place, that this epilogue concludes.

The long-held perception that Hellenistic poetry is either marginal (too late for the Golden Age of Greece) or interstitial (a thin wedge between the Golden Age of Greece and the Glory That Was Rome) results from a variety of factors, including the idealization of classical Greece at the time of the emergence of European nationalisms,[1] the conceptualization of a Hellas that would correspond with the emergence of Greece as a nation-state following the wars of the 1820s, racial biases that saw the archaic and classical Greek world as somehow culturally and also physically undiluted, and a post-Gibbon disregard for what were to become the seats of early Christian cultures. It should be obvious to the reader that none of this has very much to do with antiquity—at issue are the lenses through which antiquity is perceived, and the preferences of a much later audience. The Hellenistic period is not the only one that has suffered as a result of this myopia, as the recent growth in scholarship on the cultures of the western Greek world or the Second

---

[1] The image of a lost world, the "schöne Welt" of Schiller's "Die Götter Griechenlands," self-contained, enclosed, perfect, pervades a substantial part of mid-eighteenth- to early nineteenth-century German literature—and it is from this culture that classical philology as a discipline grew. The power and the limitations of this image continue to exert considerable, if now somewhat less dominant, influence upon the field, and upon its prejudices.

Sophistic amply demonstrate. However, it is no easy thing to attempt a shift in scholarly perception: over time doxography becomes truth, and tradition becomes convenient. But there are also times when such a shift is desirable, even necessary.

Alexander's campaigns and their aftermath brought about radical changes in the Greek world: the rise of the large, multiethnic *metropoleis*, the new portability of culture (the booty of M. Fulgentius Nobilior is a vivid example of what had already by his time been a long process of cultural deracination and refoundation), the redefinition of what it meant to be Greek. The title of R. Hunter's inaugural lecture, "On Coming After,"[2] captures the sociocultural divide that Alexander and his Successor general-kings brought about in the world of the ancient Mediterranean. It was never to be possible to return to the status quo ante; the ground had shifted.[3] Rather we move from a world often termed classical to one we might well term modern, and it is in this light that we should engage with Callimachus.

Callimachus was a polymath, an intellectual, and an author of a phenomenal amount of material in both poetry and prose. Like the philosopher Aristotle of the previous generation, also, it should be noted, not native to the center of much of his life's work, Callimachus was concerned with classification and definition; in breadth of scholarship and interests Aristotle may well be his closest parallel. And as with Aristotle, Callimachus and his work were the beneficiaries of a sovereign's generosity. Unlike Aristotle, however, Callimachus was also a poet. The term "scholar-poet" seems now dated, too suggestive of Yeats's Catullan critics. But it is certainly true that Callimachus was an intellectual, and he was a poet; and he may well be termed the first modern poet, a poet whose work is consciously, continually aware of another poetry as specifically earlier (so the *Dream* takes him back, and Hipponax comes from the then to the now). He is modern in juxtaposition to what is prior. To take his lines on his contemporary the poet Aratus as an illustration:

Ἡσιόδου τό τ' ἄεισμα καὶ ὁ τρόπος· οὐ τὸν ἀοιδῶν
ἔσχατον, ἀλλ' ὀκνέω μὴ τὸ μελιχρότατον

---

[2] Inaugural lecture as Regius Professor of Greek at Cambridge University, delivered 17 October 2001 = Hunter 2008b: 1. 8–26.
[3] The attempt in Hellenistic Sparta to recover the Sparta of an earlier period is a vivid example. See, e.g., Plut. *Cleom.* 10–11.

τῶν ἐπέων ὁ Σολεὺς ἀπεμάξατο· χαίρετε λεπταί
ῥήσιες, Ἀρήτου σύμβολον ἀγρυπνίης.

> Hesiod's is the content and the style. Not Hesiod in every regard, yet, I think, the Solean has impressed the sweetest part of his verses. Hail refined expressions, proof of Aratus' sleepless nights.
>
> *Ep.* 66 GP = 27 Pf.

Aratus' poetry is defined not only in terms of Hesiod's poetry but in terms of his use of Hesiod; it is Aratus who has put his seal on the finest of Hesiod, Aratus whose "speeches" are refined, and Aratus whose tirelessness has worked the object of praise. The epigram is not an indication of any sort of cultural belatedness; rather it is a comment on the process of composition, the model at the beginning of the epigram evolving into the later, perfected version of the final lines.

Typical too of Callimachus' poetry, and of his modernity, is the awareness of poem as text, as well as of the poem as song. As Alan Cameron and others have convincingly shown, performance occasions pervade the Hellenistic world (as indeed Hellenistic poetry itself attests), and Callimachean scholarship of an earlier period surely went too far in divorcing Callimachus' poetry from any consideration of a performative context. (Horace's *Carmen saeculare* should have suggested more restraint here.) When Callimachus, as any earlier poet, demarcates an occasion for his song, there is no reason to disbelieve him.[4] There is no reason to assume that *The Victory of Berenicei*, the poem that now opens *Aetia* 3, is not written for the specific occasion of the queen's Panhellenic victory, or that fragment 228 Pf., on Arsinoe's apotheosis, is not originally a composition performed on the death of Arsinoe II.

Yet at the same time Callimachus' poetry evokes not only the performative traditions of poetic composition but also poetry as written text, and indeed of the labor of composition (Ἀρήτου σύμβολον ἀγρυπνίης), whether understood literally or metaphorically.[5] Callimachus' poetry is replete with references to the act of composition, to his

---

[4] The material on his *Hymn to Apollo* in I. Petrovic's contribution in this volume is especially salient.

[5] It is probably always worth keeping in mind that given the prevalence of enslaved scribes in the ancient world we cannot know how literally we should take the imagery of physical writing. As with reading, the act of composition may have comprised features now unfamiliar to us—the same is of course true of how, and in what form, compositions could be made public and subsequently revised.

own poetry as the artifact of composition, and to poetic texts. Here he has no earlier precursor. I give a few examples by way of illustration.

The first is the conclusion of fragment 75 Pf. (= fr. 174 M.), the one long surviving fragment of Callimachus' elegiac narrative *Acontius and Cydippe*, an episode of the *Aetia* that was to have a long and very significant reception in Roman poetry. At lines 74–77 the poet brings together his archaic hero, the prose chronicler whom the poet names as the source of his tale, and his own poetry in a gesture that commingles *eros* and history, prose and poetry, exactly as does the *Aetia* as a whole:

> εἶπε δέ, Κεῖε,
> ξυγκραθέντ' αὐταῖς ὀξὺν ἔρωτα σέθεν
> πρέσβυς ἐτήτυμίῃ μεμελημένος ἔνθεν ὁ πα[ι]δός
> μῦθος ἐς ἡμετέρην ἔδραμε Καλλιόπην.

And, Cean, he told of your passionate love mixed together with these [cities], that old man careful of the truth, and from there the story of the child ran to my Calliope.

Fr. 75.74-77 Pf.

This short passage dramatizes several features of Callimachus' poetry. One is the use of apostrophe to mark the singer's sympathy with the object of his song; already a Homeric poeticism,[6] apostrophe for Callimachus becomes a vehicle to insert the singer's presence into his own narrative—and indeed an ongoing conceit of this episode is the later poet's temporal rapport with his subject. The poet, from a much later age, is figured as an older man in relation to his long-ago subject, figured as ὁ πα[ι]δός μῦθος, "the story of a child"; and in the final hexameter this effect is reproduced in the placement, at opposite ends of the line, of the later chronicler Xenomedes, the poet's source, the πρέσβυς of our text, and the child who is the subject of the chronicle that reaches back into the mists of time, the παῖς.[7] Acontius, the object of earlier erotic interest on the part of symposiastic revelers,[8] comes to have his "sharp" love "mixed" in with the narratives of Cean city

---

[6] Apostrophe in Homer occurs only of Eumaeus (in the *Odyssey*) and Menelaus (in the *Iliad*), interestingly two figures who are to come to have a quite complex afterlife in Hellenistic literature.

[7] The poet's implication of the imagery of old age and childhood begins already at the opening of the *Aetia*; see further Acosta-Hughes and Stephens 2002: 240 n. 9; and the chapters of Cozzoli and Payne in this volume.

[8] At fr. 69 Pf. the ἐρασταί play the κότταβος game in his honor.

foundations;[9] as he is the object of others' interest throughout much of the poem, he is the final object memorialized at its end.[10] The truth value of historical narrative—reinforced by the poet's naming his prose source, Xenomedes of Ceos—and of Callimachus' own modern re-presentation comes to the fore by being contrasted with *mythos* at the opening of the final pentameter. The child's story is figured as running from the prose chronicler's memorial to the poet's Calliope and so to his poem: the reference to his poetry in part as a physical entity is an early precursor to a trope common especially in Roman elegy. But it also reinforces the fact that books—whether of Xenomedes coming to the Alexandrian Library or the rolls of Callimachus' own poetry—are both portable and long-lasting. A few brief lines configure a wandering story that moves from archaic mythohistory to the poet's contemporary Alexandria, from prose to poetry, and from one perspective to another.

The opening of *Aetia* 3, a passage that we owe to the Lille Papyrus, first published in 1977,[11] is similarly emblematic of movement between geographical space, temporal period, and generic realm:

Ζηνί τε καὶ Νεμέῃ τι χαρίσιον ἔδνον ὀφείλω,
    νύμφα, κα[σιγνή]των ἱερὸν αἷμα θεῶν,
ἡμ[ε]τερο . [......] . εων ἐπινίκιον ἵππω[ν.
    ἁρμοῖ γὰρ Δαναοῦ γῆς ἀπὸ βουγενέος
εἰς Ἑλένη[ς νησῖδ]α καὶ εἰς Παλληνέα μά[ντιν,
    ποιμένα [φωκάων], χρύσεον ἦλθεν ἔπος.

To Zeus and to Nemea I owe a pleasing gift, Bride, Holy Blood of the Sibling Gods, our...victory of horses. For just now from the cow-birthing land of Danaus to Helen's island and the Pallenean seer, shepherd of seals, came the golden word.

Fr. 383 Pf. + *SH* 254. 1–6.

Again readers are wrapped in a rich fabric of earlier Greek poetic culture, while at the same time their attention is directed to Callimachus' contemporary Alexandria. The opening line, but for the meter, might be from an earlier epinician, but the second line reorients the

---

[9] Συγκεράννυμι is a standard term for mixing wine, though it has many other associations; for ὀξύς of wine, cf., e.g., ὀξὺν οἶνον (Alexis fr. 145.12 KA).

[10] Ultimately the whole episode is a μνήμη of Acontius, as fr. 64 Pf. is one of Simonides; references to physical memorials as well as the process of memorialization occur in both.

[11] See Massimilla's and Harder's chapters in this volume.

poem's audience—the "Sibling Gods" are Ptolemy II and his sister-wife, Arsinoe II; their "Holy Blood," their descendants in cultic succession. The next lines effect a similar transition, from Argos, original home of Io (and so of Greek investiture in Egypt) to Helen's island, Pharos, the Egyptian setting of Helen's narrative in *Odyssey* 4 and of the subsequent legend of Egyptian Helen; and to this setting, where the Egyptian women know how to mourn the death of the Apis bull (line 16, εἰδυῖαι φαλιὸν ταῦρον ἰηλεμίσαι), comes the "golden word" of Berenice II's Nemean victory. On the literary level we find a typically Callimachean juxtaposition of simple and elevated terms, but at each change of subject these lines move us toward a novel cultural amalgamation, ultimately synchronizing Argive legend and Egyptian cult practice (Stephens 2003: 9).

Among the fragments preserved for us on papyrus of Callimachus' four-book *Aetia* are ten lines conventionally regarded as the *Epilogue* to the poem. The issue of the original placement of this fragment is complex (Massimilla 1996: 34–40), one that we leave aside here; what interests us is the same movement in time and space from the earliest Greek poetry, and its archaic setting, to the Callimachean present:

>   ...]..ιν ὅτ' ἐμὴ μοῦσα τ[.....]άσεται
>   ...]του καὶ Χαρίτων [......]ρια μοιαδ' ἀνάσσης
>   ...]τερης οὔ σε ψευδον[......]ματι
>   πάντ' ἀγαθὴν καὶ πάντα τ[ελ]εσφόρον εἶπέν...[..].[
>   κείν..τῷ Μοῦσαι πολλὰ νέμοντι βοτά   5
>   σὺν μύθους ἐβάλοντο παρ' ἴχν[ι]ον ὀξέος ἵππου·
>   χαῖρε, σὺν εὐεστοῖ δ' ἔρχεο λωϊτέρῃ.
>   χαῖρε, Ζεῦ, μέγα καὶ σύ, σάω δ' [ὅλο]ν οἶκον ἀνάκτων·
>   αὐτὰρ ἐγὼ Μουσέων πεζὸν [ἔ]πειμι νομόν.

> ...when my muse...will (?)...and of the Graces...of my queen does not lie...said all good and all fulfilling...that one...pasturing many animals the Muses exchanged stories by the track of the swift horse. Farewell; come with better prosperity. Farewell, Zeus, you also are great, preserve the whole house of my lords. But I will go to the Muses' pedestrian pasture.
>
>   Fr. 112 Pf. = 215 M.

The poet moves from long-ago Helicon, from the origin of song in the *Theogony*, which recounts the beginning of the world, to the poet's contemporary Alexandria. His own song and Hesiod's are juxtaposed; ἐμὴ μοῦσα contrasts with Hippocrene, the imagery of the opening of the *Theogony*—its Muses with their "lies" contrast with the poet's queen and Graces. The queen of line 2 is generally assumed to be Berenice II. If the preceding letters are read as μαῖα δ' or "nurse,"[12] the phrase μαῖα δ' ἀνάσσης ("nurse of my queen") must be Cyrene. The restoration is especially attractive given Berenice's heritage and Callimachus' devotion elsewhere to his polis of origin;[13] it is on much firmer ground thanks to G. Massimilla's astutely noting a parallel with the funerary epigram by Dionysius of Cyzicus written for Callimachus' fellow Cyrenaean Eratosthenes (*AP* 7.78 = *HE* 1443). Dionysius' phrase, Κυρήνη | μαῖα, describes Eratosthenes' homeland. The fact that Dionysius' epigram has a number of allusions to Callimachus' poetry, and not exclusively to his *Epigrams*, strengthens the case.[14] The *Charites* of line 2 in Callimachus fragment 112 Pf., cited above, are conventionally thought to be a reference to the Parian Graces, the first *aition* of *Aetia* Book 1; but if, as we have suggested elsewhere (Acosta-Hughes and Stephens forthcoming), the association of queen and Graces is a metaphor for the four books of the *Aetia* themselves, then the poem closes with reference to the opening of the oldest poetic composition, Hesiod on the birth of the cosmos, and the one in the act of completion, Callimachus' *Aetia*.

Callimachus is, ultimately, an arbiter of culture. As he famously defines Hesiod's dictum ἐκ δὲ Διὸς βασιλῆες in terms of his own king in *Hymn* 1, so in all the passages quoted above he explicates past Hellenic culture, from its origins to his contemporary world. Whether the earliest mythic history (Minos in the opening of the *Aetia*), the Bronze Age earthquake on Ceos (fr. 75 Pf.: thought to have occurred around 1450 BC), or the apportioning of the realms between Zeus and his brothers (*Hymn* 1), all in the end comes to Alexandria. In his poetry, in all the genres in which he composes, this massive undertaking parallels what Callimachus achieved in his prose works (now all but lost to us), and in the *Pinakes* in terms of literary definition and preservation.

---

[12] The suggestion of Coppola, following Pratt; see Massimilla 2010: 512–515.
[13] Citations given by Massimilla, *ibid*.
[14] Assuming this reading of fr. 112.2 Pf. to be correct, we encounter a striking inversion of this motif, country-nurse-hero, in the opening of *Aeneid* 7, where Aeneas' nurse effectively becomes the city of Gaeta, and in an *aition* that begins this second half of the poem. That Virgil opens *Georgics* 3 with an adaptation of *The Victory of Berenice*, and includes in Aeneas' visit to the underworld an allusion (via Catullus) to *The Lock of Berenice*, suggests a use of Callimachean allusive markers in his poetry that would repay further study.

As a polymath he can, again, really be compared only with Aristotle, with the exception that Callimachus was a poet.

He was, at the same time, a poet who came after Plato, and Plato's radical redefinition (or redefinitions) of the value of poetry. As we have outlined in detail elsewhere (Acosta-Hughes and Stephens forthcoming), Plato serves as a turning point in the definition of poetry and the poet—once the poet is defined as an instrument and his song as the composition of another power, not his own, the inherent value of the poet as (to cite the title of Detienne 1996) "master of truth" is forever brought into question. It is impossible to go back; the dice are now cast. Socrates' indictment of the poet's inherent nature abides. In this regard Callimachus has an extraordinary role that has gone largely unnoticed in the scholarly histories of Greek literature, in part, perhaps, because of the way these works are usually compartmentalized. With the exception of New Comedy, a genre that is not self-reflective, Callimachus is the first extant self-reflective poet to follow Plato,[15] and his statements on his poetry and himself as poet must be appreciated in this light. An example: the poet's wish at *Hymn* 1.65: ψευδοίμην, ἀίοντος ἅ κεν πεπίθοιεν ἀκουήν. ("May I tell lies that would persuade the ear of my listener").

The allusion is of course, as scholars have long noted, to *Theogony* 27–28, but the image of poetic truth and lying is intellectually now read through Plato, and Plato's assessment of artistic dishonesty—Ion claiming that he can move his audience to tears and enjoy the prospect of his remuneration (*Ion* 535e1–6). The defense of *Iambus* 13 against those who would limit a poet to one genre not only inversely reflects Socrates' argument in the *Ion* (534b7–d4), the paradigm outlined in the poem's *diegesis* (and furnished there with the happily Socratic illustration of a carpenter and his tools), but also puts Callimachus in the position of respondent to the charge (note the Greek text of the *diegesis*: ἐν τούτῳ πρὸς τοὺς καταμεμφομένους αὐτὸν ἐπὶ τῇ πολυειδείᾳ ὧν γράφει ποιημάτων ἁπάντων φησιν, "in this he says to those who fault him for the *polyeideia* of all the poems he writes") raised by specifically Platonic principle—the figure in the courtroom here is not as it were

---

[15] One could argue that Theocritus should be included in this equation, but with the arguable exception of Lycidas = Theocritus in *Idyll* 7, Theocritus is not self-reflective to the same extent or in the same way. That said, it is very clear that Theocritus too is a close reader of Plato.

Socrates, but Callimachus,[16] and on trial is not philosophy, but poetry. Similarly articulated in response to Socrates' definition of poet and poetry in the *Ion* are the poem's most often cited lines:[17]

τίς εἶπεν αυτ[....]λε..ρ.[....].
σὺ πεντάμετρα συντίθει, σὺ δ' ἡ[ρῷο]ν,
σὺ δὲ τραγῳδε[ῖν] ἐκ θεῶν ἐκληρώσω;
δοκέω μὲν οὐδείς, ἀλλὰ καὶ το.δ..κεψαι

Who said...you compose pentameters, you the [heroic], it is your lot from the gods to compose tragedy? In my opinion no one, but [consider] also [this]

Iambus 13. 30–33

What is important here is not so much that Callimachus echoes Plato but that he takes up the gauntlet thrown down by Socrates. Callimachus responds to Plato: he defends the poet and poetic inspiration in answer to Socrates' charge in the *Ion*, and so stands first in a long, long—indeed, ongoing—line of poets to do so. In that sense, as in others, we may see Callimachus very much as the first modern.

Callimachus is the model for a long poetic tradition in both Greek and Latin literature, as illustrated in several of the chapters in this volume and in a substantial and still growing scholarship on Callimachean reception.[18] There are also, however, instances where at issue is not a question of model per se but one of aesthetic parallel, as illustrated by A.-T. Cozzoli's comparative study of Callimachus and Pascoli in this collection. I have chosen to conclude this volume with another comparative study, one with another (though much later) Greek poet from Alexandria, a later poetic voice of an also vanished culture; one who is, like Callimachus, undergoing a renaissance of interest at this time, and for many of the same reasons. This is of course C.P. Cavafy,

---

[16] Line 24, ἐρῆμος[ ].ρ ἡ ῥῆσις, is of particular interest here for its courtroom coloring.

[17] For extended discussion of this passage, see Acosta-Hughes 2002: 82–89. I am inclined now, though, to read these lines as slightly more self-referential. Whatever we should read at the end of line 31, Callimachus himself certainly composed in pentameters, and I would give more credit to his statement that he was also the author of at least one tragedy (*Ep.* 59 GP = 59 Pf.). See further my discussion in "'Nor When a Man Goes to Dionysus' Holy Contests' (Theocr. 17.112): Outlines of Theatrical Performance in Theocritus," chap. 15 in K. Bosher, ed., *Theatre outside Athens: Drama in Greek Sicily and South Italy* (Cambridge, forthcoming).

[18] In this volume, see the chapters by De Stefani and Magnelli, Barchiesi, and Citroni. Recent work on Callimachus and Roman poetry includes Hunter 2006a and Acosta-Hughes and Stephens forthcoming.

whom one can also define, in many of the senses in which we use the term, as a Hellenistic poet.[19]

There is no reason to believe that Cavafy read Callimachus; and even had he done so, this would have been a Callimachus very different from the one we know today, thanks to the papyrus finds published in the past century.[20] Yet the reader of these two Alexandrians can only be struck by the remarkable similarities that characterize their histories, their lives, their loves, and their poetry. Both poets spent the better part of their existence in Alexandria, in a Hellenic community in Egypt, and yet were newly Alexandrian. Callimachus, like many Hellenes, came to Alexandria in the early period of Ptolemaic rule. Cavafy, like many Hellenes, was part of the new Greek community that arose in Alexandria in the mid-to-late nineteenth century. Both men were scions of old Greek communities that, while in one sense part of the diaspora, had long, rich histories: the old Doric colony of Cyrene and the Greek community of Ottoman Constantinople. In the poetry of each, a place distant in both time and space is significantly, albeit differently, present. For Cavafy the Byzantine capital, for Callimachus early Cyrene, gives each in his contemporary Alexandria a sense of identity and historical continuum. Both, while they knew poverty, whether literally or figuratively, at the same time could claim aristocratic lineage. The family of Cavafy's mother included court officials of the Ottoman empire; Callimachus claims descent from Cyrenaean kings. Both were government functionaries, and while in some aspects the essence of Callimachus' *Pinakes* and Cavafy's Irrigation Office reports are, indeed, quite different, many quotidian features of their work would not have been dissimilar. Each was concerned with creating order. For two poets who both cared for the editing of their own work, this is a revealing commonality.

Both poets, as we read them in their verses, loved other men, many other men, and these loves are commemorated in their poetry. The one man's erotic experience was societally sanctioned; the other's, societally condemned; and we must necessarily take this difference into account in our reading of the erotics of each. Further, promiscuous homosexual love is an artistic convention for Callimachus. His

---

[19] For a full treatment of this comparison, see Acosta-Hughes 2003.
[20] Cavafy's library did not, according to R. Lidell's survey (2002: 121), include Callimachus.

homoerotic love poetry, especially in his *Epigrams*, derives from a long tradition of symposiastic poetry celebrating the brief passing moment of young male beauty, viewed (and desired) in public spaces by competing older men (*erastai*).[21] For Cavafy the multiplicity of desire is in some aspects rather unconventional, even daring. His erotic poetry evokes many bodies and many loves: the portrayal of the artist as single figure is frequently juxtaposed with a plurality of desires.[22] Yet there remain remarkable similarities in the two men's artistic portrayal of their erotic lives.

So, too, their poetics strikingly respond. Although informed by different temporal circumstances, aesthetic influences, and societal factors, the compelling correspondences remain. In their poetics both shun the commonplace; both seek to capture the perfect moment.[23] Characteristic of the poetry of both men is unusual poetic presence, what G.B. D'Alessio has so well termed of Callimachus in the introduction to his Biblioteca Universale Rizzoli (BUR) edition the "sfuggente poeta" (D'Alessio 2007: 6), the sudden, unanticipated poetic voice, the voice that appears from the periphery rather than the center, and that may be an amalgamation of voices. In the poetry of both, perspective is often strikingly novel: the way a subject or event is grasped, by whom, and under what circumstances.

And, of course, both Alexandrian poets have recently evolved further through the recent discovery of lost work—each is emphatically changed in his current instantiation from previous editions, Callimachus in particular through the discovery of the Lille Papyrus and the opening of *The Victory of Berenice*, of which a new fragment has only just been published;[24] Cavafy through the extraordinary publication of several lost poems by Daniel Mendelsohn in 2009.[25]

The most outstanding feature that these two Alexandrian poets share is their interactive relationship to the past. Both are readers of an earlier Hellenic experience; both refashion that experience into something novel, something that consciously calls attention to its similarity and difference. In both, earlier Greek poetry lives again. It is the

---

[21] So, e.g., Callimachus *Ep.* 1 GP (= 31 Pf.). On the conventions and evolution of the genre, see F. Buffière in Aubreton, Buffière, and Irigoin, 1994: xxxix–lx.
[22] "Their Origin" (Ἡ ἀρχή των) is a vivid example.
[23] On this aspect of Cafavy's poetry, see Jusdanis 1987: 42–44.
[24] Fr. 144 M.; cf. D'Alessio 2007: 800–803 *fragmentum novum*.
[25] C.P. Cavafy, *The Unfinished Poems*.

self-consciously scholarly character of their writing that perhaps most arrests us: not only the interweaving of allusion, the recollection of earlier authors and texts, but the references to earlier literary monuments and their reading. Yet the relationship to the past has another presence in our two poets. Both cast themselves as old men, old men looking upon younger beauty. For both, their poetic is one that looks back, one that recalls not only earlier times but earlier periods of life, one that revives earlier lived experience, one that remembers. For both poets memory—its evocation and its portrayal—is at once artistic figure and poetic stratagem.

Among the revealing coincidences in the poetry of our two Alexandrians are poems configured as reading earlier monuments, themselves physical texts: poems where an embedded text, and a remembered life, takes on a new and different life through recollection by a later reader and poet. These poems, Callimachus' *Tomb of Simonides* and Cavafy's "In the Month of Athyr," remarkably bring together other shared features of the two artists. They evoke the image of the poet as reader of other texts, and both poems play in several ways on reading and the written, and read, word. In both the text as physical object—indeed, broken object—assumes a voice of its own. And both poems derive from and highlight the two Alexandrians' scholarly interest in earlier culture and texts.

Callimachus' poem *The Tomb of Simonides* (fr. 64 Pf. = 163 M.) is one of several speaking monuments, *oggetti parlanti*, in his long, elegiac *Aetia*: part of its conceit is that the monument, the poem's narrator, narrates its own inscription, in other words engages in an act of reading an earlier poem. This is perhaps one of the more elaborate, and remarkable, evolutions of the funerary epigrammatic convention in which the monument speaks of its own inscribed letters, of inscription itself, and of its own physicality. The poem is further remarkable for its layered voice: not only does the speaking tomb speak for the poet Simonides; it is Callimachus, the later poet, who assumes the voice of the tomb, and so the voice of Simonides. The poem, *The Tomb of Simonides*, which tells of broken text, is itself fragmentary. I give only the extant full lines:[26]

---

[26] Doubtful letters marked as in Pfeiffer; Massimilla in his edition of the fragment (2010: 100) marks considerably more as doubtful.

Οὐδ' ἄ]ν τοι Καμάρινα τόσον κακὸν ὀκκόσον ἀ[ν]δρός
  κινη]θεὶς ὁσίου τύμβος ἐπικρεμάσαι·
καὶ γ]ὰρ ἐμόν κοτε σῆμα, τό μοι πρὸ πόληος ἔχ[ευ]αν
  Ζῆν'] Ἀκραγαντῖνοι Ξείνι[ο]ν ἀζόμενοι,
ἶφι κ]ατ' οὖν ἤρειψεν ἀνὴρ κακός, εἴ τιν' ἀκούει[ς   5
  Φοίνικ]α πτόλιος σχέτλιον ἡγεμόνα·
πύργῳ] δ' ἐγκατέλεξεν ἐμὴν λίθον οὐδὲ τὸ γράμμα
  ᾐδέσθη τὸ λέγον τόν [μ]ε Λεωπρέπεος
κεῖσθαι Κήϊον ἄνδρα τὸν ἱερόν, ὃς τὰ περισσά
  . . καὶ] μνήμην πρῶτος ὃς ἐφρασάμην,   10
οὐδ' ὑμέας, Πολύδευκες, ὑπέτρεσεν, οἵ με μελάθρου
  μέλλοντος πίπτειν ἐκτὸς ἔθεσθέ κοτε
δαιτυμόνων ἄπο μοῦνον, ὅτε Κραννώνιος αἰαῖ
  ὤλισθεν μεγάλους οἶκος ἐπὶ Σκοπάδας.

Not so much evil does Camarina threaten, as a holy man's grave, if moved. And yet once my tomb, which before the city the Acragantines had poured, in honor of Zeus Xenius, once a wicked man cast down, perhaps you've heard of him, Phoenix, evil leader of the city. He immured my tombstone into a [tower] nor honored the inscription that said that I, Leoprepes' son, a holy man, lay there, I who [did] amazing things...and that I first conceived of memory, nor had he any fear of you two, Polydeuces, who when that hall was about to collapse set me outside, alone of all those guests, when their Crannonian home fell down upon the great Scopadae.

Fr. 64.1–14 Pf.

The poem encompasses two acts of sin and monumental destruction: one that occurs after Simonides' death, one during his life. Phoenix, the Acragantine general, engaged in a war with Syracuse, razes the poet's monument to use the stone in a fortified tower: the city then falls to the enemy. The event that the tomb remembers, the conception of memory, occurs in the context of a party given by Scopas, a Thessalian dynast. The story, best preserved in Cicero (*De oratore* 2.86), goes as follows. Scopas gives the poet insufficient compensation for his song: the poet is summoned out of the house by a pair of divine figures (apparently the Dioscuri); the house collapses, killing all within. Only through his memory of where each guest was sitting is the poet able to recall the identity of the guests, their bodies now unrecognizable. This act of recollection is then recalled again in our poem.

The poem's reader, however we identify that figure here, engages in a multilayered act of reading. The reader of Callimachus' elegiac lines moves forward, construing speaker and context from a series of speakers and referents. First geographical setting, then period, then possessor of the tomb are revealed in a series of unveilings: indeed one of the fragment's remarkable features is the change of number, and of referent, in each distich. However, the reader of Simonides, as configured here, moves backward in sequence of narrated events: the present tomb, its destruction, its inscribing, the living Simonides, and backward through memory. Simonides' renowned mnemonic, celebrated in the tomb's inscription, is itself explained through narrated memory, hence remembered. Reading itself is variously represented in the text, whether as "writing that speaks" (τὸ γράμμα | ... τὸ λέγον) or as the dishonored inscription, one not properly read. The writing embedded in the stone is in turn embedded in the tower: what surprises us in these lines is the physicality of the text and of its inscription. And of its duration: the irony of Callimachus' poem is the recollection of a destroyed text.

Cavafy's "In the Month of Athyr" reads a fragmentary inscription: the physical act of the reading is evoked through the inscription's lacunose state, itself embedded in the poem that reads it:[27]

Μὲ δυσκολία διαβάζω στὴν πέτρα τὴν ἀρχαία.
"Κύ[ρι]ε Ἰησοῦ Χριστέ". Ἕνα "Ψυ[χ]ὴν" διακρίνω.
"Ἐν τῷ μη[νὶ] Ἀθὺρ" "Ὁ Λεύκιο[ς] ἐ[κοιμ]ήθη".
Στὴ μνεία τῆς ἡλικίας "Ἐβί[ωσ]εν ἐτῶν",
τὸ Κάππα Ζῆτα δείχνει ποὺ νέος ἐκοιμήθη.
Μὲς στὰ φθαρμένα βλέπω "Αὐτο[ν] ... Ἀλεξανδρέα".
Μετὰ ἔχει τρεῖς γραμμὲς πολὺ ἀκρωτηριασμένες·
μὰ κάτι λέξεις βγάζω— σὰν "δ[ά]κρυα ἡμῶν", "ὀδύνην",
κατόπιν πάλι "δάκρυα", καὶ "[ἡμ]ῖν τοῖς [φ]ίλοις πένθος".
Μὲ φαίνεται ποὺ ὁ Λεύκιος μεγάλως θ' ἀγαπήθη.
Ἐν τῷ μηνὶ Ἀθὺρ ὁ Λεύκιος ἐκοιμήθη.

With difficulty I read what's on this ancient stone.
"Lo[rd] Jesus Christ." I make out a "so[u]l."
"In the mon[th] of Athyr." "Leukio[s] fell a[sl]eep."
Where the age is cited, "He li[ve]d to the age of."
The Kappa Zeta indicates that he fell asleep young.
In the eroded spots I see "Hi[m] ... Alexandrian."
Three lines follow very mutilated:
though I can pick out some words—like "our te[a]rs," "pain,"
afterward again "tears" and "to [u]s his [f]riends grief."
I gather that Leukios must have been greatly loved.
In the month of Athyr Leukios fell asleep.
                               Cavafy "In the Month of Athyr"

---

[27] Text from Savidis 2000: 1.82; translation is my own.

The poem is balanced between two verbal acts that frame the read inscription, "With difficulty I read," and "I gather that Leukios" (Μέ δυσκολία διαβάζω, Μέ φαίνεται πού ὁ Λεύκιος): the Greek homonym μέ...μέ that marks this balance is of course lost in translation. In effect the one verbal act, "I read," enters the inscription; the other, "I gather," disengages from the inscription's reading. There is a revealing parallel here in the two essentials of funerary epigram itself, engagement and recognition. The reader's sympathy evolves with the awareness of the death, of a young man, an Alexandrian, one much loved. The physical act of reading is evoked through the poem's dialogic structure of reading and text read. This is very clearly laid out in the Greek original, which recreates on the page something of the figures of reader and text, as well as of distance and empathy. And reading is further evoked through the twofold valence of the bracketed letters that signal at once the absence of symbol in the physical text and the reader's own inscription of them. The language of reading—διακρίνω, "I make out," βλέπω, "I see," μὰ κάτι λέξεις βγάζω, "though I can pick out some words"—evokes not a facile, passive viewing but some effort: effort, perhaps, drawn from the reader's empathy for his text's subject. The move toward knowledge, and toward empathy, renews the inscription: in the poem's final lines, Cavafy's lines, Leukios is greatly loved, and falls asleep, again. The reading of the inscription effectively recreates its original occasion, the death of a young man. The love felt for him, and the sorrow at his death, live again in Cavafy's verses.

BIBLIOGRAPHY

Abbenes, J.G.J. 1996. "The Doric of Theocritus, a Literary Language." Pp. 1–19 in M.A. Harder, Regtuit, and Wakker, eds. 1996.
Abbenes, J.G.J., S.R. Slings, and I. Sluiter, eds. 1995. *Greek Literary Theory after Aristotle: A Collection of Papers in Honour of D.M. Schenkeveld*. Amsterdam.
Acconcia Longo, A. 1983. *Il calendario giambico in monostici di Teodoro Prodromo*. Rome.
Accorinti, D. 1996. *Nonno di Panopoli: Parafrasi del Vangelo di San Giovanni, canto XX*. Pisa.
———. 2004. *Nonno di Panopoli, Le Dionisiache, canti XL–XLVIII*. Milan.
Acosta-Hughes, B. 1996. "Callimachus, Hipponax, and the Persona of the Iambographer." *Materiali e Discussioni* 37: 205–216.
———. 2002. *Polyeideia: The Iambi of Callimachus and the Archaic Iambic Tradition*. Berkeley and Los Angeles.
———. 2003. "Aesthetics and Recall: Callimachus Frs. 226–229 Pf. Reconsidered." *Classical Quarterly* 53: 478–489.
———. 2010. *Arion's Lyre: Archaic Lyric into Hellenistic Poetry*. Princeton.
———. Forthcoming. "Il canto della cicala: Platone negli *Aitia*." In Martina and Cozzoli forthcoming.
Acosta-Hughes, B., and R. Scodel. 2004. "*Aesop Poeta*: Aesop and the Fable in Callimachus' *Iambi*." Pp. 1–22 in M.A. Harder, Regtuit, and Wakker 2004.
Acosta-Hughes, B., and S.A. Stephens. 2001. "*Aetia* Fr. 1.5 Pf.: I Told My Story like a Child." *Zeitschrift für Papyrologie und Epigraphik* 136: 214–216.
———. 2002. "Rereading Callimachus' *Aetia* Fragment 1." *Classical Philology* 97: 238–255.
———. Forthcoming. *Callimachus in Context: From Plato to Ovid*. Cambridge.
Adams, W.L., and E.N. Borza, eds. 1982. *Philip II, Alexander the Great and the Macedonian Heritage*. Washington, D.C.
Adrados, F.R. 1999. *History of the Graeco-Latin Fable*. Vol. 1 Leiden.
Ager, S.L. 2005. "Familiarity Breeds: Incest and the Ptolemaic Dynasty." *Journal of Hellenic Studies* 125: 1–34.
Agosti, G. 1997a. "Eratostene sulle Muse e il re." *Hermes* 125: 118–123.
———. 1997b. "P. Oxy. 3537r: Etopea acrostica su Esiodo." *Zeitschrift für Papyrologie und Epigraphik* 119: 1–5.
———. 2001. "L'epica biblica nella tarda antichità greca: Autori e lettori nel IV e nel V secolo." Pp. 67–104 in F. Stella, ed., *La scrittura infinita: Bibbia e poesia in età medievale e umanistica*. Florence.
———. 2003. *Nonno di Panopoli: Parafrasi del Vangelo di San Giovanni, canto V*. Florence.
———. 2004. *Nonno di Panopoli, Le Dionisiache, canti XXV–XXXIX*. Milan.
———. 2008a. "Epigrammi lunghi nella produzione epigrafica tardoantica." Pp. 663–692 in A.M. Morelli 2008.
———. 2008b. "Literariness and Levels of Style in Epigraphical Poetry of Late Antiquity." Pp. 191–213 in Carvounis and Hunter 2008.
Albert, W. 1988. *Das mimetische Gedicht in der Antike*. Frankfurt.
Albis, R.V. 1995. "Jason's Prayer to Apollo in *Aetia* I and the *Argonautica*." *Phoenix* 49: 104–110.
Aloni, A. 2001. "The Proem of Simonides' Plataea Elegy." Pp. 86–105 in Boedeker and Sider 2001.

Alpers, K. 1990. "Griechische Lexikographie in Antike und Mittelalter." Pp. 14–38 in Koch 1990.
———. 2001. "Lexikographie B/I." Pp. 194–210 in Ueding 2001.
Alster, T.B. 2005. *Sumerian Wisdom*. New York.
Amato, E. 2005. *Dionisio di Alessandria: Descrizione della terra abitata*. Milan.
Ambühl, A. 2004. "Entertaining Theseus and Heracles: The *Hecale* and the *Victoria Berenices* as a Diptych." Pp. 23–47 in M.A. Harder, Regtuit, and Wakker 2004.
———. 2005. *Kinder und junge Helden: Innovative Aspekte des Umgangs mit der literarischen Tradition bei Kallimachos*. Louvain.
———. 2007. " 'Tell, All Ye Singers, My Fame': Kings, Queens and Nobility in Epigram." Pp. 275–294 in Bing and Bruss 2007.
Ameling, W. 2001. "Ptolemaios I. Soter." Cols. 531–533 in *Der neue Pauly: Enzyklopädie der Antike*, vol. 10. Stuttgart.
Ampolo, C. 1988. "Introduzione." Pp. ix–lv in C. Ampolo and M. Manfredini, eds., *Plutarco: Le vite di Teseo e di Romolo*. Milan.
———, ed. 2006. *Aspetti dell'opera di Felix Jacoby*. Pisa.
Andrews, N.E. 1998. "Philosophical Satire in the *Aetia* Prologue." Pp 1–19 in M.A. Harder, Regtuit, and Wakker 1998.
Aneziri, S. 2003. *Die Vereine der dionysischen Techniten im Kontext der hellenistischen Gesellschaft: Untersuchungen zur Geschichte, Organisation und Wirkung der hellenistischen Technitenvereine*. Stuttgart.
Angeli Bernardini, P., ed. 2004. *La città di Argo: Mito, storia, tradizioni poetiche—Atti del Convegno internazionale, Urbino, 13–15 giugno 2002*. Rome.
Angiò, F. 2004. "Supplementum Hellenisticum 969.6." *Seminari Romani di Cultura Greca* 7: 221–223.
Ardizzoni, A. 1935. "Eracle e Tiodamante in Callimaco e in Apollonio Rodio." *Rivista di Filologia e di Istruzione Classica* 13: 452–467.
———. 1960. "Callimaco 'ipponatteo.' " *Annali della Facoltà di Lettere e Filosofia (Cagliari)* 28: 5–20.
Argentieri, L. 2003. *Gli epigrammi degli Antipatri*. Bari.
Arias, P.E. 1987. "Euthymos di Locri." *Annali della Scuola Normale Superiore di Pisa* 17: 1–8.
Arnott, W.G. 1976. "Two Functions of Ambiguity in Callimachus' *Hymn to Zeus*." *Rivista di Cultura Classica e Medioevale* 18: 13–18.
Arrighetti, G. 1994. "Un secolo di edizioni dell'*Athenaion Politeia*." Pp. 19–37 in Maddoli 1994.
Arrighetti, G., and M. Tulli, eds. 2000. *Letteratura e riflessione sulla letteratura nella cultura classica*. Pisa.
Asmis, E. 1990. "The Poetic Theory of the Stoic 'Aristo.' " *Apeiron* 23: 147–201.
———. 1992a. "Crates on Poetic Criticism. (Philodemus, *On Poems* 5, cols. 21.25–26.18." *Phoenix* 46: 138–169.
———. 1992b. "An Epicurean Survey of Poetic Theories (Philodemus, *On Poems* 5, cols. 26–36)." *Classical Quarterly* 42: 395–415.
———. 1992c. "Neoptolemus and the Classification of Poetry." *Classical Philology* 87: 206–231.
———. 1995. "Philodemus on Censorship, Moral Utility, and Formalism in Poetry." Pp. 148–177 in Obbink 1995.
———. 1998. "Hellenistic Aesthetics: Philosophers and Literary Critics." Pp. 389–391 in M. Kelly, ed., *Encyclopedia of Aesthetics*, vol. 2. Oxford.
———. 2002. Review of Janko 2000. *Classical Philology* 97: 383–394.
———. 2006. "Epicurean Poetics." Pp. 238–266 in Laird 2006a. [Originally published as pp. 15–34 in Obbink 1995.]
———. 2007. "Myth and Philosophy in Cleanthes' *Hymn to Zeus*." *Greek, Roman and Byzantine Studies* 47: 413–429.

Asper, M. 1997. *Onomata allotria: Zur Genese, Struktur und Funktion poetologischer Metaphern bei Kallimachos.* Stuttgart.
———. 2001. "Gruppen und Dichter: Zu Programmatik und Adressatenbezug bei Kallimachos." *Antike und Abendland* 47: 84–116.
———. 2004. *Kallimachos: Werke, griechisch und deutsch.* Darmstadt.
Asquith, H. 2005. "From Genealogy to Catalogue: The Hellenistic Adaptation of the Hesiodic Catalogue Form." Pp. 266–286 in Hunter 2005b.
Athanassaki, L., R.P. Martin, and J. Miller, eds. 2009. *Apolline Politics and Poetics.* Delphi.
Atti del II Congresso Internazionale Italo-Egiziano. 1995. *Alessandria e il mondo ellenistico-romano: Il centenario del Museo greco-romano, Alessandria, 23–27 novembre 1992.* Rome
Aubreton, R., F. Buffière, and J. Irigoin. 1994. *Anthologie grecque*, vol. 11. Paris.
Austin, C., and E. Stigka. 2007. "Not Comedy, but Epigram: 'Mr. Perfect' in Fr. Com. Adesp. *1036." *Zeitschrift für Papyrologie und Epigraphik* 161: 13–16.
Austin, M.M. 1986. "Hellenistic Kings, War, and the Economy." *Classical Quarterly* 36: 450–466.
———. 1981. *The Hellenistic World from Alexander to the Roman Conquest: A Selection of Ancient Sources in Translation.* Cambridge.
———. 2006. *The Hellenistic World from Alexander to the Roman Conquest: A Selection of Ancient Sources in Translation.* 2nd ed. Cambridge.
Azoulay, V. 2004. *Xénophon et les Grâces du pouvoir: De la charis au charisme.* Paris.
Bagnall, R.S. 2002. "Alexandria: Library of Dreams." *Proceedings of the American Philosophical Society* 146: 348–362.
Bagnall, R.S., and D.W. Rathbone, eds. 2004. *Egypt from Alexander to the Early Christians: An Archaeological and Historical Guide.* Los Angeles.
Bailey, C., E.A. Barber, C.M. Bowra, J.D. Denniston, and D.L. Page, eds. 1936. *Greek Poetry and Life: Essays Presented to G. Murray on His Seventieth Birthday, January 2, 1936.* Oxford.
Baines, J. 2004. "Egyptian Elite Self-Presentation in the Context of Ptolemaic Rule." Pp. 33–61 in Harris and Ruffini 2004.
Bandini, A.M. 1763. *Καλλιμάχου Κυρηναίου ὕμνοι / Callimachi Cyrenaei hymni, cum Latina interpretatione a viro cl. Ant. Mar. Salvinio Etruscis versibus, nunc primum editis, redditi.* Florence.
Bär, S. 2009. *Quintus Smyrnaeus, Posthomerica.* Volume 1, *Die Wiedergeburt des Epos aus dem Geiste der Amazonomachie: Mit einem kommentar zu den Versen 1–219.* Göttingen.
Barbantani, S. 2001. *ΦΑΤΙΣ ΝΙΚΗΦΟΡΟΣ: Frammenti di elegia encomiastica nell'età delle guerre galatiche.* Milan.
———. 2002–2003. "Callimachus and the Contemporary Historical 'Epic.'" *Hermathena* 173–174: 29–47.
———. 2005. "Goddess of Love and Mistress of the Sea: Notes on a Hellenistic Hymn to Arsinoe-Aphrodite (P.Lit.Goodsp. 2, I–IV)." *Ancient Society* 35: 133–163.
———. 2006. "Considerazioni sull'ortografia dei poemi di P.Lit.Goodspeed 2 e sulla loro destinazione." *Aegyptus* 86: 3–33.
———. 2007. "*Supplementum Hellenisticum* 969 (PSI inv. 436): In Praise of a Ptolemaic General?" Pp. 19–24 in Palme 2007.
———. 2008. "Some Remarks on the Origin and Orthography of the 'Ptolemaic Hymns,' P.Lit.Goodspeed 2." Pp. 1–32 in E. Cingano and L. Milano, eds., *Papers on Ancient Literatures: Greece, Rome and the Near East—Proceedings of the "Advanced Seminar in the Humanities," Venice International University, 2004–2005.* Padua.
Barber, E.A. 1936. "The Lock of Berenice: Callimachus and Catullus." Pp. 348–353 in Bailey et al. 1936.

Barber, E.A., and P. Maas. 1950. "Callimachea." *Classical Quarterly* 44: 96.
Barchiesi, A. 1984. *La traccia del modello: Effetti omerici nella narrazione virgiliana.* Pisa.
——. 1993. "Future Reflexive: Two Modes of Allusion and Ovid's *Heroides.*" *Harvard Studies in Classical Philology* 95: 333–365.
——. 1994. "Immovable Delos: *Aeneid* 3.73–98 and the *Hymns* of Callimachus." *Classical Quarterly* 44: 438–443.
——. 1997a. "Otto punti su una mappa dei naufragi." *Materiali e Discussioni* 39: 209–226.
——. 1997b. *The Poet and the Prince.* Berkeley and Los Angeles.
——. 2001a. "Genealogie letterarie nell'epica imperiale: Fondamentalismo e ironia." Pp. 315–354 in E.A. Schmidt 2001.
——. 2001b. "Horace and Iambos: The Poet as a Literary Historian." Pp. 141–164 in Cavarzere, Aloni, and Barchiesi 2001.
——. 2001c. *Speaking Volumes.* London.
——. 2005. "The Search for the Perfect Book." Pp. 320–342 in Gutzwiller 2005.
Barchiesi, A., J. Ruepke, and S.A. Stephens, eds. 2004. *Rituals in Ink: A Conference on Religion and Literary Production in Ancient Rome Held at Stanford University in February 2002.* Stuttgart.
Barigazzi, A. 1951. "L'epinicio per Sosibio di Callimaco." *Parola del Passato* 6: 410–426.
——. 1976. "Eracle e Tiodamante in Callimaco e Apollonio Rodio." *Prometheus* 2: 227–238.
——. 1981. "Esiodo e la chiusa degli *Aitia* di Callimaco." *Prometheus* 7: 97–107.
Barker, A. 1984–89. *Greek Musical Writings.* 2 vols. Cambridge.
——. 1988. "Che cos'era la *magadis*?" Pp. 96–107 in Gentili and Pretagostini 1988.
Barrett, W.S. 1964. *Euripides: Hippolytos.* Oxford.
Bartley, A.N. 2003. *Stories from the Mountains, Stories from the Sea: The Digressions and Similes of Oppian's "Halieutica" and the "Cynegetica."* Göttingen.
Bartoletti, V., G. Bastianini, G. Messeri, F. Montanari, and R. Pintaudi, eds. 2008. *Papiri greci e latini.* Volume 15. Florence. [*Pubblicazioni della Società italiana per la ricerca dei papiri greci e latini in Egitto.*]
Bassi, K. 1989. "The Poetics of Exclusion in Callimachus' *Hymn to Apollo.*" *Transactions of the American Philological Association* 119: 219–231.
Basta Donzelli, G. 1984. "Arsinoe simile ad Elena (Theocritus *Id.* 15, 110)." *Hermes* 112: 306–316.
——. 1991. "La seconda giovinezza di Callimaco (fr. 1, 32 ss. Pf.)." Pp. 387–394 in *Studi di filologia classica in onore di Giusto Monaco,* vol. 1. Palermo.
Bastianini, G. 1996. "Κατὰ λεπτόν in Callimaco (fr. 1, 11 Pfeiffer)." Pp. 69–80 in Funghi 1996.
——. 2000. "P.Mil.Vogl. I 18: Perché l'interruzione?" *Papyrologica Lupiensia* 9: 77–81.
——. 2006. "Considerazioni sulle *Diegeseis* fiorentine (PSI XI 1219)." Pp. 149–166 in Bastianini and Casanova 2006.
——. 2008. "Callimaco, *Victoria Berenices.*" Pp. 177–182 in Bartoletti et al. 2008.
Bastianini, G., and A. Casanova, eds. 2006. *Callimaco: Cent'anni di papiri—Atti del Convegno internazionale di studi, Firenze, 9–10 giugno 2005.* Florence.
——. 2008. *Esiodo: Cent'anni di papiri—Atti del Convegno internazionale di studi, Firenze, 7–8 giugno 2007.* Florence.
Baudelaire, C. 1964. *"The Painter of Modern Life" and Other Essays.* Ed. and trans. J. Mayne. London.
Bausi, F. 1996. *Angelo Poliziano: Silvae.* Florence.
Begg, D.J.I. 1998. "'It Was Wonderful, Our Return in the Darkness with...the Baskets of Papyri!'" *Bulletin of the American Society of Papyrologists* 35: 185–210.

Belfiore, E. 1986. "Wine and Catharsis of the Emotions in Plato's *Laws*." *Classical Quarterly* 36: 421–437.
Bellandi, F. 2007. *Lepos e pathos: Studi su Catullo*. Bologna.
Belloni, L. 2009. "Una provocazione apolloniana: Apollonio Rodio 'ἔφηβος' (*Vit*. A, 8–11 Wendel)." *Wiener Studien* 122: 37–48.
Belloni, L., L. de Finis, and G. Moretti, eds. 2003. *L'officina ellenistica: Poesia dotta e popolare in Grecia e a Roma*. Trent.
Belloni, L., G. Milanese, and A. Porro, eds. 1995. *Studia classica Iohanni Tarditi oblata*. 2 vols. Milan.
Benedetto, G. 1993. *Il sogno e l'invettiva: Momenti di storia dell'esegesi callimachea*. Florence.
———. 1997. "Il trattamento dei frammenti nell'edizione callimachea del 1761 attraverso la corrispondenza inedita di J.A. Ernesti con D. Ruhnkenius e L.C. Valckenaer (1748–1761)." Pp. 95–110 in Most 1997.
Bentley, R. 1697. "Callimachi fragmenta a Richardo Bentleio collecta." Pp. 303–429 in Graevius 1697.
Bernand, É. 1969. *Inscriptions métriques de l'Égypte gréco-romaine: Recherches sur la poésie épigrammatique des grecs en Égypte*. Paris.
Bernard, P., G.-J. Pinault, and G. Rougemont. 2004. "Deux nouvelles inscriptions grecques d'Asie centrale." *Journal des Savants*, 227–356.
Bernardini Marzolla, P. 1952. "Il testo dei *Dionysiaca* di Nonno." *Studi Italiani di Filologia Classica* 26: 191–209.
Bernsdorff, H. 1997. "Q. Sulpicius Maximus, Apollonios von Rhodos und Ovid." *Zeitschrift für Papyrologie und Epigraphik* 118: 105–112.
———. 1999. "Hesiod, ein zweiter Vergil? Bemerkungen zu P.Oxy. 3537r, 3–28." Pp. 63–83 in S. Döpp, ed., *Antike Rhetorik und ihre Rezeption*. Stuttgart.
———. 2007. "P.Oxy. 4711 and the Poetry of Parthenius." *Journal of Hellenic Studies* 127: 1–18.
Bertazzoli, V. 2002. "Arsinoe II e la protezione della poesia: Una nuova testimonianza di Posidippo." *Appunti Romani di Filologia* 4: 145–153.
Berti, M. 2009. *Istro il callimacheo*. Volume 1, *Testimonianze e frammenti su Atene e sull'Attica*. Tivoli.
Bertolini, F. 1995. "Muse, re e aedi nel proemio della Teogonia di Esiodo." Pp. 127–138 in Belloni, Milanese, and Porro 1995.
Bettini, M. 2008. *Voci: Antropologia sonora del mondo antico*. Turin.
Bicknell, P.J. 1986. "The Date of the Fall of the Eumenid Tyranny at Akragas." *Civiltà Classica e Cristiana* 7: 54–60.
Bieżuńska-Małowist, I. 1977. *L'esclavage dans l'Égypte grécoromaine, seconde partie: Période romaine*. Wrocław.
Binder, G., and B. Effe, eds. 1995. *Affirmation und Kritik: Zur politischen Funktion von Kunst und Literatur im Altertum*. Trier.
Bing, P. 1986. "Two Conjectures in Callimachus' *Hymn to Delos* v. 178 and 205." *Hermes* 114: 121–124.
———. 1988a. "A Note on the 'Musenanruf' in Callimachus: A Contribution to Greek Poetical Language." *Zeitschrift für Papyrologie und Epigraphik* 74: 273–275.
———. 1988b. *The Well-Read Muse: Present and Past in Callimachus and the Hellenistic Poets*. Göttingen. [Reprint: Ann Arbor, 2008.]
———. 1995. "*Ergänzungsspiel* in the Epigrams of Callimachus." *Antike und Abendland* 41: 115–131.
———. 1997. "Reconstructing Berenike's Lock." Pp. 78–94 in Most 1997.
———. 1998. "Between Literature and the Monuments." Pp. 21–43 in M.A. Harder, Regtuit, and Wakker 1998.
———. 2000. "Text or Performance / Text and Performance: Alan Cameron's *Callimachus and His Critics*." Pp. 139–148 in Pretagostini 2000a.

———. 2002. "Medeios of Olynthos, son of Lampon, and the *Iamatika* of Posidippus." *Zeitschrift für Papyrologie und Epigraphik* 140: 297-300.
———. 2002-2003. "Posidippus and the Admiral: Kallikrates of Samos in the Milan Epigrams." *Greek, Roman and Byzantine Studies* 43: 243-266.
———. 2005. "The Politics and Poetics of Geography in the Milan Posidippus, Section One: On Stones (AB 1-20)." Pp. 119-140 in Gutzwiller 2005.
———. 2008. See Bing 1988b.
———. 2009. *The Scroll and the Marble: Studies in Reading and Reception in Hellenistic Poetry*. Ann Arbor.
Bing, P., and J.S. Bruss, eds. 2007. *Brill's Companion to Hellenistic Epigram*. Leiden.
Bing, P., and V. Uhrmeister. 1994. "The Unity of Callimachus' Hymn to Artemis." *Journal of Hellenic Studies* 114: 19-34.
Blank, D. 1994. "Diogenes of Babylon and the KPITIKOI in Philodemus: A Preliminary Suggestion." *Cronache Ercolanesi* 24: 55-62.
———. 1995. "Philodemus on the Technicity of Rhetoric." Pp. 178-188 in Obbink 1995.
———. 1998. *Sextus Empiricus: Against the Grammarians*. Oxford.
Blass, F., A. Debrunner, and F. Rehkopf. 1976. *Grammatik des neutestamentlichen Griechisch*. 14th ed. Göttingen.
Bleisch, P. 1996. "On Choosing a Spouse: *Aeneid* 7.378-384 and Callimachus' *Epigram* 1." *American Journal of Philology* 117: 453-472.
Bliquez, L.J. 1977. "Frogs and Mice and Athens." *Transactions of the American Philological Association* 107: 11-25.
Blöbaum, A.I. 2006. *"Denn ich bin ein König, der die Maat liebt": Herrscherlegitimation im spätzeitlichen Ägypten*. Aachen.
Blomfield, C.J. 1815. *Callimachi quae supersunt*. London.
Blomqvist, J. 1990. "The Last Line of Callimachus' Hymn to Apollo." *Eranos* 88: 17-24.
Blum, R. 1977. *Kallimachos und die Literaturverzeichnung bei den Griechen: Untersuchungen zur Geschichte der Bibliographie*. Frankfurt.
———. 1991. *Kallimachos: The Alexandrian Library and the Origins of Bibliography*. Trans. H.H. Wellisch. Madison.
Blümer, W. *Interpretation archaischer Dichtung: die mythologischen Partien der* Erga *Hesiods*. Munich.
Boeckh, A. 1871. *Akademische Abhandlungen vorgetragen in den Jahren 1815-1834 in der Akademie der Wissenschaften zu Berlin*. Leipzig.
Boedeker, D., and D. Sider, eds. 2001. *The New Simonides: Contexts of Praise and Desire*. Oxford.
Boehm, S., and K.-V. von Eickstedt, eds. 2001. *ITHAKE: Festschrift für J. Schäfer zum 75. Geburtstag am 25. April 2001*. Würzburg.
Bollansée, J. 1999. *Hermippos of Smyrna*. Leiden. [Volume 4A3 continuing F. Jacoby, ed., *Die Fragmente der griechischen Historiker*.]
Bonanno, M.G. 1986. "Sul finale dell'*Ila* (Theocr. XIII 73-75)." *Quaderni Urbinati di Cultura Classica* 24: 3.29-38.
———. 1993. "Saffo 31, 9 V.: γλῶσσα ἔαγε." *Quaderni Urbinati di Cultura Classica* 43: 1.61-68.
———. 1996. "Postilla a Saffo 31, 9 V. (γλῶσσα ἔαγε)." *Quaderni Urbinati di Cultura Classica* 52: 1.173-175.
———. 1998. "Metafora e critica letteraria: A proposito di Aristofane, *Rane* 900-904." *Seminari Romani di Cultura Greca* 1: 79-87.
———. 2000. "Conclusioni." Pp. 210-212 in Pretagostini 2000a.
———. 2002. "Il *poeta doctus*: Antimaco e gli altri." Pp. 13-27 in P. Mureddu et al., eds., *Giornata di studi in memoria di Gregorio Serrao, studioso di poesia alessandrina*. Cagliari. [*Annali della Facoltà di Lettere e Filosofia della Università di Cagliari* 20.1.]

———. 2004. "Il poeta scienziato di età ellenistica: Appunti per una ridefinizione del *poeta doctus* alessandrino." Pp. 451–475 in Pretagostini and Dettori 2004.
Bond, G.W. 1963. *Euripides: Hypsipyle.* Oxford.
Bongelli, P. 2000. "Frammenti del commento di Teone a Callimaco." Pp. 281–290 in Arrighetti and Tulli 2000.
Borgonovo, P. 1996. "Callimaco frr. 238 SH e 571 Pf.: Per un aition 'attico' di Epops." *Zeitschrift für Papyrologie und Epigraphik* 110: 49–55.
Borgonovo, P., and P. Cappelletto. 1994. "Callimaco frr. 114 e 115 Pf.: Apollo 'poligonale' e Apollo delio." *Zeitschrift für Papyrologie und Epigraphik* 103: 13–17.
Bornmann, F. 1968. *Callimachi Hymnus in Dianam.* Florence.
———. 1973. "Un nuovo frammento dell'*Ecale*?" *Maia* 25: 204–206.
———. 1993. "L'invettiva di Ericio contro Partenio (*AP* 7, 377)." Pp. 85–88 in M. Bandini and F.G. Pericoli, eds., *Scritti in memoria di Dino Pieraccioni.* Florence.
———. 1996. "Callimaco." Pp. 667–668 in Mariotti 1996.
Borthwick, E.K. 1969. "The Verb ΑΥΩ and Its Compounds." *Classical Quarterly* 19: 306–313.
Bosworth, A.B. 2002. *The Legacy of Alexander: Politics, Warfare, and Propaganda under the Successors.* Oxford.
———. 2006. "Alexander the Great and the Creation of the Hellenistic Age." Pp. 9–27 in Bugh 2006.
Bowie, E.L. 1986. "Early Greek Elegy, Symposium and Public Festival." *Journal of Hellenic Studies* 106: 13–35.
———. 1990. "Greek Poetry in the Antonine Age." Pp. 53–90 in D.A. Russell, ed., *Antonine Literature.* Oxford.
———. 2000. "The Reception of Apollonius in Imperial Greek Literature." Pp. 1–10 in M.A. Harder, Regtuit, and Wakker 2000.
Braccesi, L. 1994. *Grecità di frontiera: I percorsi occidentali della leggenda.* Padua.
———. 2001a. "L'Adriatico e il concetto di Europa." Pp. 115–121 in Braccesi 2001b.
———. 2001b. *Hellenikos kolpos: Supplemento a "Grecità adriatica."* Rome.
Bramble, J. 1974. *Persius and the Programmatic Satire.* Cambridge.
Branca, V., and M. Pastore Stocchi. 1978. *Angelo Poliziano: Miscellaneorum centuria secunda.* Florence.
Brandis, V. 2002. "Zwei Dichter aus Kyrene: Maximus als Imitator des Kallimachos." *Philologus* 146: 172–178.
Branham, R.B., and M.-O. Goulet-Cazé, eds. 1996. *The Cynics: The Cynic Movement in Antiquity and Its Legacy.* Berkeley and Los Angeles.
Braund, D.C. 2003. "After Alexander: The Emergence of the Hellenistic World, 323–281." Pp. 19–34 in Erskine 2003.
Bravo, B. 1997. *Pannychis e simposio: Feste private notturne di donne e uomini nei testi letterari e nel culto.* Pisa.
Bremen, R. van. 2007. "The Entire House Is Full of Crowns: Hellenistic *agones* and the Commemoration of Victory." Pp. 345–375 in Hornblower and Morgan 2007.
Bremmer, J.N. 1980. "Two Notes on Callimachus' *Hymn to Apollo*." *Mnemosyne* 33: 176.
———. 2002. "How Old Is the Ideal of Holiness (of Mind) in the Epidaurian Temple Inscription and the Hippocratic Oath?" *Zeitschrift für Papyrologie und Epigraphik* 141: 106–108.
———. 2006. "Rescuing Deio in Sophocles and Euripides." *Zeitschrift für Papyrologie und Epigraphik* 158: 27.
Brillante, C. 1994. "Poeti e re nel proemio della *Teogonia* esiodea." *Prometheus* 20: 14–26.
Bringmann, K. 1993. "The King as Benefactor: Some Remarks on Ideal Kingship in the Age of Hellenism." Pp. 7–24 in Bulloch et al. 1993.
———. 1995. "Die Ehre des Königs und der Ruhm der Stadt: Bemerkungen zu königlichen Bau- und Feststiftungen." Pp. 93–102 in Wörrle and Zanker 1995.

Brink, C.O. 1946. "Callimachus and Aristotle: An Inquiry into Callimachus' ΠΡΟΣ ΠΡΑΞΙΦΑΝΗΝ." *Classical Quarterly* 40: 11-26.
———. 1963. *Horace on Poetry.* Volume 1, *Prolegomena to the Literary Epistles.* Cambridge.
Brioso Sánchez, M. 1974. "Nicandro y los esquemas del hexámetro." *Habis* 5: 9-23.
Brodersen, K. 1992. *Reiseführer zu den sieben Weltwundern: Philon von Byzanz und andere antike Texte.* Frankfurt.
———. 1996. *Die sieben Weltwunder.* Munich.
Bruneau, P. 1970. *Recherches sur les cultes de Délos a l'époque hellénistique et à l'époque impériale.* Paris.
Bruss, J. 2004. "Lessons from Ceos: Written and Spoken Word in Callimachus." Pp. 49-70 in M.A. Harder, Regtuit, and Wakker 2004.
Bubeník, V. 1989. *Hellenistic and Roman Greece as a Sociolinguistic Area.* Amsterdam.
Budelmann, F., ed. 2009. *The Cambridge Companion to Greek Lyric.* Cambridge.
Bugh, G.R., ed. 2006. *The Cambridge Companion to the Hellenistic World.* Cambridge.
Bühler, W. 1960. *Die Europa des Moschos.* Wiesbaden.
———. 1982. *Zenobii Athoi proverbia vulgari ceteraque memoria aucta.* Volume 1, Prolegomena. Göttingen.
———. 1987. *Zenobii Athoi proverbia vulgari ceteraque memoria aucta.* Volume 4, II 1-40. Göttingen.
———. 1999. *Zenobii Athoi proverbia vulgari ceteraque memoria aucta.* Volume 5, II 41-108. Göttingen.
Bulloch, A.W. 1973. "Tibullus and the Alexandrians." *Proceedings of the Cambridge Philological Society* 199: 71-89.
———. 1977. "Callimachus' *Erysichthon*, Homer and Apollonius Rhodius." *American Journal of Philology* 98: 97-123.
———. 1984. "The Future of a Hellenistic Illusion: Some Observations on Callimachus and Religion." *Museum Helveticum* 41: 209-230.
———. 1985. *Callimachus: The Fifth Hymn, Edited with an Introduction and Commentary.* Cambridge.
———. 2006. "The Order and Structure of Callimachus' *Aetia* 3." *Classical Quarterly* 56: 496-508.
Bulloch, A.W., E.S. Gruen, A.A. Long, and A. Stewart, eds. 1993. *Images and Ideologies: Self-Definition in the Hellenistic World.* Berkeley and Los Angeles.
Bundrick, S.D. 2005. *Music and Image in Classical Athens.* Cambridge.
Bundy, E.L. 1972. "The Quarrel between Kallimachos and Apollonios, Part I: The Epilogue of Kallimachos' *Hymn to Apollo*." *California Studies in Classical Antiquity* 5: 39-94.
Buraselis, K. 1982. *Das hellenistische Makedonien und die Ägäis.* Munich.
Burkert, W. 1985a. *Greek Religion.* Oxford.
———. 1985b. "Herodot über die Namen der Götter: Polytheismus als historisches Problem." *Museum Helveticum* 42: 121-132.
———. 2001. *Savage Energies: Lessons of Myth and Ritual in Ancient Greece.* Trans. P. Bing. Chicago.
Burstein, S.M. 1982. "Arsinoe II Philadelphos: A Revisionist View." Pp. 197-212 in Adams and Borza 1982.
Busine, A. 2005. *Paroles d'Apollon: Pratiques et traditions oraculaires dans l'antiquité tardive (IIe-VIe siècles).* Leiden.
Caccamo Caltabiano, M., and P. Radici Colace. 1987. "La moneta dell'Ade." *Annali della Scuola Normale Superiore di Pisa* 17: 971-979.
Cahen, É. 1930. *Les Hymnes de Callimaque.* Paris.
Cairns, F. 1969. "Propertius i.18 and Callimachus, *Acontius and Cydippe*." *Classical Review* 19: 131-134.

——. 1972. *Generic Composition in Greek and Roman Poetry.* Edinburgh.
——. 1979. *Tibullus: A Hellenistic Poet at Rome.* Cambridge.
——. 1984. "Theocritus' First *Idyll:* The Literary Programme." *Wiener Studien* 97: 89–113.
——. 1992. "Theocritus, *Idyll* 26." *Proceedings of the Cambridge Philological Society* 38: 1–38.
——. 2000. "A Testimonium to a New Fragment of Philoxenus of Cythera? (Machon 77–80 = Fr. 9.14–17 Gow, and Hermesianax Fr. 7.69–74 Powell)." *Zeitschrift für Papyrologie und Epigraphik* 130: 9–11.
——. 2006. *Sextus Propertius: The Augustan Elegist.* Cambridge.
Calame, C. 1988. "Mythe, récit épique et histoire: Le récit hérodotéen de la fondation de Cyrène." Pp. 105–125 in C. Calame, ed., *Métamorphoses du mythe en Grèce antique.* Geneva.
——. 1992. "Narration légendaire et programme poétique dans l'*Hymne à Apollon* de Callimaque." *Études de Lettres* 4: 41–66.
——. 1993. "Legendary Narration and Poetic Procedure in Callimachus' *Hymn to Apollo.*" Pp. 37–55 in M.A. Harder, Regtuit, and Wakker 1993.
——. 1996. *Thésée et l'imaginaire athénien.* 2nd edition. Lausanne.
Calder, W.M., H. Flashar, and T. Lindken, eds. 1985. *Wilamowitz nach 50 Jahren.* Darmstadt.
Calderón Dorda, E. 1997. "Los tópicos eróticos en la elegía helenística." *Emerita* 65: 1–16.
Calvani, G. 2000. "*Kairòs* negli scholia vetera all'*Odissea.*" *Studi Classici e Orientali* 47: 123–139.
Calvino, I. 1988. *Lezioni americane: Sei proposte per il prossimo millennio.* Milan.
——. 1995. *Saggi.* Volume 2. Milan.
Cambiano, G. 1988. "Sapere e testualità nel mondo antico." Pp. 69–98 in Rossi 1988.
Cambiano, G., L. Canfora, and D. Lanza, eds. 1994. *Lo spazio letterario della Grecia antica.* Volume 2, *La ricezione e l'attualizzazione del testo.* Rome.
Cameron, Alan. 1972. "Callimachus on Aratus' Sleepless Nights." *Classical Review* 22: 169–170.
——. 1982. "The Empress and the Poet: Paganism and Politics at the Court of Theodosius II." *Yale Classical Studies* 27: 217–289.
——. 1990. "Two Mistresses of Ptolemy Philadelphus." *Greek, Roman and Byzantine Studies* 31: 287–311.
——. 1992. "Genre and Style in Callimachus." *Transactions of the American Philological Association* 122: 305–312.
——. 1993. *The Greek Anthology: From Meleager to Planudes.* Oxford.
——. 1995. *Callimachus and His Critics.* Princeton.
——. 2004. *Greek Mythography in the Roman World.* Oxford.
Cameron, Averil. 1970. *Agathias.* Oxford.
Campanelli, M. 2001. *Polemiche e filologia ai primordi della stampa: Le "Observationes" di Domizio Calderini.* Rome.
Campbell, M. 1981. *A Commentary on Quintus Smyrnaeus,* Posthomerica *XII.* Leiden.
——. 1994. *A Commentary on Apollonius Rhodius,* Argonautica *III, 1–471.* Leiden.
Canfora, L. 1995. "Le collezioni superstiti." Pp. 95–250 in Cambiano, Canfora, and Lanza 1995.
Capovilla, G. 1967. *Callimaco.* 2 vols. Rome.
Cappelletto, P. 1995. "Le 'dee offese' nel primo libro degli *Aitia* di Callimaco." *Rendiconti dell'Istituto Lombardo* 129: 211–232.
Caprara, M. 2005. *Nonno di Panopoli: Parafrasi del Vangelo di San Giovanni, canto IV.* Pisa.

Carey, C., and P. Agocs, eds. Forthcoming. *Proceedings of "Epinician: An International Conference on the Victory Ode, University College London, Institute of Classical Studies, 5–9 July 2006."* Cambridge.
Carlier, P. 2005. "Les rois d'Athènes: Étude sur la tradition." Pp. 125–141 in Greco 2005.
Carney, E.D. 1987. "The Reappearance of Royal Sibling Marriage in Ptolemaic Egypt." *Parola del Passato* 42: 420–439.
Carrière, J. 1969. "Philadelphe ou Sôtêr? À propos d'un hymne de Callimaque." *Studii Clasice* 11: 85–93.
Carvounis, K., and R. Hunter, eds. 2008. *Signs of Life? Studies in Later Greek Poetry*. Victoria.
Casamassa, R. 2004. "Posidippo fra arte e mito: La gemma di Pegaso (Posidipp. *Ep.* 14 A–B)." *Acme* 57.1: 241–252.
Casanova, A. 2006. "Cent'anni di papiri callimachei." Pp. 1–13 in Bastianini and Casanova 2006.
Cassio, A.C. 2002 "The Language of Doric Comedy." Pp. 51–84 in Willi 2002.
———. 2007. "Alcman's Text, Spoken Laconian, and Greek Study of Greek Dialects." Pp. 29–45 in I. Hajnel, ed. *Die altgriechischen Dialekte: Ihr Wesen und Werden*. Berlin.
Castagna, G. 1981. "Il Τυρίων στρατόπεδον e lo ἱρὸν τὸ... ξείνης Ἀφροδίτης a Menfi in Herod., II, 112." *Quaderni di Lingue e Letterature* 6: 195–204.
Castagna, L., and C. Riboldi, eds. 2008. *Amicitiae templa serena: Miscellanea di studi in onore di Giuseppe Aricò*. Milan.
Castelli, C. 1995. "Poeti ellenistici nella *Periegesi* di Pausania." Pp. 711–725 in Belloni, Milanese, and Porro 1995.
———. 1998. "I *Messeniaca* di Riano: Testo ed esegesi dei frammenti." *Acme* 51.1: 3–50.
Catani, E., and G. Paci, eds. 2000. *La Salaria in età antica: Atti del Convegno di studi, Ascoli Piceno, Offida, Rieti, 2–4 ottobre 1997*. Rome.
Cataudella, Q. 1928. "Il prologo degli Aitia e Gregorio Nazianzeno." *Rivista di Filologia e di Istruzione Classica* 6: 509–510.
Cavalli, M. 1994. "Uno strano 'padre della tragedia': Il drago di Delfi." *Dioniso* 64: 9–31.
Cavarzere, A. 1996. *Sul limitare: Il "motto" e la poesia di Orazio*. Bologna.
Cavarzere, A., A. Aloni, and A. Barchiesi, eds. 2001. *Iambic Ideas: Essays on a Poetic Tradition from Archaic Greece to the Late Roman Empire*. Lanham.
Cazzaniga, I. 1961. "I frammenti poetici di Partenio da Nicea: Valutazioni critico-stilistiche." *Studi Classici e Orientali* 10: 44–53.
———. 1963. "Temi poetici alessandrini in Nonno Panopolitano: Tradizione diretta e indiretta." Pp. 626–646 in *Miscellanea di studi alessandrini in memoria di A. Rostagni*. Turin.
———. 1968. "Uno spunto dell'*Hecale* callimachea in un passo della *Vita di S. Filareto* di Niceta d'Amnia." *Parola del Passato* 23: 224–227.
Ceccarelli, P. Forthcoming. "Hellenistic Dithyrambs." In Kowalzig and Wilson forthcoming.
Ceccarelli, P., and Milanezi, S. 2007. "Dithyramb, Tragedy—and Cyrene." Pp. 185–214 in P. Wilson 2007a.
Cecchi, C. 2010. "La sequenza finale del libro III degli *Aitia* a partire da Call. frr. 80–83 Pf." *Eikasmos* 21: 175–195.
Cerasuolo, S., ed. 2004. *Mathesis e mneme: Studi in memoria di Marcello Gigante*. Volume 1. Naples.
Cerri, G. 1991. *Platone sociologo della comunicazione*. Milan.
———. 2007. "Pascoli e l'ultimo viaggio di Ulisse." Pp. 16–31 in E. Cavallini, ed., *Omero mediatico: Aspetti della ricezione omerica nella civiltà contemporanea*. Bologna.

Chambers, M. 1985. "Wilamowitz and Greek History." Pp. 228–238 in Calder, Flashar, and Lindken 1985.
———. 1990. "The Genesis of Jacoby's *Atthis.*" Pp. 381–390 in Craik 1990.
———. 2006. "La vita e la carriera di Felix Jacoby." Pp. 5–29 in Ampolo 2006.
Chamoux, F. 1953. *Cyrène sous la monarchie des Battiades.* Paris.
———. 1956. "Le roi Magas." *Revue Historique* 80: 18–34.
———. 1960. "Callimaque et Cyrène." *Revue des Études Grecques* 73: 33–34.
Chaniotis, A. 1988. *Historie und Historiker in den griechischen Inschriften.* Stuttgart.
———. 1997. "Reinheit des Körpers–Reinheit der Seele in den griechischen Kultgesetzen." Pp. 142–179 in J. Assmann and T. Sundermeier, eds., *Schuld, Gewissen und Person.* Gütersloh.
———. 2001. "Ein alexandrinischer Dichter und Kreta: Mythische Vergangenheit und gegenwärtige Kultpraxis bei Kallimachos." Pp. 213–217 in Boehm and Eickstedt 2001.
———. 2003. "The Divinity of Hellenistic Rulers." Pp. 431–445 in Erskine 2003.
———. 2006. "Rituals between Norms and Emotions: Rituals as Shared Experience and Memory." Pp. 211–238 in E. Stavrianopoulou, ed., *Ritual and Communication in the Graeco-Roman World.* Liège.
Chapouthier, F. 1935. *Les Dioscures au service d'une déesse: Étude d'iconographie religieuse.* Paris.
Cheshire, K. 2008. "Kicking ΦΘΟΝΟΣ: Apollo and His Chorus in Callimachus' Hymn 2." *Classical Philology* 103: 354–373.
Chiesa, I. 2009. "L'elegia 'in Magam et Berenicen' di Callimaco: 'in Berenices nuptias'?" *Acme* 62.2: 227–234
Chrétien, G. 1985. *Nonnos de Panopolis, Les Dionysiaques.* Volume 4, *Chants IX–X.* Paris.
Christesen, P. 2007. *Olympic Victor Lists and Ancient Greek History.* Cambridge.
Citroni, M. 1995. *Poesia e lettori in Roma antica.* Rome.
———. 1998. "Pasquali." Pp. 398–403 in *Enciclopedia oraziana,* vol. 3, *La fortuna. l'esegesi, l'attualità.* Rome.
Citti, V. 1996. "Solon e la ricezione dell'antico." *Rivista Pascoliana* 8: 63–80.
———. 1997. "La ricezione dell'antico nei *Poemi conviviali*. Pp. 99–131 in M. Pazzaglia, ed., *I "Poemi conviviali" di Giovanni Pascoli: Atti del Convegno di studi di San Mauro Pascoli e Barga, 26–29 settembre 1996.* Florence.
Clarke, K. 2008. *Making Time for the Past: Local History and the Polis.* Oxford.
Clarysse, W. 1983. "Literary Papyri in Documentary Archives." Pp. 43–61 in E. van't Dack, P. van Dessel, and W. van Gucht, eds., *Egypt and the Hellenistic World: Proceedings of the International Colloquium, Leuven, 24–26 May 1982.* Louvain.
———. 1998. "Ethnic Diversity and Dialect among the Greeks of Hellenistic Egypt." Pp. 1–13 in A.M.F.W. Verhoogt and S.P. Vleeming, eds., *The Two Faces of Graeco-Roman Egypt (P.Lugd.Bat. XXX).* Leiden.
———. 2000. "The Ptolemies Visiting the Egyptian Chora." Pp. 29–53 in L. Mooren, ed., *Politics, Administration and Society in the Hellenistic and Roman World.* Louvain.
Clarysse, W., and C. Gallazzi. 1993. "Archivio dei discendenti di Laches o dei discendenti di Patron?" *Ancient Society* 24: 63–68.
Clarysse, W., and M. Huys. 1996. "A Verse Inscription from the Temple of Ain Labakha." *Zeitschrift für Papyrologie und Epigraphik* 113: 213–215.
Clarysse, W., and G. van der Veken. 1983. *The Eponymous Priests of Ptolemaic Egypt. Chronological Lists of the Priests of Alexandria and Ptolemais with a Study of the Demotic Transcriptions of Their Names.* PLugdBat. 24. Leiden.
Classen, C.J. 1995. "Rhetoric and Literary Criticism: Their Nature and Their Functions in Antiquity." *Mnemosyne* 48: 513–535.
Clausen, W.V. 1964. "Callimachus and Latin Poetry." *Greek, Roman and Byzantine Studies* 5: 181–196.

Clauss, J.J. 1986. "Lies and Allusions: The Addressee and Date of Callimachus' *Hymn to Zeus.*" *Classical Antiquity* 2: 155-170.
———. 2000. "Cosmos without Imperium: The Argonautic Journey through Time." Pp. 11-32 in M.A. Harder, Regtuit, and Wakker 2000.
Clauss, J.J., and M.P. Cuypers, eds. 2010. *A Companion to Hellenistic Literature*. Chichester.
Clay, J.S. 1996. "Fusing the Boundaries: Apollo and Dionysus at Delphi." *Métis* 11: 83-100.
———. 2006. *The Politics of Olympus: Form and Meaning in the Major "Homeric Hymns."* 2nd ed. London.
Clayman, D.L. 1980. *Callimachus' Iambi*. Leiden.
———. 1988. "Callimachus' *Iambi* and *Aetia*." *Zeitschrift für Papyrologie und Epigraphik* 74: 277-286.
———. 1989. "Callimachus' *Iambi* and *Aetia*: Corrigenda." *Zeitschrift für Papyrologie und Epigraphik* 77: 292.
Clúa, J.A. 1991. "Euphorion's *Dionysos*: Structure and Hermeneutics." *Prometheus* 17: 111-124.
Coarelli, F. 1990. "La pompè di Tolomeo Filadelfo e il mosaico nilotico di Palestrina." *Ktèma* 15: 225-251.
Cody, J.V. 1976. *Horace and Callimachean Aesthetics*. Brussels.
Coffta, D.J. 2002. *The Influence of Callimachean Aesthetics on the Satires and Odes of Horace*. Lewiston.
Cohon, R. 1991-92. "Hesiod and the Order and Naming of the Muses in Hellenistic Art." *Boreas* 14-15: 67-83.
Collard, C., and M. Cropp. 2008. *Euripides: Fragments*. Volume 1. Cambridge, Mass.
Collombert, P. 2000. "Religion égyptienne et culture grecque: L'exemple de Διοσκουρίδης." *Chronique d'Égypte* 75: 47-61.
Colomo, D. 2009. "Scholien zu Kallimachos' *Iambus* XII in einem neuen Papyrusfragment (P. Lips. Inv. 290v, Fr. b)." *Archiv für Papyrusforschung* 55: 1-20.
Colonna, G. 2000. "I Peuceti di Callimaco e l'assedio di Porsenna." Pp. 147-153 in Catani and Paci 2000.
Colson, F.H. 1941. *Philo*. Volume 9. Cambridge, Mass.
Compton, T.M. 2006. *Victim of the Muse*. Washington, D.C.
Conca, F. 1990. *Nicetas Eugenianus: De Drosillae et Chariclis amoribus*. Amsterdam.
———, ed. 1999. *Ricordando Raffaele Cantarella: Miscellanea di studi*. Milan.
Constantakopoulou, C. 2007. *The Dance of the Islands: Insularity, Networks, the Athenian Empire, and the Aegean World*. Oxford.
Conte, G.B. 1971. "Memoria dei poeti e arte allusiva." *Strumenti Critici* 16: 325-333.
———. 1974. *Memoria dei poeti e sistema letterario*. Turin. [Rev. ed. 1985.]
———. 1986. *The Rhetoric of Imitation*. Ithaca.
———. 1992. "Proems in the Middle." Pp. 147-159 in Dunn and Cole 1992.
———. 1994. *Genres and Readers*. Baltimore.
Conti, A. 1900. *La beata riva*. Milan.
Conti Bizzarro, F. 1993-1994. "Una testimonianza di Filosseno nella commedia di mezzo: Antifane fr. 207 Kassel-Austin." *Rendiconti dell'Accademia di Archeologia, Lettere e Belle Arti di Napoli* 64: 143-157.
Coppola, G. 1930. "Callimachus Senex." *Rivista di Filologia e di Istruzione Classica* 8: 273-91.
———. 1935. *Cirene e il nuovo Callimaco*. Bologna.
Corbato, C. 1979. "La funzione delle 'fabulae' in Callimaco." Pp. 45-64 in *La struttura della fabulazione antica*. Genoa.
Costa, V. 2007. *Filocoro di Atene*. Volume 1, *Testimonianze e frammenti dell' Atthis*. Tivoli.

Costanza, S. 1991. "Motivi callimachei nel proemio dei *Cynegetica* di Oppiano d'Apamea." Pp. 479-489 in *Studi di filologia classica in onore di Giusto Monaco*, vol. 1. Palermo.
Couissin, P. 1927a. "Les armes gauloises figurées sur les monuments grecs, étrusques et romains, I." *Revue Archéologique* 25: 138-176, 301-325.
———. 1927b. "Les armes gauloises figurées sur les monuments grecs, étrusques et romains, II." *Revue Archéologique* 26: 43-79.
———. 1929. "Les armes des gaulois figurées sur les monuments grecs, étrusques et romains, III." *Revue Archéologique* 29: 235-280.
Counillon, P. 2004. "La *Périégèse de la terre habitée* et l'*Hymne à Délos* de Callimaque." *Revue des Études Anciennes* 106: 187-205.
Courtney, E. 1993. *The Fragmentary Latin Poets*. Oxford.
Cozzoli, A.-T. 1994. "Dalla catarsi mimetica aristotelica all'auto-catarsi dei poeti ellenistici." *Quaderni Urbinati di Cultura Classica* 48: 3.95-110.
———. 1996a. "Aspetti intertestuali nelle polemiche letterarie degli antichi: da Pindaro a Persio." *Quaderni Urbinati di Cultura Classica* 54: 3.7-36.
———. 1996b. "Il *Giambo* I e il nuovo ἰαμβίζειν di Callimaco." *Eikasmos* 7: 129-147.
———. 1998. "Callimaco e i suoi 'critici': Considerazioni su un recente lavoro." *Eikasmos* 9: 135-154.
———. 2000. "Callimaco, fr. 282 Pf. (= 109 Hollis)." Pp. 225-232 in M. Cannatà Fera and S. Grandolini, eds., *Poesia e religione in Grecia: Studi in onore di G. Aurelio Privitera*, vol. 1. Naples.
———. 2003. "Eustazio critico pindarico." *Studi sull'Oriente Cristiano* 7: 67-73.
———. 2006. "L'inno a Zeus: Fonti e modelli." Pp. 115-136 in Martina and Cozzoli 2006.
———. 2007. "Segmenti di epos argonautico in Callimaco." Pp. 143-163 in Martina and Cozzoli 2007.
———. Forthcoming. "Le Ninfe, le Muse e i poeti: La sacra acqua dell'ispirazione." Pp. 85-102 in G. Rati, ed., *L'acqua e i suoi simboli: Atti del Convegno S. Gemini, 19-21 settembre 2007*. Rome.
Craik, E.M., ed. 1990. *"Owls to Athens": Essays on Classical Subjects Presented to Sir Kenneth Dover*. Oxford.
Cribiore, R. 1996. *Writing, Teachers, and Students in Graeco-Roman Egypt*. Atlanta.
———. 2001. *Gymnastics of the Mind*. Princeton.
Criscuolo, L. 1990. "Philadelphos nella dinastia lagide." *Aegyptus* 70: 89-96.
———. 2000. "Nuove riflessioni sul monumento di Ptolemaios Agrios a Panopolis." Pp. 275-290 in Paci 2000.
———. 2003. "Agoni e politica alla corte di Alessandria: Riflessioni su alcuni epigrammi di Posidippo." *Chiron* 33: 311-333.
Croce, B. 1943. Review of V. Arangio Ruiz, "Estetica e filologia." *ASNP* 12 (1943: 71-74). *La Critica* 41: 223.
Crowther, N.B. 1976. "Parthenius and Roman Poetry." *Mnemosyne* 29: 65-71.
———. 1979. "Water and Wine as Symbols of Inspiration." *Mnemosyne* 32: 1-11.
Crucius, I. 1509. *Callimachi Cyrenaei hymni a I.C. Latinitate donati*. Bologna.
Csapo, E. 2000. "Later Euripidean Music." Pp. 399-426 in M. Cropp, K. Lee, and D. Sansone, eds., *Euripides and Tragic Theatre in the Late Fifth Century*. Champaign.
———. 2003. "The Dolphins of Dionysus." Pp. 69-98 in Csapo and Miller 2003.
———. 2004. "The Politics of the New Music." Pp. 207-248 in Murray and Wilson 2004.
Csapo, E., and M.C. Miller, eds. 2003. *Poetry, Theory, Praxis: The Social Life of Myth, World and Image in Ancient Greece—Essays in Honour of William J. Slater*. Oxford.
———, eds. 2007. *The Origin of the Theater in Ancient Greece and Beyond: From Ritual to Drama*. Cambridge.

Csapo, E., and P. Wilson. 2009. "Timotheus the New Musician." Pp. 277-294 in Budelmann 2009.
Cucchiarelli, A. 1994. "Sogno e prologo letterario tra alessandrinismo, precedenti enniani e dottrina epicurea: La polemica a distanza di Lucrezio (I 102-145; IV 907-1036)." *Maia* 46: 149-180.
———. 2002. "Il tramonto dell'aurora (Mus. Her. et Leand. 287-288 ≈ Callim. Epigr. 2,3)." *Museum Helveticum* 59: 61-62.
Cusset, C. 1999. *La Muse dans la bibliothèque: Réécriture et intertextualité dans la poésie alexandrine*. Paris.
———. 2001. "Le nouveau héros épique comme interface intertextuelle entre Callimaque et Apollonios de Rhodes." *Revue des Études Grecques* 114: 228-241.
———. 2003. *Ménandre ou la comédie tragique*. Paris.
Cusset, C., and É. Prioux, eds. 2009. *Lycophron: Éclats d'obscurité*. Saint-Étienne.
Cuypers, M.P. 2004. "Prince and Principle: The Philosophy of Callimachus' *Hymn to Zeus*." Pp. 95-115 in M.A. Harder, Regtuit, and Wakker 2004.
D'Alessio, G.B. 1995a. "Apollo delio, i Cabiri milesii e le cavalle di Tracia: Osservazioni su Callimaco frr. 114-115 Pf." *Zeitschrift für Papyrologie und Epigraphik* 106: 5-21.
———. 1995b. "Una via lontana dal cammino degli uomini (Parm. frr. 1+6 D.-K.; *Ol.* VI 22-27; *Pae.* VII b 10-20)." *Studi Italiani di Filologia Classica* 13: 143-181.
———. 1996. *Callimaco*. Volume 1, *Inni, Epigrammi, Ecale*; volume 2, *Aitia, Giambi, frammenti altri frammenti*. Milan.
———. 2000. "Le *Argonautiche* di Cleone Curiense." Pp. 91-112 in Pretagostini 2000a.
———. 2004a. "Past Future and Present Past: Temporal Deixis in Greek Archaic Lyric." *Arethusa* 37: 267-294.
———. 2004b. "Some Notes on the Salmakis Inscription." Pp. 43-57 in S. Isager and P. Pedersen, eds., *The Salmakis Inscription and Hellenistic Halikarnassos*. Odense.
———. 2005. "Il primo *Inno* di Pindaro." Pp. 113-149 in Grandolini 2005.
———. 2006. "Intersezioni callimachee: Callimaco, Esiodo, Virgilio, Persio." Pp. 137-162 in Martina and Cozzoli 2006.
———. 2007. *Callimaco*. Volume 1, *Inni, Epigrammi, Ecale*; volume 2, *Aitia, Giambi, frammenti minori, frammenti di sede incerta*. 2nd ed. Milan.
———. 2009. "Re-Constructing Pindar's First *Hymn*: The Theban 'Theogony' and the Birth of Apollo." Pp. 129-147 in Athanassaki, Martin, and Miller 2009.
———. Forthcoming. "The Name of the Dithyramb: Diachronic and Diatopic Variations." In Kowalzig and Wilson forthcoming.
Daverio Rocchi, G., and M. Cavalli, eds. 2004. *Il Peloponneso di Senofonte*. Milan.
Davison, J.A. 1955. "Quotations and Allusions in Early Greek Literature." *Eranos* 53: 125-140.
Dawson, C.M. 1950. "The *Iambi* of Callimachus: A Hellenistic Poet's Experimental Laboratory." *Yale Classical Studies* 11: 1-168.
Degani, E. 1984. *Studi su Ipponatte*. Bari.
———. 1995. "Ipponatte e i poeti filologi." *Aevum Antiquum* 8: 105-136. [Reprinted as pp. 131-162 in *Filologia e storia: Scritti di E. Degani*, vol. 1 (Hildesheim, 2004).]
Del Corno, D. 1962. "Ricerche intorno alla *Lyde* di Antimaco." *Acme* 15.1-2: 57-59.
———. 1969. *Graecorum de re onirocritica scriptorum reliquiae*. Milan.
Delcourt, M. 1955. *L'oracle de Delphes*. Paris.
De Marco, V. 1952. *Scholia in Sophoclis "Oedipum Coloneum."* Rome.
Demoen, K., ed. 2001. *The Greek City from Antiquity to the Present: Historical Reality, Ideological Construction, Literary Representation*. Louvain.
Depew, M. 1989. "Delian Hymns and Callimachean Imitation." *Abstracts of the American Philological Association* 69: 75.
———. 1992. " Ἰαμβεῖον καλεῖται νῦν: Genre, Occasion, and Imitation in Callimachus frr. 191 and 203 Pf." *Transactions of the American Philological Association* 122: 313-330.

———. 1993. "Mimesis and Aetiology in Callimachus' *Hymns*." Pp. 57-77 in M.A. Harder, Regtuit, and Wakker 1993.
———. 1998. "Delian Hymns and Callimachean Allusion." *Harvard Studies in Classical Philology* 98: 155-182.
———. 2000. "Enacted and Represented Dedications: Genre and Greek Hymn." Pp. 59-79 and 254-263 in Depew and Obbink 2000.
———. 2004. "Gender, Power, and Poetics in Callimachus' Book of *Hymns*." Pp. 117-138 in M.A. Harder, Regtuit, and Wakker 2004.
Depew, M., and D. Obbink, eds. 2000. *Matrices of Genre: Authors, Canons, and Society*. Cambridge, Mass.
Derchain, P. 2000. *Les impondérables de l'hellénisation: Littérature d'hiérogrammates*. Turnhout.
De Sanctis, G. 1935. "Callimaco e Orazio Coclite." *Rivista di Filologia e di Istruzione Classica* 14: 289-301.
———. 1975. *Atthís: Storia della Repubblica ateniese dalle origini alla età di Pericle*. Florence.
De Stefani, C. 1996. "Note a quattro epigrammi dell'*Antologia Greca*." *Studi Italiani di Filologia Classica* 14: 199-208.
———. 1997. "Cruces dell'*Inno a Delo* (vv. 1; 205; 249)." *Maia* 49: 93-98.
———. 2000. "Fenice di Colofone fr. 2 D³: Introduzione, testo, commento." *Studi Classici e Orientali* 47: 81-121.
———. 2002. *Nonno di Panopoli: Parafrasi del Vangelo di San Giovanni, canto I*. Bologna.
———. 2005. "Posidippo e Leonida di Taranto: Spunti per un confronto." Pp. 147-190 in Di Marco, Palumbo Stracca, and Lelli 2005.
———. 2006. "Un passo 'callimacheo' e 'licofroneo' di Nonno." *Seminari Romani di Cultura Greca* 9: 15-25.
———. 2008. "Ἀλώφητος ἔρως: Anatomy of a Late Greek Poem." Pp. 203-212 in E. Cingano and L. Milano, eds., *Papers on Ancient Literatures: Greece, Rome and the Near East*. Padua.
———. 2010. *Paulus Silentiarius, "Descriptio Sanctae Sophiae," "Descriptio Ambonis."* Berlin.
Detienne, M. 1996. *The Masters of Truth in Archaic Greece*. Trans. J. Lloyd. New York.
———. 2001. "Forgetting Delphi between Apollo and Dionysus." *Classical Philology* 96: 147-158.
Dettori, E. 2003. "Euphor. fr. 57. 5 van Gron." *Seminari Romani di Cultura Greca* 6: 219-223.
———. 2004. "Appunti sul 'Banchetto di Pollis' (Call. fr. 178 Pf.)." Pp. 33-63 in Pretagostini and Dettori 2004.
Devreesse, R. 1965. *Le fonds grec de la Bibliothèque vaticane des origines à Paul V*. Vatican City.
Di Benedetto, V. 2003. "Posidippo tra Pindaro e Callimaco." *Prometheus* 29: 97-119.
Di Castri, M.B. 1996. "Tra sfoggio erudito e fantasia descrittiva: Un profilo letterario e stilistico di Dioscoride epigrammatista (II)." *Atene e Roma* 41: 49-54.
———. 1997. "Tra sfoggio erudito e fantasia descrittiva: Un profilo letterario e stilistico di Dioscoride epigrammatista (III)." *Atene e Roma* 42: 51-73.
Di Gregorio, L., ed. 1997. *Eronda: Mimiambi I-IV*. Milan.
Di Marco, M. 2002. "Timon [2]." Cols. 592-593 in *Der neue Pauly: Enzyklopädie der Antike*, vol. 12.1. Stuttgart.
———. Forthcoming. "Baticle nel *Giambo 1* di Callimaco." In Martina and Cozzoli forthcoming.
Di Marco, M., B.M. Palumbo Stracca, and E. Lelli, eds. 2005. *Posidippo e gli altri: Il poeta, il genere, il contesto culturale e letterario—Atti dell'incontro di studio, Roma, 14-15 maggio 2004*. Pisa.

Dickie, M.W. 2001. "Exclusions from the Catechumenate: Continuity or Discontinuity with Pagan Cult?" *Numen* 48: 417–443.
———. 2002. "Who Were Privileged to See the Gods?" *Eranos* 100: 109–127.
———. 2004. "Priestly Proclamations and Sacred Laws." *Classical Quarterly* 54: 579–591.
Diehl, E. 1937. "Hypomnema: De Callimachi librorum fatis capita selecta." *Latvijas Universitates Raksti / Acta Universitatis Latviensis, Filologijas un Filosofijas Fakultates Serija (Riga)* 4: 305–476.
Diels, H. 1904. *"Laterculi Alexandrini." Abhandlungen der Königlichen Akademie der Wissenschaften zu Berlin*, Abhandlung 2.
Diggle, J. 1970. *Euripides: Phaethon*. Cambridge.
Dijk, G.-J. van. 1997. Αἶνοι, Λόγοι, Μῦθοι: *Fables in Archaic, Classical, and Hellenistic Greek Literature, with a Study of the Theory and Terminology of the Genre*. Leiden.
Diller, A. 1983. *Studies in Greek Manuscript Tradition*. Amsterdam.
Dillery, J. 2005. "Greek Sacred History." *American Journal of Philology* 126: 505–526.
Dilthey, K. 1863. *De Callimachi "Cydippa"* [...]. Leipzig.
Dionisotti, A.C. 1997. "On Fragments in Classical Scholarship." Pp. 1–33 in Most 1997.
Dobias-Lalou, C. 1987. "Dialecte et koinè dans les inscriptions de Cyrénaïque." *Verbum* 10: 29–50. [*Actes de la première Rencontre internationale de dialectologie grecque.*]
———. 2000. *Le dialecte des inscriptions grecques de Cyrène*. Paris.
Dobrov, G.W. 2002. "Μάγειρος ποιητής: Language and Character in Antiphanes." Pp. 169–190 in Willi 2002.
Döpp, S. 1996. "Das Stegreifgedicht des Q. Sulpicius Maximus." *Zeitschrift für Papyrologie und Epigraphik* 114: 99–114.
Dougherty, C., and L. Kurke, eds. 2003. *The Cultures within Ancient Greek Culture: Contact, Conflict, Collaboration*. Cambridge.
Dubois, L., ed. 1996. *Poésie et lyrique antiques: Actes du Colloque organisé par C. Meillier à l'Université Charles-de-Gaulle, Lille III, 2–4 juin 1993*. Lille.
Dunand, F. 1981. "Fête et propagande à Alexandrie sous les Lagides." Pp. 11–40 in *La fête, pratique et discours: D'Alexandrie hellénistique à la Mission de Besançon*. Paris.
———. 1986. "Les associations dionysiaques au service du pouvoir lagide (IIIe s. av. J.-C.)." Pp. 85–104 in *L'association dionysiaque dans les sociétés anciennes: Actes de la table ronde organisée par l'École française de Rome, Rome, 24–25 mai 1984*. Rome.
Dunn, F., and T. Cole, eds. 1992. *Beginnings in Classical Literature*. New Haven.
Durbec, Y. 2005a. "'Κύον, κύον': Lectures métapoétiques d'une apostrophe (Callimaque, *Aitia*, fr. 75, 4 Pfeiffer et *Hymne à Déméter* 63)." *Revue des Études Grecques* 118: 600–604.
———. 2005b. "Notes à la *Victoire de Bérénice*, SH 254–268c." *Eikasmos* 16: 161–164.
———. 2005c. "Le rapt de la boucle: Callimaque fr. 110, 50–78 Pf." *Eranos* 103: 73–77.
———. 2006a. *Callimaque: Fragments poétiques*. Paris.
———. 2006b. "Lycophron et la poétique de Callimaque: Le prologue de l'*Alexandra*, 1–15." *Appunti Romani di Filologia* 8: 81–84.
Dyck, A.R. 1993. "Aelius Herodian: Recent Studies and Prospects for Future Research." *Aufstieg und Niedergang der Römischen Welt* 2.34.1: 772–794.
Edelmann, B. 2007. *Religiöse Herrschaftslegitimation in der Antike: Die religiöse Legitimation orientalisch-ägyptischer und griechisch-hellenistischer Herrscher im Vergleich*. St. Katharinen.
Edmunds, L. 2001a. "Callimachus, *Iamb* 4: From Performance to Writing." Pp. 77–98 in Cavarzere, Aloni, and Barchiesi 2001.
———. 2001b. *Intertextuality and the Reading of Roman Poetry*. Baltimore.

Effe, B. 1970. "Προτέρη γενεή: Eine stoische Hesiodinterpretation in Arats *Phainomena.*" *Rheinisches Museum* 113: 167-182.
———. 1995. "Alexandrinisches Herrscherlob: Ambivalenzen literarischen Panegyrik." Pp. 107-123 in Binder and Effe 1995.
———. 2007. "Die Literatur als Spiegel epochalen Wandels." Pp. 260-183 and 476-478 in Weber 2007b.
Ehlers, W. 1933. *Die Gründung von Zankle in den Aitia des Kallimachos.* Dissertation, Berlin.
Ehrhardt, N. 2003. "Poliskulte bei Theokrit und Kallimachos: Das Beispiel Milet." *Hermes* 131: 269-289.
Eichgrün, E. 1961. *Kallimachos und Apollonios.* Dissertation, Berlin.
Elderkin, G.W. 1937. "The Marriage of Zeus and Hera and Its Symbol." *American Journal of Archaeology* 41: 424-435.
Ellis, W.M. 1994. *Ptolemy of Egypt.* London.
Enenkel, K.A.E., and I.L. Pfeijffer, eds. 2005. *Manipulative Mode: Political Propaganda in Antiquity—A Collection of Case-Studies.* Leiden.
England, E.B. 1921. *The Laws of Plato.* 2 vols. Manchester.
Erbse, H. 1975. "Zum Apollonhymnos des Kallimachos." Pp. 276-300 in Skiadas 1975. [Originally published in *Hermes* 83 (1955): 163-96.]
Erler, M. 1987. "Das Recht (ΔΙΚΗ) als Segensbringerin fur die Polis: Die Wandlung eines Motivs von Hesiod zu Kallimachos." *Studi Italiani di Filologia Classica* 5: 5-36.
Ernesti, J.A. 1761. *Callimachi hymni, epigrammata et fragmenta* [...]. 2 vols. Leiden.
Erren, M. 1967. *Die Phainomena des Aratos von Soloi.* Wiesbaden.
Errington, M. 1993. "Inschriften von Euromos." *Epigraphica Anatolica* 21: 15-31.
Erskine, A. 1995. "Culture and Power in Ptolemaic Egypt: The Museum and Library of Alexandria." *Greece and Rome* 42: 38-48.
———, ed. 2003. *A Companion to the Hellenistic World.* Oxford.
Fabian, K. 1992. *Callimaco: Aitia II—Testo critico, traduzione e commento.* Alessandria.
Fabri, A. 1675. Καλλιμάχου Κυρηναίου ὕμνοι, ἐπιγράμματα καὶ ἄλλα ἄττα / *Callimachi Cyrenaei hymni, epigrammata et fragmenta; eiusdem poematium "De coma Berenices" a Catullo versum.* Paris.
Fakas, C. 2001. *Der hellenistische Hesiod: Arats "Phainomena" und die Tradition der antiken Lehrepik.* Wiesbaden.
Falivene, M.R. 1990. "La mimesi di Callimaco: *Inni* II, IV, V e VI." *Studi Italiani di Filologia Classica* 65: 103-128.
Fantuzzi, M. 1981. "'Ἐκ Διὸς ἀρχώμεσθα." *Materiali e Discussioni* 5: 163-172.
———. 1985. *Bionis Smyrnaei "Adonidis Epitaphium": Testo critico e commento.* Liverpool.
———. 1988. *Ricerche su Apollonio Rodio.* Rome.
———. 1993. "Il sistema letterario della poesia alessandrina nel III sec. a.C." Pp. 31-73 in G. Cambiano, L. Canfora, and D. Lanza, eds., *Lo spazio letterario della Grecia antica*, volume 1, *La produzione e la circolazione del testo*, part 2, *L'ellenismo*. Rome.
———. 1994. "On the Metre of *Anacreont.* 19 W." *Classical Quarterly* 44: 540-542.
———. 1996. "Mythological Paradigms in the Bucolic Poetry of Theocritus." *Proceedings of the Cambridge Philological Society* 41: 16-35.
———. 2005. "Posidippus at Court: The Contribution of the Ἱππικά of P. Mil. Vogl. VIII 309 to the Ideology of Ptolemaic Kingship." Pp. 249-268 in Gutzwiller 2005.
———. 2006a. "Callimaco, l'epigramma, il teatro." Pp. 69-87 in Bastianini and Casanova 2006.
———. 2006b. "Theocritus' Constructive Interpreters, and the Creation of a Bucolic Reader." Pp. 235-262 in Fantuzzi and Papanghelis 2006.
———. 2007. "Epigram and the Theater." Pp. 477-495 in Bing and Bruss 2007.

———. 2010. "Sung Poetry: The Case of Inscribed Paeans." Pp. 181–189 in Clauss and Cuypers 2010.
Fantuzzi, M., and R.L. Hunter. 2002. *Muse e modelli: La poesia ellenistica da Alessandro Magno ad Augusto*. Rome.
———. 2004. *Tradition and Innovation in Hellenistic Poetry*. Cambridge.
Fantuzzi, M., and T.D. Papanghelis, eds. 2006. *Brill's Companion to Greek and Latin Pastoral*. Leiden.
Faraone, C., and E. Teeter. 2004. "Egyptian *Maat* and Hesiodic *Metis*." *Mnemosyne* 57: 177–207.
Farrell, F.B. 2004. *Why Does Literature Matter?* Ithaca.
Farrell, J. 1991. *Vergil's Georgics and the Traditions of Ancient Epic: The Art of Allusion in Literary History*. Oxford.
———. 2005. "Intention and Intertext." *Phoenix* 59: 98–111.
Fearn, D. 2007. *Bacchylides: Politics, Performance, Poetic Tradition*. Oxford.
Fedeli, P. 2005. *Properzio: Elegie, libro II*. Leeds.
Feeney, D. 1994. Review of P. White 1993. *Bryn Mawr Classical Review* 5: 346–349.
Fera, V., G. Ferraù, and S. Rizzo, eds. 2002. *Talking to the Text: Marginalia from Papyri to Print*. Messina.
Fernández Delgado, J.A., and J. Ureña Bracero. 1991. *Un testimonio de la educación literaria griega en época romana: IG XIV 2012 = Kaibel, EG 618*. Badajoz.
Fleming, M.L. 1981. *A Commentary on Callimachus' Fourth Hymn* (To Delos). Dissertation, University of Texas, Austin.
Floridi, L. 2007. *Stratone di Sardi: Epigrammi*. Alessandria.
Foertmeyer, V. 1988. "The Dating of the *Pompe* of Ptolemy II Philadelphus." *Historia* 37: 90–104.
Fongoni, A. 2005. "Antifane e Filosseno." *Quaderni Urbinati di Cultura Classica* 81: 91–98.
Fontenrose, J. 1968. "The Athlete as Hero." *California Studies in Classical Antiquity* 1: 73–104.
———. 1978. *The Delphic Oracle*. Berkeley and Los Angeles.
———. 1988. *Didyma: Apollo's Oracle, Cult, and Companions*. Berkeley and Los Angeles.
Ford, A. 2002. *The Origins of Criticism: Literary Culture and Poetic Theory in Classical Greece*. Princeton.
Fortenbaugh, W.W., and E. Schütrumpf, eds. 2000. *Demetrius of Phalerum: Text, Translation and Discussion*. New Brunswick.
Foster, J.A. 2006. "Arsinoe II as Epic Queen: Encomiastic Allusion in Theocritus, *Idyll* 15." *Transactions of the American Philological Association* 136: 133–148.
Fournet, J.-L. 2009. *Alexandrie: Une communauté linguistique? ou, La question du grec alexandrin*. Cairo.
Fowler, D. 1997. "On the Shoulders of Giants." *Materiali e Discussioni* 39: 13–34.
———. 2000. *Roman Constructions: Readings in Postmodern Latin*. Oxford.
———. 2009. "Horace and the Aesthetics of Politics." Pp. 247–270 in M. Lowrie, ed., *Oxford Readings in Classical Studies: Horace: Odes and Epodes*. Oxford.
Frangoulis, H. 1995. "Nonnos transposant Homère: Étude du chant 37 des *Dionysiaques* de Nonnos de Panopolis." *Revue de Philologie, de Littérature et d'Histoire Anciennes* 69: 145–168.
Frangoulis, H., and B. Gerlaud. 2006. *Nonnos de Panopolis, Les Dionysiaques*. Volume 12, *Chants XXXV et XXXVI*. Paris.
Franklin, J.C. Forthcoming. "'Songbenders of Circular Choruses': Dithyramb and the 'Demise of Music.'" In Kowalzig and Wilson forthcoming.
Fraser, P.M. 1954. "Two Hellenistic Inscriptions from Delphi." *Bulletin de Correspondance Hellénique* 73: 49–67.
———. 1972. *Ptolemaic Alexandria*. 3 vols. Oxford.
Freudenburg, K. 1993. *The Walking Muse*. Princeton.

———. 2001. *Satires of Rome*. Cambridge.
Fromm, E. 1973. *The Anatomy of Human Destructiveness*. New York.
Frösén, J., T. Purola, and E. Salmenkivi, eds. 2007. *Proceedings of the Twenty-Fourth International Congress of Papyrology, Helsinki, 1-7 August, 2004*. Helsinki.
Frost, F.J. 2005. *Politics and the Athenians: Essays on Athenian History and Historiography*. Toronto.
Fubini, M. 1973. *Critica e poesia*. Rome.
Fuhrer, T. 1988. "A Pindaric Feature in the Poems of Callimachus." *American Journal of Philology* 109: 53-68.
———. 1992. *Die Auseinandersetzung mit den Chorlyrikern in den Epinikien des Kallimachos*. Basel.
Funck, B. 1996. "Beobachtungen zum Begriff des Herrscherpalastes und seiner machtpolitischen Funktion im hellenistischen Raum: Prolegomena zur Typologie der hellenistischen Herrschaftssprache." Pp. 44-55 in Hoepfner and Brands 1996.
Funghi, M.S., ed. 1996. *ΟΔΟΙ ΔΙΖΗΣΙΟΣ: Le vie della ricerca—Studi in onore di Francesco Adorno*. Florence.
Furley, W.D., and J. Bremer. 2001. *Greek Hymns: Selected Cult Songs from the Archaic to the Hellenistic Period*. 2 vols. Tübingen.
Fusillo, M. 1988. *[Omero]: "La battaglia delle rane e dei topi" ("Batrachomyomachia")*. Milan.
Galán Vioque, G. 2001. *Dioscórides: Epigramas*. Huelva.
Gallavotti, C. 1949. "Laurentiani codicis altera analecta." *Rendiconti della Classe di Scienze Morali, Storiche e Filologiche dell'Accademia dei Lincei* 4: 352-379.
———. 1952. "Per il testo di Teocrito." *Rivista di Filologia e di Istruzione Classica* 115: 137-148.
———. 1983. "Epica religiosa in una stele siciliana." *Zeitschrift für Papyrologie und Epigraphik* 50: 1-6.
Gallazzi, C. 1990. "La 'Cantina dei Papiri' di Tebtynis e ciò che essa conteneva." *Zeitschrift für Papyrologie und Epigraphik* 80: 283-288.
———. 2003. "La prima campagna di Vogliano in Egitto: Gli scavi a Tebtynis e gli acquisti di papiri." Pp. 131-195 in Gallazzi and Lehnus 2003.
Gallazzi, C., and G. Hadji-Minaglou. 2000. *Tebtynis*. Volume 1, *La reprise des fouilles et le quartier de la chapelle d'Isis-Thermouthis*. Cairo.
Gallazzi, C., and L. Lehnus. 2001. "Due nuovi frammenti delle *Diegeseis*: Approssimazioni al III libro degli *Aitia* di Callimaco." *Zeitschrift für Papyrologie und Epigraphik* 137: 7-18.
———, eds. 2003. *Achille Vogliano cinquant'anni dopo*. Volume 1. Milan.
Garboli, C. 2002. *Giovanni Pascoli: Poesie e prose scelte*. 2 vols. Milan.
García, J.F. 2002. "Symbolic Action in the *Homeric Hymns*: The Theme of Recognition." *Classical Antiquity* 21: 5-39.
García Romero, F.A. 1989. "Las glosas homéricas en Quinto de Esmirna: Unas notas sobre Calímaco y Quinto a propósito de ἐς ἵππον κητώεντα." *Habis* 20: 33-36.
Gardthausen, V. 1922. *Die Alexandrinische Bibliothek: ihr Vorbild, Katalog*. Leipzig.
Gargiulo, T. 1992. "L'immagine della bilancia in Callimaco, fr. 1, 9-10 Pf." *Quaderni Urbinati di Cultura Classica* 42: 3.123-128.
Gärtner, T. 2007. "Zur Deutung des kallimacheischen Epigramms über die *Phainomena* des Arat." *L'Antiquité Classique* 76: 157-162.
Garulli, V. 2007. "Cleombroto di Ambracia e il 'lector in fabula' in Callimaco (Call. 'epigr.' 23 Pf.)." *Lexis* 25: 325-336.
———. 2008. "L'*epigramma longum* nella tradizione epigrafica sepolcrale greca." Pp. 623-662 in A.M. Morelli 2008.
———. Forthcoming. *Βύβλος λαινέη: Aspetti letterari degli epitafi epigrafici greci*. Bologna.
Gauthier, P. 1985. *Les cités grecques et leurs bienfaiteurs*. Paris.

Geffcken, J. 1902. *Die Oracula Sibyllina*. Leipzig. [Reprint: Leipzig, 1967.]
Gehrke, H.-J. 1982. "Der siegreiche König: Überlegungen zur hellenistischen Monarchie." *Archiv für Kulturgeschichte* 84: 247–277.
———. 2003. *Geschichte des Hellenismus*. 2nd ed. Munich.
Gelenius, S. 1532. Καλλιμάχου Κυρηναίου ὕμνοι μετὰ τῶν σχολίων [...] / *Callimachi Cyrenaei hymni cum scholiis nunc primum aeditis*. Basel.
Gelzer, T. 1982. "Kallimachos und das Zeremoniell des ptolemäischen Königshauses." Pp. 13–30 in Stagl 1982.
———. 1982–1984. "Die Alexandriner und die griechischen Lyriker: Reflexionen zur Rezeption und Interpretation." *Acta Antiqua Academiae Scientiarum Hungaricae* 30: 129–147.
Gentile Messina, R. 2000. "Un caso di *mimesis* al servizio della propaganda nell'*Epitome* di Giovanni Cinnamo." *Byzantion* 70: 408–421.
Gentili, B., ed. 1990. *Cirene: Storia, mito, letteratura*. Urbino.
———. 1992. "La Grecia antica fra cultura umanistica e scienza." *Studi Italiani di Filologia Classica* 10: 1–20.
———. 1995. *Poesia e pubblico nella Grecia antica*. 3rd ed. Rome.
Gentili, B., and R. Pretagostini, eds. 1988. *La musica in Grecia*. Rome.
George, E.V. 1974. *Aeneid VIII and the Aitia of Callimachus*. Leiden.
Gerber, D.E. 1999. *Greek Elegiac Poetry from the Seventh to the Fifth Centuries BC*. Cambridge MA and London.
Gerlaud, B. 1982. *Triphiodore: La prise d'Ilion*. Paris.
———. 1994. *Nonnos de Panopolis, Les Dionysiaques*. Volume 6, Chants XIV–XVII. Paris.
Geus, K. 2002. *Eratosthenes von Kyrene: Studien zur hellenistischen Kultur- und Wissenschaftsgeschichte*. Munich.
Giangrande, G. 1967. "'Arte allusiva' and Alexandrian Epic Poetry." *Classical Quarterly* 17: 85–97.
———. 1970. "Hellenistic Poetry and Homer." *L'Antiquité Classique* 39: 46–77.
———. 1971. "*Topoi* ellenistici nell'*Ars Amatoria*." Pp. 61–98 in I. Gallo and L. Nicastri, eds., *Cultura, poesia, ideologia nell'opera di Ovidio*. Naples.
———. 1975. *L'humour des alexandrins*. Amsterdam.
———. 1981a. *Scripta minora Alexandrina*. Volume 2. Amsterdam.
———. 1981b. "Los tópicos helenísticos en la elegía latina." Pp. 463–498 in Giangrande 1981a.
———. 1992. "The Final Line in Callimachus' *Hymn to Apollo*." *Habis* 23: 53–62.
———. 2004. "Sótades, fragmento 16 Powell, y Calímaco, fragmento 75.4 ss. Pfeiffer." *Habis* 35: 105–108.
Giannini, A. 1962. "Callimaco e la tragedia." *Dioniso* 36: 48–73.
Giannini, P. 1990. "Cirene nella poesia greca, tra mito e storia." Pp. 89–92 in Gentili 1990.
Gibson, R.K., and C.S. Kraus, eds. 2002. *The Classical Commentary*. Leiden.
Gigante, M. 1971. *L'edera di Leonida*. Naples.
———. 1997. "Considerazioni finali." Pp. 391–398 in A. Stazio and S. Ceccoli, eds., *Mito e storia in Magna Grecia: Atti del Trentaseiesimo convegno di studi sulla Magna Grecia, Taranto, 4–7 ottobre 1996*. Taranto.
Gigante Lanzara, V. 1984. "Ad Callimachi' Hymn IV 178." *Parola del Passato* 39: 279–280.
———. 1990. *Callimaco: "Inno a Delo."* Pisa.
———. 1994. "'Da Zeus i re': Poesia e potere nell'Alessandria dei Tolemei." Pp. 91–118 in Virgilio 1994.
———. 1998. "Il tempo dell'*Alessandra* e i modelli ellenistici di Licofrone." *Parola del Passato* 53: 401–418.
Gigli Piccardi, D. 1985. *Metafora e poetica in Nonno di Panopoli*. Florence.

———. 2003. *Nonno di Panopoli, Le Dionisiache, canti I–XII*. Milan.
Gilbert, C.D. 1976. "Ovid, *Met*. 1.4." *Proceedings of the Cambridge Philological Society* 26: 111–112.
Gilbert, G. 1874. "Die Quellen des plutarchischen Theseus." *Philologus* 33: 46–66.
Giuseppetti, M. 2008. *L'Inno a Delo di Callimaco: Aspetti del mito e dello stile*. Dissertation, University of Rome III.
Glei, R. 1984. *Die Batrachomyomachie: Synoptische Edition und Kommentar*. Frankfurt.
Goldhill, S. 1986. "Framing and Polyphony: Readings in Hellenistic Poetry." *Proceedings of the Cambridge Philological Society* 212: 25–52.
———. 2005. Review of Stephens 2003. *Gnomon* 77: 99–104.
Golega, J. 1960. *Der homerische Psalter: Studien über die dem Apolinarios von Laodikeia zugeschriebene Psalmenparaphrase*. Ettal.
Gomme, A.W. 1925. "Theognis 959–962." *Classical Review* 39: 101.
Gomperz, T. 1893. *Aus der Hekale des Kallimachos: Neue Bruchstücke anlässlich der XLII. Versammlung deutscher Philologen und Schulmänner in Wien*. Vienna.
Gonis, N. 2006. "Novità callimachee da Ossirinco." Pp. 29–30 in Bastianini and Casanova 2006.
Gonnelli, F. 1988. "Parole 'callimachee' nella parafrasi del Salterio." *Studi Italiani di Filologia Classica* 81: 91–104.
———. 2003. *Nonno di Panopoli, Le Dionisiache, canti XIII–XXIV*. Milan.
Gow, A.S.F. 1952. *Theocritus: Edited with a Translation and Commentary*. 2 vols. 2nd ed. Cambridge.
———. 1958. "Leonidas of Tarentum: Notes and Queries." *Classical Quarterly* 8: 113–123.
———. 1965. *Machon: The Fragments*. Cambridge.
Gow, A.S.F., and D.L. Page 1965. *The Greek Anthology: Hellenistic Epigrams*. 2 vols. Cambridge.
———. 1968. *The Greek Anthology: The Garland of Philip and Some Contemporary Epigrams*. 2 vols. Cambridge.
Gow, A.S.F., and A.F. Scholfield 1953. *Nicander: The Poems and Poetical Fragments*. Cambridge.
Graevius, T. 1697. *Callimachi hymni, epigrammata et fragmenta*. Utrecht.
Grafton, A. 1997. "*Fragmenta historicorum Graecorum*: Fragments of Some Lost Enterprises." Pp. 124–143 in Most 1997.
———. 2003. *Athenae Batavae: The Research Imperative at Leiden, 1575–1650*. Leiden.
Graindor, P. 1911. "*Akontios et Kydippè*: Nouveau fragment de Callimaque." *Musée Belge* 15: 49–64.
Grandolini, S., ed. 2005. *Lirica e teatro in Grecia: Il testo e la sua ricezione—Atti del II incontro di studi, Perugia, 23-24 gennaio 2003*. Naples.
Graziosi, B. 2002. *Inventing Homer*. Cambridge.
Greco, C. 2004. *Nonno di Panopoli: Parafrasi del Vangelo di San Giovanni, canto XIII*. Alessandria.
Greco, E., ed. 2005. *Teseo e Romolo: Le origini di Atene e Roma a confronto*. Athens.
Griffiths, F.T. 1977-78. "The Date of Callimachus' *Hymn to Delos*." *Maia* 29-30: 95–100.
———. 1979. *Theocritus at Court*. Leiden.
Grilli, A. 1979. "Antipatro di Sidone e Callimaco." *Parola del Passato* 34: 202–204.
Grimm, G., and D. Johannes. 1975. *Kunst der Ptolemäer- und Römerzeit im Ägyptischen Museum Kairo*. Mainz.
Groningen, B.A. van. 1966. *Theognis: Le premier livre*. Amsterdam.
Grube, G.M.A. 1961. *A Greek Critic: Demetrius, On Style*. Toronto.
———. 1965. *The Greek and Roman Critics*. Toronto.
Gruen, E.S. 2006. "Greeks and Non-Greeks." Pp. 295–314 in Bugh 2006.

Guarducci, M. 1967-78. *Epigrafia greca*. 4 vols. Rome.
Guéraud, O., and P. Jouguet. 1938. *Un livre d'écolier du IIIe siècle avant J.-C.* Cairo.
Guhl, C. 1969. *Die Fragmente des alexandrinischen Grammatikers Theon*. Dissertation, Hamburg.
Guimier-Sorbets, A.-M. 2007. "L'image de Ptolémée devant Alexandrie." Pp. 163-176 in F.-H. Massa Pairault et G. Sauron, eds., *Images et modernité hellénistiques: Appropriation et représentation du monde d'Alexandre à César—Actes du Colloque international, Rome, 13-15 mai 2004*. Rome.
Gutzwiller, K.J. 1992a. "Callimachus' *Lock of Berenice*: Fantasy, Romance and Propaganda." *American Journal of Philology* 113: 359-385.
———. 1992b. "The Nautilus, the Halcyon and Selenaia: Callimachus's *Epigram* 5 Pf. = 14 G.-P." *Classical Antiquity* 11: 194-209.
———. 1998. *Poetic Garlands: Hellenistic Epigrams in Context*. Berkeley and Los Angeles.
———, ed. 2005. *The New Posidippus: A Hellenistic Poetry Book*. Oxford.
———. 2007. *A Guide to Hellenistic Literature*. Oxford.
Habicht, C. 1958. "Die herrschende Gesellschaft in den hellenistischen Monarchien." *Vierteljahresschrift für Sozial- und Wirtschaftsgeschichte* 45: 1-16.
———. 1970. *Gottmenschentum und griechische Städte*. 2nd ed. Munich.
———. 1994. *Athen in hellenistischer Zeit: Gesammelte Aufsätze*. Munich.
———. 1997. *Athens from Alexander to Antony*. Trans. D.L. Schneider. Cambridge, Mass.
———. 2006. *The Hellenistic Monarchies: Selected Papers*. Trans. P. Stevenson. Ann Arbor.
Hall, A.S., and N.P. Milner. 1994. "Education and Athletics at Oenoanda." Pp. 7-47 in D. French, ed., *Studies in the History and Topography of Lycia and Pisidia: In Memoriam A.S. Hall*. London.
Hammond, N.G.L., and F.W. Walbank. 1988. *A History of Macedonia*. Volume 3, *336-167 BC* Oxford.
Harder, M.A. 1988. "Callimachus and the Muses: Some Aspects of Narrative Technique in *Aetia* 1-2." *Prometheus* 14: 1-14.
———. 1989. "Politian and the Fragments of Callimachus." *Res Publica Litterarum* 12: 77-83.
———. 1990. "Untrodden Paths: Where Do They Lead?" *Harvard Studies in Classical Philology* 93: 287-309.
———. 1992. "Insubstantial Voices: Some Observations on the *Hymns* of Callimachus." *Classical Quarterly* 42: 384-394.
———. 1993a. "Aspects of the Structure of Callimachus' *Aetia*." Pp. 99-110 in M.A. Harder, Regtuit, and Wakker 1993.
———. 1993b. "Between 'Prologue' and 'Dream' (Call. fr. 1A, 19 Pf.)." *Zeitschrift für Papyrologie und Epigraphik* 96: 11-13.
———. 1993c. "Thanks to Aristaenetus…" Pp. 3-13 in Hokwerda, Smits, and Woesthuis 1993.
———. 1998. "'Generic Games' in Callimachus' *Aetia*." Pp. 95-113 in M.A. Harder, Regtuit, and Wakker 1998.
———. 2002a. "Intertextuality in Callimachus' *Aitia*." Pp. 189-223 in Montanari and Lehnus 2002.
———. 2002b. "Papyri, literarische." Cols. 70-81 in *Der neue Pauly: Enzyklopädie der Antike*, vol. 15.2. Stuttgart.
———. 2003. "The Invention of Past, Present and Future in Callimachus' *Aetia*." *Hermes* 131: 290-306.
———. 2004. "Callimachus." Pp. 63-81 in de Jong, Nünlist, and Bowie 2004.
———. 2007. "To Teach or Not to Teach…?" Pp. 23-48 in M.A. Harder, MacDonald, and Reinink 2007.

———. Forthcoming. *Callimachus, Aetia: Introduction, Text, Translation and Commentary*. 2 vols. Oxford.
Harder, M.A., R.F. Regtuit, P. Stork, and G.C. Wakker, eds. 2002. *Noch einmal zu...: Kleine Schriften von Stefan Radt zu seinem 75. Geburtstag*. Leiden.
Harder, M.A., A.A. MacDonald, and G.J. Reinink, eds. 2007. *Calliope's Classroom: Studies in Didactic Poetry from Antiquity to the Renaissance*. Louvain.
Harder, M.A., R.F. Regtuit, and G.C. Wakker, eds. 1993. *Callimachus*. Groningen.
———. 1996. *Theocritus*. Groningen.
———. 1998. *Genre in Hellenistic Poetry*. Groningen.
———. 2000. *Apollonius Rhodius*. Louvain.
———. 2004. *Callimachus II*. Louvain.
———. 2006. *Beyond the Canon*. Louvain.
———. 2009. *Nature and Science in Hellenistic Poetry*. With the assistance of A. Ambühl. Louvain.
Harder, R. 1956. "Inschriften von Didyma Nr. 217 Vers 4." Pp. 88–97 in *Navicula Chiloniensis: Studia philologa Felici Jacoby Professori Chiloniensi emerito octogenario oblata*. Leiden.
Harding, P. 1994. *Androtion and the "Atthis": The Fragments, Translated with Introduction and Commentary*. Oxford.
———. 2006. *Didymos on Demosthenes: Introduction, Text, Translation, and Commentary*. Oxford.
———. 2008. *The Story of Athens: The Fragments of the Local Chronicles of Attika*. London.
Harris, W.V., and G.R. Ruffini, eds. 2004. *Ancient Alexandria between Egypt and Greece*. Leiden.
Harvey, A.E. 1957. "Homeric Epithets in Greek Lyric Poetry." *Classical Quarterly* 7: 206–223.
Haslam, M. 1993. "Callimachus' *Hymns*." Pp. 111–125 in M.A. Harder, Regtuit, and Wakker 1993.
Hauben, H. 1989. "Aspects du culte des souverains à l'époque des Lagides." Pp. 441–467 in L. Criscuolo and G. Geraci, eds., *Egitto e storia antica dall'ellenismo all'età araba*. Bologna.
Hausrath, A. 1940–. *Corpus fabularum Aesopicarum*. Leipzig.
d'Hautcourt, A. 2001. "Héraclée du Pont dans les *Alexipharmaca* de Nicandre de Colophon: Un nouvel indice de chronologie?" Pp. 191–198 in B. Virgilio, ed., *Studi ellenistici*, vol. 13. Pisa.
Hazzard, R.A. 1995. "Theos Epiphanes: Crisis and Response." *Harvard Theological Review* 88: 415–436.
———. 2000. *Imagination of a Monarchy: Studies in Ptolemaic Propaganda*. Toronto.
Hecker, A. 1842. *Commentationum Callimachearum capita duo*. Groningen.
Heiden, B. 2007. "The Muses' Uncanny Lies: Hesiod, *Theogony* 27, and Its Translators." *American Journal of Philology* 128: 153–175.
Heinen, H. 1983. "Die τρυφή des Ptolemaios VIII. Euergetes II. Beobachtungen zum ptolemäischen Herrscherideal und zu einer römischen Gesandtschaft in Ägypten (140/30 v. Chr.)." Pp. 116–130 in H. Heinen, ed., *Althistorische Studien: Festschrift Hermann Bengtson*. Wiesbaden.
Henderson, J. 2007. "The Hocus of a Hedgehog: Ion's Versatility." Pp. 17–44 in Jennings and Katsaros 2007.
Henrichs, A. 1975. "Die beiden Gaben des Dionysus." *Zeitschrift für Papyrologie und Epigraphik* 16: 138–144.
———. 1979. "Callimachus, *Epigram* 28: A Fastidious Priamel." *Harvard Studies in Classical Philology* 83: 207–212.
———. 1993. "Gods in Action: The Poetics of Divine Performance in the *Hymns* of Callimachus." Pp. 127–147 in M.A. Harder, Regtuit, and Wakker 1993.

———. 1994-95. "'Why Should I Dance?': Choral Self-Referentiality in Greek Tragedy." *Arion* 3: 56-111.
———. 1996. "Dancing in Athens, Dancing on Delos: Some Patterns of Choral Projection in Euripides." *Philologus* 140: 48-62.
Henry, W.B. 2005. "4711: Elegy (*Metamorphoses?*)." Pp. 46-53 in N. Gonis et al., eds., *The Oxyrhynchus Papyri*, vol. 69. London.
Hercher, R. 1858. *Claudii Aeliani De natura animalium, Varia historia, Epistolae et fragmenta; Porphyrii philosophi De abstinentia et De antro nympharum; Philonis Byzantii De septem orbis spectaculis*. Paris.
Herman, G. 1997. "The Court Society of the Hellenistic Age." Pp. 199-224 in P. Cartledge, P. Garnsey, and E. Gruen, eds., *Hellenistic Constructs: Essays in Culture, History, and Historiography*. Berkeley and Los Angeles.
Herter, H. 1929. "Kallimachos und Homer: Ein Beitrag zur Interpretation des *Hymnos auf Artemis*." Pp. 50-105 in *Xenia Bonnensia: Festschrift zum fünfundsiebzigjährigen Bestehen des Philologischen Vereins und Bonner Kreises*. Bonn. [Reprinted as pp. 371-416 in *Kleine Schriften* (Munich, 1975).]
———. 1931. Kallimachos. Cols. 386-452 in A. von Pauly et al., eds., *Real-Encyclopädie der classischen Altertumswissenschaft*, Supplementband 5. Stuttgart.
———. 1937. "Bericht über die Literatur zur hellenistischen Dichtung aus den Jahren 1921-1935, I." *Jahresbericht über die Fortschritte der Altertumswissenschaft* 63: 65-218.
Hesberg, H. von. 1981. "Bemerkungen zu Architekturepigrammen des 3. Jahrhunderts v. Chr." *Jahrbuch des Deutschen Archäologischen Instituts* 96: 55-119.
———. 1987. "Mechanische Kunstwerke und ihre Bedeutung für die höfische Kunst des frühen Hellenismus." *Marburger Winckelmann-Programm*, 47-72.
———. 1989. "Temporäre Bilder oder die Grenzen der Kunst: Zur Legitimation frühhellenistischer Königsherrschaft im Fest." *Jahrbuch des Deutschen Archäologischen Instituts* 104: 61-82.
———. 1996. "Privatheit und Öffentlichkeit der frühhellenistischen Hofarchitektur." Pp. 84-96 in Hoepfner and Brands 1996.
Heyworth, S. 1994. "Some Allusions to Callimachus in Roman Poetry." *Materiali e Discussioni* 33: 51-79.
———. 2007a. *Cynthia: A Companion to the Text of Propertius*. Oxford.
———. 2007b. *Sexti Properti elegi*. Oxford.
Hinds, S. 1988 "Generalising about Ovid." *Ramus* 16: 4-31. [Reprinted as pp. 15-50 in Knox 2006.]
———. 1992. "'Arma' in Ovid's *Fasti*." *Arethusa* 25: 81-153.
———. 1998. *Allusion and Intertext: Dynamics of Appropriation in Roman Poetry*. Cambridge.
———. 2006. See Hinds 1988.
Hinge, G. 2009. "Language and Race: Theocritus and the Koine Identity of Ptolemaic Egypt." Pp. 66-79 in J. Krasilnikoff and G. Hinge, eds., *Alexandria: A Religious and Cultural Meltingpot*. Aarhus.
Hintzen-Bohlen, B. 1992. *Herrscherrepräsentation im Hellenismus: Untersuchungen zur Weihgeschenken, Stiftungen und Ehrenmonumenten in den mutterländischen Heiligtümern Delphi, Olympia, Delos und Dodona*. Cologne.
Hoepfner, W., and G. Brands, eds. 1996. *Basileia: Die Paläste der hellenistischen Könige: Internationales Symposion in Berlin vom 16.12.1992 bis 20.12.1992*. Mainz.
Hokwerda, H., E.R. Smits, and M.M. Woesthuis, eds. 1993. *Polyphonia Byzantina: Studies in Honour of Willem J. Aerts*. Groningen.
Hölbl, G. 1994. *Geschichte des Ptolemäerreiches*. Darmstadt.
———. 2001. *A History of the Ptolemaic Empire*. London.
Hollis, A.S. 1976. "Some Allusions to Earlier Hellenistic Poetry in Nonnus." *Classical Quarterly* 26: 142-150.

———. 1982. "Teuthis and Callimachus: *Aetia*, Book 1." *Classical Quarterly* 32: 117–120.
———. 1986. "The Composition of Callimachus' *Aetia* in the Light of *P. Oxy.* 2258." *Classical Quarterly* 36: 467–471.
———. 1990a. *Callimachus. Hecale. Edited with Introduction and Commentary.* Oxford.
———. 1990b. "Epops in the Erchian Sacred Calendar and the *Aetia* of Callimachus." Pp. 127–130 in Craik 1990.
———. 1992a. "Attica in Hellenistic Poetry." *Zeitschrift für Papyrologie und Epigraphik* 93: 1–15.
———. 1992b. "The Nuptial Rite in Catullus 66 and Callimachus' Poetry for Berenice." *Zeitschrift für Papyrologie und Epigraphik* 91: 21–28.
———. 1992c. "Teuthis in Callimachus' *Aetia* (P.Mich. Inv. 6235)." *Zeitschrift für Papyrologie und Epigraphik* 92: 115–117.
———. 1994a. "Nonnus and Hellenistic Poetry." Pp. 43–62 in Hopkinson 1994c.
———. 1994b. "[Oppian], *Cyn.* 2, 100–158 and the Mythical Past of Apamea-on-the-Orontes." *Zeitschrift für Papyrologie und Epigraphik* 102: 153–166.
———. 1994c. Review of P. Chuvin, *Mythologie et géographie dionysiaques* (Clermont-Ferrand, 1991). *Classical Review* 44: 12–13.
———. 1997a. "The Beginning of Callimachus' *Hecale*." *Zeitschrift für Papyrologie und Epigraphik* 115: 55–56.
———. 1997b. "A Fragmentary Addiction." Pp. 111–123 in Most 1997.
———. 1997c. "A New Fragment on Niobe and the Text of Propertius 2.20.8." *Classical Quarterly* 47: 578–582.
———. 1998. "Callimachus, *Epigram* 9 G.-P. = 44 Pf. = *Anth. Pal.* 12,139." *Zeitschrift für Papyrologie und Epigraphik* 123: 73–74.
———. 2000. "Another Rare Epithet in Callimachus' *Hecale*?" *Zeitschrift für Papyrologie und Epigraphik* 130: 16.
———. 2002. "Callimachus: Light from Later Antiquity." Pp. 35–54 in Montanari and Lehnus 2002.
———. 2006. "The Hellenistic Epyllion and Its Descendants." Pp. 141–157 in S.F. Johnson, ed., *Greek Literature in Late Antiquity: Dynamism, Didacticism, Classicism*. Aldershot.
———. 2007. "Some Poetic Connections of Lycophron's *Alexandra*." Pp. 276–293 in P.J. Finglass, C. Collard, and N.J. Richardson, eds., *Hesperos: Studies in Ancient Greek Poetry Presented to M.L. West on His Seventieth Birthday*. Oxford.
———. 2009. *Callimachus. Hecale. With Introduction, Text, Translation, and Enlarged Commentary.* 2nd ed. Oxford.
Holmes, L. 1992. "Myrrh and Unguents in the *Coma Berenices*." *Classical Philology* 87: 47–50.
Hopkinson, N. 1984a. *Callimachus. Hymn to Demeter. Edited with an Introduction and Commentary.* Cambridge.
———. 1984b. "Callimachus' *Hymn to Zeus*." *Classical Quarterly* 34: 139–148.
———. 1984c. "Rhea in Callimachus' *Hymn to Zeus*." *Journal of Hellenic Studies* 104: 176–177.
———. 1985. "The *Hymn to Delos*." *Classical Review* 35: 249–252.
———. 1988. *A Hellenistic Anthology*. Cambridge.
———. 1994a. *Greek Poetry of the Imperial Period: An Anthology*. Cambridge.
———. 1994b. "Nonnus and Homer." Pp. 9–42 in Hopkinson 1994c.
———, ed. 1994c. *Studies in the "Dionysiaca" of Nonnus*. Cambridge.
Hörandner, W. 1974. *Theodoros Prodromos: Historische Gedichte*. Vienna.
Hordern, J.H. 2000. "Machon and Philoxenus." *Zeitschrift für Papyrologie und Epigraphik* 133: 12.
———. 2002. *The Fragments of Timotheus of Miletus*. Oxford.

Hornblower, S., and C. Morgan, eds. 2007. *Pindar's Poetry, Patrons, and Festivals: From Archaic Greece to the Roman Empire*. Oxford.
Horstmann, A.E.-A. 1976. *Ironie und Humor bei Theokrit*. Meisenheim.
Höschele, R. 2009. "Catullus' Callimachean Hair-itage and the Erotics of Translation." *Rivista di Filologia e di Istruzione Classica* 137: 118–152.
Hose, M. 1997. "Der alexandrinische Zeus: Zur Stellung der Dichtkunst im Reich der ersten Ptolemäer." *Philologus* 141: 46–64.
Housman, A.E. 1910. "Αἴτια Καλλιμάχου (*Pap.Ox.* VII, pp. 24–27)." *Berliner Philologische Wochenschrift* 30: 476–477.
Houston, G.W. 2007. "Grenfell, Hunt, Breccia, and the Book Collections of Oxyrhynchus." *Greek, Roman and Byzantine Studies* 47: 327–359.
Howe, E.A. 1990. *Stages of Self*. Athens, Ohio.
Hubbard, T.K. 1998. *The Pipes of Pan: Intertextuality and Literary Filiation in the Pastoral Tradition from Theocritus to Milton*. Ann Arbor.
Hübner, U. 1992. "Probleme der Verknüpfung in Kallimachos' Apollonhymnus." *Hermes* 120: 280–290.
Hunger, H. 1967. "Palimpsest-Fragmente aus Herodians Καθολικὴ Προσῳδία, Buch 5–7." *Jahrbuch der Österreichischen Byzantinischen Gesellschaft* 16: 1–33.
Hunt, A.S. 1910a. *The Oxyrhynchus Papyri*. Volume 7. London.
———. 1910b. "Zur Kydippe des Kallimachos." *Berliner Philologische Wochenschrift* 30: 573–574.
———. 1927. *The Oxyrhynchus Papyri*. Volume 17. London.
Hunter, R.L. 1989a. *Apollonius of Rhodes. Argonautica. Book III*. Cambridge.
———. 1989b. "Winged Callimachus." *Zeitschrift für Papyrologie und Epigraphik* 76: 1–2. [Reprinted as pp. 86–88 in Hunter 2008b.]
———. 1991. "Greek and Non-Greek in the *Argonautica* of Apollonius." Pp. 81–99 in Said 1991. [Reprinted as pp. 95–114 in Hunter 2008b.]
———. 1992a. "Callimachus and Heraclitus." *Materiali e Discussioni* 28: 113–123. [Reprinted as pp. 115–126 in Hunter 2008b.]
———. 1992b. "Writing the God: Form and Meaning in Callimachus, *Hymn to Athena*." *Materiali e Discussioni* 29: 9–34. [Reprinted as pp. 127–152 in Hunter 2008b.]
———. 1993. *The Argonautica of Apollonius: Literary Studies*. Cambridge.
———. 1996. *Theocritus and the Archaeology of Greek Poetry*. Cambridge.
———. 1997. "(B)ionic Man: Callimachus' Iambic Programme." *Proceedings of the Cambridge Philological Society* 43: 41–52. [Reprinted as pp. 311–325 in Hunter 2008b.]
———. 1999. *Theocritus: A Selection*. Cambridge.
———. 2003a. "Aspects of Technique and Style in the *Periegesis* of Dionysius." Pp. 343–356 in D. Accorinti and P. Chuvin, eds., *Des Géants à Dionysos: Mélanges de mythologie et de poésie grecques offerts à Francis Vian*. Alessandria. [Reprinted as pp. 700–717 in Hunter 2008b.]
———. 2003b. "Literature and its Contexts." Pp. 477–493 in Erskine 2003.
———. 2003c. *Theocritus: Encomium of Ptolemy Philadelphus*. Berkeley and Los Angeles.
———. 2004. "The *Periegesis* of Dionysius and the Traditions of Hellenistic Poetry." *Revue des Études Anciennes* 106: 217–231. [Reprinted as pp. 718–734 in Hunter 2008b.]
———. 2005a. "The Hesiodic *Catalogue* and Hellenistic Poetry." Pp. 239–265 in Hunter 2005b. [Reprinted as pp. 470–502 in Hunter 2008b.]
———. 2005b. *The Hesiodic* Catalogue of Women: *Constructions and Reconstructions*. Cambridge.
———. 2006a. *The Shadow of Callimachus: Studies in the Reception of Hellenistic Poetry at Rome*. Cambridge.
———. 2006b. "Sweet Nothings: Callimachus Fr. 1,9–12, Revisited." Pp. 119–131 in Bastianini and Casanova 2006. [Reprinted as pp. 523–536 in Hunter 2008b.]
———. 2008a. "Hesiod, Callimachus and the Invention of Morality." Pp. 153–164 in Bastianini and Casanova 2008. [Reprinted as pp. 559–571 in Hunter 2008b.]

———. 2008b. *On Coming After: Studies in Post-Classical Greek Literature and Its Reception*. 2 vols. Berlin.
Hunter, R., and T. Fuhrer. 2002. "Imaginary Gods? Poetic Theology in the *Hymns* of Callimachus." Pp. 143-187 in Montanari and Lehnus 2002. [Reprinted as pp. 405-433 in Hunter 2008b.]
Hurst, A. 1990. "Ménandre et la tragédie." Pp. 93-122 in A. Hurst and E. Handley, eds., *Relire Ménandre*. Geneva.
———. 1996. "La stèle de l'Hélicon." Pp. 57-71 in Hurst and Schachter 1996.
Hurst, A., and A. Kolde. 2008. *Lycophron. Alexandra*. Paris.
Hurst, A., and A. Schachter, eds. 1996. *La montagne des Muses*. Geneva.
Huss, W. 1994. *Der makedonische König und die ägyptischen Priester: Studien zur Geschichte des ptolemaiischen Ägypten*. Stuttgart.
———. 2001. *Ägypten in hellenistischer Zeit, 332-30 v. Chr.* Munich.
Hutchinson, G.O. 1988. *Hellenistic Poetry*. Oxford.
———. 2002. "The New Posidippus and Latin Poetry." *Zeitschrift für Papyrologie und Epigraphik* 138: 1-10. [Reprinted as pp. 90-108 in Hutchinson 2008.]
———. 2003. "The *Aetia*: Callimachus' Poem of Knowledge." *Zeitschrift für Papyrologie und Epigraphik* 145: 47-59. [Reprinted as pp. 42-65 in Hutchinson 2008.]
———. 2006a. "The Metamorphosis of Metamorphosis: P. Oxy. 4711 and Ovid." *Zeitschrift für Papyrologie und Epigraphik* 155: 71-84. [Reprinted as pp. 200-227 in Hutchinson 2008.]
———. 2006b. *Propertius: Carmina IV*. Cambridge.
———. 2008. *Talking Books: Readings in Hellenistic and Roman Books of Poetry*. Oxford.
Huxley, G.L. 1965. "Xenomedes of Keos." *Greek, Roman and Byzantine Studies* 6: 235-245.
———. 1980. "Βουπόρος Ἀρσινόης." *Journal of Hellenic Studies* 100: 189-190.
Imbriani, V. 1882. "Incontri, reminscenze, imitazioni, plagi." *Giornale napoletano della domenica* (June 11th). [Reprinted in V. Imbriani, *Studi letterari e bizzarrie satiriche*. Bari 1907: 350-358 and in *Quaderni di Storia* 18 (36) 1992: 141-148.]
Innes, D. 1985. "Theophrastus and the Theory of Style." Pp. 251-267 in W.W. Fortenbaugh, P.M. Huby, and A.A. Long, eds., *Theophrastus of Eresus: On His Life and Works*. New Brunswick.
Inwood, B. 1995. "Politics and Paradox in Seneca's *De Beneficiis*." Pp. 241-265 in A. Laks and M. Schofield, eds., *Justice and Generosity: Studies in Hellenistic Social and Political Philosophy—Proceedings of the Sixth Symposium Hellenisticum*. Cambridge.
Irigoin, J. 1952. *Histoire du texte de Pindare*. Paris.
———. 1960. "Sur un distique de Callimaque (fr. 496 + 533 Pfeiffer)." *Revue des Études Grecques* 73: 439-447.
———. 1994. "Les éditions de textes." Pp. 39-93 in Montanari 1994.
Ittzés, D. 2002. "*Phthonos Apollônos*: Zur Interpretation des kallimacheischen Apollon-Hymnus." *Acta Antiqua Academiae Scientiarum Hungaricae* 42: 105-123.
Jackson, S.B. 2000. *Istrus the Callimachean*. Amsterdam.
———. 2001. "Callimachus, *Coma Berenices*: Origins." *Mnemosyne* 54: 1-9.
Jackson, S.B., and D.P. Nelis, eds. 2005. *Studies in Hellenistic Poetry*. 2 vols. Dublin.
Jacoby, F. 1949. *Atthis: The Local Chronicles of Ancient Athens*. Oxford.
———. 1954. *Die Fragmente der griechischen Historiker*. Part 3b, *A Commentary on the Ancient Historians of Athens*. 2 vols. Leiden.
Jacques, J.-M. 1955. "Les *Alexipharmaques* de Nicandre." *Revue des Études Anciennes* 57: 5-35.
———. 2002. *Nicandre: Oeuvres*. Volume 2, *Les Thériaques*. Paris.
———. 2007. *Nicandre: Oeuvres*. Volume 3, *Les Alexipharmaques*. Paris.
Jan, F. von. 1893. *De Callimacho Homeri interprete*. Strassburg.
Janko, R. 1991. "Philodemus' *On Poems* and Aristotle's *On Poets*." *Cronache Ercolanesi* 21: 5-64.

———. 2000. *Philodemus. On Poems. Book 1*. Oxford.
Jennings, V., and A. Katsaros, eds. 2007. *The World of Ion of Chios*. Leiden.
Johnson, W.A. 2004. *Bookrolls and Scribes in Oxyrhynchus*. Toronto.
Joly, R. 1955. "L'exhortation au courage (θαρρεῖν) dans les Mystères." *Revue des Études Grecques* 68: 164–170.
Jong, I.J.F. de. 1987. *Narrators and Focalizers*. Amsterdam.
Jong, I.J.F. de, R. Nünlist, and A. Bowie, eds. 2004. *Narrators, Narratees, and Narratives in Ancient Greek Literature*. Leiden.
Jordan, D., and J. Traill, eds. 2003. *Lettered Attica: A Day of Attic Epigraphy*. Athens.
Jusdanis, G. 1987. *The Poetics of Cavafy: Textuality, Eroticism, History*. Princeton.
Kaczynska, E. 2001. "L'acqua cheta: Per l'esegesi di un epigramma di Callimaco (Ep. 44 Pfeiffer = 9 Gow-Page = A.P. XII 139)." *Maia* 53: 37–42.
Kahane, A. 1994. "Callimachus, Apollonius, and the Poetics of Mud." *Transactions of the American Philological Association* 124: 121–133.
Kaibel, G. 1878. *Epigrammata Graeca ex lapidibus conlecta*. Berlin.
Kakridis, J.T. 1928. "Zum neuen Kallimachos." *Philologische Wochenschrift* 48: 1214–1215.
Kambylis, A. 1965. *Die Dichterweihe und ihre Symbolik*. Heidelberg.
———. 1982. "Gregor von Nazianz und Kallimachos." *Hermes* 110: 120–122.
Kapp, I. 1915. *Callimachi Hecalae fragmenta*. Berlin.
Käppel, L. 1992. *Paian: Studien zur Geschichte einer Gattung*. Berlin.
Kassel, R. 1983. "Diologe mit Statuen." *Zeitschrift für Papyrologie und Epigraphik* 51: 1–12.
Kaster, R.A. 1988. *Guardians of Language: The Grammarian and Society in Late Antiquity*. Berkeley and Los Angeles.
Katsaros, A. 2007. "Staging Empire and Other in Ion's Sympotica." Pp. 217–240 in Jennings and Katsaros 2007.
Katsouris, A.G. 1975. *Tragic Patterns in Menander*. Athens.
Kellett, E.E. 1933. *Literary Quotation and Allusion*. Cambridge.
Kennedy, G.A., ed. 1989. *The Cambridge History of Literary Criticism*. Cambridge.
Kenney, E.J. 1976. "Ovidius Prooemians." *Proceedings of the Cambridge Philological Society* 22: 46–53.
———. 1986. *Ovid's Metamorphoses, with Introduction and Notes*. Oxford.
Kerkhecker, A. 1988. "Ein Musenanruf am Anfang der *Aitia* des Kallimachos." *Zeitschrift für Papyrologie und Epigraphik* 71: 16–24.
———. 1991. "Zum neuen hellenistischen Weihepigramm aus Pergamon." *Zeitschrift für Papyrologie und Epigraphik* 86: 7–34.
———. 1993. "Theseus im Regen: Zu Kallimachos, *Hekale* fr. 74,1 Hollis." *Museum Helveticum* 50: 1–19.
———. 1997. "Μουσέων ἐν ταλάρῳ: Dichter und Dichtung am Ptolemäerhof." *Antike und Abendland* 43: 124–144.
———. 1999. *Callimachus' Book of Iambi*. Oxford.
Keydell, R. 1953. "Metrische Bemerkungen zu den Hymnen des Isidoros." *Prolegomena* 2: 123–124. [Reprinted as pp. 313–314 in Keydell 1982.]
———. 1959. *Nonni Panopolitani Dionysiaca*. 2 vols. Berlin.
———. 1982. *Kleine Schriften zur hellenistischen und spätgriechischen Dichtung*. Leipzig.
Kidd, D. 1997. *Aratus. Phaenomena*. Cambridge.
Kidd, I.G. 1988. *The Commentary*. Volumes 2 and 3 of L. Edelstein and I.G. Kidd, *Posidonius*, 4 vols. Cambridge.
Kirk, G.S. 1985. *The Iliad: A Commentary, Volume I: Books 1–4*. Cambridge.
Kleinlogel, A. 1991. Review of Tosi 1988. *Göttingische Gelehrte Anzeigen* 243: 185–204.
Knight, W.F.J. 1944. *Roman Vergil*. London.

Knox, P.E. 1985a. "The Epilogue to the *Aetia*." *Greek, Roman and Byzantine Studies* 26: 59–65.
——. 1985b. "Wine, Water, and Callimachean Polemics." *Harvard Studies in Classical Philology* 89: 107–119.
——. 1993. "The Epilogue to the *Aetia*: An Epilogue." *Zeitschrift für Papyrologie und Epigraphik* 96: 175–178.
——, ed. 2006. *Oxford Readings in Ovid*. Oxford.
Knuf, H. 2010. "Poet und Pilger: Kallimacheische Motive in der Vision des Maximus." Pp. 273–289 in H. Knuf, C. Leitz, and D. von Recklinghausen, eds., *Honi soit qui mal y pense: Studien zum pharaonischen, griechisch-römischen und spätantiken Ägypten zu Ehren von Heinz-Josef Thissen*. Louvain.
Koch, H.-A., ed. 1990. *Welt der Information*. Stuttgart.
Koenen, L. 1977. *Eine agonistische Inschrift aus Ägypten und frühptolemäische Königsfeste*. Meisenheim.
——. 1983. "Die Adaptation ägyptischer Königsideologie am Ptolemäerhof." Pp. 143–190 in E. van't Dack, ed., *Egypt and the Hellenistic World: Proceedings of the International Colloquium, Leuven, 24–26 May, 1982*. Louvain.
——. 1993. "The Ptolemaic King as a Religious Figure." Pp. 25–115 in Bulloch et al. 1993.
Koenen, L., W. Luppe, and V. Pagán. 1991. "Explanations of Callimachean αἴτια." *Zeitschrift für Papyrologie und Epigraphik* 88: 157–164.
Kofler, W. 1996. "Kallimachos' Wahlverwandtschaften: Zur poetischen Tradition und Gattung des *Apollonhymnus*." *Philologus* 140: 230–247.
Köhler, J. 1996. *Pompai: Untersuchungen zur hellenistischen Festkultur*. Frankfurt.
Köhnken, A. 1981. "Apollo's Retort to Envy's Criticism: Two Questions of Relevance in Callimachus, *Hymn* 2, 105ff." *American Journal of Philology* 102: 411–422.
——. 1984. "'Πηλογόνων ἐλατήρ': Kallimachos, *Zeushymnos* v. 3." *Hermes* 112: 438–445.
Kolde, A. 2003. *Politique et religion chez Isyllos d'Épidaure*. Basel.
Kolde, A., A. Lukinovich, and A.-L. Rey, eds. 2006. Κορυφαίῳ ἀνδρί: *Mélanges offerts à André Hurst*. Geneva.
Kolovou, F. 1998. "Die Quellenidentifizierung als Hilfsmittel zur Textkonstitution der Briefe des Michael Choniates." Pp. 129–136 in Vassis, Henrich, and Reinsch 1998.
——. 1999. Μιχαήλ Χωνιάτης· Συμβολή στη μελέτη του βίου και του έργου του—Το Corpus των "Ἐπιστολῶν." Athens.
——. 2001 "Quellenforschung zu den Briefen des Michael Choniates." Ἑλληνικά 51: 75–99.
Körte, A. 1935. "Literarische Texte mit Ausschluß der christlichen." *Archiv für Papyrusforschung* 11: 220–283.
Kost, K. 1971. *Musaios. Hero und Leander*. Bonn.
Kotsidu, H. 2000. Τιμὴ καὶ δόξα: *Ehrungen für hellenistische Herrscher im griechischen Mutterland und in Kleinasien unter besonderer Berücksichtigung der archäologischen Denkmäler*. Berlin.
Kowalzig, B. 2007a. "'And Now All the World Shall Dance!' (Eur. *Bacch*. 114): Dionysus' Choroi between Drama and Ritual." Pp. 221–252 in Csapo and Miller 2007.
——. 2007b. *Singing for the Gods: Performances of Myth and Ritual in Archaic and Classical Greece*. Oxford.
Kowalzig, B., and P. Wilson, eds. Forthcoming. *Dithyramb and Society: Texts and Contexts in a Changing Choral Culture*. Oxford.
Kranz, H. 1939. *Kallimachos und die Sprache Homers: Eine Untersuchung der Hymnen auf Apollon und auf Delos*. Vienna.
Krevans, N. 1984. *The Poet as Editor: Callimachus, Virgil, Horace, Propertius and the Development of the Poetic Book*. Dissertation, Princeton University.
——. 1993. "Fighting against Antimachus: The *Lyde* and the *Aetia* Reconsidered." Pp. 149–160 in M.A. Harder, Regtuit, and Wakker 1993.

———. 2000. "On the Margins of Epic: The Foundation-Poems of Apollonius." Pp. 69–84 in M.A. Harder, Regtuit, and Wakker 2000.
———. 2004. "Callimachus and the Pedestrian Muse." Pp. 173–183 in M.A. Harder, Regtuit, and Wakker 2004.
———. 2005. "The Editor's Toolbox: Strategies for Selection and Presentation in the Milan Epigram Papyrus." Pp. 81–96 in Gutzwiller 2005.
Kroll, W. 1924. *Studien zum Verständnis der römischen Literatur*. Stuttgart. [Reprint: Darmstadt, 1973.]
Krüger, J. 1990. *Oxyrhynchos in der Kaiserzeit: Studien zur Topographie und Literaturrezeption*. Frankfurt.
Kuiper, K. 1896. *Studia Callimachea*. Volume 1, *De hymnorum I–IV dictione epica*. Leiden.
Kullmann, W., and J. Althoff, eds. 1993. *Vermittlung und Tradierung von Wissen in der griechischen Kunst*. Tübingen.
Kumaniecki, K. 1958. "Il periodo italiano dell'opera poetica di Filippo Buonaccorsi: I suoi epigrammi romani." Pp. 65–73 in *Il mondo antico nel Rinascimento: Atti del V. Convegno internazionale di studi sul Rinascimento*. Florence.
Kunze, C. 2002. *Zum Greifen nah: Stilphänomene in der hellenistischen Skulptur und ihre inhaltliche Interpretation*. Munich.
Kuttner, A.L. 1999. "Hellenistic Images of Spectacle from Alexander to Augustus." Pp. 97–124 in B. Bergmann and C. Kondoleon, eds., *The Art of Spectacle*. Washington, D.C.
———. 2005. "Cabinet Fit for a Queen: The Λιθικά as Posidippus' Gem Museum." Pp. 141–163 in Gutzwiller 2005.
La Penna, A. 1962. "Esiodo nella cultura e nella poesia di Virgilio." Pp. 213–252 in O. Reverdin, ed., *Hésiode et son influence*. Vandœuvres.
———. 1964. "Pasquali interprete di Orazio." Pp. vii–xxxi in Pasquali 1964b.
———. 1986. "Gli 'scritti filologici' di Giorgio Pasquali." Pp. ix–lxxiv in Pasquali 1986, vol. 1.
———. 1987. "Callimaco e i paradossi dell'imperatore Tiberio (Svetonio, *Tib.* 70, 6; 62, 6)." *Studi Italiani di Filologia Classica* 80: 181–185.
Labarbe, J. 1967. "Les aspects gnomiques de l'épigramme grecque." Pp. 351–386 in *L'épigramme grecque*. Vandœuvres.
Lacan, J. 1992. *The Ethics of Psychoanalysis, 1959–1960*. New York.
Lada-Richards, I. 1999. *Initiating Dionysus*. Oxford.
Laird, A., ed. 2006a. *Oxford Readings in Ancient Literary Criticism*. Oxford.
———. 2006b. "The Value of Ancient Literary Criticism" Pp. 1–36 in Laird 2006a.
Lallot, J. 1989. *La Grammaire de Denys le Thrace, traduite et annotée*. Paris.
Lambros, S.P. 1879–1880. Μιχαὴλ Ἀκομινάτου τοῦ Χωνιάτου τὰ σωζόμενα. 2 vols. Athens.
Lampela, A. 1998. *Rome and the Ptolemies of Egypt: The Development of Their Political Relations, 273–80 BC* Helsinki.
Lanza, D. 1992. *Aristotele: Poetica*. Milan.
Lapatin, K.D.S. 2001. *Chryselephantine Statuary in the ancient Mediterranean World*. Oxford.
———. 2010. "New Statues for Old." Pp. 126–151 in J.N. Bremmer and A. Erskine, eds., *The Gods of Ancient Greece*. Edinburgh.
Lapucci, C. 2006. *Dizionario dei proverbi italiani*. Florence.
Larivée, A. 2003. "Du vin pour le collège de veille? Mise en lumière d'un lien occulté entre le chœur de Dionysos et le νυκτερινὸς σύλλογος dans les *Lois* de Platon." *Phronesis* 48: 29–53.
Laronde, A. 1987. *Cyrène et la Libye hellénistique: Libykai historiai de l'époque républicaine au principat d'Auguste*. Paris.
Launey, M. 1949–1950. *Recherches sur les armées hellénistiques*. 2 vols. Paris. [Reprint: Paris, 1987.]

Lausberg, M. 1982. *Das Einzeldistichon: Studien zum antiken Epigramm*. Munich.
Lauxtermann, M.D. 2003. *Byzantine Poetry from Pisides to Geometres: Texts and Contexts*. Vienna.
Le Guen, B. 2001. *Les associations de technites dionysiaques à l'époque hellénistique*. Nancy.
Lefkowitz, M.R. 1981. *The Lives of the Greek Poets*. London.
Legras, B. 2001. "Entre grécité et égyptianité: La fonction culturelle de l'éducation grecque dans l'Égypte hellénistique." Pp. 133–141 in J.-M. Pailler and P. Payen, eds., *Que reste-t-il de l'éducation classique? Relire "le Marrou" Histoire de l'éducation dans l'antiquité*. Toulouse.
———. 2002. "Les experts égyptiens à la cour des Ptolémées." *Revue Historique* 304: 963–991.
———. 2006. "Καθάπερ ἐκ παλαιοῦ: Le statut de l'Égypte sous Cléomène de Naucratis." Pp. 83–102 in J.-C. Couvenhes and B. Legras, eds., *Transferts culturels et politique dans le monde hellénistique*. Paris.
Lehnus, L. 1990a. "Notizie callimachee." *Rivista di Filologia e di Istruzione Classica* 118: 26–32.
———. 1990b. "Notizie callimachee, II." *Paideia* 45: 277–292.
———. 1991a. "Callimaco fr. 1.5 Pf." *Zeitschrift für Papyrologie und Epigraphik* 89: 24.
———. 1991b. "Callimaco redivivo tra Th. Stanley e R. Bentley." *Eikasmos* 2: 285–309.
———. 1992. "Ancora su Callimaco in P.Mich. inv. 6235." *Zeitschrift für Papyrologie und Epigraphik* 91: 20.
———. 1993. "Callimaco tra la polis e il regno." Pp. 75–105 in G. Cambiano, L. Canfora, and D. Lanza, eds., *Lo spazio letterario della Grecia antica*, vol. 1, *La produzione e la circolazione del testo*, part 2, *L'ellenismo*. Rome.
———. 1994a. "Antichità cirenaiche in Callimaco." *Eikasmos* 5: 189–207.
———. 1994b. "L'ombra di Wilamowitz." *Eikasmos* 5: 401–418.
———. 1995. "Riflessioni cronologiche sull'ultimo Callimaco." *Zeitschrift für Papyrologie und Epigraphik* 105: 6–12.
———. 1996a. "Iter Callimacheum." *Eikasmos* 7: 293–307.
———. 1996b. "Notizie callimachee, III." *Acme* 49.2: 145–149.
———. 1997. "Ipotesi sul finale dell'*Ecale*." *Zeitschrift für Papyrologie und Epigraphik* 117: 45–46.
———. 1999. "In margine a un recente libro su Callimaco." Pp. 201–225 in Conca 1999.
———. 2000a. "Notizie callimachee, IV." Pp. 379–384 in M. Cannatà Fera and S. Grandolini, eds., *Poesia e religione in Grecia: Studi in onore di G. Aurelio Privitera*, vol. 2. Naples.
———. 2000b. *Nuova bibliografia callimachea, 1489–1988*. Alessandria.
———. 2000c. "Verso una nuova edizione dei frammenti di Callimaco." Pp. 21–44 in Pretagostini 2000a.
———. 2001. "Notizie callimachee, V." *Acme* 54.3: 283–291.
———. 2002. "Callimaco prima e dopo Pfeiffer." Pp. 1–29 in Montanari and Lehnus 2002.
———. 2004a. "Argo, Argolide e storiografia locale in Callimaco." Pp. 201–209 in Angeli Bernardini 2004.
———. 2004b. "A Callimachean Medley." *Zeitschrift für Papyrologie und Epigraphik* 147: 27–32.
———. 2004c. "Wilamowitz a Norden su Rudolf Pfeiffer." Pp. 313–324 in Cerasuolo 2004.
———. 2006a. "Nota sulle osservazioni di Lobel a Vitelli a proposito delle *Diegeseis*." *Quaderni di Storia* 63: 213–219.
———. 2006b. "Prima e dopo αἱ κατὰ λεπτόν." Pp. 133–147 in Bastianini and Casanova 2006.

———. 2007. "Wilamowitz a Hunt: La pace dei cento anni nel suo ultimo giorno." Pp. 201–228 in Zanetto, Martinelli Tempesta, and Ornaghi 2007.
———. 2009. "Postille inedite di Paul Maas all'*Apoteosi di Arsinoe* di Callimaco." Pp. 63–71 in Zanetto and Ornaghi 2009.
Lelli, E. 1996. "La figura del rovo nel *Giambo* IV di Callimaco." *Rivista di Cultura Classica e Medioevale* 38: 311–318.
———. 2000. "Callimaco, *Aitia* fr. 1.3–4 Pf." *Seminari Romani di Cultura Greca* 3: 73–76.
———. 2001. "La polivalenza simbolica dell'opposizione asino/cicala nel prologo degli *Aitia* di Callimaco." *Seminari Romani di Cultura Greca* 4: 242–252.
———. 2002. "Arsinoe II in Callimaco e nelle testimonianze letterarie alessandrine (Teocrito, Posidippo, Sotade e altro)." *Appunti Romani di Filologia* 4: 5–29.
———. 2003. "Elementi di folklore nei *Giambi* di Callimaco." Pp. 475–492 in Belloni, de Finis, and Moretti 2003.
———. 2004. *Critica e polemiche letterarie nei* Giambi *di Callimaco*. Alessandria.
———. 2005a. *Callimaco, Giambi XIV–XVII / Callimachi Iambi XIV–XVII: Introduzione, testo critico, traduzione e commento*. Rome.
———. 2005b. "Posidippo e Callimaco." Pp. 77–132 in Di Marco, Palumbo Stracca, and Lelli 2005.
———. 2006a. *I proverbi greci: Le raccolte di Zenobio e Diogeniano*. Trans. F.P. Bianchi et al. Soveria Mannelli.
———. 2006b. *Volpe e leone: Il proverbio nella poesia greca (Alceo, Cratino, Callimaco)*. Rome.
———. 2007. "L'onomastica del mondo italico negli alessandrini: Tra erudizione e letterarietà." *Glotta* 83: 98–112.
Lenchantin de Gubernatis, M. 1935. "Ribruscula Callimachea." *Athenaeum* 13: 101–112.
———. 1951. *Il libro di Catullo*. Turin.
Leone, P.L.M. 2002. *Scholia vetera et paraphrases in Lycophronis Alexandram*. Galatina.
Leonelli, G. 1989. *Itinerari del Fanciullino*. Bologna.
———. 2002. "Poemi di Psyche." Pp. 1157–1178 in Garboli 2002, vol. 2.
———. 2004. "Introduzione ai *Poemi conviviali*." Pp. 323–335 in G. Leonelli, *Il lettore di se stesso*. Rome.
Leroy, M. 1935. "Grégoire Magistros et les traductions arméniennes d'auteurs grecs." *Annuaire de l'Institut de Philologie et d'Histoire Orientales (Brussels)* 3: 263–294.
Leurini, L. 1985. "La *Suda*, Callimaco e la πολυείδεια di Ione di Chio." *Annali della Facoltà di Lettere e Filosofia (Cagliari)* 6: 5–13.
———. 1992. "Euphor. Fr. 57 V. Groningen e Callim. Hymn. 3, 46 ss." *Lexis* 9–10: 145–153.
———. 2000. *Ionis Chii testimonia et fragmenta*. 2nd ed. Amsterdam.
Lidell, R. 2000. *Cavafy. A Bibliography*. London.
Lightfoot, J.L. 1999. *Parthenius of Nicaea: The Poetical Fragments and the Ἐρωτικὰ Παθήματα* Oxford.
———. 2008. "Catalogue Technique in Dionysius Periegetes." Pp. 11–31 in Carvounis and Hunter 2008.
Livrea, E. 1968. *Colluto: Il ratto di Elena*. Bologna.
———. 1972. "Una 'tecnica allusiva' apolloniana alla luce dell'esegesi omerica alessandrina." *Studi Italiani di Filologia Classica* 44: 231–243.
———. 1973a. *Apollonii Rhodii Argonauticon liber IV*. Florence.
———. 1973b. *Dionysii Bassaricon et Gigantiadis fragmenta*. Rome.
———. 1979. "Der Liller Kallimachos und die Mausefallen." *Zeitschrift für Papyrologie und Epigraphik* 34: 37–42. [Reprinted as pp. 165–169 in Livrea 1991, vol. 1.]
———. 1982. Review of F. Vian, *Apollonius de Rhodes. Argonautiques*, trans. É. Delage, vol. 2 (Paris, 1980). *Gnomon* 54: 37–42.

———. 1989a. *Nonno di Panopoli: Parafrasi del Vangelo di San Giovanni, canto XVIII.* Naples.
———. 1989b. "P.Oxy. 2463: Lycophron and Callimachus." *Classical Quarterly* 39: 141–147. [Reprinted as pp. 197–205 in Livrea 1991, vol. 1.]
———. 1991. *Studia Hellenistica.* 2 vols. Florence.
———. 1992. "The Tempest in Callimachus' Hecale." *Classical Quarterly* 42: 147–151.
———. 1995. *Da Callimaco a Nonno: Dieci studi di poesia ellenistica.* Messina.
———. 1997. "Callimachus *senex*, Cercidas *senex* ed i loro critici." *Zeitschrift für Papyrologie und Epigraphik* 119: 37–42.
———. 1998. "Callimaco: Tre nuovi frammenti?" *Zeitschrift für Papyrologie und Epigraphik* 120: 28–34.
———. 2000. *Nonno di Panopoli: Parafrasi del Vangelo di San Giovanni, canto B.* Bologna.
———. 2003. "Callimachus *Iambus V.*" *Zeitschrift für Papyrologie und Epigraphik* 144: 51–58.
———. 2006a. "Un'eco callimachea in Giovenale." *Zeitschrift für Papyrologie und Epigraphik* 156: 58–59.
———. 2006b. "Il mito argonautico in Callimaco: L'episodio di Anafe." Pp. 89–99 in Bastianini and Casanova 2006.
———. 2006c. "La tomba di Simonide da Callimaco a S. Saba." *Zeitschrift für Papyrologie und Epigraphik* 156: 53–57.
Llewellyn-Jones, L., and S. Winder. 2010. "A Key to Berenike's Lock? The Hathoric Model of Queenship in Early Ptolemaic Egypt." Pp. 247–270 in A. Erskine and L. Llewellyn-Jones, eds., *Creating A Hellenistic World.* Swansea.
Lloyd-Jones, H. 1961. Review of Keydell 1959. *Classical Review* 11: 22–24.
———. 1974. "A New Hellenistic Fragment in the Archebulean Metre." *Zeitschrift für Papyrologie und Epigraphik* 13: 209–213. [Reprinted as pp. 219–222 in *Greek Comedy, Hellenistic Literature, Greek Religion, and Miscellanea: The Academic Papers of Sir Hugh Lloyd-Jones,* vol. 2 (Oxford, 1990).]
———. 1999. "The Pride of Halicarnassus." *Zeitschrift für Papyrologie und Epigraphik* 124: 1–14. [Reprinted as pp. 211–232 in Lloyd-Jones 2005.]
———. 2005. *The Further Academic Papers of Sir Hugh Lloyd-Jones.* Oxford.
Lloyd-Jones, H., and P. Parsons. 1983. *Supplementum Hellenisticum.* Berlin.
Lloyd-Jones, H., and J. Rea. 1967. "Callimachus, Fragments 260–261." *Harvard Studies in Classical Philology* 72: 125–149. [Reprinted as pp. 131–152 in *Greek Comedy, Hellenistic Literature, Greek Religion, and Miscellanea: The Academic Papers of Sir Hugh Lloyd-Jones,* vol. 2 (Oxford, 1990).]
Lobel, E. 1948. "2209A–B: Callimachus." Pp. 4–8 in *The Oxyrhynchus Papyri,* vol. 19. London.
Lobel, E., E.P. Wegener, and C.H. Roberts, eds. 1952. *The Oxyrhynchus Papyri.* Volume 20. London.
Lohse, G. 1967. "ΣΥΝΤΟΝΟΣ ΑΓΡΥΠΝΙΗ (zu Kallimachos *Epigr.* 27,4)." *Hermes* 95: 379–381.
Looijenga, A.R. 2009. "Unrolling the *Alexandra*: The Allusive Messenger-Speech of Lycophron's Prologue and Epilogue." Pp. 59–80 in Cusset and Prioux 2009.
Lord, K.O. 1990. *Pindar in the Second and Third Hymns of Callimachus.* Dissertation, University of Michigan, Ann Arbor.
Lüddecke, K.L.G. 1998. "Contextualizing the Voice in Callimachus' *Hymn to Zeus.*" *Materiali e Discussioni* 41: 9–33.
Ludwich, A. 1887. "Nachahmer und Vorbilder des Dichters Gregorios von Nazianz." *Rheinisches Museum* 42: 233–238.
Luppe, W. 1983. "Die Hypothesis zu Euripides' *Hippolytos.*" *Philologus* 127: 155–162.
———. 1985. "P.Vindob. G 29779: Ein Sophokles-Kodex." *Wiener Studien* 19: 89–104.
———. 1997. "Kallimachos, *Aitien*-Prolog V. 7–12." *Zeitschrift für Papyrologie und Epigraphik* 115: 50–54.

———. 2006. "Die Verwandlungssage der Asterie im P. Oxy. 4711." *Prometheus* 32: 55-56.
Lupu, E. 2005. *Greek Sacred Law: A Collection of New Documents*. Leiden.
Luzzatto, M.J. 1975. "La cultura letteraria di Babrio." *Annali della Scuola Normale Superiore di Pisa* 5: 17-97.
Lyne, R.O.A.M. 1987. *Further Voices in Vergil's Aeneid*. Oxford.
———. 1994. "Vergil's *Aeneid*: Subversion by Intertextuality—Catullus 66.39-40 and Other Examples." *Greece and Rome* 41: 187-204.
———. 1995. *Horace: Beyond the Public Poetry*. New Haven.
Lynn, J.K. 1995. *Narrators and Narration in Callimachus*. Dissertation, Columbia University.
Ma, J.T.C. 2003. "Kings." Pp. 177-195 in Erskine 2003.
Maas, P. 1921. "Leon Philosophos und Kallimachos." *Byzantinisch-neugriechische Jahrbücher* 2: 302 [Reprinted as "Konstantinos Rhodios und Kallimachos," pp. 419-420 in Maas 1973.]
———. 1934. "Neue Papyri von Kallimachos Αἴτια." *Gnomon* 10: 162-165.
———. 1937. "Exkurs I: Die litterarische Form der *Diegeseis* und der *Scholia Florentina*." Pp. 155-160 in Vogliano 1937.
———. 1973. *Kleine Schriften*. Munich.
Maass, E. 1892. *Aratea*. Berlin.
Macleod, C. 1973. "Catullus 116." *Classical Quarterly* 23: 304-309.
Madden, J.A. 1995. *Macedonius Consul: The Epigrams*. Hildesheim.
Maddoli, G., ed. 1994. *L'"Athenaion Politeia" di Aristotele, 1891-1991: Per un bilancio di cento anni di studi*. Naples.
Magnelli, E. 1995. "Le norme del secondo piede dell'esametro nei poeti ellenistici e il comportamento della 'parola metrica.'" *Materiali e Discussioni* 35: 135-164.
———. 1999a. *Alexandri Aetoli testimonia et fragmenta*. Florence.
———. 1999b. Review of D'Alessio 1996. *Quaderni di Storia* 50: 229-238.
———. 2002. *Studi su Euforione*. Rome.
———. 2003. "Problemi di tradizione indiretta licofronea." *Eikasmos* 14: 109-119.
———. 2004a. "Memoria letteraria in carmi epigrafici greci del Vicino Oriente." *Zeitschrift für Papyrologie und Epigraphik* 147: 51-55.
———. 2004b. "Il 'nuovo' epigramma sulle *Categorie* di Aristotele." *Medioevo Greco* 4: 179-198.
———. 2006a. "Callimaco, fr. 63 Pf.: Ambiguità sintattiche e autenticità." Pp. 47-55 in Bastianini and Casanova 2006.
———. 2006b. "Callimaco, fr. 75 Pf., e la tecnica narrativa dell'elegia ellenistica." Pp. 203-212 in Kolde, Lukinovich, and Rey 2006.
———. 2006c. "La chiusa degli *Alexipharmaca* e la struttura dei due poemi iologici di Nicandro." Pp. 105-118 in C. Cusset, ed., *Musa docta: Recherches sur la poésie scientifique dans l'antiquité*. Saint-Étienne.
———. 2006d. "Nicander's Chronology: A Literary Approach." Pp. 185-204 in M.A. Harder, Regtuit, and Wakker 2006.
———. 2006e. "On the New Fragments of Greek Poetry from Oxyrhynchus." *Zeitschrift für Papyrologie und Epigraphik* 158: 9-12.
———. 2006f. "Il proemio della *Corona* di Filippo di Tessalonica e la sua funzione programmatica." Pp. 393-404 in L. Cristante, ed., *Incontri triestini di filologia classica*, vol. 4. Trieste.
———. 2007. "Meter and Diction: From Refinement to Mannerism." Pp. 165-183 in Bing and Bruss 2007.
———. 2008. "Colluthus' 'Homeric' Epyllion." Pp. 151-172 in Carvounis and Hunter 2008.
———. 2010. "Nicander." Pp. 211-223 in Clauss and Cuypers 2010.

Malitz, J. 2007. "Von Alexander zu Kleopatra: Die politische Geschichte." Pp. 13–55 and 427–434 in Weber 2007b.
Malten, L. 1918. "Ein neues Bruchstück aus den *Aitia* des Kallimachos." *Hermes* 53: 147–179.
Manakidou, F. 1993. *Beschreibung von Kunstwerken in der hellenistischen Dichtung.* Stuttgart.
Mangoni, C. 1993. *Il quinto libro della poetica.* Naples.
Marin, M. 1979. "Sviluppi cristiani di una sentenza: Non dare la spada al folle o al ragazzo." *Vigiliae Christianae* 16: 221–236.
Marinone, N. 1997. *Berenice da Callimaco a Catullo: Testo critico, traduzione e commento.* 2nd ed. Bologna.
Mariño Sánchez-Elvira, R.M., and F. García Romero, eds. and trans. 1999. *Proverbios griegos: Menandro, Sentencias.* Madrid.
Mariotti, S. 1965. "Letteratura latina arcaica e *alessandrinismo*." *Belfagor* 20: 34–48. [Reprinted as pp. 5–20 in *Scritti di filologia classica* (Rome, 2000).]
———, ed. 1996. *Enciclopedia oraziana.* Vol. 1, *L'opera, i luoghi, le persone.* Rome.
Martina, A., and A.-T. Cozzoli, eds. 2006. *Callimachea.* Volume 1, *Atti della prima giornata di studi su Callimaco, Università di Roma III, 14 maggio 2003.* Rome.
———. 2007. *L'epos argonautico: Atti del Convegno, Università di Roma III, 13 maggio 2004.* Rome.
———, eds. Forthcoming. *Callimachea.* Volume 2, *Atti della seconda giornata di studi su Callimaco, Università di Roma III, 12 maggio 2005.* Rome.
Massimilla, G. 1993. "Callimaco fr. 115 Pf." *Zeitschrift für Papyrologie und Epigraphik* 95: 33–44.
———. 1996. *Callimaco. Aitia. Libri primo e secondo: Introduzione, testo critico, traduzione e commento.* Pisa.
———. 2000. "Nuovi elementi per la cronologia di Nicandro." Pp. 127–137 in Pretagostini 2000a.
———. 2004. "Il leone nemeo nella *Victoria Berenices* di Callimaco." Pp. 19–31 in Pretagostini and Dettori 2004.
———. 2006a. "I papiri e la tradizione indiretta medievale negli *Aitia*." Pp. 31–45 in Bastianini and Casanova 2006.
———. 2006b. "Il sepolcro di Simonide (Callimaco, fr. 64 Pf.)." Pp. 33–52 in Martina and Cozzoli 2006.
———. 2010. *Callimaco. Aitia. Libro terzo e quarto: Introduzione, testo critico, traduzione e commento.* Pisa.
———. Forthcoming. "Theudotus of Lipara (Callimachus, fr. 93 Pf.)." In D. Obbink and R. Rutherford, eds., *Culture in Pieces.* Oxford.
Masson, O. 1962. *Les fragments du poète Hipponax.* Paris.
Matelli, E. 2000. "Gli *Aesopica* di Demetrio Falereo." Pp. 413–447 in Fortenbaugh and Schütrumpf 2000.
Matthaiou, A. 2003. "Ἀπόλλων Δήλιος ἐν Ἀθήναις." Pp. 85–93 in Jordan and Traill 2003.
Matthews, V.J. 1996. *Antimachus of Colophon.* Leiden.
Mattiacci, S., and A. Perruccio. 2007. *Anti-mitologia ed eredità neoterica in Marziale: Genesi e forme di una poetica.* Pisa.
Mattingly, H. 1950. "Zephyritis." *American Journal of Philology* 54: 126–128.
Mattsson, A. 1942. *Untersuchungen zur Epigrammsammlung des Agathias.* Lund.
Mavor, C. 2007. *Reading Boyishly.* Durham.
Mazzarino, S. 1966. *Il pensiero storico classico.* Bari.
McCredie, J.R., G. Roux, and S.R. Shaw. 1992. *The Rotunda of Arsinoe.* Parts 1 (*Text*) and 2 (*Plates*). Volume 7 of *Samothrace: Excavations Conducted by the Institute of Fine Arts of New York University*, ed. P.W. Lehmann. Princeton.

McKay, K.J. 1962. *Erysichthon: A Callimachean Comedy.* Leiden.
———. 2007. *Statius' Thebaid and the Poetics of the Civil War.* Cambridge.
McKenzie, J. 2007. *The Architecture of Alexandria and Egypt, 300 BC–AD 700.* New Haven.
McLennan, G.R. 1977. *Callimachus. Hymn to Zeus: Introduction and Commentary.* Rome.
McNamee, K. 2007. *Annotations in Greek and Latin Texts from Egypt.* New Haven.
McNelis. C. 2003. "Mourning Glory: Callimachus' Hecale and Heroic Honors." *Materiali e Discussioni* 50: 155–161.
———. 2007. *Statius' Thebaid and the Poetics of the Civil War.* Cambridge.
Meijering, R. 1987. *Literary and Rhetorical Theories in Greek Scholia.* Groningen.
Meillier, C. 1979. *Callimaque et son temps: Recherches sur la carrière et la condition d'un écrivain à l'époque des premiers Lagides.* Lille.
———. 1985. "Extraits commentés d'Homère, *Odyssée*, 16 et 17." Pp. 229–238 in F. Geus and F. Thill, eds., *Mélanges offerts à Jean Vercoutter.* Paris.
———. 1990. "Callimaque, *Hymne* II, vers 113: Φθόνος ou φθόρος?" *Studi Classici e Orientali* 40: 77–95.
———. 1996. "L'éloge royal dans l'*Hymne à Délos* de Callimaque: Homère, Pindare, Callimaque—Une dialectique de l'épique et du lyrique." Pp. 129–148 in Dubois 1996.
Meissner, B. 1992. *Historiker zwischen Polis und Königshof: Studien zur Stellung der Geschichtsschreiber in der griechischen Gesellschaft in spätklassischer und frühhellenistischer Zeit.* Göttingen.
———. 2000. "Hofmann und Herrscher: Was es für die Griechen hiess, Freund eines Königs zu sein." *Archiv für Kulturgeschichte* 82: 1–36.
Meister, K. 1997. "Atthis." Cols. 232–233 in *Der neue Pauly*, vol. 2. Stuttgart.
Meliadò, C. 2004. "*PChic.* 1061 = *PLitGoodspeed* 2: Proposte di lettura ed interpretazione." *Zeitschrift für Papyrologie und Epigraphik* 150: 49–58.
———, ed. 2008. *"E cantando danzerò" (PLitGoodspeed 2): Introduzione, testo critico, traduzione e commento.* Messina.
Mendelsohn, D. 2009. *C.P. Cavafy: The Unfinished Poems.* New York.
Mercati, S.G. 1923–1925. "Intorno all'autore del carme Εἰς τὰ ἐν Πυθίοις θερμά (Leone Magistro Choirosphaktes)." *Rivista degli Studi Orientali* 10: 212–248. [Reprinted as pp. 271–309 in Mercati 1970, vol. 1.]
———. 1970. *Collectanea Byzantina.* 2 vols. Bari.
Merkelbach, R. 1969. "Zur Vision des Maximus." *Zeitschrift für Papyrologie und Epigraphik* 4: 200.
———. 1970. "Epigramm aus Chios." *Zeitschrift für Papyrologie und Epigraphik* 5: 284.
———. 1981. "Das Königtum der Ptolemäer und die hellenistischen Dichter." Pp. 27–35 in N. Hinske, ed., *Alexandrien: Kulturbegegnungen dreier Jahrtausende im Schmelztiegel einer mediterranen Grossstadt.* Mainz.
Merkelbach, R., and I. Cazzaniga. 1965. "Osservazioni critico-testuali agli inni isiaci di Isidoro." *Parola del Passato* 20: 298–300.
Merkelbach, R., and J. Stauber. 1998–2004. *Steinepigramme aus dem griechischen Osten.* 5 vols. Stuttgart and Munich.
———. 2005. *Jenseits des Euphrat: Griechische Inschriften.* Munich.
Merriam, C.U. 1993. "An Examination of Jason's Cloak (Apollonius Rhodius, *Argonautica* 1.730–768)." *Scholia* 2: 69–80.
Meschini, A. 1976. *Giano Làskaris: Epigrammi greci.* Padua.
Messeri Savorelli, G., and R. Pintaudi. 2002. "I lettori dei papiri: Dal commento autonomo agli scolii." Pp. 37–57 in Fera, Ferraù, and Rizzo 2002.
Meyer, D. 1993. "'Nichts Unbezeugtes singe ich': Die fiktive Darstellung der Wissenschaftstradierung bei Kallimachos." Pp. 317–336 in Kullmann and Althoff 1993.
———. 2001. "Apollonius as a Hellenistic Geographer." Pp. 217–235 in Papanghelis and Rengakos 2001.

———. 2005. *Inszeniertes Lesevergnügen: Das inschriftliche Epigramm und seine Rezeption bei Kallimachos.* Stuttgart.
Miguélez Cavero, L. 2008. *Poems in Context: Greek Poetry in the Egyptian Thebaid, 200-600 AD.* Berlin.
Millar, F. 1993. *The Roman Near East.* Cambridge, Mass.
Millozzi, V. 2000/2001. *I papiri di Callimaco: per la storia della tradizione di un poeta greco in Egitto.* Dissertation, Urbino.
Minas, M. 1998. "Die κανηφόρος: Aspekte des ptolemäischen Dynastiekult." Pp. 43-60 in H. Melaerts, ed., *Le culte du souverain dans l'Égypte ptolémaïque au IIIe siècle avant notre ère: Actes du Colloque international, Bruxelles, 10 mai 1995.* Louvain.
Mineur, W.H. 1979. "The Boys and the Barbarians: Some Remarks on Callimachus, H. 4,177. *Mnemosyne* 32: 119-127.
———. 1984. *Callimachus. Hymn to Delos: Introduction and Commentary.* Leiden.
Minnen, P. van. 1998. "Boorish or Bookish? Literature in Egyptian Villages in the Fayum in the Graeco-Roman Period." *Journal of Juristic Papyrology* 28: 99-184.
Miralles, C. 2004. *Studies in Elegy and Iambus.* Amsterdam.
Miralles, C., and J. Pòrtulas. 1988. *The Poetry of Hipponax.* Rome.
Molinos Tejada, T. 1990. *Los dorismos del corpus bucolicorum.* Amsterdam.
Moll, O. 1920. *Dioskorides (Vorbilder, Nachahmungen, Metrik).* Zurich.
Momigliano, A. 1971. *The Development of Greek Biography.* Cambridge, Mass.
Montanari, F. 1979. "Aristarco ad *Odissea* II 136-137: Appunti di filologia omerica antica." *Materiali e Discussioni* 3: 157-170. [Reprinted as pp. 27-40 in *Studi di filologia omerica antica*, vol. 2 (Pisa, 1995).]
———, ed. 1994. *La philologie grecque à l'époque hellénistique et romaine.* Vandœuvres.
———. 1995. "Filologi alessandrini e poeti alessandrini: La filologia sui 'contemporanei.'" *Aevum Antiquum* 8: 47-63.
———. 2000. "Demetrius of Phalerum on Literature." Pp. 391-411 in Fortenbaugh and Schütrumpf 2000.
———. 2002. "Callimaco e la filologia." Pp. 59-92 in Montanari and Lehnus 2002.
Montanari, F., and L. Lehnus, eds. 2002. *Callimaque.* Vandœuvres.
Montes Cala, J.G. 1989. *Calímaco, "Hécale": Edición revisada, traducción y comentario.* Cádiz.
———. 1991. "Tipología y técnica literaria en el epigrama fúnebre helenístico." *Excerpta Philologica* 1: 501-520.
———. 1994-1995. "Un apunte sobra *imitatio cum variatione* noniana." *Excerpta Philologica* 4-5: 63-75.
Montevecchi, O. 1973. *La papirologia.* Turin.
Morelli, A.M., ed. 2008. *Epigramma longum: Da Marziale alla tarda antichità / From Martial to Late Antiquity.* 2 vols. Cassino.
Morelli, G. 1964. "Callimaco e la legge di Naeke." *Rivista di Cultura Classica e Medioevale* 6: 140-155.
Moreschini, C., and D.A. Sykes. 1997. *St Gregory of Nazianzus: Poemata arcana.* Oxford.
Morgan, L. 2003. "Child's Play: Ovid and His Critics." *Journal of Roman Studies* 93: 66-91.
Morpurgo Davies, A. 1987. "The Greek Notion of Dialect." *Verbum* 10: 7-27. [*Actes de la première Rencontre internationale de dialectologie grecque.*]
Morpurgo-Tagliabue, G. 1980. *Demetrio: Dello stile.* Rome.
Morrison, A.D. 2007. *The Narrator in Archaic Greek and Hellenistic Poetry.* Cambridge.
Moscadi, A. 2003. "L'episodio degli uccelli parlanti nell'*Ecale* di Callimaco." *Comunicazioni dell'Istituto Papirologico "G. Vitelli"* 5: 29-43.
Mosino, F. 1996-1997. "Il bue sulla lingua: Un misterioso proverbio greco." *Atti del Sodalizio Glottologico Milanese* 37-38: 89-90.
Most, G.W., ed. 1997. *Collecting Fragments / Fragmente Sammeln.* Göttingen.

———. 2006. *Hesiod, Theogony, Works and Days, Testimonia*. Vol. 1. Cambridge, MA. and London.
Mras, K. 1938a. "Die in den neuen Διηγήσεις zu Kallimachos' *Aitia* erwähnten Kultbilder der samischen Hera." *Rheinisches Museum* 87: 277-284.
———. 1938b. "Zu den neu gefundenen Διηγήσεις des Kallimachos." *Wiener Studien* 56: 45-54.
Mueller, K. 2006. *Settlements of the Ptolemies: City Foundations and New Settlement in the Hellenistic World*. Louvain.
Müller, C.W. 1998. "Wanted! Die Kallimachosforschung auf der Suche nach einem einsilbigen Substantiv." *Zeitschrift für Papyrologie und Epigraphik* 122: 36-40.
———. 2002. "Zum Aitienprolog des Kallimachos." *Rheinisches Museum* 145: 237.
Müller, O. 1973. *Antigonos Monophthalmos und das "Jahr der Könige."* Bonn.
Müller, S. 2009. *Das hellenistische Königspaar in der medialen Repräsentation: Ptolemaios II. und Arsinoe II.* Berlin.
Murray, P. 1997. *Plato on Poetry: Ion; Republic 376e-398b; Republic 595-608b*. Cambridge.
———. 2002. "Plato's Muses." Pp. 29-46 in Spentzou and Fowler 2002.
———. 2004. "The Muses and Their Arts." Pp. 365-389 in Murray and Wilson 2004.
———. 2005. "The Muses: Creativity Personified?" Pp. 147-159 in Stafford and Herrin 2005.
———. 2006. "Poetic Inspiration in Early Greece." Pp. 37-61 in Laird 2006a.
Murray, P., and P. Wilson, eds. 2004. *Music and the Muses: The Culture of Mousike in the Classical Athenian City*. Oxford.
Musso, O. 1985. *[Antigonus Carystius]: Rerum mirabilium collectio*. Naples.
Musti, D. 1999. *I Telchini, le Sirene: Immaginario mediterraneo e letteratura da Omero e Callimaco al romanticismo europeo*. Rome.
———. 2001. "Punti fermi e prospettive di ricerca sulla cronologia della *Alessandra* di Licofrone." Pp. 201-226 in L. Braccesi, ed., *Hesperia* 14. *Studi sulla grecità di Occidente*. Rome.
Nachmanson, E. 1941. *Der griechische Buchtitel*. Göteborg.
Nachtergael, G. 1977. *Les Galates en Grèce et les Sôtéria de Delphes: Recherches d'histoire et d'épigraphie hellénistiques*. Brussels.
Naddaf, G. 2000. "Literacy and Poetic Performance in Plato's *Laws*." *Ancient Philosophy* 20: 339-350.
Naeke, A.F. 1842-1845. *Opuscula philologica*. 2 vols. Bonn.
Nagy, G. 1990. *Greek Mythology and Poetics*. Ithaca.
———. 2009. "Hesiod and the Ancient Biographical Traditions." Pp. 271-311 in F. Montanari, A. Rengakos, and C. Tsagalis, eds., *Brill's Companion to Hesiod*. Leiden.
———. 2010. "The Meaning of *homoios* (ὁμοῖος) in *Theogony* 27 and Elsewhere." Pp. 153-167 in P. Mitsis and C. Tsagalis, eds., *Allusion, Authority, and Truth: Critical Perspectives on Greek Poetic and Rhetorical Praxis*. Leiden.
Negri, M. 2009. "Oscurità e identità: Strategie licofronee di innovazione semantica nel lessico sportivo (αὐλός, νύσσα) e paternità dell'*Alessandra*." Pp. 171-191 in Cusset and Prioux 2009.
Nelis, D. 2005. "Patterns of Time in Vergil: The *Aeneid* and the *Aetia* of Callimachus." Pp. 71-83 in Schwindt 2005.
Neri, C. 1995. "Le taccole primaverili (Antip. Sid. *AP* VII 713 = LVIII G.-P.)." *Eikasmos* 6: 155-159.
———. 2003. *Erinna: Testimonianze e frammenti*. Bologna.
Nervegna, S. 2007. "Staging Scenes or Plays? Theatrical Revivals of 'Old' Greek Drama in Antiquity." *Zeitschrift für Papyrologie und Epigraphik* 162: 14-42.
Nesselrath, H.-G. 1990. *Die attische mittlere Komödie: Ihre Stellung in der antiken Literaturkritik und Literaturgeschichte*. Berlin.

Neugebauer, O., and R.A. Parker. 1969. *Egyptian Astronomical Texts*. Volume 3, *Decans, Planets, Constellations and Zodiacs*. London.
Newman, J.K. 1967. *Augustus and the New Poetry*. Brussels.
———. 1985. "Pindar and Callimachus." *Illinois Classical Studies* 10: 169–189.
Nicolai, R. 1992. "La fondazione di Cirene e i Karneia cirenaici nell'*Inno ad Apollo* di Callimaco." *Materiali e Discussioni* 28: 153–173.
Nicosia, S. 1976. *Tradizione testuale diretta e indiretta dei poeti di Lesbo*. Rome.
Nielsen, I. 1999. *Hellenistic Palaces: Tradition and Renewal*. 2nd ed. Aarhus.
———. 2001. "The Gardens of the Hellenistic Palaces." Pp. 165–187 in I. Nielsen, ed., *The Royal Palace Institution in the First Millenium BC: Regional Development and Cultural Interchange between East and West*. Aarhus.
Nightingale, A.W. 1996. *Genres in Dialogue: Plato and the Construct of Philosophy*. Cambridge.
———. 1999. "Plato's Lawcode in Context: Rule by Written Law in Athens and Magnesia." *Classical Quarterly* 49: 100–122.
Nikitinski, O. 1997. *Kallimachos-Studien*. Frankfurt.
Nikolaou, N.A. 1985. "Ἡ Ἑκάλη τοῦ Καλλιμάχου· Μιά τοπογραφική ἀνάγνωση." *Δωδώνη* 14: 131–139.
Nisbet, G. 2003. *Greek Epigram in the Roman Empire: Martial's Forgotten Rivals*. Oxford.
Nisetich, F., 2001. *The Poems of Callimachus*. Oxford.
Nocita, M. 2000. "L'ara di Sulpicio Massimo: Nuove osservazioni in occasione del restauro." *Bullettino della Commissione Archeologica Comunale in Roma* 101: 81–100.
Nock, A.D. 1958. "A Cult Ordinance in Verse." *Harvard Studies in Classical Philology* 63: 415–421.
Norden, E. 1909. *Die römische Literatur. Ein Einleitung in die Altertumswissenschaften*. Vol 1. Berlin and Leipzig.
———. 1915. *Ennius und Vergilius: Kriegsbildern aus Roms grosser Zeit*. Leipzig.
———. 1916. *P. Vergilius Maro. Aeneis. Buch VI*. 2nd ed. Leipzig. [1st ed. 1903; 3rd ed. 1927.]
Norsa, M., and G. Vitelli. 1934. "Διηγήσεις" *di poemi di Callimaco in un papiro di Tebtynis*. Florence.
Noussia, M. 2001. *Solone: Frammenti dell'opera poetica*. Milan.
Noussia-Fantuzzi, M. 2010. *Solon of Athens: The Poetic Fragments*. Leiden.
Obbink, D., ed. 1995. *Philodemus and Poetry: Poetic Theory and Practice in Lucretius, Philodemus and Horace*. Oxford.
Ogden, D. 1999. *Polygamy, Prostitutes and Death: The Hellenistic Dynasties*. London.
Oikonomakos, K. 2002. Προλεγόμενα στὴν κριτικὴ ἔκδοση τῶν Ἀλεξιφαρμάκων τοῦ Νικάνδρου. Athens.
Oliver, G.J. 2002. "Callimachus the Poet and Benefactor of the Athenians." *Zeitschrift für Papyrologie und Epigraphik* 140: 6–8.
O'Neil, J.L. 2008. "A Re-examination of the Chremonidean War." Pp. 65–90 in P. McKechnie and P. Guillaume, eds. *Ptolemy II Philadelphus and his World*. Leiden.
Oppermann, H. 1925. "Herophilos bei Kallimachos." *Hermes* 60: 14–32.
Orsi, D.P. 1995. "La storiografia locale." Pp. 149–179 in Cambiano, Canfora, and Lanza 1995.
O'Sullivan, N. 1992. *Alcidamas, Aristophanes, and the Beginnings of Greek Stylistic Theory*. Stuttgart.
Otto, A. 1890. *Die Sprichwörter und sprichwörtlichen Redensarten der Römer*. Leipzig.
Ouvré, H. 1894. *Méléagre de Gadara*. Paris.
Overbeck, J. 1868. *Die antiken Schriftquellen zur Geschichte der bildenden Künste bei den Griechen*. Leipzig.

Özbek, L., G.B. D'Alessio, G. Massimilla, and G. Bastianini. 2005. "Callimachus, *Victoria Berenices*(?)." *Comunicazioni dell'Istituto Papirologico "G. Vitelli"* 6: 3-20.
Pace, C. 1996. "Anacreonte e la palla di Nausicaa (Anacr. fr. 13 Gent. = 358 *PMG*, 1-4)." *Eikasmos* 7: 81-86.
Paci, G., ed. 2000. Ἐπιγραφαί: *Miscellanea epigrafica in onore di Lidio Gasperini*. Tivoli.
Page, D.L. 1963. "Some Metrical Rules in Meleager." Pp. 544-547 in *Miscellanea di studi alessandrini in memoria di Augusto Rostagni*. Turin.
Palme, B., ed. 2007. *Akten des 23. Internationalen Papyrologen-kongresses, Wien, 22.-28. Juli 2001*. Vienna.
Pàmias, J. 2004. "Dionysus and Donkeys on the Streets of Alexandria: Eratosthenes' Criticism of Ptolemaic Ideology." *Harvard Studies in Classical Philology* 102: 191-198.
Panno, G. 2007. *Dionisiaco e alterità nelle Leggi di Platone: Ordine del corpo e automovimento dell'anima nella città-tragedia*. Milan.
Papagiannis, G. 1997. *Theodoros Prodromos: Jambische und hexametrische Tetrasticha auf die Hauptzerzählungen des Alten und des Neuen Testaments*. 2 vols. Wiesbaden.
Papanghelis, T.D., and A. Rengakos, eds. 2001. *A Companion to Apollonius Rhodius*. Leiden.
Pardini, A. 1991. "Aconzio non era 'πολύκροτος.'" *Studi Italiani di Filologia Classica* 9: 57-70.
Parke, H.W. 1985. *The Oracles of Apollo in Asia Minor*. London.
Parke, H.W., and D.E.W. Wormell. 1956. *The Delphic Oracle*. 2 vols. Oxford.
Parker, R. 1983. *Miasma: Pollution and Purification in Early Greek Religion*. Oxford.
———. 2000. "Greek States and Greek Oracles." Pp. 76-108 in R. Buxton, ed., *Oxford Readings in Greek Religion*. Oxford.
———. 2004. "What Are Sacred Laws?" Pp. 57-70 in E.M. Harris and L. Rubinstein, eds., *The Law and the Courts in Ancient Greece*. London.
Parrhasius, I. 1567. *Liber de rebus per epistolam quaesitis*. Paris.
Parry, H. 1965. "The Second Stasimon of Euripides' *Heracles* (637-700)." *American Journal of Philology* 86: 363-374.
Parsons, P.J. 1977. "Callimachus: *Victoria Berenices*." *Zeitschrift für Papyrologie und Epigraphik* 25: 1-50.
———. 1982. "Facts from Fragments." *Greek, Roman and Byzantine Studies* 29: 184-195.
———. 1992. "Simonides' Elegies." Pp. 4-50 in E.W. Handley et al., eds., *The Oxyrhynchus Papyri*, vol. 59. London.
———. 1993a. "Identities in Diversity." Pp. 152-170 in Bulloch et al. 1993.
———. 1993b. "Poesia ellenistica: Testi e contesti." *Aevum Antiquum* 5: 9-19.
———. 1996. "ΦΙΛΕΛΛΗΝ." *Museum Helveticum* 53: 106-115.
———. 2002. "Callimachus and the Hellenistic Epigram." Pp. 99-141 in Montanari and Lehnus 2002.
Pascoli, G. 1923. *Traduzioni e riduzioni*. 3rd ed. Bologna.
———. 1929. *Lyra*. Turin.
Pasquali, G. 1913. *Quaestiones Callimacheae*. Göttingen. [Reprinted as pp. 152-301 in Pasquali 1986, vol. 1.]
———. 1915a. "Horaz C. I 18." *Hermes* 50: 304-311.
———. 1915b. Review of Norden 1915. *Göttingische Gelehrte Anzeigen* 177: 593-610. [Republished in Italian translation as pp. 223-240 in Pasquali 1994, vol. 1.]
———. 1919. "Epigrammi callimachei." *Atti della Reale Accademia delle Scienze di Torino* 54: 1132-1154. [Reprinted as pp. 302-322 in Pasquali 1986, vol. 1.]
———. 1920. *Orazio lirico: Studi*. Florence.
———. 1942. "Arte allusiva." *L'Italia Che Scrive* 25: 185-187. [Reprinted as pp. 11-20 in *Stravaganze quarte e supreme* (Venice, 1951); as pp. 275-282 in *Pagine stravaganti* (Florence, 1968), vol. 2; and as pp. 275-282 in Pasquali 1994, vol. 2.]

———. 1951. Review of Gow 1950. *Athenaeum* 29: 372–382. [Reprinted as pp. 981–993 in Pasquali 1986, vol. 2.]
———. 1964a. *Filologia e storia*. 2nd ed. Florence.
———. 1964b. *Orazio lirico: Studi*. 2nd ed. Ed. A. La Penna. Florence.
———. 1986. *Scritti filologici*. 2 vols. Ed. F. Bornmann, G. Pascucci, and S. Timpanaro. Florence.
———. 1994. *Pagine stravaganti di un filologo*. 2 vols. Ed. C.F. Russo. Florence.
Pavese, C.O. 1991. "L'inno rapsodico: Analisi tematica degli *Inni omerici*." *AION (filol)* 13: 155–178.
Payne, M. 2007. *Theocritus and the Invention of Fiction*. Cambridge.
———. 2009. "Pastoral." Pp. 117–138 in R. Eldridge, ed., *The Oxford Handbook of Philosophy and Literature*. Oxford.
Pearson, L. 1942. *The Local Historians of Attica*. Philadelphia.
Peek, W. ed. 1930. *Der Isishymnus von Andros und verwandte Texte*. Berlin.
———. 1980. *Attische Versinschriften*. Berlin.
Pelling, C.B.R. 1990. "Truth and Fiction in Plutarch's Lives". Pp. 18–52 in D.A. Russell, ed. *Antonine Literature*. Oxford.
Pennacini, A. 1968. "*Docti* e *crassi* nella poetica di Lucilio." *Atti della Reale Accademia delle Scienze di Torino* 102: 311–345.
Perdrizet P., and C. Picard. 1927. "Apollon, Bés et les Galates." *Genava* 5: 52–63.
Peremans, W. 1968. *Prosopographia Ptolemaica*. Volume 6. Louvain.
———. 1987. "Les Lagides, les élites indigènes et la monarchie bicéphale." Pp. 327–343 in E. Lévy, ed., *Le système palatial en Orient, en Grèce et à Rome*. Louvain.
Perpillou-Thomas, F. 1993. *Fêtes d'Égypte ptolémaïque et romaine d'après la documentation papyrologique grecque*. Louvain.
Perrin, B. 1914. *Plutarch, Lives: Theseus and Romulus*. Cambridge, Mass.
Perrotta, G. 1926. "Studi di poesia ellenistica." *Studi Italiani di Filologia Classica* 4: 5–280. [Reprinted as pp. 119–324 in *Poesia ellenistica: Scritti minori*, vol. 2 (Rome, 1978).]
Perry, B.E. 1952. *Aesopica: A Series of Texts Relating to Aesop or Ascribed to Him or Closely Connected with the Literary Tradition That Bears His Name*. Urbana.
Pestman, P.W. 1981. *A Guide to the Zenon Archive*. Leiden.
Petrovic, I. 2006. "Delusions of Grandeur: Homer, Zeus and the Telchines in Callimachus' Reply (*Aitia* Fr. 1) and *Iambus* 6." *Antike und Abendland* 52: 16–41.
———. 2007. *Von den Toren des Hades zu den Hallen des Olymp: Artemiskult bei Theokrit und Kallimachos*. Leiden.
———. 2010. "The Life Story of a Cult Statue as an Allegory: Callimachus' Hermes Perpheraios." Pp. 205–224 in J. Mylonopoulos, ed., *Divine Images and Human Imaginations in Ancient Greece and Rome*. Leiden.
———. Forthcoming. "Callimachus' Hymn to Apollo and Greek Metrical Sacred Regulations." In M.A. Harder, R.F. Regtuit, and G.C. Wakker, eds., *Gods and Religion: Proceedings of the Ninth Groningen Workshop on Hellenistic Poetry*. Louvain.
Petrovic, I., and A. Petrovic. 2006. "Look Who's Talking Now: Speaker and Communication in Metrical Sacred Regulations." Pp. 111–139 in E. Stavrianopoulou, ed., *Ritual and Communication in the Graeco-Roman World*. Liège.
Pette, G. 1981. "Un verso di Callimaco nella traduzione latina del Poliziano." *Sileno* 7: 205–217.
Petzl, G. 1984. "Kein Umsturz beim Galater-Überfall auf Delphi (zu *F. de Delphes* III 1,483 und Kallimachos fr. 379)." *Zeitschrift für Papyrologie und Epigraphik* 56: 141–144.
Pfeiffer, R. 1921. *Callimachi fragmenta nuper reperta*. Bonn.
———. 1922. *Kallimachosstudien: Untersuchungen zur "Arsinoe" und zu den "Aitia" des Kallimachos*. Munich.

———. 1928. "Ein neues Altersgedicht des Kallimachos." *Hermes* 63: 302–341. [Reprinted as pp. 98–132 in *Ausgewählte Schriften* (Munich, 1960).]
———. 1949–1953. *Callimachus*. 2 vols. Oxford. [Vol. 1, *Fragmenta*; vol. 2, *Hymni et epigrammata*.]
———. 1952. "The Image of the Delian Apollo and Apolline Ethics." *Journal of the Warburg and Courtauld Institutes* 25: 20–32. [Reprinted as pp. 55–71 in *Ausgewählte Schriften* (Munich, 1960).]
———. 1955. "The Future of Studies in the Field of Hellenistic Poetry." *Journal of Roman Studies* 75: 69–73. [Reprinted as pp. 148–158 in *Ausgewählte Schriften* (Munich, 1960).]
———. 1968. *A History of Classical Scholarship: From the Beginnings to the End of the Hellenistic Age*. Oxford.
Pfrommer, M. 1999. *Alexandria: Im Schatten der Pyramiden*. Mainz.
———. 2002. *Königinnen vom Nil*. Mainz.
Phillips, D.J., and D. Pritchard, eds. 2003. *Sport and Festival in the Ancient Greek World*. Swansea.
Pickard-Cambridge, A.W. 1968. *The Dramatic Festivals of Athens*. 2nd ed. Oxford.
Pitré, G. 1870. *Proverbi siciliani*. Palermo.
Platt, A. 1910. "On the New Callimachus." *Berliner Philologische Wochenschrift* 30: 477.
Platt, V. Forthcoming. *Facing the Gods: Epiphany and Representation in Graeco-Roman Culture*. Cambridge.
Podlecki, A. 1969. "The Peripatetics as Literary Critics." *Phoenix* 23: 114–137.
Poethke, G. 1993. "Fragment einer alphabetisch geordneten Wörterliste." *Archiv für Papyrusforschung und Verwandte Gebiete* 39: 17–20.
Pohlenz, M. 1962. *L'uomo greco*. Trans. B. Proto. Florence. [Originally published in German as *Der hellenische Mensch* (Göttingen, 1947).]
———. 2005. *La Stoa: Storia di un movimento spirituale*. Trans. O. De Gregorio and B. Proto. Milan. [Originally published in German as *Die Stoa: Geschichte einer geistigen Bewegung*, 2 vols., 2nd ed. (Göttingen, 1959).]
Poliakoff, M. 1980. "Nectar, Springs, and the Sea: Critical Terminology in Pindar and Callimachus." *Zeitschrift für Papyrologie und Epigraphik* 39: 41–47.
Politianus, A. [Angelo Poliziano.] 1553. *A. Politiani opera omnia*. Basel. [Reprint: ed. I. Maier, 3 vols. (Turin, 1970–1971).]
Polito, M. 2006. "Frammenti di opere in prosa conservati in poesia: Meandrio di Mileto in Callimaco." *Parola del Passato* 61: 352–370.
Pontani, A. 2000. "Niceta Coniata e Licofrone." *Byzantinische Zeitschrift* 93: 157–161.
Pontani, F. 1999. "The First Word of Callimachus' *Aitia*." *Zeitschrift für Papyrologie und Epigraphik* 128: 57–59.
———. 2001 "Le cadavre adoré: Sappho à Byzance?" *Byzantion* 71: 233–250.
———. 2002. *Angeli Politiani liber epigrammatum Graecorum*. Rome.
———. 2005. *Sguardi su Ulisse: La tradizione esegetica greca all'Odissea*. Rome.
———. 2007. "Medea's Dreams: POxy. 4712 and Beyond." *Phasis* 10: 133–149.
Porro, A. 1985. "Manoscritti in maiuscola alessandrina di contenuto profano: Aspetti grafici codicologici filologici." *Scrittura e Civiltà* 9: 169–215.
Porter, J.I. 1989. "Philodemus on Material Difference." *Cronache Ercolanesi* 19: 149–178.
———. 1994. "Stoic Morals and Poetics in Philodemus." *Cronache Ercolanesi* 24: 63–88.
———. 1995a. "Content and Form in Philodemus: The History of an Evasion." Pp. 97–147 in Obbink 1995.
———. 1995b. "*Hoi Kritikoi*: A Reassessment." Pp. 83–109 in Abbenes, Slings, and Sluiter 1995.
———. 1996. "The Philosophy of Aristo of Chios." Pp. 156–189 in Branham and Goulet-Cazé 1996.

———. 2002. "ΦΥΣΙΟΛΟΓΕΙΝ: Nausiphanes of Teos and the Physics of Rhetoric—A Chapter in the History of Greek Atomism." *Cronache Ercolanesi* 32: 137–186.
———, ed. 2006a. *Classical Pasts: The Classical Traditions of Greece and Rome*. Princeton.
———. 2006b. "Feeling Classical: Classicism and Ancient Literary Criticism." Pp. 301–352 in Porter 2006a.
———. 2007a. "Hearing Voices: The Herculaneum Papyri and Classical Scholarship." Pp. 95–113 in V. Gardner Coates and J. Seydl, eds., *Antiquity Recovered: The Legacy of Pompeii and Herculaneum*. Los Angeles.
———. 2007b. "Lasus of Hermione, Pindar and the Riddle of *S*." *Classical Quarterly* 57: 1–21.
Powell, J.U. 1925. *Collectanea Alexandrina: Reliquiae minores poetarum Graecorum aetatis Ptolemaicae 323–146 AC epicorum, elegiacorum, lyricorum, ethicorum*. Oxford.
Power, T. 2007. "Ion of Chios and the Politics of the *polychordia*." Pp. 179–205 in Jennings and Katsaros 2007.
Prauscello, L. 2006. "Looking for the 'Other' Gnesippus: Some Notes on Eupolis Fragment 148 K-A." *Classical Philology* 101: 52–66.
Pretagostini, R. 1984. *Ricerche sulla poesia alessandrina: Teocrito, Callimaco, Sotade*. Rome.
———. 1991a. "La duplice valenza metaforica di κέντρον in Sotade fr. 1 Powell." *Quaderni Urbinati di Cultura Classica* 39: 111–114.
———. 1991b. "Rito e letteratura negli inni 'drammatici' di Callimaco." *AION (filol)* 13: 253–263.
———. 1995a. "L'autore ellenistico tra poesia e 'filologia': Problemi di esegesi, di metrica e di attendibilità del racconto." *Aevum Antiquum* 8: 33–46.
———. 1995b. "L'incontro con le Muse sull'Elicona in Esiodo e in Callimaco: Modificazioni di un modello." *Lexis* 13: 157–172.
———. 1995c. "L'opposta valenza del 'tuonare di Zeus' in Callimaco e Plutarco." Pp. 617–624 in Belloni, Milanese, and Porro 1995.
———, ed. 2000a. *La letteratura ellenistica: Problemi e prospettive di ricerca—Atti del Colloquio internazionale, Università di Roma "Tor Vergata," 29–30 aprile 1997*. Rome.
———. 2000b. "La nascita di Tolomeo II Filadelfo in Teocrito, *Idillio* XVII, e la nascita di Apollo in Callimaco, *Inno a Delo*." Pp. 157–170 in Arrighetti and Tulli 2000.
———. 2000c. "Sotade e i *Sotadea* tramandati da Stobeo." *AION (filol)* 22: 275–289.
———. 2003. "La forma catalogica fra tradizione e innovazione: Il catalogo dei maestri di Eracle nell'*Idillio* 24 di Teocrito." Pp. 239–254 in Belloni, de Finis, and Moretti 2003.
———. 2006a. "Un agglomerato di similitudini: A proposito di Eracle in Callimaco, *Aitia* fr. 23 Pf." Pp. 59–70 in Martina and Cozzoli 2006.
———. 2006b. "La poetica callimachea nella tradizione papiracea: Il frammento 1 Pf. (= 1 M.)." Pp. 15–27 in Bastianini and Casanova 2006.
———. 2007. *Ricerche sulla poesia alessandrina*. Volume 2, *Forme allusive e contenuti nuovi*. Rome.
Pretagostini, R., and E. Dettori, eds. 2004. *La cultura ellenistica: L'opera letteraria e l'esegesi antica—Atti del Convegno COFIN 2001, Università di Roma "Tor Vergata," 22–24 settembre 2003*. Rome.
Prins, Y. 1999. *Victorian Sappho*. Princeton.
Prioux, É. 2007. *Regards alexandrins: Histoire et théorie des arts dans l'épigramme hellénistique*. Louvain.
———. 2008. *Petits musées en vers: Épigramme et discours sur les collections antiques*. Paris.

——. 2009a. "Fards et cosmétiques dans les sources littéraires antiques." Pp. 35–40 in I. Bardiès-Fronty, M. Bimbenet-Privat, and P. Walter, eds., *Le Bain et le Miroir: Soins du corps et cosmétiques de l'antiquité à la Renaissance*. Paris.

——. 2009b. "Machon et Sotadès, figures de l'irrévérence alexandrine." Pp. 111–127 in B. Delignon and Y. Roman, eds., *Le poète irrévérencieux*. Lyon.

——. 2009c. "On the Oddities and Wonders of Italy: When Hellenistic Poets Look Westward." Pp. 121–148 in M.A. Harder, Regtuit, and Wakker 2009.

——. 2010. "Géographie symbolique des errances de Protée: Un mythe et sa relecture politique à l'époque hellénistique." Pp. 139–164 in A. Rolet, ed., *Protée en trompe-l'œil: Genèse et survivances d'un mythe d'Homère à Bouchardon*. Rennes.

——. Forthcoming. "Images de la statuaire archaïque dans les *Aitia* de Callimaque." *Aitia* 1.

Pucci, J. 1998. *The Full-Knowing Reader: Allusion and the Power of the Reader in the Western Literary Tradition*. New Haven.

Pucci, P. 1977. *Hesiod and the Language of Poetry*. Baltimore.

Puech, A. 1910. "Acontios et Cydippé." *Revue des Études Grecques* 23: 255–275.

Puelma, M. 1982. "Die *Aitien* des Kallimachos als Vorbild der römischen *Amores*-Elegie," parts 1 and 2. *Museum Helveticum* 39: 221–246 and 285–304.

Pulleyn, S. 1997. *Prayer in Greek Religion*. Oxford.

Puricelli, F. 2004. "Antichità sicionie tra storiografia locale e poesia ellenistica." Pp. 155–177 in Daverio Rocchi and Cavalli 2004.

Quartu, B.M. 1993. *Dizionario dei modi di dire della lingua italiana*. Milan.

Quecke, H. 1997. "Eine griechisch-ägyptische Wörterliste vermutlich des 3. Jh. v. Chr." *Zeitschrift für Papyrologie und Epigraphik* 116: 67–80.

Radinger, C. 1895. *Meleagros von Gadara: Eine litterargeschichtliche Skizze*. Innsbruck.

Radke, G. 2007. *Die Kindheit des Mythos*. Munich.

Radt, S.L. 2002a. "The Importance of the Context." Pp. 348–361 in M.A. Harder et al. 2002.

——. 2002b. "Sophokles in seinen Fragmenten." Pp. 263–292 in M.A. Harder et al. 2002.

Ragone, G. 2006. "Callimaco e le tradizioni locali della Ionia asiatica." Pp. 71–114 in Martina and Cozzoli 2006.

Rauch, J. 1860. *Die Fragmente der Aitia des Kallimachos*. Rastatt.

Rawles, R. 2006. *Simonides and the Role of the Poet*. Dissertation, University College, London.

Rebuffat, E. 2001. *Ποιητὴς ἐπέων: Tecniche di composizione poetica negli "Halieutica" di Oppiano*. Florence.

Reed, J.D. 1997. *Bion of Smyrna: The Fragments and the "Adonis."* Cambridge.

——. 2000. "Arsinoe's Adonis and the Poetics of Ptolemaic Imperialism." *Transactions of the American Philological Association* 130: 319–351.

——. 2006. "New Verses on Adonis." *Zeitschrift für Papyrologie und Epigraphik* 158: 76–82.

Regenbogen, O. 1950. "Pinax." Cols. 1408–1482 in A. von Pauly et al., eds., *Real-Encyclopädie der classischen Altertumswissenschaft*, 2. Reihe, vol. 20. Stuttgart.

Rehrenboeck, G. 1987. "Bemerkungen zum Wortschatz des Pherekrates." *Wiener Studien* 100: 47–68.

Reiff, A. 1959. *Interpretatio, imitatio, aemulatio: Begriff und Vorstellung literarischer Abhängigkeit bei den Römern*. Cologne.

Reinsch, D.R. 2006. "Ein angebliches Sappho-Fragment (frg. 209 Lobel-Page) im Briefcorpus des Eustathios von Thessalonike." *Philologus* 150: 175–176.

Reinsch-Werner, H. 1976. *Callimachus Hesiodicus: Die Rezeption der hesiodischen Dichtung durch Kallimachos von Kyrene*. Berlin.

Reitzenstein, R. 1890–1891. *Inedita poetarum Graecorum fragmenta*. Rostock.

———. 1891. "Die Inhaltsangabe im Archetypus der Kallimachos-Handschriften." *Hermes* 26: 308–314.
———. 1897. *Geschichte der griechischen Etymologika*. Leipzig.
———. 1901. *Zwei religionsgeschichtliche Fragen nach ungedruckten griechischen Texten der Strassburger Bibliothek*. Strassburg.
———. 1904. Review of T. Plüss, *Das Jambenbuch des Horaz im Lichte der eigenen und unserer Zeit* (Leipzig, 1904). *Göttingische Gelehrte Anzeigen* 166: 947–961.
———. 1908. "Horaz und die hellenistische Lyrik." *Neue Jahrbücher für das Klassische Altertum* 21: 81–102. [Reprinted as pp. 1–22 in *Aufsätze zu Horaz* (Darmstadt, 1963).]
Rengakos, A. 1992. "Homerische Wörter bei Kallimachos." *Zeitschrift für Papyrologie und Epigraphik* 94: 21–47.
———. 1993. *Der Homertext und die hellenistischen Dichter*. Stuttgart.
———. 1994. *Apollonios Rhodios und die antike Homererklärung*. Munich.
———. 2000. "Aristarchus and the Hellenistic Poets." *Seminari Romani di Cultura Greca* 3: 325–335.
Rhodes, P.J. 1990. "The Atthidographers." Pp. 73–81 in Verdin, Schepens, and De Keyser 1990.
Rhodes, P.J., and R. Osborne, eds. 2003. *Greek Historical Inscriptions, 404–323 BC: Edited with Introduction, Translations, and Commentaries*. Oxford.
Rice, E.E. 1983. *The Grand Procession of Ptolemy Philadelphus*. Oxford.
Richardson, N.J. 1994. "Aristotle and Hellenistic Scholarship." Pp. 7–28 in Montanari 1994.
Robert, J. 1967. "Épigramme de Chios." *Revue des Études Grecques* 80: 282–291.
Robert, L. 1960. "Sur un décret des Korésiens au Musée de Smyrne." *Hellenica* 11–12: 132–176.
Roberts, M.J. 1989. *The Jeweled Style: Poetry and Poetics in Late Antiquity*. Ithaca.
Robertson, N. 1999. "Callimachus' Tale of Sicyon (*SH* 238)." *Phoenix* 53: 57–79.
Rodziewicz, M. 1995. "A Review of the Archaeological Evidence Concerning the Cultural Institutions in Ancient Alexandria." *Graeco-Arabica* 6: 317–332.
Rolandi, M. 2006: *Ptolemaic Dynastic Incest and Incests in Graeco-Roman Egypt: Some Aspects*. http://www.archaeogate.org/egittologia/article.php?id=538 (accessed 1/21/2011)
Rollet, C. 1994. *La sculpture grecque*. Volume 1, *La sculpture grecque archaïque*. Paris.
Rosati, G. 2009. "The Latin Reception of Hesiod." Pp. 343–374 in F. Montanari, A. Rengakos, and C. Tsagalis, eds., *Brill's Companion to Hesiod*. Leiden.
Rosenmeyer, T. 2006. "Ancient Literary Genres: A Mirage?" Pp. 421–439 in Laird 2006a.
Rosokoki, A. 1995. *Die Erigone des Eratosthenes*. Heidelberg.
Rossi, L.E. 1997. "L'Atlante occidentale degli *Aitia* di Callimaco: Mito e modi di lettura." Pp. 69–80 in A. Stazio and S. Ceccoli, eds., *Mito e storia in Magna Grecia: Atti del trentaseiesimo Convegno di studi sulla Magna Grecia, Taranto, 4-7 ottobre 1996*. Taranto.
Rossi, P., ed. 1988. *La memoria del sapere*. Rome.
Rossum-Steenbeek, M.E. van. 1997. "The So-Called 'Homeric Anthologies.'" Pp. 991–995 in B. Kramer et al., eds., *Akten des 21. Internationalen Papyrologenkongresses, Berlin, 13.-19. 8. 1995*. Stuttgart.
———. 1998. *Greek Readers' Digests? Studies on a Selection of Subliterary Papyri*. Leiden.
Rostagni, A. 1926. "Il dialogo aristotelico Περὶ ποιητῶν." *Rivista di Filologia e di Istruzione Classica* 54: 433–470.
Rubensohn, O. 1968. *Das Delion von Paros*. Wiesbaden.
Ruijgh, C.J. 1984. "Le dorien de Théocrite." *Mnemosyne* 37: 56–88.

Russell, D.A. 1981. *Criticism in Antiquity*. Berkeley and Los Angeles.
———. 2006. "Rhetoric and Criticism." Pp. 267-283 in Laird 2006a.
Russell, D.A., and D. Konstan. 2005. *Heraclitus: Homeric Problems*. Leiden.
Russo, A. 2007. *Quinto Ennio, Le opere minori: Introduzione, edizione critica dei frammenti e commento*. Volume 1, *Praecepta, Protrepticus, Saturae, Scipio, Sota*. Pisa.
Russo, L. 2001. *La rivoluzione dimenticata: Il pensiero scientifico greco e la scienza moderna*. 2nd ed. Milan.
Rutherford, I.C. 2001. *Pindar's Paeans: A Reading of the Fragments with a Survey of the Genre*. Oxford.
Rydbeck, L. 1967. *Fachprosa, vermeintliche Volkssprache und Neues Testament: Zur Beurteilung der sprachlichen Niveauunterschiede im nachklassischen Griechisch*. Uppsala.
Said, S., ed. 1991 Έλληνισμός: *Quelques jalons pour une histoire de l'identité grecque—Actes du Colloque de Strasbourg, 25-27 octobre 1989*. Leiden.
Salvadori, L. 1985. "P. Mil. Vogl. III 126: Una fonte delle *Recognitiones* pseudoclementine?" *Rivista di Filologia e di Istruzione Classica* 113: 174-181.
Salvini, A.-M. 1749. "Elegia di Catullo tradotta in greco dal Signor A.-M. Salvini." Pp. 145-152 in S. Maffei and G. Torelli, trans., *Li due primi canti dell'Iliade e li due primi dell'Eneide tradotti in versi italiani*. Verona.
Samama, É. 2003. *Les médecins dans le monde grec: Sources épigraphiques sur la naissance d'un corps médical*. Geneva.
Sánchez Ortiz de Landaluce, M. 1994. "*Acontio y Cidipa* y la novela griega: Un nuevo análisis de motivos recurrentes." Pp. 423-428 in *Actas del VIII Congreso español de estudios clásicos, Madrid, 23-28 de septiembre de 1991*. Madrid.
Santin, E. 2009. *Autori di epigrammi sepolcrali greci su pietra: Firme di poeti occasionali e professionisti*. Rome.
Savidis, G. 2000. Κ. Π. ΚΑΒΑΦΗ. ΤΑ ΠΟΙΗΜΑΤΑ. 7th ed. 2 vols. Athens.
Sbardella, L. 2000. *Filita: Testimonianze e frammenti poetici*. Rome.
Schade, G. 1999. *Lykophrons "Odyssee": Alexandra 648-819*. Berlin.
Scheidel, W. 2004. "Creating a Metropolis: A Comparative Demographic Perspective." Pp. 1-31 in Harris and Ruffini 2004.
Schenkeveld, D.M. 1964. *Studies in Demetrius On Style*. Amsterdam.
———. 1968. "OI KRITIKOI in Philodemus." *Mnemosyne* 21: 17.
———. 1993. "Pap. Hamburg. 128: A Hellenistic Ars Poetica." *Zeitschrift für Papyrologie und Epigraphik* 97: 67-80.
Schenkeveld, D.M., and J. Barnes. 1999. "Language: Poetics." Pp. 221-225 in K. Algra et al., eds., *The Cambridge History of Hellenistic Philosophy*. Cambridge.
Schepens, G. 2001. "Ancient Greek City Histories. Self-definition through History Writing." Pp. 3-25 in Demoen 2001.
Scherer, B. 2006. *Mythos, Katalog und Prophezeiung: Studien zu den "Argonautika" des Apollonius Rhodios*. Stuttgart.
Schiano, C. 2002. "Teone e il Museo di Alessandria." *Quaderni di Storia* 55: 129-143.
Schilpp, P.A., ed. 1949. *Albert Einstein: Philosopher-Scientist*. Living Philosophers, Volume 7. Evanston, Illinois.
Schizzerotto, G. 1973. "Callimaco, Angelo." Pp. 754-757 in *Dizionario biografico degli Italiani*, vol. 16. Rome.
Schlange-Schöningen, H. 1996. "Alexandria—Memphis—Siwa: Wo liegt Alexander der Große begraben?" *Antike Welt* 27: 109-119.
Schloz, S. 1994. "Das Königtum der Ptolemäer: Grenzgänge der Ideologie." Pp. 227-234 in M. Minas and J. Zeidler, eds., *Aspekte spätägyptischer Kultur*. Mainz.
Schmid, P.B. 1947. "Studien zu griechischen Ktisissagen." Diss. Freiburg (Switzerland).
Schmidt, E.A., ed. 2001. *L'histoire littéraire immanente dans la poésie latine*. Vandœuvres.
Schmidt, F. 1922. *Die "Pinakes" des Kallimachos*. Berlin.

Schmidt, S. 2004. "Kunst am Hof der Ptolemäer: Dokumente und Denkmäler." *Städel-Jahrbuch* 14: 511-524.
Schmiel, R.C. 1987. "Callimachus' *Hymn to Delos*: Structure and Theme." *Mnemosyne* 40: 45-55.
Schmitt, H.H. 2005. "Manethon." P. 670 in H.H. Schmitt and E. Vogt, eds., *Lexikon des Hellenismus*. Wiesbaden.
Schmitt, R. 1970. *Die Nominalbildung in den Dichtungen des Kallimachos von Kyrene*. Wiesbaden.
Schmitz, T. 1999. "'I Hate All Common Things': The Reader's Role in Callimachus' Aetia Prologue." *Harvard Studies in Classical Philology* 99: 151-178.
Schneider, M. 1882. *De Dionysii Periegetae arte metrica et grammatica capita selecta*. Leipzig.
Schneider, O. 1870-1873. *Callimachea*. 2 vols. Leipzig.
Scholz, P. 2007. "Philosophie und Wissenschaft: Ideen, Institutionen und Innovationen." Pp. 158-176 and 454-458 in Weber 2007b.
Schroeder, C.M. 2006. "Hesiod and the Fragments of Alexander Aetolus." Pp. 287-302 in M.A. Harder, Regtuit, and Wakker 2006.
Schröder, S. 1999. *Geschichte und Theorie der Gattung Paian*. Stuttgart.
Schultze, G. 1888. *Euphorionea*. Strasbourg.
Scodel, R. 1980a. "Hesiodus Redivivus." *Greek, Roman and Byzantine Studies* 21: 301-320.
———. 1980b. "Wine, Water and the Anthesteria in Callimachus fr. 178 Pf." *Zeitschrift für Papyrologie und Epigraphik* 39: 37-40.
———. 2001. "Poetic Authority and Oral Tradition in Hesiod and Pindar." Pp. 109-137 in Watson 2001.
Schwamenthal, R., and M. Straniero. 1991. *Dizionario dei proverbi italiani e dialettali*. Milan.
Schwartz, M.A. 1917. "Erechtheus et Theseus apud Euripidem et Atthidographos." Ph.D., University of Leiden.
Schwendner, G. 2007. "Literature and Literacy at Roman Karanis: Maps of Reading." Pp. 991-1006 in Frösén, Purola, and Salmenkivi 2007.
Schwertheim, E., ed. 1994. *Forschungen in Galatien*. Bonn.
Schwindt, J.P., ed. 2005. *La représentation du temps dans la poésie augustéenne / Zur Poetik der Zeit in augusteischer Dichtung*. Heidelberg.
Seaford, R. 1996. *Euripides: Bacchae, with an Introduction, Translation and Commentary*. Warminster
Seibert, J. 1991. "Zur Begründung von Herrschaftsanspruch und Herrschaftslegitimation in der frühen Diadochenzeit." Pp. 87-100 in *Hellenistische Studien: Gedenkschrift für Hermann Bengtson*, ed. J. Seibert. ed. Munich.
Selden, D. 1998. "Alibis." *Classical Antiquity* 17: 289-412.
Sens, A. 2006. "'Τίπτε γένος τοὐμὸν ζητεῖς;'" The *Batrachomyomachia*, Hellenistic Epic Parody, and Early Epic." Pp. 215-248 in F. Montanari and A. Rengakos, eds., *La poésie épique grecque: Métamorphoses d'un genre littéraire*. Vandœuvres.
Serrao, G. 1977. "La poetica del 'nuovo stile': Dalla mimesi aristotelica alla poetica della verità." Pp. 180-253 in R. Bianchi Bandinelli, ed., *Storia e civiltà dei greci*, vol. 9, *La cultura ellenistica: Filosofia, scienza, letteratura*. Milan.
———. 1979a. "Antimaco di Kolophòn: Primo *poëta doctus*." Pp. 299-310 in *Storia e civiltà dei greci*, vol. 5, La crisi della polis: Storia, letteratura, filosofia. Milan.
———. 1979b. "La struttura della *Lide* di Antimaco e la critica callimachea." *Quaderni Urbinati di Cultura Classica* 3: 91-98.
———. 1998. "Note esegetiche ai due prologhi degli Αἴτια callimachei (frr. 1-2 Pf.)." *Seminari Romani di Cultura Greca* 1: 299-311.
———. 2000. "Teocrito: Poetica e poesia." Pp. 45-61 in Pretagostini 2000a.

Seth-Smith, A. 1981. "Parthenius and Erucius." *Mnemosyne* 34: 63-71.
Sherk, R.K. 1992. "The Eponymous Officials of Greek Cities, Part 4." *Zeitschrift für Papyrologie und Epigraphik* 93: 223-272.
Sherwin-White, S.M. 1978. *Ancient Cos: An Historical Study from the Dorian Settlement to the Imperial Period.* Göttingen.
Shipley, G. 2000. *The Greek World after Alexander, 323-30 BC.* London.
Shorrock, R. 2001. *The Challenge of Epic: Allusive Engagement in the* Dionysiaca *of Nonnus.* Leiden.
Sider, D. 1992. "*Lekythion apolesen:* Aristophanes' Limp Phallic Joke?" *Mnemosyne* 45: 359-362.
———. 1995. "The Epicurean Philosopher as Hellenistic Poet." Pp. 42-57 in Obbink 1995.
———. 1997. *The Epigrams of Philodemus.* Oxford.
Silva Sánchez, T. 2002. *Sobre el texto de los "Cynegetica" de Opiano de Apamea.* Cádiz.
Simelidis, C., ed. 2009. *Selected Poems of Gregory of Nazianzus.* Göttingen.
Sistakou, E. 2004. Η αρνήση του έπους· Οψεις του τρωϊκού μύθου στην Ελληνιστική ποίηση. Athens.
———. 2009. "Callimachus Hesiodicus Revisited." Pp. 219-252 in Montanari, Rengakos, and Tsagalis 2009.
Skempis, M. 2008. "Ery-chthonios: Etymological Wordplay in Callimachus, *Hec.* fr. 70.9 H." *Hermes* 136: 143-152.
Skiadas, A.D. 1975. *Kallimachos.* Darmstadt.
Skinner, M. 2003. *Catullus in Verona.* Columbus.
Skutsch, O. 1986. *The Annals of Q. Ennius, Edited with Introduction and Commentary.* Oxford.
Slater, W.J. 1976. "Aristophanes of Byzantium on the *Pinakes* of Callimachus." *Phoenix* 30: 234-241.
Slings, S.R. 1989. "Anonymus, Parallel Lines from Homer and Archilochus." *Zeitschrift für Papyrologie und Epigraphik* 79: 1-8.
———. 2004. "The *Hymn to Delos* as a Partial Allegory of Callimachus' Poetry." Pp. 279-297 in M.A. Harder, MacDonald, and Reinink 2007.
Smiley, M.T. 1914. "Callimachus' Debt to Pindar and Others." *Hermathena* 18: 46-72.
Smotrytsch, P. 1961. "Le allusioni politiche nel II inno di Callimaco e la sua datazione." *Helikon* 1: 661-667.
Snell, B. 1963. *La cultura greca e le origini del pensiero europeo.* Trans. V. Degli Alberti and A. Solmi Marietti. Turin. [Originally published in German as *Die Entdeckung des Geistes: Studien zur Entstehung des europäischen Denkens bei den Griechen* (Hamburg, 1946; 2nd ed. 1955).]
Solimano, G. 1970. "Il mito di Apollo e Admeto negli elegiaci latini." Pp. 255-268 in *Mythos: Scripta in honorem M. Untersteiner.* Genoa.
Sollenberger, M.J. 2000. "Diogenes Laertius' Life of Demetrius of Phalerum." Pp. 311-329 in Fortenbaugh and Schütrumpf 2000.
Solmsen, F. 1942. "Eratosthenes as Platonist and Poet." *Transactions of the American Philological Association* 73: 192-213.
Sommerstein. A.H. 1985. *Aristophanes: Peace.* Warminster.
Sonne, W. 1996. "Hellenistische Herrschaftsgärten." Pp. 136-143 in Hoepfner and Brands 1996.
Sordi, M., ed. 1989. *Fenomeni naturali e avvenimenti storici nell'antichità.* Milan.
———, ed. 1992. *Autocoscienza e rappresentazione dei popoli nell'antichità.* Milan.
Spano, G. 2004. *Proverbi sardi tradotti in lingua italiana e confrontati con quelli degli antichi popoli.* Catania.
Spanoudakis, K. 1998. "Callimachus fr. 1, 9-12 Again." *Zeitschrift für Papyrologie und Epigraphik* 121: 59-61.

———. 2002. *Philitas of Cos*. Leiden.
———. 2004. "Adesp. Pap. Eleg. *SH* 964: Parthenius?" *Archiv für Papyrusforschung* 50: 37–41.
———. 2008. "Αποσπασματικές απολαύσεις: Ορισμένες ήσσονες μορφές." Pp. 273–324 in F.P. Manakidou and K. Spanoudakis, eds., *Αλεξανδρινή Μούσα· Συνέχεια και νεωτερισμός στην Ελληνιστική ποίηση*. Athens.
Spentzou, E., and D. Fowler, eds. 2002. *Cultivating the Muse*. Oxford.
Spina, L. 1989. "Cleombroto: La fortuna di un suicidio." *Vichiana* 18: 12–39.
Spyridakis, S. 1968. "Zeus Is Dead: Euhemerus and Crete." *Classical Journal* 63: 337–340.
Spyridonidou-Skarsouli, M. 1995. *Der erste Teil der fünften Athos-Sammlung griechischer Sprichwörter*. Berlin.
Stadtmüller, G. 1934. *Michael Choniates, Metropolit von Athen (ca. 1138–ca. 1222)*. Rome.
Stafford, E., and J. Herrin, eds. 2005. *Personification in the Greek World*. Ashgate.
Stagl, J., ed. 1982. *Aspekte der Kultursoziologie: Aufsätze zur Soziologie, Philosophie, Anthropologie und Geschichte der Kultur zum 60. Geburtstag von M. Rassem*. Berlin.
Stähelin, H. 1934. *Die Religion des Kallimachos*. Basel.
Stanford, W.B. 1968. "On the Zeta/Sigma-Delta Variation in the Dialect of Theocritos: A Literary Approach." *Proceedings of the Royal Irish Academy* 67, section C: 1–8.
Steiner, D. 2007a. "Feathers Flying: Avian Poetics in Hesiod, Pindar, and Callimachus." *American Journal of Philology* 128: 177–208.
———. 2007b. "Galloping (or Lame) Consumption: Callimachus' *Iamb* 13.58–66 and Traditional Representations of the Practice of Abuse." *Materiali e Discussioni* 58: 13–42.
Stemplinger, E. 1912. *Das Plagiat in der griechischen Literatur*. Leipzig.
Stephanus, H. 1577. *Callimachi Cyrenaei hymni (cum suis scholiis Graecis) et epigrammata*. Geneva.
Stephens, S.A. 1998. "Callimachus at Court." Pp. 167–185 in M.A. Harder, Regtuit, and Wakker 1998.
———. 2000. "Writing Epic for the Ptolemaic Court." Pp. 195–215 in M.A. Harder, Regtuit, and Wakker 2000.
———. 2002a. "Commenting on Fragments." Pp. 67–88 in Gibson and Kraus 2002.
———. 2002b. "Egyptian Callimachus." Pp. 235–269 in Montanari and Lehnus 2002.
———. 2002–2003. "Linus Song." *Hermathena* 173/174: 13–27.
———. 2003. *Seeing Double: Intercultural Poetics in Ptolemaic Alexandria*. Berkeley and Los Angeles.
———. 2004a. "Posidippus' Poetry Book: Where Macedon Meets Egypt." Pp. 63–86 in Harris and Ruffini 2004.
———. 2004b. "Whose Rituals in Ink?" Pp. 157–160 in Barchiesi, Ruepke, and Stephens 2004.
———. 2005. "Battle of the Books" Pp. 229–248 in Gutzwiller 2005.
———. 2010. "Literary Quarrels." In Martina and Cozzoli forthcoming.
Stevens, A. 2007. "Ion of Chios: Tragedy as Commodity at the Athenian Exchange." Pp. 243–265 in Jennings and Katsaros 2007.
Stewart, A. 1998. "Nuggets: Mining the Texts Again." *American Journal of Archaeology* 102: 271–282.
Stirpe, P. 2002. "Perseo nell'*Alessandra* di Licofrone e sulle monete macedoni del II secolo a.C." *Rivista di Filologia e di Istruzione Classica* 130: 5–20.
Strobel, K. 1991. "Die Galater im hellenistischen Kleinasien: Historische Aspekte einer keltischen Staatenbildung." Pp. 101–134 in Seibert 1991.
———. 1994. "Keltensieg und Galatersieger: Die Funktionalisierung eines historischen Phänomens als politischer Mythos der hellenistischen Welt." Pp. 67–96 in Schwertheim 1994.

Strootman, R. 2005a. "Kings against Celts: Deliverance from Barbarians as a Theme in Hellenistic Royal Propaganda." Pp. 101-141 in Enenkel and Pfeijffer 2005.
——. 2005b. "De vrienden van de vorst: Het koniklijk hof in de Hellenistische rijken." *Lampas* 38: 184-197.
Stroux, J. 1934. "Erzählungen aus Kallimachos." *Philologus* 43: 301-319.
Studniczka, F. 1914. *Das Symposion Ptolemaios II.* Leipzig.
Sundermann, K. 1991. *Gregor von Nazianz: Der Rangstreit zwischen Ehe und Jungfräulichkeit (Carmen 1, 2, 1,215-732).* Paderborn.
Świderek, A. 1951. "La structure des *Aitia* de Callimaque à la lumière des nouvelles découvertes papyrologiques." *Journal of Juristic Papyrology* 5: 229-235.
——. 1959-1960. "À la cour alexandrine d'Apollonius le dioecète: Notes prosopographiques." *Eos* 50: 81-89.
Swiggers, P., and A. Wouters. 1995. "Poetics and Grammar: From Technique to 'Techne.'" Pp. 17-41 in Abbenes, Slings, and Sluiter 1995.
Swinnen, W. 1970. "Herakleitos of Halikarnassos, an Alexandrian Poet and Diplomat?" *Ancient Society* 1: 39-52.
Szepessy, T. 1972. "The Story of the Girl Who Died on the Day of Her Wedding." *Acta Antiqua Academiae Scientiarum Hungaricae* 20: 341-357.
Tandy, D.W. 1979. *Callimachus, Hymn to Zeus: Introduction and Commentary.* Dissertation, Yale University.
Tanner, J. 2006. *The Invention of Art History in Ancient Greece.* Cambridge.
Tarrant, R. 1982. "Editing Ovid's *Metamorphoses*: Problems and Possibilities." *Classical Philology* 72: 342-360.
Thiel, H. van. 2001. "Die D-Scholien der Handschriften." *Zeitschrift für Papyrologie und Epigraphik* 132: 1-62.
Thissen, H.-J. 1993. "'…αἰγυπτιάζων τῇ φωνῇ…': Zum Umgang mit der ägyptischen Sprache in der griechisch-römischen Antike." *Zeitschrift für Papyrologie und Epigraphik* 97: 239-252.
Thom, J.C. 2005. *Cleanthes' Hymn to Zeus: Text, Translation, and Commentary.* Tübingen.
Thomas, Richard F. 1979. "New Comedy, Callimachus, and Roman Poetry." *Harvard Studies in Classical Philology* 83: 179-206.
——. 1983. "Callimachus, the *Victoria Berenices* and Roman Poetry." *Classical Quarterly* 33: 92-113. [Reprinted in Richard F. Thomas 1999: 68-100.]
——. 1986a. "From Recusatio to Commitment: The Evolution of the Vergilian Programme." *Papers of the Liverpool Latin Seminar* 5: 61-73. [Reprinted in Richard F. Thomas 1999: 101-113.]
——. 1986b. "Virgil's *Georgics* and the Art of Reference." *Harvard Studies in Classical Philology* 90: 171-198. [Reprinted as pp. 114-141 in Richard F. Thomas 1999.]
——. 1993. "Callimachus Back in Rome." Pp. 197-215 in M.A. Harder, Regtuit, and Wakker 1993.
——. 1999. *Reading Virgil and His Texts: Studies in Intertextuality.* Ann Arbor.
Thomas, Rosalind. 2000. *Herodotus in Context: Ethnography, Science, and the Art of Persuasion.* Cambridge.
Thompson, D.B. 1955. "A Portrait of Arsinoe Philadelphos." *American Journal of Archaeology* 59: 199-206.
——. 1973. *Ptolemaic Oinochoai and Portraits in Faience: Aspects of the Ruler-Cult.* Oxford.
Thompson, D.J. 1992. "Literacy and the Administration in Early Ptolemaic Egypt." Pp. 323-326 in J.H. Johnson, ed., *Life in a Multi-Cultural Society: Egypt from Cambyses to Constantine and Beyond.* Chicago.
——. 2000. "Philadelphus' Procession: Dynastic Power in a Mediterranean Context." Pp. 365-388 in L. Mooren, ed., *Politics, Administration and Society in the Hellenistic and Roman World.* Louvain.

———. 2005. "Posidippos, Poet of the Ptolemies." Pp. 269-283 in Gutzwiller 2005.
———. 2007. "Education and Culture in Hellenistic Egypt and Beyond." Pp. 121-137 in J.A. Fernández Delgado, F. Pordomingo Pardo, and A. Stramaglia, eds., *Escuela y literatura en Grecia antigua: Actas del simposio internacional, Universidad de Salamanca, 17-19 noviembre de 2004.* Cassino.
Timpanaro, S. 1973. "Giorgio Pasquali." *Belfagor* 28: 183-205.
Tissoni, F. 1993-1994. "L' 'ἐλεγεία περὶ κόμης Βερενίκης'" di Giuseppe Giusto Scaligero." *Studi Umanistici* 4/5: 199-257.
———. 1994. "Ancora a proposito di Callimaco Hecale fr. 51 Hollis." *Maia* 46: 299-300.
———. 1997. "*Callimachea* in Gregorio di Nazianzo." *Sileno* 23: 275-281.
———. 1998. *Nonno di Panopoli, i canti di Penteo (Dionisiache 44-46): Commento.* Florence.
———. 2000a. "Cristodoro e Callimaco." *Acme* 53.1: 213-218.
———. 2000b. *Cristodoro: Un'introduzione e un commento.* Alessandria.
Too, Y.L. 1998. *The Idea of Ancient Literary Criticism.* Cambridge.
Tosi, R. 1988. *Studi sulla tradizione indiretta dei classici greci.* Bologna.
———. 1991. *Dizionario delle sentenze latine e greche.* Milan.
———. 1994. "La lessicografia e la paremiografia in età alessandrina ed il loro sviluppo successivo." Pp. 143-197 in Montanari 1994.
———. 1997. "Callimaco e i glossografi omerici." *Eikasmos* 8: 223-240.
Traina, A. 1989. "Il Pascoli e l'arte allusiva." Pp. 239-249 in *Poeti latini (e neolatini): Note e saggi filologici*, vol. 3. Bologna.
Tress, H. van. 2004. *Poetic Memory: Allusion in the Poetry of Callimachus and the Metamorphoses of Ovid.* Leiden.
Trypanis, C.A. 1978. *Callimachus: Aetia, Iambi, Hecale and other Fragments.* 2nd ed. Cambridge, Mass. [1st ed. 1958.]
Tsantsanoglou, K. 2007. "Callimachus, *Aetia* Fr. 1,7-12 Once Again." *Zeitschrift für Papyrologie und Epigraphik* 163: 27-36.
Tsavari, I.O. 1990. Διονυσίου Ἀλεξανδρέως Οἰκουμένης περιήγησις. Ioannina.
Tueller, M.A. 2000. "Well-Read Heroes Quoting the *Aetia* in *Aeneid* 8." *Harvard Studies in Classical Philology* 100: 361-380.
Turner, E.G. 1968. *Greek Papyri: An Introduction.* Oxford.
———. 1987. *Greek Manuscripts of the Ancient World.* 2nd ed. Ed. P.J. Parsons. London.
Tziatzi-Papagianni, M. 1993-1994. "Theodoros Prodromos: Historisches Gedicht LXXVIII." *Byzantinische Zeitschrift* 86-87: 363-382.
Ueding, G., ed. 2001. *Historisches Wörterbuch der Rhetorik.* Volume 5, L-Musi. Tübingen.
Ukleja, K. 2005. *Der Delos-Hymnus des Kallimachos innerhalb seines Hymnensextetts.* Münster.
Unte, W. 2003. *Heroen und Epigonen: Gelehrtenbiographien der klassischen Altertumswissenschaft im 19. und 20. Jahrhundert.* St. Catherine.
Urban, R. 1979. *Wachstum und Krise des achäischen Bundes.* Wiesbaden.
Urso, C. 1998. "I Peucezi alle porte di Roma: Nota a Callimaco, *Diegeseis* V 25-32." *Aevum Antiquum* 11: 351-361.
Vaahtera, J. 1997. "Phonetics and Euphony in Dionysius of Halicarnassus." *Mnemosyne* 50: 586-595.
Valckenaer, L.C. 1739. *Ammonius: De adfinium vocabulorum differentia.* Leiden.
———. 1767. *Diatribe in Euripidis perditorum dramatum reliquias.* Leiden.
———. 1799. *Callimachi elegiarum fragmenta, cum elegia Catulli Callimachea.* Leiden.
Valk, M. van der. 1971. *Eustathii archiepiscopi Thessalonicensis Commentarii ad Homeri Iliadem pertinentes ad fidem codicis Laurentiani editi.* Volume 1. Leiden.
Vamvouri Ruffy, M. 2005. *La fabrique du divin: Les Hymnes de Callimaque à la lumière des Hymnes homériques et des hymnes épigraphiques.* Lausanne.

Vanderlip, V.F. 1972. *The Four Greek Hymns of Isidorus and the Cult of Isis.* Toronto.
Vassis, I., G.S. Henrich, and D.R. Reinsch, eds. 1998. *Lesarten: Festschrift für Athanasios Kambylis zum 70. Geburtstag.* Berlin.
Veneri, A. 1996. "L'Elicona nella cultura tespiese intorno al III sec. a.C.: La stele di Euthy[kl]es." Pp. 73-86 in Hurst and Schachter 1996.
Verdenius, W.J. 1983. "The Principles of Greek Literary Criticism." *Mnemosyne* 36: 14-59.
Verdin, H., G. Schepens, and E. De Keyser, eds. 1990. *Purposes of History: Studies in Greek Historiography from the Fourth to the Second Centuries BC* Louvain.
Verhoeven, U. 2005. "Die interkulturelle Rolle von Priestern im ptolemäischen Ägypten." Pp. 279-284 in H. Beck, P.C. Bol, and M. Bückling, eds., *Ägypten Griechenland Rom: Abwehr und Berührung.* Tübingen.
Vérilhac, A.-M. 1978-1982. Παῖδες ἄωροι: *Poésie funéraire.* 2 vols. Athens.
Vestrheim, G. 2005. *Construction of Voice and Addressee in the* Hymns *of Callimachus.* Bergen.
Veyne, P. 1983. *Les grecs ont-ils cru à leurs mythes?* Paris.
Vian, F. 1963-1969. *Quintus de Smyrne: La suite d'Homère.* 3 vols. Paris.
———. 1976. *Nonnos de Panopolis, Les Dionysiaques.* Volume 1, *Chants I–II.* Paris.
———. 1987. *Les Argonautiques Orphiques.* Paris.
———. 1988. "La théomachie de Nonnos et ses antécedents." *Revue des Études Grecques* 101: 275-292. [Reprinted as pp. 423-438 in Vian 2005.]
———. 1991a. "La grotte de Brongos et Cybèle: Nonnos, *Dionysiaques*, 17, 32-86." *Revue des Études Grecques* 104: 584-593. [Reprinted as pp. 457-468 in Vian 2005.]
———. 1991b. "Nonno ed Omero." Κοινωνία 15: 5-18. [Reprinted as pp. 469-482 in Vian 2005.]
———. 1995. *Nonnos de Panopolis, "Les Dionysiaques."* Volume 5, *Chants XI–XIII.* Paris.
———. 2005. *L'épopée posthomérique: Recueil d'études.* Ed. D. Accorinti. Alessandria.
Viansino, G. 1967. *Agazia Scolastico: Epigrammi.* Milan.
Virgilio, B., ed. 1994. *Aspetti e problemi dell'ellenismo: Atti del Convegno di studi, Pisa, 6-7 novembre 1992.* Pisa.
———. 2003. *Lancia, diadema e porpora: Il re e la regalità ellenistica.* 2nd ed. Pisa.
Visintin, M. 1992. *La vergine e l'eroe: Temesa e la leggenda di Euthymos di Locri.* Bari.
Vogliano, A. 1937. "*Diegeseis* di poemi di Callimaco." Pp. 66-145 in *Papiri della R. Università di Milano*, vol. 1. Milan. [Reprint: 1966.]
Vogt, M. 1902. "Die griechischen Lokalhistoriker." *Jahrbücher für classische Philologie,* Supplementband 27: 699-786.
Völcker-Janssen, W. 1993. *Kunst und Gesellschaft an den Höfen Alexanders des Großen und seiner Nachfolger.* Munich.
Vössing, K. 1997. "Bibliothek II B." Cols. 640-647 in *Der neue Pauly: Enzyklopädie der Antike*, vol. 2. Stuttgart.
———. 2004. *Mensa regia: Das Bankett beim hellenistischen König und beim römischen Kaiser.* Munich.
Voutiras, E. 1995. "Zu einer metrischen Inschrift aus Euromos." *Epigraphica Anatolica* 24: 15-20.
———. 1998. "Nachtrag zu einer metrischen Inschrift aus Euromos." *Epigraphica Anatolica* 30: 148.
Vulcanius, B. 1584. *Callimachi Cyrenaei hymni, epigrammata et fragmenta, quae exstant.* Antwerp.
Wackernagel, J. 1916. *Sprachliche Untersuchungen zu Homer.* Göttingen.
Waele, J.A. de. 1971. *Akragas Graeca: Die historische Topographie des griechischen Akragas auf Sizilien.* The Hague.

Walker, H.J. 1995. "The Early Development of the Theseus Myth." *Rheinisches Museum* 138: 1–33.
Waltz, P. 1906. *De Antipatro Sidonio*. Bordeaux.
Waltz, P., et al. 1974. *Anthologie Grecque*. Part 1, vol. 8, *Anthologie Palatine, livre IX, épigr. 359–827*. Paris. [Ed. P. Waltz, G. Soury, J. Irigoin, and P. Laurens.]
Ward, A.G., ed. 1970. *The Quest for Theseus*. London.
Watson, J., ed. 2001. *Speaking Volumes: Orality and Literacy in the Greek and Roman World*. Leiden.
Weber, G. 1992. "Poesie und Poeten an den Höfen vorhellenistischer Monarchen." *Klio* 74: 25–77.
———. 1993. *Dichtung und höfische Gesellschaft: Die Rezeption von Zeitgeschichte am Hof der ersten drei Ptolemäer*. Stuttgart.
———. 1995. "Herrscher, Hof und Dichter: Aspekte der Legitimierung und Repräsentation hellenistischer Könige am Beispiel der ersten drei Antigoniden." *Historia* 44: 283–316.
———. 1997. "Interaktion, Repräsentation und Herrschaft: Der Königshof im Hellenismus." Pp. 28–71 in A. Winterling, ed., *Zwischen 'Haus' und 'Staat': Antike Höfe im Vergleich*. Munich.
———. 1998–1999. "The Hellenistic Rulers and Their Poets: Silencing Dangerous Critics." *Ancient Society* 29: 147–174.
———. 2007a. "Der Hof Alexanders des Großen als soziales System." *Saeculum* 58: 229–264.
———, ed. 2007b. *Kulturgeschichte des Hellenismus: Von Alexander dem Großen bis Kleopatra*. Stuttgart.
———. 2007c. "Die neuen Zentralen: Hauptstädte, Residenzen, Paläste und Höfe." Pp. 99–117 and 440–445 in Weber 2007b.
Welles, C.B. 1946. "The Garden of Ptolemagrius at Panopolis." *Transactions of the American Philological Association* 77: 192–206.
Wendel, C. 1920. *Überlieferung und Entstehung der Theokrit-Scholien*. Berlin.
———. 1932. *Die Überlieferung der Scholien zu Apollonios von Rhodos*. Berlin.
———. 1934. "Theon." Cols. 2054–2059 in A. von Pauly et al., eds., *Real-Encyclopädie der classischen Altertumswissenschaft*, 2. Reihe, 5.2. Stuttgart.
West, M.L. 1966. *Hesiod: Theogony*. Oxford.
———. 1969. "Near Eastern Material in Hellenistic and Roman Literature." *Harvard Studies in Classical Philology* 73: 113–134.
———. 1971. *Iambi et elegi Graeci ante Alexandrum cantati*. 2 vols. Oxford. [2nd ed. 1989–1992.]
———. 1978. *Hesiod: Works and Days*. Oxford.
———. 1992a. Analecta Musica." *Zeitschrift für Papyrologie und Epigraphik* 92: 1–54.
———. 1992b. *Ancient Greek Music*. Oxford.
———. 1997. *The East Face of Helicon: West Asiatic Elements in Greek Poetry and Myth*. Oxford.
———. 2001. "The Fragmentary *Homeric Hymn to Dionysos*." *Zeitschrift für Papyrologie und Epigraphik* 134: 1–11.
———. 2003. *Homeric Hymns, Homeric Apocrypha, Lives of Homer*. Cambridge, Mass.
———. 2008. "The Hesiod Papyri and the Archaic Epic Language." Pp. 29–42 in Bastianini and Casanova 2008.
West, S. 1967. *The Ptolemaic Papyri of Homer*. Cologne.
Westerink, L.G. 1986. "Leo the Philosopher: *Job* and Other Poems." *Illinois Classical Studies* 11: 193–222.
Whitby, M. 1994. "From Moschus to Nonnus: The Evolution of the Nonnian Style." Pp. 99–155 in Hopkinson 1994c.
———. 2007. "The *Cynegetica* Attributed to Oppian." Pp. 125–134 in S. Swain, S. Harrison, and J. Elsner, eds., *Severan Culture*. Cambridge.

White, H. 2000. "Further Textual Problems in Greek Poetry." *Orpheus* 21: 175–188.
White, K. 1992. "Elements of Geopoetics." *Edinburgh Review* 88: 163–181.
White, P. 1993. *Promised Verse.* Cambridge, Mass.
White, S. 1994. "Callimachus on Plato and Cleombrotus." *Transactions of the American Philological Association* 124: 135–161.
———. 1999. "Callimachus Battiades (*Epigr.* 35)." *Classical Philology* 94: 168–181.
Wifstrand, A. 1926. *Studien zur griechischen Anthologie.* Lund.
Wigodsky, M. 1972. *Vergil and Early Latin Poetry.* Wiesbaden.
Wilamowitz-Möllendorff, U. von. 1893a. *Aristoteles und Athen.* 2 vols. Berlin.
———. 1893b. "Über die *Hekale* des Kallimachos." *Nachrichten von der Königlichen Gesellschaft der Wissenschaften zu Göttingen*: 731–747. [Reprinted as pp. 30–47 in *Kleine Schriften*, vol. 2 (Berlin, 1941).]
———. 1912. "Neues von Kallimachos." *Sitzungsberichte der Preussischen Akademie der Wissenschaften zu Berlin*, 524–550.
———. 1918. "Dichterfragmente aus der Papyrussammlung der Kgl. Museen." *Sitzungsberichte der Preussischen Akademie der Wissenschaften zu Berlin*: 739–742.
———. 1921. *Einleitung in die griechische Tragödie.* Berlin.
———. 1924. *Hellenistische Dichtung in der Zeit des Kallimachos.* 2 vols. Berlin.
———. 1962. *Kleine Schriften.* Volume 4, *Lesefrüchte und Verwandtes.* Berlin.
Willi, A., ed. 2002. *The Language of Greek Comedy.* Oxford.
Williams, F. 1978. *Callimachus, Hymn to Apollo: A Commentary.* Oxford.
———. 1993. "Callimachus and the Supranormal." Pp. 217–225 in M.A. Harder, Regtuit, and Wakker 1993.
Williams, G.D. 1995. "Cleombrotus of Ambracia: Interpretations of a Suicide from Callimachus to Agathias." *Classical Quarterly* 45: 154–169.
Wills, J. 1996. *Repetition in Latin Poetry: Figures of Allusion.* Oxford.
Wilson, N.G. 1983. *Scholars of Byzantium.* London.
———. 1992. *From Byzantium to Italy: Greek Studies in the Italian Renaissance.* London.
Wilson, P. 1999–2000. "Euripides' Tragic Muse." *Illinois Classical Studies* 24–25: 427–449.
———. 2000. *The Athenian Institution of the Khoregia: The Chorus, the City and the Stage.* Cambridge.
———. 2003a. "The Politics of Dance: Dithyrambic Contest and Social Order in Ancient Greece." Pp. 163–196 in Phillips and Pritchard 2003.
———. 2003b. "The Sounds of Cultural Conflict. Kritias and the Culture of *Mousiké* in Athens." Pp. 181–207 in Dougherty and Kurke 2003.
———. 2004. "Athenian Strings." Pp. 269–306 in Murray and Wilson 2004.
———, ed. 2007a. *The Greek Theatre and Festivals: Documentary Studies.* Oxford.
———. 2007b. "Performance in the *Pythion*: The Athenian Thargelia." Pp. 150–182 in P. Wilson 2007a.
Wimmel, W. 1960. *Kallimachos in Rom: Die Nachfolge seines apologetischen Dichtens in der Augusteerzeit.* Wiesbaden.
Wimsatt, W.K., and M.C. Beardsley. 1946. "The Intentional Fallacy." *Sewanee Review* 54: 468–488.
Winterling, A. 1998. "Hof." Cols. 661–665 in *Der neue Pauly: Enzyklopädie der Antike*, vol. 5. Stuttgart.
Wiotte-Franz, C. 2001. *Hermeneus und Interpres: Zum Dolmetscherwesen in der Antike.* Saarbrücken.
Wölke, H. 1978. *Untersuchungen zur Batrachomyomachie.* Meisenheim.
Wörrle, M., and P. Zanker, eds. 1995. *Stadtbild und Bürgerbild im Hellenismus: Kolloquium, München 24. bis 26. Juni 1993.* Munich.
Wyss, B. 1936. *Antimachi Colophonii reliquiae.* Berlin.

———. 1949. "Gregor von Nazianz, ein griechisch-christlicher Dichter des 4. Jahrhunderts." *Museum Helveticum* 6: 177–210.
Youtie, H.C. 1970. "Callimachus in the Tax Rolls." Pp. 545–551 in D.H. Samuel, ed., *Proceedings of the Twelfth International Congress of Papyrology*. Toronto. [Reprinted as pp. 1035–1051 in Youtie, *Scriptiunculae* (Amsterdam, 1973), vol. 2.]
Zanetto, G., S. Martinelli Tempesta, and M. Ornaghi, eds. 2007. *Vestigia antiquitatis*. Milan.
Zanetto, G., and M. Ornaghi, eds. 2009. *Argumenta antiquitatis*. Milan.
Zaninovic, M. 1994. "Tradizioni dionisiache tra Paros e Pharos." *Ktèma* 19: 209–216.
Zanker, G. 1987. *Realism in Alexandrian Poetry: A Literature and Its Audience*. London.
Zehles, F.E., and M.J. Zamora. 1996. *Gregor von Nazianz: Mahnungen an die Jungfrauen (Carmen 1, 2, 2)*. Paderborn.
Zetzel, J.E.G. 1981. "On the Opening of Callimachus, Aetia II." *Zeitschrift für Papyrologie und Epigraphik* 42: 31–33.
———. 1983. "Re-creating the Canon: Augustan Poetry and the Alexandrian Past." *Critical Inquiry* 10: 83–105. [Reprinted as pp. 107–129 in R. von Halbert, ed., *Canons* (Chicago, 1984).]
Ziegler, K. 1937. "Kallimachos und die Frauen." *Die Antike* 13: 20–42.
———. 1949. "Paradoxographoi." Cols. 1137–1166 in A. von Pauly et al., eds., *Real-Encyclopädie der classischen Altertumswissenschaft*, 2. Reihe, vol. 18. Stuttgart.
———. 1966. *Das hellenistische Epos: Ein vergessenes Kapitel griechischer Dichtung*. Leipzig.
Zinato, A. 1975. "Tecnicismi e interferenze semantiche nel linguaggio callimacheo." *Bollettino dell'Istituto di Filologia Greca (Padua)* 2: 209–229.

INDEX LOCORUM

Achilles
  Περὶ ἐξηγήσεως, 449–50
Achilles Tatius
  In Arat. isag., 100n28
Aelian
  VH
    3.26, 489
    8.8, 488n49
    8.9, 102
    8.18, 488, 488n50
Aeschylus
  Ag.
    36, 391n17
    1176, 470n31
    1624, 370
  Cho.
    968, 466
  Eum.
    721, 440n17
  Pers.
    613, 467n24
    1025–1026, 501
  Sept.
    71, 467
    106, 467
    131, 466
    644, 466
    1056, 467
  Supp.
    307–308, 468
    761, 403n41
  fr. 72 Radt, 467n24
  fr. 341 Radt, 301n61
Aesop
  Fables
    14 Perry, 376
    20 Perry, 376
    184 Perry, 381
    432 Perry, 376
    228 Hausrath, 372
    233 Hausrath, 376
Alcaeus
  fr. 42.1 V., 339n21
  fr. 343 V., 339n21
Alcman
  PMG 26, 306n80
  PMG 27, 336
  PMG 29, 449

Alexander Aetolus
  fr. 3 Magnelli, 483n28
Amelesagoras
  FGrH 330 F 1, 351
  FGrH 330 F 2, 481n19
Amphis
  Dithyrambus fr. 14 KA, 297
Anacreon
  PMG 358, 408n3
  PMG 378, 555
Antagoras of Rhodes
  fr. 1.1 Powell, 441, 442n20
  fr. 1.4 Powell, 442
Anthologia Palatina
  4.2, 550n56
  6.130, 198n64
  6.131.3, 198n62
  7.42, 185n23
  7.42.7–8, 94
  7.78, 593
  7.154, 114n90
  7.281, 549n52
  7.377.5–6, 542
  7.392, 549n52
  7.409, 540
  7.465, 549
  7.504.2, 466n23
  7.711, 539–40
  7.713, 539
  9.130, 512
  9.175, 100n26
  9.559, 320n42
  9.685, 390n14
  11.20, 543
  11.130, 542
  11.130.5–6, 104n48
  11.183.5, 550n57
  11.275.2, 94
  11.321, 104n47, 402, 550n56
  11.322, 402
  14.71, 273n24, 274–75
  14.71.1–2, 275
  14.71.3–4, 274
  14.74, 273n24, 274
  200.2, 536n4
Antigonus of Carystus
  FGrH 330 F 1, 358
  Hist. mirab. 129–173, 120, 124n15

Antimachus
  fr. 41a.7 Matthews, 197n61, 440n17
Antiphanes
  fr. 189.9 KA, 397n27
  fr. 207.7-9 KA, 290
Antoninus Liberalis
  Met. 4.5, 490
Apollonius Rhodius
  Arg.
    1.1-2, 475n1
    1.2, 343n30
    1.212-236, 475n1
    1.507-511, 184
    1.730-734, 184
    1.1213-1220, 477
    2.317-323, 126
    2.1233-1234, 184
    3.114-144, 408
    3.276-277, 468n28
    3.415, 467
    3.658, 458n7
    3.832, 461n11
    3.927-939, 559n102
    3.1323, 150
    4.110, 185
    4.259-260, 175n49
    4.272-279, 175n49
    4.303-304, 73-74
    4.452-481, 66
    4.902-911, 292
    4.911, 467n26, 475n1
    4.1001-1003, 74
    4.1177-1179, 185
    4.1201-1202, 185
    4.1561, 211
    4.1727, 74
  Σ in A.R. 1.1212-1219, 477, 477n10
    in A.R. 2.705-711, 128
    in A.R. 3.1323, 71
Apollonius Sophista
  10.13 Bekk., 111n78
Apostolius
  5.72, 391n18
  6.55, 403n43
  8.89c, 385n2
  9.89, 389n11
  16.76, 399n33
  17.32a, 389
Appendix Proverbiorum
  1.95, 396
  3.60, 397
Apuleius
  Met.
    1.14, 391n18
    11.5, 262

Aratus
  AP 11.437 (= 2 GP), 140n6
  Phaen.
    287-299, 321
    343, 467n26
    1124, 548n50
  Σ in Arat., 110n74
Archestratus of Gela
  SH 154.16, 174n45
Archilochus
  frr. 168, 185 W., 330n2
Argonautica [Orph.]
  228, 551n63
  364, 551n63
  1136-1141, 551n63
  1251, 551n63
  1265, 551n63
  1282, 551n63
Aristaenetus
  Epist.
    1.10, 69-70, 103, 114n91
    1.15, 69-70, 103
[Aristeas]
  9-10, 231n24
  10, 231
Aristophanes
  Ach.
    398-399, 428
  Av.
    687-689, 419
  Eq.
    277, 399n34
  Lys.
    435-444, 398n29
  Nub.
    1367, 318n37
  Pax
    832-837, 297
    835-837a, 294n26
    1200, 397
  Ran.
    804, 505
    939-943, 315
    1365-1368, 425
  Thesmo.
    94, 399n34
  Vesp.
    1022, 290n7
  fr. 233 KA, 146
  Σ in Aristophanem, 108n68
    ad Aves, 128
    ad Lys.
      FGrH 334 F 27, 357
    ad Nub. 260-261, 483
    ad Pac. 1067, 396

INDEX LOCORUM

Aristophanes of Byzantium
  apud IG 14.1183c, 104n45
  fr. 274 Slater, 148n18
Aristotle
  Eth. Nic.
    6.4.4, 1140a, 494
    9.7.3-4, 1167b-1168a, 494
    9.7.7, 1168a, 494
  Metaph.
    933b10-14, 289
    933b15-16, 289
    982b12-21, 423n31
  Poet.
    1448a20-24, 88
    1448b, 494
    1448b4-19, 407n1
    1450a, 496
    1451a13-14, 478n13
    1451a16-35, 418
    1452a31-32, 478n13
    1455a30-b, 421n29
    1455a-b, 495
    1457b3, 146
    1459a8-10, 146
    1460a, 495, 504
    1460a18-26, 447
    1460a-b, 500
  Pol.
    1339b6, 327
  Rh.
    1357b, 424n33
    1365a10-15, 429
    1390b27-31, 421n29
    1403b31-35, 318n37
    1405b34ff., 314n19
    1406a7, 146
    1408b11, 146
    1418b, 502
  fr. 610 R., 491n54
[Aristotle]
  On Physiognomy
    805b10-14, 368
    810b15-16, 369
Aristoxenus
  fr. 87 Wehrli, 320
Artemidorus
  1.72, 399n34
  4.84, 102
Asclepiades (attrib.)
  fr. 35 GP, 235
Athanadas of Ambracia
  FGrH 303 F1, 490
Athenaeus
  1.3a, 231n24
  2.56c, 102

3.82d, 324n55
4.144c, 10n13
5.189f, 132, 198n65
5.196e, 132n35
5.197c-203b, 132n37, 243n75
5.200f, 132
5.201a, 132
5.201d, 197
5.202c-e, 132
6.252c, 10
7.304b, 471
7.329a, 129
9.388b, 471
11.501e, 106n62
12.549e-f, 283n48
13.585b, 123
14.624e, 319
15.669c, 4
15.669c-d, 99
15.692f-693c, 183n16
16.688f-689a, 207n13

Bacchylides
  3.3, 336
  3.85, 327n66
  4.8, 336
  5, 346n37
  5.13-14, 336
  5.57, 339n21
  5.155, 339n21
  5.176-178, 336
  6.11, 336
  11.48-49, 215
  12.1-3, 336
  13.9, 336
  16.3, 336
  16.8-13, 301, 301n57
  17, 4
  228-231, 336
  fr. 20A.14, 339n21
Batrachomyomachia
  1-3, 543n36
  116-117, 543n36, 544
  179-182, 544
  180-191, 543n36
  190-191, 544
Bible
  Eccl. 5:14, 391n18
  Job 1.21, 391n18
  Judges 9:8-15, 376
  1 Kings 17.6-16, 554

Callimachus
Aetia (fragments cited by Pfeiffer number)
fr. 1 Pf., 308, 309–11, 314–16, 322, 324, 380
fr. 1.2 Pf., 332
fr. 1.3 Pf., 40n2
fr. 1.3–5 Pf., 325, 552
fr. 1.4 Pf., 554
fr. 1.5 Pf., 553n75
fr. 1.5–6 Pf., 324, 495
fr. 1.6 Pf., 413
fr. 1.6–7 Pf., 402
fr. 1.7 Pf., 402
fr. 1.9–12 Pf., 314
fr. 1.10 Pf., 403
fr. 1.13 Pf., 174
fr. 1.13–14 Pf., 318
fr. 1.16 Pf., 318
fr. 1.17–18 Pf., 325–26
fr. 1.20 Pf., 318, 403, 409n5
fr. 1.21 Pf., 543
fr. 1.21–24 Pf., 1n1
fr. 1.21–38 Pf., 496
fr. 1.23–24 Pf., 325, 409n5
fr. 1.23–28 Pf., 314, 321
fr. 1.25–28 Pf., 403
fr. 1.26 Pf., 115n94
fr. 1.26–28 Pf., 380
fr. 1.27–28 Pf., 552
fr. 1.30–31 Pf., 319, 403
fr. 1.32–36 Pf., 403
fr. 1.33–34 Pf., 373
fr. 1.35–36 Pf., 314
fr. 1.35–38 Pf., 303
fr. 1.36 Pf., 111
fr. 1.37 Pf., 319
fr. 1.37–38 Pf., 329, 382
fr. 1.39 Pf., 303
fr. 1.40 Pf., 303, 327
fr. 1a.20 Pf., 425
fr. 2 Pf., 185n23, 315, 455
fr. 2.1 Pf., 553
fr. 2.1–2 Pf., 333
fr. 2.5 Pf., 550n57
fr. 2a.10–15 Pf., 204, 208
fr. 2a.16 Pf., 425
fr. 3 Pf., 308, 334, 456
frr. 3–7 Pf., 347, 480
fr. 4 Pf., 72–73, 480
frr. 4–5 Pf., 456
fr. 5 Pf., 480
fr. 6 Pf., 112, 119, 456n3
fr. 7 Pf., 340, 456
fr. 7.6–7 Pf., 475n1
fr. 7.9–10 Pf., 112, 563
fr. 7.9–11 Pf., 258
fr. 7.13–14 Pf., 110, 347
fr. 7.19–20 Pf., 387, 475
fr. 7.19–fr. 21 Pf., 127
fr. 7.19–fr. 23 Pf., 311n6
fr. 7.20–21 Pf., 341n24
fr. 7.22 Pf., 335, 552
fr. 7.23–26 Pf., 340
fr. 7.23–29 Pf., 359
fr. 7.24–25 Pf., 347
frr. 22–23 Pf., 475
fr. 23.2–7 Pf., 341, 476
fr. 23.5–6 Pf., 516n11
fr. 23.6 Pf., 341
fr. 23.19–20 Pf., 111, 477
fr. 24 Pf., 73, 475
frr. 24–25 Pf., 475, 477
fr. 24.2–6 Pf., 341
fr. 24.6–7 Pf., 149–50
fr. 24.10 Pf., 536n4
fr. 25.21–22 Pf., 48
frr. 26–31 Pf., 129
fr. 26.5 Pf., 111
fr. 26.7 Pf., 146
fr. 27 Pf., 110n74, 341
fr. 28 Pf., 341
fr. 37 Pf., 341
fr. 41 Pf., 413
fr. 42 Pf., 109
fr. 43 Pf., 127, 159, 341–42, 362, 424
fr. 43.42 Pf., 558n95
fr. 43.46–55 Pf., 337
fr. 43.56 Pf., 335
fr. 43.57 Pf., 342
fr. 43.70–71 Pf., 78–79, 342
fr. 43.74–83 Pf., 342
fr. 43.86–87 Pf., 337
fr. 43.117 Pf., 300
fr. 44 Pf., 174
fr. 51 Pf., 365
fr. 52 Pf., 111
fr. 53 Pf., 111
fr. 54 Pf., 108n69
fr. 63 Pf., 365, 489n52
fr. 64 Pf., 488, 491, 591n10, 598–600
fr. 64.1–2 Pf., 390, 491
fr. 64.1–14 Pf., 599
frr. 64–66 Pf., 144
frr. 67–75 Pf., 482–84
fr. 67.1–2 Pf., 483
fr. 67.3 Pf., 483
fr. 67.8 Pf., 545n42
fr. 67.11–14 Pf., 483

INDEX LOCORUM

frr. 68–69 Pf., 483
fr. 69 Pf., 590n8
fr. 71.50–77 Pf., 486
fr. 72 Pf., 484
fr. 73 Pf., 108n68
fr. 73.2 Pf., 483
fr. 75 Pf., 402, 590
fr. 75.1 Pf., 540
fr. 75.1–3 Pf., 514
fr. 75.4–9 Pf., 205, 401–2
fr. 75.8–9 Pf., 424
fr. 75.9 Pf., 497
fr. 75.12–19, 69
fr. 75.13–15 Pf., 388
fr. 75.14 Pf., 484
fr. 75.15, 540
fr. 75.16 Pf., 484
fr. 75.20 Pf., 484
fr. 75.28 Pf., 550n61
fr. 75.48 Pf., 551n63
fr. 75.50 Pf., 557n93
fr. 75.53–56 Pf., 347
fr. 75.54 Pf., 311n5
fr. 75.54–55 Pf., 127, 350, 359, 485
fr. 75.58 Pf., 550n60
fr. 75.74 Pf., 158
fr. 75.74–77 Pf., 590–91
fr. 75.76–77 Pf., 127, 347
frr. 76–77 Pf., 127, 475
fr. 76.2 Pf., 252n13
fr. 77 Pf., 252n13
fr. 80 Pf., 483
frr. 80–83 Pf., 482–84
fr. 82.20 Pf., 483
frr. 84–85 Pf., 127, 486
fr. 86.1 Pf., 180
fr. 92.2 Pf., 128
fr. 98 Pf., 486
frr. 98–99 Pf., 127, 387
fr. 100 Pf., 216, 259
frr. 100–101 Pf., 259
fr. 101 Pf., 205, 216
fr. 101.53 Pf., 216
fr. 102 Pf., 488
fr. 103 Pf., 480
frr. 106–107 Pf., 159
frr. 108–109 Pf., 475n1
fr. 110.8 Pf., 207
fr. 110.44–46 Pf., 212–13
fr. 110.45 Pf., 206, 222
fr. 110.51 Pf., 208
fr. 110.53 Pf., 557n93
fr. 110.56–57 Pf., 13
fr. 110.63–64 Pf., 77–78

fr. 110.71–72 Pf., 390
fr. 110.94a–b Pf., 206, 219
fr. 110.51–58 Pf., 219
fr. 112 Pf., 6n7, 204, 315, 592–93
fr. 112.2 Pf., 200, 208, 593n14
fr. 112.8 Pf., 180
fr. 112.8–9 Pf., 563
fr. 112.9 Pf., 6, 348
fr. 113 Pf., 480
fr. 114 Pf., 258
fr. 114.2 Pf., 258
fr. 114a Pf., 216
fr. 114b Pf., 210, 216
fr. 115 Pf., 489
fr. 115.12 Pf., 537
fr. 118 Pf., 79
fr. 126.3 Pf., 335
fr. 177.8 Pf., 440n17
fr. 178 Pf., 79, 299n50, 337, 340, 361
fr. 178.1–4 Pf., 170
fr. 178.3–6 Pf., 337
fr. 178.5–7 Pf., 170
fr. 178.8–9 Pf., 361n47
fr. 178.9–10 Pf., 400
fr. 178.11–12 Pf., 321
fr. 178.15 Pf., 393
fr. 178.15–16 Pf., 400
fr. 178.21–24 Pf., 361
fr. 178.23–24 Pf., 337
fr. 178.27 Pf., 362–63
fr. 178.27–30 Pf., 423
fr. 178.32–34 Pf., 401
frr. 179–185 Pf., 362
fr. 186.13–15 Pf., 77
fr. 188 Pf., 299n50

Aetia (fragments cited by Massimilla number)
fr. 3 M, 40n2, 204
fr. 4.1–2 M., 58n31
fr. 5 M., 40n3, 308
frr. 5–8 M., 307
fr. 7.27 M., 66
fr. 9.9–14 M., 48
fr. 9.19–21 M., 47
fr. 30.5–8 M., 49
fr. 35 M., 48n15
frr. 35–38 M., 490
fr. 50.56–57 M., 45n9, 47
fr. 50.84 M., 48
fr. 50.84–87 M., 48, 48n16
fr. 50.84–92 M., 47
fr. 50.117 M., 300
fr. 53 M., 490
fr. 96.31 M., 48

fr. 110.1-11 M., 481
fr. 110.9 M., 300
fr. 144 M., 597n24
fr. 160 M, 489
fr. 174.54 M., 62n39
fr. 174.66 M., 62n39
fr. 174.76 M., 62n39
Aetia (fragments cited by SH number)
  238.8, 335
  252, 78
  253.1a-1, 101
  253.7, 345n35
  253.14, 345n35
  254, 206
  254.1, 150
  254.2, 346
  254.5, 149
  254-268c, 475, 477
  257.4, 149
  259.5-8, 478
  259.9-11, 479
  259.16-17, 544
  259.22-23, 544
  259.23, 479
  259.25, 544
  259.27-31, 544
  259.30, 479
  259.33, 150
  260A.4, 149
Σ ad Aetia, 67-68
  ad. fr. 2a5-15 (Pf. 1949-53: 2.102), 69
  ad Victoriam Berenices, 106n62
  Scholia Florentina, 67, 76, 315, 480, 485
    1-9, 14n26, 119
    7, 312
    8-9, 315
    16, 333n8
    16-19, 185n23, 554
    18, 333n8
    21-37, 72-73, 258, 480
    29-32, 307
    30, 40, 334
    30-32, 334
    30-35, 41
    32-35, 334
    51-52, 46n10
  Scholia, London, 45, 69
Epigrams
  1 Pf. (54 GP), 205, 217-18, 382, 402, 409-10, 485n34
  1.7 Pf. (54.7 GP), 562n111
  2 Pf. (34 GP), 235n47
  2.5-6 Pf. (34.5-6 GP), 549
  5 Pf. (14 GP), 12, 126, 202, 218-19, 552
  5.7 Pf. (14.7 GP), 219
  5.12 Pf. (14.12 GP), 218
  7 Pf. (57 GP), 235n47, 300n52, 465
  7.2 Pf. (57.2 GP), 300
  8 Pf. (58 GP), 300n52
  8.2 Pf. (58.2 GP), 300, 320
  8.4 Pf. (58.4 GP), 320
  9.2 Pf. (41.2 GP), 545n42
  10 Pf. (33 GP), 235n47
  13.6 Pf. (31.6 GP), 397
  14 Pf. (44 GP), 236n50
  17.1 Pf. (45 GP), 112
  21 Pf. (29 GP), 9
  21.1-2 Pf. (29.1-2 GP), 507, 546
  21.2 Pf. (29.2 GP), 192
  21.4 Pf. (29.4 GP), 530
  23.4 Pf. (53.4 GP), 548n50
  25 Pf. (11 GP), 393
  25.6 Pf. (11.6 GP), 393
  26.3-4 Pf. (47.3-4 GP), 104n50
  27 Pf. (56 GP), 314, 454-55
  27.1 Pf. (56.1 GP), 454-55
  27.4 Pf. (56.4 GP), 547
  28 Pf. (2 GP), 320, 320n42, 430-33, 436
  28.1Pf (2.1 GP), 525
  28.3 Pf. (2.3 GP), 291n10
  28.4 Pf. (2.4 GP), 432
  31 Pf. (1 GP), 432-33
  32 Pf. (7 GP), 597n21
  35 Pf. (30 GP), 507
  35.1 Pf. (30.1 GP), 192
  35.2 Pf. (30.2 GP), 401
  37 Pf. (17 GP), 13, 174n46
  42 Pf. (8 GP), 515n8
  42.5-6 Pf. (8.5-6 GP), 101
  43 Pf. (13 GP), 394
  43.6 Pf. (13.6 GP), 400n35
  44 Pf. (9 GP), 394
  44.2 Pf. (9.2 GP), 299
  44.6 Pf. (9.6 GP), 557
  46 Pf. (3 GP), 236
  46.3 Pf. (3.3. GP), 536n4
  47 Pf. (28 GP), 205, 222
  48 Pf. (26 GP), 470, 473, 505
  48.3 Pf. (26.3 GP), 470
  48.4-5 Pf. (26.4-5 GP), 470
  48.5 Pf. (26.5 GP), 300, 470
  48.6 Pf. (26.6 GP), 470
  49 Pf. (27 GP), 300n54
  51 Pf. (15 GP), 202, 209-10, 346

INDEX LOCORUM

51.3 *Pf. (15.3 GP)*, 210n15
52 *Pf. (6 GP)*, 395
55 *Pf. (16 GP)*, 13
56 *Pf. (25 GP)*, 546
57 *GP*, 235n47
58.2 *Pf. (50.2 GP)*, 545n42
59 *Pf. (59 GP)*, 595n17
fr. 395 *Pf. (66 GP)*, 589
fr. 398 *Pf. (67 GP)*, 540
fr. 400 *Pf. (70 GP)*, 571
Hecale (cited by Hollis number)
fr. 1 H., 315n27, 343n30, 353, 354, 478
fr. 2 H., 354
fr. 2.2 H., 108, 554
fr. 3 H., 354
fr. 4 H., 354
fr. 5 H., 356
fr. 7 H., 355
frr. 7–15 H., 355
fr. 9 H., 113, 557n93
fr. 17.3–4 H., 354
fr. 29 H., 113, 145
fr. 34 H., 145
fr. 35 H., 145, 151, 421, 554
fr. 36 H., 151, 559n101
fr. 36.4 H., 364n64
fr. 40.3 H., 564n123
fr. 40.5 H., 478
fr. 41 H., 295n28, 478
frr. 44–47 H., 112n81
frr. 47–49 H., 478
fr. 48.5 H., 559n102
fr. 53 H., 109
fr. 56 H., 372
fr. 65 H., 423
fr. 68 H., 559n102
fr. 69 H., 351, 418
fr. 70 H., 351
fr. 70.5 H., 550n60
fr. 70.9–11 H., 378
frr. 70–74 H., 378
frr. 70–76 H., 424
fr. 71 H., 151
fr. 73 H., 351
fr. 73.7 H., 550n60
fr. 73.13–14 H., 352
frr. 73–74 H., 357
fr. 74 H., 351
fr. 74.9 H., 357n32, 559n102
fr. 74.21 H., 559
fr. 77 H., 412
fr. 78 H., 470n31
frr. 79–83 H., 356, 478
fr. 80 H., 109, 418

fr. 80.4 H., 554
frr. 84–92 H., 357
fr. 85 H., 300
fr. 113.3 H., 115n94
fr. 116 H., 90, 469n31
fr. 117 H., 468
fr. 118 H., 552n70
fr. 132 H., 354
fr. 146 H., 109
fr. 168 H., 412
fr. 169 H., 357
fr. 176 H., 90
fr. inc. 178 H., 548n50
fr. inc. 179 H., 113, 357
Hecale (cited by Pfeiffer number)
fr. 231.2 *Pf. (= fr. 2.2 H.)*, 108
fr. 242 *Pf. (= fr. 41 H.)*, 295n28
fr. 275 *Pf. (= fr. 53 H.)*, 109
fr. 292 *Pf. (= fr. 65 H.)*, 423
fr. 299.2 *Pf. (= fr. 116 H.)*, 469n31
fr. 359 *Pf. (= fr. 146 H.)*, 109
fr. 370 dub. *Pf. (= fr. 160 inc. auct. H.)*, 564n123
fr. 371 *Pf. (= 78 H.)*, 470n31
Hymns
1.1, 385
1.1–2, 183
1.1–3, 448
1.3, 184, 187, 440, 456, 466
1.4–9, 246–47
1.4–10, 452n40
1.4–14, 186
1.5, 441
1.6–7, 443
1.6–10, 103
1.7, 184
1.7–8, 186
1.8, 103n42, 443
1.10–11, 457n5
1.11–14, 457
1.12, 458
1.13, 458, 460
1.14, 461
1.15–17, 461
1.16, 460
1.18–27, 129n28
1.19–20, 151, 460
1.19–21, 459
1.21, 460
1.22–27, 538
1.31, 557n93
1.32, 461
1.32–33, 460
1.34, 461

1.35–36, 458
1.36, 461
1.40, 458, 461
1.43, 184
1.46, 462
1.49, 462–63
1.50, 443, 462
1.52, 462
1.53, 457
1.54, 462
1.55–65, 186
1.57, 180, 184, 188, 444
1.58–59, 444, 446
1.60, 311n5, 447
1.60–67, 185, 248, 445
1.65, 443, 446–47, 594
1.65–66, 186
1.66, 463
1.66–67, 184, 462
1.67, 463–64
1.69, 189
1.69–86, 188
1.70–80, 447–48
1.74, 194n52
1.76–79, 464
1.77, 466
1.79, 464
1.79–90, 185
1.81–84, 189
1.82–83, 465
1.84, 188
1.85–90, 189, 444
1.86, 250, 444
1.87–88, 176n55
1.91, 182, 189n36
1.92, 182
1.94, 182, 189
1.95–96, 110
1.96, 189
2.1, 273
2.2, 273, 555
2.3, 273
2.5, 372
2.8, 433
2.8–11, 434
2.9–11, 263, 270, 433
2.12, 470n31
2.12–23, 433
2.17–21, 321
2.18–24, 435
2.19, 562n111
2.20–24, 250
2.25, 385
2.25–27, 250, 435

2.26, 192, 444
2.26–27, 435
2.27, 195
2.28–29, 189, 297
2.29, 191
2.32, 469n31
2.32–38, 436
2.47–54, 436
2.56–57, 191n44
2.60, 560
2.65, 10, 192
2.68, 10, 192
2.68–70, 259
2.69–71, 283
2.71, 189
2.71–72, 192
2.77–78, 284n49
2.80–83, 538–39
2.80–84, 284
2.90–95, 249
2.90–96, 211
2.91–92, 190
2.95–96, 189, 283
2.96, 192
2.100–101, 550n60
2.105–112, 543
2.105–113, 271–73, 309, 320, 322, 522
2.106, 273
2.107, 273
2.109, 273, 321
2.110–112, 275, 291n10
2.111, 273
2.111–112, 321
2.112, 276, 467, 552n73
2.113, 547
3.1, 345
3.5, 560
3.7, 560
3.8–9, 560
3.13–15, 560
3.14, 553n77
3.19–20, 560
3.20, 561n106
3.33, 559
3.48, 537
3.50, 152
3.55, 537, 551n63
3.56, 537
3.60, 551n63
3.83, 345n33
3.90–97, 559
3.91–93, 561n107
3.121–135, 185n27

INDEX LOCORUM

3.121-137, 181n10
3.148-151, 561n107
3.153, 561n106
3.154-156, 561n106
3.160-161, 477
3.183-186, 344
3.197-240, 160n12
3.245, 557n93
3.248, 553n74
3.250, 345n33
3.251-258, 196
3.252, 196
3.253, 196
3.260-267, 345
3.268, 345
4.4, 192
4.5, 343
4.6, 200
4.7, 343
4.9-10, 200
4.15, 466
4.30-33, 558
4.39, 458n7
4.82, 343, 559
4.82-85, 344-45
4.86-98, 435n7
4.96, 469n31
4.144, 537
4.160, 199
4.162-170, 188n33
4.162-204, 158
4.165-166, 196n60
4.165-190, 193
4.166-168, 199
4.166-170, 440
4.167, 200
4.168, 199
4.171, 195
4.171-187, 10
4.172, 200
4.172-173, 198
4.174, 187, 197n61
4.175-176, 196
4.183-184, 198, 199n68
4.184, 196
4.185-187, 195
4.205, 552n70
4.206-208, 199
4.210, 378
4.215, 469n31
4.229, 451
4.234, 559
4.235-255, 296-97
4.241-243, 557n93

4.242, 469n31
4.249, 372
4.249-251, 556
4.252, 343
4.257-258, 557n93
4.262, 378
4.287-288, 77
4.292, 451
4.302, 470n31
4.312-313, 301
4.316-324, 249
4.322, 378
4.325-326, 451
4.326, 452
5.14, 559
5.33, 545n42
5.34, 545n42
5.43, 467
5.56, 126n22, 486
5.83-84, 112
5.94, 470n31
5.131-137, 258
6.1, 152
6.9, 469n31, 557n93
6.44, 536n4
6.63, 205
6.70-71, 299
6.78, 564n122
6.83, 469n31
6.93, 386
6.114, 564n122
6.116-117, 386
Σ ad Hy. 2, 190
Iambi
  1 (= fr. 191 Pf.), 311, 550n59
    1.1, 330
    1.1-4, 498
    1.2, 396
    1.3-4, 330
    1.6, 396
    1.6-8, 300
    1.9, 144
    1.10-11, 13
    1.26-28, 485, 584
    1.27, 374, 396
    1.32, 397
    1.35-37, 397
    1.78-79, 397
    1.83-86, 398
    1.98, 397
  2 (= fr. 192 Pf.), 166, 550n59
    2. 8-9, 371
    2.11-12, 300n54, 318n37
  3 (= fr. 193 Pf.).37-38, 564n122

4 (= 194 Pf.), 364n64
  4.9–10, 380
  4.30, 147
  4.47–48, 372
  4.59, 398
  4.76–77, 378
  4.77, 151
  4.98–99, 379
  4.101–102, 505
5 (= fr. 195 Pf.).2–3, 62n39
  5.26–27, 549n54
6 (= fr. 196 Pf.).1, 252
  6.22, 257, 399
  6.25, 257
  6.29, 257
  6.37, 257
  6.45, 112
8 (= fr. 198 Pf.), 475n1
12 (= fr. 202 Pf.).47 Pf., 295n30
  12.69, 503
13 (= fr. 203 Pf.), 144
  13.1, 332
  13.12–14, 331
  13.17–18, 330
  13.22, 332
  13.26, 332
  13.30–33, 331, 595
  13.31–32, 294–95, 309
  13.43–45, 294
  13.47, 295
  13.52, 398
  13.54–55, 150–51
  13.58–59, 332
  13.61–62, 398
  13.62, 378
  13.64–66, 331
  13.66, 298
Iambi, unplaced fragments
  fr. 215 Pf., 300n54, 318n37, 465–66
  fr. 215.5–6, 58n31
  fr. 215.9, 56n28
  fr. 217 Pf., 106n59
  fr. 219 Pf., 300n54
  fr. 222 Pf., 110, 390
Lyric, hexameter, and elegiac fragments
  fr. 226 Pf., 166
  fr. 227 Pf., 205, 222–23
  fr. 227.6 (*Pannychis*) Pf., 399
  fr. 228 (*Apotheosis Arsinoes*) Pf., 10, 205, 222–23, 589
  fr. 228.1–4 Pf., 204
  fr. 228.5–6 Pf., 204
  fr. 228.7–39 Pf., 204

fr. 228.9 Pf., 151
fr. 228.39 Pf., 221
fr. 228.39–40 Pf., 221
fr. 228.40–75 Pf., 204
fr. 228.44 Pf., 222
fr. 228.46 Pf., 222
fr. 228.47 Pf., 211
fr. 228.47–51 Pf., 221
fr. 228.66 Pf., 211
fr. 229 (*Branchus*) Pf., 166
fr. 378 (*Galatea*) Pf., 8–9
fr. 379 Pf., 8–9, 197, 200
fr. 381 Pf., 9, 488n51
frr. 381–382 (*Ibis*) Pf., 108n69
fr. 382 Pf., 9
fr. 383.2 Pf., 206
fr. 383 Pf., 209, 346, 591–92
fr. 383.16 Pf., 109, 299n50
fr. 384 Pf., 9–10, 174n45
frr. 384 and 384a (*Sosibius*) Pf., 235–36
fr. 384.9 Pf., 147
fr. 384.35–36 Pf., 111
fr. 384.39–41 Pf., 180
fr. 384.53–56 Pf., 236
fr. 384.53–58 Pf., 180
fr. 384.57–58 Pf., 189
fr. 384a Pf., 10
fr. 385 Pf., 204
fr. 386 Pf., 204
fr. 387 Pf., 110n74, 204
fr. 388 Pf., 9, 180, 204
fr. 392 Pf. (*Marriage of Arsinoe?*), 9–10, 200, 204
Grammatical fragments
  fr. 403 Pf., 126, 486
  frr. 403–466 Pf., 98
  fr. 404 Pf., 128, 147
  fr. 405 Pf., 126, 389
  fr. 406 Pf., 129
  fr. 407 Pf., 98, 124, 125, 320
  fr. 411 Pf., 129
  fr. 413 Pf., 128
  fr. 418 Pf., 128
  fr. 419 Pf., 128
  fr. 428 Pf., 128
  fr. 454 Pf., 121
  fr. 455 Pf., 301n61
  fr. 457 Pf., 129
  frr. 457–459 Pf., 320
  fr. 458 Pf., 129
  fr. 459 Pf., 129
  fr. 460 Pf., 119, 312, 314
  fr. 464 Pf., 90

INDEX LOCORUM 669

fr. 465 Pf., 98, 413
SH 292-293, 231n25
Unplaced fragments
fr. 468 Pf., 548n50
fr. 474 Pf., 112
fr. 500 Pf., 109
fr. 515 Pf., 478n11
fr. 517 Pf., 300, 302
fr. 521 Pf., 129
fr. 523 Pf., 475
fr. 527a Pf., 109
fr. 541 Pf., 126
fr. 542 Pf., 115n94
fr. 544 Pf., 300n54
fr. 545 Pf., 115n94
fr. 548 Pf., 119n2
fr. 549 Pf., 115n94
fr. 556 Pf., 363
fr. 571.1 Pf., 564n123
fr. 598 Pf., 462n15
fr. 603, 74
fr. 604 Pf., 108n68, 300n54
fr. 612 Pf., 126n22, 454, 486
fr. 628 Pf., 469n31
fr. 631 Pf., 112
fr. 635 Pf., 112
fr. 643 Pf., 300
fr. 655 Pf., 475
frr. 661-665 Pf., 108n69
fr. 667 Pf. + SH 276, 300
fr. 668 Pf., 475n1
fr. 669 Pf., 110
fr. 672 Pf., 111
fr. 696 Pf., 112
frr. 696-699 Pf., 108n69
fr. 714 Pf., 564n123
fr. 715 Pf., 151, 174n45
fr. 741 Pf., 113
Testimonia
T 1 Pf., 11
T 1.11 Pf., 299
T 4c Pf., 11
Callixenus
FGrH 627 F 2, 176n58
Cassius Dio
69.4.6, 105
Cassius Longinus
fr. 34, 104n49
Catullus
Carm.
1, 528
51, 527
65, 527
65.16, 520n19

66 (Lock of Berenice), 70, 527
66.11-12, 179
66.11-14, 207n11
66.20, 179
66.26, 211
66.35-36, 179
66.36, 213
66.43-46, 212n19
66.63-64, 78
95, 528
116, 527
116.2, 520n19
Catulus, Lutatius
fr. 1 Courtney, 528n32
Choniates, Michael
Epist.
103.64-65, 116
110.54-55, 116
111.65-66, 116
128.4, 116
146, 115n96
173.159-160, 116
174.36-40, 117
174.37, 115
Theano
337-342, 116n99
Choricus
Or. 32.24, 104n50
Cicero
Brut. 76, 517n13
De or.
2.8-10, 256
2.86, 599
2.249, 491n55
3.177, 314n21
3.199, 314n21
3.310-312, 314n21
Tusc. 1.93, 101
Cleidemus
FGrH 323 T1, 300
Clement of Alexandria
Protr. 2.40.2, 481n19
Strom.
5.4, 102
5.8.48, 102n40
5.8.50, 94-95, 99n23
5.13.3, 268n13
Corpus Theognideum
579-582, 431
959-962, 431
Curtius Rufus, Q.
10.10.20, 230n18
Cyrenean Purity Regulation
A 1-3, 271

Cyril of Alexandria
   Adv. Iul. 6, 102

Damascius
   Isid. fr. 282, 104n52, 105n54
Damastes of Sigeum
   FGrH 5, 172n35
David
   In Ar. Categ., 103n43
[Demetrius]
   On Style
      20.1, 320n42
      36, 319n40
      38, 320n41
      54, 326
      66, 319n40
      77, 319n40
      120, 319n40
      190–239, 315
Democritus
   Peri Homeron... 68 B 20a DK, 146
Demosthenes
   De cor. 262, 318n37
Dieg. (P.Mil.18)
   IV 6–17, 487
   IV 30 Pf., 299n50
   IV 36–V 2, 488
   V 3–8, 480
   V 33–39, 475n1
   VI 1.3–4, 471
   VI 10–17, 485n34
   VIII 21–32, 475n1
   IX 32–38, 293
   IX 35–36, 295n29, 331
   X 11–13, 13n21
   XI 4–7, 478
Dieg. (P.Oxy. 2263)
   I 14–30, 129
Dinias
   FGrH 306 F 6, 393n23
Dio Chrysostom
   Or. 12, 251
Diodorus Siculus
   10, fr. 11 C.-S., 102
   13.83, 492n59
   13.86.1, 492n61
   15.7, 318n37
   18.7.1, 136
   18.14.1, 228n13
   18.28.2, 230n18
Diogenes Laertius
   1.28–33, 485
   1.79, 389
   1.80, 102

2.111, 102
2.116, 253
3.8, 312n11, 315
3.20, 11
5.78, 313n16
5.81, 313n17
9.17, 102
Diogenianus
   1.21, 393n22
   1.49, 402n40
   3.37, 393n21
   3.73, 403n43
   4.2, 391n18
   5.49, 388n7
   6.15, 387n5
   7.57, 399n33
   7.89, 398n31
   7.95, 389
   7.96, 387n5
   8.46, 389n11
Dionysius of Halicarnassus
   Comp.
      3, 323n48
      16.1, 320n43
      23, 315
   On Dinarchus 1, 98n19
Dionysius Periegetes
   Σ *in Dion. Perieget.*, 110n74
Dionysius Thrax
   Ars Gram. 1, 311n8
   Σ *in Dion. Thrac.*
      170.5, 311n8
      303.28, 311n8
      471.34–35, 311n8
      568.15, 311n8
Dio of Prusa
   Or. 36.9, 139
Dioscorides
   Ep. 14 GP, 237n51
Dioxippus
   fr. 2.1 KA, 398n28
Duris of Samos
   FGrH 76 F 6.33–34, 486

Ennius
   Ann. fr. 210 Sk., 516
Epica adespota
   4 Powell, 536n4
Epicharmus
   fr. 71.3 Kaibel, 421
   fr. 113.4115 KA, 143n11
Epimenides
   fr. 1 DK, 103n42
   fr. 5 Kinkel, 457n4

Epiphanius
   Panarion 2.169.13, 103n42, 105n52
Eratosthenes
   Erigone frr. 22–27 Powell, 299
Etymologicum Genuinum
   a 551 L.-L., 107
   a 1198, 107
   a 1279, 113
   a 1316 L.-L., 107
   b 207, 107
   Vatic. gr. 1818, 26
Etymologicum Gudianum
   239.18 Stef., 107
Eunapius
   497, 256n25
   Vit. soph. p. 494 Boiss., 104n48
Euphorion
   Dionysus
      frr. 13–18 Powell, 299
      fr. 51.8–10 Powell, 537
Euripides
   Bacch.
      111, 469n31
      142, 291n11
      494, 470
   El.
      1, 470n31
   Hec.
      84, 470n31
      509, 469n31
      661, 469n31
   Hel.
      1485, 459
   HF
      636, 469n31
      636–700, 303
      646, 306n83
      673–694, 304
      677, 307
      680–681, 305
      683–684, 307
      687–694, 305
      894–895, 303
   Hyps.
      POxy 852 fr. 1, col. III, 15, 470n31
   IA
      950–951, 398n29
   IT
      1099–1102, 378
   Med.
      92, 505
      176, 469n31
      187–188, 505
      320, 470n31
   Or.
      119, 469n31
   Phoen.
      356, 469n31
      939, 467n27
      965, 469n31
      1567, 470n31
   Supp.
      90, 469n31
   Tro.
      726–739, 370
   fr. 330b Kannicht, 320n43
   fr. 477 Kannicht, 301n61
   fr. 863 Nauck², 469n31
   Σ *in Euripidem*, 108n68
      Alcestis 1, 436n10
      Hippolytus, 356
      Medea 1334, 66
Eusebius
   Praep. evang.
      3.8.1, 101n33
      5.34.15–16, 487
      13.13.23, 102
Eustathius
   Il.
      46.3–5, 215
      522.15, 115n94
      629.55, 115n94
      781.52, 115n94
      870.6, 115n94
      985.56, 115n94
      1271.34, 115n94
      1317.19, 115n94
      1372.2, 115n94
   Od.
      1.185 (= 1.49.19), 488n50
      1778.27 (= II. 96, 7), 115n94

Galen
   Comm. 2 in Hippocr. Libr. 3 epidem.
      239, 132n34
Gellius, Aulus
   4.11.2, 102
   9.11, 197
Gregory Cyprian
   1.82, 391n18
Gregory of Nazianzus
   Carm.
      1.1.1.8–9, 555
      1.1.11.14–16, 555
      1.2.1.722–723, 556

1.2.2.172–176, 554
1.2.2.302, 554
1.2.14.101, 556–57
2.2.3.144, 563n115
Epist.
   54, 555n86

Hedylus
   Ep. 4 GP, 237
Heliodorus
   Aethiopica 4.19.3, 101n35
Heracleodorus
   On Poems 1.197.4, 315n26
Heraclitus
   Quaestiones homericae 39, 215n23
Hermesianax
   fr. 7.69–74 Powell, 291
Herodas
   Mimiambi
      1.31, 235n44
      6.101, 472
      8, 330n3
Herodian
   περὶ μονήρους λέξεως 915.17 Lentz, 103
Herodotus
   1, 212n18
   1.1–2, 213
   2.45, 174
   2.53, 246
   2.103.2–104, 175n49
   2.112, 221
   2.156, 199
   6.119, 139
Hesiod
   Op.
      11–13, 442
      17, 442n21
      160, 461
      202, 327n66
      202–212, 369
      210, 385
      213–247, 185n25
      225–247, 181n10
      250, 465
      265, 389, 550n57
      348, 386
      353, 395
      753–754, 460
   Theog.
      3–4, 333
      7–8, 333
      22, 333
      22–23, 455
      23, 333
      26–27, 443
      26–28, 327–28, 446, 456, 457n4
      27–28, 594
      31–32, 333
      32–34, 334, 336
      39–40, 333
      43, 333
      46, 246
      60, 334
      64–65, 334, 347
      73–74, 247
      77–79, 334, 336
      79, 336
      80–103, 185n24, 250
      94–96, 189, 448
      95, 464
      96, 188, 464
      105–107, 335
      108, 246
      111–112, 247
      114–115, 335
      116, 335
      158, 461n12
      187, 462n15
      199, 462
      282–283, 462n16
      385–388, 463
      390–394, 440
      424, 197n61, 440n17
      453–457, 183
      453–506, 456
      467, 460
      467–506, 185
      469–471, 460
      477, 457
      478, 183
      484, 457n5
      486, 440n17, 456
      490–491, 463
      617–719, 440
      677, 463
      801–806, 458
      820, 187, 466
      839, 320n42
      881–885, 183, 445–46
      885, 247
      907–911, 456n3
   fr. 27 M.-W., 318–19
   fr. 128 M.-W., 459
Hesychius
   κ 1123, 388n7
Hippocratic Corpus
   Art. 69, 472
Hipponax
   fr. 32.4 W. (fr. 42.4 Deg.), 472n32

INDEX LOCORUM

fr. 37 W. (fr. 46 Deg.), 472n32
fr. 78 W. (fr. 78 Deg.), 331n6
fr. 84 W. (fr. 86 Deg.), 331n6
fr. 115.8 W. (fr. 115.8 Deg.), 421
fr. 117.4 W. (fr. 196 Deg.), 472n32

Homer
  Il.
    1.9, 248
    1.36, 248
    1.169, 277n29
    1.255–258, 379
    1.324–325, 538
    1.526–527, 257
    1.528–530, 251, 499
    2.209–211, 320n43
    2.469, 485
    2.484–487, 327n66
    2.485–486, 336
    2.492, 341n23
    2.497, 326
    3.3–6, 174
    3.222, 196n59
    3.353, 197n61
    4.145, 466
    5.703–704, 344
    6.160, 479
    6.311, 257
    6.464–484, 407
    7.87, 197n61
    9.486–491, 407
    11.481, 479
    11.702, 466
    13.355, 183
    14, 216–17
    14.181, 215
    14.292–351, 215
    14.508–510, 334
    14.511, 335
    15.166, 183
    15.186–193, 183
    15.187–193, 247, 446
    15.360–364, 407
    15.607–608, 538
    16.234–235, 77
    16.259, 485
    16.259–265, 369, 407
    16.353, 479
    16.825, 467
    17.98–99, 385
    17.122, 320n43
    17.265, 320n43
    18.568–572, 408
    19.357, 196n59
    19.418, 524n27
    20.62–63, 558
    20.165, 479
    20.202, 74
    21.454, 119n2
    22.45, 119n2
    23.369, 466
    23.595, 433
  Od.
    1.1, 343n30
    3.1–66, 248
    3.348, 563n115
    3.479–480, 421
    4, 592
    4.770–771, 564n122
    6.100–101, 408, 408n3
    7.246–247, 458n7
    8.335, 189n36
    8.487–491, 327n66, 419
    11.365–368, 419
    12.109, 277n29
    13–19, 443n24
    14, 478
    15.343, 146
    17.217, 93n1
    17.218, 400
    21.154, 277n29
    23.147, 408
  Σ in Homerum, 112, 128
    ad Il., 71
    bT ad Il. 209–10, 320n43
    ad Il. 9.700, 477n11
    ad Il. 14.342–351, 500
Homeric Hymns
    7.2, 341n23
    9.1, 343n29
    14.2, 343n29
    17.1, 343n29
    18.2, 189n36
    19.1, 343n29
    20.1, 343n29
    29.8, 189n36
    31.1–2, 343n29
  Hom. Hymn Apol.
    1, 341n23
    14–15, 451
    20, 315
    158–159, 451
    187–206, 249
    334–339, 440
    538–544, 434
    546, 315
  Hom. Hymn Dem.
    459, 460
    480–482, 262
    486–489, 262n36
    495, 315

Hom. Hymn Dion.
  1-4, 261
  1-6, 452n40
  5-8, 452
  7, 261
  15, 261
  31, 263
  49, 261
  50, 261
  53, 262
  54, 262
  55, 262-63
  55-57, 261
  58-59, 262
  Mosquensis, 184n20
Hom. Hymn Merc.
  1, 343n29
  3, 187n30
  14, 187n30
  17-19, 176n55, 188
  43-46, 176n55
  265, 187n30
  377, 187n30
  423b-435, 183n18
  427-428, 247
  580, 315
Hom. Hymn Ven.
  1, 343n29
Horace
 Ars Poetica 310, 530
 Carm.
  1.3, 571
  2.20.4, 530
  4.2.5-8, 530
  4.15, 519
 Epist.
  1.19.42, 530
  2.1.225, 518
  2.2.99-101, 520, 520n19, 530
  2.2.112, 530
  2.2.120, 530
 Sat.
  1.2.101-110, 530
  1.2.105-108, 520n19
  1.4-34, 399
  1.10.31-39, 519
  2.6.14-15, 520n18
Hyginus
 Fabulae 273-277, 24n8

Ibycus
 PMGF S151.23-48, 338n18
inscriptions
 ICret. 4.243, 198n62

I.Lindos 2.484, 269
I.Lindos 2.487, 269
LSAM 20.36-41, 269n18
LSS 108, 269
LSS 115.28, 273
LSS 115.29, 273
LSS 115.30, 273
LSS 115 A 26-31, 272
OGIS 54, 179
OGIS 56, 179
OGIS 90.11, 199n67
OGIS 90.27, 199n67
SEG 9.1.23-25, 283
SEG 9.11-13, 283n47
SEG 9.11-44, 283
SEG 43.710, 268
SGO 1.01.19.01, 276-77
SGO 1.02.02.01.7-9, 277-78
SGO 1.02.02.01.9-13, 277-78
Io. Gaz. (John of Gaza)
 1.45, 562n111
Ion of Chios
 frr. 26a and 31 Leurini, 295n28
 frr. 82-84 Leurini, 297
 fr. 89.2 Leurini, 298
 fr. 93 Leurini, 296-97
 fr. 106 Leurini, 296
IEG 27.5-7, 449
Isidorus
 Hymn to Isis
  3.1-18, 185n26
  3.13, 199
Istrus
 FGrH 334 F 7, 353, 360
 FGrH 334 F 10, 353
 FGrH 334 F 50-52, 259

John Chrysostom
 PG 62.676D, 103n42
John of Damascus
 PG 95.1028B, 103n42
Justin
 16.2.7, 182n13
Juvenal
 8.32-38, 479n16

Leo the Philosopher
 Poem on Job 88-89, 562-63
 LXX Job 1.21, 563
Libanius
 Epist. 72, 399n33
Livy
 7.10.9, 197

[Longinus]
On the Sublime
3.1, 319n40
6.1, 311n8
33, 101n36, 500
33.5, 294
35.3–5, 499
Lucian
De conscr. hist. 57.9–10, 104
Pseudol. 32, 390n14
[Lucian]
Amores 48 = fr. 571 Pf., 102
Lucilius
623 Marx, 391n18
Lycophron
Alex.
21, 252, 139
1021–1026, 73
1291–1301, 213
Σ *ad Alex.*
717, 78–79
832, 326
869, 78–79
Lydus, John
Mens. 4.1, 95
Lyr. adesp. 923.4, 290n7

Machon
fr. 9.14–17 Gow, 291
Macrobius
Saturnalia 5.57, 397
Manetho
FGrH 609 F 14, 15, 174n47, 239n58
[Manetho]
Ἀποτλεσματικά
6.392, 551n63
6.690, 551n63
Martial
10.4.9–12, 104n47
10.4.11–12, 520n19
10.4.12, 94
Menander
Aspis
433–464, 142
Monost.
341, 385n2
fr. 137 KT, 398n28
Meropis
PEG 1.131–135, 152
Mnaseas
On Oracles fr. 58 Cappelletto, 393
Moschus
2.31, 461n11

Naumachius
GDRK 29.22, 550n61
Nicander
Alex. 232–234, 539
Ther.
141–143, 538
793, 466n23
950, 538
Nicetas Eugenianus
1.243–244, 564n123
3.48–49, 564n123
6.223, 564n123
7.199–200, 564n123
Nicolaus of Damascus
FGrH 90 F 52, 489
Nonnus
Dionysiaca
1.139, 557n93
1.231, 557n93
1.514–515, 557n93
2.237–238, 558
3.82–122, 559
3.324, 557n93
4.455, 558n98
6.290–291, 558n98
9.169–183, 561
9.177, 561n107
10.292–307, 560
11.54, 557n93
13.49–52, 558
13.309–392, 558
13.316–317, 558n95
15.171, 559
16.75–143, 559
16.126–130, 559–60
16.224, 557n93
17.37–86, 559n101
20.320–321, 557n93
25.18, 559
25.27, 561
36.48–57, 561
36.98–100, 558
38.145, 557n93
45.103–169, 261
45.306–307, 557n93
Paraphrase of the Gospel of John
21.142, 561n110

Oppian
Halieutica
1.114, 552n70
1.338–359, 552
2.367, 552n70
4.68, 552

[Oppian]
  Cynegetica
    1.20–21, 552
    1.28–29, 552
    2.355, 461n11
    4.322–323, 552n73
Or. Sib.
  3.737, 390n14
  5.464–467, 196n59
[Orpheus]
  Lithica 116, 550n60
Ostraca
  OBerol inv. 12605, 148n20
Ovid
  Am.
    1.1, 519
    1.15.11–15, 469
    1.15.13–14, 520n19
    1.15.14, 515
    2.4.19–20, 520n19
  Ars am.
    1.179, 523
    2.497, 483
    3.3.29, 520n19
  Fast.
    1.1, 96, 524
    1.1–2, 95
    1.7, 311n5
    1.8, 524
    1.13, 525
    1.13–14, 524
    3.543–566, 525
    3.577–578, 525
  Her.
    20–21, 521
  Ibis
    53, 520n19
    623–624, 489
    Σ in Ibidem 108n69
  Met.
    1.3–4, 524
    2.540–632, 524
    2.760–835, 523
    3.572–700, 261
    7.365–367, 524
    7.401–424, 524
    8.530–539, 523
    8.725–726, 524
    8.728–778, 523
  Pont.
    4.16.32, 520n19
  Rem. am.
    381–382, 520n19, 521
  Tr.
    2.367–368, 520n19
    2.424, 515
    5.2.67–68, 139
    5.4.38, 520n19
    5.7.51, 139
Oyster Riddle, 983–94
  Σ, 106n62

Paean Erythraeus in Seleucum Powell, 183n16
Pamphilus
  Onomasticon
    2.56c, 102
    7.284c, 102
    7.318b, 102
    7.327a, 102
    10.442f, 102
    11.477c, 102
    15.668c, 102
papyri
  Commentarius Berolinensis, 359–60, 364
  PBerol
    9571v, 322n46
    inv. 9965, 148n19
    inv. 13044, 140n7
    inv. 13417, 27n14
  PCairZen
    1.59014, 151
    2.59289, 234n41
    3.59346, 138n4
    3.59406, 138n4
    3.59501 R9, 151
    4.59534, 148
    4.59535, 137
    4.59588, 137
    4.59603, 137
    4.59651, 137
    5.59825.19, 152
  PChic col. VI, 13, 187
  PColZen 2.60, 136
  PDerveni, 152
  PEleph 1, 138
  PGiessenKuhlmann 2.9, 147n17
  PHal 1.260–65, 137
  PHamb 128, 147n13
  PHeidSieg 180, 148n18
  PHerc 1676
    col. II, 12–13, 16–17, 318
    col. VII, 8–11, 320n43
  PHib
    1.5, 148n18
    2.172, 148n22
    2.173, 147n14
    2.175, 147, 148n18
    2.183, 147n15
  PHorak 4, 38
  PKöln 6.247, 226n3

INDEX LOCORUM 677

PLille, 138, 149
  76, 106n62, 137
  76d, 89
  78a–c, 106n62
  79, 89
  82, 106n62
  82.1.2–6, 92
  83, 147n16
  84, 106n62
  111c, 106n62
PLondLit
  90, 148n18
  160, 147n17
  181.45, 204, 208
PLouvre inv. 7733v, 106n62
PMich
  4.223.2665, 150
  inv. 3499, 27n14
  inv. 6235, 89
PMilVogl
  1.18, 85
  1.19, 85
  1.20, 84
  2.44, 84n14
  2.45, 84
  2.47, 84n12
  3.120, 84
  6.262, 84
  8.309 (Posidippus Papyrus), 137, 180
  inv. 28b, 86
  inv. 1006, 86, 489
POxy
  2.222, 487n48
  7.1011, 6, 27–28, 37–38, 53, 56, 564
  9.1362, 28
  9.1380, 223n37
  10.1241, 11n14, 231n26
  11.1362, 361–62, 362n49, 363
  15.1793, 28
  17.2079, 25, 28, 101n34, 412
  18.2168, 27n14
  18.2171, 27n14
  19.2209A–B, 79
  19.2212, 53n24, 59
  19.2213 fr. 8.1–17, 56, 487
  20.2258, 28, 38, 92, 99, 99n21, 203, 206
  20.2262, 204, 208
  20.2263, 89
  22.2332.9, 199n68
  23.2376, 29
  23.2377, 29
  27.2463, 27n14
  37.2823, 27n14
  39.2886, 27n14
  50.3537r, 550n61
  69.4711, 542n30
  inv. 112/87bII, 418n19
PRev 47.16, 151
PRyl
  1.16, 148n18
  4.556.10, 152
PSI 11.1219, 89
PStrasb inv. G 2374, 147n16
SP 3.111, 180n5
Paul
  Titus 1.12, 103n42
Pausanias
  1.2.4, 481n19
  1.4.6, 198n64
  1.7.2, 194
  1.15–16, 212n18
  2.22.8, 301
  5.11.9, 254n18
  6.6, 387
  6.6.4, 487
  6.6.5–6, 487n48
  6.6.6–10, 488
  7.2.11, 484
  8.28.4–6, 101
  10.18.7, 198n64
  10.19.3, 500
  10.19.4, 198n63
  10.20.5, 197
  10.20.7, 197
  10.21.5, 198n64
  Σ *in Pausan. 8.28.6*, 481
Pausimachus
  On Poems 1.96.3–6, 315n26
Phanocles
  fr. 1 Powell, 484n30
Phanodemus
  FGrH 325 F 11, 363
  FGrH 325 F 13, 362
Pherecrates
  fr. 86 KA, 397
Pherenicus
  SH 671.3–4, 440n17
Philo of Byzantium
  Proem. 2–3, 255
  Seven Wonders
    3.1.3, 254
    3.4, 254
Philochorus
  FGrH 328 F 73–75, 364n63
  FGrH 328 F 109, 350, 478n12
  FGrH 328 F 111, 356
  FGrH 328 F 195, 357n32
  FGrH 328 T 1, 365

Philo Judaeus
    Leg. 95, 101n35
Philodamos of Scarpheia
    Paean to Dionysus
        53–63, 281
        59–60, 301
        63, 301
        105–149, 279–80
        107–108, 281
        110–112, 281–82
        146–149, 281
Philodemus
    Ad contubern. 1.3, 388n7
    De piet. 248v, 187n31
    On Poems
        1.18, 320n43
        1.21, 319
        1.33.1–5, 318n36
        1.88, 319
        1.93, 320n43
        1.108, 320n43
        1.131.8–12, 318
        1.167.16–20, 318
        1.169.16–18, 318
        1.178, 320n43
        5, 316
        5.14.5–11, 323n51
        5.14.12, 323n49
        5.21.28, 312n11
        5.23.26–33, 317
        5.27.17–21, 317n35
        5.37.2–38.15, 324n56
        7.25–9.28, 314
        11.26–12.13, 324
        15.20–21, 318
        181.8–22, 319
    On Rhetoric
        2, 325n59
Philostratus
    Her. 2, 388n7
    VA
        1.24, 139
        6.19.2, 256n24
Phoenix of Colophon
    fr. 2 Powell, 419
Photius
    Amphil. 151.27–30 Westerink, 103n42
    Bibl.
        171.17, 398n28
        265, 491b31 = fr. 446 Pf., 98n19
        279.534a, 481
        314.17, 397
    Epist.
        166, 104n52

166.181–185, 104n51, 105n52
    fr. 405 Pf., 389
Phylarchus
    FGrH 81 F 32, 379
Pindar
    Dith.
        1.15, 339n21
        2, 321–22
        2.2, 326
        fr. 150 S.–M., 345
    Hymni
        1, 4, 184n19, 307
    Isthm.
        4, 346n37
        6.8, 449n33
        6.8–9, 183n16
        8.46a–48, 339
    Nem.
        2.1–3, 385
        2.1–5, 449
        3, 344, 346n37
        3.83, 336
        5.25, 449
        7.20–23, 445n27
        7.84, 339n21
        9, 346n37
        9.33, 461n12
        9.39, 339n21
    Ol.
        1.28–29, 445n27
        2.28, 339n21
        2.83–88, 325n57
        2.84, 327n66
        3.4–5, 339
        3.40–42, 325n57
        4.1, 187
        4.1–3, 466
        4.19–22, 475n1
        6.28–30, 339
        7.54, 183
        7.54–56, 339
        9.49, 339n21
        9.100–102, 325n57
        10, 346n37
    Pyth.
        1, 184n19, 250, 439
        4.9, 191n45
        4.32, 211
        1.52, 339n21
        2.22, 339n21
        4, 346n37
        5, 191n45, 192, 192n47
        6.21, 339n21
        8.86, 502

Paeans
  fr. 5, 193
  fr. 7, 193
  fr. 7b, 4
  fr. 7b.12, 290n7
  fr. 12.9, 339n21
Parthenia
  fr. 94b.76–78, 291n10
Prosodia
  fr. 89a, 183n16, 449n32
Threni
  fr. 125, 295
Frag, Inc. Lib.
  fr. 150, 345
Σ *in Pindar.*
  ad *Ol. 2.96f*, 188n35
  ad *Pyth. 4.60–65*, 191n45
  ad *Pyth. 4.105–106*, 191n45
  ad *Pyth. 5, 1a 172*, 188n35
Plato
  Ion
    530b10–c4, 323n49
    534b5, 332
    534b7–8, 332
    534b7–d4, 594
    534c2–3, 332
    535e1–6, 594
    53414–b2, 290–91
  Leg.
    642a, 305
    653d1–5, 305
    655d, 305
    657c, 305
    664d, 306n80
    665b–667b, 305n77
    666a–c, 306
    666b3–7, 306
    666b4–6, 307n83
    666b7, 306n83
    719c, 321
    790e1–3, 300n53
    801e, 439
    828a–835a, 307
  Phd.
    117b5, 505
  Phdr.
    248c, 556
    259c5–d7, 336
    259d3, 336
    259d3–4, 336
  Phlb.
    55b–56, 425
    66d, 449n33
  Prt.
    343a–b, 374

  Resp.
    377a–378, 407n1
    377e, 447
    378d, 323n49
    392d–394d, 88
    441a5, 300n53
    549d–550b, 502
    561c7–d1, 300n53
    586b, 398n31
    607a, 439
    607b5–6, 425
  Symp.
    215a–c, 499
    221d–222a, 499
  Tht.
    155d, 423n31
  [Plato]
    Just. 374a, 445n27
Plautus
  Bacch. 675, 398n29
  Poen. 566, 398n29
Pliny
  HN
    praef. 22, 573
    4.65, 126
    7.152, 487n49
    30.4, 231n24
    34.148, 13
    36.18, 234n42
Plutarch
  De adul. et amico
    54d, 101
  De cohib. ira
    455b–c, 101
  De exil.
    602f, 101
  De Hom.
    2.8 Kindstrand, 144
  Is.
    380d, 199n68
  Lib. educ.
    19, 389n11
  Mor.
    241, 491n55
    254A, 483n25
    315C, 490
    331B, 491n55
  Mul. virt.
    253f, 101n33
  Parall. min.
    315c = fr. 45 Pf., 101n33
  Prov.
    2.31, 387n6
  Quaest. conv.
    677a–b = fr. 59 Pf., 101n33

Quaest. Rom.
    71, 398n31
Quomodo adul.
    19e–20b, 215n23
Vit. Arat.
    12–13, 132n35
Vit. Demetr.
    18, 226n3
Vit. Sol.
    25.2, 481n20
Vit. Thes.
    6.7, 354n20
    7.2, 354
    12.2, 354
    12.3, 354n21
    12.4–5, 355
    14, 355n22, 364
    14.3, 357
    17.6, 356
[Plutarch]
  Consolatio ad Apollonium
    113e = fr. 491 Pf., 101
    115a, 101
  Plac. philos.
    880d–f, 104n46
  Proverbs
    2.31, 488n50
  Vit. X orat.
    848b, 318n37
Poliziano, Angelo
  Miscellanea
    1.80, 94n6
    1.91, 95
    2.10, 99n23
    2.47, 95
    2.57, 99n23
  Praelectio on Ovid Heroides 15, 95
  Silva Nutricia
    426–33, 94n3
Pollux
  Onom.
    6.15, 449n33
    9.72, 397
Polyaenus
  8.35, 483n25
Pomponius
  In Donat. 5, 113n85
Porphyry
  Abst. 2.19, 268n13
  Homeric Questions
    1.4, p. 15.11 Sod., 99
Posidippus
  Epigrams
    8 AB, 175n52
    11 AB, 207n13
    12 AB, 207n13
    39 AB, 237
    74 AB, 175n52, 237
    78 AB, 175n52, 191n43
    79 AB, 175n52, 191n43
    80–82 AB, 175n52
    82 AB, 191n43
    87 AB, 175n52
    95 AB, 237
    113 AB (SH 978), 175n52, 237
    114 AB (SH 961), 175n52
    115 AB (GP 11), 236
    115.3 AB, 175
    116 AB (GP 12), 236
    116.8 AB, 169n26
    119 AB (GP 13), 236
Posidonius
  fr. 44 Kidd, 323
Praxiphanes
  fr. 12 Wehrli, 323n49
  fr. 13 Wehrli, 315n24
Priscian
  Grammar
    1.11, 95
    2.12, 95–96
Proclus
  Hymn 7, 550n60
  In R. 125.29, 104n49
  In Ti. 1.90.25 Diehl, 104n49
Procopius of Gaza
  Epist. 47 G.-L., 103
Propertius
  1.1, 526
  1.18, 526
  1.39–40, 526
  2.34.29–32, 520n19
  2.34.91–94, 526
  3.1–3, 520n19
  3.1.5, 518
  3.3.13–26, 519
  3.9.43–44, 520n19
  3.11, 533n40
  4.1.3–4, 519, 527
  4.1.64, 520n19
  4.1.69, 525
  4.1.133–136, 519
  4.6.1–7, 522–23
  4.6.4, 520n19
  4.6.83–84, 522
  4.8, 514
  4.8.3–16, 513
Prosopographia Ptolemaica
  III
    5406, 239n61

VI
   14596, 234n40
   14607, 234n43
   14614, 239n58
   14632, 234n42
   14645, 233n38
   14648, 232n31
   14656, 232n31
   14717, 234n41, 235n46
   15224, 237n54
   16104, 230n19
   16546, 234n39
   16640, 236n50
   16689, 235n47
   16692, 235n47
   16724, 232n31
   16725, 244n76
   16792, 235n47
   16942, 230n20
IX
   5066, 234n41
Ptolemy I
   FGrH 138, 230n20

Quintilian
   Inst. Or.
      10.1.58, 37, 99
      12.10.9, 251
Quintus Smyrnaeus
   Posthomerica
      1.33–34, 553n77
      12.308–313, 553

Rhetorica ad Herennium
   4.8.1, 314n21
Rhianus
   fr. 10 Powell, 436n10

Sappho
   fr. 58.15 V, 306n80
   fr. 94V, 207
   fr. 103.3–4 V., 215
   fr. 124V, 336
   fr. 166V., 339n21
Satyrus
   Demes of Alexandria, 91n31
Seneca
   Brev. vit.
      2.2, 104n45
   De beneficiis
      1.3.3–4.5, 210
Seneca the Elder
   Suas. 3.7, 573

Servius
   In Aen. 1.408 = *fr. 189 Pf.*, 96
   In Aen. 7.778 = *fr. 190 Pf.*, 96
Severianus
   Fragm. in epist. ad Tit. 344.15,
      105n54
Sextus Empiricus
   Math. 1.309 = *fr. 393.3–4 Pf.*, 102
Simonides
   Elegies
      fr. 11.15–17 W., 338
      fr. 11.19–22 W., 338
      fr. 11.20–21 W., 315
Solon
   fr. 25 Gentili-Prato, 445n27
Sophocles
   Aj.
      693–705, 305n74
   Phil.
      1216, 467n24
   Trach.
      205–220, 305n74
      fr. 776 Radt, 212
   Σ *in Soph. Oed. Col.*, 365
Statius
   Silv.
      5.3.156–158, 512
      5.3.156–160, 99
      5.3.157, 520n19
Stephanus of Byzantium
   Ethnika
      375.10 M., 106n62
      635.11 M (= *fr. 40 Pf.*), 96
Stesichorus
   PMG 210.1, 338n17
Stobaeus
   3.1.172, 313
   3.7.28, 491n55
   4.52.24, 324n55
Strabo
   1.1.10, 322
   1.2.3, 322n47
   1.2.17, 322n47
   1.44, 100n32
   1.46, 100n32
   5.216, 100n32
   6.1.5, 387, 488n50
   7.39f., 187n31
   7.299, 100n32
   8.3.19, 100n29
   8.3.30, 251n9, 254, 254n18, 499
   8.353–54, 100n31
   9.3.10, 301

9.438 = fr. 200a Pf., 100, 100n31
10.3.21, 222
10.4.12, 100n29
10.484, 100n32
14.1.37, 218
14.2.19, 93n2, 317n33
14.638 = Ep. 6 Pf. = 55 GP, 100n30
17.1.8, 229n17
17.3.22 (test. 16 Pf.), 93n2
17.805 = fr. 715 Pf., 100n30
Strato
   fr. 1.43 KA, 146
   fr. 1 KA, 141
Strattis
   fr. 72 KA, 391n17
Suda, 465
   a 166, 8, 412
   a 3215, 107n66
   a 3419, 106n62
   a 4105, 111
   a 4259, 113n85
   k 227 = test. 1 Pf., 98
   l 25, 198
   m 194 = test. 24 Pf., 95, 100n24
   n 375, 111
   o 64, 387n6, 488n50
   t 522, 389n11
   t 813, 398n28
   u 108, 393n22
Suetonius
   Tib. 70, 111n77
Supplementum Hellenisticum
   Adespota
      922.9, 194n52
      958, 141n8, 196
      961, 137, 141n8
      964, 542n30
      969, 141n8, 237n54
      977, 136, 233n35
      979, 137, 141
      979.6-7, 194n52
      985, 137

Tatian
   Or. adv. Gr. 31.130, 316n31
Telestes
   Asclepius
      fr. 806 PMG, 295
      fr. 808 PMG, 295
      fr. 810 PMG, 295
Terpander
   PMG 698, 449

Theocritus
   Id.
      1, 408
         1.71, 548n50
         1.115, 548n50
      2, 414
         2.106-110, 414
      7, 330n3, 408
         7.44, 503
         7.93, 503
      11.53-79, 498
      14, 414
         14.31-32, 414
         14.48-49, 393n23
      15, 142, 235n44, 243, 414-15
         22-24, 241
         24, 151
         46-50, 175
         52-59, 415
         60, 241
         65-86, 241
         87-88, 142
      16, 292, 292n16
         44-46, 292
      17, 13, 175n51, 185, 188-89,
         195, 195n54, 195n57,
         196n60, 197, 207, 327, 440,
         449
         13-15, 188
         18-19, 199, 450
         19, 197
         39-42, 207n11
         56, 194n52, 196n60
         57, 209n15
         64-72, 159n8
         66-67, 196n60
         74-75, 188
         77-120, 185
         90, 195
         95, 189
         103, 194n52
         133-134, 215
      22
         9-10, 78
         116-117, 345
         212, 190
      24, 13
         105, 476
         105-134, 476
      29, 571
   Σ in Theocritum
      ad Id. 7, 503

ad Id. 17.58, 92
ad Id. 17.128, 206
Theodore Prodromus
  Calend. iamb.
    17 March, 564n122
  Carm. hist.
    30.274-275, 563-64
  Tetrast. VT
    32b.2, 564n122
    218b.3, 564n122
Theodoret
  PG 82.861.17, 103n42
Theognis
  19, 327n66
  30, 129-130 West, 189
  681-682 W, 327
  687, 385n2
  769-772, 327n66
  789-794, 327n66
  815, 391n17
  911a1., 564n122
Theophrastus
  On Drunkenness fr. 576 F., 302, 305
Theophylact Simocatta
  Epist. 65.4 Zanetto, 103n41
  Hist. pp. 20.9-20.11 de Boor, 103
Thucydides
  2.41.4, 424n33
Tibullus
  1.4.79-80, 413
Timaeus
  FGrH 566 F 148, 388n8
Timocles
  fr. 6.12 KA, 397n27
Timon of Phlius
  SH 786, 233n37
Timotheus
  Pers.
    202-205, 297n38
    202-240, 321n45
    236-240, 297n38
    229-231, 296
  PMG 802, 300n52
Triphiodorus
  Sack of Troy
    3, 553
    5, 553
    78-79, 553n74
    119, 553n74
    310, 553n74
    342, 553n74
    386, 553n74
    415, 553n74
    420, 553n74
    430, 553n74
    450-451, 553n74

    513, 553n74
    557, 553n74
    637, 553n74
    643, 553n74
    656-669, 553n74
    666-667, 553n75
Tzetzes, John
  Epist.
    34 Leone, 115n94
  Hist.
    8.834, 115n94

Valerius Aedituus
  fr. 1 Courtney, 528n32
Virgil
  Aen.
    2.15, 501
    2.52-53, 501
    2.258, 501
    3.94-98, 522
    7, 528, 593n14
    7.41-45, 522
  Ecl.
    6, 522, 528
    6.1-8, 520
    6.3-8, 519
    6.5, 518
    10.50, 520
  Geo.
    3, 528, 533, 593n14
Vita Eur.
  36-45, 488n49
Vita Isid.
  fr. 276 Zintzen, 105n52
Vita Nicandri
  1, 106n62

Xenomedes
  FGrH 442, 486n41
Xenophanes
  DK 21 B 1.22, 445n27

Zenobius
  1.11, 388
  1.48, 393n22
  1.51, 402n40
  2.55, 390n15
  2.73, 403n41
  2.95, 403n43
  3.49, 393n21
  4.75, 398n28
  4.95, 387n5
  5.18, 390n14
  6.18, 403
Zenobius Rec. Ath.
  3.175, 387n

INDEX RERUM

Abdera, 53, 164
Abusir el-Melek, 136
accent, spoken, 138–39, 141–42. *See also* dialects, Greek; *koinai*
Acciarini, Tideo, 96
Achaean League, 159n10
Achelous, 523
Achilles Tatius, 98, 449
  Isagoge, 110n74
Acontiadae, 51–52
Acontius, 51–52, 158, 482–84, 526, 590–91
Acosta-Hughes, B., 207–8, 215
acropolis (Athens), 164
Acte, Isthmus of, 212–13
Actium, battle of, 522
act of composition, 589–93, 589n5
Adrastea, 90
Aeetes, 475n1
Aegeus, 352–55
Aegina, 166
Aelian, 102
Aeneas, 522
Aenus, 166
Aeschylus, 137
  and allusion, 569
  influence on Callimachus, 466–68
Aesop, 13, 370, 373–74, 526n30. *See also* fables
aesthetic conflict, in Callimachus' poetry, 309–10
Aethra, 354
Aetia (Callimachus), 5, 223, 291. See also *Aetia* (Callimachus), sections of
  and aetiological paroemiography, 386–92
  and Attic presences, 365
  Banquet of Pollis, 170, 400–401, 423
  Book 1, 35, 39–42, 44–45, 127, 391
    book fragments, 71–72
    diegeseis for, 89
    geographic settings, 163
    Heracles in, 475
    influence, 553
    reconstruction of, 67–68
  Book 2, 35–36, 39–40, 42–45, 127, 365, 490
  Book 3, 35–36, 49–53, 258, 361, 390, 482–85, 591–92
    diegeseis for, 88
    Euthycles son of Astycles, 487
    geographic settings, 163
    influence, 526
    and Roman setting, 169
  Book 4
    diegeseis for, 88
    geographic settings, 163–64
    Heracles in, 475
  book fragments, 70–74
  Books 1 and 2
    Graces in, 347
    influence, 552
    Muses in, 333–37, 340–43
  Books 3 and 4
    aetiological aspects, 57–58
    connections among elegies, 58–60
    Muses in, 345–48
  chronopoetics of, 172–73
  commentaries on, 107
  content and structure, 35–36
  dialect of, 144
  dynastic discourse in, 206–8
  episodes featuring sacred games, 127
  and exclusion of Egypt, 174–75
  fable of Donkey and Cicada, 380–82
  and fables, 370–71
  geographic settings of episodes, 161–65
  geopoetics of, 169
  Hesiod in, 484–85
  influence, 513–17, 524–27, 529, 546, 558, 562–63, 565
  and kingship ideology, 179–80
  lengths of elegies, 46, 56–57
  local histories in, 349
  murder of Androgeos, 480–81
  Muses in, 329
  as object of scholarly study, 72
  papyrus fragments, 74–80
  proverbs in, 386–92
  reception of, 65–66
  and royal incest, 215–16
  Schneider's view of, 24
  Strabo and, 100

structure of, 65, 416–17, 455–56
subjects and arrangement of elegies, 46
title of, 94–96
transition in, 48
viewed through papyri, 39–62
Aetia (Callimachus), sections of
Book 1
1.1 Against the Telchines (Prologue),
40, 90, 119, 178, 275, 318–20,
402, 415–17, 423, 429–30, 437,
471, 494, 511n2, 544, 555, 571
childhood in, 495–97
influence, 515, 518–19, 522, 528,
531, 543, 552, 555
plain style in, 315
and poetics of childhood, 425–27
1.2 Invocation to the Muses, 40,
415n15, 425
1.3 The Dream, 40, 208–9, 389,
415n15
1.4 The Graces, 40–41, 45
*1.5 Return of the Argonauts and the
Rite of Anaphe*, 41, 46, 66, 416
1.6 Sacrifice at Lindus, 41
1.7 Thiodamas the Dryopian, 41–42
1.8 Linus and Coroebus, 42, 48–49
1.9 Artemis of Leucas, 42
Book 1 or 2
1/2.1 Icos, 44–45
1/2.2 The Hyperboreans, 44, 77
1/2.3 End of a Muse's speech?, 44, 47
1/2.4 Poverty?, 44
*1/2.5 Bandaged Statue of Athena at
Teuthis*, 44–45, 89n25, 481–82
Book 2
2.1 Sicilian Cities, The, 42–43,
45–47, 49
2.2 Haliartus and Crete, 43, 47
2.3 Busiris and Phalaris, 43, 46, 174
2.4 Merciful Athens, 43
Book 3
3.1 Victory of Berenice, 10, 50, 57,
68, 79–80, 89, 127, 149, 179–80,
191n43, 202–3, 206, 208–9, 211,
217, 221, 345, 477, 533, 544, 597
3.2 Phalaecus of Ambracia, 35n40,
51, 51n22, 490
3.3 The Attic Thesmophoria, 51, 365
3.4 The Tomb of Simonides, 51, 58,
390, 598–600
3.5 The Fountains of Argos, 51
3.6 Acontius and Cydippe, 51–52,
57, 62–64, 68–69, 75, 127, 158,
163, 345, 347, 387–88, 401–2,
514, 540, 590–91

3.7–9 Three unknown subjects, 52
3.10 The Nuptial Rite of the Eleans,
52
3.11 The Isindian Guest, 52
*3.12 Artemis the Goddess of
Childbirth*, 52, 57
3.13 Phrygius and Pieria, 52, 69–70,
156, 163
3.14 Euthycles the Locrian, 52–53
Fragments 157 and 158, 50
Onnes and Tottes, 51
Statue of Apollo at Delos, 51
Uncertain Thracian Story, 51
Book 4, 36, 49–50, 53–56, 180, 259,
387
4.1 Invocation to the Muses, 53
4.2 The Delphic Daphnephoria, 53
4.3 Abdera, 53
4.4 Melicertes, 53, 128
4.5 Theudotus of Lipara, 54
4.6 Limone, 54
4.7 The Boastful Hunter, 54
4.8 The Pelasgian Walls, 54
4.9 Euthymus, 54
*4.10 The Primordial Statue of Hera
at Samos*, 54, 216, 259–60
*4.11 The Other Statue of Hera at
Samos*, 54, 216, 259–60
4.12 Pasicles of Ephesus, 55
4.13 Androgeos, 55
4.14 The Thracian Oesydres, 55
4.15 The Dragging of Antigone, 55
4.16 The Roman Gaius, 55, 490–91
*4.17 The Anchor of the "Argo" Left
at Cyzicus*, 55
4.18 The Lock of Berenice, 10, 12,
55–56, 68, 75, 80, 164, 176n54,
179–80, 191, 202–3, 206–8, 211–
14, 218, 235, 346
audience for, 163n17
as hymn to Arsinoe-Aphrodite,
219
proverbs in, 390–91
time frame of, 172
4.19 Epilogue, 56, 180, 201, 208,
348, 592–93
aetiological stories
in Aetia, 170
in Iambi, 166–67
aetiology, 120–21, 126–28
and Alexandrian pathology, 131
Atthidographers and, 361
Callimachus and, 334, 337, 341–42,
387–88, 455–56, 474
and chronopoetics, 171–73

for cult of Muses in Rome, 516
and Panhellenism, 171–73
of proverbs, 386–89, 391
of Rome and Italy, 514
Aetolia, 161
Against Praxiphanes (Callimachus), 119–20, 312, 314
Agathias, 562
Agias, 127, 350, 359
Agrigentum, 163, 492
Ai Khanoum, 136
Aiora festival, 337
Alcaeus, 529–30
Alcman, 449
Alcmeon, 397
Alexander (son of Alexander the Great), 225
Alexander Aetolus, 118, 118n1, 233
Alexander the Great, 183n14, 197, 225, 230–31, 588
Alexandria, 164, 596
  Callimachus and, 9–14
  construction of, 229
  dialect of, 135
  dual identity of, 131n33
  foundation of, 1
  as geographical setting in *Aetia*, 167
  Library (*See* Library of Alexandria)
  monuments, 12–13
  Museum (*See* Museum of Alexandria)
  and New Music, 291–93
  and Pergamum, 317
  and Peripatetic critics, 313
  Serapeum, 12–13, 138
  as setting in *Iambi*, 166–67, 166n21
  war with Cyrene, 11
Alexandria-in-Arachosia (Kandahar, Afghanistan), 545
"Alexandrian," as category, 530–33
"Alexandrian pathology," 130–33
Alexandrian perspective, 167–70
alienation, and Alexandrian literary world, 131
allegory, in Hellenistic literary criticism, 327
allusion, 566–86
  as artistic process, 575
  Conte's typology of, 581
  integrative, 581
  as recovery and renovation, 575–76
  reflexive, 581, 585
  use of term, 583
Amarantus, 108n67
Amasis, 240
ambiguity, in fable, 371

Ambracia, statue of Artemis at, 490
Ambühl, A., 209
Amelesagoras, 351, 358–59, 363–64
Ammonius, 109
  De adfinium vocabulorum differentia, 95n7
Amphitres, 488–89
anabasis, 471–72
Anacreon, 338, 408
Anaphe, 161
ancient and modern
  polarization between, 518–19
  union of, 568, 572
ancient authors, as characters in Callimachus, 484–86
Androcles (father or uncle of poet Callimachus), 284
Androgeos, 40, 55, 480–81, 481n19
Andromenides, 316–22, 318n37, 319, 323, 323n53
Andros, hymn to Isis from, 548n50
Anna, 525
Anniceris, 11, 284
Anspielung, 573–75, 574n7
Antagoras of Rhodes, 3, 441, 441n18, 442
  Hymn to Eros, 184, 441
Anthesteria, 299n50, 361, 363
Anti, Carlo, 82, 82n3, 82n5, 85n16
Antigone, 55
Antigonids, 157, 238n55
Antigonus Gonatas of Macedon, 14, 158–59, 184, 194, 197, 366, 367n79
Antigonus of Carystus, 120, 124–25, 351, 358
anti-intentionality, 583
Antimachus, 105, 146–48, 152, 321, 417, 540
Antinoopolis, 76
Antiochus I, 194, 197, 233
Antipater of Sidon, 536, 539–41, 551
Antipater of Thessalonica, 543, 543n34
Antiphanes, 104
  Tritogonistes, 290
antiquarianism, 171
Antoninus Liberalis, 490
Apama, 191, 191n43
Aphrodite, 56, 215–16, 221
Apion, 107n66
Apis bull, 174n45, 220n31
Apocaucus, John, 116
Apollinarius of Laodicea, 551
Apollo, 42, 67–68, 158, 204, 485, 485n35, 522
  and Aeneas, 522

and Augustan poets, 519
in Callimachus' poetry, 292–93, 296
  Aetia Prologue, 430
  Hymns, 2–4, 189–200, 433–37, 439–40
Carneius, 283, 302n62
cult of
  on Anaphe, 41
  in Cyrene, 283–85
  at Didyma, 7–8
  cult statues of, 216, 258
  and Cyrene, 211, 283
  Delius, 302
    temple at Athens, 305
  Delphic, 302
  and fable of Laurel and Olive, 377
  on hymn, 276–82
  Maleatas, 437–38
  and Muses, 345
  oracles of, 267, 276n27
  Pythius, 302n69, 305
    sanctuary at Athens, 302
    temple at Delos, 303n69
Apollodorus (son of Dionysius of Lampsacus), 232
Apollodorus of Athens, 107
  Grammatical Inquiries into Book XIV of the "Iliad," 85
Apollonius, 135, 233, 233n35, 408–9
Apollonius Dyscolus, 71, 104, 111–12
Apollonius of Rhodes, 71, 99, 108, 171n30, 175, 233, 292, 477, 535
  Argonautica, 14, 126, 170n29, 171–72, 172n39, 184–85, 240n63, 343n30, 524
apostrophe, 590, 590n6
appropriation of enemy culture, Romans and, 533
Apsyrtus, 66
Aratus, 118, 184n21, 321, 526n30, 588–89
  Phaenomena, 3, 14, 441, 449, 454
Arcadia, as birthplace of Zeus, 442–43, 457, 459
Arcesilas IV, 191
Arcesilaus of Pitane, 294
Archaic and Classical periods, in works of Callimachus, 482–84
Archelaus, 125n19
Archelaus of Priene, *Apotheosis of Homer*, 336
Archelaus Relief, 173
Archibius, commentary on Callimachus' *Epigrams*, 111

Archilochus, 136, 147, 369, 471, 484, 529–30
  Fox and the Eagle, 373
Archimedes of Syracuse, 233
aretalogy, 438
Arethas of Caesarea, 114n90
Argives, and "Lamb Month," 42
Argonautica, Orphic, 550
Argonauts, 41, 55, 475n1
Argos, 51, 159n10, 163, 167, 219–20, 592
Aristaenetus, 25, 69–70
Aristarchus, 257n26, 294
Aristo, 322
Aristonicus, 107
Aristonous, paean to Apollo, 279n35
Aristo of Chios, 316
Aristophanes, 318n37
  Banqueters, 146
  Frogs, 314n20, 315, 427–28, 469
  influence, 423, 425, 428
Aristophanes of Byzantium, 107, 146, 316n31, 450n36
Aristotle, 88, 289, 314n19, 323n49, 422, 429, 500, 504
  Athenaion politeia, 350–51
  Didascaliae, 121
  Nicomachean Ethics, 494
  Poetics, 146, 494
  Politics, 327
Aristotle, Ps.-
  De mirabilibus, 126n20
  On Physiognomy, 368–69
Aristoxenus, 312n12
Arsinoe-Aphrodite, 12, 218
  temple at Cape Zephyrium, 202, 235–37
Arsinoe I, repudiated by Ptolemy II, 206
Arsinoe II, 7, 9–10, 151, 179, 201, 205, 223–24, 366, 592
  as Aphrodite, 218
  death of, 232n34
  as Helen, 219–22
  marriage to Ptolemy II Philadelphus, 206
  as Sibling Gods (with Ptolemy II), 230n18
  statue in Olympia, 234n43
  as tenth Muse, 208, 210
Arsinoe III, 173
Arsinoeum (Alexandria), 204
Artemidorus, 102
Artemis, 52, 163, 483
  in *Hymns*, 2–3, 451
  as Muse, 344–45

prayer to, 44
statues of
    at Ambracia, 490
    in Leucas, 42
Artists of Dionysus, 299
Asclepiades of Myrlea, 100n28, 235, 392
Asclepiades of Samos, 14, 233
Asclepius, 437–38
    at Epidaurus, 267–69, 437–38
Asineis, 42
Askren, David L., 82, 82n6
Asmis, E., 317, 324
Aspendus, 166
Asper, M., 363
astronomy, in *Lock of Berenice*, 203, 213–14, 235
Astyages, 113, 113n85
Athanadas of Ambracia, 490
Athena, 44–45, 359
    and fable of Laurel and Olive, 377
    in *Hymns*, 2, 4
    statue of, at Teuthis, 44–45, 481–82
Athenaeus, 10, 98, 102, 123, 129, 132, 353, 471
    Deipnosophistae, 99
Athens, 164
    and cults of Apollo and Dionysus, 302
    Pelasgian Walls, 54
    Sanctuary of Apollo Pythius, 302
    temple of Apollo Delius, 305
Athens/Attica, 157–58
    as setting for *Hecale*, 157–58
athletes, portrayed by Callimachus, 486–88
Athos, Mount, 204, 212–13, 222
Attalus I, 194, 538n14
Attalus III, 538n14
Atthidographers, 8, 127, 349–67
    and the *Aetia*, 357–63
    defined, 350
Atthis, as title of works by Atthidographers, 350–51, 358, 366
Attica, 163. *See also* Athens
attribution, problems of, 122
audience, 170n28
    for *Aetia*, 163
    of Alexandrian poets, 155–56
    for court poetry, 241–44
Auditorium of Maecenas, 515n8
Augeas, king of Elis, 52
"Augustan age," 512
aulos, 301, 304–5
authority, of Apollo, 435–36
autobiography, as literary genre, 239

autopsy (sightseeing), 254–56
    rejection of, 254–56

Babrius, 550
Bactria, 545
Bagnani, Gilbert, 81–82, 82n5, 84
Bagnani, Stewart, 82–83
Barbarian Customs (Callimachus), 98, 126, 389
barbarians
    in *Aetia*, Book 3, 169
    in *Hymn 4 "To Delos,"* 194–98
Barchiesi, A., 156n2
    La Traccia del modello, 585
Bardanes, Georgius, 116
Barthes, Roland, 582–83
Basileia (Alexandria), 183, 183n14
basileus, 226, 228–29, 238. *See also* kings; Ptolemies
Batavi, the, 25
Baton of Sinope, 294
Batrachomyomachia, 536, 543–45
Battiades, Callimachus as, 525
Battiads, 283
Battus, 190–91, 283–84, 507, 525
Baudelaire, Charles, 497
    "A Philosophy of Toys," 493
bee imagery, 186–87, 463
bees, used for priestesses of Demeter, 275–76
Bentley, Richard, 23–24
Berenice I, 92, 179n4, 183, 201
Berenice II, 9–10, 55–56, 80, 150, 179–80, 191n43, 204–5, 209, 224, 345–46, 592–93
    as daughter of Arsinoe II, 206–8
    dedication of lock of hair, 203, 235
    as Grace, 210, 346
    in *Hymn 2 "To Apollo,"* 190–91
    as surrogate Muse, 346
Berenice Syra, 223
Bernand, Étienne, 145
Bias, 485n34
bibliographic works (Callimachus), 121–24. *See also Pinakes* (Callimachus)
bibliography, 120–21
Bilistiche, 232, 234–35
Bing, Peter, 130–31, 199
    Well-Read Muse, 586
biological model, of poetic invention, 494–95
Bion, 536
    Epitaph on Adonis, 536n4

birds
　dialogue of, 351–52
　in fable of Laurel and Olive, 374–80
Bisalti, 55
Bleisch, P., 217
Blomfield, C.J., 24
Blum, Rudolf, 119–21
Bonn school, 25
book fragments, 70–74
Bornmann, Fritz, 152
Bosporus, 213
Bouphonia (Delos), 483
bramble, in fable of Laurel and Olive, 377
Brennus, 9, 181
Bruss, Jon, 347
bucolica, 520
Bull of Phalaris, 43
Buonaccorsi, Filippo (Callimachus Experiens), 97n15
Busiris, 174

Cabiri, 222–23
Caius. *See* Gaius
Calderini, Domizio, 94
Callicrates of Samos, 12, 179n3, 215n21, 224, 233–34, 234n43, 236, 237n52
Callimacheanism
　history of, 534–35
　Roman, 511–33, 534n2
Callimachean models, Roman appropriation of, 511–33
Callimachus
　on act of composition, 589–93
　and aetiology, 334, 337, 341–42, 387, 455–56, 474
　in Alexandria, 9–14
　and Apollo, 292–93, 296
　as arbiter of culture, 593–94
　arrangement of poetic works, 36–38
　arrival at court, 231n26
　and Atthidographers, 349–67
　background of, 9–10, 182n13
　as *Battiades*, 525
　and Cavafy, 595–601
　and characterization, 474–92
　cited by ancient authors, 93–117
　collected editions, 18–19, 23–26, 36–38
　and contemporary religion, 264–85
　as court poet, 61, 80, 192, 225–44
　critiqued by ancient authors, 104–5, 309–28, 469
　dates, 10
　dialogue with Muses, 45, 47–49, 61, 334, 336–37, 347

　and Dionysus, 292–93, 299–300
　and epic, 542–43, 543n33
　epitaph for his father, 507
　as erotic epigrammatist, 393–95
　and euphony, 318–22
　and exclusion of Egypt, 174–75
　extant works, 1–9 (*See also separate entries under titles of works*)
　and fable, 368–83
　as first modern poet, 588–95
　as "fragment," 63–80
　and geopoetics, 155–77
　and humor, 224
　influence of (*See* Callimacheanism)
　interest in cult, 12–13
　on kings and kingship, 178–200
　and *koinai*, 134–52
　and later Greek poetry, 534–65
　and Latin poets, 511–33
　linguistic ambience, 135–38
　and linguistic collage, 420–23
　as literary critic, 395–99
　literary inheritance, 134–35
　lost works, 9, 119–21, 126, 299, 465 (*See also separate entries under titles of works*)
　as love poet, 521, 530, 595–97
　and metaliterary speech, 429–33
　as model to imitate, 512, 528
　and the Muses, 329–48
　and New Music, 289–308
　as object of scholarly study, 107–17
　and Peripatetics, 312–13
　and philology, 118–33
　and plain style, 315
　as *poeta philologus*, 61
　and poetic autobiography, 326–27
　poetic persona in *Aetia*, 61–62
　and poetics of verisimilitude, 446–47
　poetic voice, 134, 429–53
　and "politics of Olympus," 440, 452–53
　as polymath, 588, 594
　and Posidippus, 224
　and presentation of the divine, 245–63
　as *princeps elegiae*, 520, 527
　as programmatic model, 527–28
　on queens, 201–24
　quotation of Hipponax, 471–73
　range of sources, 15
　range of voices, 15
　read in schools, 99–100
　and recovery of youth, 426–28
　rediscovered in papyri, 23–38

Romanized reading of, 531
self-fashioning, 409–10
self-presentation
  as child, 407–28
  as cicada, 380–82, 402–3
  as Cyrenaean, 191–92
  as self-reflective poet, 594
self-revelation through use of proverbs, 399–403
  as *senex*, 400–403
study of Homer, 98–99
as teacher/scholar, 11
and tragedy, 505–6, 595n17
travel to Athens, 12, 157–58
treatment of Ptolemies, 68
use of dialect, 142–43
use of proverbs and popular sayings, 384–403
use of size imagery, 324–26
use of water imagery, 275–76, 425
vocabulary, 71
"Callimachus" (narrator), 40, 45, 329, 333
Callimachus (general; father or uncle or grandfather of poet), 284
Callimachus (nephew and namesake of poet), 89, 125n19
Callimachus' family, and Cyrenean cult of Apollo, 283–85
Callimaco, Angelo, 97n15
Calliope, 47, 335–36, 340–41, 347, 552
  in *Aetia*, Book 1, 41
Callixenus of Rhodes, 132, 132n35, 238, 243–44
Calvino, Italo, 428
Camarina, 491
Cameron, Alan, 11, 89, 189, 191, 284, 360, 531, 589
Canopus, 164
  temple complex of Isis and Anubis, 234
Cantina dei Papiri, 82
Cape Zephyrium temple, 12–13
Carducci, Giosuè, *Odi barbare*, 568
Carneia festival, 3, 189
cartonnage, 135–38, 147
Cassander, 10n13
Catalogue of Women, 36
Catullus, 179, 203, 211, 213, 512, 521, 525, 527–28
  and ancients *vs.* moderns, 518–19
Cavafy, C.P., 595–601
  "In the Month of Athyr," 598, 600–601
Ceos, 158, 163, 427

Ceramicus, 481n19
Chalcidice, 213, 222
Chamaeleon of Heracles, 312n12, 316n31
Chamoux, Françoise, 283–84
chancery training, evidence of, 86, 86n20
Chapouthier, F., 223
characterization
  in Callimachus, 474–92
  through proverbs, 389–90
Charis, 204
charis, 209–11
Charites, 593
child, poet as, 407–28. See also family dynamics
childhood, poetics of, 409–10, 422–28
  in *Aetia Prologue*, 495–97
  in *Iambi*, 497–505
Chilon, 485n34
Choeroboscus, 71
Choes, 363
Choniates, Michael, 115–17, 115n97, 353, 564
Choniates, Nicetas, 117
chora, Egyptian, 135–38
  and *koine*, 138–41
Choricius, 104
Chremonidean War, 195, 365–67
Chremonides, 366
Christodorus, 562
chronopoetics, 171–73
  and Panhellenism, 176–77
cicada, 380–82, 402
Cicero, 103, 251
Cilicia, 161
Cinnamus, John, 114n91
citations of Callimachus, in ancient authors, 93–117
Civici Musei del Castello Sforzesco, 83
Clarke, K., 358n33
Clauss, James, 187
Cleanthes, 184n21, 442
  Hymn to Zeus, 316
Cleidemus, 359–60, 363–64
Clement of Alexandria, 66, 99
  Protrepticus, 102
Cleobulus, 485n34
Cleomenes of Naucratis, 228n13
Cleon of Curium, *Argonautica*, 531
Clio, 40, 43, 45, 47, 334–36, 341–42
code model, 581
coins, Ptolemaic, 198, 223
Colchis, 161

Collection of Marvels throughout the World...(Callimachus), 120, 124, 129
collectors
  royal, 132–33
  scholarly, 133
Colluthus, 562
Colomo, Daniela, 38
comedy, Attic, 364, 421
coming after, 586
Companions. See also *Philoi*, 227
competition between nonhuman contenders, as form of folk narrative, 376–79
conjugal love, as royal virtue, 179
connections among elegies in *Aetia*, 58–60
Conon of Samos, 214, 233, 235
Constantine Cephalas, 114n90
Constantine the Sicilian, 563
Conte, Gian Biagio, 580–86
contemporary figures, in works of Callimachus, 488–90. *See also names of kings and queens*
content and form, contrast of, 323–26
context, lack of, in book fragments, 73–74
Conti, Angelo, 415, 420
Corcyra, 161
Coresia/Arsinoe, 158
Coroebus, 42
Coronis, 41
Corycus, 398
Cos, 158–59, 194
  as birthplace of Ptolemy II Philadelphus, 195
  in *Hymn 4 "To Delos,"* 194–95, 199
cosmology, Egyptian, 213–14
court
  development of, 227–28
  as military camp, 227n7
courtiers. See *Philoi*
court poetry, 80, 174, 197, 241–44
  and court society, 234–38
  and dynastic discourse, 207
  and exclusion of Egypt, 175–76
court poets, 182, 192, 225–44
  and truth poetry, 186
court society, 231–41
  and court poetry, 234–38
  location of, 235n44
Cozzoli, A.-T., 595
Crantor, 441n18
Crataemenes of Chalcis, 43

Crates, 316–17, 317n33
Crete, 43, 461–62
  as birthplace of Zeus, 442–43, 457
Crinito, Pietro, 95
crisis of the subject, 583
Croatian coast, 161
Croce, Benedetto, 576, 578
Cronus, 457
Crotopus, 42
crow, 412, 419
Crusius, Otto, 27
Ctesibius, 237–38
cult titles, 252
Cydippe, 521
Cyrenaic philosophers, 322
Cyrene (city), 9, 167, 271–73
  and Delphi, 302
  founding of, 283
  inscriptions from, 301–2
  Pythium, 302n63
  temple to Apollo, 189–93
  war with Alexandria, 11
Cyrene (nymph), 3, 190, 211
Cyril of Alexandria, 71–72, 102
Cyzicus, 55, 164

D'Alessio, Giovan Battista, 303, 307, 597
Damasichton, 484
Danaids, 475
Danaus, 220, 475
Daphne, 379
Daphnephoria, Delphic, 53, 163–64
Darius II, 488, 488n51
death of the author, 583
Deianeira, 477
Delia festival, 4
Delos
  cult statue of Apollo, 258
  temple of Apollo Pythius, 303n69
Delos (Apollo), 216
  in *Hymns*, 2–4
Delphi, 42, 164
  cults of Apollo and Dionysus, 300–301
  and Cyrene, 302
  in *Hymn 4 "To Delos,"* 196–97
  Pythian Games at, 301
  statue of Ptolemy II, 234n42
Delphic Oracle, 42–43, 53, 55, 271, 276
  and approval of hymns, 278–82
  and foundation of Cyrene, 283
Demeter, 2, 4
Demetrius Chlorus, 106n62
Demetrius of Byzantium, 233

Demetrius of Phalerum, 10–11, 13, 230, 312n12, 313–14, 314n19, 369, 372
  On Dreams, 313
  On Old Age, 313
  On Poems, 102n36
Demetrius the Fair, 191n43
demiourgoi, 283
Demophon, 363
Depew, Mary, 580
Dercylus, 127, 350, 360
De Sanctis, G., 491
de Waele, J.A., 492
diagramma, of new constitution of Cyrene, 283–84
dialects, Greek, 134, 138, 141–45
  Alexandrian, 135
  Attic-Ionic, 138
  Cyrenean, 142
  Cyrenean Doric (subdialect), 143
  Doric, 138, 143, 145
  of *Hymns*, 2, 4
  Ionic, 472
  literary, 142
  mixing of, 143–44
  poets' choice of, 144–45
dialektos, use of term, 141
diasporic identity, Ennius and, 516
Dicaearchus of Messana, 312n12
Dicte, Mount, 462
Didyma, 276
Didymus Chalcenterus, 110–11
Diegeseis (PMilVogl 1.18), 6–7, 12, 34–38, 49–50, 53, 53n24, 57–59, 68–69, 76, 78, 81–92, 163, 293, 360, 488–89
  archaeological context, 81–86
  contents, 88–92
  defined, 88
  editio princeps, 85
  format, 86–88
  physical description, 85–86
  revised edition, 85
diegesis, 221, 352–53, 377, 418, 504, 594
Diehl, E., 110
Diels, Hermann, 27
difficult words, study of, 145–49
Dilthey, Karl, 25
Dio Chrysostom, *Olympic Oration*, 251
Diodorus, 136
Diogenes Laertius, 11, 98, 102, 253
Diogenianus, 109
Diomedon, 400n36

Dionysiac inspiration, Ion of Chios and, 298
Dionysiac music, 290–91. *See also* New Music
Dionysiac ritual experts, guild or company of, 244
Dionysius, 550n61
Dionysius of Cyzicus, 593
Dionysius of Halicarnassus, 98, 98n19, 320n42
Dionysius of Lampsacus, 232
Dionysius of Phaselis, 106n62
Dionysius Periegetes, 551
Dionysius Thrax, 311
Dionysus, 41, 217
  in Callimachus' poetry, 292–93, 298–300, 300n55
  as Ptolemaic divine ancestor, 299
Dionysus Phallen, 500
Dioscorides, 233, 235n47, 536
Dioscuri, 7, 204, 221–23
Diphilus of Laodicea, 108n67
diplomats and diplomacy, 243
  role of queens, 211–14
discontinuity, geographical, in *Aetia*, 161–65
divine action, poets and, 246–51
divine epiphany, 260–63
divine epithets, in *Hymns*, 436
divinities
  Greek
    images of, 251–60
    as literary figures, 265
    origins and genealogies of, 245–51
  linked to queens, 205
  in work of Callimachus, 245–63
division of poetic art, 323–26
Djed-Hor, 239
Dodona, oracle at, 45
Dositheus of Pelusium, 233–34
Drimys, Demetrius, 116
Dryopes, 41–42, 477
Duris of Samos, 322, 486
  On Contests, 127
Du-Stil, 2
dynastic discourse, role of queens in, 206–14

Edmunds, Lowell, 584
education, of literary audience, 243
educational texts, and *koine*, 145–49
Egypt
  circulation of Callimachus' poems in, 99

exclusion of, in Panhellenism, 173–76
"intertextual," 175n50
power relations in, 244
under Ptolemies, 228–31, 228n12, 238–41
Egyptian culture, Ptolemy I and, 238–39
Egyptian language, 138
Egyptian Museum, 83
Egyptians, in court society, 238–41
Einstein, Albert, 423
Eleans, 52
elegies (Callimachus), 46, 204. See also *Aetia* (Callimachus)
Lock of Berenice as, 203
elegy, Latin, 520–21
Eleusinian rites, 269n18
elevation of style, through allusion, 569
El Hibeh, 147
Eliot, T.S., 577–78
Elis, 163
elitism, poet's preference for, 430–33
embeddedness, of fables, 369
Empedocles, 516
emulation, 570, 570n1
open, 573–74
Ennius, 528, 533
Annales, 515–17
as possible post-Callimachean, 515–17
Envy, 523
Epaphroditus of Chaeronea, 109
commentary on Callimachus' *Aetia*, 111
Epeius, 500–501
Epharmostus, 136
Ephesus, 163–64, 331
Ephorus, 316n31
epic, 542–43
Callimachus and, 542–43, 543n33
Ennian, 517
Hellenistic, 531
Homeric
absence of fables in, 369
and representations of childhood, 407–9
Ovid and, 524–25
Epicharmus, *Pyrrha*, 143
Epicurean criticism, 316
Epicurus, 316
Epidaurus, temple of Asclepius at, 267–69, 437–38
epigram collections, 4, 14, 137
epigrammatists, 14, 392
epigrams
funerary, 392n20

from Oenoanda, 547–48
on Pillar of Ptolemagrius (Panopolis), 183n17
as testimonia, 65
written for poets, 471
Epigrams (Callimachus), 4–5, 223, 329n1, 597
on Cleombrotus, 103
influence, 515, 519, 546
proverbs in, 389, 392–95
Strabo and, 100
Epimenides of Crete, 184, 184n22, 441–43
epitaphs
in Antipater, 539
in Callimachus, 388, 400, 507
from Chios, 546–47
imitating Callimachus, 545
written for poets, 471
from Zeno Archive, 136
epithalamium, for Ptolemy II and Arsinoe II, 201
Epopeus, 44
epyllion, *Hecale* as, 8
Equicola, Mario, 96
Erasistratus of Ceos, 233
Erato, 44, 47, 335
Eratosthenes, 233, 233n38, 322, 536, 537n8
Erigone, 157, 299, 537
Erechtheus, 353
Erichthonius, 351, 357, 359
Erigone, 363
Erigonus, 475n1
Ernesti, J.A., 24, 24n4
Eros, 408
as *erotodidaskalos*, 483
Erotian, 109
erotic poetry, 430–32, 483–84, 519–20
Erycius, 542
Erysichthon, 4, 523
Eteocles, 55
Ethnikai onomasiai (Callimachus), 98, 147
Etymologicum genuinum, 26, 71, 106n59, 107, 113, 129
Etymologicum magnum, 23
etymologies, Byzantine, 108–9
euergesia, royal, 189
euergetes, 236
Euergetes II, 283
Euhemerus, 3, 13, 184

eulogy, 438–48
Eumaeus, 590n6
Eunapius, 104, 256n25
euphonist criticism, 316–22, 324
Euphorion, 520, 536–39, 541
  Dionysus, 299
Euphrates, 522–23, 528
Euripides, 99, 136–37, 569
  Bacchae, 261, 469–71, 473
  Licymnius, 301n61
  Madness of Heracles, 303–5
  quoted by Callimachus, 469–71
Eurydice (wife of Ptolemy I Soter), 183
Eurypylus, 211
Eusebius, 487
Eustathius of Thessalonica, 114, 316n31, 389
Euthycles, 52–53, 486–87
Euthymus of Locri, 54, 387, 486–88
evocation, as function of allusion, 569–70, 581
exclusion, as poetic practice, 173–76
exegesis, Callimachean, and *Diegeseis*, 88–92
exemplary model, 581, 585

fable, 368–83
  defined, 368
fables
  Corinna, 376
  Donkey and Cicada, 380–82
  Fox and Eagle, 373
  Hawk and Nightingale, 369–70
  Laurel and Olive (talking trees), 374–80, 398, 502–3
  talking animals, 371–74, 524
Fabri, Anna (Mme. Dacier), 23
family dynamics, in *Iambi*, 493–507
family tree, of Callimachus' family, 284
Fantuzzi, Marco, 292, 330, 586
Fasti triumphales, 491
father, Lacanian model of, 506–7
fertility images, 215–16, 216n24
festival culture, 242–44
festival of Apollo Maleatas and Asclepius, 278
festivals, Greek, 243. *See also names of festivals*
First Punic War, 517n13
Florence, papyri in, 34–35
form and content, contrast of, 323–26
Foundations of Islands and Cities...(Callimachus), 126

founding hero, 191n44
fox, in fable, 372–73
fragmentary poems (Callimachus), 8–9, 63–80
  and kingship ideology, 180–81
fragment collection, 93–97
framing narrative
  in *Aetia*, Books 3 & 4, 163
  in *Iambus 4*, 375–76
Fraser, P.M., 126n20
Freud, Sigmund, *The Future of an Illusion*, 497n6

Gaia, 460
Gaius (Roman), 55, 57, 60, 169, 490–91
Galatea, 8–9, 181
Galatea (Callimachus), 181, 196–97
Galatians, 181
  as new Titans, 197–98, 440
  revolt of, in Egypt, 194–98
Galen, 102
Gallio, 573
games, children's, 407–9
Gauls, 8–9, 181
Gellius, Aulus, 102
generic contamination, in *Iambus 13*, 293–98
generic figures, portrayed by Callimachus, 490–92
generic model, 581, 585
generic self-awareness, in paean for Dionysus by Philodamos of Scarpheia, 281–82
generic syncretism, 301
genre, literary
  and dialect, 144
  hierarchy of, 385, 392, 519
  hymn, 438–48
  multiple, 293–98, 515
  variety of, 242
Gentili, Bruno, 392n20
geographic dream space, 220–22
geography, in *Aetia*, 161–65
geopoetics, 155–77. *See also* Panhellenism
  and exclusion, 173–76
  political, 156–60, 170
  spatial, 160–70
Georgius Choeroboscus, 112
Germanicus, 526n30
Giangrande, Giuseppe, 578–79
gifts to the gods, 275–76
Glaucon, 232, 234, 234n40

glossai, Homeric, 146–47
glossary, Greek-Egyptian, 140
Gomperz, Theodor, 27, 351–52, 358
Gow, A.S.F., 5
Graces, 40–41, 48, 58–59, 67–68, 258, 334, 346, 391, 455–56
   cult at Paros, 308
   genealogy of, 40–41, 334
   and Muses, 347
   queens as, 209–11
grammarians, 71
Grand Procession of Ptolemy II Philadelphus, 132, 173, 176, 176n58, 197, 238
Greece, imaginary, 160–61. *See also* geopoetics
Greek culture
   Egyptians and, 240, 240n64, 240n66
   and geopoetics, 167–70
   preservation of, in Alexandria, 230–31
   role of fable in, 368–70
Greek settlement, 164
Greeks/Macedonians, in court society, 228–29, 231–38, 240
Gregorius Magister, 114n89
Gregory of Nazianzus, 105, 554–57
groups of related stories, in *Aetia*, 58–60, 68–69
Grube, G.M., 313
Guéraud-Jouguet schoolbook, 140–41, 148

Haliartus, 43
Harder, Annette, 334, 434n6, 481n21
Harding, P., 360n39
Hecale, 353, 418, 478, 478n13, 479
Hecale (Callimachus), 8, 358, 421, 478
   as *aition* of local cult of Zeus Hecaleius, 350
   and Atthidographers, 352–57
   and Attic comedy, 364
   commentaries on, 107
   dialect of, 144–45
   dialogue of the birds, 351–52, 378, 418–19
   diegesis for, 88, 92
   geopoetics of, 169
   influence, 523–24, 545–46, 553–54, 559, 565
   Muses in, 343n30
   narrative structure, 417–19
   opening of, 353–54
   proverbs in, 385–86, 423

   set in Athens/Attica, 157–58
   Theseus in, 479–80
   tragic voice in, 468
Hecataeus of Abdera, 239n59
Hecker, A., 25–26, 73, 101n34
Hecker's law, 25–26, 113, 113n88
Hedylus of Samos, 107, 218, 235n47, 237–38
Hegesias, 158
Helen, Arsinoe II as, 219–22
Helicon, Mount, 40, 161, 164n18
Helladius, 109
Hellanicus, 351
   Barbarian Customs, 127
Hellenism, Roman, 531–33
"Hellenistic," as category, 530–33
Hellenization, of Egyptian elements, 224
Henrichs, Albert, 260, 305
Hephaestion, 71, 412–13
   Enchiridion, 413
   handbook of Greek meter, 112
Hera, cult statue on Samos, 54, 216–17
Heracleodorus, 315n26, 316, 318
Heracles, 52, 67–68, 163, 217
   Bouthoinas, 476
   cult of, at Lindus, 41
   and Nemean Lion, 202–3, 209, 478
   portrayed by Callimachus, 475–79
   Twelve Labors, 477, 477n11
Heraclides of Pontus, 312n12, 314, 316, 316n32, 319
Heraclitus of Halicarnassus, 549
Hercules Musarum, temple of, 516n11
Herennius Philo, 109
Hermann, Gottfried, 25
Hermes, 188, 408, 500–501
   Hermes Perpheraeus, 500
Hermesianax, 291
Hermippus, 89, 123, 322, 360n40
Hermocrates of Iasus, *On Accents*, 311n7
Hermopolis, 76
Herodas of Cos, 233, 411
Herodian, *Katholike prosodia*, 112
Herodotus, 174–75, 245–46
Hero of Temesa, 387
Hero of the Stern (Androgeos), 55
Herophilus of Chalcedon, 233
Herse, 357
Hersephoria, 357
Herter, Hans, 575
   "Kallimachos und Homer," 585–86
Hesiod, 318–19, 389–90, 395, 441, 484, 589

and Callimachus' *Hymns*, 2
as Callimachus' model, 178–79, 185
Hymn to the Muses, 335
influence, 454–65
and kingship ideology, 187
on origins and genealogies of the
    gods, 246–51
Theogony, 185, 246, 250, 327–28,
    333–37, 445–46, 456, 553, 592
Works and Days, 185
    fable of Hawk and Nightingale,
    369–70
Hesychius, 71, 109, 128, 148
hierarchy, of literary genres, 385, 392,
    519
hieroglyphics, 239
Hieronymus of Rhodes, 312n12
hieros gamos, 215–18
Hinds, Stephen, 583–84
Hippocrene, 164n18
Hippomedon of Sparta, 233
Hipponax, 5–6, 12, 369, 471–73, 484
    in *Iambi*, 330–32, 340, 374, 397,
    497–98, 517, 571
Hollis, Adrian, 100n26, 116, 352–53,
    357, 556
"Holy Blood," 592
Homer, 484, 498–99, 528
    and allusion, 569
    Callimachus' study of, 98–99
    and dialects, 144
    and Ennius, 517
    Iliad, 141, 248, 257, 407
        episode of Shield of Achilles, 408
        Muses in, 334–37
        scholia minora on, 84
    as object of scholarly study, 106, 137
    and Oceanus, 321
    Odyssey, 8, 141, 407–8, 416, 478
    on origins and genealogies of the
        gods, 246–51
Homeric Catalogue of Ships, 161
Homeric Hymns, 2, 184, 260–63, 339,
    341, 343, 408, 440, 452
    Hymn to Apollo, 193, 249, 315, 321,
        437
    Hymn to Dionysus, 184, 184n20,
        260–63, 452
    Hymn to Hermes, 189n36
Homeric poems, language of, 146
homosexuality and homoeroticism, 299,
    595–97
Hopkinson, Neil, 152

Horace, 398–99, 519, 529–30
    Ars Poetica, 323n51
    Epodes, 529
    Odes, 568
    and Pasquali's *Orazio lirico*, 570–73
Horatius Cocles, 491
horn of plenty, 216–17, 223
hospitality, theme of, 8, 170n27, 478–80,
    524, 554–55
humor, 224
    in treatment of Heracles, 475–79
hunger, 523
Hunt, A.S., 27
Hunter, Richard, 292, 314, 330, 432n5,
    531–33, 586
    "On Coming After," 588
Hutchinson, Gregory, 340
Huxley, G.L., 212
Hyginus, 24
Hyllus, 41–42
hymnic genre, and eulogistic intent,
    438–48
Hymns (Callimachus), 2–4, 223, 249–51,
    260–63, 291, 329n1
    arrangement of, 166n19
    audience for, 163n17
    chronopoetics of, 173
    commentaries on, 113
    dialect of, 144
    divine children in, 408
    geographical settings of, 167
    geopoetics of, 169
    Hymn 1 "To Zeus," 3, 14, 103, 176n54,
        246–48, 250, 327, 448–50, 593
        diegeseis for, 88
        and influence of Hesiod, 456–65
        and kingship ideology, 182–89
        sententiae in, 385
        tragic voice in, 466–67
    Hymn 2 "To Apollo," 3, 10, 119, 169,
        176n54, 205, 211, 248, 263–85, 345,
        380, 430, 450–51
        and Cyrenean Purity Regulation,
        271–73
        dating of, 191–92
        diegeseis for, 88
        influence, 519, 522, 528, 539
        and kingship ideology, 189–93
        and metrical sacred regulations,
        276–82
        and *programmata*, 270
        voice in, 433–39, 467
        water imagery in, 320–21

Hymn 3 "To Artemis," 3, 259, 451, 477
  influence, 559–61
  Muses in, 344–45
Hymn 4 "To Delos," 3–4, 10, 158, 176n54, 181, 249–50, 345, 378, 427, 439–40, 451, 466
  dating of, 196
  Greek-Egyptian elements, 199–200
  and kingship ideology, 193–200
  Muses in, 343–44
  tragic voice in, 467
Hymn 5 "To Athena" (Bath of Pallas, Loutra Pallados), 4, 91, 143–44, 167, 252, 257
  influence, 548
  tragic voice in, 467–68
Hymn 6 "To Demeter," 4, 143, 169, 523
  proverbs in, 386
  influence, 546, 553, 565
  kingship ideology, 181–200
  mimetic hymns, 167–69, 266
  Muses in, 343–45
  ordering of, 2, 448–53
  performance, 241
  proverbs in, 385–86
  Strabo and, 100
Hyperboreans, 44
hypomnemata, 106, 120
Hypomnemata (Callimachus), 90, 92

Iambi (Callimachus), 5–6, 12–17, 106n59, 204, 235n47, 326
  arrangement of, 166
  chronopoetics of, 173
  commentaries on, 107
  dialect of, 144
  diegeseis for, 88
  and exclusion of Egypt, 174–75
  and fables, 370–71
  family dynamics in, 493–507
  geographical settings of, 166–67
  geopoetics of, 169
  Hipponax in, 330–32, 340, 374, 397, 484–85, 497–98, 517, 571
  Iambus 1, 110n74, 156, 166, 184, 281n38, 311, 374, 471, 484–85
    proverbs in, 396–98
    story of cup of Bathycles, 373–74
  Iambus 2, 382, 505
    fable of talking animals, 371–74
  Iambus 4, 166n21, 505
    fable of laurel and olive, 374–80, 502–3
    proverbs in, 398

Iambus 6, 144, 166, 252–60, 399, 506
Iambus 7, 144, 166, 258, 500–501
Iambus 8, 144, 166
Iambus 9, 222, 258, 500
Iambus 10, 166
Iambus 11, 144, 166, 388
Iambus 12, 184n22, 276n28, 504
Iambus 13, 119, 293–98, 330, 380, 430, 485, 594
  Ion of Chios in, 504–5
  proverbs in, 398–99
Iambus 15 (Pannychis), 399
Iambus 17 (Branchus), 7–8, 156, 380
  influence, 515, 529, 546
  proverbs in, 395–99
  role of Muses in, 329–32
  sources for, 313
  Strabo and, 100
iambus, as literary genre, 395–96
Icos, 44, 361–63
idealistic aesthetics, 576
identity, Greek, 130, 131n33
Imbriani, Vittorio, 577n13
imitation, 519, 528, 567. *See also* Callimacheanism
Imperial age, and influence of Callimachus, 550–57
"implied grammatical interpretation," 579
indirect tradition, 97n18, 106n58–106n59. *See also* citations of Callimachus; fragment collection
  medieval, 39
individual figures, in Callimachus, 474–92
inscriptions
  and Callimachus' influence, 545–49
  from Cyrene, 301–2
  at Epidaurus, 437–38
  language of, 142, 142n10
  and occasional poetry, 145
  as record of divine words and deeds, 267
Insula of the Papyri (Tebtynis, near Umm-el-Breigât), 81–86
intentional fallacy, 583
intentionality, of allusion, 577, 582–84
intention of the text, 583
internal narrator, 61
intertextuality, 224. *See also* allusion; quotation
  and allusion, 582
  in Callimachus' *Hymns*, 448–53
  of Hesiod and Callimachus, 454–65

of Hipponax and Callimachus, 471–73
of Latin poets and Callimachus,
    511–33
Roman, 522
Io, 219–20, 220n31
    equated with Isis, 213
Ion, 359
Ion, threefold, in *Iambus 13*, 293–98
Ion of Chios, 293–98, 331, 485, 504–5
    elegies, 296–98
    foundation narratives, 127
    lyric poems with sympotic settings,
        298
Ion of Ephesus, 504
Isidorus, hymns to Isis, 185, 548
Isindus, 52, 163–64
Isis, 213, 219, 220n31
    sanctuary at Medinet Madi, 548
Isis and Anubis, temple complex in
    Canopus, 234
Isocrates, 315
Istrus, 89, 353, 355n22, 357, 360
    Appearances of Apollo, 259
    Synagoge ton Atthidon, 366
Isyllus, 278–79, 437–38
Italia Che Scrive, L', 567
Italy, 164
Iulis, 51–52

Jackson, S.B., 219
Jacoby, Felix, 350, 357–58, 361, 361n44,
    362, 364, 366, 490
Jakobson, Roman, 134
Janko, Richard, 313, 316
Jason, 475n1
"jeweled" style, Nonnus and, 557–62
John of Gaza, 562
Julian the Egyptian, 562

Kapp, Ida, 26
katabasis, 471–72
Kellett, E.E., 577–78
Kenyon, F.G., 350
Kerkhecker, A., 472
Kidd, I.G., 323n50
kings. *See also basileus; names of rulers;*
    Ptolemies; queens
    as both *basileus* and pharaoh, 228–29
    characteristics of, 226
    compared to Zeus, 439, 444–45, 464
kingship ideology, 175–76, 178–200
Kirk, G.S., 248
Knight, W.F. Jackson, 577–78
Knox, P., 6n7

Koenen, Ludwig, 176
Köhnken, Adolf, 187
koinai. *See also* dialects, Greek
    Callimachus and, 134–52
    regional, 134, 139
koine, 138–41
    emergence of, 130
    Ennius and, 515
    low *vs.* high, 139
    as minority language, 139
    poetic, 145–49
    and poetry, 149–52
Krevans, Nita, 321
Kristeva, Julia, 582
kritikoi, 317–18, 320, 482
Kroll, Wilhelm, 254
    *Studien zum Verständnis der
        römischen Literatur*, 583
Kybernesia, 356

Lacan, Jacques, 499–500, 506
Lagus, 228
Lanuvium, snake ritual at, 513–14
Laronde, André, 284
Lascaris, Ianos, 91
Lasus of Hermione, *Hymn to Demeter*,
    316n32
Latin sources, mediatory role of, 97
Latin studies, and intertextuality/
    allusion, 584–85
laurel, 377, 398, 502–3
League of Corinth, 133n38
Leander of Miletus, 62
Lechantin, M., 491
leges sacrae, use of term, 265n5
Lehnus, Luigi, 97, 284
Leipzig Scholia, 38
Leleges, 53
Lelli, E., 106n59, 372, 484n31
Lemnian women, 7
Lemnos, 166, 222
Leodamas, 489
Leonidas of Tarentum, 536
Leo the Philosopher, 562
Lesbos, 161, 164
Leto, 3–4, 451
Leucas, 161
lexicons, ancient, 71
Library of Alexandria, 10–11, 13–14, 62,
    123, 132, 230–31. *See also* collectors;
    Pinakes (Callimachus)
    collections, 132n34
Life of Aratus, 312n10
Lightfoot, Jane, 111, 542

Lighthouse of Alexandria, 234
lightness, in poetry, 427–28
Lille Papyrus, 591, 597
Limone, 54
Lindus, 41
  cult of Heracles at, 475–76
linguistic collage, 420–23
Linus, 42, 476
Lipara, 54, 164
literary criticism, Hellenistic
  Callimachus and, 309–28
  and cultivation of literary judgment, 311–12
  extant works, 310–11
  in *Iambi*, 395–99
literary judgment, 311–12
  and euphonism, 317
literary language, 142
Livrea, Enrico, 74, 79–80, 579
Lobel, Edgar, 28–29, 79
local cults, 259
local histories, used by Callimachus, 350. *See also* Atthidographers
local history, Hellenistic revival of interest in, 171
Local Month Names (Callimachus), 129
locations
  in book fragments, 72
  in papyrus fragments, 78
"lock of Isis," 219
Locri, Calabrian, 163
London Scholia, 69, 76
Longinus, 104, 499–500
lost works
  Callimachus, 9, 119–21, 126, 299, 465
  discovery of, 597
lost world, 587n1
love poets, Roman, 519–20
Lowes, Livingston, 578
Lucian, 102, 104
Lucilius, 515, 523
Lucillius of Tarrha, 108n67, 550
luxury, as characteristic of Hellenistic kings, 227n8
Lycophron, author of *Alexandra*, 100, 139, 536
Lycophron of Chalcis, 118, 118n1, 233
Lycurgus, 438
Lynceus, 322
Lyne, R.O.A.M., 585
lyre, 304–5
  in New Music, 296–97
Lysanias of Cyrene, *On the Iambic Poets*, 471
Lysimachus of Macedon, 206, 218

Maas, Paul, 27–28, 36n41, 88, 563
Maas's law, 87
Macedonians, 157
Macedonius Consul, 562
Machon, 291
Magas, 9–10, 180, 183, 191
Magdola, 137
Mallarmé, Stéphane, 505
Malten, L., 362
Manetho, 174, 239n59, 241
  Egyptian History, 239
Manethoniana, 550
maps, 161, 161n15
  geographic settings in *Aetia*, 162, 165
  geographic settings in *Iambi*, 168
Marcus Aurelius, 99
Marianus of Eleutheropolis, 38, 65, 100n24
marriage. *See also* royal incest
  of Ptolemy III Euergetes and Berenice, 201–2
  of Ptolemy II Philadelphus and Arsinoe II, 201–2, 204, 214–18
Martial, 65–66, 72, 104
Massimilla, Giulio, 303, 307, 477, 593
materiality, of deities, 258–60
Maximus, *Peri katarchon*, 550
Mazzarino, S., 491
McLennan, G.R., 187
Meandrius of Miletus, 128n26, 350
measurability, in poetry, 423, 426
measurement, in *Iambus 6*, 498–500
Medea, 524
Medeius, 234, 237
Medinet Madi, sanctuary of Isis, 548
Megaclides of Athens, 316, 316n31
Megara, 393
Mele (Callimachus), 7–8
  and *Aetia*, 208
  Apotheosis of Arsinoe, 7, 202, 204, 207–8, 211, 220–22, 250
  audience for, 163n17
  Branchus, 7–8, 156, 380
  Fragment 225 Pf., 7
  and *Iambi*, 166, 166n20
  Pannychis/Night Revel, 7
Meleager, 528, 536, 551
Meliae, 462, 462n15
Melicertes, 53
Memphis, 137
Menander, 99, 104
Mendelsohn, Daniel, 597
Menelaus, 590n6

Meropis, 152
metaliterary speech, Callimachus and, 429–33
Metaphrasis of the Psalms, 551
metapoetics, and criticism of Latin poetry, 519–26
meter
  hexameter, 541
  of *Hymns*, 2, 4
  of *Iambi*, 6, 331
  iambic trimeter scazon, 472
  inner metric, 541
  of *Mele*, 7
  of metrical sacred regulations, 266
Methodius, lexicon, 109
Methymna, 500
mice, 203, 209, 478–79, 544
Milan *Diegeseis*. See *Diegeseis* (PMilVogl 1.18)
Miletus, 52, 156–57, 163–64, 166, 484
mimetic hymns (Callimachus), 167–69, 266
Mimnermus, 431, 520, 530
Minnen, P. Van, 83n10
minority language, *koine* as, 139
Minos, 40, 480–81
Minyans, 475n1
Mnaseas, *On Oracles*, 393
modernity
  of Callimachus, 588–95
  Ennius and, 516
Molorchus, 203, 209, 478–79, 544
monarchies, Hellenistic
  establishment of, 225–28
  structure of, 244
monarchy. See also kings
  bicultural, 186–88, 199–200
  divinized, 444
  dual, as both *basileus* and pharaoh, 228–29, 238
monuments. See also inscriptions
  dedication of, 234, 234n42–234n43, 236
  speaking, 598–600
mortuary temple of Arsinoe (Alexandria), 13
Moschus, 536
motto, Pasquali's concept of, 571–73, 575
Mouseion (Callimachus), 120
Müller, S., 206
multigeneric composition, 515
mummies, Egyptian, 135–36
mummification, 136
Murray, Penelope, 291n9, 342

Musaeus, 562
Musea, 343
Muses, 40–41, 45, 58–59, 67–68, 204, 382, 391, 455–56, 471
  Callimachus and, 329–48
  development into goddesses, 342
  as goddesses of learning, 342–43
  iconography of, 336
  naming of, 334
  Roman temple of, 516
  tenth Muse, 208–9
  traditional division of, 336
Museum of Alexandria, 132, 176, 230
  and the Muses, 343
music. See New Music
Myontus, 484
Mysteries, 4
Mysteries of Demeter, 51
mythological cycles
  Argonauts, 41, 55, 475, 475n1
  Heracles, 41, 52, 67–68, 163, 202–3, 209, 217, 475–79, 477n11, 478
  Theseus, 8, 417–19, 479–81
Myus, 52

Naeke, A.F., 25
Naeke's law, 551
names of deities, 246, 246n2
Names of Fishes (Callimachus), 129
narrative frame
  in *Aetia*, 45, 47–49
  interruption of, 48–49
Naumachius, 550
nautilus, offered by Selenaea, 218–19
Naxos, 163
Nectanebus, 239
Neda, 461
Nemean Games, 163, 202
Neoplatonic philosophers, 103
Neoptolemus of Parium, 237n54, 316, 316n31, 323, 323n51, 324
neoteroi, 529
New Comedy, 137
New Critics, 123
New Dithyrambic language, 291–92, 307
New Music
  Callimachus and, 289–308
  rise of, 289–91
Nicander, 108, 536, 538–39, 538n14, 541
  Heteroeumena, 173
  Theriaca, 84, 126
Nicanor of Alexandria, 111
Nicetas Eugenianus, *Drosilla and Charicles*, 564

Nicias, 107
Nicolaus of Damascus, 489
Niobe, 435n7
nomenclature, treatises on, 120, 128–30
Nonnus of Panopolis, 105, 261
   Dionysiaca, 557–61
   and influence of Callimachus, 557–62
   Paraphrase of St. John's Gospel, 557
Norden, Eduard, 572–75
   Ennius und Vergilius, 573
Norsa, Medea, 28, 85
number seven, associated with Apollo, 297

occasional poetry
   and *koine*, 145–49
   Lock of Berenice as, 203
Oceanus, 321
Odysseus, 483, 498
Oenoanda, 547–48
olive, 398, 502–3
   in fable of Laurel and Olive, 377
Olympia, 166, 215n21
   statue of Zeus by Phidias, 252–60
   statues of Ptolemy II and Arsinoe II, 234n43
Olympic Games, 52
On Contests (Callimachus), 126, 486
Onnes, 222, 489
On Nymphs (Callimachus), 128
onomastics, 120–21
On the Marvels and Wonders of the Peloponnese and Italy (Callimachus), 124n16
On the Rivers of the Inhabited World (Callimachus), 128–29, 129n28
On the Selections (Callimachus), 120
On the Sublime, 101
On Winds (Callimachus), 128
Oppian of Cilicia
   Cynegetica, 552
   Halieutica, 551–53
oppositio in imitando, 579
oppression by the past, Bloomian-Freudian model of, 496–97, 497n5
Oracle of the Potter, 199n68
oracular responses, 273
   and Callimachus' *Hymn 2 "To Apollo,"* 276–82
   as sacred regulations, 267–68
oral performance, and geopoetics of *Aetia*, 163. *See also* performance
originality, impossibility of, 577, 577n13
Orion, 44, 113n85
   Etymologicum, 109

Orphic hymns, 2
Orphism, 516
Orus, *Peri ethnikon*, 109
Ovid, 96, 261, 261n33, 489, 519, 521, 523–25, 528–29, 573, 585
   on Callimachus, 469
   Fasti, 516n11, 524–26, 529
   Metamorphoses, 173, 517–18, 529
owl, 412
Oxford, papyri in, 34–35
Oxyrhynchus, 34, 76

Page, D.L., 5
Pagine stravaganti, 578
Palatine Anthology, 4, 273–75
Palladas, 550
Palladium (statue of Athena), 4
Pallantidae, 355–56
Pallene, 220
Pamphilus, 109
   Onomasticon, 102
Pamprepius, 562
Pandion, 356
Panhellenism, 160–70, 176–77
   and aetiology, 171–73
   and exclusion of Egypt, 173–76
papyri. *See also* list in Index Locorum
   as annotated "editions," 76
   challenge of working with, 76–77
   dates and locations, 34–35
   of *Hymns*, 2
   list of, 29–34
   literary, from Tebtynis, 83–86
   and reconstruction of *Aetia*, 39–62
   subliterary, 76
papyrus discoveries, 23–38, 76, 135–38, 511n2, 531, 596. *See also* Zeno Archive
   Diegeseis, 81–86
papyrus fragments. *See also* fragment collection
   of *Aetia*, 74–80
   collection and edition of, 75
parade, 132–33
paradoxography, 120–21, 124–26
   principles of, 125
parainetic elegy, 491
Parallelüberlieferung, 89
Pardini, A., 483
Parians, 55
paroemiography, 102, 102n38, 122n8, 386–94, 396–97, 399, 401, 403
Paros, 40, 161
   cult of Graces at, 308
Parrasio, Aulo Giano, 96

Parsons, Peter, 29, 79–80
Parthenius of Nicaea, 536, 541–43
  Metamorphoses, 173n41, 542n30
Pascoli, Giovanni, 414n10–414n11, 577
  Child, The, 413–14, 420
  Civetta, La (The Owl), in *Convivial Poems*, 410–14
  Convivial Poems, 414, 420
  Reflections on the Art of Poetry, 412
Pasicles, 55, 488–89
Pasquali, Giorgio
  "Arte allusiva," 566–86
  Orazio lirico, 568–73, 585
past
  oppression by, Bloomian-Freudian model of, 496–97, 497n5
  and present, interaction between, 248–51 (*See also* ancient and modern)
pastoral song, 408
patronage, imperial, 13, 192, 230, 235, 299, 299n47
Paul the Silentiary, 562
Pausanias, 101, 360, 500
Pausimachus of Miletus, 311n7, 315n26, 316, 319
Pearson, L., 360, 367n78
pedantry, in Hellenistic literature, 130–33
Peithagoras (granduncle of poet Callimachus), 284
Pelasgians, 245
Peleus, 44
Pelops of Macedonia, 233–34
performance, 589. *See also* ritual performance
  and New Music, 291
  of poetry, 241–44
perfume, 207, 207n13, 210
Pergamum, and Alexandria, 317
Periander, 485n34
Peri anemon (Callimachus), 98
Perieres of Cyme, 43
periodization, literary, Romans and, 531–33
Peri orneon (Callimachus), 98
Peripatetic criticism, 312–16
periplus, 161
Peri potamon (Callimachus), 98
Peri pronoias, 492
Perseus, 475
Persian Wars, 197
personality, literary, and dialect, 145
Petosiris, 239

Peucetii, 55, 490
Pfeiffer, Rudolf, 5, 7, 24, 27–29, 35, 38, 75, 77, 79, 127–28, 303, 361, 363, 466, 472, 525, 535
  and *Diegeseis*, 83, 88–89, 92
  on *Fragmenta grammatica*, 120
Phaedrus, 526n30
Phalaecus, 488, 490
Phalaris, 43, 488, 490
Phalerum, 481n19
Phanias of Eresus, 312n12
Phanodemus, 362–64
pharmakos, 481
Pharos, 220, 592
Phidias, statue of Zeus at Olympia, 252–60, 498–500
Philadelphia, 136–37
Philemon and Baucis, 524
Philetas, 118, 122, 148, 152, 232, 317n33, 322, 520, 521
  Ataktoi glossai, 145–46
Philicus of Corcyra, 233, 244, 244n76
Philip (doctor), 233, 236
Philip II of Macedon, 438
Philip III of Macedon (Arrhidaeus), 225, 438
Philip V of Macedon, 438
Philip of Thessalonica, 104, 550
Philo (granduncle of poet Callimachus), 284
Philochorus, 316n31, 350, 352–53, 355, 355n23, 356–57, 364–66, 366n72, 367, 478
Philodamos of Scarpheia, paean for Dionysus, 279–82
Philodemus, 311, 316, 319, 324n56
  On Poems, 314, 316–17
Philogenes, 108n67
Philoi, 189, 189n38, 231–34, 232n32, 240
philology, 574, 587n1
  Callimachus and, 118–33
Philo of Byblus, 109
Philo of Byzantium, 253–56
Philostephanus, 360, 360n40
Philotera, 204, 206
Philoxenus, 107
  Peri monosyllabon rematon, 107n65
Philoxenus of Cythera, 290n5
Phoenix, 491–92, 599
Photius, 104, 389
  summary of Conon, 171n30
Phrygius, 52, 483–84
Phrynis, 289, 290n3
Pieria of Myus, 52

Pillar of Ptolemagrius (Panopolis), epigrams on, 183n17
Pinakes (Callimachus), 10–11, 90, 98, 120, 122–24, 130–31, 231, 231n25, 313, 313n14, 358, 366–67, 593
Pinax and Register of the Dramatic Poets...(Callimachus), 120–21
Pinax of the Glosses and Writings of Democritus (Callimachus), 119–20
Pindar, 61, 184, 317n32, 321–22, 325, 339, 385, 390, 417, 449
   Alexandrian poets and, 471
   and allusion, 569
   and Callimachus' *Hymns*, 2
   commentary to, 110
   as influence, 423
Piraeus, 164
Pittacus, 389, 485n34
Pittheus, 354
Pius, I.B., 95n11
place, in poetry. *See* geopoetics
place names
   in Callimachus' works, 156–65
   Greek, 174–75
plain style, Callimachus' use of, 315
Planudean Anthology, 4
Plato, 88, 315, 323n49, 594–95
   Ion, 290–91, 331–32, 425
   Laws, 305–8
   as model for Callimachus, 422, 425
   Phaedo, 420
   Phaedrus, 335–36, 425
      myth of cicadas, 381–82
   and poetic truth, 594–95
Platonism, 516
Platt, V., 501n14
Pliny, 13, 102n37, 126–27
Plutarch, 100–101, 108n67
   and Atthidographers, 353
   Life of Theseus, 350, 352–57, 364
poetae docti, 241
poetic authority, sources of, 330, 340
poetic exchange, 14
poetic invention, biological model of, 494–95
poetic memory
   in Callimachus and Cavafy, 597–98
   as system, 582
Poetics (anon.), 147
poetics, Roman, 512
poetic truth, Plato and, 594–95
poetry
   Augustan, allusion in, 568–69

   Byzantine, and influence of Callimachus, 562–65
   Greek, and influence of Callimachus, 534–65
   Hellenistic
      as *arte allusiva*, 578–79
      "derivative" character of, 585–86
      historical perceptions of, 587–88
      Pascoli and, 410–14
      and poetics of childhood, 422–28
      as *techne*, 330, 423, 426, 469
      theology of, 245
   Latin
      realism, 518
      satire, 518
poetry (Callimachus). *See also titles of works*
   erotic, 393–95, 521, 530, 595–97
   and *koine*, 149–52
   other poetic voices in, 454–73
   on queens, 202–5
   as *techne*, 331
poets. *See also names of poets*
   Alexandrian
      audience of, 155–56
      and quality of lightness, 427–28
   Archaic, role in creation of Greek theology, 246–51
   Augustan, 515
   Greek, and influence of Callimachus, 534–65
   Hellenistic
      and influence of Callimachus, 536–45
      as object of scholarly study, 106, 106n60
   Latin
      and Callimachus, 76, 511–33
      love poetry, 519–20
      pre-Neoteric, 515
politics
   and geopoetics, 156–60
   of Olympus, 440, 452–53
Poliziano, Angelo, 93–96, 108n70
   Epistulae, 95n9
   Greek epigram 23, 94
   Miscellanea, 94
Pollianus, 542
Pollux, 109
polyeideia, of Callimachus, 122n8, 298, 421, 427, 485, 515, 594
Polymnia, 47, 335
Polynices, 55

Polyphemus, 9
polyphony, in Callimachus' *Hymns*, 429–53
Porphyry of Tyre, *Homeric Questions*, 99
Posidippus, 14, 175, 200, 218, 233, 392
  and Callimachus, 224
  Epigrams, 14, 126, 236–37
  Hippica, 180
  Lithica, 207, 212, 216n24, 550
Posidonius, 323
poststructuralism, 582
Power, Tim, 297
powerful figures, portrayed by Callimachus, 490–92
praise poems, 235
Praxiphanes, 312, 312n10, 314n19
prayer, Greek, 248, 248n8
prepon, 385
Pretagostini, R., 476
priestesses, of Demeter, 275–76
Priscian, 96
Proclus, 104
  Hymns, 2, 550
Procopius of Gaza, 103
programmata, 267–69, 433. *See also* inscriptions; monuments
  in Callimachus' *Hymn 2 "To Apollo,"* 270, 273–75
  in Rhodes, 269
  at Temple of Asclepius at Epidaurus, 268
  at Temple of Zeus Lepsynus, 268–69
programmatic writing, Augustan poets and, 519–21
Prometheii, 484
Propertius, 512, 519–23, 525–27
  as new Callimachus, 513–14
prorrheseis (priestly proclamations), 269–70
prose works (Callimachus), 11, 171n30. *See also titles of works*
  and philology, 119–30
Proteus, 219–20, 220n30
proverb collections, 384
proverbs and popular sayings, 384–403
  derived from oracles, 393
  erotic function, 393–95
  and poet's self-revelation, 399–403
Psamathe, 42
Ps.-Demetrius, *On Style*, 312–16, 324
Ps.-Epicharmus, 137
pseudonyms, in Callimachus' *Iambi*, 371–72
Ptolemaea, 132, 180, 197, 238

Ptolemaic dynasty, 228
Ptolemaic empire, 155–77, 211–14
  and Panhellenism, 173
Ptolemies, 68
  and Athens/Attica, 157, 365–67
  as bicultural monarchs, 186–88, 199–200
  as both *basileus* and pharaoh, 228–29
  claim of Dionysus as divine ancestor, 299
  cult of deified rulers, 230n18
  and dynastic continuity, 206, 208–9
  and geography of power, 160
  and island of Cos, 158–59
  and Library collections, 131n33, 132
  and Miletus, 157
  and Panhellenism, 176–77
  as patrons, 13, 192, 230–31, 235, 299, 299n47
  and Rome, 159
  and Seleucids, 211–14
Ptolemy Ceraunus, 183, 228
Ptolemy I Soter, 3, 177n59, 179n4, 180, 182–83, 188, 194n52, 444–45
  death of, 183n14
  and *diagramma* of new constitution of Cyrene, 283–84
  and Egyptian culture, 238–39
  and Milesians, 157
  as ruler, 228–32
Ptolemy II Philadelphus, 3–4, 10, 91–92, 132, 135, 150, 177n59, 179, 179n4, 180–82, 211, 366–67, 444–45, 592. *See also* Grand Procession of Ptolemy II Philadelphus
  accession to coregency, 182–84
  accession to sole rule, 183n15
  and Achaean League, 159n10
  and Cos, 158
  and court society, 232–33
  and death of Arsinoe II, 232n34
  and divinization, 195
  dynastic issues, 206
  and Egyptian culture, 239–40
  and encouragement of Greek culture, 137
  in *Hymn to Delos*, 193–200, 439–40
  marriage to Arsinoe II, 201–2, 204, 214–18
  and Milesians, 157
  as patron, 230–31
  as Sibling Gods (with Arsinoe II), 230n18

statues
- in Delphi, 234n42
- in Olympia, 234n43
- truce with Athenians, 157

Ptolemy III Euergetes, 9–10, 55–56, 179, 190, 191n43, 206, 223, 234n40
- and court society, 233–34
- and Egyptian culture, 240
- and liberation of Athens from siege by Antigonids, 157
- marriage to Berenice, 201–2
- and Third Syrian War, 235

Ptolemy IV, 137, 173, 194n52
Ptolemy V, 199n67
Pucci, Joseph, 584
Punic War, 159
purity regulations, 268–69, 433
- in Callimachus' *Hymn 2 "To Apollo,"* 271–73
- Cyrenean Purity Regulation, 271–73

Pythagoras of Rhegium, 488
Pythagoreanism, 516
Pythian Games, 301, 500

queens, Ptolemaic, 201–24
- and/as Graces, 209–11
- as divinities, 218–24
- as patrons of the arts, 209
- poems on, 202–5
- praise of, 223–24
- role in dynastic discourse, 206–14
- role in war and diplomacy, 211–14

Quintilian, 251
Quintus of Smyrna, *Posthomerica*, 553
quotations. *See* book fragments; citations of Callimachus

readers' digests, 84
reading, in Cavafy's "In the Month of Athyr," 600–601
reading public, 170n28, 177, 241–42. *See also* audience; performance
- as audience for *Aetia*, 163
- and New Music, 291
realism, Alexandrian, 399–403
recusatio, 528
reference, 580
Reitzenstein, R., 26, 570, 572–73
religion, Hellenistic
- and Callimachus' *Hymn 2 "To Apollo,"* 264–85
- and poetic performance, 241
religious syncretism, 281n39, 301
reminiscence, as category, 567

Rhadamanthys, 43
Rhea, 460–61
rhetorical handbooks, 101n36
Rhianus, 536
Rhodes, 161
Rice, Ellen, 133
Riddle of the Oyster, 137
ritual, Greek
- hymns and, 266, 276–82
- sacred regulations and, 266
ritual libation, in Callimachus' *Hymn 1 "To Zeus,"* 448–49
ritual performance
- of Callimachus' *Hymn 1 "To Zeus,"* 448–49
- fiction of, 190
rituals
- local, 169
- universal, 169
Rivers of Asia (Calllimachus), 129
Romantics, 575, 577
Rome, 159, 164, 490
Rossum-Steenbck, Monique van, 84
royal couple, in *Aetia*, 179–80
royal incest, 179, 202, 206, 214–18
royal mistresses, 232
royal tutors, 232–33, 322
Ruhnkenius, David, 24n4
Ruijgh, C.J., 143
ruler cult, Hellenistic, 250–51
rupture, and Alexandrian literary world, 130–31

Sacadas of Argos, 301
sacred regulations, Greek, 265–69
- metrical, 266–67, 276–82
- oracular responses as, 279
- use of term, 265n5
- varieties of, 265–66
Sallustius, 113n87
- commentary on Callimachus' *Hecale*, 113
Salustios, 26
Samos, 216
- sanctuary of Hera, 164
Sappho, 207, 498, 527, 529
- Alexandrian poets and, 471
Satyrus of Callatis, 233, 322
Savior Gods (Theoi Soteres), 179n4, 195, 222n35
Schneider, Otto, 24, 70, 75, 535
scholarly works (Callimachus). *See also titles of works*
- citation of, 98–99

scholars
  Alexandrian, 106
  Byzantine, 114–17
  Hellenistic, 88–89
  modern, and collection of Callimachus citations, 93–97
school curriculum, Callimachus' works in, 4, 99–100, 100n24
schools, 137
  and *koine*, 139–41
Schubart, W., 359
Schwartz, Eduard, 27
Schwendner, G., 151
science, Hellenistic, 423–24
Scirus of Salamis, 356
Scopadae, 488
seer, poet as, 425
Selden, D., 130–31, 176, 213–14
Selenaea, 218–19
Seleucids, 157, 238n55
Seleucus, 108
Seleucus II, 235
self-fashioning
  of Callimachus, 409–10
  Ptolemaic, 242
Selinus, 166
Seller, Abednego, 24n3
Seneca, 102n37
  De beneficiis, 210
Seneca the Elder, 573
senex, poet as, 400–403
Senoucheri, 239, 239n63
sententiae, of Homeric and Hesiodic influence, 385–86
sequence of elegies in *Aetia*, Books 3 & 4, 59–60
Serapeum (Alexandria), 12–13, 138
Serapis, temple of, in Canopus, 13, 13n22
Servius, 96
Seven Sages, 374, 485, 485n34, 498
Seven Wonders of the World, 253–54
Severianus of Gabala, 104–5, 105n54
Sextion, 108n67
Sextus Empiricus, 102–3
shield, as trophy, 198
Short Account of Dr. Bentley's Humanity and Justice…, 24n3
Sibling Gods (Ptolemy II and Arsinoe II), 10, 592
sibling marriage, 179. *See also* royal incest
Sicily, 161
  weight of, on Enceladus, 382

Sicyon, 44
Sicyonians, revolt against Macedonian rule, 159n10
sightseeing (autopsy), 254–56
Simelidis, Christos, 555–56
Simias, 118, 122
Simonides, 51, 390, 484, 591n10, 598–600
  Plataea Elegy, 338
size imagery, 324–26
Smendes, 239–40
Smotrytsch, P., 191
Smyrna, 218–19
Snell, Bruno, 409, 427
Solon, 338, 431, 485n34
Sophocleius, 108n67
Sophocles, 212, 469
Soranus, *On the Parts of Human Body*, 109
Sosibius, 9–10, 180, 189, 233–34
Sosii, 85
Sostratus of Cnidus, 233–34, 234n42, 236
Sotades of Maronea, 233
Soteria (Delphi), 181n7, 197
sound, in poetry. *See* euphonist criticism
"source," of poetry, 576–77
space, geopoetics and, 160–70
speaker. *See also* voice
  animals as, 371–74, 524
  in Callimachus' Hymn 2 "To Apollo," 282–83
  monument as, 598–600
  trees as, 374–80, 398, 502–3
spoken language, 142. *See also* accent, spoken; dialects, Greek; *koinai*
Spurius Carvilius, 491
Stanley, Sir Thomas (Stanleius), 23
Statius, 99
statues
  aniconic, 498–501
  of Apollo on Delos, 258
  of Artemis
    at Ambracia, 490
    in Leucas, 42
  of Athena at Teuthis, 44–45, 481–82
  of deities, 251–60
  of Euthymus, 487–88, 487n49
  of Glaucon in Olympia, 234n40
  of Hera on Samos, 54, 216–17
  of Ptolemy II and Arsinoe II in Olympia, 234n43
  of Ptolemy II in Delphi, 234n42

of Zeus by Phidias at Olympia, 252–60, 498–500
Stemplinger, Eduard, 573–74, 577
Stephanus, Henricus (Henri Estienne), 23, 89
Stephanus of Byzantium, 96, 101, 109, 362–63
Stephens, Susan, 175n50, 176, 186
Stesichorus, 417
Stilpo of Megara, 253
Stobaeus, 102n38, 313, 413
   Florilegium, 72
Stoic criticism, 316, 324
Stoics, 322
Strabo, 100, 254, 499
Strato, 146
Strato of Lampsacus, 232, 322
Strato of Sardis, 550
Street of the Papyri, 84
Stroux, J., 491
structuralism, 582
stylistics, 314–16
subject, literary, and dialect, 144–45
Successors, 225–26, 228, 230
Suda, 9, 11, 25–26, 98, 113, 119–20, 123, 124n16, 129, 151, 226, 299, 300n54, 317n33, 322, 365–67
Sulpicius Maximus, Quintus, 548–49
supplements to text, 77–78
Supplementum Hellenisticum, 77
swan, associated with music and with Apollo, 372
symposium, 326
   Banquet of Pollis, 361–63, 400–401
   held by *basileus*, 242
   in *Hymn 1 "To Zeus,"* 183, 450

Tabula Vindobonensis, 27–28, 351–52, 358, 363
Taranto krater (Taranto, Nat. Mus. IG 8263), 302n62
Tarentum, 516n11
Tatian, 316n31
Taurinus, 234
teaching, as purpose of *Diegeseis*, 88
Tebtynis, 34, 76, 81–86
techne, poetic, 325–26, 330–31, 423, 426, 468–69
Telchines, 178, 312, 312n10, 318, 327, 332, 402, 416–17, 426–27, 495, 518
   identity of, 90
Temesa, 54, 164
Tempe, Thessalian, 164
Tenedos, 53, 164

Terpander, 449
Tertullian, *De corona*, 101n33
testimonia, to *Aetia*, 65–70
Teuthis, 44, 481–82
textual comparison, Pasquali's typology of, 567
Thales, 485, 485n34
   and golden cup, 374
Thargelia festival, 302
Thasos, 164
Thaumaton synagoge (Callimachus), 98
Theaetetus, 108n67, 465
theater mask, 470–71, 473
Thebes, 164, 435n7
Theocritus, 99, 108, 143, 175, 233, 411, 498, 503, 535, 594n15
Theodaisia, 43, 337
Theodore Prodromus, 563
Theognis, 137, 338, 431
Theon of Alexandria, 107–10, 107n66
Theophrastus, 142, 311n7, 312n12, 323, 323n53
   On Drunkenness, 302
Theophylact Simocatta, 103
Theoxenia, 281, 281n39
Theseus, 352–57
   and Marathon Bull, 8, 480
   portrayed by Callimachus, 479–81
   reception at house of Hecale, 417–19
Thesmophoria, 4, 51, 489n52
Theudorus (father or uncle of poet Callimachus), 284
Thiodamas, 41–42, 477
Third Syrian War, 179, 191, 203, 208, 213, 223
Thomas, Richard, 533, 534n2, 579–80
Tiberius, Emperor, 111
Tibullus, 521, 527
Timaeus, 127
Timon of Phlius, *Silloi*, 233
Timotheus, 290n3, 296
Timpanaro, Sebastiano, 567
Titans, 187, 440
titles, instability of, 122
Tmolus, Mount, 166n21
Tornices, Euthymius, 116
Tottes, 222
tragedy, Greek, 8
   Callimachus and, 505–6, 595n17
tragic voices, in Callimachus' works, 465–71
transition, in *Aetia*, 48–49
trees, fable of, 374–80, 398, 502–3
Tress, H. van, 581

Triphiodorus, *Sack of Troy*, 553
Tripodiscus, 42
Trojan War, Callimachus and, 481–82
truth poetry, 185–86
Turner, Eric, 89
Tydeus, 475
Tyrrhenians, 54
Tyrtaeus, 431
Tzetzes, John, 114–15

Umm-el-Breigât, 81–86

Valckenaer, L.C., 24, 24n4
  Diatribe in Euripidis perditorum dramatum reliquias, 25
Varius, 569
Varro Atacinus, 569
Virgil, 501, 519–20, 528, 573
  Aeneid, 522
  and allusion, 569
Vitelli, Girolamo, 28, 83, 85
vividness, in Hellenistic literary criticism, 327
Vogliano, Achille, 34, 82, 85, 85n16
voice, poetic. *See also* polyphony
  of Callimachus, 134, 597
    in Latin poets, 526–30
    in fable of talking animals, 371–74
    in *Hymn 2 "To Apollo,"* 282–83, 433–39
    in *programmata*, 268–70
    of speaking monument, 598–600
    strategic fragmentation of, 437
voices
  of children, 409–12
  of other poets, in works of Callimachus, 454–73
  tragic, in Callimachus' works, 465–71
Vulcanius, Bonaventura, 23
vulgarity, poet's rejection of, 430–33

Wackernagel, Jacob, 543
Wagner, Richard, *Die Meistersinger*, 568
water imagery, in poetry, 320–21, 425
  Callimachus' use of, 275–76
weaving, 209
Wennofer, 239

West, M.L., 36
White, K., 156n2
Wilamowitz, Ulrich von, 27, 184, 350, 352, 359, 367
Williams, Frederick, 275
Wilson, P., 297, 302
wine, and Dionysiac inspiration, 290–91
wine aesthetic, Ion of Chios and, 298
wonder, role of, 423–24
word lists, 146–49
World War I, 27
World War II, 28

Xenomedes of Ceos, 62, 127, 158, 350, 359, 363, 485–86, 590–91
Xenophantus, 233
Xenophon of Ephesus, *Ephesiaca*, 483n26
Xerxes, 212–13

Youtie, Herbert, 150

Zaleucus of Locri, 438
Zancle, 42–43
Zeno Archive, 135–37, 148
Zenodotus, 118
  Glossai, 146
Zenodotus of Ephesus, 232, 322
Zeno of Caunus, 135–37, 233n35
Zephyrus, 56
Zeugma, 523
Zeus
  birthplace of, 441–42, 457–64
  as charioteer or driver-away, 187–88, 466
  as giver of wealth, 189
  in *Hymns*, 2–3, 182–89, 439–48
  as ideal critic, 327
  as "king of bees," 186–87
  origin of his power, 444–48
  statue by Phidias at Olympia, 252–60, 498–500
Zeus and Hera, as model for sibling marriage, 179, 215
Zeus Basileus, 183
Zeus Hecaleius, 350